W9-CQG-596

PARENT
PARTICIPATION

STAFF
CONFERENCE

COMMUNITY
CONTACT

GUIDANCE

American School
CURRICULUM

Frontispiece—

Education can no longer be considered the sum of specific learnings. In arithmetic specific learnings must result in quantitative thinking in all phases of life.

Photograph from the Cleveland Press, Cleveland, Ohio

Photographs used in the end papers were supplied by the public schools, Chattanooga, Tennessee

American School

CURRICULUM

THIRTY-FIRST YEARBOOK

AMERICAN ASSOCIATION OF SCHOOL ADMINISTRATORS

A DEPARTMENT OF THE NATIONAL EDUCATION ASSOCIATION OF THE UNITED STATES
1201 Sixteenth Street, Northwest, Washington 6, D. C.

COMMISSION ON AMERICAN SCHOOL CURRICULUM

LAWRENCE G. DERTHICK

Superintendent of Schools, Chattanooga, Tennessee
CHAIRMAN

GUY T. BUSWELL

Professor of Education, University of California
Berkeley, California

STANLEY E. DIMOND

Professor of Education, University of Michigan
Ann Arbor, Michigan

FRANCIS L. DRAG

Assistant Superintendent, Curricular Services
San Diego County Schools, San Diego, California

ERNEST HORN

Professor of Education, The State University of Iowa
Iowa City, Iowa

RAYMOND H. OSTRANDER

Superintendent of Schools, Mineola, Long Island, New York

DAVID H. PATTON

Superintendent of Schools, Syracuse, New York

NOEL WICAL

Education Reporter, The Cleveland Press, Cleveland, Ohio

FRANK L. WILLIAMS

Assistant Superintendent in Charge of Instruction
Dallas Independent School District, Dallas, Texas

HARRY H. WILLIAMS

Assistant Principal, Horace Mann School, New York, New York

FOREWORD

IN 1925—some 25 years before the present yearbook commission was appointed—the AASA (then the Department of Superintendence) issued its first yearbook on the curriculum. It is interesting to note that even in those so-called benighted times superintendents were aware of the necessity of cooperation among classroom teachers, school administrators, and laymen, of the importance of a friendly, open-minded approach by the administrative officers, of the value of research in supplying the basis for curriculum improvement, and of the wisdom of organization within the school system in order to have unified curriculum action. Thus it is apparent that the idea of democratic and intelligent leadership is not a product only of the past decade.

When President Warren Travis White appointed the 1952 commission, he was of the opinion that a critical need of superintendents was for a straightforward statement on a number of the current issues in the curriculum field. This has been a difficult assignment. In the past two decades educational research has turned up more information than school systems can readily appraise and use. Classroom teachers have made tremendous strides forward in professional preparation, including the everyday application of new knowledge as to the nature and needs of children. Parents too have advanced both in scientific knowledge and in their desire to share in decisions concerning the education of the children. Laymen in general and special interest groups have awakened to the significance of education in the development of the nation's future citizens. Among the laymen there are both individuals and groups who, for reasons both clear and obscure, have by destructive methods sought to limit the school curriculum. Under such conditions, both orderly and chaotic, it has not been easy to select yearbook materials with assurance that they would be equally useful in all parts of the country.

Nevertheless the Commission has faced its assignment squarely. It has sought to restate the values in American life to which we all owe enduring allegiance and then by principle and example to indicate ways in which the superintendent can play his essential role. At some points the Commission has rather definite views and has said so; at other places the text suggests that many acceptable roads lead to the same constructive ends. The Commission has not attempted to outline a curriculum for the nation as a whole or to touch even lightly the entire range of current curriculum problems. The volume centers upon the school administrator in an effort to help him give leadership to curriculum improvement in the midst of the overwhelming tasks of today's superintendency.

This yearbook, like most in the past, has drawn upon the experience and knowledge of many educators and laymen. It is not a document written in an ivory tower about a never-never world. To some so-called "frontier thinkers" the pace of the volume may seem pedestrian, but they are not the audience. The volume is addressed to the superintendent, his immediate staff, classroom teachers, graduate students in school administration and laymen, particularly members of boards of education. Many will see that curriculum improvement, a highly technical process, offers each of them opportunities for satisfying, constructive endeavors.

The chapters of the yearbook have been developed from an outline worked out cooperatively at the first meeting of the Commission. Drafts of the chapters, prepared by members of the Commission, have been submitted again and again to group scrutiny. No one was more helpful in this process than the layman, a member of a board of education and education writer of the *Cleveland Press*. Noel Wical lived up to the honors he has won as a friend and as a discerning observer of the schools.

The Commission expresses its debt to all who have helped to make the volume possible. Among these are the Washington staff, such as Worth McClure, executive secretary, who handled the necessary business phases and provided wise counsel from his rich experience. The coordination of the production and final editing for publication has been ably handled by Frank W. Hubbard, director of the NEA Research Division. During the first part of this work he was assisted by Ivan A. Booker, assistant director. Other members of the Research Division included Bernice Brigham, who handled the secretarial work, and Mabel T. Smith and Beatrice Crump, who helped in the production and editing. Proofreading and related matters have been the responsibilities of Jesse S. Cowdrick and Violet Argent of the NEA Division of Publications.

CONTENTS

As educators we believe—

1. That the purpose of education in the United States of America is the development of each individual for the fullest participation in the American democratic way of life.

2. That universal free education must be made available by and to all peoples in the interests of world understanding, citizenship, and peace.

3. That the American democratic way of life may be perpetuated—

a. Through universal free education fitted to the abilities, interests, and needs of each person and of the society in which he lives, and

b. Through teaching the individual how free America permits him to choose and plan his own goals, provides him increasing equality of opportunity to reach these goals, allows him to keep the rewards for his work, and matches these privileges with serious duties of citizenship.

4. That the school program should emphasize the worth and dignity of all essential work.

5. That the quality of education will be determined principally by the quality of the persons who teach.

6. That the structure of American school systems should be adaptable enough to meet the educational needs of a changing society.

7. That the total educational experience of each individual must be designed to contribute to the development of effective ethical character.

8. That spiritual, social, civic, economic, and vocational competencies are as important as academic literacy.

—From the Platform of the American Association of School Administrators, 1951 revision

CHAPTER ONE

What Schools Are For

THE continuance of our American way of life depends upon the way our citizens are educated. As the problems of society become more complicated, the education of our people becomes more difficult and requires more time. A hundred years ago, when mastery of the rudiments of the Three R's was sufficient, the necessary schooling could be obtained in a few years. Now many years of school attendance are necessary. And, more and more our people, to meet changing demands of life, are supplementing their schooling with adult education.

The professed confidence and faith of the American people in the public schools has been strongly in evidence since early pioneer days. This faith in education is founded in the basic fact that education does something beneficial to people and for them.

Among the national resources of America are our natural or material wealth, the latent ability of our people, and the acquired ability and high ideals of our people. The first group includes our valuable forests, mines, broad fertile lands, water power, and favorable climates. For the second group, we think of the native ability of our people, including their health and physical vigor. The third group represents what we have been able to do with the intelligence and capacities of people and what intellectual gains we can successfully pass on to future generations.

The broad concept of American education is to develop the art of using *all* our resources advantageously. Only brief reflection on the growth of our country suffices to assure one that this is a great and successful nation—successful in business and industrial developments, in cultural growth, and in high standards of living. These achievements are the results of the creative power of man and the ingenuity that is fostered and nurtured thru education.

The American people have wisely and generously invested their earnings in education so that larger and larger benefits may accrue to us as a nation. It is the belief of America that by helping people to use intelligence for the general welfare the destinies of our country will be fulfilled.

9

Schools Accept New Requirements

Advancement in culture necessitates change. Almost any change in the life of an individual brings forth major or minor resistance. The characteristic of the American people to expect firm and deliberate appraisals makes for slow progress but gives greater assurance of stability. In our free dynamic society this process is ever at work. Even many of those who oppose change, by their very resistance, produce adjustments in our way of life. Education has been and always will be a major resource in resolving conflicts as we move from the old to the new.

Since change in a dynamic society, such as we cherish, is inevitable and inescapable, education will always be playing an important part. As it plays this role, we will find that what education was intended to be or do in the past does not necessarily include what it should be or do in the future. Schools accept the new patterns of society growing organically and continually out of the old in response to human emotional forces and human intelligence.

Good administrative practice involves cooperative deliberation by teachers, parents, and the community at large. Altho less than half of the homes in a given community are directly affected by having children in the schools, all other homes are affected indirectly. The school program should give parents and the community something positive and constructive to believe about the schools. This constructive belief stimulates faith in them. It also protects the educational system from insincere people and from the attacks of the demagog. It avoids the confusion which may be developed from statements written or spoken by radical propagandists who, posing as educators, may be clamoring for a place to be heard, and from those who seek to impair the strength of America by undermining the public-school system.

Every individual's philosophy is expressed in his words and deeds—the way he lives. Likewise, every school system has a philosophy either in documentary form or expressly implied in the daily activities of its program. Every school system should have a *stated* philosophy which clarifies the full meaning of its program. The philosophy of an individual, school, or enterprise gives color, direction, and vitality.

Our program of public education can and should provide for every educable child, youth, and adult. Each individual should have the kind and amount of education which will (a) make him most useful to himself and to others according to the principles of American democracy, (b) lead him to understand the principles and goals of our democratic way of life so that he may have a basis for his beliefs and loyalties, (c) help him to be an active and discerning participant in local, state, and national concerns so that this country may have exemplary leadership in its governmental affairs, (d) stimulate him to contribute all he can to the development and preservation of peaceful, cooperative, and equitable world relationships, and (e) help him to recognize and understand the operation of natural laws in his environment.

To achieve these things for all individuals, educators must arouse the interest of our total population. Every individual should be cognizant of the fact that he is a part of the world drama. He cannot afford to sleep thru the performance by devoting the major part of his time to reading comic strips, playing with crossword puzzles, or reading cheap fiction.

Education should stimulate devotion to our way of life; it should also guard zealously against its imperfections.

We should so direct educational processes that human behavior will present a pattern of harmony and tolerance. The first prerequisite to this social scene will involve a loyalty to a cause or purpose—respect for man and his importance in our society.

Education Takes Root

Second only to building their first church the Pilgrim fathers turned their earliest attention to building a school, so that the children of the little colony might have enough education to read the Bible and copy its verses. From such humble beginnings has developed modern American public education of the twentieth century with its myriad complexities. During the intervening years the objectives of the schools have changed and expanded. Yet thruout their history has run the dominant purpose of developing happy and competent citizens qualified to meet the current needs of useful members of a democratic society.

Early in the existence of the Massachusetts Bay Colony it became evident that a curriculum of reading and writing was not sufficient for the day. True, it was many years later before the schools became

11

significant factors in helping to solve the problems of all the people, but even in colonial days there was an ever-increasing need for ministers, teachers, and lawyers. Hence Latin, mathematics, and rhetoric soon were added to the curriculum.

Expanding Fundamental Principles

As the population grew and life became more and more complex, the demands for more education outside the home gradually produced a demand for compulsory and universal instruction. In a few places, towns not providing any type of educational facilities were compelled by their colonial assembly to pay a fine to those neighboring towns which did make such provision. As a matter of fact, certain taxes for educational purposes were levied here and there. The type of financial support varied with the productive resources of the several communities. These isolated examples of compulsory attendance and compulsory financial support were forerunners of the common pattern thruout the United States.

It was not without long and vigorous debate, however, that these attitudes were incorporated into fundamental principles of American education and the basic state laws. It was argued that publicly supported schools were impractical and visionary, that education would become too common and would break down long-established and desirable social distinctions, that most children were already being as well educated in the home as they deserved, that public authorities had no right to intervene between parent and child in the matter of education, that it was unjust to tax one man's property to educate his neighbor's child, and that taxes would be so increased that no colonial government could long survive. These contentions were countered by the arguments that expanding colonial civic duties and responsibilities required universal schooling; that increased immigration to the colonies demanded a system of common learnings; that publicly supported education was a natural right of all children; that social, moral, political, and economic benefits would more than compensate for the cost; and that publicly supported education was not for the sake of economy but rather for the welfare of the individual and society.

The framers of the Constitution, altho recognizing the problem as vital, left the control and regulation of education to the states, thru the indirection of the Tenth Amendment of the Bill of Rights. Thus they established the principle that the national government should not use the schools as instruments for directing the lives of its citizens. And so it was, nearly 175 years ago, that a clear line of demarcation was drawn by our forebears between the objectives of public education in a free and democratic society and the recent objectives of education in totalitarian or communistic societies.

The Nation Grows

The westward movement beyond the Alleghenies, which culminated in the election of Andrew Jackson as President of the United States, placed a new emphasis on educational objectives and inaugurated an epoch-making period of popular and universal public education. If the common people could, at last, elect one of their own number as President, certainly it was high time that they and their children enjoyed the benefits of education at public expense. One-room rural schools sprang up, built frequently from lumber hewed from virgin forests, even as that first little school in Old Massachusetts. But there the likeness ceased, for the objectives of these later schools were as different as the times. The primary purpose no longer was to produce teachers, preachers, and lawyers from the ranks of the "rich, the well-born, and the able"; that task was left to the private schools on the seaboard. Rather the public school was to teach "readin', 'ritin', and 'rithmetic" to the children of common folk, to boys and—revolutionary indeed— to girls. These little schools were actively responsive to the wants of their patrons. The schoolmaster was an integral part of the frontier community. He "boarded 'round" and life bound him so tightly to his locality and to his neighbors that their ideas and their thoughts were his ideas and his thoughts and guided what he taught and how he taught it.

Paralleling the westward agrarian movement was the rapid growth of cities along the Atlantic coast. Agriculture long continued in first place among the occupations, but the development of industry and manufacturing, resulting in the building of factories and the invention of machinery, drew thousands of families from the eastern farms to the cities, producing new and unprecedented challenges to education in those congested centers. Extended

13

transportation and communication facilities cleared horizons for educational vision far beyond the potentialities of the early private schools and academies. As the organized labor movement developed, its leaders demanded that the' educational opportunities of the children of the common man, even tho provided at public expense, should equal those afforded the children of the wealthy at private expense.

After 1850 far-reaching events developed in rapid succession. Gold was discovered in California, silver in Colorado and Nevada, iron in Minnesota, and public lands were opened to veterans for settlement. Power presses stimulated the publication of books, magazines, and papers to flood proportions. Labor-saving inventions began to increase not only production but also leisure time. The means of transportation and communication were multiplying with fantastic speed, trade and commerce were taking our ships to all corners of the world, and immigrants were arriving in ever-growing numbers.

And Educational Needs Change

No longer could unsystematic educational facilities meet or cope with the challenges of the day. While the purpose of education still remained the service of the individual and society of his time, the objectives had long since ceased to be those characteristic of English colonies, or of the times of Jackson, or even of pre-Civil War America. They were now characteristic of a great, vigorous, and growing agricultural, commercial, and industrial nation. The new school objectives were not at all within the scope of small district schools, with their single curriculum and often untrained teachers. There was in truth educational chaos into which order had to be brought. And so state, city, and district school systems were evolved to correlate and coordinate the services of the individual schools. The principle that the wealth of a state should be taxed to afford equal educational opportunity to all children became a fundamental reality. Permissive educational policies became mandatory standards. Compulsory attendance laws, fixed length of the school year, regulation of school-building construction, statewide certification of teachers, determination of the general curriculum, establishment of minimum salary laws gradually became the order of the day.

The old Three-R curriculum of the elementary school and the classical college-preparatory courses were expanded to include courses of study in agricultural, commercial, technical, industrial, and scientific fields.

While the number and the quality of the elementary schools increased and while in many cities kindergartens were established, nevertheless the change of greatest significance was the unprecedented growth of secondary education. In 1880 there were about 800 public high schools in the entire United States; 20 years later in 1900, there were 6005. In 1889-90 public and private high schools enrolled only 7 percent of the boys and girls between 14 and 17 years of age as compared with 73 percent in 1949-50. Between 1900 and 1950 the number of youth increased 60 percent but total high-school enrolment increased by more than 1600 percent.

Paralleling the many economic and industrial developments, social changes of a fundamental nature were also in the making. The attitude of individual responsibility, so characteristic of the American home of the seventeenth and eighteenth centuries, was being supplemented by an attitude of group interdependence of the twentieth century. In the early days of our history the home life of boys and girls provided most of the practical instruction necessary to equip them for the occupational pursuits of the times. The family was the unit of sufficiency. Father and the boys, assisted by kindly neighbors at "raising" time, built their own houses of lumber split and sawed with their own hands from the giant pines, oaks, and maples of the forest. Most of the furniture, too, they made. The mother and daughters spun the wool and flax and wove cloth for the family clothing. Logs from the nearby woods furnished heat for warmth and cooking, homemade tallow candles burned for light, and deep-dug wells brought forth water. The assembly line had not yet come. Factory prefabricated homes, apartment buildings, and penthouses with their gas heat, electric lights, and water at the turn of a faucet from reservoirs miles away were many generations in the future.

With the arrival of new inventions, the challenges and objectives of education changed again. Society demanded that its schools keep pace with other areas of national progress. The task of the school multiplied a thousandfold between the time when the aim of education was only enough reading instruction to enable one to read the Bible, and enough writing and arithmetic for simple trading and today's technological developments, centralization of industry, specialization of occupations, compulsory age retirements, state and federal labor regulations, and a shorter work week coupled with leisure-time activities. Educational leaders have responded to the changing demands of a dynamic society. The curriculum of today is in a continuous process of change in order that all boys and girls may be offered an education designed to produce free, responsible, and competent men and women. It is not sufficient that young people grow as citizens of a pioneer colony; they must grow as citizens of a complex world.

The little district schoolhouse is all but gone and in its stead are consolidated and central schools, both urban and rural. Audio-visual aids have replaced the hornbook and slate. Schools and classes for the physically and mentally handicapped, nursery schools, summer schools, radio schools of the air, television, evening schools, adult classes—all these, in response to the demands of the present, are making their contribution to the growth of intelligent citizens—the men and women of tomorrow's America.

What Schools Do for Society

Schools, like other social institutions, are a product of the society in which they exist. They tend, therefore, to reflect in their objectives the needs and desires of that society. Schools do have an active role to play for they should and do influence social progress, at least by improving the functioning of the members of society.

Schools Change as Society Changes

Most institutions, including the schools, do not easily adapt to change. The planning and substance of change tend to block instantaneous adjustment and create a lag between the operations of social institutions and society's needs and desires. However, this slowness of adaptation also provides society with a degree of desirable stability, especially necessary in emergencies.

Many of the fundamental knowledges, abilities, attitudes, and ideals require relatively little adjustment from year to year. Much of the past has stood the test of time. The successes of the past must not be discarded until we have assurance of something better. Altho the future rests with our imaginations, and science is constantly changing the world drama, we must guard against illusions. As we plan to meet the future, we should strive to do better the worthwhile things we have been doing. We can do better, for education embraces a science in itself and research is improving this science.

Invention, discoveries, research, and methods of production are contributing to the needs of man in an ever accelerated degree. Educators must be alert to evaluate the product of these accomplishments in terms of the effect on the lives of the people. Education must preserve a balance between the new and the old. It must interpret these achievements thru continuous curriculum adjustments.

Basically all curriculums attempt to meet the demands and the needs of our people. Therefore, for any curriculum to be correct in its volume and scope, great care must be given in accurate observation of individual and group needs. It is obvious here that extensive research should be a continuous part of our curriculum planning. Once the findings have been made, the next steps are interpreting and activating the program adjustments. We are, at present, attempting to bring the schools into closer alignment with our presentday industrialized, democratic society. Education is challenged continuously to fit its objectives to the needs and desires of the times.

American education cannot be satisfied with the present and emerging future, but rather it shall give full recognition to the important contributions of the total social heritage. Our scope of vision shall be both national and international.

No community or country can be self-contained or isolated from the rest of the world. New inventions not only bring the people of every nationality closer together but the eyes of television bring into many homes the events, the customs, and the people of every land. The responsibility for wise interpretation of national and worldwide events and affairs will depend on the extent education gives to every citizen understandings and knowledge which will enable him to translate these rationally.

The task is no small one. It is not, as it once was, merely a matter of adding new areas to the curriculum. Today's needs require some fundamental readjustment commensurate with the profound changes

17

taking place in society. Those changes often had their origin in the Industrial Revolution and in the resulting social revolution. It is not the fact that we are living in an atomic age which requires us to re-evaluate our educational objectives, but it is the rapid adjustment in our social structure with all that it implies. The problems of the atomic age are only one part of this larger social problem. Since valid educational objectives should be in harmony with the needs and desires of the society in which the schools are found, a brief analysis is given here of some of the requirements resulting from the industrial and social upheavals of the recent past.

Effective specialization—One of the keys to the successful functioning of our society is specialization. It has made possible mass production and a tremendous increase in our material standard of living. Specialization has done this, however, not without cost to those who have benefited. It has impersonalized many human relationships. There is a tremendous gap between employer and employee in the steps between the processing of a product and its distribution in finished form.

This gap has resulted in lack of mutual understanding with resulting conflict and tension; it has caused a loss of a sense of responsibility and of pride in good workmanship. Often those conditions have created a philosophy that puts a premium on dependence and security instead of on independence and enterprise. To this dependence specialization has also contributed for it requires interdependence and cooperative effort.

Group living—Schools must also provide youth with opportunities to learn and practice the technics of living and working together cooperatively and democratically. Thru their school studies they should gain an understanding of, and faith in, the processes of group action. Our lives must function thru this faith. The orderliness of modern traffic control comes about thru mutual understanding so automatic that we seldom think about it. We approach a green light with confidence that our fellow travelers will also respect its signal and not cross our path. We travel at high speed on our highways sure that on-coming traffic will keep to our left. Only by such faith can we travel so far and so fast with safety.

Our system of business and credit likewise functions successfully only as its members have confidence in one another. We put our money in a bank knowing that it will be returned to us when we want it. We buy a product unquestioningly accepting the weight and qualities stated on its label.

Freedom for leisure—Another major development resulting from the Industrial Revolution is an increase in the amount of leisure time. Here again, we find both benefits and hazards. People, freed from full-time employment in making a living, have had time to promote the growth of American culture. Leisure time has given people opportunities to enrich their lives and the lives of others in myriad ways.

On the other hand, free time—including time for added schooling—challenges educational leadership to provide training that will make worthwhile activity the goal of each individual rather than worthless activity or nonactivity. We Americans may become a nation of passive spectators instead of active participants in leisure-time activities. We may lack sufficient preparation and skill to use, in constructive, worthwhile ways, the time at our disposal.

Speed and tension—Today's complex, impersonal, and high-speed world, in spite of more leisure time, has produced a feeling of tension, strain, and frustration thruout the population. Good mental health is recognized to be as important a factor in successful living as physical health. In fact, the two have merged together in surprising ways. Schools, for years a major influence in setting good physical health standards and habits, today are challenged to meet the increased mental hazards of modern civilization. Both mental health and physical health very dramatically affect the educational process. Schools help with the problem by encouraging pupils to develop proper attitudes and habits thru real-life situations in the schools, and by the personal examples of teachers who themselves face the world with poise and confidence.

Technological changes—The amazing strides in transportation and communication have been awe-inspiring but sometimes appalling because of the problems they make. Thus safety education has been developed to help us keep alive in this era of speed. Its job is only begun, if the accident statistics are correct. Communication has been climaxed with television and the tremendous impact of this new influence on our society as yet can only be guessed. The effect of the automobile on our way of life has been astounding, but

19

the effect of television may be more far-reaching. But regardless of the exact effects we may be sure that the schools must meet the issue squarely. The least we can do will be to help youth develop a sense of values, an understanding of the technics of developing public opinion, and an ability to weigh a situation with an open mind.

Revision, Not Accretion

The complex social, economic, and political problems of our present world necessitate clear, critical thought and analysis. Clear thinking requires improved reading ability, better problem-solving ability, and an understanding of both scientific methods and basic scientific knowledge. Reading must result in understanding, not simply the facts, but the implications of those facts. Many economic problems, including personal ones, are caused in part by a lack of thoro understanding of our number system and its functioning. The nation's credit system requires a better knowledge of interest and budgeting than ever before. Scientific principles determine much of our everyday living. We should teach youth what these principles are and how to live with them. Conservation education needs more emphasis for we court disaster when we ignore the scientific relationships in nature in our eagerness to exploit resources.

It would be a mistake to assume that the answer to these many implications is to teach more facts or even to teach them better. It does imply that facts are important and that basic skills need to be motivated by attitudes and understandings. We must be sure that these attitudes and understandings are based upon moral, ethical, and spiritual values and are not perverted to selfish or mean ends.

Discovering the Individual

A social system based on group action begins to disintegrate and the whole of society suffers when mutual faith and trust are lost. Basic to this faith in group action is the mutual trust of the *individuals* who compose the group. Major emphasis in the curriculum must be placed upon the worth and importance of the individual and his responsibilities to society, as well as the rights which he

Cleveland Press, Cleveland, Ohio

Our schools teach the moral principles of our pattern of government, the privileges it confers, the duties it entails, and the sacrifices that were made for it.

should expect from it. Youth should be taught that there is no social group apart from the individuals that compose it, and that the strengths and weaknesses of these individuals are the strengths and weaknesses of the group.

The discovery and stimulation of the creative mind has become a recognized part of the responsibility of education today. Schools should put a premium on originality. Young people must be freed to discover their talents and guided in using and developing their abilities. More needs to be done in this area so that not only leisure time, but all time, may be more constructively employed for the benefit of the individual and his social group. In the same way that we use imagination and skill and provide the conditions by which the power of the atom is unlocked, so we must in our schools apply imagination and skill and provide the conditions by which the power of the creative minds of youth may be unlocked and used to benefit society. This job is part of the schools' obligations.

What Schools Do for the Individual

The schools provide a great part of the influence leading to a better life for all. Teachers and the curriculum are concerned with the worth and dignity of each individual, the creative talents of youth, good mental health and group relationships, critical thinking and objective appraisal, and the ideals of good sportsmanship and fair play. Thru all of these, and undergirded with a faith in the ultimate goodness of the universe and man's divine rights and responsibilities as a part of it, the schools promote a better society.

Belief in the essential worth of each individual demands educational opportunities for all. However, universal education in itself will not assure the democratic way of life. We are providing more people with more education than ever before in American history, and yet we are in a most critical period in our national life. We must remember that even the dictators have relied on universal education and used it to foster their ends. We must define our purposes in terms of the democratic ideal, then put those purposes to work. Here is where we so often run into trouble. It is so much easier to define the goals than to put them into practice. Especially difficult is the building of the attitudes necessary to motivate these practices.

If we are realistic, we must admit that the home is the foundation of citizenship and our social structure. Monarchs may not need educated citizens, but a republic cannot succeed without them. The job of maintaining a high order of citizenship is a primary obligation of the home and the school. Along with the home and school we find a broad and flexible array of community influences sharing in giving direction and quality to our citizens. Indeed, education is a vast enterprise interlinked with the total dramatic scene of community life.

In any community the character of all the people is improved by their participation in the desirable activities which make up community life. The sharing of civic and family responsibilities, the giving of service as an official or a citizen, the assumption of social obligations and amenities, should be stressed in our schools.

We must make clear the ethical and moral ideals which sustain our pattern of government, the privilege it confers, the duties it entails, the sacrifices that have been made for it, the achievements it has made, and the problems it must face.

Our society is an evolving one based on the freedom of the individual. We must help students understand that the aggregate of the actions of each individual determines the success or failure of our government. Altho it is committed to the fundamental doctrine that life, liberty, and the pursuit of happiness is each citizen's right, we must also indicate to him his responsibilities and obligations.

The school curriculum and its processes of development should stimulate faith in our form of government. Such teaching does not mean that it shall be regarded as perfect, but rather as the finest code of national behavior ever created by man. As fast as we grow in stature as citizens, as rapidly as we merit improvement in government, we will get it. Our pattern of government represents the highest point which has been reached in a long hard climb toward human freedom.

What Makes Society Work?

If society is to be an enduring and cooperating social group, so functioning as to maintain itself adequately, then it must: (a) determine the factors in the total situation that maintain society vigor-

23

ously, and (b) discover the fundamental components of a workable society. The factors will include: (a) the desirable social, ethical, and other human traits contributing to the success of society, (b) the economic and industrial potentials that maintain social groups, and (c) the essential civic and ideological elements.

After determining these factors, the means for attaining these ends must be organized. This problem involves educating the citizens so that they will be imbued with the ideals and behavior patterns necessary for the continuance of the social order. It involves training in the practical aspects of government, industry, and scientific developments, so that society can produce the things necessary to sustain the economy and provide the means for its survival. In our democracy, it also involves the free development in each citizen of the factors which allow him to become an individual in his own right, with freedom to grow morally, physically, mentally, and spiritually. He needs to satisfy those inner desires and needs so fundamental for self-expression.

The Good Citizen

The effectiveness of the educational program in any society determines, in large measure, the society's strength and ability to survive. This means that society must (a) give opportunity for every member to develop to the maximum as an individual and (b) prepare every member to contribute to the fullest to the welfare of that society. To whatever extent this is accomplished we then have the "good" citizen, who not only contributes to society but lives a full and abundant life. Each individual will be expected, therefore, to avail himself of the educational advantages in his environment that contribute to his attainment of the qualities and accomplishments characteristic of the effective citizen. The degree to which he attains these ends will be determined by his innate capacities and by the impact of the aggregate of external conditions and influences upon him.

What then are the essentials that our citizens should possess in order to fulfil these requirements?

Civic competence—The "good" citizen performs his civic duties in a satisfactory manner, not only locally but on a national and international basis as well. He acquires knowledge of civic problems and weighs this knowledge without prejudice. He realizes that the welfare of the people and of the state is more important than party allegiances. He realizes that he should do his duty at the polls. He understands that should he be elected to public office, his major duty is to serve the best interests of the people and that integrity of action and service are of utmost importance.

He believes in the principles of American democracy, and works for the advancement of the ideals which have made this country what it is today. He takes an interest in world affairs and learns to understand the ideologies of other peoples so that he may interpret their actions wisely. He also acquaints himself with the social, industrial, and economic growth of other nations, thus becoming more tolerant of differing attitudes in the solution of world problems.

Educational flexibility—The "good" citizen gives attention to his educational and mental development. He avails himself of the educational facilities. He then outlines a program, as early as is practical, in order that he may develop these capacities to the fullest possible extent. He understands, since life is a period of change and adjustment, that he must condition himself so as to make these adjustments with calmness and good judgment. He realizes that education is a continuing process thruout his life.

Social understanding—The "good" citizen demonstrates concern about the welfare of others, knowing that as he contributes to the betterment of his neighbor, his social groups, and to others, he thereby contributes to society as a whole. His social consciousness leads him to cooperate with others and to work with them harmoniously. He enjoys being with others and is a member of one or more social groups which have desirable activities as their objectives. He realizes that individuals differ in their reactions to all types of situations and have differing viewpoints and attitudes. He is considerate of these differences. He realizes that there are many factors in the solution of any problem and that dogmatic statements or opinions will not solve them. He is open-minded and listens to others, giving recognition to their ideas and contributions. He controls his personal relationships so that his self-satisfactions and activities do not predominate.

Occupational efficiency—The "good" citizen seeks an occupation in which he can find maximum satisfaction and attain maximum production. He thinks of this occupation not only as a means whereby he can provide for the needs of himself and his family but as a contributing factor in the total economy. He is able to get along with his fellow workers and to take part in their activities. He participates constructively in the relationships between employer and employee. He strives to be not a mere worker but a functioning part of a productive enterprise. He does not forget, if his occupation is a profession in which service is above monetary reward.

Home loyalty—The "good" citizen makes his home the cornerstone of society. He so conducts his marital relationships that they promote understanding, consideration, sympathy, compatibility, and companionship. He does his part in the practical aspects of maintaining and conducting the affairs of that home. He contributes to the care and upbringing of the children and sets examples before them which gain their continued respect. He cultivates the child's respect for old age.

He plans for and with his children for their education. He helps them develop those qualities and attitudes necessary for their development as normal individuals in the community. He preserves the sanctity of the home and all those intimate and individual characteristics which make it a haven for a family.

Religious consciousness—The "good" citizen views the religious aspects of his life as of paramount importance. He understands religion as the expression of an innate tendency to aspire to those things that satisfy man's inner needs and consciousness of the existence of a Supreme Being. He realizes that religion's codes of moral and ethical concepts contribute to desirable civic behavior.

He knows that the interpretations of the concepts of religious beliefs differ in many ways, and that for centuries different concepts have been handed down from generation to generation and accepted as satisfying many sincere fellow citizens. Therefore, he is tolerant and unprejudiced in his attitudes, realizing that freedom of worship is fundamental to our way of life.

No program of education is adequate which neglects this large area of human concern. Traditionally the American people have been a God-loving and a God-fearing people, and in many ways we say, "In God we trust." Therefore, the public schools should not be godless—and they are not.

Among the great problems of our culture, two are paramount in importance: the relation of man to his spiritual needs, and the relation of man to his fellow men. These problems are interrelated.

American culture provides a congenial climate for individual approval, development, and participation in the spiritual life of one's own choice. It is not the business of public education to secure adherence to any particular creed, but public education should acquaint youth with the significance of religion in our culture. An inherent goodness is within the life of every normal person.

We must find procedures that bring this attribute to forceful expression. Almost no one achieves the good life to the fullest of his potential, yet we are conscious of the power and influence of any one good man or woman. Education should stimulate youth with an impelling conviction that religion has a place in the life of every individual. Good teaching will point up, or identify in the curriculum, that which spiritual values have done for our culture.

Leisure-time opportunities—The "good" citizen realizes that leisure time is an opportunity for growth and development; that it should be a time for self-expression, recreation, and the advancement of social contacts; that it is time to devote to one's family and to many of the responsibilities pertaining thereto. He uses his leisure time judiciously, not only for his own needs but in cooperative efforts with others. He seeks to apportion his leisure time in such a way that his activities will be wholesome for himself and for society.

The citizen looks forward to the time when his work career is ended and he is free from the demands of his regular occupation. He realizes that the span of life has greatly increased and also that it may be prolonged to a still greater degree because of man's increasing knowledge. He prepares for this eventuality by discovering and training himself to engage in activities that will sustain him by producing both tangible accomplishments and social and recreational benefits.

Education Lights the Way

Educational gains have brought man from illiteracy to literacy. It is a common philosophy of our schools that each individual, thru his initiative and creative power, should rise above the present goals of man. Quoting Ruskin, "Education does not mean teaching people what they do not know; it means teaching them to behave as they do not behave." This emphasis points to the responsibility of the schools to develop well-adjusted people. It means bringing order into society which otherwise could be only some form of chaos. It implies that a well-adjusted individual achieves balance of personality between self-adjustment and social adjustment.

Self-adjustment is based on personal security that comes from a feeling of self-reliance, personal worth, personal freedom, and of belonging. Social adjustment is based on feelings of group security and includes a knowledge of social standards and social skills, freedom from antisocial tendencies, desirable family relations, and satisfactory community relations.

The character and basic integrity of a people are priceless ingredients. We need to pause only briefly to observe how men of our nation have graced it in its economic development. We no longer look with favor upon the schemes of the merchant of the trading post where people were taught, "Your eyes are your market." Today, business operates on the principle of service. Trademarks, licenses, and other forms of evidence give the people confidence of a wholesome relationship with their fellow men. This honesty has stimulated the morale of our people. We stand strongly against offenders who take advantage of the weak. It may be appropriately said that the doctrine of fair play is permeating our economic life.

We are conscious that human beings thruout the world are suffering from their inability to associate together successfully to produce social, political, and economic harmony. We also witness the individual tension, prejudice, hatred, conflict, and other stubborn human strains, or hostilities. In spite of all these symptoms of maladjustment, we believe that the science of human relations can master the powers within and among men. We concur in the famous statement of Horace Mann that the human race is capable of accelerating improvability. We endorse national crusades against tuberculosis, cancer, infantile paralysis, and heart disease, which endanger our common welfare. But we should be just as vigorous to remove or to inhibit such destructive human traits as dishonesty, selfishness, envy, hate, malice, revenge, intolerance, fear, and cowardice. These present a threat to society.

Improvements come slowly because people are reluctant to make full use of education. The accumulations of educational research are extensive. This research becomes a national resource only when it gains popular understanding and acceptance. But man seems less sure today of mastery of his problems than when he had less knowledge in a less complicated world. It remains the task of education to give direction to man thru a broader understanding of the world in which he must live and contribute a sustaining influence.

Whatever great achievements have taken place in business, industrial, social, and economic life, we cannot escape the force of education which has in some manner given direction to the activity. Indeed, it is no figment of imagination, but rather a realistic statement of fact, to say that the past half century has witnessed a miracle of achievement on all educational fronts. This record cannot be equaled by any other nation, or any other political or economic system.

A myriad of intertwined technological advancements have come thru the wisdom and application of scientific research, all of which have contributed, in turn, to cultural and social developments. The potentialities that lie ahead, from further scientific studies and discoveries, may bring us an even more amazing record during the next half century. All these things receive their great stimulus from training men to live in a free society and operate in a system of free enterprise. Competition and opportunity are always the challenge. It is almost fantastic to think of the responsibilities that education has carried in developing this nation.

It is safe to assume that the American people will be willing to further expand the opportunities of our nation. The wisdom and intelligence of our people add both zest and enthusiasm to this whole job of providing more benefits to man thru a higher standard of living. Perhaps the miracle of America for the past half century is only the first episode of a great unfolding of the promise of our nation—a nation where men are permitted to strive for their greatest achievement within their respective capacities. To recount only briefly a few symbols of our freedom and progress during the past half century: we have increased our supply of electrical energy for industry nearly fiftyfold; we have more than doubled the man-hour production in manufacturing; we have more than doubled the real annual income of the industrial worker; and we have reduced the average work week in manufacturing by almost 20 hours. It is even more fantastic to think of the responsibilities that education must assume as its counterpart of past performance in the next long-distance run than to think of its role in the past.

The walls of the minds of men are covered with many scribblings; these scribblings can be made legible if only there is enough light.[1] Whatever may be the hopes, desires, aspirations, or ambitions of American society, be they only in the formative or scribbling state, education will light the way to their ultimate realization.

---

[1] Paraphrased from Emerson who wrote: "The walls of rude minds are scrawled all over with facts, with thoughts. They shall one day bring a lantern and read the inscriptions." See the *New Dictionary of Thoughts*, New York: Classic Publishing Co., 1934. p. 646. The quotation from Ruskin, earlier in the chapter, is on page 151.

SELECTED REFERENCES

AMERICAN ASSOCIATION OF SCHOOL ADMINISTRATORS. *The American School Superintendency*. Thirtieth Yearbook. Washington, D. C.: the Association, a department of the National Education Association, 1952. 663 p.

AMERICAN COUNCIL ON EDUCATION. *Emotion and the Educative Process*. Washington, D. C.: the Council, 1938. 323 p. (See especially Chapters 2, 3, 4, and 10 by Daniel A. Prescott and others.)

COMMAGER, HENRY S. *Documents of American History*. (Colonial Period.) Fifth edition. New York: F. S. Crofts and Co., 1949. 759 p.

ELSBREE, WILLARD S. *The American Teacher*. New York: American Book Co., 1939. 566 p. (See especially Chapters 1, 2, and 11.)

GWYNN, J. MINOR. *Curriculum Principles and Social Trends*. New York: Macmillan, 1943. 630 p. Revised 1950. (See especially Chapter 1.)

KRUG, EDWARD A. *Curriculum Planning*. New York: Harper and Brothers, 1950. 306 p. (See especially Chapters 1, 2, and 9.)

NATIONAL EDUCATION ASSOCIATION AND AMERICAN ASSOCIATION OF SCHOOL ADMINISTRATORS, EDUCATIONAL POLICIES COMMISSION. *Education for ALL American Youth. A Further Look*. Washington, D. C.: the Commission, 1952. 402 p. (See especially Chapters 1, 2, and 5.)

NATIONAL EDUCATION ASSOCIATION AND AMERICAN ASSOCIATION OF SCHOOL ADMINISTRATORS, EDUCATIONAL POLICIES COMMISSION. *Learning the Ways of Democracy*. Washington, D. C.: the Commission, 1940. 486 p. (See especially Chapters 5 and 8.)

NORTON, JOHN K., and NORTON, MARGARET A. *Foundations of Curriculum Building*. Boston: Ginn and Co., 1936. 599 p. (See especially Chapter 1.)

CHAPTER TWO

How Children Learn and Grow

T HE outstanding characteristic of childhood is growth. From birth to approximately age 20, children are passing thru a period of continuous change which differentiates these years from the more stable period of adulthood. One of the main difficulties of the school is that of devising a curriculum which will be effective at successive levels of maturity. To build such a curriculum successfully one must understand how children learn and grow.

First Things First

Children have certain inalienable rights. They have the right to live by a set of values that seem important to their age. To the four-year-old, playing tag is more important—has more value—than learning to read a book. For the ten-year-old, playing ball contributes more to full living than does learning grammatical rules. Children, at each age, have a right to try to experience what is important for them, just as adults of any age have a similar right. The curriculum must take these rights of childhood into account. Perhaps the most successful curriculum would be one which enables children to experience a rich, full, satisfying life each year until they reach maturity. By then they should have learned, from practicing effective living, how to carry on independently as adults. The school should help children to live effectively at each age level. This does not imply that there should be no preparation for future living but rather that preparation for the future should make sense to the child.

Social Outcomes Determine Content

How children learn and grow is not the main factor in determining what the content of the curriculum should be. Rather, what the school puts into its curriculum is decided by the outcomes that society expects from its schools. However, the effectiveness of the curriculum depends in large measure on how well it is adapted to the abilities and interests of children, year by year, as they grow toward maturity. In large part, the child's abilities are the products of growth, but the school must so study children that these abilities may be increased thru the processes of education. While all interests are learned, the child's level of maturity has a marked bearing on the relative ease of developing them. Within rather broad limits set by growth, it is the function of the school thru its curriculum to stimulate interests toward the outcomes set by society.

Learning makes no headway without interest; but interest, per se, does not determine what should be learned. One of the important functions of a school is to interest children in experiences which result in outcomes that are important for them as individuals and as members of society. For example, society has determined that children must learn to read; illiteracy is not compatible with democratic processes. With this policy determined, it is the function of the school to find the level of maturity at which reading may be begun and then to devise ways to interest children in learning to read. With some children the school has been very successful in stimulating interests; with others more ingenuity is required than has so far been exhibited. The psychology of learning has an important part to play in the selection of materials and in determining the sequence and organization of what is to be learned.

Something Is Learned

One basic fact regarding the relationship of the curriculum and the learning process should be made clear at the start. The verb *learn* requires an object. One cannot learn without learning *something*. This "something to be learned" is the curriculum. The determination of the nature of the content to be learned is the primary concern of the curriculum maker. This content may be defined in such terms as school subjects or activities or experiences, but in any case the school must be clear as to *what* is to be learned. The failure to be clear about this has resulted in confusing slogans such as "teach the child, not the subject." There can be no such thing as teaching a child without at the same time teaching him some kind of content, of whatever kind the school may decide. A specific answer to the question, "How do children learn?" can be given only in terms of a curriculum that is to be learned.

How Children Learn

From the very large number of studies of learning, eight important principles will be discussed:

Learning Is an Active Process

Children learn from the things that they do. For more than 50 years psychological studies have emphasized this important principle. What is presented to children in school results in worthwhile learning only if the pupils respond in worthwhile ways. If the curriculum is dull, the child learns to look out the window and daydream to escape boredom. If the curriculum is stimulating, children respond by active thinking and understanding.

In effective schools pupils are continually doing something. It is important to understand, however, that doing something does not always involve overt physical activity. When pupils listen attentively or when they think actively as they read, they are "doing something" just as truly as when they use their muscles. The proponents of the activity movement in education have frequently failed to see this distinction and have emphasized a large amount of physical movement in school.

Certainly there is a place for a normal amount of physical activity in the classroom, but to overlook the importance of intellectual activity in the process of learning is to miss the essence of the "activity movement." It was a reaction against the dull monotony of the intellectual boredom in many classrooms even more than against the admittedly bad practice of keeping pupils seated in rows during most of the school day. Children learn in school the things that they do with their minds as well as with their muscles.

Children learn to solve problems by attacking real problems appropriate to their level of maturity. They learn facts by making use of facts. The facts children cannot use in what they do are soon forgotten. Children learn personality traits, such as fair play, by engaging in many play activities where doing the fair thing is expected and practiced. They do not learn fair play by reading a book about it. They learn to appreciate fine ways of living and things of beauty not only by art instruction but also by living in a school atmosphere where fine living is practiced and where the school environment affords good taste and beauty. Moral and spiritual values are learned thru situations in which the child experiences the satisfying effects of doing the right thing and in which he feels the inner warmth that great moments can bring. In all of these ways the principle of learning by doing is illustrated, whether the doing is mainly physical or intellectual or emotional. The learning process is an active process.

In most schools of 50 years ago the curriculum took little account of this principle of learning by doing. There was no freedom for physical activity and the methods of teaching gave little more freedom for active mental exploration. The tendency to conceive of schools as laboratories for active learning rather than as rooms where children are to sit and be taught is giving a new challenge to the curriculum maker. The possibilities of this vital principle of "learning by doing" are still far from being fully realized.

Learning Is Affected by the Total Situation

One of the classic pieces of research in psychology is Pavlov's experiment on the conditioned response with dogs. Pavlov showed how the flow of saliva, first caused by the sight or smell of food, could then be produced by associating the food stimulus with the sound of a bell. This "conditioned response" of secreting saliva has frequently been described as tho it were entirely due to the stimulus of the sound of the bell. However, if, as the bell sounds, a pair of rabbits were suddenly to race across the room, or if a vicious dog fight were to occur in front of the door, the probabilities are slight that the dog would simply stand still and secrete saliva. The specific response of secreting saliva will result only when the total situation approximates that of the laboratory.

One of the outstanding contributions of research in psychology in the last quarter of a century has been a demonstration of the fact that learning is a product of the total situation in which it occurs as well as of the specific situations which constitute the center of attention. To be effective, learning must be focused and centered on the particular outcomes to be attained. But the total situation in which learning occurs is also a potent factor. Many a specific learning exercise in school has been thwarted by the "rabbits" that flit thru the pupils' minds while the teaching is under way.

34

No curriculum can be effective unless the situation in which it is presented is appropriate to the learning outcomes that are desired. Studies of classroom "climate" have shown how important are friendly relations between the classroom teacher and his pupils. It is difficult to stimulate effective learning in an atmosphere of fear or worry. Good social relationships in a school are important assets to the school's equipment for learning. Likewise, good adjustment at home and in the community outside the school are reflected in the learning accomplished in school. Personality frustrations and inner conflicts produce barriers to learning which even excellent methods of teaching cannot overcome. School counselors often make an important contribution to learning in the classroom by producing adjustments in a child's life which otherwise would frustrate his learning.

The importance of the total situation as it affects learning is equally significant within the area of academic study. The time is gone when education is conceived as a sum total of many specific learnings. The present psychology of learning emphasizes relating specifics to larger areas in order to give greater meaning to education. The correlation and integration of subjectmatter is becoming increasingly common. Specific learnings in the arithmetic class must somehow be accompanied by and result in a kind of quantitative thinking in the total area of social living. The science learned in the high school must be related to the attitudes and beliefs of adults outside the school. One of the very difficult problems of the curriculum maker is to translate this concept of the influence of the total situation on learning in such a way that the program of the schools will be less open to the criticism of being "academic" and "ivory-towered." Some of these points are illustrated by the examples given in Chapters V and VI.

Learning Should Be Meaningful

Children learn best when they understand what they learn. It is, of course, true that they may also learn, in a verbatim way, things that have no meaning at all. Certain nursery jingles of a meaningless variety have been learned by successive generations of children. There is no particular objection to letting children learn nursery rhymes, altho it is the pleasing sound sensation which catches their interest rather than the ideas contained in the verses. However, the serious purposes of the school do not include meaningless outcomes.

If the ultimate outcomes of education are to be meaningful, there is considerable evidence that learning activities should be meaningful at every stage of the process. This implies that the content of the curriculum must be appropriate for the successive maturity levels of childhood. Herein lies a problem of real difficulty.

Much of the recent discussion of the importance of meaningful learning has centered upon the subject of arithmetic because, in the past, it was one of the best examples of a school subject which was taught by the application of memorized rules and by drill on processes that were not understood. Such drill teaching was true at all levels from the primary grades up to high-school mathematics. Children were told to "learn" it now and understand it later when they were more mature. The results were poor retention and a high percent of failure in the subject.

Within the present generation it has been demonstrated that arithmetic may be so organized and taught that it is meaningful to pupils at all grade levels. Furthermore, children not only understand it but they also like it. Understanding and learning are reciprocal. This principle of making learning experiences meaningful is spreading over the whole curriculum. The learning of facts is still important, but an effective curriculum provides for the use of the facts in functional situations where real problems are solved. Recently, several movements have been concerned with producing a more functional curriculum. Their objectives are in line with the concept of meaningful learning (see Chapter III).

Learning Must Be Adjusted to Individual Differences

One of the firmly established facts of psychology is that there are wide individual differences among children in their ability to learn and in their methods of learning. One of the difficult problems of the school is to adjust its work to the individual differences among children who are grouped into a single school grade. For example, the school has a curriculum for Grade IV and yet the individual members of a Grade IV class may vary in ability and achievement from those normally found in Grades II to VI. Furthermore, the individual variations from child to child are extremely complex in character. The oldest child may not be the brightest; the brightest may not be the tallest; the tallest may not be the best reader; and the best reader is not always the best in handwriting. With such an amazing complexity in ability and achievement, the problem of organizing a suitable curriculum for each child seems almost hopeless. However, certain facts stand out rather clearly.

In the main, the correlations among various abilities are positive, even tho often quite low. There are few negative correlations. There is certainly no justification for the popular idea that the beautiful are also dumb; that those possessed of strong backs also have weak minds. It is therefore practical to make some subgroupings to facilitate learning.

Also, within a given grade, individual differences in any trait are distributed somewhat normally. As the deviations from the mean increase, the number of cases becomes fewer and fewer. Teachers must learn to expect a wide spread in the results of learning. In any school grade above the second, approximately one-fourth of the pupils will be as poor or poorer in school achievement than the average in the grade just below and about one-fourth will be as good or better than the average in the grade just above. Beyond Grade IV there is usually a spread of six years or more in any trait that we know how to measure. Test makers have long since learned that specific grade norms must give way to norms that vary as does the group.

Still further, individual differences in ability or achievement are, per se, causes for neither praise nor blame. They simply reflect differences that exist, some of which can and some of which cannot be changed by the school. Terms, such as high and low or good and bad, should give way to terms which simply express the nature of the differences. Individual differences in learning ability should be considered in the same objective way as are color of eyes, height, and such physical factors. Also, individual differences in achievement and ability should be considered in relation to each other. The school should be concerned about average achievement from those of high ability fully as much as with failure of those with low ability. Under the commonly used system of assigning school marks, dull pupils never receive A marks in academic courses. Bright pupils do not deserve any special rank for doing what for them is easy.

In our conception of a democratic society every individual has value, yet our schools sometimes contribute little or nothing to the feeling of personal dignity which even the dull and maladjusted need to develop. An effective testing and guidance program is one method of helping meet the problems occasioned by individual differences among pupils. But the school must also modify or adjust its curriculum and methods of teaching to fit the ways that individual children learn.

A "good" curriculum must be thought of in terms of what is desirable for each type of child. One particular fallacy to be avoided is to assume that the education that was good for teachers is good for every one else. In view of the stated democratic aims of American education, present curriculums still fall far short of meeting the differences in learning ability that are found among people.

Some very significant experiments have shown that generalizations previously thought to be too difficult for dull children to learn may be learned thoroly and be retained when presented in units of reasonable size and by methods appropriate to their level of ability. Dull children deserve a great deal of sympathy in schools, particularly where teachers lack both knowledge of suitable methods and a concern for such pupils. We need to know still more about the ways that children of different ability actually learn and also what motives may stimulate their desire to learn.

Learning Should Result in Versatile, Adaptable Behavior

In a free society the schools do not try to blueprint the way the next generation should think and live. Rather, the purpose of the school is to help each succeeding generation learn how to be versatile and adaptable in adjusting to the new situations that it must face. What kind of education enables children to be versatile? This question is part of the old but crucial issue of transfer of training. The psychology of learning has many studies bearing on transfer and versatility.

In the normal process of learning outside of school, children develop a high degree of versatility. A brief observation of children at play furnishes many examples of this. Nothing is more common than to find even small children using their playthings in ways and for purposes never conceived of by the manufacturer. A tin pan becomes a helmet in war games. Lacking an automobile, the child builds his own soap-box conveyance from an amazing collection of odds and ends. The important point is that the child never was *taught* to do things in these ways. The child learns many specific, concrete ways of doing things, but he soon extends his activities into forms of behavior that were never learned as such. He does this by seeing the relationships that exist in his concrete experiences and then applying these relationships or generalizations to new problems never encountered before.

The school, at its best, should enable pupils to extend their learning in the same way that is normally done outside of school. Certainly no school can teach all the specifics that will be needed thruout life. It must teach the important things that are needed for independent, versatile living. The main job of the curriculum maker is to find what content is most valuable in leading to these ends. What skills, what facts, what generalizations must be learned? There is considerable agreement at some points and a great deal of uncertainty at others. This question is discussed further in Chapters III, XI, and XII.

No one can be versatile and adaptable in our society unless he can read and write. Illiterates are blocked at every turn of the road. The ability to read gives one an amazing freedom in finding solutions to problems. Arithmetic, if it is really learned, also supplies a tool for independent behavior, not only in enabling one to make the frequent computations necessary but also to do a type of quantitative thinking that is essential to adjustment in a technological age. Education has a solid foundation in subjects such as these, altho there are other important, less tangible goals.

There is much more difficulty in reaching other goals of education. For example, how do children learn to adjust their inner conflicts so that they may find mental poise, peace of mind, and inner happiness when they encounter the unpredictable frustrations and troubles that life holds for everyone? How do children learn interpersonal relations that lead to good family and community living? How do people learn to meet new social, economic, and political problems? These things are not attained by learning specific patterns of behavior to be followed as stereotypes, but rather by learning general principles of behavior that can be applied in a great variety of specific new situations.

A good example of the difference between stereotyped (specific) learning and versatile (general) learning is the way one learns good manners. Many people attempt to learn good manners by reading a book on etiquette and then behaving in stereotyped ways according to the specific instructions in the book. Other people may or may not read a book on etiquette, but soon discover a general principle of behavior in social situations, namely, that good manners always require kindness and consideration to the other person. Kindness and consideration are thus learned as a generalized pattern of behavior which is then applied in a variety of particular ways but always so that the other person will be made to feel at ease. In fact, on some occasions the kindest thing to do is to violate a specific rule of etiquette.

It is easy and satisfying to teach specifics. Things that are concrete are easier to learn than things that are abstract and general. A basic amount of concrete learning is needed because such learning is the necessary foundation for generalizations. Furthermore, as one of our elder statesmen recently pointed out, each new generation must learn for itself that the stove is hot. However, it is the generalizations, not the specifics, that furnish the tools for versatile and adaptable behavior. It is as important that the curriculum end with the abstract and general as it is that it begin with the concrete and particular. This is the way children learn normally outside of school.

The function of the school is to so improve on everyday experience that a child will learn in twelve years what would require many life-times to learn outside of school. Furthermore, one of the most important objectives of education is to learn how to learn, so that after leaving school one will be equipped to continue to learn thruout life. The reasons why the old concept of formal discipline was rejected need to be understood clearly. Too many people still think that one kind of curriculum content is as good as another just so it exercises or "disciplines" the mind. However, it is not a case of "strengthening" the mind but rather of giving the learner habits of work and kinds of content that have such wide, general values that they may be transferred broadly.

The selection and organization of curriculum content are keys to a superior education. They are important in the classroom (Chapter VIII) as they are in the school system as a whole (Chapter III).

There Are Various Types of Learning

It helps to understand the way children learn if one analyzes the learning process into a number of rather clearly differentiated types. It should be understood, of course, that such a classification into categories is artificial in the sense that the number of divisions may be increased or decreased and also that certain similarities characterize all types of learning, such as the need for motivation, the necessity of active participation, and the necessity of practice in most cases. A common classification of types of learning uses the following four subtypes, but a given learning situation may involve several types.

1. *Learning which includes those forms of behavior that involve overt muscular responses;* for example: learning to swim, ride a bicycle, do handwriting, play a piano, and operate a lathe.

2. *Learning that is mainly verbal and involves association and memory;* for example: learning number facts, the spelling of words, foreign language vocabularies, names, places, dates, and formulas.

3. *Learning characterized by the process of thinking, either in the development of new concepts and understandings or in the solving of problems;* for example: the inductive development of concepts in a science class or the deductive reasoning in solving problems in geometry. Learning of this type requires more generalizing than do the former two.

4. *Learning involving the acquisition of taste or appreciation for those values which society holds high;* for example: learning to appreciate good music or to develop a taste for good art or literature. Less is known about this type of learning than the other three, but it is of major importance for a good society.

All children do not learn skills, facts, methods of thinking, and standards of appreciation in the same ways. Different methods of teaching, different equipment, and different purposes characterize these four types of learning. Learning to appreciate good music is not accomplished simply by reading a book; and learning to solve problems is more than memorizing rules. In Type 4 learning, it is of special importance that schools pay attention to the role played by peer groups, as related to the development of attitudes, personality, and character.

The curriculum can be planned effectively only when the types of learning necessary for implementing it are clearly understood. The classroom teacher must apply this conclusion with his pupils as well as the general curriculum committee in reaching its decisions.

Limiting Factors Govern What Can Be Learned

The child learns only by responding to stimulations which he receives thru his sense organs. Of the various possible sense avenues, the eyes and the ears are the child's main contacts in the school. Furthermore, the great bulk of the education carried on in the schools is acquired thru the medium of language, and the major part of this is attained thru reading. In the history of the human race, reading is quite a recent accomplishment. Only within the last 200 years has the quantity of material to be read posed a problem.

A typical eighth-grade pupil, reading the usual length of line, will make approximately eight eye-movements per line. On a 30-line page this means 240 consecutive precise adjustments of the eye. Reading 10 pages requires 2400 such movements; an hour's reading frequently mean 50,000 such muscular adjustments. Never in the whole history of the race has such a burden of close work for eyes been remotely approached. Yet the school expects children to do such work many hours per week.

Prior to the middle of the past century courses of study for high schools and for colleges were the same for all students with no electives offered. Furthermore, there was little library reading to do. A few textbooks contained the content to be learned. Now, with the advent of the elective system, the programs in high schools and colleges have become heavy and complex. With the immense increase in knowledge, new chapters and new courses have been added to what was included before. When the load became impossibly heavy, resort was made to "survey courses," in which a whole field of knowledge was condensed into a one-year or one-semester course.

Yet, in the face of all this increase in content to be learned, the human individual has evolved no new powers to cope with it. There is no evidence that children have more native mental ability now than when the content of education was less. In basic structure they have essentially the same eyes, ears, and nervous systems that children in simpler cultures have had. How far can the school increase the load of learning that pupils are expected to acquire? What sacrifice in terms of superficial understandings is to be made in order to cover broader areas of content? How much pressure can pupils take?

Cleveland Press, Cleveland, Ohio

No one can be versatile and adaptable in our society unless he can read and write. The ability to read gives one an amazing freedom in finding solutions to problems.

It is a cruel thing to press students to learn more than their ability permits. It is not only cruel but also stupid. There is a relationship among such factors as amount to be learned, time available for learning, and ability to learn. With an optimum relationship among these three factors the outcome may be thoro understanding at a level of relative permanence. Under poor relationships among the three factors the outcome may be a superficial confusion with no permanent values. Many of our "experiments" with the curriculum are not experiments in the scientific sense. There are no controls and there is no body of precise evidence from which generalizations are possible. The reaction against specialization has often produced such a condensing of content into short periods of time that the only result is another form of specialization—a specialization in superficialities. At the high-school and college levels survey courses have frequently imposed loads on students without concern for their ability to carry such loads and with no provision for individual differences among the group of learners.

One of the really serious problems of the curriculum maker is to resolve the impasse between increasing amounts of new knowledge and the student's rather static biological ability to learn. In part, schools are trying to solve the problem by improving the technics of teaching. But the possibilities in this direction are quite severely limited. The nub of the problem is what to do with the great increase in knowledge that is still accelerating rather than tapering off. What is most important to learn? Is it preferable to learn thoroly what is learned, even tho the scope is less, and trust to transfer and versatility for the remainder? The main hope seems to be in this direction.

Emotional and Social Learning Are Important

The last 30 years have witnessed a marked increase in studies of the emotions in relation to education. The nature of emotional development is still not too clearly understood and the measurement of emotional maturity is at about the same stage as was the measurement of intelligence when the Binet tests were first used in this country. Both motivation of learning and social adjustment have their origins in the emotions. The nonacademic curriculum of the school not only is motivated by the emotions but its very content

44

has to do with the education of the emotions and the development of personal-social adjustments.

Society is interested in the quality of the person graduating from its schools quite as much as in his academic competence. The quality of the person is, however, not solely an outcome of academic learning. The personal traits which are esteemed, such as courage, self-reliance, unselfishness, and the characteristics which make for good human relationships, are all qualities that are learned. Altho schools have been urged repeatedly to provide for these learnings, there is still little systematic provision for them in the curriculum.

At the present time the principal method of providing for improved personal-social education is thru counseling and guidance services. These have accomplished much, but in the main they operate only after there is sufficient maladjustment to produce referrals to the counseling service. The schools cannot forever let such maladjustments continue to the breaking point before attempting to meet the problem. Sooner or later, there must be an effective curriculum for personal-social education that parallels the academic curriculum.

The school teaches such subjects as spelling, reading, and arithmetic by a sequential organization of subjectmatter by which the child is carried, grade by grade, to the final goals of accomplishment. While the education of emotional and personal traits may involve different modes of learning than in the case of academic learnings, there is no reason to be complacent with the lack of experimentation with some organized and sequential attack on the problem. We need to know the kinds of experiences by means of which such traits are learned and also the levels of development, grade by grade, that are reasonable.

Obviously one would expect different levels of behavior in personal-social traits with successive stages of maturity, but such levels are as yet undefined. Eventually they must be as clearly understood as are stages of development in reading and arithmetic. An experimental approach to a curriculum of experiences that will lead to desired outcomes in respect to quality of the person being educated is as necessary as has been the experimental approach to the academic curriculum. Personal-social traits are learned and the school must intensify its efforts to develop curriculum experiences which help to develop superior personal characteristics.

How Children Grow

It is difficult to draw a sharp line between changes brought about by growth and those brought about by learning. In some ways it is not important to attempt a differentiation; but in other ways it is quite important that the distinction be drawn in order that lines of responsibility may be clear. The number and approximate time of eruption of the permanent teeth are controlled by *growth*. A child cannot learn to have more than the normal number nor can he learn how to get them all at age six. Biological growth is the controlling factor here. On the other hand, children do not acquire the ability to read simply by growing in a normal, healthy way. Children *learn* to read; the alternative is illiteracy.

It is true that learning and growth are related. One recognition of this relationship is found in the concept of "readiness" to learn. The curriculum maker must give serious attention to the sequence of the different kinds of content that are introduced in the school. While stage of maturity is one factor in determining readiness, there are also others, such as background experience and method by which the new content is to be taught. Fortunately, one of the valuable contributions of the last quarter of a century has been a large increase in our knowledge of how children mature and of the relationship between maturity and learning.

The school is greatly interested in providing conditions that facilitate growth, but beyond this the responsibility is nature's. On the other hand the school, not nature, is responsible for a good program of learning for children. The school will succeed better in its part of the task if it understands the nature of growth and if it sets its objectives in accord with interests and abilities that characterize the successive maturity levels. The school must accept and respect these characteristics of maturity levels. Its program must be flexible enough to harmonize with the basic facts of growth.

Growth Is Gradual but Not Uniform

Drawings of children found in books published a century ago often look like miniature adults. In fact, it was not until about that period that many artists became aware of the differences in body proportions between children and mature persons. The usual concept of the growth process was that growth was similar to the

46

stretching of a rubber band—uniform in all parts. One of the important findings of students of the growth process is that while growth as a whole is a gradual process, it proceeds at different rates for different body parts and at different ages. These segmental differences in growth are of great importance to the school, because it is thus that children vary in body types from age to age. The "stripling" appearance of children during early adolescence is due to a relationship between limb length and body length which characterizes that particular stage of maturity.

Furthermore, individual differences in body build at the same level of maturity reflect varying combinations of segmental development. The growth process is far more complex than that suggested by an analogy of stretching a rubber band. Children frequently seem to be more aware of these body differences than are adults, as indicated by the commonness of such nicknames as Skinny, Tubby, Slim, and Shorty. These physical differences are found within a single class as well as among various grade levels.

Girls and Boys Mature at Different Rates

Studies of physical and physiological growth show that girls mature at a more rapid rate than do boys. This fact is shown clearly in growth curves for various aspects of development. For example, x-ray photographs of the carpal bones in the wrist, show differences in rate of development between boys and girls as early as age three. The greater maturity of the girls' wrist bones increases year by year until by age 16 the girls' bones, on the average, are from one and one-half to two years more mature than those of boys of equal age. Likewise in eruption of teeth and in physiological development girls are consistently more mature than boys of the same age until full maturity is reached for both. There is of course wide overlapping between the sexes for all growth factors but, in general, girls mature at a more rapid rate than boys. This difference in physical maturation rate is reflected in intellectual and social interests, and should receive more attention from the school than is ordinarily the case.

For a period of about three years, from age 11½ to 14½, the average girl is taller and heavier than the average boy of corresponding age, owing to the earlier arrival of the adolescent spurt

47

in growth. The maturity differences at these ages are great enough to produce a problem of social adjustment between boys and girls on the same chronological age, as classroom teachers in Grades VII, VIII, and IX are well aware. In spite of the fact that girls are farther along in their growth cycle than are boys, the school usually places the same load of work on both and measures their achievement by the same standards. Some of the advantages of coeducation are lost when teachers fail to give consideration to the maturity differences between boys and girls of the same age.

Individual Differences in Rate of Maturing Are Wide

Even more striking than the differences between the sexes are the individual differences in rate of maturing for both boys and girls. For example, in one high school the school physician reported a range of five years in date of first menstruation among 487 girls, the earliest occurring at age 12 and the latest at age 17. This means that one girl of 12 and another of 17 were at the same level of physiological development. Differences of three years are common. Comparison of maturity differences by use of numbers fails to indicate the many ways in which the effects of such differences are apparent in the interests and activities of children. The games they play, the books they enjoy reading, their choice of companions, the spread of their interests are definitely related to level of maturity. Such individual differences, overlapping in marked degree from grade to grade, not only impose difficulties for curriculum construction but also require great sensitivity and flexibility among classroom teachers in adjusting a curriculum to individual needs. One of the marked contributions of the child development movement of the last two decades has been an increased understanding of children, particularly in respect to individual differences which are due to different rates of growth.

One further aspect of individual differences needs special mention. Children are sometimes judged to be brighter or duller than they actually are, owing to precocity or retardation in growth. Many classroom teachers confuse maturity with intelligence and many school principals have listened to mothers' explanations that their children are not really dull but are only slow in developing. Sometimes they are right, but not always. Research studies show positive,

48

but very low, correlations between level of intelligence and physical maturity at any given age. Curriculum adjustments for learners who are dull must be differentiated from adjustments for pupils who are only slow in maturing.

Growth Affects Learning in Many Fields

Since language is a learned activity, it furnishes a good example of the close relationship between growth and learning. Language is a mode of expression which can develop only as the individual has something to express. Studies of language have traced in great detail the changes that occur from the first physiological cry, thru the vocal expression of emotional feelings, the stage of babbling, the imitative expression of a few words, the slow and difficult organization of speech units, until eventually a mature language is attained. While learning is an important factor in language development, it must proceed in harmony with the growth stages of the child. The language arts program is dependent to a large degree on the stage of development and the readiness of the child. Evaluation procedures also are related to language development (see Chapter XI).

Studies of the development of drawing ability and of number ability also show clearly marked levels of development that correspond with the maturity of the learner. In drawing, children pass thru stages of scribbling, schematic representation, logical realism where they show both ears in a facial profile, two dimensional representation, and finally visual realism with perspective. Likewise in learning numbers, children begin with a stage of one-to-one representation and proceed thru rather clearly marked levels to the stage of dealing competently with the four fundamental operations. Learning programs must have respect for the process of maturation if they are to be successful.

Dilemmas of Curriculum Construction

The task of constructing a curriculum encounters certain dilemmas in over-all strategy which this yearbook makes no pretense of having resolved. However, any serious effort to improve the curriculum cannot overlook choices which must be made nor the resulting problems which such choices entail.

Adjusting to the Increase in Knowledge

One of the perennial obligations of schools in any society is to preserve and transmit to the next generation the gains in knowledge and skill which the race has achieved up to the present time. This is no static function; it is not preserving the "dead past." Rather, it is preserving the means of growth. By thus inheriting a body of scientific knowledge, a highly developed language, and intricate mathematics, a wealth of art and literature, each new generation is able to ride on the shoulders of previous generations.

However, the very extent of this inherited intellectual capital poses one of the most difficult problems for the curriculum maker. No longer can he simply add a new chapter to the textbooks in history and science to record new achievements. The school program has long since become too crowded to permit the addition of new courses to keep pace with the accumulation of new knowledge. The elective system, which 50 years ago seemed to offer some relief, has so narrowed the scope of knowledge and experience common to all learners that, even now, communication among the educated becomes difficult. The question, "What knowledge is of most worth?" can no longer be evaded.

General education and survey courses provide current answers to the dilemma. Yet, these may become so packed with more and more content, much of it abstract in character, that the learning which results faces the danger of becoming more and more superficial. If, for the sake of thoroness in learning, a smaller curriculum coverage is chosen, what will be omitted and what retained? These are issues which go to the heart of anyone's theory of education. The answers cannot be given arbitrarily or quickly, but they must be sought earnestly. This is the "great debate" in education.

Individual Differences in Our Society

We are committed to the concept that every individual has dignity and worth. What does this mean for the curriculum? The schools have accepted differentiation thru the elective system, but with no very clear principles to guide the choice of content. We have often passed on to the pupil the important and difficult decision as to what to elect. We have defined equality of opportunity in terms of years of schooling with the simple faith that if pupils stay in school until age 16 or 18 society is meeting its democratic obligations. Honest thinking prevents the acceptance of so simple a solution.

We are committed to equality of educational opportunity. What then constitutes such equality? Does opportunity to take the present high-school program satisfy? We have provided certain alternatives, chiefly of a vocational nature. But difference in vocational outlook is only one of the many differences among learners. We have had 40 years of study of the psychology of individual differences, resulting in findings that are important for the curriculum maker. Yet there is no agreement on what education should be common to all learners and what differentiations should be made to meet variations in ability. The proposed remedies range from a still further extension of the elective system to a curriculum which is, at heart, the same for all people at any time and in any place. This dilemma must be included in the great debate.

Academic Subjects and Personality

A third major dilemma for the curriculum maker is how to provide a curriculum which meets the demand for scientific knowledge in the various fields of learning and also for the development of desirable personal characteristics. Certainly in a society such as ours the demands for a scientific education are well grounded. But equally strong are the arguments for developing those spiritual and moral values that are needed to develop a superior person. How can a curriculum meet both of these needs? As of now, the academic program seems to be in more healthy shape than the program for personality development. Both must be strengthened.

Three major curriculum issues have just been mentioned. Others, equally important, could be added. With the heavy load of knowledge and skills that now crowds the curriculum, and with a future that holds only more and more such content, what is the school to do? Keeping in mind that the total curriculum will always be limited by what an individual mind can learn, the school may have to discover some new hypothesis to solve the problem. Perhaps we must give up the belief that all of this content *can* be learned in school. As an alternative we might examine the hypothesis that the most important obligation of all is to help the child *learn how to learn* and develop a desire to continue learning. If this could be done thru helping him learn a limited sample consisting of the most significant part of the available knowledge and experience, and to do this with thoroness, he might then leave school with confidence that he knows how to learn other things as the necessity arises. If the sample were well chosen, the learnings might transfer to the unpredictable experiences that life will bring, so as to produce a versatility of behavior more valuable than the superficial understandings that are the outcome of an overcrowded curriculum. Obviously, there must be always a content to be learned, but there is no possibility of complete coverage.

There are things that are learned directly and are used in the same form as they are learned. Spelling, typewriting, the name of the capital of the United States are learnings of this kind. There is a considerable total of this specific type of learning and it is important. However, the great bulk of the learning that is carried on in schools is not of this directly applicable kind. Rather, it is learning which has its chief value in general understandings, general methods of work, general habits of thinking, and general attitudes and values which are widely transferable to specific needs that no school can foresee. General understandings, habits, and values must be developed thru many specific experiences, but they will endure, if learned thoroly, long after the specifics thru which they were learned are forgotten. An effective curriculum must rest on a clear understanding of the nature of learning.

SELECTED REFERENCES

ANDERSON, G. LESTER, and GATES, ARTHUR I. "The General Nature of Learning." *Learning and Instruction*. Forty-Ninth Yearbook, Part I, National Society for the Study of Education. Chicago: University of Chicago Press, 1950. Chapter 1, p. 12-35.

ANDERSON, JOHN E. "Child Development and the Growth Process." *Child Development and the Curriculum*. Thirty-Eighth Yearbook, Part I, National Society for the Study of Education. Bloomington, Ill.: Public School Publishing Co., 1939. Chapter 1, p. 15-49. (Now available from the University of Chicago Press, Chicago, Ill.)

ANDREWS, T. G.; CRONBACH, LEE J.; and SANDIFORD, PETER. "Transfer of Training." *Encyclopedia of Educational Research*. Revised edition (Edited by Walter S. Monroe.) New York: Macmillan Co., 1950. p. 1483-89.

BROWNELL, WILLIAM A., and MOSER, HAROLD E. *Meaningful vs. Mechanical Learning*. Research Studies in Education, No. 8. Durham, N. C.: Duke University Press, 1949. 207 p.

DOUGLASS, HARL R., and SPITZER, HERBERT F. "The Importance of Teaching for Understanding." *The Measurement of Understanding*. Forty-Fifth Yearbook, Part I, National Society for the Study of Education. Chicago: University of Chicago Press, 1946. Chapter 2, p. 7-26.

HILGARD, ERNEST R. *Theories of Learning*. New York: Appleton-Century-Crofts, 1948. 409 p.

MELTON, ARTHUR W. "Learning." *Encyclopedia of Educational Research*. Revised edition. (Edited by Walter S. Monroe.) New York: McMillan Co., 1950. p. 668-90.

NATIONAL SOCIETY FOR THE STUDY OF EDUCATION. *Adolescence*. Forty-Third Yearbook, Part I. Chicago: University of Chicago Press, 1944. 358 p.

OLSON, WILLARD C. *Child Development*. Boston: D. C. Heath Co., 1949. 417 p.

PERKINS, HUGH V., JR. "Effects of Climate and Curriculum on Group Learning." *Journal of Educational Research* 44: 269-86; December 1950.

CHAPTER THREE

Organizing the Curriculum

A WRITER describing the curriculum is in much the same position as the stranger from abroad who asked an American
political scientist how, in the few days at his disposal, he could get
the best understanding of a large city. The political scientist replied:

> Understanding any large city presents difficult problems. Probably the most
> important thing for you to do is to look at the city from several different vantage
> points. Spend some time in the downtown business area. Then be driven out a
> mile or two from the business district and travel thru the blighted area. Later,
> move out perhaps ten miles to the new residential areas and drive around the
> outer circumference of the city. Perhaps, with these samplings you may get some
> understanding of the social forces that make up a large city.

Similar advice seems good for the school administrator alert
to curriculum problems. Looking at the curriculum from several
vantage points will give a better understanding than an attempt
to use a single focus.

Curriculum problems are knotty, complex, difficult. Few school
administrators will be able to devote full time and energy to these
problems. The administrator, like the foreign visitor, must strive
for perspective. The issues are numerous, the times uncertain,
and the evidence inadequate. Under such conditions a clear view
of a few prominent issues is essential. This chapter attempts to
help in obtaining such a view by discussing four questions: (a)
What learning experiences are of most value? (b) What are the
patterns of curriculum organization? (c) How are experiences
organized for teaching? and (d) Where are the experiences provided?

What Learning Experiences Are of Most Value?

In recent years the curriculum has been most commonly defined
as all of the directed learning experiences of children and youth
under the influence of the school. Stated another way, such a
definition indicates that "the school's curriculum is the total of
those situations which are purposely used to produce favorable

learning responses."[1] Such definitions imply that some school experiences are of more worth than others and that someone must decide which experiences will be "purposely used" or "directed." This raises the fundamental curriculum question: What learning experiences are of most value?

Herbert Spencer propounded almost the same question nearly a century ago when he asked: What knowledge is of most worth? The years since Spencer asked this question have brought forth new knowledge at a tremendously accelerating pace. In Spencer's time, one man might be able to develop an acquaintance with most knowledge. Today we recognize this dream as an impossibility. No man today can know all that is known. Each individual exercises choice in what he decides to learn. Schools have difficult choices to make as they plan the curriculum.

How are these choices to be made? In simple terms, the formula is as follows:

1. Decide on the school's objectives.
2. Determine what learning experiences will best achieve these objectives.
3. Organize the experiences for teaching and learning.
4. Judge whether the objectives are attained.

Stating the formula is easy. Getting the formula into functional operation is very difficult. The goals, the learner, the classroom teacher, the instructional materials, and methods of evaluation must all be considered—as they are elsewhere in this yearbook. But the fundamental question is: What are the objectives? Until that question is answered, no decision can be reached on what learning experiences are of greatest value.

Objectives are value judgments. They represent choices by human beings. Accordingly, objectives will be determined from a variety of sources because people are influenced by many different factors (see Chapters XI and XII on evaluation).

Earlier chapters have provided a general background for the consideration of general objectives of education. A few examples will suffice to illustrate the sources from which such objectives can be selected.

[1] Buswell, Guy T. "Organization and Sequence of the Curriculum." *The Psychology of Learning*. Forty-First Yearbook, Part II, National Society for the Study of Education. Bloomington, Ill.: Public School Publishing Co., 1942. Chapter 13, p. 446.

One source of objectives is the accumulated knowledge of the scholars. Subjectmatter specialists, particularly, have developed a vast reservoir of knowledge. From this reservoir, information to be learned and understandings to be gained can be selected. Schools have always used the writings of specialists to aid in the selection of objectives that are geared to subjectmatter.

Other scholars, too, have provided sources for objectives. Philosophers and psychologists, for example, are particularly helpful. A philosophy that stresses maintaining the status quo will emphasize objectives of obedience, while a philosophy of change will emphasize independence. Psychologists contribute to the determination of objectives by aiding with studies of grade placement, forgetting, and transfer of training.

Another source for objectives is an analysis of society. Our society is a democratic one. We believe in human freedom. Because of the nature of our society, schools consider teaching democracy as a fundamental objective.

Our society is confronted with difficult problems growing out of technological factors, the international situation, the findings of science, and the nature of rural and urban life. Because of these contemporary problems, schools emphasize the use of intelligence in solving problems as another objective.

Our society finds many people in conflict. Strife is prevalent in families, between races, among nations. Schools, as a consequence, stress objectives that attempt to improve the quality of human relationships.

The nature of the learner provides another source for educational objectives. The findings described in the previous chapter lead to accepting the child as he is and assisting his growth and development. This concern for the individual tends to emphasize objectives of personal growth, physical well-being, personal integrity, vocational skills, and esthetic expression as in music, art, or literature. The recognition of the emotional problems of children and youth causes objectives of emotional adjustment and meeting basic needs to receive greater attention.

Educational objectives provide the foundation for all curriculum planning. There is danger, however, that objectives will be stated as generalized platitudes which may have little influence on the individual classroom teacher or the particular school. Increasingly, therefore, after decisions have been made on general objectives, these generalizations are separated into statements of anticipated behavior. The objective "to develop critical thinking" yields subordinate objectives such as these: understanding how to define a problem, how to state alternative solutions, how to reach a conclusion; developing *skills* in selecting sources of data, in taking notes, in reading charts; gaining *attitudes* of respect for evidence, of respect for the opinions of others, of willingness to submit one's opinions to group study and group judgment.

Another problem in stating objectives will be to maintain a reasonable balance between social and individual objectives. This issue of individual versus society will also arise in connection with individual and group learning experiences and with organizing these educational experiences. The frequent recurrence of this problem in curriculum matters should not be surprising, however, since our democratic society is based on a twofold search for the "blessings of liberty" and a concern for the "general welfare."

What learning experiences are of most value? One answer is those experiences which will best attain the objectives agreed upon.

What Are the Patterns of Curriculum Organization?

A great variety of curriculum patterns can be noted in American schools. *The Dictionary of Education* defines 12 patterns of curriculum organization based on the type of learning situation and includes more than a dozen other expressions which are commonly used in discussions of curriculum organization.[2]

The permutations and combinations possible among this variety of patterns may not all have been tried in the schools. Observers, however, are struck by the fact that many different combinations are being tried. Sometimes different names are applied to the same general practice with resultant confusion. There are certainly semantic difficulties when school people discuss the patterns of curriculum organization.

Numerous attempts have been made to classify the bases of curriculum organization. A realistic classification encounters diffi-

[2] Good, Carter V., editor. *Dictionary of Education*. New York: McGraw-Hill Book Co., 1945. p. 113-14. For our purposes here the 12 curriculum patterns defined are: activity, broad-fields, child-centered, community-centered, core, correlated, experience, fused, integrated, pupil-teacher planned, subject (traditional), and unified.

culty because pure theory is not found in practice. Actual school practices sometimes do not win the hearty support of those primarily concerned with theory. Within a single school different plans of curriculum organization are occasionally found. In spite of these difficulties, certain issues about curriculum planning are clarified by an analysis of current curriculum patterns. The role of subject content, the place of activity or experience, the relation of planning by teacher and pupils, attitudes toward pupil interest, and viewpoints toward time allotments can be noted by examination of the common methods of curriculum organization.

Observation of school practice gives some clues or trends that may assist in analyzing the many curriculum plans that are found. Four central patterns seem to be in use:

1. The subject curriculum
2. The broad-fields curriculum
3. The core curriculum
4. The experience curriculum.

Listed in this way, as discrete patterns, one might get the erroneous impression that the subject curriculum avoids experience or that the experience curriculum does not employ subject content. One might, similarly, get the idea that broad-fields or core programs have by some magic avoided subjects or experience. Such implications miss the point of the analysis. Each curriculum pattern employs subjectmatter; each pattern makes use of experience. In every curriculum plan, content is employed, pupils engage in some type of activity, the interest of pupils is sought, teacher-pupil planning can be done.

One could, also, in viewing these four patterns assume that they represented a hierarchy or a continuum—that somehow as a teacher improved in educational skill he moved from "subjects" along a road with stations at "broad-fields" and "core," arriving finally at full maturity to "experience." This assumption would be considered false by some educators. These patterns represent distinctive ways of organizing a curriculum. While there are relationships, priority can be given only by individual judgment until more scientific evidence is available. The analysis by patterns is valuable in bringing out the central emphases and the relative weighing of the significant elements.

While the present, healthy tendency seems to be to seek ways of unifying the strengths claimed by proponents of different plans, it is well to realize that some of the major cleavages of educational opinion for past decades have been over matters of curriculum organization. The search for new patterns grew out of protests against actual school practices that were blamed for inadequate pupil learning. Protesting groups usually have vigor and vehemence. Clashes are inevitable. In the final evaluation, conflicting claims will have to be judged on the basis of available evidence.

The Subject Curriculum

The subject curriculum is the most widely used type in American schools. It is the oldest form of curriculum organization and maintains a vigorous, healthy existence in spite of continuous attack from critics. In this pattern each subject, or subject field, exists as a relatively independent teaching area. Each subject receives a time allotment. Each subject is believed to have a logic and organization of its own. As pupils grow in maturity, it is assumed that each subject can be studied systematically in successive years.

Mathematics, language, history, geography, science, and the other subjects are viewed as essential features of both elementary and secondary schools.

Because the subject curriculum has been in existence for a long time, there is danger that critics may attack practices that either no longer exist or are gradually disappearing. Curriculum workers in the subject fields have been unusually active over a long period of time. As a result, while retaining the advantages of logical systems of knowledge, these experts have also made innumerable studies of organization and content until today it is possible to teach subjects by psychologically sound methods and to use content that is defensible both in terms of social values and in terms of pupil maturity.

The chief purpose of the subject curriculum is for the pupil to gain information and understanding altho he may also learn skills and appreciations when the teaching is effective. Explanation has been the chief teaching method but is no longer the only teaching method. Problem solving, units, and laboratories are used by many subject teachers.

The continued persistence of the subject curriculum can be attributed to the following factors:

1. The scholarly disciplines from which the subject content is drawn represent the accumulated reservoir of human experience. The heritage of the race is included in language, mathematics, science, art, literature, history, and other subjects.

2. Organized subjects provide a coherent, logical, systematic plan which aids the classroom teacher and the learner. Orderly continuity is provided, since learning can proceed from the simple to the complex. Subjects can be taught in creative, psychologically sound ways and the content can be related to the daily life of the child.

3. The subject curriculum has strong public support because parents and other school patrons understand this organization. It is the kind of school pattern with which they are familiar.

4. The training and certification of teachers and the consequent habits of teachers tend to reinforce the subject pattern.

5. The habits and training of school administrators give similar reinforcement. Most administrators were at some time classroom teachers of a subject. The scheduling of classes under subject patterns rarely requires attempting any unusual innovations. The strongest consultation service administrators can get frequently comes from subject specialists.

6. Textbooks, pamphlets, audio-visual aids, tests, and the other instructional aids are more readily available for teaching particular subjects than for other types of organization.

7. Associations of subject teachers give valuable help thru their magazines, conventions, yearbooks, and other useful sources.

In spite of the age, popularity, and strengths of the subject curriculum, several objections are commonly made:

1. Much of the subjectmatter taught in a given field may be meaningless for children. Since systematic study of the subject is the central vehicle in daily practice, the learners' interests and special abilities may be neglected. Children may be studying matters about which they have little experience or interest. Under such conditions learning becomes memorization and understanding is not developed.

2. The subjectmatter may be compartmentalized and fragmentary. In life situations, knowledge from several subject fields is usually required. A study of taxation, for example, requires not only knowledge of arithmetic, but knowledge of history, government, economics, sociology, plus the ability to use language.

Subject teaching tends to deal with pieces rather than with wholes. There are so many important subjects today that the daily program of the child may become broken up into too many tiny pieces.

3. Logically-organized subjects may neglect significant social problems. Recent events may not have found a place in the subject as taught. Science may be out of date. History may not deal adequately with the twentieth century. It is hard to disrupt the old for the new. Students may know more about feudalism than they do about labor unions. They may know more about algebra than they do about wise purchasing. Race relations, safety education, and atomic energy may be neglected.

4. The classroom teacher who is well informed on a particular subject may not understand enough about the pupils being taught. With the center of teaching focused on a subject, that subject may become more important than the child. The teacher may not be as well grounded in child growth and development as he is in art, music, or geometry. Since the pupils may be with the teacher for only a portion of each hour of the day, it may be impossible really to know the children well enough to help them.

5. Teaching by subjects often does not emphasize thinking. Memory, drill, and understanding the thoughts of others tend to be more prominent than individual thinking. The search for evidence, the analysis of alternate solutions to problems, the testing of conclusions may take a subordinate role. The mastery of facts and principles may satisfy teacher and student; the use of facts and principles may not receive attention.

To all these criticisms the advocates of the subject curriculum reply, "Most of these defects may also be true for other types of curriculum organization. Good teaching will negate these difficulties." Their search, therefore, is to find ways of improving the quality of teaching. Their wrath is turned against the classroom teacher who still assigns "five pages for tomorrow."

Others, however, respond to these criticisms in a different way. They say in effect, "The persistence of these criticisms over a fairly long period of time is evidence that there is some truth on the side of the critics. Maybe, there is a better way." They turn their energies toward developing other patterns of curriculum organization.

The Broad-Fields Curriculum

The accusation that subject teaching was fragmentary and compartmentalized gained support as new subjects were added to the curriculum. The newer subjects decreased the time available for any one subject. Fragmentation grew worse. More compartments were necessary. One answer seemed possible—combine subjects.

61

These efforts at combining subjects took several directions. Correlation, fusion, integration, and broad-fields approaches were tried. Unfortunately, in practice the terms were used almost synonymously depending upon the current fad in a particular locality.

Correlation—This plan usually means an honest attempt to bring out the reciprocal relationships among subjects. A standard example is to teach United States history and American literature so that they reinforce each other. The literature teacher stresses the historical background or setting for a piece of literature. The history teacher makes use of historical novels and points up the influence of literary writers on historical events. These relationships may be taught incidentally, but in best practice, thru committees, teachers plan definitely to achieve as large a degree of correlation as possible.

Fusion—The fusion pattern usually means that several subjects previously taught separately have been combined into a single course. Thus the American problems course is a combination of government, economics, and sociology. Biology is a combination of botany and zoology. The physical science course is a combination of astronomy, physics, chemistry, and geology. In some cases social studies have been fused with English, or social studies, science, and art have been combined. Sometimes these courses represent actual fusion, sometimes the parts are only taught as related units and really represent a correlated approach.

Integration—The term "integration" usually has meant a fused course that combines content from diverse subject fields as in the example of social studies, science, and art in the paragraph above. Ignoring subjectmatter boundaries has been the key concept. Actually there has been considerable criticism of the use of the word "integration" as a curriculum pattern.[3] Those who object contend that "integration" applies to a process which occurs within an individual and should not be applied to the process of combining subjects. Nevertheless, the term continues to be used.

Correlation, fusion, and integration are not really patterns of curriculum organization. They are rearrangements applied to the subject pattern. The type and character of these rearrangements have been significant factors in the improvement of instruction, but

---

[3] For example, *see:* Hopkins, L. Thomas, and others. *Integration.* New York: D. Appleton-Century Co., 1937. 315 p.

rarely have the readjustments gone far enough to justify the idea of a "pattern." The readjustments have been widely made in the broad-fields curriculum.

The so-called "broad-fields curriculum" stresses relationships among subjects. Under this pattern the curriculum is built around a small number of major areas instead of the many subjects. By grouping related subjects the number of fields taught is reduced from more than a dozen to five, six, or seven. Under the broad-fields plan each subject actually loses its identity and becomes an integral part of the newly created field.

The broad-fields pattern is not new. Its history can be traced backward for nearly 80 years.[4] Thruout the twentieth century the idea has received attention at the college, secondary-school, and elementary-school levels.

In the public schools a typical broad-fields curriculum might consist of these six areas:

1. Social studies
2. General science
3. Language arts
4. Health and physical education
5. General mathematics
6. General arts.

The chief purpose of the broad-fields curriculum is to retain the values of logical, systemized knowledge while achieving freedom of action within the broad fields. Thus, in the language-arts field, spelling is reinforced because it is related to reading and to writing. Spelling learned in isolation is believed to have less value. The principal advantages claimed are: (a) there are fewer compartments in the curriculum so that teachers spend longer periods of time on any one field; (b) topics for study tend to be more general in nature; and (c) understanding of generalizations or developmental processes are emphasized instead of memorizing isolated details.

The chief criticisms of the subject curriculum apply in modified form to the broad-fields pattern. Altho compartmentalization and fragmentation are reduced, they still exist. The subjectmatter may be devoid of meaning for the children. Significant social problems may be neglected. Teachers may not get to understand pupils. Thinking may be neglected.

The severest critics contend that broad fields, in practice, are too frequently glorified subjectmatter departments which have merely

---

[4] Smith, Bonnie Othanel; Stanley, William; and Shores, J. Harlan. *Fundamentals of Curriculum Development.* Yonkers-on-Hudson, N. Y.: World Book Co., 1950. p. 403-404.

changed their labels in order to retain vested interests. Some who recognize the merits of the broad-fields approach are critical because the field of study is still more important than the learning process or the needs and interests of the pupil.

Fundamentally, it must be recognized that the broad-fields curriculum is basically planned around organized human knowledge. The worth of this form of curriculum organization depends ultimately upon the judge's opinion of the worth of subjectmatter organized into systematic fields.

The Core Curriculum

At the present time the phrase "core curriculum" is used in so many ways that it is impossible to know what the user means by it until the actual practices in his school are examined. The core curriculum has been used to describe a group of required subjects. The broad fields are sometimes, erroneously, called core courses. Correlated, fused, and integrated courses have been designated as core courses. Courses which have been developed by a system of free planning of pupils and teacher are called core courses. Administrative plans which leave pupils with one teacher for longer periods of time have used the same name. At one stage the term core seemed to be acquiring the meaning "any type of curriculum innovation which differs from a strict subjectmatter approach." Such a term, meaning only "something different," is not satisfactory as a basis for classifying curriculum organization.

Is there anything fundamental about the core pattern? Does it differ from the subjectmatter, the broad-fields, or the experience patterns? In some actual practice, as well as in the minds of some theorists, the core *is* a distinct form of curriculum organization. The contention is that the distinctive feature lies in the emphasis upon the presentday needs of America and the world. The uniqueness of the core pattern is that it is centered upon life today, according to these educators.

Advocates of the core curriculum believe that schools should deal with socially significant content—especially in a time of great social transition. They abhor, particularly, subjectmatter which is unrelated to current social needs. They believe that teachers should employ methods that stress reflection about the essential needs of a democratic society. At the same time they are opposed to "turning the school over to the kids." They believe that adults, especially classroom teachers, make a major contribution to the planning of an educational program. They recognize that having pupils share in the planning of classroom and school activities is sound educational practice, but insist that teachers participate in this process, too (see Chapter VIII).

The core curriculum represents a reaction against the "subject-centered" patterns and the "child-centered" school. The core curriculum is not new; it has merely attracted unusual attention during the past decade in the secondary schools. Core-type programs have been employed fairly extensively for the past two decades in elementary schools under such names as "areas-of-living," "integrative core," "social living themes," or "centers of interest." The core idea has gained strength, undoubtedly, because of the uncertain social times of this century.

The core idea represents a reaction against the neglect of such important phases of living as home and family life, diet, housing, accident prevention, and technology. It is a product, in part, of the plea that schools assume greater social responsibility so that democracy may survive. Advocates of the core idea point out that "many of the most pressing social needs faced by our society were almost completely ignored by the school."[5]

On the secondary level, core programs are usually organized around units or problems, such as: propaganda, universal military training, marriage and family, unemployment, housing, making machines serve mankind, and civil liberties.

In the elementary school, areas of living or centers of interest have included: (a) protecting life and health, (b) living in and improving the home, (c) conserving and improving material conditions, (d) cooperating in social and civic action, (e) getting a living, (f) securing an education, (g) expressing religious impulses, (h) enjoying and expressing beauty, and (i) engaging in recreation.[6]

The primary purpose of the core, then, is to provide a common body of socially significant experience for all pupils, emphasizing social values or social problems (see Chapters V and VI).

---

[5] Caswell, Hollis L., and Foshay, A. Wellesley. *Education in the Elementary School.* Second edition. New York: American Book Co., 1950. p. 241.

[6] Frederick, O. I., and Farquear, Lucile J. "Areas of Human Activity." *Journal of Educational Research* 30: 672-79; May 1937.

Because the "common body of socially significant experience" is believed to be necessary for *all* pupils, the "core" usually is required of all pupils and occupies a considerable portion of the school time, usually from one-third to one-half the day.

To the query, "Are not reading, arithmetic, history, literature, and science socially significant?" the believer in core would reply in the affirmative but would stress that some decision has to be made as to whether pupils will read about comic heroes, Eskimos, the Middle Ages, or transportation. It is in this type of decision that the core proponent wants greater influence.

Advocates of the core curriculum emphasize the following values:

1. Socially significant content represents the best content of the subject fields because selection is made in terms of social need.

2. The recognized values of pupil planning and sharing are conserved but not carried on to absurdity as may happen in some child-centered schools.

3. The nature and length of the classes enables teachers to understand pupils better, so that guidance becomes an actuality and not a plan on paper.

4. The pupils experiencing core classes are able to cope with presentday social problems because they have learned to think within a democratic framework.

Critics of the core pattern, often defenders of the subject, broadfields, and experience patterns, argue that:

1. In actual practice content is exceedingly meager. Subjectmatter is not well selected in terms of problems. There is "a watering-down" process. The coverage of important experiences is inadequate.

2. Most schools do not have adequate instructional materials to conduct core classes. Some critics are doubtful that the materials exist at present.

3. Classroom teachers are not trained for core teaching. So much general knowledge is required of the core teacher that no one person can know enough to deal adequately with all the problems studied. Not enough teachers are well equipped to handle discussion, guidance, and reference activities.

4. Either there is not enough recognition of pupil interest, or there is too much recognition, depending on the critic's point of view.

5. There is no adequate provision for sequential learning. Pupils do the same things year after year and grow toward maturity in a haphazard manner.

Resolving the conflicts between critics and supporters of the core is probably impossible at the present time. Core programs have not been tried under a sufficient variety of conditions to evaluate results

In preparing for the business world this young student has learned to operate a ton of machines, mastered 500 keys and levers, and written 12 miles of shorthand.

fairly. The theoretical premise that a distinctive curriculum pattern can be developed around problems of presentday life is sound and justifies continued exploration and experimentation.

The Experience Curriculum

The idea that pupil needs and interests should provide the basis for the curriculum has been a catalytic agent in American education. The idea has influenced each of the curriculum patterns discussed above. Proponents of separate subjects, broad-fields, and core programs have attempted to make adjustments so that pupil needs and interests, would be utilized. Important modifications in school practice can be traced to this idea.

These curriculum patterns, however, have not been satisfactory to the believers in the fundamental nature of pupil needs and interests. For them, the needs and interests of pupils are the only sound basis for the curriculum (see Chapter II).

From observation of the practices in American schools, however, it appears that this is more of a theoretical pattern of organization than an actual one. The school that really operates solely on the basis of pupils' needs and interests is rare. Except for the strictly experimental schools, this plan of organization has not been widely used. It is more talked about than practiced. Activity curriculum, child-centered curriculum, and experience curriculum are names that have been used to designate this pattern. The name *core* has been applied to some of these programs on the secondary level.

The basic purpose of this pattern is to insure learning by engaging only in those activities that are related to the real interests or needs of the pupil. Granted this fundamental purpose, another aspect of the activity curriculum becomes apparent: the curriculum can be planned *only* by a teacher with a particular class. Any other planning will be restrictive of pupil needs and must therefore be eliminated. The classroom teachers must be free to assist pupils with those activities which they think are desirable. Any curriculum guide, course of study, or general framework is considered undesirable. The curriculum is not to be considered planless since pupils and teacher spend many hours in careful planning.

Does this complete emphasis on pupil interest as the center of the curriculum mean that there is an unawareness of social problems and values? No. Frequently, supporters of this pattern are among the most socially-minded people. Their position, however, is that any personal need leads naturally to issues of social problems and social values, but that a child can get social understanding only by starting with his own interests or needs. In fairness, it should be noted that these interests are not to be confused with whims, fancies, or fleeting interests. Significant interests lead to worthwhile action.

Since pupil-teacher planning predominates in this curriculum pattern, certain methods are essential. These methods emphasize problem solving, group activity, and laboratory technics.

The major criticisms of the experience pattern center around two questions:

1. How are decisions made as to which needs will provide the basis for the curriculum?

2. Does this approach assure that the child will receive a well-rounded education?

When a classroom teacher tries to develop an experience curriculum, decisions have to be made as to what the needs of a child are and which ones shall be selected for emphasis. How is this to be done? The theory is that the classroom teacher and class will do this together. The critics are suspicious that much of this decision-making is really done by the teacher—unconsciously or thru cunning devices. As evidence they point to the fact that successive classes of a particular teacher seem to be doing similar things year after year. They reason, therefore, that actually the decisions are based on the classroom teacher's experience and that he is really using some basis other than pupil needs. This other basis, they contend, is really borrowed from some other pattern of curriculum organization. The logical conclusion from such criticism is that it is not possible to have an activity program because, at one extreme, one cannot really tell what pupils' needs and interests are or at the other extreme, individual differences in needs will be so great as to prevent using interest as the major emphasis.

The other major criticism starts with the assumption that pupil interest can provide the basis for sound teaching. These critics point out, however, that pupils tend to follow certain interests over very long periods of time. As a result, other experiences which may be more important are neglected. An interest in athletics or movie stars, if pursued persistently, can be so time-consuming that art, music, or contemporary affairs are neglected. If these things are not explored during childhood and youth, they may never be developed. Observers point out that children learn "interests" much as they do other things, hence the establishment of interests is one of the tasks of the school.

To these criticisms the supporters of the activity program have one reply. The needs and interests of children represent the only fundamental basis of learning. Neglect these needs and interests and learning does not take place. They point to an adult's lack of interest in science, literature, history, or social problems and say, "This adult went thru your preplanned curriculum. Look at the result. All he knows today is what grew out of genuine interest. Everything else that you planned so carefully has been forgotten. Why do you persist in imposing these wasteful procedures?"

What Questions Must We Answer?

The schools are engaged in a titanic struggle as they attempt to increase the efficiency of learning. Disagreements are plentiful. The search for evidence is increasing. What are the crucial questions that administrators are trying to answer as they experiment with different patterns of curriculum organization? Around what issues will the decisions on the fundamental worth of each pattern be reached? The following questions seem to be among the most pertinent:

1. Who decides what is to be taught in a school? What is the appropriate role of the pupil, the classroom teacher, the school administrator, and the layman?

2. What is the proper relationship between subject and child? How are individual need and social need brought into harmonious relationship?

3. How can contemporary social life and its problems be best utilized in the curriculum? When is it of most value for pupils to analyze social problems?

4. Should the curriculum for a school system be organized by a single pattern from Grade I thru Grade XII? Would there be advantages to using different patterns at different grade levels?

5. How is information acquired? How can the understanding gained from books be enriched by other kinds of experiences?

6. How is thinking taught? Can habits of effective thinking be developed?

7. How long should one teacher be with a given group of pupils? Part of a day? All day? One period? A semester? Several years? Can a teacher really understand pupils without watching them grow over long periods of time?

8. Can the virtues of subjectmatter, social significance, and pupil interest be brought into better harmony?

The manner in which the foregoing questions are answered will determine the future patterns of curriculum organization.

How Are Experiences Organized for Teaching?

The curriculum viewed from another level shows variation in the ways experiences are organized for teaching. In some schools the classroom teacher relies chiefly on the textbook as the organizing guide. In other schools, courses of study or curriculum guides of various types are available. In many schools some types of units are employed. There seems to be general recognition that a teacher requires and deserves some assistance in the organization of experiences for teaching.

The Textbook

American schools certainly have not discarded the textbook. The observer of many schools is impressed that the textbook is still the most widely used device for organizing teaching experiences. Its use is apparent at the elementary-school level; it is dominant at the secondary-school level.

The textbook writers are the experts who have largely decided how materials should be organized for instructional purposes. The persistent use of textbooks is a tribute to the textbook publishing industry and to their authors. As new ideas have gained acceptance, textbooks have been modified to keep abreast of these advances. Parents who have not seen a textbook since their own school days usually have been impressed by the quality and attractiveness of modern books. These books, however, are not infallible. It would be a rare author who would contend that he had included all the desirable ideas in one book. Most authors encourage wide reading plus other learning activities. In view of recognized limitations of the textbook, it is startling to find so many mature and experienced teachers still using one book as the single basis for organizing instruction.

In spite of the educational zeal that has been used to improve the curriculum, it may be that not enough attention has been given to effective ways of using textbooks. A significant literature has developed concerning ways to use audio-visual materials. One who searches for similar guidance on using a textbook encounters disappointment. Little has been done with this subject for the past 10 years.[7] Teachers, however, have continued to use textbooks as their main source of instruction. Perhaps it is time to revive some of the materials, on how to teach by a textbook, that were used effectively more than a quarter of a century ago.

Courses of Study and Curriculum Guides

For many years the course of study was the chief aid given to classroom teachers for organizing instruction. Recent changes in form, purpose, and methods of producing these guides are well known. Preparation by central-office authorities has been supplanted by production by teachers either thru committee procedures or by the participation of all teachers. The newer courses of study take the form of suggested ideas rather than compulsory ones.

As curriculum revision programs have concentrated on getting people to work together on common problems, questions have been raised about the efficacy of courses of study, curriculum bulletins, and other guides. Do they serve a useful purpose?

While it may be true that older courses of study have been merely "dust collectors," this should not be interpreted to mean that these materials are worthless and that schools should abandon their production. Such materials are especially valuable for:

1. The classroom teachers who participate in the preparation of the materials.

2. The teachers who are seeking help on the things they are teaching. If good curriculum guides are not available, they may choose their help from less desirable places.

3. The classroom teachers who are new to the profession or new to a school system. These beginning teachers find security in having courses of study to assist them with their planning. By means of courses of study these teachers can be stimulated to prepare their own material since they need not follow such courses slavishly.

4. The school patrons who are worried about what is being taught in the schools.

The course of study and the curriculum guide still serve useful purposes. Their preparation should not be eliminated. Produced by

---

[7] Notable exceptions are: Cartwright, William H. *How To Use a Textbook*. Washington, D. C.: National Council for the Social Studies, 1950. 6 p. ¶ Phi Delta Kappa. "What Are Textbooks For: A Symposium." *Phi Delta Kappan* 33: 241-306; January 1952.

group procedures and supplemented by other good, inservice education procedures, these carefully planned aids give help to many classroom teachers.

Unit Plans

The unit as a means of organizing instruction has come into widespread use. As with other educational movements, a host of types of units exist. Most of these units, in spite of different names, can be grouped into two types: (a) teaching units and (b) resource units. The essential difference between these units is in their purpose, altho they differ also in content and form.

The teaching unit is designed as a teaching plan—somewhat akin to the lesson plans of an earlier day. In contrast, the resource unit is not designed as a specific teaching guide. Rather, it is a compilation of a wide variety of materials, activities, and teaching aids, prepared for classroom teachers—to assist in their plans for teaching a specific unit. The resource unit is used as a basis for classroom-teacher preplanning; this preplanning is essential before pupil-teacher planning in a classroom is undertaken. Put another way, the resource unit supplies a reservoir of ideas to assist the teacher in the process of developing specific plans for teaching a unit.

Because the resource unit is currently one of the most acceptable types of supplementary assistance available to classroom teachers, the usual contents of it are mentioned here briefly:

1. *An introduction* provides an overview of the central problem or topic of the unit and an indication of the reasons for its study. The significance of the unit in relation to the total school program or a specific course is usually stressed.

2. *A statement of objectives* or learning outcomes of a rather comprehensive nature is usually developed under three divisions—understandings, attitudes, and skills. From these the teacher and class plan the objectives to be emphasized in their own study of the unit.

3. *An outline of the content,* or of the problems to be considered, is included. The intent of this part is to give an indication of the range of material which may be included in the unit rather than to present a logical teaching outline.

4. *A list of suggested activities* of considerable length is developed. These suggested activities help account for the popularity and usefulness of resource units. There are many more activities than one teacher with one class can possibly use. The activities represent the most workable ideas that successful teachers are sharing with other teachers. The activities are self-contained in the sense that all pertinent information needed to use the suggestions with a class are

included. Frequently the activities are divided into three groups: those for introducing the unit, those for working on the unit, and those for culminating the unit.

5. *Evaluation materials* also form a useful part of the resource unit. A variety of types of evaluation instruments are sometimes included. More samples are available than a teacher can use. Ideas for evaluation of outcomes that cannot be measured by paper and pencil tests are usually suggested.

6. *A bibliography* of useful books, pamphlets, and visual aids comprises another portion of the resource unit. These bibliographical items usually have been tested by the contributing teachers in actual classroom situations. Ordinarily, therefore, they are quite useful to the teachers. Many hours of previewing materials are avoided thru the pooled experiences and judgments of teachers as represented in the bibliography.

An important element in the success of the resource unit has been the sharing of the ideas of classroom teachers. Some of the better resource units have been prepared in workshop sessions by classroom teachers brought together for this purpose. This method of preparation has been effective but there is still a scarcity of resource units. This raises a serious question: Who should prepare resource units?

At present, resource units are being prepared by local school systems, state systems, business, labor, and governmental organizations, as well as individual schools participating in special studies. Nevertheless, resource units are not plentiful. There is need for bringing together able classroom teachers and scholars for the production of resource units. A well-organized effort with adequate financial support could render a service to teachers if resource units could be increased in number and made more generally available. The possibility of a national commission, created to develop resource units, merits careful consideration. One approach might be to free outstanding teachers and scholars from their teaching duties and bring them together for lengthy periods of work to develop these units.

One unique feature of some resource units should be noted. This feature is the scholar's presentation of the content.[8] As the first part of a unit, a recognized scholar has prepared an accurate, up-to-date, summary statement about the topic. This statement supplies the latest and the most reliable information for teachers. This portion

---

[8] For example, see the resource units developed by the National Association of Secondary-School Principals and the National Council for the Social Studies, *The Problems in American Life Series,* and the resource units on local government published by the National Council for the Social Studies in cooperation with the Maxwell School of Citizenship.

of the unit refreshes the classroom teacher's previous knowledge and brings recent information to her attention. This scholar's presentation can assist materially in meeting the criticism that a teacher cannot possibly know enough to teach effectively under some of the newer patterns of curriculum organization. The knowledge of the scholar is brought to the aid of the teacher. The scholarly presentation as a part of the resource unit is a recognition that classroom teachers need help—not only *with teaching methods* but with basic subject content, too.

Where Are the Experiences Provided?

A child learns by experience, both direct and vicarious. The school tries to provide significant experience. Where does this experience take place? The answer to the question provides another perspective on the problem of organizing the curriculum.

From the preceding discussion of curriculum patterns and curriculum aids one might get the impression that teaching in the classroom is the only important place for pupils to gain experience. Subjects, textbooks, units, and activities tend to call to mind classroom experiences. In recent years, however, there has developed a general recognition that learning experiences other than classroom experiences have educative value.

Look across America. Where are the pupils getting their experience? In schools, of course. But what about the bus load of pupils leaving the county courthouse? Are those children in school? What about those boys working in that auto factory? Are they students? What about those girls leaving school at noon to serve as secretaries in business offices during the afternoon? Are they getting their experiences in school or out of school? Those children at the "tot lot" in the city slums—are they in school or are they playing hooky? Is a class visit to the zoo education or recreation?

Where are the learning experiences provided for our children? Investigators for the Educational Policies Commission, reporting on their search for effective civic education practices, grouped school practices into three major categories: classroom activities, out-of-class school activities, and school activities in the community.[9] They

---

[9] National Education Association and American Association of School Administrators, Educational Policies Commission. *Learning the Ways of Democracy.* Washington, D. C.: the Commission, 1940. p. 127-328.

found, as other observers have, that the school walls are no longer a demarcation line between school and nonschool activities. The modern school provides experiences for children in many places, mostly in the school, but frequently away from school.

Experiences Within the Classroom

The classroom is the center of instruction. Here reading and arithmetic are learned. History, mathematics, literature, music, art, and vocational education also are taught in classrooms. Sometimes these classrooms are barren places with little equipment and slight contact with the real world. Ideally, they are places rich in such equipment as books, pamphlets, and audio-visual aids.

At their best, classrooms are laboratories of democratic living. The atmosphere is friendly. Students and classroom teachers feel at home. There is respect for individual worth. Working together is emphasized. The individual classroom is the heart of the curriculum (see Chapter VIII).

Experiences in the School but Not in the Classroom

School life outside the classroom has become a powerful educative force. The out-of-class activities of the secondary school are well known. Student government, athletics, musical events, clubs, and school publications have captured the fancy of youth and adults. The school cafeteria and the school corridor have achieved status as places where education takes place.

Less well recognized, perhaps, are similar activities on the elementary-school level. Yet, a study in Texas showed that more than 40 different activities were carried on by Texas elementary schools *outside the classroom.*[10] Assembly programs, safety patrols, student councils, clubs, and the Junior Red Cross are examples of the fact that elementary schools now have a thoro-going out-of-class program.

Life in the school but outside the classroom has become an important part of the curriculum pattern.

The examples given in Chapters V and VI touch upon some of the first-hand experiences within the school and outside in the community.

[10] Otto, Henry J. *Principles of Elementary Education.* New York: Rinehart and Co., 1949. p. 228.

Experiences Away from School

The slogans "the community school" and "youth serving the community" have underlined the educational truth that out-of-school experiences give vitality to school activities. Spectacular achievements with housing, neighborhood beautification, and safety projects have dramatized the educational power that exists when youth is mobilized for social good.

Work-experience programs have demonstrated that the job and the school program can be brought into harmony for the benefit of pupil, school, and industry.

Field trips have shown their power to enrich learning but the failure to provide these direct experiences for many pupils has been noted.[11] Camping, as a school activity, is gaining momentum. The community is part of the school curriculum.

From the Past to the Future

Decisions on curriculum patterns and ways of organizing experiences for teaching need to be made with consideration of where experiences will occur. Limiting experiences to the classroom type neglects some valuable learnings. Advocates of experience programs and proponents of core plans tend to emphasize the facility with which out-of-class and out-of-school experiences can be included within their plans. But many teachers using subject or broad-fields patterns have found effective ways to develop experiences that go far beyond classroom activities. Regardless of the curriculum pattern, these efforts to make greater use of a variety of experience help to achieve more effective learning.

From this attempt to get perspective on curriculum matters the Commission now turns to the question: What will the future of curriculum organization be? What directions should be taken in the years immediately ahead? Perhaps the best general agreement can be had on these propositions:

1. Teaching by subjects now predominates in American education and will probably continue to predominate in the foreseeable future. Consequently, it is imperative that curriculum workers assist class-

---

[11] Collings, Miller R. "Exploring Your Community: A Direct Experience Study." *Journal of Educational Research* 44: 225-30; November 1950.

room teachers to teach subjects more effectively than has been done in the past. Some of the criticism of subject teaching is deserved, but could be avoided by improved preservice and inservice education. Able classroom teachers teach pupils effectively thru subjects.

2. The vitality of the American school is in part a result of freedom of experimentation and exploration that has existed during this century. The variety of curriculum patterns noted is a healthy symptom of this freedom. No one pattern has been proved distinctly better than all the others. The tendency of some lay organizations to attempt to force a return to the traditional subject curriculum of an earlier date is, therefore, cause for deep concern. In terms of the best interests of children, schools should be encouraged to try different patterns of curriculum organization.

3. The curriculum worker must continue to recognize that learning occurs in places other than classrooms. Experiences in school but not in the classroom and experiences away from school deserve more attention in modern schools than they now get.

4. Classroom-teacher participation in these curriculum activities has proved to have great value. As participation has increased, the quality of instruction usually has improved.

5. Classroom teachers need assistance with their curriculum problems. Textbooks, courses of study, and units are of help to teachers. It appears that the resource unit has merits that have not been adequately explored. This type of unit has important possibilities for bridging the widening gap between the scholar and the public-school teacher, to the end that schools may be provided with the best available instruction.

SELECTED REFERENCES

ALBERTY, HAROLD B. *Reorganizing the High School Curriculum.* New York: Macmillan Co., 1947. 458 p.

CASWELL, HOLLIS L., and OTHERS. *Curriculum Improvement in Public School Systems.* New York: Teachers College, Columbia University, 1950. 462 p.

FAUNCE, ROLAND C., and BOSSING, NELSON W. *Developing the Core Curriculum.* New York: Prentice-Hall, 1951. 311 p.

GWYNN, J. MINOR. *Curriculum Principles and Social Trends.* New York: Macmillan Co., 1950. 768 p.

HANNA, PAUL R., and OTHERS. *Youth Serves the Community*. New York: D. Appleton-Century Co., 1936. 303 p.

KRUG, EDWARD A. *Curriculum Planning*. New York: Harper and Brothers, 1950. 306 p.

NATIONAL EDUCATION ASSOCIATION AND AMERICAN ASSOCIATION OF SCHOOL ADMINISTRATORS, EDUCATIONAL POLICIES COMMISSION. *Education for ALL American Youth—A Further Look*. Washington, D. C.: the Commission, 1952. 402 p. $2.

NATIONAL EDUCATION ASSOCIATION AND AMERICAN ASSOCIATION OF SCHOOL ADMINISTRATORS, EDUCATIONAL POLICIES COMMISSION. *Learning the Ways of Democracy*. Washington, D. C.: the Commission, 1940. 486 p. $2.

PIERCE, PAUL R. *Developing a High-School Curriculum*. New York: American Book Co., 1942. 367 p.

SMITH, BONNIE OTHANEL; STANLEY, WILLIAM O.; and SHORES, J. HARLAN. *Fundamentals of Curriculum Development*. Yonkers-on-Hudson, N. Y.: World Book Co., 1950. 780 p.

SPEARS, HAROLD. *The Emerging High School Curriculum and Its Direction*. New York: American Book Co., 1940. 400 p.

STRATEMEYER, FLORENCE B., and OTHERS. *Developing a Curriculum for Modern Living*. New York: Teachers College, Columbia University, 1947. 558 p.

TYLER, RALPH W. *Basic Principles of Curriculum and Instruction*. Chicago: University of Chicago Press, 1950. 83 p.

WRIGHT, GRACE S. *Core Curriculum Development, Problems and Practices*. U. S. Office of Education, Federal Security Agency, Bulletin 1952, No. 5. Washington, D. C.: Superintendent of Documents, Government Printing Office, 1950. 104 p. 30¢.

WRIGHT, GRACE S. *Core Curriculum in Public High Schools*. U. S. Office of Education, Federal Security Agency, Bulletin 1950, No. 5. Washington, D. C.: Superintendent of Documents, Government Printing Office, 1950. 32 p. 15¢.

CHAPTER FOUR

Mobilizing for Curriculum Improvement

CHANGE is inevitable. The nature of organized society and its progress demands change. The school is a part of society. As society changes the school must likewise change. The big question, then, is "What kind of change in the school is necessary in order that it may play its part in society?" The task of the educator is to see that the changes are constructive and point to the desired end. Curriculum planning, in the light of presentday demands of society, is the school superintendents' means of causing the school system to meet the needs of the times.

The Superintendent Should Lead

Essential as it is for every school superintendent to have a clear concept of the purposes of education, it is quite another thing to put into effect, thru organizational structure, the things that he knows to be good. Many school administrators who desire to improve the instructional program, generally spoken of as the curriculum, never get around to it on an organized all-school basis. Indifference, and sometimes a belief that the instructional program is a function of the classroom teacher only, account for some of these failures. Many capable superintendents, however, desire to conduct programs of curriculum study and improvement but lack the actual knowledge of how to get started and how to proceed to a successful conclusion. Many feel that they cannot employ a specialist to conduct the work.

The brief discussion of practices which follows is intended to give the busy school administrator quick reference to a few plans of operation for which he himself can furnish leadership and in which he can have confidence. It is unlikely, however, that any specific plan should be expected to meet the full needs in any given situation without proper adjustment. By adapting general principles to local needs the superintendent can demonstrate his leadership.

Some Outstanding Organizational Plans

There are many acceptable types of curriculum planning and improvement. Outstanding among them is the systemwide plan of causing the entire school system to move toward improvement with everybody working in the program. The theory behind this plan is that there is learning thru participation; that instruction improves with classroom teacher growth. The systemwide plan lends itself especially well to the process of changing the curriculum design or pattern in a school system as discussed in Chapter III. A school system, characterized by specific subject emphasis but desiring to move into one of the more recent curriculum patterns (e.g., broad fields, core, or experience), will find this plan quicker and probably better than some of the others. Other school systems that have been conducting excellent curriculum-improvement programs for years and that are now well launched upon a particular philosophy of instruction may find more help in an approach thru the type initiated by the classroom teacher or the individual school type of curriculum improvement.

In any event, a reasonable amount of systemwide unity should prevail. Even in the individual school approach, there is no need for several schools to be "way out in front" while other schools in the same system remain far behind. An effective program, whether all-school or individual school, will allow for diversity, flexibility, and individual school initiative and still retain unity under administrative leadership. Unity of purpose and function, operating under the same educational philosophy and administrative policy, should enable any individual school to progress at its own rate in the way of educational program, but no individual school within a modern school system should be allowed to remain static and ineffective. The school system should provide an educational "floor" below which no school should be allowed to remain, but each school should establish its own "ceiling." Unity—not uniformity, is desired.

The various plans for initiating curriculum improvement in a school system, in the order discussed in this chapter, are: (a) the systemwide plan, (b) the inservice growth programs, (c) the practices that begin in the classroom, (d) the programs that begin in individual schools, and (e) the special-interests beginning. Each of these will be given brief attention.

The Systemwide Plan

In organizing for the systemwide or all-school type of curriculum planning, it is wise to establish a policy of procedure if the school system does not already have one. Such procedures will encourage conformity to the general educational philosophy of the school system and facilitate unity of purposes. Cooperative preplanning of this type will reduce the amount of revision and correctional work later. Caution should be exercised at this point, however, to guard against the major program becoming the development of policy or the preparation of principles or objectives. School systems have been known to spend so much time planning that they never reached the main program.

Guides for curriculum planning—Statements of policy differ widely in content and in form, but for illustrative purposes a brief set, which draws from several lists, is given below. Many good sets may be found in recent literature.[1]

1. The purpose of curriculum improvement is to lift the quality of all the activities carried on under school auspices, looking toward an increase in pupil growth and achievement.

2. The curriculum should be so planned as to produce the kind of education desired for the school; that is, it should be in conformity with the evolving philosophy of the school.

3. The entire community—school staff, lay citizens, and pupils where they can play a part—should assist in determining the nature of the curriculum.

4. Since the actual methods and technics of getting desired results from the curriculum are highly complicated, the selection and application of these constitute a professional job.

5. Curriculum improvement, including research and evaluation, is a continuous process.

6. There is no substitute for administrative leadership in curriculum improvement.

7. Curriculum improvement must be meaningful and promising to classroom teachers.

8. Findings of scientific research should be respected and incorporated into curriculum plans.

9. Learning activities should be selected on the basis of pupil needs, if these needs are interpreted broadly enough to include society's needs as well.

---

[1] For example: Caswell, Hollis L., and others. *Curriculum Improvement in Public School Systems.* New York: Teachers College, Columbia University, 1950. p. 38-40, 242. *See also:* Barr, A. S.; Burton, William H.; and Brueckner, Leo J. *Supervision.* New York: D. Appleton-Century Co., 1947. p. 629-55.

10. The curriculum should be sufficiently flexible to enable each classroom teacher to plan in accordance with new situational demands and changing needs of pupils. Teaching units, materials, aids, and supervisory assistance should replace some of the more rigid courses of study. At the same time, these individual classroom adjustments would revolve around certain basic, over-all policies.

11. The sequence of learning experiences must be in accordance with the developmental level and readiness of the child.

12. The curriculum should provide for differentiated teaching and learning.

As the curriculum work proceeds, those who are involved will find that frequent reference to the policy or guiding principles will improve direction, continuity, and unity. The superintendent of schools should find his part in the program facilitated by establishing such guides as a part of the school function. Direction will be found in them, yet there will be sufficient leeway to provide for initiative and creativity. It must be remembered also that curriculum policies and principles may change as conditions change.

Providing leadership—After principles have been established, or possibly even before, the most likely question to loom before the superintendent is: Who is to take charge and direct the program? One essential is that someone be in charge who is clothed with sufficient administrative authority to get things done. Principle 6 above states "there is no substitute for administrative leadership." If the school system is not too large, the superintendent himself may find genuine enjoyment and professional satisfaction in directing the program. The work is interesting and refreshing and it usually draws him into a closer relationship with classroom teachers. As the superintendent launches the program, his job becomes one of discovering and developing leadership, calling conferences, authorizing or appointing necessary committees, providing money and materials for operation, securing assistance, and giving participants a feeling of satisfaction and security in the accomplishment of valuable work.

In a large school system the superintendent may have to delegate actual leadership to an assistant superintendent, a curriculum director, a coordinator, or regardless of title, to a person who is qualified to coordinate and direct the program. In some situations, it may be necessary to place a local person in administrative charge and bring in a specialist from a nearby college or university to provide expert instruction and guidance.

Many school systems that have engaged in large-scale curriculum programs recently have found it expeditious to establish a curriculum council which is representative of all divisions and levels of the educational staff. In Battle Creek, Michigan, where a program of this general type has been in operation, the representation is by buildings, and the council is a policy-making body which utilizes sub-committees for working on specific problems. Such a council can be very valuable in planning, serving as a clearinghouse, and in providing motivation and encouragement.

Creating the machinery—After the basic principles have been agreed upon and adequate leadership has been established, machinery must be organized to provide opportunity for achieving expected improvement. Each school will likely find a pattern of organization to fit its own purposes, but some rather characteristic plans have been used. In discussing such plans it should be kept in mind that this particular type of curriculum-improvement program under consideration at present is the systemwide one which is very effective in changing curriculum design. In such a plan the chief hypothesis is that all participate. After all, curriculum improvement can take place only in the classroom. As teachers change their beliefs and practices—as teachers grow in knowledge and concepts—instruction improves. By encouraging all teachers to participate in the curriculum program, growth takes place in and thru teachers. They must have conviction that change is desirable and will result in improvement and they must learn how to guide the new curriculum as it develops.[2]

In order to provide the opportunity for everyone to participate, school systems have organized the entire faculty into committees according to teaching fields. All fourth-grade classroom teachers, for example, may constitute horizontal committees. Among other tasks, horizontal committees sometimes work on the scope of the curriculum while vertical committees may consider the sequence. This kind of committee organization may work well when the major task is that of constructing curriculum guides or resource materials.

Other school systems have found success in organizing by buildings with the principal or an outstanding classroom teacher in charge. As pointed out earlier in this chapter, on an all-school basis,

---

[2] Caswell, Hollis L., and others, *op. cit.*, p. 49.

this plan should work well if sufficient coordination is provided. It is usually considered undesirable for wide degrees of difference to exist between schools in such a program, in that no school should continually lag far behind.

Another plan of operation is that of the organization of committees by types of work choices. Classroom teachers who desire to work on related interests may be grouped together.

Still another plan is that of having suggestions originate with the curriculum council after which committees are appointed or elected to do the work.

Regardless of the machinery agreed upon, it must be adapted to the situation and to the nature of the program in each individual case. Furthermore, constant watchfulness with adjustments from time to time is essential for continued success. The examples in Chapters V and VI illustrate some of these points.

Producing materials—To considerable extent the production of materials, such as curriculum guides, units, and resource materials, is a technical job. Some classroom teachers have had training and experience for such work but for others considerable "know-how" will be required. Practically all teachers, however, can soon learn to produce creditable materials. Participation tends to increase knowledge and understanding on the part of the classroom teacher and also pride in accomplishment sufficient to insure usage of the materials thus produced. On occasion it may be economical in time to arrange instructional sessions, seminars, and short courses under the direction of specialists in order to gain momentum in the developmental process. Expert consultation as the work progresses is also extremely valuable. Sometimes the plan is followed of having all the production work done by small committees of specialists, but to do so lessens the probability of the materials being used by those who had no hand in their production.

If the production of curriculum guides and resource units is a part of the objectives, the results of the work of all classroom teachers or of all committees should be coordinated and thoroly discussed by all concerned, and finally approved by the curriculum council.

During the process of unit building, a set of suggestions and principles furnished to classroom teachers can be a great help. Curriculum development programs in Denver and Dallas provided an optional outline form which listed suggested divisions of the unit and left blank spaces under each division to be developed by teachers. Units prepared in such a manner may be submitted to a central committee (in large school systems) where selection, revision, and editing are done and the units are assembled into curriculum bulletins for the school system. Those well prepared in curriculum work, such as the specialists in the school system, should belong to this committee.

Evaluating the continuing program—Suppose a curriculum study and improvement program has been in operation for some time, much good has resulted, and new practices are in effect. Now what? Are we now "out of the woods" and may we relax our efforts? The answer is, "No." Curriculum improvement is a continuing process (Guide 5). The next essential is to test the value of what has been done and to refine the processes and results. Evaluation and improved efficiency are now the goals.

Altho classroom teachers may have gained understanding of the theory and practices of the improvement program, there will be a few who have "missed the boat" entirely. Others will not yet be sufficiently skilled in handling the new practices they are attempting. Effective and constant guidance is essential in order to improve the technical operation of all. Supervisors, key teachers, teacher visitation, conferences, and various other influences can be used to advantage at this stage of development.

Evaluation is also a continuing process. Taking stock should be done frequently, especially at key points in the program. It is especially necessary to view the entire situation periodically. Do the new practices really produce increased learning? Is there improvement in the children's ability to do their own work? Is there any favorable change in behavior? Unless these and many other questions can be answered in the affirmative, curriculum study and improvement really do not result in advancement. Any curriculum study and improvement program that is done well, with consideration given to classroom teacher, parent, and pupil participation, will stand up under careful evaluation. Specific information on processes of evaluation will be found in Chapters X and XI of this yearbook.

The systemwide curriculum improvement plan as described above is largely that designed for the purpose of changing the curriculum pattern of a school system. Philadelphia has used a plan of system-wide curriculum improvement in which many ideas, projects, and special studies have moved along simultaneously.[3] There is no reason why, under a systemwide plan, many specialized improvement programs cannot operate at the same time. Some may be systemwide, others may function in individual schools or in groups of schools, and still others may operate in the form of experimental activities, yet all may constitute parts of the general systemwide curriculum improvement program for which general leadership is furnished on a citywide basis from the central office. These activities may include reading improvement, cumulative records, guidance and counseling, child study, the school health program, improving human relations, and many others.

Curriculum Improvement thru Inservice Growth Programs

The second source of curriculum programs is to be found in inservice education. There is a tendency to refer to "inservice education" as a special program and to give it a special label. Rather, we should view as inservice study the various programs that may be in operation, such as extension courses, workshops, and committees. Evaluation programs, child-study movements, and general curriculum-improvement programs fall under the inservice stipulation in many schools. Inservice activities frequently serve as the start of varied and important curriculum movements, as for example, the improved curriculum practices resulting from child-study programs. It is possible for curriculum improvement and related work in a school system to go on effectively yet never to be labeled as inservice education. Labels and magical formulas are not as important as activities which win the cooperation of classroom teachers.

The child-study program has been one of the foremost prompters of curriculum improvement. When classroom teachers study the growth, development, and activities of children, they are less likely to isolate such matters as cumulative records, health programs, guidance improvement, physical and emotional needs, and the adjustment of the curriculum to child needs. These items just naturally fall into perspective. Referring to a recent child-study program in his school system, one superintendent made the statement: "There

---

[3] Caswell, Hollis L., and others, *op. cit.*, p. 286-316.

is just no way to tell how much good came from that program. New ideas and practices kept popping up. Teachers were constantly changing their classroom practices after learning how to observe and interpret child behavior."

Frequently all-school evaluation programs, initiated as the school inservice work, point up areas which need strengthening. These areas, when studied by the faculty, lend themselves to improvement. They may be in reading, improvement of the school plant, community relations, or any other pressing problem.

General curriculum-study programs also prompt subsequent fields of endeavor that sometimes continue for years.

School systems have followed the plan of inviting a specialist, usually from a college, to come in and conduct an inservice education program without knowing what the program was to be. In such cases the practice was for the participants, under the leadership of the specialist, to choose the area of work that appeared most in need of improvement at the moment. Good programs often have had their beginnings in this way. Arlington County, Virginia, reported a major curriculum-improvement program that had its beginning in an extension course conducted by a field coordinator from New York University. From the extension course sprang several workshops in various fields of instruction. The program, still in operation, is gaining momentum with time.

The foregoing examples are sufficient to indicate how many and varied accomplishments may result from one or more activities that had their beginnings in an inservice education program.

Conferences, surveys, local school faculty meetings, institutes, and all other inservice activities can be used to advantage in continuously working on selected problems and in increasing teacher growth. A surprising amount of progress can be made over a period of a few years, if a faculty keeps at it.

Practices That Begin in the Classroom

In recent years considerable discussion has been given to curriculum improvement that has originated in classrooms. Some educators have the feeling that all curriculum improvement must begin in the classroom. This idea is frequently referred to as the "grass-roots" origin. Undoubtedly teacher initiative that produces improvement in the classroom is commendable and may lead to schoolwide acceptance. Certainly the classroom teacher is in contact with the pupils and should be able to see opportunities for improvement. An example of such practices is a school cleanliness and lunchroom campaign that began when a class raised the question of manners and courtesy in the lunchroom. In another instance the science class studying water purification was responsible for a school and communitywide water testing program that produced startling results.

Frequently a classroom teacher will place in operation a new idea or practice which he learned in summer school, in a study group, or from his own classroom procedures. The introduction of a large unit of work, in which the children exhibit interest and for which they help to provide motivation, may spread quickly to other classroom teachers and classes and then from school to school within the district. Often a classroom teacher asks the art teacher to help with certain phases, the music teacher aids with the direction of folk songs, and before long the unit involves many people and resources.

Another teacher may originate, develop, and complete a unit entirely within the class but word goes around and other classroom teachers follow the example. This stimulus may lead to a general school curriculum improvement program in which many classroom teachers ask for help in learning how to do the same thing.

Classroom-initiated projects often go beyond the school into the community. One class was instrumental in initiating a successful mosquito-extermination project for an entire community. A communitywide network of playgrounds was the result of another class study.

Programs That Originate in Individual Schools

Another major type of curriculum organization emphasizes the individual school. The use of such a plan is sometimes spoken of as curriculum improvement on a "broken-front" basis and utilizes the concept that not all schools need to, or should, move in the same direction at the same time. The individual school plan recognizes that the curriculum often requires development so as to meet the community needs known by each school staff to exist in the neighborhood. This plan is further supported by the belief that activities of a systemwide nature develop out of work in the individual schools, especially in a general curriculum improvement program.

Baltimore has been cited as a city system that has used the individual school as the operational and planning unit in curriculum development.[4] Advantages attributed to this plan are principally these: (a) local school needs are met; (b) the school principal is brought into the forefront of the program and becomes a key worker, instead of being bypassed as is sometimes the case in system-wide plans; and (c) the primary concern for all classroom teachers becomes development of the best possible program for their pupils.

Individual schools are also frequently used as pilot, or "try-out" schools. In such cases a new idea may be tested in a few schools in order to obtain observations and reactions before being introduced into the entire school system. Experimental work may be done on this basis and sometimes it leads to systemwide improvement.

Special-Interests Beginnings

Still another type of curriculum-improvement program has its beginning in special interests. These interests may be initiated by individuals, either classroom teachers or school administrators, but usually are fostered and developed by groups. This type of activity can, of course, be classified also as inservice development, as can practically every other worthwhile activity in a school, but there is a difference between the two ideas, especially in initiation and in purposes.

Among these special interests may be such things as a survey of community resources for the improvement of classroom instruction. What institutions, enterprises, businesses, public utilities, welfare organizations, parks, and museums are in the community? Which of these potential resources have materials that may be brought into the classroom and to which may the class be taken? Schools often have developed excellent bulletins which include listings, annotations, and descriptions of all such community resources. From such a special interest may come almost any kind of curriculum improvement.

---

[4] Caswell, Hollis L. "Postwar Trends in Curriculum Development." *NEA Journal* 41: 93-95; February 1952.

Camping, or the outdoor classroom, is another example, as in Tyler (Texas) public schools, where the entire school program has been influenced by year-round camp activities. This program was instituted and organized by cooperative administration-teacher-community planning of the highest type.

The extended school year also offers promise, especially in the direction of recreational activities and creative programs. Teachers frequently acquire special interest in handicapped children and desire to find out ways and means of classifying them, planning special programs for their benefit, and improving their opportunities.

The Civil Aeronautics Administration has done a great deal in stimulating curriculum improvement by providing stimulus and materials in the field of aviation. In the Bromwell School, in Denver, Colorado, a Grade II class developed an extensive unit of work on the theme of "aviation in our lives." The program was set forth in a film strip under the title, *Second-Graders Try Their Wings,* which gives both the experiences of the class and the teaching procedures that were used.[5]

Many other ideas may be found just as beneficial. Included among them are such experiences as school library improvement, audio-visual aids, expansions of radio and television activities, and studies in nutrition. Any one or all of these special interests can and have led to general improvement within their own departmental areas and in the total school curriculum.

Adjusting the Program to Schools of Various Sizes

No school system is too small for curriculum improvement. In fact, the smaller the school system, sometimes the less difficult the task. In a one-teacher school instructional improvement may be done by the classroom teacher getting a vision and proceeding to do something about it. In a school system of not more than a few dozen teachers the curriculum plans may be incorporated within the regular faculty meetings. In systems with several buildings the organizational structure becomes more and more complicated until in large systems it becomes a major movement. The primary premise,

---

[5] The film strip (35 mm., 64 frames, 9 minutes) may be borrowed from the Civil Aeronautics Administration, Audio-Visual Aids, Washington 25, D. C. The procedure is described in a 32-page bulletin (50¢) issued by the Department of Elementary School Principals, NEA, 1201 Sixteenth St., N.W., Washington 6, D. C.

however, is that any school system, regardless of how small or how large it may be, is usually in need of curriculum study and improvement. The degree of need is not determined by size but by the initiative and educational desires of its superintendent and other administrators, the faculty, and the community. The only important advantage held by large school systems is the greater likelihood that there are staff members who are fundamentally curriculum workers, and persons who are qualified to direct major curriculum programs. There is also frequently a supervisory staff and, in some cases, more money for operation and materials. Reports of large-city curriculum programs are to be found in the professional literature.[6]

The small school that desires to act can organize for action and get action. Frequently, there is someone in the school—superintendent, principal, supervisor, or classroom teacher—who has sufficient training to direct the program. If such a person is not available, the state and county offices may be asked for the services of one or more supervisors or consultants. In case these offices cannot supply staff members, the possibility should be explored of employing an outside specialist from a nearby college or university on a part-time consultation basis. Still another plan is to organize a college extension class in curriculum development. Where the school system cannot afford the cost of a special course, there are usually enough classroom teachers who desire college credit and who are willing to pay the regular tuition fee to make the course possible. In some instances two or even three adjacent schools or school districts combine in order to secure greater numbers of interested teachers. In such cases the meetings may be rotated among the participating school systems.

Large school systems are in a sense a combination of many small community schools banded together for administrative and organizational expediency. Systemwide supervision and coordination are provided, of course, but the quality of education actually received by the child depends almost entirely upon what goes on in the classrooms of the individual or neighborhood school. What goes on in one school may be different from what goes on in another school in the same system. There are many justifiable reasons for diversity. Any individual school may initiate its own curriculum program and

---

[6] For example: Caswell, Hollis L., and others, *op. cit.*, p. 105-316. See publications of other authors listed at the end of this chapter.

profit from it even tho other schools are doing different things, but the system as a whole must provide coordination, management, leadership, and unity. There is no justification for one or more schools within a system choosing to "not participate" in a current curriculum program. To do so is to not "belong" to the system. When such isolated cases exist, the schools should be encouraged to initiate a study and improvement program of their own or to join a larger movement of a group of schools or of the system as a whole.

Countywide Programs

Curriculum improvement can be especially effective, where the county serves as an intermediate unit of school administration, if the county superintendent's office provides leadership characterized with both vision and competence. Striking examples of county work in Arlington County, Virginia, and Dade County, Florida, are described in Chapter V; Garrett County, Maryland, is explained in Chapter VI.

The county unit of administration enables many small districts to receive curriculum services which often are found only in city districts. Because of the unique relationship of the county office of education to the districts it serves, curriculum activity is enhanced in a threefold way. *First,* as an intermediate unit, the county office offers as a service to the individual schools—personnel, materials, and facilities for curriculum improvement—resources which the local districts because of size and finances cannot provide for themselves. *Second,* because of this service relationship, the program of educational improvement is built around the voluntary participation of school administrators, classroom teachers, and others in curriculum activities. *Third,* thru this intermediate relationship, the county office serves the advancement of education by offering a coordinated approach to curriculum improvement, thus striving for a unity as to purposes and major goals or outcomes, rather than a uniformity as to specific technics and curriculum practices.

To an increasing extent in rural schools, programs of curriculum improvement are taking place upon a countywide basis. Closely resembling the city organization are those that have been worked out by county-unit districts. There are 12 states with the county-

CURRICULUM

unit pattern, including the parish type in Louisiana. In three states the county units are complete units including all the cities; in the other nine states there are a few independent districts, mostly cities. In the county-unit states the county board acts as the policy-making body and the superintendent functions much as he would in a large city system.

In the New England states and New York there are large administrative-supervisory areas often including both rural and urban schools. In some respects these units function as county units and in some ways as intermediate units.

The intermediate unit is basically the "old pattern" of county organization. In the past it has been chiefly a record-keeping and money-distributing agency of the state. There are 28 states with this pattern. In these states, the county—as an intermediate unit— is taking on new obligations and services. California is one of the best examples of this new development where by means of state funds and added expert staff the county office is performing many services for the administrative units thruout the county even tho the county superintendent has relatively little administrative authority over the local districts.

Ascension Parish, Louisiana—This parish illustrates the possibilities of leadership in a rural area organized into a single school unit.[7] The total area is about 300 square miles, about 55 percent of which is in farms. The people live in small towns and villages, and scattered thruout the open country on farms. The total population in 1945 was about 22,500 of which approximately 25 percent lived in urban areas.

The parish superintendent got the idea of a coordinated program in 1942 from the cooperative programs of the war years. After the war, it was decided that many people and agencies could work toward some common goals in improving rural living. The living standards of the people were generally low; diet and cooking habits were poor; few people had any idea of "good living" at home. The schools, teaching the traditional subjects, had little effect upon the homes and the community life.

The program began slowly with the expansion of the school lunch programs. The mothers pitched in to improve the lunchroom

---

[7] This section based upon *Improve Rural Living Through Education* by E. J. Niederfrank; issued by the Division of Agricultural Extension, Louisiana State University (no date, mimeo), 35 p.

94

facilities and to provide better food. Another factor was the change in the school instruction. Work conferences were held with the classroom teachers to develop plans for teaching nutrition, health, home improvement, and better farming. Consultants came in from the extension service, health agencies, and units of the parish government.

A research project was started with the help of the Agricultural Experiment Station of Louisiana State University. The purpose of the research program was to find ways to teach more effectively about nutrition as a means of improving health. This program was independent of the coordinated school program but it supplemented and reinforced what the schools were attempting to do.

It was not necessary to have a coordinating council. All of the agencies worked informally thru the office of the parish superintendent of schools. Meetings of the leaders of various groups were held from time to time and all agencies were called upon when they could help. Annual meetings of teachers in workshops made possible the exchange of information of the programs in various schools.

As a result of these efforts the school programs were broadened and related to life at home and in the community. School attendance improved, and physical examinations of the children showed improvement in personal health and in health habits. Parents became conscious of nutrition. Agencies in the area worked together as never before. Many more people developed the feeling that the schools belonged to them and believed, more than ever before, that they could do things for themselves.

Los Angeles County, California—The counties of California are of the intermediate type. The county superintendent has few if any administrative duties involving the actual operation of schools. Rather the county office is becoming a service center exerting influence by the quality of the guidance given to individual teachers in small schools and to large groups in the urban centers. What is said here about Los Angeles County is true in many ways also of San Diego County, Santa Clara County, Alameda County, and a number of the other larger counties in the state.

Several years ago the state made available to the county superintendents funds to develop the staff and the services which the schools in their counties needed. Most superintendents proceeded with care so as not to disturb the basic control and interest of the people in their schools. The idea was to serve the various districts, not to attempt to run the schools for them.

Some idea of how the Los Angeles County office affects the school curriculum may be shown by several of the services now provided:

1. Continuous help is given to the local districts with instructional and curriculum programs. Coordinators spend a great deal of time in the field with classroom teachers, principals, and superintendents to ascertain needs, suggest resources, and to get ideas of materials which the county office might supply.

2. Each summer the county office organizes a four-week workshop with the assistance of the state department of education and the nearby colleges.

3. The county office provides housing, transportation, and supervision of a visual-aids library. The materials are purchased by annual contributions made by each district of 50 cents per child. The library consists of motion picture films, film slides, recordings, and study prints which are made available to every district in the county.

4. The county operates a cooperative library service.

5. A number of psychologists are available to help local districts in organizing guidance programs and in giving attention to the most serious individual cases.

6. A special director of trade and industrial education is employed to help local districts develop and operate trade and industrial education programs.

7. A coordinator of speech education gives diagnostic services to children in the local administrative units.

8. Two special schools are maintained at hospitals to meet the special needs of handicapped children.

Santa Clara County maintains an audio-visual center supplying aids to local school systems. The curriculum laboratories, bookmobiles, and mobile shop units in San Diego County have enriched the curriculum opportunities of rural youngsters.

Other rural areas—Leadership in organizing, planning, and operating programs for the improvement of the curriculums of rural schools are described in several of the publications of the NEA Department of Rural Education.[8] Three yearbooks of the American Association of School Administrators bear on the subject.[9]

---

[8] National Education Association, Department of Rural Education. *The Rural Supervisor at Work.* Yearbook 1949. Washington, D. C.: the Department, 1949. p. 17-21; 95-118. ¶ National Education Association, Department of Rural Education. *The County Superintendent of Schools in the United States.* Yearbook 1950. Washington, D. C.: the Department, 1950. p. 76-140.

[9] American Association of School Administrators. *Schools in Small Communities.* Seventeenth Yearbook. Washington, D. C.: the Association, a department of the National Education Association, 1939. p. 150-83. ¶ American Association of School Administrators. *Schools for a New World.* Twenty-Fifth Yearbook. Washington, D. C.: the Association, a department of the National Education Association, 1947. p. 177-95. ¶ American Association of School Administrators. *The American School Superintendency.* Thirtieth Yearbook. Washington, D. C.: the Association, a department of the National Education Association, 1952. p. 196-226 and 361-78.

Statewide Programs

Within the past two decades many states have conducted successful statewide curriculum programs.[10] One of the best results has been the development of general educational policies and procedures to which small schools may look for guidance, for direction, and for confidence and security. Such statewide coordinating and unifying programs usually provide for local school autonomy thru which sufficient local initiative and flexibility may be obtained.

The state is the recognized source of responsibility for public education in the United States. It is, therefore, the duty of the state to provide an educational system for its people. In so doing, the function of instructional leadership includes the provision of curriculum guides, teaching aids and materials, and many other special features. In many cases the personnel of state departments of education are available for conferences, workshops, and curriculum programs in local school districts. In other instances itinerant consultation is a possibility. Many schools avail themselves of all the desirable services at their disposal thru the state organization. Two examples of statewide programs, Florida and Illinois, are given in Chapter VI.

Regional Planning

Some worthwhile contributions have been made by still another geographical delineation of group activities—that of regional planning thru work conferences, cooperative movements, and study groups. These efforts extend over state lines and include special interests and areas. A representative list of such programs is as follows:

Cooperative Curriculum Research Conference (Sponsored by the Association for Supervision and Curriculum Development, NEA)

Metropolitan School Study Council (A group of schools centering around New York City)

National and regional conferences sponsored by the Home Economics Education Service of the U. S. Office of Education

National Conference of County and Rural Area Superintendents (Sponsored by the NEA Department of Rural Education)

[10] Caswell, Hollis L., and others, *op. cit.*, Chapter 13, "The Florida State Curriculum Program," p. 364-98; and Chapter 14, "The Michigan Curriculum Program—A Case History," p. 399-423.

National Conference on Citizenship (Sponsored by the NEA and the U. S. Department of Justice)

National Conference on Life Adjustment Education for Youth (Held in cooperation with the U. S. Office of Education)

National Conference on Higher Education (Sponsored by the Association of Higher Education, NEA)

National Conference on Teacher Education and Professional Standards (Sponsored by the National Commission on Teacher Education and Professional Standards, NEA)

National Training Laboratory in Group Development (Sponsored by the NEA and the Research Center for Group Dynamics at the University of Michigan)

Southern States Work Conference (Sponsored by the state departments of education and the state education associations of Alabama, Arkansas, Florida, Georgia, Kentucky, Louisiana, Mississippi, North Carolina, Oklahoma, South Carolina, Tennessee, Texas, Virginia, and West Virginia)

Three annual regional conferences on science teaching in the schools (Sponsored by the National Science Teachers Association, NEA).

The Role of Different Groups in Curriculum Development

Current educational literature is practically unanimous in the opinion that in the curriculum-improvement program "nearly everyone"—both staff and laymen—should participate. Such a statement is a pleasing democratic gesture but it is decidedly more difficult to accomplish than to describe. Considerable planning, organization, and ingenuity are necessary to get each person into the program, to get him into the proper place, and to enable him to contribute constructively. Occasionally it becomes necessary to prevent a person from being destructive, perhaps a pupil, classroom teacher, or parent who wants to ride a hobby, or desires to emphasize unduly a minor personal irritation. What is meant by total participation, however, is that school administrators, classroom teachers, pupils, parents, and other lay persons should be brought into the program and that there is a place for representatives of the many interests.

The Superintendent

Since this book is written primarily for school superintendents, and because the work of curriculum improvement is fundamentally the responsibility of the superintendent, his sphere of activity will be outlined first. Contrary to some educational opinion it is the prime responsibility of the superintendent of schools to see that the instructional program of the school is sound and effective, that it remains that way, and that it is constantly being studied and improved, especially thru curriculum revision.

Many contemporary writers explain at great length that improvement must begin with the classroom teacher and work up thru the school system—not down from the administration. The idea is enticing, but to put all curriculum study and improvement on that basis would tend to reduce drastically the amount of work done and it would make many otherwise good programs both spotty and intermittent. Many good projects are conceived and started in the classroom and frequently they lead to successful results. Actually, the plans sometimes described as the "administrative approach" and "grass-roots approach" are, when combined, almost identical with the systemwide plan presented here.[11] Whatever distinguishing characteristics there are undoubtedly lie quite largely in the methods of operation, for the plans do not stand out as being greatly different in general structure and development.

It is gratifying when a faculty suggests, or even demands, a program of large-scale curriculum improvement. But while the superintendent is waiting for a program to be generated, he had best begin some stimulation and motivation himself. If he is a wise administrator, he will soon have the faculty implementing the program from within the ranks and not from the top. He may sometimes take his cue from an opportunity to assist some classroom teacher in a small movement, or some school in a special project. These opportunities will give him an excuse to ask, "Why don't we continue this activity into something bigger?"

Once launched, the program demands much from the superintendent.[12] It requires, first of all, sanction and approval. It must have support in the face of possible opposition. It needs to be explained to the board of education and have official approval. Financial aid and adequate working materials are essential. Constant encouragement and motivation must be provided. All of these things only the superintendent can guarantee. In the final analysis

---

[11] For example, *see:* Smith, B. Othanel; Stanley, William O.; and Shores, J. Harlan. *Fundamentals of Curriculum Development.* Yonkers-on-Hudson, N. Y.: World Book Co., 1950. p. 622-26.

[12] A number of specific examples of what the superintendent can do are to be found in *The American School Superintendency,* Thirtieth Yearbook, American Association of School Administrators, 1952. See Chapter 8, "Improving Curriculum and Instruction," p. 196-226.

he can make or break any program. It is unfortunate, indeed, when the parents in a community wake up after a number of years to the realization that their school is outmoded and their children are not getting their rightful educational portion. Sooner or later the superintendent who allows deterioration and decadence to develop is relieved of his responsibilities. The tragedy is that he could have looked after the educational progress of his school along with the financial and management ends. The first job of the superintendent is to work for a modern and effective educational program. Without that, he cannot justify his existence.

The Principal

The principal is the responsible head of the individual school, including the instructional program.[13] He is responsible for seeing that the basic systemwide philosophy, policies, and principles are observed. He is the local school representative in the systemwide program. He must, in his school, provide some of the elements of leadership given by the superintendent to the system as a whole. He points out strengths and weaknesses, obtains materials, adjusts programs, assists classroom teachers, appoints committees, makes reports, stimulates interest, and maintains morale. All the time he must demonstrate a sufficient knowledge of curriculum procedure to command respect in educational work for his school.

The type of curriculum-improvement program under way will of necessity dictate the specific role of the principal. If the systemwide type is in progress, the principal should be a key figure. If the entire system moves to improvement at once, each principal must be established in a role of leadership and he must accept and exercise that role. Altho there may be an adequate supervisory staff, the failure of the principal to provide stimulation as well as educational consultation and know-how to the classroom teachers in his building will constitute a gap in the total program. He can't afford not to play his proper role.

Experience has shown that principals are willing and eager to accept the comparatively new responsibility for the educational program in their buildings. In the Dallas systemwide improvement

---

[13] This point of view is developed in the publications of the NEA Department of Elementary School Principals and the National Association of Secondary-School Principals, NEA.

program many principals have voluntarily joined their faculties from the beginning as students in orientation and technics and quickly prepared themselves for the tasks ahead. Others assumed technical leadership based upon previous experience but all have conducted improvement programs of some kind in their respective buildings. These activities have made possible the success of the systemwide program.

In school systems that use central councils, principals are usually well represented, and on individual school curriculum committees the principal is an essential figure. He may choose not to serve as chairman but his membership on the committee is essential.

On the individual school improvement basis, the principal is especially important. In this type of program he must furnish leadership for initiation, assist in determining the exact nature of the program, and also provide know-how and assistance in its execution. Here, each school shines in the local setting in proportion to the nature and the success of its own curriculum activities. The school either succeeds or it does not. A school may be known as a leader in the system, it may be characterized as doing nothing, or it may be anywhere between the two extremes, depending to some extent upon the initiative and the ability of the principal.

In classroom-teacher initiated programs, the principal is still a necessary and important person. He must assist with the appointment of committees, see that planning is effected, provide materials, secure assistance, and make the program generally operative.

In any event, altho the principal cannot hand out ready-made experiences to the children, he can make it possible for many things to happen. In the words of the Educational Policies Commission:

What the administrator can do, however, is to fling wide open the door of opportunity for children and teachers to live. He can help the school envision its role in society. He can help interpret this role in experiences for children at their levels by giving wise counsel and allowing thoughtful staff members to use initiative. He can help to make every school activity fully available for use in teaching children. He can administer the whole school so that children can learn with and from other children in the school. He can have some part of the community brought into the school and can arrange for children to go to other parts. In short, he can help to make the school a place of excellent living.[14]

---

[14] National Education Association and American Association of School Administrators, Educational Policies Commission. *Education for ALL American Children.* Washington, D. C.: the Commission, 1948. p. 193.

The Classroom Teacher

The classroom teacher, of course, is the backbone of the program. The improved curriculum must be evident in the classroom and must be reflected in improved learning. Curriculum changes will be most evident in the changed concepts, principles, and practices of the teacher. The place of the classroom teacher in curriculum development and improvement is discussed in Chapter VIII and need not be more than mentioned at this point.

Teachers Associations

Teachers collectively, too, have expressed interest in curriculum improvement thru their various associations, local, state, and national. Many associations have written into their constitutions or platforms references to curriculum improvement and most of them have made concrete recommendations thru their publications. Some have produced specific teaching and curriculum guides or aids, as for example, yearbooks, handbooks, and courses of study. A few of the organizations are the National Education Association, the NEA Department of Classroom Teachers, the National Society for the Study of Education, the National Council for the Social Studies, the National Council of Teachers of Mathematics, and others (see Chapter VI of this yearbook).

Teachers associations have been active, with a considerable degree of success, in obtaining recognition of curriculum work by classroom teachers as a substitute for rather than an addition to regular teaching duties. The matter of released time for conferences, teacher-teacher planning, workshops, faculty meetings, and other curriculum duties has been emphasized practically all over the nation. Undoubtedly classroom teachers have a point and many school administrators have come to realize that tired and overworked teachers cannot do constructive thinking on curriculum matters. It must be borne in mind, however, that the schools are organized on a limited time basis for actual classroom instruction and if too much pupil class time is used for any other purpose, there can be a serious public relations problem with school patrons. In a few school systems the public's reaction has had a devastating effect on good curriculum programs. It does not seem unreasonable to suppose that organizational machinery can be devised which will allow teachers time for constructive curriculum work without depriving children of the educational opportunities the school should provide.

The Pupils

Effective curriculum planning takes the learners into partnership. In the elementary school the children may appropriately assist in planning immediate activities. The responsibility always rests with the classroom teacher to see that those activities are well selected and that they result in meaningful experiences that produce learning. Furthermore, the learning must be pointed in the direction of the school's major objectives and must be in conformity with the school's philosophy.

In the secondary school also, pupils can take a constructive part in pointing out their own needs, citing choices, and helping to plan ways of achieving their goals. Group planning and group participation can be used to great advantage and should be brought into practice wherever possible by teachers at all levels.

Parent Participation and Lay Participation

Parents and lay citizens in general should have a voice in determining the *kind* of education produced in the community school. They should be brought into general discussions of philosophy and policy formation. They should assist in determining *what* is taught in the schools and in planning many of the processes. It is the task of educators, however, to determine *how* the teaching is to be done. One excellent example of school and community curriculum planning is given in the 1950 Yearbook of the American Association of School Administrators.[15] Chapter IX of the present volume also discusses the importance of lay participation in curriculum development and directs attention to some of the critical problems involved. If the professional staff and the community work together, mutual trust and confidence can be created as well as a better understanding on the part of each concerning what the other is trying to do. For best results parents should be included from the beginning, not just

---

[15] American Association of School Administrators. *Public Relations for America's Schools.* Twenty-Eighth Yearbook. Washington, D. C.: the Association, a department of the National Education Association, 1950. p. 90-94.

brought in at the conclusion to be told what has gone on and asked for their stamp of approval.

Consultants and Agencies

Some of the work of curriculum development is so technical that it must be done by specialists. The place of the curriculum director, the college professor, the consultant, and other specialists is to transmit the know-how, or at least to make suggestions in that direction. They plan over-all strategy and assist with organization. They meet with groups on a consultative basis and are resource people to whom classroom teachers may go for assistance. Finally, they organize materials and put them into shape for publication.

Several other worthwhile sources of assistance and information should not be overlooked. They include our state departments of education, state, regional, and national committees, the state and national education associations, and the U. S. Office of Education. They frequently furnish information, statistics, and reports and in some cases provide technical consultation service.

Translating Theory into Practice

One of the outstanding charges that has been hurled against curriculum-development programs is that the end does not justify the means. That is, the good things done, the new philosophies and principles developed, the changes made in teacher thinking, and the new written materials do not result in changed practices in the classroom. To whatever extent this charge is true, Principle 1 among those listed at the beginning of this chapter has been violated. Undoubtedly the charge sometimes is partially true. Yet, there is no need for a curriculum program to bog down and end in committee structure, in the formation of objectives, and in the writing of units.

If classroom teachers actually participate in the entire movement and really work on curriculum materials, those who thought the materials worthy of production will also think they are worthy of use. If the preliminary orientation program of understanding is well done, classroom teachers should be eager to put the new program into practice. They will want to "try out their own stuff." This is the reason why a classroom teacher gains more by going thru a curriculum-study program than by merely using materials that were written by someone else.

If the proper teacher growth results from the study, teachers will begin, consciously or unconsciously, to use new ideas in the classroom as the study progresses. Written materials will become only guides which the highly competent classroom teacher can often do without, but which are sometimes handy to have around. The constant development of new materials will result from a great deal of the class planning and procedure.

The conclusion should not be drawn, however, that written units and other documents are not worth the writing. There are many uses to which they can be put to advantage. The classroom teacher new to the school system can use them for guidance; the inexperienced classroom teacher will find them an invaluable aid; and even the best classroom teacher of the experience curriculum can use written reports of his previous units or other work as a guide, as resource material, and as a labor saver in the development of new units. Then, too, most schools need something to send out when fellow school superintendents write in for sample curriculum materials. It helps the ego to be able to say, "This is what we do in our school system."

If the emphasis has been properly placed during a curriculum study and improvement program, the results *will be used* in classrooms. Much of the material developed in the study will have been produced there. At this point, however, the school administration may be forced to assume further direct responsibility. The school organizational plan, the daily schedule, the provision for materials and supplies, the physical equipment, and the administrative "go ahead" signal—all are necessary before the classroom teacher can get desired results from study findings.

Suppose, for example, that a school which is accustomed to teaching individual subjects as such decides to accept the broad-fields, the core, or the experience curriculum pattern. Suppose further that the daily schedule continues to be chopped up into 20- or 30-minute periods, or that there is no library available, or that no provision is made for a classroom library, or that an administrator complains that the children should not move around in the classroom, or that a parent complains, "My child hasn't had a spelling lesson in three days." What is the classroom teacher to do? Obviously, certain patterns of curriculum organization demand parallel adjustments and provisions to make their operation possible.

In a curriculum-development program that originates properly and is guided carefully, with adequate teacher growth constantly evident, there will be no particular stage at which the "new curriculum" is "introduced." The introduction will be gradual and constant. It will follow changed ideas and concepts as well as careful teacher-pupil planning. It will get into operation in the classroom and it will result in improved practices and improved learning.

SELECTED REFERENCES

ALBERTY, HAROLD B. *Reorganizing the High-School Curriculum.* New York: Macmillan Co., 1947. 458 p.

AMERICAN ASSOCIATION OF SCHOOL ADMINISTRATORS. *Schools for a New World.* Twenty-Fifth Yearbook. Washington, D. C.: the Association, a department of the National Education Association, 1947. 448 p. $2.

AMERICAN ASSOCIATION OF SCHOOL ADMINISTRATORS. *Schools in Small Communities.* Seventeenth Yearbook. Washington, D. C.: the Association, a department of the National Education Association, 1939. 608 p. (Out of print.)

NATIONAL EDUCATION ASSOCIATION AND AMERICAN ASSOCIATION OF SCHOOL ADMINISTRATORS, EDUCATIONAL POLICIES COMMISSION. *Education for ALL American Children.* Washington, D. C.: the Commission, 1948. 292 p. $1.

NATIONAL EDUCATION ASSOCIATION AND AMERICAN ASSOCIATION OF SCHOOL ADMINISTRATORS, EDUCATIONAL POLICIES COMMISSION. *Education for ALL American Youth. A Further Look.* Washington, D. C.: the Commission, 1952. 402 p.

NATIONAL EDUCATION ASSOCIATION, DEPARTMENT OF RURAL EDUCATION. *The County Superintendent of Schools in the United States.* Yearbook 1950. Washington, D. C.: the Department, 1950. 188 p. $2.50.

NATIONAL EDUCATION ASSOCIATION, DEPARTMENT OF RURAL EDUCATION. *The Rural Supervisor at Work.* Yearbook 1949. Washington, D. C.: the Department, 1949. 242 p.

NATIONAL SOCIETY FOR THE STUDY OF EDUCATION. *Learning and Instruction.* Forty-Ninth Yearbook, Part I. Chicago: University of Chicago Press, 1950. 352 p.

SMITH, BONNIE OTHANEL; STANLEY, WILLIAM O.; and SHORES, J. HARLAN. *Fundamentals of Curriculum Development.* Yonkers-on-Hudson, N. Y.: World Book Co., 1950. 780 p.

CHAPTER FIVE

Curriculum Developments in
Elementary Schools

IN EDUCATION, as in other institutions of a democratic society, pioneers are pushing forward into new areas. The curriculum in the elementary schools is one of these areas, and improving the curriculum is a teamwork task both stimulating and satisfying to all who engage in it—classroom teachers, school administrators, scholars, pupils, and patrons.

The Commission, in reporting the following illustrations of efforts to improve the curriculum in the elementary school, does so with the full realization that these examples do not necessarily meet with the full approval of individual Commission members, or for that matter with readers of this yearbook. The reports have been included here because (a) they represent, for the most part, practices which harmonize with the principles of curriculum improvement stated thruout the yearbook; and (b) they have been reported by school systems to be important activities of promise because those who were involved received benefits and encouragement to continue their efforts. In addition the examples are current and specifically describe the processes involved when classroom teachers, school administrators, parents, and others work cooperatively for curriculum improvement. Readers may see how the plans outlined can be improved upon in their own school systems.

The Purpose of Curriculum Change

It is generally accepted that educational leadership has the responsibility for accelerating curriculum change so that instruction and learning can be improved. What are some of the marks of effective action to this end? Miel has stated that "the changes involved when the school curriculum is really modified are actually changes in the attitude and behavior of persons." [1]

---

[1] Miel, Alice. *Changing the Curriculum.* New York: Appleton-Century-Crofts, 1946. p. 14.

Desirable changes in attitudes and behaviors are those which result in the effective and enthusiastic application of improved practices in classroom work with boys and girls. Such changes are achieved when there is involvement and active participation in curriculum improvement activities of all concerned. When the participation is voluntary and comes because teachers believe they can benefit, the changes are more likely to be lasting and effective. When individuals or groups become immersed in a problem at their point of interest and need, and then work together in a voluntary atmosphere, their working relationships are more likely to be harmonious, their satisfactions enduring, and their efforts productive.

In contrast to the conditions which accelerate curriculum change are those which impede progress. Inconsistency in approach—the failure to square the means used with the ends desired—may occur when decisions by the central office are substituted for responsible group planning. Much waste results when sporadic effort replaces careful planning for continuous and orderly work, or when provision is not made for communication among all persons and groups concerned. Effective action becomes difficult when we neglect to recognize praiseworthy effort, neglect to provide the time and funds for the curriculum project at hand, or neglect to develop community understanding of changes in curriculum practices.

The purpose of all curriculum effort is, of course, more effective and efficient learning, that is, changed behavior of pupils. To determine whether or not new practices are successful in improving learning is the responsibility of those involved in the activity, and the nature of the activity will govern the method, the teaching aids, the extent, and the measurement. For example, a project to improve the reading of children with undeveloped phonetic skills can be controlled and be of short duration, therefore lending itself to precise measurement. On the other hand, a project to improve learning in the primary grades by keeping a group of children with the same teacher for two or more years is much more difficult to measure precisely.

Each example in this chapter describes change, in a particular situation, toward some desired goal of classroom teachers, school administrators, or others who had a need, planned an attack, and followed thru on it. They represent successes—large and small—which have come about because someone was moved to do something about an existing need and because one or more of the conditions for effective curriculum improvement were recognized. They show that, altho many methods and plans have been used, there are common elements making for success. Those who attempt similar programs should keep in mind the problems of evaluation as discussed in Chapters XI and XII of the present yearbook.

A Program Grows from Teacher Interests

In the Des Moines elementary schools,[2] a group of principals and central office personnel capitalized upon classroom teacher interest in first-grade readiness activities to bring about a citywide study of readiness on all levels.[3] This activity has continued for more than four years with heightening interests and gratifying results. It is significant because it demonstrates to all of us—superintendents, principals, and instructional leaders—that oftentimes important and worthwhile movements begin in a small way, and while they are not envisioned in their entirety at the beginning, open-minded and flexible leadership permit them to grow at their own pace and in their own way. But here is the story; this is how it began.

Principals Alert to Needs

What is readiness? What pupils have it? How is it recognized? These and other similar questions had been asked by Des Moines elementary-school teachers and principals as they became increasingly aware of the need to adapt their schools to the children, not children to the schools. Many of the teachers began to try to do something in their classrooms. As the teachers turned to the principals for support and guidance, the principals found that they, too, needed to clarify their own understanding of the meaning of readiness for learning. At a principals meeting it was decided to begin the study with reading readiness in Grade I. This was in October of 1947. The study which began so simply has continued and developed

[2] This account of curriculum improvement practice and those that follow thruout the chapter concern but one phase of the total curriculum improvement program in the system. The purpose here is to describe in some detail a selected project within the school system rather than to attempt to outline the entire program.

[3] Reported by Adelene E. Howland, Education Section, General Mills (formerly assistant director, Elementary Education, Des Moines Public Schools); George W. Hohl, director of elementary education; N. D. McCombs, superintendent, Des Moines Public Schools, Des Moines, Iowa.

into a citywide activity involving classroom teachers on all grade levels, principals, supervisors, parents, and education specialists. This activity illustrates how a beginning study of reading readiness in the first grade became one of readiness for learning in all grades and learning areas.

A Four-Year Span

In October the principals visited a classroom to observe a teacher who had attained success in providing a reading-readiness program for slowly maturing children. They saw the teacher at work with the children, the kinds of activities they were engaged in, the children's own stories and charts, and the teacher-prepared materials, including pictures, objects, stories, and games designed to build readiness.

During November, first-grade teachers from approximately half the Des Moines elementary schools observed the same teacher and examined the materials she had found useful. A discussion with the teacher generated much interest and resulted in plans for meetings to be attended by these first-grade teachers.

In January, first-grade teachers from the remainder of the schools asked to meet and discuss problems in reading readiness. At this point, because of the increased involvement, first-grade teachers decided to plan and hold their meetings in seven geographic areas within the city. Usually the meetings were held monthly, from 4:00 to 5:00 p. m. The groups studied current literature, materials, visual aids, and children's needs. Also of concern were the testing program, grade standards, and ways of informing parents of the possible changes in emphasis which might occur as a result of these teachers developing readiness in pupils.

By May the groups began to feel that there should be some means of communicating and sharing ideas citywide, and that teachers of the second grade should be invited to participate. A committee was formed, consisting of one teacher from each of the seven geographic areas.

In September, at the beginning of the 1948-49 school year, the committee sent a questionnaire to all first-grade teachers and elementary-school principals. Guided by the responses, which indicated a strong interest in readiness for learning on a much broader base than readiness for reading, the central committee became a "Committee on Readiness for Learning," and has since then been concerned with the total readiness problem. The next activity of the committee was the organization of a series of workshops which had been requested as a part of the year's readiness study activity.

Public Schools, Mineola, New York

Outside the four walls of the school are material and human resources whereby both instruction and the curriculum may be enriched thru first-hand experiences.

Four workshops were held, one each month from January to April. Teachers engaged in projects which were designed to give them background information as well as specific technics and useful classroom materials in several areas of children's needs and interests. These included building readiness for literature, science, social studies, music and rhythm, and numbers, and developing readiness materials for use by the children as quiet time activity.

The staff for the workshops consisted of three classroom teachers, three principals, and two supervisors. Attendance was voluntary, but was greater than the committee anticipated. Teachers were urged to participate in at least two areas during the four sessions. The only complaints received indicated the need for more time, clock time as well as calendar time. There were not enough hours in a day or days in a month. But the work of the teachers reflected the influence of the workshops, limited in time tho they were. Resumés written by the workshop leaders provided a permanent record of the content of each section.

A dinner meeting in May served as a summary and evaluation session for the year's work. At this meeting a consultant was employed to help appraise the work of the group and to suggest future activities. The consultant's evaluation, together with the results of an evaluation questionnaire which the committee had prepared for use by all teachers involved in the study, served as the basis for planning the program for the third year.

The third-year period saw an enlargement of the citywide committee to bring building participation into sharper focus. This resulted in a recommendation by the steering committee that each school faculty, including teachers for all elementary grades, center its study of readiness in problems and needs of teachers locally. The year's study culminated in a joint meeting planned by the committee and the local Association for Childhood Education. Participants in a planned panel included the superintendent, principals, classroom teachers, instructional coordinators, parents, a pediatrician, and a newspaper columnist.

In the fourth year the building program continued as the study took on a new aspect: the involvement in the readiness problem of the Social Studies Club for the city. The study has become further refined thru the setting up of two subcommittees to consider problems of the gifted child and to plan a series of workshop meetings covering such areas as creative arts, music, dramatics, and literature.

Thus, from a beginning made by a few primary-school teachers, the activity expanded to include many teachers on all elementary-grade levels in the Des Moines schools. From the special interest in reading readiness, the study expanded to a concern with readiness for all types of learning. Teachers' interests led them from discussion to observation, to study and workshop activities, and to improved classroom practices.

Child Study Leads to Primary Block Plan

Wayne, Michigan, is another school system which has developed a systemwide activity from small beginnings.[4] The philosophy of educational leadership in this community may be expressed as follows: "Our focal point is the child; our approach to the child is thru the teacher; our job is to help the teacher be as consistently sound in her teaching as resources and facilities will permit. In other words, we believe in starting where we are, stepping carefully along the way, but always making progress." This policy of building carefully is worth noting.

Time Is a Factor

In 1945 a few teachers who had engaged in a child study activity expressed an interest in staying with the same group of children during their second year in school. The movement which finally developed came to be known as the Primary Block Plan. Each year a few more teachers became interested. No pressure was exerted on them, but after they had entered into the child-study activities, they were encouraged to consider the Primary Block Plan. Wherever the opportunity afforded, parents were made acquainted with the program and helped to consider its advantages. By 1948 several classroom teachers chose to go all the way thru the primary block for the first three grades, and by 1951 the first sequence of the Primary Block Plan in the Wayne Public Schools was completed.

Difficulties Surmounted

The idea of assigning a teacher to stay with a group of children for more than one year is not new. In the rural school this practice is quite common, but in graded school systems the practice is not too frequently carried on. Many school systems have considered such a move; some have actually tried it with success, while others have tried and reverted to previous practice. Wayne is one of the systems which has succeeded, and not because Wayne teachers did not encounter obstacles, for they did. They reported them:

Teachers were reluctant at times because they felt they were not prepared to move from grade to grade.

---

[4] Reported by Stuart L. Openlander, superintendent, Wayne Public Schools, Wayne, Michigan.

It meant changes in the curriculum and, therefore, changes in teaching methods and procedures.

Because of unsettled times, teacher turnover was approximately 25 percent, thus presenting another block to continuity.

There were other blocks and difficulties to be surmounted. But, too, there were advantages and satisfactions which were sufficiently compelling to keep the plan operating. In the first place, the whole program was approached in a permissive manner; no one had to participate. Those who did were encouraged and recognized; those who did not were not censured or criticized.

Parents Support Program

Another significant factor was the relationship which the classroom teachers and administrators had with the parents. Parents were a part of the venture; the plan was as much theirs as it was the teachers. Then, too, the administrative and supervisory leadership realized that no plan, no matter how good, will grow without proper nurture. The whole philosophy of the Primary Block Plan as Wayne saw it centered in the teacher's understanding of the child. The teachers were given opportunity to study child development, they were encouraged and assisted to confer with parents about their children's progress in school, and they were helped to evaluate learning in terms of individual needs and individual progress.

Teachers React

Values accruing from this inservice program of curriculum improvement are implicit in the teachers' own reactions. This is the way five teachers have expressed themselves:

1. There is less time wasted in the fall assigning children to rooms and no time is wasted as far as getting children started in suitable activities. The teacher knows their needs and abilities.

2. One of the main advantages of the Primary Block Plan is that it enables the school to adapt itself to the individual. Individual differences are expected and accepted, as well as varying rates of growth. The teacher is relieved of pressure to get quick results, and therefore does not need (nor feel the urge) to push a child faster than he can go.

3. I think relations with parents, being continuous, are improved. Parents have a clearer concept of our objectives and philosophy.

4. I also feel quite strongly that there is a greater interaction among primary-school teachers. I feel their problems are more freely discussed with one another. They share ideas more, and often plan work together.

5. Children benefit from the Primary Block Plan thru understanding definite goals from year to year. Some examples are the development of good audience attitude, spirit of cooperation, and attitudes toward work. Thru having one teacher over a period of time these attitudes are more likely to be achieved.

Under the Primary Block Plan the teacher becomes more alert to the types of things her children need, and endeavors to include these things in the program. She can introduce new ideas and learning situations in the manner best accepted by the children.

A Different Approach—Similar Results

The Normal Park School in Chattanooga, Tennessee, is an example of how a school community, thru a cooperative study which included school leadership, classroom teachers, and parents, arrived by a somewhat different avenue at a point similar to that reached in Wayne, Michigan.[5] A year of intensive work began with the raising of questions by primary-school teachers concerned with reading readiness and attempts by consultants from the central office to answer these questions. It was decided that the classroom teachers should constitute a committee to study the problem and to formulate recommendations for changes in instruction and administration.

After a series of meetings, the classroom teachers decided that community participation was necessary. They asked a group of seven parents to meet with a like number of teachers representing Kindergarten thru Grade VI. Meetings of this joint committee continued thruout the school year. Other teachers were invited from time to time by the committee to sit with the study group and to think with them on the problems occurring at various stages of progress. Likewise parent members of the group took opportunities to discuss their work with neighbors and other persons in the community.

Community Involvement Planned

The committee arranged to present periodically its thinking on reading-readiness problems to the local Parent-Teacher Association. Two open meetings were held with community people. The first

---

[5] Reported by Robert N. Grove, administrative assistant; Lawrence G. Derthick, superintendent of schools, Chattanooga Public Schools, Chattanooga, Tennessee.

was to apprise parents of the problem with which the committee was working and to solicit their understanding, suggestions, and support. The second meeting, at the close of the school term, was to ascertain whether or not the community in general favored the introduction of what the group had named "The Normal Park Plan for Normal Progress." This plan called for teachers to continue thru two and three years with the same group of children. Other related aspects of the plan included a revised method of reporting to parents consistent with the philosophy of normal progress, setting up a preschool workshop program the following September for teachers interested in preparing themselves to teach under the new plan, planning new room arrangements to meet the new need, and planning for the necessary teaching materials which would be recommended for purchase during the next school year.

Time Plus Communication Equals Success

Those who are participating in the Normal Park project stress two important considerations which contributed to this successful activity. The first of these is good communication: "There was continuous interpretation by the mothers and teachers on the committee; they discussed the plan with other members of the community at every opportunity." The second is providing time: "It proved of utmost value that sufficient time was given to the joint curriculum committee activity so that the natural evolution of ideas occurred."

Approach to the Open Mind

An illustration of a systemwide activity in a special area of curriculum study is the Philadelphia Schools Open-Mindedness Study.[6] Classroom teachers and administrators undertook a study of "ways of improving those practices thru which pupils may be taught to think effectively." At the beginning, a group of 10 classroom teachers and school administrators began to collect and classify illustrations from their own teaching situations of closed-mindedness in pupils which impeded, beclouded, or sidetracked thinking. At the end of the first year and a half the group was enlarged to

---

[6] Reported by C. Leslie Cushman, associate superintendent and David A. Horowitz, acting assistant to the associate superintendent, Philadelphia Public Schools, Philadelphia, Pennsylvania.

include representatives from all areas within the city and from all instructional levels.

Classroom Problems Lead to Open-Mindedness

More than 200 teachers representing all levels of instruction have become involved. They have worked with boys and girls in everyday problem situations; they have conferred and cooperated in trying to identify the characteristics of the open mind. They have consulted experts, and they have, above all, striven thru their daily relationships with children to find answers to many questions. That they have found answers is attested by the following two excerpts taken from their most recent report,[7] which includes hundreds of anecdotal accounts of classroom activities involving problem solving and critical thinking.

1. The 7A class had just learned a new process in arithmetic. They were working out examples. Marsha sat quietly at her desk, but she made no attempt to do the work. When Miss Fisher asked her if she needed some help, Marsha replied, "No, I can't do arithmetic. I never could do it. Even my mother and father say I just can't do it."

Miss Fisher thought she recognized signs of a closed mind. She discussed with Marsha her difficulty with arithmetic and suggested a course of action which began with doing easier examples successfully.

Marsha followed Miss Fisher's advice during the following weeks, and was pleased with her success. Under Miss Fisher's guidance, she realized that she could do arithmetic.

2. The school is in an underprivileged neighborhood. Many of the children in the fourth-grade class have known what it means "to do without." They agreed with the statement Carl made during a social studies lesson, "I like Abraham Lincoln because he was poor. I don't like rich people. They're greedy. They always try to get more money for themselves. They don't care about anybody else."

Judy wasn't so sure about this. "Some rich people are good," she said. "I heard about a rich man who gave money to help poor people."

Mrs. Kent seized upon Judy's answer to direct the class to examine Carl's statement more closely. She raised two pertinent questions: "Do any of you know anything good that a rich person has done for the people of Philadelphia?" and "Do you think there are any poor people who are greedy?"

The replies of the pupils to these two questions led Rachel to say, "Maybe there are rich people who are greedy and poor people who are greedy, and rich people who aren't and poor people who aren't." The class, including Carl, was inclined to agree.

---

[7] Philadelphia Public Schools, Curriculum Office. *Toward the Open Mind*. The Open-Mindedness Study. Philadelphia, Pa.: Board of Education, 1951. p. 8.

A Fourfold Approach

From their experiences in classrooms, group meetings, workshops, and work with consultants, the classroom teachers discovered that open-mindedness is an attitude of mind and that it can be fostered in many ways. Four areas of approach to the study of open-mindedness were eventually identified by the group in its search for clues to effective teaching. These were: creating good climate, making decisions, thinking critically, and building desirable values.

The participants explored each of these four approaches. Creating good climate, for example, could be used as an illustration of the approach made to improved thinking in each of the four areas identified above. From the conclusion reached from observations in classroom situations thruout the city that "good climate provides the atmosphere in which the open mind has an opportunity to function," the study was directed toward the discovery of the specific conditions or elements in good climate. Synthesized from observations, discussions, and study these elements were found to be constant in all classroom situations where good climate existed: (a) self-respect on the part of each individual, (b) mutual respect among all members, (c) meaningful and purposeful activities to be engaged in, and (d) a pleasant and comfortable environment.

The teachers involved in the experiment subjected these four elements to penetrating scrutiny in hundreds of daily situations to discover, if possible, just how a child behaved. In regard to self-respect they found that a boy or girl who was at ease with himself, who knew and was able to use his abilities, and who was aware of his limitations and accepted them, had some of the essential attributes.

The question arose: How can we help our pupils develop self-respect? Some of the answers were:

We can help the individual gain the feeling that he is valued as a person.
We can give the pupil work at a level where he can show his ability.
We can use the things in which the pupil is interested in order to stimulate his desire to improve.
We can show the pupil wherein he is making progress and help him evaluate his growth.

And so on—questions, discovery, application, refinement, further questions, and discovery. "We saw," said several classroom teachers, "that pupils by examining the ways in which they make decisions and by increasing their skill in the process of critical thinking were developing the inquiring mind." "We have seen," reported other teachers, "that pupils provided with certain kinds of experiences will build higher values as bases for improved thoughts and actions."

Action-Research Affects Curriculum Change

Increasingly in recent years, school systems thruout the country are using services afforded them by agencies conducting systematic and long-range experimentation in education. Among these organizations are the Metropolitan School Study Council in New York; the Metropolitan Detroit Bureau of Cooperative School Studies in Michigan; the Horace Mann-Lincoln Institute of School Experimentation of Teachers College, Columbia University; the Center for Intergroup Education, University of Chicago; and the University of Maryland Child Study Project.

Such experimentation programs, in most cases, are a combination of the effort of college and university departments of education and widespread participation by practicing classroom teachers and administrators. The unique feature of the programs is the gearing of research with application in the field. Consultants provided by the agencies are the link in this process: persons practicing in the field bring their needs to the attention of the researchers, the researchers tailor their work to the satisfaction of these needs, and findings are tested at various stages by applying them in the field. As a result, research is made more precise and realistic and practice benefits thru the enlargement of vision and insights. Because of this interaction of researcher and practitioner, these programs are often referred to as "action-research" programs.

Cooperative Approach Evolves

One such systemwide curriculum improvement program is that of the West Orange, New Jersey, Public Schools.[8] It involves the classroom teachers and school administrators of the school system and consultants from the Horace Mann-Lincoln Institute of School

---

[8] Reported by Ronald C. Doll, administrative assistant, Department of Curriculum and Guidance; Eleanor Noyes, supervisor of elementary education; and Milton W. Brown, superintendent of schools, West Orange Public Schools, West Orange, New Jersey.

Experimentation. Together they have developed a program of group activities which stems from the interest of teachers in attempting to discover patterns of organization, teaching technics, and materials to meet more effectively the needs of pupils. The program is guided by a Central Curriculum Committee of 24 members, including representatives from the Institute. There are a number of study groups whose approach tends toward action research. These are called study groups because the plan of work centers in classroom experimentation and in developing good group processes in solving educational problems. Seven of these existing in the early stages of the program were: social studies—kindergarten to Grade III; social studies—Grades IV to VI; English and language arts; youth attitudes; high school pupils' interests and needs; reading; and problems of instructional supervision.

Prior to the present cooperative effort curriculum improvement in West Orange consisted primarily of course-of-study preparation by a select few, with the rank and file of classroom teachers having little to do with it. As a consequence many of the materials were little used in the classroom. Along with this, inservice improvement was left to special supervisors operating chiefly within their own spheres and there was little effort toward coordination of approach or teacher involvement in planning.

Teachers Express Opinions

In the fall of 1949, the superintendent asked that the classroom teachers and principals consider ways by which current problems in curriculum might be approached on a cooperative basis. Thru informal discussions the groups began to express satisfactions and dissatisfactions with present programs of teaching and learning.

After several months of these informal discussions certain needs were crystallized. Some of these needs were: more direct experiences for younger children; remedial reading; better use of community resources; improved method and content in science, social studies, and arithmetic; more attention to problems facing pupils of extremely low or high mental ability; improved study skills; greater continuity of instruction thru coordination of the three levels of the school system. The group now had a working basis for extensive discussion, exploration, and research.

Principles and Criteria Determined

All staff members were involved thru discussions and questionnaires in laying out a plan of approach for cooperative study of the problems. Six general principles of organization were agreed upon for the organization of a central representative committee and its procedures. These were:

1. Curriculum study would begin on the front or fronts where needed
2. Activities of groups would be coordinated by one central representative committee
3. Members of the central representative committee would be selected upon the basis of function and usefulness
4. Lay members would be involved where feasible
5. Pupils would be involved where this was consistent with effective pupil-teacher relationships
6. Members of the central representative committee would be elected by fellow staff workers with criteria for services as a committee member specified.

By mid-January 1950, criteria for membership and the setting up of the Central Curriculum Committee was completed. In February the committee met with representatives of the Horace Mann-Lincoln Institute of School Experimentation. Two major ideas emerged: (a) the need for recognizing and encouraging innovations and experiments that were already under way in West Orange schools, and (b) the importance of identifying among teachers feelings of need for curriculum improvement. Following this meeting, there were several months during which the Committee and school faculties exchanged ideas. They identified three problem areas which they agreed upon for immediate action. The three areas were improving pupils' attitudes and sense of values, improving the social studies program in the lower elementary grades, and improving reading and study skills.

Joint Enterprise Given Approval

At this juncture the West Orange Board of Education, acting on the suggestion of the superintendent, made a formal arrangement with the Horace Mann-Lincoln Institute of School Experimentation for a joint enterprise curriculum improvement study on a long-term basis. An essential part of this arrangement was that either party could, whenever it desired, discontinue its relationship to the other.

121

The Committee, in evaluating the results of the work to this point, found that the cooperative plan had the support and approval of teachers and administrators. Reasons given were that the program had not been hurried, classroom teachers had participated on a voluntary basis (much of the work to this point had been done by teachers volunteering to serve on one or another action group), teacher's interests and concerns had been given central importance, there was evidence of the desire to make this curriculum activity a continuous one, and there was the promise that curriculum work would be shared so that only some of the teachers in the school system would have responsibilities at any one time.

Thru this gradual and unforced manner the groundwork was laid for cooperative curriculum work in the West Orange schools. It had begun in a preliminary, exploratory way in 1949 and continued thru that school year. It was not until the fall of 1950 that action groups were organized in the seven areas listed earlier. These action groups have since operated on the principles which won the plan its original approval—gradualism, volunteering, and recognizing the central importance of teachers' actual problems and concerns.

How do action groups operate? What methods do they use? How do the members of the groups feel about their efforts? What results are they getting? These questions perhaps may best be answered by following the activities of one of the groups.

How One Group Worked

The Kindergarten-Grade III Social Studies group was one of the first to be organized, 13 teachers forming the group in October 1950. Its organization rose out of dissatisfaction with a program in social studies which, as one teacher said, "called for teaching about Indians, cavemen, dinosaurs, and little else." She continued, "I doubted all along that study about dinosaurs was appropriate for children of this age. For instance, when I told the children that dinosaurs were 70 feet long, not only they, but I also couldn't visualize a 70-foot animal. We were fortunate enough to be close to a New York museum, so we could get an idea of size, but then I thought, how about the time concept? Isn't there something these children could learn which is more nearly within the range of their experience?"

122

This feeling was shared by other members of the group which met eight times within the ensuing school year. They agreed that time placement of certain content needed study and that much of the content was inappropriate.

The first action proposal was for each teacher to observe the children in her classroom to determine their interest in and attitudes toward the content of the social studies. Discussions of these observations followed, and a chart was made on which the classroom teachers recorded examples of social learnings which they observed. This chart called for a description of the situation, an indication of whether the responses of the children seemed to be on a verbal or functional level, and the social learning or learnings which seemed to result.

Following the study of these observations the group agreed that it needed to learn more about the physical, emotional, and social characteristics and needs of these children. Arrangements were made for a conference on child development with an Institute consultant.

As a result of this conference, the group decided that they should explore children's interests and capacities more fully, using technics which would reach beyond observations of attitudes toward materials in the social studies. Thru an "interest finder" teachers conducted a series of interviews with pupils based upon the following topics:

1. My three wishes
2. What I'd like to know more about
3. What I like best in school
4. What I like best outside of school
5. What I want to be when I grow up
6. One of the places I'd like to go.

Several such interview experiences were engaged in, first by a subcommittee and later by the entire group. Results were charted. The group felt that this interview technic was helpful in identifying children's interests, but that it should be refined and that continued effort should be made to study interests thru other technics. Among these are dramatic play, having children make pictures of open questions about their interests and desires, planned interpretation of pictures by the classroom teacher and other children, arranging for children to compose a group study called "the story of Jack" (an imaginary child), and having children write autobiographies. The group continued its exploration of child interests.

123

It had collected data, by a variety of methods, relating the pupils' interests and unconscious needs. The next major step was the drawing together and interpretation of the data. Following interpretation of the data, tentative conclusions were drawn regarding the social studies program for kindergarten thru Grade III.

The experimentation which has been conducted to date has inevitably affected the experiences of children in the classroom since they have been important participants in the research. The group has now prepared a written guide which emphasizes technics which classroom teachers may use in determining social-studies content.

This expression of how, after nearly two years, an action group views its activities, reveals the unique features of this plan. The study which began with an expression of classroom-teacher needs has grown into an effort on the part of teachers to find out more about the actual needs of children. Classroom teachers are equipping themselves to be more objective in relating themselves to the human as well as course material with which they work, and they are finding satisfactions in the process of discovery. They have had additional satisfactions in sharing their action research with specialists from outside their own schools.

A Small-Size City Utilizes Local Resources

We have seen how a school system may profit by using educational resources made available on a national or regional scale. In contrast, here is an example of how a school district in a small-size city is undertaking successfully a comprehensive curriculum improvement program, using its own and local resources.

La Mesa-Spring Valley School District has developed design both for curriculum improvement and organization.[9] Both are based on the policy of helping classroom teachers use their own creative energies in the solution of problems which stem from situations immediately at hand. This implies that all—principals, classroom teachers, instructional coordinators—recognize that "curriculum change in the classroom sometimes comes about informally." How this policy works may be seen in the development of a fruitful activity in a third grade.

---

[9] Reported by Dorothy L. Harding, director of education and Glenn E. Murdock, superintendent of schools, La Mesa-Spring Valley School Districts, La Mesa, California.

A Unit Emerges

The curriculum steering committee, working with the science committee, was urging more definite use of the immediate environment. Committee reports suggesting ways of doing this were distributed for discussion by building groups, but it was a casual comment which set off the chain of events leading to a unit on "Our New School." This third-grade teacher was quick to capitalize on pupil curiosity aroused by the bustle and noise of workmen beginning construction which would eventually greatly enlarge the school.

Pupils had begun immediately to ask questions. "How large would the addition be?" "Who decided what it was to look like?" "Who hired the workers?" "When would it be finished?"

Here, in the thinking of this teacher, was a project ready-made to satisfy curriculum committee suggestions. She set about to develop a unit, receiving the immediate cooperation of the principal, instructional coordinator, and the curriculum committee. During the project, pupils employed many skills. They interviewed workmen. They drew plans. They calculated labor hours, number of bricks, tons of equipment. They learned to spell names of tools and materials. They experimented with mixing cement. They made to scale a miniature foundation of the new plant. They kept a diary of construction progress. They asked the music supervisor to help them put down the rhythms of manual labors. By the end of the project they had used the Three R's, human relations, creative skills, and had gained a store of new information.

This, it was agreed, was curriculum change of the sort that was not preplanned, but yet fitted the school's design for curriculum improvement.

Such informal developments are part of La Mesa-Spring Valley's over-all program for curriculum improvement. This program, described in the following sketch, utilizes the district's own resources and consultant service from the local college's education department and the facilities of the office of the county superintendent of schools.

Determining Processes

In this community three underlying hypotheses determine the broad framework of activity and govern the processes of curriculum organization in the district:

1. Curriculum changes are best brought about by those who are most generally involved—the classroom teachers. Therefore, changes for the most part should be planned by teacher groups.

125

2. Curriculum changes are brought about slowly on broken fronts, not in large sections. Therefore, such changes should begin with the immediate problems of classroom teachers.

3. Curriculum changes should be subject to constant evaluation and flexibility should be safeguarded. Therefore, curriculum improvement should be a continuous process.

A few of the applications of these guides are shown by the following brief descriptions of committees and classroom experimentation.

Steering committee a clearinghouse—The organization provides for a curriculum steering committee whose membership and function are constituted as follows:

A districtwide steering committee of six members works with the director of education in the over-all planning of curriculum development activity. Membership, selected by cooperative appointment by the administration and the teachers' association, is composed of two teachers from the primary level, two from the elementary level (Grades IV, V, and VI), and two from the intermediate level (Grades VII and VIII).

The committee acts as a clearinghouse for suggestions from the staff for needed curriculum revision and for reports of progress. It acts as a coordinating agency for the work of the various committees.

Work committees flexible—Curriculum work committees vary as to type, membership, and function according to the needs of teachers and the planning of the curriculum steering committee:

Curriculum committees may involve a subject area (arithmetic, social studies), an area of living (family-life education, discipline), and may either be geared to one grade or level, or may cut across several or all grade levels.

Committees may produce materials for district use or may function as discussion groups for the growth of members directly involved. They may meet for a specific short term project, such as preparing material for distribution (parents' handbook).

Membership on curriculum committees is voluntary. Since suggestions for such committees arise from the needs of staff members, it is inevitable that interest be present before a group is formed. There is a special, and up to this time successful, attempt to involve lay participation.

Teachers encouraged to experiment—Classroom teachers are given freedom and assistance in making use of the environmental and the dominant interests of classroom groups, as seen in the following experiences:

An upper-grade group working on problems of taxation in their arithmetic became interested in the construction of a new school to house junior-high pupils, with a resulting series of experiences including not only taxation on the

126

local level but a study of bonds, budgets, community planning, and legal procedures as these matters related to their community.

A fifth- and sixth-grade group, stimulated by daily hearing of jet planes flying overhead, branched into a project in navigation involving considerable scientific investigation, astronomy, and history.

Teacher Workshops

The background information, materials, and teaching methods necessary for such classroom activities are provided for interested teachers by district workshops held thruout the school year. Recently these workshops included one in which teachers and the music coordinator met after school for a series of sessions. Teachers had firsthand experiences in learning folk dances appropriate to their units and in the construction and use of percussion instruments. In another workshop classroom teachers and parents constructed needed classroom equipment, such as large blocks, doll houses, puzzles, and quiet-time developmental seatwork games. A third workshop involved the production by teachers and interested parents of manipulative materials to aid in the instruction of arithmetic.

In all of these activities, from those in which teacher and pupils plan out a unit in the classroom to those in which long-range, district-wide programs are developed, the La Mesa-Spring Valley School District seeks to organize all local resources which fit actual current interests and needs of the teachers and their pupils. This example should be re-examined in terms of the suggestions in Chapter IV.

Curriculum Improvement Centers in the School-Community

In Oak Ridge, Tennessee, a dual approach is taken to curriculum improvement. There is a systemwide program in curriculum development, and also a program in the elementary schools which is centered in the educational needs and problems of each school community.[10] Classroom teachers and school administrators in the separate schools are assisted by the instructional division to carry on workshop activities during the school term, but each faculty sets up its own workshop program to explore those problems and needs it considers as a group to be most significant at the time. In an area

[10] Reported by Raymond H. Ostrander, superintendent of schools, Mineola, New York (formerly superintendent of schools at Oak Ridge, Tennessee).

such as Oak Ridge, where new social forces were making impact on settled ways of life, this procedure was most important, as can be seen in the example of Linden School.

School-Community Readiness

The teachers at Linden School had for some time been concerned with the types of learning experiences provided for citizenship education. This concern was of prime interest to a community which had grown in just a few years "into a city where none before had existed." The Manhattan Project established in 1943 replaced a rural-farm area and three small schools with an urban community having over 7000 children. In a relatively few months thousands of people had come to live in the new community, bringing with them different habits and values. In all, living had become quite different. All members of the community had to learn ways of getting along and living together. The schools were no exception, and the classroom teachers felt this need. Following a series of preliminary discussions with the superintendent and an outside consultant, the faculty decided that the problem might be approached by making the study of "responsibility" a schoolwide project. The teachers felt that the study should be a cooperative endeavor thruout the community, and that it should involve not only the teaching and administrative staff but pupils and community people as well, all seeking for ways in which they could better learn to carry on their everyday relationships thru assuming individual and group responsibilities for improved home, school, and community living.

Workshops for Teachers and Parents

A committee of three classroom teachers chosen by the faculty served with the principal to coordinate the program of workshops and other activities. One of the first jobs was to compile a questionnaire designed to discover those activities already being undertaken to help children become aware of and accept their responsibilities to one another and their responsibilities in their school and in their homes. In workshop groups lists of present and possible activities were refined and extended, and served as the basis for discussion and further planning.

128

At this stage of the project the teacher group decided that parents' participation was essential if the best results were to be obtained. Parents were invited to attend the workshops and to consider with teachers the problem of developing responsibility thru the school program of activities. This was expanded later to include ways of building responsibility in the home as well as in the school, when parents and classroom teachers met in smaller groups according to the classroom attended by pupils.

Numerous Activities

In a second series of workshops items of responsibility were grouped under six general headings—personal, family, school, community, spiritual, and moral. Attention was then given to developing specific inschool activities which offered opportunities for the exercise of responsibility by individual pupils and the group. These cut across all school functions. They included activities in the school cafeteria, such as assisting in the preparation of meals, serving, and care of the cafeteria; in the classroom including classroom management; in hall and playground activities; in the use and care of school materials and equipment; in the library; and in regard to safety patrols and the bus schedule. Other activities included the school garden, the Junior Red Cross and CARE programs, secretarial assistance, and operating the lost and found department. Suggestions were given for various ways in which children might be helped to develop value standards relating to the responsibilities in these activity areas. This resulted in the development of helper-responsibility charts, making lists of duties, making posters, dramatizing and role-playing situations, puppetry, and classroom discussion.

An interesting outgrowth of parent participation in the planning of inschool activities was their own assumption of responsibilities outside the home. They began to assist at school clinics with immunization and with the dental program for sodium fluoride treatment of children's teeth, they participated in dramatizations for parent education programs, served as instructors in bicycle safety programs, and helped teachers in conducting classes on field trips. This lay participation in school activities took many forms; it is always a serious problem to find ways that satisfy both parents and classroom teachers.

129

Values Noted

In order to assure that the growth which was taking place would not be lost, and that effort in this area would continue, a check was made to determine the progress being made by teachers in the classroom and the parent and pupil reactions. Suggestions were requested as to how the idea of responsibility could be extended thru the summer vacation period ahead. Children by their comments showed new understandings of the importance of responsibility.

A sixth-grader wrote, "We grow in responsibility beginning at home, and from home to school, and from school to community. It is our responsibility to try to understand people and to get along with people of other nations. It is also our responsibility to learn to live and work together." Another said, "Our responsibilities are to keep our work up, and when the other boys are not caught up we help them. We should be polite and friendly to all people or visitors who come to our school." One fifth-grader commented regarding the conduct of a group of people at a public meeting: "If they had been at Linden, they would have learned the responsibility of behaving in public places."

Parents also indicated that they had gained insight. One parent said, "I didn't realize I had this much responsibility in raising my daughter as I now see that I have." One mother remarked, "Since you have started this program, I have discovered many new duties to my children and ways of accomplishing them." Parents repeatedly spoke of the carry-over value of the program, particularly their learning of how important it is to apply the word "responsibility" to the specific task required of the child. They have noted that responsibility was more acceptable to the children if they took part in the planning. In some classrooms it was noted that after the program started there was more cooperation from the home in the way of getting the children to school on time, returning permission slips, and general interest in what children had done that day in school. Teachers have this to say about the program:

We often wonder if our efforts are successful when occasionally regression calls our attention to lacks in our program. Then we are reminded of the huge task confronting us and of the fact that neither we adults nor the children learn responsibility in a day, a month, or a year. Only thru patient, helpful guidance can we establish a foothold, a beginning on which to build a meaningful understanding of responsibility.

Curriculum Materials—A Means to an End

In the past, and to an extent even today, much of the curriculum work which has been carried on in school systems over the country has been limited to preparation of course-of-study materials or curriculum guides. Too often such activity involves only the central staff members or small committees set up for this sole purpose. The object has been to produce a publication, but do the classroom teachers use it? The weakness of such a procedure is generally recognized —the materials offer little more than previous guides or courses of study, they are not accepted by those who are to use them, and they are soon "forgotten and put on the shelf."

Chapter VIII emphasizes that the *real* curriculum is what takes place in the individual classrooms. There is little point in having elaborate course of study bulletins and printed guides if these are not of interest and use to the teachers. Often it is necessary, as this Richland example indicates, to begin with the immediate needs of teachers so as to develop the guides teachers will use.

Beginning a Long-Term Project

The Richland, Washington, elementary schools provide an example of a school system which in setting out to prepare guides for the social studies, recognized that the duplicated materials themselves were but the physical byproduct of a considerable effort engaged in by the staff to work out new approaches to their social studies activities.[11] Such effort involves the cooperative thinking of classroom teachers and school administrators and continues over a long period of time—in this case, five years—and the project is still going on. It has resulted in three tentative guides for the social studies—the first one culminating two years of intensive work in 1948, with a revision appearing in 1949 and a restatement in 1951.

At the beginning of the 1948-49 school year all classroom teachers in the system were invited to examine the first guide critically. It was realized that only a beginning had been made and that there were many aspects of the guide which needed revision and improvement as a result of the teachers' classroom experiences in the two

---

[11] Reported by Anne Hospers, director of curriculum, Richland Elementary Schools; P. A. Wright, superintendent, Richland Public Schools, Richland, Washington.

years during which it had been in preparation. Teachers' suggestions for revision included such items as these: (a) there was need for a more flexible time schedule for the several units on certain grade levels; (b) in some instances too many units were included for a given grade; (c) the sequence of introducing the units of work should be altered; (d) more current problems and materials should be included; (e) the framework should be revised so that subject content did not crowd out challenging problem areas which utilize content; and (f) teaching materials, including films and books, should be brought up to date, with specific emphasis on the availability of materials.

A Flexible and Functional Framework

As a consequence the framework devised in 1949 gave more emphasis to the child and his experiences and greater provision for flexibility in number, sequence, and length of units. The revision process, by enlisting the thinking of the entire staff, enabled teachers to attain new insights into the social studies and improved their use of the guide. As a result of continued study upon the problem, the 1951 guide for Grades I, II, and III has been developed around problems, experiences, and social understandings suggested by the majority of the classroom teachers. The problems and experiences are within the area of the child's immediate interest and environment. They serve as an aid to teachers rather than stereotyped direction, since they are designed to serve as a springboard from which departures can be made, depending upon the interest and needs of children and the judgment of the teacher.

The success of the inservice procedures used in Richland is attested by the fact that in five years of work the classroom teachers themselves have moved forward on a continuous program of revising the social studies guides. Starting with a social studies course of study which reflected a teaching practice rather formal, academic, and content centered, they developed current guides which reflect practices based upon activities which are centered in the needs of the children and which utilize problems and experiences designed to attain the outcomes of what is generally considered a forward-looking approach to the social studies.

Two County Systems Organize for Change

Cooperative activity in curriculum improvement is facilitated when the office of the county superintendent of schools is well organized and directed. Resources for concerted and coordinated study, research, and application are provided as a service to the several districts and schools in a way consistent with acceptable methods of cooperative planning for curriculum improvement. The following two illustrations indicate what is happening in county-level curriculum improvement thruout the country in those states which provide the intermediate district service.

Arlington County, Virginia

This county is representative of increasing numbers of counties which, because of enlightened professional leadership, are offering greatly augmented educational services to their schools as well as curriculum improvement activities centered in a cooperative and coordinated county-level program.[12]

Arlington County has developed a philosophy of work that holds that all curriculum organization and procedures must stem from the situation in which they are to be used. The Arlington County Teachers' Council on Instruction, composed of a teacher representative from each of the 38 schools in the county and two representatives each from the supervisory and administrative staff of the county office, serve as the countywide curriculum coordination committee. The purposes of this committee are to consider problems reported by the representatives of each school, to formulate from these countywide policies and plans, and to transmit to the county superintendent suggestions for implementing them.

In addition to the teachers council on instruction, there is a second countywide curriculum group known as the Arlington Public Schools Study Council. This study council also consists of a classroom teacher representative from each of the 38 schools and representatives from the supervisory and administrative staff. Its major function is to hear reports of curriculum improvement activity being undertaken in all the schools of the county and, thru its members,

---

[12] Reported by C. Glen Hass, associate superintendent and director of instruction; William A. Early, formerly superintendent, Arlington County Schools, Arlington, Virginia; now superintendent of schools at Savannah, Georgia.

to carry back to the individual schools ideas which may further contribute to improved practices locally.

The teachers council on instruction has engaged in a wide range of activities. Some of the jobs which it has pursued recently include the preparation of a handbook for parents of children just starting to school, evaluation of textbooks, the addition of reading consultants to the staff of the county superintendent, the publication of a periodic curriculum bulletin, and projection of an education summer workshop, a language arts guide, and a system for the use of cumulative records on a countywide basis. The teachers' council does not undertake such projects itself; after planning, the work is done by committees of volunteer participants with the assistance of persons they request from the county superintendent's office.

It is significant that in Arlington County there is a countywide parents council on instruction which includes parent representatives from each of the schools within the county. The purpose of the parents council is to study the existing curriculum. It meets monthly, hears reports on various curriculum activities, raises questions, and makes suggestions which are passed on to the teachers council on instruction and to the superintendent. There is a close working relationship between the lay and professional groups, which reaches down to the various work groups in the school centers.

Dade County, Florida

Florida has the county unit pattern similar to Maryland and West Virginia. As indicated in Chapter IV, the county unit has unique possibilities for mobilizing for curriculum improvement.

Dade County has instituted an over-all curriculum improvement program.[13] Like Arlington County, it has a central county instructional planning committee. Organized activities for the inservice professional growth of teachers are provided thru the cooperation of the University of Miami and other institutions under the general direction of the county instructional planning committee. Executive responsibility for this program is shared by the office of the county superintendent of schools, thru its instructional division, and representatives of the university.

[13] Reported by William Alexander, professor of education, University of Miami, and curriculum advisor, Dade County Schools, Dade County, Florida.

These activities, for which classroom teachers receive credit from the university, are of five general types:

1. *Practicums*—These are provided for those faculties desiring to work on a particular school problem. In 1950-51 five practicums were offered in the county, including one dealing with evaluation of elementary schools, one in the general field of guidance, and a third on unit planning and teaching.

2. *Workshops*—The workshops range in length from one to three weeks and cover such topics as language arts, curriculum planning, and problems identified by individual schools.

3. *Inservice courses*—The courses have been organized for teachers in co-operation with the university. Courses cover such areas as elementary school art, music, children's literature, health education, and physical education.

4. *Institutes*—Several special two-week institutes have been set up in cooperation with the University of Miami and the Florida Agricultural and Mechanical College. These institutions meet after school for an hour and a half each day for two weeks and deal with music, art, elementary science, mental health, guidance, and instructional materials.

5. *Evening division courses*—Several on-campus courses are arranged for and offered to Dade County teachers and are planned with special reference to their needs.

In a system as large as Dade County there are a large number of professional activities in addition to those offering formal credit which have inservice educational values. Some of the more frequent of these include conferences and clinics. As an example, the reading conference, a joint university-county committee affair, has been conducted annually for several years. Program meetings of the 42 professional organizations also offer many opportunities for professional growth. These include reports of curriculum planning committees, demonstrations with pupil groups, demonstrations and exhibits of materials, panel discussions, and social programs. Well-planned faculty meetings, thru discussion, demonstrations, planning, and other means, deal with specific problems of individual schools. Many of these meetings occur in preschool and postschool planning periods. Consultants are available to the faculty groups thru the county instructional planning committee.

Sometimes, in a school system the size of Dade County, problems involve several schools, so that the faculties from these schools need to meet together. For this purpose the "school group organization" plan divides the county into 13 groups of schools, each organized around a senior high school. During the postschool planning period, the elementary schools in each group plan for next year's joint meetings. Certain days are designated as planning days when all instructional personnel in the 13 groups may come together for inservice programs. Another activity for teachers provides for curriculum planning committees, which yearly involve upwards of 900 people. These groups engage in the preparation of materials, the study of materials for children, the analysis of teaching procedures, the preparation of lists of equipment and supplies, and the planning of inservice programs for groups of teachers.

The programs in Arlington and Dade Counties illustrate how the county level of school administration serves a coordinating function in pooling resources for currriculum improvement. Thru these service functions wider participation in curriculum work is made possible and greater unity in purpose and goals as well as in instructional practices is achieved.

Curriculum Action To Meet Special Needs

Curriculum change occurring in a school need not be novel and startling in order to be significant. Practices, long accepted and used successfully by other schools, may be new to this school and therefore the first order of business for classroom teachers and school administrators who are alert to the needs of children.

According to a study made in 1951 and reported in the 1952 Yearbook of the American Association of School Administrators,[14] only 11 percent of the approximately 3000 rural and urban superintendents of schools reporting had in their districts reading clinics for diagnosis and counseling of pupils; however, 85 percent stated that they would like to provide such clinical services.

Remedial Reading Clinic

Two years ago the Cheboygan, Michigan, City Schools[15] established a remedial reading clinic because "our teachers had noticed for some time that students who were having difficulty in various areas of schoolwork almost invariably also had some sort of reading difficulty." A remedial reading specialist heads the clinic work,

---

[14] American Association of School Administrators. *The American School Superintendency.* Thirtieth Yearbook. Washington, D. C.: the Association, a department of the National Education Association, 1952. p. 205.

[15] Reported by Harold Wetherell, superintendent, and Dorothy Fredberg, remedial reading specialists, Cheboygan City Schools, Cheboygan, Michigan.

doing the diagnostic testing of individual reading problems and remedial teaching of the extreme cases. As much as possible, this specialist works with classroom teachers in an inservice program of reading improvement thruout the school system. However, during the first year, the clinic worked mostly with special cases in Grades III and VIII to keep the work of the specialist from being spread too thin while the program was still being developed.

In the second year 39 elementary-school pupils, 18 junior high-school pupils, and one high-school pupil received special attention in reading at the clinic. These pupils generally are given 30 minutes of instruction three times per week, either in groups of two to four pupils, or individually as their need may require. Results have been gratifying, not only in view of average gains, which have equaled 0.8 of a grade during the most recent four-month period, but more especially in view of teachers' reports of children's over-all improvement in schoolwork. Typical statements are: "These pupils appear confident in classwork for the first time," and "They are beginning to volunteer frequently in class activities which include reading skills," and "John now reads without hesitation and stammering." Both individual and group evaluations should be made of curriculum developments (see Chapters XI and XII).

Inservice Education Program

In conjunction with the development of the reading clinic, an inservice program has been organized for elementary-school teachers who are interested in improving the teaching of reading in the classroom. An extension course in this area is offered by the University of Michigan. Under the direction of the reading specialist, after-school meetings are held to discuss the problems of classroom teachers, such as the adjustment of the reading program to meet individual differences, causes for reading failures, prevention of severe reading disabilities, methods of building readiness for reading, grouping for instruction in silent reading, and problems of reading instruction for the slow reader at the high-school level.

It is reported that "teachers and community people are sold on the program and at the present time we are in the process of expanding our facilities. We feel that this project in remedial reading is going to be of lasting benefit to the children of Cheboygan."

137

A Project To Improve Method in Arithmetic

Much of the curriculum improvement work most productive and helpful to the classroom teacher consists in beginning on actual specific problems or needs of teachers, applying sound technics of study, and utilizing in the classroom the positive results of the investigation.

Locating Specific Instructional Problems

During the past two years, the San Diego City Schools have made a unified effort to strengthen the mathematics program at all levels.[16] The Mathematics Steering Committee, made up of classroom teachers, principals, and central office staff members, approved the development of new diagnostic tests and new arithmetic drill sheets which are now being used from Grades II to VI. An arithmetic guide was developed, stressing the meaning approach as well as the need for effective drill so that each child may achieve mastery in accordance with his ability. Three master teachers were released as teacher-consultants to help all elementary-school teachers in classroom work in arithmetic. Elementary-school principals held study-group meetings in arithmetic with consultant assistance so that they might provide more help for their teachers.

One phase of the citywide inservice training activity in arithmetic was an intensive classroom-centered workshop in teaching multiplication of whole numbers. A pilot study had been conducted previously, so materials and procedures were available and the success of the project was fairly well assured. Fifty-nine fifth-grade teachers accepted the invitation to participate. A graduate student was enlisted to refine the materials and directions, and to evaluate the children's improvement as a topic for his master's thesis.

Pretests in several aspects of multiplication and division were given to the pupils of the 59 teachers and to control groups. The teachers scored the papers and then met with the consultant to study results and to receive instruction regarding the teaching procedure to follow. Two days later the group met again to discuss progress and to clarify misunderstandings which had been revealed during their

---

[16] Reported by Robert E. Jenkins, assistant superintendent in charge of instruction, San Diego City Schools; and Richard Madden, chairman of graduate studies, San Diego State College; and Will C. Crawford, superintendent, San Diego City Schools, San Diego, California.

teaching. Further instruction on method and on analysis of pupils' work was given.

A supplementary bulletin on specific procedures, the need of which was revealed by the supervisors who followed the project day by day, was produced at the beginning of the second week.

Evaluation of the Results

At the close of the 10-day period the teachers retested and then reassembled to check results. Before the results were determined, an unsigned response card was used to secure the teachers' individual evaluations. They were not only almost universally favorable, but laudatory. Test results showed over 20 percent over-all gain in achievement, with children at some levels of achievement gaining 100 percent. A few children moved from 0 percent of examples correct to 100 percent correct.

At the final meeting, plans were made to apply the same method of instruction to division. Further, two types of follow-up activities were initiated: (a) principals made every effort to make it possible for all teachers to profit from the results of this workshop, and (b) similar workshops were planned for other grade levels.

This project is meritorious, particularly in that teachers saw a need, quantified it by testing, received specific instruction, ascertained the results personally, and generalized the method for wider application. A meaningful approach to teaching the number system rather than a drill approach was stressed. The teachers saw results immediately. The methods at once became teaching practice, and provision was made to extend the program on a wider base thruout the system.

Significant Changes Are Possible

The examples given in this chapter are representative of the kinds of significant curriculum change which result in changed behavior and attitudes on the part of classroom teachers, pupils, school administrators, parents, and others. Each group, according to *its* peculiar needs, has achieved results because certain conditions prevailed. There has been that permissiveness which makes it possible to try out new ideas, to take a new line of attack. There has been conscious effort to provide flexibility in planning and work. Activities have begun with the needs of teachers and pupils, so that the ensuing programs of curriculum improvement have been soundly backed by those who have to carry them out in the classroom. Time has been provided—time to explore needs and interests, time to plan, time to communicate, and time to work, to try results, and to evaluate. Finally, there has been understanding leadership exercised thru coordinating groups and administrative organizations built with the voluntary cooperation of all participants.

The curriculum will change—the changing nature of our society ensures this. The kind of change depends upon what happens to all those persons involved in it. Need creates opportunity by challenging individuals or groups to action. Good leadership is sensitive to the appearance of these opportunities and makes the most of them. In the democratic situation, leadership does not merely reside in a select few, or in a hierarchy. It may arise in an individual classroom, in a committee, a teachers club, a parents group, or in individuals anywhere along the line of service. It may emerge in the course of an organized attempt to solve problems, or it may come before organization has taken place. In any of its appearances it is recognized and encouraged.

The responsibility for creating these conditions of opportunity and for encouraging the emergence of leadership lies in the superintendent. Behind most successful curriculum improvement programs there is a superintendent of schools with vision and understanding. He backs the groups working on curriculum problems by providing encouragement and material support. He understands and practices good group processes, knowing that the conditions for successful curriculum change are the same in nature as those for successful learning in the classroom. Finally, such a superintendent has developed the necessary skills for making operative thruout the total program of his school system those conditions which create orderly progress thru democratic participation.

SELECTED REFERENCES

ASSOCIATION FOR SUPERVISION AND CURRICULUM DEVELOPMENT. *Action for Curriculum Improvement.* 1951 Yearbook. Washington, D. C.: the Association, a department of the National Education Association, 1951. 248 p. $3.50.

ASSOCIATION FOR SUPERVISION AND CURRICULUM DEVELOPMENT. *Growing Up in an Anxious Age.* 1952 Yearbook. Washington, D. C.: the Association, a department of the National Education Association, 1952. 263 p. $3.50.

ASSOCIATION FOR SUPERVISION AND CURRICULUM DEVELOPMENT. *Instructional Leadership in Small Schools.* Washington, D. C.: the Association, a department of the National Education Association, 1951. 88 p.

ASSOCIATION FOR SUPERVISION AND CURRICULUM DEVELOPMENT. *Toward a New Curriculum.* 1944 Yearbook. Washington, D. C.: the Association, a department of the National Education Association, 1944. 192 p. (Out of print.)

ASSOCIATION FOR SUPERVISION AND CURRICULUM DEVELOPMENT. *Toward Better Teaching.* 1949 Yearbook. Washington, D. C.: the Association, a department of the National Education Asscociation, 1949. 282 p. $3.

BOWEN, GENEVIEVE. *Living and Learning in a Rural School.* New York: Macmillan Co.. 1944. 324 p.

COOK, LLOYD A., and COOK, ELAINE F. *A Sociological Approach to Education.* Second edition. New York: McGraw-Hill Book Co., 1950. 514 p.

FAUNCE, ROLAND C., and BOSSING, NELSON L. *Developing the Core Curriculum.* New York: Prentice Hall, 1951. 311 p.

MIEL, ALICE. *Changing the Curriculum.* New York: Appleton-Century-Crofts, 1946. 242 p.

NATIONAL EDUCATION ASSOCIATION, DEPARTMENT OF ELEMENTARY SCHOOL PRINCIPALS. *Community Living and the Elementary School.* Twenty-Fourth Yearbook. Washington, D. C.: the Department, 1945. 351 p. $2.

NATIONAL EDUCATION ASSOCIATION, DEPARTMENT OF RURAL EDUCATION. *The County Superintendent of Schools in the United States.* 1950 Yearbook. Washington, D. C.: the Department, 1950. 188 p. $2.50.

NATIONAL EDUCATION ASSOCIATION, DEPARTMENT OF RURAL EDUCATION. *The Child in the Rural Environment.* 1951 Yearbook. Washington, D. C.: the Department, 1951. 253 p. $2.

TABA HILDA, director. *Elementary Curriculum in Intergroup Relations.* Washington, D. C.: American Council on Education, 1950. 248 p.

TABA, HILDA, director. *With Focus on Human Relations.* Washington, D. C.: American Council on Education, 1950. 227 p.

CHAPTER SIX

Curriculum Developments in Secondary Schools

OUR secondary schools, particularly the senior high schools, constitute what is commonly considered the most static segment of the American educational scene. Nevertheless, the diligent inquirer is likely to be surprised or even amazed by the variety and volume of curriculum change being effected each year in our junior and senior high schools. For example, a survey, made in New Jersey, revealed that of the 190 approved public secondary schools 119 reported recent changes in their curriculums.[1] The report concluded that while some of the changes "are not revolutionary in scope . . . they do reveal that public secondary education in New Jersey is responding to changing pupil needs and is not completely frozen in a traditional pattern which permits no change."

However, even those who are encouraged by the amount of curriculum development currently in progress are well aware of the fact that a large fraction of our secondary schools lack a curriculum development program of any consequence. Moreover, it can be safely said that curriculum change in the secondary schools has not kept pace with the highly accelerated changes that have been taking place in our nation and in the world.

A recent report issued by the U. S. Office of Education succinctly describes the situation in regard to the high schools:

A review of the history of secondary education in the United States suggests some challenging generalizations:

1. Our conception of the nature and purposes of secondary education has undergone far-reaching and almost continuous changes.

2. High-school programs and operations are critically in need of further changes. The rate of social change in this country is rapid and it tends to outrun the capacity of the schools for making needed adaptations.

3. The basic philosophy and promising patterns for changing the schools to bring them abreast of the times have been developed during recent decades.

---

[1] New Jersey Secondary School Teachers' Association. *We Look at Curriculum Growth in New Jersey's High Schools.* 1952 Yearbook. Plainfield, N. J.: Lester D. Beers, 1035 Kenyon Ave., 1952. 96 p.

They have been widely discussed and frequently tested, and they are widely approved by educational leaders.

4. Ways must be found to accelerate changes in our secondary schools needed to gear them more closely to the rapid changes in our social and economic life.[2]

As the introduction of Chapter II indicates, those who determine the content of the curriculum should be guided by an understanding of the outcomes that society expects from its schools. The curriculum workers, who have recognized the needs and defined the problems dealt with in the following examples, have given evidence of an acceptance of this basic principle. As the examples also make clear, the enlightened curriculum participant may be a classroom teacher or school administrator in the local school or he may hold an office that enables him to exert his influence on a county, state, region, or nationwide scale. The illustrations also reveal ways in which curriculum workers of all levels can and do cooperate in getting the job done. It should not be inferred that the examples given conform in all respects to the views of all members of the Yearbook Commission. The examples should be considered in the light of principles stated in other chapters, such as Chapter IV.

One of the following descriptions indicates that curriculum development has been aimed at a reorganization of the basic structure of the curriculum. As yet, at least, efforts in this direction have made but small headway in the secondary schools. Dominant among the plans which involve major reorganization of the structure of the curriculum is perhaps, the so-called core-curriculum plan. A recent inquiry by the U. S. Office of Education has shown that the core-curriculum organization, as defined, has been adopted in only about 3.5 percent of all public secondary schools of the United States.[3] The study showed that the senior high school has remained practically unaffected; almost all core programs are in junior high schools. In many of these it is doubtful that the adopted programs yet involve much more than a process of putting subjects together into larger blocks.

While this chapter deals with ways in which curriculum changes have been brought about in secondary schools, it should be stated

---

[2] The first Commission on Life Adjustment Education for Youth. *Vitalizing Secondary Education.* U. S. Office of Education, Federal Security Agency, Bulletin 1951, No. 3. Washington, D. C.: Superintendent of Documents, Government Printing Office, 1951. p. 2.

[3] Wright, Grace S. *Core Curriculum in Public High Schools.* U. S. Office of Education, Federal Security Agency, Bulletin 1950, No. 5. Washington, D. C.: Superintendent of Documents, Government Printing Office, 1950. p. 6.

immediately that what follows is the story of how a few selected curriculum programs have developed. Practical considerations make it impossible for a chapter such as this to be comprehensive.

Guidance Committee Sponsors an Occupational Survey

More than a hundred secondary schools in Michigan and practically all of the state's colleges cooperate in a plan called the Michigan College Agreement Plan. This interesting development is one of the outgrowths of the Michigan Study of the Secondary School Curriculum begun in 1937. Its objective is to improve education so that the needs of youth may be more effectively satisfied.

Secondary schools which are members of the College Agreement have agreed to apply what the parties concerned believe to be the best modern theory in the areas of guidance and curriculum development. On their part the colleges agree not only to help the schools improve themselves but also to admit their graduates upon the recommendation of the local authorities regardless of the pattern of subjects taken in high school by the candidates for college admission.

Getting the Facts

Schools cooperating under the Michigan College Agreement Plan are urged to conduct frequent occupational surveys.[4] As its initial survey under the plan, Dowagiac Central High School decided to conduct a survey of stenographers, bookkeepers, and general office clerks in Dowagiac, Michigan. The over-all purpose of this occupational survey was as follows: to evaluate occupational training, placement, and adjustment of students enrolled in the business education department. The specific purposes of the survey were:

1. To determine the number of jobs in Dowagiac included in the following job classifications: stenographer, bookkeeper, and general office clerk

2. To ascertain the number and percentage of new workers needed in each office occupation in Dowagiac each year

3. To survey the office occupational opportunities in the community in order to indicate changes and trends in employment opportunities and in the occupations themselves

---

[4] Based on a 1949 report, *A Survey of Office Occupations in Dowagiac, Michigan,* directed by Elaine Sheltraw, Business Education Coordinator, working with the Dowagiac High School Guidance Committee, 1949. 27 p. (Mimeo.)

Public Schools, Chattanooga, Tennessee

Our nation's success in business and industrial development, cultural growth, and high standard of living is the result of man's creative power nurtured by education.

4. To secure pertinent information relating to the school's success in job placement, quality and adequacy of instruction in basic educational and occupational skills, and other data essential to evaluating and improving the school's offerings.

5. To obtain information about job opportunities for students now enrolled in the cooperative business education program of the school

6. To improve school-business relationships so as to meet more fully the responsibilities of the business training program in the school.

The Dowagiac survey was conducted under the immediate supervision of the high-school guidance committee consisting of eight teachers appointed by the director of guidance. This committee, in turn, chose the business education coordinator to serve as the survey director.

Preparation for the survey included a public relations program. The prospective survey was publicized in the *Dowagiac Daily News* at various intervals while preliminary work was being completed. Plans of the survey were discussed with many businessmen so that their ideas could be incorporated in the study. Cooperative trainees as well as other business students were prepared for the survey thru class discussions. The value of this preparation can be seen in the fact that 40 percent of the employers returned their completed questionnaires during the first week of the survey and within a month 83 percent of the questionnaires had been returned.

Facing the Facts

After summarizing the data obtained from these questionnaires, the committee and its director drew up a list of conclusions and recommendations as follows:

CONCLUSIONS

1. Eighty-four percent of the businessmen in Dowagiac require high-school graduation for employment in their firms. Therefore, the business education department of the Dowagiac Central High School should be regarded primarily as a terminal training center.

2. Office employees are deficient in the spelling and computation skills. These were two of the most common weaknesses found in young employees, and employers also considered them the two most serious weaknesses.

3. Personality factors ranked high among the outstanding weaknesses of office workers. Employers regard young employees' lack of interest in their work as one of their most serious weaknesses.

4. Dowagiac employers consider an employable personality, over and above occupational competency, as essential for a successful office worker.

5. The occupational survey in Dowagiac served as an excellent medium of public relations. Contacts made during the study resulted in the placement of several students on the cooperative training program.

1. Since there are almost twice as many general office clerk jobs available in Dowagiac as those specializing in stenography and bookkeeping, it is recommended that a program in clerical office training be evolved to supplement the present stenographic and bookkeeping courses.

2. It is recommended that special attention be given to preparing students for employment in the wholesale-retail and manufacturing industries. Since over half of the office jobs in Dowagiac are in these two occupational groupings, it is suggested that concentrated vocabularies in these areas be presented to vocational business students.

3. It is recommended that the cooperative work experiences program in office occupations be extended to give better terminal training for business graduates of the Dowagiac Central High School.

4. It is recommended that special remedial courses in spelling and arithmetic be offered to all business students deficient in these skills. It is further suggested that all business students be given an achievement test in these fundamentals at the end of their sophomore year to aid in selecting students for the remedial courses.

5. Personality development should be incorporated into all commercial courses and stressed in all classes.

6. It is recommended that this type of survey become a continuous endeavor of the Dowagiac Central High School business education department.[5]

The above survey was believed by the teacher committee to be the first survey of local office occupations ever to have been conducted in Dowagiac. Since it was an initial survey, the committee decided that it was advisable to narrow its scope to a small concentrated field. It is hoped that by reporting it here we may suggest how the guidance committee of a school and other aspects of instruction can join to improve school community relations.

Cooperative Occupational Education

In 1949 the four departments—homemaking, family life education, industrial arts, and vocational education—joined forces and became an Educational Division in the Kansas City (Missouri) Schools. This in itself is a curriculum step of no mean proportions.

---

[5] Balance Sheet. "Survey of Office Occupations." *Balance Sheet* 32: 28; September 1950.

In discussing the challenge that it presented, the head of the division wrote, "In the comparatively short time we have been working together, we have proved again that the whole is greater than the sum of its parts and that a number of individuals who are able to coordinate their efforts and work together as a team can accomplish much more than the same individuals working separately."

Toward Functional Work Experience

Work education or work experience has been recognized for some time as an integral part of the total program of education for youth. Those school systems that have sought a more functional and realistic program of education, especially for those youth of high-school age who do not intend to go to college or enter the highly skilled occupations, are finding the answer in work experience. The school district of Kansas City in an effort to extend the educational opportunities offered to youth and to promote a closer working relationship between the public schools and business and industry, launched such a program in 1945.[6] The program was named Cooperative Occupational Education and was designed as an extension of the high-school program to include on-the-job occupational training.

In this plan the student spends approximately half of each school day pursuing his high-school courses, one of which is directly related to his employment. The other half of the school day, or a minimum of 15 hours each week, is spent on the job where his training is supervised and controlled by the school.

The objectives of Cooperative Occupational Education are:

1. To provide opportunities for advanced high-school students to continue their high-school work and at the same time prepare themselves for a vocation

2. To provide a much wider range of training experience than would be possible if all training were attempted within the school

3. To bridge the gap between the regular classroom and actual occupational practice by providing supervised on-the-job work experience

4. To provide a means of keeping students in school who might otherwise quit to enter employment.

---

[6] Based upon materials submitted by V. L. Pickens, chairman, Division of Practical Arts, Vocational, and Family Life Education, Public Schools of Kansas City, Missouri.

From the applicants for a COE program, a group of juniors, seniors, or postgraduates 16 years of age or older is carefully selected by the school authorities. These students register for two and one-half units of regular high-school subjects and one unit of instruction related to their employment. This schedule, as stated above, is compressed into one-half day so that the workers may spend the remaining half day in supervised work experience on the job. Their employment is carefully supervised by a coordinator who is a regular member of the high-school faculty. The supervision is designed to insure that the pupils are in a learning situation and that they are following a planned training schedule previously agreed to by the coordinator, employee, and employer. For successfully discharging the requirements of employment, the workers receive another unit of high-school credit. This rounds out their normal four and one-half units of credit per year. The areas of occupations used in the COE program in Kansas City were:

1. Distributive occupations such as retail selling
2. Clerical occupations such as stenography
3. Skilled occupations such as junior machinists or dental assistants
4. Service occupations such as beauty operator assistants or hospital attendants.

Many Gains from the Program

The program has very definite values which accrue to the learner, the school, the employer, and the community. These make it a truly cooperative one:

1. *To the student*
   a. He is enabled to continue his high-school work for graduation while carrying on part-time employment.
   b. He is more able to bridge the gap between school and employment.
   c. He receives on-the-job training which will give him advanced standing in employment after he has completed his high-school work.

2. *To the school*
   a. It helps to keep students in school who must otherwise leave to enter employment.
   b. It enables the school to assist the student in adjusting himself to employment.
   c. It serves as a tie between the school and employer.
   d. It furnishes an opportunity to meet the special needs of pupils.

3. *To the employer*

    a. He has the aid and the benefit of the experience of the coordinator in training young people for entrance into full-time employment.

    b. He is given the opportunity to select new employees on a learner basis.

    c. He has an opportunity to suggest specific training for the learner.

    d. The coordinator, the learner, and the employer working together should develop a more valuable worker in a shorter period of time.

4. *To the community*

    a. Better citizens should be developed as the young workers begin to understand the real worth of honest labor and their obligation to fellow workers and employers.

    b. The whole community benefits from better trained and more responsible workers.

    c. The community and the school are partners in a COE program. They have a stake in the young workers—all three benefit.

In developing this COE program and in offering it to high-school students and to employers, three basic principles are recognized:

1. The program should be presented as an integral part of the curriculum of the public schools of Kansas City, Missouri.

2. The program must be presented as an organized training plan with value for both students and employers. This program must not be an ordinary type of part-time employment but a definite learning situation for high-school students.

3. All employment selected for use in this program must be evaluated in advance in terms of definite criteria.

The program is now in its seventh year with an enrolment of 450 girls and boys. Every high school in Kansas City is participating and requests are already in for more coordinators to handle the growing demand. Placements have been made in 40 different occupations with 95 different employers. A few of the occupations in which the pupils are working are: advertising, accounting, store sales, office work, telephone operating, tabulating machine operating, drafting, cabinet making, and service station helper.

Cooperation Brings Results

The success of the program hinges upon cooperation. The employer, the school, and the family must all understand and work toward a common goal—the training of an individual for proper job adjustment. A recent survey of participating employers and parents indicated enthusiasm and interest in the continuation of cooperative education as a part of the secondary-school program of Kansas City.

A revealing evaluation of this COE program was made by one of the high-school counselors who wrote,

> The Cooperative Occupational Education program is serving a real purpose in Kansas City, Missouri. The program is planned for normal or average high-school boys and girls who want work-experience training. However, the co-ordinator does not hesitate to take students who have problems of various kinds, emotional as well as financial. I can think of many examples of students who would not have had a high-school education without the assistance of the COE program. One example I recall was of a girl who came from a small town in another state who had intelligence above average, a broken spirit (which was probably because she came from a broken home), little money, no place to live, and a strong desire for an education. This girl enrolled in the COE program. She now is filling a real place in industry, and with the money earned from working is a respected school citizen. She has blossomed under the re-sponsibility placed on her by her employer. She would hardly be recognized as the same person we saw a year ago last fall. She will be graduated this June and will, without a doubt, continue to advance on the job she now has. I can recall examples of other students who had attendance problems, as well as disciplinary problems, who have been able to adjust so that they have matured enough socially and emotionally to have very high job ratings. They are not school problems now.

Cooperative Revision of Senior English

In 1947 the Commissioner of Education of New York informed the school administrators and classroom teachers of the secondary schools of a new regulation that would make possible considerable change in the English programs of the twelfth grade. This regulation, which became effective in September 1951, proposed that hence-forth the comprehensive Regents examination in English be given at the end of the eleventh grade, i.e., a year earlier than formerly. The aim was to encourage greater flexibility in the twelfth-grade program.

Procedures and Processes

During the 1948-49 school year several schools in central New York conducted a comprehensive study of a new English 12 pro-gram thru their school study council and have since reported the

151

results of their study.[7] During 1948-49, this study council was an organization of 46 public-school systems allied with the Syracuse University Graduate School of Education for the purpose of carrying on cooperative study of common educational problems. Among the schools represented were 22 central schools, 14 city schools, 4 union free schools, and 6 village schools. Teachers from 40 of these schools took part in the study of English 12. A steering committee, which the council authorized its president to appoint, organized and directed the study.

The general plan followed during the study included three general conferences open to all teachers of English 11 and 12 in schools that were members of the council. Between the general conferences teachers in neighboring schools met as regional work committees. Syracuse University, the New York State Department of Education, and other agencies provided a total of ten consultants for the study. The steering committee edited the reports of the committees which were published for distribution to all of the council's schools. The proposals of the study are now being evaluated as they are tried out in actual classroom situations.

Appraisal and Evaluation

During the study the questionnaire technic was used to determine what students, graduates, and English teachers thought should be included in the English 12 course as topics and activities. Five of the regional committees of the study prepared a resource unit each for the proposed course. In preparing these they followed a work form which one of the research assistants developed to guide the groups in preparing such units. These units were all designed to develop social competence, civic responsibility, and cultural growth and dealt with five major forms of communication, namely, the magazine, the motion picture, the newspaper, the radio, and the theater. Another committee made a study of the workshop-type class which they thought of as a means of introducing a desirable flexibility into teaching by using student interest as an approach to meeting student needs. It was not thought of as a classroom procedure that will solve all the problems of teaching.

---

[7] Committee on English 12. *A Guide for the Teaching of English.* Report of the Central New York School Study Council. Syracuse, N. Y.: the Council, 1949. 125 p. (Mimeo.)

Still another regional committee worked in the area of evaluation. It pointed out the objectives of the English program and their relation to the major objectives of education and outlined the specific skills and understandings relating to reading, writing, speaking, and listening. Also listed were procedures that have been used by teachers in attempting meaningful evaluation of students. In this difficult area it seems fair to say that the study was more suggestive than comprehensive. As in other areas, a bibliography of reference materials was prepared.

Curriculum Revision by a Teachers Association

Hinsdale, Illinois, is a residential village of 9000 people, lying 17 miles southwest of Chicago's Loop. It has two school districts. The township high-school district has a population of approximately 17,000. The grade-school district, servicing Hinsdale and Clarendon Hills, includes 12,500 residents. Both districts have identical personnel on the boards of education and have a common administrative staff. Both districts have identical salary schedules for teachers, a common educational philosophy and curriculum program, and many of the benefits of the unit system.[8]

Unique Features of the Plan

The Hinsdale Public Schools Curriculum Program was characterized in certain ways:

1. The program is truly fundamental in that it was begun by the teachers association and has remained its major project for the past six years.

2. Most of the work is done on released time from school.

3. Laymen have played an important part in the group discussions and decisions.

4. The curriculum program has united the efforts of teachers of two separate school districts in planning courses from kindergarten thru the twelfth grade.

5. Preschool workshops lasting two weeks have become an integral part of the program.

6. The Illinois Curriculum Program thru providing consultant help, organizing curriculum conferences, and making available the results of research has contributed greatly to the progress made.

---

[8] Based on a report by Clifford Durman, curriculum coordinator, Hinsdale Public Schools, Hinsdale, Illinois.

153

The Hinsdale Teachers Association was organized in 1946. Since the classroom teachers considered themselves a professional group, they decided to produce on a professional level. With the permission and cooperation of the administration and the board of education they took curriculum revision as their major project. Not only have the years since 1946 witnessed the improvement of education in the community, but the experience has been a valuable means for the inservice growth of teachers.

Planning, Program, and Progress

A committee of teachers and laymen working for several months with ideas from the community and teaching staff drew up a philosophy of education which proved to be an extremely valuable guide. Work began in subject-area groups where classroom teachers seemed to have the feeling of greatest security. The goal was to provide a 12-year program in social studies, language arts, and other subject-fields. Each group consisted of teachers from the primary grades, the middle grades, and the high school. The elected group leaders from each of seven groups, plus the president of the teachers association and four administrators made up the planning committee. Groups all met on released time, one-half day a month. The planning committee met once a month.

Very early the classroom teachers felt the need for preschool workshops. They volunteered to give a week of time and to pay for consultants from the University of Chicago for the first workshop; they also paid for consultants for the next workshop lasting two weeks. Soon the board of education extended the pay period to cover the workshops and gave teachers credit toward the salary schedule requirements of periodic summer-school attendance.

One of the early workshops was devoted to intergroup education. Thru the influence of the teachers in the elementary school, the high-school teachers agreed to have a workshop on child development. As a result of the interest aroused, the next year was spent in grade-level groups working on child study. Other workshops have been devoted to education for family living, general problems selected by the teachers, and meeting the challenge of national security. Many interested parents have participated in group work and in summer workshops.

After the program had functioned for two years, the Hinsdale Schools were selected by the Illinois Secondary Schools Curriculum Program, as it was then called, as one of the eight school systems in the state to receive special help. Thru the cooperation of the University of Chicago and the state program, Hinsdale now receives consultative service from the University of Chicago for its workshops and for group sessions thruout the school year. Consultants from other institutions of higher learning are available upon request. Hinsdale's curriculum coordinator reports that the state curriculum conferences and the various studies have been most valuable.

The program, thru democratic planning, has progressed thru three stages. The first two years emphasized subject areas. The next step was child study, lasting about a year and a half. For the past two years the program has been problem centered. The problems have been selected by the classroom teachers and have been varied, as for example, improving school-community citizenship, educating the exceptional child, improving public relations, and many others. At the present time all teachers are working in subject-area groups to insure that the school program promotes the national security.

During the past six years the Hinsdale teachers have either borrowed or developed certain guides that have proved most valuable in their local situation. These are:

1. Curriculum revision must take place thru group planning by the teachers concerned. Teachers should begin where they are—they must feel secure in their efforts.

2. The local school or local school system is the most desirable place for the work to begin.

3. Curriculum development is a continuous process.

4. A necessary step is the agreement by all participants in a clearly defined philosophy of education, subject to change but acting as a guide to all groups.

5. Evaluation is a part of each step in curriculum development and should always be made in terms of the stated philosophy or aims of education.

6. Group work to be effective should include classroom teachers, administrators, laymen, and students. It should be based upon principles of group dynamics. No group should be "loaded" with administrative personnel. Each group should know its specific function, its responsibilities, and its authority.

7. Channels of communication must be established and maintained between groups, coordinating committees, consultants, and the community.

8. Curriculum revision offers a remarkable opportunity for the inservice growth of teachers.

9. Research and experimentation is a part of cooperative curriculum revision and should be encouraged.

10. Beautifully written courses of study should not be regarded as the end result of curriculum planning. The end result is the improved behavior of boys and girls and their ability to meet the problems of life.

11. If curriculum work is important, it cannot be done by tired teachers at the end of a busy day. If it is important, released time from school should be given to do the job.

12. Teachers should assume the responsibility for curriculum revision as their major professional obligation.

13. Groups cannot function most effectively until teachers have had experience in group dynamics or group interaction.

14. Progress in getting started is slow, almost frustrating, but sure and extremely valuable.

15. A teacher-selected professional library is of great value.

16. Consultants are of value if they neither dominate the group nor "just sit back and listen." There seems to be a happy medium where teachers and consultants can work together for common gains to each.

17. Preschool workshops make valuable and inspirational contributions if adjusted to local needs as determined by teachers.

18. You cannot move faster than your community is willing to move. A good public relations program is essential.

19. Wherever the program starts, in subject areas or problem groups, if geared to the needs of the child, some time must ultimately be given to the study of child development.

20. Great gains come if representatives from elementary, secondary, and higher education work together. The elementary and secondary teachers can work best if aided by consultants from the normal colleges and universities. The experience results in mutual gain to each.

21. Great faith should be placed in the pooled thinking and research of teachers. By making use of their total training and experience, education can be improved. We firmly believe that "several heads are better than one."

Professional and Public Relations Dividends

What has Hinsdale gained thus far from its cooperative efforts in curriculum revision? The curriculum coordinator of Hinsdale answers this question as follows:

1. *Pride of our teachers in producing on a truly professional level.* If teachers want recognition as a profession by laymen and other professional groups, they must first develop the professional feeling in their own ranks. That has been developed in Hinsdale thru the cooperative efforts of our teachers in im-

proving the educational program. Problems are no longer considered on a personal basis but rather in terms of what is best for the boys and girls. The continuance of our program over a six-year period is proof of the professional zeal of Hinsdale teachers.

2. *An improved educational program.* The thinking of teachers has changed, resulting in improved educational offerings. The emphasis on subjectmatter has given way to a consideration of the needs of the individual students. Every attempt is being made to equip boys and girls to meet the problems of today's world. Units and courses have been changed, added, or dropped. Educational standards and the behavior of boys and girls have improved.

3. *Pride of the community in the Hinsdale schools and the feeling that they have a part in the project.* Thru the participation of laymen in our group work and workshops the community has developed more interest and pride in education. The lay participants also help interpret and explain the program to parents. They are an excellent source of improved public relations. Many times we have found the thinking of laymen not only of value but far ahead of professional thought on educational matters.

4. *The professional growth of our teachers in service.* Teachers new to our schools have told us that more was gained in professional growth thru participating in a preschool workshop than in a year of formal training. Teachers with many years experience have become alert to the needs of the students and the community and to newer methods and technics of teaching.

5. *Development of leadership within our teaching staff.* Thru the opportunity of leadership training offered in our curriculum program several members of our staff have served as consultants and leaders in other workshops in the state, the country, and Canada. The opportunity to be of service is highly prized.

6. *Direct benefits to teachers.* The Hinsdale community has shown its interest and appreciation for the work being done by the teachers in several ways. A good salary schedule has been provided with identical schedules for teachers in the grades and high school. A new high school has been completed and bonds approved for two new grade schools and the improvement of two other buildings. Ten new homes have been purchased by the board of education and made available to teachers.

Every Hinsdale teacher can claim a share of the credit for the progress that is being made. That is justifiable professional pride!

Self-Evaluation by a New Administration

The advent of a new administration has sometimes proved to be an auspicious time to begin or accelerate a program of curriculum development. Even then, however, it is essential that the program grow from within rather than be imposed from without. The following example illustrates effective use of a transition period.

Statesmanship in Administration

In 1949 the Horace Mann School of New York City entered upon such a developmental period. The principal of the school was to retire the following year and the head of a neighboring school was designated as his successor. Prior to assuming the principalship, the newly appointed administrator made contact with members of the administration and staff of the school and obtained from each a written analysis of the strengths and weaknesses of the schools as that staff member saw them. He also held a number of conferences with the faculty as a group and with individual staff members. All this was done with the permission and cooperation of the retiring principal. The extent and type of cooperation was unusual but it illustrates what should be possible in a professional group.

Next the principal-elect designated one of the Horace Mann staff to serve as chairman of a faculty curriculum committee which he commissioned to analyze the faculty recommendations and to draw up a blueprint to guide future development of the school. Other committees were set up to study other aspects of the school, for example, its business administration. As Chapter VII emphasizes, curriculum development may be helped or hindered by business and purchasing methods.

When the school opened in the fall of 1950, the curriculum committee was ready with a tentative report. It had already completed a survey of other schools similar in function to Horace Mann and had visited a number of them. It had been able to carry on its work during the summer since key members of the committee also taught in the school's summer session. When school reopened in September, the tentative report of the committee was discussed by the entire faculty and then revised. The report included recommendations both for every subjectmatter department of the school and for matters of a more general nature. They ranged from the addition of new curriculum offerings and dropping of others to a general reorganization of the school's guidance setup and the institution of a much more elaborate remedial program within the school.

The committee recommended that a curriculum coordinator be appointed and systematic curriculum study become a more vital process within the school. This step can be significant in public school systems (see Chapter IV).

Evidence of Progress

Next the committee arranged to have its study reviewed critically by experts. These were university professors known generally for their work in the field of secondary education. Again the report was revised by the faculty in the light of the recommendations made. Actually the revision at this point was very slight. Then the report was presented by the principal to the trustees of the school who adopted it as the general plan of development for the years ahead.

In the intervening years it has been possible to carry out most of the recommendations of this first report and to move on to later recommendations. The school program has been enriched by the addition of such offerings as driver education, precollege typing, theater arts, studio arts, and mechanical drawing; a newly instituted remedial program embraces the areas of reading, speech, English mechanics, and mathematics. Another result of the re-evaluation has been an overhauling of the comprehensive records system and an expansion of the guidance program so that practically every teacher serves as the guidance counselor to a small group of students. Students ordinarily retain the same guidance counselor during their stay in the school. Meetings of the school's faculty committee on curriculum development are now held weekly on school time. Joint student-faculty subcommittees are set up from time to time. Those dealing with school citizenship and discipline have been particularly rewarding. Close cooperation of students and faculty has characterized the program thruout.

Functional Mathematics

The Florida State Department of Education has played a leading role in curriculum development in that state for about 25 years. As a result of sustained efforts over these years, the state now has a well-developed program called the Florida Program for Improvement of Schools. Most of the members of the state department are concerned with curriculum development. While some are involved in this phase of the department's activities to greater extent than others, the coordination of the program is under the curriculum director, called the director of instruction. This example should be considered in terms of the suggestions in Chapter IV.

Inservice Education of Teachers

While exerting strong leadership itself the state department has made the development of leadership within the state one of the major purposes of its curriculum program. It has stressed the inservice education of teachers and has given its support to various measures for promoting their professional growth. Under its guidance and with the help of consultants, teachers have produced during the last 10 years more than 50 curriculum bulletins which the state department has published and distributed. Local, county, and state workshops and conferences have been sponsored and participation in regional and national workshops and conferences has been encouraged. The universities of the state have cooperated with the state department of education and the local and county units in developing many of the conferences and workshops.

Planning and Study

The operation of the Florida program is well illustrated by that portion of it which resulted in the development of a functional mathematics program for the state's secondary schools. The impetus for a restudy of the secondary mathematics program in Florida arose when the belief became prevalent that an earlier attempt to do the same thing had not been productive. As a result of a study made some 25 years earlier, general mathematics had been introduced into the schools as a substitute for algebra. The hope had been that such a course would reduce the number of failures in mathematics, that it would provide materials within the interest and understanding of the less mature students, and that it would provide a course of special value to those students who did not take mathematics after the ninth grade. However, after the prolonged efforts of many capable teachers over the years, it was felt that "general mathematics in the ninth grade is an overloaded, unproductive, dead-end course; and that constructive work aiming toward this weak spot should be started at once." Such was the conclusion of a committee which the director of the division of instruction of the state department of education had appointed to study the existing secondary mathematics curriculum. This committee was composed of three mathematics teachers: one was chairman of the mathematics section of the Florida Education Association, one representative of the state department of education, and the third from the University of Florida.

The next step in this development, after proper authorization had been obtained, was the setting up of a mathematics workshop. Thirty-six secondary mathematics teachers representing all sections of the state, all areas of mathematical subjectmatter, and all types of schools met during the summers of 1948 and 1949. They worked out the detailed program at the Curriculum Laboratory of the University of Florida, and this has been made available to the schools of the state by the Florida State Department of Education.[9]

This study proposes that all pupils take the same work in mathematics thru the eighth grade and that a two-track program be set up for the following grades. One track would be the traditional Algebra I, Algebra II, Plane Geometry, Solid Geometry, and Trigonometry sequence. The other track would be the new general mathematics sequence. For the latter, the workshop participants developed lists of basic mathematical concepts and principles, grade placement charts, and content materials with teaching aids and references for Grades IX thru XII. In the bulletin that it prepared for the schools, the workshop group refers to the new courses as Mathematics 9, Mathematics 10, Mathematics 11, etc. The functional program proposed for Grades IX thru XII is quite different from the traditional courses for the same years. Thus in Mathematics 9 such portions of algebra, geometry, and trigonometry as contribute to the mathematical development of the functional ideas presented in this grade are used freely. Emphasis is on understanding thru experimentation and application rather than by formal proof.

From Paper to Practice

Altho it had stated its philosophy, defined the problem, and worked out in detail what it wished to propose for trial, the workshop group realized that its job was not done. One of the most important steps remained. The new program was as yet only a plan on paper. It realized that some group would have to carefully outline plans for implementing it. The workshop group accepted this responsibility.

---

[9] Florida State Department of Education. *Functional Mathematics in the Secondary Schools.* Florida Program for Improvement of Schools. Bulletin No. 36. Tallahassee: the Department, June 1950. 117 p.

The plan for administering the proposed twofold program was thought thru with the help of outside consultants. It is included here because it gives considerable insight into much of the thinking of the workshop group. The plan recommended:

1. That pupils should be encouraged to take at least two years of mathematics—Mathematics 9 and Mathematics 10 (described above). This is deemed necessary in order:
   a. To spread the basic concepts, skills, and materials essential to effective living over a longer period of time
   b. To place materials in grade levels compatible with the level of maturity of the pupils
   c. To provide spiral learning of the mathematical concepts
   d. To remove the overload from the ninth-grade course.

2. That many pupils should choose the four-year sequence of functional courses.

3. That a pupil who completes the functional courses Mathematics 9 and 10 will be qualified and may choose to elect any traditional course on the upper level considered necessary for specialized work.

4. That a pupil who completes Mathematics 9 and 10 and elects to take only one additional functional course should be advised to take Mathematics 11.

5. That the smaller high school consider using the proposed functional program when it is inadvisable to offer more than one sequence. This latter recommendation is based upon the belief of the workshop group and its advisers that the functional program can be made to serve "the other eighty-five percent" better, and at the same time will be adequate for the smaller number who wish to continue in specialized fields.

Curriculum Development in a County System

Until recently most school systems in Maryland had only 11 grades. In 1945 the legislature authorized extension to a 12-grade system thruout the state. This change set off a statewide program of curriculum development, initiated by the state superintendent of schools. An over-all framework for the state was developed cooperatively, and state curriculum workshops were held in 1945 and 1946. Bulletins and resource units were prepared. Next, selected teachers from various sections of the state carried ideas developed thus far into their own classrooms and attempted to develop functional educational programs. Following this, these teachers came together during the summer of 1947 and prepared reports of their experimental experiences. These reports were distributed thruout the state.

Since 1947 much of the curriculum development program has been county-centered. First, a state committee, and then later the state department of education, served as the coordinating and promoting agency. State conferences are held and there are cooperative enterprises such as the one concerned with the development of evaluative instruments. There is also a state testing program. These are aimed to considerable extent at keeping the county programs moving. Attention will be focused here on a sample of county-level curriculum development at the secondary level.

Early Steps in the Plan

In 1948 the curriculum development program got under way in full force in Garrett County.[10] The county was confronted with the problem of changing from an 11-year program to a 12-year program and was considering the adoption of a junior high-school program. It was planning to consolidate five high schools into two new high-school plants. These and other factors, such as the groundwork that had been done on a state level, produced a favorable opportunity for a complete curriculum development program in the county. The steps in this development were:

1. In 1948, February to August, each school faculty developed a statement of its philosophy of education. A composite of these philosophies was made for the entire county by an over-all county committee.

2. A county junior-senior high-school supervisor was appointed to coordinate the work of all the schools of the county.

3. Experimentation with the core program was carried to all five high schools. Heretofore, in 1946-47 and in 1947-48, this program was attempted in only two high schools, in Grades VII and VIII. The program in these two schools was based upon an experimental program that grew out of a county workshop in 1946 when resource units were developed for these grades.

Five resource units, such as *How Maryland's Historical Background Affects and Reflects the American Way of Life, Discovering How Our Colonial Forefathers Founded and Expanded the Nation,* and *Skills in Communication,* were the bases for a core program in early grades of the junior high school. The units were largely subject-matter and merely attempted to correlate English and history. Also

---

[10] Based on an over-all account of curriculum development in Garrett County, Maryland, prepared thru the courtesy of R. Bowen Hardesty, county superintendent of schools.

during the year 1948-49 a wide variety of reference materials, current materials, books, pamphlets, visual aids, conference tables, bulletin boards, and files were provided for each core class teacher. A double class period for the core program was scheduled for each junior high-school grade.

Outside Help Enlisted

During the school year 1948-49 a consultant from Ohio State University visited the schools and spoke to the teachers in a general meeting about the extent to which we meet the needs for common learnings of all boys and girls. This general meeting of teachers was aimed at setting up a "where-we-are" agreement and a "where-we-want-to-go" program. Questions of the following type were raised:

What are the needs of young people?

What are the needs of society?

What kind of teaching results in the most effective learning?

Is it possible for pupils to learn the meaning of democracy in any other than a democratically operated classroom and school?

Twenty-four Garrett County teachers visited the University School at Ohio State in Columbus. They were given the opportunity to visit classes and discuss their observations with the administrators and curriculum coordinator.

Workshops for Teachers

Plans were developed for a workshop for the summer of 1949. A consultant from the University School was secured to serve as director. Resource people included three members of the state department of education. Thirty-two classroom teachers representing most of the areas of the curriculum participated from August 1 to August 20. A small sum toward defraying their expenses was allowed by the board of education. The purposes of the workshop were: (a) to set up a continuous program in general education for Grades VII thru XII; (b) to organize a curriculum structure for Grades VII thru XII, based on needs and interests of adolescent people, that will enable them to solve life problems in a way consistent with the accepted philosophy and purposes of secondary education; (c) to

164

develop resource units for teachers at each grade level; and (d) to provide inservice training for teachers.

The classroom teachers had considerable preparation for the workshop. *First,* they made a study of the population of their schools, and of the environment and of the economic and cultural status of the people of the community. *Second,* they formulated a composite philosophy that they felt met the needs of the people of their community. *Third,* they observed a school where an effort is made to meet the common needs of young people. *Fourth,* thru the use of a problem checklist for junior and senior high-school pupils, they attempted to discover what pupils regard as their common needs. *Fifth,* many of the classroom teachers had one or more years of child study under the supervision of the University of Maryland. *Sixth,* they had had the benefit of several years of teaching experience.

In the light of the pupils' needs as identified thru the *Mooney Problem Check List,*[11] the predicted needs as indicated by teachers, and the biological needs as evidenced by teachers thru experience and their child-study work, a list of 17 problem areas was designated as the basis for the core program.

Bulletins and Resource Units

The scope of these areas, the philosophy of the program, a detailed list of the needs of adolescent boys and girls, and points of continuing emphasis (referred to frequently as threads) are the major parts of a general bulletin, *Cooperating, Organizing, Reasoning, and Experiencing with Garrett County Youth.* This bulletin was the result of the first cooperative efforts of the workshop group. It contains outlines of general discussions of topics such as: (a) technics and procedures in working in the core class, (b) problems regarding the implementations of the core program, (c) evaluation of the core program, (d) pupil progress reports to parents, and (e) a public relations program.

In addition to the general bulletin, eight resource units were produced. The resource units were: *The American Heritage, Leisure and Recreation, Making a Living, Knowing Garrett County, Communicating Ideas, Consumer Problems,* and *Intercultural Relations.* The component parts of each unit are: (a) a statement of the major

---

[11] Published by the Psychological Corporation, 522 Fifth Ave., New York 36, N. Y.

purposes of the unit, (b) the scope of the unit written in paragraph form and giving the possibilities in the problem area for learning units and points of emphasis, (c) learning activities, (d) evaluating outcomes, and (e) teaching materials and aids.

Staff and Facilities Increased

Teacher-counselors in arts and crafts and in music were added to the staff to work in individual classrooms with core teachers.

Modern buildings and facilities have not yet been provided to house the educational program being developed in Garrett County. To ease the situation, rooms have been equipped with upright filing cabinets, conference tables, extra bulletin boards, and additional shelving. Each core room has access to a tape recorder, a 16 mm motion picture projector, a filmstrip projector, a three-speed phonograph, a science kit, and two or three copies of numerous references. Each core room has a set of encyclopedias. An arts-crafts counselor is available to help in the core classes. A school bus is available for field trips.

Inservice Education Continued

Small-group meetings in the different schools were held with the principal and supervisor to exchange ideas and to discuss problems that arose from time to time. Some of these problems were: how to initiate a unit, standards that should be required for different types of work, how to get materials at the right time, how to prepare for group work, and how to close a unit. During the early part of the year a general meeting of all classroom teachers was held to discuss ways by which teachers in special areas can help to enrich the general education program. Principals and county supervisors conducted inservice education meetings which increased teacher security in the general program.

Approximately 50 of the 70 high-school teachers participated in a second workshop in June 1950. All high-school teachers attended except those not returning to the system the next school year and those excused for summer-school work. The purposes were: (a) to complete the curriculum structure for a program in general education for Grades VII to XII in line with work done in the 1949 workshop, (b) to promote further the development of cooperative teacher-teacher planning for the entire faculty, and (c) to provide inservice training for all the teachers. After reconsideration of the problem areas, the group decided to write several additional resource units and to place each unit according to grade level.

The discussion of the general session in this workshop pertained largely to the sharing of responsibilities by the entire staff. Among the topics discussed were: What are the common responsibilities of the entire staff to the child and to the public? What is the librarian's responsibility in sharing materials? What is the teacher's responsibility in sharing materials? What is the value of teachers' visits to other classes?

The inservice education program for the third year (1950-51) included a half-day of released time once a month for all members of the county staff. A comprehensive program was worked out jointly by the administration and a steering committee composed of classroom teachers, principals, supervisors, teachers association officers, and PTA members. This program called for visiting consultants in secondary curriculum, science, arts, child study, guidance, and evaluation. In addition to these consultants, at least one staff member from the Maryland State Department of Education attended each meeting. The purposes of this series of meetings were: (a) to study the various areas of curriculum endeavor, as suggested by the fields of specialization of the consultants; and (b) to give attention to the general over-all theme of learning, working together as a county staff.

During the period of curriculum development, teachers supplemented the inservice education program with summer-school work and participation in child-study groups. Special provision was made for books, professional pamphlets, and magazines in order that teachers might be up to date on the most recent developments in secondary education.

Another phase of inservice education which paralleled the monthly meetings during the past year was the use of teacher-parent committees. Teachers and parents volunteered to serve on committees such as: inservice education, unmet needs, know-how bulletin, extra-curriculum activities, adult education, new school furniture, teacher welfare, reporting to parents, child welfare, assisting new teachers, school calendar, and materials specifications. At the close of the school year these committees reported to the entire teaching staff and to a representative lay group consisting of officers of civic groups, representative professional people, members of the state general assembly, and county officials.

In addition to the activities already mentioned, approximately 50 classroom teachers met with principals and supervisors in five different groups to study child growth and behavior. These classes met 15 times during the school year for two-hour periods under the direction of the University of Maryland. Anecdotal records were kept and analyzed. The university granted two hours of graduate credit for this work.

During the summer, June 25 to August 3, 1951, the University of Maryland, the office of the county superintendent of schools, and the state department of education jointly conducted a summer school in Garrett County. Forty-seven teachers from Grades I thru XII attended. Demonstration classes of the elementary- and junior high-school levels were among the special features of this program. The course was designed to present a continuous program for Grades I to XII, to give teachers an opportunity to examine some of the principles of human development that should be the bases for curriculum building, to help new teachers succeed, to give teachers an opportunity to observe successful classroom practices, and to focus attention and crystallize the thinking of teachers on what Garrett County schools would be doing in 1951-52.

Progress Evaluated

In evaluating the Garrett County program, the junior-senior high-school supervisor of the county reported:

In way of appraisal or estimation of our program, as developed so far, the following points can be brought out in the light of (a) our belief in how learning takes place, and (b) the reaction of pupils, parents, and teachers. Hugh Laughlin's doctorate dissertation on *An Evaluation of the Core Program in Garrett County* gives us pertinent information based on questionnaires to parents, pupils, and classroom teachers:

1. Next to physical-education classes pupils like the core classes.
2. Parents think that the school is doing a satisfactory job in teaching writing and spelling.
3. Teachers feel that skills (Three R's) should be emphasized more. Fundamental skills beyond the Three R's are not readily recognized.

168

4. Special area teachers value the core program equally as satisfactory as core teachers.

5. Parents feel that the core program is doing a good job in citizenship training.

6. The core program affords excellent opportunities for speech improvement.

7. Beginning core teachers need considerable help. (A committee of teachers is preparing a bulletin for new teachers.)

8. Teachers are gradually accepting a continuous program for Grades I-XII.

9. There is more need for smaller group inservice training.

10. Teachers must acquire knowledge of and more respect for local environment.

11. Teachers must recognize and be more appreciative of learnings important to the adolescent youth.

12. More effective interpretation of the program must be made to the public.

13. Teacher leadership and initiative must be accepted by members of the teaching staff.

14. Procedure in the classroom is more compatible with our philosophy of democratic social living.

15. Core teachers do not confine their goals to subject mastery. They are also interested in the total development of the pupil, including improvement in attitudes, understandings, and social adjustment.

16. Good subjectmatter teachers generally make good core teachers.

17. Elementary trained teachers are good prospects for teachers in the core program.[12]

Statewide Cooperation in Curriculum Planning

The Illinois Curriculum Program is an outstanding example of a highly successful attempt to marshal on both the statewide and the local level all who are, or should be, interested in the high-school curriculum.

State-Level Steering Committee

Until February 9, 1952, it was known as the Illinois Secondary School Curriculum Program. The change of name indicates the future emphasis that the program plans to give to elementary education. For 11 years the Illinois Secondary-School Principals Association had tried unsuccessfully to introduce an organized curriculum program thruout the state. Then in 1947, such a program got under way when the state superintendent of public instruction launched it

---

[12] Laughlin, Hugh D. *A Study of the Curriculum Development Program of the Secondary Schools of Garrett County, Maryland.* Columbus, Ohio: Ohio State University, 1951. (Doctor's thesis)

at the request of the principals association. The state-level steering committee consists of representatives of the state superintendent's office, the secondary-school principals association, colleges and universities, numerous professional organizations of teachers and administrators, the Illinois Association of School Boards, the Illinois Congress of Parents and Teachers, business, agriculture, industry, and the service organizations.

In line with the avowed policy of the ICP that curriculum development is a grass-roots job to be done largely at the local level, the chief functions of the state steering committee are: (a) to formulate general policies, (b) to provide services and materials to local schools, and (c) to coordinate the general program. Local high schools may decide to participate, or not to participate, in the program according to their own wishes. At local levels representative committees usually have been formed according to the same general plan followed in the statewide committee.

Starting at the Grass Roots

Local schools are encouraged to start on curriculum development by working on problems of vital interest to them. They can call upon consultants from the state department, the colleges and universities, and from other schools. They also receive help thru workshops which are an important feature of the program. For example, prior to the spring of 1951 more than 700 school administrators had attended one or more three-day workshops; 29,703 administrators and teachers had attended one of 51 county meetings. During the summer of 1950 teachers colleges and universities conducted workshops.

The program carries on what it calls "basic studies." Thus, 79 local schools participated in a study of holding power; 13 schools, on a selected-sample basis, in a study of participation in extra-class activities; 79 schools in a study of hidden tuition costs; 93 schools in a study of guidance; and 95 schools in a follow-up study. Other projects have dealt with various aspects of the "need-meeting function" of the secondary school, with ways of lending more effective assistance to those who are working on experimental projects in local schools, and with the development of a sound program of relationships between high schools and higher institutions of learning.

The procedure in these studies had been to furnish all materials free of charge to participating schools, to analyze all data centrally

170

without charge, to send each school's findings to it, and to publish statewide findings. An outgrowth of these studies is a second type of publication in the form of suggestions and guides for investigation at the local level and for curriculum development procedures. These have been issued as circulars and bulletins under such titles as *Guide to the Study of the Curriculum in the Secondary Schools of Illinois, How To Conduct the Participation in Extra-Class Activities Study,* and *The Story in Nineteen Schools.*[18]

Consultants and Specialists Participate

The ICP is also cooperating with local school systems in the development of numerous curriculum improvement projects. The colleges and universities provide some 350 faculty members as consultants to these schools. One hundred seventy of these projects deal with the improvement of courses in science, social studies, and other subject areas. Others are concerned with developing new courses such as common-learnings courses. Still others are making studies of their total programs. The consultants for the nine across-the-board projects are furnished entirely, or largely, by one higher institution of learning. Thus, the University of Illinois provides the consultant team for the Bloomington schools, Northern Illinois State Teachers College for the De Kalb schools, and the University of Chicago for the Hinsdale schools. As many as 35 faculty members have constituted the consultant team for a single school system. Consultants commonly visit a school project twice or more each month. The project itself may last from three to five years. Much of the consultants' time is spent in meetings of local curriculum committees altho the consultants also work with individual teachers as needs arise. A consultant team includes specialists in service areas, such as guidance, testing, and evaluation, as well as in subjectmatter areas. Some of the consultants are relieved of certain on-campus duties in order to have time for these local projects. Their services are provided to the school systems without charge. Curriculum

---

[18]Houston, Victor M.; Sanford, Charles W.; and Trump, J. Lloyd. *Guide to the Study of the Curriculum in the Secondary Schools of Illinois.* Circular Series A, No. 51, Illinois Secondary School Curriculum Program Bulletin No. 1. Springfield, Ill.: State Superintendent of Public Instruction, August 1948. 42 p. ¶Hand, Harold C. *How To Conduct the Participation in Extra-Class Activities Study.* Circular Series A, No. 51, Illinois Secondary School Curriculum Program Bulletin No. 5. Springfield, Ill.: State Superintendent of Public Instruction, May 1949. 66 p. ¶Sanford, Charles W., and others. *The Story in Nineteen Schools.* Circular Series A, No. 51, Illinois Secondary School Curriculum Program No. 10. Springfield, Ill: State Superintendent of Public Instruction, September 1950. 369 p.

development in Hinsdale, one of the schools cooperating in the Illinois Curriculum Program, has already been reviewed in some detail in an earlier section in this chapter.

A Nationwide Project on Citizenship

The Citizenship Education Project is an example of curriculum development undertaken on a nationwide basis for a special purpose. The idea for such a project came from an annual report of the Carnegie Corporation in which its president indicated that the corporation would welcome proposals for the improvement of citizenship education in the schools. As a follow-up to this suggestion, Teachers College, Columbia University, has become the center of a program which has been financed by large grants from the corporation.

Broad Base for Planning

The Citizenship Education Project plans were drawn up with the help of experts from the National Education Association, state departments of education, universities, local school systems, and other sources, in addition to staff members from the sponsoring institution. No attempt was made to outline a new curriculum or to devise specific courses. Early developments were: (a) a clear statement of the premises of liberty; (b) lists of topics in American history, current problems, and government courses; and (c) lists of projects or laboratory practices in citizenship which have been tried out with success in American schools or in connection with them.[14]

The next steps were to initiate and then evaluate programs of citizenship education in eight pilot schools. Experimental classes engaged in such activities as a study of local labor-management relations, a study of a local public housing project which apparently had stalled, the reorganization of school student government, a community survey, a study of the Hoover plan for governmental reorganization and its application to local conditions, and a study of election procedures. The results obtained from a carefully admin-

---

[14] Russell, William F. "The Citizenship Education Project." *Teachers College Record* 52: 83; November 1950.

Cleveland Press, Cleveland, Ohio

Grandpa's pencil box could not contain the educational tools of this machine shop student whose skill in handling them assures him a place in our industrial world.

istered program of evaluation were deemed gratifying in terms of pupil behavior and the enthusiasms of pupils, teachers, and parents.

Functional Materials Developed

The project has broadened as it has developed. Formerly the plan was to confine it to the "American History" or "Problems of American Democracy" classes of the twelfth year of the senior high schools. Now materials are being provided to help teachers of English, science, and business education to cooperate more effectively in citizenship training. These materials are being used in many (approximately 400) schools thruout the country. Enrolment in the project is effected thru workshops. A number of schools of education also have become affiliated with the project and it is hoped that plans and procedures of value to all teacher-education institutions will result.

Specific helps that have been developed for the use of classroom teachers and pupils include: (a) an organization guide, (b) laboratory-practice (activity) descriptions, and (c) the materials card file. References in the materials card files are extensive in number and are cross-indexed. They contain full bibliographical data and annotations on books, pamphlets, periodicals, films, film strips, and recordings concerned with various aspects of citizenship. All are coded to the list of premises and issues previously developed. Laboratory-practice descriptions have been prepared in booklet form under the following titles: *Knowing and Serving the School, Participating in School Responsibilities, Student Government and Student Elections, Discovering the Community, Participating in Political Work and Elections, Our Government Machinery in Operation, Reporting on and to the Community, Student Service in the Community, Understanding the Economic Community, Science and Community Problems, Citizenship Education and the National Emergency.* These booklets range in length from 22 pages to 55 pages and were published in 1951 and 1952 by the project. At present they are available only to cooperating schools.

Applications to Life Situations

Perhaps the most characteristic feature of the Citizenship Education Project is its attempt to tie together citizenship knowledge and action. Activities or laboratory practices form the real core of the program. Schools are encouraged to adapt them to the local situations. Thus the students of one town, where a bond issue for a new school had failed at election time by $2\frac{1}{2}$ to 1, decided that they would study the situation. This led them to conclude that they needed the new school building. They translated their decision into such actions as conferring with the mayor, talking with citizens, conducting radio programs, and using other means of calling their need to the attention of the voters. They were sure that they had no small part when the school bond issue carried in the next election by 16 to 1.

In another laboratory practice a twelfth-grade English class entered into a signed agreement with the principal, the head of the English department, and the librarians. This agreement commissioned them to survey the school and decide what new books should be purchased for the library with a sum of money that was made available to them. Within certain limits the group was allowed to carry on its activities and was responsible to the whole school for its actions.

With the help of their classroom teacher they employed various questionnaires to determine the types of books the student body liked. They examined book reviews and checked books against the criteria which they had agreed upon. They used the public library. Finally, they drew up their list and then the books were purchased. To acquaint their fellow students with the new books, these students then decided to conduct a series of assembly programs in which some of the books were reviewed. These programs were well attended altho attendance was purely voluntary. When the activity was completed, the students who had participated thought it a valuable experience. To quote one of them: "I have learned how to plan a program of action and how to carry out that program to the fullest advantage of the class and the individual. I have learned how important books are in our everyday life, and I have learned how to get the most out of the power I was permitted to use." The files of the Citizenship Education Project contain many such instances of putting the results of study to work.

The personal feelings and opinions of the students is one important type of appraisal of any curriculum project. However, there are other more objective methods which can be used (see Chapters XI and XII).

A National Commission Initiates Change

The National Commission on Life Adjustment Education for Youth at its conference in Chicago in May 1947 stated that "the purpose of the Commission shall be to promote in every manner possible, ways, means, and devices for improving the life adjustment education of secondary school youth."[15] This conference grew out of the Prosser Resolution introduced in 1945 at a conference on vocational education. In directing this resolution to the U. S. Commissioner of Education, Prosser called for a conference or a series of regional conferences for representatives of general and vocational education to consider the failure of the high schools to provide adequate educational opportunity to that large section of American youth who leave school before high-school graduation.

First Steps Broadly Conceived

The Commissioner of Education accepted responsibility for getting the program under way. First, regional conferences were called thruout the United States. Then the Commissioner and his staff appointed a National Commission consisting of one representative for each of nine national educational organizations. A steering committee from the U. S. Office of Education was assigned to work with this Commission.

Among early decisions of the Commission were: (a) that life adjustment is for all, and (b) that the Commission would function in the states only in cooperation with state departments of education. In regard to the first of these decisions, special concern was felt for the 60 percent of the students who later engage in occupational pursuits for which extensive periods of training in special types of education are not prerequisite. To implement its second decision, the Commission thru the U. S. Office of Education circulars offered detailed suggestions in which state departments of education, state committees, teacher-education institutions, and others might cooperate in the program.

Numerous workshops, conferences, and publications have resulted from the efforts of the Commission and cooperating agencies. Thus at one meeting there gathered more than 200 participants from 31 states. The U. S. Office of Education has distributed on a large

---

[15] Jones, Galen, and Gregory, Raymond W. *Life Adjustment Education for Every Youth.* Washington, D. C.: U. S. Office of Education, Federal Security Agency, 1948. p. 40.

scale copies of such bulletins as *Life Adjustment Education for Every Youth* and *Developing Life Adjustment Education in a Local School.*[16] Private organizations have contributed funds and have published and distributed other brochures. Altho the Commission has had little direct contact with local schools, it has stressed the fact that the program becomes valuable only as it affects procedures in local schools.

Results Produced at State and Local Levels

According to the Commission, 20 states had as of July 1950 appointed or designated cooperating committees; other states have been carrying on curriculum revision of the kind recommended by the Commission. Examination of the reported life-adjustment activities within the various states indicates that it has been common procedure to hold conferences and workshops, to make available the services of consultants, and to issue guides and bulletins for teachers. A few states have had experimental projects in pilot schools.

The 1952 Yearbook of the New Jersey Secondary School Teachers' Association reports, as a recent trend in New Jersey secondary schools, an emphasis upon preparing the student to meet the problems of life in a realistic fashion.[17] It relates how this so-called Life Adjustment Education has led to greater use of free and frank discussion in the classroom and to expanded use of field trips and community resources; how it has resulted in a better understanding of the problems youth must face. Descriptions are given of curriculum development in Life Adjustment Education which has led to special courses in eight of the high schools of the state which were selected for reporting in the yearbook. These courses usually were planned by committees working with teachers, parents, students, and various community groups. They have been given such titles as *General Education, Modern Living, Family Living,* and *Human Relations.* In these courses the topics for discussion may include such items as manners, dress, recreation, social behavior, vocational planning, consumer education, family relations, boy-girl relationships, citizenship, health, and how we learn. Those of the schools which have

---

[16] U. S. Office of Education, Federal Security Agency. *Developing Life Adjustment Education in a Local School.* Circular No. 253, revised. Washington, D. C.: the Office, 1951. 24 p.

[17] New Jersey Secondary School Teachers' Association, *op. cit.*

included statements of evaluation with the descriptions of their new courses have expressed enthusiasm for the course in the improvement of student-behavior patterns, greater interest among parents and students, and desirable character and personality changes that have been effected thru them. A number of the schools reported that interest in these courses has grown to the point where plans have been made for an expansion of the offerings in this area which has recently come to be known as Life Adjustment Education.

Those who attempt to evaluate these programs should keep in mind that the primary purpose of the Life Adjustment Education movement in the local school, as reported by the National Commission, is not to promote the development of new means for meeting the needs of youth, but to stimulate the use of means already known.

Curriculum Change Is Widely Practiced

If space were available, it would be possible to continue with descriptions to show how all areas of the curriculum are undergoing change. Many forces are at work.

Cooperation Among Professional Groups

In the social studies, for example, the National Council for the Social Studies (NEA) and the National Association of Secondary-School Principals (NEA) have jointly sponsored a *Problems in American Life Series* of resource units which have pointed up new curriculum materials, and ways of using them to further modern educational objectives. Indeed, many well-known organizations, such as the National Society for the Study of Education and the National Education Association including its various departments and Research Division, have greatly influenced all aspects of the curriculum thru their reports, curriculum materials, and yearbooks. State governments also have a direct influence on the curriculum thru their laws and regulations. New Jersey, for example, now requires that all high schools of that state include in their curriculums two years of American History to be taken by all secondary-school students before graduation.

Many schools are now engaged in developing physical-science courses for the later high-school years. These are in addition to the usual chemistry and physics courses and are designed either to replace the latter courses or, as is more commonly the case, to reach students who do not elect to take chemistry or physics. In its magazine, *Science Teacher*, the National Science Teachers Association recently published the outlines of six such courses as a sampling of the many in process of development in various parts of the country.

Associations of teachers, such as those by subjectmatter areas, can and do affect curriculum development in a number of ways. The National Science Teachers Association, for example, besides keeping its membership informed of developments in science and the teaching of science, also sponsors the publishing of curriculum materials and cooperates with industry to develop and bring to teachers and students publications of value as resource materials. It and various other organizations have also promoted the "junior research" type of student project. While commonly aimed, as far as the student is concerned, at getting the student started as a potential scientist, such programs have affected both teaching practice and curriculum content. No doubt efforts of this kind have expanded the use of problem-solving by scientific methods in secondary-school science. The program is "down to earth" and close to the everyday problems of science teachers.

Music Education Essential

In music, developments point toward a greater realization that music cannot or at least should not stand alone and apart from the other areas of learning in the school curriculum.[18] While those in charge of the music education program have specific outcomes which they expect to attain at each level, much of what the children do grows out of demands from various sources. The music teacher must in such a program evaluate the demands made upon the music program in terms of their inherent worth, their value for pupil growth, and the time available. A recent curriculum bulletin prepared by the music-education staff of the public schools of Dallas, Texas, shows the over-all picture of the music program in a system where

---

[18] See the *Music Educators Journal* of the Music Educators National Conference (NEA). The conference, in cooperation with other NEA departments, is preparing publications on music education in secondary schools, in elementary schools, and for the handicapped child. These reports are planned for 1953.

179

the teachers have accepted this point of view and cooperatively worked on its implementation.[19]

Music education is more and more thought of as one of the basic parts of the curriculum. It is definitely not a frill or fringe subject. The readiness of communities to accept music education has been witnessed in Louisiana in recent years; it was almost nonexistent early in the 1930's. Only two parishes (counties) in the state could then boast of a parishwide music instruction program. Today practically all the parishes have organized programs of music instruction. This rapid development began when state authorities became convinced of the need for music in schools and offered to help defray the costs of meeting this need. Both the music program and the financial help were received enthusiastically by the local schools.

Guidance and Curriculum Related Activities

Developments point to a growing tendency to think of the curriculum planning function and the guidance function as being substantially one and the same. The Dowagiac and Kansas City examples already cited illustrate this point of view. It was the guidance committee of Dowagiac which sponsored the occupational survey. One of its specific purposes, you will recall, was to secure pertinent information relating to the school's success in job placement, to improve the quality and adequacy of instruction, and to obtain other data essential to evaluating and improving the school's offerings. Similarly, Cooperative Occupational Education in Kansas City shows how teachers cooperated to deal directly with the problems and needs of individual students. Vocational guidance and curriculum development went hand in hand.

Conclusion

The review of curriculum changes in secondary schools, summarized in this chapter, points to the following conclusions:

1. There is a widespread conviction that those at the local level who will use a curriculum should also have a major share in its development.

[19] Dallas Independent School District. *Growth Through Music.* A Teaching Guide for Grades I-XII. Dallas, Texas: Board of Education. 1952. 47 p.

2. There is great need for inservice education of classroom teachers and school administrators as they embark upon a program of curriculum revision.

3. The services of consultants from state departments, institutions of higher education and other sources are commonly used in curriculum development programs.

4. There is inadequate evaluation of the product of curriculum improvement and also of the process itself. Available evaluation is usually stated in terms of what classroom teachers, principals, pupils, and parents think of any change that is made. Important as these opinions are they do not take the place of other methods of evaluation. Objective evidence should be in hand to assure all concerned that the strong points of previous curriculum programs have been retained and that new gains have been made. There are those who believe that too much tinkering with the curriculum is done today without regard for the past findings of research, educational and otherwise. The use of the services of expert consultants and a follow-up evaluation program should minimize whatever amount of energy is at present put into poorly conceived projects.

5. It is clear that curriculum development and improvement must be accompanied by changes in instructional methods and in the extent and quality of teaching aids.

6. State leadership is readily accepted at the local level when it suggests and supplements local leadership but does not prescribe. Such leadership tends to extend educational planning to all fronts within the state.

7. The idea that adequate provision must be made for continuous curriculum planning as a necessary part of the total program of the local school system has widespread acceptance.

SELECTED REFERENCES

AMERICAN ASSOCIATION FOR HEALTH, PHYSICAL EDUCATION, AND RECREATION. *Developing Democratic Human Relations Through Health, Physical Education, and Recreation.* First Yearbook. Washington, D. C.: the Association, a department of the National Education Association, 1951. 562 p. $4.25.

AMERICAN ASSOCIATION OF SCHOOL ADMINISTRATORS. *Community Leadership.* Washington, D. C.: the Association, a department of the National Education Association, 1950. 24 p. 25¢.

CASWELL, HOLLIS L., and OTHERS. *Curriculum Improvement in Public School Systems.* New York: Teachers College, Columbia University, 1950. 462 p.

DOUGLASS, HARL R., editor. *Education for Life Adjustment.* New York: Ronald Press, 1950. 491 p.

KELLEY, EARL C. *The Workshop Way of Learning.* New York: Harper and Brothers, 1951. 169 p.

KRUG, EDWARD A. *Curriculum Planning.* New York: Harper and Brothers, 1950. 306 p.

LAWLER, MARCELLA R. *The Work of the Consultant.* New York: Teachers College, Columbia University, 1949. 187 p. (Doctor's thesis)

MACKENZIE, GORDON N., and BEDELL, CLIFFORD. "Curriculum Development." *Review of Educational Research* 21: 227-37; June 1951.

MIEL, ALICE. *Changing the Curriculum, a Social Process.* New York: Appleton-Century-Crofts, 1946. 242 p.

NATIONAL ASSOCIATION OF SECONDARY-SCHOOL PRINCIPALS. *Planning for American Youth.* An Educational Program for Youth of Secondary-School Age. Washington, D. C.: the Association, a department of the National Education Association, 1951. 63 p. 50¢.

NATIONAL ASSOCIATION OF SECONDARY-SCHOOL PRINCIPALS. *Life Adjustment in the Secondary-School Curriculum.* No. 171. Washington, D. C.: the Association, a department of the National Education Association, 1950. 248 p. $1.50.

NATIONAL COUNCIL FOR THE SOCIAL STUDIES. *Social Studies for Young Adolescents.* Programs for Grades VII, VIII, and IX. Curriculum Series No. 6. Washington, D. C.: the Council, a department of the National Education Association, 1951. 87 p. $1.50.

NATIONAL EDUCATION ASSOCIATION, NATIONAL COMMISSION ON SAFETY EDUCATION. *The High School Principal and Safety.* Safety Series, No. 1. Washington, D. C.: the Association, 1948. 32 p. 35¢.

NATIONAL SCIENCE TEACHERS ASSOCIATION. *Physical Science Today.* Symposium on present practices. Washington, D. C.: the Association, a department of the National Education Association, 1951. 10 p. 25¢.

STOREN, HELEN F. *Laymen Help Plan the Curriculum.* Washington, D. C.: Association for Supervision and Curriculum Development, a department of the National Education Association, 1946. 76 p. $1.

CHAPTER SEVEN

Better Aids to Instruction

BANG went the gavel! "Adopted unanimously," said the chairman, as the board of education approved the recommendation of the professional staff for increasing the budget for audiovisual aids. Each week similar actions of local boards of education are determining, in large measure, the kind of instruction that takes place in schools. Without appropriate materials, a modern educational program is an impossibility. Upon the superintendent and other school administrators falls the task of *getting* better aids and *making them available* to classroom teachers.

Before discussing ways to obtain better instructional materials it should be emphasized that the most suitable aids can be selected only after decisions have been made as to the learning expected of pupils. As a background to any discussion of instructional materials, it is desirable: (a) to define the terms used; (b) to gain some comprehension of the materials now available; (c) to study the need for new, improved materials and the methods for determining the deficiencies, and (d) to consider possible plans of action that may result in the production of more functional teaching aids.

In dealing with the problem of how to obtain more resources of instruction, various aspects may be considered: (a) how resources can be chosen to obtain the most suitable ones, (b) how teachers can be helped to seek and discover new instructional aids and to use the old ones in new and better ways, (c) how materials may be gotten to the right place at the right time, (d) how they can be used most effectively, (e) what can be done to obtain materials when funds are limited, and (f) how sufficient funds can be obtained.

Instructional Materials Now Available

Instructional materials, as considered in this chapter, are those physical properties of a movable nature which may be used by classroom teachers as aids to learning. Excluded from consideration are the usual classroom furniture and pieces of equipment normally attached to or constructed as an integral part of the school building itself. It should be noted, however, that the newer conception of materials needed for instruction will affect the design of school buildings. Included within the scope of the above definition are such diverse items as art construction paper and opaque projectors, encyclopedias, and saws. The terms instructional materials, instructional aids, teaching materials, teaching aids, aids to learning, and resources of instruction are used interchangeably in this chapter.

Textbooks and Films

Even a cursory examination of the teaching materials now available leaves one awe-stricken over their number, complexity, and diversity. The American Textbook Publishers Institute, for example, reports more than 1000 separate new titles of textbooks published in the United States in the single year 1951. Titles of texts range from *Alcohol and Human Affairs* to *Outline of Zoology* and from *Appreciation of Music* to *Soil Management*. There are books covering horticulture and others dealing with good grooming. Few areas of learning have been omitted.

The variety of commercial helps to teachers is further emphasized by the fact that over 8000 separately titled 16 mm films are available to schools in the United States.[1]

Television and Radio

Many schools use radio programs as a regular part of their instructional procedures; some have recently added television. A few radio stations have transcriptions, particularly of local history, available for school use. School systems are developing files of radio transcriptions. Local boards of education and state education departments are establishing their own FM radio and television stations for use in the educational programs.

Free and Inexpensive Printed Materials

Usable teaching aids are by no means limited to those prepared for sale. Increasingly, special-interest groups are preparing such

---

[1] U. S. Office of Education, Federal Security Agency. *General Catalog of Educational Films.* Washington, D. C.: the Office, 1950. 4 p. (Mimeo.)

items as brochures, films, and filmstrips for free distribution to teachers for classroom use. In some instances a single manufacturing company prepares and distributes pamphlets patterned after the resource units of specific subjects. Illustrative of such publications are: *Time Telling—and Its Importance in Our Daily Lives,*[2] by the Hamilton Watch Company; and *An Outline of Transportation,*[3] distributed by the Fisher Body Corporation. In other cases the various major manufacturers of an industry pool their efforts. Such industrywide brochures are: *What It Takes To Make Your Car,*[4] published by the Automobile Manufacturers Association; and *The Nation's Wood Supply,*[5] distributed by the American Forest Products Industries. These are but a few of the many that could be cited.

Many printed materials are available either free or at cost from agencies organized for the public welfare. The pamphlet, *Facing the Facts about Cancer,*[6] for example, is one of a series on major health problems that can be obtained from the Public Affairs Committee of New York. The National Commission on Safety Education of the National Education Association, in cooperation with other NEA departments and with industry, has prepared a well-illustrated series of instructional documents emphasizing the safe use of all kinds of objects in the daily lives of children, such as bicycles, electric appliances, toys, and matches.

Departments of the federal government produce many authoritative monographs purchasable at low cost from the Superintendent of Documents, Government Printing Office, Washington 25, D. C. Particular attention should be given to the population reports of the Census Bureau, the consumer's price index of the Bureau of Labor Statistics, the national income and other economic materials of the Department of Commerce, and the many phases of agriculture treated in pamphlets of the Department of Agriculture.

The Research Division of the National Education Association has prepared resource information on teaching about light and

[2] Zim, Herbert S. *Time Telling—and Its Importance in Our Daily Lives.* Lancaster, Pa.: Hamilton Watch Co., Educational Service Dept., 1949. 16 p.

[3] Boulton, Archibald L. *An Outline History of Transportation.* Detroit: General Motors Corporation, Fisher Body Division, 1934. 70 p.

[4] Automobile Manufacturers Association. *What It Takes To Make Your Car.* Detroit: the Association, 1950. 48 p.

[5] American Forest Products Industries. *The Nation's Wood Supply.* Washington, D. C.: the Industries, 1951. 24 p.

[6] Johnson, Dallas. *Facing the Facts about Cancer.* Public Affairs Pamphlet, No. 38. New York: Public Affairs Committee, 1947. 31 p.

sight. Using this bulletin as a base, the Better Light—Better Sight Bureau, 420 Lexington Avenue, New York City, has provided supplementary study leaflets and filmstrips on the same topic.

So many free and inexpensive instructional materials are available that numerous selected lists have been prepared to assist educators in locating and evaluating them.[7] These free materials often contain advertising and other content not appropriate for school use. A screening committee made up of classroom teachers, principals, and possibly a few parents is a necessity (see pages 196-200).

The intense interest of children in the so-called "comic" books has encouraged the use of a similar style in some supplementary printed materials designed for school use (see Chapter IX).

Newer Materials Now Accepted

While the printed word is still a dominant resource in American classrooms, other mediums are gaining in use. Children work with their hands. They observe at close range. Lumber and nails, plastics and leather now appear on the supply list for the art room along with the water colors. The wooden orange box and the packing carton nowadays team up in primary classrooms when pupils build stores and post offices. Timmy, the white angora rabbit, and Tommy, the hamster, are vital contributors to the development of children's understanding and knowledge. A collection of shells or of early American cooking utensils may properly have a place in the instructional program. The electric sewing machine and the automobile equipped with dual controls, are necessities for the tasks now set for education. It may be necessary for children to make a trip to a farm to see a cow, but second-graders can make butter in their own classroom—if a churn (or an egg beater) can be found.

An increased emphasis is being placed upon audio-visual aids, maps and globes, half-tones and colored prints. Films and filmstrips, correlated with textbooks, are gaining increased acceptance. Compact kits of laboratory equipment are assisting in extending science instruction in elementary schools.

[7] Association for Supervision and Curriculum Development. *List of Outstanding Teaching and Learning Materials.* 1951 edition. Washington, D. C.: the Association, a department of the National Education Association, 1951. 20 p. ¶ American Association of School Administrators. *Conservation Education in American Schools.* Twenty-Ninth Yearbook. Washington, D. C.: the Association, a department of the National Education Association, 1951. 527 p. ¶ American Association of School Administrators. *Safety Education.* Eighteenth Yearbook. Washington, D. C.: the Association, a department of the National Education Association, 1940. 544 p.

Teaching Aids Dealing with Methods

Up to this point, the discussion of materials available for classroom use has been concerned only with those dealing primarily with content or subjectmatter. A wide variety of materials is also available on the process of teaching and the philosophy of education. State departments of education, local school systems, and individual authors have published documents devoted to the nature of learning, methods of teaching, and facts on child growth and development. Teaching guides and courses of study are included in this group.

Materials Prepared by Study Councils

In recent years the "study council" has substantially increased the availability of teaching materials prepared by classroom teachers themselves and evaluated by them. These councils are established by school systems united to discover better educational practices, to quickly disseminate the knowledge about them, and to extend the use of effective practices. The movement has been pioneered by the Metropolitan School Study Council composed of about 70 school systems and school communities of varying sizes, located in New Jersey, Connecticut, New York, and Pennsylvania. It has spread rapidly thruout the Northeast, to the Middle West, to the South, and thru the Associated Public School Systems has become a nationwide movement. While each council sets up its own goals and purposes, all possess the common element of providing for the systematic exchange of information about educational improvements.

Both Content and Process Needed

An educational program may be looked upon as the instrument thru which an educational philosophy is translated into changes in human beings. The tools used include both those devoted to content and those concerned with process. Thus materials of both types should be used. Frequently, school systems have found it advantageous to develop instructional aids locally on a cooperative basis. This practice has been particularly effective in meeting the unique

187

needs of a local situation. Numerous school systems have prepared statements of philosophy and curriculum guides.

In San Diego County, California, the county superintendent's office has established a model science laboratory where teachers learn how science equipment may be constructed at home. Workshops designed to assist teachers in preparing such audio-visual materials as film slides, study prints, charts, and exhibits are becoming popular.

It is hazardous to try to make curriculum changes without providing the requisite accompanying materials. When the materials are not available, teachers and pupils are frustrated. There is grave danger that only superficial instruction will take place.

The Need for New and Improved Materials

Perhaps on first thought it would seem that such a galaxy of helps for teaching should be more than adequate to meet the needs of the most unusual child or the most critical educator. Unfortunately, such is not the case. In spite of rapid progress there continues to be a definite need for better materials of instruction.

Most young teachers graduate from teachers colleges with enthusiasm for types of teaching that provide opportunities for children to learn at different rates according to their individual abilities and previous achievement. It is frustrating to such beginners in the profession to discover, in many of their first assignments, that their skills are greatly restricted because of a lack of appropriate tools needed for accomplishing their instructional tasks.

Books and Pamphlets Related to Varied Abilities

Classroom teachers complain that they need many, many more printed pamphlets and books written in varied style and language to meet the greatly different abilities of their pupils. If children are to grow into emotionally and socially acceptable citizens, they must associate with other young people of similar physical, social, and emotional maturity. Such grouping in schools inevitably results in a wide range of intellectual achievement and ability within each class. Teachers, well educated in child psychology and child development, can devise efficient ways of leading these groups of mixed

188

abilities into satisfying mental, social, and emotional growth. Their work becomes easier, however, as more instructional materials become available to meet the needs and interests of individual pupils.

Materials Required for Social Studies

In the middle grades there is a shortage of printed information, for many areas of the social studies, prepared with the format, style, and content that is suitable for the varying levels of pupil ability. Ample and carefully prepared material on the European nations may be available for the average sixth-grader, but what happens to the sixth-grader whose reading ability is about equal to that of the average fourth-grader? He needs books that he can read with ease and understanding if he is to continue to have zest for learning. Studies of the textbooks now available in the social science field indicate that greater emphasis should be placed upon such topics and problems as minority groups, international relations, and life under other cultures.[8] Other vacuums in suitable aids for classrooms are the lack of source materials dealing with individual states and specific regions. In spite of notable exceptions there is a dearth of sources giving economic and social facts about local communities.

Teachers of less privileged children look in vain for materials on consumer education designed for lower income families. While most of the consumer education aids are helpful to middle-class buyers, little is available for those families who buy second-hand furniture, radios, and automobiles.

The resourceful classroom teacher is able to lead his pupils into most satisfying and intellectually developing experiences growing out of special interests. Capable teachers, however, find that students could use more resource materials than are currently available. It is impossible to teach many phases of the social studies in the most desirable way simply because of a lack of materials. If a class becomes interested in an industry—for example, clothing, iron, or plastics—the need for sources of printed information is soon apparent. In some cases, industry and business have a few excellent pamphlets available. Encyclopedias may supply many answers. But the number of books or monographs written for students with

---

[8] Quillen, I. James. *Textbook Improvement and International Understanding.* Washington, D. C.: American Council on Education, 1948. p. 64.

varied reading and vocabulary abilities is still inadequate. Films and filmstrips, fortunately, are helping to fill some of these gaps.

Unsolved Problems

The needs are easier to chronicle than to meet. The cold facts are that producers of the instructional materials classroom teachers use as tools of learning must be concerned with profits. Volume of sales is, of necessity, a major factor in determining whether materials are to be published or manufactured. Publishers, for example, report that the small volume of sales that must be expected is a major deterrent to producing printed materials on a given topic in different reading levels, as would be required to meet the demands expressed by classroom teachers.

Another obstacle to the preparation of books for fifth-grade children, who have third-grade reading skill, is to determine the concepts such children can grasp. The textbook publishers claim that books prepared on fifth-grade topics and on a third-grade reading level must present the subjectmatter in third-grade concepts. Such books have not been accepted by teachers, it is said.

Even on the process side of education further information is to be desired. Altho there is an abundance of printed material concerning the growth and development of children of the preschool and primary school ages, there is a shortage of information about children in the intermediate grades.

Supplementary Books Poorly Bound

While textbooks are usually bound for long service, librarians say that many of the supplementary books published on the reading levels of school children and youth are bound in relatively cheap materials. Such volumes cannot withstand the rigors of school library usage. Poorly bound books may be made serviceable for library circulation by having them reconstructed, often using the original covers. Recently a process known as prebinding has gained favor. Prebound books are prepared from publishers' sheets with specially constructed covers, usually of buckram. A number of publishers are now selling books of the same title in two different bindings, a trade edition and a library edition.

The Division of Libraries of the Chicago Board of Education has taken the lead in preparing a list of books recommended for purchase only in prebound editions.

These illustrations of apparent omissions in the commercially prepared tools of learning indicate some of the things that still should be done in order to provide adequate materials. Especially short are social studies materials with subjectmatter and reading difficulty adapted to the pupils' reading abilities.

Curriculum development and the production of teaching materials should proceed simultaneously. Classroom teachers should be major participants in the preparation of both. This type of coordination tends to promote efficiency and progress.

Establishing Criteria

The instructional materials needed in a given classroom will vary with the philosophy of education that is followed in that classroom and with the environment. In establishing criteria for the determination of those needs, common purposes or goals should be agreed upon. On the basis of the accepted philosophy, criteria for unmet needs in materials may be established. Such criteria may be for a local school system or even a larger geographic area.

In order to establish criteria for many types of materials, there is need for a professional analysis of the types of concepts that require mediums of the nonverbal type.

Specific criteria, dealing with details such as forms and raw materials for the various types and tools of learning, are beyond the scope of this yearbook. There are, however, general criteria which seem applicable. Instructional materials should be:

1. In harmony with a stated philosophy of education as developed by educators, laymen, and students
2. In keeping with the specific, desired learnings
3. In accord with the latest research on efficient methods of learning and the ways in which human beings grow and develop
4. Accurate in factual content.

Criteria such as these can be prepared by committees in any school system. These committees should include classroom teachers of all grade levels and of the many subject and experience fields. Principals and supervisors also should be represented. Scholars from various fields can help establish the accuracy of the content (see Chapter III for a discussion of the role of scholars).

Ways of Obtaining New and Better Materials

If the classrooms of America's schools are to have a continuous supply of improved teaching aids, then two general lines of approach must be tried. The first is to improve the sources from which the materials come; the second is to improve the methods whereby materials are selected for school use.

Cooperation Between Educators and Publishers

At the present time, most new instructional equipment and supplies appear only when manufacturers and publishers are impressed sufficiently with the prospects of a profitable market. This practice creates a time-lag between the discovery of a need and the actual production of materials to meet it. It is hoped that various educational groups will tackle this problem with increasing vigor. The greater the agreement among educators regarding what is to be taught, the easier it is for publishers to supply suitable material. Among the possible ways educators may reduce the time-lag are:

1. National, state, regional, and local educational organizations of either the general type or those devoted to special interests (music, physical education, etc.) could take the lead in encouraging classroom teachers to report the kinds of new materials they want as soon as the need arises. By a system of sampling, the extent to which a given article or publication might be purchased, if available, could be estimated. The organization could approach representatives of publishers or manufacturers with the information collected. As the system might be refined thru experience, it is presumed that those producing instructional items would accept the suggestions of the cooperating educational organizations.

2. Educational associations could provide additional opportunities in their meetings for the study of instructional materials. The audio-visual aids sections of a few teachers associations are already providing opportunities for the study of the use of new or unfamiliar materials. Exhibits of textbooks and other teaching aids are standard practice with many associations. Besides making classroom teachers acquainted with newer articles, the various sectional meetings could obtain firsthand reports from teachers as to their needs. If these procedures were extended, supplies could be produced with this information as a guide.

3. Representatives of national education associations might cooperate with similar groups representing those whose business is the publishing or manufacturing of schoolbooks, equipment, and supplies. While some efforts have been made in this area, the full possibilities appear to be unexplored.

4. For the preparation of informational materials about a particular region or state, universities and other institutions of higher education in the area might well take the leadership. An example is the preparation of materials of a regional nature by the Universities of Kentucky, Florida, and Vermont in cooperation with the Sloan Foundation.

5. Local school systems, or groups of schools in cooperation, may enlist the cooperation of industry, agriculture, labor, and business in the preparation of printed booklets, pictures, films, and slides dealing with topics of local interest. This method is a good point of departure for a program of curriculum revision.

6. Committees of educators, school supply distributors, and school equipment producers might work in cooperation with representatives of the major business, industrial, and labor organizations interested in providing educational materials. The combined committees might prevent unnecessary duplication of materials as well as encourage the preparation of needed materials by those in the most favorable position to produce and disseminate them.

7. Controlled experiments to determine the relative effectiveness of various instructional aids could be conducted in classroom situations. Such projects could involve cooperation among local school systems, state departments of education, university specialists, and laboratory schools.

Members of the NEA Department of Audio-Visual Instruction report increasingly closer cooperation between producers and distributors of the newer types of audio-visual aids and their organization. Manufacturers' representatives and directors of audio-visual aids now exchange views at the Department's meetings.

Another step in the right direction is reported by the American Textbook Publishers Institute. Certain industries have offered to provide material for textbook publishers and to assist the publisher in determining the accuracy of the data used.[9]

Possibly the Advisory Council on Industry-Science Teaching Relations of the National Science Teachers Association may lead the way to closer cooperation between industry and education in the preparation of source materials containing basic information. The plan, in effect since 1948, is based upon the work of a committee of 10 representatives of industry and 10 science educators. "Its continuing purpose," stated a president of the National Science Teachers Association, "is to promote good science teaching by improving industry offerings and by teaching teachers to make the best use of this material in the classrooms of the nation."[10] As the

[9] American Textbook Publishers Institute. *Newsletter.* No. 55. New York: the Institute, March 27, 1951.
[10] Neal, Nathan A. "A Step in Industry-Education Cooperation." *Science Counselor* 13: 17-18; March 1950.

National Science Teachers Association evaluates industry-prepared materials, and sets its stamp of approval only on those found acceptable according to the specifications, increasing prestige should come to its Advisory Council.

The 61-page report of the Consumer Education Study, *Specifications for Commercial Supplementary Teaching Materials for Science,* is still another step forward.[11]

The Fresno County (California) schools report a thrilling adventure in preparing stories of local industry and agriculture. About 20 firms and individuals were asked to prepare basic material on their industries. After rewriting the first drafts, the professional educators got the reactions of pupils thru six weeks of classroom use of mimeographed copies. After further revision in vocabulary and content by both teachers and industrial leaders the stories were printed with ample illustrations.

The materials are accompanied by about 25 flat mounted pictures, 11 inches by 14 inches. Fresno County children may now study even at the third- and fourth-grade level about such complicated local industries as petroleum, dairying, grain crops, and cotton. An exciting byproduct is the enthusiastic support of the schools by the industrial, petroleum, and agricultural leaders who cooperated on the project.

The NEA National Commission on Safety Education has succeeded notably in producing instructional materials in cooperation with industry. In most instances industrial groups have provided the Commission with funds, free of all controls, which have been used to pay the expenses of professional committees. These committees have included classroom teachers, school administrators, audio-visual specialists, and experts from industry. In other cases the Commission has worked with representatives of industry in preparing publications and films but with the distinct understanding that no approval would be given to the product until it met acceptable educational standards.

Worthwhile in establishing criteria for the cooperation of industry with educators, including the preparation of industry-sponsored instructional materials, is the research study conducted by the

---

[11] National Association of Secondary-School Principals, Consumer Education Study. *Specifications for Commercial Supplementary Teaching Materials for Science.* A report prepared by the National Science Teachers Association. Washington, D. C.: National Association of Secondary-School Principals, a department of the National Education Association, 1946. 61 p. (Offset)

public-relations firm of Hill and Knowlton of New York. This study, financed by the American Iron and Steel Institute, is well explained in an illustrated booklet, *Education and Industry Cooperate*.[12]

The success which the late Isaac Bildersee had in New York City in basing the content of a science course on the 12,000 questions asked by 32,000 children would imply the need for more pupil participation in the discovery of new materials.[13] Pupils could appraise the instructional aids in controlled experiments of learning.

Foundations interested in education may be the source of funds for the preparation of badly-needed materials that publishers and manufacturers may consider doubtful commercial risks.

Evidence of Progress

Fortunately, there is some indication that even the present relatively chaotic condition is improving. A number of discernible trends can be noted: (a) increasingly materials are being selected in conformity with previously determined educational objectives; (b) materials and equipment are improving, both mechanically and functionally, especially in the audio-visual field; (c) more local and regional teaching materials are being produced; (d) classroom teachers are participating more widely in the preparation of such materials; (e) audio-visual aids are being more closely integrated with such well-established types of instructional materials as textbooks; (f) the visual-aids movement has exerted a wholesome influence upon book publishers, as evidenced by the prevalence of dynamic charts and maps and pictographs in many recently printed texts; (g) the language of the printed page to an increasing degree is approaching the style, and hence the interest, of a private conversation; (h) emphasis is being placed upon comprehensive study of relatively small bodies of subjectmatter rather than upon an attempt to cover all of the facts in a cursory manner; (i) mass mediums of communication outside of school, such as television and radio, are receiving greater attention by educators; and (j) educational publishers, manufacturers and salesmen have become increasingly professional and helpful.

---

[12] Hill and Knowlton, Inc. *Education and Industry Cooperate*. New York: the Company (350 Fifth Ave.), July 1951. 44 p.

[13] Educator's Washington Dispatch. "Teacher's Exchange of Ideas, Facts, and Aids." *Teacher's Letter*, February 17, 1951. p. 4.

To suggest closer coordination in the production of instructional materials does not imply either national or state regimentation. All activity on national, regional, and state levels should be entirely voluntary. Any other approach might result in thought control and stifling of local initiative and resourcefulness. Cooperative action, within the framework of free enterprise, is a great need of the day.

Better Selection of Instructional Aids

With a multitude of materials of diverse types available, both commercial and free, the educator is confronted with a critical problem when he attempts to choose the items that will prove most beneficial to the specific purposes of the learners in a given classroom. Good teaching involves the use of a wide variety of carefully selected materials. Such selection may be accomplished in many ways.

The classroom teacher is faced daily with the task of choosing the reference books and pamphlets, maps and globes, and the pictures and other teaching aids which will best serve the needs of the pupils in his classes. Less frequently, but just as significantly, someone in the school system must decide what textbooks to purchase, what library books to order, how many and what kind of opaque projectors to buy. These and similar decisions are of such vital importance to the success of an educational venture that the greatest of care should be exercised not only in the actual requisitioning but also in organizing for making the selections.

Local plans for selecting materials—Some school systems have well-organized plans for selecting materials of instruction.

The Detroit public schools adopt secondary-school textbooks for at least a five-year period. The principals decide by ballot what areas will be opened for adoption. All publishers are notified when a new adoption is to be considered. Representatives of the publishers discuss their books with the principals, heads of departments, and with the classroom teachers who are chosen for this committee assignment. Classroom teachers and department heads make recommendations to the principals, who in turn make recommendations to the superintendent. The superintendent obtains final approval from the board of education. This process usually consumes a considerable period of time, frequently seven or eight months or longer.

The choice of elementary-school textbooks for the Detroit public schools follows essentially the same pattern. Supervisors, however, rather than department heads serve on the committees. Supplementary books are chosen upon the recommendation of committees of classroom teachers or principals. All such books must be thoroly read and approved by at least three people before they will be accepted by the superintendent and board of education and placed on the approved list. Library books are similarly chosen, except that only two people are required to read each book. Library lists are revised twice a year. Schools have freedom in selecting from the approved lists, providing they keep within budgetary allotments.

Since free and low-cost materials also have a vital influence upon instruction, the same care is exercised by Detroit in determining which shall be permitted in the classrooms. Classroom teachers, principals, and department heads aid in making the decisions. The final recommendation to the superintendent is made by a committee composed of two assistant superintendents and the supervising director of instruction.

The Cincinnati public schools follow procedures only slightly different from Detroit. One conference only by each publisher's representative with each committee member is permitted. Professional credit leading to salary adjustment is granted for committee work involved in the selection of textual material if the time required meets the established standards. Central office supervisors and directors advise but do not appraise individual items or vote.

Other school systems have equally well-organized but different plans for selecting materials. Some ask publishers to submit books and supporting documents for the use of a committee whose identity is kept secret. Proponents of such a scheme claim that the committee can act more objectively and without being influenced by personalities. It is also held that the possibility of collusion, or plausible charges of collusion, are lessened. Those who oppose secret committees say that complete secrecy is impossible. They claim that the insistence upon secret meetings could be construed as a reflection upon the integrity of the people involved. Even more forcefully it is asserted that if publishers' representatives are excluded from the deliberations of a selection committee, important features of the books might be overlooked. Local plans will vary; the important thing is *careful appraisal* of materials.

Still other school systems involve every classroom teacher and every principal in the selection of the materials used. Choices within the scope of the centrally prepared lists are made by the classroom teachers of a given grade, or subject, by individual schools under the leadership of the principal. Overlapping membership on committees making final decisions at different times promotes consistency with respect to types of aids chosen. Where there is universal participation by the staff, it is strongly urged that the school librarian serve on all individual school committees charged with the responsibility of selecting teaching aids. In small school systems the classroom teachers concerned and the principal usually make all the choices. Better materials and a richer variety are more likely when there is participation in the selection by those close to the learning situations.

Adoptions by state departments—Many departments of education take into account the recommendations of local committees in adopting textbooks for inclusion on state-approved lists, where such lists are still required by law. Greater freedom is being granted to local school systems in the selection of other aids to learning.

The history of state participation in the selection of textbooks reveals a movement from prescription to cooperation. Two or more decades ago the trend was toward statewide adoption and uniform basic materials. Some states published their own books. It has even been charged that a few state education departments were unduly influenced in their choices. Books, it is claimed, have been written especially for adoption by a particular state and sometimes even with a local author. These practices impaired the general instructional movement toward a variety of books, recognition of individual differences, and greater freedom for the classroom teacher. In recent years state departments of education have sponsored workshops to help teachers prepare curriculum materials, to choose instructional aids, and to assist the state in making selection policies in harmony with state law and current professional trends.

Lay participation in selection of materials—Separation of the political subdivisions of our planet into two groups with conflicting ideologies has created a special problem for publishers and producers, and for those who use textbooks, library books, films, and slides. The public is particularly sensitive to charges of subversive teach-ings. Books that were considered quite appropriate for classroom use a few years ago have recently come under attack. The usual pattern is to quote isolated passages from which generalizations are drawn. In some communities the emotional turmoil generated by enemies of public schools, modern education, or both, has reached catastrophic proportions.

Positive steps can be taken. An example is the work of the Committee of the American Legion, Department of Michigan, on the Evaluation of Instructional Materials.[14] First approved by the Legion, Department of Michigan, the Committee report was unanimously adopted by the National Convention as the criteria of American Legion policy, Resolution No. 291. These criteria are proving of invaluable assistance to school people and laymen alike both in selecting printed materials and in avoiding hasty, ill-advised criticism of teaching.

A Committee on Evaluation of Instructional Materials, democratically chosen from lay, teaching, and pupil groups, has tackled the problem in Oak Ridge, Tennessee. One of the statements appearing in the minutes of its meetings is indicative of the committee's approach to its task: "Its purpose is not to delete materials, but to help detect propaganda in order that the materials may be used wisely. Materials are not to be banned, but to be identified."

Criteria for selection of teaching aids—Regardless of who chooses the books and other resources, the choices should be based on the established goals of the school. Selections should be made not only upon the quality of the material itself, but also upon the following characteristics of the learner: (a) interests and activities; (b) reading ability; (c) achievement level; and (d) mental, physical, and emotional maturity.

Any teaching device is valuable if it fits into a well-planned program. If it is extraneous to the plan, its showing tends to become entertainment, not education. A general principle then is: to use only those teaching materials which contribute effectively to a carefully planned learning situation.

The planning, of course, is best when it involves the learners. It will not always occur greatly in advance of the need for materials, since pupil discussion may raise questions that can best be answered

---

[14] American Legion, Department of Michigan. "Evaluation of Instructional Materials." *Michigan Education Journal* 27: 218-20; November 1949.

by study or observation. Only in rare cases, when a most unusual opportunity arises, is a classroom teacher justified in inviting pupils to share experiences that have not been specifically planned for and with them.

When classroom teachers and principals choose materials that are complementary, the efficiency of learning tends to be improved. The taxpayer actually gets more for his money. Books and audio-visual aids should be purchased to supplement each other and the other resources available. It is in terms of the varied abilities of pupils and the characteristics of the local community that the wise teacher will write his specifications for aids to teaching. He will keep in mind that most of their use will be by individuals rather than groups.

Inservice Education of Staff

The best of plans for selecting globes, maps, books, films, slides, and other materials will prove insufficient unless the personnel who use them are alert to ways of discovering new materials and to new ways of using old ones. Leadership in appropriate inservice education along these lines is the responsibility of those in administrative and supervisory positions.

Day by Day Help for Classroom Teachers

If teachers are to develop a consciousness of a need for new devices, books, and films, they should become thoroly familiar with desirable ways of using those already accessible. Principals and supervisors can give inestimable help to classroom teachers on the use of various pieces of equipment. Many teachers actually are afraid to operate a movie projector or tape recorder in front of a class. Supervisors need to help them overcome that fear thru thoro instruction and by assuring them that assistance will be available, if needed, as long as the fear persists.

Some school systems have developed a plan whereby a classroom teacher is chosen as the audio-visual aids representative in each building. That teacher is then the one in the most favorable position for helping other teachers.

Librarians report that classroom teachers need to be reminded again and again about the availability of materials. They say that teachers who accompany their classes to the library are the ones who make the most effective use of what the library has to offer.

Teachers of ninth-grade social living classes in the Jefferson Junior High School, Oak Ridge, Tennessee, found that a list of the instructional materials available, along with a statement of objectives, content, and suggested procedures, resulted in the more effective use of instructional aids. In the Pine Valley School teachers added an evaluation of the reading level of the various books and pamphlets to the list of materials suitable for use in their teaching units. By using loose-leaf notebooks, they are able to keep their information up to date.

Curriculum Laboratories

Local and regional curriculum laboratories, or materials centers, are beginning to exert a major influence. Not only do they help teachers to acquire needed information about available equipment and materials of instruction, and their uses, but also they help teachers learn how to make their own materials and to discover needs for new aids.

The centers should be adequately housed for the various functions they are expected to perform. Rooms are needed for the different services such as library, audio-visual, and curriculum development. A place for previewing films and slides is essential. A professional library is a must. But here a word of caution should be given. If the professional library is used as a conference room, it will not be used as a library. Those who have tried it say that teachers or parents who come to borrow books on education usually will not break into a conference to do so. Only occasionally will those who have found a conference group in the library attempt again to borrow a book. Subjectmatter books, publications devoted to the professional aspects of education, sample textbooks, and resource materials all have a place in a library designed for the staff.

Curriculum laboratories are most prevalent in the teachers colleges of the larger universities. Some are located in state departments of education and in a few local school systems. Teachers College, Columbia University, was a pioneer in the movement as early as 1924. The functions of its laboratory have changed, but it continues as a center for curriculum study and evaluation. In response to the expressed wishes of teachers a science workshop has been added to the curriculum center of the school system of San Diego County, California. Here teachers have the opportunity to learn the facts of science and to discover interesting ways to use equipment and materials to foster learning experiences. They learn how to construct science laboratory equipment from free and inexpensive materials.

Unfamiliar terminology often is confusing to the uninitiated. Undoubtedly many of the functions of a curriculum center are carried on in numerous school systems under different names. Libraries of books and magazines on the professional side of education exist to a greater or lesser degree in most school systems. Preview rooms are likewise available, as well as conference rooms. In some instances school administrators would do well to coordinate these services in a unified center. In some of the smaller school systems all might be coordinated under the direction of a materials counselor, a person trained both in library science and in the use of audio-visual aids.

Homemade Materials

Many simple but effective devices can be made by the classroom teacher and his students. Games designed to facilitate the learning of the arithmetic processes are easily prepared. Models for high-school mathematics classes can be made by students in the school shops. Science equipment for elementary schools and junior high schools can be built at home or in the school. Examples of this type of homemade equipment range from animal cages to convection boxes and from specimen boxes to periscopes. Hartig and Powers have prepared an illustrated, duplicated bulletin of specifications for many items for the science laboratory.[15]

Waste materials should not be overlooked as potential resources for many classroom activities. Dad's old shirt makes a suitable smock for painting. A cylindrical cereal box can become a doll carriage or cradle. The bulletin, *Uses for Waste Materials,* prepared by the Association for Childhood Education International, contains a multitude of suggestions.[16]

---

[15] Hartig, Hildergarde, and Powers, Chester. *Simple Homemade Science Equipment.* San Diego, Calif.: Office of the County Superintendent, September 1950. 28 p.
[16] Association for Childhood Education International, Committee on Equipment and Supplies. *Uses for Waste Materials.* Revised edition. Washington, D. C.: the Association, 1949. 24 p.

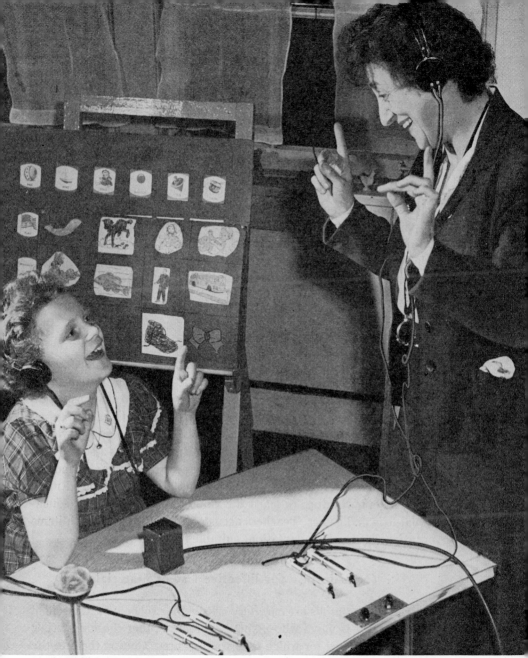

The child with impaired hearing can find happiness and success in the modern school where curriculum and method are adjusted to the ways individual children learn.

Parents can assist teachers in preparing some of these materials. The goodwill and understanding of education which the parents should gain may be of even greater value than the instructional items produced. Frequently pupil-prepared materials are of lasting worth and, where storage space is available, can be used by other groups of students.

The more experience that classroom teachers and principals have with various resources, the better choices they will make in terms of particular groups of pupils and of curriculum goals. The selection of materials should be made on the basis of a sound philosophy of education, supported by a reasonably clear concept of the growth and learning process, rather than on the mere accessibility of books, maps, films, and test tubes.

Exhibits

Exhibits of various types involving teaching aids can be helpful to both teachers and parents. Books, toys, and games designed for their instructional value; homemade materials; and demonstration exhibits with pupils, classroom teachers, and parents participating, illustrate kinds of exhibits that may assist in extending knowledge of instructional materials. These may be sponsored by a school system, the teachers association, the parent-teacher organization, or by any other interest group. Both parents and teachers need more frequent opportunities to learn the value and availability of educational toys and games. Teachers accustomed to the use of such items occasionally develop adaptations suitable for their own pupils.

Organization for Effective Use of Materials

Even tho materials are carefully selected for school use, the school administrator is naive who assumes, therefore, that those materials are filling the need for which they were secured. Getting them to the right place at the right time is a problem as yet only partially solved in most school systems that involve more than one building.

Even such standard items as paper and chalk, it is said, are sometimes missing when desperately needed. Principals and classroom teachers have the responsibility of making certain that these as well as other supplies are present whenever and wherever required.

Plans should be carefully laid in advance whenever specialized equipment is to be employed. The classroom teacher will have fewer disappointments in carrying out plans if he finds out in advance whether an electric outlet is available, whether the electric cord is long enough, and whether the projector is in working condition. For the audio-visual requirements of the classroom consult the 1949 AASA Yearbook and publications of the NEA Department of Audio-Visual Instruction.

The Library: Nerve Center of the School

In many individual schools the library is considered the nerve center for many classroom activities.[17] Not only are books and periodicals circulated from this center but many other types of teaching aids are under the supervision of the librarian. Textbooks, when not assigned to pupils, are frequently placed in the library or in a storeroom adjacent to it.

The more alert librarians store supplementary pictures and clippings in vertical files by subject. To avoid having the material damaged by fraying along the edges as file drawers are opened and closed, some are now using oversized files which will take paper up to 14 inches by $18\frac{1}{4}$ inches. These files are marketed under various trade designations such as "jumbo."

Collecting and filing supplementary materials is by no means the exclusive duty of the school librarian. In one school the entire teaching staff cooperated in after-hours work in assembling the original items included in what they called the materials bureau. Modern classrooms should be designed to provide the individual teacher with files and storage space.[18]

The Librarian as Materials Counselor

The argument between advocates of classroom libraries and those favoring central libraries seems to be waning. Efficient utilization of materials decrees the allocation to classrooms of those in daily use and the allocation to central depositories of those materials used irregularly. The practice of assigning groups of library books

[17] National Education Association, Department of Elementary School Principals. *Elementary-School Libraries Today.* Thirtieth Yearbook. Washington, D. C.: the Department, 1951. 415 p.
[18] American Association of School Administrators. *American School Buildings.* Twenty-Seventh Yearbook. Washington, D. C.: the Association, a department of the National Education Association, 1949. p. 88-104.

to classrooms on a rotating basis has proved both effective and economical. As classroom teachers look more and more to the library specialist for help in choosing and using materials of various types, the question may well be asked whether the term "librarian" properly describes the duties. Perhaps such a term as "materials counselor" would more nearly connote the multiplicity of skills and responsibilities expected of presentday school librarians, many of whom have had classroom teaching experience.

To be efficient, libraries and materials centers must establish businesslike procedures and must strictly follow them. In moderate to large-sized systems a central cataloger can save much valuable library time and reduce duplication of work. Regardless of who does the job, materials that are centrally stored must be cataloged if they are to be used efficiently.

Good equipment and supplies justify good care. A definite location for the storage of each item and proper maintenance go a long way towards stretching budgets. A dry room for the storage of laboratory equipment lengthens its life. Damp storage invites rust and corrosion. Early repair of instructional materials may prolong life and extend the effectiveness of public funds.

In the audio-visual field it is usually recommended that the items of most frequent use be stored in the separate schools. In cases where funds are extremely limited, or in very small schools, two schools may share such materials. Articles of less frequent use and needing specialized care, for example, school-owned films, can most efficiently be circulated from a central office.

The Role of the Audio-Visual Specialist

As the types of equipment for classroom use have multiplied, the need for technical assistance for the classroom teacher has become more and more apparent. In smaller school systems classroom teachers look to the principal for help in setting up the new gadgets, in learning how to run them, and in selecting appropriate films, filmstrips, and the like. In large schools, not having the services of a specialist, the principal may find it necessary to free a classroom teacher of duties and have that person assume the duties of coordinator of audio-visual education. In some school systems additional assistance is provided for the school librarians so that the newer aids can take their place in the library along with the more thoroly established printed materials.

In some communities, particularly the larger ones, a full-time co-ordinator of audio-visual aids is appointed for the school system as a whole. He serves as a resource person, available for help in the various schools.

Best use of commercially prepared audio-visual materials is ef-fected when teachers use the manuals and study guides designed to accompany the films or other aids. Those with experience in the field have found it advantageous to store the guides in bound folders in the library for circulation on the same basis as other publications.

Teachers say they need help from someone: the principal, the coordinator of audio-visual aids, or some other person. They want to learn how to operate visual equipment so that they can use it with confidence in their classrooms. They want help in selecting materials. They want to know what materials are available. They want to know which are best for specified uses. Many want to learn how to make their own materials. They want support from the public so that the community will understand the what and why of class-room activities.

Developing New Curriculum Resources

In the past teachers thought of instructional aids as confined largely to textbooks. Gradually the horizon widened to include many types of supplementary publications. Models, exhibits, firsthand experiences, pictures, maps, and films gradually assumed a signifi-cant place among the teacher's tools. Recently, the school adminis-trator has tried to facilitate the teacher's efforts to enrich instruc-tion by the support given officially to tap many material and human resources outside the four walls of the school.

Tapping Community Resources

Increasingly classroom teachers are using the many learning experiences that can be made available to children and youth out-side the classroom. Field trips of many types provide firsthand knowledge on many subjects. The teacher may arrange a trip to a farm, museum, bank, store, post office, labor union hall, factory, or to the department of public welfare. Wherever trips may take the pupils, if they are well planned by students, teachers, and parents in accordance with established educational goals and practices, they are exceedingly valuable learning situations. Like all other teaching devices, they must be well integrated with other phases of student endeavor in order to be effective.

Educational trips do not need to be limited to the local community. Journeys of senior classes to the nation's capital are traditional in many smaller communities. Recently trips by students of high-school age have been arranged on an exchange basis, not only within the United States but even with foreign nations. The usual plan is for students to spend a period of time living with other students in their homes. Not only are educationally significant side trips arranged, but students attend classes in the schools they visit.

It cannot be emphasized too strongly that all trips must be preceded by a period of preparation. Students and teachers can discuss what they will be looking for and how what they will see ties in with their classroom activities. It must be clearly understood that the behavior of students affects the attitude of the public toward schools and toward modern instructional methods.

Museums for Children

A children's museum can be a rare storehouse of interesting and highly educational displays. These museums usually are privately sponsored but depend for their effectiveness upon the support of professional educators. Exhibits may be circulated to schools. Loan collections from other museums permit wider use. Even a very small space, donated by a school system to an interested group of laymen and teachers, has paid rewarding dividends in better instruction for pupils. Pioneers in the children's museum movement include Detroit, Boston, Brooklyn, Nashville, and St. Louis.

The Crow Island School of Winnetka, Illinois, has a "Pioneer Room" equipped in the colonial manner. Included are a wardrobe of early American style costumes and cooking facilities appropriate for the period.

Fortunate indeed are the pupils who reside near the larger museums of natural history and art. Alert teachers will take full advantage of such resources whenever the subjectmatter is appropriate and transportation can be arranged.

School Camps and Farms

School camps and school farms are beginning to play an important role in developing pupils' firsthand knowledge of the out-of-doors.[19] Some are owned by boards of education, acquired by purchase or by gift. Camping experience may be provided only during the summer, as in Albuquerque, New Mexico; or it may be available thruout the school year, as in Battle Creek, Michigan; Salisbury, North Carolina; San Diego County, California; Tyler, Texas; and the Demonstration School of George Peabody College for Teachers, Nashville, Tennessee.

School systems unable to maintain school farms in some instances are providing limited agricultural experiences for children in school gardens which may be on the school grounds or in the neighborhood of the school. Sometimes nonschool agencies, and individuals, supply the land for such projects. Even the nation's largest city, New York, has been able to use vacant lots for school gardens.

Human Resources

Classroom teachers often may draw upon the out-of-school experiences of pupils. Those who take trips may serve as resource persons for other pupils. If there is an opportunity for group planning in advance of a pupil's trip, questions may be posed which will encourage him to secure desired information. Skilful class management can also produce worthwhile home-learning television and radio experiences that carry over into the classroom.

The human resources of many communities remain virtually untapped so far as classroom use is concerned. Other communities have worked out plans for the utilization of many of the talents of laymen and teachers. Questionnaires have been filled out and card catalogs prepared. Laymen lead discussions on "career" days. They teach handicrafts. Some show pictures of China. Others discuss family life in Australia. Leaders in industry discuss management problems. Labor leaders point out that they have problems, too. Teachers who have special talents or knowledge are released from their regular duties as needed so that they may assist in other classes.

[19] American Association of School Administrators. *Conservation Education in American Schools.* Twenty-Ninth Yearbook. Washington, D. C.: the Association, a department of the National Education Association, 1951. p. 133-35, 153-54, and 164-66.

Among the school systems that have pioneered in this area are: Bronx Park Community in New York City; Garden City, Great Neck, Manhasset in New York; Essex Fells, New Jersey; and Oak Ridge, Tennessee. Others are described in the references cited at the end of this chapter.

Talents need not be spectacular to be helpful. Fathers can build a playhouse for their children's class. Mothers can transport and supervise children on field trips. The wise teacher will use as many of the talents as are available so long as a satisfactory contribution is being made to the growth and development of the pupils.

Long-Range Plans for Enough Resources

A school system may place greater emphasis on ways of selecting printed materials than upon plans for obtaining and maintaining enough resources. However, plans similar to those already described may be used in establishing long-range programs for the purchase of equipment; for example, as musical instruments and audio-visual aids. Committee work may involve making an inventory of existing equipment besides the desirable equipment goals. The goals should be based upon: (a) the needs of children in the local situation; (b) the nature of the instructional program; (c) the training, experience, and interests of the adult personnel involved; (d) the availability of other materials to be used with this equipment; and (e) the recommendations and findings of authorities.

The extent of use and the types of use are more reliable standards than just the numbers of pupils or teachers. From a consideration of the equipment currently owned, the goals established, and the funds likely to be available, a realistic program of purchasing and maintaining needed equipment can be established. Here as elsewhere, as far as possible, all those who use the equipment should participate in the planning for it.

Even with an ever-increasing supply of teaching aids available and the discovery of many potential human and material resources in the community, most schools still have difficulty in securing enough resources. Many teachers would do better work if the tools they use were available in greater variety and abundance. It is up to school administrators to make sure that planning and budget procedure provide these tools.

Careful Planning

Educators have not always obtained the most instructional materials and equipment possible for the money available. An annual or perpetual inventory which indicates the condition of school equipment is an important part of a long-range plan for its economical and efficient maintenance and replacement. Long-term programs are particularly advantageous in purchasing instructional equipment such as typewriters, motion picture projectors, and tape recorders. It is often surprising how much equipment of this type can be obtained even with meager funds, if a definite plan is formulated and followed. Of course, the administration of the program should be flexible enough to meet changing conditions.

Wise Use

Well-planned utilization of materials and other resources stretches the value of the dollars expended. Material lying in a storeroom contributes nothing to the education of children and youth.

In many classrooms there is an obstacle to good teaching that cannot be overcome by providing aids of great variety and sufficient quantity. If there is insufficient space for a reading corner or a terrarium, books and plants will not solve the teacher's problem. The only solutions are a reduction in the number of pupils in the room or providing a larger room, either thru new construction or remodeling operations.

Importance of the Purchasing Agent

An exceedingly important member of the curriculum team is sometimes overlooked. Purchasing agents often feel that teachers are inflexible because they object to savings made by grouping orders or substituting cheaper brands of supplies that seem to the purchasing agent to offer equal advantages educationally. Teachers, on the other hand, frequently say that those who do the buying show little understanding of the uses to which their purchases will be put. To assure the purchase of the best materials, those consistent with both cost and function, there should be the closest kind of cooperation between the purchasing agent and those who

211

will use the product. All purchasing should be related to the philosophy of the school system. Requisitions for classroom supplies, equipment, and books should be initiated by classroom teachers with the advice and counsel of principals.

Purchasing agents and school administrators have a major responsibility to keep in mind that supplies must be delivered promptly to the point where they are to be used or they will be of little or no value. Teachers and principals, likewise, should understand that they must submit their requisitions well in advance of the probable time of use. The principal, the classroom teacher, and the central office need to have clearly stated understandings and timetables if the most efficient purchasing and utilization of instructional materials are to be possible.

An Adequate Budget

Even in the well-planned, well-administered school system there is still no substitute for dollars. These, of course, may be either public or private. For public schools, the taxpayers may pay the entire bill, parents may bear most of the burden, or parents may share the cost of instructional materials. While the latter course is one frequently followed, the trend is toward complete provision of the materials needed in the classrooms by purchase from public funds.

It is axiomatic that the best schools spend the most for teaching aids. Superior teachers can use many free and inexpensive articles in classroom instruction, but their effectiveness is multiplied many times over if they have suitable and sufficient books, maps, globes, sand tables, aquariums, and the multitude of other resources. Such materials can transform a schoolroom from a lecture hall into a challenging, stimulating, and enjoyable place of learning.

To discover the amount of money that school systems are spending for their materials program, the NEA Research Division requested 134 cities report their expenditures in some detail. These cities were scattered over the country and most of them were over 10,000 in population according to the 1950 Census. Information was returned by 107 of them. An over-all description is provided in Table 1 by showing the median expenditure and the highest expenditure per pupil in average daily attendance for the school year 1950-51. Only those cities that *actually reported* expenditures in any particular classification entered into the calculation of the median. The lowest expenditures in all cases was a negligible amount and therefore is not listed.

It will be noted that the medians of the total expenditures for all items were $6.27 for elementary schools, $9.00 for junior high schools, and $10.90 for senior high schools. Since few investigators have attempted to get the cost of *all* instructional materials, these totals cannot be readily compared with other research studies.

The American Textbook Publishers Institute has suggested a "reasonable" standard for the cost of elementary textbooks as $5.53 at 1951-52 wholesale price levels.[20] This amount was designed to cover the cost of basal textbooks, teacher's manual, selected workbooks, supplementary books, standardized tests, and classroom references. It did not cover teachers' professional books, school library books, maps, globes, charts, and periodicals. In other words, the Institute's proposed "reasonable" standard for textbooks is more than *double* the median per-pupil expenditure for books and magazines (not including library books) reported by the 107 cities for elementary schools in 1950-51.

These same superintendents were also given an opportunity to rate their stock of instructional materials *before* 1950-51 schoolyear purchases were made. Of the 107 who did this, 18 felt their stock was "rather meager," 62 thought their stock was "about average," and 26 were of the opinion their stock was "above average." Their opinion on 1950-51 expenditures for books and other instructional supplies fell in similar fashion. Seventeen thought expenditures were a "bare minimum," 66 said expenditures were "fairly satisfactory," and 23 indicated expenditures were "rather generous." Both of these expressions of opinion could be said to reveal a reasonable degree of satisfaction with the instructional materials program.

However, there was enough dissatisfaction with the 1950-51 expenditure level that 63 superintendents offered a *realistic* estimate of what they thought should have been spent to provide a *desirable* or forward-looking program. A comparison of the actual expenditures made in these systems with the desirable estimates is given in

[20] American Textbook Publishers Institute. *Per Pupil Cost of Printed Materials of Instruction.* New York: the Institute, 1952. 11 p.

TABLE 1.— MEDIAN AND HIGHEST EXPENDITURE PER PUPIL IN AVERAGE DAILY ATTENDANCE FOR INSTRUCTIONAL MATERIALS AND SUPPLIES, 1950-51*

Purpose	Elementary		Junior High School		Senior High School		Median All Grades
	Median	Highest	Median	Highest	Median	Highest	
1	2	3	4	5	6	7	8
1. Books, magazines and other publications....	$2.09	$7.24	$3.64	$9.28	$3.91	$10.13	$2.86
a. Textbooks....	1.73	6.00	2.25	7.36	2.67	8.04	2.12
b. Supplementary books....	.52	2.53	.38	2.26	.35	4.61	.45
c. Library books....	.65	2.35	.89	3.06	1.10	4.48	.89
2. Audio-visual materials....	.27	1.28	.35	1.61	.38	2.64	.38
3. Audio-visual equipment....	.21	1.79	.39	1.21	.36	1.33	.25
4. Other instructional materials and supplies....	3.13	11.52	4.80	12.31	6.39	16.37	4.21
Median of total expenditures....	$6.27		$9.00		$10.90		$7.68

* Based on replies from 107 city school systems.

TABLE 2.—MEDIAN ACTUAL EXPENDITURE AND MEDIAN ESTIMATED DESIRABLE EXPENDITURE PER PUPIL IN AVERAGE DAILY ATTENDANCE FOR INSTRUCTIONAL MATERIALS AND SUPPLIES, 1950-51*

Purpose	Elementary			Junior high school			Senior high school			Total		
	Actual	Desirable	Percent of increase	Actual	Desirable	Percent of increase	Actual	Desirable	Percent of increase	Actual	Desirable	Percent of increase
1	2	3	4	5	6	7	8	9	10	11	12	13
1. Books, magazines, and other publications	$2.09	$2.86	37%	$3.64	$4.50	24%	$3.91	$4.55	16%	$2.86	$3.54	24%
a. Textbooks	1.73	2.21	28	2.25	3.06	36	2.67	3.33	25	2.12	2.50	18
b. Supplementary books	.52	.65	25	.38	.60	58	.35	.63	80	.45	.63	40
c. Library books	.65	.88	35	.89	1.31	47	1.10	1.40	27	.89	1.09	22
2. Audio-visual materials	.27	.44	63	.35	.78	123	.38	.75	97	.38	.58	53
3. Audio-visual equipment	.21	.38	81	.39	.65	67	.36	.48	33	.25	.40	60
4. Other instructional materials and supplies	3.13	3.69	18	4.80	5.00	4	6.39	5.83	–9	4.21	4.29	2
Median of total expenditure	$6.27	$8.75	40%	$9.00	$11.20	24%	$10.90	$12.38	14%	$7.68	$9.06	18%

* Columns 2, 5, 8, and 11 based upon replies of 107 city school systems; columns 3, 6, 9, and 12 based upon 63 replies.

Table 2 by listing the median amount reported for the various types of instructional materials. Only those cities that actually made an estimate for any particular classification entered into the calculation of the median. The increase of the medians for *desirable* expenditures over the medians of *actual* expenditures ranges from 4 to 123 percent in the various categories. The median estimate of desirable expenditure for elementary textbooks, supplementary books, and library books (Item A) is only $2.86; an amount considerably below the $5.53 of the American Textbook Publishers Institute.

The difference between the actual amounts spent and the amounts given as forward looking does suggest some goals for strengthening the instructional programs of school systems. In general, these superintendents expressed a strong wish to increase expenditures for audio-visual aids and equipment and for supplementary books.

Today, as never before in the memory of most school administrators, any discussion of expenditures for supplies must take into account price trends. An expenditure of $5.00 per pupil for instructional supplies in 1950-51 actually represented a purchasing power of $2.75 in 1935-1939 dollars. To have had the same purchasing power in the summer of 1952, one would have to increase the $5.00 to $5.20—and the outlook at the beginning of the school year 1952-53 was for still further price increases.

A Look Ahead

In spite of the availability of a variety of instructional materials, classroom teachers find it difficult to provide pupils with appropriate learning tools. Still urgently needed are instructional aids useful in promoting the educational growth and development of individuals of varying abilities and interests. Curriculum and instructional helps for teachers themselves also are lacking or in need of improvement.

On the favorable side there is evidence that materials are being improved. There is even an occasional attempt at cooperation among national agencies toward the production of functional teaching aids. More aggressive leadership by educational organizations toward such cooperation is overdue.

The materials needed for teaching should be wisely chosen. Classroom teachers should be encouraged to locate new materials and to make better use of the materials already available. Plans should be devised for each school and each school system to facilitate the circulation, distribution, and use of the articles available. Free and inexpensive materials are sometimes of greater educational value than commercial items, but they should be selected by professional committees. Community resources, both human and material, may supplement the regular staff and equipment.

In spite of all these possibilities there is no substitute for an adequate budget. It is the joint responsibility of superintendents, principals, supervisors, classroom teachers, boards of education, parents, and all other citizens to see that children have the best possible opportunities by wise use of all the available resources. No plan of curriculum improvement is complete without a parallel program for better instructional aids.

SELECTED REFERENCES

AMERICAN TEXTBOOK PUBLISHERS INSTITUTE. *Textbooks in Education.* New York: the Institute, 1949. 139 p.

ASSOCIATION FOR CHILDHOOD EDUCATION INTERNATIONAL, COMMITTEE ON EQUIPMENT AND SUPPLIES. *Uses for Waste Materials.* Revised edition. Washington, D. C.: the Association, 1949. 24 p.

ASSOCIATION FOR SUPERVISION AND CURRICULUM DEVELOPMENT. *Action for Curriculum Improvement.* 1951 Yearbook. Washington, D. C.: the Association, a department of the National Education Association, 1951. 248 p. $3.50.

ASSOCIATION FOR SUPERVISION AND CURRICULUM DEVELOPMENT. *List of Outstanding Teaching and Learning Materials.* 1951 edition. Washington, D. C.: the Association, a department of the National Education Association, 1951. 20 p. 75¢.

AUDIO-VISUAL EDUCATION ASSOCIATION OF CALIFORNIA. *Setting Up Your Audio-Visual Education Program.* Stanford University, Calif.; Stanford University Press, 1949. 34 p.

DRAG, FRANCIS L. *Curriculum Laboratories in the United States.* San Diego, Calif.: Office of the County Superintendent of Schools, 1947. 172 p.

FOWLKES, JOHN GUY, and OTHERS. *Elementary Teachers Guide to Free Curriculum Materials.* Randolph, Wis.: Educators Progress Service, 1951. 357 p.

GEORGE PEABODY COLLEGE FOR TEACHERS, DIVISION OF SURVEYS AND FIELD SERVICES. *Education and Industry Cooperate.* A study of education-industry cooperation by Hill and Knowlton, Public Relations Counsel. New York: Hill and Knowlton (350 Fifth Ave.), July 1951. 44 p.

GEORGE PEABODY COLLEGE FOR TEACHERS, DIVISION OF SURVEYS AND FIELD SERVICES. *Free and Inexpensive Learning Materials.* Nashville, Tenn.: the College, 1952. 194 p.

HOLLAND, CLEMENT, compiler. *Catalog of Free and Inexpensive Teaching Aids for High Schools.* Consumer Education Study. Washington, D. C.: National Association of Secondary-School Principals, a department of the National Education Association, 1948. 104 p.

HORKHEIMER, MARY FOLEY, and DIFFOR, JOHN W., compilers. *Educators Guide to Free Films.* Twelfth edition. Randolph, Wis.: Educators Progress Service, 1952. 508 p.

METROPOLITAN SCHOOL STUDY COUNCIL, COMMITTEE ON HUMAN RESOURCES. *Fifty Teachers to a Classroom.* New York: Macmillan Co., 1950. 44 p.

NATIONAL ASSOCIATION OF SECONDARY-SCHOOL PRINCIPALS. *Commercial Supplementary Teaching Materials.* Consumer Education Study. Washington, D. C.: the Association, a department of the National Education Association, 1945. 24 p.

NOEL, ELIZABETH G., and LEONARD, J. PAUL. *Foundations for Teacher Education in Audio-Visual Instruction.* Series II, Motion Pictures in Education, No. 9. Washington, D. C.: American Council on Education, 1947. 60 p.

UNESCO. *A Handbook for the Improvement of Textbooks and Teaching Materials as Aids to International Understanding.* Publication No. 368. New York: Columbia University Press, 1949. 172 p.

CHAPTER EIGHT

Teacher's Role in Curriculum Improvement

BECAUSE the curriculum is the sum total of classroom and school activities, the curriculum is shaped and made effective by the classroom teacher. Not only is the curriculum affected by the teacher but, in all probability, the classroom teacher is the most important person in the total curriculum study and improvement process. The school philosophy is and should be determined by group and community participation. Over-all curriculum planning, involving the selection of policies and patterns, should be done by joint action.

Teaching guides and materials may be provided by many workers, but ultimately one person—the classroom teacher—must accept the responsibility for directing the learning of the child. The teacher is the connecting link between the child and the curriculum; the curriculum is the link between the child and the educational philosophy of the school.

The Teacher as an Individual

It is granted that the classroom teacher has many helpers and several avenues of assistance, but what he does in the classroom and how he does it are mainly dependent upon himself. Some factors that loom large in the ability of the teacher to be effective are: (a) the teacher's personality, (b) his philosophy, and (c) his professional preparation.

His Personality

The place of the classroom teacher has been glorified by many writers. Such tributes have been justified because it is practically impossible to over-emphasize the importance of a competent teacher.

Many adults recall with fervor the effective teachers they have had and can point out the valuable influences left on their lives

219

long after they have forgotten what those teachers taught. There is sometimes more good in the person than in what he teaches. The first essential of the classroom teacher is that he should represent and reflect the qualities essential to America's ideals, such as: character, religious faith, regard for right, honesty and sincerity of purpose, and loyalty to country. Above all, he must have faith in the cause he represents, that of leading all children to grow in the knowledge, appreciations, and skills of good citizenship.

His Philosophy

An effective teacher has both a personal and a professional philosophy. When his major beliefs are in keeping with the general philosophy of the school system, then both his and the system's philosophies unite in producing the best teaching. The classroom is the place where the curriculum really comes to life, and it is the teacher who brings it to life. By his ingenious ability to lead and direct the activities of the children, the classroom teacher produces the kind of education to which the school system and the community have subscribed.

The competent teacher relates himself to the total curriculum and helps to make that curriculum dynamic and effective in proportion to his own feelings concerning the purposes of the school. On any grade level, the classroom teacher views the children as living, growing, and energetic persons. Each individual is unique. Each has his own potential values. In the primary grades, the middle grades, the junior high school, and the senior high school, children have characteristic growth and development stages, as outlined in Chapter II of this yearbook. The school seeks to direct the natural energetic and personal tendencies of these individuals into learning experiences in accordance with their respective developmental stages and to guide the behavior of these children into socially and educationally acceptable behavior patterns.

His Preparation

Society expects every classroom teacher to be a well-educated, professionally competent person. The obligations of the profession require the teacher to keep himself informed on research and trends in educational practice, to participate actively in local school system projects, and to work continuously for better instruction. Such demands can be met only by carefully planned and enriched professional preparation.[1]

Within the four years of preservice college education the prospective teacher should expect to secure the basic core of general education. Within this core should be included adequate courses in English, history, mathematics, science, languages, and cultural interests to qualify the student teacher to take his place in society as an educated person.

In addition to the general education core the student teacher should obtain specific learning and adequate knowledge in two or more teaching fields to enable him to teach content material successfully. He needs also a professional core of knowledge and experiences in the art of teaching. This core should include a knowledge of child growth and development, methods of teaching, and the use of instructional materials.

College preparation alone cannot provide the professional equipment needed by the fully prepared and mature teacher. Many concepts and understandings must necessarily come after regular teaching experience. In classrooms and school systems one deepens his philosophy, improves his skill with methods, broadens the scope of his general knowledge, and mellows his understanding of human nature. Much of the best and more advanced preparation must come as professional growth in service and not as preservice education. The truly professional classroom teacher cannot be prepared fully prior to the experience of a regular teaching position. He must continue to expand his training and his efficiency thru additional college courses, workshops, classroom experience, and other inservice improvement programs, such as those mentioned in Chapter IV.

Developing the Curriculum of a Class

At a given time, in developing the curriculum for and with a particular group of children, the classroom teacher necessarily assumes a highly creative role. He is confronted with the problem of reconciling multiple factors. He wants his group to gain certain

[1] Many recent publications of professional groups have re-emphasized the essential qualities and important role of the classroom teacher; for example, *Goals for 1960 in Elementary Education,* 1950 Yearbook of the Texas Association of School Administrators (address Fred Kaderli, Superintendent, San Marcos, Texas).

221

knowledges, common understandings, skills, and attitudes, but the group has varying degrees of readiness. He wants to make learning meaningful for all, but each pupil has a different combination of experiences from which to derive meaning in new experiences.

In order for each pupil to develop in the way best for him, the classroom teacher must find processes that foster individual initiative without violation of the common good. Teaching aids must be localized according to circumstance and focused upon a particular class. To keep interest alive, to bring each learner to purposes of his own, and to keep each identified with group problems, he seeks a variety of appeals and motivations.

How can he reach one pupil without imposing on another? How can he be an effective task master and win respect for his understanding? What can he do about the many factors beyond his immediate control? How can he make each day meaningful for every child?

Within the framework of the stated philosophy and policies of the school system, the teacher strives to relate forces and factors both without and within his classroom. He tries to bring something to his pupils and to get something from them. He goes into his room with some plans. In accordance with major educational objectives he seeks to guide his pupils within the process of further planning. Using a framework of content and planned-in-advance learning experiences as points of departure, the teacher and his group proceed as learners together. Thus, within the framework of a planned curriculum, the classroom group evolves a curriculum that cannot be foreseen in detail by curriculum committees, school administrators, or authors of textbooks. It is the classroom teacher who reconciles many conditions and develops the *actual* curriculum.

Framework for Planning

Effective planning rests upon school organization and the climate of the classroom. No teacher can reconcile the many factors and forces previously mentioned without a permissive, flexible, and functional teaching situation.

Exploring and sharing—The emphasis in modern teaching may be suggested by such words as "introduce," "explore," and "share." In teaching spelling, for instance, the teacher may introduce a standard word list and principles involved in the spelling of each word. That is not all of the spelling activity, however. Pupils are encouraged to explore continuously for the new words they would like to own. They check back thru their own writings every few days to list words they did not spell correctly. They share with others their findings concerning the rules of spelling and types of difficulties most common.

Similarly, in science the classroom teacher may effect introductions to principles and factors in balance. Pupils explore the thoughts projected—enlarging, discovering, verifying, and sharing.

Flexibility in time and content organization—With exploration and sharing there must be long blocks of time and close grouping of kindred elements to be learned. Instead of teaching spelling as an isolated, separately scheduled subject, it might be dealt with as one phase of the broad field of language arts. The whole family of communicative arts might occupy a single long block of time. In all phases the classroom teacher carries forward a program of "introductions," and all together explore, or investigate and share almost without ceasing. The same principles apply in high-school course work. Periods should be long enough and the outlook big enough for the introduce-explore-share emphasis.

Individualization of opportunities—The class cannot be taught simply as tho it were one individual. Some of the "introductions" will be to the whole class at one time. Part of the exploring and sharing will be done as a whole group, but the problem of individualization always prevails. If the time block is adequate and the outlook is broad, procedures may be employed which will allow each individual to proceed according to his own readiness and need and at the same time maintain identity with the group projects.

Individualization can be illustrated by an upper elementary-school social studies project. The teacher introduced to the class several outstanding aspects of pioneering in new American frontiers. With social studies defined broadly as the study of mankind and his problems thru time and space, new frontiers were simply a window thru which the group would look to see universal problems. Pioneering in general was immediately in focus. The "here and now" of pioneering became a convenient pivot point. Soon the detailed, action-filled aspects of our geographical frontiers in the

223

westward movement were located. The map was studied, names of leaders were introduced, household equipment, transportation, occupations, and Indians were given attention.

Small groups, with special interests, explored thoroly several of the most prominent phases of frontier life. They became real resource committees, working at their respective individual levels, and sharing among themselves in preparation for bigger sharings with the entire class. Their exploring and sharing activities included experiences in reading, writing, conversing, painting, dramatizing, displaying, modeling, and formal reporting. Each pupil was identified with the project. Each could work up to his full capacity. Each benefited from the accomplishment of others. Thru it all, the classroom teacher was introducing, exploring, sharing, thus enlarging concepts, leading each to needed information, bringing each to the creative level, and coordinating to help each serve all.

There were many extensions into and from other learning areas. Being conscious of principles to which the group had been introduced in the skills areas, the teacher was able to ascertain where each was with respect to what he had been taught. The teacher was better able, therefore, to help or "pick-up" each child on the basis of his own needs. The sequence scale became a slide rule; for example, groups were formed for those with special needs in the language arts. This diversity of subgrouping avoided fixed. or labeled subgroups. There was little likelihood that the group working together this week would be together next week. *Tomorrow's* group even might not be the same as *today's*. Whenever subgrouping was effected, it was for an understood purpose. Groups with special interests held together longer than groups with special needs.

It will be understood that the program of sequences was carried forward in the formal, teacher-carries-it-to-pupils manner; "pickups" brought teaching and learning nearer to individual needs.

Adjustment to various areas—Perhaps in bookkeeping, or typing, or Latin, or mathematics, the processes described would not be applicable without changes. The same basic principles should apply, however, in any area. For best results, the teaching-learning situation will allow for flexible, functional, creative, individualized procedures of whatever nature is becoming to the area; the time blocks and classroom atmosphere will be appropriate to the needed

224

procedures; and the teaching procedures will include introductions, explorations, and sharings in whatever proportions appear proper at a given time for the course or area and with a particular group.

Discovering Pupil Interests and Needs

During the "introduce" phases of teaching, the classroom teacher watches for individual reactions. Thru observation he ascertains the various interests prevailing within his groups. He notes particularly the characteristics and inclinations of individual pupils which might lead them into the participations necessary for building or justified interests. Also thru exploring and sharing there are real opportunities for the discovery of both interests and needs.

A fourth-grade project—A fourth-grade teacher found some special interests and needs of her pupils in a study of Australia. By introducing many facts concerning the people and the country and by reading, telling, and allowing open discussion, individuals began to show interest in particular phases. Some had a real interest in animals after a brief introduction to the kangaroo. Following some reports from a member of the class who had lived for a brief period in Australia, some wanted to know more about the daily experiences of children there. This question led to others about homes, play, clothing, food, cities and occupations.

Groups were formed around items of special interest, on a free choice basis. Many interests were common to the majority of the pupils and were typical of the age group. Some of the interests were engendered within the group. As the groups explored and shared, however, many related interests, rather personal in nature, were reflected. There were indications of some things particular individuals liked most or least. Some interests seemed more justified than others. Special needs and talents became increasingly evident, too. Some wanted to have recreational reading, some liked the more factual, some did not want to read at all, while some others could not read. Poor coordination, poor vision, inclination to promptness, neatness, disorder, nervousness, extent of abilities to work cooperatively, and to use language effectively were evidenced.

A seventh-grade project—In a unit on homes a seventh-grade social studies teacher found a variety of interests. A few pupils

225

wanted to build miniature homes, some wanted to furnish them, some wanted to make charts or draw, and some wanted to create murals. Still others were more inclined to collect. A few took photographs in various areas of the city and talked with people living in different types of homes. One pupil need revealed was the necessity of understanding and tolerance with regard to people in various parts of the city. From these activities came an appreciation of "family pride" in homes and an understanding of the effect when such pride was lacking.

A special student project—When given an opportunity to do a term project in American history her own way and in an area of her choosing, rather than do a term theme on one of several suggested topics, a girl who had not made a good academic record in high school revealed a dominating interest in clothing design. Her fashion book, indicating how mass psychology and social, political, and economic trends could influence expression thru dress, brought out her own personal and occupational interests. In guiding her in the development of the project, the classroom teacher found a definite lack of reading ability, emotional difficulties, an extreme desire to be attractive and accepted, willingness to be helped stifled by a fear of being exposed in her shortcomings, and a vague discernment of values in academic studies.

Interests develop from vital activities—A language arts teacher found that a study of elements in the daily news uncovered many interests and needs. In the upper grades of elementary school another teacher found that pupils will reveal their interests and needs if challenged to find their own applications of arithmetic principles taught. Girls often discover problems having to do with chinaware, silverware, clothing, design, bargains, and other things relating to their personal and social roles. Boys tend more to sports, industries, banking, management, and similar interest areas in their applications. Attempts to make applications result in a discovery of the extent to which understandings have been gained. Problems of the "teaser type" are believed by some to be valuable in finding interests and needs.

Among incidental devices in discovering interests and needs is that of keeping mail-order catalogs available for perusal by pupils. Also, choice of friends and kinds of out-of-school activities engaged in have implications. Reading choices, reaction to various arts, personal habits, kinds of escapes and identities sought, all should be studied.

Marshaling Resources

Effective teaching requires setting the stage for effective learning. Learning requires that something be learned. One of the principal tasks of the classroom teacher, then, is to be sure that proper and adequate content material or subjectmatter is included in the teaching unit and that proper materials and experiences are provided to enable the pupils to learn. There must be a close relationship between the objectives of learning and the activities or experiences thru which the pupils are expected to accomplish the learning objectives. It is essential that the teacher be thoroly conscious of this relationship in order that he can evaluate progress and know when the objectives have been attained.

It is also essential that in introducing a unit of work the classroom teacher have a thoro understanding of what is to be done and how to do it. He should have an adequate background of knowledge in the subject at hand, altho it is granted that in the process of exploration he will himself profit from the findings in the immediate area.

In any teaching situation an important function of the classroom teacher is that of effecting availability of the numerous resources or materials appropriate for the learning desired. Some frequently mentioned resources are textbooks, encyclopedias, almanacs, trade books, newspapers, magazines, pamphlets, films, slides, maps, models, specimens, teachers, community places and people and the pupils themselves.

Special bureaus—In getting ready for the unit on Australia referred to above, books, pamphlets, pictures, maps, and other materials were placed on a classroom table. A story from a reader brought a desire on the part of pupils to examine some of the other materials. At the beginning of the term the study and some of the materials had been planned by the teacher. Valuable materials were secured from the Australian News and Information Bureau in New York. A wide range and variety of materials were necessary in exploring the various facets of Australian life and the classroom teacher accepted responsibility before and during the study for securing materials and locating sources which could be made available to the group during their searching and sharing.

Individuals and community groups—The teacher may find resource persons outside the school. While studying the Rocky Mountains and their part in the story of America, one teacher invited into his class a parent who had served as bus driver and guide in the Rocky Mountain National Park. While studying the oil industry, another teacher invited a pupil's father to discuss the physics of oil and its production and after his visit the library was searched for more reading material on oil. The classroom teacher asked the librarian to help pupils find material and the librarian became a resource person. A similar experience was noted by a teacher who invited a U. S. Department of Agriculture poultry inspector to class during the studies in agriculture.

In high-school mathematics a teacher became concerned about mathematics used in the vocations in which his students had expressed an interest. He organized some community sponsors in the respective vocations on whom he could call for consultation with pupils. There were times when subgroups would have the benefit of a vocational advisor in the classroom; for example, five students might be in one corner with an architect and four in another with a pharmacist. Since the students were having on-the-job experiences, the project also provided vocational counseling. The mathematics teacher made the most of circumstances in marshaling resources for his area.

Field trips and other means of using community resources are universally accepted by teachers. Usually it takes initiative of one teacher in making resources available, altho all teachers may be continuously on the search for aids of all types. Any effort to obtain community resources should be school initiated and should have the approval of the school principal because of the obligations which may arise.

Sometimes the most useful aids may be overlooked. An art teacher had a standing agreement with merchants that she could direct committees of pupils in searching their scrap piles for bits of needed materials. Discarded neon (not fluorescent) lamp tubes proved to be a real value. The lumber dealer knew always that scraps of lumber could be used by this art teacher. A science teacher found his community ready to save just about anything he needed for experimentation.

Students as resources—Perhaps the most valuable resource of all lies in the talents and experiences of the pupils themselves. A skilful teacher can arrange to make each pupil's abilities serve the learning purposes of all. Primary teachers have found that reading becomes much more meaningful when the children create their own reading matter from their own experiences. A second-grade boy came into his room glowingly announcing his experiences with a turtle which he had caught as he was coming to school. After he related his experience, the teacher guided the class in creating a story which all read and copied into their Treasure Book. In almost every undertaking some child, because of his talents or the nature of his experiences, can be a resource person or part of a resource group. Pupils as resources become increasingly helpful thru their years in school.

The classroom teacher is the key person in making any and all resources available to her classes.

Effective Use of Guides

Such teaching aids as teaching guides, courses of study, and textbooks supply common points of reference in teaching. For various teachers concerned with like elements of content, or similar ideas to be dealt with in effecting learning experiences, they serve as cue sources. They facilitate the use of major aspects of a learning area in a diversity of approaches and procedures. The particular uses to which such aids may be put might be suggested more definitely in separate considerations of those named.

Curriculum guides—Within recent years the curriculum guide and the teaching guide have come into prominence, possibly because of their flexibility. The term "curriculum guide" generally means a statement of what is to be taught in the curriculum and where it is to be taught. By referring to such a guide a beginning teacher, a teacher new to the system, a regular teacher, or a lay person may know the content of the curriculum in a particular school system. It may be said that the curriculum guide is a statement of the scope and sequence of the curriculum.

A *teaching* guide is more specific than the *general* curriculum guide. It may, for example, be a prepared statement or bulletin on the teaching of music in the school system or any other subject under consideration. The purpose of the teaching guide is to give the individual teacher an understanding of the purposes, philosophy, methods, and to some extent, the content of the courses in question.

Both curriculum guides and teaching guides differ from courses of study in that the old type traditional course of study gave the teacher specific and definite instructions as to what should be done in the classroom and when it should be done. Under the newer plans of teaching, specific and definite instructions issued from above, either by school administrators or supervisors, cannot always be followed in the classroom to the best advantage. The flexibility and permissive nature of guides should be more helpful to the classroom teacher (see Chapter III).

Using courses of study—There is general agreement today that it is not acceptable practice to follow a course of study in a lock-step fashion. As a result, the common tendency is to replace the old outline-of-content-to-be-taught type document with the more flexible aid referred to as a "framework-of-reference." Yet, the nature and intent of courses of study might vary, justifiably, according to the level or area of instruction for which they were developed. The intended purpose the aid is to serve will determine the best uses which may be made of it.

A teaching guide in algebra, for instance, might be less flexible than one for world history. The sequences in the one are more nearly fixed than in the other. The steps in algebra follow more systematic patterns than in history. Similarly, in shop and trade courses the course of study might be more prescriptive and more nearly in step-by-step sequence than in social studies or most phases of the creative and recreative arts. The teaching of grammar or arithmetic invites a closer adherence to preplanned sequences than the more exploratory areas of health-science or social studies.

The curriculum guide may reflect the logical order of sequences. In arithmetic it will list addition at an earlier point in the sequence than long division. It will bring attention to the *function* of verbs before definite consideration is given to the *kinds* of verbs. It will indicate that from the standpoint of experience the home and school environment represents the child's world before the United States of America is his world. The first-grade pupil will gain new experiences largely in his home and school environment. The scope will become progressively wider until in about his fifth school year he is led to see problems of living in the light of how they affect us in the United States. It will reflect the "what" of teaching and often it indicates that "this" is passed necessarily on the way to "that."

Yet, the "how" of teaching is at best merely suggested. Never can the matter of technic or approach be definitely scheduled. The exact sequence of the "what" cannot be always scheduled. The classroom teacher working with a particular group at any given time will relate the elements of content in such a way as to gain the greatest understanding in terms of the purposes evolved by the group. He will capitalize upon the experiences children have had and are having to find springboards for new learnings. He may "introduce" to the class certain elements in a rather orderly sequence. The applications that may be made of the principle or skills introduced may be found much of the time during explorings and sharings and enlargements in which the skill employed is not the primary consideration. Too, not all elements of content located in a guide need follow any particular order. The guide may reflect that customs, cultures, recreation, transportation, cities, products, industries, natural resources and features, types of people, and population factors will all be considered in studying Western Europe. They need not be studied in that order or as separate entities. Each element is a part of the other. The circumstances at the time, the nature of the group, and the purposes of the study are factors that influence the treatment of a topic.

Briefly, then, the classroom teacher remains flexible in his use of courses of study. He remains as flexible as the purposes in his teaching and the nature of the course or area will allow.

Using textbooks—There are still too many classroom teachers who make exclusive use of the textbook as the course of study. This failing may be caused by a lack of planning time in the daily schedule. When teachers have too heavy teaching loads, frequently they resort to the sole use of the textbook because they do not have time for better curriculum planning. The textbook is a summary source or a particular outline of content that may be approached in

231

any number of ways. It is one of many sources. While in some courses, such as mathematics, it is a primary source, in other classes the textbook is used as a reference. Experiences necessary for a full realization of knowledge about anything come outside the textbook. The textbook merely gives order and arrangement to elements dealt with. Often readiness activities are advisable before going to the textbook even as a summary or reference source.

A pupil of sixth-grade social studies had listened to stories and conversations about recreation in Czechoslovakia before even attempting to read from his geography book. The teacher observed that since the child was below his grade level in reading skill attainment, and since the textbook was so tightly packed with content and vocabulary new to him, he was able to get meaning from it only after a number of experiences that prepared him to read it. A book in Latin might be more meaningful after certain conditioning experiences before dealing with a particular element in the study of the language. The same is true for physics, mathematics, or any other textbook. A guide other than the textbook may be the primary source. The textbook in any area may be simply another source to pass thru on the way to fulfilment of objectives derived independently of the book.

Then, too, no one source, however basic or primary, is sufficient. If discernment in what is learned is to prevail, different approaches, presentations, and points of view should be studied.

Guiding Pupil Activities

The effective teacher is always looking for opportunities to capitalize upon events and experiences which may be used as natural leads into desired areas of new experiences. The art teacher may know that a group of his pupils are studying the importance of trees in man's daily living. In accordance with the readiness of the pupils and the purposes of the art area, he initiates several art activities relating to the tree study which are at the time opportune and appropriate. The mathematics teacher knows that problems in design are under consideration in homemaking classes. In terms of whatever mathematical principles he is dealing with at the time, and to whatever extent they apply, he builds upon the prevailing experiences and understanding to gain meaningful application in his area and to encourage extensions of all learning.

232

Public schools, Chattanooga, Tennessee

The curriculum really comes to life in the classroom, and it is the teacher who brings it to life by viewing each child as a unique, living, growing, active person.

More than following noses—To coordinate pupil interest as developed in many school areas does not mean that any classroom teacher is driven only by circumstance. In guiding and adapting pupils' activities, the teacher necessarily assumes considerable initiative. The role of the teacher is not that of a caterer to whim. Teaching is not a matter of engaging people in a process of just following their noses. Indeed violence may be done to purposeful learning if the types of activities entered into are either promiscuous or superficially imposed. Forced correlations, piecemeal teaching, or incoherent, purposeless floundering may result in patronizing, get-by, hurdle-jumping tactics on the part of the pupils.

Elsewhere in this chapter it has been proposed that the classroom teacher should have some purposes and plans in order to bring ideas and information to the pupils. It has been noted, on the other hand, that he wants ever to inspire pupil purposing and to maintain a flexible, permissive setting that will give pupils opportunity for development of their own characteristics and needs. Guidance of learning activities is in terms of the processes demanded by purposes, needs, and situations. Many experiences in school and out of school form the basis for other desired experiences.

So it is that the classroom teacher rotates much of his work around experiences and events that offer opportunity for individuals to make contributions peculiar to them, but related to the interests, needs, and purposes of others. Each thus can relate learning to general experience and all can benefit from the abilities of everyone.

Individual teaching involves process—Process is the key word perhaps, in adapting learning to the needs of individuals. Spelling has been pointed to as an area in which individualization is necessary. Individualization does not consist of simply teaching one child at a time. Employing processes that allow each to discover his own needs and then proceed as an individual in meeting them amounts to individualization.

It has been observed that however thoro and necessary the teaching of a standard word list may be, it still is not enough. When words expected to be used extensively by a group in exploring any topic or problem are introduced and analyzed, group and individual needs are being met. But that, too, is presumptive and not enough. The teacher who gets a pupil to find his own errors in whatever vocabulary he is trying to use in writing, and thus helps him to discover his particular pattern of errors is leading him to recognize causes behind his difficulties. This procedure can be used with a whole class, and with little time spent on particular individuals. The teacher has directed his efforts toward establishing work procedures that help each pupil discover and meet his own particular needs. The plan amounts to guidance that results in adaptation of learning to individual needs without interference of the teacher-generated progression thru sequences.

The classroom teacher is challenged, then, to become skilful in processes that allow interests, needs, and abilities of individuals to be seen; to capitalize upon experiences that will inspire desired activities; to "introduce" carefully in the light of known characteristics and needs; to use a variety of approaches, materials, and processes that will allow pupils to make adaptations for themselves. The obligations are many and the load heavy. The classroom teacher must expect from the school administrator both sympathetic understanding and effective action toward lifting the burden of many school tasks.[2]

Evaluating Progress and Performance

The creative role of the classroom teacher places a premium on his ability to evaluate the whole teaching-learning process as it relates to a particular group of learners, individuals within the group of learners, and the situation. Evaluation is related to the total teaching-learning situation (see Chapter XI).

Many ways to use tests—The conception of evaluation operating in the classroom determines in a very large measure the effectiveness of the total teaching-learning situation. An example may help to clarify this statement. In a certain mathematics classroom the teacher was observed to confine testing to marking (grading). Periodically he gave a test to establish a mark. In conversation he complained about the inability of individuals to do the work assigned. Across the hall, another mathematics teacher used the test in an entirely different way. Periodically this teacher

---

[2] National Education Association, Research Division, "Teaching Load in 1950." *Research Bulletin* 29: 1-51; February 1951. See especially pages 40-48.

presented to the class a test with the intention of discovering individual learning difficulties and with a clear teacher-pupil understanding that no mark was being established. In conversation he was expressive concerning the development of individuals and pointed out how he had discovered needs for understanding and consequently helped individuals over difficult spots.

In the first classroom situation, students who were not successful with the test, showed tension and expressed dislike for the study of mathematics. In the second classroom, students who experienced the same types of difficulties were quick to express interest in the study of mathematics, while admitting their difficulties. They had confidence in the help given by the teacher, who understood the differences among members of the class and worked patiently, and in the main successfully, to ease pupils over their difficulties. Evidences of tension simply were not present in the second classroom. Instead, there was a belief by pupils and teacher that together they could solve their difficulties.

Evaluation aids instruction—The comparison of the two classrooms serves to point up the main features of what has come to be understood by the term "evaluation." Evaluation from the point of view of the classroom teacher is the careful analysis of a teaching-learning task or situation to find out salient features to improve. Evaluation, when applied to the individual pupil, means finding out the strengths and weaknesses of the pupil with a view toward improving upon his responses to a particular learning task.

In setting up the test situation as a device to create awareness of difficulty the second teacher emphasized evaluation as it is related to the learner. Evaluation is inseparable from the learner. The learner must realize a relationship between his evaluation of his learning and his desire to learn. He must have a desire to learn and to continue to learn. The teacher can do much toward creating and stimulating this desire. Learning is something that the pupil does for himself, and the better he understands what he is about, the more surely will his learning progress.

Desirable practices in evaluation take into consideration the principles established in the above comparison; that is, evaluation is part and parcel of the teaching-learning process; and evaluation is a joint undertaking shared by both the classroom teacher and the pupil. Teachers who come into a clear understanding of these principles plan from the very beginning of every teaching-learning situation to make evaluation operative thruout the learning activity and always cooperative. Cooperation comes when the teacher and pupils plan together from the very beginning of a unit to evaluate progress in terms of agreed-upon objectives. Evaluation, based upon clearly understood and accepted purposes, results in the pupils' assuming responsibility for their achievement.

Evaluation is concerned with evidences of learning. For this reason the classroom teacher may keep a folder for each child, in which to place samples of his work as a record of his activities. This easy device helps in the idea of cooperation between pupil and teacher in evaluation. One fifth-grade teacher kept such a folder, and used it at the time a mark had to be established for the report card. She and the individual pupil evaluated together the samples of work and, upon that basis, discussed the report card marks.

The teacher who uses the folder idea for gathering evidence to evaluate progress will find many opportunities to indicate progress by means other than examples of work and test papers. Besides schoolwork, a record of outside activities would indicate development on the part of the pupil; for example, voluntary reading, club membership, and hobbies. Anecdotal records of pupils' reactions in certain school situations may be most revealing, especially where attitudes and resourcefulness are concerned.

Tests furnish one of the most common evaluative devices. Too often test items relate only to the recall of information on the assumption that the possession of the information guarantees understanding. To find out whether understanding really exists the teacher is compelled to create test items that demand the use of the higher mental processes; that is, the application of principles, the exercise of judgment values, and weighing of facts as evidences of cause and effect.

Testing the intangibles—It is a challenge to teachers to attempt evaluations of such intangibles as initiative, dependability, resourcefulness, cooperation, and attitudes. Actually the challenge is to teach for these so-called intangibles. Too often they are listed as objectives of teaching without any definite attempt to teach them. Clearly they cannot enter into the classroom teacher's scheme for

237

evaluation unless there is a teaching-learning situation in which they can really manifest themselves.

The first step in evaluation is to decide the situation for learning; for example: cooperativeness as a skill has to be learned (see Chapter XI). The teacher must recognize possible classroom opportunities for teaching cooperative group action if cooperativeness is to enter into evaluation of pupil growth. If initiative is to be evaluated, the teacher must create situations in which initiative may become operative. It is a waste of time for the teacher to look for cooperation and initative if he establishes a teaching-learning situation that allows only obedience and the following of directions.

Correlating Class and Nonclass Experiences

The significance of the need to correlate classroom experiences of pupils is emphasized when the classroom teacher realizes that new learning results only in as far as the pupil is able to relate the new to previous experiences. The primary-school teacher who has this understanding will relate all that is attempted in early classroom activities to the experiences the pupils have had in the home. Correlating classroom experiences of primary-school pupils with out-of-school relationships with parents, other boys and girls, neighbors, and pets is an established practice. For example, as was pointed out previously, in developing a vocabulary for reading the teacher works with the pupils in building stories based on their experiences. This practice is done by arranging situations in which pupils are encouraged to tell incidents out of their experience. Under the guidance of the teacher, telling about experiences leads into writing and reading experiences.

Reading and writing thus developed become functional and there is little chance of the pupil's learning to repeat words without understanding. The functional aspect of inschool learning is best assumed when the experience situation is in some way connected with the on-going life experiences of the learner. The teacher of arithmetic, for example, who plans a teaching unit in money management will be concerned with the kinds of experiences with money matters the pupils have had in the home. Work with the spending of allowances, for example, places the study of money management in a context that may be real and meaningful to class members.

The pupil who can think in abstract terms or who finds it easy to recognize and manipulate symbols, tends to deal with them without arriving at applications in terms of his own experience. This application is another reason for correlating classroom learning with experiences pupils have outside the classroom. It is an assurance against mere verbalization.

The learning experiences of the child are by no means confined to the school. The total curriculum, as it relates to any particular child, consists of all learning experiences occurring both in and out of school. The school's function in furthering the life-curriculum of individuals is to develop the individual's abilities to deal with home and community experiences in a way satisfactory to the democratic society in which the school exists. Helping pupils to deal with such problems can be done best when there is cooperation between the home and the school in handling actual situations important to youth in the school.

The classroom teacher who becomes concerned with the problem of developing and guiding out-of-classroom learning experiences will look for opportunities to involve these experiences in constructive classroom learnings. Such experiences will aid the pupil in developing a desire for continued learning.

The alert teacher never loses sight of the real aim of teaching; that is, to continue to identify all classroom learning with the ongoing experiences of the individual.

Planning His Own Teaching Unit

Unit teaching is largely a matter of planning and organizing around a large idea for emphasis. The importance of planning is stressed in all curriculum improvement programs. Curriculum guides prepared in more recent improvement programs encourage classroom teacher planning by being flexible enough to allow adaptation to the class situation and the most obvious teaching job.

Units Based on Group Needs

Teaching units cannot be well planned without regard for the group that is to learn. Good planning is shaped to meet the actuality of the situation and the job to be done. Many classroom teachers

239

realize the truth of this statement and begin their plans for teaching units with a study of the class group. The classroom teacher aims in this study to find out about individual levels of development, abilities, interests, and group and individual responses and to contemplate possibilities for the class as a group and as individuals.

Discovering the individual—Aside from making use of school records teachers use various technics to learn about their class members. One teacher reported that during the period when the main objective is to find out about class members no textbooks are given out. Several days are spent in just getting acquainted, visiting, and encouraging individual class members to tell about themselves. A part of these early class periods is planned for students to converse in small groups in order to get members of the class thoroly acquainted and so there will be no hesitancy to talk in the larger group. This type of procedure calls for skill in group dynamics, but it offers excellent possibilities for the teacher to become acquainted with class members. It has advantage over the device of having pupils write about themselves in that it provides for individual and group development in an important area of human relations.

Recognizing group needs—A teaching unit is planned with a particular class in mind. Activities are planned with the individual levels of development, abilities, interests, and needs in mind. In the preplanning period the teacher thinks thru pupil purposes for doing the unit, that is, possible activities that will attract individuals and at the same time will develop the objectives the teacher has in mind. The classroom teacher in upper-grade social studies may well have planned in advance for the little interest groups that developed in the unit on American Frontiers. The kinds of things that students did in this unit developed abilities in research, in organizing materials, in sharing learnings, and in cooperative effort. These abilities were thought thru in planning, and suggested activities were listed by the teacher. All of this suggests that the teacher has in mind the objectives or outcomes of the unit in knowledge, skill in using knowledge, attitudes, and appreciations as plans are made for the kinds of things pupils will do during the progress of the unit.

Assistance thru the school system—Many school systems are furnishing aids to teachers in the form of resource units, which are of material help in planning teaching units.

In planning a teaching unit from a resource unit, a teacher selects from it objectives, problems, activities, materials, subjectmatter, and evaluative procedures that meet the needs of a particular class group at the time the unit is planned. The selections made from the resource unit may be supplemented from the teacher's background of experience and the uniqueness of the class.[3]

Working with Other Teachers

Modern curriculum improvement programs are making extensive use of the resource unit. The resource unit provides concrete and practical help for the teacher in building teaching units. They may be developed by individual teachers for their own use; but any one teacher finds it time consuming to develop all the resource units needed. It is, therefore, important for school systems to provide ways for classroom teachers to share in the development of resource units. But first a system may be interested in developing total participation in resource unit production. Participation has been accomplished by enlisting the efforts of each teacher in resource unit production, thus emphasizing the importance of the uses of the design becoming familiar with details thru being a part of the designing. This plan has the advantage of making each classroom teacher familiar with the importance of research and over-all planning so important to the development of a teaching unit.

Plans for Group Work

A school system, interested in developing resource units for teacher use, finds it necessary to institute group processes that encourage teachers to think thru areas for resource unit development. Once areas are isolated, groups of teachers may assume responsibility for developing resource units. Groups organize materials for resource units thru discussion, research, and getting together and organizing what has already been experienced. Ideas result from group discussions which stimulate teachers to think of better ways of doing the work of the classroom.

---

[3] From *Manual for Using the Form for Planning and Developing a Resource Unit*, Dallas, Texas, 1951. Dallas Independent School District. p. 1.

The main value of resource units is in the variety of suggestions offered to teachers for planning. Group development of resource units tends to assume greater variety in suggestions. Teachers have said that growth comes mainly from actual doing. Among the values listed by classroom teachers from the experience of working together in curriculum planning are these: (a) conserving time and energy by bringing together the experiences of the group in the way of suggestions for procedures, valuable reference, and ways of evaluating; (b) gaining knowledge of ways of directing classroom activities to allow for varying needs, interests, and capabilities of pupils; (c) becoming acquainted early with change which encourages experimentation in its use and is likely to insure success; and (d) the feeling of security that comes from planning with the group (see Chapters III and IV).

Participating in the Systemwide Program

The classroom teacher is responsible for bringing the planned curriculum to life in the classroom. This fact alone makes the teacher an important figure in the systemwide program of curriculum development. No modern school system would contemplate for even a moment's time leaving the classroom teacher out of plans for curriculum improvement. To make the most of planning for bringing the curriculum to life in the classroom, the teacher needs a thoro understanding of the total planning that goes into curriculum development. This knowledge can be gained thru an orientation program, but it is best gained thru participation in the total program. The classroom teachers gain understanding from the first-hand experience of serving on committees, and from membership in study or discussion groups.

SELECTED REFERENCES

ALBERTY, HAROLD B. *Reorganizing the High-School Curriculum.* New York: Macmillan Co., 1947. 458 p.

ASSOCIATION FOR SUPERVISION AND CURRICULUM DEVELOPMENT. *Leadership Through Supervision.* 1946 Yearbook. Washington, D.C.: the Association, a department of the National Education Association, 1946. 163 p. $2.

ASSOCIATION FOR SUPERVISION AND CURRICULUM DEVELOPMENT. *Toward Better Teaching.* 1949 Yearbook. Washington, D. C.: the Association, a department of the National Education Association, 1949. 282 p. $3.

BURTON, WILLIAM H. *The Guidance of Learning Activities.* New York: Appleton-Century-Crofts, 1948. 601 p.

GWYNN, J. MINOR. *Curriculum Principles and Social Trends.* New York: Macmillan Co., 1950. 768 p.

JERSILD, ARTHUR T., and OTHERS. *Child Development and the Curriculum.* New York: Teachers College, Columbia University, 1946. 274 p.

KRUG, EDWARD A. *Curriculum Planning.* New York: Harper and Brothers, 1950. 306 p.

LEE, J. MURRAY, and LEE, DORRIS MAY. *The Child and His Curriculum.* Revised edition. New York: Appleton-Century-Crofts, 1950. 710 p.

LEONARD, J. PAUL. *Developing the Secondary School Curriculum.* New York: Rhinehart and Co., 1946. 560 p.

MIEL, ALICE. *Changing the Curriculum.* New York: Appleton-Century-Crofts, 1946. 242 p.

NATIONAL SOCIETY FOR THE STUDY OF EDUCATION. *Adolescence.* Forty-Third Yearbook, Part I. Chicago: University of Chicago Press, 1944. 358 p.

NATIONAL SOCIETY FOR THE STUDY OF EDUCATION. *Learning and Instruction.* Forty-Ninth Yearbook, Part I. Chicago: University of Chicago Press, 1950. 352 p.

OTTO, HENRY J. *Principles of Elementary Education.* New York: Rhinehart and Co., 1949. 430 p.

STRATEMEYER, FLORENCE B., and OTHERS. *Developing a Curriculum for Modern Living.* New York: Teachers College, Columbia University, 1947. 558 p.

STRICKLAND, RUTH G. *How To Build a Unit of Work.* U. S. Office of Education, Federal Security Agency, Bulletin 1946, No. 5. Washington, D. C.: Superintendent of Documents, Government Printing Office, 1946. 48 p.

WALTERS, T. L. "The Unit Plan of Instruction." *Bulletin of the National Association of Secondary-School Principals* 34: 85-90; May 1950.

CHAPTER NINE

Home and Community Influence Instruction

A LWAYS influenced by home and community, education today is and should be increasingly affected by the rapidly mounting complications of social and economic life in this last half of the twentieth century. Yet unless foresight is exercised, unplanned changes may be wrought in the instructional program of schools, merely in an attempt to adjust to pressures from the home, the community, and the world.

The hit-and-miss methods of community pressures on the curriculum are all too familiar. The school administrator, working with the instructional staff, finds it difficult to harmonize such demands. For example, one group would like to have more early American history taught; another thinks that there should be greater emphasis upon recent events such as the United Nations. Some are much concerned about the need for more individualized instruction. Others contend that the world is going downhill because children no longer obey their parents and teachers; and they want the schools to remedy that difficulty.

Still others declare that the schools are getting out of their proper sphere when they attempt to teach morals and family life or deal with the vital issues of the economic system. There are employers of school graduates who would have the schools teach only "the fundamentals"—as *they* define the term. A few contend that the technics needed for production in the factories can be taught better under actual working conditions than in the schools. Still other employers are interested in expanding the program of vocational education, so as to prepare young people for specific jobs in factories. Similarly, the question of sex education has been discussed over and over again, with parents and community groups fighting on both sides of the issue, one group arguing for sex education in the public schools, and one against it.

These examples are only a few of the issues which classroom teachers and administrators regularly meet as they attempt to develop curriculum programs which reflect the thinking of the community and the democratic ideals of our republic. Some educators use inaction to counterbalance all these pressures. They feel that since so many people have conflicting ideas about what the schools should or should not do, it is best just to ignore all of them and run the schools as they have been run for years. This "easy way out" of the dilemma certainly is not the way that leads to progress in education. Therefore, while this chapter deals with the general operation of home and community influences on the curriculum, it is concerned primarily with the positive changes which can be produced by design thru the cooperative effort of pupils, classroom teachers, school administrators, boards of education, and other citizens.

Positive Guidance of Influences

Since it is natural for citizens to be interested in the education of their children, it is important for each school system to have a positive program for discovering, analyzing, and channeling these interests. Unless they are used constructively to strengthen and enrich a developing curriculum, they may become destructive forces that impair the efforts of teachers. Citizens whose energies and abilities are directed against certain aspects of the school program, with the proper encouragement and direction, may in time become constructive critics and effective champions of the public schools. A positive program of channeling home and community influences also meets the needs of persons who sincerely want to do something for the schools, either because their children are pupils, or because they think education is important. What, then, are some of these positive approaches?

Approaching thru the Pupils

A happy and satisfied pupil is the school's most effective public relations person. Parents' opinions about the school are determined largely by their children's feeling of success or failure, and what they think about what goes on. Dissatisfaction with the school program, perhaps growing out of a student's unfavorable reaction to a particular subject or to the marking system, may start a public attack on the school. But just as surely other citizens are strong supporters of the schools because their children enjoy success and happiness in their studies.

Happy and achieving pupils are the products of effective instruction by an understanding classroom teacher. And the earmarks of the curriculum in such a setting have to do with pupils who are participating in planning and who are engaging in important tasks to solve problems which for them are significant and worthwhile. These pupils take seriously such opportunities as arousing interest in voting, improving sanitary conditions, beautifying homes and schools, interviewing public officials for needed information, or reporting findings and recommendations to clubs and other civic groups. In such endeavors they work enthusiastically. Their zeal is contagious and their parents are proud of their accomplishments. They work steadily at all hours and thru the week end. Their teacher is the one who "can't wait for Monday to come."

To be satisfied, the pupil must also know that he is steadily sharpening the tools for learning—his ability to use the dictionary and reference material, to write, to read, and to work with numbers so that he has an increasing sureness in dealing with the accumulated knowledge of the world for use in attaining his objectives. Such a pupil, with a sense of growth and development, has a profoundly positive effect upon parents.

When pupils thus understand and approve of the school program, parents usually are pleased and are willing to cooperate constructively for its continuous improvement. Thus, the *pupil* is a key person in the channeling of home and community influences upon instruction.

Approaching thru the Classroom Teacher

A first requisite of effective education is for a classroom teacher to have technical skill and a sincere love of children. Thru these qualities and his genuineness there is nourished a natural bond of confidence and friendship. But if the classroom teacher is to guide home and community influences, his traditional sphere of activity must be broadened. When he plans the educational program around the needs of children and relates it to local problems and life in the community, he will find more and more resources outside the classroom. Often he will make himself available for community leadership and service. By such participation he develops an inner drive to help the community with its problems, in school and out, whenever he can be of service. In this capacity the classroom teacher helps the community to identify its problems as well as the children to identify theirs. He engenders within all a desire to do something to solve their problems and to find answers to their questions. He becomes a guide to community growth and development and, in this role, can often give a constructive turn to community thinking about the school program.

The success of the community approach calls for a great amount of vision on the part of school administrators, classroom teachers, and all citizens of the community. Teachers and pupils may spend part of the school day working on community problems outside of school. Teachers participate with lay groups in civic, social, and cultural enterprises. This interaction between the community and the school results not only in community improvements, thru the efforts of the school, but also in improvements in the school program growing out of the increased interest of the citizens. School-community contacts serve as two-way streets for the exchange of ideas. Teachers interpret the school program; laymen explain their views of education. From these informal exchanges of ideas come changes in the instructional program, as the schools adopt and adapt some of the better suggestions offered by fellow citizens.

A natural phase of these processes will be to accelerate the practice of selecting local citizens to assist with instruction. At times the widely traveled business man or lawyer can dramatize a lesson in geography; a local labor leader or a commercial salesman can enliven the economics class. There are citizens with hobbies and vast stores of information on countless subjects who, by being called upon to help classroom teachers, increase their interest in the school system. Indeed it has been said there can be "fifty teachers to the classroom," [1] and in few other ways can community influences be harnessed more positively than by the enlistment of laymen who are qualified to enrich instruction.

---

[1] Metropolitan School Study Council, Committee of Human Resources. *Fifty Teachers to a Classroom.* New York: Macmillan Co., 1950. 44 p.

Schools sometimes fail to profit from the use of resource persons because of a lack of technics for identifying and screening ideas and people. Planning and systematic procedures are required to identify areas in which aid is needed and to locate persons competent enough to make constructive contributions. Each process helps the other and both can be advanced by pooling and cataloging the ideas of groups of classroom teachers and parents and drawing upon the acquaintance of all persons who understand the purposes involved. The process is endless but it becomes increasingly effective as it continues. Time is also well invested in the advance orientation of resource persons who are chosen. In this way the effectiveness of their service is much improved. Friendly and informal preclass conferences with the teacher by the resource person will usually suffice to furnish background and to supply simple suggestions. Many resource persons may become interested in associating themselves together with teachers for the sharing of experiences and the mutual exchange of ideas on content and method. Rewarding indeed can this plan become when wisely used.

Approaching thru the Visiting Teacher

The school social worker or visiting teacher, with specialized knowledge of the meaning of behavior as an expression of human need, provides one of the newer and certainly one of the more important connecting links between home and school. This staff member is sometimes known by other titles, such as, "visiting teacher." In this discussion the concept applies to a school social worker who is trained for both teaching and social work with successful experience as a classroom teacher. As these visiting teachers become intimately acquainted with the needs of individual children and as they work in cooperation with classroom teachers, parents, and others to rearrange environmental forces and to correct maladjustments, they have unique opportunities to interpret the school to the home and the home to the school. Often by their efforts alone, conditions and points of view that exist in home and community are translated into curriculum adjustments and other changes at school.

The fact that school practices and procedures often lag far behind scientific knowledge of child growth and development is highlighted by the referrals made to school social workers. Consider the cases of children who have learned to plan intelligently and to carry out meaningful jobs which challenge their imagination and interest but who are baffled and confused when given rote assignments with no opportunity to make the slightest decision for themselves. Such children find themselves out-of-step with the school because the school is out-of-step with life in home and community. When this happens, the visiting teacher or school social worker can help to interpret the feelings and ideas of parents and children who vaguely sense that something is wrong. What could be a critical demand for change becomes a partnership venture in school improvement, with classroom teachers and parents meeting one another halfway. As study by the visiting teacher individualizes the instructional program for certain children, classroom teachers become increasingly sensitive to individual differences in all children and adjust their work to varying needs as fully as possible within the framework of the group process which is inherent in the organization of the school system and the individual school.

There are children's agencies other than the school, such as the family service agency and the community guidance clinic, which have workers skilled in the area of emotional development. They have definite contributions to make in planning the curriculum. Yet these agencies and the schools all too often exist side by side with no channel for interchanging ideas and information. The school social worker, with training in both social work and education, is in a favorable position to facilitate this exchange. If this is not done, schools and social agencies, which have many common responsibilities and each of which has a vital relationship to the other, may never learn to share knowledge and resources for the benefit of children. A child's problem usually is best solved in the environment of a regular school, provided the curriculum and other school experiences are properly adapted to his needs. The visiting teacher is second to none as a liaison person thru whom to channel the influences of helpful nonschool agencies on the curriculum.

In some situations it has been thru community and home influences thus channeled, that special education classes have been added, reading clinics organized, and work-experience programs introduced. In others, these forces have encouraged part-time schools for employed boys and girls, in which classes, schedules, and scholastic requirements are highly flexible.

"We cannot expect to perfect our democratic way of life if we have one set of goals and processes for the school and a conflicting set for the home and still another in the community." [2] Since school social workers or visiting teachers are in continuous contact with home and community groups, they have an unusual opportunity to help reconcile conflicting goals and processes, to marshall and coordinate all local resources, and to help give unified direction to the educational program.

Approaching thru the Board of Education

A board of education, made up of persons of vision and prestige, obviously can have a major role in channeling home and community influences constructively. One instance is the handling of the question of whether or not the schools shall deal with issues concerning which there are sharp divisions of opinion. Many organized groups refuse to agree that points of view contrary to their own can be presented by teachers. These are forces to be reckoned with, for there are classroom teachers and school administrators who submit to voluntary censorship in order to avoid conflicts with such groups. There is involuntary censorship, too, that threatens freedom, when state legislatures, yielding to the demands of vested interest groups, prescribe what shall or shall not be taught. Some pressure groups by excluding studies of current social and economic problems and confining the curriculum to the glorious past, would have education fail in preparing youth to reinterpret American ideals in the light of changing conditions. Fortunately, there are many school systems which deal with controversial issues because the board members are unafraid in their convictions about the mission of education in a democracy. They insist upon the conditions where learning and teaching can be free.

The board of education, by adopting a clear-cut policy, can set the stage for dealing with this critical problem. Reports from communities in which such policies have been adopted indicate that this is a most effective and satisfactory method of counteracting attacks.[3]

[2] New York Board of Education, the Board of Superintendents. *Guiding Principles in Curriculum Development*. Curriculum Bulletin No. 2. New York: Board of Education, 1942. p. 20.

[3] The instructional aspects of dealing with controversial issues have been elaborated in the publications of the National Council for the Social Studies, a department of the National Education Association. Consult the NEA *Publications List*.

An interesting example of this method is found in Elizabeth, New Jersey. There the board of education defines a controversial issue as "one in which there exists conflicting opinions among the citizens of the community, of the nation, or among the nations of the world."

The Elizabeth Policy gives the responsibility of the classroom teacher and school administrator with respect to the teaching of controversial issues.[4] An abstract from the statement is as follows:

A teacher in a free society has the obligation to uphold, protect, and defend the fundamental freedoms as documented in the history of our American democracy and to maintain a classroom atmosphere conducive to the free, spirited, and friendly interplay of ideas. Teachers shall see that all facts, evidence and aspects of a controversial issue are presented honestly and shall acquaint pupils with books, newspapers, and other materials which present reliable data on all sides of the issue under discussion.

It is the duty of the teacher to create in students the habit of basing statements or opinions about controversial issues on substantiated facts or creditable evidence and to help children learn to identify propaganda in its many forms. In all discussions the teacher has the right to express his opinion on controversial issues providing students understand that it is his own opinion and is not to be accepted by them as the authoritative answer.

The Elizabeth Policy also gives guides basic to the administration of such a policy. They are:

That the teacher is competent in her field, the principal is responsible for the total program in the school and the citizen has a right to expect the proper teaching of controversial issues. Questions concerning the teaching of controversial issues are referred to the principal, who, if a solution cannot be found, refers them to the Division of Instruction and ultimately to the superintendent if necessary. Teachers are encouraged with approval of principal and/or superintendent to invite representatives of both sides of a controversial issue to discuss their point of view with the class.

In dealing with the problem of controversial issues, partisan groups must be helped to understand (a) that the learners must have access to *all* the facts bearing upon problems, and (b) that unless youth have practice in solving current problems using democratic technics, they will not be prepared to live in the modern world.[5]

---

[4] Elizabeth Public Schools. *A Policy for the Handling of Controversial Issues in the Elizabeth Public Schools.* Elizabeth, N. J.: Board of Education, 1950. 5 p.

[5] Courter, Claude V., chairman. *An Educational Platform for the Public Schools.* Report of Special Committee of school superintendents of large cities in the United States and Canada. Chicago: Inland Press, 1952. p. 11.

Schoolboards in some communities are asking representatives of organizations with differing views to cooperate in working out an acceptable educational policy for teaching controversial issues. They are helping citizens understand that to study about communism, for example, does not mean to advocate it. As an editorial in the *NEA Journal* put it, "A doctor cannot undertake to rid the world of cancer by refusing to study the facts concerning it. He wants the facts, not the cancer." [6]

Youth in school, with all the facts, come to understand the evils of communism by an analysis of its characteristics and by comparing the blessings of democracy as they examine its imperfections. There is no reason to fear that such youth at any time will be weaned away from the democratic system by honeyed words and half truths or by criticisms that magnify the imperfections of the democratic way.

A helpful approach in dealing with controversial issues is a movement sponsored by the Joint Council on Economic Education designed to promote sound economic education. [7] The sharpening of the conflicts between capital and labor during the past 15 years, the hatreds generated, the misunderstandings fostered, the failure to recognize the relative values that each side has to contribute to the American economic system, the selfishness on both sides, the irresponsibility of some labor leaders, and the greed on the part of some representatives of management—all of these things are dangerous. If the schools continue to turn out generations of youth who are unprepared to understand and deal with these issues, controversies will be heightened and this country will suffer from internal threats to our strength and security.

Beginning in a small way but expanding rapidly, boards of education have encouraged classroom teachers to come together with enlightened leaders of labor and management to work out policies and plans whereby the schools may prepare successive generations of youth for cooperation as they participate in the American economic system. In communities where this has been done, schools have introduced modern programs in economic education with the approval of all elements of the community. Boys and girls of all the people are learning about the values in our economic system which have

---

[6] Pesognelli, Mary Ann. "The Erosion of Freedom." *NEA Journal* 40: 321-22; May 1951. From a statement prepared by the NEA Committee on Tenure and Academic Freedom.

[7] Balance Sheet. "Economic Education Report." *Balance Sheet* 33: 324-25; March 1952.

made this country great. They are comparing its fruits with conditions in communistic countries. They are learning the essential values of the contributions of both labor and management and they are sensing the deep significance to the common welfare of cooperation by all. Youth in these schools are learning how to make the American economic system work better, and they are emphasizing the fine examples of cooperation currently achieved by labor and management instead of dealing only with sensational news about discord and trouble. Current curriculum ventures, such as this in economic education, point the way in which schools may win community support in dealing with all controversial issues.

Approaching thru Citizen Participation

The role of laymen in the development of the school curriculum has varied from era to era and also from locality to locality. Today administrators are bending every effort to increase lay-professional relationships in planning curriculums that truly satisfy the needs of their communities. While some laymen still believe that the main function of schools is to teach reading, writing, and arithmetic, the majority have broader views. Most citizens recognize that a primary function of modern education is training for citizenship in today's world, while transmitting at the same time those values, habits, and skills which are important parts of our cultural heritage. For persons who subscribe to this philosophy of education, lay participation becomes an important factor in educational planning. Only thru cooperative planning, which involves the student, the layman, and the teacher, can a curriculum be developed which provides these desirable outcomes.

The nationwide quickening of interest by citizens in their public schools is a development of deep significance with most encouraging possibilities. The schools belong to the people. To the degree that the people assert their ownership by intelligent inventories and wise participation in planning policies in the light of the historic mission of education, good results will accrue for children and youth. In fact, educational progress is much greater in those communities with the wisdom and know-how for stimulating the general participation of citizens in school affairs.

253

Pitfalls and the Board of Education

In any great venture there are pitfalls. The citizens movement in behalf of the schools is no exception. A basis for misunderstanding has to do with relations with the board of education and conflicts concerning respective spheres of operation. The schoolboard and staff with judgment and leadership can avoid these pitfalls and add strength to the local citizens movement by working for understanding and by observing simple principles of cooperation in a common course.

Boards have the legal responsibility for the schools and this they cannot delegate to citizens committees. But citizens committees can study school and community conditions so as to understand better the problems and handicaps of the board. They can discuss purposes and objectives and examine community resources. They can hold forums to interpret and crystallize public opinion. And they can make recommendations and bring support to the board of education as their legal agency for deciding upon and carrying out the will of the community for the schools.

Altho procedures will vary in different communities as to detail, it is fundamental that citizens groups be broadly representative of the community and that they not approach the board or school officials in an antagonistic mood, being certain to respect the role that each has to play. This danger all must avoid to prevent a wall of separation which will divide the very forces upon whom the children have to depend.

While boards of education may profitably enlist the participation of citizens thru the appointment of advisory committees for particular tasks, a major citizens movement in behalf of the schools should have its origin apart from the board, else it may be regarded as a mere mouthpiece of the board. The relationship is one of coordination and cooperation on both sides instead of control. The citizens committee that regards itself as a strong but independent right arm to supplement and strengthen the work of the board holds great promise for the public schools.[8] For years the parent-teacher movement has been a constructive influence for better schools; other movements have developed in recent years, such as citizens committees and community councils.

---

[8] American Association of School Administrators. *Lay Advisory Committees.* Washington, D. C.: the Association, a department of the National Education Association, 1951. 23 p.

Leadership by the National Citizens Commission

The movement to encourage the formation of independent citizens groups in local communities for the purpose of improving local public schools has often been led by the National Citizens Commission for the Public Schools. This Commission is a nonprofit organization whose members are citizens not professionally identified with education, religion, or politics. The Commission has set for itself two immediate goals:

1. To help Americans realize how important our public schools are to our expanding democracy.

2. To arouse in each community the intelligence and will to improve our public schools.

In striving toward these goals, the Commission acts as a clearinghouse so that all groups may benefit from the experience of others, so that community effort now being carried on in isolation can benefit from continued encouragement and a widespread pooling of information. The Commission and the local groups associated with it differ from certain pressure groups in that they work closely with the professional staff of the school or school system. They seek to understand the educational program in all its aspects before offering constructive suggestions for improvement. Out of the wide experience of the Commission there have evolved many guides for local groups desiring to organize citizens committees according to a sound and functional plan, which avoids the pitfalls and magnifies the merits of an essential partnership between citizens and their schools.

Parent-Teachers Associations and Citizens Surveys

The parent-teacher association is in many respects the closest partnership with the schools for citizens who are also parents and patrons. The PTA with its more than a half century of experience characteristically plays a leading role in coordinating community influences. Its ways of work are commonly known and appreciated for their soundness and effectiveness. An excellent example of a relatively new departure of the PTA is that of conducting a citizens survey on a statewide basis to determine what the people think about their schools and what they want their schools to be. Such a survey was done by the Mississippi Congress of Parents and Teachers in cooperation with educational agencies and many other patriotic, cultural, civic, and labor organizations thru the Mississippi Citizens Council on Education.

About 55,000 copies of the section of the survey on curriculum and instruction were distributed by parent-teacher organizations. The questions were varied. They sought opinions from the people of Mississippi about which grades and what services should be included in tax-supported public-school programs. Inquiry was made concerning the educational opportunities that should be offered for out-of-school youth and adults. The questionnaire asked what factors were chiefly responsible for drop-outs. There were questions about the effect of college entrance requirements on curriculum offerings to the exclusion of experiences that would better meet the needs of high-school pupils. Opinions were sought on many controversial issues. Inquiry was made as to whether the people of Mississippi wanted children to study community problems. There were questions about the core curriculum, about whether or not religious training should be offered, and about the place of competitive athletics in the school program. Investigation was made concerning criticisms of the schools, undesirable practices, alleged unfairness, lack of attention to the individual pupils, and poor discipline.

This venture in Mississippi was undertaken in the belief that "a good school program must spring from the people. They provide the children, the schools, and the financial support necessary to maintain an educational program." [9]

Returns on the questionnaire were evaluated by a committee, whose recommendations were then sent to the Mississippi Council. From these findings the Council is now developing plans, based upon the best thinking of the people. The Council is to be a permanent organization, planning continuously for better schools in Mississippi, for schools that reflect the ideals of the people.

The survey of the public schools of Denver, Colorado, is another illustration of a constructive approach in determining what the people expect of their schools. In that city the educational authorities realized that the school draws its strengths and weaknesses, in large part, from the community which it serves. They knew that the citizen's concept of the character of a good school plays a vital role

[9] National Congress of Parents and Teachers. *Examples of School-Community Cooperation*. Chicago: the National Congress, 1947. (Mimeographed Report.) 10 p.

256

in establishing and maintaining a dynamic educational program. To determine how the citizens felt about their schools, a private research organization was employed to conduct an impartial survey.

This survey revealed that the people generally felt that the educational program was providing the type of experiences they desired for their children. Perhaps the most significant feature of the Denver survey was the fact that the majority of the people, on the basis of this representative sampling, approved of most of those features of a modern educational program which some critics refer to as "fads and frills." There were, of course, a number of constructive criticisms and recommendations for improvements. The findings of the research organization were published and the school administration, recognizing that certain weaknesses revealed by the survey needed to be corrected, announced that the educational program would be changed in line with the results of this study. This example is one of the best of its kind in showing how a school system may seek and respond to community views.[10]

Strengthening the Citizens Movement

When a school administrator accepts responsibility for aiding and encouraging groups which have organized and indicated their desire to participate in educational planning, his first and perhaps most important job is one of analyzing the community to determine just where it is with respect to a common philosophy of education. He must begin at that point, working with the forces which show the most promise, but always being careful not deliberately to antagonize others. These groups will be encouraged to move on to higher levels as rapidly as new concepts and philosophies are developed. It must be kept in mind that the process of growth is often a long and difficult one. In many cases backtracking is necessary to bring certain groups up to the level of the entire community. In working with lay groups, the professional staff must be qualified to observe, interpret, and guide the committees as they progress. Many of the technics described in publications on group dynamics and democratic school administration will prove effective in working with lay groups.

Successful promotion of growth and development on the part of lay groups often requires help for the individual layman to find his

---

[10] Research Services. *Denver Looks at Its Schools.* Denver, Colo.: Board of Education, 1950. 31 p.

place in the process. He may need to be encouraged to improve his ability by participating as a member of a committee. In some instances, every effort must be made to help the layman analyze his own concept of education, in order to evolve a workable philosophy about the type of curriculum that should be developed. Such a philosophy enables him to participate freely without a feeling of being lost, for he can always return to this point of reference when new developments tend to confuse him.

In organizing a layman's committee for curriculum study and improvement, another consideration is important. Before there is actual participation in building the curriculum, the committee should reach an agreement on certain standards or requirements for the finished product. Thus, while each individual's own philosophy serves as his personal point of reference, the committee as a whole agrees upon its general objectives and purposes.

After a committee has evolved the general purposes, much work remains to be accomplished thru cooperative planning. General purposes serve only as a guide or outline. The actual identification of needs within each area must still be undertaken. Then, the committee must select the types of experiences that will satisfy these needs. Also the process involves continuous evaluation of the program.

Lay participation assumes many forms and is possible under many different types of organization. In this endeavor the school administrator will find value in a concise discussion of lay advisory committees. Information on what committees do, methods of selecting members, community readiness, and method of operation will be found in the pamphlet, *Lay Advisory Committees*.[11]

Pressure Groups and Attacks as Factors of Influence

As has often been said, social change does not occur on a broad, even front; this is particularly true of change in the schools. On the contrary, it moves ahead in one area or in one community, and lags behind in another. If this pattern of change could be visualized, it would have a jagged appearance. There are at work at all times small liberal influences that tend to push ahead in one area and strong conservative forces in another area that try to maintain the status

---

[11] American Association of School Administrators, *op. cit.*, p. 13-18.

quo. Actually, however, the opposing liberal and conservative forces usually represent only a small percent of the total public, and this is where confusion arises. The remainder of the people are largely uninformed of the particular issues at stake and, therefore, are at a loss to determine what course of action to follow.

How Pressure Groups Develop

Conflict, tension, and misinformation often promote the development of special interest groups of people who join together to defend a certain position or perhaps to advocate some change in practice. By any number of methods they try to influence the general public to accept their points of view. When special interest groups present their differing points of view to the public, conflict usually results. The struggle may grow stronger as the opposing points of view gain followers. Gradually the original interest groups become pressure groups, fighting vigorously to convince the larger and often disinterested public of the merits of their respective views. The schools offer a fertile field for the operation of such contending forces, with the school administrator frequently the target for attacks from both the so-called liberal groups and the conservative groups. Often he appears to each group to be the key person working for the opposing force.

It is characteristic of groups with a negative approach to separate themselves completely from the schools and to attack them, as it were, from afar off. Often the attacking group uses a name which suggests that its adherents actually are friendly toward public education even tho their whole program is designed to undermine faith in the public schools. There have been instances in which selfish promoters have engaged in a form of racketeering by enlisting members "to save" the schools from "wicked forces" that threaten to influence these "foundation stones of democracy." By playing upon fears, and by lies and slander, such schemes have brought much loot to the promoters and much harm to the schools. Frequently they have misled unsuspecting citizens. Other negative groups simply strive to bring about their own brands of change in the school program. In the case of groups which resort to unscrupulous attacks by criticism of one kind or another, the aim is to influence changes in the curriculum by arousing public opinion to the point at which reason is discarded and demands for changes in the schools are made without thought of their effect on the schools and on children. The school administrator needs to be sensitive to these various forces and to know how to cope with them.

Both constructive and destructive critics with their differing motives have had certain common points of criticism and attacks centering around charges that: the public schools do not teach the Three R's properly, school costs are too high, progressive education contains too many frills and fads, or textbooks are infiltrated with communistic propaganda. Other targets are the developments in modern education which strive to improve intergroup and human relations as well as the classroom teacher's devices for teaching youngsters to live harmoniously in the world. Workshops for teachers also are criticized on the grounds that these ventures are means of spreading frills, fads, and false doctrines.

The Effect of Attacks and Criticisms

Altho the negative and underhanded attacks have not been widespread, they have, together with the genuine concerns of honest critics, stimulated educational forces to action and to self-evaluation. They have invited examination by competent and impartial agencies. There has been some evidence that classroom teachers have drawn away from discussions of controversial issues, have closed fields of knowledge to the learner, and have denied pupils experiences in dealing with questions they must face later in life.

On the other hand there have been some healthy effects. Educators have quickly put together impressive evidence to show that the schools are doing a much better job in teaching the Three R's; that education is making progress in curriculum adaptations for equipping children and youth to live in the modern age, and that effective use is made of vast new knowledge concerning the nature of children and the way they learn. Efforts and technics have been accelerated to help the layman understand and participate in shaping the program and policy for his child's school. These and other positive approaches have been demonstrated as successful methods for dealing with attacks and criticisms. The result of both positive and negative influences upon the curriculum depends upon the quality of the available educational leadership.

Public Relations and Administrative Leadership

Capable administrative leadership is reflected almost always in effective public relations. Editors and reporters are recognized as able partners who are entitled to courteous and helpful treatment. Every effort is made to provide releases written in newspaper style. Channels exist for prompt and efficient communication (see Chapter X).

Many Public Relations Technics Available

Frequently, educators have the unpleasant experience of preparing newspaper releases which are not used. Since the school usually is at fault when this occurs, the person in charge of publicity should carefully analyze all releases to determine the cause. Those experiencing this difficulty might consider the following explanation of why school and college news releases often go to the wastebasket: "The release isn't really news, it's advertising. It contains too many superlatives, plugs and puffs. It fails to give the names of those who could supply more information. It tries to palm off old stuff as new. It's a technical abstract rather than a simple explanation of a development or trend. It was sent to several editors at once without angling the news to the specific publication. Finally, any news release that's a carbon copy, singlespaced, or so poorly typed that it's illegible, is doomed." [12] An increasing number of school systems in addition to taking full advantage of press and radio facilities are developing attractive brochures, pamphlets, posters and cartoon booklets of all types to tell their story.[13] These printed materials are designed to meet specific as well as general needs for interpretation. If, for example, there are criticisms of the Three R's and nostalgic comparisons with the good old days, then comes a dynamic and convincing brochure telling the story of "Today's Schools" and asking the question, "Are they as good as yesterday's?" In picture and story the layman quickly finds that his schools are doing a better job with the Three R's. Moreover, he is astonished and stirred by the modern practices and facilities developed and engineered for a tremendously ex-

[12] *Educator's Washington Dispatch.* August 2, 1951. p. 4.

[13] The National School Public Relations Association, a department of the National Education Association, has both newsletters and handbooks dealing with public-relations methods and publications.

panded curriculum. He learns that today, more than in the past, the curriculum involves a much more complex society, a greatly increased period of schooling, and a school population growing steadily larger.

Some of the methods are unique for distributing the kind of materials just described. In one community a pamphlet on arithmetic was placed on a morning train. Cards promoting a successful bond campaign have gone right into the homes with the milk delivery (a convenient hole slips over the bottle's neck). Public-spirited organizations with vast mailing lists have been willing to insert the story of the children at school. Those with the imagination and zeal to produce these valuable public-relations aids will find equally clever methods for placing them in the hands and the hearts of citizens.

Assigned Personnel Essential

With the growing significance of positive school-community relations as an important factor in curriculum building, there is a tendency to add to the superintendent's staff the position of director of school-community relations. Such a director might have other duties, such as research, adult education, or curriculum planning. In smaller communities the superintendent, with the help of qualified staff members and teachers, must undertake full direction of the public-relations program.

Wherever a director of school-community relations is employed, he is responsible for effective communication between the office of the board of education, the individual schools, and the community. All his planning must be done in terms of developing the best educational opportunities for the child. A superintendent of schools is sometimes referred to as a social engineer; the director of public relations should qualify likewise.

An important consideration in school-community relations programs, whether a director or the superintendent is in charge, is that the person be close to all phases of community activities as well as to the curriculum planning activities of the school system. His office should be a two-way street between the community and the school system. When problems of curriculum development or enrichment

*Spiritual values arise from many sources, such as creative
artistic expression. The modern school recognizes the need
for expressing and evoking the inner life of the spirit.*

arise, which call for cooperation between homes and schools, he should be in a position to call upon those persons in the community who can make the most valuable contribution.

The director's door should always be open to the community as well as to school personnel. He should be familiar with the various community services which are available to the schools and the many school services which can be used by the community. He should be in a position to expedite the process of exchanging these services. In short, whoever it is that coordinates community relations is also largely responsible for making the schools a vital and important part of the community and for drawing strength and constructive influence from the community for the public schools.

It cannot be overemphasized that the role of the school administrator is a strategic one. Potential forces and resources in the community, which could otherwise be utilized as constructive influences upon instruction, remain untapped when the administrator lacks vision or otherwise fails to release these powers. His failure likewise can give free rein to negative activities which result in hurtful pressures. The times require alertness and know-how on the part of leadership in dealing with home and community influences.

Minor Problems with Major Agitations

Consideration of the problems which follow in which both teachers and laymen have similar headaches will point up even more sharply the need for cooperative action.

Homework, an Age-Old Issue

For many school generations some parents have insisted that actually they are doing the teaching at home whereas the classroom teachers only listen to the children recite their lessons. These parents have wanted at least to reverse the situation. Other parents have demanded homework and have complained if the children did not have enough of it. The children take hope in the current controversy on the merits of homework, wishing that it might be eliminated. Possibly they would be willing for a longer school day, if all school work could be completed, leaving their evenings free.

Opponents of homework point to the strains it puts on family living, to the curtailment in family activities, and to development of pupil fatigue. Often a better attack upon lessons could be made the next day at school, under much more suitable study conditions. The critics cite cases of unreasonable assignments and of the overly conscientious pupil who stays up late desperately attempting to complete homework, thus impairing his efficiency at school and damaging his health. Besides, they say, the child should have as much right as an adult to close his desk and enjoy an evening of relaxation, provided he chooses to practice piano lessons, help with home duties, attend club or church meetings, or engage in any one of many other worthy out-of-school pursuits.

The homework die-hards insist that regular study hours at home are essential because school-time study opportunities are too restricted. They believe that after instruction by the classroom teacher, out-of-school study is needed for full learning and that valuable attitudes and habits are engendered when pupils develop work habits and a sense of responsibility for independent study. The argument on this side also insists that homework brings parents into closer touch with the school and keeps children out of mischief. To have longer school hours in order to eliminate homework, it is also contended, would not be readily accepted by the pupils not to mention the adverse effects on school finance and personnel.

The competition for the pupil's time in the evening is tremendous. Television is but the latest in a long series of distracting influences which seems to have crystallized the issue of homework. The results of research studies already completed or in process are having their influence. They give evidence in carefully controlled experiments that youngsters without homework under good instruction and supervised study do as well as those under good instruction with homework. Prominent among the studies showing this result is that conducted by the Connecticut Fact-Finding Commission.[14] Instead of the traditional homework, this Commission offered suggestions for using after-school hours to stimulate growth in good citizenship. Typical of these suggestions are the following: participating in community activities, forums, concerts, and community chest drives;

---

[14] Governor's Fact-Finding Commission on Education. *Do Citizens and Education Mix?* The Connecticut Report: A Guide to School Study. Hartford: the Commission, 1951. 159 p. Summarized in: Fine, Benjamin. "No More Homework? the Pros and Cons." *New York Times Magazine*, January 13, 1952. p. 16, 39, and 41.

taking part in family activities; discussing and reporting on radio and TV programs; developing and enjoying worthwhile hobbies; and learning how to derive lasting satisfaction from great books.

Even tho the opponents of homework appear to be leading in the debate with their arguments based upon impressive and increasing scientific data, homework cannot easily be terminated—such is the tradition of the American school. But a broader definition of homework than the traditionally accepted concept would help resolve the sharp differences of opinion presently prevailing and lead to sounder practices with increased harmony and understanding.[15] Certainly there is no wisdom in long assignments and conflicting demands which not only are poor teaching but harmful public relations.

One superintendent has defined homework as "those experiences in the lives of children which occur outside the schoolroom which tend to foster desirable physical, social, emotional, spiritual, and mental growth. Such experiences, under the guidance of parents, supplement and extend the school experiences." [16] This definition takes into account the vast resources outside the school for educational development. Perhaps a definition of this nature should point up more specifically the guidance that effective teachers also give in utilizing and adapting these enriching experiences outside the classroom.

While this broader definition is in harmony with the new views regarding homework, it does not exclude the older practices tho obviously it curtails their extent and implies needed modifications. Those who are conserving best the values of the older types of homework are avoiding unreasonable assignments and are planning practical applications of these activities related to home and community interests such as budgeting, interviews, family discussions and radio programs.[17]

A definition of terms then is one method for avoiding controversies concerning this issue. Another would be to hold "talk it over" sessions with parent groups in order to clarify such questions as reasons for and values of homework, time allotments, cautions and disadvantages, research findings, and the responsibilities involved for classroom teachers, pupils, and parents. By this means much can

[15] Specific suggestions will be found in *It Starts in the Classroom*, published by the National School Public Relations Association, a department of the National Education Association, 1951. p. 29-34.
[16] Ostrander, R. H. "Homework in the Modern Manner." *School Executive* 68: 48; October 1948.
[17] Courter, Claude V., Chairman, *op. cit.*, p. 10-11.

be accomplished in developing insights and understandings about best ways to help children.

The Comics

All of us say "comics" because this form of picture story at the outset of its modern appearance, about 1900, was intended to be funny. The name has stuck even tho most comics have long since become continued and colorfully illustrated stories, filled with adventure, human interest, and pathos. Despite current criticisms, the comics may have had ancient beginnings, for on the walls of his cave, early man pictured the fantasies and events of his life and times. Man's desire to pictorialize his ideas has been expressed in many ways thru sculpture, painting, stained glass windows, and the art forms directly related to the so-called "comic" strip or booklet.

Today the production of comics is big business. Sixty million comic books are printed every month in this country. Millions of children in school and out of school spend uncounted hours poring over them. They are the despair of some parents and teachers. Tho certain of them are suitable for children, others range from objectionable to very objectionable. All of them materially influence the curriculum by absorbing substantial amounts of the energies and attention of children, by exciting them emotionally and filling their minds with lurid stories and vivid pictures, or in other instances, by reinforcing and supplementing school studies and experiences.

This medium has affected enormously the reading habits of a great part of the American people. Surveys of the reading audience do not agree as to their conclusions except that comics are widely read. One study reported 7 in 10 adult men and 5 in 10 adult women as regular readers. Nearly 2 in 10 of the adult readers were college graduates.[18] Therefore, forward-looking schools are taking a constructive view of the comics by analyzing and seeking to modify and eliminate harmful effects by providing substitute attractions, and by turning the potentialities of the comics toward educational purposes.

Those who have scorned and despaired of the comics have emphasized such objections as: the content is unethical and cheap;

[18] Zorbaugh, Harvey W. "The Comics—There They Stand!" *Journal of Educational Sociology* 18: 196-203; December 1944.

the pictures are contrary to artistic standards; the superhuman characters use fascist methods; they lead to day dreaming rather than normal thinking; they incite readers to crime; and the shallow plots emphasize impossible situations. While authorities disagree as to the harmful effects of the comics and while some feel there is no cause for alarm, still there is general agreement that children should not have a steady diet of horror stories. On a nationwide basis more needs to be done to eliminate the destructive features.

An outstanding example of an intelligent and successful community attack on the problem of comics and their influences upon the growth and development of children and youth is found in Cincinnati. Interest was initiated by the publication of a portion of a sermon, given during National Family Week, pertaining to the undesirable influence of certain types of comic books. So much interest was aroused that a community committee was organized. This committee undertook to evaluate the comic books. Policies of action were developed, involving a program based upon cooperation rather than criticism and coercion. The committee's approach was to work with publishers and distributors so that the quality of comics available to children might be improved. The committee then developed criteria by which to determine the acceptability of a comic book. Ultimately the evaluations based upon these criteria were published. The first evaluation indicated that only 57.47 percent of the books were suitable for children and young people. The second rating, following efforts with publishers and public, revealed that 69 percent were suitable.[19]

Another effective approach is to provide substitute attractions to insure a balanced diet of things to do. A wealth of good books should surround the child and these should be within his reading ability range. Methods of interesting him in these books need to be employed. Fishing excursions, live pets, and games and work in happy family companionship can be much more interesting than bad comics. Association with the Scouts and other youth groups and absorption in hobbies will leave the child little time for less worthy pursuits. Parents who are alert and informed, instead of banning comics, will help youngsters schedule their time for reading them and together with teachers help them select the better comics.

---

[19] Murrell, Jesse L. "Cincinnati Rates the Comic Books." *Parents Magazine* 25: 38-39, 80, 83, 85-87; February 1950, and in the October 1950 issue, pages 44-45 and 120-24.

A third way to deal with the problem is to capitalize on the values in comics by turning them to educational purposes. Those who emphasize the values [20] say that thru comics vocabularies and a liking for reading may be increased; interest in adventure and a sense of humor may develop; moral lessons may be impressed; hobbies may develop; and factual information may accrue. One teacher, very critical of comics, found to his surprise after research using one popular series as a sample, that the vocabulary is on a high level, thus teaching words he wanted his students to master.[21] He learned that some comics encouraged reading and increased speed and that the values being stressed are wholesome. He concluded, since comic books are reaching and intriguing a large audience, including many children not doing so well in school, that they might well be utilized for educational purposes.

Classroom teachers who continually confiscate comic books acknowledge the power of the cartoon technic. It would be better to enlist the cooperation of more cartoonists and comic book publishers as was done in producing the historical comics which have been widely accepted. For many children this device gives history's fascination to their favorite comic book characters. In these cases the characters really live and their adventures are indeed true stories which have affected the lives of all the readers.

This medium of expression, relatively new to the schools, is by no means limited to the historical comic. "Why hasn't someone written an arithmetic book," it has been suggested, "in which a sympathetic comic cartoon character meets and conquers animated problems at every turn of his thrilling life?" Why hasn't someone, by means of cartoons, freed English grammar from its mysteries and from the drabness of technical wordage? Why not use vivid comics as personifications in science? [22] Some of the popular "scientific" TV programs of space ships are similar in story form to the comic strip. They often initiate scientific interest.

Other positive applications of the values in comics are workbooks by Harold Downes and work games using Superman to teach grammar. Plans by these authors will extend these methods to his-

[20] Armstrong, David T. "How Good Are the Comic Books?" *Elementary English Review* 21: 283-85, 300; December 1944.
[21] Frank, Josette. *Comics, Radio, Movies and Children*. Public Affairs Pamphlet No. 148. New York: Public Affairs Committee, 1949. 32 p.
[22] Musial, Joseph W. "Edu-Grafs: New Vitamins for the Schools." *Education* 70: 228-33; December 1949.

tory, geography, social sciences, and mathematics. Subjectmatter for Bible stories has been given similar treatment.

Classroom teachers have turned their pupils to critical analysis of comic books. The results of these evaluations can help both parents and classroom teachers. Under the criteria usually developed the comics are classified as "informational," "harmless," and "unwholesome." Certainly by critical study and comparison with standards, comics can be made to serve educational purposes.

Comics are here to stay. They have become an important social factor among the American people.[23] Consequently, schools and communities must learn to deal intelligently and positively with the problems and challenges they present so that their harmful effects may be restricted and their potential values may be utilized. The superintendent can take leadership in making intelligent surveys.

Television and Radio

With the coming of television, as was the case with the movies, the radio, and other new types of communication, there has been much objection by parents and classroom teachers about the way the new medium interferes with school and family life. But television, also, is here to stay and there is little point in merely objecting. The sensible thing is to accept it and make it a constructive influence.

When television changes substantially the patterns of home and family life, this trend has an important impact upon the schools. One study of high-school students showed that they watched television programs more than 25 hours each week.[24] This time was the equivalent of seeing a double feature movie every day in the week. Other research investigations speak of the decline in magazine reading, newspaper reading, and movie attendance. These conditions further emphasize the problem of the new competition faced by the schools.

To curtail the bad features and to magnify the promising possibilities of television, one must consider the disadvantages and the advantages which so far have been identified. Those who disapprove

---

[23] Marston, William Moulton. "Why 100,000,000 Americans Read the Comics." *American Scholar* 13: 35-44; January 1944.

[24] Cousins, Norman. "The Time Trap." (Editorial) *Saturday Review of Literature* 32: 20; December 24, 1949.

think that most of the programs are too stimulating and action-packed and that they are not educational. They say that television creates countless problems at bedtime and mealtime and conflicts with home duties; that it interferes with physical development and other recreation of children; and that it impairs vision. On the affirmative side television is said to keep the family at home together; to stimulate thought; to increase vocabularies and imagination; and to acquaint children with many personalities, events, and topics to which they would otherwise not be exposed.

Of course television competes with home duties, and with many out-of-school but school-related activities. However, there are better ways of dealing with the problem than that of complaining. School-community planning groups by careful study and investigation can find new and better ways for adapting these out-of-school experiences to the needs of youth and the requirements for a balanced program of activities.

Experience has shown that the extraordinary amount of time which children are inclined to devote to the new TV set rather quickly adjusts itself as the novelty wears off, especially if parents assume their responsibility for supervision and regulation.

The educational use of radio as a community force is still in its early stages despite its start over television. Like television, the radio exerts certain influences that must be counteracted. During the time that television is in its infancy is the time to accelerate efforts to improve radio programs and services.

A constructive approach in guiding children in the use of both radio and television is that of helping them plan listening time and instructing them in methods of good listening. Much can be done, too, to coordinate these programs with curriculum activities. For example, the school may offer guidance to homes with newly purchased television sets. Directions may be given about how to schedule listening time while the set is new, and before the novelty wears off, so that good habits of listening and viewing are established.

The courageous and commendable action of the Federal Communications Commission in allocating 242 TV channels to education offers great opportunities but also serious difficulties. Financing and programming are major problems. A few communities are attacking these problems vigorously and have educational stations on the air. Others are using educational time on commercial stations. Already there is tangible evidence that these programs are effective in promoting good public relations and, when properly co-ordinated, can be especially useful in teaching current events, science, social science, languages, music, literature, vocational guidance, and health.

As in radio there are many do's and don'ts to be learned for good results but the promises make effort inviting. Teachers need to be selected for special studies on ways and means for capitalizing the educational possibilities in the field of electronics. Specialists in the fields of radio and television may be enlisted by school people to plan jointly for programs, particularly those bearing upon cur-riculum experiences. Educators also can stand with parents in opposing unworthy exploitation of audiences by either radio or television.

Curriculum workers, in addition to coordinating school programs with the field of electronics and devising ways and means to cultivate appreciation of good programs, should re-examine the existing cur-riculum with a view to removing outmoded materials and making room for new and vital educational possibilities. In all of this, school administrators need to keep in balance, remembering that radio and television are primarily supplementary resources and that the best teaching involves the direct interplay of teacher-children relation-ships.

Contests, Athletic and Nonathletic

Most of the present generation of school administrators have seen athletic programs evolve from a dominant interest on the fringe of the school program to becoming an integral part of the curriculum. Some educators of today are the boys and girls of yesterday who oftentimes had to bootleg sport activities and events. Those were the days when outside community interests frequently exerted negative influences; at best they were working at cross purposes with the schools. The account of the great transition in this area is a familiar story but it is too significant to overlook in relation to the theme of this chapter.

Perhaps in no area other than athletics has experience compelled the establishment of such clear channels of participation and control as between school and community. But the very nature of athletic contests demands constant vigilance and the continuous re-examination of standards and policies so that community support may be positive in all respects. Here again it is essential for citizens, under wise guidance, to help develop the necessary controls. Participation under capable leadership breeds understanding, and understanding of basic ideals and principles is particularly important today when America's love for athletics is multiplying out-of-school leagues in untold numbers. These leagues include all age groups down even to the eight-year-olds. The coordination of school and community thought regarding the curriculum urgently calls for intelligent direction of out-of-school athletic programs.

In self-defense, schools find it necessary to control the never-ending demand for art, essay, forensic, and scholarship contests. Nearly every worthy organization—and some not so worthy—have the notion that their objectives can best be achieved by imposing contests upon school children. Scarcely a week goes by that a new proposal is not competing for the attention of pupils.

Notable among control measures has been the work of the National Contest Committee of the National Association of Secondary-School Principals.[25] This committee has gained in prestige and influence since its organization in 1940. By its annual listing of approved national contests it has relieved schools from local pressures for participation in unworthy ventures. In addition the committee has developed standards for offering worthy educational results for all participants over and above the prizes and awards which may be involved. Among the benefits are the public-relations values for schools with citizens who realize the effectiveness of immediate contact with the millions of boys and girls thru worthy contests. When citizens are thus related to the educational program, an honest interest in the welfare of the schools should increase correspondingly among sponsoring groups.

Essay contests, in particular, can get out of hand. They may have merit if properly controlled and supervised. An important safeguard is a special committee, which checks subjects, rules, and prizes; gives advice concerning needed adjustments; insists that participation be voluntary; and devises ways and means for relieving classroom teachers of unreasonable burdens in judging papers. Thru

[25] Manning, George A. "What Are Sound Policies for Controlling Non-Athletic National Contests and Activities Offered in Schools by Outside Organizations?" *Bulletin of the National Association of Secondary-School Principals* 36: 29-38; March 1952.

properly conducted essay contests boys and girls may find worthy opportunities for growth in self-expression, creative work, and ability to acquire useful information. The recognition won sometimes provides new incentive for school instruction. Such gains must be weighed against the obvious disadvantages of nonschool contests.

Eternal Vigilance the Price of Freedom

The forces and factors bearing constantly upon the public schools can only be touched upon in a single chapter. Each community has its unique combination of pressures and even these change their forms from time to time. Most of these outside groups are interested in the curriculum for thru it they hope to capture the minds of children.

Since the schools exist "to teach all of the children of all of the people" and since children are required by law to attend school, there is an obligation upon school administrators and classroom teachers to be eternally vigilant against attempts to exploit children or to use the schools for narrow, selfish ends. At the same time the schools cannot be quarantined from life. Many of the pressures upon the schools are motivated by wholly constructive purposes and the proposals made by groups may be educationally acceptable. The problem of administrative leadership, in cooperation with the staff and the people of the community, is to identify and to act upon those principles and practices which will build an educational program of the highest possible quality.

SELECTED REFERENCES

ADAMS, J. HARRY, and RAFERTY, GERALD. "A Policy for Handling Controversial Issues." *Nation's Schools* 47: 31-34; May 1951.

AMERICAN ASSOCIATION OF SCHOOL ADMINISTRATORS. *Lay Advisory Committees.* Washington, D. C.: the Association, a department of the National Education Association, 1951. 24 p. 25¢.

CARY, STURGES F. " 'Hot Potatoes' in the Classroom." *Senior Scholastic* 55: 16-17; September 21, 1949.

CHURCH, HAROLD H. "How Shall Superintendents Be Judged?" *Nation's Schools* 45: 32-33; May 1950.

ENGLEMAN, FINIS E. "We Must Teach the Truth." *School Executive* 70: 61-63; March 1951.

FRANK, JOSETTE. "Is Television Good or Bad for Children?" *Woman's Home Companion* 77: 70-71; November 1950.

HULBURD, DAVID L. *This Happened in Pasadena.* New York: Macmillan Co., 1951. 166 p.

KANDEL, I. L. "Comics to the Rescue of Education." *School and Society* 71: 314-15; May 20, 1950.

MC GOWAN, WILLIAM N. "Time's Up." *Clearing House* 25: 491-93; April 1951. Condensed in: *Education Digest* 17: 1-2; September 1951.

MUMFORD, LEWIS. *Culture of Cities.* New York: Harcourt, Brace and Co., 1938. 586 p.

NATIONAL EDUCATION ASSOCIATION AND AMERICAN ASSOCIATION OF SCHOOL ADMINISTRATORS, EDUCATIONAL POLICIES COMMISSION. *Education for ALL American Youth: A Further Look.* Revised edition. Washington, D. C.: the Commission, 1952. 402 p. $2.

NORTON, JOHN K. "Emerging Demands on Administrative Leadership in Education." *School and Society* 72: 433-34; December 30, 1950.

STOREN, HELEN F. *Laymen Help Plan the Curriculum.* Washington, D. C.: Association for Supervision and Curriculum Development, a department of the National Education Association, 1946. 76 p. $1.

STRATEMEYER, FLORENCE E., and OTHERS. *Developing a Curriculum for Modern Living.* New York: Teachers College, Columbia University, 1947. 558 p.

YAUCH, WILBUR A. *How Good Is Your School?* New York: Harper and Brothers, 1951. 213 p.

CHAPTER TEN

Building Public Understanding

N O SCHOOL system can have too much goodwill in order to ward off and withstand the major anti-schools bombardments. Even to counter the pot shots of criticism, often delivered sincerely by members of a community, the schools must keep a healthy community-school relations plan to win and maintain the public's approval and support.

Patient merit alone will not produce this desired condition, regardless of the quality of the schools. Sound classroom accomplishment provides a cornerstone—but is only the beginning—of solid public relations for the public schools. Their shortcomings and failures, real or alleged, can easily get into the public eye during a headline-spotted controversy. But the news of school achievements, often lacking in dramatic conflict and combat, is harder to tell.

Educators are challenged to put the schools' accomplishments before the public, with regularity and attention-catching imagination, so that the schools can rely on an informed public, rather than one that is uninformed and therefore possibly doubtful, dissatisfied, and even hostile toward what its schools are doing. The everyday story of the American classroom, while seldom melodramatic, can compete favorably for public attention when the educational epic—the trials and triumphs of a pupil and his teacher—is imaginatively presented.

What the schools can do to inform the public about curriculum and instruction—fostering public understanding and confidence— is suggested in this chapter. The chapter does not supersede the 1950 yearbook, *Public Relations for America's Schools.*[1] It does add to and amplify such parts of that book as are saliently related to the school's daily story: What happens to the child when the child and the curriculum come together. This chapter discusses the growing need for telling the public what the schools are teaching; it reports public-relations practices that have become more widely adopted, for curriculum-explaining purposes, since the 1950 yearbook appeared.

---

[1] American Association of School Administrators. *Public Relations for America's Schools.* Twenty-Eighth Yearbook. Washington, D. C.: the Association, a department of the National Education Association, 1950. 497 p.

The Public Asks Blunt Questions

The public, with certain widely-headlined exceptions, appears willing to leave curriculum organization and teaching style up to the educators. These parents and taxpayers have shown greatest concern for the schools' results, regardless of the professional methods. Other citizens, however, have spoken out against certain teaching patterns, including "progressive education."

What are the pupils learning? Why? How much are they learning? Are they benefited by it? Are the community and nation benefited? These are among the questions raised in communities from Maine to Oregon, from Minnesota to Louisiana. The public desires, often clamors, for the answers.

Behind most of the questions is a desire for better schools. In some instances the questions have been suggested, even planted, by remote control by individuals and groups who, for reasons not always apparent, have sought to try public education in a court of public opinion. After throwing the court into a furor, a calm verdict is almost impossible.

There are few educators today who do not recognize the curriculum areas which have been made sensitive thru the friction caused by criticism and controversy. To begin the list, the Three R's lead off, followed but not necessarily in order, by the social studies, extra-curriculum activities, "progressive education," and the frills as labeled and defined by each critic. And at family dinner tables, other detonations have been set off by such matters as homework and report cards.

Other "tender spots" that trouble education today can be added to the list by school administrators who have faced the numerous questions and criticisms, often arising from a community's lack of information, or a surplus of misinformation, regarding the purposes and practices of the schools. The best way to heal such a tender spot, or to avoid one, according to authoritative advice, is to treat it where it starts—in the classroom.

Pupils Tell the Curriculum Story

What is taught, how well it is taught, and how thoroly the public is informed about why it is taught—these lay much of the groundwork, firm or faulty, on which a large segment of the community bases its ideas about the schools.

The Pupil's Role

The child, the living hub of the curriculum, has a central role in the outgoing school story (see Chapter IX). Providing effective instruction is merely the first step in citizen-school relations. Schools boast of a "dynamic" curriculum, having as its goals the cultivation of wholesome attitudes, insights, habits, as well as the mastery of skills and facts essential for living successfully and happily in today's world. Many taxpayers want to know what they are getting for their school taxes besides the adjective "dynamic." To many others, the modern school appears strange and newfangled, conditioned as they are by their own schoolroom experiences or their romantic image of a schoolroom pervaded by the Three R's. To approve and support the goals and purposes of today's schools, the public often demands to know—and to have spelled out—just how a "dynamic" school program benefits the child, the community, and—the taxpayer.

The Teacher's Responsibility

Not only do classroom teachers have a strategic opportunity to strike the spark of school-community understanding but, because of their preparation and contacts, they must assume a major responsibility for the task. Alert classroom teachers find numerous ways to make classroom activities mean something real to their pupils and, consequently, carry meaning to the pupils' families. Publications of the National School Public Relations Association, including its handbook for teachers, *It Starts in the Classroom*, bristles with things to do and how to do them.[2]

The child, for instance, can get a better notion of what his teacher is doing, and why, thru teacher-pupil planning of lessons. Another valuable carry-home result can be produced by a discussion of the question, "What have you learned and why?" asked by the teacher at the close of a session.

---

[2] National School Public Relations Association. *It Starts in the Classroom.* Washington, D. C.: the Association, a department of the National Education Association, 1951. 64 p.

Among the routine opportunities for classroom teachers to interpret education to create Grade-A public relations, the following are cited:

1. *The "why" of the curriculum may be dramatized.* By putting mice on different diets, for example, pupils see the value of instruction in nutrition for themselves.

2. *A field trip,* whether to a factory, airfield, state capital, or to Washington, becomes a lesson instead of a lark when the classroom teacher, pupils, and parents share in the preparations, discussing not only tour arrangements but also the things to be seen and their importance and value.

3. *Community studies,* including traffic surveys around schools, the use or lack of recreation facilities, grounds, or observations of courts, are bound to attract the attention of parents to social-studies aims.

4. *Family response* may be obtained by home assignments that bring parents into the act. Teachers have asked parents to evaluate their children's newspaper and book-reading habits and their telephone skills.

Every assignment, giving parents a picture of the school and its work, can be an uninteresting or a vivid picture. In Schenectady, high-school students conducted a study of recreation facilities which brought a promise of improvements. Street and traffic reforms were made in Paris, Illinois, in line with findings turned up by civics students. In other "assignments of significance," a classroom teacher tested her pupils' abilities to follow directions by asking each to make a simple kind of cookie and to bring one to class as a test-sample. Pupils have interviewed aged citizens or prominent leaders, polled neighbors to discover opinions on current school or civic problems, and made reports on local industries and customs.

When classroom teachers use community resources in their planned assignments, the school and community are linked in a common endeavor, making for kindred understanding. It makes an appeal, thru skilful public relations, for the education-for-living program of modern schools. It makes the point, for all to observe, that education must go beyond the Three R's and carry children toward the nature of things for which they use words and figures in their reading, writing, and arithmetic.

The People Should Share

Since the schools *are* the community, the people must share always in the basic decisions affecting the schools. If wise and wholesome choices are to be made, and if decisions are to be acceptable to both educators and laymen, there must be a constant back-and-forth flow of ideas between the schools and community. The two-way communication is unlike commercial advertising which usually beams messages in but one direction—toward the consumer. Commercial advertising expects little back-talk, but the school-relations program must anticipate back-talk, even foster it.

Whetting the public's appetite for a particular breakfast food, or fostering goodwill for the entire railroad industry may seem like passive results beside the public reaction which the school administrator seeks to elicit thru his system's public-relations efforts.

The school, with its "institutional advertising," must seek approval that leads to action today or maybe tomorrow. The school must persuade, not distant customers, but the close-at-hand "stock-holders," the citizens. They must be given the information upon which they can base their decisions as to whether the schools deserve the support of public money and public opinion.

The People Roll Up Their Sleeves

Important channels for an exchange of information between the classroom and the living room are the nationwide groups working for school improvement. These movements, when achieving worthy purposes, have brought mutual assistance along with mutual knowledge. Such helpful organizations as the National Congress of Parents and Teachers and the National School Boards Association have been long at work in this field. In recent years, citizens committees have taken a more active, at least a more noticeable, part in school affairs in many communities.

Many professional-lay committees have been organized since World War II. Other groups, already in existence, have become more active or have been suddenly "discovered" by newspaper and radio reporters. Interest in community participation in school affairs has been stimulated by the Advertising Council of America and by professional educational groups and government agencies. Forward-looking citizens thruout the nation have begun to realize more fully the part which the public schools must play in a free society. Because of the part of the individual voter in making community choices and decisions, many childless persons have joined with parents in forming school-community partnerships. Since 1949, the National Citizens Commission for the Public Schools has striven to give the movement a voice without dictating any specified course of action for local committees. In January 1952 the Commission estimated that 5000 communities had citizens school advisory committees, including 1600 that were in touch with the Commission.[3]

Citizens committees can and do build a broad road for school public relations but, as some superintendents have learned, the same road can suddenly be bumpy and hard to travel. In a Midwestern city, a lay advisory committee recently smoothed the path for the superintendent and schoolboard by supporting their recommendation for a sixth-grade "art-of-living course," which vocal individuals had criticized after newspaper headlines, bluntly and incorrectly, referred to it as "sex education." In a near-by village, a citizens group calling itself a "school betterment league" served their board of education with an ultimatum that it would campaign to defeat a bond issue for school construction. The league rejected the proposal despite the fact it was recommended by a school-planning specialist who was hired, at the league's behest, to make the survey and submit a recommendation.

People Like What They Work For

Like the prodigal's parents, citizens often feel strong loyalty for the thing which worries them most. Citizens advisory committees tend to spread the schools' worries. The worries, in turn, often create greater public interest, thereby enlisting citizens to help educators solve their problems. The opposite result, and it can occur, is one of the calculated risks that must be weighed in any attempt to broaden the base of understanding and support of a community's school program.

The nettling issue of homework was met cooperatively and constructively in Glencoe, Illinois. Formal assignments of homework were a source of confusion and annoyance to Glencoe parents and pupils. Parents did not demand that homework be abolished. They wanted to know, specifically, what the homework was all about; they wanted to know how they could help their children with it.

---

[3] National Citizens Commission for the Public Schools. *Citizens and Their Schools.* Third Annual Dinner, St. Louis, Missouri, January 25, 1952. New York: the Commission, 1952. p. 12.

A selected group of parents visited classrooms for six weeks, discussing what they observed with classroom teachers and school administrators. As a result, the parents helped develop a homework guide, *Together We Learn*.[4] Short on theory, the guide was long on workable tips. It spelled out ways in which the home and school could work together to serve the child a bigger and more palatable slice of learning. Turning into zestful public relations, the project overcame the parents' annoyance and made them enthusiastic about the pupil's home assignments.

A workshop sponsored by parent-teacher groups wrote a creed for the schools of Hasbrouck Heights, New Jersey. The creed, important for its ideals and inspiration, was valuable before the first word was ever put on paper. Representative lay citizens, including childless taxpayers, had joined the parents and teachers in the series of workshops. They all shared the "ownership" of the schools and the Hasbrouck children by the time the first draft of the creed was written. By using the pronoun, "our,"—our schools, our children—the citizens with and without children made a pact of mutual responsibility. It is far-sighted public relations to have community representatives put a sense of unity on record somewhere besides in the poll books on the day a school-bond issue or levy is up for a vote.

Taking the Offensive with Information

Not every member of the public—in any of the community's various "publics"—is knocking on school doors, eager to participate in school decisions. Nor is everyone eager to get information on education at firsthand. Every community has its share of citizens whose interest in schools, as in other civic affairs, is ordinarily passive. They stay in the back row, apparently indifferent, until they are stimulated by the officials and supporters of the school system or by its opponents.

Sudden bursts of criticism leveled at education confront the schools with acute problems in public relations. So many times lately the outbreaks have caught the uninformed citizen off balance, an easy prey for sensational charges because he lacks the ballast

---

[4] Misner, Paul J. "The Parent's Role in Curriculum Planning." *Journal of the National Education Association* 37: 157; March 1948.

of facts necessary to stand against a storm of allegations. School administrators and boards of education repeatedly have found that no matter how far they hold the curriculum above reproach, the attacks can cut a destructive swath in community opinion before the charges can be met and completely answered.

"Don't wait for a tornado of criticism to strike; beat the school-attackers to the initiative," advises Harold C. Hand of the University of Illinois.[5] Building a new school calls for many community decisions. If the people, with teachers and school officials, decide its cost and what it is to be like, then the new structure will belong psychologically, as well as legally, to everybody. Most citizens will resent attacks upon what they have helped to build; they certainly are not easily fooled when they have acquired understanding thru participation.

Polls and Surveys

The curriculum, in many instances, is not built that way. "It's made by 'experts,' frequently behind closed doors," Hand said. "The people are kept out of the decisions. When the new curriculum decisions are announced, patrons have a right to suspect, to question, even attack. To prevent such attacks, the instructional program should be built together with the people." [6]

To ward off or to blunt any attack, many school administrators gird their schools with the armor of public opinion—in advance of any possible blow. Dr. Hand suggests:

1. *Poll your community now* to find out what parents think about the schools. In most polls made before trouble occurs, parents say they're generally satisfied with the schools. "I do not know of any city in which, after its survey results were reported, any local critic has attempted to persuade the community there is dissatisfaction with the schools."

2. *Gather evidence* showing how much better schools are today than a generation ago. Simplify data, make them available to parents. Facts must be local. They must show that pupils in your schools are learning more today than pupils who attended the same schools 20 or 30 years ago. If parents have this evidence they are almost certain to resist the critic who would have them pressure the school to turn back the clock.[7]

---

[5] Quoted from the *Educator's Washington Dispatch* of March 13, 1952, p. 2. (His views are amplified in: Hand, Harold C. *What People Think about Their Schools.* Yonkers-on-Hudson, N. Y.: World Book Co., 1948. 219 p.)

[6] *Ibid.*, p. 3.

[7] Educator's Washington Dispatch., *op. cit.* p. 3.

A data-gathering project in Denver, resulting in favorable news for the Denver schools, is mentioned in Chapter IX. There are suggestions in Chapter XII for appraising the school's product and for making follow-up opinion surveys among school graduates. Such studies provide a reservoir of information on which to base news stories and annual or special reports that show vividly and persuasively what the schools are doing to benefit the pupils and the community now and in the future.

According to data from the National School Service Institute, obtained from 51,000 opinionnaires, there is substantial support for the objectives and performances of today's classrooms. The survey form, a leaflet entitled *Just a Second,* was distributed in many communities to check on local attitudes. In the sampling analyzed, from 250 large and small school districts, one-half of the respondents were property owners, two-thirds were women, and a large percentage had children in school.[8]

Only 1 person out of 14 preferred that his child be taught a trade while in school. Sex education was favored by 85 percent. Teaching of art and foreign languages was approved by 97 percent. Personality development and family-living courses received a 96 to 98 percent endorsement, along with history. Only 300 out of 51,000 persons thought teaching of good manners and intelligent spending of money had no place in the school. No one thought that schools today cost too much money. Only 5 percent preferred the hickory stick to self-discipline.[9]

Using the Results

Results of similar surveys, made on the home grounds, should make "good reading," as the city editors say, and also provide interesting program material for local radio and television stations and for parents—teacher meetings and civic clubs. The announced results should do more than assure the public that the schools are on the right, at least the popular track. The results provide an informal progress report, which should be most welcome to the citi-

[8] Crosby, Otis A. "The Nation Reaches a Verdict in the Case of the People vs. Today's Schools." *Nation's Schools* 47: 34-37; January 1951.

[9] *Ibid.,* summarized in National School Public Relations Association. " 'Just a Second' Survey Reveals Public Attitudes." *Trends (in Public School Relations).* Washington, D. C.: the Association, a department of the National Education Association, September 1950. p. 2.

zen-stockholders who like to identify themselves with a successful enterprise.

In the National School Service Institute sampling, however, only 1 person in 4 felt that children today read as well or better than a generation ago. This opinion may be explained partly by the parents judging a child's reading skill only by *oral* reading and ignoring the research evidence that children today read better silently than ever they did in bygone days. The apprehension of parents indicates that a vital part of the curriculum story is not getting across to the public. The situation challenges everyone who is responsible for school public relations, to make better use of pupils' performances on standardized reading tests, and their comparative rating with students across the nation. There is another part of the reading story too often neglected, that is, the increasing reading experiences required of today's pupils.

The term, "counter attack," is too strong and inexact to explain what should be done, and in many places is being done, to answer the critics, many of whom are sincere tho misinformed about their schools. "Counter act" is a more descriptive watchword. The job is to counteract the misinformation and the half-information, with the facts—terse and dramatized—before the criticisms cut devastating inroads into a community's confidence in its schools.

Current Criticisms and Recommended Cures

Parents have picked at real and imaginary flaws in education since the first teacher stood before the first pupil. In our society, citizens not only possess the right to criticize the schools, but they *must* do so. In recent years, however, the schools have faced an increasing, at least a more noticeable, amount of criticism from self-appointed and "professional" critics of education, much of it making newspaper headlines.

Criticisms Reported by Newspapers

To discover what was being put before the public by the newspapers, the NEA Research Division examined 256 items which appeared in 168 different newspapers during a 12-week period in 1951. The items, containing information, opinions and reports of citizens' criticism of the schools, were divided among news stories, editorials, columnists' articles, and letters to the editor. The NEA tabulators grouped the items in these categories and found the facts shown in the following tables.

The findings, according to the NEA research staff, indicated that newspaper reporters, editors, and columnists appeared to be most interested in the possibility of teachers' spreading subversive

REFERENCES TO ATTACKS ON PUBLIC SCHOOLS BY NEWSPAPERS[10]

Type of attack	Percent of articles
Alleged subversive teaching	44%
Three R's or fundamentals	27
General and miscellaneous	23
Teaching methods	21
U. S. history, geography, and citizenship	19
Moral and spiritual values	16
Cost of schools	12
Fads and frills	9

[10] National Education Association, Research Division. *Current Criticisms of Schools and How They Are Being Met.* Washington, D. C.: the Division, February 1952. 16 p. The items studied appeared in newspapers during the period from August 22 to November 16, 1951. The District of Columbia and all the states except Missouri and South Dakota were represented.

NUMBER OF REFERENCES TO ATTACKS ON PUBLIC SCHOOLS AS FOUND IN NEWSPAPERS BY TYPE OF ATTACK[11]

Type of attack	News stories	Edito-rials	Colum-nists' articles	Letters to the editor	Total
1	2	3	4	5	6
Three R's	18	17	22	12	69
Fads and frills	3	7	5	8	23
Cost of schools	8	9	6	7	30
Moral and spiritual values	14	5	7	14	40
U.S. history, geography, and citizenship	14	22	5	8	49
Subversive teaching	32	41	28	12	113
Teaching methods	10	11	23	11	55
Lay partnership	5	3	3	. .	11
General and miscellaneous	12	29	8	10	59
Number of items	60	93	47	56	256

[11] NEA Research Division, *Ibid.,* p. 6.

propaganda thru textbooks and/or thru the manner in which they conduct classroom discussions. So far as the letters to the editors can be assumed to be an indication, the public is mostly concerned with the teaching of moral and spiritual values in the schools. The figures should be used cautiously, the NEA information memorandum advises, owing to the short span of time and the small percentage of American newspapers used in the study.

Criticisms Reported by School Principals

Those in charge of elementary schools were asked to report the common criticisms of education thru a questionnaire sent in November 1951 to 1000 members of the NEA Department of Elementary School Principals, the sampling being made by taking each tenth addressograph plate from a membership list of over 10,000. The project was sponsored by the NEA Research Division, the Department of Elementary School Principals, and the National School Public Relations Association. Replies received from 415 of the principals—a 41.5 percent return—reported the most prevalent criticisms in this order:

1. The schools do not teach the Three R's properly.
2. The public schools cost too much money.
3. There are too many "fads and frills" in the school program.
4. The schools neglect moral and spiritual values.
5. The schools are carrying on "subversive" teaching and/or they are not teaching enough about American history and ideals.[12]

Noting the differences between the newspaper items and the principals' reports, the NEA Research Division said several things should be considered. It is "good business" for newspapers to reflect controversial issues as a boost to circulation. Since the Three R's is a primary objective of elementary schools, the principals may be extra sensitive to criticisms on this point. Opinions of elementary-school principals are based on personal contacts and reflect grass-roots gripes. It is probable that many newspaper items reflect attacks on schools elsewhere, but not in their own particular communities—as a result of the state and national programs of attack.

---

[12] NEA Research Division. *Ibid.*, p. 8.

Counteracting Criticism

The elementary-school principals in the NEA Research Division study were asked to report the "most effective" steps taken in their own schools to ward off or to clear up the criticisms.[13] The principals ranked the steps as follows:

1. We invite parents to visit the school, see what it is doing, and ask for explanations of anything not understood.
2. We arrange for parents and teachers to confer about children's work and problems so that they plan together what to do for children.
3. We keep parents and public informed about the school program thru letters, reports, and other materials sent to them from time to time.
4. We invite critics to present their opinions at meetings of parents and teachers where the questions can be discussed.
5. We invite newspaper reporters to visit the school and tell about its program.

The principals were requested to tell which public-relations procedures had obtained the best results for their school system, not necessarily their own schools. They voted as follows:

1. Organization of study and advisory groups of parents and other laymen 28.6%
2. Distribution of pamphlets and other printed materials.......... 26.2
3. Public meetings of the schoolboard......................... 16.9
4. Frequent conferences with newspaper reporters.............. 15.2
5. Appointment of committees of laymen and educators to investigate 9.3
6. Other procedures (including parent-teacher study groups, citizens advisory groups, and exchange visits)...................... 3.8

100.0%

Treating the "Tender Spots" of Curriculum

Rarely does an hour pass, on a superintendent's or a principal's clock, without bringing a question, suggestion, or objection regarding schools. It may come from a parent around the corner or a taxpayer just down the street. The school administrator, besieged at times by what appears to be a myriad of public doubts about education, may feel somewhat like the African hunter who also was plagued with little troubles. Bold and alert, the old hunter felt no fear of big game which he could spot in the distance or

---

[13] NEA Research Division. *Ibid.*, p. 11-12.

could hear trampling toward him. "I can take care of the elephants," he prayed one night, "but I sure could stand some outside help with all these pesky gnats."

Many of the common welts on modern education—and the old education, too—were put there by ordinary public anxiety, not by elephant attacks on the schools. Adults like what they found—or think they found—in school yesterday and hope to find it in the same place today and tomorrow. Educators must strive to find more and more convincing methods to save the curriculum from fly-bite doubts.

Can Today's Pupils Read

Announcements and news stories giving the results of tests showing that pupils today read faster and with more comprehension than a previous generation provide a satisfactory answer for many adults. Yet statistics leave a considerable number of citizens unresponsive and unimpressed. Taking a cue from modern advertising, the San Diego County Schools presented graphic evidence that reading is being taught successfully there. In a magazine-style report, the staff included a large photograph of an eighth-grade boy standing behind two stacks of books that towered above his head. Under the picture appeared the caption: "The books he and his classmates have read since they started kindergarten."

Similar eye-arresting pictures have appeared recently in many sections of the country. Here is how the idea was worked out in Cleveland: A reporter and his cameraman asked for help in planning a picture to show all the reading that would be required, as a minimum, for a student to progress thru the grades and graduate from high school in an academic course. The system's curriculum director, assisted by subject supervisors, gathered the prescribed lists of textbooks and supplementary readings. The result was a 16-foot stack of books touching the ceiling at the city's school-board headquarters. On one side, the photographer posed a boy about to graduate, a top-notch twelfth-grade student. On the other side of the book stack stood a five-year-old ready to enter kindergarten. The before-and-after situation, pictorially emphasized, showed reading as a cumulative process and "measured" the First R for newspaper scanners.

289

Investing time and imagination, the educators who have arranged such pictures have come up with the graphic argument, instead of any table of tedious figures, that pupils do read widely and proficiently these days. In Cleveland, the idea got a better news play than would probably have been given to any expert's testimony on the amount and quality of reading in schools today. Accompanied by human-interest copy relating the troubles and progress of the older boy in his school career, the picture stayed on the front page thruout the day. It was syndicated, with explanatory cutlines, and appeared in numerous papers thruout the nation.

The findings of the National School Service Institute underscore the need for graphic reports showing pupils' mastery of reading skills.[14] Such findings also indicate the worth of open-house programs, public demonstrations, and direct action, especially with skeptical newspapermen, to show what pupils are doing in the realm of the revered Three R's.

How to get the public to take a look is often a problem. Technics of good teaching will draw a sizeable audience to the school when the demonstration is imaginatively promoted. Citizens came from miles around to see the use of visual aids and other demonstrations at Edmore Rural Agricultural School, Edmore, Michigan. Promotion was strongly emphasized since Edmore schools, like so many others nowadays, compete with movies, television, and assorted diversions for the citizen's time. The Edmore faculty sent boxholder mailings to residents, blanketing the whole community, instead of relying on take-home notices which go out only to families of pupils in the community.

This effective type of school advertising, that of having laymen see for themselves, has been given an unusual twist in several communities where school systems, unable to bring the desired number of people to the schools, virtually took the classrooms to the people. During American Education Week, teachers in a Midwestern town conducted classes in a furniture store window. The voices of the pupils and classroom teacher were piped to the sidewalk over a public-address system. The project turned out to be a crowd-stopper, collecting in the street-side audience citizens who never had gone inside a classroom since their own school days. Most schools have

---

[14] National School Public Relations Association. *Trends*. September 1950. p. 2.

nothing to fear in demonstrating what they do or do not accomplish. The problem is to make the program or demonstration so accessible and so painless that the ordinarily indifferent members of a community will, along with any doubting Thomases, take a long and considered look.

A see-for-yourself technic was used for removing any doubt about the children's mastery of the Three R's in the schools of Washington, D. C. In this instance, newspaper editors questioned the how and why of the instruction. The school administrators invited them to make a sampling. Spot checks were conducted in which pupils' papers involving reading, arithmetic, spelling, and writing were selected from desk tops and submitted to members of the editorial staff making the inquiry. In every case, the school administrators said, the materials "proved satisfactorily" that the teaching of the basic subjects was adequate. The technic might be improved by inviting newspaper editors and other key citizens, first, before questions were formally raised. Their seal of satisfaction, stamped on a school program in advance, could be valuable if and when criticism came from other sources. The schools then would have potential and influential allies on record before well-organized attackers struck from the flank.

The Three R's—Lost in the Shuffle?

Many laymen believe the Three R's are submerged, even lost, in today's maelstrom of education. For this troublesome opinion, the profession must accept some blame. Educational terminology, such as that being used necessarily in this book, helps to feed the public's misapprehension about the schools. The schoolyard is cluttered with "core curriculum, motivation, integration," terms an average citizen does not trust because he does not understand them, or which he cannot feel much enthusiasm for. He would feel greater confidence and less resentment if he heard more about the things he is acquainted with, and believes in, such as spell-downs and multiplication tables (not number combinations).

Fortunately, pedagese appears on the decline in school prepared public-relations materials. It should fade even faster, perhaps, to hasten the time when the schools once again can have their common touch. Helpful articles dealing with the art of clear, useful language appear in magazines.[15] Books on the subject enjoy a wide sale, often finding their way to educators' shelves.[16] Writers of school bulletins and annual reports, as happily reported in the newsletter, *It Starts in the Classroom*,[17] often find the language of the neighborhood most eloquent for their purposes. The Three R's still live and breathe when not smothered by educators' professional prose.

Another difficulty is that the school story when related in newspapers, radio, television, and in bulletins is often told piece-meal. The public is presented with a myriad of goings-on such as classroom banking, student government, train trips for transportation units, and mock grocery stores. Reported singly, and in procession, the activities tend to add up to a lot of unrelated commotion. With each phase separated in print from the over-all pattern of instruction, the activities can look like mere play instead of learning. And equally disastrous, the "fundamentals," if they appear at all in the text and pictures or speech, may seem to have gotten in thru sheer accident.

One answer, being provided by school systems or sponsoring citizens groups able to afford it, is to produce booklets on the system's whole program. Such publications draw together the aims, steps, and development of the program and sets them forth on successive pages. Distribution of the booklets may pose a problem. It is fairly easy, but valuable, to put copies in the hands of parents and key citizens. Getting mass readership is another matter. Several school organizations, including those in Syracuse and Detroit, have come up with a partial and inexpensive solution. They put such materials in the offices of physicians and dentists. Other school systems circulate reports to beauty parlors and other waiting rooms frequented by persons with time on their hands to browse thru available print and pictures.

A 48-page bulletin, *Print It Right*, published by the National School Public Relations Association in February 1953, offers many suggestions on printing and distribution of school publications.

[15] A noteworthy example is the article, "The Case Against 'Gobbledygook,'" by Maury Maverick. *New York Times Magazine.* May 21, 1944. p. 11, 35-36. The same article, abridged, with the title, "Curse of Gobbledygook." *Reader's Digest* 45: 109-10. August 1944.

[16] Prominent among such books is: Flesch, Rudolph. *The Art of Plain Talk.* New York: Harper and Brothers, 1946. 210 p.

[17] *It Starts in the Classroom* is a public relations newsletter for classroom teachers published by the National School Public Relations Association, a department of the National Education Association, Washington, D. C. In 1953, NSPRA will issue a handbook on the preparation of booklets and similar public relations materials.

Among the mass media, newspapers still provide the chief outlet and the one most frequently used for giving the public a glimpse into classrooms. Few newspapers today keep aloof from the schools, packed as schools are with vested-interest story possibilities. The papers cover the schools—sometimes exploit them— for child interest, youthful accomplishments, public concern over taxation, controversy and conflict and, in instances when schools have swimming carnivals, even sex interest. Also, the newspaper, if responsive to the heritage of the American press, recognizes its responsibility to share with educators the job of affording the public a general view of education. It is seldom any task to enlist newspapers to allow space for school news. Getting a quantity of stories into print is seldom a problem; the problem is one of "quality." It involves, for the educator, the job of helping reporters find stories that are beneficial to education—yet so interesting they can compete with sensation, violence, entertainment, and Hollywood cheesecake for news space. So many school stories appearing today, while not directly harmful to education, do not benefit it much either. They break the school scene into bits as tho it were a jig-saw picture which readers were only entitled to receive a scrap at a time. The Hollywood beauty would lack interest, too, if her picture were cut to pieces and printed for readers in daily or weekly bits.

The fault of "fragmentizing" the drama of education can turn it into pretty dull reading. Fragmentary accounts reveal little or no connection between what the child is doing and what he is supposed to learn from it. Sight of the "fundamentals" and also the goals can be blurred or completely lost. In a popular primary classroom unit, combining studies of health, diet, arithmetic, and language arts, the pupils often include dairy products and, as one activity, they churn butter. The scene is eye-catching in a newspaper picture, but it creates more interest—and makes more sense —when it is pointed out to readers that the pupils are "churning" arithmetic along with the butter.

School administrators may have to enlist the editor, or whoever is the paper's policy-maker, along with the reporter, to accept the challenge of giving the public an over-all view of the school's instructional program. It is worth the effort for both the schools and the newspaper. The paper can perform an important civic service. In many communities, there is a sore need for a public over-view of the school curriculum so that citizens, fairly and thoroly, can make up their minds at the ballot box about the operation and needs of schools.

Offsetting fragmentary accounts of instruction, newspapers in various sections of the country recently published running, chapter-by-chapter stories on the progressive activities in classrooms. The papers used a reporting formula, certainly not new, but one that is consistently effective. Reporters and their photographers have gone back to school, "enrolling" in kindergarten, then moving up until they "graduated" from the twelfth grade. The news teams often started with five-year-olds on the kindergarten floor. Day by day, or week after week, they produced a continuing text-picture feature. The series have carried such titles as "Your Child in School." The articles related the big problems of little folks, their troubles and successes, and progressed to the little problems of the bigger pupils. The text usually was sprinkled with human interest and seasoned with nontechnical methodology, to give adults a fair idea of what children were learning, or were expected to learn, particularly in the Three R's. At least one superintendent considered the project of sufficient value to warrant assigning a headquarters supervisor to guide the reporter to classrooms with teachers who could explain articulately the classroom processes so the writer, in turn, could report those processes in household words.

The curriculum has widespread reader interest, school representatives can remind editors, providing the subject is treated with imagination. Newspapermen themselves have so testified. The Education Writers Association, comprising school-beat reporters, annually presents awards for outstanding reports by newspaper, magazine, and radio, interpreting what children learn in the classroom. Many local units of the American Newspaper Guild annually bestow honors for special-fields reporting, including the field of education.

While many reporters seek to write serious articles on education, those catchy little stories of novel classroom activities will continue to appear in print, for the editors will want them. The circulation-wise editor tries to catch the eye of the average reader, not necessarily the eye of the professor of education. But the classroom teacher, when opportunity presents itself, should not let the newspaper reporter leave without offering to acquaint him with the background and the end-product of the activity he is observing for story purposes. The reporter should understand that the make-believe dairy is a failure if the pupils merely taste butter but do not digest some arithmetic. Without the connection being made known, the classroom activity can look like undirected motion.

Answering the Fundamentalists

Perhaps the time has come to answer more eloquently the charge that schools are neglecting the fundamentals by turning back the critics' own word—"fundamental."

How the term, "fundamental," can be broadened, so that citizens should see its full breadth and meaning, was offered in a publicly recorded speech by a metropolitan school superintendent to his headquarters staff. But he spoke beyond the auditorium to the newspapers and their readers when he said:

> In the minds of some, the fundamentals never change—they continue to be the so-called Three R's and nothing more. But, in the minds of most people, education for living in the world we have with us today must extend its base over wider areas. Especially, living in a democratic society makes much greater demands upon the individual than skill in the Three R's, which in no way is saying that the Three R's do not continue high priority in the levels of objectives.
>
> Even the first two of the Three R's have become four, thru the addition of speaking and listening. Actually, we don't read what someone else writes, or write nearly as much these days as we speak and listen. . . . The ability to listen and to know what is said is a skill which everyone should have.
>
> But the fundamentals today do not end at this point. If an atomic attack were imminent, the most fundamental teaching we might do would be in teaching children what to do to minimize the effect of the bomb upon them. . . . It would be no time to stop and make certain that the names of the capitals of all the states were known by all the pupils.[18]

Other presentday fundamentals, as stated by this superintendent and others, included sound family life, health and physical fitness, and ability to earn a living. Any reasonable listener or reader could easily conclude that such "fundamentals" must have a place in schools with the classic Three R's. Professional views on the rudiments can draw an audience and be persuasive when the views are put into dramatic terms and street-corner metaphor. Delivered before Mr. or Mrs. Fundamentalist speaks up, the explanation has already given them an answer.

---

[18] From an address to the Cleveland, Ohio, principals and supervisory staff by Mark C. Schinnerer, superintendent of schools, as quoted by the *Cleveland Press*. September 28, 1951.

Palatable Pupil Reports

The pupil report, like the department store bill and credit letter, is one of the most sensitive contacts between the school and its patrons. Like a muddled "past due" notice, the report card can arouse a high degree of irritation if the child's standing is rendered in terms that puzzle the community or affront the parent.

Traditional one-way reports for elementary-school pupils were dropped by the school system of San Jose, California. Instead of the take-home, no-further-comment reports, the San Jose administrators announced the start of conferences between parents and classroom teachers to discuss a child's problems and progress. School sessions during the "report periods" were shortened, giving teachers time to meet parents on a friendly and informal basis. They were to discuss not only the child's accomplishments, but also his attitude toward other children and toward school life in general, plus ways in which the child's attitude might be improved if deemed desirable.

The first editorial comment in a San Jose newspaper was critical. It indicated, according to school officials, that the writer did not understand the program. The superintendent then took an outline of the program to the editorial writer. In a subsequent Sunday issue, the same newspaper devoted an entire editorial page to the conference-type reports. It displayed pictures of the steps of the new program, along with two columns of extrasize type explaining and praising the innovation.

The printed endorsement was gained thru the few hours spent by San Jose school administrators in gathering the facts and spreading them before a receptive, but previously uninformed, editorial writer. Besides the published approval, the schools obtained a news note on the popularity of the news reports which were bringing 95 percent of the parents to the school. The second article could, and should, have appeared in the first place if the schools and newspaper had prepared together to publicize the transition.

In Long Beach, California, a newspaper columnist complained in print of not being able to understand his child's report. The superintendent called in the newspaperman and one of his colleagues, asking them to sit down with school staff members and thoroly study the system's elementary-school report cards. One of

Public schools, Norfolk, Virginia

The arts have become basic parts of the modern school curriculum. To an increasing extent they are woven like golden threads thru the fabric of many school activities.

the newspapermen wanted to know why a report card should not be as attractive as some of the literature used in Long Beach's school-bond campaigns.

The swapping of ideas brought forth a two-color, six-page report card, not only including a simple yet thoro reporting table, but also providing space for comments by teachers—and parents. In a public-relations-wise introduction, the Long Beach schools give the purpose of the card, pointing up the joint teacher-parent responsibility.

Newspaper writers, radio commentators, and the stand-by public draw conclusions about report cards, as for other matters, from the facts at hand. The school administrator or his information director can save headaches by passing along in advance to the various news and public-relations channels explanations of pending changes.

Perils in Progressive Education?

Sporadic alarm over "progressive education" somewhat follows the pattern of the flying saucer fright. Every time the phenomena have been reported, they have appeared differently and caused varying degrees of anxiety to different people.

So great can be the concern over "progressive education," with or without a capital P, that those alarmed often stick the label on any kind of instruction that looks merely modern. Those skeptical of modern education want to know, as in the case of the flying saucer, Is it really ours? Is it home-grown American education or is it something out of this world? Their fears may not be allayed until they have a full explanation from an authority whom they trust, who talks in terms they understand. A suggestion that school administrators explain up-to-date instruction, publicly, articulately, and frequently would be superfluous. The question is how to get about it—what words to use.

Modern education appeared native, just as native to America as modern medicine and modern engineering, in articles written by a Kansas superintendent and published in the newspaper of his city just before American Education Week. The editor had invited the superintendent to write a by-line series on "progressive or modern education" which had been discussed in the community. "The progress of today's schools," he wrote, "is in fact a proof of the effectiveness of the educators of former times, for if the schools . . . failed to adapt to changing times, then the schools would have become the brake on all scientific, social, political, and economic progress."[19]

Meeting a rhetorical argument that schools should recapture the educational virtues of former times, he continued: "It would then be necessary to decide which former period we should choose and how far backward we should go. Should we choose the Gay Nineties era, or the Civil War period, or go back to the Colonial Days and pre-Revolutionary times?"

The guest writer then presented a recipe of modern education, containing many of the ingredients in this book, showing it to be as American as apple pie. The Kansan, as other educators have done, left any reader rejecting his explanation with a real burden —that of deciding just which components of education he would toss aside in order to turn around and go backward.

Moving head-on against complaints, Denver schools set about to find out if "progressive education" was hampering children there as it was charged. The school staff listened carefully to the critics, then immediately began surveying basic skills of Denver pupils in comparison with those in other cities. Even tho the Denver children compared favorably, re-evaluation tests were given to determine any weaknesses in the teaching of spelling, arithmetic, and grammar. The findings caused the superintendent to recommend to the board of education that more emphasis be placed on English drill, spelling training, and social studies work. The project fostered community-school relations. The press and public, kept fully informed, recognized that something was being done to improve education, regardless of the name—or the nickname—that it carried.

Make Curriculum Claims in Concrete Terms

Educators may find a lesson in the advertising of a tobacco firm selling its cigarettes on claims of "proof positive" of the merits of the product. A prove-it attitude toward education is held by a

---

[19] Lafferty, Charles. "The Schools of Today," an article in *The Atchison*, Atchison, Kansas, November 12, 1951.

considerably large number of citizens who want "proof positive" that something beneficial happens to the child while he is in the classroom. For them favorable testimony, either for tobacco or education is not enough. They can be skeptical of testimony, particularly from an educator, considering him a vested-interest source of opinion. Besides, so many testimonials on the merits of schools are long and abstract. The public wants "evidence" so it can make up its own mind. It wants the "evidence" delivered in concrete terms, and delivered with the speed of a radio or television commercial.

Publicizing the Product

The best evidence of a school's effectiveness probably is the graduate. How he develops as a citizen, jobholder, and personality reflects favorably and unfavorably on the schools. School systems with the staff resources can profitably gather long-term data on former students, eventually presenting it, along with the graduates' collective opinions as to the school's contribution to their careers. Newspapers would find the material rich in story angles.

More immediately, the development of the child before he leaves school could show, if skilfully dramatized, the processing of the "product." The assembly-line "growth" of an automobile and the manufacture of a baseball make fascinating sequence stories in film or on the rotogravure page. The child, undergoing educational processing and growth, offers an equally interesting sequence, if it can be imaginatively recorded and presented.

A metropolitan school staff, at a reporter's suggestion, recently started to gather case histories and pictures of a score of pupils from as many schools. An educational aide will keep records of the students, starting in kindergarten. They will be photographed annually and the pictures will be filed away with specimens of their handwriting, arithmetic papers, and spelling papers. There will be brief summaries filed each year on the subjects they studied, the skills and learnings they mastered in the various grades.

At the end of their elementary or high-school years the material will be used to make well-documented and lively copy, showing their physical growth, and indicating their mental growth, from stage to stage. Photographs will accompany the feature, along with the reproductions of their progressively improving handwriting and arithmetic papers. The newspaper suggesting the idea thinks it will make a bell-ringing story. The idea was born by accident. The paper once published the art work of a half-dozen kindergarten pupils. Because of the universal appeal, a city editor decided next year to display the same students, picturing them with their art work for the first and second year. It was repeated annually with the same then-and-now examples of art, and brought increasing reader interest. The next step will be to try the formula on education generally.

Displaying the Samples

A variation of the above formula can be worked out by organizing a newspaper feature story, radio or television program, or picture booklet around a subject field. It could be "Language Arts in Our Schools," "History in Our Schools," or any field. This technic often is used, but seldom to the fullest extent. Representative pupils in every grade—but only one from each grade to give dramatic punch and unity—should be presented as they face the learnings and skills which they must master, say, in English, at their particular level. The dozen pictures, the dozen stories, presented together, eloquently tell the story of growth and development that pupils experience, and which their teachers must guide and nurture, as children move along in school. It is the story of curriculum in personal, graphic terms which laymen can appreciate and understand.

To show a student's past or anticipated development in mathematics, a news photographer recently assembled six students from the third to twelfth grades, the largest number he could get into the picture he wanted. The boys and girls, seated on a gymnasium floor, were snapped from 10 feet overhead, with large placards displaying their own sample math problems directly in front of them. Tips of the placards touched, making an eye-pleasing six-sided design, and the picture—with its "proof" of their progressive learning—was equally pleasing to parents, teachers, and taxpayers.

In one city where books were stacked to indicate reading achievement, their 270 pounds, and their 73,297 pages were woven into the newspaper story. At an institute of newspapermen meeting at

Columbia University, the idea drew favorable comment, another indication that mass media are receptive to positive stories about education when they are appealing.

Other published examples of concrete school results include a newspaper picture of a technical high-school student surrounded by the 60 tools he learned to use in the school shop; a stenographer-trainee seated in a semicircle of typewriters and office machines, totaling a ton, which she learned to operate in addition, as the story said, to practice-writing 12 miles of shorthand in the course; a twelfth-grade girl from a vocational high school pictured running a four-spool sewing machine, with the text explaining that her 2700 feet of practice stitches equaled the distance between (for a graphic comparison) two well-known landmarks in the community.

Meet the Press—More than Halfway

School news is a valuable commodity for a circulation-wise newspaper. Nearly 1 in 5 persons in the nation is a pupil in the first 12 grades. Add the parents to this pool of vested reader interest, then include the teachers and other school employees and their friends, and the school news audience has risen to three-fifths or more of the population. Count in the taxpayers who finance the schools, plus the adults who once were pupils themselves, and it is unanimous.

School News Has Appeal

It is almost inconceivable that any newspaper editor, from the city to the crossroads, should be unaware of this tremendous reader potential in school news. Yet the figures have been brought to the attention of news directors on more than a few occasions in order to obtain greater news coverage for schools. The Education Writers Association has used the statistics to stress the editorial importance of school news.

The newspaper, despite the competition of radio, and lately of television, remains the chief medium of public information in practically every community. Many persons get most of what they know about their schools from what they read in the newspaper.

Newspapers are alert to conflict; it is a basic element of news. A community argument over the schools, a board of education meeting filled with pro-and-con debate—these are bound to get a play in a newspaper that knows the circulation value of controversy. The school organization will have no trouble getting its "noisy" news into print.

Getting It Printed

Getting space for the "quiet" news, the school's day-to-day accomplishments, the curriculum in action is another matter. It requires alertness, imagination and perseverance on the part of administrators and classroom teachers, and a friendly, working arrangement between them and the school-beat reporters and, at times, the reporter's boss, the city editor.

Story tips about various phases of the school system are welcomed by the newsgatherers. The suggestions call attention to "favorable" news and help further to familiarize the reporters with the system. School public-relations specialists offer a checklist of school news tips, putting child-and-curriculum ideas high on their list. Their suggestions include:

Success stories
Scholarships won
Learning to read and cipher
Good citizenship, character building activities
Curriculum improvement to meet local needs
Class projects, such as exchange of letters with other cities or countries
Unusual organizations; knitting clubs, reforestation clubs, good-reader clubs
Exhibits of fine work done, especially in vocational classes
Back-to-school night, Dad's night
Hobby shows
Unusually talented pupils and classes; national, regional, or state recognition
Pupils studying and making good despite handicaps such as blindness
Educational field trips
Honor students.[20]

Give your help and understanding to the school news reporter who often wishes that his material were as dramatic as that of the medical writer. The latter's copy can contain life-or-death suspense; he has readers following his paragraphs to learn whether the miracle drug did its work, whether the patient did or did not recover.

---

[20] American Association of School Administrators. *The Superintendent, the Board and the Press.* Washington, D. C.: the Association, a department of the National Education Association, 1951. p. 16-17.

Reporting how the student responded to educational "treatment" can be far more difficult. For drama, the school reporter often must be satisfied with undramatic anonymity—the student's triumph as measured, collectively, when a classroom's test results are compared with remote and unnamed children who took the same standardized test elsewhere.

Competition Makes Drama

The competition may be on the football field or in a classroom. Many educators have been reluctant to publicize the comparisons of classroom achievements of their own students with any students close enough to their district to put spice in the news. Occasionally, however, comparisons are printed in a circumspect manner that still gives zest to the story.

Chicago parents recently were informed that their elementary-school pupils were above average for the nation in the mastery of the Three R's; for example: 73 percent of 8-A pupils were at or above the reading norm for that grade.[21] A similar report, released by the superintendent to reporters in another Midwestern city, got front-page attention in a story hailing that city's "young champions" of classroom endeavor.

The Nature and Nurture of Reporters

While helping look for stories on the curriculum and its results, the superintendent and his various aides-de-camp for public relations will have the responsibility of maintaining easy relations with newspapermen, the latter bent on finding any and all types of "copy."

To meet the press—amiably, frankly, often—these pointers are suggested:

1. Know the names of the editor, city editor, and schools reporter of each newspaper serving your district. A personal acquaintance with at least one person on the staff of each paper is invaluable.

2. Invite the editor or the schools reporter to speak to the faculty or to a school assembly. Such an experience gives him a personal feeling about the school.

---

[21] Chicago Public Schools. *Today's Schools: Are They as Good as Yesterday's?* Chicago: Chicago Public Schools, 1952. p. 7.

3. Win the respect of the schools reporter. He observes and remembers, and his impressions could color his stories about the school.

4. Always be available. At least, show the reporter you are trying to be accessible and the chances are he will make allowances. Everyone resents a brush-off treatment, and a reporter is in a position to do something about it. Make reporters feel welcome. Do not keep them waiting. They have deadlines to make. If they miss today's deadline (if it is a big-city paper), the story may never run. Make a telephone available for calls to their city editors. If you do not have the facts about a story, admit it frankly. Offer to get the facts and call back—and be sure to call back.

5. Watch your language! Do not use technical terms not understood by laymen. Pedagese is disappearing but there is still too much used to assure that the schools are fully understood.

6. Admit the existence of unfavorable news. Explain reasons why the story should not be published. Offer, meanwhile, to help the reporter round up the missing facts. Remember that reporters are allergic to flat demands to keep a story out of the paper.

7. Assume that every representative of the press is a responsible person. Go along on projects and even stunts if they are in good taste. Be understanding when a reporter asks for a "pretty valedictorian." He knows that beauties, beasts, and babies have the highest looking-interest in pictures. A photographer cannot make 30 or 40 faces stand out clearly on pulp newsprint unless the editor gives him an entire page, which seldom happens.

8. Pat the editor or the reporter on the back occasionally. He is human like the rest of us. A word of commendation is remembered as long as a protest. Once in a while a protest, if well supported by sound reasoning, is in order. It will not help the current story but may do some good in the future.

9. Call papers to report human interest stories. Do not limit calls to requests for space announcing plays, concerts, and items of pure advertising. Study the kind of stories carried by each newspaper for clues in releasing items.

Telling It by Television

Television and radio news bulletins about school happenings provide only a fraction of the opportunities for fostering school-community relations over the flash-quick media. For a score or so of years, only radio, among all media, could report the curriculum story firsthand. Radio gave listeners the voices of students in the classroom, thinking aloud, as they accomplished lessons or other learning activities. Now, with eyes installed in the air, the television screen brings to parents and other watchers the motions, the skill of students' hands, the expressions of young faces. It provides an animated visual report, along with all the learning sounds, of what happens when child, curriculum, and classroom instructor are combined.

A video report from the actual classroom, or from a simulated classroom, can be described as an electronic version of Citizens Night at the school. Lounging near TV sets, more persons are "visiting" schools than could ever be accommodated in one shift at the building itself.

As television facilities march across the nation, additional school systems fall in with those in New York, Philadelphia, St. Louis, Chicago, Cleveland, and other previously established TV centers. They use "sight and sound" to communicate to thousands the work going on inside the schools.

Mirroring the Classroom

In Dallas, Texas, where the young medium is still younger, school administrators said they already regard television "as the prime medium of educating the general public concerning presentday classroom technics, curriculum patterns and public education trends." Schools in the Texas city last year (1952) completed a 138-program series, "Adventures in Learning," combining a short film relating to a specific teaching area augmented by "live" performances of teachers and pupils. The 15-minute program was telecast three times weekly. Another Dallas station started telecasts of a half-hour program each Saturday morning, the "show" usually simulating a classroom situation. School supervisors said the show made no effort at entertainment other than what is provided by a skilful classroom practice when presented for its intrinsic worth. "The reaction to the shows," Dallas educators said, "was prompt and favorable, most of it coming from parents."

Inside the Schools

The paragraph title identifies a series of programs produced on more than a dozen of the nation's TV stations with the help of *Life*. The idea, conceived by Roy E. Larsen, president of Time, Incorporated, and chairman of the National Citizens Commission for the Public Schools, is described by the *Life* staff "as a method of alerting the citizens of a community to the accomplishments and needs of their schools so that they will become sufficiently interested" to help plan and support the program of their local schools. "Inside Our Schools," according to its creators, shows parents and taxpayers a community's children working "naturally and unrehearsed" with their teachers.

The series was first produced by local television stations, *Life*, and boards of education in Schenectady, St. Louis, Louisville, Cleveland, and New York. The sponsor planned to extend the series to 11 other cities by the end of 1952. In addition to telecasts from classrooms, the programs have included the appearances of prominent guests, school administrators, classroom teachers, and civic leaders discussing the regular school program, plus special school-related problems. In New York City, an adult panel traded opinions on "Humanities Versus Sciences" and "How Should Communism Be Taught in Our Schools?" The syndicated radio-television critic, John Crosby, called the New York programs, which drew 1800 letters, "one of the most extensive public examinations of the school system ever undertaken."

Commenting on a trip by a cameraman to New York City's Public School 168 for the story "Inside Our Schools," a newspaper columnist wrote: "There was a fascinating demonstration of the sixth grade and its teacher, Miss Louise Anderson, showing how the principle of coordinated curriculum worked in practice. The integration of history, science, geography, economics, writing, and current events in a study of Japan was helpful, clear and revealing to a parent." [22] Such "inside the schools" stories can be told in most school systems with good public-relations results.

Televising to Taxpayers

Observing that the housetops were luxuriant with antennas, Cleveland school administrators decided, as have others where the opportunity was afforded, to use the new medium to reveal the schools to their owners, the community. With a pioneer school-owned radio station, the Cleveland system already had a trained staff of writers, radio teachers, and specialists to create TV programs for

[22] Gould, Jack. "Radio and Television: Balanced Understanding of the School System in New York Presented by NBC and Life." *New York Times*, April 4, 1952. p. 34.

a 15-minute spot allotted one evening a week by one of the city's three television stations.[23]

The radio education specialists turned to the task of televised public relations. In the series, "Meet Your Schools," they endeavored to educate the watching public in the purposes, problems, and methods of public education. Altho the programs had their origin in the studio, not an actual classroom, the Cleveland program—like those in several other cities—presented classroom lessons taught in a reasonable facsimile of an everyday school situation. There was no attempt to add dramatic trimmings, except to tailor the dramatic materials to the television medium.

Activity in reading, writing, mathematics, spelling, social studies, music, art, and, for a change of pace, such topics as basketball, Christmas, Lincoln's Birthday, and hobbies—all were included in "Meet Your Schools." The Cleveland schools' television recipe is itemized here, not because it is unique, but because it is fairly typical of what other schools are doing with the medium.

As for casting, the Cleveland schools, as other systems, had plenty of actors, the pupils of all ages, sizes, and descriptions and their teachers. Even tho a classroom teacher and pupil are not necessarily actors, the Cleveland show, catching them at work in the "studio classroom," gave the programs a spontaneity that carefully rehearsed actors might never provide. The school TV producers found "audience interest of the keenest sort in the face of a child thinking, trying to find the answer, solve the problem, arrange the blocks, or fill a test tube." [24]

The material used on the telecast was new to the student group, as far as that was possible. There was a rehearsal each time of a similar unit of learning for the purpose of fixing a pattern. There were errors, too, on the program, which the Cleveland staff felt made it more convincing and gave opportunities for correction by the teacher or by other students.

Policy and general guideposts for the programs were outlined each week by a planning committee—the superintendent, an assistant superintendent, the curriculum director, two visual-aids specialists, a supervisor of English, the school radio station director,

[23] Cameron, James B. "Cleveland Citizens Meet Their Schools via Television." *Nation's Schools* 49: 84, 86, 88, 90; June 1952.

[24] Cameron, James B. *Ibid.*, p. 86.

and various subject consultants. These two-hour sessions became the most regular, if not the most important, public-relations sessions of the school organization over the entire school year.

The school administrators believe that their effort, tho not bringing spectacular results, did give good returns for the talent and time expended. Pulse ratings for the program averaged more than 12 points, never falling below 11 points, meaning that the program had 150,000 viewers, one out of every 10 persons in the community. The accomplishment, they feel, should help increase public understanding of the teaching processes and problems.

SELECTED REFERENCES

AMERICAN ASSOCIATION OF SCHOOL ADMINISTRATORS. *Public Relations for America's Schools.* Twenty-Eighth Yearbook. Washington, D. C.: the Association, a department of the National Education Association, 1950. 497 p. $4.

AMERICAN ASSOCIATION OF SCHOOL ADMINISTRATORS. *The Superintendent, the Board, and the Press.* Washington, D. C.: the Association, a department of the National Education Association, 1951. 23 p. 25¢.

APPLEGATE, MAUREE. *Everybody's Business—Our Children.* Evanston, Ill.: Row, Peterson and Co., 1952. 310 p.

BRAMMEL, P. ROY. *Your Schools and Mine.* New York: Ronald Press Co., 1952. 438 p.

DOOB, LEONARD W. *Public Opinion and Propaganda.* New York: Henry Holt and Co., 1948. 600 p.

FINE, BENJAMIN. *Educational Publicity.* Revised edition. New York: Harper and Brothers, 1951. 561 p.

FITZGERALD, STEPHEN E. *Communicating Ideas to the Public.* New York: Funk and Wagnalls Co., in association with *Modern Industry Magazine,* 1950. 267 p.

JONES, JOHN PAUL. *The Modern Reporter's Handbook.* New York: Rhinehart and Co., 1949. 430 p.

KALISH, STANLEY E., and EDOM, CLIFTON C. *Picture Editing.* New York: Rhinehart and Co., 1951. 207 p.

LESLY, PHILIP, editor. *Public Relations Handbook.* New York: Prentice-Hall, 1950. 902 p.

LEVENSON, WILLIAM B., and STASHEFF, EDWARD, editors. *Teaching Through Radio and Television.* New York: Rhinehart and Co., 1952. 560 p.

MACDOUGALL, CURTIS D. *Interpretative Reporting.* Revised edition. New York: Macmillan and Co., 1948. 751 p.

POWELL, NORMAN J. *Anatomy of Public Opinion.* New York: Prentice-Hall, 1951. 619 p.

CHAPTER ELEVEN

How To Appraise Classroom Achievement

THE more important the objectives of education are held to be, the more mandatory it is to discover whether or not they have been achieved. Neither the necessity for evaluation nor decisions as to the methods of evaluation to be used can be taken lightly. Valid appraisals are difficult to make, whether they are based on the classroom teacher's informal, day-by-day questions and observations in guiding learning, on the results of informal objective examinations, or on the results of standardized tests. The problems of evaluation and the problems of curriculum construction are intricately interwoven. What is to be evaluated and the method of evaluation both depend on what schools teach or should teach, and what is evaluated and the methods of evaluation inevitably affect instruction.[1]

Evaluation an Essential Part of Curriculum Planning

The term "evaluation" as used in this chapter includes all means for ascertaining and interpreting the results of instruction. It is not limited to standardized tests. Evaluation of instruction may be defined as the process by which one reaches a judgment as to its quality and effectiveness. This process involves (a) defining the ultimate objectives of the entire educational program in terms of specific behaviors, (b) establishing desired standards of attainment, (c) describing the extent to which objectives have been attained by individual students at various grade levels, (d) deter-

---

[1] For an extended and helpful discussion of the relations between appraisal and instruction, see Lindquist, E. F., editor. *Educational Measurement*. Washington, D. C.: American Council on Education, 1951. Chapter 1, "The Functions of Measurement in the Facilitation of Learning," by Walter W. Cook, p. 3-46; Chapter 2, "The Functions of Measurement in Improving Instruction," by Ralph W. Tyler, p. 47-67; and Chapter 5, "Preliminary Considerations in Objective Test Construction," by E. F. Lindquist, p. 119-58.

mining the discrepancies between the results actually obtained and the standards set for each objective, and (e) interpreting the results.

This chapter is chiefly concerned, however, with such evaluations as are made during the time pupils are in school. Evaluations of instruction thru investigations of the reasons why students drop out, and follow-up studies of graduates are treated in Chapter XII and the evaluations of the curriculum in terms of the social function of the school are made in Chapter I.

For practical reasons, evaluation must be based primarily on the immediately observable behavior of the school pupil; that is, on the observable acts or performances of the pupil while he is still in school. It is obvious that we cannot wait until the child becomes an adult to make decisions concerning present curriculum changes in content and organization. Rather, we must rely upon our subjective judgment to infer from the child's presently observable behavior what his future behavior will be like. These subjective inferences, often of doubtful validity, constitute an outstanding weakness in the whole evaluation process. Evaluation based on the attainment of immediate objectives of instruction is valid only to the extent that these immediate objectives contribute to achieving the ultimate goals of instruction.

It is easy to drift into the unwarranted assumption that a student's achievement in a given area is to be attributed solely to what he learned in school. This assumption is not justified even in the case of abilities in the Three R's, for the development of which the schools have long had the chief responsibility. In other areas, such as leisure activities, moral behavior, and mental and physical health, the school may not play even the major role. On the other hand, critics are quick to impute shortcomings in the behavior of the graduates of our schools or, indeed, the ills of the world at large, to alleged neglects or inefficiencies in school instruction.

Schools, in their concern for the all-round development of students, have assumed an increasing number of responsibilities as well as a greater degree of responsibility for achievements which are obviously shared with the home, the community, and the church. As a result, curriculums are badly overcrowded. The time has come to assess realistically the specific responsibilities and the degree of responsibility which schools can and should assume. However, Cureton points out that ". . . responsibility has no meaning in the absence of some method for determining whether it has been discharged effectively or ineffectively. If the school wants to accept some responsibility, but lacks either the necessary authority to discharge it or the ability to evaluate, however crudely, the results of its proposed efforts, we must conclude that it is unable to accept this responsibility." [2]

The preceding statement implies that decisions as to what achievements should be evaluated and as to how they are to be evaluated should not be delayed until after the curriculum has been constructed, and certainly not until after instruction has been completed. Rather, it implies that, both in formulating objectives and in devising means for the attainment, decisions as to how and what to evaluate play an important part. In other words, curriculum construction and plans for evaluation should go hand in hand. A realistic consideration of how the achievement of any objective can be appraised will contribute markedly to its clarification and aid in determining whether or not its achievement is a responsibility which the school should accept. It will also tend to focus attention upon important matters and so increase the efficiency of instruction. The more classroom teachers and pupils know about what achievements are to be evaluated and, in a general way, about what form the evaluation will take, the more intelligent and motivated their efforts are likely to be.

Conditions Essential to an Efficient Program of Evaluation

If the program of evaluation is to realize its full potentialities, certain conditions must be established. The most essential conditions, highly interrelated, are merely listed below, but they are discussed in detail in the pages which follow.

There must be a clear understanding that the controlling purpose of evaluation is to guide and facilitate learning experiences designed to develop those behaviors required to deal effectively with important situations in the pupils' present and future lives.[3] All

---

[2] Lindquist, E. F., editor, *op. cit.*, Chapter 16, "Validity," by Edward E. Cureton, p. 657.

[3] The word "behavior" is here used in the general sense assigned to it in current literature on evaluation, which assumes that evaluation must be based on the observable acts of students. It includes symbolic behavior (such as thinking and communication), perhaps the most important type of behavior that schools can develop. It also implies such knowledge, attitudes, abilities, and habits as are essential to effective performance. Whenever such terms as "knowledge" and "abilities" appear in the following pages, it should be understood that they are to be considered in relation to some desired type of behavior.

other purposes are subordinate to this one. It is necessary, therefore, that:

1. The objectives set up to guide instruction should specify unambiguously and realistically the behaviors for the development of which the schools accept responsibility. These are the ultimate objectives.

2. The selection, organization, and sequential arrangement of learning experiences (for example: immediate objectives, units of instruction, and course content) should be clearly relevant to the attainment of these ultimate objectives. Appraisals, in turn, should be relevant to the immediate objectives so determined.

3. Evaluation, as an integral part of the instructional program, should be as comprehensive as that program. It must embrace all important behaviors and must show periodically the degree to which these behaviors have been achieved. It will utilize all technics which perform important services.

4. The data obtained from evaluation should be fully utilized for the improvement of instruction.

5. The staff responsible for instruction should have the primary responsibility for the program of evaluation; that is, for determining what should be tested, what forms of evaluation are appropriate, and how the results are to be interpreted and used. It should, however, include persons with special competence in the technics of evaluation.

6. Classroom teachers should participate in the program of evaluation to the fullest practicable extent, not only because of the contributions they can make to it but also because of the beneficial effect on their teaching.

7. Pupils should share in the appraisal of their achievements.

Evaluation in Relation to Ultimate Objectives

In order to guide learning experiences, it is necessary to discover periodically and systematically the degree to which students have developed the behaviors constituting the goals of instruction. These behaviors may be termed criterion behaviors; that is, they are the criteria for planning instruction and for appraising its results.

The behaviors most frequently and crucially needed in life should be reflected in broad outline in the objectives set up to guide instruction. This requires that they be grouped in terms of major life needs and that there be clear definition of the most important types of behavior needed for competence in each group. The statements of objectives must be comprehensive, realistic, and unambiguous if they are to afford a guide either to planning instruction or to planning evaluation. Any failure to meet these requirements in the formulation of objectives will constitute a serious obstacle to devising adequate means of appraising results.

313

How, for example, would one set out to evaluate the achievement of such objectives as the following:

1. To develop within learners the best social and spiritual attitudes and appreciations
2. To build character which will insure the basis for rich ethical living in a society promoting the common welfare
3. To develop the power to create and respond to the environment
4. To integrate the whole life of the child within the group
5. To prepare students for life in a complex industrial society dedicated to democracy, equality of opportunity, and the peaceful achievement of social ends
6. To extend the depth and breadth of our experiences
7. To insure the transmutation of the elemental instincts and passions into high ideals, worthy purposes, and true standards of conduct
8. To appreciate how our present everyday life has grown out of time and space
9. To aid individuals to meet adequately an ever-changing world.

Such objectives afford little guidance for either teaching or testing, unless they are broken down into the desired behaviors essential for their attainment. This breakdown was not done in the courses of study from which these objectives were taken. No one would quarrel, for example, with the importance of developing "the best social and spiritual attitudes and appreciations," but if the statement of the general objectives is to be serviceable, the situations in which these attitudes and appreciations are to function must be specified and the desired behaviors in each type of situation should be clearly defined.

Such statements afford little guidance to either teaching or testing. Nor are their implications for specific objectives pointed out in the courses of study from which they were taken.

The examples of objectives quoted above are selected, of course, rather than representative. On the other hand, it is not easy to find statements of objectives which are indicative of a careful and comprehensive analysis of social needs and are also stated clearly enough to guide evaluation. Fragmentary, ambiguous, or pretentious statements of objectives appear frequently in current courses of study, even in the statements of objectives for specific units or areas of the curriculum.

Fortunately, however, not all statements of objectives have these weaknesses. Many are realistically conceived, clearly stated, and broken down into the implied behaviors. An excellent example is the pamphlet on solving social problems issued by the Citizenship Education Study.[4] It identifies the sources of problems (situations), ranging from relatively simple social adjustments of individuals to problems of the nation and the world; it gives specific suggestions on (a) how to define and set up a problem, (b) how to gather data, (c) how to draw logical conclusions, and (d) how to carry out the conclusions. Or consider this one: "To develop the behaviors, including reading abilities and study skills, needed to work with printed materials." This statement suggests immediately the necessity of identifying the most important behaviors needed in working with printed materials, and when they have been unambiguously described, the degree to which they have been developed can be appraised. Among these specific behaviors might be included: how to find information, including use of the dictionary, atlases, encyclopedias, other standard reference works, the index, and the library; how to interpret and appraise what is read and to select important information bearing on the specific purpose for which the reading is done; how to organize the selected information for achieving the purpose; and how to remember what is read.[5]

The grand strategy of the program of evaluation is determined, as earlier suggested, by ultimate objectives; that is, by the criterion behaviors frequently and crucially needed in life situations now and in the foreseeable future. Objectives so defined may or may not coincide with the objectives stated in the curriculum materials. There may be wide discrepancies between what is taught and what should be taught. The fact that such discrepancies do sometimes exist not only justifies the direct evaluation of the achievement of criterion behaviors but constitutes an obligation to do so quite apart from whether these behaviors are listed among the stated objectives.

For example, assume that it is thought desirable for students to be able to read such graphs and tables as appear in general reading. It would be entirely possible to construct a valid test of the abilities involved. It would be necessary, first, to make a comprehensive investigation of the types of abilities needed and, second, if com-

---

[4] Citizenship Education Study. *Problem Solving*. Detroit, Mich.: Wayne University Press, 1948. 11 p.

[5] For suggestions on the relation of the development of these knowledges and abilities to the total curriculum see: *Suggestions for the Testing of Reading*, Philadelphia Public Elementary Schools, Curriculum Office, Philadelphia Public Schools, Philadelphia, Pennsylvania, 1949.

parison with other schools is desired, to secure norms of achievement for a representative population. Such a test would be a valid measure of this particular achievement in any school regardless of whether or not the school had specifically planned for the development of these abilities; in other words, entirely apart from whether the development of the ability to read graphs and tables was a specified objective in that school. If, however, students are shown to be weak in this ability, it may be not because they and their teachers have not worked faithfully or efficiently on such contracts as they were asked to undertake but because those responsible for preparing the curriculum guides had neglected to set up this objective and to suggest efficient learning experiences for its attainment.

Specialists in test construction have been increasingly concerned with the direct analysis of social needs and to a considerable extent, particularly in the so-called basic skills, have included in their tests measures of behaviors not commonly included in instructional programs. There is considerable evidence to show that this practice has had the effect of calling attention to these needed behaviors and with beneficial results upon instruction.

It should be recognized that some of the behaviors for which the school accepts responsibility may not be needed until after schooling has been completed. Some follow-up studies have been made of the needs of out-of-school youth, and the data provided from these investigations may have some significance for the reconstruction of the curriculum. However, the efficiency with which the students meet these delayed needs is affected not only by what they learned or did not learn in school and out, up to the time they left school, but also by influences operating in the intervening years. It is, of course, impossible to anticipate every situation to which each student may wish or need to respond. Neither in the case of any individual can we prophesy when any situation will be met. But we can discover, by analysis of social needs and pupil behavior, what important situations are found commonly and persistently year after year.

For purposes of appraisal these situations can be presented vicariously, usually by verbal descriptions, and we can at least make sure (a) that the student understands the principal factors involved in a given situation and (b) that he has the knowledges, abilities, and attitudes required to meet it. On the other hand, many criterion

316

situations and the accompanying criterion behaviors are present in the lives of children in the early grades, such as, catching colds, home accidents, choice of radio and television programs, group singing, the choice and adaptation of clothing suitable to the occasion, and the gracious introduction of strangers to friends. This overlap of present and future needs is the most important principle in determining grade sequence of instruction and is highly significant, therefore, in determining what achievements should be appraised at each grade level. It is to be expected, of course, that these recurring situations will be met with more efficiency with each succeeding year. Some of these situations are met in school and some outside. While the school is not directly responsible for the behavior of students out of school, it can help students, thru instruction and thru the cooperation of parents, to meet present life situations more effectively. An important part of any evaluation program should be to ascertain at each grade level the degree to which the student has developed the knowledges and abilities needed to solve his present problems.

Difficulties arising from lack of pertinence of immediate to ultimate goals—The evaluation of students' progress year by year and even day by day is frequently difficult because of the irrelevance of the immediate learning experiences to the ultimate objectives. Having stated the ultimate goals, one would assume that the next step would be to design learning experiences by means of which pupils may be expected to progress efficiently toward these goals. These are the immediate objectives. Actually the statements of ultimate objectives and the designing of the means to their achievement appear in many instances to have been two separate tasks. But if day-by-day instruction is not to be haphazard, the relevance of each learning experience as a means to attaining desired criterion behaviors (objectives) must be critically established. What achievements should be appraised at any grade level are, of course, influenced by the immediate learning experience designed as a means of attaining the ultimate objectives.

The choice of immediate objectives can be made in several ways: (a) by common-sense, logical analysis in which the pertinence of the proposed immediate objectives to the ultimate objectives is carefully examined; (b) by a critical analysis of the experimental evidence on the effectiveness of the various means proposed; and (c) by a careful consideration of the present abilities and behavior needs of students. That these procedures are not always followed or used effectively is evidenced by the large amount of material in curriculums of every type which seems to have little or no relevance to ultimate objectives as well as by the omission of many learning experiences of undoubted value.

There was a time, for example, when the chief means to the attainment of correctness in written and spoken English was held to be the teaching of grammar in heavy doses, beginning relatively early in the grades. Many patrons as well as teachers still hold this opinion. Extensive experiments, however, have failed to show that the teaching of grammar leads to correct usage as efficiently as do learning experiences specifically designed for this purpose.[6] It may be argued, of course, that the teaching of grammar has relevance to behaviors other than correctness of speech and writing and that its contributions would be greater if it were taught more extensively and effectively. This might, on the other hand, be done at the expense of more valuable learning experiences. But whatever objective it is presumed to serve, its value as a means to the attaining of that objective must be appraised by ascertaining the degree to which the objective has been reached.

Fallacies, not usually resulting from common-sense analysis, may be induced by erroneous or at least debatable educational theories. It is not uncommon to find classroom teachers and supervisors who put a high estimate upon methods of teaching which have been clearly shown to be inefficient and to cherish activities that have slight relevance, if any, to important life needs.

As matters stand today, the chief difficulties involved in appraising the progress of students at various grade levels arise not so much from shortcomings in the theory and technics of measurement as from the lack of clear relevance of what is taught year by year to important ultimate objectives. There is no acceptable excuse for failing to identify the knowledges and abilities most frequently and crucially needed in life or for failing to ascertain from time to time the degree to which these knowledges and abilities have been developed.

---

[6] Monroe, Walter S., editor. *Encyclopedia of Educational Research.* Revised edition. New York: Macmillan, 1950. p. 392-93.

Chapter III describes four of the most common patterns of curriculum organization. For convenience in discussion the learning experiences in any type of curriculum are designated "course content." There is no value in course content *per se*, whether it be the content of a subject, an activity, a unit, a core, or a broad field. The only significance of a learning experience in any instance is its relevance to ultimate objectives. It must contribute to some present or future criterion behavior, and it is this contribution that should be evaluated. There are so many knowledges and abilities of major importance in meeting life needs that efforts in appraisal should be focused upon them, whether the appraisals be oral questions, teacher-made pencil-and-paper examinations, observational technics, or standardized tests. Tests of insignificant or minor facts or abilities are not merely a waste of time; they are actually detrimental since they distract attention from really important matters. Anyone who will examine a sampling of standardized tests, say for social studies, or of teacher-made objective tests, or of stenographic reports of teachers' oral questions will be impressed by the number of trivial items, many requiring only the recall of verbal statements about facts of low significance.

But unfortunately much of the course content is taught either because it has traditionally been taught or because it is a current pedagogical fashion, with little concern for its relevance to ultimate objectives. In many schools the textbook determines the course content. For example, an investigation [7] of the teaching of the social studies in 100 cities showed that page-by-page assignments to a single textbook were the practice in over 90 percent of the schools—no problems, not even topics—and that in most classes the appraisals in the succeeding recitations consisted of oral questions which could be answered by parroting the text. One method of combating this atrocious practice would be to emphasize, both in teaching and in testing, only those items which are clearly pertinent to criterion needs.

However, the demand that any course content that is taught have relevance to ultimate objectives is not enough. One must also ascertain whether all important criterion behaviors are being developed. The content of traditional subjects tends to lag behind life needs,

---

[7] Thompson, Oscar E. *Social Studies Instruction in Iowa Schools.* Doctor's thesis. Iowa City: State University of Iowa, 1945. 388 p. (Typewritten)

and units included in other types of curriculums, because of their spottiness, often omit or underemphasize very important types of behavior. In other words, it is necessary to make sure not only that what is taught is relevant to ultimate objectives, but also that no course content is omitted which is indispensable for the attainment of the ultimate objectives.

The need for looking beyond course content to ultimate objectives in evaluating achievement is so important that it deserves more specific illustration. Since 1946 the Canada-United States Committee on Education has been concerned with the improvement of relations between these two countries. One of its activities has been to investigate what is included and what should be included about Canada in United States history textbooks. The amount of space devoted to Canada in these textbooks was found to be strikingly smaller than the importance of Canada to this country would dictate.[8] Moreover, the periods covered and the knowledges emphasized are out of all proportion to their significance. In junior high-school textbooks, for instance, 76 percent of the space devoted to Canada deals with the period from 1497 to 1763 and only 24 percent with the later periods in which the most significant developments in the relation between Canada and the United States have occurred. In all periods, including the period before 1763, many of the most important matters are neglected. It is not strange that the results of tests on what students know about Canada have shown that they are not only uninformed but actually misinformed on matters so important that every intelligent American citizen should know about them.[9] Obviously a test limited to what students are taught from their textbooks (that is, to the immediate course content) will not show what students should know and, on the other hand, a test on what they should know would not be a valid test of what they are taught.

Still another illustration may help to show the difficulty of evaluation because of the lack of pertinence of course content to

---

[8] American Council on Education, Canada-United States Committee on Education. *A Study of National History Textbooks Used in the Schools of Canada and the United States.* Publication No. 2. Washington, D. C.: American Council on Education, 1947. 81 p.

[9] Gell, Kenneth. *What Every High School Graduate Should Know about Canada.* Doctor's thesis. Cambridge, Mass.: Harvard University, 1944. (Typewritten.) ¶ Hauck, Arthur A. "Education and Canadian-United States Relations." *Social Education* 9: 67-70; February 1945. ¶ Lattin, Richard D. *An Evaluation of Elementary School Pupil's Knowledge of Canada as Related to the Opinion of Authorities.* Doctor's thesis. Iowa City: State University of Iowa, 1952. 252 p. (Typewritten)

ultimate objectives. A consideration of the creative behaviors in visual arts in which most people commonly engage in life outside the school will disclose that such behaviors as are involved in photography; planning a house; planning a garden; arranging a room; reconditioning furniture; redecorating, choosing, making, adapting, or designing clothing; landscaping a yard; and arranging flowers are more widespread than painting and drawing, which in comparison, are much less common among the creative activities of most persons. Yet in most schools painting and drawing constitute the bulk of the course content. Even if we had highly valid and reliable means of appraising achievement of creative efforts in painting and drawing, such tests would measure only a small proportion of the creative activities in which most persons engage.[10]

Lack of relevance of test content to what is or should be taught— The preceding paragraphs pointed out the difficulty of constructing evaluation instruments when the course content is not relevant to criterion behaviors. An equally disturbing situation arises when the evaluation instrument itself lacks relevance either to what is taught in a given school or to what should be taught. Consider first this problem in relation to the use of standardized tests. The knowledges and abilities which these tests seek to measure have been, for the most part, selected from the analysis of textbooks and courses of study in order to choose items dealing with matters that are most widely taught. This tends to perpetuate both curriculums and methods of doubtful quality, and of course tends to penalize schools which deviate from common practice. Such tests may operate as a conservative influence but what is conserved may or may not be good. They should be used with full knowledge of their limitations and used very cautiously lest schools be discouraged in the attempts to construct curriculums more responsive to life needs and to experimenting with learning procedures which, in the light of evidence, seem likely to promote achievement.

The lack of relevance of test items to what is taught is less serious in such areas as basic skills than in the so-called content subjects, but even in these instances there is sometimes a lack of

---

[10] For a view of the ramifications of visual arts in American life, see Chapters 1 to 20 in the Fortieth Yearbook, National Society for the Study of Education. *Art in American Life and Education.* Public School Publishing Co., 1941. Bloomington, Ill., 819 p. (Now available from University of Chicago Press,, Chicago, Ill.)

relevance to what should be taught at a given grade level. For example, authorities in the teaching of arithmetic hold that facility in dealing with the quantitative situations in life requires an understanding of the number system itself and practice in using numbers to solve practical problems. They advocate, particularly in the early grades, that the chief emphasis be put upon meaning rather than upon drill. Nevertheless, intensive formal drill in computation is commonly found even in the early grades, partly because of the way classroom teachers themselves were taught, partly because they have been more accustomed to drill methods than to the meaning approach, and partly because of their desire to have pupils make high scores. Consequently test norms based on a wide sampling of the school population will be higher for early grades than they should be, in terms of valid objectives. Schools which, following the recommendations of authorities, stress meaning in the early grades, are likely to be discouraged because their achievement in these grades, as measured by these tests, is lower even tho achievement in later grades reaches or surpasses standard norms. Yet low scores on pencil-and-paper computations in Grade III may be evidence of good teaching while high scores may indicate either a poor choice of learning experiences or an inordinate expenditure of time on formal drill.

The discussion up to this point should have made clear that the criteria for determining what should be taught and what should be tested are the same; that is, both should be relevant to criterion behaviors which constitute the ultimate objectives. Only confusion can result when either or both of these tasks are not guided by these ultimate criteria. Ideally, the program of instruction and the program of evaluation will be planned together so that what is taught and what is tested will coincide. Unfortunately, however, this practice is not commonly found.

Suppose, for example, that the criterion behaviors selected as objectives to guide instruction have been carefully chosen and specifically described and that the immediate learning experiences for attaining these objectives have been chosen both because of their close relevance to these objectives and because of substantial evidence of their efficiency. Assume, furthermore, that classroom teachers and pupils have worked faithfully in fulfilling the contracts which they have assumed. It would be obviously unfair to evaluate their achievement by means of a test which was in large part unrelated to the criterion behaviors with which the instructional program had been concerned. In other words, such a test would measure neither what pupils should have learned nor what they did learn. On the other hand, suppose that the test does measure important criterion behaviors but that these behaviors were largely ignored in instruction. In such a case the test would be valid as a measure of the degree to which the objectives have been realized but it would not be a measure of the degree to which children learned what they had uncritically been encouraged to learn.

These are extreme cases, of course, since in actual practice varying degrees of relevance to ultimate behaviors are found both in instruction and in the instruments of evaluation. They do illustrate, however, the need for the close integration of the program of instruction and the program of evaluation.

The Necessity of Comprehensiveness in Evaluation

Since the purpose of evaluating achievement is to guide and facilitate learning, the program of evaluation should be as comprehensive as is the instructional program itself. It should be comprehensive in four respects: (a) achievement in all curriculum areas should be appraised; (b) evaluation should provide meaningful data thru which the students' growth from year to year in desirable behaviors can be shown; (c) all children in all the schools in a system should be included; and (d) the technics of appraisal which perform the most useful service should be used. However, in stressing the need for a comprehensive program of evaluation, it should be kept in mind, as previously emphasized, that the controlling purpose of evaluation is to guide and facilitate essential learning experiences. The criteria for determining the amount and nature of evaluation are (a) the need for evidence and (b) the uses to which the obtained evidence is to be put.

The need for balance—Achievement in all areas of the curriculum should be evaluated in order to ascertain the degree to which the objectives in each area are being attained, and in order to insure balance or well-roundedness in the students' development. The influence of what is tested upon what is taught and studied has long been noted. Aside from this fact, it is important to discover the degree of achievement of the objectives in all areas, both the achievement of individual pupils and the general level of achievement in schools as a whole. We need to discover how well Johnny reads, what progress he has made in science, and also to determine the levels of achievement in reading and science for all the schools in the system. Such appraisals should be as valid and objective as they can be made. But the degree of confidence which can be placed in them varies widely from area to area.

Conspicuous progress has been made in securing objectivity and validity in measuring achievement in such basic abilities as reading, arithmetic, and correctness of written English and in measuring specific items of knowledge. We can meaningfully describe, by means of the results of standardized tests, what progress a student in Grade V has made in reading or arithmetic, and if we desire to do so, can compare meaningfully his achievement with that of other fifth-grade pupils in his class, in the entire system, or in the country at large. Only limited confidence can be placed, however, in descriptions of his attainment in such areas as music, visual arts, and social adjustment. When tests rendering numerical scores are not available or are inapplicable, other methods of appraisal, involving qualitative description, must be used, including anecdotes, diaries, and impartial judgments. The use of judgments in the appraisal of values is not new, of course. It has been used and continues to be used widely in various situations in life, in spite of the well-known fact that subjective judgments may be limited in their reliability. Recent studies have shown that, if the behavior to be judged is explicitly defined and the judgments are made according to established rules, the reliability of the appraisals can be greatly increased.[11] Whatever may be the limitations of measurement in a given area, the school must make the best appraisals it can. Every type of behavior that it seeks to develop is amenable to some kind and degree of objective appraisal. The more objective the appraisal, the better it is, of course. It is always possible to secure evidence which is acceptable in the court of enlightened professional opinion and such evidence will usually be acceptable to patrons.

---

[11] Engelhart, Max D. Article on "Examinations" in *Encyclopedia of Educational Research*. Revised edition, 1950, p. 407-14.

Even in the case of basic abilities such as reading or arithmetic, not all important abilities are tested and, as will be shown later, numerical scores may be, and frequently are, sadly misinterpreted. Moreover, the scores obtained from the most carefully constructed test are not a substitute for critical judgment but an aid to it. There is a certain compelling force about achievements that are described by numerical scores that tends to overemphasize them in the total program of instruction. Hence the need for obtaining and publicizing evaluations of achievements of other areas so that the educational program will not be distorted.

The need for comparable results—It is highly desirable that the evaluation technics yield results by which achievement in one area can be meaningfully compared with achievement in others. To do this the evaluation technics must have high objectivity and validity. Comparable results are chiefly limited, therefore, to those secured from standardized tests, and even then only in case of test batteries so constructed that the norms for achievement in one area are comparable with the norms in another. In such instances achievement in reading can be meaningfully compared with achievement in arithmetic and correctness in written English. It is not possible at the present time, however, to make meaningful comparisons of achievement in music with that in visual arts or the achievement in either of these subjects with achievement in arithmetic.

Comparisons of the students' growth and achievement from year to year likewise require comparable test results. Meaningful but limited comparisons can be made of the students' progress in reading and arithmetic thru the use of standardized tests which have been so constructed that the scores from year to year are comparable in a statistical sense. Satisfactory evidence of growth from year to year is much more difficult to obtain in other areas. How, for example, would one compare achievement in the geography of the United States in Grade V with achievement in the geography of Latin America or Europe in Grade VI? A student's performance on a valid test in one year could, of course, be compared with his performance on an equally valid test in another, but this might throw little light on his growth. It would be possible, of course, to show growth in the ability to read maps or growth in basic concepts, such as the effect of altitude on temperature, or on any abilities or concepts that are needed thruout the course. It would also be possible to test the student each year on the total range of content included in the course of study in geography for all grades, but this would not be practicable and it would, moreover, violate the principle that what is tested in a given year should be relevant to what is taught. The difficulties of showing growth in the mastery of a subject, here illustrated by geography, apply also, and probably with greater force, where the course of study consists of a series of units such as conservation, transportation, and world peace. The sequence of such units within a grade and from year to year is often gratuitous and arbitrary.

Records of appraisal—Ideally, the student's development in each of the curriculum areas should be a matter of record as on a profile chart. Such records, however, are difficult to interpret except in a case of achievements to which numerical scores can be validly attached. At the present time, therefore, the types of relationships which can be satisfactorily portrayed in the form of a profile for certain abilities in such areas as reading, arithmetic, and correctness of written English cannot be so satisfactorily portrayed in the case of music, art, and the social studies. This lag arises from the greater difficulty of assigning meaningful numerical measures to performances in these areas or to the low reliability of any measure that is assigned. In spite of these limitations, the records should contain the best obtainable estimate of achievement in each of the curriculum areas. Qualitative judgments are better than no appraisal, if recognized as such. Ultimately, as desired behaviors in the various fields have been identified, unambiguously described, and efficiently taught, marked developments in the measurement of achievement may be expected. Some progress has already been made even in art, music, personality traits, and social adjustment.

Comparability in the results of appraisals from subject to subject and from year to year is also required for the coordination of the instructional program for all the pupils in all schools in a system. The results of classroom teachers' appraisals are of some use, of course, but these vary so widely in amount, kind, and quality that they afford very limited evidence for the coordination of instruction in the school system as a whole. Standardized tests can be used for this purpose, in the case of abilities which they measure

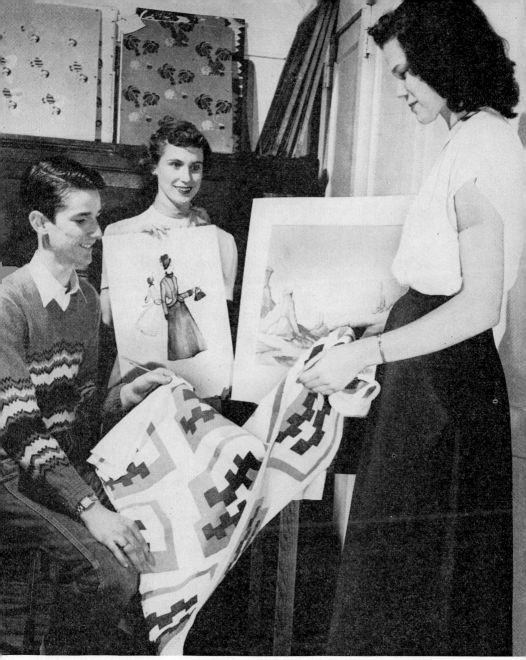

Public schools, Dallas, Texas

Everyone must have freedom to grow physically, mentally, and spiritually. He must satisfy his need for self-expression in ways wholesome for himself and society.

and insofar as these abilities coincide with local objectives. Locally constructed tests could also be given to all schools. Only the results of standardized tests, however, afford a reasonably satisfactory basis for comparing local progress with that in other school systems.

Designing effective technics of evaluation in such fields as music, visual arts, and social studies has lagged not so much because we do not know how to measure achievement in these fields as because of lack of agreement as to what should be taught. For example, as far as technical problems of test construction are concerned, it would be entirely possible to construct a standardized test in the social studies. Other limitations, however, make it virtually impossible to construct satisfactory tests for general use, such as: failure to identify the objectives, failure to state them unambiguously and break them down into essential behaviors, and the great variety of contents, grade sequences and patterns in the curriculums of different school systems. If these limiting conditions could be removed, there is no more reason why satisfactory standardized tests could not be produced for social studies than for reading and arithmetic.

The need for tests on units widely taught—One of the greatest opportunities for improving instruction thru evaluation is the construction of standardized tests on units which either are or should be included in the curriculum. Classroom teachers and pupils as well as patrons of the school presumably would like to have, after a unit has been taught, dependable evidence on what has been accomplished. There are a great number of units the value and content of which would not vary greatly from community to community. For example, Sidhanta, now a member of the faculty in Lucknow University in India, with the aid of distinguished scholars in India, England, and the United States, has listed the main concepts which an intelligent American should possess about India and the erroneous concepts which should be corrected.[12] What an intelligent citizen in Rockford, Illinois, should know about India would not be expected to vary from what should be known by a citizen of Fresno, California. It would be entirely feasible to construct a useful standardized test on this unit which would be advantageously used thruout the country.

---

[12] Sidhanta, Ranjana. *A Study of Basic Concepts Relating to India.* Doctor's thesis. Iowa City: State University of Iowa, 1950. 299 p. (Typewritten)

Yates, after an extensive investigation of cases of libel and slander, found the majority of students with "serious misconceptions and unethical attitudes toward many of the issues involved in the conflicts between the right to the enjoyment of a good name and the privilege of free speech." [13] The more serious shortcomings were shown in the attitude to be taken toward malice as a factor in truthful statements, the concepts of qualified and absolute privilege, and the responsibilities of talebearers. She also found that pupils' concepts and attitudes on many matters deteriorated rather than improved with advancing grades. The ethical as well as the legal principles involved in slander and libel are well established. It is again entirely feasible to construct a test on this unit for general use. Such a test would be an example of the direct evaluation of ultimate criterion behavior. In view of the harm done by careless and malicious gossip, slander, and libel, it seems desirable that a unit in this field be taught and the results critically evaluated.

Standardized tests could be constructed for most units that are or should be commonly included in the curriculum, such as, the formulation of the Constitution, care of the teeth, prevention of home accidents, the actual and potential production of oil, and the use of the dictionary. Such tests, if properly constructed, would not only aid classroom teachers in their appraisals but also constitute a valuable guide as to what to teach about these units.

The Coordination of Different Types of Evaluation

In the earlier sections of this chapter considerable emphasis has been given to the use of standardized tests. But the means of evaluating the results of instruction are not limited to these tests. They include also objective tests locally designed for systemwide use, objective tests made by teachers to evaluate their own instruction, essay tests, the appraisal of exhibits of work such as themes, standard scales in handwriting, interest inventories, records of out-of-school activities such as choice of radio programs, teachers' oral questions, observational technics, and anecdotal records. Each of these technics of appraisal serves a useful purpose.

Tests must be valid—The most fundamental problems pertaining

[13] Yates, Ida M. "Concepts and Attitudes Concerning Slander and Freedom of Speech." *University of Iowa Studies in Education*, Vol. 9, No. 1. Iowa City: State University of Iowa, 1934. p. 183-206.

to any of these technics of evaluation are not the technical problems of designing the technics, important as these are, but the problems of defining and selecting the specific behaviors (that is, knowledges and abilities) that are to be appraised and of deciding upon the uses to which the results of evaluation are to be put. In fact, decisions on these matters must first be made before the method of evaluation can be intelligently chosen.

In the case of any method of appraisal it is desirable to achieve the greatest possible validity.[14] The validity of a test or other appraisal technic is commonly defined as the extent to which the test measures what it purports to measure, but this in turn depends upon the reliability of the instrument; that is, the degree of validity is determined by the degree of relevance plus the degree of reliability. Reliability is defined in terms of the accuracy and consistency with which a test measures whatever it does measure. A test may be reliable altho low or lacking in validity with reference to a given criterion behavior; that is, with reference to the achievement to be evaluated, it may consistently get wrong, irrelevant, or inadequate answers. Any criterion behavior that can be unambiguously defined as a goal for teaching can be evaluated with some objectivity but of course with varying degrees of validity according to the technic used.

Much has been said about the impossibility of measuring intangibles in education. But if an objective is intangible, we cannot teach it confidently, and if we try, we cannot know, without dependable evaluation, how successful our efforts have been. In general, if we can define an objective in terms of the specific behaviors which we desire to develop, we can devise a method of appraisal that is valid enough to be of considerable use.

Validity, moreover, has no meaning except in terms of purpose. A given technic of evaluation may have high validity for some purposes and low validity for others. It is important, therefore, to examine each type of evaluation in terms of the purpose or purposes which it purports to serve.

Limitations of standard tests—Attention has already been called to the use and limitations of standardized tests in providing data which make possible (a) a comparison of the student's achievement in one area with his achievement in another, (b) a description of his

---

[14] For a penetrating discussion of validity see: Lindquist, E. F., editor, *op. cit.*, Chapter 16, "Validity," by Edward E. Cureton, p. 621-94.

growth from year to year, and (c) a coordination of the instructional program in the school system as a whole. These tests also make it possible, in areas such as basic skills, to compare achievement in one school system with achievement in other representative schools. In fact, standardized tests provide the only convincing basis for such comparisons altho, as will be shown later, such comparisons must be made very cautiously.

Standardized tests in reading, arithmetic, study skills, and correctness of written English deal with common learnings; that is, with behaviors which all schools seek to develop. Critics of the schools have a special interest in achievement in these areas. There will be differences, of course, from school system to school system in the methods of teaching to be used in emphasis, and in the grade sequences of learning experiences. It is to be expected that each local school system will select the test which most closely fits its own program.

Two points should be kept in mind in selecting standardized tests: (a) choose tests that give the best description of achievements of the most important behaviors to be evaluated and (b) choose tests with norms that have been established on a wide and appropriate school population. There may be a temptation to choose the tests which give the most favorable rating to local achievement but this temptation can be resisted by keeping in mind that the purpose of the test is to get the truest possible estimate of local achievement in relation to norms established from representative populations.

Standardized tests often are given annually. The annual evaluations in curriculum areas for which suitable standardized tests are not available, as well as evaluations for shorter periods, of necessity are almost wholly the task of local school systems because of the wide variation in the country at large in the content, organization, and grade sequence of courses of study.

Valuable as annual evaluations are for the purposes cited above, their influence on child development and in guiding learning is less potent than appraisals made by classroom teachers day by day or at short intervals. Appraisals of the latter type provide evidence of achievement of agreed-upon goals—goals set up cooperatively by teachers and pupils. Their purposes are more easily understood, they make possible the intelligent redirection of effort as occasion demands, and, since they show students both their achievements and shortcomings, they make substantial contributions to motivation. There is, however, one common defect in the appraisals by classroom teachers; namely, they take the value of the immediate course content for granted. They do not appraise it in terms of its relevance to ultimate objectives.

Improving teachers' appraisals—In the early days of the development of objective testing, and serving to some extent as a stimulus to it, many studies were made, the results of which indicated serious shortcomings in the practices of classroom teachers in evaluating the achievement of their pupils. Teachers were shown to ask too many questions, and especially too many that required mere verbal memory of statements from the texts; the questions included on essay examinations were little better; the quality of the answers to questions was poorly appraised; grades recorded on report cards could not be taken as dependable evidence of the true achievement of the pupils. These limitations still hold for many classroom teachers today. In recent years, however, serious attempts have been made, and with considerable success, to help teachers to improve the quality of their appraisals. In cases where this help has been carefully provided, the quality of teachers' appraisals has been markedly increased. For purposes of guidance, the evidence provided by the teachers' evaluations is, in many instances, of great importance since, in face-to-face relations with the pupils, the classroom teacher can take into consideration more factors than can the maker of a standardized test. Since teachers' appraisals, good or bad, operate willy-nilly in every classroom every day, and since these appraisals are so influential upon achievement, it is important that, both in the preparation of teachers and in the development of teachers in service, help be given for the improvement of these technics.

Use of paper-pencil tests—Two types of pencil-and-paper tests in common use are the essay examination and the teacher-made objective test. The problems involved in their construction need not be discussed here since they are amply treated in standard references on measurement.[15] It is important, however, to point out two

---

[15] Lindquist, E. F., editor. *Educational Measurement, op. cit.,* Chapters 7, 9, 12, and 13. ¶ Greene, Harry A.; Jorgensen, Albert N.; and Gerberich, J. Raymond. *Measurement and Evaluation in the Secondary School.* New York: Longmans, Green and Co., 1943. 670 p. ¶ Weitzman, Ellis, and McNamara, Walter J. *Constructing Classroom Examinations.* Chicago: Science Research Associates, 1949. 153 p.

requirements for their effective use: (a) to select only knowledges and abilities that have high relevance to ultimate objectives, and (b) to place the emphasis on questions in essay examinations and on items in objective examinations that test understanding rather than verbal memory. A student's understanding of a fact or a principle is best measured by requiring him to use it. The significant result of testing knowledge and skills by requiring their use, especially if the use is related to a criterion behavior, is that it tends automatically to discourage emphasis, in learning and in testing, upon matters that have low utility.

No plan for evaluating results is satisfactory which depends solely, or perhaps even chiefly, on pencil-and-paper tests, no matter how carefully these tests have been constructed. These tests, standardized or otherwise, must be supplemented by other technics of appraisal. If one had to choose a single instrument from among such alternatives as standardized tests, informal pencil-and-paper tests, and face-to-face appraisals made in the process of instruction, he would be wise, as far as the effect upon the student's development is concerned, to choose the face-to-face appraisals. Fortunately, we do not have to make this choice, but it is of major importance not to underestimate oral questioning and observational technics.

Many types of behaviors, as well as aspects of behavior, cannot be evaluated adequately either by pencil-and-paper tests or by teachers' oral questioning. Such instruments must be supplemented by observational technics, including the making of anecdotal records. It is possible, for example, to discover by pencil-and-paper tests whether students know how to use the dictionary, but it is not possible thru such tests to discover whether pupils do habitually use the dictionary when they need to do so. A student may make a high score on a pencil-and-paper test dealing with tolerance toward the opinions of others, but only by observation of his behavior can the teacher discover whether he does in fact possess such tolerance.

Use of anecdotal records—Unfortunately evaluations based on observational technics and anecdotal records are often lacking in reliability. They should be made and used very cautiously, particularly if the evaluations are to be recorded in the student's permanent record. The inclusion of any appraisal or even any incident suggesting moral deficiency is open to serious question because of the known tendency for classroom teachers to treat pupils as if they actually have either the desirable or undesirable trait they have been alleged to possess. Anecdotal records are always subject to the operation of errors in sampling. A reported incident may be unique in the life of the student to whom it is ascribed. Indeed, it is likely to be recorded because it is unique, but the fact that it has been recorded is a temptation for his teacher and for subsequent teachers to generalize upon it. Pupils make mistakes and outgrow them, and such mistakes should not be a matter of permanent record.

Interpretation and Use of Results

The following discussion of the interpretation and use of results of evaluation is limited to the results obtained from certain standardized tests, in such areas as reading, arithmetic, study skills, and correctness of written expression. Results of such tests deal with abilities that every school seeks or should seek to develop. They represent areas in which the critics of schools have special interest. They furnish data that are sufficiently precise to make possible dependable comparisons with results obtained in other schools. In many schools they are the only evaluation results that are kept in the central office.

These tests deal, however, with only one part of the curriculum, altho a very important part. Moreover, they do not measure all the abilities even in the areas tested, and the data that they provide must be supplemented and validated by other evidence. In other words, they are an aid to judgment in evaluation but not a substitute for it.

As earlier indicated, the controlling purpose for an evaluation program is to provide data for the improvement of instruction. To accomplish this purpose the data must be used. One of the commonest misuses of the results of tests is to make no real use of them at all except to satisfy the curiosity of the administrative and supervisory staff as to how the local school stands in relation to the test norms, after which the tests are filed away and forgotten. When this occurs, the time and money expenditure involved in giving the tests cannot be justified. The results must be used. Use involves a critical interpretation of the pertinence and adequacy of the test results in relation to the local program of instruction and a careful study of the implications of the test scores for the improvement of the program. Several problems arise in connection with these two processes.

Preventing Misunderstanding of Test Results

It should be clearly understood that the purpose of giving these tests is to obtain evidence on the achievement of individual pupils—not on the efficiency of classroom teachers. This distinction is important because it affects the attitudes of teachers toward evaluation.

The scores made by pupils in a given class are the result of many influences, of which the classroom teacher's efficiency is only one. Achievement also depends upon such factors as the intelligence of the pupils, their instruction in earlier years, their socio-economic background, the adequacy of instructional equipment, the teaching load, and the nature of the methods which the teacher is encouraged or required to use. The student's behavior at any given time is a function of all of his experiences to date, both in school and out of school. For example, his poor arithmetic performance in the eighth grade may be heavily influenced by his learning experiences in arithmetic in Grades V and VI. Evaluation of a given unit of instruction must, therefore, be based on *changes* in the student's behavior during a given period of instruction, not just on his status at the close of the period.

Interpreting Local Achievement in Relation to Standard Norms

The significance of the norms on standard tests should be clearly understood. These norms merely depict the achievement in the school populations from which the norms have been developed. They do not indicate the degree of ability needed in life, nor do they represent the level of achievement which could readily be reached if the best available procedures were used. They are not standards to be set up as goals to be reached. Therefore, the results obtained by giving a standardized test in a local school system merely describe local achievement in relation to the norms. They do not necessarily tell whether the achievement is excellent or poor. Each school must decide, in terms of its total program, what level of achievement in a given area is desirable and is reasonable to expect its pupils to reach.

Utilizing the Data on Individual Differences

Perhaps the most significant evidence provided by standard tests is the evidence on individual differences. Wide ranges of ability have been repeatedly shown in every grade in every ability which has been adequately measured. Cook, for example, reported the range of achievement from the 2nd to the 98th percentile at the sixth-grade level to be between seven and eight years in "reading comprehension, vocabulary, the mechanics of English composition, literary knowledge, science, geography, and history," and between six and seven years in arithmetic. These facts have suggested to some the policy of retarding weak students and promoting the bright, but in a carefully controlled experiment Cook found that schools following this practice did not raise the level of their achievement or, in general, reduce the range of abilities. They did, however, succeed in increasing retardation! [16]

The data on ranges of achievement in reading are especially significant because achievement in other fields is so heavily dependent upon the degree of reading ability which students have developed. The range of scores in one standardized reading test of nearly 6809 seventh-grade pupils was more than eight times the difference between the medians of the seventh and eighth grade. The range of scores from the 25th to the 75th percentile was nearly three times as great as the difference between the medians of the sixth and seventh grades and greater than the difference between the medians of Grade VI and Grade VIII. Altho the range in reading ability in a single grade is usually somewhat less than this, it is always so great that it constitutes a serious problem.[17]

One of the most feasible solutions to this problem is to provide for each grade books with a range of reading difficulty commensurate with the range of reading ability. There is no better evidence of the failure to use test results than the fact that altho wide ranges of ability have been known since the first reading tests were given, this one essential requirement for meeting individual differences has in most school systems not yet been met.

It is possible that the impressions which some patrons form regarding deficiencies in achievement in such subjects as spelling,

---

[16] Lindquist, E. F., editor, *op. cit.*, Chapter 1, "The Functions of Measurement in the Facilitation of Learning," by Walter W. Cook, p. 3.

[17] Horn, Ernest. *Methods of Instruction in the Social Studies.* New York: Charles Scribner's Sons, 1937. p. 45-47.

arithmetic, and reading are gained from their experiences with graduates who are low in the general distribution of ability. Obviously, the lower fourth of students in any one of these abilities constitutes a considerable population. Some of these students, upon leaving school, are undoubtedly employed in positions where deficiencies in basic abilities are readily noted.

Utilizing Test Results for Curriculum Reconstruction

The worth of any curriculum must be appraised in terms of the desirable changes it makes in the behavior (such as, knowledge and abilities) of students. The results of standardized tests provide valuable data, in the behaviors measured, for making these appraisals. These data, however, must be used judiciously. Attention was called earlier to the need of careful interpretation of achievement in arithmetic in the primary grades as measured by standard tests, the norms of which are heavily influenced by traditional drill practices.

The scores made on standardized reading tests also require critical interpretation. Suppose, for example, that achievement in a local school system is found to be low in comparison with the norms on an adequately descriptive reading test. How shall these low scores be interpreted? The whole program for the development of reading ability needs to be re-examined. The low scores may be due in part to the way in which reading is taught in periods specifically set apart for the development of reading abilities, but, to a much larger extent, they are likely to be due to the failure to provide in other curriculum fields, as in social studies, conditions favorable to the development of these abilities.

Particularly objectionable is the widespread practice of giving page assignments to a single textbook followed by an oral quiz in which the questions may be answered by parroting the words of the text. There are many reasons why such practice is unfavorable to the development of reading abilities: (a) it does not set up purposes for which pupils should read; (b) it gives no opportunity for learning how to find and utilize references; (c) it provides no criteria as to which facts to select and which to disregard; (d) it provides no criteria for the organization of these facts; and (e) most important, it does not provide for differences in reading ability. So intimately is reading bound up with successful learning in other fields that poor reading scores on an adequately analytical and well-balanced reading test are almost certain proof of poor teaching in other curriculum fields where books are used.

Those Responsible for Evaluation

The discussion up to this point should show how intricately related are the problems of evaluation and the problems of curriculum construction. This fact suggests that the staff responsible for evaluation should either be a part of or closely affiliated with the staff responsible for instruction.

Competent and Enthusiastic Leaders Needed

A wide variety of administrative plans are in vogue for selecting and utilizing the staff members who are to guide the evaluation of instruction. But if the program of evaluation is to be comprehensive and effective, competent and enthusiastic leaders are needed. The problems of evaluation are complex and, in certain respects, exceedingly technical, such as the selection of appropriate tests, the preparation and interpretation of manuals for testing, plans for scoring, tabulating and reporting results, and ways of helping classroom teachers to improve their own appraisals. All these require a high degree of specialized training, experience, and sound judgment. The need for technical competence is obvious, but this competence will be largely wasted or misdirected unless guided by a substantial grasp of problems of teaching and problems of curriculum construction.

The Importance of Participation by Classroom Teachers

It is now fairly common practice for classroom teachers to share the responsibility for curriculum construction. All the rights, benefits, and limitations applicable to this practice are applicable to teacher participation in evaluation. However, such participation has lagged behind participation in curriculum making. There are more curriculum workshops than evaluation workshops. The two types of participation should be closely integrated. Effective teacher participation, however, as previously pointed out, requires competent and inspiring leadership.

Among the more important reasons for teacher participation in the evaluation program are the following:

1. Classroom teachers can make valuable contributions, often indispensable, in determining what behaviors should be evaluated, the degree of accomplishment which it is reasonable to expect at the various grade levels, the appropriateness of proposed evaluation instruments as measures of the curriculum objectives, and particularly the relevance of proposed measures to the objectives that guide instruction in their own classes.[18]

2. They can aid in the experimental tryout of standardized tests and of other technics of appraisal. In many cities such tests are not chosen for systemwide use until they have been tried out in a number of classrooms in order to secure the judgment of teachers as to their appropriateness in terms of the school objectives, difficulties of administration and scoring, and the interpretation and use to be made of results. Such preliminary tryouts are equally valuable for any form of appraisal intended for citywide use.

3. Committees of teachers, with the aid of the central staff, may undertake to devise methods of evaluating special units and to assist in planning for the evaluation of areas not now adequately measured by standardized tests.

4. Participation in the evaluation program is one of the best methods of helping classroom teachers clarify their own objectives as well as their understanding of the ultimate objectives set up for the entire curriculum.

5. Participation also helps classroom teachers to grow in their understanding of the purpose of evaluation and to improve their own evaluation procedures. It goes a long way toward removing the distrust and uneasiness which teachers have when the evaluation program is planned solely in the central office.

6. The most compelling argument for the participation of classroom teachers is that the effective utilization of the results of any type of evaluation largely depends upon them. Moreover, the teacher's attitude toward evaluation is certain to be reflected in the attitudes of the students.

The Importance of Participation by Pupils

The basic thesis of the preceding pages of this chapter is that the controlling purpose of evaluation is to guide, facilitate, and safeguard the development of behaviors needed to deal effectively with the most important situations in the pupils' present and future life. It is not enough that school administrators and classroom teachers appreciate and understand that this is the purpose of the program

---

[18] In this connection one may ponder Plato's statement: "When a man cannot measure, and a great many others who cannot measure declare he is four cubits high, can he help believing what they say." From *Plato's Republic*, Jowett Translation, Modern Library Edition, Book IV, 426, p. 138.

of appraisal; it should be understood and appreciated also by the students. Probably the most important factor in determining the validity and usefulness of the results of any type of appraisal is the attitude of the pupils toward it. Unless the pupils understand the purpose of the appraisal and take it seriously, the appraisal will fall far short of its potential influence upon their learning. This statement holds whether the appraisal is a standardized test, a teacher-made test, or an appraisal made by the pupils themselves.

Since the turn of the century, classroom teachers in our best schools have sought increasingly to encourage the participation of pupils in setting up problems, in planning the attack upon them, and in the general management of their school activities. It is equally important that pupils understand the purposes for which different types of appraisals are made and share, as far as is practicable, in the processes of appraisal. In fact, the setting up of a purpose to be accomplished implies that both teachers and pupils will want to know whether or not their goal has been reached.

The participation of pupils should be encouraged in many ways. Consider first the appraisals instituted by others, whether the appraisal instrument is a standardized test, a teacher-made test, or a rating of a performance, as in music. The pupil should understand the purpose of the appraisal, the results should be reported to him and carefully interpreted with him, and they should be used as the basis for planning future work. If the appraisal deals with behaviors not specifically set up by teachers and pupils as immediate objectives, the pupils should understand this fact. Suppose, for example, that the pupils in a given school have had only limited instruction regarding Canada. The teacher may say: "We have spent only a little time in the study of Canada. Perhaps there are some important problems that we did not consider. Leading scholars who know about Canada think that there are certain important things that every citizen of the United States should understand about our neighbor. Some of the most important things have been included in this test. Shall we see how many of these things we have learned?" Time devoted to making clear the nature of an appraisal is well spent.

But it is not enough that students understand the purposes of tests instituted by others or that the results be reported to them. The pupil should be encouraged and helped to make appraisals on his own initiative. Whether or not he forms the habit of self-appraisal

340

is one good index of the vitality of the total appraisal program. It is difficult to describe the inspiring morale in a school in which students share in setting up their goals, accept the responsibility for attaining them, and participate in appraising the success of their efforts. But no one who has known such schools is likely to be satisfied with any other kind.

SELECTED REFERENCES

AMERICAN EDUCATIONAL RESEARCH ASSOCIATION. "Educational and Psychological Testing." *Review of Educational Research* 20: 5-97; February 1950. $1.50.

DRESSEL, PAUL L., and SCHMID, JOHN. *Evaluation of the Tests of General Educational Development*. Washington, D. C.: American Council on Education, 1951. 57 p.

GREENE, HARRY A.; JORGENSEN, ALBERT N.; and GERBERICH, J. RAYMOND. *Measurement and Evaluation in the Secondary School*. New York: Longmans, Green and Co., 1943. 670 p.

LINDQUIST, E. F. *Educational Measurement*. Washington, D. C.: American Council on Education, 1951. 819 p.

MICHEELS, WILLIAM J., and KARNES, M. RAY. *Measuring Educational Achievement*. New York: McGraw-Hill Book Co., 1950. 496 p.

NATIONAL SOCIETY FOR THE STUDY OF EDUCATION. *The Measurement of Understanding*. Forty-Fifth Yearbook, Part I. Chicago: University of Chicago Press, 1946. 338 p.

SEGEL, DAVID. *State Testing and Evaluation Programs*. Circular No. 320. Washington, D. C.: U. S. Office of Education, Federal Security Agency, 1951. 38 p. Single copy free.

WEITZMAN, ELLIS, and MCNAMARA, WALTER J. *Constructing Classroom Examinations*. Chicago: Science Research Associates, 1949. 153 p.

WRIGHTSTONE, J. WAYNE. "Evaluation." *Encyclopedia of Educational Research*. Revised edition. (Edited by Walter S. Monroe.) New York: Macmillan Co., 1950. p. 403-407.

CHAPTER TWELVE

Appraising the School's Total Effectiveness

THE curriculum is influenced by many varieties of evaluation. A penetrating comment by a parent may help to bring about the introduction of a new course. Concern over the number of students who do not graduate from high school may lead to a change in teaching method. Study of mental health statistics may induce changes in teacher-pupil relations. Not all evaluation is or can be done by the careful scientific procedures described in Chapter XI. While educators must continue to evaluate as much of the curriculum as they can by technical and objective methods, attention also should be given to the other useful methods of appraisal.

This chapter is a plea for a broad, common-sense type of evaluation of the large, important and over-all matters. It suggests that we look not only at classroom teaching but at our total product. The chapter attempts to relate evaluation to three important issues: (a) Is the school keeping abreast of changing social conditions? (b) Can the effect of the school on youth be measured? and (c) Can the effectiveness of the school administrator be measured?

The Curriculum and Social Change

There is a genuine concern on the part of many adults to know more about the quality of the young people who are a product of the American schools. Adults are aware of the enormous changes which the automobile, radio, television, atomic energy, and airplanes are making in modern living. They wish assurance that the school is able to adjust to these new conditions and still maintain a high level of literacy, morality, ambition, and productivity among our young people. Many parents and other citizens want to know how to make their community a place where constructive influences will reinforce the school's program.

People Ask Questions

How loyal are our youth to the ideals of democracy? Why do so many young persons enter careers of crime? With the greater number of high-school graduates, why, still, do so few people vote? What about the moral fiber of youth? Were the basketball scandals and cheating revelations of recent years merely episodes? Or were they significant trends?

Educators confronted with these questions must admit that they cannot be sure how much influence schools have on the human behavior illustrated by such queries. Social conditions and educational efforts are intertwined. Cause and effect relations are too enmeshed to guarantee that a certain school procedure will result in a specific behavior years later. Home, church, television, and companions exert educative force as well as schools. The "condition of the times" may be more powerful than schools. These things are not known with certainty.

Questions Partly Answered

Most educators would agree with a recent comment of Bertrand Russell's:

I think a certain standard of good manners is essential to the smooth running of social and family life. I should concede to the modern educator that a parent should not be rude to his child, but I do not think it follows that the child should be rude to his parent. This is one of the many limitations on the doctrine that the child's impulses should remain unchecked.[1]

It would take a modern Diogenes to locate a classroom teacher, principal, or superintendent who did not want boys and girls to be well-mannered. Modern educators desire boys and girls to be courteous, respectful to their elders, orderly, honest, and punctual. They have lost none of their zeal for these time-honored traits. While placing emphasis on self-discipline, individual initiative, and creative thinking, they have continued to try to develop boys and girls who are not "rude to parents." But just as the distinguished British philosopher appraised the boys and girls of the current generation, so too, do others judge the work of the schools. School leadership must find ways to answer these judgments.

[1] Russell, Bertrand. "As School Opens—The Educators Examined." *The New York Times Magazine,* September 7, 1952. p. 9, 44-45.

Consider another example. The facts revealed by physical and health examinations of American youth during World War II caused a number of changes in the physical education programs in American schools. In spite of protests that low standards of living, inadequacy of medical care, and faulty food habits were potent causes of youth's physical defects, many schools revised their programs of health education under the impact of criticism. Questions have been raised as to whether some of these changes were desirable.[2] The fact is that the school curriculum was changed even tho accurate data about the relations of school procedures to health conditions were not known. Some indication of these changes will be found in *Health in Schools,* revised AASA yearbook issued in 1951.

Similar pressures for curriculum change are occurring in other important areas. Higher divorce rates bring pleas for more home and family life education. Poor turnouts at elections cause demands for better citizenship education. Traffic accident rates emphasize the need for driver training. In spite of the difficulty of evaluating the work of the school in these broad social areas, appraisals are made and curriculum changes are urged.

Election time is usually a period when educators can look for this type of social appraisal. Each election results in pleas for the schools to help get to the polls a larger percent of the voting public. The facts here are clearer than in some other social data. The more education a person has the more likely it is that he will vote. The percent of college graduates voting is greater than that of high-school graduates; the percent of high-school graduates voting is greater than that of elementary-school graduates.[3] The process of education, apparently, is influential in getting people to vote.

Along with voting records, some people are concerned about the lack of knowledge of the American people on many important issues. Is ignorance a product of social conditions or of inadequate schools? Public opinion polls periodically show that the American people have an appalling ignorance of current affairs, geography, history, and election issues. Thoughtless critics infer that schools are not

---

[2] See, for example: Hunsicker, Paul. "The Importance of Physical Fitness." *The University of Michigan School of Education Bulletin* 23: 54-55; January 1952.

[3] See "Interview with George Gallup." *United States News and World Report* 32: 57; May 23, 1952.

producing results. Yet, public opinion experts examine these facts and conclude:

Interviewers who gather public opinion are accustomed to hearing the expression of apathetic, narrow, uninformed viewpoints, but it is significant that many . . . gradually tend toward sympathy for persons of this type. They talk so often with families who are weighed down by a pressing burden of personal problems, with women who wear themselves out daily with the care of large families in substandard living quarters; they encounter abject poverty, crushing illness. . . . We should not be too critical, nor too impatient. And it would be well to realize that the remedy does not always and necessarily lie in the realm of mere information and education. Sometimes the task is only to free people from their pressing concern with personal problems so that they may have occasional opportunities to look out to broader horizons.[4]

Startled by the arrests of youth, some critics condemn the schools for the crime rate. Yet one student searching for evidence of the school influence on crime reduction concluded: "The causes of crime are myriad and too complex to permit the blame for them to be placed on one social force or individual source. To blame the school for the current high rate of crime, for instance, would be to discount the influences of the home, church, the community, the recreational programs—in fact, the influences of all the social forces at work in the incidental or accidental education of the American citizen today. . . ."[5]

Continuous Community Records Needed

Divorce rates, election returns, juvenile-delinquency rates, the manners of youth, and crime records make interesting reading. They reveal sometimes startling human weaknesses, but they have not been useful for the individual school system. One reason for the inability to use such data effectively has been that the causes behind the behavior of persons are exceedingly complex and are different for different individuals. We need studies and continuous records of individual behavior as related to social factors.

Another reason for not establishing clearer relationships between school procedures and later behavior is that most data of these types are available chiefly on a national basis. Rarely are

[4] National Council for the Social Studies. *The Teaching of Contemporary Affairs.* Twenty-First Yearbook. Washington, D. C.: the Council, a department of the National Education Association, 1950. 233 p. (See especially, Chapter 2, "The Current Status of American Public Opinion" by Herbert H. Hyman and Paul B. Sheatsley, p. 34.)

[5] Lauck, Marie T. "A Search for Evidence That Guidance in School Prevents Delinquency in Adults." *School Review* 56: 26-35; January 1948.

such data collected for the individual school or school district. How many graduates of School X are divorced? How many young people who once attended School X have entered careers of crime? Until such information is collected by schools in differing localities, schools are not going to know enough about the relationship of total educational programs to later adult behavior.

There is need for a few schools to pioneer in the collection of pertinent community data. Records of broken windows, broken street lamps, and destruction of public property by vandals—if systematically collected by a few individual schools—might give clues to the effectiveness of the school program. Analysis of police records, voting returns, health data, and juvenile court records, if limited to the students who attended particular schools, may help provide better understanding of the cause and effect relationship of individual school programs to these highly important social behaviors that are ultimately reflected in broad social trends.

At the present moment analyses of the 1950 Census data are becoming available. The United States at mid-century will be studied for changes in social conditions. Schools will be judged, rightly or wrongly, in terms of these social trends. Educators, while striving to get better information about specific school situations, will need to re-examine the curriculum to be sure that schools are not lagging behind the times.

Appraising the School's Product

The search to know more about the effect of schooling upon youth has been a persistent appraisal technic. Several significant attempts have been made to get a better understanding of the long-time effect of school practices. The Eight-Year Study influenced high-school education thru a careful analysis of the work of high-school graduates while they were in college.[6] The Maryland Study of Youth during the depression years revealed weaknesses in civic and vocational education.[7] These and similar studies have pointed to paths that may lead to better appraisal of our school's product. A few promising evaluation practices which are currently receiving attention will be summarized at this point.

[6] Aikin, Wilford M. *The Story of the Eight-Year Study.* New York: Harper and Brothers, 1942. 157 p.

[7] Bell, Howard M. *Youth Tell Their Story.* Washington, D. C.: American Council on Education, 1938. 273 p.

346

Drop-out Studies

The loss of approximately 50 percent of our youth between Grade V and high-school graduation has brought about serious studies of those who are "early-school-leavers." West Virginia, Syracuse, Louisville, Detroit, Denver, and other places have studied these early school drop-outs.[8] A number of studies of school drop-outs have been made but others are needed to bring out specific factors which will result in curriculum improvements.

The Denver procedure was fairly typical. At North High School a questionnaire was mailed to a sampling of one-fourth of the graduates and of the drop-outs during the years between 1942 and 1950. All students from these classes attending college received another questionnaire. The students enrolled at the high school during the year 1949-50 replied to the Illinois Inventory of Pupil Opinion.[9] Based on the replies, the conclusions reached were:

1. More boys than girls left school

2. More mid-year entry students were lost than fall entry students

3. Drop-outs showed a lack of participation in activities

4. Mid-year students participated less in school activities than did fall entry students

5. Boys were more dissatisfied with the number and variety of school subjects than were girls

6. Teachers need to make increased efforts to know students well and to be interested in their problems.[10]

The North High School Study did not show much adverse criticism of the courses offered. Improved teacher-pupil relationships seemed to be of greater importance.

Other studies have shown that dissatisfaction with school loomed larger. Dillon found that among the reasons for disliking school to the point of leaving were: preferred work to school, not interested in schoolwork, could not learn and was discouraged, was failing and did not want to report grade, disliked a certain teacher, disliked

---

[8] See: Boyer, Phillip A.; Desing, Minerva F.; and Laird, Mary Alice. "Conditions Affecting the Guidance Program." *Review of Educational Research* 21: 89-90; April 1951.

[9] Hand, Harold C.: Finlay, Gilbert C.: and Dolio, Ardwin J. *Illinois Inventory of Pupil Opinion.* Secondary-school form. Yonkers-on-Hudson: World Book Co., 1948. 6 p.

[10] Summarized from materials submitted by Superintendent Kenneth E. Oberholtzer. *Report of Life Adjustment Study, North High School.* Denver, Colorado, June 29, 1951. (Mimeo.)

a certain subject, and could learn more out of school than in school.[11] In the Syracuse study, 61 percent of the reasons checked by drop-outs were school situations.[12]

The drop-out study has become an appraisal device that is especially useful at the initial stages of curriculum change. The Illinois Study of the Secondary School Curriculum provides helpful information on methods of conducting such holding power studies.[13]

Follow-up Studies

Follow-up studies of high-school graduates have been employed to evaluate the relation of school programs to later activities of young people. The early studies of this type were limited to attempts to determine vocational interests and types of employment. This information has helped curriculum committees to ascertain if the schools were adequately preparing graduates for their jobs. Many of these studies, made in the 1930's, are not of great value today in suggesting curriculum changes.

More recent follow-up studies have gathered information about marital status, number of children, religious, social, and civic activities. These broader types of studies seem to yield refreshing insights into the total effect of the school program.[14]

For many years colleges and universities have invited secondary-school personnel to participate in freshman conferences. A purpose of these conferences has been to ascertain how well freshmen were getting along in the university environment. By means of conferences with faculty members and interviews with former students, some high-school principals and counselors have found ways by which they could improve their college preparatory work.

This same technic has been useful when applied to business and industrial life. Employers, personnel managers, and labor union leaders are willing to set up similar conferences for young workers who are in their "freshman year" in the business world. Such

[11] Dillon, Harold J. *Early School Leavers*. New York: National Child Labor Committee, 1949. p. 50.

[12] Smith, Harry P. *Syracuse Youth Who Did Not Graduate*. Syracuse, N. Y.: Board of Education, 1950. 61 p. (Mimeo.)

[13] Allen, Charles M. *How To Conduct the Holding Power Study*. Circular Series A, No. 51, Illinois Secondary School Curriculum Program Bulletin No. 3. Springfield, Ill.: State Department of Public Instruction, May 1949. 128 p.

[14] Ann Arbor Public Schools. *The Second Follow-up Report of the 1947 Graduation Class of the Ann Arbor High School*. Ann Arbor, Michigan, August 1950. (Duplicated)

conferences and related interviews of younger employees also aid classroom teachers and school administrators to locate strengths and weaknesses in the school curriculum and in the school product.

Opinion Surveys

Attempts to get the judgment of adults about the results of education have been frequent in recent years. Gallup, Roper, and others have demonstrated the usefulness of polling technics in many types of situations. They have evolved a tool which educators have found useful. Weaknesses in knowledge about geographic information, election issues, international affairs and other public questions have caused a search for improved ways to teach social studies.[15] The shortcomings brought out in such surveys have been a powerful defense against those who would limit schools to teaching about past events.

Questionnaires and opinion polls are used increasingly to get data about adult attitudes toward schools.[16] The Michigan State Department of Public Instruction distributed a questionnaire, *How Would You Answer This?* to thousands of persons in many communities. Prepared by specialists at the request of the Michigan Educational Policies Commission, a committee of prominent lay and educational leaders, the four-page questionnaire was designed to determine how valid were current criticisms of the schools. Results from a variety of communities indicate that there is substantial support for the schools and that critics are in the minority. To such questions as the following 75 to 90 percent gave replies favorable to schools while only 10 to 25 percent were critical:

1. In your opinion, are today's youngsters who have finished grammar school as well educated as those you knew when you were a child?

2. How about those who graduate from high school nowadays—do you believe they are as well educated as high-school youngsters were when you were of that age?

3. Some people have the feeling that *too many* new ideas, experiments and changes are made in the schools of today. Do you agree?

---

[15] See, for example: Gallup, George H. "What We Don't Know *Can* Hurt Us." *The New York Times Magazine.* November 4, 1951. p. 12.

[16] Hand, Harold C. *What People Think About Their Schools.* New York: World Book Co., 1948. 217 p.

4. How do you feel about today's teachers? Do you consider them well-trained and up-to-date? [17]

Other instruments of this type which have been used in other places are:

1. *What Do We Know about Our Schools?*—Questions raised by some 200 people as they themselves have become involved in studying their schools. Published by the National Citizens Commission for the Public Schools, 2 West 45th Street, New York 19, New York, 1951. 15¢ each.

2. *15 Ways To Find Out*—A list of 15 questions proposed by Wilbur A. Yauch in his article, "How Good Are Your Schools?" *American Magazine* 62:41; September 1951.

3. *Just a Second*—A questionnaire which purports to find out, "How would you do it if you had the job of planning the very best schooling for your boys and girls?" Published by the National School Service Institute, Chicago, Illinois. 2¢ each.

4. *How Good Are Your Schools?*—Presents six qualities as the basis for evaluating your schools, and describes three levels—Grade C, Grade B, and Grade A—of desirability for each of the six. Prepared by William G. Carr of the National Education Association and distributed by the National Citizens Commission for the Public Schools, 2 West 45th Street, New York 19, New York. 10¢ each.

5. *Schools Are What We Make Them, A Handbook for Citizens*—Presents a checklist to help you judge how much you know about your schools. Offers suggestions as to the kinds of things you should know and where to get some of the answers. Prepared by the NEA Research Division and published by Bell and Howell Company, 7100 McCormick Road, Chicago 45, Illinois. Single copy free.

6. *Characteristics of a Good School*—Presents in question form standards for evaluating a school, its facilities, its staff, and its program. Pamphlet No. 7 of School Board Reference Library. Prepared for and distributed by the Illinois Association of School Boards, First National Bank Building, Springfield, Illinois. 35¢ each.

7. *How Good Is Your School?*—A "test" of 63 questions prepared by *Life* magazine as a practical way to measure the education children are getting. *Life* 29: 54-55; October 16, 1950.

These instruments aid school administrators to gauge the general climate of opinion with which schools have to deal.

Less formal methods of gathering opinions are also beneficial. One superintendent made a practice of personally inviting prominent citizens to accompany him on school visits. The appraisals growing out of the conversations which followed these visits helped

---

[17] Thurston, Lee M. *How Would You Answer This?* Lansing, Mich.: State Department of Public Instruction, 1951. 4 p.

the citizens to understand the school, but they also aided the superintendent to understand the types of activities and problems which were worrying the thoughtful citizens.

Other superintendents have made use of panels of parents, classroom teachers, and pupils to evaluate the school program at a variety of public meetings. Lay advisory committees have been useful, too, for evaluation purposes. Informal conferences with parents, teachers, and pupils are commonly employed also.

Opinions are not entirely valid or reliable for the appraisal of the total program of the school. But, until better devices are developed, the school as a social institution will be judged by many types of persons. The school curriculum can be improved if school people are aware of the kinds of judgments which exist and honestly attempt to ascertain these judgments by devices as objective as are available.

The School Administrator's Effectiveness

A third aspect of the total appraisal of the school product is receiving increasing attention—the measurement of the school administrator's effectiveness. Is a school system better or worse today than it was five years ago? How influential was the superintendent during those five years? This aspect of school evaluation has not received major attention. The effectiveness of classroom teaching has been a matter of serious study; the effectiveness of the supervisory and administrative services has not been subjected to such careful evaluation procedures.

If an administrator desires to determine whether a school is a better school today than it was five years ago, what technics are available to aid him? Two general methods exist: testing programs and judgments of people.

Regular Testing Programs

School systems maintaining annual testing programs have some basis for deciding whether progress or retrogression is taking place. If the same tests are given to successive classes as they progress thru school, some accurate statements can be made concerning the learning of pupils. If the median score in reading moves upward

351

from a grade level of 3.5 to 4.6 and so on to 7.2 in successive years, with the group remaining fairly constant, it is apparent that the group as a whole is improving each year. While the variations from year to year may be accounted for by several factors, the fact remains that growth is taking place. Certain difficult questions still remain unanswered: Are the gains the result of natural growth? Are they results of changed teaching methods? But, despite these questions, the public has some evidence on which to base its conclusions about the effectiveness of the school.

If, in addition to the evidence on the class's growth, comparisons can be made with previous classes, another type of evidence is obtained. If the Senior Class of 1953 had a median score of 12.3 in reading and the Class of 1948 had a median score of 12.2, both classes being about equal in size, ability, and cultural background, then most citizens would concede that the school was doing as well in reading in 1953 as in 1948. Since this illustrates a common worry among parents, the school administrator is justified in trying to collect the necessary evidence. It is one measure of his effectiveness as a school executive.

Testing programs when used for such purposes should include tests of more than one type. Tests of basic subjectmatter are essential. In addition, since modern educational programs receive a major support because they contribute to other worthwhile objectives, two other types of tests should be included: (a) tests of emotional or social adjustment, and (b) tests of specific skills such as critical thinking. A balanced testing program gives the opportunity to get evidence on a variety of objectives. Not all tests need to be given each year. A cycle system has merits when tests are repeated at intervals of two to five years.

The use of testing programs has certain dangers as discussed in Chapter XI. One of the greatest of these is that schools and administrators may be judged exclusively by national or state norms. It should be recognized that the norms for some tests have not been carefully described and that one cannot always know whether the pupils used to standardize the tests are comparable to those in a specific school. It is desirable, therefore, for schools to develop base lines for comparison purposes from their own data. Such comparisons are more defensible than statements that a particular school is above or below the published, national norm.

Opinion Polls and Checklists

The school administrator striving to determine the effectiveness of his own work can also make use of the judgments of people. One superintendent of a large city school system commented that he was grateful he did not have to be a candidate for election every four years as was true of the mayor of the city. The fact that superintendents are appointed has given professional status to school administration and has been beneficial to school systems. It has not, however, removed the desirability of keeping in touch with the general reactions of the people.

Some devices for obtaining reactions of citizens were described earlier in this chapter. In addition to the use of questionnaires with adult lay citizens, the use of checklists and polling devices with classroom teachers and students seems particularly justifiable by the administrator who is trying to discover the effectiveness of his own work.

The thoughtfully prepared questionnaire in which the superintendent honestly asks teachers how well he is doing may be his most effective device for determining his own status. When the replies to such devices are unsigned, but give evidence of thoughtful answers, the results give some indication of an administrator's status and progress. Used in successive years at periodic intervals, the cumulative effect can be to reveal strengths and weaknesses in the school system and in the administrative and supervisory practices.

Similar opinion research tools, when given to students in successive graduating classes, can be equally effective. As students are leaving a school, requests for their help in evaluating school practices usually meet with intelligent, thoughtful responses. The insights of students when compared over a period of several years can aid in measuring the effectiveness of one's work.

Better Evaluations Are Essential

The qualities of the young people of this generation are being evaluated by many different types of persons. One parent, whose child has become a useful citizen, points with pride to the accomplishments of home, church, and school. Another parent, whose first-born has been in trouble with the law, is bewildered by his own failure and wonders why the church and the school did not have more influence on his boy. One religious scholar contends that schools are producing "a nation of Henry Aldriches." [18] Another college professor points out that "No other people ever demanded so much of education as have the American. None other was ever served so well by its schools and educators." [19]

As adults look at young people today they seem to be deeply concerned with the question: How well are our schools doing? Sometimes they are interested solely in the competence of young people in the Three R's. Sometimes they are scrutinizing the ability of young people to help solve today's deep-seated social problems. Educators are well aware that the general public today is appraising the school's product.

This chapter has suggested that in the over-all appraisal of the school it is well to recognize that evaluation can be made in terms of three large questions:

1. Is the curriculum keeping up with changing social conditions?

2. Are the products of today's schools better, worse, or as good as those of earlier periods?

3. How effective is a school administrator over a given period of time?

There are no easy answers to these questions. Cause and effect relations are difficult to trace. Procedures are not refined. Data are difficult to gather. In spite of these obstacles, answers to such questions are being given constantly. The educator concerned about improving instruction strives to find better answers by using the most refined methods available.

---

[18] Bell, Bernard Iddings. "Know How vs. Know Why." *Life* 29: 89; October 16, 1950.
[19] Commager, Henry Steele. "Our Schools Have Kept Us Free." *Life* 29: 46; October 16, 1950.

SELECTED REFERENCES

CASWELL, HOLLIS L., editor. *The American High School.* Eighth Yearbook, John Dewey Society. New York: Harper and Brothers, 1946. 264 p. (See especially, Chapters 1-4, p. 1-69.)

FEATHERSTONE, WILLIAM B. *A Functional Curriculum for Youth.* New York: American Book Co., 1950. 276 p.

GRIZZELL, E. DUNCAN, and GARBER, LEE O., issue editors. "Critical Issues and Trends in American Education." *Annals of the American Academy of Political and Social Science* 265: 1-231; September 1949. Philadelphia: American Academy of Political and Social Science.

HOLLINGSHEAD, AUGUST B. *Elmtown's Youth.* New York: John Wiley and Sons, 1949. 480 p.

MILLER, VAN, and SPAULDING, WILLARD B. *The Public Administration of American Schools.* Yonkers-on-Hudson: World Book Co., 1952. 606 p. (See especially, Chapter 18, "How To Get a Community To Evaluate Its Schools," p. 451-74.)

SMITH, BONNIE OTHANEL; STANLEY, WILLIAM O.; and SHORES, J. HARLAN. *Fundamentals of Curriculum Development.* Yonkers-on-Hudson: World Book Co., 1950. (See especially, Chapter 24, "Experimental Appraisal of Curriculum Patterns," p. 583-617.)

TYLER, RALPH W. *Basic Principles of Curriculum and Instruction.* Chicago: University of Chicago Press, 1950. 83 p.

Venturing in Education

O UR COUNTRY began as an exciting venture which tempted explorers and stirred imagination. Children respond to the thrilling stories of how their nation came into being and adults should keep these memories ever before them. Our heritage is not only a new world but a new way of life which has not ceased to be a continuous venture of discovery, of sacrifice, of service, and of rewards.

Today the United States is still a land of promise for millions of people around the world because nowhere else are the opportunities so great for the common man, nor is there any land where the freedoms we cherish are so secure. Visitors from other countries marvel at the high standard of living—new homes, educational opportunities, numerous automobiles, good roads, great cities, abundant crops, and the vast length and breadth of this nation with its wide variety of rich resources. They admire the friendliness of the people and, beyond the imperfections which we recognize, they see democratic ideals in everyday operation. They understand that democracy does work.

It is the ventures of the past in the climate of democracy by an educated people which have made us creative and powerful. Nevertheless, there are in these times threats to our country both from within and without and with these threats we should be seriously concerned. But we should not for a moment despair, for the hazards that beset us today, like the uncharted waters of 1492, are simply challenges to beckon modern explorers to venture in a cause no less exciting than that which gave us birth. Such is the nature of freedom that only the unwillingness or inability of the people impose limitations upon their possibilities for strength and growth. And in the schools are the processes upon which we depend to tune the spirits and sharpen the abilities of the rising generation including the leaders who will be the explorers of each tomorrow.

The fundamental task of education, therefore, is unchanged; the complexities of this age simply make its success more vital. Patriots from the beginning have earnestly and repeatedly stressed the mission of free public schools for the preservation of country. Plato was among those who knew that the republic would perish if a single generation of youth were not instructed. Jefferson, Horace Mann, Theodore Roosevelt and countless leaders in our own country have preached "a crusade against ignorance" and have sought "to establish and improve the law for educating the common people" under the conviction "that the people alone can protect us against evils of misgovernment."

Such great truths as those just quoted from Thomas Jefferson, voiced by so many of our greatest statesmen, are magnified many fold in an age which has given us a startling new source of energy with both disturbing and inspiring vistas of new ways of life to follow. To insure positive directions, character, ideals, and spiritual awareness are essential, as never before. The how-to-think process must be extended, the ability to distinguish between truth and propaganda must be sharpened; and understanding and goodwill must be spread to make good neighbors of all people.

In such an age the school superintendent faces stirring ventures—a job with tremendous potentialities and grave responsibilities. All of the currents and cross-currents of the community touch his office. He must excel as a teacher, a businessman, a personnel director, a general manager skilled in public relations, a radio and television performer, a public speaker, a counselor in human relations, a positive force in race relations, and a leader in government and public affairs. Often these pressures have distracted his attention from his primary function as a professional leader.

To help the superintendent venture in curriculum development with staff and public, this yearbook has been prepared. Its chapters are keys to venturing. They present a platform for American education, a philosophy, a point of view. They stress that the nature of the child as well as the needs of society must be considered. Learning experiences are evaluated and patterns for organizing them are reviewed; the role of the classroom teacher and influences of home and community are examined. Ideas are given for setting action machinery in motion. Illustrations are supplied showing how changes have been made in elementary and secondary programs. Valuable are the aids for securing and using the materials of instruction. Evaluation is treated as an integral part of the program with principles, methods, and cautions explained. The ap-

357

praisal of the schools' product is not overlooked, and due attention is given the public's stake in the curriculum.

Here then is a call to action for educational statesmanship in this perilous period of our history. How well we meet this challenge will determine whether we shall keep and expand our freedoms in peace and prosperity or whether we shall be compelled to yield to enemies both within and without. In the struggle the youth of America constitute our best resource and our greatest hope. The responsibility is overwhelming to nurture them in body, mind, and spirit, and to give them faith.

This age brings democracy great opportunities as well as dangers. The same lines of attack will promote the one and curtail the other, provided educational leadership will keep open the channels of learning and enlightenment for American youth thru the stewardship of the free public schools.

OFFICIAL RECORDS

OFFICERS 1952-53

AMERICAN ASSOCIATION OF SCHOOL ADMINISTRATORS

A Department of the National Education Association of the United States

President

VIRGIL M. ROGERS, Superintendent of Schools, Battle Creek, Michigan

President-Elect

LAWRENCE G. DERTHICK, Superintendent of Schools, Chattanooga, Tennessee

Vicepresident

PEARL A. WANAMAKER, State Superintendent of Public Instruction, Olympia, Washington

Executive Secretary

WORTH MC CLURE, 1201 Sixteenth Street, N.W., Washington 6, D. C.

Assistant Secretary

SHIRLEY COOPER, 1201 Sixteenth Street, N.W., Washington 6, D. C.

Executive Committee

HERBERT B. BRUNER, Professor of Education, New York University, New York, N. Y.

PAUL D. WEST, Superintendent, Fulton County Schools, Atlanta, Georgia

G. ARTHUR STETSON, Superintendent of Schools, West Chester, Pennsylvania

WILL C. CRAWFORD, Superintendent of Schools, San Diego, California

THE PRESIDENT, PRESIDENT-ELECT, AND VICEPRESIDENT, ex officio

ROSTER OF MEMBERS

AMERICAN ASSOCIATION OF SCHOOL ADMINISTRATORS

A Department of the
National Education Association of the United States

Corrected to November 1, 1952

* Indicates the Life Members

This roster is arranged by states, and lists for each member his name, educational degrees, present position, and the year he assumed his present position. It does not indicate street addresses except where no other information is available.

ALABAMA

INDIVIDUAL MEMBERS

Alverson, Roy T., B.S.'28, M.S.'29, Ala. Polytech. Inst.; Supvr., Local Sch. Acctg., Montgomery, Ala., since 1948.

Armstrong, Louis E., B.S.'28, Southeastern State Col., Durant, Okla.; M.A.'31, Okla. Agrl. and Mech. Col.; Ph.D.'40, George Peabody Col. for Tchrs.; Pres., Ala. Educ. Foundation, and Dir., Indian Springs Sch., Helena, Ala.

Balch, B. L., B.S.'18, Ala. Polytech. Inst.; M.A.'28, Univ. of Ala.; Co. Supt. of Educ., Tuskegee, Ala., since 1946.

Banks, L. Frazer, A.B.'11, Univ. of Colo.; Officier d'Academie '19, Republic of France; M.A.'28, George Peabody Col. for Tchrs.; LL.D.'33, Birmingham-Southern Col.; Supt. of Sch., Birmingham, Ala., since 1942.

Baxter, Solomon, B.S.'29, Univ. of Ala.; M.S.'45, Ala. Polytech. Inst.; Co. Supt. of Sch., Dothan, Ala., since 1933.

Boyd, G. Robert, A.B.'31, Western Ky. State Tchrs. Col., Bowling Green; M.A.'38, Ph.D.'43, Univ. of Ky.; Dean, State Tchrs. Col., Troy, Ala., since 1947.

Brewster, C. M., A.B.'27, Howard Col.; Supt. of Sch., Sheffield, Ala., since 1927.

Brooks, Joseph T., A.B.'23, Morehouse Col.; A.M.'34, Atlanta Univ.; Asst. to the Pres., Alabama State Col., Montgomery, Ala., since 1950.

Browder, I. J., B.S.'28, Univ. of Ala.; Supt. of City Sch., Gadsden, Ala., since 1951.

Brown, LeRoy, B.S.'35, State Tchrs. Col., Jacksonville, Ala.; M.A.'39, Univ. of Ala.; Ed.D.'48, Tchrs. Col., Columbia Univ.; Dir., Gadsden Center, Univ. of Ala., Gadsden, Ala., since 1947.

Bryan, John Edwards, A.B.'15, Hampden-Sydney Col.; LL.D.'37, Howard Col.; L.H.D. '37, Birmingham-Southern Col.; Pres., Ala. Inst. for Deaf and Blind, Talladega, Ala., since 1948.

Burns, Cranford H., B.S.'36, M.A.'41, Univ. of Ala.; Ed.D.'48, Columbia Univ.; Asst. Supt. in chg. of Instr., Pub. Sch., Mobile, Ala.

Bynum, L. D., B.S.'17, Univ. of Ala.; M.A.'39, Tchrs. Col., Columbia Univ.; Co. Supt. of Educ., Troy, Ala., since 1947.

Campbell, T. J., A.B.'25, Univ. of Ala.; Supt. of Sch., Attalla, Ala., since 1942.

Carter, O. B., B.S.'29, Ala. Polytech. Inst.; M.A.'41, Univ. of Ala.; Supt. of Sch., Eufaula, Ala., since 1942.

Carter, R. A., A.B.'24, Talladega Col.; M.S.'35, Univ. of Mich.; Head, Dept. of Natural Science, and Dean, Ala. Agrl. and Mech. Col., Normal, Ala., since 1927.

Clark, Kenley J., B.A.'09, Univ. of Richmond; M.A.'21, Harvard Univ.; Supt. of Sch., Mobile, Ala., since 1944.

Coleman, Hulda, A.B.'40, Huntingdon Col.; Co. Supt. of Sch., Hayneville, Ala., since 1939.

Collins, Baxter W., B.S.'32, Ala. Polytech. Inst.; M.A.'37, George Peabody Col. for Tchrs; Co. Supt. of Sch., Selma, Ala., since 1950.

Creel, John Paul, B.S.'21, Ala. Polytech. Inst.; M.A.'32, Tchrs. Col., Columbia Univ.; Supvr., Sch. Transportation and Sch. Plant Maintenance, Co. Board of Educ., Talladega, Ala., since 1948.

*Culp, Delos P., B.S.'37, M.S.'40, Ala. Polytech., Inst.; Ed.D.'49, Tchrs. Col., Columbia Univ.; Assoc. Prof. of Educ., Ala. Polytech. Inst., Auburn, Ala., since 1952.

Dannelly, Clarence Moore, B.Ped.'07, State Tchrs. Col., Troy, Ala.; A.B.'12, L.H.D.'31, Birmingham-Southern Col.; M.A.'26, George Peabody Col. for Tchrs.; Litt.D.'31, Southwestern Univ.; LL.D.'32, Centenary Col.; Ph.D.'33, Yale Univ.; Supt. of Sch., Montgomery, Ala., since 1936.

Davis, Alonzo J., B.S.'31, M.S.'32, Howard Univ.; Ph.D.'47, Univ. of Minn.; Dean, Sch. of Educ., Tuskegee Inst., Tuskegee Institute, Ala., since 1949.

Davis, Harwell Goodwin, LL.B.'03, LL.D.'39, Univ. of Ala.; Pres., Howard Col., Birmingham, Ala., since 1939.

Deason, J. Powell, B.S.'37, State Tchrs. Col., Jacksonville, Ala.; M.A.'47, George Peabody Col. for Tchrs.; Supvg. Prin., Redmill Sch., Jasper, Ala., since 1942.

Dickinson, James O., B.Ped.'12, State Normal Col., Troy, Ala.; B.S.'30, M.A.'40, Univ. of Ala.; Co. Supt. of Sch., Gadsden, Ala., since 1948.

Drake, Joseph Fanning, B.A.'16, Talladega Col.; M.A.'26, Columbia Univ.; Ph.D.'38, Cornell Univ.; Pres., Ala. Agrl. and Mech. Col., Normal, Ala., since 1927.

Eddins, William N., B.A.'39, Henderson Col.; M.A.'46, Univ. of Ala.; Deputy Supt. of City Sch., Gadsden, Ala., since 1951.

Elliott, Woodrow W., A.B.'38, Howard Col.; M.A.'46, Univ. of Ala.; Co. Supt. of Educ., Columbiana, Ala., since 1951.

ALABAMA

*Fisher, Rayburn J., A.B.'29, Howard Col.; M.A.'35, Univ. of Ala.; Ed.D.'50, Tchrs. Col., Columbia Univ.; Asst. Supt. of Sch., Jefferson Co., Birmingham, Ala., since 1949.

Floyd, James P., B.S.'28, M.A. 36, Univ. of Ala.; State Supvr. of Temperance Educ., State Dept. of Educ., Montgomery, Ala., since 1951.

Flurry, Bruce, A.B., M.A.'27, Univ. of Ala.; Supt. of City Sch., Dothan, Ala., since 1935.

Formby, J. R., B.S.'28, M.S.'38, Ala. Polytech. Inst.; Co. Supt. of Educ., Wetumpka, Ala., since 1948.

Garrett, William Silas, A.B.'38, Huntingdon Col.; M.Ed.'48, Duke Univ.; Admin. Asst. to Supt. of Sch., Montgomery, Ala., since 1950.

Gibson, Roy, B.S.'26, M.A.'35, Univ. of Ala.; Co. Supt. of Sch., Ashville, Ala., since 1938.

*Glenn, Charles B., B.S.'91, M.S.'92, Ala. Polytech. Inst.; A.B.'96, Harvard Univ.; LL.D.'18, Univ. of Ala.; Litt.D.'31, Birmingham-Southern Col.; Pres., American Assn. of Sch. Admin., 1937-38; Honorary Life Member, American Assn. of Sch. Admin.; Supt. Emeritus of Sch., 3349 Dell Road, Birmingham, Ala., since 1943.

Gonce, Wilson F., B.S.'34, Middle Tenn. State Col.; Murfreesboro; M.A.'40, Univ. of Ala.; Supt. of City Sch., Ft. Payne, Ala., since 1948.

Greene, John Tom, B.S.'32, M.S.'35, Ala. Polytech. Inst.; Supt. of City Sch., Lanett, Ala., since 1946.

Greenhill, Noble F., B.A.'14, Univ. of Ala.; M.A.'25, Tchrs. Col., Columbia Univ.; Ph.D. '32, New York Univ.; Supvr. of Textbooks and Instr. Supplies, State Dept. of Educ., Montgomery, Ala., since 1944.

Greer, Hugh G., B.S.'17, Miss. Col.; A.M.'27, Univ. of Chicago; Co. Supt. of Sch., Monroeville, Ala., since 1930.

Grove, Frank L., A.B.'09, Univ. of Ala.; A.M.'17, Columbia Univ.; Secy., Ala. Educ. Assn., Montgomery, Ala., since 1928.

Hadley, J. H., B.S.'38, M.A.'41, Univ. of Ala.; Ed.D.'46, Columbia Univ.; Supt. of Sch., Tuscaloosa, Ala., since 1946.

Hamner, Herman B., Russell Co. Supt. of Sch., Phenix City, Ala., since 1920.

Hatch, Robert C., B.S.'35, Ala. State Col.; A.M.'39, Fisk Univ.; Ed.D.'46, Tchrs. Col., Columbia Univ.; Exec. Secy., Ala. State Tchrs. Assn.; State Supvr. of Instr., Ala. State Dept. of Educ.; and Prof. of Educ. (summer), Ala. State Col., Montgomery, Ala., since 1945.

Hicks, Delbert Gilford, B.S.'46, Ala. State Tchrs. Col.; Florence; M.A.'49, George Peabody Col. for Tchrs.; Co. Supt. of Sch., Scottsboro, Ala., since 1949.

Hill, W. W., A.B.'29, Oglethorpe Univ.; M.A.'35, Univ. of Ala.; Ed.D.'42, Columbia Univ.; Pres., State Tchrs. Col., Livingston, Ala., since 1944.

Howard, George, A.B.'12, Davidson Col.; M.A.'22, Ph.D.'24, Columbia Univ.; Prof. of Educ., Univ. of Ala., University, Ala., since 1946.

Jackson, Walter M., B.S.'20, Georgetown Col., Ky.; M.A.'27, Tchrs. Col., Columbia Univ.; Supt. of Sch., Decatur, Ala.

James, L. L., B.S.'39, George Peabody Col. for Tchrs.; M.S.'41, Ala. Polytech. Inst.; Supt. of Sch., Roanoke, Ala., since 1919.

Jeffcoat, Roy E., B.S.'36, State Tchrs. Col., Troy, Ala.; M.S.'41, Ala. Polytech. Inst.; Supt. of Sch., Troy, Ala., since 1946.

Johnson, Joseph H., A.B.'23, Univ. of Ky.; M.A.'32, Univ. of Ill.; Supt. of Sch., Andalusia, Ala., since 1943.

*Johnson, Kermit Alonzo, Certificate '34, State Tchrs. Col., Jacksonville, Ala.; B.S. in Ed.'38, M.A. in Ed. Adm.'44, Univ. of Ala.; Ed.D.'49, Tchrs. Col., Columbia Univ.; Co. Supt. of Sch., Tuscaloosa, Ala., since 1945.

Jones, W. J., B.S.'29, Univ. of Ala.; M.A.'34, Columbia Univ.; Co. Supt. of Educ., Camden, Ala., since 1923.

Judd, Zebulon, Ph.B.'03, Univ. of N. C.; A.M.'14, Columbia Univ.; L.H.D.'35, Birmingham-Southern Col.; Dean, Sch. of Educ., Ala. Polytech. Inst., Auburn, Ala., since 1915.

Kirby, T. H., A.B.'24, Birmingham-Southern Col.; M.S.'37, Ala. Polytech. Inst.; Supt. of Sch., Opelika, Ala., since 1946.

Lawrence, Rianzo Jay, B.A.'24, M.A.'38, Univ. of Ala.; Co. Supt. of Sch., Union Springs, Ala., since 1944.

Lawson, T. A., B.S.'32, Tuskegee Inst.; Dir. State Voc. Trade Sch., Birmingham, Ala., since 1948.

Leeman, Hafford R., M.A.'42, Univ. of Ala.; Co. Supt. of Educ., Decatur, Ala., since 1947.

Letson, John W., B.S.'32, Ala. Polytech. Inst.; M.A.'40, Ed.D.'49, Columbia Univ.; Supt. of Sch., Bessemer, Ala., since 1949.

McCall, W. Morrison, A.B.'23, Westminster Col.; A.M.'26, Ph.D.'30, Univ. of Mo.; Dir., Div. of Instr., State Dept. of Educ., Montgomery, Ala., since 1937.

McKee, Walter T., B.S.'33, M.A.'36, Univ. of Ala.; Asst. Supt. of Sch., Montgomery, Ala., since 1942.

Martin, Charles L., A.B.'18, Howard Col.; M.A.'40, Univ. of Ala.; Supt. of Sch., Sylacauga, Ala., since 1943.

Mellown, Elgin W., B.S.'25, Birmingham-Southern Col.; M.A.'28, Univ. of Ala.; Co. Supt. of Educ., Livingston, Ala., since 1939.

Moore, R. E., A.B.'23, Birmingham-Southern Col.; B.D.'25, Drew Theological Sem.; M.A.'42, Univ. of Ala.; Co. Supt. of Educ., Cullman, Ala., since 1929.

Mullins, David W., A.B.'31, Univ. of Ark.; M.A.'34, Univ. of Colo.; Ed.D.'41, Tchrs. Col., Columbia Univ.; Exec. Vicepres., Ala. Polytech. Inst., Auburn, Ala.

Myer, P. G., A.B.'22, Birmingham-Southern Col.; M.A.'35, Univ. of Ala.; Supt. of Sch., Alexander City, Ala., since 1948.

Nelson, Byron B., A.B.'28, Howard Col.; M.S.'35, Ala. Polytech. Inst.; Supt. of Sch., Tallassee, Ala., since 1935.

Nelson, Carey, Patterson, B.S.'25, M.A.'29, Univ. of Ala.; Ed.D.'46, Tchrs. Col., Columbia Univ.; Supt. of City Sch., Anniston, Ala., since 1951.

Nipper, Henry L., A.B.'21, Howard Col.; M.A.'39, Univ. of Ala.; Supt. of Sch., Florala, Ala., since 1944.

Norton, Elbert B., A.B.'23, L.H.D.'42, Birmingham-Southern Col.; LL.D.'42, Ala. Polytech. Inst.; Pres., State Tchrs. Col., Florence, Ala., since 1948.

Nunn, G. Virgil, B.S.'32, M.S.'35, Ala. Polytech. Inst.; Supt. of Sch., Fairfield, Ala., since 1946.

Nunnelley, Newman Franklin, B.S.'35, M.A.'40, Univ. of Ala.; Co. Supt. of Sch., Talladega, Ala., since 1947.

Parker, W. A., A.B.'25, Howard Col.; Supt. of Sch., Tarrant, Ala., since 1930.

Patrick, G. T., B.S.'37, Univ. of Ala.; Supt. of Sch., Jasper, Ala., since 1933.

Patterson, F. D., D.V.M.'23, M.S.'27, Iowa State Col.; Ph.D.'32, Cornell Univ.; Pres., Tuskegee Inst., Tuskegee Institute, Ala., since 1935.

362

Peacock, Otis L., B.S.'31, Univ. of Fla.; M.A.'37, George Peabody Col.; Dir. of Extension, State Tchrs. Col., Florence, Ala., since 1946.

Puryear, Boyd, B.S. in Ed.'39, Univ. of Ala.; M.A.'47, George Peabody Col. for Tchrs.; Supt. of City Sch., Tuscumbia, Ala., since 1945.

Raines, Vincent, A.B.'21, A.M.'22, Univ. of Ill.; Asst. Secy., Ala. Educ. Assn., Montgomery, Ala., since 1943.

Richardson, Creel, A.B.'25, Univ. of Alabama; A.M.'28, Trinity Col.; Hartford, Conn., Supt. of Sch., Ozark, Ala., since 1949.

Robinson, Ewell W., B.S.'30, Auburn Col.; Owner, Standard Sch. Serv., 3827 1st Ave., N. Birmingham, Ala., since 1934.

St. John, Vernon L., B.S.'28, M.A.'48, Univ. of Ala.; Supt. of Sch., Opp, Ala., since 1945.

Scarborough, C. L., D.E.'51, Columbia Univ.; Asst. Supt. of Sch., Mobile, Ala., since 1950.

Simmons, Ira Fred, A.B.'14, Howard Col.; A.M.'24, Ph.D.'34, George Peabody Col. for Tchrs.; Co. Supt. of Sch., Birmingham, Ala., since 1948.

Smith, Charles Bunyan, B.S.'22, M.A.'27, George Peabody Col. for Tchrs.; D.Ed.'41, Tchrs. Col., Columbia Univ.; Pres., State Tchrs. Col., Troy, Ala., since 1937.

Smith, Martha W., B.S.'23, M.A.'24, Univ. of Mo.; State Supvr., Sch. Attendance and Community Relations, State Dept. of Educ., Montgomery, Ala., since 1938.

Snellgrove, J. R., B.S.'38, State Tchrs. Col., Troy, Ala.; M.S.'43, Ala. Polytech. Inst.; Supt. of City Sch., Enterprise, Ala., since 1948.

Snuggs, William E., B.S.'20, Ala. Polytech. Inst.; M.A.'28, Tchrs. Col., Columbia Univ.; Supt. of Sch., Selma, Ala., since 1943.

Stone, Ernest, M.A.'38, Univ. of Ala.; Supt. of Sch., Jacksonville, Ala.

Taylor, Hugh L., B.S.'26, M.A.'31, Univ. of Ala.; Co. Supt. of Educ., Andalusia, Ala., since 1942.

Terry, W. J., B.S. in Ed.'25, M.A. in Ed.'31, Univ. of Ala.; LL.D.'51, Birmingham-Southern Col.; State Supt. of Educ., Dept. of Educ., Montgomery, Ala., since 1951.

Tharp, S. M., A.B.'09, Univ. of Ala.; Co. Supt. of Sch., Bay Minette, Ala., since 1918.

Thomas, Ralph C., A.B.'16, Univ. of Ala.; M.A.'24, Tchrs. Col., Columbia Univ.; Supt. of City Sch., Russellville, Ala., since 1928.

Tidwell, Robert E., B.S.'05, LL.D.'27, Univ. of Ala.; LL.D.'23, Birmingham-Southern Col.; M.A.'25, Columbia Univ.; Dean of Extension and Prof. of Educ., Univ. of Ala., University, Ala., since 1930.

Trenholm, H. Councill, A.B.'20, Morehouse Col.; Ph.B.'21, A.M.'25, Univ. of Chicago; LL.D., Allen Univ.; Pres., Ala. State Col. for Negroes, Montgomery, Ala., since 1925.

Turner, Rex A., B.A.'36, Howard Col.; M.S.'46, Ala. Polytech. Inst.; Pres., Montgomery Bible Col., Montgomery, Ala., since 1942.

Waldrop, Amos I., B.S., M.A. in Ed.'26, Univ. of Ala.; Co. Supt. of Educ., Jasper, Ala., since 1947.

White, Raymond H., B.S. in Ed.'18, Southwest Mo. State Tchrs. Col., Springfield; A.B.'19, Drury Col.; A.M.'24, Univ. of Chicago; Ed.D.'36, Columbia Univ.; Prof. of Sch. Admin., Ala. Polytech. Inst., Auburn, Ala.

White, Stephen Reece, B.S.'34, M.S.'39, Ala. Polytech. Inst.; Dir. of Admin. and Finance, State Dept. of Educ., Montgomery, Ala., since 1951.

Wood, C. R., B.S.'12, M.S.'14, Ala. Polytech. Inst.; Ph.D.'28, George Peabody Col. for Tchrs.; Dean, State Tchrs. Col., Jacksonville, Ala.

Woodward, H. B., Jr., A.B.'32, Howard Col.; M.A.'46, Univ. of Ala.; Ed.D.'48, Tchrs. Col., Columbia Univ.; Prof. of Educ. and Dir., Bur. of Educ. Research, Univ. of Ala., University, Ala.

Yates, L. W., B.S.'39, Ala. Polytech. Inst.; M.A.'44, George Peabody Col. for Tchrs.; Supt. of Sch., Cullman, Ala., since 1948.

INSTITUTIONAL MEMBER

Library, Ala. Polytech. Inst., Auburn, Ala.

ALASKA

INDIVIDUAL MEMBERS

Anderson, C. L., B.S. in Ed.'35, M.S. in Ed.'49, Univ. of Idaho; Supt. of Sch., Skagway, Alaska, since 1946.

Carlson, Carl R., B.A.'28, Univ. of Wash.; Supt. of Sch., Seward, Alaska, since 1947.

*Erickson, Everett R., A.B.'26, M.S.'33, Univ. of Idaho; Deputy Commr. of Educ. for Alaska, P.O. Box 586, Juneau, Alaska, since 1949.

Morgan, A. W., B.S.'28, Utah State Agric. Col.; M.S.'41, Univ. of Idaho; Supt. of Sch., Anchorage, Alaska, since 1951.

Shuff, Robert V., B.Ed.'45, Univ. of Toledo; Supt. of Sch., Hoonah, Alaska, since 1950.

ARIZONA

INDIVIDUAL MEMBERS

Abbott, A. D., B.A.'30, Hanover Col.; M.A.'36, Ed.D.'51, Univ. of Colo.; Supt., Yuma Union H. S. Dist., Yuma, Ariz., since 1951.

Adams, A. D. Lon, B.S.'34, M.A.'51, Ariz. State Col.; Supt. of Pub. Sch., Bagdad, Ariz., since 1945.

Ashe, Robt. W., M.A.'42, Ariz. State Col., Tempe; Supt. Glendale Union H. S., Glendale, Ariz., since 1946.

Austin, Wilfred G., A.B.'26, Univ. of Ariz.; M.A.'33, Stanford Univ.; Supt. of Sch., Chandler, Ariz., since 1937.

Best, (Mrs.) Bessie Kidd, M.A.'48, Ariz. State Col.; Co. Supt. of Sch., Flagstaff, Ariz., since 1929.

Booth, Raymond E., B.S.'29, Kansas State Tchrs. Col., Pittsburg; M.A.'35, Univ. of Ariz.; Supt. of Sch., Winslow, Ariz., since 1939.

Bowie, Arthur J., B.A.'38, Ariz. State Col., Tempe; M.A.'42, Ariz. State Col., Flagstaff; Supt. of Sch., Williams, Ariz., since 1945.

Burggraaf, Stanley R., A.B.'28, Rutgers Univ.; M.Ed.'36, Harvard Univ.; Supt. of Sch., Florence, Ariz., since 1949.

Carmody, John F., Area Dir. of Sch., Window Rock, Ariz.

Carlson, Charles A., A.B.'21, Univ. of Ariz.; M.A.'24, Stanford Univ.; Asst. Supt. of Sch. in charge of Sec. Educ., Tucson, Ariz., since 1934.

Case, Arthur Maurice, B.S. in Ed., M.S. in Ed.'40, Univ. of Southern Calif.; Prin., Lower Miami Sch., Miami, Ariz., since 1934.

Case, Randolph V., B.A.'39, Ariz. State Col., Flagstaff; Prin., Washington Elem. Sch., Sonora, Ariz., since 1944.

Clark, James J., M.S. in Ed.'37, Univ. of Southern Calif.; Supt. of Osborn Sch., Phoenix, Ariz., since 1946.

Coor, L. F., M.A.'46, Colo. State Col. of Educ., Greeley; Prin., Avondale Sch., Avondale, Ariz., since 1936.

Crites, Kenneth K., A.B.'32, B.S.'38, Salem Col. (W. Va.); Supt. of Sch., Navaho Serv., Ganado, Ariz., since 1945.

Cromer, Sturgeon, A.B.'32, Ariz. State Col., Flagstaff, Ariz.; M.A.'40, Univ. of Ariz.; Supt. of Sch., Flagstaff, Ariz., since 1947.

Curtis, Loren S., A.B.'32, M.A.'37, Univ. of Ariz.; Supt. of H. S., Casa Grande, Ariz., since 1948.

Dingess, L. C., Asst. Supt. in chg. of Bus. Affairs, Yuma H. S., Yuma, Ariz.

Donaldson, Marion, Supt., Amphitheater Sch., Tucson, Ariz.

Dyer, Kenneth, B.A.'32, Ariz. State Col.; Supt., Elem. Sch., Tolleson, Ariz., since 1942.

Eastburn, Lacey A., Ed.D.'36, Stanford Univ.; Pres., Ariz. State Col., Flagstaff, Ariz., since 1947.

Fairbanks, Joseph Harrison, B.S.'21, Univ. of Del.; M.S.'35, Univ. of Southern Calif.; Dist. Supt. of Sch., Morenci, Ariz., since 1939.

Fulghum, Ruby E., Co. Supt. of Sch., Bisbee, Ariz., since 1931.

Gammage, Grady, B.A.'16, M.A.'22, LL.D.'27, Univ. of Ariz.; Ed.D.'40, New York Univ.; Pres., Ariz. State Col., Tempe, Ariz., since 1933.

Gardner, Gladys, Educ. Specialist-Home Econ., Bureau of Indian Affairs, Phoenix, Ariz.

Garretson, Oliver K., A.B.'18, Univ of Okla.; A.M.'26, Univ. of Texas; Ph.D.'29, Columbia Univ.; Dean, Col. of Educ., Univ. of Ariz., Tucson, Ariz., since 1950.

Gear, Harold L., A.B., B.S. in Ed.'34, Kent State Univ. (Ohio); M.A.'37, The Ohio State Univ.; Ed.D.'50, Grad. Sch. of Educ., Harvard Univ.; Asst. Supt., Phoenix Union H. S. and Phoenix Col., Phoenix, Ariz., since 1952.

Guitteau, Paul E., M.A.'37, Univ. of Ariz.; Pres., Eastern Ariz. Jr. Col., Thatcher, Ariz.

Hall, Chester A., B.S.'26, Southwest Mo. State Tchrs. Col., Springfield; M.A.'34, Univ. of Ariz.; Supt. of Sch., Bisbee, Ariz., since 1942.

Harkins, Clifton L., B.A.'32, Ariz. State Col., Flagstaff; M.A.'51, Ariz. State Col., Tempe; Supt. of Sch. Dist. 38, Madison Elem. Sch., Phoenix, Ariz., since 1949.

Hendrickson, H. A., M.A.'47, Ariz. State Col., Flagstaff; Prin. Union H. S., Snowflake, Ariz., since 1946.

Herrera, John K., Supt., Tolleson Union H. S., Tolleson, Ariz.

Hickerson, Carl W., B.S.'26, Southwestern State Tchrs. Col., Weatherford, Okla.; M.A. '37, Univ. of Ariz; Co. Supt of Sch., Prescott, Ariz., 1933-51. Address: Box 1752, Prescott, Ariz.

Hostetler, Ivan P., B.S. in Ed.'19, State Tchrs. Col., Emporia, Kansas; M.A. in Ed.'26, Stanford Univ.; Supt., Lower Miami and Inspiration Pub. Sch., Miami, Ariz., since 1934.

Jones, James Joseph, B.S.Ed.'46, M.Ed.'49, Univ. of Ga.; D.Ed.'52, Ind. Univ., (Bloomington); Asst. Prof. of Educ., Ariz. State Col., Tempe, Ariz., since 1952.

Joy, O. B., B.A.'39, M.A.'46, Ariz. State Col., Flagstaff; Prin., Inspiration Addition Sch., Miami, Ariz., since 1943.

Judd, Abia W., A.B.'36, Ariz. State Col.; M.A.'42, State Univ. of Iowa; Supt. of Sch., Prescott, Ariz., since 1951.

Larson, Emil Leonard, B.S. in Ed.'20, Kansas State Tchrs.; M.A.'23., Ph.D.'25, Tchrs. Col., Columbia Univ.; Prof. of Educ., Univ. of Ariz., Tucson, Ariz., since 1926.

Lewis, Edmund L., B.A.'49, Univ. of Ariz.; Co. Supt. of Sch., Prescott, Ariz., since 1951.

McDonald, Lewis J., A.B.'31, M.A.'41, Ariz. State Col., Flagstaff; Supt. of Sch., Jerome, Ariz., since 1949.

McKemy, Harvey M., A.B.'30, Univ. of Ariz.; M.S.'34, Univ. of Southern Calif.; Supt. of Sch., Tempe, Ariz., since 1934.

Maxwell, Walter, B.S. in Ed.'38, Ariz. State Col., Tempe; M.S. in Ed.'41, Univ. of Southern Calif.; Exec. Secy., Ariz. Educ. Assn., Phoenix, Ariz., since 1942.

*Menke, Robert F., B.S. in Ed.'42, State Tchrs. Col., Oshkosh, Wis.; M.A.'45, Ph.D.'51, Northwestern Univ.; Dir. of Placement, and Assoc. Prof. of Educ., Ariz. State Col., Tempe, Ariz., since 1947.

Montgomery, E. W., A.B.'09, A.M.'13, Ind. Univ.; H.D.'46, Col. of Osteopathic Physicians and Surgeons, Los Angeles, Calif.; LL.D.'49, Univ. of Ariz.; Supt. of Union H. S. and Pres., Phoenix Col., Phoenix, Ariz., since 1925.

Morelock, Charles E., A.B.'25, Mo. Wesleyan Col.; M.Ed.'32, Univ. of Kansas; Area Dir. of Schs., Bureau of Indian Affairs, Phoenix, Ariz.

Morrow, Edward O., B.S. in Ed.'41, State Tchrs. Col., Maryville, Mo.; Reservation Prin. of Hopi Sch., Oraibi, Ariz., since 1951.

Morrow, Robert D., B.A.'28, George Wash. Univ.; M.A.'28, Gallaudet Col.; M.A.'40, Univ. of Ariz.; Supt. of Sch., Tucson, Ariz., since 1941.

O'Brien, Mary C., Co. Supt. of Sch., Florence, Ariz.

Payton, Lee, M.A.'36, Northeastern State Col.; Sch. Supt., Dept. of Interior Ind. Service, Chinle, Ariz., since 1950.

Peters, George E., Prin. of Educ., Fort Apache, Ariz.

Plotts, (Mrs.) Sylvia F., B.A.'23, State Univ. of Iowa; M.S.'47, Drake Univ.; Graduate Student, Univ. of Ariz., Tucson, Ariz.

Riggs, Edwon L., A.B.'34, Ariz. State Col., Tempe; M.A.'39, Colo. State Col. of Educ.; Prin., Creighton Sch., Phoenix, Ariz., since 1945.

Ryan, Carson V., B.S.Ed.'32, Univ. of Okla.; Reservation Prin. of Sch., Pajago Indian Agency, Sells, Ariz., since 1949.

Shepherd Rulon T., M.S.'34, Univ. of Southern Calif.; Supt. of Elem. Sch., Mesa, Ariz., since 1946.

Smith, Harold W., A.B.'16, East Texas State Normal Sch., Commerce; M.A.'30, Univ. of Calif.; Supt. of Grammar Sch., Glendale, Ariz., since 1925.

Stevenson, H. E., A.B.'29, Ariz. State Col., Flagstaff; A.M.'30, Stanford Univ.; Supt. of Sch., Douglas, Ariz., since 1948.

Sullivan, William R., B.S. in Ed.'36, Univ. of Southern Calif.; M.A. in Adm.'40, Univ. of Ariz.; Supt., Murphy Elem. Sch., Phoenix, Ariz., since 1940.

Sutton, J. B., B.A.'34, State Col., Tempe; M.A. '38, Univ. of Ariz.; Supt., Isaac Sch., Phoenix, Ariz., since 1925.

Taylor, Harvey L., A.B.'21, Univ. of Utah; M.A.'25, Columbia Univ.; Supt. of H. S., Mesa, Ariz., since 1946.

Tommaney, Thomas A., A.B.'38, Univ. of Kansas; M.S.'50, Okla. A. & M. Col.; Prin., Phoenix Indian Sch., Phoenix, Ariz., since 1952.

Townsend, W. A., M.A.'39, Ariz. State Col., Flagstaff, Ariz.; Supt. of Santa Cruz Valley Union H. S., Eloy, Ariz., since 1948.

Walters, Hallie O., B.S.'37, M.A.Ed.'48, Northeast Mo. State Tchrs. Col.; Reservation Prin., San Carlos, Ariz., since 1949.

Witzleben, Leo E., B.A.'27, State Tchrs. Col., Valley City, N. Dak.; M.A.'47, Ariz. State Col.; Reservation Prin., Colo. River Indian Sch., Parker, Ariz., since 1951.

Wochmer, Raymand E., B.S.'34, York Col.; M.A.'40, Univ. of Nebr.; Ph.D.'47, Univ. of Wyo.; Prof. of Educ. Admin., Ariz. State Col., Tempe, Ariz., since 1952.

Wolfenbarger, O. K., Co. Supt. of Sch., Peoria, Ariz.

ARKANSAS

INDIVIDUAL MEMBERS

Bailey, Wallace, B.S.'34, M.S.'46, Univ. of Ark.; Supt. of Sch., Russellville, Ark., since 1946.

Bedwell, Robert L., Ph.B.'10, Miss. Col.; M.A.'18, Univ. of Miss.; Ph.D.'29, George Peabody Col. for Tchrs., Supt. of Sch., Hot Springs, Ark., since 1943.

Bell, C. E., A.B.'34, Ouachita Col.; M.A.'40, Univ. of Ark.; Supt. of Sch., Parkin, Ark., since 1941.

Benson, George S., B.S.'25, Okla. Agrl. and Mech. Col.; A.B.'26, LL.D.'30, Harding Col.; M.A.'31, Univ. of Chicago; Pres., Harding Col., Searcy, Ark., since 1936.

Blackburn, Clifford S., B.S.Ed.'25, Univ. of Ark.; M.A.'30, Univ. of Ill.; Ph.D.'51, George Peabody Col. for Tchrs.; Supt. of Sch., North Little Rock, Ark., since 1951.

Blackmon, Donald E., B.A.'37, Henderson State Tchrs. Col., Arkadelphia, Ark.; M.S.E.'40, Univ. of Ark.; Supt. of Sch., Wynne, Ark., since 1946.

Blossom, Virgil T., B.S.E.'30, Mo. Valley Col.; M.S.'39, Univ. of Ark.; Supt. of Sch., Fayetteville, Ark., since 1941.

Bonds, A. B., Jr., A.B.'35, Henderson State Tchrs. Col., Arkadelphia, Ark.; A.M.'36, La. State Univ. and A. and M. Col.; State Commr. of Educ., Little Rock, Ark., since 1949.

*Bruce, Imon E., B.A.'32, Henderson State Tchrs. Col.; M.A.'37, La. State Univ.; Ed.D.'52, Ind. Univ.; Dir. of Student Tchg., Ark. State Tchrs. Col., Conway, Ark., since 1949.

Bunn, H. G., B.A. and B.S.'23, Ouachita Col.; M.S.,'46, Univ. of Ark.; Asst. Supt., Co. Special Sch. Dist., Little Rock, Ark., since 1951.

Burrough, Rudolph V., B.S.E.'46, Ark. State Tchrs. Col.; M.A.'47, Tchrs. Col., Columbia Univ.; Supt. of Elem. Educ., Little Rock, Ark., since 1951.

Castleberry, G. F., B.S.'37, Ark. State Col., M.S.'50 Univ. of Ark.; Supt. of Pub. Sch., Newport, Ark., since 1951.

Chitwood, R. B., M.S.'46, Univ. of Ark.; Supt. of Sch., Danville, Ark., since 1947.

Coats, Earl, B.A.'46, Col. of the Ozarks; M.S.'50, Univ. of Ark., Supt. of Sch., Alma, Ark., since 1951.

Davis, Lawrence A., A.B.'37, Agrl., Mech., and Normal Col.; A.M.'41, Univ. of Kansas; LL.D.'48, Lane Col.; Pres., Agrl., Mech., and Normal Col., Pine Bluff, Ark., since 1943.

Deer, Philip J., M.A.'41, George Peabody Col. for Tchrs.; Supt. of Sch., Wilson, Ark., since 1948.

Doss, Vernon L., B.S.E.'50, Univ. of Ark.; Prin., Drew Central H.S., Monticello, Ark., since 1952.

Forrest, M. D., B.A.'32, Hendrix Col.; M.A.'35, Univ. of Colo.; Supt. of Sch., Corning, Ark., since 1949.

Garrett, S. K., A.A.'23, Texas Military Col., Terrell; B.S.E.'29, M.S.'45, Univ. of Ark.; Supt. of Sch., Gurdon, Ark., since 1946.

Gibson, Hays, B.S.'29, Erskine Col.; M.S.'47, Univ. of Ark.; Supt. of Sch., Conway, Ark., since 1949.

Goff, Lloyd L., A.B.'25, Ark. Col.; M.A.'36, Univ. of Mo.; Supt. of Sch., Jonesboro, Ark., since 1946.

Gray, Julius C., B.A.'16, M.S.'29, Univ. of Ark.; Supt. of Sch., Eudora, Ark., since 1933.

Haizlip, Ralph H., B.S.E.'28, M.A.'41, Univ. of Ark.; Supt. of Sch., Paragould, Ark., since 1945.

Hull, Joseph William, M.A.'30, George Peabody Col. for Tchrs.; Pres., Ark. Polytech. Col., Russellville, Ark., since 1932.

Jeffers, Leo D., B.A.'33, Lane Col.; M.S.'50, Ind. Univ.; Prin. Richard B. Harrison H.S., Blytheville, Ark., since 1952.

Kelly, J. O., M.S.'38, Univ. of Ark.; Supt. of Sch., Springdale, Ark., since 1944.

Kirksey, B. L., Supt. of Sch., Rogers, Ark.

Lewis, Russell A., A.B.'22, Abilene Christian Col.; M.A.'28, Ph.D.'38, Univ. of Texas; Asst. to the Pres., Harding Col., Searcy, Ark., since 1951.

Little, Harry A., A.B.'19, Hendrix Col.; M.A.'28, George Peabody Col. for Tchrs.; Ph.D.'34, Columbia Univ.; Supt. of Sch., Little Rock, Ark., since 1948.

Locke, W. M., Supt. of Sch., Texarkana, Ark., since 1942.

McCuistion, Ed T., A.B.'17, Hendrix Col.; M.A.'22, George Peabody Col. for Tchrs.; State Dir. of Negro Sch., State Dept. of Educ., Little Rock, Ark., since 1938.

McKenzie, A. R., B.A.'24, M.S.'49, Univ. of Ark.; Supt. of Sch., Sheridan, Ark., since 1933.

Middleton, W. E., M.S.'44, Univ. of Ark.; Supt. of Consol. Sch., Mena, Ark., since 1925.

Newman, J. Marion, A.B.'34, Ark. State Tchrs. Col., Conway; M.A.'40, George Peabody Col. for Tchrs.; Supt. of Sch., Pocahontas, Ark., since 1949.

Nicholson, W. B., B.S.'17, M.A.'28, Peabody Col.; Supt. of Sch., Blytheville, Ark., since 1943.

Norman, Loyal V., B.S.'37, Ark. Agrl. and Mech. Col.; M.S.'40, Okla. Agrl. and Mech. Col.; M.Ed.'50, George Peabody Col. for Tchrs.; Supt. of Sch., Searcy, Ark., since 1947.

Payne, Ralph J., B.S. in Ed.,'31, Ark. State Tchrs. Col.; M.S. in Ed.'48, Univ. of Ark.; Prin., Joe T. Robinson H. S., Little Rock, Ark., since 1946.

Perrin, Basil Howard, B.A.'27, State Tchrs. Col., Conway, Ark.; M.A.'32, Univ. of Colo.; Supt. of Sch., Benton, Ark., since 1936.

Petty, Paul V., B.S. in Ed.'36, Ark. State Tchrs. Col.; M.A.'41, Duke Univ.; Ph.D.'51, Univ. of Texas; Assoc. Prof. of Educ., Univ. of Ark., Fayetteville, Ark., since 1950.

Poteet, Custer, L.I.'17, Col. of the Ozarks; B.S.E.'44, Ark. State Tchrs. Col., Conway; Co. Supvr. of Sch., Morrilton, Ark., since 1945.

Pyle, H. R., B.S.'30, M.S.'39, Univ. of Ark.; Exec. Secy., Ark. Educ. Assn., Little Rock, Ark., since 1947.

Rainwater, A. W., B.A.'30, State Tchrs. Col., Conway, Ark.; M.S.'43, Univ. of Ark.; Supt. of Sch., Walnut Ridge, Ark., since 1930.

Ramsey, James William, A.B.'13, LL.D.'46, Ouachita Col.; M.A.'21, George Peabody Col. for Tchrs.; Supt. of Sch., Fort Smith, Ark., since 1923.

Reng, Carl R., D.Ed.'48, Univ. of Mo.; Pres., Ark. State Col., State Col., Ark., since 1951.

Reuter, George S., Jr., B.S. in Ed.'41, M.S. in Ed.'49, Central Mo. Col.; Ed.D.'52, Univ. of Mo.; Assoc. Prof. of Educ., Ark. A. & M. Col., College Heights, Ark., since 1952.

Ritchie, J. Bryan, B.A.'26, Ouachita Col.; M.A.'38, Tchrs. Col., Columbia Univ.; Co. Sch. Supvr., Prescott, Ark., since 1950.

Roelfs, Robert Max, B.S.'41, Kansas State Col. of Agric. and Applied Science; M.Ed.'48, Ed.D.'51, Univ. of Colo.; Asst. Prof., Univ. of Arkansas, Fayetteville, Ark., since 1951.

Rozzell, Forrest, A.B.'31, Col. of the Ozarks; LL.B.'41, Ark. Law Sch.; M.A.'48, Univ. of Ark.; Dir. of Field Serv., Ark. Educ. Assn., Little Rock, Ark., since 1940.

Sage, T. Raymond, B.A.'24, Hendrix Col.; M.S.'50, Univ. of Ark.; Supt. of Sch., Cotton Plant, Ark., since 1950.

Sanders, Claude Franklin, B.S.'35, Memphis State Col.; M.A.'47, George Peabody Col. for Tchrs.; Supt. of Sch., Osceola, Ark., since 1946.

Scott, Emma, A.B.'29, Univ. of Ark.; M.A.'39, Ind. Univ.; Editor, *Journal of Ark. Educ.*, and Asst. Dir. of Field Serv., Ark. Educ. Assn., Little Rock, Ark., since 1948.

Shannon, Avon G., B.A.'27, Ark. Col.; M.A.'30, Univ. of Mo.; Supt. of Sch., Carlisle, Ark., since 1947.

Smith, C. B., B.S.'27, Ark. Tech. Col.; B.S.E.'30, Okla. A. and M. Col.; Supt. of Sch., Greenwood, Ark., since 1927.

Smith J. Ed, Supt. of Sch., Prescott, Ark.

Smith, Milton S., A.B.'15, Ark. Col.; M.A.'39, George Peabody Col. of Tchrs.; Supt. of Sch., Forrest City, Ark., since 1919.

Smith, Robert L., B.S.'34, East Central State Col., Ada, Okla.; M.A.'44, Univ. of Mo.; Supt. of Sch., Harrison, Ark., since 1942.

Smith, Vivian Thomas, A.B.'16, Greenville Col.; M.A.'29, Ph.D.'33, Univ. of Ill.; LL.D. '43, Cornell Col.; Dean, Col. of the Ozarks, Clarksville, Ark., since 1952.

Snow, Silas D., B.A.'29, Ark. State Tchrs. Col., Conway; M.A.'46, George Peabody Col. for Tchrs.; Supt. of Sch., Crossett, Ark., since 1944.

Stubblefield, Garland A., B.S.E.'24, M.S.'31, Univ. of Ark.; Supt. of Sch., El Dorado, Ark., since 1944.

Sugg, B. A., B.S.E.'25, M.S.'35, Univ. of Ark.; Co. Sch. Supvr., Helena, Ark., since 1943.

Summitt, W. K., A.B.'25, Union Univ.; M.A.'28, George Peabody Col. for Tchrs.; Ph.D.'33, Univ. of Mo.; Prof. of Educ. and Registrar, Harding Col., Searcy, Ark., since 1933.

Teeter, Charles R., M.A.'47, Univ. of Ark.; Supt., Pub. Sch., Star City, Ark.

Terrell, M. T., A.B.'27, Ouachita Col.; M.A.'30, George Peabody Col. for Tchrs.; Supt. of Sch., Bauxite, Ark., since 1948.

Thomasson, C. W., Ph.D.'40, George Peabody Col. for Tchrs.; Chmn., Dept. of Educ., Henderson State Tchrs. Col., Arkadelphia, Ark., since 1947.

*Tietjen, Charles H., A.B.'47, M.A. in Ed.'48, Univ. of N. C.; Ed.D.'49, Tchrs. Col., Columbia Univ.; Supt. of Sch., Malvern, Ark., since 1951.

Tinnin, (Mrs.) G. C., B.S.E.'40, John Brown Univ.; Supt. of Sch., Bentonville, Ark., since 1943.

Wahl, James Frank, B.A.'20, Hendrix Col.; M.A.'26, George Peabody Col. for Tchrs.; Supt. of Sch., Helena, Ark., since 1928.

Walker, Fred A., A.B.'26, D.D.(Hon.)'47, Col. of the Ozarks; M.A.'31, McCormick Theol. Sem.; Pres., Col. of the Ozarks, Clarksville, Ark., since 1949.

Ward, Henry H., B.A.'37, Northeastern State Col.; M.A.'49, Univ. of Ark.; Supt. of Sch., Stephens, Ark., since 1946.

Warren, B. Davis, B.A.'38, Univ. of Ark.; M.A.'48, Univ. of Texas; Supt. of Sch., Emerson, Ark., since 1948.

Wetherington, A. B., M.S.'38, Univ. of Ark.; Dir. of Finance and Transportation, Dept. of Educ., Little Rock, Ark., since 1948.

Whiteside, Frederick W., A.B.'12, Univ. of Chicago; Supt. of Sch., Camden, Ark., since 1926.

Whitten, A. L., B.S.E.'31, Ark. State Tchrs. Col., Conway; M.S.'40, Univ. of Ark.; Supt. of Sch., Marianna, Ark., since 1944.

Williams, Ben G., B.A.'41, Agrl., Mech., and Normal Col.; M.S.'50, Ind. Univ.; Supt. of Sch., Magnolia, Ark., since 1946.

Williamson, Horace, M.S.'44, Univ. of Ark.; Co. Supvr. of Sch., El Dorado, Ark., since 1942.

Wilson, John L., B.S.'23, Kansas State Col. of Agr. and Applied Science; M.A.'34, Univ. of Kansas; Dean of Col. and Prof. of Chemistry, Agrl., Mech., and Normal Col., Pine Bluff, Ark., since 1946.

INSTITUTIONAL MEMBERS

General Library, Univ. of Ark., Fayetteville, Ark.

Torreyson Library, Ark. State Tchrs. Col., Conway, Ark.

CALIFORNIA

INDIVIDUAL MEMBERS

Abbott, John L., Asst. Supt. of Sch., Los Angeles, Calif.

Adams, Harold W., Ph.B.'17, Linfield Col.; M.S. in Ed.'28, Univ. of Idaho; Supt. of Sch., Eureka, Calif., since 1943.

Adams, Roland R., B.A.'31, Occidental Col.; M.A.'51, Univ. of Southern Calif.; Dist. Supt., Old River Sch. Dist., Downey, Calif., since 1942.

Addicott, Irwin Oliver, A.B.'22, Univ. of Calif.; M.A.'24, B.D.'25, Pacific Sch. of Religion; Ed.D.'39, Stanford Univ.; Prof. of Educ., Fresno State Col., Fresno, Calif.

Allison, LeRoy, Ph.B.'29, Creighton Univ.; M.A.'35, Univ. of Nebr.; Supt. of Sch., Pomona, Calif., since 1946.

Amerman, Alwyn R., A.B.'30, Chico State Col.; Dist. Supt. of Sch. and Pres., Sacramento Co. Bd. of Educ., Isleton, Calif., since 1942.

Anderson, Godfrey Tryggve, Ph.D.'44, Univ. of Chicago; Pres., La Sierra Col., Arlington, Calif., since 1946.

Armacost, George Henry, B.A.'26, LL.D.'47, Dickinson Col.; M.A.'30, Ph.D.'40, Columbia Univ.; Pres., Univ. of Redlands, Redlands, Calif., since 1945.

Arnheim, Roy L., B.S.'19, Univ. of Calif.; M.S. in Ed.'36, Univ. of Southern Calif.; Prin., Virgil Jr. H. S., Los Angeles, Calif., since 1942.

Atkins, Charles H., Diploma '09, San Jose State Col.; Co. Supt. of Sch., Jackson, Calif., since 1946.

Babcock, George Thomas, A.B.'15, Pomona Col.; M.A.'16, Univ. of Calif.; Pacific Coast Mgr., D. C. Heath and Co., San Francisco, Calif., since 1937.

Bacon, Francis Leonard, A.B.'12, LL.D.'31, Southwestern Col.; A.M.'16, Columbia Univ; L.H.D.'37, Williams Col.; Consulting Supt. of Twp. Sch., Evanston, Ill. and Prof. of Educ., Univ. of Calif., Los Angeles, Calif., since 1949.

Barnes, B. H., B.S.'20, Wesleyan Col.; Deputy Supt. of Sch., Burbank, Calif., since 1941.

Bartky, A. John, Ph.D.'37, Northwestern Univ.; Dean, Sch. of Educ., Stanford Univ., Stanford University, Calif., since 1946.

Barton, (Mrs.) Virginia Rocca, A.B.'40, San Jose State Col.; Dist. Supt. of Sch., Salinas, Calif., since 1947.

Baum, Paul B., A.B.'19, Aurora Col.; M.A.'21, Univ. of Wis.; Dean, La Verne Col., La Verne, Calif., since 1952.

Baxter, Bernice, A.B.'28, San Francisco State Col.; Ph.D.'35, Yale Univ.; Dir. of Educ. in Human Relations, Pub. Sch., Oakland, Calif., since 1949.

Beacock, Curtis O., A.B.'42, San Jose State Col.; Dist. Supt., Coastside Union Elem. Sch., Half Moon Bay, Calif., since 1947.

Beaumariage, George N., Jr., B.S. in Ch.E.'42, Georgia Inst. of Tech.; M.A. in Ed.'51, Stanford Univ.; Coordinator of Educ., Sonora, Calif., since 1951.

Beckner, Howard B., B.A.'23, La Verne Col.; M.S. in Ed.'35, Univ. of Southern Calif.; Dist. Supt. of Sch., Temple City, Calif., since 1945.

Beeman, (Mrs.) Alice Lucille, A.B.'35, San Diego State Col.; Prin., West View Elem. Sch., Palm City, Calif., since 1951.

Begg, Foster A., B.S.'28, Univ. of Ill.; M.A.'31, New York Univ.; Dist. Supt. of Sch., Manhattan Beach, Calif., since 1937.

Beleal, A. P., M.S.'34, N. Dak. Agr. Col.; Dist. Supt. of Sch., Escondido, Calif., since 1947.

Bell, George H., B.S.'12, M.S.'13, Univ. of Calif.; Ed.D.'31, Univ. of Southern Calif.; Pres., Mt. San Antonio Col., Pomona, Calif., since 1946.

Bell, Hilton D., Supt. of Sch., Visalia, Calif.

Bell, Ralph Rogers, B.S.A.'44, B.Ed.'47, Univ. of British Columbia; M.S.'49, Oregon State Col.; Prin., Dist. Supt. of Sch., Saugus, Calif., since 1951.

Benedetta, Mother Mary, M.A. in Ed.'34, DePaul Univ.; Prin., Villa Cabrini Acad., Burbank, Calif., since 1943.

Berg, Selmer H., B.A.'17, St. Olaf Col.; M.A.'24, Univ. of Minn.; Supt. of Sch., Oakland, Calif., since 1949.

Berry, Aubrey L., A.B.'31, M.A.'47, Ed.D.'48, Univ. of Calif. at Los Angeles; Asst. Prof. of Educ. and Head, Office of Tchr. Placement, Los Angeles, Calif., since 1939.

Berry, Godfrey G., B.S.'27, Kansas State Tchrs. Col., Pittsburg; M.A.'37, Univ. of Mo.; Dist. Supt., South Bay Union Sch., Palm City, Calif., since 1947.

Bessire, M. Ethel, Pres., Mar-Ken Sch., Sherman Oaks, Calif.

Bessire, Wm. Kent, Co-Dir., Mar-Ken Sch., Sherman Oaks, Calif.

Bettinger, George Edward, A.B.'15, M.A.'28, Univ. of Southern Calif.; Supt. of Sch., Alhambra, Calif., since 1934.

Bewley, Fred W., A.B.'34, Whittier Col.; M.S.'38, Univ. of Southern Calif.; Dist. Supt. of Elem. Sch., Whittier, Calif., since 1949.

Beyer, Fred C., M.A.'39, Stanford Univ.; Co. Supt. of Sch., Modesto, Calif., since 1950.

Billington, Lillian E., Ed.D.'47, Stanford Univ. Address: P.O. Box 113, Stanford Univ., Stanford University, Calif.

Bishop, Frank Edward, B.A.'16, Nebr. Wesleyan Univ.; M.A.'30, Stanford Univ.; Ed.D.'49, Univ. of Calif., Los Angeles; Assoc. Prof. of Educ., Univ. of Redlands, Redlands, Calif.

Bishop, Henry F., A.B.'27, Fresno State Col.; M.A.'31, Stanford Univ.; Dist. Supt. of Coalinga-Huron Elem. Sch., Coalinga, Calif., since 1946.

Blair, Maurice Guernsey, B.S. in Ed.'27, M.A. in Ed.'33, Univ. of Southern Calif.; Assoc. Supt., Curriculum Div., City Sch., Los Angeles, Calif., since 1945.

Blomquist, C. Leonard, A.B.'37, San Diego Col.; Viceprin., Union H.S., Corning, Calif.

Boortz, Nathan H., B.S.'39, M.A.'43, Univ. of Minn.; Grad. Student, Stanford Univ., 1952-53. Address: 311-1 Stanford Village, Stanford, Calif.

Bowman, Frank L., A.B.'30, Univ. of Calif., Berkeley; LL.B.'34, San Francisco Law Sch.; Pres., Bd. of Educ., Santa Ana, Calif., since 1949.

Branigan, John, Field Rep., Div. of Pub. Sch. Admin., State Dept. of Educ., Los Angeles, Calif.

Bratton, J. Wesley, A.B.'35, Seattle Pacific Col.; M.S. in Ed.'38, Ed.D.'51, Univ. of Southern Calif.; Dean, Educ. Serv. and Summer Sessions, Long Beach State Col., Long Beach, Calif.

Bretsch, Howard S., Ph.D.'48, Syracuse Univ.; Asst. Prof., Univ. of Calif., Berkeley, Calif., since 1952.

Bridges, Joe W., A.B.'25, Central State Col. (Okla.); Prin., Campo Elem. Sch., Lakeside, Calif., since 1950.

Brierley, Wallace H., A.B.'32, San Jose State Col.; M.S. in Ed.'50, Univ. of Southern Calif.; Dist. Supt. of Elem. Sch., McFarland, Calif., since 1947.

Briscoe, Charles A., B.A.'38, Univ. of Wash.; M.A.'49, Stanford Univ.; Bus. Mgr., Unified Sch. Dist., Alameda, Calif., since 1946.

Briscoe, William S., A.B.'23, Univ. of Idaho; A.M.'27, Stanford Univ.; Supt. of City Sch., Santa Monica, Calif., since 1948.

Brooks, Harold Bennett, A.B.'19, Occidental Col.; M.A.'26, Univ. of Calif.; Ed.D.'38, Univ. of Southern Calif.; Prin., Benjamin Franklin Jr. H. S., Long Beach, Calif., since 1929.

Brown, Forrest L., A.B.'39, Fresno State Col.; M.A.'51, Claremont Graduate Sch.; Dist. Supt. of Sch., Greenfield, Calif., since 1951.

Brown, Paul D., Vice-Prin. Unified Sch., Montebello, Calif.

Brown, Prentiss, A.B.'16, Univ. of Oregon; M.A.'31, Stanford Univ.; Dist. Supt. of Sch., Los Gatos, Calif., since 1931.

Brown, T. Malcolm, B.S.'15, Univ. of Minn.; M.A.'31, Univ. of Calif.; Asst. Supt. in chg. of Sec. Sch., San Diego, Calif., since 1949.

Brown, William Bartholomew, Master's'33, Univ. of Southern Calif.; Asst. Supt. in chg. of Personnel, Bd. of Educ., Los Angeles, Calif., since 1947.

Brownell, W. A., A.B.'17, LL.D.'42, Allegheny Col.; A.M.'23, Ph.D.'26, Univ. of Chicago; Dean, Sch. of Educ., Univ. of Calif., Berkeley, Calif., since 1950.

Bruce, Robert, A.B.'28, Chico State Col.; M.A.'30, Columbia Univ.; Dist. Supt. of Sch., Santa Maria, Calif., since 1927.

Bryan, Paul C., A.B.'24, M.A.'25, Stanford Univ.; Ed.D.'47, Univ. of Calif.; Supt. of Sch., Albany, Calif., since 1941.

CALIFORNIA

Buchser, Emil R., A.B., San Jose State Col.; Supt. of City Sch., and Prin., Union H. S., Santa Clara, Calif., since 1939.

Bunker, James G., M.A.'35, Univ. of Calif.; Supt., Coalinga Sec. Sch., Coalinga, Calif.

Burke, Joseph W., B.S.'32, M.S.'34, Univ. of Idaho; Dir. of Educ. Serv., Troop Information and Educ. Section, Hq., 6th Army, Bldg. 558, Presidio of San Francisco, Calif., since 1947.

Burkhard, William J., B.S.'21, M.A.'30, Univ. of Calif.; Supt. of Sch., Sacramento, Calif., since 1948.

Burnight, Ralph F., A.B.'18, A.M.'20, Univ. of Southern Calif.; Supt., Excelsior Union H. S. Dist., Norwalk, Calif., since 1930.

Bursch, Charles Wesley, B.S.'18, Kansas State Tchrs. Col.; M.A.'26, Ed.D.'30, Stanford Univ.; Chief, Div. of Pub. Sch. Admin., in charge of Sch. Planning, State Dept. of Educ., Sacramento, Calif., since 1934.

Burrell, Clarence, B.A.'26, San Jose State Col.; M.A.'41, Stanford Univ.; Supt. of City Sch., San Leandro, Calif.

Butler, Henry D., A.B.'33, Chico Col.; M.E.'46, Univ. of Oregon; Dist. Supt. of Sch., Delano, Calif., since 1945.

Butler, Paul C., A.B.'39, Whittier Col.; M.S.Ed. '48, Univ. of Southern Calif.; Supt., Elem. Sch. Dist., La Cañada, Calif., since 1948.

Butterbaugh, Wayne L., B.A.'43, La Verne Col.; M.A.'51, Claremont Grad. Sch.; Dist. Supt. of Sch., Stanton, Calif., since 1949.

Bystrom, Theodore L., A.B.'27, M.A.'28, Univ. of Mich.; Supt. of Sch., Piedmont, Calif., since 1947.

Campbell, A. B., B.S.'23, M.A.'33, Univ. of Calif.; Asst. Supt. of Sch., Berkeley, Calif., since 1938.

Campion, Howard A., A.B.'23, Univ. of Calif.; M.A.'25, Ed.D.'41, Univ. of Southern Calif.; Assoc. Supt. of Sch., Los Angeles, Calif.

Carr, Ellis G., A.B.'23, Wichita Univ.; Dist. Supt. of Sch., LeGrand, Calif., since 1951.

Carson, Charles Hamilton, M.S.'41, Univ. of Southern Calif.; Supt., Ranchito Sch. Dist., Pico, Calif., since 1946.

Cartwright, Donovan F., B.A.'26, M.A.'42, Univ. of Oregon; Prin. and Dist. Supt. of Sch., Tulare, Calif., since 1946.

Casier, Roger, B.A.'34, Santa Barbara Col.; Dist. Supt. of Sch., Carpinteria, Calif., since 1950.

Cassidy, Rosalind, B.A.'18, Mills Col.; M.A.'23, Ed.D.'37, Tchrs. Col., Columbia Univ. Address: Women's Physical Educ. Bldg., Univ. of Calif. at Los Angeles, Los Angeles, Calif.

Castle, Clayton A., A.B.'26, M.A.'47, Univ. of Calif.; Dist. Supt. of Sch., Lindsay, Calif., since 1941.

Caywood, Hal D., A.B.'30, Chico State Col.; Co. Supt. of Sch., Santa Barbara, Calif., since 1946.

Chaffey, George P., B.S.'39, Univ. of Calif.; Deputy Supt. of Sch., Vallejo Unified Sch. Dist., Vallejo, Calif., since 1951.

Chase, Frank M., Jr., M.S.'36. Univ. of Southern Calif.; Supt. of Oceanside-Carlsbad Union H. S. and Jr. Col., Oceanside, Calif., since 1950.

Ching, John Frederic, Ed.D.'32, Univ. of Calif.; Supt. of Sch., Salinas, Calif., since 1947.

Clark, Edith M., B.S.'30, Univ. of Cincinnati; M.A.'35, Univ. of Southern Calif.; Asst. Supt., Div. of Extension and Higher Educ., City Sch., Los Angeles, Calif., since 1950.

Clark, George W., B.A.'19, M.A.'36, Univ. of Calif.; Co. Supt. of Sch., Merced, Calif., since 1951.

Claypool, Vincent B., B.S.'24, Univ. of Calif.; M.A.'35, Claremont Col.; Ed.D.'48, Univ. of Calif. at Los Angeles; Prin., Sequoia H. S., Redwood City, Calif., since 1952.

Clish, Herbert C., B.S.'26, M.A.'27, Ed.D.'40, Columbia Univ.; LL.D.'49, St. Mary's Col., Calif.; Supt. of Sch., San Francisco, Calif., since 1947.

Cobb, Wilbur Kirkpatrick, A.B.'17, Pomona Col.; M.A.in Ed.'32, Univ. of Southern Calif.; City Supt., Woodland Pub. Sch., Woodland, Calif., since 1952.

Cohen, Milton S., A.B.'46, San Jose State Col.; Dist. Supt., Owens Valley Unified Sch., Independence, Calif., since 1952.

Collins, Margaret, Dist. Supt. of Sch., Pinole, Calif., since 1944.

*Compton, John L., A.B.'25, Whittier Col.; M.A.'29, Univ. of Southern Calif.; Supt. of Sch., Bakersfield, Calif., since 1940.

Conner, Jay Davis, A.B.'28, San Diego State Col.; M.A.'30, Stanford Univ.; Ed.D.'46, Univ. of Southern Calif.; Assoc. Supt. of Pub. Instr. and Chief, Div. of Instr., State Dept. of Educ., Sacramento, Calif., since 1948.

Cook, L. T., M.A.'39, Stanford Univ.; Prin. and Dist. Supt., Sierra Joint Union H. S., Auberry, Calif., since 1948.

Corey, Arthur F., A.B.'24, Whittier Col.; A.M.'32, Univ. of Southern Calif.; LL.D.'49, La Verne Col.; State Exec. Secy., Calif. Tchrs. Assn., San Francisco, Calif., since 1947.

Cornick, Homer H., A.B.'20, M.A.'22, Univ. of Calif.; Supt. of Sch., Santa Cruz, Calif., since 1940.

Corson, James Hunt, A.B.'27, Ped.D.'48, Col. of the Pacific; M.S. in Ed.'36, Univ. of Southern Calif.; Supt. of Sch., Modesto, Calif.

Cowan, James R., A.B.'37, Chico State Col.; M.S. in Ed.'48, Univ. of Southern Calif.; Supt., Arcade Sch. Dist., Sacramento, Calif., since 1939.

Cowan, William A., A.B.'34, San Jose State Col.; M.A.'39, Ed.D.'50, Stanford Univ.; Assoc. Prof. of Educ., San Francisco State Col., San Francisco, Calif., since 1946.

Crabb, Paul E., A.B.'26, M.A.'33, Stanford Univ.; Supt. of Sch., Vallejo, Calif., since 1951.

Cragen, (Mrs.) Dorothy C., Co. Supt. of Sch., Independence, Calif.

Cralle, Jefferson, M.A.'24, Univ. of Calif.; Supvr. and Prin., H. S., Crockett, Calif., since 1942.

Cralle, Robert E., A.B.'22, M.A.'26, Univ. of Calif., Berkeley; Ed.D.'44, Univ. of Southern Calif.; Exec. Secy., Calif. Assoc. of Sch. Admin.; 1041 Rancho Rd., Arcadia, Calif., since 1952.

Crandall, Earle P., A.B.'27, Col. of the Pacific; A.M.'42, Ed.D.'46, Stanford Univ.; Supt. of Unified Sch. Dist., San Jose, Calif., since 1951.

Crawford, Bruce M., A.B.'34, M.S.'37, Univ. of Southern Calif.; Dist. Supt. of Sch., Shafter, Calif.

Crawford, Lynn H., A.B. and M.A.'25, Stanford Univ.; Supt. of Sch., Santa Ana, Calif., since 1946.

Crawford, Will C., A.B.'13, Pomona Col.; A.M.'15, Columbia Univ.; Ed.D.'40, Univ. of Southern Calif.; Supt. of Sch., San Diego, Calif., since 1934.

Critser, Loren A., A.B.'29, M.A.'46, Univ. of Calif.; Prin. of San Leandro H.S., San Leandro, Calif., since 1952.

Croad, J. R., A.B.'28, Chico State Col.; M.A.'29, Stanford Univ.; Supt. of Sch., Burbank, Calif.

Crooke, Charles R., A.B.'33, San Jose State Col.; A.M.'35, Leland Stanford Jr. Univ.; Dist. Supt. of Sch., Union H. S., Mountain View, Calif., since 1936.

Crossley, John B., A.B.'29, Pomona Col.; M.A.'40, Claremont Col.; Litt.D.'45, Howard Col.; Ed.D.'50, Univ. of Calif. at Los Angeles; Supt., Ventura Union H. S. Dist., Ventura, Calif., since 1950.

Cruickshank, (Mrs.) Ruby S., Pres., Los Angeles Elem. Tchrs. Club, 202 Embassy Auditorium Bldg., Los Angeles 17, Calif., since 1951.

Cunliffe, J. William, B.A.'33, Pomona Col.; M.A.'40, Claremont Graduate Sch. Address: 463 W. 7th St., Claremont, Calif.

Curtis, James E., B.S.'28, Univ. of Minn.; M.S.'32, Univ. of Wis.; Ed.D.'48, Univ. of Calif.; Assoc. Prof. of Educ., San Jose State Col., San Jose, Calif., since 1950.

Dailard, Ralph C., A.B.'28, Nebr. State Tchrs. Col.; A.M.'36, Univ. of Nebr.; Ph.D.'39, Columbia Univ.; Assoc. Supt. of Sch., San Diego, Calif., since 1939.

Dann, Erwin A., Asst. Supt. of Sch., Fresno, Calif.

Danner, Don S., A.B.'27, Univ. of Calif. at Los Angeles; Dist. Supt. of Sch., Orange, Calif., since 1939.

Darby, Francis C., A.B.'31, Pomona Col.; M.Ed.'40, Univ. of Oregon; Asst. Supt., Bus. Serv., San Diego Co. Sch., San Diego, Calif., since 1946.

Davis, Albert M., A.B.'26, Univ. of Colo.; M.A.'33, Ed.D.'50, Stanford Univ.; Supt., Laguna Beach Unified Sch. Dist., Laguna Beach, Calif., since 1950.

Davis, B. E., B.A.'50, George Pepperdine Col.; Coordinator of Health, Physical Educ. and Recreation, Garvey Sch. Dist., Garvey, Calif., since 1950.

Demaree, Paul H., A.B.'17, Ky. Wesleyan Col.; M.A.'35, Univ. of Southern Calif.; Prin. and Dist. Supt., Anaheim Union H. S., Anaheim, Calif., since 1941.

Denison, Alan M., A.B.'39, Col. of the Pacific; Co. Supt. of Sch., Sonora, Calif., since 1943.

Denlay, Raymond E., A.B.'30, Chico State Col.; M.A.'39, Leland Stanford Jr. Univ.; Dist. Supt. of Sch., Santa Paula, Calif., since 1942.

Dent, James W., A.B.'29, M.A.'37, Univ. of Calif.; Supt. of Mt. Diablo Unified Sch. Dist., Concord, Calif., since 1948.

de Reschke, Oscar, A.B.'30, San Jose State Col.; Supt., Franklin-McKinley Sch. Dist., San Jose, Calif., since 1944.

Dice, Norvell R., A.B.'28, Santa Barbara State Col.; M.S.'33, Ed.D.'50, Univ. of Southern Calif.; Dist. Supt. of Sch., Arcadia, Calif., since 1948.

Dickerson, Elizabeth, A.B.'32, Whittier Col.; M.A.'40, Univ. of Calif.; Dist. Supt. of Sch., Cypress, Calif., since 1947.

Dickey, Levi H., B.A.'26, La Verne Col.; M.A.'28, Univ. of Southern Calif.; Dist. Supt. of Sch., Chino, Calif., since 1945.

Diggs, William Lloyd, B.S.'30, McPherson Col.; M.S. in Ed.'39, Univ. of Southern Calif.; Prin., H. S., Orosi, Calif., since 1943.

Digneo, Elmer J., B.S.'45, La Sierra Col.; Prin., Prep. Dept., La Sierra Col., Arlington, Calif., since 1947.

Donegan, (Mrs.) Olive M., Chmn., Affiliated Tchr. Organizations of Los Angeles, Los Angeles, Calif., since 1952.

Dotson, George E., A.B.'26, San Diego State Col.; M.A.'27, Ed.D.'39, Stanford Univ.; Asst. Supt. of Sch., Long Beach, Calif., since 1944.

Downing, George M., A.B.'37, San Jose State Col.; Dir. of Special Serv., Pub. Sch., San Jose, Calif., since 1948.

Dreier, (Mrs.) Grace M., B.S. in Ed.'32, Univ. of Southern Calif.; Asst. Supt. of Sch., Los Angeles, Calif.

Dunlavy, V. A., Dist. Supt., Sonora Union H. S., Sonora, Calif.

Dunn, E. F., Supt. of Sch., Little Rock, Ark.

Ehret, Paul D., A.B.'37, Univ. of Calif.; Supt. of Sch., San Lorenzo, Calif., since 1948.

Elliott, Robert E., A.B.'39, La Verne Col.; Dist. Supt., Lakeside Union Elem. Sch., Bakersfield, Calif., since 1949.

Elliott, Robert Thomas, A.B.'34, San Jose State Col.; M.A.'38, Univ. of Calif.; Admin. Asst. to Supt. of Sch., Modesto, Calif., since 1947.

Ellis, Stanley B., B.S.'30, Northeast Mo. State Tchrs. Col., Kirksville; A.M.'40, Univ. of Mo.; City Supt. of Sch., Sunnyvale, Calif., since 1944.

Engvall, Willard R., Supt. of Sch., San Bruno, Calif.

Ensz, Elmer, M.A.'38, Stanford Univ.; Ed.D.'50, Univ. of Southern Calif.; Coordinator of Curriculum, Alhambra City Sch. Dist., Alhambra, Calif., since 1951.

Erickson, Leonard C., B.S.'32, Univ. of Minn.; M.S.'48, Univ. of Southern Calif.; Asst. Supt. and Bus. Mgr., City Sch., Compton, Calif., since 1948.

Everly, Roger B., A.B.'37, Univ. of Calif. at Los Angeles; M.S. in Ed.'46, Univ. of Southern Calif.; Dist. Supt. of Sch., El Segundo, Calif., since 1948.

Eyring, Edward, A.B.'26, Univ. of Ariz.; M.A.'27, Ph.D.'32, Univ. of Calif.; Pres., New Mexico Highlands Univ., 1939-52. Address: 304 Perkins St., Oakland, Calif.

Falk, Charles J., Assoc. Prof. of Educ., Occidental College, Los Angeles, Calif.

Fawcett, Claude W., A.B.'33, Southwest Mo. State Tchrs. Col., Springfield; Ph.D.'43, Yale Univ.; Educ. Dir., Western Div., National Assoc. of Manufacturers, San Francisco, Calif.

Fikes, Edith E., Co. Supt. of Sch., Santa Cruz, Calif.

Findlay, Bruce A., B.A.'17, Pomona Col.; M.A.'20, Univ. of Southern Calif.; Assoc. Supt. of Sch., Los Angeles, Calif.

Finley, E. S., B.S. in Ed.'20, Mo. State Tchrs. Col.; M.S. in Ed.'41, Univ. of Mo.; Dist. Supt. of Sch., Holtville, Calif., since 1945.

Fitts, (Mrs.) Lucile Derr, Pres., H. S. Tchrs. Assn. of Los Angeles City, Inc., Los Angeles, Calif.

Flamson, George H., A.B.'18, Park Col.; M.S.'21, Pennsylvania State Col.; Supt. of Sch., Paso Robles, Calif., since 1945.

Florell, David M., B.A.'35, M.A.'39, Univ. of Minn.; Ed.D.'46, Univ. of Calif.; Dist. Supt. of Sch., Lompoc, Calif., since 1947.

Fontes, (Mrs.) Eleanor, A.B.'31, San Francisco State Col.; M.A.'49, Stanford Univ.; Dist. Supt. of Sch., Freedom, Calif., since 1946.

Fox, Rollin C., A.B.'28, Univ. of Ala.; M.A.'34, Tchrs. Col., Columbia Univ.; Ed.D.'46, Univ. of Calif. at Los Angeles; Supt. of Sch., Needles, Calif., since 1951.

Freese, Theron, A.B.'32, A.M.'41, Univ. of Southern Calif.; Asst. Supt. of Sch., in chg. of Instr., Long Beach, Calif.

Friedrich, Kurt, A.B.'35, M.A.'39, Columbia Univ.; Ed.D.'48, Tchrs. Col., Columbia Univ.; Asst. Prof. of Educ. San Diego State Col., San Diego, Calif., since 1949.

369

Fugate, Ben Fred, A.B.'37, Ed.M.'37, Univ. of Okla.; Dist. Supt. of Sch., Oceanside, Calif., since 1951.

Fuller, Merle L., A.B.'30, San Jose State Col.; Dist. Supt. of Elem. Sch., Chowchilla, Calif., since 1936.

Gaertner, (Mrs.) Reita I., Admin. Credential '51, Univ. of Calif., Santa Barbara; Dist. Supt. of Sch., Ventura, Calif., since 1951.

Gansberg, Lucille, M.Ed.'48, Mills Col. (Calif.); Supt. of Co. Sch., Susanville, Calif., since 1951.

Garrison, Elra Gell, B.S.'20, M.S.'28, Univ. of Calif., Berkeley; Dist. Supt. of Sch., Oceanside, Calif.

Geyer, George H., A.B.'27, Pomona Col.; A.M.'30, Univ. of Calif.; Ed.D.'40, Tchrs. Col., Columbia Univ.; Asst. Supt., Unified Sch. Dist., San Diego, Calif., since 1949.

Gilchrist, Robert S., A.B.'27, A.M.'28, Colo. State Col. of Educ., Greeley; Ph.D.'38, New York Univ.; Asst. Supt. of Sch., Pasadena, Calif., since 1949.

Gillingham, Robert Cameron, B.A.'21, M.A.'22, Pomona Col.; Ph.D.'49, Univ. of Southern Calif.; Chmn., Social Science, Compton Jr. Col., Compton, Calif., since 1936.

Glass, Sidney L., A.B.'30, Fresno State Col.; M.S.'36, Univ. of Southern Calif.; Asst. Supt. of Co. Sch., Fresno, Calif., since 1946.

Glick, Dale I., A.B.'27, La Verne Col.; M.A.'29, Claremont Col.; Dist. Supt. of Sch., Placentia, Calif., since 1947.

Goodell, Earl A., A.B.'33, San Jose State Col.; Supt. of Sch., Hilmar, Calif., since 1947.

Goodwill, Glen T., B.A.'29, Univ. of Redlands; M.A.'38, Univ. of Southern Calif.; Supt. of Sch., Monterey, Calif., since 1944.

Goold, J. Vernon, A.B.'20, Stanford Univ.; Dist. Supt., Wash. Union H. S., Centerville, Calif., since 1942.

Gore, Walter R., A.B.'39, M.A.'40, Univ. of Denver; Ed.D.'47, Univ. of Colo.; Prof. of Educ. Admin., Col. of the Pacific, Stockton, Calif., since 1951.

Grant, Al, M.A.'28, Univ. of Chicago; Curriculum Coordinator, City Sch., Inglewood, Calif., since 1951.

Graves, Albert D., A.B.'26, A.M.'32, Ed.D.'48, Stanford Univ.; Prof. of Educ., Los Angeles State Col., Los Angeles, Calif.

Gray, C. Delmar, A.B.'31, State Col. of Wash.; M.A.'34, Claremont Col.; Dist. Supt. of Sch., Escondido, Calif., since 1934.

Gregory, Carl E., A.B.'39, Univ. of Washington; M.A.'46, Ed.D.'48, Columbia Univ.; Chairman, Div. of Social Science, Long Beach State Col., Long Beach, Calif., since 1951.

Gridley, (Mrs.) Louise B., Exec. Secy., Calif. Tchrs. Assn., San Francisco, Calif.

Griffin, Herschel R., Exec. Secy., Affiliated Tchrs. Organizations of Los Angeles, Los Angeles, Calif.

Grover, Charles C., B.S.'08, Baker Univ.; M.A.'16, Univ. of Denver; M.A.'27, Stanford Univ.; Asst. Supt. of Sch., Oakland, Calif., since 1947.

Gunn, Henry M., B.S.'29, M.A.'31, Univ. of Oregon; Ed.D.'40, Stanford Univ.; Supt. of Sch., Palo Alto, Calif., since 1950.

Gustafson, LeRoy E., A.B.'32, Fresno State Col.; M.A.'49, Stanford Univ.; Supt. of Sch., Kingsburg, Calif., since 1937.

*Gwinn, Joseph Marr, A.B.'02, Univ. of Mo.; A.M.'07, Tchrs. Col., Columbia Univ.; LL.D. '26, Univ. of Mo.; Pres., Dept. of Superintendence, 1927-28; Honorary Life Member, American Assn. of Sch. Admin.; Prof. Emeritus of Educ., San Jose State Col., San Jose, Calif., since 1940. Address: 160 S. Euclid Ave., Pasadena 5, Calif.

*Hall, George V., B.S.'31, M.A.'34, Univ. of Minn.; Ed.D.'49, Tchrs. Col., Columbia Univ.; Asst. Supt. in chg. of Instr., Pub. Sch., San Diego, Calif., since 1952.

Hamm, Hal W., M.A.'30, Colo. Col. of Educ.; Prin. and Dist. Supt., Santa Ynez Valley Union H. S., Santa Ynez, Calif., since 1944.

*Hanna, Paul Robert, B.A.'24, D.Ped.'39, Hamline Univ.; A.M.'25, Ph.D.'29, Columbia Univ.; Prof. of Educ., Stanford Univ., Stanford University, Calif., since 1935.

Hannah, Stanford, B.S.'22, Mont. State Col.; M.A.'30, Univ. of Calif.; Dist. Supt., Jefferson Union H. S., Daly City, Calif., since 1944.

*Hardesty, Cecil D., A.B.'28, Kansas Wesleyan Univ.; M.A. in Ed.'32, Ed.D.'33, Univ. of Southern Calif.; Supt. of Co. Sch., San Diego, Calif., since 1950.

Harmer, Ralph L., A.B.'27, M.A.'29, Colo. State Col. of Educ., Greeley; Supt., Plumas Unified Sch. Dist., Quincy, Calif., since 1943.

Harper, Laurence, A.B.'26, Univ. of Calif.; Dist. Supt. of Sch., South Pasadena, Calif., since 1946.

Harris, Ben M., A.B.'48, M.Ed.'51, Univ. of Calif.; Coordinator, Elem. and Sec. Educ., Independence, Calif., since 1951.

Harris, Richard F., A.B.'34, Whittier Col.; Dist. Supt. of Sch., Westminster, Calif.

Haskell, Eugene Ryan, B.A.'30, Stanford Univ.; M.A.'43, Univ. of Calif. at Los Angeles; Box 806, Boulder Creek, Calif.

Hatch, H. Thurston, A.B.'22, Western State Col. of Colo., Gunnison; M.A.'30, Ed.D.'49, Univ. of Calif.; Supt. of Sch., Chico, Calif., since 1950.

Hayhurst, Normal C., B.S.'15, Univ. of Ariz.; M.E.'34, Univ. of Southern Calif.; Supt. of Sch., Glendale, Calif., since 1947.

Heffernan, Helen, B.A.'24, M.A.'25, Univ. of Calif.; Asst. Chief, Div. of Instr., in charge of Elem. Educ., State Dept. of Educ., Sacramento, Calif.

Heisner, H. Fred, A.B.'29, Univ. of Redlands; M.A.'32, Ed.D.'47, Univ. of Southern Calif.; Supt., Centinela Valley Union H. S. Dist., Inglewood, Calif., since 1948.

Hemphill, Franklin C., A.B.'22, Colo. State Col. of Educ., Greeley; M.A.'33, Univ. of Southern Calif.; Asst. Supt., Compton Jr. Col., Compton Calif., since 1930.

Henzie, C. Russell, Pres., San Diego Tchrs. Assn., San Diego, Calif.

*Hepner, Walter R., A.B.'13, A.M.'16, Ed.D. '37, Univ. of Southern Calif.; Pres., San Diego State Col., San Diego, Calif., since 1935.

Hicks, Robert S., A.B.'21, Occidental Col.; M.A.'31, Univ. of Southern Calif.; Dist. Supt., El Monte Union H. S. Dist., 1936-52 (retired). Address: Whitney Portals, Lone Pine, Calif.

Hiebert, Lester L., A.B.'46, Univ. of Calif.; M.S.Ed.'51, Univ. of Southern Calif.; Dist. Supt., Pixley Union Elem. Sch., Pixley, Calif., since 1952.

Hilburn, Robert F., A.B.'40, Ariz. State Col.; M.S.'49, Univ. of Southern Calif.; Supt. of Sch., Inglewood, Calif., since 1951.

Hildreth, Elon E., Pres., Palomar Col., Vista, Calif.

Hill, Harold P., A.B.'28, Stanford Univ.; M.A.'39, Univ. of Calif.; Dist. Supt. of Sch., St. Helena, Calif., since 1946.

Hill, (Mrs.) Margaret Ford, B.A.'39, Santa Barbara Col., Univ. of Calif.; Tchr., Lincoln Sch., Santa Barbara, Calif., since 1947.

Hodges, J. Allen, A.B.'28, Univ. of Calif.; Exec. Secy., San Diego City Sch. Retirement System, San Diego, Calif., since 1940.

Hoff, Arthur G., B.Ed.'28, State Tchrs. Col., Superior, Wis.; M.A.'30, State Univ. of Iowa; Ph.D.'38, Univ. of Minn.; Supt., Unified Sch. Dist., Palm Springs, Calif., since 1948.

Hoggatt, Vernon A., B.S.'33, M.S.'44, Kansas State Tchrs. Col., Pittsburg; Jr. Past ATOLA Chmn., 329 Diamond St., Arcadia, Calif.

Holbrook, C. Ray, B.A.'19, M.A.'22, Univ. of Wash.; Ed.D.'39, Stanford Univ.; Admin. Consultant, Kern Co. Sch., Bakersfield, Calif., since 1950.

Holstein, Walter E., A.B.'25, M.A.'31, Univ. of Southern Calif.; Prin., Phineas Banning Evening H. S., Los Angeles, Calif., and Supvg. Prin. Day Adult Classes, Los Angeles Harbor Area, Wilmington, Calif., since 1933.

*Holy, Thomas C., A.B.'19, Des Moines Univ.; M.A.'22, Ph.D.'24, State Univ. of Iowa; Special Consultant in Higher Educ., Univ. of Calif., Berkeley, Calif., since 1952.

Homfeld, Melville J., Dist. Supt. of Sch., Menlo Park, Calif., since 1947.

Hopkins, Frank O., B.S. in Ed.'32, M.S. in Ed.'46, Univ. of Southern Calif.; Supt. Brea-Olinda Union H. S. Dist., Brea, Calif., since 1946.

Horning, John L., A.B.'32, San Jose State Col.; M.A.'34, Stanford Univ.; Prin., Cragmont Sch., Berkeley, Calif., since 1943.

Houseman, Richard A., B.S.'36, Central Michigan Col. of Educ.; M.A.'41, Ed.D.'45, Tchrs. Col., Columbia Univ.; Assoc. Prof. of Educ., San Diego State Col., San Diego, Calif., since 1948.

Howell, Harry M., B.A.'24, M.S. in Ed.'37, Ed.D.'50, Univ. of Southern Calif.; Assoc. Supt. of Sch., Los Angeles, Calif., since 1938.

Hoyt, Guy M., Ph.B.'16, M.A.'21, Univ. of Chicago; Assoc. Supt. of Sch., Los Angeles, Calif.

Hubbard, O. S., Supt., Santa Clara Co. Sch., San Jose, Calif.

Hughes, Harold G., A.B.'28, Pacific Univ.; M.A.'33, Univ. of Oregon; Asst. Supt., Grossmont H. S. Dist., Grossmont, Calif., since 1947.

Hull, J. Henrich, A.B.'30, Univ. of Redlands; M.A.'32, Colo. State Col. of Educ., Greeley; Ed.D.'49, Univ. of Southern Calif.; Supt. of City Sch., Torrance, Calif., since 1947.

Hull, Osman R., B.S.'13, M.S.'14, Ph.D.'25, Univ. of Calif.; Prof. in Educ. Admin., since 1924 and Dean, Sch. of Educ., Univ. of Southern Calif., Los Angeles, Calif., since 1945.

Hummel, Edward John, A.B.'13, Univ. of Southern Calif.; A.M.'14, Columbia Univ.; Ed.D.'45, Univ. of Southern Calif.; Deputy Supt. of Sch., Beverly Hills, Calif., since 1939.

Hunt, (Mrs.) Lucy, Co. Supt. of Sch., Redding, Calif., since 1949.

Hurlburt, Edwin N., B.S.'29, Western Mich. Col. of Educ., Kalamazoo; M.A.'46, Claremont Grad. Sch.; Dist. Supt., Soledad Union Elem. Sch., Soledad, Calif., since 1949.

Hutchens, Jens H., A.B.'34, San Diego State Col.; M.S.'38, Univ. of Calif.; Ed.D.'50, Univ. of Calif. at Los Angeles; Asst. Supt. of Special Serv., San Diego Co. Sch., San Diego, Calif., since 1943.

Huxtable, Ethel E., Art Supvr., Pub. Sch., San Mateo, Calif.

Ingalls, Rosco C., A.B.'09, McPherson Col.; A.M.'11, Univ. of Kansas; LL.D.'38, McPherson Col.; LL.D.'42, Col. of Osteopathic Physicians and Surgeons; Pres., East Los Angeles Jr. Col., Los Angeles, Calif., since 1945.

Jack, Walter A., A.B.'37, Humboldt State Col.; M.A.'41, Stanford Univ.; Supt., Elem. Sch. Dist., San Mateo, Calif., since 1946.

Jacobsen, Einar William, B.A.'16, M.A.'23, Univ. of Calif.; Ph.D.'30, Columbia Univ.; Supt. of Sch., Santa Barbara, Calif., since 1948.

Jacobson, Lawrence, A.B.'34, Fresno State Col.; Dist. Supt. of Sch., Bakersfield, Calif., since 1936.

Jarvis, Ellis A., Asst. Supt. of Sch., Los Angeles, Calif.

Jaster, Vincent E., M.S.'36, Univ. of Southern Calif.; Dist. Supt. of Elem. Sch., Brea, Calif., since 1943.

Jensen, Gerald L., Ed.D.'49, Stanford Univ.; Coordinator, Sec. Educ., Imperial Co. Sch., El Centro, Calif., since 1948.

Jensen, Harry T., B.S.Ed.'25, Genl. Beadle State Tchrs. Col., Madison, S. Dak.; M.S.'30, Univ. of Minn.; Ed.D.'41, Stanford Univ.; Prof. of Educ., San Jose State Col., San Jose, Calif., since 1940.

Johnson, Donald W., A.B.'36, Beloit Col.; M.A.'48, Ed.D.'50, Univ. of Calif.; Supvg. Prin. of Sch., Needles, Calif., since 1951.

Johnson, Frank R., A.B.'36, Chico State Col.; M.S.'40, Univ. of Southern Calif.; Dist. Supt. of Sch., Guadalupe, Calif., since 1927.

Johnson, (Mrs.) Laura M., A.B.'27, M.A.'29, Univ. of Calif., Berkeley; Co. Supt. of Sch., Downieville, Calif., since 1947.

Johnson, Lloyd G., A.B.'30, Chico State Col.; Co. Supt. of Sch., Colusa, Calif., since 1950.

Johnson, Loaz W., A.B.'28, N. Mex. State Tchrs. Col.; M.A.'31, Univ. of Wyo.; Ed.D.'38, Univ. of Calif.; Coordinator of Curriculum, Court House Annex, Oroville, Calif., since 1939.

Johnson, Ray W., A.B.'27, Col. of Emporia; M.S.Ed.'40, Ed.D.'52, Univ. of Southern Calif.; Supt. of Sch., Riverside, Calif., since 1950.

Johnson, Reuben E., A.B.'33, Bethany Col.; A.M.'38, Univ. of Southern Calif.; Asst. Supt. of Sch., Monterey, Calif., since 1951.

Johnston, Eugene M., A.B.'23, Univ. of Dubuque; M.A.'37, Univ. of Southern Calif.; Supt., Taft Union H. S. Dist., Taft, Calif., since 1944.

Jones, L. L., A.B.'33, Pomona Col.; M.A.'40, Claremont Graduate Sch.; Supt. of Sch., Watsonville, Calif., since 1948.

Jones, Lowell Butler, B.A.'39, La Verne Col.; M.A.'49, Claremont Graduate Sch.; Yorba Linda, Calif., since 1947.

Jones, Marston E., B.Arch.'31, M.S.Ed.'42, Univ. of Southern Calif.; Coordinator, Instrl. Materials, Orange Co. Sch., Santa Ana, Calif., since 1947.

Joyal, Arnold E., A.B.'25, M.A.'26, Ph.D.'31, Univ. of Calif.; Pres., Fresno State Col., Fresno, Calif., since 1948.

Kaar, Harold W., A.B.'23, M.A.'27, Univ. of Calif., Berkeley; Asst. Supt., Educ. Serv., Contra Costa Co. Sch., Martinez, Calif., since 1949.

Keenan, Ethel, B.S. in Ed.'40, Univ. of Southern Calif.; Dist. Supt. of Sch., Puente, Calif., since 1932.

371

Kemp, Charles B., B.A.'35, Whittier Col.;
M.S. in Ed. '40, Univ. of Southern Calif.;
Dir. of Special Serv., Montebello Sch. Dist.,
Montebello, Calif., since 1951.

Kendall, Glenn, A.B.'25, Western Ky. State
Tchrs. Col., Bowling Green; M.A.'31, Univ. of
Ky.; Ed.D.'41, Tchrs. Col., Columbia Univ.;
Pres., Chico State Col., Chico, Calif., since
1950.

Kennedy, (Mrs.) Pearl M., B.S.'46, Univ. of
Southern Calif.; Supt., Lawndale Sch., Los
Angeles, Calif., since 1948.

Kepley, Ruth A., Co. Supt. of Sch., El Centro,
Calif.

Kibby, George M., A.B.'34, M.A.'42, Univ. of
Calif.; Dist. Supt. of Sch., Corona, Calif.,
since 1948.

Kibby, Harold V., A.B.'37, San Jose State Col.;
M.S.'42, Univ. of Southern Calif.; Dist. Supt.,
and Prin., Union H. S., Orange, Calif., since
1947.

Kirkpatrick, W. Bruce, A.B.'20, Occidental Col.;
A.M.'30, Univ. of Southern Calif.; Prin., John
Marshall H. S., Los Angeles, Calif., since 1941.

Kitch, Donald E., A.B.'27, Southwestern Col.;
M.A., Northwestern Univ.; Chief, Bur. of
Guidance Serv., State Dept. of Educ., Sacra-
mento, Calif., since 1947.

Knapp, Roy A., B.S.'23, Huron Col.; M.A.'33,
Claremont Col.; Supt., Antelope Valley Joint
Union H. S. Dist., Lancaster, Calif., since
1934.

Knowles, Willard B., B.S.'24, Utah State Col.;
Dist. Supt., Pub. Sch., Martinez, Calif., since
1950.

Kramer, Carlisle H., A.B.'40, San Jose State
Col.; M.A.'41, Stanford Univ.; Dist. Supt. of
Sch., Hillsborough, San Mateo, Calif., since
1951.

Kratt, Edwin C., A.B.'24, Linfield Col.; M.A.'29,
Stanford Univ.; Supt. of Sch., Fresno, Calif.,
since 1944.

Kratt, William E., A.B.'27, Linfield Col.; M.A.'33,
Univ. of Oregon; LL.D.'46, Linfield Col.;
Pres., Menlo Sch. and Col., Menlo Park,
Calif., since 1945.

Krogh, Thor, Ph.B.'29, Univ. of Vt.; M.A.'34,
Univ. of Wash.; Sequoia Union H. S., Redwood City, Calif.

La Fleche, Rock, Asst. Supt., Alameda Co.
Sch., Oakland, Calif., since 1949.

*Laird, J. David, A.B.'28, Colo. State Col. of
Educ., Greeley; Supt. of Sch., Tulare, Calif.,
since 1943.

Landis, Ira C., Supt. of Sch., Riverside, Calif.,
1928-51 (retired).

Langston, Roderick G., Ed.D.'48, Stanford Univ.;
Prof. of Educ., Los Angeles State Col., Los
Angeles, Calif., since 1952.

Larsen, Ansgar J., A.B.'30, Santa Barbara State
Tchrs. Col.; M.S. in Ed.'48, Univ. of Southern
Calif.; Supt. Hueneme Elem. Sch. Dist.,
Port Hueneme, Calif., since 1943.

Lauderbach, John Calvin, B.A.'20, M.A.'31,
Ed.D.'48, Univ. of Calif. at Los Angeles; Supt.
of Sch., Chula Vista, Calif., since 1935.

Laugesen, Roy M., A.B.'39, San Francisco State
Col.; M.A.'49, Stanford Univ.; Dist. Supt. of
Sch., Mill Valley, Calif., since 1947.

Lawson, Jalmar W., Diploma '17, Western
Mich. Col. of Educ., Kalamazoo; A.B.'28,
San Diego State Col.; A.M.'32, Univ. of
Southern Calif.; Supt., Elem. Sch., Ventura,
Calif., since 1946.

Lawson, Oliver C., A.B.'26, M.A.'35, Stanford
Univ.; Asst. Supt. of Sch., Santa Ana, Calif.,
since 1948.

Lee, Edwin A., B.S.'14, M.A.'15, Ph.D.'32,
Columbia Univ.; Prof. of Educ. and Dean,
Sch. of Educ., Univ. of Calif., Los Angeles,
Calif., since 1940.

Leonard, J. Paul, A.B.'23, Drury Col.; A.M.'27,
Ph.D.'29, Columbia Univ.; Pres., San Francisco State Col., San Francisco, Calif., since
1945.

Lewis, Harvey, Jr., Member, since 1944, and
Pres., Bd. of Educ., Unified Sch. Dist., San
Diego, Calif.

Lewis, James A., B.S.'36, Univ. of Oregon;
M.A.'41, Col. of the Pacific; Supt. of Sch.,
King City, Calif., since 1948.

Lindquist, Tom B., A.B.'33, Univ. of Calif.;
Dist. Supt. of Sch., Bakersfield, Calif., since
1946.

Lindsay, Frank B., A.B.'21, Indiana Univ.;
A.M.'34, Claremont Col.; Asst. Chief, Div. of
Instr., State Dept. of Educ., Sacramento,
Calif., since 1938.

Little, Wilson, B.S.'31, North Texas State Tchrs.
Col., Denton; M.A.'38, Ph.D.'42, Univ. of
Texas; Dir., Regional Project in Sec. Educ.,
Sacramento State Col., Sacramento, Calif.

Lockwood, Charles W., A.B.'26, Univ. of Calif.,
Los Angeles; M.A.'31, Univ. of Southern
Calif.; Dist. Supt. of Sch., San Jacinto, Calif.,
since 1944.

Lones, Philip T., A.B.'36, M.A.'41, Univ. of
Calif.; Asst. City Supt. of Sch., San Leandro,
Calif., since 1952.

Long, H. B., A.B.'25, M.A.'32, Ed.D.'49, Stanford, Univ.; Dist. Supt. of Sch., Gilroy, Calif.,
since 1946.

Long, Watt, A., B.A.'24, Pacific Univ.; M.A.'32,
Univ. of Oregon; Assoc. Supt. of Sch., San
Francisco, Calif.

Lonsdale, Bernard J., Ed.D.'50, Univ. of Calif.;
Consultant in Elem. Educ., State Dept. of
Educ., Sacramento, Calif., since 1946.

Loomis, Arthur Kirkwood, A.B.'09, Baker Univ.;
A.M.'17, Univ. of Kansas; Ph.D.'26, Tchrs.
Col., Columbia Univ.; L.H.D.'44, Baker
Univ.; Chief, Educ. Div., G-5, HQ, FEC,
APO 500, c/o P. M., San Francisco, Calif.,
since 1949

Lounsbury, John L., A.B.'19, B.S. in Ed.'21,
Southwest Mo. State Col., Springfield;
M.S.'22, Stanford Univ.; Ed.D.'39, Univ. of
Southern Calif.; Pres., San Bernardino Valley
Col., San Bernardino, Calif., since 1942.

Lucas, Dan Broox, B.A.'24, Univ. of Oregon;
M.A.'38, Univ. of Southern Calif.; Dist. Supt.
of Elem. Sch., Baldwin Park, Calif., since
1945.

Lucas, Frank L., A.B.'41, Univ. of Calif.; Dist.
Supt., Amador Valley Joint Union H. S. and
Pleasanton Elem. Sch., Pleasanton, Calif.,
since 1948.

Lucas, Frederick E., Supt., Fall River Unified
Sch. Dist., Fall River Mills, Calif., since 1949.

Lydell, Dwight M., Diploma '17, Chico State
Tchrs. Col., Chico, Calif.; Supt. of Elem. Sch.,
Monrovia, Calif., since 1939.

McCammon, Oliver, B.A.'32, Humboldt State
Col.; M.A.'36, Univ. of Calif. at Berkeley;
Dist. Supt. of Sch., Hawthorne, Calif., since
1943.

McCandless, Harry P., A.B.'22, Nebr. Wesleyan
Univ.; M.A.'32, Univ. of Southern Calif.;
Supt. of Sch., Redondo Beach, Calif., since
1935.

McComb, Stuart F., A.B.'32, Ariz. State Col.;
M.S.'39, Ed.D.'47, Univ. of Southern Calif.;
Supt., Compton Union H. S. and Jr. Col. Dist.
and Pres., Compton Col., Compton, Calif.,
since 1950.

McCuen, Theron L., A.B.'28, M.A.'29, Stanford Univ.; Dist. Supt., Kern Co. Union H. S. Dist., Bakersfield, Calif., since 1945.

McCunn, Drummond J., A.B.'27, Occidental Col.; M.S. in Ed.'38, Univ. of Southern Calif.; Supt., Contra Costa Co. Jr. Col. Dist., Martinez, Calif., since 1949.

McDonald, Howard, B.S.'21, Utah State Agrl. Col.; M.A.'25, Ed.D.'49, Univ. of Calif. at Berkeley; Pres., Los Angeles City Col. and Los Angeles State Col. of Applied Arts and Sciences, Los Angeles, Calif., since 1949.

McDonald, John M., A.B.'13, B.S. in Ed.'14, A.M. in Ed.'23, Univ. of Mo.; Dist. Supt. of Sch., National City, Calif., since 1932.

McDonell, Kenneth A., A.B.'36, San Francisco State Col.; M.A.'50, Stanford Univ.; Supt., Union Sch. Dist., Los Gatos, Calif., since 1946.

McGaugh, J. H., Supt. of Sch., Seal Beach, Calif.

McGinnis, J. Clark, A.B.'33, San Jose State Tchrs. Col.; Dist. Supt. and Prin., Rosedale Union Sch., Bakersfield, Calif., since 1937.

McIntosh, Donald H., B.A.'16, Occidental Col.; Dist. Supt. of Sch., Colton, Calif., since 1930.

McKay, Henry W., A.B.'33, Univ. of Calif.; M.S.'34, Univ. of Southern Calif.; Deputy Supt., City Sch., Compton, Calif., since 1950.

McKibben, Howard J., A.B.'30, Santa Barbara Col.; M.S.'43, Univ. of Southern Calif.; Supt. of Sch., Whittier, Calif., since 1948.

McLaughlin, James O., A.B.'05, A.M.'09, Grove City Col.; Ed.D.'30, Stanford Univ.; Instr. in Sch. Admin., Claremont Graduate Sch., Claremont, Calif., since 1950.

McNaughton, Daniel Charles, B.S.'29, Colo. Agrl. and Mech. Col.; M.A.'35, Univ. of Chicago; Ed.D.'42, Stanford Univ.; Dir., Santa Ana Col., Santa Ana, Calif., since 1949.

McPherson, H. M., Ed.D.'38, Univ. of Calif.; Dist. Supt. of Sch., Napa, Calif., since 1940.

MacConnell, James D., A.B.'31, Central Mich. Col. of Educ., Mt. Pleasant; M.A.'40, Ed.D.'44, Univ. of Mich.; Assoc. Prof. of Sch. Admin. and Assoc. Dean, Stanford Univ., Stanford University, Calif., since 1949.

MacGregor, John I., A.B.'35, San Jose State Col.; M.A.'52, Stanford Univ.; Dist. Supt. and Prin. of Sch., Newark, Calif., since 1937.

Magee, Lawrence Thomas, B.A.'35, Ariz. State Col., Tempe; M.A.'37, Univ. of Southern Calif.; Dist. Supt. of Sch., Rivera, Calif., since 1948.

Malloch, James Morrow, A.B.'17, M.A.'20, Univ. of Calif.; G.Th.'33, Church Divinity Sch. of the Pacific; D.D.'43, Col. of the Pacific; Dean, St. James' Cathedral, since 1937, and Vicepres., Bd. of Educ., Fresno, Calif.

Mannatt, (Mrs.) Earnestyne W., B.S. in Ed. '30, M.S.'33, Univ. of Southern Calif.; Dist. Asst. Supt. of Sch., Los Angeles, Calif., since 1945.

Mapes, E. P., Co. Supt. of Sch., Willows, Calif., since 1927.

Marsee, Stuart E., B.S.'39, M.S.'42, Univ. of Oregon; Ed.D.'47, Univ. of Southern Calif.; Asst. Supt. of Sch. in chg. of Bus. Service, Pasadena, Calif., since 1951.

Martin, Edwin L., A.B.'23, M.A.'35, Univ. of Southern Calif.; Prin. of Belmont Adult Educ. Center, Los Angeles, Calif., since 1929.

Martin, Walter G., A.B.'14, Ottawa Univ.; M.A.'16, Univ. of Calif.; Co. Supt. of Sch., Fresno, Calif., since 1945.

Mattox, Clifford J., A.B.'25, Univ. of Wash.; A.M.'39, Stanford Univ.; Asst. Supt. of City Sch., San Bernardino, Calif., since 1945.

Meade, (Mrs.) Agnes Weber, Co. Supt. of Sch., Marysville, Calif., since 1927.

Melbo, Irving R., A.B.'30, M.A.'32, N. Mex. State Tchrs. Col., Silver City; Ed.D.'34, Univ. of Calif.; Prof. of Educ. Admin., Univ. of Southern Calif., Los Angeles, Calif., since 1939.

Melendy, Ruth W., M.A.'34, Univ. of Oregon; Supt. of Sch., San Carlos, Calif., since 1943.

Mennet, Earl F., M.S.'37, Univ. of Idaho; Dir. of Research, Oakland, Calif., since 1946.

Mette, Wilda Carter, B.A.'27, San Jose State Col.; Supt., Russell Elem. Sch. Dist., Hayward, Calif., since 1945.

Michell, Forrest C., M.A.'34, Univ. of Calif.; Admin. Asst., Pub. Sch., Oakland, Calif., since 1946.

Miller, Bruce, A.B.'34, San Diego State Col.; M.A.'44, Claremont Col.; Supt. of Sch., Ontario, Calif., since 1940.

Milliken, Daniel B., B.A.'26, Pomona Col.; M.B.A.'28, Harvard Univ.; Supt. of Chaffey Union H. S., and Pres., Chaffey Col., Ontario, Calif., since 1949.

Miner, George D., B.A.'22, Carleton Col.; M.A.'29, Ed.D.'40, Univ. of Calif.; LL.D.'45, Ursinus Col.; Supt. of Sch., Richmond, Calif., since 1949.

Mitchell, R. G., B.A.'26, Univ. of Calif. at Los Angeles; M.A.'27, Univ. of Calif.; Supt. of Sch., Beverly Hills, Calif.

Mock, Thomas M., B.S. in Ed.'20, Kansas State Tchrs. Col.; M.S.'32, Univ. of Southern Calif.; Prin., Horace Mann Sch., Beverly Hills, Calif., since 1929.

Montgomery, G. Millage, B.S.'13, Oregon State Col.; Assoc. Supt. of Sch., Los Angeles, Calif., since 1944.

Morgan, Edward D., A.B.'36, San Francisco State Col.; Supt. of Sch., Dinuba, Calif., since 1951.

Morgan, Miles Evan, A.B.'15, M.A.'22, Ph.D.'33, Univ. of Washington; Asst. Supt. of Sch., Santa Monica, Calif., since 1948.

Morgan, Richard J., A.B.'39, Whittier Col.; M.S.'46, Univ. of Southern Calif.; Prin. of Elem. Sch., Bell Gardens, Calif., since 1948.

Morphet, Edgar L., A.B.'18, Ind. State Tchrs. Col., Terre Haute; M.A.'26, Ph.D.'27, Tchrs. Col., Columbia Univ.; Prof. of Educ., Univ. of Calif., Berkeley, Calif., since 1949.

Morris, A. B., Dist. Supt. of Sch., Castro Valley, Calif.

Morrisett, Lloyd N., A.B.'17, Univ. of Okla.; M.A.'30, Ph.D.'34, Columbia Univ.; Prof. of Educ., Univ. of Calif., Los Angeles, Calif., since 1941.

*Muelder, Wallace Richard, B.S.'46, Western Ill. State Col.; M.S.Ed.'47, Ed.D.'52, Univ. of Southern Calif.; Asst. Co. Supt. of Sch., Riverside, Calif., since 1950.

Mueller, Frederick Eugene, B.A.'28, Iowa State Tchrs. Col., Cedar Falls; M.A.'34, State Univ. of Iowa; Supt. of Sch., San Bernardino, Calif.

Murdock, Forrest G., B.A.'16, State Col. of Wash.; M.Ed.'32, Univ. of Wash.; Pres., El Camino Col., El Camino College, Calif., since 1947.

Murdock, Glenn E., B.A.'28, Univ. of Redlands; M.A.'36, Stanford Univ.; Supt. of Elem. Sch., La Mesa, Calif.

Murphy, Edward V., A.B.'31, Fresno Col.; Dist. Supt. of Sch., Norwalk, Calif., since 1943.

Murray, Earl, A.B.'18, Whittier Col.; M.A.'28, Univ. of Southern Calif.; Prin., Burroughs H. S., Kern Co. Union H. S. Dist., and Supt., Elem. Sch. Dist., U. S. Naval Ordnance Test Sta., China Lake, Calif., since 1945.

Myers, Arno E., Dist. Supt., Moorpark, Calif.

Myers, Newell Dixon, A.B.'33, Stanford Univ.; M.A.'36, Univ. of Calif.; Dist. Supt. of Sch., Palos Verdes Estates, Calif., since 1939.

Neil, James W., Ed.D.'49, Univ. of Calif.; Asst. Prof. of Educ., Sacramento State Col., Sacramento, Calif., since 1950.

Nelson, Ada Shuman, B.E.'06, Bloomsburg State Tchrs. Col.; Life Admin. '24, Univ. of Southern Calif.; Dist. Supt. of Sch., Los Nietos, Calif., since 1912.

Nelson, (Mrs.) Myra Banta, Master's '29, Univ. of Calif. at Los Angeles; Dist. Asst. Supt. of Sch., Los Angeles, Calif., since 1946.

Nelson, Thomas L., B.S.'16, M.A. in Ed.'25, Ed.D.'33, Univ. of Calif.; Supt. of Sch., Berkeley, Calif., since 1945.

Netzley, Byron L., Dist. Supt. of Sch., Lemon Grove, Calif.

Newcomb, Douglas A., B.S.'18, Univ. of Rochester; M.A.'27, Stanford Univ.; LL.B.'38, Univ. of Southern Calif.; Supt. of Sch., Long Beach, Calif., since 1947.

Nichols, Leroy, A.B.'12, Southwestern Col.; A.M.'14, Univ. of Southern Calif.; Dist. Supt. of Sch., Lodi, Calif., since 1932.

Noel, Francis W., A.B. in Ed.'32, Univ. of Calif.; M.S. in Ed.'35, Univ. of Southern Calif.; Chief, Bur. of Audio-Visual Educ., State Dept. of Educ., Sacramento, Calif., since 1945.

Nopel, John H., A.B.'35, Chico State Col.; M.A.'41, Univ. of Calif.; Admin. Asst. of Chico City Sch., Chico, Calif., since 1950.

Norby, Theo J., Diploma '28, Western Wash. Col. of Educ., Bellingham; B.S.'35, M.Ed.'39, Univ. of Oregon; Supt. of Sch., Inglewood, Calif., since 1951.

Northrup, Orville I., A.B., B.E.'39, Univ. of Calif. at Santa Barbara; Supvg. Prin. of Sch., Tustin, Calif.

Norwood, Olive A., Dist. Supt. of Sch., Delano, Calif., since 1944.

Nuttall, Drayton B., A.B.'36, M.A.'41, Univ. of Utah; Dir. of the Sch. Facilities Survey, Calif. State Dept. of Educ., Sacramento, Calif., since 1952.

Odell, William R., B.S., B.A.'27, Univ. of Southern Calif.; M.A.'30, Ph.D.'32, Tchrs. Col., Columbia Univ.; Prof. of Educ. Admin., Standard Univ., Stanford University, Calif., since 1949.

Ogden, Clyde L., A.B.'29, M.A.'33, Ed.D.'49, Univ. of Calif.; Supt., Sequoia Union H. S. Dist., Redwood City, Calif., since 1948.

Oliver, Parke C., A.B.'21, Pomona Col.; Prin., Sr. H. S., Bell Gardens, Calif., since 1947.

Olson, H. R., B.S.'23, Oregon State Col.; M.A.'32, Univ. of Calif.; Supt., Delano Joint Union H. S., Delano, Calif., since 1932.

Paden, William G., A.B.'08, M.A.'20, J.D.'12, Univ. of Calif.; Supt. of Sch., Alameda, Calif., 1925-52 (retired).

Palmer, John H., A.B.'28, Chico State Col.; Supt. of Elem. Sch. Dist., Marysville, Calif., since 1944.

Parks, D. Russell, B.S.'36, M.S.'48, Univ. of Southern Calif.; Dist. Supt. of Sch., Fullerton, Calif., since 1945.

Parsons, Neil M., A.B.'24, Col. of Pacific; M.A.'44, Univ. of Calif.; Dist. Supt. of Sch., Lafayette, Calif., since 1945.

Partridge, Jay E., Co. Supt. of Sch., Oroville, Calif., since 1927.

Pattee, Howard Hunt, B.A.'22, Pomona Col.; M.A.'26, Stanford Univ.; Exec. Secy., Calif. Assn. of Independent Sch., Claremont, Calif., since 1942.

Paulsen, O. B., M.A.'32, Univ. of Calif.; Dist. Supt., Union H. S., Hayward, Calif., since 1942.

Pearson, (Mrs.) Nora L., Pres., Dept. of Classroom Tchrs., South Pasadena, Calif.

Pence, Edith E., B.A.'12, M.A.'13, Univ. of Calif.; Prin., Lowell H. S., San Francisco, Calif., since 1950.

Peterson, P. Victor, A.B.'17, Iowa State Tchrs. Col., Cedar Falls; A.M.'21, Ph.D.'30, Stanford Univ.; Pres., Long Beach State Col., Long Beach, Calif., since 1949.

Pisor, Carl E., B.A.'30, Fresno State Col.; Dist. Supt. of Sch., Fowler, Calif., since 1942.

Pollich, Raymond E., Ed.D.'43, Univ. of Southern Calif.; Asst. Supt. of Sch., Elem. Educ. Div., Los Angeles, Calif., since 1945.

Porter, (Mrs.) Florence C., Exec. Secy., Calif. Sch. Trustees Assn., Bakersfield, Calif., since 1930.

Potter, (Mrs.) Gladys L., B.E.'27, Univ. of Calif. at Los Angeles; M.A.'35, Univ. of Calif. at Berkeley; Deputy Supt. of Sch., Long Beach, Calif., since 1947.

Powell, Earle B., Dist. Supt. of Sch., Banning, Calif.

Poytress, Frank H., A.B.'24, Univ. of Calif.; M.A.'40, Stanford Univ.; Dist. Supt. of Sch., Merced, Calif., since 1944.

Price, Jackson, B.S.'23, Utah State Agric. Col.; M.A.'49, Univ. of Calif.; Dist. Supt., Shasta H. S. and Jr. Col., Redding, Calif., since 1934.

Price, Thomas B., Co. Supt. of Sch. and Supt. of Mariposa Co. Unified Sch. Dist., Mariposa, Calif.

Pulliam, Nolan D., A.B.'25, Central Col.; A.M.'32, Ed.D.'46, Stanford Univ.; Supt. of Sch., Stockton, Calif., since 1951.

Ranson, Mae, Prin. Elem. Sch., Alhambra, Calif.

Redding, Ray G., A.B.'27, Univ. of Redlands; M.A.'38, Claremont Col.; Dist. Supt. of Sch., Julian, Calif., since 1935.

Rees, Jack D., M.A.'41, Univ. of Calif.; Dist. Supt. of Elem. Sch., Hayward, Calif., since 1945.

Reeves, Claude L., M.A.'27, Univ. of Southern Calif.; Asst. Supt. of City Sch., Los Angeles, Calif., since 1949.

Regier, J. N., M.A.'32, Univ. of Nebr.; Supt, of Sch., San Luis Obispo, Calif., since 1948.

Reid, John Lyon, B.A.'29, M.A.'29, Univ. of Calif.; M.Arch.'31, Mass. Inst. of Tech.; Architect, 1069 Market St., San Francisco, Calif., since 1946.

Reller, Theodore L., B.S. in Ed.'28, A.M.'30, Univ. of Pa.; Ph.D.'33, Yale Univ.; Prof. of Educ., Univ. of Calif., Berkeley, Calif., since 1948.

Rhodes, Alvin E., A.B.'31, San Jose State Col.; M.A.'41, Stanford Univ.; Co. Supt. of Sch., San Luis Obispo, Calif., since 1947.

Riddlebarger, Clifford G., A.B.'38, Whittier Col.; M.S. in Ed.'47, Univ. of Southern Calif.; Dist. Supt. of Sch., Lawndale, Calif., since 1952.

Rinehart, (Mrs.) Gladys C., 2225 E. Orange Grove Ave., Pasadena, Calif.

Roberts, Harold B., Ed.D.'50, Stanford Univ.; Dean of Educ. Serv. and Summer Session, Sacramento State Col., Sacramento, Calif., since 1949.

Roberts, Roland J., A.B.'35, M.A.'45, Univ. of Calif.; Supt. of Sch., Felton, Calif., since 1950.

Roberts, W. E., A.B.'33, San Jose State Col.; Supt. of Co. Sch., Yreka, Calif., since 1951.

Robertson, Gus C., A.B.'40, San Jose State Col.; Dist. Supt. of Sch., Irvington, Calif., since 1943.

Robinson, Jack, B.A.'29, Chapman Col.; Supt. of Elem. Sch., Paramount, Calif., since 1949.

Robinson, (Mrs.) Margaret R., Member, Fresno City Bd. of Educ., Fresno, Calif., since 1939.

Roehe, Rev. Patrick J., Asst. Supt. of Parochial Sch., Los Angeles, Calif.

Roderick, Donald M., A.B.'34, Chico State Col.; M.A.'38, Ed.D.'46, Stanford Univ.; Supt. of Sch., Alameda, Calif., since 1952.

Rogers, Paul J., A.B.'27, Chapman Col.; Dist. Supt. of Sch., Colton, Calif., since 1944.

Rolff, Everett I., A.B.'33, Univ. of Calif.; Bus. Mgr., Unified Sch. Dist., Vallejo, Calif., since 1947.

Ross, John G., B.A.'32, San Jose State Col.; Deputy Co. Supt. of Sch., Bakersfield, Calif., since 1943.

Ross, Milton G., B.A.'37, Univ. of Calif. at Santa Barbara; Supt. of Sch., Taft, Calif., since 1949.

Ross, Thomas, A.B.'30, Chico State Col.; Dir. of Educ., Yuba Co. Sch., Marysville, Calif., since 1949.

Royse, Clarence W., B.A.'28, Col. of the Pacific; Dist. Sup. of Sch., Oakdale, Calif., since 1942.

Rudholm, Melvin P., A.B.'34, Fresno State Col.; Dist. Supt. of Sch., Pixley, Calif., since 1936.

Ruppenthal, Bruce M., A.B.'46, Ariz. State Col.; Dist. Supt. of Sch., San Marcos, Calif., since 1950.

Rusk, James H., A.B.'24, M.A.'34, Stanford Univ.; Supt. Natl. Sch. Dist., National City, Calif., since 1942.

Ryan, Thomas L., A.B.'29, Univ. of Santa Clara; Supt., East Side Union H. S., Alum Rock Union Elem. Sch., San Jose, Calif., since 1933.

Samuels, Charles T., A.B.'31, M.S. in Ed.'35, Univ. of Southern Calif.; Dist. Supt., East Whittier Sch., Whittier, Calif., since 1938.

Schaefer, Amos E., M.A.'36, Univ. of Southern Calif.; Supt. of Pub. Sch., Coronado, Calif., since 1948.

Schei, Ben I., Prin. of Sch., La Mesa, Calif.

Scheiber, Frank, B.A.'43, Humboldt State Col.; Dist. Supt. of Sch., Santa Rosa, Calif.

Schmidt, (Mrs.) Blanche, A.B.'20, San Jose State Col.; Prin., since 1928, and Dist. Supt., Elem. Sch., Dos Palos, Calif., since 1943.

Schnepple, Stanley O., B.A.'41, Stanford Univ.; Supt., Ravenswood Elem. Sch. Dist., East Palo Alto, Calif., since 1948.

Sears, Jesse Brundage, A.B.'09, Stanford Univ.; Ph.D.'20, Tchrs. Col., Columbia Univ.; Prof. of Educ., Emeritus, Stanford Univ., since 1949. Address: 40 Tevis Pl., Palo Alto, Calif.

*Seidel, Vaughn D., Co. Supt. of Sch., Oakland, Calif.

Selland, Arthur L., Mgr., E. F. Hutton and Co., Fresno Branch, and Member, Bd. of Educ., Fresno, Calif.

Sewell, Nelson B., A.B.'32, Univ. of Calif. at Los Angeles; M.A.'33, Univ. of Calif.; Prin., Salinas Union H. S., Salinas, Calif., since 1942.

Seyler, Louise Wood, A.B.'27, M.A.'38, Ed.D.'45, Univ. of Calif. at Los Angeles; Asst. Supt. of Sch., Div. of Elem. Educ., Los Angeles, Calif., since 1946.

Shafer, Paul F., B.A.'21, Pomona Col.; M.Ed.'32, Univ. of Southern Calif.; Litt.D.'48, Univ. of Louisville; Asst. Supt., Elem. Sch. Dist., Los Angeles, Calif., since 1947.

Shambaugh, Clifford F., A.B.'32, A.M.'36, Colo. State Col. of Educ., Greeley; Dist. Supt. of Sch., Downey, Calif., since 1947.

Shaver, Stanley B., A.B.'23, M.A.'24, Pomona Col.; Prin., Union H. S., and Dist. Supt. of Sch., Covina, Calif., since 1946.

Sheldon, Donald R., B.S.'26, Kansas State Tchrs. Col., Pittsburg; M.A.'31, Stanford Univ.; Deputy Supt. of Sch., Stockton, Calif., since 1951.

Shimmin, Irvin A., B.S.'28, Univ. of Calif. Address: Box K 302, Newhall, Calif.

Shively, Dean L., B.A.'37, Whittier Col.; Dist. Supt. of Sch., El Monte, Calif., since 1942.

Silbaugh, (Mrs.) Della M., 835 Middlefield Rd., Palo Alto, Calif.

Silverbrand, Edmund, M.A.'51, Stanford Univ.; Dist. Supt., Elem. Sch., Salinas, Calif., since 1947.

Simmons, Linton T., B.S.'21, Univ. of Ariz.; M.S.'41, Univ. of Southern Calif.; Orange Co. Supt. of Sch., Santa Ana, Calif., since 1945.

Simpson, Roy E., M.A.'31, Claremont Colleges; Litt.D.'48, Chapman Col.; State Supt. of Pub. Instr., Sacramento, Calif., since 1945.

Singer, Jack R., A.B.'31, Univ. of Redlands; M.S.'41, Univ. of Southern Calif.; Supt. of City Sch., Culver City, Calif., since 1947.

Skaggs, Darcy A., A.B.'33, M.A.'40, Ariz. State Col., Tempe; Ed.D.'49, Univ. of Southern Calif.; Dist. Supt. of Sch., Artesia, Calif., since 1946.

Skutt, Charles A., M.S.'37, Univ. of Southern Calif., Supt. of City Sch., Sierra Madre, Calif., since 1946.

Slocum, Darrel Hugh, Ed.B.'32, Superior State Tchrs. Col.; A.M.'38, Western State Col. of Colo.; Field Representative, State Dept. of Educ., Los Angeles, Calif., since 1951.

Smith, Don M., Supt., Wiseburn Sch. Dist., Hawthorne, Calif.

Smith, Gerald A., B.A.'37, M.A.'39, Univ. of Redlands; Dist. Supt. of Sch., Bloomington, Calif., since 1946.

Smith, H. Lawson, A.B.'40, San Jose State Col.; M.A.'49, Stanford Univ.; Supt. of Elem. Sch., Herlong, Calif., since 1947.

Smith, Irving Wright, B.S.'10, Trinity Col.; M.A.'13, Yale Univ.; Ed.M.'27, Harvard Univ.; Consultant in Research, P.O. Box 1352, Richmond, Calif.

Smith, Lewis F., Ph.B.'31, Univ. of Wis.; M.A. '40, Ohio State Univ.; Dist. Supt. of Sch., Grossmont, Calif., since 1944.

*Smith, Lewis Wilbur, A.B.'02, LL.D.'28, Denison Univ.; A.M.'13, Ph.D.'19, Univ. of Chicago; Research Fellow, Univ. of Calif.; Berkeley, Calif., since 1941.

Smith, W. Max, A.B.'34, Fresno State Col.; M.S.'35, Univ. of Southern Calif., Supt., Merced City Sch. Dist., Merced, Calif., since 1933.

Snow, Irene, Dist. Supt. of Elem. Sch., Napa, Calif., since 1937.

Sparks, Fred M., A.B.'27, Tusculum Col.; M.S.'35, Univ. of Idaho; Supt., Hudson Sch. Dist., Puente, Calif., since 1945.

*Spaulding, Frank E., A.B.'89, LL.D.'20, Amherst Col.; A.M., Ph.D.'94, Leipzig Univ., Germany; A.M.'20, Yale Univ.; Honorary Life Member, American Assn. of Sch. Admin.; Prof. Emeritus of Educ., Yale Univ., since 1935. Address: 2901 Hill Dr., Los Angeles, Calif.

Spears, Harold, A.B.'24, Wabash Col.; M.A.'31, Ed.D.'39, Tchrs. Col., Columbia Univ.; Asst. Supt. of Sch., San Francisco, Calif.

Spencer, Edward M., B.S.'24, Iowa State Col.; M.A.'37, Ph.D.'40, State Univ. of Iowa; Educ. Dept., Fresno State Col., Fresno, Calif., since 1950.

Spiess, Henry R., A.B.'21, Willamette Univ.; A.M.'31, Stanford Univ.; Supt. of Sch., Antioch, Calif., since 1942.

Spinas, Andrew, A.B.'30, Humboldt State Col; Dist. Supt. of Sch., Redwood City, Calif., since 1937.

Staffelbach, Hubert W., B.A.'36, San Jose State Col.; M.A.'42, Ph.D.'51, Stanford Univ.; Asst. Prof. of Educ., San Francisco State Col., San Francisco, Calif., since 1951.

Stafford, Gordon, Architect, 102½ J St., Sacramento, Calif.

Stanton, Robert, Architect, A. I. A., State of Calif., Carmel, Calif., since 1934.

Steed, Eli R., B.A.'35, Brown Univ.; Dist. Supt. of Sch., Barstow, Calif., since 1944.

Stevens, A. C., Jr., Dist. Supt., Fremont Union H. S., Sunnyvale, Calif.

Stockton, Jesse D., A.B.'20, Univ. of Calif. at Berkeley; Co. Supt. of Sch., Bakersfield, Calif., since 1947.

*Stoddard, Alexander Jerry, B.S.'22, LL.D.'40, Univ. of Nebr.; A.M.'24, Columbia Univ.; Ed.D.'32, R. I. Col. of Educ., Providence; L.H.D.'39, Beaver Col.; LL.D.'39, Temple Univ.; L.H.D.'40, Univ. of Pa.; LL.D.'47, Bucknell Univ.; Pres., Dept. of Superintendence, 1935-36; Honorary Life Member, American Assn. of Sch. Admin.; Chmn., Educ. Policies Commn., 1936-46; Supt. of Sch., Los Angeles, Calif., since 1948.

Stoffer, Robert J., M.A.'36, Stanford Univ.; B.A.'30, San Jose State Col.; Asst. Supt. of Sch., San Francisco, Calif., since 1947.

Stokesbary, Maurice R., M.S.'35, Univ. of Southern Calif.; Deputy Supt. of Sch., Alhambra, Calif., since 1940.

Stone, Gladys, Co. Supt. of Sch., Salinas, Calif.

Stowers, Cecil B., B.S.'42, Central State Tchrs. Col., Edmond, Okla.; M.S.'51, Univ. of Southern Calif.; Dist. Supt., Carmenita Sch. Dist., Norwalk, Calif., since 1951.

Sullivan, Evalyn Dobyns, M.S.'47, Univ. of Southern Calif.; Prin., Fries Ave. Sch., Wilmington, Calif., since 1948.

Sullivan, J. Graham, A.B.'30, Stanford Univ.; M.A.'50, Univ. of Calif.; Asst. Supt. and Dir. of Curriculum, Contra Costa Jr. Col. Dist., Martinez, Calif., since 1950.

Sutcliffe, Paul, Jr., A.B.'47, San Jose State Col.; M.Ed.'51, Univ. of Calif.; Teaching Asst., Educ. Dept., Univ. of Calif., Los Angeles, Calif., since 1950.

Sweeney, Mary J., Asst. Prin., Argonne-Cabrillo Sch., San Francisco, Calif., since 1938.

Sweeney, William G., A.B.'30, San Jose State Col.; M.A.'34, Ed.D.'41, Stanford Univ.; Chmn., Div. of Educ. and Tchr. Tr., San Jose State Col., San Jose, Calif., since 1946.

Sweet, Hugh W., B.S.'25, Huron Col.; M.A.'36 Univ. of Minn.; Dist. Supt., Eastside Union Sch. Dist., Lancaster, Calif., since 1946.

Taber, Theron S., Jr., A.B.'27, M.A.'28, Stanford Univ.; Deputy Supt., Kern Co. Union H. S. Dist., Bakersfield, Calif., since 1945.

Taft, Chester A., A.B.'25, Stanford Univ.; M.A.'30, Univ. of Southern Calif.; Acting Supt. of City Sch. Dist., Inglewood, Calif., since 1951.

Tallman, Norman O., A.B.'31, Occidental Col.; M.A.'36, Ed.D.'51, Univ. of Southern Calif.; Asst. Supt., Unified Sch. Dist., Montebello, Calif., since 1947.

Tannehill, H. M., Prin., Lincoln Sch., South Pasadena, Calif.

Taylor, John Walter, A.B.'31, Univ. of Calif.; Co. Supt. of Sch., Ukiah, Calif., since 1935.

Thecla, Sister Mary, B.A.'41, Immaculate Heart Col.; M.A.'46, Ph.D.'52, Catholic Univ. of America; Pres., Immaculate Heart Col., Los Angeles, Calif., since 1951.

Thomason, J. A., B.S. and M.S.'30, Univ. of Idaho; Dist. Supt. of Sch., North Fork, Calif., since 1935.

Thompson, Byron E., A.B.'33, Univ. of Redlands; Dist. Supt. of Sch., El Monte, Calif., since 1947.

*Thompson, Carroll W., A.B.'23, Chapman Col.; A.M.'25, B.D.'27, Univ. of Southern Calif.; Ed.D.'49, Tchrs. Col., Columbia Univ.; Prin., Evening H. S., Glendale, Calif.

Thornton, James W., Jr., Ph.D.'41, Stanford Univ.; Vicepres., Orange Coast Col., Costa Mesa, Calif.

Thrall, C. Burton, Co. Supt. of Sch., San Bernardino, Calif.

Thyberg, Clifford S., B.A.'35, Whittier Col.; M.S. in Ed.'48, Univ. of Southern Calif.; Dist. Supt., West Covina Sch., Covina, Calif., since 1948.

Tibby, (Mrs.) Ardella Bitner, A.B.'22, M.A.'28, Univ. of Southern Calif.; Supt. of Sch., Compton, Calif., since 1934.

Tierney, (Mrs.) Hallie M., B.A.'10, Lawrence Col.; Co. Supt. of Sch., Alturas, Calif., since 1935.

Tiffany, Burton C., M.A.'38, Tchrs. Col. Columbia Univ.; Curriculum Coordinator, Co. Sch., San Diego, Calif., since 1947.

Tiner, Hugh M., A.B.'29, Abilene Christian Col.; M.A.'29, Stanford Univ.; Ph.D.'44, Univ. of Southern Calif.; Pres., George Pepperdine Col., Los Angeles, Calif., since 1939.

Titus, Robert C., A.B.'25, A.M.'29, Stanford Univ., Address: 429 Pope St., Menlo Park, Calif.

Toddhunter, Lawrence E., Asst. Supt. of Sch., Fresno, Calif.

Tormey, James R., B.A.'32, San Jose State Col.; M.A.'51, Stanford Univ.; Co. Supt. of Sch., Redwood City, Calif., since 1950.

Triggs, Dean E., A.B.'33, Whittier Col.; M.S.'48, Univ. of Southern Calif.; Co. Supt. of Sch., Ventura, Calif., since 1944.

Trillingham, Clinton C., A.B.'21, Southwestern Col.; A.M.'31, Ed.D.'33, Univ. of Southern Calif.; Co. Supt. of Sch., Los Angeles, Calif., since 1942.

Trombetta, J. C., Asst. Supt. of Sch., Fresno, Calif.

Troxell, (Mrs.) Naomi S., Ph.B.'26, Univ. of Chicago; M.Ed.'37, Loyola Univ.; Coordinator, Psych. and Guidance Serv., Pub. Sch., Oakland, Calif., since 1949.

Turner, George W., Pres., Bd. of Educ., Fresno, Calif., since 1938.

Turner, Lawrence E., B.A.'30, McPherson Col.; A.M.'41, Ph.D.'46, Univ. of Calif. at Berkeley; Exec. Dean, Humboldt State Col., Arcata, Calif.

Turner, Rex H., B.A.'24, State Col. of Wash.; M.A.'28, Stanford Univ.; Ed.D.'36, Univ. of Calif.; Asst. Supt. of Sch., Oakland, Calif., since 1946.

Turner, Thomas R., Supt., Pacific Grove Unified Sch. Dist., Pacific Grove, Calif.

Ulrich, Robert P., B.A.'28, Ohio Wesleyan Univ.; M.A.'33, Ohio State Univ.; Elem. Dist. Supt. of Sch., Mojave, Calif., since 1950.

Updegraff, Harlan, Ph.B.'94, Cornell Col. (Iowa); A.M.'98, Ph.D.'08, Columbia Univ.; LL.D.'26, Syracuse Univ. Address: 1596 E. Mountain St., Pasadena, Calif.

Vanderveer, Lonnie T., B.S.'28, Southwestern State, Weatherford, Okla.; M.Ed.'39, Okla. Univ.; Head, Dept. of Educ., Pepperdine Col., Los Angeles, Calif., since 1951.

Van Dyke, Willard H., B.S.'25, Oregon State Col.; M.A.'46, Univ. of Calif.; Dist. Supt. of Sch., Tamalpais Union H. S. Dist., San Anselmo, Calif., since 1944.

Vaniman, Glenn G., A.B.'29, LaVerne Col.; M.A.'31, Univ. of Southern Calif.; Dist. Supt.; Citrus H. S. and Jr. Col., Azusa, Calif., since 1945.

Van Matre, (Mrs.) Clara E., Co. Supt. of Sch., Weaverville, Calif., since 1931.

Van Wyk, A. C., B.A.'26, Hope Col.; M.A.'37, Univ. of N. Dak.; Supt., Santa Maria Union H. S. and Jr. Col., Santa Maria, Calif., since 1952.

Vasche, Joseph Burton, A.B.'31, San Jose State Col.; M.A.'35, Ed.D.'47, Stanford Univ.; Assoc. Supt. of Pub. Instr. and Chief, Div. of State Colleges and Tchr. Educ., State Dept. of Educ., Sacramento, Calif., since 1952.

Vasconcellos, John Bernard, B.S. in E.E.'26, Univ. of Santa Clara; A.B. in Ed.'28, San Jose State Col.; Dist. Supt. of Sch., Rodeo, Calif., since 1944

Walker, A. Glenwood, B.S. in Ed.'38, Pa. State Tchrs. Col.; Ed.M.'40, Univ. of Pittsburgh; Ed.D.'46, Tchrs. Col., Columbia Univ.; Dir., Pacific Coast Office, Educ. Testing Serv., Los Angeles, Calif.

Walker, Elmer M., A.B.'28, Univ. of Calif.; M.A.'52, Univ. of Southern Calif.; Dist. Supt. of Sch., Lakeside, Calif., since 1946.

Walker, Robert Edwin, B.S.'34, State Tchrs. Col.; Slippery Rock, Pa.; M.A.'40, Univ. of Pittsburgh; Dist. Supt. of Sch., San Dimas, Calif.

Walker, Stephen L., A.B.'29, M.A.'36, Ed.D.'49, Univ. of Calif.; Dean of Instr., Sacramento State Col., Sacramento, Calif., since 1949.

Walkup, Frank R., LL.B.'17, Univ. of Iowa; B.A.'26, Univ. of Colo.; M.S.'47, Univ. of Southern Calif.; Acting Supt. of Sch., Pasadena, Calif., since 1950.

Walter, Robert Bruce, B.S. in Ed.'29, M.S. in Ed.'39, Ed.D.'51, Univ. of Southern Calif.; Chief Deputy Co. Supt. of Sch., Los Angeles, Calif., since 1942.

Walters, Paul E., A.B.'36, Fresno State Col.; Dist. Supt. of Elem. Sch., Soquel, Calif., since 1945.

Walton, H. L., M.A.'42, Colo. State Col. of Educ., Consultant in Audio-Visual Educ., Fresno, Calif., since 1948.

Wampler, W. Norman, A.B.'29, Intermountain Union Col.; A.M.'33, Univ. of Wash.; Ph.D.'46, Univ. of Southern Calif.; Supt. of Sch., Bellflower, Calif., since 1946.

Warburton, T. Stanley, B.A.'32, Pomona Col.; M.A.'33, Claremont Col.; Supt. of Union H. S., Jr. Col., and Adult Educ. Program, Fullerton, Calif.

Ward, E. W., Dist. Supt. of Sch., Alameda Sch. Dist., Downey, Calif., since 1923.

Ward, (Mrs.) Ethel S., Asst. Supt. of Alameda Co. Sch., Piedmont, Calif.

Washburn, David M., B.S.'32, M.S.'33, Oregon State Col.; Dir. of Educ. Serv., Co. Office of Educ., Riverside, Calif., since 1951.

Wassum, Clara E., Dist. Supt. of Sch., Empire, Calif.

Watson, Norman E., A.B.'38, Pomona Col.; M.A.'40, Univ. of Southern Calif.; Dist. Supt. of Sch., San Juan Capistrano, Calif., since 1948.

Weakley, Guy A., A.B.'20, Baker Univ.; Supt. of Elem. Sch., El Centro, Calif.

Weibel, H. Z., B.S.'32, M.A.'36, Univ. of Nebr.; Dist. Supt. of Sch., Daly City, Calif., since 1951.

Wennerberg, Carl Herbert, A.B.'37, Univ. of Redlands; Supt., Union H. S. Dist., Whittier, Calif., since 1949.

Wheeler, (Mrs.) Geraldine R., A.B.'41, Fresno State Col.; Member, Bd. of Educ., Fresno, Calif., since 1949.

Whinnery, John Carroll, A.B.'32, Univ. of Calif. at Los Angeles; M.A.'34, Occidental Col.; Dist. Supt. of Sch., Montebello, Calif., since 1945.

White, George V., A.A.'23, San Jose State Col.; A.B.'28, Stanford Univ.; Dist. Supt. of Elem. Sch., Burlingame, Calif., since 1945.

White, Lawrence B., Ed.D.'44, Univ. of Calif. at Los Angeles; Dist. Supt. of Sch., San Gabriel, Calif., since 1949.

Wiemers, Lawrence A., Dist. Supt., Union H. S., Oxnard, Calif.

Wiens, Jacob F., A.B.'31, Fresno State Col.; M.S.'42, Ed.D.'50, Univ. of Southern Calif.; Dist. Supt. of Sch., Hemet, Calif., since 1951.

Willey, Walter O., M.A.'42, Univ. of Calif. at Los Angeles; Prin., El Rodeo Elem. Sch., Beverly Hills, Calif., since 1936.

Willhoit, Dist. Supt. of Sch., Fontana, Calif.

Williams, Dan T., B.S.'29, Univ. of Utah; M.A.'31, Univ. of Calif., Berkeley; Ed.D.'43, Univ. of Southern Calif.; Supt. of Sch., Garvey, Calif., since 1945.

Williams, James H., B.A.'29, Hardin-Simmons Univ.; M.S.'34, Ed.D.'43, Univ. of Southern Calif.; Deputy Supt. of City Sch., Richmond, Calif., since 1950.

Williams, Joseph Post, A.B.'33, Univ. of Colo.; Supt., Tulare Co. Sch., Visalia, Calif., since 1949.

Wilson, Bryan O., B.A.'28, Univ. of Mont.; M.A.'36, Univ. of Calif.; Co. Supt. of Sch., Martinez, Calif., since 1932.

Wilson, Glen A., A.B.'36, M.A.'41, Occidental Col.; Supt., Perris Union H. S. Dist., Perris, Calif., since 1948.

Wilson, James H., A.B.'13, Sterling Col.; A.M.'28, Univ. of Chicago; Coordinator of Curriculum, Vista H. S., Vista, Calif., since 1952.

Wilson, William M., A.B.'27, Univ. of Calif.; Supt., City Sch., Grass Valley, Calif., since 1952.

Wise, James I., Prin. Grandview Elem. Sch., Monterey Park, Calif.

Wohlheter, Walter P., A.B.'40, Univ. of Redlands; M.A.'48, Whittier Col.; Prin., Bell Gardens Evening H. S., Bell Gardens, Calif., since 1950.

Wolfson, Leo, B.S.'27, Univ. of Ariz.; M.S.'33, Univ. of Southern Calif.; Dist. Supt., Jt. Union H. S. Dist. and Reedley Col., Reedley, Calif., since 1950.

Wollen, Lloyd P., B.S.'31, Kansas State Tchrs. Col.; Prin. and Dist. Supt. of Sch., Bishop, Calif., since 1949.

Wolzak, Heiltje, Co. Supt. of Sch., Bridgeport, Calif., since 1950.

Wood, Lloyd K., B.S.'25, M.A.'31, Univ. of Calif.; Supt. of Sch., Santa Rosa, Calif., since 1941.

Wright, Frank Moore, A.B.'16, Whittier Col.; M.A.'30, Ed.D.'50, Univ. of Southern Calif.; Assoc. State Supt. of Pub. Instr., Sacramento, Calif., since 1947.

Wright, Henry L., 816 W. 5th St., Los Angeles 13, Calif.

Wyland, Ray O., A.B.'15, Univ. of Ill.; B.S.'18, Garrett Biblical Inst.; M.A.'28, Ph.D.'34, Columbia Univ. Address: P. O. Box 502, Tujunga, Calif.

Wynn, William J., B.A.'47, Univ. of Calif. at Los Angeles; Dist. Supt., Big Bear Lake Elem. Sch., Big Bear Lake, Calif., since 1947.

Yost, Harold, Asst. Supt., Santa Ana, Calif.

Youngs, Grant Barton, A.B.'29, Univ. of Calif., Berkeley; Asst. Supt., Plumas Co. Unified Sch. Dist., Quincy, Calif., since 1949.

Ziegler, Walter J., A.A.'38, Fullerton Jr. Col., Fullerton, Calif.; A.B.'41, Santa Barbara Col.; Supt., Reef-Sunset Union Elem. Sch. Dist., Avenal, Calif., since 1945.

INSTITUTIONAL MEMBERS

California State Library, Mabel R. Gillis, Libn., Sacramento, Calif.

California Test Bureau, Ethel M. Clark, Pres., Los Angeles, Calif.

Claremont College Library, Periodicals Lib., Harper Hill, Claremont, Calif.

Division of Library and Textbook Activities, H. S., 1205 W. Pico Blvd., Los Angeles 15, Calif.

Herlong Elem. Sch. Dist., Lassen County, Herlong, Calif.

Library, Chico State Col., Chico, Calif.

Library, Loyola Univ., Los Angeles, Calif.

Library, Mills College, Oakland, Calif.

Library, San Diego State Col., San Diego, Calif.

Long Beach Unified School District, c/o D. A. Newcomb, Supt., Long Beach, Calif.

Santa Barbara County Schools, Library, Educ. Serv. Center, Goleta, Calif.

Superintendent, San Diego County Sch., 209 Civic Center, San Diego, Calif.

Teachers Library, Kings Co. Free Lib., Harriet S. Davids, Libn., Hanford, Calif.

Teachers Professional Library, c/o Bd. of Educ., Long Beach, Calif.

University Library, Univ. of Calif., Los Angeles, Calif.

Walnut Creek Grammar School, Attn.: Dist. Supt. Sheldon Rankin, Walnut Creek, Calif.

Westwood Junior and Senior High School, Lassen Co., Westwood, Calif.

CANAL ZONE

INDIVIDUAL MEMBERS

Johnson, Lawrence, Supt. of Canal Zone Sch., Balboa Heights, Canal Zone.

Wright, George C., B.A.'29, State Tchrs. Col., Valley City, N. Dak.; M.A.'36, Northwestern Univ.; Dir. Vocational Educ., Balboa, Canal Zone.

COLORADO

INDIVIDUAL MEMBERS

Allen, Herbert E., B.A.'30, Nebr. State Tchrs. Col., Chadron; M.A.'36, Colo. State Col. of Educ., Greeley; Supt. of Sch., Rifle, Colo., since 1948.

Anderson, A. Helen, A.B.'14, A.M.'31, Univ. of Denver; Dir. of Publications, Pub. Sch., Denver, Colo., since 1929.

Anderson, Ruth, Prin., Gove Jr. H. S., Denver, Colo.

Andrews, Sterling M., B.S.'04, Valparaiso Univ.; Supt. of Sch., Walsenburg, Colo., since 1908.

Angevine, Merrill L., A.B.'27, M.A.'36, Univ. of Denver; Supt. of Sch., Lafayette, Colo., since 1934.

Armstrong, Charles E., Pub. Sch., Denver, Colo. Address: 251 So. Washington St., Denver, Colo.

Arnold, Leta, Prin., Fairview Sch., Denver, Colo.

Arnold, Paul R., M.A.'48, Denver Univ.; Dir. of Guidance and Counseling for Trinidad State Jr. Col., Pub. Sch., and Las Animas Co. Pub. Sch., Trinidad, Colo., since 1950.

Asfahl, William D., M.A.'27, Univ. of Okla.; M.A.'30, Univ. of Colo.; Ed.D.'44, Tchrs. Col., Columbia Univ.; Mgr., Rocky Mountain Educ. Consulting Serv., Denver, Colo.

Babitz, Barto, B.Ed.'39, Southern Ill. Univ.; M.A.'40, Univ. of Ill.; M.Sc. in Ed.'46, Western Ill. State Tchrs. Col., Macomb; Supt. of Sch., Silverton, Colo., since 1949.

Bader, Ernest H., B.S.'15, Colo. Agrl. and Mech. Col.; M.S.'32, Colo. Univ.; Supt. of Sch., Berthoud, Colo., since 1950.

Bain, Francis M., A.B.'30, Univ. of Colo.; Member, Bd. of Educ., Denver, Colo., since 1949.

Baird, Dwight C., B.S.'28, Colo. Agrl. and Mech. Col.; M.S.'36, Univ. of Colo.; Pres., Trinidad State Jr. Col., Trinidad, Colo., since 1946.

Barbiero, Samuel M., A.B.'39, Colo. State Col.; M.A.'44, Colo. Univ.; Supt. of Sch., Louisville, Colo., since 1944.

Barrett, Lawrence Adams, B.S.'25, Kansas State Tchrs. Col., Pittsburg; M.S.'29, Univ. of Colo.; Ph.D.'41, McKinley Roosevelt Foundation; Supt. of Sch., Salida, Colo., since 1941.

Baumunk, Lowell, Supt. of Sch., Yuma, Colo., since 1952.

Baxter, Dave, A.B.'41, M.A.'45, Western State Col.; Supt. of Sch., Hotchkiss, Colo., since 1948.

Bell, Theodore S., B.A.'40, M.A.'45, Colo. State Col. of Educ., Greeley; Supt. of Prospect Valley Sch., Keensburg, Colo., since 1950.

Bennett, Charles Willis, A.B.'39, M.A.'46, Colo. State Col. of Educ., Greeley; Supt. of Sch., Saguache, Colo., since 1943.

Bethke, Paul G., M.A.'48, Colo. State Col. of Educ., Greeley; Supt. of Sch., Timnath, Colo., since 1947.

Bishop, William E., A.B.'31, Cotner Col.; M.A.'39, Colo. State Col. of Educ., Greeley; Supt. of Elem. Sch., Jefferson Co., Golden, Colo., since 1951.

Black, Lorenzo George, A.B.'24, Grand Island, Nebr., A.M.'32, Colo. State Col. of Education; Supt. of Sch., Cheraw, Colo., since 1951.

Boltz, Idris K., B.S.'29, Kansas State Tchrs. Col., Pittsburgh; M.A.'36, Colo. State Col. of Educ., Greeley; Supt. of Sch. Dist. 51, Grand Junction, Colo., since 1943.

Boyd, Earl J., D.D.S.'19, Univ. of Denver; Member of Bd. of Educ., Denver, Colo., since 1951.

Braun, Louis H., A.B.'30, A.M.'31, Colo. State Col. of Educ., Greeley; Prin. East H. S., Denver, Colo., since 1946.

Britton, Russell K., B.S.'35, M.S.'40, Colo. A. & M. Col.; Dir. of Instr., Pub. Sch., Denver, Colo., since 1944.

Brown, A. A., A.B.'21, Wheaton Col.; M.A.'26, Univ. of Colo.; Supt. of Sch., Littleton, Colo., since 1946.

Bruce, James H., Centennial Sch. Supply Co., Box 5224, Denver 17, Colo.

Brumfield, Carl A., A.B.'23, M.A.'25, Colo. Col.; Supt. of Sch., Monte Vista, Colo., since 1925.

Bundy, W. Wilson, A.B.'36, M.A.'40, Univ. of Colo.; Supt. of Sch., Manitou Springs, Colo., since 1946.

Bunner, Ray, B.A.'34, Western State Col. of Colo.; M.A.'46, Colo. State Col. of Educ., Greeley; Supt., Yuma Co. H. Schs., and Sch. Dist. 2, Wray, Colo., since 1949.

Burbank, Natt B., A.B.'25, Univ. of Vt.; M.A.'31, Tchrs. Col., Columbia Univ.; Supt. of Sch., Boulder, Colo., since 1949.

Burkhard, Elmer L., M.A.'41, Colo. State Col. of Educ., Greeley; Supt., Las Animas Pub. Sch. and Bent Co. H. S., Las Animas, Colo., since 1945.

Butler, Leo William, A.B.'27, M.A.'31, Colo. State Col. of Educ., Greeley; Supt. of Sch., Fort Lupton, Colo., since 1935.

Carlson, C. J., Centennial Sch. Supply Company, 3012 Huron, Denver, Colo.

Carroll, R. J., B.S.'25, Olivet Col., A.B.'27, Univ. of Dubuque; M.A.'34, State Univ. of Iowa; Supt., Logan Co. H. S. System, Sterling Pub. Sch. and Northeastern Jr. Col., Sterling, Colo., since 1947.

Carson, (Mrs.) Esther D., A.A., Colo. State Col. of Educ., Greeley; Co. Supt. of Sch., Kiowa, Colo., since 1946.

Cavanaugh, Elizabeth, B.A.'48, Colo. State Col. of Educ., Greeley; Co. Supt. of Sch., Leadville, Colo., since 1951.

Chamney, John S., Supt. of Sch., Colorado Springs, Colo.

Chase, Merle V., B.S.'32, M.S.'37, Kansas State Col. of Agr. and Applied Science; Supt., Elem. and Co. H. S., Walsenburg, Colo., since 1952.

Chollar, William F., A.B.'35, Friends Univ.; M.A.'41, Univ. of Wichita; Supt. of Sch., Florence, Colo., since 1950.

Cole, Alton, M.Ed.'40, Univ. of Okla.; Supt., Telluride Sch., Telluride, Colo., since 1949.

Davis, Charles H., Jr., A.B.'33, M.A.'40, Univ. of Nebr.; Supt. of Sch., Pueblo, Colo., since 1952.

Davis, (Mrs.) Frances R., A.B.'41, Univ. of Denver; Prin., Beach Ct. Sch., Denver, Colo., since 1941.

Douglass, Harl R., A.B.'15, M.A.'21, Univ. of Mo.; Ph.D.'27, Stanford Univ.; Dir., Col. of Educ., Univ. of Colo., Boulder, Colo., since 1940.

Duncan, Carl G., A.B.'21, Cedarville Col.; A.M.'38, Univ. of Colo.; Prin., Avondale Sch., Avondale, Colo., since 1940.

Dunning, Howard, B.A.'37, Northwestern State Col., (Okla.); M.A.'49, Western State Col. of Colo.; Supt. of Sch., Cripple Creek, Colo., since 1950.

Edwards, Walter L., B.S.'34, Iowa Wesleyan Col.; M.A.'50, Univ. of Iowa; Supt. of Sch., Estes Park, Colo., since 1952.

Ehrenkrook, W. J., 1178 S. Race St., Denver, Colo.

Fitz Simmons, Warren B., A.B.'40, M.A.'45, Colo. Col.; Derby, Colo.

Fowler, Homer, M.A.'41, Colo. State Col. of Educ., Greeley; Supt. of Sch., Fowler, Colo., since 1949.

Franzen, Carl B., A.B.'36, Nebr. State Tchrs. Col., Kearney; M.A.'39, Univ. of Colo.; Supt. of Sch., Fort Morgan, Colo., since 1952.

Freeman, Charles W., B.S.'37, Fort Hays Kansas State Col.; Supt. of Sch., La Porte, Colo., since 1951.

Garrison, Lloyd A., A.B.'26, M.A.'32, Colo. State Col. of Educ., Greeley; Ph.D.'40, Yale Univ.; Prof. of Educ. since 1946; Dean, Grad. Col., and Dir., Sch. of Educ., Univ. of Denver, Denver, Colo., since 1949.

Gerken, Edna A., A.B.'14, Washburn Col.; M.P.H.'26, Mass. Inst. of Tech. Address: Route 1, Grand Junction, Colo.

Glendinning, Katherine S., B.S.'26, M.A.'48, Tchrs. Col., Columbia Univ.; Elem. Prin., Bryant Webster Sch., Denver, Colo., since 1949.

Gordon, C. F., A.B.'51, Colo. State Col. of Educ., Greeley; Prin., Grade Sch., Haxtun, Colo., since 1949.

Grant, John A., B.S.'14, M.Ed.'45, Colo. A. & M. Col.; Supt., Co. H. S., Julesburg, Colo., since 1945.

Greear, Harold L., B.S.'28, M.S.'29, Colo. A. & M. Col.; Supt. of Sch., Yampa, Colo., since 1949.

Grieder, Calvin, B.A.'27, Univ. of Dubuque; M.A.'36, Ph.D.'38, State Univ. of Iowa; Prof. of Sch. Admin., Col. of Educ., Univ. of Colo., Boulder, Colo., since 1940.

Grimes, Leslie K., A.B.'22, A.M.'34, Univ. of Mo.; Ed.D.'44, Wash. Univ.; Supt. of Sch., Greeley, Colo., since 1951.

Hall, James Alonzo, A.B.'28, Univ. of Denver; M.A.'32, Tchrs. Col., Columbia Univ.; Ed.D. '48, Univ. of Denver; Dir. of Instr., Pub. Sch., Denver, Colo., since 1949.

Hargrave, Charles Howard, B.A.'51, Univ. of Colo.; Supt., Peyton Consol. Sch., Peyton, Colo., since 1952.

Hatcher, William H., M.A.'48, Colo. State Col. of Educ., Greeley; B.A.'33, Peru State Tchrs. Col., Nebr.; Supt. of Sch., Sargent, Colo., since 1952.

Heacock, Elizabeth H., 420 Ivanhoe, Denver, Colo.

Hinderman, Roy A., B.S.'28, Univ. of Minn.; M.S.'29, Ph.D.'38, Univ. of Wis.; Asst. Supt. of Sch. in charge of Sec. and Adult Educ., Denver, Colo., since 1946.

Hinkley, William C., M.A.'38, Univ. of Mich.; Supt. of Sch., Aurora, Colo., since 1949.

Holm, Peter C., A.B.'20, Colo. Col.; M.A.'27, Univ. of Denver; Asst. Supt. of Sch., Denver, Colo., since 1950.

Homsher, Ruth Ann, A.B.'30, Colo. State Col. of Educ., Greeley; Elem. Sch. Prin., Denver, Colo., since 1947.

Hopper, J. Victor, B.Ed.'41, Western Ill. State Col.; M.A.'47, Stanford Univ.; Asst. Prof. of Educ., Colo. Col., Colorado Springs, Colo., since 1951.

Hughes, Mary E., Prin., Emerson Sch., Denver, Colo.

Irwin, Frank L., B.S.'20, M.S.'39, Kansas State Tchrs. Col., Emporia; County Supt. of Sch., Fort Collins, Colo., since 1948.

Jeffrey, Harold C., A.B.'30, Nebr. State Tchrs. Col., Wayne; M.A.'41, Univ. of Colo.; Supt. of Sch., Gunnison, Colo., since 1948.

Jenkins, Ralph D., A.B.'28, Colo. State Col. of Educ., Greeley; A.M.'33, Tchrs. Col., Columbia Univ.; Supt. of Sch., Englewood, Colo., since 1934.

Jones, Harold D., B.S.'41, Northern State Tchrs. Col., Aberdeen, S. Dak.; M.Ed.'50, Univ. of Colo.; Supt. of Sch., Simla, Colo., since 1950.

Kantor, Leon L., Supt. of Sch., Wiley, Colo., since 1951.

Kaupp, (Mrs.) Eugenia, Baker Jr. H. S., Denver, Colo.

COLORADO

Kellenbenz, George L., A.B.'31, Western State Col. of Colo.; M.A.'42, Denver Univ.; Supt. of Sch., Idaho Springs, Colo., since 1946.

Kettle, Frances E., B.S.'17, Colo. Agrl. and Mech. Col.; Co. Supt. of Sch., Westcliffe, Colo., since 1948.

Kimmel, Grace G., Prin., Alcott Sch., Denver, Colo.

Kitchen, B. F., A.B.'13, Univ. of Colo.; A.M.'47, Colo. State Col. of Educ.; Supt. of Sch., Loveland, Colo., since 1950.

Kunsmiller, Dorothea, B.A.'47, Univ. of Denver; Member, Bd. of Educ., Denver, Colo., since 1931, and Vicepres., since 1951.

Lacewell, D. Boone, B.A. in Ed.'44, Eastern N. Mex. Univ.; Supt. of Sch. Dist. 50, Pagosa Springs, Colo., since 1950.

Lackemann, Luise M., A.B.'38, Denver Univ.; Prin., Steck Elem. Sch., Denver, Colo., since 1948.

Leake, James D., A.B.'25, B.S.'25, Drury Col.; M.A.'30, Univ. of Colo.; Ed.D.'49, Univ. of Denver; Supvr., Evaluation and Testing, Pub. Sch., Denver, Colo., since 1951.

Leftwich, Stanley A., A.B.'40, Univ. of Denver; Co. Supt. of Sch., Pueblo, Colo., since 1947.

Leise, George, B.S.'39, Colo. Agrl. and Mech. Col.; Supt. of Sch., Waverly, Fort Collins, Colo., 1951-52.

Lesher, D. B., A.B.'21, Colo. Col.; M.A.'33, Univ. of Denver; Ed.D.'46, Colo. State Col. of Educ., Greeley; Supt. of Sch., Fort Collins, Colo., since 1944.

Lester, Vincil S., M.A.'41, Colo. State Col. of Educ., Greeley; Supt. of Sch., Cortez, Colo., since 1945.

McDivitt, W. L., M.A.'47, Colo. State Col. of Educ.; Dean, La Junta Jr. Col., La Junta, Colo., since 1952.

Marshall, Homer K., B.A.'48, Univ. of Colo., Prin. Mesa Valley Sch. Dist. #51, Grand Junction, Colo.

Mathias, Henry Edwin, A.B.'23, A.M.'24, Univ. of Mo.; Dean of the Lower Div. and Dir. of Admissions, Colo. Col., Colorado Springs, Colo.

Mickelson, Peter Palmer, A.B.'35, State Tchrs. Col., Mayville, N. Dak.; A.M.'39, Ph.D.'41, Univ. of Colo.; Pres., Western State Col. of Colo., Gunnison, Colo., since 1946.

Miller, Eugene, B.S.'38, Central State Col. (Okla.); M.A.'42, Western State Col. of Colo.; Prin. of Elem. Sch., Rangely, Colo., since 1951.

Miller, Fletcher M., A.B.'15, Univ. of Ohio; M.A.'28, Western State Col. of Colo.; Asst. Supt., Jefferson Co. Pub. Sch., Golden, Colo.

Miller, Graham R., Asst. Supt. of Sch., in chg. of Bus. Admin., Denver Colo.

Minear, Craig P., A.B.'23, Iowa Wesleyan Col.; M.A.'30, State Univ. of Iowa; Exec. Secy., Colo. Educ. Assn., Denver, Colo., since 1944.

Monell, Ralph P., A.B.'26, A.M.'39, Colo. Col.; Supt., Sch. Dist. 1, Canon City, Colo., since 1950.

Moore, Harold E., A.B.'24, State Tchrs. Col., Terre Haute, Ind.; M.A.'29, Ed.D.'45, Ind. Univ.; Prof. of Educ. and Dir. of Educ. Research, Univ. of Denver, since 1951; and Dir. of State Sch. Bldg. Survey, State Dept. of Educ., Denver, Colo., since 1951.

Morie, Alvin L., M.Ed.'49, Univ. of Colo.; Supt. of Sch., Springfield, Colo., since 1952.

Morrison, Gaylord D., B.S.'37, Northwest Mo. State Tchrs. Col., Maryville; M.A.'43, Univ. of Nebr.; Ed.D.'51, Univ. of Mo.; Asst. Prof. of Educ. Admin., Colo. State Col. of Educ., Greeley, Colo., since 1951.

380

Mullins, Cecil, B.S. in Ed.'31, Univ. of Ark.; M.A.'34, Univ. of Colo.; Supt. of Sch., Del Norte, Colo., since 1946.

Naylor, Robert G., B.A.'40, M.A.'50, Univ. of Denver; Supt. of Sch., Kremmling, Colo., since 1951.

Needham, Elza, B.S.'14, Valparaiso Univ.; M.S. in Ed.'45, Univ. of Southern Calif.; Supt. of Sch., Durango, Colo., since 1943.

Newlon, Carl B., A.B.'13, Ind. Univ.; M.A.'17, Tchrs. Col., Columbia Univ.; Dir., Div. of Tchr. Welfare, Colo. Educ. Assn., Denver, Colo., since 1937.

Nolte, M. C., A.B.'37, Simpson Col.; M.S.'48, Drake Univ.; Supt., Washington Co. H. S. System, Akron, Colo., since 1950.

Oberholtzer, Kenneth E., B.S.'24, Univ. of Ill.; M.S.'28, Agrl. and Mech. Col. of Texas; Ph.D.'37, Tchrs. Col., Columbia Univ.; Pres., American Assn. of Sch. Admin., 1951-52; Supt. of Sch., Denver, Colo., since 1947.

Park, James D., B.A.'33, Southeastern State Col., Durant, Okla.; Supt., Sargent Consol. Sch. Dist. 3, Monte Vista, Colo.

Pendleton, Claud B., A.B.'21, A.M.'22, Univ. of Denver; Asst. Supt. of Sch., in chg. of Elem. Educ. and Special Sch., Denver, Colo., since 1946.

Penttila, Rayno William, B.S.'31, Mont. State Col.; Supt., Ute Voc. Sch., Ignacio, Colo., since 1947.

Peters, Joseph B., B.S.'39, Colo. Agrl. and Mech. Col.; M.E.'48, Mont. State Univ.; Supt., Rio Blanco Co. H. S. System, Sec. Sch. Dist. 1 and Elem. Sch., Meeker, Colo., since 1950.

Pillep, Edwin R., B.S.'47, Univ. of Colo.; Supt. of Sch., Ridgway, Colo., since 1950.

Porter, Stanley M., A.M.'35, Colo. State Col. of Educ.; Supt. of Sch., Byers, Colo., since 1952.

Powell, Rolland, M.E.'42, Colo. Agrl. and Mech. Col.; Supt. of Sch., Fruita, Colo., since 1942.

Pratt, Philip S., A.B.'28, Western State Col. of Colo.; M.S.'38, Univ. of Southern Calif.; Supt., Sch. Dist. 1, Montrose, Colo.

Ranum, Iver C., B.A.'34, Luther Col.; M.A.'46, Denver Univ.; Supt. of Sch., Westminster, Colo., since 1948.

Rea, Charles Dale, B.S.'36, Colo. A. and M. Col.; M.S.'40, Univ. of Southern Calif.; Ed.D.'50, Univ. of Colo.; Pres., Fort Lewis A. and M. Col., Hesperus, Colo., since 1948.

Rebell, Milton C., M.S.'39, Denver Univ.; Admin. Asst., Pub. Sch., Denver, Colo., since 1946.

Reiva, James T., 614 Ogden St., Denver, Colo.

Reyhner, Theodore O., B.S.'37, Newark Col. of Engineering; A.M.'38, Columbia Univ.; Ph.D.'50, New York Univ.; Assoc. Prof. of Civil Engineering, Col. of Engineering, Univ. of Denver, Denver, Colo., since 1949.

Rishel, John B., Ph.B.'15, M.A.'26, Bucknell Univ.; Prin., Westwood Jr. H. S., Denver, Colo., since 1950.

Robertson, Estil G., B.A.'38, M.A.'41, Colo. State Col. of Educ., Greeley; Supt. of Rio Blanca Co. Dist. 1, Meeker, Colo., since 1952.

Ross, William R., B.S.'21, M.S.'24, Colo. Agrl. and Mech Col.; Ph.D.'40, Colo. State Col. of Educ., Greeley; Pres., Colo. State Col. of Educ., Greeley, Colo., since 1948.

Rugg, Earle U., A.B.'15, A.M.'17, Univ. of Ill.; Ph.D.'23, Columbia Univ.; Head, Div. of Educ., Colo. State Col. of Educ., Greeley, Colo., since 1923.

Rule, Philip, B.A.'31, M.A.'38, Univ. of Colo.; Supt. of Sch., La Junta, Colo., since 1951.

Samuels, Isadore, A.B.'12, Park Col.; LL.B.'18, Univ. of Kansas City; Member, Bd. of Educ., Denver, Colo., since 1948.

Sanborn, Kent L., A.B.'12, Clark Univ.; A.M.'30, Univ. of Colo.; Supt. of Sch., Longmont, Colo., since 1934.

Sauer, George P., B.A.'43, Colo. State Col. of Educ., Greeley; M.A.'47, Univ. of Denver; Supt. of Sch., Steamboat Springs, Colo., since 1949.

Simmons, L. V., B.A.'32, M.Ed.'47, Univ. of Buffalo; Supt. of Sch., Rocky Ford, Colo., since 1948.

*Slonecker, Lyle Nelson, B.S.'24, M.S.'33, Colo. A. & M. Col.; Member, Dept. of Educ., and Dir. of Placement, Colo. A. & M. Col., Fort Collins, Colo.

Smith, Gerald L., B.S.'40, Univ. of Kansas; M.Ed.'51, Univ. of Colo.; Supt., Pub. Sch. Dist. 1, Trinidad, Colo., since 1951.

Snyder, Clarence A., B.S.'25, M.S.'37, Colo. A. & M. Col.; Admin., Jt. Sch. Dist. 50, Delta, Colo.

Spitzer, Ben R., A.B.'26, McPherson Col.; M.A.'44, Colo. State Col. of Educ., Greeley; Supt. of Central Pub. Sch., Clifton, Colo., since 1946.

Spratlen, Frank P., Jr., 3200 Brighton Blvd., Denver, Colo.

Stafford, George E., A.B.'32, Whittier Col.; A.B.'33, M.A.'35, Western State Col. of Colo., Gunnison; Supt. of Sch., Paonia, Colo., since 1943.

Stevens, Paul C., A.B.'26, M.A.'36, Univ. of Denver; Supt. of Sch. Dist. R-1, Golden, Colo.

Stone, Clark H., A.B.'19, A.M.'33, Univ. of Denver; Prin., Jr. H. S., Denver, Colo., since 1939.

Summers, Hugh O., A.B.'37, Ariz. State Col. at Tempe; M.A.'46, Ariz. State Col. at Flagstaff; Supt., Co. H. S. System, Montrose, Colo., since 1950.

Swartz, R. D., B.A.'40, Nebr. State Tchrs. Col., Wayne; M.Ed.'43, Univ. of Mont.; Supt. of Lewis-Palmer Consol. Sch., Monument, Colo., since 1949.

Tabery, Norbert F., B.S.'38, Northern State Tchrs. Col., Aberdeen, S. Dak.; M.A.'50, Univ. of Colo.; Instructor, Univ. of Colo., Boulder, Colo., since 1951.

Taylor, Burtis E., A.B.'38, M.S.'39, Fort Hays Kansas State Col.; Ed.D.'51, Univ. of Denver; Dir. of Sch. Facilities Survey, State Dept. of Educ., Denver, Colo., since 1951.

Thomann, F. C., Supt. of Pub. Sch., Eaton, Colo.

Tozer, George E., A.B.'14, Nebr. Wesleyan Univ.; M.A.'28, Colo. State Col. of Educ.; Supt. of Sch., Windsor, Colo., since 1931.

Traylor, Frank A., Member, Bd. of Educ., Denver, Colo., since 1947.

Troxel, Oliver L., B.S.'14, North Central Col.; A.M.'22, Ph.D.'26, Univ. of Minn.; Prof. of Educ. Admin., Colo. State Col. of Educ., Greeley, Colo., since 1929.

Vikan, Walter L., B.A.'21, Univ. of N. Dak.; M.Ed.'40, Univ. of Colo.; Supt., Sch. Dist. No. 27, Brighton, Colo., since 1942.

Waggoner, Jess W., B.A.'40, Colo. A. & M. Col.; M.A.'45, Univ. of Denver; Asst. Supt. of Sch., Palisade, Colo., since 1951.

Waldman, Sam, 1221 S. Fillmore St., Denver 10, Colo.

Walker, Cary D., Pub. Sch., Denver, Colo. Address: 2945 Pontiac St., Denver, Colo.

Walters, Newell B., A.B.'32, M.A.'40, Univ. of Denver; Exec. Secy., Denver Pub. Sch. Employees' Pension and Benefit Assn., Exec. Secy., Denver Sch. Employees' Council, Denver, Colo., since 1945.

Wasson, Roy J., B.A.'20, Cornell Univ.; M.A.'29, Columbia Univ.; Ph.D.'40, Colo. State Col. of Educ.; Supt. of Sch., Colorado Springs, Colo., since 1942.

Way, C. A., B.S., M.Ed., Ohio Univ.; Supt. of Sch., Ignacio, Colo., since 1946.

Weber, Joseph C., B.A.'34, St. Ambrose Col.; M.A.'39, Colo. State Col. of Educ., Greeley; Supt. of Sch., Leadville, Colo., since 1947.

Welch, Tano E., A.A.'40, Trinidad Jr. Col.; A.B.'42, A.M.'46, Adams State Col.; Prin., H. S., Trinidad, Colo.

Wilson, Glenn T., A.B.'18, Geneva Col.; M.S.'34, Univ. of Southern Calif.; Commr., Colo. H. S. Activities Assn., Denver, Colo., since 1948.

Winkler, Pauline C., 654 S. Washington St., Denver, Colo.

Wishard, C. M., B.S. in Ed.'37, Central Mo. State Tchrs. Col., Warrensburg; M.A.'43, Colo. State Col. of Educ., Greeley; Supt. of Sch., Castle Rock, Colo., since 1947.

Worley, Vivienne S., M.A.'31, Univ. of Denver; Prin., Whittier Sch., Denver, Colo.

Young, Alfred R., B.S.'29, Baker Univ.; M.A.'36, Univ. of Kansas; Supt. of Sch., Lamar, Colo., since 1943.

INSTITUTIONAL MEMBER

Library, Colo. State Col. of Educ., Greeley, Colo.

CONNECTICUT
INDIVIDUAL MEMBERS

Albohm, John C., B.A.'34, M.A.'37, Ed.D.'46, New York Univ.; Supt. of Sch., New London, Conn., since 1948.

Baer, Joseph A., Ph.B.'10, Hiram Col.; M.A.'18, Univ. of Chicago; Ph.D.'28, Ohio State Univ.; Chief, Bureau of Research and Planning, State Dept. of Educ., Hartford, Conn., since 1938.

Barrows, Mildred K., B.S.'33, Boston Univ.; M.A.'39, Trinity Col.; Asst. Prof., Tchrs. Col. of Conn., and Prin., Stanley Lab. Sch., New Britain, Conn., since 1937.

Barstow, Robbins W., Jr., A.B.'41, Dartmouth Col.; M.A.'45, New York Univ. Sch. of Educ.; Spec. in Field Serv., Conn. Educ. Assoc., Hartford, Conn., since 1950.

Bartman, (Mrs.) Julia H., A.B.'13, Hunter Col.; M.A.'43, Univ. of Conn.; Dir. of Extension and Field Serv., State Tchrs. Col., Willimantic, Conn., since 1950.

Bennet, Elizabeth M., 64 Benton St., Manchester, Conn.

Bixby, Arthur P., B.S.E.'35, State Tchrs. Col., Fitchburg, Mass.; Ed.M.'42, Boston Univ.; Dist. Supt., State Dept. of Educ., Pomfret, Conn.

Black, Robert H., Supt. of Sch., Hartford, Conn., since 1951.

Brown, Edward J., B.A.'23, Col. of the Holy Cross; M.A.'42, Yale Univ.; Pres., Arnold Col., Milford, Conn., since 1948.

Brown, Robert H., Jr., B.S.'31, Springfield Col.; M.A.'39, Columbia Univ.; Supt. of Sch., Madison, Conn., since 1942.

Brownell, Samuel M., A.B.'21, Univ. of Nebr.; A.M.'24, Ph.D.'26, Yale Univ.; Prof. of Educ. Admin., Grad. Sch., Yale Univ., since 1938, and Pres., New Haven State Tchrs. Col., New Haven, Conn., since 1947.

Butler, Huldah Anne, B.S. in Ed.'36, M.E.'43, Boston Univ.; Supvg. Prin., Nathan Hale Sch., Manchester, Conn., since 1951.

Butler, S. B., B.A.'13, Yale Univ.; M.A.'28, Tchrs. Col., Columbia Univ.; Supt. of Sch., Groton, Conn., since 1928.

Carson, J. O., B.Ed.'39, Southern Ill. Univ.; M.A.'40, George Peabody Col. for Tchrs.; Dir. of Elem. Educ., Dept. of Educ., Stratford, Conn.

Chaffee, Charles E., B.S.'27, Susquehanna Univ.; A.M.'31, Bucknell Univ.; D.Ed.'39, New York Univ.; Supt. of Sch., Stratford, Conn., since 1946.

Champlin, George R., B.S.'30, R. I. State Col.; Ed.D.'38, Tchrs. Col., Columbia Univ.; Supt. of Windham Sch., Willimantic, Conn., since 1948.

Chatterton, Arthur E., Ph.B.'16, Yale Univ.; M.A.'47, Univ. of Conn.; Supt., Vernon Pub. Sch., Rockville, Conn., since 1945.

Chittenden, Harold E., A.B.'09, Yale Univ.; Supt. of Sch., Naugatuck, Conn., since 1918.

Chubbuck, R. Daniel, B.S.'31, Univ. of Conn.; M.A.'47, Ph.D.'51, Yale Univ.; Supt. of Rural Sch., Willimantic, Conn., since 1950.

Coulter, Isabel M., B.S.'38, M.A.'45, Tchrs. Col., Columbia Univ.; Supt. of Sch., Waterford, Conn., since 1946.

Coulter, Kenneth C., A.B.'30, Ohio Univ.; M.A.'34, Ed.D.'47, Tchrs. Col., Columbia Univ.; Asst. Supt. of Sch., Greenwich, Conn., since 1952.

Cox, A. W., B.S.'30, Mass. State Col., Amherst; M.A.'45, Yale Univ.; Supt. of Sch., Guilford, Conn., since 1940.

Crouch, T. Allen, A.B.'32, Brown Univ.; M.A.'37, Tchrs. Col., Columbia Univ.; Supt. of Sch., Stonington, Conn., since 1945.

Curran, Timothy Edwin, B.A.'14, Col. of the Holy Cross; M.A.'48, Yale and State Tchrs. Col.; Asst. Supt. of Sch., in chg. of Elem. Sch., New Haven, Conn., since 1950.

Curtis, William H., B.S.'30, Tufts Col.; M.S. in Ed.'44, Univ. of Conn.; Supt. of Sch., Wallingford, Conn., since 1944.

Davis, Stewart G., A.B.'42, Westminster Col. (Pa.); M.A.'47, N. Y. State Tchrs. Col., Albany; Admin. Asst. to Supt. of Sch., Stratford, Conn., since 1951.

Doherty, Joseph B., A.B.'31, Boston Col.; Ed.M. '42, Harvard Univ.; Supt. of Sch., East Hampton, Conn., since 1951.

Dorsey, Margaret M., Prin., Waltersville Sch., Bridgeport, Conn., since 1945.

Duckworth, Irene G., Agency Mgr., *The Grade Teacher*, Darien, Conn., since 1947.

Dustin, Richard H., Prin., Middlefield Sch., Middlefield, Conn.

Engleman, Finis Ewing, B.S.'20, Southwest Mo. State Col., Springfield; M.A.'26, Univ. of Mo.; Ph.D.'34, Yale Univ.; Commr. of Educ., State Dept. of Educ., Hartford, Conn., since 1948.

Farr, John C., A.B.'31, Bowdoin Col; M.Ed.'41, Univ. of N. H.; Asst. Prin., Southington H. S., Southington, Conn., since 1952.

Fay, Raymond J., A.B.'29, M.A.'31, Tufts Col.; Ph.D.'43, Yale Univ.; Consultant, State Dept. of Educ., Hartford, Conn., since 1949.

Fisher, Royal O., A.B.'23, B.S. in Ed.'24, Univ. of Vt.; M.A.'31, Bates Col.; Supvg. Prin., George Hersey Robertson Sch., South Coventry, Conn., since 1952.

Flaharty, William H., B.S.'28, Franklin and Marshall Col.; Ed.M.'32, Rutgers Univ.; Ed.D.'47, Columbia Univ.; Deputy Commr. of Educ., State Dept. of Educ., Hartford, Conn., since 1949.

Flanagan, Russell J., B.A.'27, M.A.'40, Yale Univ.; Asst. Supt. of Sch., in chg. of Bus. Affairs, New Haven, Conn., since 1948.

Fontane, Patrick Earl, Jr., B.S.'37, Univ. of Conn.; M.A.'42, Columbia Univ.; Supvr. and Dir., Univ. of Conn., Waterbury, Conn., since 1948.

Foran, Joseph A., B.A.'37, M.A.'43, Yale Univ.; Supt. of Sch., Milford, Conn., since 1946.

Forbes, Ernest F., B.S.'23, Ed.M.'34, Univ. of N. H.; Supt. of Sch., New Britain, Conn., since 1947.

Fuller, Edward H., A.B.'12, A.M.'16, Bates Col.; M.A.'32, Ed.D.'37, New York Univ.; Supt. of Sch., Ridgefield, Conn., since 1948.

Fuller, Harvey, B.B.A.'28, Boston Univ.; M.A.'35, Yale Univ.; Supt. of Sch., Wethersfield, Conn., since 1945.

Getchell, Gordon C., Supvg. Prin., Pub. Sch., Ellington, Conn., since 1952.

Gillis, William E., B.S.'18, R. I. State Col.; B.Ed.'37, New Haven State Tchrs. Col., Conn.; M.Ed.'42, Univ. of Conn.; Supt. of Sch., East Haven, Conn., since 1930.

Gilmartin, John G., A.B.'12, L.H.D.'39, Col. of the Holy Cross; Supt. of Sch., Waterbury, Conn., since 1945.

Goodrich, John W., B.S.'25, Univ. of Conn.; A.M.'32, Tchrs. Col., Columbia Univ.; Supt. of Sch., Middletown, Conn., since 1948.

Graff, George E., M.S. in Ed.'31, N. Y. State Col. for Tchrs., Albany; Supt. of Rural Educ., State Dept. of Educ., Rockville, Conn., since 1948.

Griffin, Orwin Bradford, A.B.'15, A.M.'17, Boston Univ.; Ph.D.'28, Columbia Univ.; Supt. of Sch., Litchfield, Conn., since 1929.

Griswold, Wilber R., B.S.'38, Trinity Col.; M.A.'47, Univ. of Conn.; Supvr., Hartford Branch, Univ. of Conn., Hartford, Conn., since 1946.

Gustin, Margaret Catherine, B.S. in Ed.'19, Univ. of Mo.; M.A.'26, Tchrs. Col., Columbia Univ.; Supvr. of Elem. Sch., State Dept. of Educ., Unionville, Conn., since 1931.

Hay, George A. F., M.A.'27, Colo. State Col. of Educ., Greeley; Supt. of Sch., Old Lyme, Conn., since 1950.

Hays, R. Vernon, B.Sc.'26, M.A.'33, Univ. of Nebr.; Ed.M.'38, Harvard Univ.; Supt. of Sch., Danielson, Conn., since 1945.

Hellman, Walter H., Asst. Supt. of Sch., Fairfield, Conn.

Hill, Clyde Milton, A.B.'10, Drury Col.; A.M.'15, Ph.D.'26, Columbia Univ.; Sterling Prof. of Educ. and Chmn., Dept. of Educ., Yale Univ., New Haven, Conn., since 1926.

Hill, Owen F., B.S.'42, Gorham State Tchrs. Col. (Maine); M.A.'49, Ed.D.'51, Tchrs. Col., Columbia Univ.; Asst. Supt. of Sch., New Britain, Conn.

Hirst, Eric A., B.S. and M.A.'39, Tchrs. Col., Columbia Univ.; Supt. of Rural Educ., State Dept. of Educ., Waterbury, Conn., since 1950.

Homicki, Joseph J., B.S.Ed.'42, Westfield State Tchrs. Col.; M.S.Ed.'49, Springfield Col.; Supvg. Prin. of Sch., Somersville, Conn., since 1951.

Hoyt, Carlyle G., B.S.'26, Middlebury Col.; Ph.D.'44, Yale Univ.; Supt. of Sch., Fairfield, Conn., since 1947.

Idleman, Hillis K., Ph.B.'31, Brown Univ.; M.A.'39, Tchrs. Col., Columbia Univ.; Supt. of Sch., Norwalk, Conn.

Illing, Arthur H., B.S.'20, Wesleyan Univ.; Ed.M.'42, Boston Univ.; Supt. of Sch., Manchester, Conn., since 1935.

CONNECTICUT

Isham, Charlotte H., B.E.'35, Danbury State Tchrs. Col., Conn.; M.E.'47, Yale Univ.; Elem. Sch. Supvr. for Towns of Bethlehem, Woodbury and Southbury, Woodbury, Conn.

*Jakob, Philip A., Ph.B.'13, Yale Univ.; M.A.'22, Tchrs. Col., Columbia Ur'v.; Ed.D.'39, New York Univ.; Supt. of Sch., Norwalk, Conn., 1932-49 (retired). Address: 130 East Ave., Norwalk, Conn.

James, Henry J., B.A.'24, Wesleyan Univ.; M.A.'33, Univ. of N. H.; Supt. of Sch., Simsbury, Conn., since 1934.

Jeffery, Joseph E., A.B.'10, Ped.D.'47, Morningside Col.; M.A.'12, Washington Univ.; Supt. of Sch., Bridgeport, Conn., since 1945.

Joel, Lewin G., Jr., A.B.'39, Dartmouth Col.; M.A.'46, Yale Univ.; Supt. of Sch., Clinton, Conn., since 1950.

Johnson, Eleanor M., Ph.B.'25, Univ. of Chicago; M.A.'31, Tchrs. Col., Columbia Univ.; American Educ. Publications Editorial Offices, Middletown, Conn., since 1952.

Johnson, Ralph M. T., Ph.B.'21, Sheffield Scientific Sch., Yale Univ.; M.A.'40, New York Univ.; Supt. of Sch., Bethel, Conn., since 1946.

Jorgensen, Albert N., B.A.'21, Coe Col.; M.A.'25, Ph.D.'27, State Univ. of Iowa; LL.D.'42, Coe Col.; Pres., Univ. of Conn., Storrs, Conn., since 1935.

Ketchum, G. Wesley, B.S.'34, N. Y. State Tchrs. Col., Buffalo; M.S.'39, Sch. of Educ., N. Y. Univ.; State Supvr. of Industrial Arts, Bur. of Youth Service, Hartford, Conn., since 1945.

King, A. Kurtz, B.S.'28, Juniata Col.; M.Ed.'32, Rutgers Univ.; Ed.D.'50, Univ. of Pa.; Supt., Regional H. S. Dist. 4, Chester, Conn., since 1950.

Kingsley, Percy, Supt. of Sch., Shelton, Conn., since 1943.

Knoblauch, Arthur Lewis, B.S.'29, Mich. State Col.; M.A.'33, Univ. of Mich.; Ed.D.'42, Harvard Univ.; Dir., Div. of Univ. Extension, Summer Session and Educ. by Radio, and Prof. of Educ. Admin., Univ. of Conn., Storrs, Conn., since 1942.

Knox, Francis S., A.B.'08, Amherst Col.; M.A.'33, Tchrs. Col., Columbia Univ.; Supt. of Sch., Glastonbury, Conn., since 1917.

Knox, Weldon R., B.S.'28, Colby Col.; M.A.'49, Univ. of Conn.; Supt. of Sch., New Milford, Conn., since 1943.

Langford, John A., A.B.'30, Holy Cross Col.; M.S.'33, Mass. State Col.; M.A.'42, Yale Univ.; Supt. of Sch., East Hartford, Conn., since 1949.

Lawler, Frank D., B.S. in Ed.'33, Univ. of Maine; M.A. in Ed.'46, Univ. of Conn.; Supt. of Sch., Winsted, Conn., since 1948.

Lee, Karl Dayton, A.B.'14, Ed.M.'38, Bates Col.; Supt. of Enfield Schs., Thompsonville, Conn., since 1941.

LeGrow, Carl A., B.S.'21, Univ. of Maine; M.A.'33, Tchrs. Col., Columbia Univ.; Supt. of Sch., Newtown, Conn., since 1950.

Lewis, (Mrs.) Dorothy Shanley, Secy., Conn. Tchrs. Retirement Bd., Hartford, Conn., since 1924.

Light, N. Searle, B.A.'08, Yale Univ.; Chief, Bureau of Sch. and Community Serv., State Dept. of Educ., Hartford, Conn.

Lojko, Joseph Peter, A.B.'34, Boston Col.; M.A.'50, Univ. of Conn.; Supt. of Sch., Jewett City, Conn., since 1949.

Lumley, Raymond A., A.B.'28, Dickinson Col.; M.A.'35, Columbia Univ.; Supvr. in Sec. Educ. and Dir. of Safety Educ., State Dept. of Educ., Hartford, Conn., since 1942.

McAlister, R. D., B.A.'17, Univ. of Maine; A.M.'27, Tchrs. Col., Columbia Univ.; Supt. of Sch., Suffield, Conn., since 1927.

McCrann, Leo M., B.S.E.'35, Boston Univ.; M.A.'39, Trinity Col., (Conn.); Asst. Supt. of Sch. in chg. of Admin., Hartford, Conn., since 1951.

McFarland, John Joseph, B.A.'14, Yale Univ.; M.A.'28, Grad. Sch. of Educ., Yale Univ.; Asst. Supt. of Sch., Bridgeport, Conn., since 1951.

McKelvie, C. L., B.S.'27, A.M.'29, Univ. of Pa.; American Educ. Publications Editorial Offices, Middletown, Conn., since 1952.

MacKenzie, Kenneth L., B.S. in Ed.'37, Ed.M.'38, Boston Univ.; Supt. of Sch., Kensington, Conn., since 1952.

MacLaughlin, Marlin V., A.B.'27, Univ. of Maine; Supt. of Berlin Sch., Kensington, Conn., since 1941.

MacVittie, Robert William, B.Ed.'44, N. Y. State Tchrs. Col., Oneonta; M.A.'46, New York Univ.; Supvg. Prin., Montowese Elem. Sch., North Haven, Conn., since 1948.

Magoun, Creighton F., B.S.'29, R. I. State Col.; M.A.'47, Yale Univ.; Supt. of Sch., Portland, Conn., since 1948.

Mahan, Thomas W., A.B.'21, Col. of the Holy Cross; M.Ed.'35, Harvard Univ.; Supt. of Sch., Norwich, Conn., since 1942.

Mahoney, Robert H., A.B.'17, Holy Cross Col.; A.M.'18, Ph.D.'22, Catholic Univ.; Asst. Supt. of Sch., Hartford, Conn., since 1951.

Marland, S. P., Jr., A.B.'36, Univ. of Conn.; Supt. of Sch., Darien, Conn., since 1948.

Mathers, Albert P., B.S.'35, A.M.'43, Boston Univ.; Supt. of Sch., New Canaan, Conn., since 1946.

Mendel, Augusta, B.S.'34, M.A.'44, New York Univ.; Asst. Supt. of Sch., Bridgeport, Conn., since 1951.

Metlicka, Albert J., B.S.'37, M.A.'38, New York Univ.; Supt. of Sch., Southbury, Conn., since 1952.

Monson, Harold, B.A.'32, St. Olaf Col.; M.A.'45, Ph.D.'50, Yale Univ.; Supt. of Sch., Thomaston, Conn., since 1945.

Moody, Van Buren, A.B.'12, A.M.'15, Harvard Univ.; Supt. of Sch., Middletown, Conn., since 1925.

Moon, Glenn W., B.A.'24, Iowa State Tchrs. Col.; Cedar Falls; M.A.'31, Columbia Univ.; Prin., Walter R. Dolan Jr. H. S., Stamford, Conn., since 1949.

Moore, Simon H., B.S. in Ed.'34, State Tchrs. Col., Bridgewater, Mass.; M.A.'47, Univ. of Conn.; Supt. of Sch., Cromwell, Conn., since 1950.

Moroney, Helen G., B.S.'32, M.A.'40, Tchrs. Col., Columbia Univ.; Supvg. Prin., Salem Sch., Naugatuck, Conn., since 1933.

Morris, Richard Knowles, A.B.'40, Trinity Col.; M.A.'49, Ph.D.'51, Yale Univ.; Instr. in Educ., Trinity Col., Hartford, Conn., since 1951.

Morse, Seavey D., B.S.'30, St. Lawrence Univ.; Supt. of Sch., Woodstock, Conn., since 1950.

Murphy, Albert J., B.S.'28, Bridgewater Tchrs. Col.; Ed.M.'31, Boston Univ.; Supt. of Sch., Putnam, Conn., since 1949.

Murphy, Charles E., B.S.'31, Univ. of Conn.; M.A.'39, Columbia Univ.; Supt. of Uncasville Sch., Montville, Conn., since 1946.

Nason, Doris E., B.S. in Ed.'47, Ed.M.'48, Ed.D.'51, Boston Univ.; Asst. Prof. of Educ., Univ. of Conn., Storrs, Conn., since 1950.

Neuwien, Reginald, B.A.'26, Loyola Col.; M.A.'32, Tchrs. Col., Columbia Univ.; Supt. of Sch., Stamford, Conn.

383

Nichols, Marjorie H., B.S. in Ed.'37, State Tchrs. Col., North Adams, Mass.; M.A.'42, Tchrs. Col., Columbia Univ.; State Supvr., Dept. of Rural Educ., North East Dist., Putnam, Conn., since 1949.

Nolan, Thomas F., A.B.'13, Holy Cross Col.; A.M.'50, Univ. of Conn.; Asst. Supt. of Sch., Waterbury, Conn., since 1945.

Nybakken, Ernest O., B.A.'28, Concordia Col.; M.A.'36, Univ. of Minn.; Chief, Bur. of Rural Supvy. Serv., State Dept. of Educ., Hartford, Conn., since 1949.

O'Brien, Justin L., B.A.'26, Holy Cross Col.; M.A.'37, New York Univ.; Supt. of Sch., New Haven, Conn., since 1940.

O'Hara, James L., A.B.'25, A.M.'32, Bates Col.; Ph.D.'36, Yale Univ.; Supt. of Sch., Derby, Conn., since 1944.

Palapoli, Leonard G., B.S. in Ed.'31, State Tchrs. Col., Bridgewater, Mass.; Ed.M.'46, Boston Univ.; Supt. of Sch., Plainfield, Conn., since 1951.

Patterson, Helen, B.S.'33, Boston Univ.; M.A.'40, Tchrs. Col., Columbia Univ.; Elem. Supvr., West Ave. Sch., South Norwalk, Conn., since 1947.

Penley, Ferdinand J., B.S.'18, Univ. of Maine; M.A.'26, Columbia Univ.; Supt. of Rural Educ., Unionville, Conn., since 1919.

Perkins, Raymond E., B.S. in Ed.'36, Univ. of Maine; M.S.'43, Univ. of Ark.; Supt. of Sch., Bloomfield, Conn., since 1947.

Perry, William Russell, B.E.'39, Willimantic State Tchrs. Col., Conn.; M.Ed.'51, Hillyer Col.; Deputy Dir., Pub. Sch. Bldg. Commn., Hartford, Conn., since 1950.

Pierpont, Donald W., Provost, Avon Old Farms, Avon, Conn.

Pike, Irving L., B.S. in Ed.'40, Gorham State Tchrs. Col., Maine; M.A.'47, Prof. Diploma in Elem. Sch. Admin. '48, Tchrs. Col., Columbia Univ.; Supvg. Prin., Saugatuck Elem. Sch., Saugatuck, Westport, Conn.

*Pillsbury, W. Howard, A.B.'06, Carleton Col.; L.H.D.'39, Union Col.; Pres., American Assn. of Sch. Admin., 1941-42; Honorary Life Member, American Assn. of Sch. Admin. Address: 194 Central Ave., New Haven, Conn.

Pinkham, Raymond, Supt. of Sch., Branford. Conn.

Poehler, Paul F., Jr., Prin., Jr. H. S., Wilton, Conn., since 1950.

Pratt, Lyndon U., B.S.'23, Dartmouth Col.; A.M.'30, Tchrs. Col., Columbia Univ.; Exec. Secy., Conn. Educ. Assn., Hartford, Conn., since 1942.

Price, S. Willard, B.S.'27, Univ. of Idaho; Ph.D.'32, Yale Univ.; Supt. of Sch., Greenwich, Conn., since 1946.

Rast, Gerhardt E., Ph.B.'28, M.A.'33, Univ. of Chicago; Ed.D.'51, Tchrs. Col., Columbia Univ.; Supt. of Sch., Westport, Conn., since 1945.

Reed, Nona B., M.A.'29, Columbia Univ.; State Dir. of Elem. Educ., Bridgeport, Conn., since 1929.

*Reiche, Karl A., B.L.'09, M.A.'38, Trinity Col.; Supt. of Sch., Bristol, Conn., since 1913.

Reilly, John C., Rural Supt. of Sch., Willimantic, Conn.

Reuben, Gabriel, B.A.'48, State Tchrs. Col., New Paltz, N. Y.; M.A.'49, New York Univ.; Supvg. Prin., Bolton Elem. Sch., Manchester, Conn., since 1951.

Rice, Cecil L., B.S.'32, State Tchrs. Col., Pittsburg, Kansas; M.A.'38, Ed.D.'44, Tchrs. Col., Columbia Univ.; Prof. of Educ., Advanced Sch. of Educ., Univ. of Pa., Philadelphia, Pa.; and Supt. of Sch., North Haven, Conn., since 1950.

Richardson, Thomas F., M.A.'26, Yale Univ.; B.A.'17, Miss. Col.; Asst. Supt., in chg. of Sec. Sch., New Haven, Conn., since 1948.

Riggs, Frank J., Jr., B.S.'49, Univ. of Bridgeport; B.S.'51, New Haven State Tchrs. Col.; Deputy Dir., Conn. Pub. Sch. Bldg. Commn., Hartford, Conn., since 1951.

*Ritch, Charles F., Jr., A.B.'34, Columbia Univ.; A.M.'40, Harvard Univ.; Dir., Pub. Sch. Bldg. Commn., State Office Bldg., Hartford, Conn., since 1950.

Robertson, Martin Brown, B.S.'18, Trinity Col.; M.A.'20, Pa. State Col.; M.A. in Ed. Adm. '21, Tchrs. Col., Columbia Univ.; Supt. of Rural Educ., Willimantic, Conn., 1925-52. Address: 944 Middle Turnpike, Manchester, Conn.

Rogers, Malcolm B., B.A.'26, M.A.'32, D.Ed.'44, Univ. of Mich.; Supt. of Sch., Meriden, Conn., since 1949.

Roselle, Ernest N., Supt. of Tr. Sch., Southbury, Conn., since 1936.

Roth, Friedrich G., Ph.B.'19, Yale Univ.; M.A.'27, Columbia Univ.; Prin., Bassick H. S., Bridgeport, Conn., since 1945.

Russell, Earle S., B.S.'19, Tchrs. Col., Columbia Univ.; Ed.M.'22, Harvard Univ.; Ph.D.'34, Yale Univ.; Supt. of Sch., Windsor, Conn., since 1934.

Ryscavage, Jerome J., B.S.'31, M.A.'32, Mt. St. Mary's Col.; Supt. of Thompson Schs., North Grosvenordale, Conn., since 1946.

Saunders, Robert E., B.A.'36, Bates Col.; M.A. '47, Tchrs. Col., Columbia Univ.; Supt. of Sch., Unionville, Conn., since 1949.

Schneider, Bernhard W., M.A. in Ed.'48, New York Univ.; Supt. of Rural Educ., Winsted, Conn., since 1950.

Seidel, Ida E., B.S.'22, Northeast Mo. State Tchrs. Col., Kirksville; M.A.'27, Tchrs. Col., Columbia Univ.; Supvr., Div. of Instr., State Dept. of Educ., Willimantic, Conn., since 1935.

Shaheen, T. A., A.B.'38, M.Ed.'49, Boston Univ.; Supt. of Sch., Terryville, Conn.

Shattuck, George E., Ph.B.'22, Brown Univ.; M.A.'33, New York Univ.; Prin., Norwich Free Academy, Norwich, Conn., since 1940.

Sheehan, Wilfred Joseph, B.S.'31, Trinity Col., Conn.; M.S.'39, Univ. of N.H.; Ph.D.'47, Yale Univ.; Research Specialist, Conn. Educ. Assn., Hartford, Conn., since 1949.

Shultz, Wilmer L., B.S.'28, Susquehanna Univ.; M.A.'42, New York Univ.; Dist. Supt., State Dept. of Educ., Canaan, Conn., since 1949.

Sibley, Ernest, Sch. Archt., 7 S. Main St., West Hartford, Conn., since 1907.

Sibley, Ernest, Jr., 7 S. Main St., West Hartford, 7, Conn.

Stanley, Calvin, B.A.'24, Univ. of Tenn.; M.A.'28, George Wash. Univ.; M.A.'30, Columbia Univ.; Consultant, State Dept. of Educ., Hartford, Conn., since 1950.

Stanne, Leon J., B.S.'31, M.S.'36, Univ. of Mass.; Supt., Edison Sch., Trumbull, Conn., since 1950.

Stevens, John J., Supt. of Sch., Ansonia, Conn.

Stoddard, Paul W., B.A.'24, M.A.'29, Ph.D.'47, Yale Univ.; M.A.'28, Columbia Univ.; Supvg. Prin., Housatonic Valley Regional H. S., Falls Village, Conn., since 1939.

Strong, William M., B.S.'13, Tufts Col.; Ed.M.'29, Harvard Univ.; Supt. of Sch., Southington, Conn., since 1934.

Summerton, Edward, B.S.'38, N. J. State Tchrs. Col., Trenton; M.A.'41, Tchrs. Col., Columbia Univ.; Supt. of Weston Sch., Westport, Conn., since 1947.

Sweet, Walter Prescott, B.S.'17, Tufts Col.; Ed.M.'30, Harvard Univ.; Supt. of Sch., Danbury, Conn., since 1941.

Swett, Donald B., A.B.'18, Bates Col.; A.M.'26, Tchrs. Col., Columbia Univ.; Asst. Supt. of Sch., West Hartford, Conn., since 1949.

Swift, Gordon C., A.B.'11, Yale Univ.; A.M.'17, Tchrs. Col., Columbia Univ.; Supt. of Sch., Watertown, Conn., since 1919.

Thompson, Roger M., A.B.'17, Ind. State Normal Sch., Terre Haute; A.M.'23, Tchrs. Col., Columbia Univ.; State Dir., Fed.-State-Local Relations, State Dept. of Educ., Hartford, Conn., since 1947.

Thorne, Edmund H., B.S. in Ed.'29, M.A.'32, Ph.D.'44, Univ. of Mich.; Supt. of Sch., West Hartford, Conn., since 1947.

Thorp, John H., B.S.'28, Stout Inst.; M.S.'31, Univ. of Wis.; Ed.D.'45, New York Univ.; Supt. of Sch., Cheshire, Conn., since 1945.

Tobin, Helen A., B.S.'34, M.A.'41, Tchrs. Col., Columbia Univ.; Asst. Supt. of Sch., Stamford, Conn.

Trask, Ervin E., B.A.'20, Bates Col.; Supt. of Sch., Plainville, Conn.

Umberger, Willis H., A.B.'29, Ph.D.'51, Yale Univ.; M.A.'40, Tchrs. Col., Columbia Univ.; Supt. of Rural Sch., State Dept. of Educ., Norwich, Conn., since 1950.

Urban, Herman F., B.A.'30, Bowdoin Col.; M.Ed.'43, Bates Col.; Supt. of Sch., Seymour, Conn., since 1945.

Vincenti, E. John, B.S.'50, Hillyer Col.; Asst. to Supt. of Sch. for Bus., Glastonbury, Conn., since 1950.

Wagner, Melvin E., B.Ed.'32, State Tchrs. Col., Whitewater, Wis.; M.A.'42, New York Univ.; Supt. of Sch., West Haven, Conn., since 1951.

Wallace, John W., B.A.'30, Syracuse Univ.; M.E.'40, Univ. of Vt.'; Supt. of Sch., Newington, Conn., since 1951.

Walsh, Joseph W., M.A.'44, Yale Univ.; Supt. of Sch., Saybrook, Conn., since 1942.

Waters, Roy A., B.S.'32, M.A.'36, Columbia Univ.; Prin., Rogers Jr. H. S., Stamford, Conn., since 1944.

Weber, C. A., Ph.D.'43, Northwestern Univ.; Prof. of Educ., Univ. of Conn., Storrs, Conn.

White, Wesley Dale, B.S.'37, N. Y. State Col. for Tchrs., Buffalo; M.S.'46, N. Y. State Col. for Tchrs., Albany; Ed.D.'52, Tchrs. Col., Columbia Univ.; Dir. of Educ. and Tr., Southbury, Conn., since 1951.

Wish, Fred D., Jr., A.B.'13, Bowdoin Col.; Supt. of Sch., Hartford, Conn., 1923-51 (retired). Address: 200 Sylvan Knoll Rd., Stamford, Conn.

Witt, Earl M., B.S.'24, M.S.'45, Univ. of Mass.; Supt. of Sch., Stafford Springs, Conn., since 1934.

Wolffer, Wilfred C., B.Ed.'46, Keene Tchrs. Col., N. H.; M.A.'49, Ed.D.'51, Tchrs. Col., Columbia Univ.; Bus. Mgr., Havermeyer Pub. Sch., Greenwich, Conn.

Woodmansee, Merle B., M.A.'45, Univ. of Conn.; Supt. of East Windsor and South Windsor Sch., Warehouse Pt., Conn., since 1944.

Wyllie, David, M.A.'38, N. Y. Univ.; Asst. Supt. of Sch., Hamden, Conn., since 1951.

INSTITUTIONAL MEMBERS

Library, Gilbert and Bennett Sch., Georgetown, Conn.

State Teachers College, Willimantic, Conn.

Wilbur L. Cross Library, Univ. of Conn., Storrs, Conn.

DELAWARE

INDIVIDUAL MEMBERS

Adams, Albert W., A.B.'36, Univ. of Del.; M.A.'46, Bucknell Univ.; Supvg. Prin., John M. Clayton Sch., Dagsboro, Del., since 1948.

Atkinson, Donald Eugene, B.S.'48, State Tchrs. Col., Lock Haven, Pa.; M.S.'50, Okla. A. & M. Col.; Prin., Elem. Sch., Lewes, Del., since 1951.

Baltz, Austin D., B.S.'31, Allegheny Col.; M.Ed.'38, Univ. of Pittsburgh; Prin., Oak Grove Sch., Elsmere, Wilmington, Del., since 1948.

Brewer, Joseph H., B.S. Indus. Ed.'35, Carnegie Inst. of Tech.; Ed.M.'48, Temple Univ.; Prin., William P. Bancroft Sch., Wilmington, Del., since 1947.

Bricker, Rodney E., B.S.'35, State Tchrs. Col., Millersville, Pa.; M.S.'47, Univ. of Pa.; Prin., Oak Grove Sch., Elsmere, Del.

Clark, Zenas R., B.A.'20, Oberlin Col.; M.A.'29, Ph.D.'31, Tchrs. Col., Columbia Univ.; Admin. Asst., Pub. Sch., Wilmington, Del., since 1930.

Cobbs, Ramon C., D.Ed.'50, Temple Univ.; Supt. of Sch., Milford, Del., since 1948.

Cummings, C. W., Prin., Henry C. Conrad H. S., Woodcrest, Wilmington, Del.

Durkee, Robert L., B.S.'35, Pa. State Col.; M.A.'49, Lehigh Univ.; Exec. Secy., State Educ. Assn., Dover, Del., since 1948.

Green, David M., B.S.'28, M.S.'34, Temple Univ.; Supt. of Sch., Dover, Del., since 1952.

Heck, (Mrs.) Phyllis Mason, Ph.B.'15, Dickinson Col.; M.A.'26, Tchrs. Col., Columbia Univ.; Supvr. of Rural Schools, State Dept. of Pub. Instr., Wilmington, Del., since 1923.

Heiney, John F., B.S.'28, Gettysburg Col.; M.A.'35, Columbia Univ.; Supt., Mt. Pleasant Special Sch. Dist., Wilmington, Del., since 1949.

Holloway, H. V., A.B.'95, A.M.'98, LL.D.'32, Washington Col. (Md.); Ph.D.'14, Univ. of Pa.; State Supt. of Pub. Instr., Dover, Del., 1921-46. Address: 10 King's Highway, Dover, Del.

Howie, Thomas W., B.S.'23, Lafayette Col.; M.S.'31, Temple Univ.; Ed.D.'43, New York Univ.; Supt., Alexis I. duPont Special Sch. Dist., Wilmington, Del., since 1936.

Hunt, John L., B.S.'29, Col. of Wooster; B.D.'36, Union Theol. Sem.; Coordinator of Pub. Relations, Pub. Sch., Wilmington, Del., since 1949.

Keen, George H., B.S.'29, State Tchrs. Col., East Stroudsburg, Pa.; M.A.'32, Univ. of Mich.; Supt. of Sch., Lewes, Del., since 1952.

King, Harry Brandt, A.B.'17, Franklin and Marshall Col.; A.M.'23, Columbia Univ.; Ph.D.'28, New York Univ.; Asst. State Supt. of Pub. Instr. in chg. of Elem. Sch., Dover, Del., since 1922.

Kleckner, Joseph R., B.S.'28, State Tchrs. Col., West Chester, Pa.; M.Ed.'39, Temple Univ.; Supt. of Sch., New Castle, Del., since 1946.

Lawless, Thomas A., A.B.'10, S.T.L.'12, D.D.'14, Pontifical Roman Univ.; LL.D.'31, LaSalle Col.; Rector, Salesianum Sch. for Boys, Wilmington, Del., since 1943.

Lecrone, Ellis K., A.B.'21, Susquehanna Univ.; M.Ed.'38, Temple Univ.; Supvg. Prin. of Sch., Middletown, Del., since 1944.

McMenamin, David, A.B.'24, Washington Col.; M.A., Columbia Univ.; Prin., Alfred I. duPont Sch. Dist., Wilmington, Del., since 1930.

385

DELAWARE

Madden, Kenneth C., B.S.'39, State Tchrs. Col., Shippensburg, Pa.; M.A.'46, Univ. of N. C.; Ed.D.'50, Pa. State Col.; Supt. of Sch., Seaford, Del., since 1952.

Messner, J. C., A.B.'16, Franklin and Marshall Col.; B.D.'19, Eastern Theological Sem. of the Reformed Church in the U. S.; M.A.'24, Columbia Univ.; Supt. of Sch., Harrington, Del., since 1926.

Miller, George R., Jr., A.B.'15, Lafayette Col.; M.A.'21, Tchrs. Col., Columbia Univ.; Ed.D. '43, New York Univ.; State Supt. of Pub. Instr., Dover, Del., since 1946.

Miller, Ward I., A.B.'14, A.M.'15, Univ. of Denver; Ed.D.'41, Tchrs. Col., Columbia Univ.; Supt. of Sch., Wilmington, Del., since 1946.

Mitchell, Edith L., B.S.'30, M.A.'31, Tchrs. Col., Columbia Univ.; State Dir. of Art Educ., Dover, Del., since 1938.

Moore, James A., B.S.'41, State Tchrs. Col., Oswego, N. Y.; M.A.'50, Syracuse Univ.; Prin. of H. S., Lewes, Del., since 1950.

Omwake, H. Geiger, Certificat '26, Univ. de Poitiers, Tours, France; A.B.'29, Franklin and Marshall Col.; M.Ed.'48, Duke Univ.; Supvg. Prin. of Sch., Greenwood, Del., since 1952.

Parsons, M. James, B.S.'32, Wash. Col.; M.S.'35, Univ. of Pa.; Mngt. Tr. Consultant, Parkway, Bethany Beach, Del., since 1950.

Penrose, William O., Ed.D.'48, Harvard Univ.; Dean, Sch. of Educ., Univ. of Del., Newark, Del., since 1949.

Pillard, Matthew J., A.B.'38, Univ. of Rochester; M.A.'42, Ed.D.'51, Tchrs. Col., Columbia Univ.; Assoc. Prof., Educ. Admin., Univ. of Del., Newark, Del., since 1951.

Shue, Wilmer E., B.S.'29, Franklin and Marshall Col.; M.A.'33, Tchrs. Col., Columbia Univ.; Supt. of Sch., Newark, Del., since 1945.

Simpson, William B., B.S.'30, Univ. of Del.; M.S. in Ed.'36, Cornell Univ.; Ed.D.'51, Temple Univ.; Supt. of Sch., Camden, Del., since 1938.

Slaybaugh, J. Paul, A.B.'21, Dickinson Col.; A.M.'33, Univ. of Pa.; LL.D.'42, Waynesburg Col.; Pres., Wesley Jr. Col., Dover, Del., since 1951.

*Stahl, Harvey E., A.B.'14, Ind. Univ.; A.M.'18, Tchrs. Col., Columbia Univ., Dist. Supt. of Sch., Claymont, Del., since 1922.

Stewart, Robert C., B.S.'35, Ursinus Col.; M.A.'42, New York Univ.; Ed.D.'50, Univ. of Pa.; Dir. of Research and Publications, State Dept. of Pub. Instr., Dover, Del., since 1947.

Taliaferro, John Arthur, B.S.'35, Cheyney State Tchrs. Col.; Prin., Absalom Jones Sch. Dist. 106, Newport, Del., since 1943.

Thomas, Joseph D., B.A.'23, Univ. of Utah; M.A.'30, Columbia Univ.; Supt. of Sch., Georgetown, Del., since 1943.

Timmons, Leslie E., B.S.'26, Washington Col.; M.S.Ed.'38, Tchrs. Col., Columbia Univ.; Supvg. Prin. of Sch., Millsboro, Del., since 1938.

Vansant, Joseph A., B.A.'26, Haverford Col.; M.A. in Eng.'29, Univ. of Pa.; Ed.D.'41, Columbia Univ.; Supt. of Special Sch. Dist., Rehoboth, Del., since 1952.

Wagner, M. Channing, B.A.'13, Wittenberg Col.; A.M.'23, Columbia Univ.; Asst. Supt. of Sch., Wilmington, Del., since 1929.

Wangler, Frank A., B.S.A.'17, Syracuse Univ.; M.A.'31, Tchrs. Col., Columbia Univ.; Supvg. Prin. of Sch., Delaware City, Del., since 1948.

White, William E., Prin., H. Fletcher Brown Voc. H. S., Wilmington, Del.

Wright, George W., B.S., Rider Col.; Ed.M., Temple Univ.; Supt. of Sch., Smyrna, Del., since 1943.

INSTITUTIONAL MEMBER

Library, Univ. of Del., Newark, Del.

DISTRICT OF COLUMBIA

INDIVIDUAL MEMBERS

Adams, Arthur S., Sc.D.'27, Colo. Sch. of Mines; Pres., American Council on Educ., Washington, D. C., since 1951.

Albright, Roger, A.B.'14, Colgate Univ.; B.D.'17, Union Theological Seminary; Dir., Educ. Services, Motion Picture Assn. of America, Washington, D. C., since 1935.

Amidon, Edna P., B.S.'19, M.S.'27, Univ. of Minn.; Chief, Home Economics Educ. Serv., Office of Educ., Federal Security Agency, Washington, D. C., since 1938.

*Ballou, Frank Washington, B.S.'04, Tchrs. Col., Columbia Univ.; M.A.'08, Univ. of Cincinnati; Ph.D.'14, Harvard Univ.; LL.D.'41, Marietta Col.; LL.D.'43, George Washington Univ.; Pres., Dept. of Superintendence, 1925-26; Honorary Life Member, American Assn. of Sch. Admin.; Supt. of Sch., Washington, D. C., 1920-43 (retired). Address: 3130 Wisconsin Ave., N. W., Washington 16, D. C.

Barber, Joseph E., B.S.'26, M.S.'33, Syracuse Univ.; Ed.D.'48, Univ. of Buffalo; Educ. and Training Research Spec., Bur. of Navy Personnel, Washington, D. C., since 1952.

*Beach, Fred F., B.S.'26, M.S.'27, Syracuse Univ.; M.A.'28, Ph.D.'33, Columbia Univ.; Chief, State Sch. Systems, Office of Educ., Federal Security Agency, Washington, D. C., since 1947.

Bedell, Ralph, B.S.'26, Central State Col. (Mo.); A.M.'29, Ph.D.'32, Univ. of Mo.; Chmn., Dept. of Psych. and Educ., American Univ., Washington, D. C., since 1950.

Berns, Karl H., B.S. in Ed.'24, Kent State Univ.; M.A.'27, Univ. of Akron; LL.B.'37, William McKinley Sch. of Law; Ph.D.'42, Ohio State Univ.; Asst. Secy. for Bus., Natl. Educ. Assn., Washington, D. C., since 1948.

*Booker, Ivan Albert, A.B.'25, Ind. State Tchrs. Col., Terre Haute; M.A.'27, Ph.D.'34, Univ. of Chicago; Asst. Dir., Div. of Press and Radio Relations, Natl. Educ. Assn., Washington, D. C., since 1952.

Bragdon, Helen Dalton, B.A.'18, Mt. Holyoke Col.; Ed.M.'25, Ed.D.'28, Harvard Univ.; LL.D.'46, MacMurray Col.; L.H.D.'49, Bowling Green State Univ.; LL.D.'50, Lake Erie Col.; Genl. Dir., American Assn. of Univ. Women, Washington, D. C., since 1950.

Brodinsky, B. P., B.A.'32, Univ. of Del.; M.A.'34, Univ. of Pa.; Editor, *Educator's Washington Dispatch*, Washington, D. C., since 1945.

Brown, Francis J., A.B.'18, State Univ. of Iowa; M.A.'23, Columbia Univ.; Ph.D.'32, New York Univ.; Litt.D.'49, Muhlenberg Col.; Staff Assoc., American Council on Educ., Washington, D. C., since 1940.

Burnett, Lewie W., B.A.'37, Central Wash. Col. of Educ.; Ed.D.'48, Stanford Univ.; Sch. of Educ., George Wash. Univ., Washington, D. C.

Burr, Samuel Engle, Jr., Litt.B.'19, Rutgers Univ.; M.A.'25, Univ. of Wis.; M.A.'27, Tchrs. Col., Columbia Univ.; Ed.D.'36, Univ. of Cincinnati; Chmn., Dept. of Educ., Col. of Arts and Sciences, and Dir., Inst. on World Affairs, American Univ., Washington, D. C., since 1947.

Cantrell, Lawson J., A.B.'26, M.A.'27, George Washington Univ.; Assoc. Supt. of Sch., Washington, D. C., since 1939.

Carlton, Harold O., Educ. Consultant, Driver Educ. and Tr. Program, American Automobile Assn., Washington, D. C., since 1945.

Carney, Norfleet Lynn, B.A.'10, Southwestern Univ.; B.S.'13, Univ. of Tenn.; M.S.'32, Univ. of Kansas; Sch. Facilities Survey Rep., Office of Educ., Federal Security Agency, Washington, D. C., since 1951.

Carr, William G., A.B.'24, M.A.'26, Ph.D.'30, Stanford Univ.; Exec. Secy., Natl. Educ. Assn., Washington, D. C., since 1952.

Clark, Lois M., A.B.'28, Western Mich. Col. of Educ., Kalamazoo; M.A.'31, Tchrs. Col.; Columbia Univ.; Asst. Dir. of Rural Serv., Natl. Educ. Assn., Washington, D. C., since 1945.

Coleman, William H., A.B.'09, Nebr. Wesleyan Univ.; M.A.'16, Univ. of Nebr.; Ph.D.'31, Columbia Univ.; Chief Educ. Officer, Veterans Educ. Facilities Program, Office of Educ., Federal Security Agency, Washington, D. C., since 1940.

Cooper, Shirley, A.B.'34, Davis and Elkins Col.; M.A.'39, W. Va. Univ.; Ph.D.'43, Cornell Univ.; Asst. Secy., American Assn. of Sch. Admin., Washington, D. C., since 1949.

Corning, Hobart Munson, Ph.B.'11, A.M.'12, Dickinson Col.; A.M.'31, Tchrs. Col., Columbia Univ.; Ed.D.'31, Colo. Col.; Supt. of Sch., Washington, D. C., since 1946.

Cramer, (Mrs.) Bessie Wood, M.A.'40, Univ. of Md.; Dir. of Elem. Educ. in chg. of Special Serv., Peabody Sch., Washington, D. C., since 1947.

Cummings, James E., A.B. in Ed.'32, George Washington Univ.; L.H.D.'43, St. Francis Col.; Asst. Dir., Dept. of Educ., Natl. Catholic Welfare Conf., Washington, D. C., since 1928.

*Davis, Hazel, B.S.'32, Tchrs. Col., Columbia Univ.; M.A.'36, Univ. of Chicago; Ph.D.'40, Tchrs. Col., Columbia Univ.; Asst. Dir. of Research, Natl. Educ. Assn., Washington, D. C., since 1937.

Dawson, Howard A., B.S. and M.A.'24, Ph.D.'26, George Peabody Col. for Tchrs.; Dir. of Rural Serv. and Exec. Secy., Dept. of Rural Educ., Natl. Educ. Assn., Washington, D. C., since 1936.

Deering, Elmer C., M.A.'28, Univ. of Texas; Sch. Facilities Survey Rep., Office of Educ., Federal Security Agency, Washington, D. C., since 1951.

Devine, John M., Major General, USA, B.S.'17, United States Military Academy; M.S.'22, Yale Univ.; Chief, Armed Forces Information and Educ. Div., Dept. of Defense, Washington, D. C., since 1950.

Elicker, Paul Edgar, A.B.'14, Ursinus Col.; A.M.'21, Columbia Univ.; Ed.M.'31, Harvard Univ.; Sc.D. in Ed.'41, Boston Univ.; Exec. Secy., Natl. Assn. of Sec.-Sch. Prin., Washington, D. C., since 1940.

Eliot, Martha M., A.B.'13, Radcliffe Col.; M.D.'18, Johns Hopkins Univ.; Chief, Children's Bureau, Federal Security Agency, Social Security Admin., Washington, D. C., since 1951.

Elstad, Leonard M., B.A.'22, LL.D.'46, St. Olaf Col.; M.A.'23, Gallaudet Co.; Pres., Gallaudet Col., Washington, D. C., since 1945.

Exton, Elaine, B.S.'33, Columbia Univ.; M.A.'34, Univ. of Southern Calif. Address: 1200 16th St., N. W., Washington, D. C.

Farley, Belmont Mercer, Ph.D.'29, Columbia Univ.; Dir. of Press and Radio Relations, Natl. Educ. Assn., Washington, D. C., since 1929.

Faust, Wilda Freebern, A.B.'29, Iowa State Tchrs. Col., Cedar Falls; M.A.'43, Univ. of Fla.; Natl. Secy., Future Tchrs. of America, Natl. Educ. Assn., Washington, D. C., since 1948.

Featherston, E. Glenn, B.S.'29, M.A.'31, Ed.D. '41, Univ. of Mo.; Asst. Dir., Admin. of State and Local Sch. Systems, Office of Educ., Federal Security Agency, Washington, D. C., since 1951.

Fenton, J. Nelson, B.S. in Ed.'42, State Tchrs. Col., Shippensburg, Pa.; M.A.'47, Univ. of Pa.; Asst. Dean, Marine Corps Inst., Washington, D. C., since 1951.

Fitzwater, C. O., A.B.'36, W. Va. State Col.; M.A.'41, W. Va. Univ.; Ph.D.'46, Cornell Univ.; County and Rural Sch. Administration, U. S. Office of Education, Washington, D. C., since 1951.

Fox, James Harold, A.B.'25, A.M.'26, Univ. of Western Ontario; Ed.M.'36, Ed.D.'37, Harvard Univ.; Dean, Sch. of Educ., George Washington Univ., Washington, D. C., since 1938.

Franseth, Jane, B.A.'30, Western Mich. Col. of Educ., Kalamazoo; M.A.'36, Univ. of Mich.; Ph.D.'50, Univ. of Chicago; Specialist for Rural Sch., Office of Educ., Federal Security Agency, Washington, D. C., since 1947.

Frutchey, Fred P., A.B.'22, Ursinus Col.; M.A. '30, Colo. State Col. of Educ., Greeley; Ph.D. '32, Ohio State Univ.; Educ. Analyst, Div. of Field Studies and Tr., Extension Serv., U. S. Dept. of Agriculture, Washington, D. C., since 1938.

Fuller, Alma Deane, B.S.'42, Kansas State Col.; Dir., Educ. Div., American Forest Products Indus., Washington, D. C., since 1950.

Fuller, Edgar, A.B.'27, Brigham Young Univ.; J.D.'32, Univ. of Chicago; Ed.D.'40, Harvard Univ.; Exec. Secy., Natl. Council of Chief State Sch. Officers, Washington, D. C., since 1948.

Gabbard, Hazel, B.S.'27, Univ. of Cincinnati; Specialist for Extended Sch. Serv., Office of Educ., Federal Security Agency, Washington, D. C., since 1942.

Gibbs, Andrew H., A.B.'39, M.A.'44, George Wash. Univ.; Chief Educ. Asst. in State Sch. Admin., Office of Educ., Federal Security Agency, Washington, D. C., since 1936.

Giddings, Ernest, A.B.'25, Western Mich. Col. of Educ.; A.M.'40, Mich. State Col.; Asst. Dir., Div. of Legislation and Fed. Relations, Natl. Educ. Assn., Washington, D. C., since 1945.

Givens, Willard E., A.B.'13, LL.D.'38, Ind. Univ.; M.A.'15, Columbia Univ.; Diploma '16, Union Theol. Sem.; Ed.D.'41, Miami Univ.; Honorary Fellow of the Educ. Inst. of Scotland '47; Doctor of Humanities '50, Col. of Idaho; Exec. Secy., Natl. Educ. Assn., Washington, D. C., 1935-52 (retired). Address: 4329 Blagden Ave., N. W., Washington, D. C.

Good, Paul H., A.B.'23, Friends Univ.; A.M.'29, Columbia Univ.; Secy., Com. on Educ., Chamber of Commerce of the U. S., Washington, D. C., since 1944.

Goodykoontz, Bess, B.A.'20, M.A.'22, State Univ. of Iowa; D.Ped.'35, N. Y. State Col. for Tchrs., Albany; Asst. Dir. for Program Coord., Office of Educ., Federal Security Agency, Washington, D. C.

Grigsby, Rall I., A.B.'18, D.Ed.'49, Cornell Col.; M.A.'28, Drake Univ.; Deputy Commr., Office of Educ., Federal Security Agency, Washington, D. C., since 1949.

387

Hager, Walter E., B.S.'16, Univ. of Nebr.; A.M.'27, Ph.D.'31, Columbia Univ.; Pres., Wilson Tchrs. Col., Washington, D. C., since 1941.

Halberg, Anna D., B.S.'22, A.M.'24, Columbia Univ.; Prof. of Educ., Wilson Tchrs. Col., Washington, D. C., since 1927.

Hamon, Ray Laforest, B.S.'22, Univ. of Fla.; A.M.'25, George Peabody Col. for Tchrs.; Ph.D.'30, Tchrs. Col., Columbia Univ.; Chief, Sch. Housing Section, Office of Educ., Federal Security Agency, Washington, D. C.

Hansen, Carl F., A.B.'27, M.A.'40, Univ. of Nebr.; Ed.D.'44, Univ. of Southern Calif.; Assoc. Supt. in chg. of Elem. Sch., Div. 1-9, and Curriculum Planning, Div. 1-13, Washington, D. C., since 1947.

*Haycock, Robert Lee, B.A.'11, M.A.'12, George Washington Univ. Address: 1893 Ingleside Terr., N. W., Washington, D. C.

Haynes, Harold A., E.E.'10, Univ. of Pittsburgh; M.A.'30, Univ. of Chicago; Ed.D.'46, New York Univ.; First Asst. Supt. of Sch., Washington, D. C.

Hill, Wilhelmina, B.S. in Ed.'30, Univ. of Kansas; M.A.'33, Ed.D.'39, Tchrs. Col., Columbia Univ.; Specialist in Social Science, Elem. Div., Office of Educ., Federal Security Agency, Washington, D. C.

Hochwalt, Frederick G., A.B.'31, LL.D.'48, Univ. of Dayton; M.A.'40, Ed.D.'44, Catholic Univ. of America; LL.D.'47, Mount Mary Col.; LL.D.'48, St. Mary's Col.; LL.D.'48, Villanova Col.; Secy. Genl., Natl. Catholic Educ. Assn., Washington, D. C., since 1944.

Holmes, Thomas J., M.A.'30, George Washington Univ.; Assoc. Supt. of Sch., Washington, D. C., since 1950.

Horn, Francis H., A.B.'30, Dartmouth Col.; M.A.'34, Univ. of Va.; M.A.'42, Ph.D.'49, Yale Univ.; Exec. Secy., Assn. for Higher Educ., Natl. Educ. Assn., Washington, D. C., since 1951.

Hornbostel, Victor O., B.S.'42, Kansas State Tchrs. Col., Emporia; M.S.'47, Univ. of Wis.; Asst. Dir. of Research, Natl. Educ. Assn., Washington, D. C., since 1952.

Hubbard, Frank W., A.B.'22, M.A.'26, Univ. of Calif.; Ph.D.'31, Tchrs. Col., Columbia Univ.; Dir. of Research, Natl. Educ. Assn., Washington, D. C., since 1940.

Hull, J. Dan, Ph.D.'33, Yale Univ.; Asst. Dir., Div. of Elem. and Sec. Sch., Office of Educ., Federal Security Agency, Washington, D. C., since 1947.

*Hunt, Rolfe Lanier, B.A.'24, Millsaps Col.; M.A.'27, Ph.D.'37, George Peabody Col. for Tchrs.; Chief, Publications Section, Office of Educ., Federal Security Agency, Washington, D. C., since 1952.

*Hutchins, Clayton D., B.A. and B.S.'22, M.A.'27, Ph.D.'38, Ohio State Univ.; Specialist in Sch. Finance, Office of Educ., Federal Security Agency, Washington, D. C., since 1950.

Hypps, Irene C., A.B.'26, Howard Univ.; M.A.'32, Ph.D.'43, New York Univ.; Assoc. Supt. of Pub. Sch., Research Dept., Wilson Sch., Washington, D. C., since 1952.

Isenberg, Robert M., B.S. in Ed.'41, N. Y. State Col. for Tchrs. at Buffalo; M.S. in Ed.'48, Ph.D.'52, Cornell Univ.; Asst. Dir., Div. of Rural Serv., Natl. Educ. Assn., Washington, D. C., since 1952.

Kearns, Carroll D., B.M.'23, M.M.'25, Mus.D. '48, Chicago Musical Col.; B.S.'33, Westminster Col.; M.E.'38, Univ. of Pittsburgh; Member of Congress from Pa., House Office Bldg., Washington, D. C., since 1947.

Keith, Paul J., B.S.'29, Central Mo. State Col.; M.A.'35, Univ. of Mo.; Sch. Facilities Survey Rep., Office of Educ., Federal Security Agency, Washington, D. C., since 1951.

Key, Norman, A.B.'38, Howard Col.; M.A. in Ed.'47, George Washington Univ.; Exec. Secy., Natl. Commn. on Safety Educ., Natl. Educ. Assn., Washington, D. C.

Lambert, Sam M., B.S.'35, M.A.'38, W. Va. Univ.; Asst. Dir., Research Div., Natl. Educ. Assn., Washington, D. C., since 1950.

Lloyd, George W., M.A.'28, Clark Univ.; Pres., Mount Vernon Seminary, Washington, D. C., since 1931.

Lyle, Robert S., A.B.'29, Dartmouth Col.; M.S. in Ed.'40, Cornell Univ.; Headmaster, Sidwell Friends Sch., Washington, D. C., since 1949.

McClure, Worth, A.B.'08, D.Ed.'38, Simpson Col.; A.M.'20, Univ. of Wash.; LL.D.'32, Col. of Puget Sound; D.Ed.'42, Columbia Univ.; Pres., 1943-44; and Exec. Secy., since 1946, American Assn. of Sch. Admin., Washington, D. C.

McGrath, Earl James, A.B.'28, M.A.'30, Univ. of Buffalo; Ph.D.'36, Univ. of Chicago; L.H.D.'46, Coe Col.; Litt.D.'49, Muskingum Col.; LL.D.'49, Univ. of Louisville; LL.D.'49, Alfred Univ.; LL.D.'50, St. Bonaventure Col.; Sc.D. in Ed.'50, Boston Univ.; LL.D.'50, Univ. of Toledo; LL.D.'50, Bethany Col.; Ped.D.'50, Bradley Univ.; U. S. Commr. of Educ., Office of Educ., Federal Security Agency, Washington, D. C., since 1949.

Maas, Leroy John, B.S. in Ed.'28, Oakland City Col.; M.A.'45, George Wash. Univ.; Pres., Southeastern Univ., Washington, D. C., since 1946.

Mackintosh, Helen K., Ph.D.'31, State Univ. of Iowa; Chief, Instr. Problems, Elem. Div., Office of Educ., Federal Security Agency, Washington, D. C., since 1938.

Marks, Sallie B., A.B.'23, Southwestern State Tchrs. Col., Weatherford, Okla.; M.A.'24, Tchrs. Col., Columbia Univ.; Chief, Elem. Educ., 499 Pennsylvania Ave., Washington 25, D. C., since 1944.

Mehrens, Harold E., A.B.'28, N. Mex. State Tchrs. Col., Silver City; M.A.'31, N. Mex. Highlands Univ., Las Vegas; M.S.'36, Ed.D. '39, Univ. of Southern Calif.; Chief, Aviation Educ. Div., Civil Aeronautics Admin., Washington, D. C., since 1945.

Mobley, M. D., B.S.A.'23, Univ. of Ga.; M.S.'30, Cornell Univ.; LL.D.'45, Piedmont Col.; Exec. Secy., American Voc. Assn., Inc., Washington, D. C., since 1951.

Myer, Walter E., A.B.'10, Southwestern Col.; A.M.'13, Univ. of Chicago; LL.D.'34, Southwestern Col.; Dir., Civic Educ. Serv., Washington, D. C., since 1925.

Nelson, Norman J., A.B.'17, George Washington Univ.; A.M.'30, Harvard Univ.; First Asst. Supt. of Sch. in chg. of White Sr. H. S. and Wilson Tchrs. Col., Washington, D. C., since 1947.

Oxnam, G. Bromley, A.B.'13, Univ. of Southern Calif.; S.T.B.'15, Boston Univ. Sch. of Theology; D.D.'25, Col. of the Pacific; LL.D.'29, Ohio Wesleyan; LL.D.'29, Wabash Col.; Litt.D.'30, Boston Univ.; LL.D.'31, Univ. of Southern Calif.; D.Sc.'35, Rose Polytechnic Inst.; L.H.D.'38, DePauw Univ.; Litt.D.'41, Northeastern Univ.; D.D.'46, Wesleyan Univ.; S.T.D.'46, Yale Univ.; LL.D.'46, Allegheny Col.; LL.D.'50, Dickinson Col.; LL.D.'52, Bennett Col.; Bishop of the Methodist Church, 100 Maryland Ave., N. E., Washington, D. C., since 1952.

Pepper, Margaret R., B.A.'28, M.A.'32, George Washington Univ.; Exec. Asst. to the Supt. of Sch., Washington, D. C.

Peterson, Gladys Tignor, M.A.'34, Howard Univ.; M.A.'40, Ed.D.'49, Columbia Univ.; Educationist in the office of the First Asst. Supt. of Sch., Div. 2, Washington, D. C., since 1949.

Pinkston, Eva G., Exec. Secy., Dept. of Elem. Sch. Prin., Natl. Educ. Assn., 1931-50 (retired). Address: 3600 Brandywine St., N. W., Washington, D. C.

Reason, Paul L., B.Ed.'37, Keene Tchrs. Col.; Ed.M.'47, Harvard Univ.; Specialist, Educ. Records and Reports, Office of Educ., Federal Security Agency, Washington, D. C.

Reed, Wayne O., B.A. in Ed.'35, Nebr. State Tchrs. Col., Peru; M.A.'40, Ph.D.'49, Univ. of Nebr.; Asst. Commr. of Educ., in charge of Div. of State and Local Sch. Systems, Office of Educ., Federal Security Agency, Washington, D. C.

Rees, Conard N., Ph.D.'49, Univ. of Nebr.; Dean, Washington Missionary Col., Takoma Park, Washington, D. C., since 1949.

Rice, Harold A., A.B.'20, A.M.'26, W. Va. Univ.; Ed.D.'38, New York Univ.; Sch. Facilities Survey, Sch. Housing Section, Office of Educ., Federal Security Agency, Washington, D. C., since 1951.

Roblee, Dana B., B.S.'27, St. Bonaventure Univ.; M.S.'33, N. Y. State Col. for Tchrs., Albany; Sch. Relations Officer, Federal Civil Defense Admin., Washington, D. C., since 1952.

Rulkoetter, A. H., A.B.'36, Union Col.; M.A.'39, Ph.D.'48, Univ. of Nebr.; Assoc. Secy., International Religious Liberty Assn., Washington, D. C.

Savoy, A. Kiger, A.B. in Ed.'29, Howard Univ.; M.A.'34, Columbia Univ.; Assoc. Supt. of Sch., Washington, D. C. since 1930.

Shephard, William H., B.A.'29, Washington Missionary Col.; M.A.'36, Univ. of Va.; Pres., Washington Missionary Col., Takoma Park, Washington, D. C., since 1946.

Smith, (Mrs.) Josephine C., A.B.'30, Howard Univ.; M.A.'37, Columbia Univ.; Dir. of Elem. Educ., in chg. of Admin., Div. 10-13, Public Sch., Washington, D. C., since 1947.

Snearline, Paul Albert, A.B.'37, Univ. of Akron; A.M.'38, Univ. of Mich.; Admin. Asst. to First Asst. Supt. of Sch., Washington, D. C., since 1950.

Taylor, James L., B.S.E.'30, Arkansas State Tchrs. Col.; M.A.'36, George Peabody Col.; Specialist, Sch. Plant Management, U. S. Office of Educ., Washington, D. C., since 1951.

Viles, N. E., A.M.'30, Ph.D.'34, Univ. of Mo.; Specialist, Sch. Plant Management, Office of Educ., Federal Security Agency, Washington, D. C., since 1946.

Webster, Marjorie Fraser, B.A.'33, George Washington Univ.; M.A.'35, American Univ.; Pres. and Founder, Marjorie Webster Jr. Col., Washington, D. C., since 1920.

Wells, George C., B.S.'23, Univ. of Okla.; A.M.'27, Columbia Univ.; Educ. Spec., Bur. of Indian Affairs, Washington, D. C.

*Whitelaw, John B., Ph.B.'29, Ph.D.'35, Yale Univ. Address: 7205 Harwick Rd., Wood Acres, Washington 16, D. C.

Wilkinson, Garnet C., A.B.'02, Oberlin Col.; LL.B.'09, LL.D., Howard Univ.; M.A.'32, Univ. of Pa.; Ed.D., Morgan Col.; LL.D., Wilberforce Univ.; First Asst. Supt. of Sch., in charge of Colored Schs., Washington, D. C., 1924-51 (retired).

Wilson, Roy K., B.E.'36, Eastern Ill. State Col.; A.M.'43, Univ. of Ill.; Asst. Dir. of Press and Radio Relations, Natl. Educ. Assn., Washington, D. C., since 1946.

*Woofter, James, A.B.'41, Glenville State Col.; A.M.'48, Univ. of Ala.; Ed.D.'50, Columbia Univ.; Educ. Consultant, Office of Educ., Federal Security Agency, Washington, D. C., since 1950.

Wyman, Harry B., B.S. in Ed.'18, M.A.'27, Ph.D.'31, Ohio State Univ.; Chief, Program Sec., Training Activities Br., International Exch. Ser., Dept. of State, Washington, D. C.

INSTITUTIONAL MEMBERS

Civil Aeronautics Admin., Dept. of Commerce, Aviation Education Div., Office of Aviation Devel., Washington, D. C.

Library, Miner Tchs. Col., Washington, D. C.

Library, Wilson Tchrs. Col., Washington, D. C.

Watson Automotive Equipment Company, C. P. Lineweaver, Branch Mgr., 1042 Wisconsin Ave., N. W., Washington 7, D. C.

FLORIDA

INDIVIDUAL MEMBERS

Alexander, William M., B.A.'34, Bethel Col.; M.A.'36, George Peabody Col. for Tchrs.; Ph.D.'40, Tchrs Col., Columbia Univ.; Prof. of Educ., Univ. of Miami, Coral Gables, Fla., since 1950.

Altman, R. D., M.A.'38, Univ. of Fla.; Co. Supt. of Sch., Crawfordville, Fla., since 1949.

*Anderson, Homer W., B.A.'10, Highland Park Col.; M.A.'15, Ph.D.'25, State Univ. of Iowa; Pres., American Assn. of Sch. Admin., 1942-43; Honorary Life Member American Assn. of Sch. Admin. Address: 613 Francis Blvd., Lakeland, Fla.

Badger, William V., B.S.'35, M.A.'36, George Peabody Col.; D.Ed.'52, Florida State Univ.; Research Project, Tallahassee, Fla.

Bailey, Thomas D., A.B.'19, Wofford Col.; M.A.E.'39, Univ. of Fla.; LL.D.'49, Fla. Southern Col.; Supt. of Pub. Instr., State Dept. of Educ., Tallahassee, Fla., since 1949.

Baird, J. Pope, B.S.C.'30, Bowdoin Col.; State Supvr. of Transportation, State Dept. of Educ., Tallahassee, Fla., since 1946.

Bamberger, Florence E., B.S.'14, M.A.'15, Ph.D.'21, Tchrs. Col., Columbia Univ.; Visiting Prof., Univ. of Fla., Gainesville, Fla., since 1949.

Beery, John R., A.B.'30, Juniata Col.; A.M.'34, Univ. of Chicago; Ph.D.'42, Columbia Univ.; Dean, Sch. of Educ., Univ. of Miami, Coral Gables, Fla., since 1947.

Bennett, Ulric J., A.B.'09, B.L.'14, A.M.'26, Univ. of Ga.; Co. Supt. of Pub. Instr., Ft. Lauderdale, Fla., since 1931.

Blackburn, J. Hartley, A.B.'30, Fla. Southern Col.; M.Ed.'42, Duke Univ.; Co. Supt. of Sch., Bradenton, Fla., since 1945.

Boland, Ardney J., M.S.'48, Fla. State Univ.; B.S.A.'43, Univ. of Fla.; Co. Supt. of Pub. Instr., Monticello, Fla., since 1949.

Christian, Floyd T., A.B.'37, M.A.'50, Univ. of Fla.; Co. Supt. of Pub. Instr., Clearwater, Fla., since 1949.

Cook, Denton L., A.B.'35, Nebr. State Tchrs. Col.; M.A.'40, Univ. of Fla.; Ed.D.'52, Colo. State Col. of Educ.; Supvg. Prin. of Sch., Plant City, Fla., since 1943.

389

FLORIDA

Dean, Harris William, Ed.B.'29, Ill. State Normal Univ., Normal; A.M.'36, State Univ. of Iowa; Ed.D.'47, Univ. of Ill.; Prof. of Educ. Admin., Fla. State Univ., Tallahassee, Fla., since 1948.

Dominick, H. B., B.S.'37, Univ. of Fla.; Co. Supt. of Pub. Instr., Wauchula, Fla., since 1949.

Efferson, H. Manning, Dean of Admin., Fla. Agrl. and Mech. Col., Tallahassee, Fla.

Eggert, C. Lee, Dir. of Lab. Sch., Prof. of Sch. Admin., Univ. of Fla., Gainesville, Fla.

Ersoff, Samuel, 3424 S. W. 4th St., Miami, Fla.

Farnell, J. Crockett, B.S.'37, Univ. of Tampa; M.A.E.'51, Univ. of Fla.; Co. Supt. of Pub. Instr., Hillsborough Co., Tampa, Fla., since 1949.

Godby, Amos, A.B.'30, Mercer Univ.; Co. Supt. of Pub. Instr., Tallahassee, Fla., since 1944.

Gore, George William, Jr., A.B.'23, De Pauw Univ.; Ed.M.'28, Harvard Univ.; Ph.D.'40, Columbia Univ.; Pres., Fla. Agrl. and Mech. Col., Tallahassee, Fla.

Greene, Crawford, A.B. and B.S.'21, Henderson-Brown Col.; M.A.'26, George Peabody Col. for Tchrs.; Bus. Mgr., Hillsborough Co. Bd. of Pub. Instr., Tampa, Fla.

Hall, Ernest W., A.B.'39, Asbury Col.; Co. Supt. of Pub. Instr., Everglades, Fla., since 1949.

Hamilton, Marshall W., B.S.'36, M.A.'48, Univ. of Ky.; Prin., H. S., Crawfordville, Fla., since 1951.

Harden, Claude M., B.S.E.'36, M.A.'38, Fla. Southern Col.; Supt. of Pub. Instr., Polk Co., Bartow, Fla., since 1949.

Harper, C. L., Jr., B.S.'31, Howard Col.; M.A.'45, Univ. of Fla.; Asst. Supt. of Pub. Instr., Jacksonville, Fla., since 1948.

Henderson, Ed, Exec. Secy., Fla. Educ. Assn., Tallahassee, Fla.

Huskey, D. C., A.B.'30, Florida Southern Col.; M.Ed.'40, Duke Univ.; Co. Supt. of Sch., Ft. Pierce, Fla., since 1945.

Hutzler, Damon A., B.A.'30, M.A.'47, Univ. of Fla.; Co. Supt. of Sch., Titusville, Fla., since 1937.

*Jeffrey, F. J., B.Sc.'00, Ohio State Univ. Address: 923 N. Thornton St., Orlando, Fla.

Johns, Roe L., B.S.'23, Southeast Mo. State Col.; Cape Girardeau; M.A.'27, Ph.D.'28, Tchrs. Col., Columbia Univ.; Prof. of Sch. Admin., Dir., Div of Field Serv., Col. of Educ., Univ. of Fla., Gainesville, Fla., since 1946.

Kimbrough, Verman, A.B.'25, Birmingham-Southern Col.; Co. Supt. of Pub. Instr., Sarasota, Fla., since 1945.

Koepke, William Charles, Ph.B.'13, Univ. of Wis.; M.A.'27, Columbia Univ.; Ph.D.'31, Marquette Univ. Address: 2501 13th Ave., W., Bradenton, Fla.

Lawler, Eugene S., B.A.'14, Trinity Univ.; M.A.'22, Ph.D.'32, Tchrs. Col., Columbia Univ.; Fla. State Univ., Tallahassee, Fla., since 1951.

Lawton, T. W., A.B.'03, Pd.D.(Hon.)'45, Rollins Col.; Co. Supt. of Pub. Instr., Sanford, Fla., since 1917.

Leps, Joseph M., A.B.'20, Hampden-Sydney Col.; M.A.'38, Fla. Southern Col.; Ed.D.'42, Columbia Univ.; Prof. of Sch. Admin., Univ. of Fla., Gainesville, Fla., since 1943.

Lovell, Broward, A.B., M.A.E.'38, Univ. of Fla.; Co. Supt. of Pub. Instr., Ocala, Fla., since 1941.

McLaughlin, F. S., A.B.'21, Maryville Col., (Tenn.); M.A.'32, Columbia Univ.; Supvg. Prin. of Sch., Lake Wales, Fla., since 1934.

March, Leland S., A.B.'23, Univ. of Maine; B.P.E.'28, Springfield Col.; Ed.M.'34, Boston Univ.; Asst. Co. Supt. of Sch., Key West, Fla.

Marks, George W., A.B.'14, Univ. of Kansas; Co. Supt. of Pub. Instr., DeLand, Fla., since 1923.

Mills, (Mrs.) Lula C., A.B.'07, M.A.'36, Winthrop Col.; Prin., Tomlin Jr. H. S., Plant City, Fla., since 1943.

Morse, C. Marguerite, B.S.E.'33, Univ. of Fla.; Genl. Supvr. of Sch., Clearwater, Fla.

Moseley, Nicholas, B.A.'19, Ph.D.'25, Yale Univ. Address: Route 2, Box 1083, Pompano Beach, Fla.

Nance, Ellwood C., Pres., Univ. of Tampa, Tampa, Fla.

O'Bryant, Horace, 'B.S.'22, A.M.'32, Univ. of Fla.; Co. Supt. of Pub. Instr., Key West, Fla., since 1949.

Phillips, O. K., B.S. in Ed.'20, Southeast Mo. State Col.; M.A.'27, Univ. of Mo.; Supt. of Pub. Instr., Broward Co., Fort Lauderdale, Fla., since 1952.

Purcell, Wilbur Hallam, A.B.'30, John B. Stetson Univ.; M.A.'37, Duke Univ.; Area Supv. Prin., Mulberry Area Sch., Mulberry, Fla., since 1936.

Puryear, Royal W., A.B.'33, Howard Univ.; M.S.'39, Univ. of Ind.; Pres., Fla. Normal Indus. and Memorial Col., St. Augustine, Fla., since 1950.

Rhodes, Francis Arlington, A.B.'30, M.A.'46, Ed.D.'48, Univ. of Fla.; Specialist in Surveys, State Dept. of Educ., Tallahassee, Fla., since 1951.

Rumph, A. H., Supt. of Pub. Instr., Columbia Co., Lake City, Fla.

Simmons, Russell, A.B.'41, Univ. of Fla.; Co. Supt. of Sch., Chipley, Fla., since 1945.

Simpson, A. M., B.Ed.'38, Southern Ill. Univ.; M.A.'41, Univ. of Ill.; Prin., Seacrest H. S., Delray Beach, Fla., since 1952.

Thompson, Alvin H., B.S.'47, State Tchrs. Col., Livingston, Ala.; M.S.'50, Fla. State Univ.; Prin., H. S., Sopchoppy, Fla., since 1951.

Walker, Judson B., A.B.E.'22, M.A.E.'24, Univ. of Fla.; Co. Supt. of Sch., Orlando, Fla., since 1932.

Watkins, Howell L., A.B.'16, M.A.'36, Emory Univ.; Co. Supt. of Pub. Instr., West Palm Beach, Fla., since 1948.

White, Joseph Benton, A.B.'27, Wofford Col.; M.A.'32, Duke Univ.; Ph.D.'46, George Peabody Col. for Tchrs.; Dean, Col. of Educ., Univ. of Fla., Gainesville, Fla.

Wild, Fred, B.S.E.'34, Fla. Southern Col.; Co. Supt. of Pub. Instr., Sebring, Fla., since 1945.

Wilson, James T., B.S.'20, Miss. State Col.; M.S.'33, Tchrs. Col., Columbia Univ.; D.Ed. '44, Univ. of Miami; Supt., Bd. of Pub. Instr. of Dade Co., Miami, Fla., 1937-52.

*Withers, John W., B.S.'90, B.A.'91, Pd.D.'96, Natl. Normal Univ.; M.A.'02, Ph.D.'04, Yale Univ.; LL.D.'17, Washington Univ.; LL.D.'18, Univ. of Mo.; L.H.D.'38, New York Univ.; Honorary Life Member, American Assn. of Sch. Admin.; Dean Emeritus, Sch. of Educ., New York Univ., New York, N. Y., since 1939. Address: 1813 First Ave., Bradenton, Fla.

INSTITUTIONAL MEMBERS

Audio Visual Dept., 275 N. W. 2nd St., Miami, Fla.

Library, Rollins Col., Winter Park, Fla.

390

GEORGIA

INDIVIDUAL MEMBERS

Adams, George Walter, A.B.'26, Mercer Univ.; M.A.'43, Emory Univ.; Prin., High and Elem. Sch., Roswell, Ga., since 1938.

Aderhold, Omar Clyde, B.S.A.'23, M.S.'30, Univ. of Ga.; Ph.D.'38, Ohio State Univ.; Pres., Univ. of Ga., Athens, Ga., since 1950.

Agnew, Donald C., Head, Soc. Science Dept., Oglethorpe Univ., Oglethorpe, Ga., since 1952.

Armsler, O. L., B.S.'18, North Ga. Col.; M.A. in Ed.'31, Oglethorpe Univ.; Supt. of Sch., Decatur, Ga., since 1944.

Antley, Shuler, B.S.'22, The Citadel; LL.B.'30, Atlanta Law Sch.; Supt. of Sch., Marietta, Ga., since 1942.

Ayers, Fred, A.B.in Ed.'29, M.A.'34, Univ. of Ga.; Supt. of Sch., Athens, Ga., since 1948.

Barnes, Jarvis, B.S.'38, Clemson Col.; M.A.'38, George Peabody Col. for Tchrs.; Dir. of Research and Pupil Personnel, Bd. of Educ., Atlanta, Ga., since 1942.

Battle, L. H., Ph.B.'15, M.A.'32, Emory Univ.; Supt. of Sch., Dublin, Ga., since 1945.

Blakeney, Revis Duin, M.A.'48, Univ. of Ala.; Supt. of City Sch., Thomasville, Ga., since 1950.

Boddiford, Joseph Knapp, B.S. in Ed.'38, Ga. Tchrs. Col., Collegeboro; M.A.'39, Ohio State Univ.; Co. Supt. of Sch., Sylvania, Ga., since 1949.

Bradley, Harry M., Dir., Peabody Laboratory Sch., Ga. State Col. for Women, Milledgeville, Ga., since 1952.

Brewster, William R., B.S.'20, U. S. Military Acad.; Pres., Ga. Military Acad., College Park, Ga., since 1939.

Burgess, John Evans, A.B.'34, Emory Univ.; M.Ed.'40, Duke Univ.; Prin., H. S., Avondale Estates, Ga., since 1940.

Calhoun, Hazel, Owner-Mgr., Calhoun Co., 235 Ponce de Leon Ave., N. E., Atlanta 5, Ga.

Carpenter, K. L., B.S.'34, M.S.'35, Stetson Univ.; Supt. of Sch., Americus, Ga., since 1947.

Carter, (Mrs.) G. L., A.B.'35, Univ. of Ga.; Co. Supt. of Sch., Talbotton, Ga., since 1944.

Cherry, Jim D., B.S.'36, Ga. Tchrs. Col., Collegeboro; M.A.'40, Univ. of N. C.; Co. Supt. of Sch., Decatur, Ga., since 1949.

Cheves, Charles Judson, A.B.'19, Mercer Univ.; A.M.'30, Tchrs. Col., Columbia Univ.; Supt. of Sch., Gainesville, Ga., since 1934.

Clark, Reuel Stafford, A.B.'42, Berry Col.; M.Ed.'45, Univ. of Ga.; Co. Supt. of Sch., LaGrange, Ga., since 1949.

Clement, Rufus E., A.B.'19, Livingstone Col.; B.D.'22, Garrett Biblical Inst.; A.M.'22, Ph.D.'30, Northwestern Univ.; Pres., Atlanta Univ., Atlanta, Ga., since 1937.

Collins, M. D., A.B.'31, M.A.'32, Ped.D.'33, Oglethorpe Univ.; LL.D.'38, Mercer Univ.; H.D.'44, Bob Jones Col.; State Supt. of Sch., Atlanta, Ga., since 1933.

Connell, Cater Lloyd, B.S.'39, Univ. of Ga.; Co. Supt. of Sch., Cairo, Ga., since 1949.

Cordell, J. J., A.B.'28, Mercer Univ.; M.A.'38, Univ. of S. C.; Supt. of Sch., Albany, Ga., since 1948.

Cutts, Harvey C., A.B.'20, Mercer Univ.; M.S. in Ed.'41, Univ. of Ga.; Supt. of Sch., Greenville, Ga., since 1933.

Drake, Walter Homer, M.A.'36, Univ. of Ga.; Supt. of Sch., Newnan, Ga., since 1941.

Drum, Woodard Glenn, A.B.'28, Asbury Col.; M.S.'39, Univ. of Ga.; Pres., Emmanuel Col., Franklin Springs, Ga., since 1949.

Early, William Ashby, Diploma '23, Randolph-Macon Academy; A.B.'27, Emory and Henry Col.; M.Ed.'41, Duke Univ.; Supt. of Sch., Savannah and Chatham Co., Ga., since 1952.

Gant, George F., A.B.'30, M.A.'31, Univ. of Nebr.; Ph.D.'34, Univ. of Wis.; 4525 Stella Dr., N. W., Atlanta, Ga.

Gauerke, Warren E., Ph.D.'49, Univ. of Chicago; Assoc. Prof., Emory Univ., Atlanta, Ga., since 1951.

Hale, Clifford G., Supt. of Sch., Dalton, Ga.

Highsmith, Edwin McKoy, Ph.B.'07, A.M.'14, Ph.D.'23, Univ. of N. C.; A.M.'15, George Peabody Col. for Tchrs.; Chmn., Div. of Educ., Mercer Univ., Macon, Ga., since 1937.

Hodges, C. V., B.S.'34, Ga. Tchrs. Col., Collegeboro; M.Ed.'39, Duke Univ.; Supt. of Sch., Fitzgerald, Ga., since 1948.

Hodgson, Prince A., B.S.Voc.Ed.'20, Univ. of Ga.; Co. Supt. of Sch., Elberton, Ga., since 1949.

Hood, R. E., Co. Supt. of Sch., Brunswick, Ga.

Jarrell, (Miss) Ira, A.B.'28, M.A.'31, Oglethorpe Univ.; Supt. of Sch., Atlanta, Ga., since 1944.

Lamb, W. L., B.S.'22, Univ. of Ga.; Co. Supt. of Sch., Bainbridge, Ga., since 1949.

Lewis, L. W., A.B.'23, M.A.'45, Mercer Univ.; Prin., Lanier Jr. H. S., Macon, Ga., since 1941.

Little, Thomas C., A.B.'37, Eastern Ky. State Col.; M.A.'41, Univ. of Ky.; Ph.D.'48, George Peabody Col. for Tchrs.; Chmn., Div. of Educ., Georgia Tchrs. Col., Collegeboro, Ga., since 1948.

McCord, George M., B.Ph.'27, M.A.'36, Emory Univ.; Prin., Murphy H. S., Atlanta, Ga., since 1942.

Martin, A. G., A.B.'15, Union Col.; Prin., Joseph E. Brown Jr. H. S., Atlanta, Ga., since 1923.

Miller, William Starr, B.S. in Ed.'47, M.S. in Ed.'47, Univ. of Ga.; Bessie Tift Col., Forsyth, Ga.

Moss, W. A., A.B.'32, M.A.'36, Univ. of Ga.; Co. Supt. of Sch., Hartwell, Ga., since 1937.

Norvell, (Mrs.) Florence Crane, B.S.'38, Ga. State Col. for Women; M.A.'41, Tchrs. Col., Columbia Univ.; Prin., Pape Sch., Savannah, Ga., since 1944.

Nunn, W. G., Supt. of Sch., Valdosta, Ga.

Payne, W. K., A.B.'23, Morehouse Col.; A.M.'27, Columbia Univ.; Pres., Savannah State Col., Savannah, Ga.

Peters, Edmund Clarke, B.A. and B.S.A.'16, Univ. of Tenn.; M.A.'25, Univ. of Chicago; Pres., Paine Col., Augusta, Ga., since 1929.

Read, Florence M., A.B.'09, Litt.D.'29, Mt. Holyoke Col.; LL.D.'39, Oberlin Col.; Pres., Spelman Col., Atlanta, Ga., since 1927.

Rehberg, W. H., A.B.'29, M.A.'35, Mercer Univ.; Co. Supt. of Sch., Thomasville, Ga., since 1944.

Rollins, Roy E., B.A.'32, Elon Col.; M.A.'38, Duke Univ.; Supt. of Sch., Augusta, Ga., since 1951.

Rowley, Kerman, B.S.'41, Southern Univ.; M.Ed.'49, Harvard Univ.; Morris Brown Col., Atlanta, Ga.

Salter, J. D., A.B.'28, Mercer Univ.; M.S. in Ed.'41, Univ. of Ga.; Supt. of Sch., Waycross, Ga., since 1947.

Saxon, J. Harold, A.B.'14, Emory Univ.; M.A.'31, Mercer Univ.; Exec. Secy., Ga. Educ. Assn., Atlanta, Ga., since 1944.

GEORGIA

Scott, Wilton C., A.B.'40, Xavier Univ.; LL.B.'48, Blackstone Col.; Dir. of Pub. Relations and Supvr. of Adult Educ. Evening Program, Ga. State Col., Savannah, Ga., since 1947.

Senkbeil, Anna E., A.B.'36, M.A.'37, Oglethorpe Univ.; Prin., George W. Adair Sch., Atlanta, Ga., since 1942.

Shaw, William Henry, B.A.'28, M.Ed.'33, Duke Univ.; Supt. of Educ., Columbus, Ga., since 1945.

Shepard, Jack D., A.B.'32, Asbury Col.; M.S. in Ed.'41, Univ. of Ga.; Supt., Randolph Co. Sch., Cuthbert, Ga., since 1944.

Smith, Doyne M., B.S.'40, M.S.'47, Univ. of Ark; Ed.D.'49, Univ. of Colo.; Assoc. Prof. of Educ., Univ. of Ga., Athens, Ga., since 1949.

Smith, Mark A., B.S.'15, Clemson Agrl. Col.; LL.D.'39, Mercer Univ.; D.Ed.'48, Clemson Col.; Co. Supt. of Sch., Macon, Ga., since 1941.

Smith, William Frank, A.B. and M.Ed.'45, Univ. of Ga.; Co. Supt. of Sch., Cordele, Ga., since 1944.

Smith, William S., A.B.'35, Glenville State Col., Glenville, W. Va.; M.S. in Ed.'39, Univ. of Ga.; Co. Supt. of Sch., Folkston, Ga., since 1945.

Sprayberry, W. P., A.B.'31, Univ. of Ga.; Co. Supt. of Sch., Marietta, Ga., since 1943.

Sprowles, Lee, A.B.'39, M.A.'46, Ed.D.'47, Univ. of Ky.; Assoc. Prof. of Educ., Univ. of Ga., Athens, Ga., since 1951.

Still, Dennis D., B.S.A.'17, A.B. in Ed.'32, M.A.'34, Univ. of Ga.; Ph.B.'32, Piedmont Col.; Co. Supt. of Sch., Monroe, Ga., since 1949.

Strickland, A. J., A.B.'35, Wofford Col.; M.Sc. in Ed.'40, M.Ed.'40, Univ. of Ga.; Supt. of City Sch., Trion, Ga., since 1948.

*Sutton, Willis Anderson, Ph.B.'03, LL.D.'04, LL.D.'38, Emory Univ.; Ped.D.'24, Oglethorpe Univ.; LL.D.'37, Tusculum Col.; Pres., Natl. Educ. Assn. 1930-31; Honorary Life Member, American Assn. of Sch. Admin.; Supt. Emeritus, Atlanta Pub. Sch., 930 Drewry St., N. E., Atlanta, Ga., since 1944.

Vick, Alfred Teasdale, B.S.E.E.'31, Clemson Agrl. Col.; M.S.Ed.'47, Univ. of Ga.; Co. Supt. of Sch., Savannah, Ga., since 1949.

Walker, Knox, A.B.'15, Mercer Univ.; M.A.'25, Columbia Univ.; Asst. Co. Supt. of Sch., Atlanta, Ga.

Wells, Guy H., A.B.'15, Mercer Univ.; A.M.'25, Columbia Univ.; Pres., Ga. State Col. for Women, Milledgeville, Ga., since 1934.

West, Paul D., Ph.D.'24, M.A.'40, Emory Univ.; Co. Supt. of Sch., Atlanta, Ga., since 1947.

Whelchel, Emmett V., M.A.'37, Mercer Univ.; Supt. of Sch., Moultrie, Ga., since 1946.

Williams, B. B., A.B.'41, M.A.'45, Oglethorpe Univ.; Supt. of Sch., Canton, Ga., since 1949.

INSTITUTIONAL MEMBERS

Library, Ga. State Col. for Women, Milledgeville, Ga.
Library, Ga. Tchrs. Col., Collegeboro, Ga.
Library, North Ga. Col., Dahlonega, Ga.
Library, Univ. of Ga., Serials Division, Athens, Ga.

GUAM

INDIVIDUAL MEMBERS

DeGood, K. C., A.B.'38, Findlay Col.; M.A.'46, Univ. of Mich. Address: c/o George Washington H. Sch., Agana, Guam.

Palomo, Jose R., B.S. in M.E.'22, Carnegie Inst. of Tech.; M.A.'28, Ph.D.'38, Ohio State Univ.; Dir. of Educ., Dept of Educ., Agana, Guam, since 1951.

Tabery, Norbert F., Dept. of Educ., Guam.

HAWAII

INDIVIDUAL MEMBERS

Crosson, John, B.A.'40, Washington Square Col., New York Univ.; Prin., Puuhale Sch., 336 Mokauea St., Honolulu, T. H.

Fox, John F., B.S.in Ed.'29, Univ. of Mo.; M.A.'31, Ph.D.'36, New York Univ.; Pres., Punahou Sch., Honolulu 24, T. H., since 1944.

Kent, Harold W., B.S.'21, M.S.'35, Northwestern Univ.; Pres., The Kamehameha Sch., Honolulu, T. H., since 1946.

Loper, W. Harold, B.S.'21, Univ. of Redlands; Ed.M.'25, Grad. Sch. of Educ., Harvard Univ.; Ed.D.'39, Tchrs. Col., Columbia Univ.; Supt. of Public Instr. and Exec. Officer, Territorial Bd. for Voc. Educ., Territorial Office Bldg., Honolulu 4, T. H., 1946.

Parmiter, Charles A., Jr., B.A.'32, Harvard Univ.; M.A.'36, Clark Univ.; B.D.'44, Episcopal Theol. Sem.; Rector of Iolani Sch., Honolulu, T. H., since 1950.

IDAHO

INDIVIDUAL MEMBERS

Alexander, James B., A.B.'22, Drury Col.; A.N.'31, Univ. of Wash.; Supt. of Sch., Salmon, Idaho, since 1944.

Booth, Clarence L., A.B.'17, Otterbein Col.; M.A.'27, State Col. of Wash.; Supt. of Sch., Lewiston, Idaho.

Broadhead, W. R., B.A.'47, M.A.'50, Univ. of Idaho; Supt. of Sch., Payette, Idaho, since 1951.

Christensen, W. W., B.S.'23, M.S.'33, Utah State Agrl. Col.; Supt. of Sch., Idaho Falls, Idaho, 1934-52.

Clem, (Mrs.) Beryl E., B.A.'51, Northern Idaho Col. of Educ., Lewiston; Co. Supt. of Pub. Instr., Lewiston, Idaho, since 1948.

Finch, Jack, B.A.'49, Northern Idaho Col. of Educ., Lewiston; Supt. of Sch., Lapwai, Idaho, since 1950.

Foy, Zed L., A.B.'21, Univ. of S. C.; A.M.'29, Tchrs. Col., Columbia Univ.; Ed.D.'38, Stanford Univ.; Supt. of Sch., Boise, Idaho, since 1940.

Gale, Clair E., Supt. of Sch., Idaho Falls, Idaho, since 1952.

Godfrey, W. W., A.B.'23, Col. of Idaho; Supt. of Sch., Hansen, Idaho, since 1951.

Gruwell, Melvin, B.S.'41, M.S.'48, Utah State Agrl. Col.; Supt., Fremont Co. Joint Sch. Dist. A-215, St. Anthony, Idaho.

Hartvigsen, Milton F., B.S.'30, M.Ed.'39, Utah State Agrl. Col.; Supt. of Sch., Joint Class A Sch. Dist. 148, Grace, Idaho, since 1948.

Honeyman, Roger B., M.A.'51, Brigham Young Univ.; Supt., Rural H. S. Dist. 1, Paris, Idaho, since 1951.

Hulme, Amos B., Co. Supt. of Sch., Paris, Idaho.

Ingersoll, Leigh, M.S.Ed.'50, Univ. of Idaho; Supt. of Sch., Gooding, Idaho, since 1945.

Likeness, George M., B.A.'25, Hanover Col.; M.A.'33, Univ. of Kansas; Supt. of Sch., Buhl, Idaho, since 1937.

Martin, Dan W., M.S.'43, Univ. of Idaho; Asst. Supt. of Sch., Pocatello, Idaho, since 1944.

392

Mechan, Onan T., B.S.'37, Univ. of Utah; Supt., North Gem Class B Sch. Dist. 22, Bancroft, Idaho.

Merrill, Donald P., B.S.'30, Brigham Young Univ.; Supt., Class A Sch. Dist. 251, Rigby, Idaho, since 1949.

Olds, W. V., B.S.'25, Ottawa Univ.; Supt., Joint Class A Sch. Dist. 261, Jerome, Idaho, since 1944.

Porter, Arthur, B.S.'96, Brigham Young Univ.; Co. Supt. of Sch., Rexburg, Idaho, since 1949.

Ragland, Ernest H., B.S. in Ed.'36, Southwest Mo. State Col., Springfield; M.A. in Ed.'49, Tchrs. Col., Columbia Univ.; Supt., Class A Sch. Dist. 411, Twin Falls, Idaho.

Riggs, Dorcey S., B.A.'42, Col. of Idaho; M.S.Ed. '49, Univ. of Idaho; Supt. of Class A Sch. Dist. 241, Grangeville, Idaho, since 1948.

Robinson, L. C., A.B.'14, Ed.M.'24, Harvard Univ.; Supt. of Sch., Moscow, Idaho, since 1946.

Shoun, H. Maine, A.B.'22, Carson-Newman Col.; State Supvr. of H. S., State Dept. of Educ., Boise, Idaho, since 1952.

Simmons, W. Horland, B.S.'28, Univ. of Idaho; M.S.'36, Colo. State Col. of Educ.; Supt., Eastside Class A Sch. Dist. 201, Preston, Idaho, since 1944.

Snyder, Raymond H., B.A.'12, Ind. Univ.; M.A.'19, Univ. of Chicago; Dir., Div. of Educ., Col. of Idaho, Caldwell, Idaho, since 1951.

Thatcher, J. Kenneth, B.S.'25, Univ. of Utah; M.S. in Ed.'36, Univ. of Idaho; Supt., Joint Class A Sch. Dist. 322, Sugar City, Idaho, since 1944.

Thomas, L. A., B.A.'21, M.S. in Ed.'36, Univ. of Idaho; Supt., Consol. Class A Sch. Dist. 2, Meridian, Idaho, since 1947.

Thomas, William, B.S.'43, Utah State Agrl. Col.; Supt. of Joint Independent Sch. Dist. 60, Shelley, Idaho, since 1947.

Warner, Carl W., B.S. in Ed.'35, M.S. in Ed.'50, Univ. of Idaho; Co. Supt. of Sch., Rupert, Idaho, since 1951.

Welsh, Maurice J., B.S.'27, N. Dak. State Col.; M.S.'44, Univ. of N. Dak.; Supt. of Sch., Filer, Idaho, since 1951.

Weston, Roy A., B.A.'20, Univ. of N. Dak.; Supt. of Sch., Aberdeen, Idaho, since 1929.

Wrigley, Bernell, B.S.'41, Utah State Agrl. Col.; Co. Supt. of Sch., Joint Class A Sch. Dist. 151, Burley, Idaho, since 1949.

INSTITUTIONAL MEMBER

Independent Sch. Dist. 8, Shoshone Co., Wallace, Idaho.

ILLINOIS

INDIVIDUAL MEMBERS

Abell, Theodore L., B.Ed.'31, Ill. State Normal Univ.; M.A.'41, State Univ. of Iowa; Prin., Octavia Sch., Colfax, Ill., since 1949.

Adams, L. R., M.S.'30, Univ. of Ill.; Supt., Community H. S., Hillsboro, Ill., 1950-52.

Alderfer, Henry F., B.S.'23, Muhlenberg Col.; M.A.'40, New York Univ.; Dir. of Educ. and Prin., H. S., Mooseheart, Ill., since 1951.

Alexander, E. L., A.B.'35, Shurtleff Col.; M.A.'37, Wash. Univ.; Supt. of Sch., Edwardsville, Ill., since 1937.

Allen, B. Leslie, Bd. of Educ., Proviso Twp. H. S., Melrose Park, Ill.

Allen, Beatrice Ona, B.S.'40, Northwestern Univ.; M.A.'46, Univ. of Chicago; Elem. Prin., Waters Sch., Chicago, Ill., since 1947.

Allen, Edward B., B.S.'29, M.S.'36, Univ. of Ill., Supt. of Community Unit Sch., Warrensburg, Ill., since 1948.

Allen, Edward L., M.S. in Ed.'47, Southern Ill. Univ.; Supt. of Sch., Belleville, Ill., since 1949.

Ames, Clarence E., A.B.'24, Morningside Col.; M.A.'46, Northwestern Univ.; Sr. Class Prin., Community H. S., Blue Island, Ill., since 1932.

Ancel, Louis, Attorney, Bd. of Educ., Proviso Twp. H. S., Maywood, Ill.

Anderson, Archibald W., B.S.'32, M.A.'33, Tchrs. Col., Columbia Univ.; Ph.D.'38, Ohio State Univ.; Prof. of Educ., Univ. of Ill., Urbana, Ill.

Anderson, Ervin A., B.A.'29, St. Olaf Col.; M.A.'39, Univ. of Wis.; Supt., V. I. T. Unit Sch. Dist. 2, Table Grove, Ill., since 1949.

Anderson, Harry D., LL.B.'22, Univ. of Ill.; B.D.'25, Western Ill. State Tchrs. Col.; M.A.'32, Univ. of Ill.; Supt., Maine Twp. H. S., Des Plaines, Ill., since 1949.

Anderson, Robert Henry, B.A.'39, M.A.'42, Univ. of Wis.; Ph.D.'49, Univ. of Chicago; Supt. of Sch. Dist. 163, Park Forest, Ill., since 1949.

Aniceta, Sister M., Ph.D.'39, Univ. of Ill.; Pres., Col. of St. Francis, Joliet, Ill., since 1938.

Armstrong, Leland R., A.B.'28, Friends Univ.; M.A.'36, Tchrs. Col., Columbia Univ.; Dir. of Bus. Affairs, Bd. of Educ., Oak Park, Ill., since 1948.

Arnspiger, Varney Clyde, A.B.'17, Texas Christian Univ.; Ph.D.'33, Tchrs. Col., Columbia Univ.; Exec. Vicepres., Encyclopaedia Britannica Films, Inc., Wilmette, Ill., since 1929.

Aspinall, Richard, A.B.'11, W. Va. Wesleyan Col.; D.B.'14, Drew Univ.; A.M.'14, Ph.D.'26, New York Univ.; Supt. of Mooseheart, Mooseheart, Ill.

Atteberry, L. L., Co. Supt. of Sch., Pekin, Ill.

Augspurger, Harry F., A.B.'27, Ill. Wesleyan Univ.; M.S.'38, Univ. of Ill.; Supt. of Elem. Sch., Lincoln, Ill., since 1941.

Aurand, David B., B.S.'32, Coe Col.; M.Ed.'40, Univ. of Colo.; Supt. of Sch. Dist. 105, La Grange, Ill., since 1945.

Aurand, E. D., B.E.'33, Northern Ill. State Tchrs. Col., De Kalb; M.S.'36, Northwestern Univ.; Supt. of Sch., Lyons, Ill., since 1940.

Austin, Kent C., B.Ed.'39, State Tchrs. Col., Whitewater, Wis.; M.S. in Ed.'49, Univ. of Wis.; Prin., Lakewood Elem. Sch., Park Forest, Ill., since 1952.

Baber, Eric R., M.A.'35, New York Univ.; Supt., Rich Twp. H. S. Dist., Park Forest, Ill., since 1951.

Badders, D. R., M.A.'48, George Peabody Col. for Tchrs.; Supt., Wauconda Community Consol. Sch., Wauconda, Ill., since 1951.

*Bailey, Francis B., A.B.'28, Univ. of Ill.; M.Ed. '43, Loyola Univ.; Dist. Supt. of Sch., Oak Lawn, Ill., since 1947.

Baker, Clara Belle, A.B.'09, A.M.'11, Northwestern Univ.; Dir., Children's Sch., Natl. Col. of Educ., Evanston, Ill., since 1926.

Baker, Herbert H., B.Ed.'31, Ill. State Normal Univ., Normal; M.S.'39, Univ. of Ill.; Supt., Community Unit Dist. 206, Stockton, Ill.

Baker, I. D., M.Ed.'47, Univ. of Ill.; Supt. of Sch., Moweaqua, Ill., since 1948.

Bannister, Thurlow H., B.S.Ed.'45, Southern Ill. Univ.; M.S.Ed.'50, Univ. of Ill.; Supt. of City Sch., Dist. 50, Vandalia, Ill., since 1948.

Barlow, Charles C., Supt. of Sch., Roodhouse, Ill.

Barnhart, Elizabeth, 1710 N. 31st St., East St. Louis, Ill.

Barr, George O., B.A.'17, Ill. Wesleyan Univ.; M.A.'40, Columbia Univ.; Supt. of Sch., Silvis, Ill., since 1928.

Bartels, Martin H., B.A.'30, Capital Univ.; M.A.'35, Ph.D.'49, Ohio State Univ.; Dir. of Placement, Northern Ill. State Tchrs. Col., De Kalb, Ill.

Batchelder, Mildred L., A.B.'22, Mt. Holyoke Col.; B.L.S.'24, N. Y. State Lib. Sch.; Exec. Secy., Div. of Lib. for Children and Young People, American Lib. Assn., Chicago, Ill., since 1949.

Battershell, B., M.S.'42, Univ. of Ill.; Supt., Shelby Co. Sch., Shelbyville, Ill., since 1951.

Beane, Don, A.B.'29, Ill. Col.; M.A.'37, Wash. Univ.; Supt., Community H. S., Hillsboro, Ill., since 1952.

Beasley, K. B., Ph.B.'29, Shurtleff Col.; M.A.'36, Univ. of Ill.; Supt. of Sch., Kewanee, Ill., since 1946.

Beebe, Ralph Edwin, B.A.'13, Winona Col.; M.A.'16, Ind. Univ.; Supt. of Sch., Naperville, Ill., since 1927.

Beem, Harlan D., M.A.'40, Univ. of Ill.; A.B.'28, DePauw Univ.; Field Secy., Ill. Assn. of Sch. Bds., Springfield, Ill., since 1949.

Bell, Millard D., A.B.'26, State Tchrs. Col., Peru, Nebr.; M.A.'30, Univ. of Nebr.; Ed.D.'39, Tchrs. Col., Columbia Univ.; Supt. of Sch., Wilmette, Ill., since 1942.

Bell, Robert M., B.S.'33, M.A.'35, Northwestern Univ.; Prin., Pulaski Elem. Sch., Chicago, Ill., since 1948.

Belsly, Josephine, Prin., Lincoln Elem. Sch., River Forest, Ill.

Benben, John S., M.A.'38, Northwestern Univ.; Instr., Sch. of Educ., Northwestern Univ., Evanston, Ill.

Benne, Kenneth D., B.S.'30, Kansas State Tchrs. Col.; M.A.'36, Univ. of Mich.; Ph.D.'44, Columbia Univ. Address: c/o Adult Leadership, Chicago, Ill.

Benner, Thomas E., A.B.'14, A.M.'16, Ed.M.'23, Ed.D.'24, Harvard Univ.; Prof. of Sch. Admin., Univ. of Ill. Address: 615 Hessel Blvd., Champaign, Ill.

Berry, Dale L., B.Ed.'47, M.S.'52, Southern Ill. Univ.; Supt. of Sch., Milford, Ill., since 1948.

Betcher, Mabel R., B.S.'39, M.E.'42, DePaul Univ.; Prin., Washington Sch., Maywood, Ill., since 1950.

Bezek, John D., B.S.Ed.'41, Concordia Col.; M.A.Ed.'43, Northwestern Univ.; Supt. of Sch., La Grange, Ill., since 1951.

Biester, Fred L., A.B.'14, North Central Col.; M.A.'38, Univ. of Chicago; Prin., Glenbard Twp. H. S., Glen Ellyn, Ill., since 1918.

Birkhead, Theodore R., B.Ed.'30, Ill. State Normal Univ.; M.S.'36, State Univ. of Iowa; Supt., Thornton Twp. H. S. and Jr. Col., Harvey, Ill., since 1950.

Bishop, S. D., B.S.'25, Univ. of Ill.; M.S.'32, Northwestern Univ.; Prin., Community H. S. Dist. 94, West Chicago, Ill., since 1926.

Black, H. B., M.A.'24, Univ. of Ill.; Prin., Signal Hill Sch., East St. Louis, Ill., since 1948.

Black, Luther J., B.E.'31, Eastern Ill. State Tchrs. Col., Charleston; M.S.'37, Univ. of Ill.; Secy., Tchrs. State Examining Bd., Springfield, Ill., since 1943.

Blair, Clarence D., B.Ed.'30, Ill. State Normal Univ., Normal; Co. Supt. of Sch., Belleville, Ill., since 1939.

Blodgett, Darrell R., Ph.B.'24, Shurtleff Col.; M.A.'35, Ed.D.'46, Wash. Univ.; Supt. of Sch., Wheaton, Ill., since 1952.

Blundell, W. Irvin, B.S.'38, Bradley Univ.; M.A.'46, Ed.D.'51, Tchrs. Col., Columbia Univ.; Secy.-Bus. Mgr., Twp. H. S., Evanston, Ill., since 1951.

Blythe, G. V., B.Ed.'34, Western Ill. State Col.; M.S.'38, Univ. of Ill.; Supt., Community Sch., Vandalia, Ill., since 1943.

Bohn, Julius Edward, A.B.'20, Heidelberg Col.; M.A.'26, Ohio State Univ.; Supt. of Sch., Springfield, Ill., since 1947.

Bolin, Paul L., B.E.'30, Ill. State Normal Univ., Normal; M.A.'35, George Peabody Col. for Tchrs.; Supt. of Sch., East Peoria, Ill., since 1929.

Bonar, Hugh S., B.Acc'ts.'16, B.A.'18, Mt. Morris Col.; M.A.'24, Univ. of Chicago; Supt. of Twp. H. S. and Jr. Col., Joliet, Ill., since 1947.

Bone, Paul L., B.Ed.'37, Ill. State Normal Univ.; M.A.'41, State Univ. of Iowa; Supt. of Sch., Princeton, Ill., since 1944.

Booth, H. G., B.E.'27, Northern Ill. State Tchrs. Col., De Kalb; M.S.'37, Northwestern Univ.; Supt. of Elem. Sch., West Chicago, Ill., since 1943.

Bossert, Edward O., B.A.'38, North Central Col.; M.A.'47, Univ. of Chicago; Supt. of Twp. H. S., Lemont, Ill., since 1950.

Bottino, Louis F., B.A.'30, Beloit Col.; M.A.'35, Columbia Univ.; Supt., Twp. H. S., Lockport, Ill.

Bowyer, Vernon, S.B.'21, A.M.'23, Univ. of Chicago; Dir. of Americanization and Adult Educ., Pub. Sch., Chicago, Ill., since 1938.

Bozarth, W. A., B.Ed.'41, Southern Ill. Univ.; M.A.'43, Univ. of Ill.; Co. Supt. of Sch., Tuscola, Ill., since 1943.

Bozeman, Estelle, B.S.'25, Univ. of Ga.; Natl. Dir. of Narcotic Educ., Woman's Christian Temperance Union, Evanston, Ill., since 1943.

Brach, Wallace Roy, B.Ed.'28, Ill. State Normal Univ.; M.S.'35, Univ. of Ill.; Supt. of Sch., Pearl City, Ill., since 1949.

Brackman, Walter, Ph.B.'27, M.A.'34, Univ. of Chicago; Editor in Chief, Row, Peterson and Co., Evanston, Ill., since 1949.

Bradley, Joseph F., B.S.'32, Mich. State Normal Col.; Dir. of Physical Educ., Glencoe, Ill., since 1942.

Braeuninger, W. B., B.S.'31, M.S.'36, Univ. of Ill.; Supt. of Sch., Athens, Ill., since 1948.

Brewick, Gayheart Millard, B.Ed.'40, Northern Ill. State Tchrs. Col., De Kalb; M.A.'45, Northwestern Univ.; Supt. of Sch., Schiller Park, Ill., since 1940.

Brien, Aaron, B.S. in Ed.'46, St. Louis Univ.; M.S. in Ed.'48, Ill. Univ.; Supt., Cahokia Commonfields Pub. Sch., East St. Louis, Ill., since 1950.

Bright, Orville T., Ph.B.'35, M.A.'39, Univ. of Chicago; Supt. of Sch., Lake Bluff, Ill., since 1943.

Bronson, Marian H., B.A.'10, Iowa State Col.; Mgr., Midwest Territory, The A. N. Palmer Co.; 221 East Cullerton Rd., Chicago 16, Ill., since 1946.

Brown, Eric E., B.E.'37, Eastern Ill. State Col., Charleston; M.S.'41, Indiana Univ.; Supt. of Sch., Calumet City, Ill., since 1936.

Bruce, M. E., A.B.'22, Harris Tchrs. Col., St. Louis, Mo.; Ph.M.'28, Univ. of Wis.; Supt. of Sch., East St. Louis, Ill., since 1942.

Brunjes, Orville O., B.Ed.'37, Ill. State Normal Univ.; M.A. in Ed.'41, Washington Univ.; Asst. Supt. of Sch. Dist. 104, Hartford, Ill., since 1948.

Buford, John Lester, B.Ed.'28, Southern Ill. Univ.; M.A.'39, Univ. of Mich.; LL.D.'44, McKendree Col.; City Supt. of Sch., Mt. Vernon, Ill., since 1937.

Bush, Charles Austin, M.S.'51, Ind. State Tchrs. Col.; Supt. of Unit C-2, H. S., Marshall, Ill., since 1952.

Buskirk, Roy E., B.A.'40, Western Ill., State Tchrs. Col., Macomb; M.A.'46, Univ. of Ill.; Supt. of Sch., Libertyville, Ill., since 1947.

Butler, Albert F., A.B.'31, A.M.'33, Univ. of Mich.; Mgr., H. S. and Col. Dept., Ginn and Co., Chicago, Ill., since 1948.

Buzzard, Robert Guy, S.B.'16, S.M.'17, Univ. of Chicago; Ph.D.'25, Clark Univ.; A.M.'38, Univ. of Ill.; Pres., Eastern Ill. State Col., Charleston, Ill., since 1933.

Byerly, C. C., A.B.'18, Manchester Col.; M.A.'34, Univ. of Chicago; First Asst. State Supt. of Pub. Instr., Springfield, Ill., since 1943.

Calhoun, George B., Ed.B.'36, Southern Ill. Univ., Carbondale; M.A.'40, Northwestern Univ.; Supt. of Sch., Elmwood Park, Chicago, Ill., since 1944.

Carlton, Everett, Supt. of Sch., Bloomington, Ill.

Carrington, J. W., B.S.'22, M.A.'34, Univ. of Ill. Address: Ill. State Normal Univ., Normal, Ill.

Carruthers, William H., Ed.B.'29, Southern Ill. State Normal; M.A.'39, Univ. of Ill.; Supt. of Sch., Murphysboro, Ill., since 1933.

Cassell, George F., First Asst. Supt. of Sch., Chicago, Ill. (retired). Address: 136 S. Hamlin Ave., Chicago 24, Ill.

Challand, Harold U., M.A.'36, State Univ. of Iowa; Supt. of Elem. Sch., Sterling, Ill., since 1944.

Chapman, A. Hunter, Ph.B.'30, Shurtleff Col.; M.A.'39, Univ. of Ill.; Dist. Supt. of Sch., Arenzville, Ill.

Chase, Francis S., B.S.'27, M.S.'31, Univ. of Va.; Dir., Rural Editorial Serv., and Lecturer in Educ. Admin., Univ. of Chicago, Chicago, Ill.

Childress, Jack R., B.Ed.'41, Ill. State Normal Univ.; M.S.'45, Univ. of Ill.; Ph.D.'50, Northwestern Univ.; Dir., The Univ. Col., Northwestern Univ., Chicago, Ill., since 1951.

Chitty, Arthur L., Ed.B.'37, Southern Ill. Univ.; M.A.'42, Univ. of Ill.; Co. Supt. of Sch., Vienna, Ill., since 1951.

Christ, (Mrs.) Alice Louise, Supt., Rhodes Sch. Dist. 84½, River Grove, Ill.

Chute, Oscar M., B.S.'29, Colby Col.; Ed.M.'34, Harvard Univ.; Ed.D.'46, Univ. of Ill.; Supt. of Elem. Sch. Dist. 75, Evanston, Ill., since 1947.

Clabaugh, Ralph E., M.A.'37, Univ. of Ill.; Supt. of Sch., Arlington Hgts., Ill., since 1943.

Clark, Charles W., B.S.'25, Ill. Wesleyan Univ.; M.A.'40, Univ. of Ill.; Supt. of Community Unit Sch. Dist. 8, Colfax, Ill., since 1949.

Clark, John F., B.Ed.'36, Northern Ill. State Tchrs. Col., De Kalb; M.A.'38, Northwestern Univ.; Supt. of Sch., Villa Park, Ill., since 1949.

*Clettenberg, Joseph E., B.S.'31, Univ. of Ill.; M.S.'36, Northwestern Univ.; Supt., Sch. Dist. 83, Melrose Park, Ill.

Clift, David H., Exec. Secy., American Libr. Assn., Chicago, Ill.

Cochran, Frank Lee, B.S.'36, Univ. of Mich.; Architect, Perkins and Will, Chicago 6, Ill., since 1945.

Cohen, Theresa T., Ph.B.'26, Univ. of Chicago; M.E.'36, Loyola Univ.; Prin., Jefferson Sch., Chicago, Ill., since 1952.

Cohler, Milton J., B.S.'23, Univ. of Wis.; M.A.'36, Ph.D.'40, Northwestern Univ.; Prin., Waller H. S., Chicago, Ill., since 1946.

Conklin, Paul S., B.S.'17, Univ. of Ill.; M.S.'31, Univ. of Wis.; Co. Supt. of Sch., Rockford, Ill., since 1938.

Connelly, George W., A.B.'37, A.M.'40, Northwestern Univ.; Acting Chairman, Dir. of Student Tchg., Dept. of Educ., Chicago Tchrs. Col., Chicago, Ill., since 1950.

Cook, Paul M., A.B.'18, Central Wesleyan Col.; M.A.'27, Univ. of Chicago; LL.D.'47, Phillips Univ.; Exec. Secy., Phi Delta Kappa, Homewood, Ill., since 1928.

Cook, Raymond Mack, Dean, Chicago Tchrs. Col., Chicago, Ill., since 1948.

Coplan, Franklin, B.S.'31, Eureka Col.; M.S.'44, Univ. of Ill.; Supt. of Sch., Community Unit Dist. No. 4, Edinburg, Ill., since 1943.

Cordis, William Reynold, B.S.'27, M.S.'35, Univ. of Ill.; Supt. of Sch., Princeville, Ill., since 1932.

Cornell, Francis G., A.B.'27, M.A.'31, Ph.D.'36, Columbia Univ.; Dir., Bur. of Educ. Research, Col. of Educ., Univ. of Ill., Urbana, Ill., since 1947.

Cornwell, G. E., B.Ed.'39, Eastern Ill. Tchrs. Col., Charleston; M.S.'41, Univ. of Ill.; Supt., Community Unit Sch. Dist. 3, Taylorville, Ill., since 1948.

Courtenay, Mary E., B.A.'10, M.A.'37, Univ. of Chicago; Asst. Supt. of Sch., Dept. of Special Educ., Chicago, Ill., since 1949.

Crackel, Verne E., A.B.'37, M.A.'40, Univ. of Chicago; Supt., Will Co. Sch., Joliet, Ill., since 1952.

Crafton, Paul M., B.S.'25, Lincoln Col.; M.S.'35, Univ. of Ill.; Supt. of Sch., Monmouth, Ill., since 1946.

Crakes, Charles R., B.A.'30, M.A.'40, Northwestern Univ.; Educ. Dir., De Vry Corporation, Chicago, Ill.

Cravens, Aaron W., A.B.'30, Central Wesleyan Col.; Ph.M.'42, Univ. of Wis.; Supt. of Sch., Galena, Ill., since 1952.

Crawl, Lester P., B.S.'34, Ind. State Tchrs. Col.; M.S. in Ed.'36, Ind. Univ.; Supt. of Sch., Lansing, Ill., since 1932.

Crawshaw, Clyde, B.Ed.'29, Southern Ill. Univ.; M.A.'41, Univ. of Ill.; Supt. of Sch., Marseilles, Ill., since 1947.

Crescencia, Sister Mary, Madonna H. S., Chicago, Ill.

Crum, J. E., B.S. in Ed.'44, M.S. in Ed.'47, Ill. State Normal Univ.; Supt. of Elem. Sch., Streator, Ill., since 1950.

Cunningham, Daniel F., A.B.'16, M.A.'18, Loyola Univ.; LL.D.'32, De Paul Univ.; Supt. of Catholic Sch., Chicago, Ill., since 1927.

Dahle, Casper O., M.A.'32, Ph.D.'40, State Univ. of Iowa; Supt., Sch. Dist. 107, Highland Park, Ill., since 1946.

Darling, D. K., M.S.'45, Univ. of Ill.; Supt., Collinsville Community Unit Dist. 10, Collinsville, Ill., since 1944.

Darnall, James D., A.B.'16, Univ. of Ind.; M.A.'17, Univ. of Chicago; Supt., Community Unit. Sch. Dist. 228, Geneseo, Ill., since 1919.

Daugherty, Arthur C., B.S.'22, Knox Col.; M.S.'33, Univ. of Ill.; Prin., Community H. S., Dupo, Ill., since 1943.

Davis, Melvin G., B.A.'14, Ind. Univ.; M.A.'20, Univ. of Wis.; Ph.D.'35, State Univ. of Iowa; Supt. of Sch., Peoria, Ill., since 1944.

Davis, Milton J., B.S. in Ed.'48, Northern Ill. State Tchrs. Col., De Kalb; Prin., Grade Sch., Gurnee, Ill., since 1945.

395

DeAtley, Glenn O., B.Ed.'31, Ill. State Normal Univ., Normal; M.A. in Ed.'37, Washington Univ.; Supt. of Elem. Sch., Dist. 104, Wood River, Ill., since 1922.

Dekum, Sister Mary Ethelbert, A.B.'28, Loras Col.; M.A.'34, Univ. of Notre Dame; Supt., Community Unit Sch. 50, Teutopolis, Ill., since 1948.

Delabar, L. B., B.S.'30, Monmouth Col.; M.A.'35, State Univ. of Iowa; Supt. of Sch., Spoon River Valley Community Unit 4, Fairview, Ill., since 1948.

DeLaurenti, John C., A.B.'29, Greenville Col.; M.A.'40, New York Univ.; Dist. Supt. of Sch., Highland, Ill., since 1942.

Dent, Ellsworth C., B.S. in Ed.'23, Kansas State Tchrs. Col., Emporia; Dir. of Distribution, Coronet Instrl. Films, and Vicepres., Ideal Pictures Corp., Chicago, Ill., since 1946.

Diel, J. Harold, M.S.'39, Univ. of Ill.; Supt., Community Unit Sch., Dist. 5A, Stewardson, Ill., since 1948.

Di Leonarde, Joseph H., B.S.'32, Univ. of Ill.; A.M.'39, DePaul Univ.; Ph.D.'52, Northwestern Univ.; Prin., Hendricks Sch., Chicago, Ill., since 1950.

Dimmett, W. S., Ph.B.'31, M.A.'36, Univ. of Chicago; Supt. of Sch., Forest Park, Ill., since 1930.

Dintelman, Charles J., B.Ed.'37, Southern Ill. Univ.; M.S.'40, Univ. of Ill.; Dist. Supt. of Sch., Seward, Ill., since 1948.

Dolan, Francis H., B.A.'28, M.A.'32, Univ. of Minn.; Supt., Twp. H. S. and Oglesby Jr. Col., LaSalle, Ill., since 1947.

Dorland, Z. Harold, B.Ed.'29, Ill. State Normal Univ., Normal; M.A.'33, State Univ. of Iowa; Supt., Twp. H. S., Streator, Ill., since 1946.

Downey, Helen M., M.Ed.'36, Loyola Univ.; Prin., Kellogg Elem. Sch., Chicago, Ill., since 1941.

Doyle, Sister M. Timothea, B.A.'17, M.A.'18, Univ. of Minn.; Pres., Rosary Col., River Forest, Ill., since 1949.

Drechney, (Mrs.) Hyacinth G., Mus.M.'27, Chicago Musical Col.; Ph.B.'31, M.A.'36, De Paul Univ.; Prin., Chopin Sch., Chicago, Ill., since 1939.

Driscoll, Lucy E., M.A.'33, State Univ. of Iowa; Asst. Supt. of Co. Sch., Chicago, Ill., since 1951.

Duffie, Burton, B.S.'31, M.A.'34, Univ. of Chicago; Dir. of Bur. of Educ. Extension, 228 N. LaSalle St., Chicago 1, Ill., since 1948.

Eades, Roscoe, B.S.'21, Eureka Col.; M.A.'38, Columbia Univ.; Supt., Sterling Twp. H. S., Sterling, Ill., since 1931.

Eater, J. W., B.Ed.'37, Southern Ill. State Normal Univ., Carbondale; M.S.'45, Univ. of Ill.; Supt. of Sch., Rantoul, Ill., since 1945.

Eaton, O. R., Ph.M.'35, Univ. of Wis.; Supt., Community Unit Sch. Dist. 4, Paris, Ill., since 1948.

Eberly, Wade L., B.E.'32, Ill. State Normal Univ.; M.A.'37, Univ. of Iowa; Prin., Grant Community H. S., Fox Lake, Ill., since 1948.

Eckhardt, Edward E., B.S.E.'42, Concordia Tchrs. Col.; M.A.'52, DePaul Univ.; Supt. of Sch., Morton Grove, Ill., since 1947.

Edman, V. Raymond, A.B.'23, Boston Univ.; M.A.'30, Ph.D.'33, Clark Univ.; LL.D.'41, Houghton Col.; Pres., Wheaton Col., Wheaton, Ill., since 1941.

Edward, Sister Mary, A.B.'40, DePaul Univ.; Prin. and Supvr. of Sch., 2901 W. 43rd St., Chicago, Ill., since 1944.

Edwards, LaVerne, Prin., Elem. Sch., Mount Morris, Ill.

Ege, Louise N., Ph.B., DePaul Univ.; M.E., Loyola Univ.; Prin., Morris Sch., Chicago, Ill., since 1944.

*Eichelberger, James W., A.B.'04, Livingstone Col.; A.M.'23, Northwestern Univ.; Secy. of Christian Educ., African Methodist Episcopal Zion Church, Chicago, Ill., since 1932.

Elliott, R. H., Co. Supt. of Sch., Danville, Ill.

Ellis, Homer C., B.S.'23, Mt. Union Col.; M.A. '30, Oberlin Col.; 6901 Madison St., Niles, Ill.

Ellis, Raymond S., M.A.'38, Northwestern Univ.; Supt., Round Lake Consol. Sch. Dist. 43, Round Lake, Ill., since 1927.

Elzay, Jack, B.A.'35, B.S. in Ed.'36, Ohio Northern Univ.; M.A.'41, Tchrs. Col., Columbia Univ.; Supt. of Sch., Downers Grove, Ill., since 1949.

Endicott, Frank S., B.A.'27, Cornell Col.; M.A. '29, Ph.D.'38, Northwestern Univ.; Dir. of Placement and Assoc. Prof. of Educ., Northwestern Univ., Evanston, Ill., since 1935.

Endres, (Mrs.) Mary P., B.E.'42, Western Ill. State Tchrs. Col., Macomb; M.A.'46, Univ. of Chicago; Supt. of Community Consol. Sch. Dist. 10, Woodstock, Ill., since 1946.

Erickson, Albin H., B.S.'33, M.S.'36, Univ. of Minn.; Dean, North Park Col., Chicago, Ill., since 1949.

Erzinger, John F., B.S.'29, M.S.Ed.'35, Northwestern Univ.; Prin., Lovett Elem. Sch., Chicago, Ill., since 1948.

Ewert, H. W., Bd. of Educ., Proviso Twp. H. S., Maywood, Ill.

Fairchild, R. W., A.B.'14, M.A.'19, Univ. of Mich.; Ph.D.'32, Northwestern Univ.; Pres., Ill. State Normal Univ., Normal, Ill., since 1933.

Faulkner, Elizabeth, A.B.'85, Univ. of Chicago; Prin., Faulkner Sch. for Girls, Chicago, Ill., since 1909.

Fearn, Harold, B.Ed.'39, Eastern Ill. State Col., Charleston; M.A.'46, Univ. of Ill.; Supt., Community Unit Sch. Dist. 1, Charleston, Ill., since 1950.

Fearn, Logan W., B.Ed.'39, Eastern Ill. State Col.; M.S.'47, Univ. of Ill.; Supt. of City Sch., Litchfield, Ill., since 1948.

Fegley, Paul V., M.A.'38, Washington Univ.; Supt., Community Unit Sch. Dist. 8, Pana, Ill.

Ferentchak, Martin, Pres., Bd. of Educ., Argo, Ill., since 1933.

Ferguson, J. C., Ginn and Co., Wheaton, Ill.

Fierke, W. F., Supt. of Sch., Tinley Park, Ill.

Finley, Elden D., B.S.'23, Knox Col.; M.A.'28, Columbia Univ.; Asst. Supt. of Pub. Instr., Springfield, Ill., since 1949.

Fischer, E. E., B.S.'32, Eureka Col.; M.S.'37, Univ. of Ill.; Supt. of Sch., Alpha, Ill., since 1948.

Fishback, Woodson W., Ph.D.'48, Univ. of Chicago; Assoc. Prof. of Educ., Southern Ill. Univ., Carbondale, Ill., since 1948.

Fisher, William O., B.Ed.'46, M.Ed.'47, Univ. of Okla.; Supt., Community Unit Sch. Dist. 84, Wolf Lake, Ill., since 1948.

Fitzgerald, Eleanor M., Ph.B.'29, M.A. in Ed.'37, DePaul Univ.; Prin., Barton Sch., Chicago, Ill., since 1937.

Fitzgerald, Matthew L., Ph.B.'24, Univ. of Chicago; J.D.'34, Loyola Univ.; M.Ed.'36, DePaul Univ.; Dist. Supt., Lake View H. S., Chicago, Ill., since 1951.

Fitzhugh, Harry L., B.Ed.'34, Eastern Ill. State Col., Charleston; A.M.'41, Univ. of Ill.; Supt. of Sch., Morgan Co. Unit Dist. 1, Franklin, Ill., since 1948.

Foster, Charles W., B.E.'42, Ill. State Normal Univ.; M.A.'49, Northwestern Univ.; Bus. Mgr., Thornton Twp. H. S. and Jr. Col., Harvey, Ill.

Fowler, Oscar F., Ph.B.'24, Univ. of Chicago; M.A.'35, Northwestern Univ.; Dist. Supt. of H. S., Chicago, Ill., since 1937.

Fox, Elvira, Ph.B.'28, Loyola Univ.; M.S. in Ed. '32, Northwestern Univ.; Prin., Spry Elem. Sch., Chicago, Ill.

French, Floyd, B.Ed.'30, Ill. State Normal Univ., Normal; M.A.'36, Univ. of Chicago; Co. Supt. of Sch., Princeton, Ill., since 1935.

Frey, Sydney W., B.S.'25, McKendree Col.; M.S.'34, Univ. of Ill.; Asst. Supt., Community Unit H. S., Roxana, Ill.

Friedli, F. J., B.S.'16, McKendree Col.; M.S.'33, Univ. of Ill.; Asst. Supt. of Sch., Belleville, Ill., since 1942.

Fristoe, Dewey, B.Ed.'31, Ill. State Normal Univ., Normal; A.M.'36, Colo. State Col. of Educ., Greeley; Ed.D.'41, New York Univ.; Supt. of Sch., Flossmoor, Ill., since 1943.

Fullmer, C. E., A.S.'21, Blackburn Col.; B.S.'23, M.S.'32, Univ. of Ill.; Prin., Wadsworth Elem. Sch., Chicago, Ill., since 1951.

Fullmer, M. F., M.A.'35, State Univ. of Iowa; Supt. of Sch., Winchester, Ill., since 1948.

Gaffney, Matthew P., B.S.'12, Litt.D.'42, Colgate Univ.; M.A.'19, Columbia Univ.; Supt., New Trier Twp. H. S., Winnetka, Ill., since 1931.

Galloway, Geraldine, B.S. in Ed.'41, M.A. in Ed.'42, Univ. of Ill.; Supt., Kane Community Sch., Fairfield, Ill.

Ganster, William A., B.S.'30, M.S.'35, Univ. of Ill.; Architect, 222 Washington St., Waukegan, Ill.

Gard, W. L., B.S.'21, M.S.'28, Univ. of Ill.; Supt. of Sch., Beardstown, Ill., since 1928.

Gates, John Wesley, A.B.'28, Washburn Municipal Univ. of Topeka; A.M.'38, Ph.D.'45, Univ. of Chicago; Supt., East H. S., Aurora, Ill., since 1946.

Geiger, C. Harve, Ph.B.'22, Univ. of Chicago; Ed.M.'28, Harvard Univ.; Ph.D.'39, Columbia Univ.; Pres., North Central Col., Naperville, Ill., since 1946.

Geppert, Otto Emil, Secy.-Treas., Denoyer-Geppert Co., Chicago, Ill., since 1916.

Gillet, Harry O., Genl. Editor, United Educators Inc., Chicago, Ill.

Gilson, Harry V., B.S.'30, D.Sc. in Ed.'45, Temple Univ.; M.A.'34, Tchrs. Col., Columbia Univ.; Educ. Dir., Natl. Soc. for Crippled Children and Adults, Chicago, Ill., since 1951.

Goodier, Floyd T., A.B.'03, Colgate Univ.; A.M.'09, Tchrs. Col., Columbia Univ.; Dir. of Integration, Ill. State Normal Univ., Normal, Ill., 1937-50 (retired). Address: 603 Broadway, Normal, Ill.

Goodrich, (Mrs.) Lucille, Co. Supt. of Sch., Pontiac, Ill.

Gordon, Claude T., B.S.'39, Ill. Inst. of Tech.; M.Ed.'42, DePaul Univ.; Supt. of Sch., Bartlett, Ill., since 1951.

Gore, J. H., B.Sc.'10, Blackburn Col.; M.A.'28, Univ. of Chicago; Supt. of Sch., Venice, Ill., since 1935.

Goreham, Wilfred John, A.B.'24, Ill. Wesleyan Univ.; M.A.'33, Univ. of Ill.; Prin., Twp. H. S., Sidell, Ill., since 1927.

Graham, James C., A.B.'25, Park Col.; B.Ed.'32, Western Ill. State Tchrs. Col., Macomb; M.A.'37, Univ. of Wyo.; Supt. of Sch., Morrisonville, Ill., since 1949.

Graham, Verne O., Prin. Pub. Sch., Chicago, Ill.

Grant, Lester J., Ed.B.'34, State Normal Univ., Normal, Ill.; M.S.'36, Univ. of Ill.; Supt. of Sch., Decatur, Ill., since 1950.

Grant, Robert C., B.S.'32, Bradley Univ.; M.A.'37, Univ. of Ill.; Prin., Consol. H. S., Watseka, Ill., since 1944.

*Gray, William S., S.B.'13, Ph.D.'16, Univ. of Chicago; M.A.'14, Columbia Univ.; Prof. of Educ., Emeritus, Univ. of Chicago, Chicago, Ill., since 1950.

Green, Harry B., Supt. of Sch., Pekin, Ill.

Griffin, Lee H., Ph.B.'16, Univ. of Chicago; Mng. Dir., Ginn and Co., Chicago, Ill.

Grigsby, Paul A., A.B.'22, Central Col. (Mo.); A.M.'29, Univ. of Mo.; Supt., Community Unit Sch. Dist. 9, Granite City, Ill., since 1950.

Gum, B. E., A.M.'37, Univ. of Ill.; Supt. of Sch., Salem, Ill., since 1937.

Haebich, I. E., B.A.'15, Baldwin-Wallace Col.; M.S.'33, Univ. of Chicago; Supt. of Riverside-Brookfield Twp. H. S., Riverside, Ill., since 1939.

Hall, Hal O., B.Ed.'30, Southern Ill. Univ.; M.B.A.'34, Northwestern Univ.; Ed.D.'43, New York Univ.; Supt. of Sch., Belleville, Ill., since 1945.

Hall, Ruel, B.Ed.'29, Eastern Ill. State Col., Charleston; M.A.'39, Univ. of Chicago; Co. Supt. of Sch., Kankakee, Ill., since 1941.

Hamlin, Milford M., Dept. of Educ., American Type Founders, Chicago, Ill.

Hammer, Kenneth S., A.B.'37, Cornell Col.; M.Ed.'40, Univ. of Colorado; Supt. of Sch., Morris, Ill., since 1951.

Hand, Harold C., B.A.'24, D.Sc.'49, Macalester Col.; M.A.'30, Univ. of Minn.; Ph.D.'33, Columbia Univ.; Prof. of Educ., Univ. of Ill., Urbana, Ill., since 1946.

Handlin, William C., A.B.'09, Univ. of Ill.; M.A.'28, James Millikin Univ.; Prin., Community H. S., Lincoln, Ill., since 1919.

Hanke, Robert H., B.S.'35, North Central Col.; M.S.'39, Univ. of Wis.; Prin., Elem. and Primary Sch., Mooseheart, Ill., since 1949.

Hanna, David C., B.S.'43, M.A.'46, Ph.D.'50, Ohio State Univ.; Dir. of Attendance and Research, Pub. Sch., Springfield, Ill.

Hannum, James M., B.S. in Ed.'46, Phillips Univ.; M.A. in Ed.'48, Northwestern Univ.; Supt., Oak Lawn Elem. Schs., Oak Lawn, Ill., since 1952.

Hanson, Earl H., A.B.'24, Augustana Col.; M.A.'33, Columbia Univ.; Supt. of Sch., Rock Island, Ill., since 1937.

Hanson, Ernest M., B.S.'22, M.A.'28, Univ. of Minn.; Supt., Thornton Twp. H. S. and Jr. Col., Harvey, Ill., since 1952.

Harlan, Willard M., B.S.'36, M.S.'41, Univ. of Ill.; Supt., Community Consol. Sch., Sheffield, Ill., since 1942.

Harris, John Harper, B.S.'39, Bradley Univ.; M.A.'40, Ed.D.'49, Columbia Univ.; Asst. Supt. of Sch., Peoria, Ill., since 1943.

Harris, Latham E., M.A. in Ed.'42, Washington Univ.; Supt., Elem. Sch., Roxana, Ill., since 1940.

Harris, Verne B., M.A.'36, Tchrs. Col., Columbia Univ.; B.S.'30, Ind. State Tchrs. Col., Terre Haute; Supt. of Sch. Dist. 156, Calumet City, Ill., since 1946.

Harshbarger, Ernest M., B.S.'34, Univ. of Ill.; Co. Supt. of Sch., Urbana, Ill., since 1931.

Hatcher, James G., B.S.'27, Univ. of Mo.; M.S.'42, Ed.M.'46, Univ. of Ill.; Prin., Morton Twp. H. S., Morton, Ill., since 1941.

Hatfill, Harlie Alvin, B.S. in Ed.'45, Greenville Col.; M.A. in Ed.'48, Washington Univ. (Mo.); Supt. of Sch., Paris, Ill.

397

Hattenhauer, M. E., B.Ed.'29, Ill. State Normal Univ., Normal; M.A.'38, Northwestern Univ.; LL.B.'39, Kent Law Sch.; Supt. of Sch., Bellwood, Ill., since 1932.

Hauser, Ludwig J., B.A.'19, M.A.'28, Univ. of Minn.; Ed.D.'39, Columbia Univ.; Supt. of Sch., Riverside, Ill., since 1931.

Haussler, A. G., LL.B.'23, Ill. Wesleyan Univ.; B.Ed.'39, Ill. State Normal Univ., Normal; M.A.'42, New York Univ.; Vicepres., Bradley Univ., Peoria, Ill.

Hawley, Ray C., A.B.'24, Morningside Col.; A.M.'33, Univ. of Ill.; A.M.'41, Tchrs. Col. Columbia Univ.; Co. Supt. of Sch., Marseilles, Ill.

Heffernan, David J., M.A.'47, DePaul Univ.; First Asst. Cook Co. Supt. of Sch., Chicago, Ill.

Hegner, Herman H., Ph.B.'25, Univ. of Wis.; Pres., Pestalozzi Froebel Tchrs. Col., Chicago, Ill., since 1937.

Heider, Louis N., Prin., Community H. S., Jerseyville, Ill.

Hein, Fred V., Ph.B.'29, Ripon Col.; M.S.'34, Ph.D.'46, Univ. of Wis.; Consultant in Health and Fitness, Bureau of Health Educ., American Medical Assn., Chicago, Ill., since 1946.

Hendricks, Frank D., A.B.'33, Univ. of Ill.; M.S.Ed.'46, Drake Univ.; Supt., Huntley Consol. Sch. 158, Huntley, Ill., since 1947.

Henniger, K. V., A.B.'29, James Millikin Univ.; A.M.'33, Univ. of Ill.; Supt., Lakeview Community Sch. Unit 4, Decatur, Ill.

Henry, N. B., Prof. Emeritus of Educ., Univ. of Chicago, Chicago, Ill.

Henry, Virgil, Ed.B.'32, Southern Ill. Univ.; M.S.'38, Univ. of Ill.; Ed.D.'48, Tchrs. Col., Columbia Univ.; Supt. of Sch., Orland Park, Ill., since 1949.

Herbster, William E., B.Ed.'37, Ill. State Normal Univ.; M.A.'40, Northwestern Univ.; Supt. of Sch., North Chicago, Ill., since 1951.

Herr, Ross, B.S. in Ed.'20, Bowling Green State Normal Col.; A.M. in Ed.'22, Univ. of Chicago; Prin., Harrison Tech. H. S., Chicago, Ill., since 1949.

Herron, Harry H., Ph.B.'21, Univ. of Chicago; Registrar, Office Supvr., and Pur. Agt., New Trier Twp. H. S., Winnetka, Ill., since 1922.

Hester, Vance C., M.A.'39, Univ. of Colo.; Supt. of Sch., Franklin Park, Ill., since 1941.

Hexter, Edward G., A.B.'16, McKendree Col.; A.M.'30, Univ. of Ill.; Registrar, Twp. H. S. and Jr. Col., Belleville, Ill.

Heybeck, Frank D., B.S.'42, Ill. Inst. of Tech.; Supt. of Comm. Consol. Sch., Lake Zurich, Ill., since 1947.

Hill, Alvin F., B.S.'37, M.A.'50, Univ. of Ill.; Supt., Fairmont Sch., Lockport, Ill., since 1940.

Hill, E. Lynn, A.B.'27, James Millikin Univ.; M.A.'34, Univ. of Ill.; Supt., Unit Sch. Dist. 200, Roseville, Ill., since 1948.

Hoff, Harold A., Ph.M.'33, Univ. of Wis.; Prin., Community H. S., Mount Morris, Ill., since 1938.

Hollmeyer, Lewis H., A.B.'20, Hanover Col.; M.A.'37, Tchrs. Col., Columbia Univ.; Asst. Supt. of Pub. Instr., Springfield, Ill., since 1945.

Holmes, Leslie A., B.S.'26, M.S.'28, Ph.D.'42, Univ. of Ill.; Pres., Northern Ill. State Tchrs. Col., De Kalb, Ill., since 1949.

Horn, Earl G., M.S.'34, Iowa State Col.; Supt., Lee Co. Community Unit Sch. Dist. 271, Ashton, Ill., since 1948.

Howard, Harriet, M.A.'16, Columbia Univ.; Dir., Supvn. Dept., Natl. Col. of Educ., Evanston, Ill., since 1923.

Howell, John Marion, B.A.'25, Emmanuel Missionary Col.; M.A.'38, Ph.D.'42, Univ. of Nebr.; Prin., Broadview Acad., La Grange, Ill.

Hufford, Gayle N., Ph.D.'37, Univ. of Chicago; Supt. of Sch., Joliet, Ill., since 1937.

Hughes, James Monroe, A.B.'16, Ind. Univ.; M.A.'22, Columbia Univ.; Ph.D.'24, Univ. of Minn.; Dean, Sch. of Educ., Northwestern Univ., Evanston, Ill., since 1941.

Hummel, M. W., Supt. of Sch. Dist 95, Brookfield, Ill.

Hunt, Herold C., A.B.'23, A.M.'27, Univ. of Mich.; Ed.D.'40, Tchrs. Col., Columbia Univ.; Pres., American Assn. of Sch. Admin., 1947-48; Genl. Supt. of Sch., Chicago, Ill., since 1947.

*Huth, Oscar Walter, B.Ed.'35, State Tchrs. Col., Milwaukee, Wis.; M.A.'39, Northwestern Univ.; Supt. Sch. Dist. No. 162, Matteson, Ill., since 1940.

Igoe, Celestine, B.E.'30, DePaul Univ.; M.E.'35, Loyola Univ.; Dir., Spalding Sch. for Handicapped, Chicago, Ill., since 1942.

Jacobs, H. D., B.S. in Ed.'21, Kent State Univ.; M.A.'33, Columbia Univ.; Supt., Community Unit Sch. Dist. 300, Dundee, Ill., since 1947.

Jardine, Alex, A.B.'26, M.A.'34, Ind. State Tchrs. Col.; Supt. of Sch., Moline, Ill., since 1946.

Jeffries, U. B., A.B.'20, Ind. Univ.; M.A.'31, Univ. of Wis.; Supt., Twp. H. S., Carmi, Ill., since 1950.

Jennings, Robert C., B.S.'22, M.A.'27, Col. of William and Mary; Supt. of Sch. Dist. 83, Melrose Park, Ill., since 1950.

Jensen, Elmer A., B.Ed.'23, Ill. State Normal Univ., Normal; M.S.'38, Univ. of Ill.; Ed.D.'42, Univ. of Mo.; Supt. of Sch., Knoxville, Ill., since 1943.

John-Michael, Sister Mary, B.V.M., M.A.'39, Univ. of Mich.; Pres., Mundelein Col., Chicago, Ill.

Johnson, Eugene L., B.S.'28, Central Mo. Col., Warrensburg; M.A.'33, Tchrs. Col., Columbia Univ.; Supt. of Sch., Kankakee, Ill.

Johnson, James B., M.A.'37, Univ. of Ill.; Supt. of Sch., Alton, Ill., since 1947.

Johnson, K. Richard, B.S.'29, Knox Col.; M.S. '32, Ph.D.'39, Univ. of Colo.; Pres., Natl. Col. of Educ., Evanston, Ill., since 1949.

Johnson, Russell D., A.B.'25, Augustana Col.; Asst. Supt. of Sch., Granite City, Ill., since 1934.

Johnson, Stella M., B.S.'20, Univ. of Chicago; M.E.'36, Loyola Univ.; Prin., Park Manor Sch., Chicago, Ill., since 1939.

Johnson, Wesley Albert, B.A.'21, Aurora Col.; M.A.'31, Univ. of Wis.; Supt. of Sch., Bensenville, Ill., since 1943.

Jones, Guy M., Pub. Relations Dir., Natl. Sch. Studios of Minneapolis, since 1947. Address: Natl. Sch. Studios, Inc., Chicago, Ill.

Jones, J. Morris, A.B.'17, C.M.'18, Univ. of Wales; Mng. Editor, World Book Encyclopedia and Childcraft, Chicago, Ill., since 1940.

Jordan, Marion, B.S.'33, Northwestern Univ.; M.S.'36, Univ. of Chicago; Supt. of Sch., Palatine, Ill., since 1947.

Jordan, Roy W., A.B.'32, Ill. Col.; M.A.'45, Unv. of Ill.; Supt. of Sch., Carmi, Ill., since 1940.

Judge, Virgil H., M.A.'40, Univ. of Ill.; Supt. of Sch., Albion, Ill., since 1948.

Katzenmaier, A. J., B.S.'33, Lake Forest Col.; Supt. of Sch., North Chicago, Ill., since 1944.

Kaula, F. Edward, A.B.'04, Tufts Col.; First Vicepres., World Book Co., Chicago, Ill., since 1933.

398

Keenan, Robert C., A.B.'20, J.D.'25, M.Ed.'37, Loyola Univ.; Dist. Supt. of Elem. Sch., Chicago, Ill., since 1941.

Keener, Edward E., A.B.'14, Piedmont Col.; M.A.'17, George Peabody Col. for Tchrs.; Asst. Supt. of Sch., Chicago, Ill., since 1948.

Kennedy, Wendell C., Asst. Dir., Professional and Pub. Relations, Ill. Educ. Assn., Springfield, Ill.

Kenney, Frances M., Editor, Natl. League of Tchrs. Assns. Bulletin, Chicago, Ill.

Kerr, Everett F., A.B.'35, M.A.'40, Univ. of Chicago; Supt. of Sch. Dist. 130, Blue Island, Ill.

Kich, Elmer G., B.S.'23, Capital Univ.; M.A.'41, Northwestern Univ.; Dist. Supt. of Elem. Sch., Blue Island, Ill.

Kietzman, Ben, B.A.'18, N. Central Col.; M.Ph. '26, Univ. of Wis.; Supt. of Educ., Canton, Ill., since 1935.

King, Floyd E., B.S.'26, Eureka Col.; M.S.'32, Univ. of Ill.; Supt., Harvard Community Unit Sch. Dist. 50, Harvard, Ill., since 1949.

Kingsland, George M., B.S. in Ed.'31, M.S. in Ed.'38, DePaul Univ.; Supt. of South Holland Sch., Harvey, Ill., since 1948.

Kirchhoff, E. L., B.S.'39, M.S.'41, Butler Univ.; Supt., Sch. Dist. 123, Oak Lawn, Ill., since 1951.

Kistenbroker, Arthur W. III, Member, Bd. of Educ., Forest Park, Ill.

Kizer, M. E., Supt., Community Unit Sch. 9, Medora, Ill.

Knecht, W. W., B.S.'37, Southern Ill. Univ.; M.S.'41, Univ. of Ill.; Prin., H. S., East St. Louis, Ill., since 1951.

Knoeppel, Leroy J., B.A.'27, Carthage Col.; M.A.'35, State Univ. of Iowa; Prin., Twp. H. S., Arlington Heights, Ill., since 1947.

Koelling, Harry C., A.B.'29, Elmhurst Col.; M.A.'37, Washington Univ.; Supt. of Community Unit Sch. Dist. 132, Red Bud, Ill., since 1943.

Korty, Hester L., B.Ed.'34, Ill. State Normal Univ., Normal; Co. Supt. of Sch., Winchester, Ill., since 1949.

Kramer, William G., Secy., Sch. Bd., Dist. 91, Forest Park, Ill., since 1942.

Krantz, Beatrice V., A.B.'29, Lake Forest Col.; A.M.'30, Columbia Univ.; Admin. Asst. and Dean of Girls, York Community H. S., Elmhurst, Ill.

Krantz, LaVern L., B.S.'29, M.A.'30, Univ. of Minn.; Supt. of Sch., Community Unit Dist. 2, Mattoon, Ill., since 1949.

Krause, Victor C., B.S.'40, Concordia Tchrs. Col.; M.A.'47, Tchrs. Col.; Columbia Univ.; Asst. Prof. of Educ., Concordia Tchrs. Col., River Forest, Ill., since 1950.

Krutsinger, L. V., M.S.'33, Univ. of Ill.; Supt. of Sch., East Richland Community Unit Dist. 1, Olney, Ill., since 1948.

Kuster, Warren D., B.Ed.'30, Ill. State Normal Univ., Normal; A.M.'37, Univ. of Ill.; Supt. of Sch., Dwight, Ill., since 1948.

LaGesse, Earle G., B.S.'41, M.Ed.'48, Loyola Univ.; Acting Supt. of Sch. Dist. 148, Dolton, Ill., since 1947.

Lakemacher, Robert E., B.S.'25, Bradley Univ.; M.S.'35, Northwestern Univ.; Prin., Carl Schurz H. S., Chicago, Ill., since 1950.

Lally, Ann M., B.A.'35, Mundelein Col.; M.A.'39, Ph.D.'50, Northwestern Univ.; Dir. of Art, Bd. of Educ., Chicago, Ill., since 1948.

Lambird, Don K., B.A.'38, Carthage Col.; M.A.'47, Peabody Col.; Supt. of Sch., Virginia, Ill., since 1952.

Lancaster, Allen H., B.S.'18, Univ. of Ill.; M.S.'38, Univ. of Wis.; Supt. of Sch., Dixon, Ill., since 1932.

Lang, Charles E., Ph.B.'20, Univ. of Chicago; M.A.'38, Northwestern Univ.; Supt., Elem. Sch. Dist. 5, Chicago, Ill., since 1943.

Larsen, Arthur Hoff, B.Ed.'29, State Tchrs. Col., Superior, Wis.; Ph.M.'31, Ph.D.'39, Univ. of Wis.; Dean, Ill. State Normal Univ., Normal, Ill., since 1949.

Lau, John A., LL.B.'03, Univ. of Wis.; Ph.B.'18, Univ. of Chicago. Address: Scott Foresman and Co., Chicago, Ill.

Lauby, Cecilia J., Ed.D.'49, Ind. Univ.; Assoc. Prof. of Educ. and Coordinator of Off-Campus Student Tchg., Ill. State Normal Univ., Normal, Ill., since 1949.

Lawson, Douglas E., A.B.'32, M.A.'33, Colo. State Col. of Educ., Greeley; Ph.D.'39, Univ. of Chicago; Dean, Col. of Educ., Southern Ill. Univ., Carbondale, Ill., since 1948.

Lechimski, (Mrs.) Regina G., M.A.'46, DePaul Univ.; Prin., Chappell and Sauganash Sch., Chicago, Ill., since 1948.

Lehr, Edgar I., A.B.'26, M.A.'30, Ind. Univ.; Supt. of Sch., Rock Falls, Ill., since 1930.

Leinauer, (Mrs.) Marjorie B., B.S. in Ed.'44, Northern Ill. State Tchrs. Col., De Kalb; Co. Supt. of Sch., Sycamore, Ill., since 1941.

Leist, Mary G., M.A.'26, Univ. of Chicago; Prin., Shepard Sch., Chicago, Ill., since 1937.

Leonard, James H., A.B.'21, Lake Forest Col.; LL.B.'33, Chicago Kent Col. of Law; M.S.'47, Ind. Univ.; Supt., Thornton Fractional Twp. H. S., Calumet City, Ill., since 1948.

Lewis, (Mrs.) Virginia F., B.S. in Ed.'37, M.A.'42, Northwestern Univ.; Prin., Wendell Phillips H. S., Chicago, Ill., since 1950.

Lichty, Elden A., Ed.D.'43, Univ. of Mo.; Assoc. Prof. of Educ., Ill. State Normal Univ., Normal, Ill., since 1945.

Lieb, George W., B.S.'37, M.A.'40, Northwestern Univ.; Supt., Sch. Dist. 122, Oak Lawn, Ill., since 1948.

Lindsey, Richard V., B.E.'10, Ill. State Normal Univ., Normal; Ph.M.'26, Univ. of Wis.; Supt. of Sch., Galesburg, Ill., since 1938.

Lindstrom, Stan C., Pres., Superior Coach Sales Co., Evanston, Ill.

Lineberger, Clarence, A.B.'09, LL.D.'39, Lenoir-Rhyne Col.; A.M.'11, Univ. of N. C.; Dist. Supt. of Sch., Chicago, Ill., since 1938.

Litchfield, Vernon B., B.E.'35, Western State Col.; M.A.'52, Bradley Univ.; Supt. of Sch., Creve Coeur, Ill., since 1947.

Litle, Lester O., B.S. in Ed.'26, Southwest Mo. State Col.; A.M.'30, Ed.D.'43, Univ. of Mo.; Supt. of Sch., Quincy, Ill., since 1949.

Littlepage, H. S., B.S.'24, Eureka Col.; M.S.'37, M.Ed.'44, Univ. of Ill.; Supt., Community Unit Sch. Dist., Carlinville, Ill., since 1948.

Litwiller, O. J., A.B.'26, Bluffton Col.; M.A.'34, Ohio State Univ.; Supt. of Lena-Winslow Community Unit Sch., Lena, Ill., since 1949.

Loew, C. C., A.B.'28, Ill. Col.; M.A.'38, Wash. Univ.; Supt. of Sch., Urbana, Ill., since 1948.

Loomis, Orson E., B.A.'17, Beloit Col.; M.A.'28, Univ. of Wis.; Prin., Hononegah Community H. S., Rockton, Ill., since 1929.

Lovelass, Harry Donald, B.Ed.'36, Eastern Illinois State Col.; M.A.'38, Ed.D.'49, Univ. of Illinois; Prin., University H. S., Ill. State Normal Univ., Normal, Ill., since 1949.

Luhtala, Viona H., Ph.B.'37, Chicago Univ.; M.A.'41, Northwestern Univ.; Prin., Roosevelt Sch., Maywood, Ill., since 1942.

Lundahl, Arthur W., B.E.'26, Northern Ill. State Tchrs. Col.; M.A.'35, Univ. of Minn.; Dir. of Bus. Affairs, Pub. Sch., Rockford, Ill., since 1948.

Lundahl, Leon J., B.E.'33, Univ. of Ill.; M.A.'35, Northwestern Univ.; Supt. of Elem. Sch., Crystal Lake, Ill., since 1935.

Lusson, Mary G., M.A.Ed.'34, Loyola Univ.; Dir. of Curriculum Development, Pub. Sch., Chicago, Ill., since 1936.

Lyon, Jared T., A.B.'24, Carthage Col.; M.A.'35, State Univ. of Iowa; Supt. of Sch., Hoopeston, Ill., since 1947.

McAllister, W. E., Ed.B.'43, Eastern Ill. State Tchrs. Col., Charleston; M.A.'49, Univ. of Ill.; Supt. of Sch., Centralia, Ill., since 1949.

McCahey, Marie A., Ph.B.'27, Univ. of Chicago; M.Ed.'36, Loyola Univ. (Ill.); Prin., Hirsch H. S., Chicago, Ill., since 1942.

McCain, Hadley D., B.Ed.'39, Eastern Ill. Tchrs. Col., Charleston; M.A.'42, M.Ed.'45, Univ. of Ill.; Supt. of Sch., Madison, Ill., 1949-52.

McCall, H. R., B.S.'25, Southwest Mo. State Col.; A.M.'29, Ed.D.'43, Univ. of Mo.; Dist. Supt. of Sch., Dist. 61, Waukegan, Ill., since 1941.

McCallister, James M., B.S. in Ed.'21, Central Mo. Col., Warrensburg; A.M.'22, Ph.D.'29, Univ. of Chicago; Dean, Herzl Branch, Chicago City Jr. Col., Chicago, Ill., since 1948.

McCannon, Roland, B.S.'38, Univ. of Ill.; M.A.'41, Univ. of Chicago; Secy.-Mgr., Ill. Pupils Reading Circle, Ill. Educ. Assn., 203 W. Kelsey St., Bloomington, Ill.

McCleery, Wayne E., B.S.'30, M.S.'35, Univ. of Ill.; Supt. of Sch., Aurora, Ill., since 1950.

McElroy, Gerald A., B.A.'27, Upper Iowa Univ.; M.A.'34, State Univ. of Iowa; Prin., Twp. H. S., Palatine, Ill., since 1944.

McGaughy, (Mrs.) Jean Barker, Ph.B.'18, Univ. of Chicago; Supt., Community Consol. Sch. Dist. 1, Barrington, Ill., since 1947.

McIntosh, William Ray, B.S.'20, M.A.'23, Northwestern Univ.; M.S.'32, Univ. of Ill.; Supt. of Sch., Rockford, Ill., since 1950.

McKibben, J. D., B.S.'28, Univ. of Chicago; M.S.'40, Univ. of Ill.; Supt., R. O. V. A. Sch. Dist. 208, Oneida, Ill.

McKnelly, Oren H., B.S.'39, Southwest Mo. State Col.; M.S.'41, Univ. of Ill.; Supt. of Sch., Shelbyville, Ill., since 1952.

McKnight, William W., Jr., B.S. in Commerce '38, Northwestern Univ.; McKnight and McKnight Educ. Publishers, Bloomington, Ill., since 1938.

McLure, William Paul, M.A.'32, Univ. of Ala.; Ph.D.'46, Tchrs. Col., Columbia Univ.; Prof. of Educ. and Dir., Bur. of Educ. Research, Univ. of Ill., Urbana, Ill., since 1948.

McMahon, (Mrs.) Edna T., Prin., Bennett Sch., Chicago, Ill.

McSwain, E. T., B.A.'19, Newberry Col.; M.A. '28, Ed.D.'38, Tchrs. Col., Columbia Univ.; Dean, Sch. of Educ., Northwestern Univ., Evanston, Ill., since 1948.

MacDonald, Manley E., B.A.'23, Greenville Col.; M.A.'27, Ph.D.'44, Univ. of Mich.; Dean, Col. of Educ., Bradley Univ., Peoria Ill., since 1947.

Mackenzie, Harold, A.B.'09, Wheaton Col.; A.M.'22, Univ. of Chicago; Supt. of Sch., Savanna, Ill., since 1940.

MacLean, William P., Ph.B. in Ed.'26, M.A. in Ed.'28, Univ. of Chicago; Supt., J. Sterling Morton Schs., Cicero, Ill., since 1940.

Mader, Melvin, 226 Elgin, Forest Park, Ill.

Magan, Isabel L., Ph.B.'26, M.A.'35, Univ. of Chicago; Ph.D.'47, Columbia Univ.; Prin., South Shore H. S., Chicago, Ill., since 1949.

Main, George O., B.Ed.'28, Western State Col. of Colo.; M.A.'33, State Univ. of Iowa; Supt. of Sch., Reddick, Ill.

Malan, William Russell, A.B.'22, Park Col.; M.A.'30, Univ. of Mich.; Supt. of Sch., Harrisburg, Ill., since 1935.

Mann, J. A., A.B.'28, Evansville Col.; A.M.'34, Univ. of Ill.; Supt. of Sch., Jacksonville, Ill.

Marinaccio, Anthony, B.Ed.'37, Tchrs. Col. of Conn., New Britain; M.A.'39, Ohio State Univ.; Ph.D.'49, Yale Univ.; Asst. Supt. of Sch., Peoria, Ill., since 1949.

Martin, C. Lewis, B.S. in Ed.'41, Ohio Univ.; M.A.'47, Ohio State Univ.; Adm. Asst., Sch. Dist. 102, La Grange, Ill., since 1948.

Martin, Cecil W., A.B.'25, Ill. Col.; M.S.'31, Univ. of Ill.; Ed.D.'42, Tchrs. Col., Columbia Univ.; Supt. of Elem. Sch., Cicero, Ill., since 1948.

Martz, Lorene Laingor, B.S.'31, Univ. of Ill.; M.S.'37, Ind. Univ.; Supt., Justice Park Sch., La Grange, Ill., since 1940.

Masiko, Peter, Jr., B.A.'36, Lehigh Univ.; M.A.'37, Ph.D.'39, Univ. of Ill.; Dean, Wright Jr. Col., Chicago, Ill., since 1950.

Mason, J. A., B.S.'37, Bradley Univ.; M.S.'41, Ed.M.'49, Univ. of Ill.; Supt., Miles Twp. H. S., Skokie, Ill.

Mattiazza, Dominic Louis, B.S.'46, Univ. of Ill.; M.A.'50, Colo. State Col. of Educ., Greeley; Supt. of Pub. Sch., Oglesby, Ill., since 1950.

Meek, Paul, B.Ed.'39, Southern Ill. Univ.; M.S.'45, Univ. of Ill.; Asst. Supt., Community Unit Sch. Dist. 5, Waterloo, Ill.

Mees, John D., Ed.D.'50; Prin., Univ. Sch., Southern Ill. Univ., Carbondale, Ill.

Mellon, E. H., B.S.'23, Ill. Col.; M.S.'32, Univ. of Ill.; Ed.D.'42, Colo. State Col. of Educ., Greeley; Supt. of Community Unit Sch. Dist. 4, Champaign, Ill., since 1943.

Mercer, Lloyd V., B.A. in Ed.'20, Western Ill. State Tchrs Col., Macomb; M.A.'38, Univ. of Ill.; Supt. of Sch., Community Unit 223, Orion, Ill., since 1948.

Meyer, Carl S., B.D.'30, Concordia Theol. Sem.; M.A.'31, Univ. of Chicago; Pres., Luther Inst., Chicago, Ill., since 1943.

Meyer, Fred E., Bd. of Educ., Proviso Twp. H. S., Maywood, Ill.

Michael, Lloyd S., Ph.B.'25, M.A.'26, Denison Univ.; Ed.D.'41, New York Univ.; Supt., Twp. H. S., Evanston, Ill., since 1948.

Middleton, B.D., B.S.Ed.'44, M.S.Ed.'46, Southern Ill. Univ.; Supt., Columbia Community Unit, Columbia, Ill., since 1951.

Miller, C. E., B.S.'18, A.M.'42, Northwestern Univ.; Supt. of Sch., Westmont, Ill., since 1931.

Miller, Earl G., M.A.'32, Univ. of Minn.; Supt. of Sch., La Salle, Ill., since 1939.

Miller, James Roscoe, B.A.'25, LL.D.'49, Univ. of Utah; M.D.'30, M.S.'31, LL.D.'49, Northwestern Univ.; LL.D.'50, Williams Col.; Pres., Northwestern Univ., Evanston, Ill., since 1949.

Miller, Ralph E., B.Ed.'40, M.S.'52, Ill. State Normal Univ.; Supt. of Sch. Dist. 177, Georgetown, Ill., since 1940.

Miller, Van, A.B.'29, Hastings Col.; M.A.'35, Univ. of Nebr.; D.Ed.'42, Harvard Univ.; Prof. of Educ., Univ. of Ill., Urbana, Ill., since 1950.

Mills, Clyde W., M.A.'42, Univ. of Ill.; Supt., Community Unit Sch. Dist. 10, Altamont, Ill., since 1946.

Mills, Russel J., B.E.'36, Superior State Tchrs. Col. (Wis.); M.A.'47, Northwestern Univ.; Supt., Fairview Sch., Skokie, Ill., since 1951.

Milward, Arthur, B.S.'37, M.S.Ed.'41, Purdue Univ.; Prin., Twp. H. S., Mt. Vernon, Ill., since 1950.

Misner, Paul J., A.B.'26, Mich. State Normal Col., Ypsilanti; A.M.'27, Ph.D.'35, Univ. of Mich.; Supt. of Sch., Glencoe, Ill., since 1935.

*Mitchell, William D., M.A.'38, Univ. of Mo.; Co. Supt. of Sch., Quincy, Ill., since 1935.

Monson, Martin Thomas, B.A.'27, St. Olaf Col.; M.A.'35, Northwestern Univ.; Ed.D.'44, Colo. State Col. of Educ., Greeley; Supt. of Sch., Community Unit Dist. 316, Elvaston, Ill., since 1948.

Montag, Karl A., B.S.'39, M.A.'42, Northwestern Univ.; Supt., Berkeley Sch. Dist. 87, Bellwood, Ill., since 1940.

Moon, James, M.S.'46, Northwestern Univ.; Supt. of Sch., Western Springs, Ill., since 1949.

Moore, Byron R., B.Ed.'31, Ill. State Normal Univ.; M.Ed.'35, Columbia Univ.; Prin., Community H. S., East Peoria, Ill., since 1928.

Moore, Hollis A., Jr., A.B.'46, Baylor Univ.; Assoc. Editor, *The Nation's Schools*, Chicago, Ill., since 1952.

Moore, R. D., B.S.'32, M.S.'39, Univ. of Ill.; Supt., Melvin-Sibley Community Sch. Unit, Melvin, Ill., since 1949.

Moore, Raymond, A.B.'20, Ped.D.'45, Lake Forest Col.; Ed.M.'30, Harvard Univ.; Supt., H. S., Lake Forest, Ill.

Morgan, Lewis V., Co. Supt. of Sch., Wheaton, Ill.

Morris, J. Russell, B.Ed.'30, Western Ill. State Col., Macomb; M.S.'48, Univ. of Ill.; Supt., Brown Co. Community Unit Sch., Mt. Sterling, Ill., since 1947.

Morris, Lee M., M.S.'41, Univ. of Ill.; Supt. of Sch., Harvey, Ill., since 1950.

Muffley, E. J., B.S.'17, Eureka Col.; A.M.'45, Univ. of Ill.; Prin., Roosevelt Jr. H. S., Decatur, Ill., since 1943.

Mullen, (Mrs.) Frances Andrews, Ph.B.'23, M.A.'27, Ph.D.'39, Univ. of Chicago; Dir., Bureau of Mentally Handicapped Children, Chicago, Ill., since 1949.

Mullen, Mary M., 4250 N. St. Louis Ave., Chicago, Ill.

Muller, (Mrs.) Emma Fleer, Mus.B.'18, Marquette Univ.; S.B.'23, Univ. of Chicago; Dir. of Personnel and Registrar, Chicago Tchrs. Col., Chicago, Ill., since 1928.

*Muns, Arthur C., M.S.'35, Univ. of Ill.; Supt. of Sch., Sycamore, Ill., since 1952.

Murphy, L. R., M.A.'41, Univ. of Chicago; Supt. of Sch., Mt. Prospect, Ill., since 1948.

Murray, L. D., B.Ed.'36, Ill. State Normal Univ., Normal; M.S.'41, Univ. of Ill.; Prin., Community H. S. Dist. 310, Bartonville, Ill.

Myer, C. J., B.S.'31, Ill. Wesleyan Univ.; M.A.'42, Univ. of Ill.; Supt. of Sch., Assumption, Ill., since 1950.

Myers, Dallas, B.S.'31, Ill. Wesleyan Univ.; M.A.'39, Univ. of Kansas; Supt., Comm. Unit Sch., Lexington, Ill., since 1946.

Nelson, Clarence J., B.E.'36, Wis. State Tchrs. Col., Eau Claire; M.Ph.'42, Univ. of Wis.; Supt. of Sch., Niles, Ill., since 1950.

Nelson, John B., A.B.'19, Wheaton Col.; M.A.'28, Univ. of Chicago; Supt. of Sch., Batavia, Ill., since 1938.

Nettleship, O. R., B.E.'40, Ill. State Normal Univ., Normal; M.S.'48, Univ. of Ill.; Supt., Sch. Dist. 95, Hillsboro, Ill., since 1949.

Neubauer, Wilson O., A.B.'31, Carthage Col.; M.A.'39, Univ. of Ill.; Supt. of Community Unit Sch., Liberty, Ill., since 1950.

Nevosad, Franklyn W., B.S.'36, M.A.'38, Northwestern Univ.; Asst. Supt. of Sch., Chicago Heights, Ill., since 1948.

Newcomer, John M., Secy., Bd. of Educ., Proviso Twp. H. S., Maywood, Ill.

Newenham, R. L., B.S.'26, Univ. of Ill.; M.A.'30, Univ. of Chicago; Supt. of Elem. Sch., Zion, Ill., since 1947.

Newman, Chas. C., B.Ed.'43, Eastern Ill. State Col.; M.A.'46, Univ. of Ill.; Supt. of Sch., Edgar Co. Unit 2, Hume, Ill., since 1948.

Nichols, Everette C., B.Ed.'31, Ill. State Normal Univ.; M.A.'37, Univ. of Ill.; Prin., Community H. S., Marengo, Ill., since 1949.

Nickell, Vernon L., B.Ed.'29, Ill. State Normal Univ., Normal; M.A.'32, Univ. of Ill.; Ed.D.'46, Ill. Wesleyan Univ.; State Supt. of Pub. Instr., Springfield, Ill., since 1943.

Niehus, W. G., B.Ed.'31, Ill. State Normal Univ., Normal; M.A.'38, Univ. of Iowa; Supt. of Consol. Sch., Plainfield, Ill., since 1948.

Nitsche, Vivian J., Asst. Co. Supt. of Sch., Chicago, Ill.

Oates, Forrest R., B.Ed.'32, Southern Ill. Normal Univ.; M.A.'41, Univ. of Detroit; Supt., Community Unit Sch. 348, Mt. Carmel, Ill.

Oestreich, Arthur H., B.A.'33, Ripon Col.; M.A.'39, Ph.D.'49, Northwestern Univ.; Supt. of Sch., Kenilworth, Ill., since 1949.

Olsen, George S., Supt.-Prin., Lyons Twp. H. S. and Jr. Col., La Grange, Ill.

Olsen, Hans C., A.B.'20, Nebr. State Tchrs. Col., Kearney; A.M.'22, Ph.D.'26, Columbia Univ.; Prof. of Educ., Eastern Ill. State Col., Charleston, Ill., since 1938.

O'Malley, Very Rev. Comerford J., S.T.D.'29, Collegio Angelico, Rome, Italy; Pres., De Paul Univ., Chicago, Ill., since 1944.

Osborn, L. G., B.S.'12, Shurtleff Col.; A.B.'14, M.A.'18, Univ. of Ill.; Ph.D.'38, Wash. Univ.; Asst. Supt. of Sch., East St. Louis, Ill., since 1942.

Osborn, Ralph A., M.S.'42, Butler Univ.; Supt., Unit Sch. Dist. 226, Annawan, Ill., since 1947.

O'Shea, Dennis, Vicepres., Rand McNally and Co., Chicago, Ill.

O'Sullivan, Daniel L., A.B.'13, A.M.'28, De Paul Univ.; Supt. of Sch., Lemont, Ill., since 1931.

Page, William J., Diploma '07, Chicago Tchrs. Col.; Ph.B. in Ed.'21, Univ. of Chicago; M.A. in Soc. Sci., Loyola Univ.; Supt., Parental Sch., Chicago, Ill., since 1937.

Palmer, Lester H., A.B.'27, M.A.'42, Univ. of Ill.; Dir. of Educ. Materials, Pub. Sch., Blue Island, Ill., since 1952.

Parmenter, L. E., A.B.'14, Syracuse Univ.; Exec. Mgr., Natl. Sch. Service Inst., Chicago, Ill., since 1940.

Patterson, O. F., B.S.'25, M.S.'30, Univ. of Ill.; Supt., St. Elmo Comm. Unit Sch., St. Elmo, Ill., since 1946.

Patterson, Warren W., B.E.'31, Northern Ill. State Tchrs. Col., De Kalb; M.A.'47, Northwestern Univ.; Supt. of Sch., River Grove, Ill., since 1948.

Patton, James E., B.Ed.'30, Ill. State Normal Univ.; M.S.'36, Univ. of Ill.; Supt. of Elem. Sch., Steger, Ill., since 1936.

Pearce, H. W., M.S.'44, Univ. of Ill.; Prin., Zion-Benton Twp. H. S., Zion, Ill., since 1942.

Pearson, Irving F., B.S. in Ed.'22, Univ. of Ill.; M.S. in Ed.'30, Northwestern Univ.; Exec. Secy., Ill. Educ. Assn., Springfield, Ill., since 1938.

401

Pease, James E., A.B.'29, Central State Tchrs. Col., Mt. Pleasant, Mich.; M.A.'37, Univ. of Mich.; Dist. Supt. of Sch., since 1940, and Pres., Ill. Educ. Assoc., La Grange, Ill., since 1952.

Peck, Jesse R., B.E.'38, Western Ill. State Tchrs. Col., Macomb; Co. Supt. of Sch., Galesburg, Ill., since 1939.

Peek, E. R.; Supt. of Sch., Kewanee, Ill.

Perkins, Lawrence B., B.Arch.'30, Cornell Univ.; Partner, Perkins and Will, Chicago, Ill., since 1935.

Perne, Anton W., A.B.'31, Knox Col.; A.M.'39, Univ. of Ill.; Prin., H. S., Livingston, Ill., since 1944.

Perz, Robert E., B.Ed.'40, Chicago Tchrs. Col.; A.M.'46, Univ. of Chicago; Prin. of H. S., Springfield, Ill., since 1951.

Petersohn, (Mrs.) Mathilde, 7642 Adams, Forest Park, Ill.

Peterson, F. M., B.S.'24, M.S.'27, Univ. of Ill.; Prin., Community H. S., Pekin, Ill., since 1938.

Petty, W. C., B.E.'31, Ill. State Normal Univ.; M.A.'38, Univ. of Chicago; Co. Supt. of Sch., Waukegan, Ill., since 1931.

Pfisterer, Thomas R., B.S.'21, Beloit Col.; Co. Supt. of Sch., Freeport, Ill., since 1935.

Pierce, Paul R., Ph.B.'14, A.M.'27, Ph.D.'34, Univ. of Chicago; Asst. Supt. in Charge of Instr. and Guid., Chicago, Ill., since 1949.

Pinkstaff, Hugh E., M.S. in Ed.'40, Ind. Univ.; Supt. of Bond Co. Community Unit 2, Greenville, Ill., since 1947.

Pittman, Kenneth C., M.A.'38, Univ. of Ill.; Supt. of Sch. Dist. 61, Havana, Ill., since 1950.

Platt, Frank K., B.E.'36, Northern Ill. State Tchrs. Col., De Kalb; M.A.'41, Northwestern Univ.; Supt. of Elem. Sch., Peru, Ill., since 1945.

Plimpton, Blair, S.B.'30, A.M.'38, Univ. of Chicago; Supt. of Sch., Park Ridge, Ill., since 1947.

Poppenheimer, Charles W., B.A.'38, Iowa State Tchrs. Col.; M.A.'41, Northwestern Univ.; Supt. of Sch., Warrenville, Ill., since 1952.

Preston, K. L., Ph.B.'31, Univ. of Chicago; M.S.'35, Northwestern Univ.; Dist. Supt. of Sch., Berwyn, Ill., since 1945.

Price, Alfred J., Asst. Supt. of Sch., Hampshire, Ill.

Prichard, Clarence E., A.B.'12, Butler Univ.; M.A.'13, Ind. Univ.; M.A.'27, Univ. of Chicago; Supt., Twp. H. S., Waukegan, Ill., since 1950.

Puffer, Noble J., B.S.'23, LL.D.'50, Ill. Wesleyan Univ.; M.A.'32, Northwestern Univ.; Co. Supt. of Sch., Chicago, Ill., since 1951.

Pygman, Clarence Huston, A.B.'28, James Millikin Univ.; M.A.'34, Univ. of Chicago; Supt. of Sch., Cook Co. Dist. 89, Maywood, Ill., since 1940.

Quinlan, Frederick F., B.S.'33, M.A.'39, Columbia Univ.; Supt. of Sch., Lake Forest, Ill., since 1944.

Rader, Ralph K., M.A.'41, Northwestern Univ.; Prin., Roxana Grade Sch., Roxana, Ill., since 1949.

Randolph, Paul H., Ed.B.'28, Southern Ill. Univ.; M.A.'36, Univ. of Ill.; Supt., Community Unit Dist. 425, Shabbona, Ill., since 1952.

Randolph, Victor, B.Ed.'35, Southern Ill. Univ.; M.A.'37, Columbia Univ.; Ph.D.'42, George Peabody Col. for Tchrs.; Assoc. Prof. of Educ., Southern Ill. Univ., Carbondale, Ill.

Rathbun, Ruth M., A.B.'14, Univ. of Chicago; M.A.'32, Northwestern Univ.; Prin., Jamieson Sch., Chicago, Ill., since 1928.

Reaugh, William L., B. of Ed.'35, Ill. State Normal Univ., Normal; M.A.'48, Univ. of Ill.; Supt., Cook Co. Sch. Dist. 148, Dolton, Ill., since 1941.

Reavis, George Harve, B.S.'11, Univ. of Mo.; M.A.'16, Ph.D.'20, Columbia Univ.; Educ. Counselor, Field Enterprises, Inc., Chicago, Ill., since 1948.

Reavis, William C., Ph.B.'08, A.M.'11, Ph.D.'25, Univ. of Chicago; Prof. Emeritus of Educ., and Chmn., Com. on Appointments and Field Serv., Univ. of Chicago, Chicago, Ill.

Redmond, James Francis, M.A.'40, Ed.D.'48, Tchrs. Col., Columbia Univ.; Dir. of Purchases, Pub. Sch., Chicago, Ill., since 1952.

Reed, Frederick, B.S.'22, Ohio State Univ.; M.S.'23, Purdue Univ.; Prin., S. S. Greeley Sch., Winnetka, Ill., since 1934.

Reed, J. McLean, B.A.'23, B.S.'25, D.Ph.Ed.'44, Ohio Northern Univ.; M.A.'31, Ohio State Univ.; Supt. of Sch., Danville, Ill.

Reeves, Floyd W., Ph.D.'25, Univ. of Chicago; Prof. of Admin., Univ. of Chicago, Chicago, Ill., since 1929.

Reichert, Edwin C., B.A.'31, Univ. of Wis.; Ph.D.'39, Univ. of Minn.; Head, Educ. Dept., and Dir., Evening Session, Lake Forest Col., Lake Forest, Ill., since 1946.

Reid, George L., Jr., B.S. in Ed. '48, Southeast Mo. State Col.; Prin., Stallings Sch., Granite City, Ill., since 1951.

Reinhardt, Emma, Ph.D., Univ. of Ill.; Prof. of Educ. and Head, Dept. of Educ., Eastern Ill. State Tchrs. Col., Charleston, Ill.

Renwick, Harold A., A.B.'30, Univ. of Ill.; M.A.'34, State Univ. of Iowa; Supt. of Bushnell-Prairie City Sch., Bushnell, Ill., since 1946.

Reusser, John L., Ph.D.'32, State Univ. of Iowa; Prin., Ill. Soldiers' and Sailors' Children's Sch., Normal, Ill., since 1944.

Rice, Arthur H., Ph.D.'47, Univ. of Mich.; Editor, *Nation's Schools*, Chicago, Ill., since 1951.

Rich, Franklin A., B.Ed.'27, Southern Ill. Univ.; M.S.'36, Univ. of Ill.; Supt. of Sch., Bunker Hill, Ill., since 1934.

Richards, Harold L., B.S. in Ec.'20, B.Mil.Sci.'24, D.Sc.'49, Pa. Military Col.; Ph.B.'31, A.M.'33, Univ. of Chicago; Supt., Community H. S., Blue Island, Ill., since 1935.

Ricketts, Robert E., B.S.'26, Parsons Col.; M.A.'38, Univ. of Chicago; Supt., Evergreen Park Pub. Sch., Chicago, Ill., since 1945.

Riedel, Mark T., B.S. in Ed.'33, Northeast Mo. State Tchrs. Col., Kirksville; A.M. in Ed.'36, Univ. of Mo.; Supt. of Sch. Dist 41, Glen Ellyn, Ill., since 1948.

Robb, Ralph, A.B.'11, Ill. Col.; A.M.'48, Univ. of Colo.; Dist. Supt. of Sch., Clinton, Ill.

Robertson, Harris M., B.S.'25, Ill. Col.; M.A.'34, Univ. of Ill.; Supt. of Sch., Community Unit Dist. 224, Galva, Ill., since 1948.

Robinson, Truman, Asst. Supt., Clinton Community Unit Sch. Dist 15, Clinton, Ill.

Rochfort, Marcella T., Diploma '29, Chicago Tchrs. Col., Ill.; Ph.B.'32, M.Ed.'35, Loyola Univ.; Prin., Edgebrook and Wildwood Sch., Chicago, Ill.

Rogers, Don C., B.A.'16, M.A.'21, Ph.D.'23, State Univ. of Iowa; Asst. Supt. of Sch., Chicago, Ill., since 1944.

Ross, Paul, A.B.'24, Oakland City Col.; M.S. in Ed.'39, Ind. Univ.; Supt., Community Unit Sch. Dist. 5, Macon, Ill., since 1948.

Roth, Gus F., M.A.'37, Univ. of Ill.; 521 W. Pearl St., Jerseyville, Ill.

Rouse, Lawrence H., M.A.'46, Northwestern Univ.; Prin., Community H. S., Grayslake, Ill., since 1947.

Rowe, John R., A.B.'19, Beloit Col.; M.A.'22, Univ. of Chicago; Educ. Dir., *Encyclopedia Britannica*, Chicago, Ill., since 1940.

Rowe, Lester, M.A.'42, Northwestern Univ.; Supt., Holmes Sch., Warrenville, Ill., since 1948.

Rush, John J., Supt. of Sch., Rossville, Ill.

Sansone, Amerigo R., B.S. in M.E.'28, Ill. Inst. of Tech.; M.A.'37, Northwestern Univ.; Prin., Carver High and Elem. Sch., Chicago, Ill., since 1944.

Savage, George F., B.S. in Ed.'32, Univ. of Ill.; M.A.'41, Northwestern Univ.; Supt. of Sch. Dist. 69, Skokie, Ill., since 1950.

Schauer, (Mrs.) Lois E., B.S.'32, Lewis Inst.; M.A.'33, De Paul Univ.; Prin., Gillespie Elem. Sch., Chicago Ill., since 1944.

Schloerb, Lester J., B.A.'19, North Central Col.; Ed.M.'34, Harvard Univ.; Asst. to Genl. Supt., Bd. of Educ., Chicago, Ill.

*Schniepp, Albert E., A.B.'24, Central Wesleyan Col.; M.A.'30, Univ. of Mo.; Prin., Jr. and Sr. H. S., Cerro Gordo, Ill.

Schriner, Don D., B.Ed.'31, Eastern Ill. State Tchrs. Col.; M.S.'46, Univ. of Ill.; H. S. Prin., New Athens, Ill., since 1950.

Schultz, Elmer H., M.Ed.'41, Loyola Univ.; B.A.'38, Y.M.C.A. Col.; Supt. of Sch., Homewood, Ill., since 1950.

Scott, E. J., A.B.'29, Westminster Col.; M.Ed.'39, Univ. of Mo.; Asst. Supt. of Sch., Quincy, Ill., since 1948.

Scott, Willis H., A.B.'17, Oberlin Col.; Exec. Vicepres., Scott Foresman & Co., Chicago, Ill.

Seay, Maurice F., A.B.'24, M.A.'26, Transylvania Col.; Ph.D.'43, Univ. of Chicago; LL.D. '43, Union Col.; Chairman, Dept. of Educ., Univ. of Chicago, Chicago, Ill., since 1951.

Selleck, Eugene R., Ph.B. in Ed.'29, Univ. of Wis.; M.S. in Ed. '32, Northwestern Univ.; Supt., Sch. Dist. 98, Berwyn, Ill., since 1949.

Seney, John E., M.A.'37, Northwestern Univ.; Prin., Fenger H. S., Chicago, Ill., since 1948.

Seybold, Harley J., M.S.'31, Univ. of Ill.; Supt. of Sch., Chenoa, Ill., since 1944.

Shafer, B. F., M.A.'23, Univ. of Chicago; Supt. of Sch., Freeport, Ill., since 1929.

Shafer, P. F., M.A.'38, Univ. of Ill.; Supt. of Sch. Dist. 185, Macomb, Ill., since 1941.

Shane, Harold G., B.Ed.'35, State Tchrs. Col., Milwaukee, Wis.; M.A.'39, Ph.D.'43, Ohio State Univ.; Prof. of Educ., Northwestern Univ., Evanston, Ill., since 1949.

Shannon, MacRae, B.S.'33, M.A.'37, Univ. of Ill.; Prin., Twp. H. S., Ottawa, Ill., since 1948.

Shapiro, Leo, Ph.B.'35, M.A.'36, De Paul Univ.; Ph.D.'47, Northwestern Univ.; Natl. Dir., Dept. of Educ., Anti-Defamation League, Chicago, Ill., since 1944.

Shea, Varian M., Ph.B.'16, A.M.'21, Univ. of Chicago; Dist. Supt. of H. S., Chicago, Ill., since 1948.

Sheehan, William E., B.S.'42, M.A.'44, Northwestern Univ.; Supt. of Sch., Deerfield, Ill., since 1945.

Shepherd, Warren P., M.S.'32, Univ. of Ill.; Supt. of Elem. Sch., Ottawa, Ill., since 1943.

Shute, Don D., M.S.'38, Univ. of Ill.; Asst. Supt. of Sch., East Peoria, Ill., since 1951.

Sifert, E. R., A.B.'13, Des Moines Univ.; M.A.'26, State Univ. of Iowa; Ph.D.'42, Univ. of Minn.; Supt., Proviso Twp. H. S., Maywood, Ill., since 1936.

Simmonds, E. S., B.S. in Ed.'23, M.S. in Ed.'31, Univ. of Ill.; Supt. of Sch., Morrison, Ill., since 1943.

Simmons, W. O., B.A.'27, Westminster Col.; M.A.'38, Univ. of Ill.; Dist. Supt. of Sch., Carlyle, Ill., since 1948.

Simpson, Richard L., Pres., Chas. A. Bennett Co., Inc., Peoria, Ill., since 1952.

Sires, Ely, B.S. in Ed.'39, Milwaukee State Tchrs. Col.; M.S. in Ed.'48, Univ. of Ill.; Supt. of Sch., Hazel Crest, Ill., since 1951.

Skinner, Kate E., B.A.'21, Cornell Col.; M.A.'38, State Univ. of Iowa; Elem. Supvr., Ginn and Co., Chicago, Ill., since 1936.

Smaage, Leon, B.A.'30, Buena Vista Col.; M.A.'36, Northwestern Univ.; Supt. of Sch., Des Plaines, Ill., since 1946.

Smiley, Rachel Turnbull, Ph.B.'31, Univ. of Chicago; M.A. in Ed.'46, De Paul Univ.; Prin. of Helen C. Peirce Sch., Chicago, Ill.

Smith, A. Edson, Ph.B.'20, Shurtleff Col.; M.A.'37, Univ. of Chicago; Prin., East Alton-Wood River Community H. S., Wood River, Ill., since 1949.

Smith, Bertrand LeRoy, B.S. and A.B.'34, Southwest Mo. State Tchrs. Col., Springfield; M.A.'37, Ed.D.'42, Tchrs. Col., Columbia Univ.; Supt. of Sch., Oak Park, Ill., since 1946.

Smith, Cecil E., B.Ed.'39, Eastern Ill. State Tchrs. Col., Charleston; M.S.'44, Univ. of Ill.; Supt., Community Unit Sch. Dist. 5, Chrisman, Ill.

Smith, James McKinnon, A.B.'21, McMaster Univ.; A.M.'22, Univ. of Chicago; Supt. of Twp. H. S., Lockport, Ill., since 1925.

Smith, Tilman R., A.B.'28, Goshen Col.; M.A.'32, State Univ. of Iowa; M.S.'39, Univ. of Ill.; Supt. of Sch., Community Unit Dist. 140, Eureka, Ill., since 1949.

Smola, Frank A., M.A.'32, Northwestern Univ.; Educ. Dir., Natl. Dairy Council, Chicago, Ill., since 1946.

Sohrbeck, Harold M., B.S.'29, Bradley Univ.; M.A.'40, Colo. State Col. of Educ., Greeley; Supt. of Grade Schs., East Moline, Ill., since 1940.

Sommers, Hobart H., Ph.B.'18, Univ. of Chicago; M.Ed.'31, Loyola Univ. (Ill.); Ed.D.'47, Iowa Wesleyan Col.; Asst. Supt. of Sch. in charge of Voc. Educ., Chicago, Ill., since 1948.

Spalding, Willard B., B.B.A.'26, Boston Univ.; Ed.M.'32, Univ. of N. H.; Ed.D.'42, Harvard Univ.; LL.D.'47, Pacific Univ.; Dean, Col. of Educ., Univ. of Ill., Urbana, Ill., since 1947.

Spearman, Cecil E., A.B.'32, M.A.'39, Univ. of Ala.; Ed.D.'43, Tchrs. Col., Columbia Univ.; Supt. of Sch., Hinsdale, Ill., since 1945.

Speltz, Arthur F., B.S.'19, Mich. State Univ.; M.A.'30, Univ. of Mich.; Supt. of Sch., Pontiac, Ill., since 1929.

Springman, John H., A.B.'31, Albion Col.; A.M.'34, Wayne Univ.; Ed.D.'44, Colo. State Col. of Educ., Greeley; Supt. of Sch., Glenview, Ill., since 1948.

Sprouse, Denson, B.Ed.'37, Eastern Ill. State Col., Charleston; M.A.'40, Univ. of Ill.; Supt., Panhandle Unit Sch. Dist. 2, Raymond, Ill., since 1948.

Spurgin, William H., B.S.'10, Illinois Wesleyan Univ.; M.A.'30, Univ. of Chicago; Dir. of Educ. Expenditures, Bd. of Educ., Chicago, Ill., since 1948.

Stack, Eileen C., Ph.D.'50, Northwestern Univ.; Prin., Foreman H. S., Chicago, Ill.

Stancliff, Glen, B.S.'28, Monmouth Col.; M.A.'36, State Univ. of Iowa; Supt. of Sch., La Harpe, Ill., since 1948.

Starke, Louis E., A.B.'26, Culver-Stockton Col.; A.M.'37, Univ. of Mo.; Supt. of Sch., Normal, Ill., since 1946.

Stateler, C. B., Sales Mgr., A. J. Nystrom & Co., Chicago, Ill.

Stead, Olin W., B.S.'27, Univ. of Ill.; M.S.'37, Univ. of Wyo.; Supt. of Sch., Carrollton, Ill., since 1940.

Steele, Maurice E., Pg.B. and A.B.'15, Valparaiso Univ.; Ph.B.'27, Univ. of Chicago; M.A.'33, Columbia Univ.; Supt. of Sch., Mendota, Ill., since 1927.

Steinmetz, Kathryn E., S.B.'25, A.M.'30, Univ. of Chicago; Dist. Supt. of Elem. Sch., Chicago, Ill., since 1948.

Stoddard, George Dinsmore, A.B.'21, Pa. State Col.; Diplôme '23, Univ. of Paris; Ph.D.'25, State Univ. of Iowa; Litt.D.'42, Colgate Univ.; LL.D.'42, St. Lawrence Univ.; LL.D.'42, Syracuse Univ.; LL.D.'42, Hobart Col.; LL.D.'43, New York Univ.; LL.D.'43, Skidmore Col.; L.H.D.'43, Alfred Univ.; LL.D.'44, Union Col.; LL.D.'46, Yeshiva Col.; LL.D.'48, Univ. of Fla., Lake Forest Col., and Wash. Univ.; Pres., Univ. of Ill., Urbana, Ill., since 1946.

Stork, Nelson N., B.S. in Ed.'28, Oakland City Col.; M.S. in Ed.'34, Ind. Univ.; Supt. of Elem. Sch. Dist. 72, Woodstock, Ill., since 1947.

Sturm, Mary Mark, Ph.B.'35, Univ. of Chicago; M.A.'39, Northwestern Univ.; Dir., Div. of Home Ec., Pub. Sch., Chicago, Ill., since 1945.

Sugden, W. E., M.A.'37, Colo. State Col. of Educ., Greeley; Supt. of Sch., River Forest, Ill., since 1950.

Sullivan, Samuel B., M.A.'33, State Univ. of Iowa; Supt. of Sch., De Kalb, Ill., since 1943.

Sumption, Merle R., Ph.D.'40, Ohio State Univ.; Head, Field Serv. Div., Bureau of Research and Serv., Col. of Educ., Univ. of Ill., Urbana, Ill., since 1946.

Sweat, Clifford H., A.B.'29, Knox Col.; M.A.'34, Univ. of Chicago; Asst. Supt. of Sch., Park Ridge, Ill., since 1944.

Sylla, Ben A. Ph.B.'28, M.A.'33, Univ. of Chicago; Supt. of Sch., Chicago Heights, Ill., since 1933.

Tabor, Forrest L., B.Ed.'39, Western Ill. State Col.; M.A.'41, Univ. of Ill.; Prin., Twp. H. S., Rock Falls, Ill., since 1950.

Taggart, Charles C., B.S.'14, Ohio Wesleyan Univ.; M.A.'35, Univ. of Chicago; Asst. Supt., Proviso Twp. H. S., Maywood, Ill., since 1937.

Taylor, Lillian, Ph.B.'29, M.A.'37, Univ. of Chicago; Prin., Pub. Sch., Chicago, Ill., since 1948.

Tazewell, R. L., M.A.'40, Northwestern Univ.; Co. Supt. of Sch., Woodstock, Ill., since 1949.

Theman, Viola, Ph.D.'42, Northwestern Univ.; Assoc. Prof., Sch. of Educ., Northwestern Univ.; Evanston Ill., since 1944.

Thokey, Carl, B.A.'25, DePauw Univ.; M.A.'36, Univ. of Wis.; Supt. of Reavis Comm. H. S., Oak Lawn, Ill., since 1950.

Thomas, Franklin C., B.A.'25, Mt. Morris Col.; M.A.'31, Univ. of Ill.; Supt. of Sch., Barrington, Ill., since 1944.

Thomasson, A. L., A.B.'25, Western Ky. State Tchrs. Col.; M.A.'28, George Peabody Col. for Tchrs.; Ph.D.'43, Univ. of Ill.; Prin., Jr. H. S., Champaign, Ill., since 1934.

Thompson, G. E., A.B.'15, Defiance Col.; A.M. '34, Univ. of Chicago; Supt. of Sch., St. Charles, Ill., since 1919.

Thompson, Orrin G., B.E.'33, Northern Ill. State Tchrs. Col., De Kalb; M.S.'36, Northwestern Univ.; Supt. of Sch., Elgin, Ill., since 1946.

Thornton, Kenneth W., Supt. of Sch., Williamsfield, Illinois.

Tibbetts, Keim Kendall, A.B.'10, Oberlin Col.; A.M.'31, Univ. of Chicago; Bus. Mgr., Pub. Sch., Wheaton, Ill., since 1928.

Tigard, Paul E., M.Ed.'42, Univ. of Wyo.; Supt., Community Consol. Sch. Dist. 19, Hebron, Ill., since 1943.

Torrens, John A., M.S.'34, Univ. of Ill.; Supt. of Co. Sch., Dixon, Ill., since 1939.

Traughber, T. Lloyd, Supt. of Sch., Oswego, Ill.

Travelstead, Clyde O., Supt. of Sch., Munderlein, Illinois.

Trimpe, Wilbur R. L., B.Ed.'42, Western Ill. State Tchrs. Col., Macomb; M.A.'45, Univ. of Ill.; Genl. Supt. of Sch., Community Unit Dist. 8, Bethalto, Ill., since 1950.

Troxel, Russell B., A.B.'23, Ill. Wesleyan Univ.; M.A.'34, Univ. of Ill.; Supt. of Sch., Farmington, Ill., since 1939.

Tureman, Cuba M., Co. Supt. of Sch., Hardin, Ill.

Turner, Maurice C., B.E.'27, North Ill. State Tchrs. Col.; M.A.'37, Northwestern Univ.; Supt. of Elem. Sch., Elmhurst, Ill., since 1950.

Tuttle, Edward M., B.S.A.'11, A.B.'13, Cornell Univ.; Exec. Secy., Natl. Sch. Bds. Assn., Chicago, Ill., since 1949.

*Tyler, Ralph W., A.B.'21, Doane Col.; A.M.'23, Univ. of Nebr.; Ph.D.'27, Univ. of Chicago; Prof. of Educ., since 1938, Univ. Examiner, since 1942, and Dean of Social Sciences, Univ. of Chicago, Chicago, Ill., since 1948.

Underbrink, Henry E., M.A.'30, Univ. of Chicago; Prin., Twp. H. S., Libertyville, Ill., since 1922.

Urquhart, Margaret, Prin., Elem. Sch., Chicago, Ill.

Urquhart, Mary, Ph.B.'30, Univ. of Chicago; M.E.'32, DePaul Univ.; Elem. Sch. Prin., Chicago, Ill., since 1944.

Van Hettinga, H., M.A.'32, State Univ. of Iowa; Mgr., Elem. Textbk. Dept., Ginn and Co., Chicago, Ill., since 1949.

Vick, Claude E., B.S.'25, M.S.'29, Univ. of Ill.; Ed.D.'35, Washington Univ.; Dir. of Professional and Pub. Relations, Ill. Educ. Assn., Springfield, Ill., since 1943.

Von Brock, Carl Edward, B.S.M.'31, DePauw Univ.; M.S. in Ed.'52, Southern Ill. Univ.; Supt. of Sch., Caseyville, Ill., since 1951.

Voshall, J. Harold, B.Ed.'29, Western Ill. State Tchrs. Col., Macomb; M.S.'35, Univ. of Ill.; Supt. of Pittsfield Community Unit Sch. Dist. 10, Pittsfield, Ill., since 1948.

Wagner, Paul Alexander, A.B.'38, Univ. of Chicago; A.M.'40, Yale Univ.; LL.D.'49, John B. Stetson Univ.; Exec. Dir., Film Council of America, Evanston, Ill., since 1952.

Wallschlaeger, Theo W., Prin., John Palmer Sch., Chicago, Ill., since 1948.

Walters, C. L., B.S.'27, M.S.'34, Univ. of Ill.; Supt. of Sch., Peotone, Ill., since 1933.

Walton, Eldred L., B.Ed.'41, Eastern Ill. State Col., Charleston; M.S.'46, Univ. of Ill.; Supt. of Sch., Community Unit 3, Kansas, Ill., since 1948.

Watson, Norman E., Ph.D.'42, Northwestern Univ.; Supt., Northfield Twp. H. S., Northbrook, Ill., since 1947.

Weaver, Paul H., A.B.'21, Heidelberg Univ.; M.A.'27, Ohio State Univ.; Supt., Sch. Dist. 143, Midlothian, Ill., since 1950.

Welch, W. M., B.S.'17, Univ. of Mich.; Sc.D.'22, Univ. de Blattereau, France; Pres., W. M. Welch Manufacturing Co., Chicago, Ill., since 1937.

Wells, George Newton, Diploma'21, Southern Ill. State Tchrs. Col., Carbondale; Ph.B.'28, M.A.'33, Univ. of Chicago; Supt. of Sch., Bloomington, Ill., since 1944.

Wendlandt, Elver H., M.Ed.'46, Univ. of Minn.; Supt. of Sch., Yates City, Ill., since 1951.

West, Byron, M.A.'40, Univ. of Mo.; Prin., Community H. S., Dist. 312, Carthage, Ill., since 1949.

Westlake, Glenn, B.E.'36, Northern Ill. State Tchrs. Col., De Kalb; M.A.'46, Northwestern Univ.; Supt. of Sch., Lombard, Ill., since 1944.

Wheeler, Bruce E., Diploma '22, Ill. State Normal Univ., Normal; A.B.'23, Carthage Col.; A.M.'29, Univ. of Chicago; Asst. Supt. of Sch., Springfield, Ill., since 1944.

White, Arthur L., B.Ed.'28, Western Ill. State Tchrs. Col., Macomb; M.A.'39, State Univ. of Iowa; Co. Supt. of Sch., Cambridge, Ill., since 1947.

Wilcox, Clifford G., Diploma '31, Ill. State Normal Univ., Normal; B.Ed.'36, Western State Tchrs. Col., Macomb, Ill.; M.A.'40, Univ. of Ill.; Supt., Twp. H. S., Savanna, Ill., since 1944.

Wilkins, George T., B.E.'37, Southern Ill. Univ.; Co. Supt. of Sch., Edwardsville, Ill., since 1947.

Willey, Gilbert S., B.S.'20, Univ. of Ill.; Ph.D.'26, Univ. of Wis.; Supt. of Sch., Winnetka, Ill.

Williams, Omer Stewart, Ph.D.'39, Northwestern Univ.; Dean, Woodrow Wilson Branch, Chicago City Col., Chicago, Ill., since 1948.

Williams, Ralph R., B.S.'17, M.A.'28, Univ. of Chicago; Prin., Yale Sch., Chicago, Ill., since 1935.

Wilson, Charles H., A.B.'34, Ohio Northern Univ.; M.A.'38, Northwestern Univ.; Ph.D.'49, Ohio State Univ.; Dist. Supt. of Sch., Highland Park, Ill.

Wilson, D. Clarence, B.Arch.'25, Univ. of Manitoba, Canada; Architect, 1108½ Main St., Mount Vernon, Ill., since 1938.

Wilson, Kenneth D., B.S.'24, Univ. of Ill.; M.A.'37, State Univ. of Iowa; Prin., Elem. Sch. Dist. 140, Marengo, Ill., since 1945.

Wilson, O. A., Jr., A.B.'33, Central Col. (Mo.); A.M.'39, Univ. of Mo.; Co. Supt. of Sch., Jerseyville, Ill., since 1951.

Wilson, William G., B.S.'25, Armour Inst. of Tech.; M.A.'32, Univ. of Chicago; Dist. Supt. of Sch., Chicago, Ill., since 1951.

Winegarner, J. Lewis, Ed.B.'34, Ill. State Normal Univ.; M.A.'40, Univ. of Ill.; Supt. of Sch., Harvey, Ill., since 1947.

Wingo, Charles E., B.A.'24, Furman Univ.; M.A.'37, Cornell Univ.; Supt. of Sch., Argo, Ill., since 1942.

Winkler, Clyde V., Ed.B.'29, Southern Ill. Univ.; M.A.'34, Univ. of Mich.; Supt. of Sch., Carbondale, Ill., since 1948.

Witt, Earl R., 245 Elgin, Forest Park, Ill.

Woellner, Robert Carlton, B.S.'15, Bradley Univ.; B.S.'22, Univ. of Cincinnati; M.A.'24, Univ. of Chicago; Dir., Voc. Guid. and Placement, Assoc. Prof. of Educ., Asst. Dean of Students, Univ. of Chicago, Chicago, Ill.

Wolters, A. E., B.S.'23, Iowa State Col.; M.S. in Ed.'34, Northwestern Univ.; Prin., H. S., Highland Park, Ill., since 1944.

Worst, Glenn C., Ph.B.'32, M.Ed.'34, Loyola Univ.; Prin., Calumet H. S., Chicago, Ill., since 1939.

Wright, Roe M., B.Ed.'33, Southern Ill. Univ.; M.A.'39, Univ. of Ill.; Supt., Central Unit Sch., Robinson, Ill.

Yates, Harry D., B.S.'32, Nebr. State Tchr. Col., Kearney; M.A.'37, Colo. State Col. of Educ., Greeley; Supt. of Elem. Sch., Lockport, Ill., since 1949.

Ylvisaker, Herman L., B.A.'15, Luther Col.; M.A.'24, Univ. of Chicago; Prin., Leyden Community H. S., Franklin Park, Ill., since 1940.

Young, Paul Arlington, B.S.'27, Iowa State Tchrs. Col., Cedar Falls; A.M.'43, Doctorate '47, Northwestern Univ.; Supt., York Community H. S., Elmhurst, Ill., since 1950.

Youngert, Eugene, A.B.'20, Augustana Col.; A.M.'37, Ed.D.'39, Columbia Univ.; Ed.D.'45, Cornell Col.; Supt., Twp. H. S., Oak Park, Ill., since 1941.

INSTITUTIONAL MEMBERS

Acquisitions Department, Univ. of Chicago Libr., Chicago, Ill.

Bell and Howell Company, 7100 McCormick Rd., Chicago 45, Ill.

Board of Education, Dist. #104, Argo, Ill.

The Chicago Public Library, 78 E. Washington St., Chicago 2, Ill.

F. E. Compton and Company, C. S. Jones, Vicepres., 1000 N. Dearborn St., Chicago 10, Ill.

Department of Registration and Education, Southern Ill. Univ., Carbondale, Ill.

Division of Libraries, Bd. of Educ., Chicago, Ill.

Illinois State Library, Springfield, Ill.

The Joseph Schaffner Library, Northwestern Univ., Chicago, Ill.

Librarian, Science Research Associates, 57 W. Grand Ave., Chicago 10, Ill.

Library, Eastern Ill. State Tchrs. Col., Charleston, Ill.

Library, Natl. Col. of Educ., Evanston, Ill.

Library, Northwestern University, Evanston, Ill.

Library, Western Ill. State Tchrs. Col., Macomb, Ill.

Natl. Congress of Parents and Tchrs., 600 South Michigan Blvd., Chicago, Ill.

Northern Illinois State Teachers College, De Kalb, Ill.

Periodical Division, Univ. of Ill. Lib., Urbana, Ill.

Riverside-Brookfield Twp. High School, Riverside, Ill.

INDIANA

INDIVIDUAL MEMBERS

Abbett, Merle J., A.B.'07, LL.D.'49, Franklin Col.; A.M.'18, Columbia Univ.; Supt. of Sch., Fort Wayne, Ind., 1932-52 (retired).

Alexander, Gerald, A.B.'25, Wabash Col.; A.M.'30, Ind. Univ.; Supt. of Sch., Greensburg, Ind.

Allen, Frank E., A.B.'16, A.M.'23, Ind. Univ.; Supt. of Sch., South Bend, Ind., since 1931.

Allman, H. B., B.S.'10, Tri-State Col.; M.A.'31, Ind. Univ.; Prof. of Sch. Admin. and Dir., Summer Sessions, Ind. Univ., Bloomington, Ind., since 1946.

Asbell, Ernest, B.S., A.B., M.A.'36, Butler Univ.; Supt. of Community Sch., Shoals, Ind., since 1951.

Baker, John Emerson, A.B.'31, DePauw Univ.; M.A.'37, Univ. of Minn.; Ph.D.'52, Univ. of Chicago; Prof. of Educ., Ball State Tchrs. Col., Muncie, Ind., since 1948.

Banks, Ralph H., A.B.'27, Ind. State Tchrs. Col.; M.S.'33, Ind. Univ.; Supt. of Sch., Vincennes, Ind., since 1943.

Bechdolt, Burley V., A.B.'30, De Pauw Univ.; M.S. in Ed.'35, Ind. Univ.; Dir. of Research, Ind. State Tchrs. Assn., since 1940, and Study Dir., Ind. Sch. Study Commn., Indianapolis, Ind., since 1949.

Becker, Ralph, A.B.'28, Hastings Col.; M.A.'35, Tchrs. Col., Columbia Univ.; Supt. of Sch., Evansville, Ind., since 1947.

Beckes, Isaac K., B.S. in Ed.'35, Ind. State Tchrs. Col.; B.D.'38, McCormick Theol. Sem.; Ph.D.'45, Yale Univ.; Pres., Vincennes Univ., Vincennes, Ind., since 1950.

Bennett, Paul E., B.S.'33, Manchester Col.; M.S.'39, Ind. Univ.; Supt., Wayne Twp. Sch., Fort Wayne, Ind., since 1951.

Berger, Lowe, B.A.'19, Columbia Univ.; M.A.'21, Univ. of Mich.; Vicepres., Bobbs-Merrill Co., Indianapolis, Ind., since 1928.

Bergwall, Evan H., A.B.'39, Taylor Univ.; B.D.'43, Yale Divinity Sch.; Pres., Taylor Univ., Upland, Ind., since 1951.

Binford, H. E., A.B.'17, Ind. State Tchrs. Col., Terre Haute; A.M.'23, Tchrs. Col., Columbia Univ.; Supt. of Sch., Bloomington, Ind., since 1935.

Blackburn, Elisha Phillips, A.B.'24, Oakland City Col.; M.S.'35, Ind. Univ.; Supt. of Sch., Hartford City, Ind., since 1946.

Blasingham, Sue, Member, Bd. of Educ., Logansport, Ind., since 1949.

Boehm, Myron P., B.Ed.'42, Central YMCA Col., Chicago, Ill.; M.Ed.'49, Ind. Univ.; Supt. of Pub. Sch., Campbellsburg, Ind., since 1950.

Boomershine, Howard, M.S.'42, Purdue Univ.; Supt. of Sch., Angola, Ind., since 1947.

Boston, Paul F., A.B.'17, Ind. State Tchrs. Col., Terre Haute; A.M.'25, Columbia Univ.; Supt. of Sch., La Porte, Ind., since 1943.

Brock, Dale E., B.S.'39, M.S.'41, Ind. Univ.; Supt. of Sch., Connersville, Ind., since 1952.

Bulleit, Robert B., A.B.'33, DePauw Univ.; M.S.'40, Ind. Univ.; Supt. of Sch., Salem, Ind., since 1949.

Burt, Carl W., A.B.'27, Manchester Col.; A.M. '30, Univ. of Chicago; Supt. of Sch., Warsaw, Ind., since 1943.

Bush, George H., B. S. in E.E.'22, Kansas State Col. of Agr. and Applied Science; M.S. in Ed. '37, Ind. Univ.; Assoc. Prof. in Trade and Indus. Educ., Purdue Univ., Lafayette, Ind., since 1938.

Caldwell, Lee L., A.B., Simpson Col.; B.A., Iowa State Tchrs. Col., Cedar Falls, Iowa; Supt. of Sch., Hammond, Ind., since 1922.

Campbell, James A., A.B.'26, DePauw Univ.; M.S.'42, Ind. Univ.; Supt. of Sch., Seymour, Ind., since 1951.

Carpenter, Leewell Hunter, A.B.'24, Miami Univ.; A.M.'28, Univ. of Chicago; Supt. of Sch., Wabash, Ind., since 1946.

Castor, E. S., A.B.'33, M.A. in Ed.'38, Ball State Tchrs. Col.; Supt. of Sch., Rochester, Ind., since 1949.

Chadd, Archie R., B.A.'28, M.A.'42, Butler Univ.; Supt. of Sch., Anderson, Ind., since 1942.

Chambers, J. W., M.S.'45, Ind. State Tchrs. Col.; Supt. of Sch., French Lick, Ind., since 1949.

Christian, Thomas L., A.B.'17, A.M.'22, Wabash Col.; Supt. of Sch., Lebanon, Ind., since 1943.

Church, Harold H., A.B.'18, Albright Col.; A.M.'29, Tchrs. Col., Columbia Univ.; Ph.D. '43, Ohio State Univ.; Dir., Div. of Research and Field Services, Sch. of Educ., Ind. Univ., Bloomington, Ind., since 1949.

Collins, Vance B., M.S.'36, Ind. Univ.; Supt. of Sch., North Vernon, Ind., since 1945.

Cory, Frank Mirl, A.B.'17, Ind. Univ.; A.M.'23, Tchrs. Col., Columbia Univ.; Supt. of Sch., Hagerstown, Ind., since 1926.

Craw, J. R., A.B.'27, M.A.'36, Butler Univ.; Supt. of Sch., New Castle, Ind., since 1944.

Cunningham, Clyde, B.S.'24, Ind. State Tchrs. Col., Terre Haute; M.A.'32, Tchrs. Col., Columbia Univ.; Supt. of Sch., Peru, Ind., since 1947.

Curtis, Glenn M., M.S.'40, B.S.'30, Ind. State Tchrs. Col., Terre Haute; Supt. of Sch., Martinsville, Ind., since 1948.

Davidson, Harry R., A.B.'28, Ind. Central Col.; M.S.'37, Ind. Univ.; Supt. of Sch., New Albany, Ind., since 1944.

Dilley, Norman E., B.S.Ed.'41, State Tchrs. Col., Edinboro, Pa.; M.A. in Ed.'47, Washington Univ.; Teaching Fellow, Sch. of Educ., Ind. Univ., Bloomington, Ind., since 1952.

Driver, H. E., A.B.'09, Ind. Univ.; Supt. of Sch.. Aurora, Ind., since 1931.

Eash, C. E., B.A.'10, M.A.'27, Ind. Univ.; Prin., Warren Central H. S., Indianapolis, Ind., since 1924.

Eberhart, Elder J., A.B.'24, Ind. Univ.; M.A.'32, Columbia Univ.; Co. Supt. of Sch., Evansville, Ind., since 1948.

Eikenberry, Wayne, A.B.'30, Manchester Col.; M.S.'36, Ind. Univ.; Supt., Delphi-Deercreek Twp. Consol. Sch., Delphi, Ind., since 1949.

Eiler, C. Emmet, A.B.'27, Manchester Col.; A.M.'36, Univ. of Chicago; Asst. State Supt. of Pub. Instr., Indianapolis, Ind., since 1951.

Elliott, Edward Charles, B.Sc.'95, A.M.'97, LL.D.'36, Univ. of Nebr.; Ph.D.'05, LL.D. '29, Columbia Univ.; LL.D.'28, De Pauw Univ.; LL.D.'28, Butler Univ.; LL.D.'30, Oregon Agrl. Col.; LL.D.'40, Ind. Univ.; Litt.D.'41, Hahnemann Med. Col. and Hospital; L.H.D.'43, Univ. of Pittsburgh; D.Sc.'44, Ill. Inst. of Tech.; LL.D.'47, Purdue Univ.; D.Sc.'48, Temple Univ. Address: 538 S. Seventh St., Lafayette, Ind.

Emens, John R., A.B.'25, State Normal Col., Ypsilanti, Mich.; M.A.'26, Ph.D.'36, Univ. of Mich.; Pres., Ball State Tchrs. Col., Muncie, Ind., since 1945.

Eskew, Phil N., A.B.'29, Oakland City Col.; M.S.'33, Ind. Univ.; Supt., City Sch., Sullivan, Ind., since 1951.

Estell, Edwin Randolph, B.S.'38, M.S.'41, Ind. Univ.; Supt. of Sch., Washington, Ind., since 1946.

Eve, Lee L., A.B.'24, Manchester Col.; A.M.'28, Ind. Univ.; Supt. of Sch., Crawfordsville, Ind., since 1950.

Eyster, Elvin S., B.S.'26, M.S.'31, Ed.D.'45, Ind. Univ.; Prof. of Bus. Admin. and Assoc. Dir. of Guidance and Placement Bureau, Sch. of Bus., Ind. Univ., Bloomington, Ind., since 1941.

Fechtman, Fred D., B.S.Ed.'37, M.S.Ed.'44, Ind. Univ.; Supt. of Sch., Tell City, Ind., since 1949.

Floyd, William, M.S. in Ed.'36, Butler Univ.; Supt. of Sch., West Lafayette, Ind., since 1945.

Foster, Isaac Owen, B.S. in Ed.'21, M.S. in Ed.'22, Ph.D.'25, Univ. of Ill.; Assoc. Prof. of Educ., Ind. Univ., Bloomington, Ind., since 1926.

Franklin, William E., B.A.'35, Hanover Col.; M.S.'39, Ind. Univ.; Supt. of Sch., Milan, Ind., since 1949.

Franzén, Carl Gustave Frederick, A.B.'08, Univ. of Pa.; M.A.'12, Ph.D.'20, State Univ. of Iowa; Prof. of Sec. Educ., Ind. Univ., Bloomington, Ind., since 1923.

French, Clifford, M.A.'26, Ind. Univ.; Prin. of Royerton Sch., Muncie, Ind., since 1928.

Galey, F. Stanton, B.S.'16, Purdue Univ.; M.A. '37, Ind. Univ.; Supt. of Sch., Fairmount, Ind., since 1929.

Gallagher, Bernard, M.A.'34, Ind. Univ.; Supt. of Sch., Jasper, Ind., since 1946.

Garrison, Paul C., B.S. in Ed.'31, Oakland City Col.; M.S. in Ed.'36, Ind. Univ.; Supt. of Sch., Richmond, Ind., since 1946.

Garver, Harlie, B.S.'14, Hiram Col.; M.A.'26, Columbia Univ.; Supt. of Sch., Hobart, Ind., since 1940.

Gerichs, George W., A.B.'30, Central Normal; M.S.'41, Butler Univ.; Co. Supt. of Sch., Winamac, Ind., since 1946.

Gillespie, F. H., B.A.'27, DePauw Univ.; M.S. '32, Purdue Univ.; Supt., Monticello and Union Twp. Sch., Monticello, Ind., since 1941.

Gladden, Robert F., A.B.'32, M.S.'44, Butler Univ.; Co. Supt. of Sch., Indianapolis, Ind., since 1944.

Glenn, Edward E., A.B.'32, Oakland City Col.; M.S.'35, Ind. Univ.; Supt. of Sch., Boonville, Ind., since 1949.

Goldman, Ray, A.B.'26, Oakland City Col.; M.S.'32, Ind. Univ.; Supt. of Sch., Huntingburg, Ind., since 1938.

Grayson, Cecil A., A.B.'15, Indiana Univ.; Co. Supt. of Sch., Crown Point, Ind., since 1937.

Grinnell, Melvin Walter, B.S.'28, Evansville Col.; M.A.'36, Ind. Univ.; Head of Bus. Central H. S., Evansville, Ind., since 1918.

Gunn, Cyrus L., Supt. of Sch., Mt. Vernon, Ind.

Hamer, O. Stuart, A.B.'13, Mt. Morris Col.; A.M.'14, Univ. of Chicago; Ph.D.'30, Univ. of Iowa; Prof. of Educ., Manchester Col., North Manchester, Ind., since 1931.

Harris, Ernest A., A.B.'22, Hanover Col.; M.A. '27, Univ. of Chicago; H. S. Prin., Pendleton, Ind., since 1950.

Harrison, H. P., M.Ed.'44, Univ. of Cincinnati; Supt. of Sch., Lawrenceburg, Ind., since 1942.

Hiatt, J. Russell, B.S.'41, Ball State Tchrs. Col.; M.S.'46, Ind. Univ.; Supt. of Sch., Lafayette, Ind., since 1952.

Hodges, Thomas F., M.S.'41, Ind. Univ.; Co. Supt. of Sch., Spencer, Ind., since 1943.

Holden, John W., B.S.'28, M.S.'41, Ind. State Tchrs. Col., Terre Haute; Supt. of City Sch., Rockport, Ind., since 1946.

Holmstedt, Raleigh Warren, A.B.'24, Hastings Col.; M.A.'27, Ph.D.'32, Tchrs. Col., Columbia Univ.; Prof. of Educ., Ind. Univ., Bloomington, Ind., since 1929.

Hopkins, Lowell, M.A.'31, Univ. of Mo.; Dir. of Elem. Educ., Evansville, Ind., since 1951.

Hughes, Otto, A.B.'28, Franklin Col.; M.A.'30, Ed.D.'50, Ind. Univ.; Prin., Univ. Sch., Ind. Univ., Bloomington, Ind., since 1945.

Huntington, Ira Leo, Supt. of Sch., Rensselaer, Ind.

Ireland, Leonard, B.S.'32, M.A.'47, Ball State Tchrs. Col. (Ind.); Supt. of Sch., Edinburg, Ind., since 1952.

Jacob, Lewis S., A.B.'33, Hanover Col.; M.S.'39, Butler Univ.; Supt. of Metropolitan Sch. Dist., Pendleton, Ind., since 1950.

Johnshoy, Howard G., B.A.'40, Concordia Col.; M.A.'47, Ed.D.'51, Tchrs. Col., Columbia Univ.; Admin. Asst. to Pres., Ball State Tchrs. Col., Muncie, Ind., since 1951.

Jordan, Richard C., A.B.'33, Manchester Col.; M.A.'39, Ball State Tchrs. Col.; Supt. of Sch., Speedway, Indianapolis, Ind., since 1948.

Kashner, William H., B.S.C.E.'41, Purdue Univ.; Supt., Physical Plant, City Sch., Lafayette, Ind., since 1949.

Kendall, William R., B.S.'34, Ind. State Tchrs. Col., Terre Haute; M.A. in Ed.'39, Ind. Univ.; Supt. of Sch., Nappanee, Ind., since 1949.

Kerr, A. G., B.S.'26, Ball State Tchrs. Col.; M.S.'34, Ind. Univ.; Supt. of Sch., Columbia City, Ind., since 1935.

Kinsey, Clarence V., A.B.'23, Ind. State Tchrs. Col., Terre Haute; M.S.'33, Butler Univ.; Supt. of Sch., Beech Grove, Ind., since 1945.

Kirklin, Curtis D., Prof. of Educ., Franklin College, Franklin, Ind.

Klitzke, Lyle K., B.A.'29, State Univ. of Iowa; M.A.'34, Univ. of Chicago; Supt. of Sch., Plymouth, Ind., since 1949.

Knapp, M. L., A.B.'19, Ind. Univ.; A.M.'26, Columbia Univ.; Supt. of Sch., Michigan City, Ind., since 1939.

Kraft, Milton Edward, Ph.D.'34, Univ. of Ill.; Prof. of Educ., Earlham Col., Richmond, Ind., since 1948.

Lambert, John W., Trustee, Pub. Sch., Daleville, Ind., since 1947.

Laughlin, Harvey, A.B.'26, A.M.'34, Ind. State Tchrs. Col., Terre Haute; Supt. of Sch., Mooresville, Ind., since 1949.

Light, J. Everett, B.S.'34, Ball State Tchrs. Col.; M.A.'41, Columbia Univ.; Supt. of Sch., Rushville, Ind., since 1945.

Lindley, Aaron T., A.B.'25, Earlham Col.; M.S. '30, Butler Univ.; Supt. of Sch., Fort Wayne, Ind., since 1952.

Lockwood, Luther A., A.B.'17, Ind. State Tchrs. Col.; M.A.'39, Univ. of Chicago; Supt. of Sch., Columbus, Ind., since 1945.

Loper, William F., A.M.'30, Ind. Univ.; Supt. of Sch., Shelbyville, Ind., since 1934.

Love, H. D., A.B.'32, M.S.'39, Ind. Univ.; Supt. of Sch., Scottsburg, Ind., since 1950.

Loveless, Edward E., B.S.'40, M.S. in Ed., Purdue Univ.; Supt. of Sch., Brook, Ind., since 1952.

Lutz, Charles D., M.A.'32, Univ. of Chicago; Supt. of Sch., Gary, Ind., since 1941.

McCann, Lloyd E., A.B.'35, Nebr. State Tchrs. Col., Peru; M.A.'39, Ed.D.'51, Colo. State Col. of Educ., Greeley; Asst. Prof. of Educ. Admin., Butler Univ., Indianapolis, Ind., since 1952.

McClelland, Mary M., M.S.'44, Butler Univ.; Prin., Ben Davis Grade Sch., Indianapolis, Ind., since 1943.

McKenney, H. L., B.S.'07, A.B. in Ed.'22, Valparaiso Univ.; A.M. in Ed.'31, Univ. of Cincinnati; Supt. of Sch., Auburn, Ind., since 1923.

McReynolds, George W., A.B.'15, Ind. Univ.; Supt. of Sch., Lawrenceburg, Ind., since 1949.

Maier, John V., A.B.'20, A.M.'29, Ed.D.'40, Ind. Univ.; Prin., Wilson Jr. H. S., Muncie, Ind., since 1934.

Miller, Ernest Edgar, A.B.'17, Goshen Col.; M.A.'27, Ph.D.'39, New York Univ.; Pres., Goshen Col., Goshen, Ind., since 1940.

Minniear, E. V., B.Pd.'17, Tri-State Col.; B.S.'28, Ball State Tchrs. Col.; M.S. in Ed.'34, Ind. Univ.; Supt. of City Sch., Garrett, Ind., since 1947.

Mitchell, James Russell, B.S.'30, M.S.'35, Ind. Univ.; Dir. of Tchr. Placement and Assoc. Prof. of Educ., Purdue Univ., Lafayette, Ind., since 1945.

Monbeck, Lon P., A.B.'34, Manchester Col.; M.A.'36, Columbia Univ.; Supt. of Sch., Highland, Ind., since 1950.

Morgan, Hedley G., A.B.'25, Ind. State Tchrs. Col., Terre Haute; A.M.'29, Univ. of Mich.; Supt., Montpelier-Harrison Twp. Sch., Montpelier, Ind., since 1933.

Morland, John B., A.B.'40, Valparaiso Univ.; A.M.'41, Univ. of Ky.; Supvg. Prin. of Pub. Sch., Bremen, Ind., since 1950.

Mourer, Harry H., A.B.'13, A.M.'23, Ind. Univ.; Supt. of Sch., Bedford, Ind., since 1938.

407

Muncie, E. O., Supt. of City Sch., Madison, Ind.

Neff, Gerald R., B.S. in Ed.'38, Manchester Col.; M.S. in Ed.'40, Ind. Univ.; Asst. Supt. of Sch., Mishawaka, Ind., since 1947.

Nicely, Paul W., M.S.'41, Ind. Univ.; Prin., Francis Willard Sch. 80, Indianapolis, Ind.

Patterson, Ruth, Diploma '04, Tchrs. Col. of Indianapolis; B.S.'33, A.M.'39, Tchrs. Col., Columbia Univ.; Asst. Prof. of Kdgn. Educ. and Supvr. of Kdgn. Student Tchg., Butler Univ., Indianapolis, Ind., since 1930.

Peregrine, Donald, A.B.'22, Valparaiso Univ.; M.S.'36, Purdue Univ.; Co. Supt. of Sch., Knox, Ind., since 1945.

Phillips, G. Warren, A.B.'30, De Pauw Univ.; M.S.'35, Ind. Univ.; Supt. of Sch., Valparaiso, Ind., since 1944.

Phillips, L. V., A.B.'15, Ind. Univ.; M.A.'27, Columbia Univ.; Commr. of H. S. Athletics, Indianapolis, Ind., since 1945.

Pitts, Kenneth E., M.S. in Ed.'34, Ind. Univ.; Supt. of Sch., Corydon, Ind., since 1949.

Porter, Stanley, A.B.'25, Franklin Col. of Ind.; M.S.'30, Ind. Univ.; Supt. of Sch., Greenwood, Ind., since 1950.

Pound, Clarence A., B.S.'27, Ind. State Tchrs. Col., Terre Haute; M.A.'31, Univ. of Chicago; Assoc. Prof. of Educ., Purdue Univ., Lafayette, Ind., since 1948.

Pruett, J. W., M.S.'39, Ind. Univ.; Supt. of Sch., Princeton, Ind., since 1947.

Purcell, Borden R., B.S. and M.S.'34, Ind. Univ.; Dir. of Field Serv. and Placement, Ind. State Tchrs. Assn., Indianapolis, Ind., since 1944.

Purcell, William E., A.B.'28, M.A.'42, Ind. State Tchrs. Col.; Co. Supt. of Sch., Terre Haute, Ind., since 1948.

Rapp, Earl W., A.M.'30, Univ. of Wis.; Supt. of Sch., New Harmony, Ind., since 1930.

Rayburn, Russell H., B.S.'29, M.S.'33, Ind. State Tchrs. Col.; Dir. of Sch. Inspection, State Dept. of Pub. Instr., Indianapolis, Ind., since 1946.

Rice, Joe C., M.S.'36, A.B.'37, Ind. Univ.; Supt. of Sch., Elkhart, Ind.

Riordan, Emmet L., A.B.'14, Ind. State Tchrs. Col., Terre Haute; M.S. in Ed.'37, Ind. Univ.; Supt. of Sch., Whiting, Ind., since 1949.

Robbins, Clarence E., A.B.'35, DePauw Univ.; A.M.'43, Ind. State Tchrs. Col.; Supt. of Sch., Spencer, Ind., since 1951.

Rogers, L. E., A.B.'19, A.M.'27, Ind. Univ.; Supt. of Sch., Knightstown, Ind., since 1920.

Ross, Frank A., A.B.'31, De Pauw Univ.; M.A.'38, Ind. Univ.; Supt. of Sch., Union City, Ind., since 1946.

Roudebush, Earl D., A.B.'12, M.S.'27, Ind. Univ.; Supt. of Sch., Winamac, Ind., since 1925.

Salisbury, Charles B., A.B.'28, Franklin Col.; M.A.'38, Ball State Tchrs. Col.; Supt. of Sch., Dunkirk, Ind., since 1951.

Sargent, Galen B., A.B.'23, Manchester Col.; A.M.'36, Northwestern Univ.; Bus. Mgr., South Bend, Ind., since 1951.

Schafer, Dan A., B.S.'40, Manchester Col.; M.S.'47, Ind. Univ.; Supt. of City Sch., Rensselaer, Ind., since 1952.

Schulte, Harold F., A.B.'27, Ind. Univ.; M.A.'31, Ind. State Tchrs. Col.; Supt. of Sch., Jeffersonville, Ind., since 1951.

Scott, Keith, A.B.'31, Ind. State Tchrs. Col., Terre Haute; M.A.'41, Ball State Tchrs. Col.; Supt. of Sch., Elwood, Ind., since 1947.

*Seagers, Paul William, A.B.'27, Cornell Univ.; M.A.'32, Ed.D.'50, Columbia Univ.; Assoc. Prof. of Educ., Sch. of Educ., Ind. Univ., Bloomington, Ind.' since 1947.

Senour, Alfred C., B.A.'17, Ind. State Tchrs. Col.; M.A.'27, Univ. of Chicago; Supt. of Sch., East Chicago, Ind., since 1943.

Shaffer, Roscoe D., A.B.'24, Ball State Tchrs. Col.; M.Sc. in Ed.'33, Ind. Univ.; Supt. of Sch., Muncie, Ind., since 1946.

Sharp, William B., B.A.'32, Col. of Wooster; M.S. in Ed.'36, Ind. Univ.; Supt. of Sch., Rockville, Ind., since 1946.

Shibler, Herman L., A.B.'29, M.A.'32, Ph.D.'41, Ohio State Univ.; Supt. of Sch., Indianapolis, Ind., since 1950.

Shipman, Stuart C., Supt. of Sch., Cambridge City, Ind., since 1949.

*Smith, Henry Lester, A.B.'98, A.M.'99, Ind. Univ.; A.M.'10, Ph.D.'16, Columbia Univ.; LL.D.'40, Butler Univ.; Pres., Natl. Educ. Assn., 1934-35; Consultant on Schoolhouse Planning, State Dept. of Pub. Instr., Bloomington, Ind., since 1946.

Snider, R. Nelson, A.B.'22, Ball State Tchrs. Col.; M.A.'30, Columbia Univ.; Prin., South Side H. S., Fort Wayne, Ind., since 1926.

Sonner, Cecil B., A.B.'35, Ind. State Tchrs. Col., Terre Haute; M.S.'39, Ind. Univ.; Supt. of Sch., Charlestown, Ind., since 1948.

Sparks, Frank Hugh, A.B.'35, Butler Univ.; A.M.'37, Ph.D.'41, Univ. of Southern Calif.; LL.D.'41, Butler Univ.; LL.D.'41, Hanover Col.; L.H.D.'45, Bucknell Univ.; LL.D.'47, De Pauw Univ.; Pres., Wabash Col., Crawfordsville, Ind., since 1941.

Standley, James W., B.S.'30, Ind. State Tchrs. Col., Terre Haute; M.S.'35, Ind. Univ.; Prin., Tolleston H. S., Gary, Ind., since 1935.

Stapley, M.E., B.A.'28, State Univ. of Iowa; M.S. in Ed.'38, Ed.D.'47, Ind. Univ.; Assoc. Prof. of Educ., Ind. Univ., Bloomington, Ind.

Stemen, C. B., A.B.'24, A.M.'25, Ind. Univ.; Supt. of Sch., Tipton, Ind., since 1950.

Stephan, Burton, M.A.'29, Ind. Univ.; Supt. of Sch., Huntington, Ind., since 1941.

Stinebaugh, Virgil, A.B.'21, LL.D.'45, Manchester Col.; A.M.'27, Tchrs. Col., Columbia Univ.; Supt. of Sch., Indianapolis, Ind., 1944-50. Address: 150 N. Meridian St., Indianapolis 4, Ind.

Strickland, Ruth G., B.S.'25, M.A.'32, Tchrs. Col., Columbia Univ.; Ph.D.'38, Columbia Univ.; Assoc. Prof. of Educ., Ind. Univ., Bloomington, Ind., since 1939.

Sutton, Clyde S., B.S.'33, Central Normal Col.; M.S.'42, Butler Univ.; Co. Supt. of Sch., Goshen, Ind., since 1949.

Swain, Charles I., M.S.E.'49, Ind. Univ.; Supt. of Sch., Cannelton, Ind., since 1950.

Swalls, J. Fred, A.B.'32, Ind. State Tchrs. Col.; M.S.'39, Ed.D.'50, Ind. Univ.; Assoc. Prof. of Educ., Ind. State Tchrs. Col., Terre Haute, Ind., since 1946.

Swanson, Dale V., B.S.'27, Purdue Univ.; M.S.'35, Ind. Univ.; Supt. of Sch., Noblesville, Ind., since 1950.

Swihart, O. M., A.B.'28, N. Manchester Col.; M.S.'36, Ind. Univ.; Supt. of Sch., Kokomo, Ind., since 1946.

Swingley, Clarence E., A.B.'28, Ball State Tchrs. Col.; M.A.'31, Ph.D.'50, Univ. of Chicago; Prin., Edison Elem. and H. S., Gary, Ind., since 1943.

Thompson, Gordon, Dir., Orchard School, Indianapolis, Ind.

Tirey, Ralph Noble, A.B.'18, A.M.'27, LL.D.'45, Ind. Univ.; Pres., Ind. State Tchrs. Col., Terre Haute, Ind., since 1934.

Tower, J. Harold, A.B.'22, Ind. State Tchrs. Col., Terre Haute; M.S.'39, Ind. Univ.; Co. Supt. of Sch., LaPorte, Ind., since 1945.

Trible, Dierdre, Supt. of Special Educ., Evansville, Ind.

Ulery, Cloyce B., M.A.'27, Ohio State Univ.; Editor, Educ. Dept., Bobbs-Merrill Co., Indianapolis, Ind., since 1944.

Van Slyke, Frank A., B.S.'37, Canterbury Col.; M.S.'40, Ind. Univ.; Supt. of Sch., Griffith, Ind., since 1947.

Walker, Deane E., A.B.'22, Tri-State Col.; A.M.'28, Tchrs. Col., Columbia Univ.; State Supt. of Pub. Instr., Indianapolis, Ind., 1949-51. Address: 404 East Shore St., Culver, Ind.

Walker, Robert R., Pres., Robert R. Walker, Inc., South Bend, Ind., since 1946.

Walsh, J. Hartt, Ed.B.'27, State Tchrs. Col., Eau Claire, Wis.; Ph.B.'27, Ripon Col.; M.A.'34, Univ. of Minn.; Ph.D.'44, Univ. of Wis.; Dean, Col. of Educ., Butler Univ., Indianapolis, Ind., since 1948.

Watson, Wayne P., M.S.'30, Ind. Univ.; Supt. of Sch., Terre Haute, Ind., since 1946.

Weaver, Robert B., A.B.'22, De Pauw Univ.; A.M.'26, Univ. of Chicago; Supt. of Sch., Goshen, Ind., since 1942.

Weller, D. S., A.B.'20, Ind. Univ.; A.M.'23, Columbia Univ.; Supt. of Sch., Portland, Ind., since 1940.

Wells, Herman B., B.S.'24, A.M.'27, Ind. Univ.; LL.D.'39, Butler Univ., Rose Polytech. Inst., De Pauw Univ.; LL.D.'42, Wabash Col.; LL.D.'46, Univ. of Wis.; LL.D.'48, Earlham Col.; Pres., Ind. Univ., Bloomington, Ind., since 1937.

Wesner, Philip M., B.S.'28, M.S.'33, Ind. Univ.; Supt. of Sch., Paoli, Ind., since 1951.

Westfall, Byron L., B.S. in Ed.'29, A.M.'32, Ph.D.'35, Univ. of Mo.; Prin. of Lab. Sch. and Dir., Div. of Tchg., Ind. State Tchrs. Col., Terre Haute, Ind., since 1946.

Whiteman, Harris, A.B.'31, Western State Tchrs. Col., Kalamazoo, Mich.; M.A.'37, Columbia Univ.; Prin., Jr. H. S., Goshen, Ind., since 1932.

Whiteman, Kelro, B.S.'29, Ball State Tchrs. Col.; M.S.'33, Ind. Univ.; Supt. of Sch., Alexandria, Ind.

Whitmer, Dana P., Asst. Supt., in charge of Educ. Admin., Pub. Sch., Gary, Ind., since 1950.

Wilson, William E., A.B.'20, Hanover Col.; M.S.'31, Ind. State Tchrs. Col., Terre Haute; Co. Supt. of Sch., Jeffersonville, Ind., since 1933.

Wisehart, Charles S., B.S.Elem. Ed.'40, Ball State Tchrs. Col.; M.S.Ed.Adm.'42, Ind. Univ.; Supt. of Sch., Greenfield, Ind.

Wood, Earl L., A.B.'25, Central Normal Col., Danville, Ind.; M.S.'30, Ind. Univ.; Supt. of City Sch., Franklin, Ind.

Woodruff, S. M., B.S.'30, Ind. State Tchrs. Col., Terre Haute; M.S.'35, Purdue Univ.; Supt. of Sch., Frankfort, Ind., since 1949.

Wright, Wendell William, A.B.'16, Ind. State Tchrs. Col., Terre Haute; Ph.D.'29, Tchrs. Col., Columbia Univ.; Dean. Sch. of Educ., Ind. Univ., Bloomington, Ind., since 1946.

Wyatt, Robert H., A.B. and M.A.'25, Ind. Univ.; Exec. Secy., Ind. State Tchrs. Assn., Indianapolis, Ind., since 1938.

Yoder, Harry T., A.M.'27, Manchester Col.; M.S. in Ed.'34, Ind. Univ.; Co. Supt. of Sch., Columbia City, Ind., since 1937.

Young, John J., B.S.'33, Ball State Tchrs. Col.; M.S.'36, Ind. Univ.; Supt. of Sch., New Haven, Ind., since 1949.

Young, John J., A.B.'21, Ind. State Tchrs. Col., Terre Haute; M.A.'24, Univ. of Wis.; Ph.D.'35, New York Univ.; Supt. of Sch., Mishawaka, Ind., since 1948.

Zeller, Ernest M., B.S.'33, M.S.'41, Indiana State Tchrs. Col.; Supt. of Sch., Butler, Ind., since 1951.

Zimmerman, Carl A., A.B.'28, A.M.'32, Ind. Univ.; Supt. of Sch., Logansport, Ind., since 1945.

Zuck, Charles L., A.B.'22, Ind. Univ.; A.M.'28, Columbia Univ.; Supt. of Sch., Brookville, Ind., since 1929.

INSTITUTIONAL MEMBERS

Indiana State Library, 140 N. Senate Ave., Indianapolis, Ind.

Library, Ball State Tchrs. Col., Muncie, Ind.

Library, Butler Univ., Indianapolis, Ind.

Library, Purdue University, c/o J. H Moriarty, Lafayette, Ind.

Primary Council of Indiana, Miss O'Connor, Secy.-Treas., Huntington, Ind.

Teachers' Special Library, Indianapolis, Instr. Center, 1644 Roosevelt Ave., Indianapolis, Ind.

IOWA

INDIVIDUAL MEMBERS

Ackerman, Kenneth K., B.A.'30, Iowa State Tchrs. Col., Cedar Falls; M.A.'40, State Univ. of Iowa; Supt. of Consol. Sch., Clemons, Iowa, since 1945.

Albers, Martin Z., A.B.'15, Hope Col.; A.M.'19, Des Moines Col.; Co. Supt. of Sch., Eldora, Iowa, since 1936.

Amen, Clarence E., B.S.'33, Northeast Mo. State Tchrs. Col., Kirksville; M.Ed.'40, Univ. of Mo.; Co. Supt. of Sch., Mt. Pleasant, Iowa, since 1948.

Ballantyne, S. A., B.A.'41, Iowa State Tchrs. Col., Cedar Falls; M.S.'43, Drake Univ.; Supt. of Sch., West Union, Iowa, since 1951.

Becker, Conrad H., B.S.'35, M.S.'38, Colo. State Col. of Agrl. and Mech. Arts; D.D.'48, Wartburg Theol. Sem.; Pres., Wartburg Col., Waverly, Iowa, since 1945.

Berg, Ben Conrad, B.A.'16, Univ. of Ill.; M.A.'23, Columbia Univ.; Supt. of Sch., Newton, Iowa, since 1922.

Bielefeldt, Arthur J., B.S.'34, Iowa State Tchrs. Col.; M.E.'50, Colorado A. & M. Col.; Supt.; Orange Twp. Consolidated Sch., Waterloo, Iowa, since 1945.

Block, Arthur R., M.A.'35, State Univ. of Iowa; Supt. of Sch., Storm Lake, Iowa, since 1945.

Boss, Henry T., B.A.'40, Lawrence Col.; M.Ed. '46, Harvard Univ.; Supt. of Sch., Colfax, Iowa, since 1951.

Bracewell, Ray H., B.S.'15, Ill. Col.; M.A.'25, Univ. of Chicago; Supt. of Sch., Burlington, Iowa, since 1937.

Bredall, A. J., M.A.'48, Univ. of Iowa; Supt. of Sch., New Hampton, Iowa, since 1949.

Briggs, L. V., B.A.'24, William Penn Col.; M.A. '36, State Univ. of Iowa; Supt. of Sch., Hampton, Iowa, since 1944.

Brooke, George M., B.A.'39, Parsons Col.; M.S.'46, Drake Univ.; Supt. of Sch., Lisbon, Iowa, since 1948.

Bryan, Gerald C., Supt. of Sch., Corydon, Iowa.

Bryson, Morris E., Supt. of Sch., Exira, Iowa.

Buerkens, Clarence C., A.B.'20, State Univ. of Iowa; M.S.'22, Iowa State Col.; Supt. of Sch., Pella, Iowa, since 1936.

Burns, W. R., M.A.'47, Univ. of Iowa; Supt. of Sch., Eldon, Iowa, since 1947.

Camp, Frances M., M.A.'24, State Univ. of Iowa; Coordinator of Placement Serv. and Dir. of Educ. Placement Office, State Univ. of Iowa, Iowa City, Iowa, since 1924.

Carter, Charles Wayne, B.A.'39, Iowa Wesleyan Col.; M.A.'47, State Univ. of Iowa; Supt. of Sch., Wayland, Iowa, since 1951.

Christiansen, C. J., B.A.'21, Cornell Col.; M.A. '36, Drake Univ.; Supt. of Sch., Clarion, Iowa, since 1932.

Clark, Max R., B.S.'31, Iowa State Tchrs. Col.; Cedar Falls; M.A.'36, State Univ. of Iowa; Supt. of Sch., Dubuque, Iowa, since 1946.

Coen, Edwin, B.A.'34, Iowa State Tchrs. Col.; M.A.'39, State Univ. of Iowa; Co. Supt. of Sch., Denison, Iowa, since 1951.

Colbert, E. Allen, B.S.'39, M.S.'48, Drake Univ.; Supt. of Sch., Scranton, Iowa, since 1948.

Cooper, Dan H., B.S.'34, Northwestern Univ.; M.A.'38, Ph.D.'46, Univ. of Chicago; State Univ. of Iowa, Iowa City, Iowa.

Cottrell, C. A., M.A.'30, Univ. of Colo.; Supt. of Sch., Mt. Pleasant, Iowa, since 1937.

Cox, John B., B.S.'38, Northwest Mo. State Tchrs. Col., Maryville; M.A.'50, State Univ. of Iowa; Supt. of Sch., Mapleton, Iowa.

Creel, R. E., Supt. of Sch., Cherokee, Iowa.

Cushman, M. L., A.B.'32, Western Mich. Col. of Educ., Kalamazoo; A.M.'37, Univ. of Mich.; Ph.D.'43, Cornell Univ.; Prof. of Rural Educ., Iowa State Col. of Agr. and Mech. Arts, Ames, Iowa.

David, Floyd A., A.B.'25, Nebr. State Tchrs. Col., Chadron; M.A.'37, Univ. of Nebr.; Supt. of Sch., Knoxville, Iowa, since 1945.

Davis, George W., M.A.'39, Univ. of Mo.; Supt. of Sch., Des Moines, Iowa, since 1947.

*Davis, Harvey H., A.M.'23, Ph.D.'28, State Univ. of Iowa; Prof. of Educ., since 1936, Chmn., Dept. of Educ., since 1937, and Provost, State Univ. of Iowa, Iowa City, Iowa, since 1950.

DeKock, H. C., B.A.'26, Central Col. (Iowa); M.A.'34, State Univ. of Iowa; Supt. of Consol. Sch., Tipton, Iowa, since 1946.

Doolin, Ruie B., M.Ed.'47, Univ. of Mo.; Dir. of Special Serv., Cedar Rapids, Iowa, since 1951.

Douma, Frank W., A.B.'16, Hope Col.; M.A.'38, State Univ. of Iowa; Supt. of Sch., Ottumwa, Iowa, since 1936.

Dunlavy, Donald Dewitt, B.A.'33, M.S.Ed.'41, Drake Univ.; Supt. of Sch., Corning, Iowa, since 1946.

Eastman, H. J., M.A.'35, State Univ. of Iowa; Supt. of Sch., Vinton, Iowa, since 1948.

Edgar, William John, B.A.'32, Upper Iowa Univ.; M.A.'36, State Univ. of Iowa; Supt. of Sch., Grand Junction, Iowa, since 1947.

Edie, Irwin W., B.A.'26, Upper Iowa Univ.; M.A.'32, State Univ. of Iowa; Supt. of Sch., Rudd, Iowa, since 1929.

Eriksen, Walter B., B.S.'28, Western Mich. Col. of Educ., Kalamazoo; M.A.'34, Univ. of Mich.; Supt. of Sch., Bettendorf, Iowa, since 1948.

Fallgatter, Florence A., B.S.'17, Univ. of Minn.; M.A.'27, Tchrs. Col., Columbia Univ.; Head, Home Economics Educ., Iowa State Col., Ames, Iowa, since 1938.

Fannon, E. W., Supt. of Sch., Centerville, Iowa, since 1918.

Fatka, Wilbur W., B.A.'41, Westmar Col.; M.S. Ed.'50, Drake Univ.; Supt. of Sch., Anita, Iowa, since 1950.

Faust, C. E., B.A.'41, Central Col. (Iowa); M.E.'49, Univ. of S. Dak.; Supt. of Sch., Garden Grove, Iowa, since 1950.

Feelhaver, Carl T., M.A.'31, Columbia Univ.; Supt. of Sch., Fort Dodge, Iowa, since 1947.

Ferguson, Court L., B.A.'37, William Penn Col.; M.A.'41, Univ. of Iowa; Supt. of Sch., Panora, Iowa, since 1951.

Findley, W. C., A.B.'14, Bellevue Col.; M.A.'25, State Univ. of Iowa; Asst. Supt. of Sch., Des Moines, Iowa, since 1941.

Forney, W. Paul, B.A.'27, M.A.'42, State Univ. of Iowa; Supt. of Independent Sch., Sibley, Iowa, since 1946.

Fuller, Albert C., B.A.'11, State Univ. of Iowa; Iowa State Tchrs. Col., Cedar Falls, Iowa.

Galbreth, W. Henry, B.A.'29, Upper Iowa Univ.; M.A.'36, State Univ. of Iowa; Asst. Exec. Secy. and Dir. of Publications, Iowa State Educ. Assn., Des Moines, Iowa, since 1941.

Garbee, Eugene E., B.S.'31, Southwest Mo. State Col.; M.A.'33, George Peabody Col. for Tchrs.; Ed.D.'49, New York Univ.; Pres., Upper Iowa Univ., Fayette, Iowa, since 1952.

Gettys, Joe L., B.A.'19, Grinnell Col.; M.A.'32, State Univ. of Iowa; Supt. of Sch., Oskaloosa, Iowa, since 1947.

Gibson, Robert W., M.A.'31, Univ. of Mich.; Supt. of Sch., Eagle Grove, Iowa, since 1944.

Goltry, Keith, Dean, Parsons Col., Fairfield, Iowa.

Goss, Leslie C., Ph.B.'30, Ripon Col.; M.A.'42, Colo. State Col. of Educ., Greeley; Dir. of Purchasing and Maintenance, Pub. Sch., Davenport, Iowa, since 1927.

Graeber, B. H., M.A.'34, State Univ. of Iowa; Supt. of Sch., Waukon, Iowa, since 1943.

Green, R. J., B.S.'29, Iowa State Tchrs. Col., Cedar Falls; M.A.'38, Columbia Univ.; Supt. of Sch., Greenfield, Iowa, since 1940.

Griewe, C. S., B.A.'23, Morningside Col.; M.A.'37, Univ. of Colo.; Supt. of Sch., Sac City, Iowa, since 1946.

Hadley, Charles G., B.A.'24, Parsons Col.; M.A.'36, Univ. of S. Dak.; Co. Supt. of Sch., Sioux City, Iowa, since 1933.

Haehlen, J. K., B.A.'28, Western Union Col.; M.A.'29, State Univ. of Iowa; Supt. of Sch., Waverly, Iowa.

Hagman, Harlan Lawrence, B.E., Northern Ill. State Tchrs. Col., DeKalb; M.A., Ph.D., Northwestern Univ.; Dean, Col. of Educ., Drake Univ., Des Moines, Iowa, since 1950.

Hahn, Charles W., B.A.'39, Coe Col.; M.S.E.'48, Drake Univ.; Supt. of Sch., Ackley, Iowa, since 1951.

Halverson, B. G., B.S.'33, Iowa State Col.; Co. Supt. of Sch., Carroll, Iowa, since 1948.

Hamilton, Holmes, Ed.B.'34, Western Ill. State Tchrs. Col., Macomb; M.A.'43, State Univ. of Iowa; Supt. of Consol. Sch., Hudson, Iowa, since 1948.

Hancher, Virgil M., B.A.'18, J.D.'24, State Univ. of Iowa; B.A.'22, M.A.'27, Oxford Univ., England; LL.D.'41, Grinnell Col.; LL.D.'41, St. Ambrose Col.; L.H.D.'43, Cornell Col.; LL.D.'44, Northwestern Univ.; Litt.D.'44, Beloit Col.; LL.D.'49, Univ. of Southern Calif.; Pres., State Univ. of Iowa, Iowa City, Iowa, since 1940.

Hansen, C. Arthur, B.S.'36, Buena Vista Col.; M.A.'47, State Univ. of Iowa; Supt. of Sch., Earlham, Iowa, since 1950.

Harrison, Albert E., B.A.'04, Parsons Col.; Co. Supt. of Sch., Storm Lake, Iowa, since 1915.

Hartman, W. Harold, B.A.'28, Iowa State Tchrs. Col., Cedar Falls; M.A.'38, State Univ. of Iowa; Co. Supt. of Sch., Waterloo, Iowa, since 1948.

Hartzell, Wylie W., B.A.'20, Simpson Col.; M.A.'37, State Univ. of Iowa; Supt. of Sch., Albia, Iowa, since 1937.

Hatfield, D. H., M.S.'43, Drake Univ., Des Moines, Iowa; Supt. of Sch., West Bend, Iowa, since 1952.

*Hawk, Rupert Adam, A.B.'24, Grinnell Col.; M.A.'34, State Univ. of Iowa; Assoc. Prof. of Econ., Controller and Bus. Mgr., Grinnell Col., Grinnell, Iowa, since 1947.

Hedemann, R. F., M.A.'42, State Univ. of Iowa; Supt. of Sch., West Branch, Iowa, since 1947.

Hendrickson, Abner A., B.A.'26, Luther Col., Decorah, Iowa; M.A.'40, Univ. of Minn.; Co. Supt. of Sch., Cresco, Iowa, since 1943.

Hetzel, Walter L., B.A.'29, Upper Iowa Univ.; M.A.'34, LL.B.'39, State Univ. of Iowa; Supt. of Sch., Decorah, Iowa, since 1951.

Hilburn, W. C., B.S.'28, M.S.'40, Iowa State Col. of Agrl. and Mech. Arts; Supt. of Sch., Iowa Falls, Iowa, since 1945.

Hoglan, John C., B.A.'23, M.A.'32, State Univ. of Iowa; Supt. of Sch., Marshalltown, Iowa, since 1946.

*Horn, Ernest, B.S.'07, A.M.'08, Univ. of Mo.; Ph.D.'14, Columbia Univ.; Prof. of Educ. and Dir., Univ. Elem. Sch., State Univ. of Iowa, Iowa City, Iowa, since 1915.

Hoth, Donald L., B.A.'37, Upper Iowa Univ.; M.A.'48, State Univ. of Iowa; Supt. of Sch., Lamont, Iowa, since 1950.

Howell, Fannie G., B.A.'24, Marion Col., Ind.; Co. Supt. of Sch., Charles City, Iowa, since 1933.

Hoyt, C. O., A.B.'18, Grinnell Col.; M.A.'30, Columbia Univ.; Asst. Supt. of Sch., Des Moines, Iowa, since 1941.

Hungerford, J. B., Supt. of Sch., Coggon, Iowa, since 1940.

Hurwitz, John J., Supt. of Sch., Central City, Iowa.

Isenberger, W. W., M.A.'48, State Univ. of Iowa; Supt., Norway Consol. Sch., Norway, Iowa, since 1950.

Iverson, Lowell I., Supt. of Sch., Rockwell City, Iowa.

Johansen, Marvin J., B.A.'29, Iowa State Tchrs. Col., Cedar Falls; M.A.'45, State Univ. of Iowa; Supt. of Sch., West Liberty, Iowa, since 1947.

Johnson, Wiert G., B.S.'34, Iowa State Tchrs. Col.; M.A.'38, State Univ. of Iowa; Prin., H. S., Sioux City, Iowa, since 1951.

Johnson, Winfred Foote, A.B.'20, Aurora Col.; M.A.'27, Univ. of Wis.; Supt. of Sch., Spencer, Iowa, since 1940.

Johnsten, Carsten T., B.A.'30, Iowa State Tchrs. Col., Cedar Falls; M.A.'41, Colo. State Col. of Educ., Greeley; Supt. of Sch., Osage, Iowa, since 1948.

Johnston, C. J., M.A.'39, State Univ. of Iowa; Supt. of Sch., Bloomfield, Iowa, since 1948.

Jones, Benjamin, B.A.'22, Coe Col.; M.A.'32, State Univ. of Iowa; Supt. of Sch., Tama, Iowa, since 1942.

Jones, Burton Robert, M.A.'28, State Univ. of Iowa; Supt. of Sch., Creston, Iowa, since 1933.

Jones, Kyle C., B.A.'28, M.A.'38, State Univ. of Iowa; Supt. of Sch., Emmetsburg, Iowa, since 1946.

Jorgensen, R. H., B.A.'32, Simpson Col.; M.A. '39, Tchrs. Col., Columbia Univ.; Supt. of Sch., Ankeny, Iowa, since 1952.

Kann, Sister Jean Marie, O.S.F., Ph.D.'39, Yale Univ.; Pres., Briar Cliff Col., Sioux City, Iowa, since 1943.

Kaskadden, Alfred A., B.A.'30, Penn Col., Oskaloosa, Iowa; M.A.'36, Univ. of Iowa; Supt. of Sch., Oelwein, Iowa, since 1948.

Killion, Ray A., B.A.'30, Drake Univ.; M.A.'32, State Univ. of Iowa; Supt. of Sch., Harlan, Iowa, since 1946.

Kinsey, Eldon O., B.A.'30, Buena Vista Col.; M.A.'42, State Univ. of Iowa; Supt. of Sch., Sioux Center, Iowa, since 1944.

Koch, Kenath B., B.A.'28, Westmar Col.; M.A. '38, State Univ. of Iowa; Supt. of Sch., Denison, Iowa, since 1951.

Lagomarcino, Virgil Seth, B.A.'43, Coe Col.; M.A.'48, Drake Univ.; Supt. of Sch., Anamosa, Iowa, since 1949.

Laing, Otto B., M.A.'30, State Univ. of Iowa; Supt. of Sch., Algona, Iowa, since 1932.

Lapham, P. C., A.B.'12, Des Moines Col.; A.M. '16, Univ. of Chicago; Supt. of Sch., Charles City, Iowa, since 1927.

Laughrige, Robert S., B.A.'23, Parsons Col.; M.A.'37, State Univ. of Iowa; Prin. H. S., Bloomfield, Iowa, since 1948.

Lee, Amos C., B.A.'22, Drake Univ.; M.A.'34, State Univ. of Iowa; Supt. of Sch., West Des Moines, Iowa, since 1942.

Lillard, D. R., B.A.'27, Morningside Col.; M.A. '36, State Univ. of Iowa; Supt. of Sch., Winterset, Iowa, since 1942.

Littell, D. R., B.A.'28, Upper Iowa Univ.; M.A. '49, Drake Univ.; Supt. Sch., Manning, Iowa, since 1951.

Logan, Jack M., A.B.'15, Drake Univ.; M.A.'27, State Univ. of Iowa; Supt. of Sch., Waterloo, Iowa, since 1942.

Logan, Lawrence A., B.A.'29, Drake Univ.; M.A.'35, State Univ. of Iowa; Supt. of Sch., Shenandoah, Iowa, since 1945.

Lown, Jack A., B.A.'42, Iowa State Tchrs. Col.; M.S.'47, Iowa State Col.; Supt., Marquette-McGregor Sch., Clayton Co., Iowa, since 1952.

Lunan, Frank A., B.A.'17, Tarkio Col.; M.A.'24, State Univ. of Iowa; Supt. of Sch., Chariton, Iowa, since 1945.

Lynch, E. B., B.A.'21, Iowa State Tchrs. Col., Cedar Falls; M.A.'27, State Univ. of Iowa; Supt. of Sch., Red Oak, Iowa, since 1944.

McBurney, John H., A.B.'20, Morningside Col.; M.A.'26, State Univ. of Iowa; Supt. of Sch., Webster City, Iowa, since 1944.

McCombs, Newell D., A.B.'20, D.Ed.'43, Simpson Col.; M.A.'27, State Univ. of Iowa; LL.D. '44, Drake Univ.; Supt. of Sch., Des Moines, Iowa, since 1941.

McCurdy, Melvin B., B.A.'29, Parsons Col.; M.A.'39, State Univ. of Iowa; Supt. of Sch., Hansell, Iowa.

McKinley, F. G., B.A.'33, M.A.'51, State Univ. of Iowa; Supt. of Sch., Dunkerton, Iowa, since 1948.

McPhail, Harry R., B.S.'32, Baker Univ.; M.A. '38, State Univ. of Iowa; Supt. of Sch., Ames, Iowa.

Macaulay, William B., B.A.'32, Cornell Col.; M.S.'39, Drake Univ.; Supt. of Sch., Andrew, Iowa, since 1950.

Martens, Leston C., B.A.'34, Grinnell Col.; M.A.'44, Drake Univ.; Supt. of Sch., Traer, Iowa, since 1950.

Martin, Charles Francis, B.A.'15, State Univ. of Iowa; Exec. Secy., Iowa State Educ. Assn., Des Moines, Iowa, since 1946.

Martin, Harold W., M.S. in Ed.'47, Drake Univ.; Supt. of Sch., Albion, Iowa, since 1950.

411

Maucker, J. W., Pres., Iowa State Tchrs. Col., Cedar Falls, Iowa, since 1950.

Mease, Clyde D., M.A.'36, State Univ. of Iowa; Supt. of Sch., Humboldt, Iowa, since 1947.

Miller, Earl L., B.A.'39, Nebr. State Tchrs. Col., Wayne; M.Ed.'45, Univ. of Colo.; Supt. of Sch., Britt, Iowa.

Mogok, Edwin T., M.A.'37, Univ. of Iowa; Supt. of Sch., Glidden, Iowa.

Molsberry, W. W., M.S.'39, Iowa State Col.; Co. Supt. of Sch., Sigourney, Iowa, since 1951.

Morse, A. S., A.B.'16, Knox Col.; M.A.'27, Univ. of Minn.; Supt. of Co. Sch., West Union, Iowa, since 1944.

Mounce, James Rex, B.A.'19, Coe Col.; M.A.'24, State Univ. of Iowa; Supt. of Sch., Clinton, Iowa, since 1944.

Mourer, Russel J., B.S.'18, Purdue Univ.; M.A.'28, Tchrs. Col., Columbia Univ.; Supt. of Sch., Council Bluffs, Iowa, since 1948.

Moyers, A. Edison, B.A.'12, Tabor Col.; M.S.'22, Iowa State Agrl. and Mech. Col.; Supt. of Sch., Menlo, Iowa.

Murray, Arlo Adrian, A.B.'37, Upper Iowa Univ.; M.A.'49, Univ. of S. Dak.; Supt. of Sch., Lohrville, Iowa, since 1947.

Naffziger, R. A., B.S.'24, Parsons Col.; M.A.'49, Univ. of Iowa; Supt. of Sch., Carroll, Iowa, since 1948.

Nodland, Marvin T., B.A.'26, Cornell Col.; M.A.'35, State Univ. of Iowa; Supt. of Sch., Sioux City, Iowa, since 1946.

Norris, Ralph C., B.A.'28, M.A.'34, Colo. State Col. of Educ., Greeley; Co. Supt. of Sch., Des Moines, Iowa, since 1945.

Obermeier, M. H., B.S.'24, Iowa Wesleyan Col.; M.A.'39, Univ. of Mo.; Supt. of Sch., Tingley, Iowa, since 1950.

Ojemann, Ralph H., B.S.'23, M.S.'24, Univ. of Ill.; Ph.D.'29, Univ. of Chicago; Iowa Child Welfare Research Sta., State Univ. of Iowa, Iowa City, Iowa, since 1929.

Opstad, Iver A., B.A.'11, Luther Col.; M.A.'19, State Univ. of Iowa; Supt. of Sch., Iowa City, Iowa, 1920-52. (Retired.)

*Parker, Clyde, A.B.'30, Franklin Col.; A.M.'31, Ind. State Tchrs. Col., Terre Haute; Supt. of Sch., Cedar Rapids, Iowa, since 1946.

Parker, Jessie M., A.B., Des Moines Univ.; B.Pd., Valparaiso Univ.; LL.D., Buena Vista Col.; State Supt. of Pub. Instr., Des Moines, Iowa, since 1938.

Palmer, Donald D., B.S.'29, Iowa State Tchrs. Col., Cedar Falls; M.A.'39, State Univ. of Iowa; Supt. of Brooklyn Independent Schs., Brooklyn, Iowa, since 1952.

Paschal, Harland L. R., B.S.'36, Parsons Col.; M.A.'40, State Univ. of Iowa; Supt. of Sch., Fort Madison, Iowa, since 1945.

Peet, John Herbert, B.A.'16, Cornell Col.; M.A.'28, Univ. of Chicago; Supt. of Sch., Cedar Falls, Iowa, since 1935.

Pence, W. G., A.B.'12, B.S.'21, Northeast Mo. State Tchrs. Col., Kirksville; M.S.'22, Univ. of Chicago; Supt. of Sch., Fairfield, Iowa, since 1927.

Peterson, Clifford C., A.B.'30, Iowa State Tchrs. Col.; M.A.'41, Iowa Univ.; Supt. of Sch., Indianola, Iowa, since 1951.

Peterson, Elmer T., A.B.'17, Augustana Col.; A.M.'22, Tchrs. Col., Columbia Univ.; Ph.D. '27, State Univ. of Iowa; Dean, Col. of Educ., State Univ. of Iowa, Iowa City, Iowa, since 1946.

Petty, Walter T., A.B., B.S., B.S. in Ed.'40, Central Mo. State Col.; M.A.'50, State Univ. of Iowa; Co. Supt. of Sch., Leon, Iowa, since 1948.

Pickett, Louis L., A.B.'21, Mo. Wesleyan Col.; M.S.'23, Iowa State Col. of Agrl. and Mech. Arts; Supt. of Sch., Ruthven, Iowa, since 1948.

Polton, Russell C., M.A.'40, Univ. of Iowa; Supt. of Sch., Tabor, Iowa, since 1939.

Pope, Farnham G., B.S.'42, M.S. in Ed.'47, Ph.D.'49, Cornell Univ.; Instr., Dept. of Educ., Iowa State Tchrs. Col., Cedar Falls, Iowa, since 1949.

Prehm, Ernest A., B.A.'17, Grinnell Col.; M.A.'29, Univ. of Iowa; Supt. of Sch., Jefferson, Iowa, since 1947.

Rand, Sidney A., B.A.'38, Concordia Col. (Moorhead, Minn.); C.T.'43, Luther Theol. Sem.; Pres., Waldorf Col., Forest City, Iowa, since 1951.

Reppe, F. N., B.A.'36, Luther Col.; Ed.M.'47, Univ. of S. D.; Supt., Consol. Sch., New London, Iowa, since 1949.

Rew, Orra K., B.A.'39, Iowa State Tchrs. Col.; M.A.'49, Colo. State Col. of Educ.; Supt. of Sch., Winfield, Iowa, since 1951.

Rice, Harold H., A.B.'35, M.A.'43, Colo. State Col.; Supt. of Sch., Audubon, Iowa, since 1950.

Ritter, Elmer L., A.B.'14, Ind. Univ.; M.A.'16, Ph.D.'20, State Univ. of Iowa; Dir. of Extension, Iowa State Tchrs. Col., Cedar Falls, Iowa, since 1948.

Rupert, Charles L., B.S.'34, State Tchrs. Col., Maryville, Mo.; M.A.'38, Univ. of Mo.; Co. Supt. of Sch., Fort Madison, Iowa, since 1951.

Schindler, Elmer Paul, B.A.'23, Iowa State Tchrs. Col.; M.A.'30, State Univ. of Iowa; Story Co. Supt. of Sch., Nevada, Iowa, since 1937.

Schmidt, Frederick K., B.S.A.'21, Purdue Univ.; M.A.'27, State Univ. of Iowa; Supt. of Sch., Eldora, Iowa, since 1933.

Schuler, A.H., B.A.'32, Westmar Col.; M.A.'42, Colo. State Col. of Educ., Greeley; Supt. of Sch., Atlantic, Iowa.

Seaton, Donald F., B.S. in Ed.'29, Iowa State Col.; M.A.'38, State Univ. of Iowa; Supt. of Sch., Boone, Iowa, since 1949.

Seydel, E. Paul, B.A.'32, Cornell Col., Mt. Vernon, Iowa; M.A.'46, Univ. of S. Dak.; Supt. of Sch., Maquoketa, Iowa, since 1947.

Shannon, S. Boyd, B.A.'30, M.A.'36, State Univ. of Iowa; Supt. of Sch., Monticello, Iowa, since 1944.

Shepoiser, Lawrence H., B.A.'32, Iowa State Tchrs. Col., Cedar Falls; M.A.'39, State Univ. of Iowa; Supt. of Sch., Mason City, Iowa, since 1947.

Shupp, Walter A., B.A.'17, Coe Col.; M.A.'42, State Univ. of Iowa; Co. Supt. of Sch., Cedar Rapids, Iowa, since 1936.

Smith, John Edgar, M.A.'25, Univ. of Minn.; Co. Supt. of Sch., Emmetsburg, Iowa, since 1950.

Smith, Lloyd H., B.S. in Ed.'25, Southeast Mo. State Col., Cape Girardeau; M.A.'31, Univ. of Mo.; Co. Supt. of Sch., Winterset, Iowa, since 1948.

Smith, Merrill E., B.A.'30, Union Col.; Supt., Oak Park Academy, Nevada, Iowa, since 1946.

Snider, Frank J., B.S.'19, Iowa Wesleyan Col.; M.A.'28, State Univ. of Iowa; Co. Supt. of Sch., Iowa City, Iowa, since 1937.

Speas, Richard M., A.B.'27, William Penn Col.; M.A.'49, Univ. of Iowa; Supt. of Sch., Delmar, Iowa, since 1948.

Sperry, M. K., B.A.'22, Upper Iowa Univ.; M.A.'32, State Univ. of Iowa; Supt. of Sch., Greene, Iowa, since 1938.

Spitzer, Herbert F., B.S.'30, North Texas State Col.; A.M.'32, Ohio Univ.; Ph.D.'38, State Univ. of Iowa; Assoc. Prof. of Educ. and Prin. of Univ. Elem. Sch., State Univ. of Iowa, Iowa City, Iowa, since 1940.

Staven, LaVier L., B.A.'43, Carroll Col.; M.S.'50, Drake Univ.; Supt. of Sch., Jordan, Iowa, since 1948.

Swanson, (Mrs.) L. W., B.S.'33, Simmons Col.; Member, Bd. of Educ., Mason City, Iowa, since 1951.

Tubbs, Earl L., B.S. in Math.'40, Iowa State Tchrs. Col., Cedar Falls; M.S. in Ed.'45, Drake Univ.; Supt. of Sch., Dows, Iowa, since 1946.

Tweed, S. T., B.A.'29, Luther Col.; M.S.'40, Univ. of Iowa; Co. Supt. of Sch., Forest City, Iowa, since 1948.

Van Cleave, Arlene R., B.S.'20, Coe Col.; Co. Supt. of Sch., Logan, Iowa, since 1929.

Vanderlinden, J. S., B.S.'21, M.A.'28, State Univ. of Iowa; Supt. of Sch., Perry, Iowa, since 1935.

Van Dyke, R. F., B.A.'30, Drake Univ.; M.A.'36, State Univ. of Iowa; Supt. of Sch., Bedford, Iowa, since 1945.

Van Horn, Keith W., B.A.'43, M.S. in Ed.'47, Drake Univ.; Supt. of Sch., Forest City, Iowa, since 1951.

Varner, Carl Lee, B.S.'47, M.S.'50, Drake Univ.; Supt. of Sch., Strahan, Iowa, since 1949.

Varner, Charles S., B.A.'33, MacAlester Col.; M.A.'46, Drake Univ.; Supt. of Sch., Johnston, Iowa, since 1946.

Vasey, Hamilton G., A.B.'36, Ill. Col.; M.A.'38, State Univ. of Iowa; Supt. of Sch., Independence, Iowa, since 1947.

Vernon, Chester B., A.B.'14, Baker Univ.; A.M. '20, Columbia Univ.; Ed.D.'35, Univ. of Southern Calif.; Supt. of Sch., Marion, Iowa, since 1926.

Voigt, Edwin E., B.S.'17, M.A.'22, Northwestern Univ.; B.D.'21, D.D.'42, Garrett Biblical Inst.; Ph.D.'24, Yale Univ.; Pres., Simpson Col., Indianola, Iowa, since 1942.

Wallace, Paul E., B.S.'30, Parsons Col.; M.S.'41, Drake Univ.; Supt. of Sch., Adel, Iowa, since 1944.

Wezeman, Frederick H., LL.B. and J.D.'14, John Marshall Law Sch.; B.S. in Ed.'22, Lewis Inst.; B.D.'26, Univ. of Chicago; Prin., Chicago Christian H. S., Chicago, Ill., 1927-51. Address: Orange City, Iowa.

Williams, Harold J., B.S.'16, Iowa State Col.; M.A.'30, State Univ. of Iowa; Supt. of Sch., Davenport, Iowa, since 1947.

Wise, Roy W., B.A.'33, Parsons Col.; M.A.'45, State Univ. of Iowa; Supt. of Sch., Mediapolis, Iowa, since 1950.

Wood, Wallace, Dir. Elem. Educ., Davenport, Iowa.

Woodruff, Leonard L., B.A.'23, Parsons Col.; M.S.'32, State Univ. of Iowa; Co. Supt. of Sch., Burlington, Iowa, since 1932.

Wright, James C., A.B.'27, Drake Univ.; M.A.'36, State Univ. of Iowa; Supt. of Sch., Keokuk, Iowa, since 1940.

Yestness, C. T., Supt. of Sch., Doon, Iowa.

Ylvisaker, J. W., B.A.'21, Luther Col.; C.T.'25, Luther Theol. Sem.; M.Th.'26, Princeton Theol. Sem.; Pres., Luther Col., Decorah, Iowa, since 1948.

INSTITUTIONAL MEMBERS

Drake University, Cowles Lib., Des Moines, Iowa.

Midland Laboratories, C. F. Hillyard, Vicepres., 210 Jones St., Dubuque, Iowa.

KANSAS

INDIVIDUAL MEMBERS

Anderson, Earle T., A.B.'25, Friends Univ.; M.A.'30, Univ. of Kansas; Supt. of Sch., Herington, Kansas, since 1948.

Anderson, Ernest Mitchell, B.S.'18, Tchrs. Col., Columbia Univ.; M.A.'22, Univ. of Colo.; Ph.D.'28, Univ. of Mo; Prof. of Educ., Kansas State Tchrs. Col., Pittsburg, Kansas, since 1929.

Andree, Paul H., B.S.'29, M.S.'38, Fort Hays Kansas State Col.; Supt. of Sch., Nes City, Kansas, since 1949.

Arnold, A. S., B.S. in Ed.'34, M.S. in Ed.'39, Kansas State Tchrs. Col., Emporia; Supt. of Sch., Cimarron, Kansas, since 1948.

Ayers, Solon G., M.B.A.'33, Univ. of Texas; Supt., Haskell Inst., Lawrence, Kansas, since 1942.

Baker, H. H., Ph.D.'47, Univ. of Colo.; Prof. of Educ., Univ. of Wichita, Wichita, Kansas, since 1947.

Berges, William R., A.B.'18, Southwestern Col.; A.M.'26, Univ. of Chicago; Prin., Mathewson Jr. H. S., Wichita, Kansas.

Bergman, Frank V., B.S.'17, Kansas State Tchrs. Col., Emporia; M.A.'29, Univ. of Colo.; Supt. of Sch., Manhattan, Kansas, since 1942.

Bevan, Earl R., B.S. in Ed.'29, Kansas State Tchrs. Col., Emporia; M.S. in Ed.'36, Univ. of Kansas; Supt. of Sch., Pittsburg, Kansas, since 1951.

*Bigler, Frank William, A.B.'27, Southwestern Col.; M.A.'36, Univ. of Wichita; Prin., Jr. H. S., El Dorado, Kansas, since 1946.

Black, William Albert, B.S.'26, M.S.'34, Kansas State Tchrs. Col., Emporia; Ph.D.'42, Univ. of Colo.; Head, Dept. of Educ. and Dir. of Tchr. Tr., Kansas State Tchrs. Col., Pittsburg, Kansas, since 1947.

Brandner, Daniel C., M.A.'41, Northwestern Univ.; Supt. of Sch., Plains, Kansas, since 1949.

Briner, Francis William, B.S. in Ed.'23, Kansas State Tchrs. Col., Emporia; M.A. in Ed.'32, Tchrs. Col., Columbia Univ.; Supt. of Sch., Harper, Kansas, since 1941.

Brogan, Hugh, B.S.'23, Kansas State Tchrs. Col., Emporia; A.M.'40, Colo. State Col. of Educ., Greeley; Supt. of Sch., Great Bend, Kansas, since 1947.

Brown, Minter E., A.B.'22, Southwestern Col.; M.A.'31, Univ. of Kansas; Dir. of Professional Relations, Kansas State Tchrs. Assn., Topeka, Kansas, since 1944.

Bryan, Hugh, B.S.'25, Kansas State Col. of Agrl. and Applied Science; M.S.'37, Kansas State Tchrs. Col., Emporia; Supt. of Sch., Leavenworth, Kansas, since 1943.

Buchanan, James H., A.B.'28, Univ. of Denver; A.M.'32, Ed.D.'49, Univ. of Colo.; Dir. of Graduate Div., Kansas State Tchrs. Col., Emporia, Kansas, since 1950.

Buhler, Arnold, Supt., Consolidated Sch., Preston, Kansas.

Carr, Wilmot D., A.B.'24, Ottawa Univ.; M.A.'37, Univ. of Kansas; Supt. of Sch., Anthony, Kansas, since 1944.

Cashman, Lee R., M.S.'48, Kansas State Col.; Prin. of Sch., Effingham, Kansas, since 1951.

Chandler, H. E., A.B.'11, Washburn Col.; A.M.'27, Tchrs. Col., Columbia Univ.; Assoc. Prof. of Educ. and Dir. of Tchrs. Appointment Bur., Univ. of Kansas, Lawrence, Kansas, since 1934.

Chrisman, Paul G., B.S.'36, M.S.'40, Kansas State Tchrs. Col., Pittsburg; Supt. of Sch., Baxter Springs, Kansas, since 1947.

Colvin, C. F., B.S. in Ed.'37, Kansas State Tchrs. Col., Emporia; M.A.'42, Colo. State Col. of Educ., Greeley; Supt. of Planeview Pub. Sch., Wichita, Kansas, since 1945.

Cooper, Paul B., B.S.'20, Kansas State Tchrs. Col., Emporia; M.S.'38, Univ. of Kansas; Supt. of Sch., Derby, Kansas, since 1948.

Cullison, Jess O., B.S.'37, Northwestern State Col.; Ed.M.'40, Phillips Univ.; Supt. of Sch., Larned, Kansas, since 1946.

Cunningham, Morton C., B.A.'26, Westminster Col. (Mo.); M.Ed.'37, Ed.D.'44, Univ. of Mo.; Pres., Ft. Hays Kansas State Col., Hays, Kansas, since 1949.

Cushman, George L., M.S.'39, Kansas State Tchrs. Col., Pittsburg; Supt. of Sch., Protection Kansas, since 1949.

Dawson, Floyd Harold, B.S.'26, M.S.'37, Kansas State Tchrs. Col., Emporia; Supt. of Sch., Kinsley, Kansas, since 1947.

Dedrick, Lillian I., A.B.'33, A.M.'34, Univ. of Wichita; Co. Supt. of Sch., El Dorado, Kansas, since 1943.

Deever, Harold, A.B.'33, Southwestern Col.; A.M.'38, Greeley State Tchrs. Col.; Supt. of Sch., Osage City, Kansas, since 1947.

Degan, Sister Mary Pauline, S.C.L., Ph.D.'50, Catholic Univ. of America; Head of Educ. Dept., St. Mary Col., Xavier, Kansas, since 1950.

DeLay, Calvin W., B.S.'35, Kansas State Tchrs. Col., Emporia; M.S.'40, Univ. of Kansas, Lawrence; Supt. of Sch., Yates Center, Kansas, since 1947.

Dellett, Fred, A.B.'32, M.S.'46, Fort Hays Kansas State Col.; Supt. of Sch., Garfield, Kansas, since 1945.

Dixon, Paul T., B.S. in Ed.'39, Central State Tchrs. Col. (Mo.); M.Ed.'43, Ed.D.'48, Univ. of Mo.; Coordinator of Sec. Educ., Kansas State Tchrs. Col., Pittsburg, Kansas, since 1950.

Duncan, Ralph L., B.A.'30, Univ. of Kansas; M.A.'38, Univ. of Colo.; Prin., Sublette Rural H. S., Sublette, Kansas, since 1948.

Edgerton, Dene R., M.S.'39, Univ. of Kansas; Prin., Hickory Grove Sch., Mission, Kansas, since 1943.

Engelhardt, J. L., A.B.'22, Southwestern Col.; M.A.'23, Univ. of Kansas; Supt. of City Sch., Kingman, Kansas, since 1926.

Esping, K. O., A.B.'38, Bethany Col.; M.S.'46, Kansas State Col. of Agrl. and Applied Science; Supt. of Sch., Council Grove, Kansas, since 1948.

Evans, Evan E., A.B.'20, Baker Univ.; A.M.'28, Univ. of Chicago; Supt. of Sch., Hickory Grove-Overland Park Dist. No. 110, Overland Park, Kansas, since 1952.

Fisher, Buford E., M.S. in Ed. Admin.'47, Kansas State Tchrs. Col.; Supt. of City Sch., Chanute, Kansas, since 1951.

Fitzgerald, Sister Mary Paul, B.A.'29, Kansas Univ.; M.A.'32, Ph.D.'37, St. Louis Univ.; Vicepres. of St. Mary Col., Xavier, Kansas, since 1949.

Foote, Oscar E., A.B.'37, Municipal Univ. of Wichita; M.E.'41, Univ. of Kansas; Supt. of Sch., Lyons, Kansas, since 1947.

Forker, Marvin P., B.S. in Ed.'37, Ft. Hays Kansas State Col.; M.S. in Ed.'41, Univ. of Kansas; Supt. of Sch. Dist. 2, Liberal, Kansas, since 1952.

Fowler, Wade C., B.S. in Ed.'21, Central Mo. State Tchrs. Col., Warrensburg; M.A.'31, Ed.D.'38, Tchrs. Col., Columbia Univ.; Supt. of Sch., Wichita, Kansas, since 1945.

Gahnstrom, Ruth, Co. Supt. of Sch., Salina, Kansas.

Galle, K. R., A.B.'21, Bethel Col.; A.M.'24, Univ. of Chicago; Dean, Jr. Col., Arkansas City, Kansas, since 1945.

Gammon, Delore, B.S.'29, Kansas State Tchrs. Col., Emporia; M.A.'37, Tchrs. Col., Columbia Univ.; Dir. of Elem. Educ., Pub. Sch., Wichita, Kansas, since 1943.

Giffin, Walter C., M.A.'43, Univ. of Kansas City; Supt., Roesland and Roeland Park Schs., Kansas City, Kansas, since 1944.

Gilbaugh, John W., B.S.'47, M.S.'48, Kansas State Tchrs. Col., Pittsburg; Supt. of Sch., Humboldt, Kansas, since 1950.

Gill, Howard, B.S.'27, M.S.'38, Kansas State Tchrs. Col., Pittsburg; Supt. of Sch., Cherryvale, Kansas, since 1944.

Glad, Amos W., A.B.'16, Bethany Col. (Kansas); A.M.'24, Univ. of Kansas; Supt. of Sch., Pratt, Kansas, since 1931.

Godwin, Wendell R., A.B.'26, De Pauw Univ.; M.A.'32, Univ. of Chicago; Supt. of Sch., Topeka, Kansas, since 1951.

Golladay, Edna Lois, B.S. in Ed.'52, State Tchrs. Col.; Co. Supt. of Pub. Instr., Fort Scott, Kansas, since 1947.

Green, Finis M., Ed.D.'50, Univ. of Colo.; Head, Dept. of Educ., Kansas State Col., Manhattan, Kansas, since 1951.

Gump, Carl F., M.S.'48, Kansas State Tchrs. Col.; Prin., H. S., Paola, Kansas, since 1948.

Guthridge, Wallace H., M.A.'28, Univ. of Kansas; M.S.'36, Kansas State Tchrs. Col., Pittsburg; Supt. of Sch., Parsons, Kansas, since 1941.

Harnly, Paul W., A.B.'15, McPherson Col.; A.M.'16, Univ. of Kansas; A.M.'32, Tchrs. Col., Columbia Univ.; Ed.D.'38, Stanford Univ.; Dir. of Sec. Educ., Pub. Sch., Wichita, Kansas, since 1945.

Harris, Frank C., B.S. in Ed.'30, Kansas State Tchrs. Col., Emporia; M.Ed.'47, Univ. of Kansas; Supt. of Sch., Cheney, Kansas, since 1945.

Harris, Wylie V., M.S.'41, Kansas State Tchrs. Col.; Prin. of Sch., Kansas City, Kansas, since 1947.

Harrison, Mabel B., Prin., Overland Park Sch., Overland Park, Kansas.

Harrison, Raymond H., B.S.'39, Central State Col., Edmond, Okla.; M.S.'41, Okla. Agrl. and Mech. Col.; Supt. of Sch., Elkhart, Kansas, since 1945.

Hawk, Herbert C., A.B.'22, Midland Col., (Nebr.); M.A.'24, Univ. of Wis.; Supt. of Sch., Winfield, Kansas, since 1952.

Hawkins, Paul W., B.S. in Ed.'29, M.S.'35, Kansas State Tchrs. Col., Pittsburg; Supt of Sch., El Dorado, Kansas, since 1950.

Hayden, Murle M., B.S.'25, M.S.'35, Kansas State Tchrs. Col., Emporia; Supt. of Sch., Lincoln, Kansas, since 1940.

Heller, Ray E., B.S.'33, M.S.'38, Kansas State Tchrs. Col., Pittsburg; Supt. of Sch., Neodesha, Kansas, since 1951.

Henrie, M. W., B.S.'37, M.S.'50, Kansas State Tchrs. Col.; Supt. of Sch., Sterling, Kansas, since 1951.

Hesser, P. C., B.S.'36, M.A.'44, Phillips Univ.; Supt. of Sch., Fredonia, Kansas.

Hill, Kenneth S., B.S.'36, Kansas State Tchrs. Col., Pittsburg; M.S.'39, Univ. of Kansas; Supt. of Sch., Meade, Kansas, since 1943.

Hines, Walter, B.S.'36, Kansas State Col. of Agrl. and Applied Science; M.A.'41, Univ. of Colo.; Prin., Highland Park Rural H. S., Topeka, Kansas, since 1946.

Horn, Nelson Paxson, B.A.'16, Mo. Wesleyan Col.; B.D.'18, D.D.'37, Garrett Biblical Inst.; M.A.'19, Northwestern Univ.; Pres., Baker Univ., Baldwin, Kansas, since 1936.

Horn, William Robert, Prin. Rural H. S., Hoyt, Kansas.

Horst, Orville, M.A.'50, Columbia Univ.; Supt. of Sch., Walton, Kansas, since 1949.

Hughes, Rees H., Pres., Kansas State Tchrs. Col., Pittsburg, Kansas.

Huyck, Claude A., M.E. and M.S.'40, Univ. of Ark.; Prin., Washington Rural H. S., Bethel, Kansas, since 1936.

Iden, Thomas L., A.B.'22, Kansas Wesleyan Univ.; A.M.'29, Western State Col. of Colo.; Supt. of Sch., Russell, Kansas, since 1939.

James, Carl A., A.B.'29, Col. of Emporia; M.S.'35, Univ. of Southern Calif.; D.Ed.'50, Univ. of Kansas; Supt. of Sch., Concordia, Kansas, since 1947.

Johnson, C. Ray, B.S.'47, M.Ed.'49, Phillips Univ.; Supt. of Sch., Hardtner, Kansas, since 1950.

Jones, J. R., A.B.'20, Hamline Univ.; M.A.'36, Univ. of Colo.; Supt. of Sch., Garden City, Kansas, since 1940.

Kampschroeder, W. C., B.S.'27, M.S.'31, Univ. of Kansas; Dir., Sch. Facilities Serv., State Dept. of Educ., Topeka, Kansas, since 1951.

Kelley, Thomas D., M.S.'38, Kansas State Tchrs. Col., Pittsburg; Admin. Asst. to Supt. of Sch., Wichita, Kansas, since 1949.

Kier, Hazel A., B.S.'34, Univ. of Kansas; M.A.'39, Univ. of Minn.; Dir. of Intermediate Grades and Sec. Educ., Kansas City, Kansas, since 1940.

King, Boyd, B.S.'36, M.S.'41, Kansas State Tchrs. Col., Pittsburg; Prin., Grant Co. Rural H. S., Ulysses, Kansas, since 1949.

Kintigh, W. B., A.B.'25, York Col.; M.E.'37, Univ. of Kansas; Supt. of Sch., Olathe, Kansas, since 1936.

Kittle, Ruth, A.B.'29, Washburn Col.; Penmanship Supvr., Pub. Sch., Topeka, Kansas, since 1924.

Klemm, D. F., B.S.Ed.'19, B.S.'36, M.S.Ed.'37, Ft. Hays Kansas State Col.; Prin. of H. S., Gove, Kansas, since 1949.

Kliewer, Orville P., B.S. in Ed.'48, M.S.'51, Kansas State Tchrs. Col., Emporia; Head of Bus. Educ. Dept., Hillsboro, Kansas, since 1948.

Klotz, V. A., M.A.'33, Univ. of Kansas; Supt. of Sch., Coffeyville, Kansas, since 1950.

Knox, Carl S., M.S. in Ed.'46, Univ. of Kansas; Supt. of Sch., Eureka, Kansas.

Krieger, Robert H., Supt. of Sch., Burlington, Kansas.

Kroesch, Edward D., A.B.'15, Ottawa Univ.; A.M.'16, Univ. of Kansas; Supt. of Sch., Hoisington, Kansas, since 1925.

Lafferty, Charles W., B.S.'37, M.S.'40, Kansas State Tchrs. Col., Pittsburg; Supt. of Sch., Atchison, Kansas, since 1950.

Lamb, Clara S., B.S.'30, Kansas State Tchrs. Col.; M.A.'36, Tchrs. Col., Columbia Univ.; Prin., Stanley Sch., Kansas City, Kansas, since 1931.

Lidikay, Donald R., B.S.'27, Baker Univ.; M.E.'34, Univ. of Kansas; Prin., Trego Community H. S., Wakeeney, Kansas, since 1947.

Loveless, Paul C., Supt. of Sch., Scott City, Kansas.

Lowe, E. E., Supt. of Sch., Sedan, Kansas.

Lowe, Harold E., M.A.'51, Univ. of Kansas City; Supt., Elem. Sch., Merriam, Kansas.

McConnell, Donald A., B.S.'20, Kansas State Tchrs. Col., Emporia; M.A.'27, Tchrs. Col., Columbia Univ.; Supt. of Sch., Junction City, Kansas, since 1939.

MacFarlane, David L., B.A.'16, S.T.B.'17, Northwestern Univ.; Ph.D.'31, Univ. of Edinburgh, Scotland; Pres., Kansas State Tchrs. Col., Emporia, Kansas, since 1945.

Martin, Joel N., A.B.'30, Bethany Col.; M.S.'39, Kansas State Tchrs. Col., Emporia; Supt. of Sch., Ellsworth, Kansas, since 1947.

Mase, Wayne E., B.S.'32, M.S.'39, Kansas State Tchrs. Col., Emporia; Supt. of Sch., St. John, Kansas, since 1945.

Menhusen, A. T., Co. Supt. of Sch., Mankato, Kansas, since 1951.

Miller, Clifford D., B.S.'29, M.S.'35, Ft. Hays Kansas State Col.; Coordinator, Audio-Visual Educ., Bd. of Educ., Wichita, Kansas, since 1939.

Morrell, John S., B.S. in Agrl.'23, Univ. of Mo.; Supt. of Sch., Beloit, Kansas, since 1930.

Munson, Willard D., A.B.'24, Col. of Emporia; M.S.'34, Kansas State Col.; Supt. of Sch., Mulvane, Kansas.

Nicholson, John H., B.S.E.'30, State Tchrs. Col., Emporia, Kansas; M.S.E.'40, Colo. State Col. of Educ.; Ed.D.'45, Tchrs. Col., Columbia Univ.; Dir. of Instr., State Dept. of Educ., Topeka, Kansas, since 1950.

Niehaus, Dorothy, Prin., Bird City Grade Sch., Bird City, Kansas.

Ostenberg, Joe W., A.B.'24, Bethany Col.; A.M.'33, Univ. of Kansas; Supt. of Sch., Iola, Kansas, since 1946.

Ostenberg, W. M., A.B.'24, Bethany Col.; A.M.'39, Colo. State Col. of Educ., Greeley; Supt. of Sch., Salina, Kansas, since 1950.

Palmer, Florence, B.S.'17, Kansas State Tchrs. Col.; M.A.'26, Columbia Univ.; Dir. of Home Economics, Kansas City, Kansas, since 1936.

Palmquist, T. R., A.B.'25, Ottawa Univ.; Prin., H. S., Turner, Kansas, since 1938.

Parker, Henry A., B.S.'29, Kansas State Tchrs. Col., Pittsburg; M.A.'35, Univ. of Kansas; Supt. of Sch., Ottawa, Kansas, since 1948.

Parsons, Paul D., A.B.'36, Friends Univ.; M.Ed.'51, Univ. of Colo.; Prin., Jr. H. S., Chanute, Kansas, since 1946.

Phillips, Clyde U., B.S.'18, Kansas State Tchrs. Col., Pittsburg; A.M.'26, Univ. of Chicago; Supt. of Sch., Hays, Kansas, since 1931.

Pitts, Harold C., A.B.'38, Ottawa Univ.; M.Ed. '46, Univ. of Kansas; Prin., H. S., Lincoln, Kansas, since 1946.

Plath, Ernest C., B.S.'44, M.S. in Ed.'47, Univ. of Kansas, Lawrence; Supt., Pub. Sch., Madison, Kansas.

Potwin, R. W., A.B.'10, Univ. of Kansas; A.M.'27, Univ. of Chicago; Supt. of Sch., McPherson, Kansas, since 1915.

Powell, Jackson O., Ph.D.'50, Syracuse Univ.; Dean, Col. of Educ., Univ. of Wichita, Wichita, Kansas, since 1950.

Reed, Albert J., A.B.'18, Washburn Municipal Univ.; M.A.'36, Univ. of Kansas; Supt. of Sch., Kiowa, Kansas, since 1937.

Reichley, E. V., B.S.'32, Baker Univ.; M.A.'40, Univ. of Colo.; Supt. of Sch., Wellington, Kansas, since 1947.

Richards, W. M., B.Sc.'19, Kansas State Tchrs. Col., Emporia; M.Sc.'26, Univ. of Kansas; Supt. of City Sch., Emporia, Kansas, since 1935.

Riggs, John Forest, B.S.'25, Ottawa Univ.; M.A.'42, Colo. State Col. of Educ., Greeley; Prin., Rural H. S., Lakin, Kansas, since 1949.

415

Robinson, H. H., M.S.'34, Univ. of Kansas; Supt. of Pub. Sch., Augusta, Kansas, since 1940.

Robinson, William C., A.B.'26, Ph.B.'35, Washburn Municipal Univ.; M.A.'38, Tchrs. Col., Columbia Univ.; Supt. of Sch., Abilene, Kansas, since 1940.

Roth, Anthony E., A.B.'27, St. Benedicts Col.; Co. Supt. of Sch., Hays, Kansas, since 1943.

Russell, Robert H., B.S.'35, Kansas State Col.; M.S.'44, Kansas State Tchrs. Col., Pittsburg; Prin., H. S., Paxico, Kansas.

Salser, George Alden, A.B.'16, Southwestern Col.; M.A.'24, Univ. of Chicago; Prin., Horace Mann Sch., Wichita, Kansas, since 1941.

Schadt, R. Marvin, B.A.'34, Park Col.; M.A.'36, Univ. of Mich.; Supt. of Sch., Ellinwood, Kansas, since 1946.

Schlagle, F. L., B.S.'16, Kansas State Tchrs. Col., Emporia; M.A.'23, Tchrs. Col., Columbia Univ.; Pres., Natl. Educ. Assn., 1944–46; Supt. of Sch., Kansas City, Kansas, since 1932.

Schroedermeier, A. G., M.A.'35, Univ. of Kansas; A.B.'18, North Central Col.; Supt. of Sch., Dodge City, Kansas, since 1935.

Scott, G. Ogden, B.S.Ed.'29, Kansas State Tchrs. Col. (Emporia); M.A.Ed.'41, Univ. of Colo., (Boulder); Prin., Jr. H. S., Salina, Kansas, since 1944.

Scott, H. W., B.A.'23, Baker Univ.; M.B.A.'32, Denver Univ.; Supt. of Sch., Newton, Kansas, since 1951.

Selby, Paul J., B.S. in Ed.'28, Ft. Hays Kansas State Col.; Supt., Rozel Consol. Sch., Rozel, Kansas.

Shaw, John, Asst. Prin., H. S., Paola, Kansas.

Shenk, Clifford M., B.S. in Ed.'40, M.S. in Ed.'48, Kansas State Tchrs. Col., Pittsburg; Supt. of Sch., Halstead, Kansas, since 1950.

Simmonds, Ivan, M.A.'51, Kansas State Col.; Supt. of Pub. Sch., Hill City, Kansas, since 1951.

Sloan, Clair M., B.S.'33, M.S.'41, Kansas State Tchrs. Col., Emporia; Supt. of Sch., Minneapolis, Kansas, since 1945.

Small, Lowell A., B.S.'27, Kansas Wesleyan Univ.; M.A.'35, Univ. of Colo.; Supt. of Sch., Hutchinson, Kansas, since 1951.

Smith, Cecil Edwin, B.S. in Ed.'28, Kansas State Tchrs. Col., Emporia; M.A.'31, Ohio State Univ.; Prin., Lakeside Jr. High and Elem. Sch., Pittsburg, Kansas, since 1948.

Smith, Harold W., B.S. in Ed.'31, Kansas State Tchrs. Col., Emporia; M.S. in Ed.'41, Kansas State Tchrs. Col., Pittsburg; Supt. of Sch., Cullison, Kansas, since 1951.

Soderstrom, LaVern W., A.B.'24, Bethany Col.; M.A.'34, Univ. of Kansas; Supt. of Sch., Lindsborg, Kansas, since 1931.

Spong, Clarence R., Sc.B.'32, Ottawa Univ.; M.A.'39, Univ. of Kansas; Supt. of Sch., Syracuse, Kansas, since 1950.

Stark, M. F., B.S. in Ed.'22, Kansas State Tchrs. Col., Emporia; Ed.M.'33, Harvard Univ.; Supt. of City Sch., Hiawatha, Kansas, since 1935.

Stevens, Evan Ray, M.S.'25, Univ. of Kansas; Supt. of Sch., Independence, Kansas, since 1946.

Strange, C. E., B.S.Ed.Adm.'26, Kansas State Tchrs. Col., Emporia; M.A.Ed.Adm.'36, Univ. of Chicago; Prin., Wichita H. S., North Wichita, Kansas, since 1945.

Sward, John I., A.B.'23, Bethany Col.; A.M.'38, Colo. State Col. of Educ., Greeley; Supt. of Sch., Valley Center, Kansas, since 1937.

Swartz, Daniel V., A.B.'31, Southwestern Col.; M.A.'38, Univ. of Colo.; Supt. of Sch., Fort Scott, Kansas, since 1946.

Taylor, Roy H., A.B.'25, Colo. State Tchrs. Col.; A.M.'41, Univ. of Wichita; Prin., Ingalls Elem. Sch., Wichita, Kansas, since 1945.

Terrell, B. E., B.S. in Ed.'34, Ft. Hays Kansas State Col.; M.S. in Ed.'39, Univ. of Kansas; Supt. of Sch. Dist. 20, Caldwell, Kansas, since 1943.

Tharp, Orval C., B.S.'25, Southwest Mo. State Col.; A.M.'36, Univ. of Mo.; Supt. of Sch., Blue Rapids, Kansas, since 1947.

Thomas, Frank, A.B.'30, Col. of Emporia; A.M.'40, Kansas Univ.; Supt. of Sch., Valley Falls, Kansas, since 1945.

Throckmorton, Adel F., A.B.'20, Southwestern Col.; M.A.'29, Univ. of Kansas; State Supt. of Pub. Instr., Topeka, Kansas, since 1949.

Tracy, Lester L., A.B.'39, Drury Col.; M.Ed.'49, Ed.D.'51, Univ. of Mo.; Dir. of Placement, Kansas State Tchrs. Col., Pittsburg, Kansas, since 1951.

Trimmell, Sidney E., B.S.'38, M.S.'46, Kansas State Tchrs. Col., Pittsburg; Supt. of Sch., Howard, Kansas, since 1946.

Twente, John W., A.B.'10, Central Wesleyan Col.; M.A.'16, Univ. of Kansas; Ph.D.'23, Tchrs. Col., Columbia Univ.; Prof. of Educ., Univ. of Kansas, Lawrence, Kansas, since 1925.

Vineyard, Jerry J., A.B.'21, William Jewell Col.; A.M.'27, D.Ed.'46, Univ. of Mo.; Supt. of Sch., Arkansas City, Kansas, since 1947.

Wallace, J. W., B.S. in Ed.'24, Kansas State Tchrs. Col. (Emporia); Supt. of Pub. Instr., Mound City, Kansas, since 1947.

Wantland, Clarence L., B.S.'49, M.S.'49, Kansas State Tchrs. Col., Pittsburg; Supt. of Sch., Galena, Kansas, since 1949.

Ward, Elmer W., B.S.'45, Northwestern State Col., Alva, Okla.; M.S.'47, Ft. Hays Kansas State Col.; Supt. of Sch., McDonald, Kansas.

Ward, Victor O., A.B.'35, Northwestern State, Alva, Okla.; Prin., H. S., Lenora, Kansas, since 1950.

Watkins, George Earl, A.B.'18, McPherson Col.; M.A.'30, Univ. of Kansas; Supt. of Sch., Paola, Kansas, since 1948.

Watson, Clifford R., A.B.'15, Friends Univ.; Co. Supt. of Sch., Topeka, Kansas, since 1951.

Webb, Harold V., M.S. in Ed.'49, Kansas State Tchrs. Col., Emporia; Supt. of Sch., Bucklin, Kansas, since 1950.

Wedelin, George H., B.S.'24, Kansas State Tchrs. Col., Emporia; M.E.'34, Univ. of Kansas; Supt. of Sch., Stafford, Kansas, since 1946.

Welch, Claude A., A.B.'31, Sterling Col.; M.S.'43, Kansas State Tchrs. Col., Emporia; Prin., Greeley Co. Community H. S., Tribune, Kansas, since 1949.

Wilbur, L. E., A.B.'28, Friends Univ.; Asst. Supt. in charge of Bus. Affairs, Bd. of Educ., Wichita, Kansas, since 1947.

Wolfe, William D., A.B.'17, Ed.D.'35, Col. of Emporia; M.E.'29, Univ. of Kansas; Supt. of Sch., Lawrence, Kansas.

Wolgast, D. E., B.S.'22, Ottawa Univ.; M.E.'42, Univ. of Kansas; Supt. of Sch., Marysville, Kansas, since 1933.

Wood, W. Clement, B.S.'35, Colo. Agrl. and Mech. Col.; M.A.'39, Colo. State Col. of Educ., Greeley; Head, Dept. of Educ., Ft. Hays Kansas State Col., Hays, Kansas, since 1949.

Woodin, James C., B.S.'28, Kansas State Tchrs. Col. (Pittsburg); M.S.'38, Colo. A.&M. Col.; Dir., Industrial and Adult Educ., Pub. Sch., Wichita, Kansas, since 1933.

Wright, C. O., A.B.'20, A.M.'21, Univ. of Mo.; Exec. Secy., Kansas State Tchrs. Assn., Topeka, Kansas, since 1941.

Wright, W. W., Dir. of Finance, Topeka, Kansas.

Yeargan, Gordon A., A.B.'32, M.S.'40, Kansas State Tchrs. Col., Pittsburg; Supt., Goodland Elem. Sch., and Sherman Community H. S., Goodland, Kansas, since 1952.

York, George A., B.S. in Ed.'24, Kansas State Tchrs. Col., Pittsburg; M.E.'35, Univ. of Kansas; Supt. of City Sch., Osawatomie, Kansas, since 1924.

Zink, Clarence L., B.S.'30, McPherson Col.; M.A.'36, Univ. of Kansas; Supt. of Sch., Mt. Hope, Kansas, since 1948.

INSTITUTIONAL MEMBERS

City Teachers Club, City Bldg., Salina, Kansas.

Forsyth Library, Fort Hays Kansas State Col., Hays, Kansas.

Kansas State Teachers College, Pittsburg, Kansas.

The McCormick-Mathers Publishing Company, C. W. Park, 1501 E. Douglas, Wichita, Kansas.

KENTUCKY

INDIVIDUAL MEMBERS

Arnett, Edgar, A.B.'25, Univ. of Ky.; M.A.'30, Columbia Univ.; Supt. of Sch., Erlanger, Ky., since 1930.

Atwood, Rufus B., A.B.'20, Fisk Univ.; B.S.'23, Iowa State Col. of Agrl. and Mech. Arts.; M.A.'34, Univ. of Chicago; LL.D.'36, Lane Col.; Pres., Ky. State Col., Frankfort, Ky., since 1929.

Belt, R. A., B.S.'20, M.A.'37, Univ. of Ky.; Supt. of Sch., Dawson Springs, Ky., since 1936.

Burkhead, G. C., B.S.'29, Western Kentucky State Tchrs. Col., Bowling Green; Co. Supt. of Sch., Elizabethtown, Ky., since 1934.

Burns, F. T., Co. Supt. of Sch., Owensboro, Ky.

Caldwell, L. C., A.B.'25, Marshall Col.; M.A.'27, George Peabody Col. for Tchrs.; Supt. of Sch., Ashland, Ky., since 1946.

Carmichael, Omer, A.B.'14, Univ. of Ala.; A.M.'24, Columbia Univ.; Supt. of Sch., Louisville, Ky., since 1945.

*Carr, John Wesley, A.B.'85, A.M.'90, Ind. Univ.; Ph.D.'13, New York Univ.; Pres., Dept. of Superintendence, 1905-06; Honorary Life Member, American Assn. of Sch. Admin. Address: State Tchrs. Col., Murray, Ky.

Cherry, Ralph W., A.B.'30, Maryville Col. (Tenn.); M.A.'38, Univ. of Ky.; Ed.D.'42, Tchrs. Col., Columbia Univ.; Supt. of Sch., Owensboro, Ky., since 1949.

Coffman, Ben F., A.B. in Ed.'29, M.A.'40, Univ. of Ky.; Supt. of Sch., Russell, Ky., since 1940.

Coslow, William F., B.S.'23, Univ. of Ky.; M.A.'28, Tchrs. Col., Columbia Univ.; Asst. Supt. in charge of Sec. Educ., Bd. of Educ., Louisville, Ky., since 1947.

Craft, Dave L., A.B.'40, Georgetown Col.; Supt. of Co. Sch., Whitesburg, Ky., since 1950.

Crosthwait, Ted L., B.S.'38, Morehead State Col.; M.S.'43, Calif. Inst. of Tech.; Dir., Purchases and Stores, Louisville Public Sch., Louisville, Ky., since 1952.

Dale, C. S., B.S. and M.A.'21, Univ. of Ill.; Supt. of Sch., Bellevue, Ky., since 1942.

Davis, Mitchell, M.A.'50, Western Ky. State Col.; Co. Supt. of Sch., Glasgow, Ky., since 1946.

Dickey, Frank G., A.B.'39, Transylvania Col.; M.A.'42, Ed.D.'47, Univ. of Ky.; Dean, Col. of Educ., Univ. of Ky., Lexington, Ky., since 1950.

Dodson, James Marvin, A.B.'39, M.A.'42, Western Ky. State Col.; Dir., Pub. Relations, Ky. Educ. Assn., Louisville, Ky., since 1950.

Dunn, D. Y., B.S. in Agr. '22, M.A.'29, Univ. of Ky.; Co. Supt. of Sch., Lexington, Ky., since 1929.

Estes, Kenneth A., M.A.'48, George Peabody Col. of Tchrs.; Bus. Mgr., City Sch., Owensboro, Ky., since 1948.

Farley, C. H., B.S.'28, Eastern Ky. State Tchrs. Col., Richmond; Co. Supt. of Sch., Pikeville, Ky., since 1934.

Farley, Gene C., A.B.'50, M.A.'50, Eastern Ky. State Col.; Prin. H. S., Glasgow, Ky., since 1951.

Fiser, H. Barton, B.S.'41, M.A.'48, Murray State Col.; Co. Supt. of Sch., Hopkinsville, Ky., since 1948.

Fossit, F. J., A.B.'21, Transylvania Col.; M.A.'28, Univ. of Ky.; Asst. Supt. of Sch., Covington, Ky., since 1950.

Gatton, Harper, A.B.'12, LL.D.'36, Georgetown Col.; A.M.'26, Univ. of Chicago; Supt. of Sch., Madisonville, Ky., since 1914.

Gilbert, Ted C., A.B.'39, M.A.'47, Eastern Ky. State Col.; Supt. of Pub. Sch., Maysville, Ky., since 1950.

Gotherman, Edward E., A.B.'19, M.A.'23, Univ. of Ky.; B.P.Th.'19, Col. of the Bible; Prin., Jefferson Davis Elem. Sch., Lexington, Ky., since 1928.

Hager, Cornelius R., A.B.'34, Asbury Col.; B.D.'38, Asbury Theol. Sem.; M.A.'41, Univ. of Ky.; Co. Supt. of Sch., Nicholasville, Ky., since 1947.

Hall, Floyd, B.S.'32, Murray State Col.; A.M.'42, Marshall Col.; Co. Supt. of Sch., Catlettsburg, Ky., since 1949.

Hall, Weldon, M.A.'50, Murray State Col.; Supt. of Sch., Columbia, Ky., since 1950.

Hamilton, Thomas F., M.A.'42, Univ. of Ky.; Supt. of Sch., Campbellsville, Ky., since 1945.

Harding, Kenneth H., A.B.'24, M.A.'28, Univ. of Ky.; Supt. of Sch., Mt. Sterling, Ky., since 1943.

Hartstern, Fred J., Architect, 200 McDowell Bldg., 505 S. 3rd St., Louisville, Ky.

Herr, Ben B., A.B.'20, Transylvania Col.; M.A. '23, Columbia Univ.; Bus. Dir., since 1934, and Acting Supt. of Pub. Sch., Lexington, Ky., since 1949.

Hopkins, P. H., B.A.'07, Georgetown Col.; Supt. of Sch., Somerset, Ky., since 1927.

Hopper, Robert L., B.S.'41, North Texas State Tchrs. Col., Denton; M.Ed.'47, Harvard Univ.; Assoc. Prof., Dept. of Admin., Col. of Educ., Univ. of Ky., Lexington, Ky.

Knuckles, W. L., Jr., A.B.'31, Union Col. (Ky.); M.A.'51, Univ. of Ky.; Supt. of Sch., Brooksville, Ky., since 1951.

Koffman, Gladstone, A.B.'15, Union Univ., Jackson, Tenn.; A.M.'28, Univ. of Chicago; Supt. of Sch., Hopkinsville, Ky., since 1932.

Lassiter, Alford Lee, B.S.'19, Col. of William and Mary; M.A.'30, Columbia Univ.; Supt. of Sch., Richmond, Ky., since 1941.

McCormick, Charles Edward, B.S. in Ed.'41, Univ. of Cincinnati; Co. Supt. of Sch., Alexandria, Ky., since 1943.

KENTUCKY

McGuire, Heman H., A.B.'38, Morehead State Col.; Co. Supt. of Sch., Grayson, Ky., since 1938.

McQuown, James B., Supt. of Pub. Sch., Ashland, Ky.

Maynard, Fred, A.B.'27, M.A.'40, Univ. of Ky.; Co. Supt. of Sch., Greenup, Ky., since 1942.

Meece, L. E., A.B.'31, M.A.'32, Ph.D.'38, Univ. of Ky.; Prof. of Educ., Univ. of Ky., Lexington, Ky., since 1941.

Melton, Monroe Joel, A.B.'15, Ind. State Tchrs. Col., Terre Haute; A.M.'33, Univ. of Colo.; Asst. Supt. of Sch. in charge of Bus. Affairs, Louisville, Ky., since 1946.

Milburn, Joda, M.A. in Ed.'50, Eastern Ky. State Col.; Supt., Lincoln Co. Sch., Stanford, Ky., since 1950.

Moore, W. J., A.B.'25, A.M.'28, Ph.D.'31, Univ. of Ky.; Dean, Eastern Ky. State Tchrs. Col., Richmond, Ky., since 1945.

Noe, Samuel VanArsdale, A.B.'22, Centre Col.; M.A.'28, Columbia Univ.; Admin. Asst., Bd. of Educ., Louisville, Ky., since 1950.

O'Donnell, William F., A.B.'12, LL.D.'43, Transylvania Col.; M.A.'32, Tchrs. Col., Columbia Univ.; Pres., Eastern Ky. State Col., Richmond, Ky., since 1941.

Owens, Anderson D., B.A.'18, M.A.'25, Transylvania Col.; Ed.D.'39, Univ. of Cincinnati; Supt. of Sch., Newport, Ky., since 1925.

Pitt, Felix Newton, A.B.'16, M.A.'17, St. Mary's Univ.; Ph.D.'33, Univ. of Fribourg, Switzerland; Supt. of Catholic Sch., Louisville, Ky., since 1925.

Ray, (Mrs.) Willie C., A.B.'13, M.A.'30, Transylvania Col.; Supt. of Sch., Shelbyville, Ky., since 1930.

Rayburn, J. D., B.S.'35, Murray State Col.; M.A.'50, George Peabody Col. for Tchrs.; Supt. of City Sch., Providence, Ky., since 1949.

Redding, C. D., A.B.'19, Georgetown Col.; M.A.'23, Univ. of Ky.; Supt. of City Sch., Frankfort, Ky., since 1939.

Reiley, William Traver, B.S. in Ed.'42, Univ. of Cincinnati; M.A. in Ed.'46, Xavier Univ.; Supt. of Pub. Sch., Dayton, Ky., since 1950.

Reneau, R. C., A.B.'28, Berea Col.; Supt., Clinton Co. Sch., Albany, Ky., since 1934.

Ridgway, John M., B.A.'31, State Tchrs. Col., Morehead, Minn.; M.A.'36, Univ. of Ky.; Supt. of Sch., Lexington, Ky., since 1951.

Ross, Alton, B.S.'35, M.A.'48, Murray State Col.; Supt., Oldham Co. Sch., La Grange, Ky., since 1950.

Rubado, Clarence A., Ph.D.'29, Tchrs. Col., Columbia Univ.; Asst. Supt. of Sch., Louisville, Ky., since 1929.

Scott, Frank D., M.A.'30, Univ. of Ky.; Co. Supt. of Sch., Flemingsburg, Ky., since 1944.

Scully, Mark F., B.S. in Ed.'35, Southeast Mo. State Tchrs. Col., Cape Girardeau; M.A.'36, George Peabody Col. for Tchrs.; Supt. of Sch., Paducah, Ky., since 1947.

Slaughter, Horace B., Bus. Dir., Louisville Pub. Sch., Louisville, Ky.

Smith, H. L., B.S.'25, George Peabody Col. for Tchrs.; M.A.'30, Tchrs. Col., Columbia Univ.; Supt. of Sch., Henderson, Ky., since 1947.

Snapp, Carlos V., A.B.'23, M.A.'32, Univ. of Ky.; Supt. of Sch., Jenkins, Ky., since 1929.

Spain, Charles R., A.B.'36, Bethel Col. (Tenn.); M.A.'37, George Peabody Col. for Tchrs.; Ed.D.'41, Columbia Univ.; Pres., Morehead State Col., Morehead, Ky.

Sublett, James L., A.B.'39, Transylvania Col.; M.A.'48, Univ. of Ky.; Dir. of Instr., Jefferson Co. Sch., Louisville, Ky., since 1950.

Swearingen, Orville L., A.B.'29, Univ. of Ky.; Co. Supt. of Sch., Somerset, Ky., since 1946.

Swing, Glenn O., B.A.'16, M.A.'17, Ohio State Univ.; Supt. of Sch., Covington, Ky., since 1927.

Taylor, H. C., M.A.'29, George Peabody Col. for Tchrs.; Supt. of Sch., Elizabethtown, Ky., since 1931.

Taylor, Herman W., B.A.'29, Lincoln Memorial Univ.; M.A.'39, George Peabody Col. for Tchrs.; Supt. of Sch., Franklin, Ky., since 1945.

Thomasson, R. Case, A.B.'25, Centre Col.; M.A.'36, Univ. of Ky.; Supt. of Sch., Middlesboro, Ky., since 1944.

True, Roy T., Co. Supt. of Sch., Frankfort, Ky., since 1934.

Turner, (Mrs.) Marie R., A.B.'29, Morehead State Col., Ky.; Co. Supt. of Sch., Jackson, Ky., since 1931.

Turpen, Noah C., B.S.'29, Middle Tenn. State Col.; M.A.'32, George Peabody Col. for Tchrs.; Ed.D.'41, Tchrs. Col., Columbia Univ.; Co. Supt. of Sch., Lexington, Ky., since 1949.

Van Hoose, Richard, A.B.'35, Georgetown Col.; M.A. in Ed.'39, Univ. of Ky.; Co. Supt. of Sch., Louisville, Ky.

Ward, Edwin R., M.A.'36, Univ. of Ky.; Asst. Supt., Bus. Mgr., Fayette Co. Sch., Lexington, Ky., since 1949.

Ward, (Mrs.) Emma B., A.B.'36, Univ. of Ky.; Supt. of Co. Sch., Lawrenceburg, Ky., since 1948.

Wells, J. Evelyn, A.B.'24, Univ. of Louisville; M.A.'34, Columbia Col.; Asst. Prin., Shawnee H. S., Louisville, Ky., since 1930.

Woods, Ralph H., Ph.B.'21, Berea Col.; B.S. in Agrl.'23, M.A.'27, Univ. of Ky.; Ph.D.'30, Cornell Univ.; Pres., Murray State Col., Murray, Ky., since 1945.

INSTITUTIONAL MEMBER

Library, Eastern Ky. State Col., Richmond, Ky.

LOUISIANA

INDIVIDUAL MEMBERS

Aiken, Ewell S., A.B.'23, Northwestern State Col. of La.; M.S.'29, La. State Univ.; Supt., Rapides Parish Sch., Alexandria, La., since 1949.

Babin, Larry J., B.A.'11, La. State Univ.; Supt. of Sch., Donaldsonville, La., since 1925.

Barrow, Clark L., B.A.'23, M.A.'34, La. State Univ.; M.A.'35, Ph.D.'39, Columbia Univ.; Pres., Southeastern La. Col., Hammond, La., since 1952.

Becker, Ernest O., B.A.'16, M.A.'18, B.B.A.'20, Tulane Univ.; Asst. Supt. of Sch., New Orleans, La., since 1944.

Bond, George W., B.S.'20, Univ. of Ark.; M.A.'23, Univ. of Chicago; Ed.D.'38, Columbia Univ.; Dean, Sch. of Educ., La. Polytech. Inst., Ruston, La., since 1945.

Bourgeois, Lionel J., Sr., B.A., Jefferson Col.; M.A., Tulane Univ.; LL.B., Loyola Univ.; Supt. of Sch., New Orleans, La., 1946-51.

Caldwell, S. A., Dean, Jr. Div., Allen Hall, La. State Univ., Baton Rouge, La.

Carmouche, Norman Edward, B.A.'27, M.A.'44, La. State Univ.; Parish Supt. of Sch., Plattenville, La.

Cayer, L. A., B.A.'25, La. Col.; Parish Supt. of Sch., Marksville, La., since 1937.

418

Clark, Felton G., A.B.'24, Beloit Col.; A.M.'25, Ph.D.'33, Columbia Univ.; Pres., Southern Univ., Baton Rouge, La., since 1938.

Eley, Edwin William, B.A.'18, Earlham Col.; First Asst. Supt. of Sch., New Orleans, La., since 1932.

Emmons, Morelle, B.A.'37, La. Polytech. Inst.; M.A.'40, La. State Univ.; Parish Supt. of Sch., Ruston, La., since 1948.

Ferran, Rose Marie, B.A.'25, M.A.'29, Tulane Univ.; Dir., Kdgn.-Prim. Grades, Pub. Schs., New Orleans, La., since 1943.

Foote, John M., M.A.'23, George Peabody Col. for Tchrs.; D.Ed.'36, La. State Univ. Address: 1853 Blouin Ave., Baton Rouge, La.

Ford, G. W., A.B.'26, Northwestern State Col. of La.; M.A.'31, La. State Univ.; Supt. of City Sch., Lake Charles, La., since 1948.

Frazar, Lether Edward, A.B.'28, Southwestern La. Inst.; M.A.'32, La. State Univ.; Pres., McNeese State Col., Lake Charles, La., since 1944.

Hanchey, K. R., M.S.'36, La. State Univ.; Supt. of Sch., Beauregard Parish, De Ridder, La., since 1930.

Higgins, L. W., M.A.'38, Tulane Univ.; Parish Supt. of Sch., Gretna, La., since 1940.

Israel, M. J., B.A.'28, M.A.'32, La. State Univ.; Supt. of Sch., Bogalusa, La., since 1939.

Janvier, Carmelite, B.A.'11, M.A.'13, Tulane Univ. Address: 1130 Eighth St., New Orleans, La.

Johns, William Christy, B.S.'28, George Peabody Col. for Tchrs.; M.A.'40, La. State Univ.; Asst. Supt. of Caddo Parish Sch., Shreveport, La., since 1945.

Jordan, A. L., Central Memorial H. S., Bogalusa, La.

Koonce, John D., B.A.'34, La. Polytech. Inst.; M.E.'46, La. State Univ.; Supt., Jackson Parish Sch., Jonesboro, La., since 1948.

Landry, J. C., B.A.'22, Southwestern La. Inst.; M.A.'33, La. State Univ.; Parish Supt. of Sch., Lafayette, La., since 1948.

Landry, Thomas R., B.A.'31, Southwestern La. Inst.; M.A.'39, La. State Univ.; State Supvr. of Elem. Sch., State Dept. of Educ., Baton Rough, La., since 1949.

Lavergne, Remi, Parish Supt. of Educ., Port Allen, La.

Lee, E. A., A.B.'24, La. State Normal Col., Natchitoches; Parish Supt. of Sch., Natchitoches, La., since 1925.

Lucky, S. G., M.A.'39, La. State Univ.; Parish Supt. of Sch., Bastrop, La., since 1949.

Marquette, M. L., Div. Mgr., The South Coast Corp., Franklin, La., since 1941.

Marshall, Donald, B.A.'07, M.A.'09, La. State Univ.; Asst. Supt., Orleans Parish Sch. Board, New Orleans, La., since 1942.

Martin, H. G., B.S.'08, Univ. of Mo.; Dir., Isaac Delgado Central Trades Sch., New Orleans, La., since 1920.

Moncla, Robert O., Parish Supt. of Educ., Thibodaux, La.

Moncla, Samuel A., B.A.'26, Southwestern La. Inst.; M.A.'37, La. State Univ.; Parish Supt. of Sch., Opelousas, La., since 1943.

Newton, J. H., Jr., B.S.'25, Southwestern Presbyterian Univ.; M.A.'40, La. State Univ.; Parish Supt. of Sch., Amite, La., since 1944.

Olinde, Patrick, B.A.'31, M.A.'39, La. State Univ.; Supt., Plaquemines Parish Sch., Pointe-a-la-Hache, La., since 1942.

Perry, Currie L., B.A.'31, Northwestern State Col. of La.; M.A.'45, La. State Univ.; Asst. Supt., Caddo Parish Sch. Bd., Shreveport, La., since 1948.

Pitcher, J. E., B.S.'18, La. State Univ.; Parish Supt. of Sch., Minden, La., since 1936.

Prather, H. Lee, A.B.'10, LL.B.'12, Univ. of Mo.; Pres., Northwestern State Col., Natchitoches, La., since 1950.

Robertson, J. B., B.A.'28, M.A.'40, La. State Univ.; Dir., Elem. and Sec. Educ., State Dept. of Educ., Baton Rouge, La.

Robertson, Minns Sledge, B.A.'21, Northwestern State Col. of La.; M.A.'23, Ph.D.'25, George Peabody Col. for Tchrs.; Research Prof. of Educ. and Assoc. Dir., Bureau of Educ. Research, La. State Univ., Baton Rouge, La., since 1948.

Shows, S. M., B.A.'26, Northwestern State Col.; Supt. of DeSoto Parish Sch., Mansfield, La., since 1926.

Sigler, A. L., B.A.'31, La. State Normal Col.; M.A.'40, La. State Univ.; Parish Supt. of Educ., Coushatta, La., since 1941.

Smith, L. L., Allen Parish Sch., Oberlin, La.

Solis, Paul J., Asst. Supt., Jefferson Parish Sch. Bd., Gretna, La.

Taylor, Elizabeth, B.S.'28, George Peabody Col. for Tchrs.; M.A.'37, Columbia Univ.; Asst. Parish Supt. of Sch., Shreveport, La., since 1945.

Terrebonne, L. P., A.B.'21, Southwestern La. Inst.; M.A.'21, Ph.D.'40, La. State Univ.; Parish Supt. of Educ., Plaquemine, La., since 1929.

Thatcher, Fred G., B.I.'04, La. Polytech. Inst.; Exec. Secy., La. Sch. Bd. Assn., Baton Rouge, La., since 1947.

Walker, O. Perry, B.E.'22, Tulane Univ.; M.S. '39, La. State Univ.; Acting Supt. of Sch., New Orleans, La., since 1951.

Walsworth, M. M., B.A.'30, La. Polytech. Inst.; M.A.'36, La. State Univ.; Parish Supt. of Sch., Lake Providence, La., since 1949.

White, Roscoe H., A.B.'23, A.M.'26, Univ. of Colo.; Parish Supt. of Sch., Shreveport, La., since 1943.

Wright, Howard W., Exec. Secy., La. Educ. Assn., Baton Rouge, La., since 1939.

INSTITUTIONAL MEMBERS

Louisiana Education Association, Baton Rouge, La.

Materials Library, Richland Parish Sch. Bd., c/o Mrs. Selma W. Tomb, Supv., Rayville, La.

Russell Library, Northwestern State Col., Natchitoches, La.

Stephens Memorial Library, Southwestern La. Inst., Lafayette, La.

MAINE

INDIVIDUAL MEMBERS

Additon, Loring R., B.S.'26, Bates Col.; M.A.'39, Univ. of Maine; Supt. of Sch., Bath, Maine, since 1944.

Aikins, Frederick H., B.S.'17, Univ. of Maine; M.Ed.'37, Bates Col.; Supt. of Sch., South Windham, Maine, since 1926.

Andrews, Roland B., B.S.'28, Colby Col.; M.Ed. '41, Univ. of Maine; Supt. of Sch. Union 121 Presque Isle, Maine, since 1943.

Bagley, Laurence P., A.B.'26, M.A.'37, Bates Col.; Supt. of Sch., Union 114, Island Falls, Maine, since 1944.

Bailey, Francis Louis, B.A.'21, A.M.'24, Univ. of Mich.; Ph.D.'39, Columbia Univ.; Pres., Gorham State Tchrs. Col., Gorham, Maine, since 1940.

MAINE

Beal, George E., A.B.'16, Bowdoin Col; A.M.'34, Bates Col.; A.M.'41, Bowdoin Col.; Supt. of Sch., South Portland, Maine, since 1940.

Brackett, Anthony G. L., B.S.'33, Middlebury Col.; Ed.M.'42, Harvard Univ.; Supt. of Sch., Westbrook, Maine, since 1947.

Bracy, Alfred A., B.S.'37, Tufts Col.; M.S.'39, Univ. of Mass.; Supt. of Sch., Canton, Maine, since 1951.

Carpenter, Roland J., B.S.'22, M.Ed.'39, Bates Col.; Supt. of Sch., Bangor, Maine, since 1943.

Clifford, Harold B., A.B.'16, M.A.'41, Bates Col.; Supt. of Sch., Union 49, East Boothbay, Maine, since 1925.

Crabtree, Paul L., Secy.-Treas., Assoc. Exhibitors of the Natl. Educ. Assn., Island Falls, Maine, since 1936.

Crawford, John R., B.A.'24, Culver-Stockton Col.; M.A.'29, Ph.D.'31, State Univ. of Iowa; Prof. of Educ. and Dir., Bur. of Educ. Research and Serv., Univ. of Maine, Orono, Maine, since 1930.

Cyr, Albert A., A.B.'31, Harvard Univ.; Supt. of Sch., Fort Kent, Maine, since 1948.

Day, Lorey Clifford, B.A.'13, M.A.'16, Clark Univ.; Union Supt. of Sch., Kittery, Maine, since 1945.

Fernald, Waldron E., A.B.'27, Univ. of Maine; A.M.'40, Brown Univ.; Supt. of Sch., Danforth, Maine, since 1951.

Gallagher, Erwin A., B.S. in Ed.'47, Univ. of Maine; Supt. of Sch., Skowhegan, Maine.

Grant, Buford L., B.S.'43, Univ. of Maine; Supt. of Sch., Camden, Maine, since 1951.

Greene, Porter C., B.S. in M.E.'28, M.Ed.'42, Univ. of Vt.; Headmaster, Thornton Academy, Saco, Maine, since 1946.

Hale, William Wallace, B.S.'25, Colby Col.; M.Ed.'43, Univ. of Maine; Supt. of Sch., Millinocket, Maine, since 1945.

Harriman, Alonzo Jesse, B.S.E.'20, Univ. of Maine; M.Arch.'28, Harvard Univ.; Treas., Alonzo J. Harriman, Inc., Auburn, Maine, since 1945.

Hincks, Edward W., Supt. of Sch., Calais, Maine.

Kent, Frank H., B.S.'39, M.Ed.'49, Univ. of Maine; Supt. of Sch., Guilford, Maine, since 1946.

Kinney, Bruce J., B.S.'48, Univ. of Maine; Supt. of Sch., Union 27, Dixfield, Maine, since 1949.

Leonard, Joseph A., A.B.'27, Tufts Col.; M.Ed. '45, Harvard Univ.; Supt. of Sch., Old Town, Maine, since 1938.

Libby, Philip C., B.S.'40, Univ. of New Hampshire; Supt. of Sch., Belfast, Maine, since 1950.

Lord, Carl B., B.S.'15, Colby Col.; Ed.M.'36, Bates Col.; Supt. of Sch., Union 52, North Vassalboro, Maine, since 1924.

Lunt, Robert B., B.S.'30, Colby Col.; M.A. in Ed.'33, Univ. of Maine; Supt. of Sch., Union 10, Scarborough, Maine, since 1949.

Lyseth, Harrison C., B.A.'21, Bowdoin Col.; Ed.M.'28, Ed.D.'41, Harvard Univ.; Supt. of Sch., Portland, Maine, since 1942.

McGuire, Harvey C., B.S. in Ed.'33, Univ. of Maine; Supt. of Sch., Ridlonville, Maine, since 1944.

McMonagle, Edward L., A.B.'32, Holy Cross Col.; Dir. of Schooling in Unorganized Territory, State Dept. of Educ., Augusta, Maine, since 1946.

Martin, Edgar P., B.A.'41, Colby Col.; M.S. in Ed.'46, Butler Univ.; Union Supt. of Sch., Van Buren, Maine, since 1946.

Nickerson, Kermit S., A.B.'26, Dartmouth Col.; M.A.'34, Univ. of Maine; Supt. of Sch., Waterville, Maine, since 1945.

Peakes, Lawrence A., A.B.'28, Colby Col.; M.A.'40, Bates Col.; Union Supt. of Sch., Rumford, Maine, since 1944.

Perkins, Henry G., B.S.'25, Univ. of Maine; Supt. of Sch., Union 92, Ellsworth, Maine, since 1946.

Puffer, Charles, B.A. in Ed.'32, Univ. of Maine; Supt. of Sch., South Paris, Maine, since 1945.

Redding, Hubert Ervin, B.R.E.'26, Atlantic Union Col.; A.M.'28, Boston Univ.; Supt. of Sch., Union 53, Oakland, Maine, since 1948.

Russell, Clyde, B.A.'22, M.A.'26, Colby Col.; Ed.M.'33, Harvard Univ.; Exec. Secy., Maine Tchrs. Assn., Augusta, Maine, since 1945.

Russell, Garland B., A.B.'33, A.M.'35, Brown Univ.; D.Ed.'43, Boston Univ.; Assoc. Prof. of Educ., Univ. of Maine, Orono, Maine, since 1949.

Russell, J. Weldon, B.S.'32, M.E.'49, Univ. of Maine; Supt. of Sch., Union 70, Rockland, Maine, since 1948.

Shibles, Mark R., B.A.'29, Colby Col.; M.Ed.'35, Boston Univ.; Dean, Sch. of Educ., Dir. of Summer Session and Dir. of Extension Div., Univ. of Maine, Orono, Maine, since 1947.

Shibles, Perry F., Supt. of Sch., Augusta, Maine.

Small, Elmer O., A.B.'15, Bates Col.; Ed.M.'37, Harvard Univ.; Supt. of Sch., Union 30, Lisbon Falls, Maine, since 1943.

Smith, Gwyeth T., B.S.'27, Colby Col.; M.A.'37, Columbia Univ.; Supt., Sch. Union 54, Fairfield, Maine, since 1945.

*Smith, Payson, A.M.'03, Tufts Col.; LL.D.'08, Univ. of Maine; Litt.D.'09, Bates Col.; Litt. D.'11, Bowdoin Col.; D.Ed., R. I. Col. of Educ.; LL.D., Norwich Univ.; LL.D., Northeastern Univ.; LL.D.'35, Springfield Col.; D.Ed., Colby Col.; Pres., Dept. of Superintendence, 1923-24; Honorary Life Member, American Assn. of Sch. Admin.; Lecturer, Sch. of Educ., Univ. of Maine, Orono, Maine.

Sullivan, Neil V., B.S.E.'39, State Tchrs. Col., Fitchburg, Mass.; M.A.'41, Columbia Univ.; Supt. of Sch., Sanford, Maine, since 1950.

Veayo, Galen I., B.A.'31, M.A.'42, Univ. of Maine; Supt. of Sch., Auburn, Maine, since 1946.

Violette, Lawrence A., A.B.'25, Marist Col., Washington, D. C.; Supt. of Sch., Madawaska, Maine, since 1946.

*Webber, Elmer Harrison, Diploma '07, State Normal Sch., Farmington, Maine; B.Pd.'15, Univ. of Maine; A.M.'23, Bates Col.; Pres., Webber Inst., Mt. Vernon, Maine, since 1945.

Wenners, Paul Joseph, A.B.'24, A.M.'26, Boston Col.; Ed.M.'44, Ed.D.'52, Harvard Univ.; Prin., Robert W. Traip Academy, Kittery, Maine, since 1944.

Wieden, Clifford O. T., B.S.'23, Acadia Univ.; Ed.M.'34, Bates Col.; Pres., Aroostook State Tchrs. Col., Presque Isle, Maine, since 1952.

Wiggin, Harold A., B.B.A.'23, Ed.M.'34, Boston Univ.; Supt. of Sch., Union 75, Union, Maine, since 1949.

Woodman, Orlando C., B.A.'16, Bates Col.; Union Supt. of Sch., Gardiner, Maine, since 1944.

Woodworth, A. Alden, Supt. of Sch., Lewiston, Maine.

420

MARYLAND

INDIVIDUAL MEMBERS

Adams, Mary A., B.S.'25, M.A.'30, Johns Hopkins Univ.; Asst. Supt. of Sch., Baltimore, Md., since 1942.

*Allan, Harold A., A.B.'06, Bates Col.; Honorary Life Member, American Assn. of Sch. Admin.; Asst. Secy. for Bus., Natl. Educ. Assn., 1923-49; Trustee, Natl. Educ. Assn., 1948-52. Address: 6211 Georgia St., Chevy Chase 15, Md.

Beall, Irl H., M.E.'49, Univ. of Md.; Prin., Gray Manor Elem. Sch., Dundalk, Md., since 1950.

Bender, Charles O., Pres., Bd. of Educ., Grantsville, Md.

Bennett, J. M., A.B.'10, Western Md. Col.; Co. Supt. of Sch., Salisbury, Md., since 1917.

Blackwell, Jefferson Davis, B.S.'14, Univ. of Mo.; A.M.'23, Tchrs. Col., Columbia Univ.; Ph.D.'29, Johns Hopkins Univ.; Pres., State Tchrs. Col., Salisbury, Md., since 1935.

Boston, William Theodore, B.A.'30, Washington Col.; M.A.'46, Univ. of Md.; Co. Supt. of Sch., Cambridge, Md., since 1938.

Brish, William Murray, A.B.'28, Franklin and Marshall Col.; M.A.'32, Tchrs. Col., Columbia Univ.; Co. Supt. of Sch., Hagerstown, Md., since 1947.

Broening, Angela M., A.B., Goucher Col.; A.M., Ph.D., Johns Hopkins Univ.; Asst. Dir. of Research, Pub. Schs., Baltimore, Md.

Broome, Edwin W., LL.B.'16, A.B.'20, George Washington Univ.; Co. Supt. of Sch., Rockville, Md., since 1916.

Brown, Edward W., B.S.'23, Princeton Univ.; Head Master, Calvert Sch., Baltimore, Md., since 1940.

Buchwald, Leona C., Asst. Dir., Guid. and Placement, Pub. Schs., Baltimore, Md.

Busick, James G., Supt. of Sch., Dorchester Co., Cambridge, Md.

Byrd, Harry Clifton, B.S.'08, Univ. of Md.; LL.D.'36, Washington Col.; LL.D.'38, Dickinson Col.; D.Sc.'38, Western Md. Col.; Pres., Univ. of Md., College Park, Md., since 1936.

Carlson, C. Allen, B.Ped.'14, State Tchrs. Col., Mansfield, Pa.; B.S.'36, A.M.'38, Univ. of Md.; Co. Supt. of Sch., Princess Anne, Md., since 1940.

Carpenter, Richard E., Bachelor's '35, Dartmouth Col.; Master's '46, Ed.D.'51, Tchrs. Col., Columbia Univ.; Asst. Supt., Montgomery Co. Sch., Rockville, Md., since 1947.

Certain, (Mrs.) Julia L., Enoch Pratt Free Libr., Baltimore, Md.

Chapman, Harold Benjamin, B.A.'11, Yale Univ.; M.A.'24, Tchrs. Col., Columbia Univ.; Ph.D.'26, Ohio State Univ.; Asst. Dir., Bureau of Research and Statistics, Pub. Schs., Baltimore, Md., since 1926.

Compton, Lillian C., B.A.'14, W. Va. Univ.; M.A.'28, Columbia Univ.; Pres., State Tchrs. Col., Frostburg, Md., since 1945.

Cooper, Paul D., B.S.'39, Western Md. Col.; M.Ed.'43, Univ. of Md.; Co. Supt. of Sch., Snow Hill, Md., since 1948.

Cooper, William P., A.B.'23, Western Md. Col.; M.A.'32, Univ. of Md.; Dir. of Cafeterias, Co. Bd. of Educ., Cumberland, Md., since 1943.

Corr, Reade W., A.B.'26, Univ. of Richmond; M.A.'38, Columbia Univ.; Supt. of Sch., Chestertown, Md., since 1947.

Davis, James Willard, A.B.'15, Washington Col.; M.A.'24, Tchrs. Col., Columbia Univ.; Co. Supt. of Sch., Easton, Md., since 1935.

Dawson, Walter W., Co. Bd. of Educ., Oakland, Md.

Dent, Lettie Marshall, A.B.'15, Western Md. Col.; Co. Supt. of Sch., Leonardtown, Md., since 1928.

Diehl, William C., A.B.'23, Gettysburg Col.; M.Ed.'46, Univ. of Md.; Asst. Supt. of Sch., Hagerstown, Md., since 1947.

Dorn, Wesley N., A.B.'33, Gettysburg Col.; M.Ed.'47, Univ. of Md.; Special Asst., Bus. Div., Dept. of Educ., Baltimore, Md., since 1943.

Drazek, Stanley Joseph, B.S.'41, N. Y. State Tchrs. Col., Oswego; M.A.'47, Ph.D.'50, Univ. of Md.; Asst. Dean, Col. of Special Continuation Studies, Assoc. Prof. of Educ., Univ. of Md., College Park, Md., since 1950.

Dunn, Wendell E., A.B.'16, A.M.'27, Univ. of Wis.; Prin., Forest Park H. S., Baltimore, Md., since 1935.

Fischer, John Henry, B.S.'40, Johns Hopkins Univ.; M.A.'49, Ed.D.'51, Tchrs. Col., Columbia Univ.; Deputy Supt. of Pub. Instr., Baltimore, Md., since 1952.

Fitzgerald, W. Stewart, A.B.'13, St. John's Col.; M.A.'29 Tchrs. Col., Columbia Univ.; Co. Supt. of Sch., Denton, Md., since 1940.

Fockler, Edwin B., B.S.'23, Univ. of Del.; M.A.'35, Univ. of Pa.; Supvr. of H. S., Elkton, Md., since 1947.

Froelicher, Hans, Jr., A.B.'12, Haverford Col.; LL.B.'17, Univ. of Md.; Headmaster, Park Sch., Baltimore, Md., since 1932.

Gerstmyer, Eva E., B.S.'28, M.E.'33, Johns Hopkins Univ.; Dir., Primary Grades and Kdgns., Dept. of Educ., Baltimore, Md., since 1933.

Grau, Mary L., B.S.'31, D.Ed.'45, Johns Hopkins Univ.; M.A.'36, Tchrs. Col., Columbia Univ.; Supv. of Elem. Educ., Bd. of Educ., Montgomery Co., Rockville, Md., since 1948.

Hale, Helen E., A.B.'35, Goucher Col.; M.A.'52, Johns Hopkins Univ.; Supvr., Secondary Aigburth Manor, Towson, Md., since 1949.

Hall, R. Milton, D.Ed.'37, Johns Hopkins Univ.; Prin., Clifton Park Jr. High Sch., Baltimore, Md., since 1947.

Hardesty, R. Bowen, A.B.'32, Randolph-Macon Col.; M.A.'34, Columbia Univ.; Co. Supt. of Sch., Oakland, Md., since 1948.

Hawkins, Earle T., A.B.'23, LL.D.'48, Western Md. Col.; M.A.'28, Columbia Univ.; Ph.D.'42, Yale Univ.; Pres., State Tchrs. Col., Towson, Md., since 1947.

Hawkins, Elmer T., A.B.'26, Morgan State Col.; A.M.'34, Hampton Institute; Prin., Garnett Sch., Chestertown, Md., since 1926.

Healy, Katharine L., B.S.'21, M.A.'29, Johns Hopkins Univ.; Instrl. Supvr., Dept. of Educ., Hagerstown, Md.

*Henderson, Elmer A., Asst. Supt. of Sch. in chg. of Colored Schs., Baltimore, Md., since 1945.

Henry, William E., A.B.'23, Va. Union Univ.; M.A.'29, Ed.D.'45, Univ. of Pa.; Pres., Md. State Tchrs. Col., Bowie, Md., since 1942.

Hughes, Harry R., Co. Supt. of Sch., Prince Frederick, Md., since 1932.

Hurley, Charles F., B.S.'34, Mo. State Tchrs. Col., Maryville; M.A.'41, Tchrs. Col., Columbia Univ.; Prin., Sec. H. S., East New Market, Md., since 1943.

Jackson, Houston R., A.B.'27, Morgan State Col.; A.M.'37, Univ. of Pa.; Asst. Supt. of Sch., Baltimore, Md., since 1951.

Jenkins, David S., B.A.'30, St. Johns Col. (Md.); M.A.'42, Ed.D.'49, Univ. of Md.; Co. Supt. of Sch., Annapolis, Md., since 1946.

Jenkins, Martin David, B.S.'25, Howard Univ.; A.B.'30, Ind. State Tchrs. Col., Terre Haute; M.S.'33, Ph.D.'35, Northwestern Univ.; Pres., Morgan State Col., Baltimore, Md., since 1948.

Jenness, Samuel M., B.S.'22, Wash. Col.; A.M. '29, Univ. of Md.; Co. Supt. of Sch., Westminster, Md., since 1946.

Johannes, Dana B., Architect, 855 Pershing Drive, Silver Spring, Md.

King, Oliveine C., M.Ed.'49, Univ. of Md.; Supvg. Prin., Elem. Sch., Havre de Grace, Md., since 1947.

Kopp, Charles L., A.B.'09, Gettysburg Col.; A.M.'25, Tchrs. Col., Columbia Univ.; Ed.D. '34, Gettysburg Col.; Co. Supt. of Sch., Cumberland, Md, 1928-52 (retired).

Lamborn, Robert L., A.B.'38, Stanford Univ.; Ed.M.'41, Harvard Univ.; Ed.D.'51, Johns Hopkins Univ.; Headmaster, McDonogh Sch., McDonogh, Md., since 1952.

Lemmel, William H., A.B.'22, M.A.'28, State Univ. of Iowa; D.Ed.'40, Tchrs. Col., Columbia Univ.; Supt. of Sch., Baltimore, Md., since 1946.

Lewis, John W., A.B.'17, Colgate Univ.; Asst. Supt. of Sch., Baltimore, Md., since 1927.

McCann, R. Harold, Dir., Transportation and Maintenance, Bd. of Educ., Annapolis, Md.

McCormick, Leo Joseph, A.B.'21, St. Mary's Sem.; S.T.L.'27, Propaganda Univ., Rome, Italy; Ph.D.'43, Catholic Univ. of America; Supt., Bur. of Catholic Educ., Archdiocese of Baltimore, Baltimore, Md., since 1943.

Martin, T. Carlyle, B.A.'22, Berea Col.; B.S. in Agr.'24, Univ. of W. Va.; M.A. in Ed.'26, Univ. of Md.; Supt. of Sch., La Plata, Md., since 1951.

Mason, Elwood B., A.B.'31, Washington Col.; M.A.'40, Duke Univ.; Prin., Leland Jr. High Sch., Chevy Chase, Md., since 1943.

Mauck, Willfred, 689 Rollingwood Dr., Chevy Chase 15, Md.

*Murphy, Harry T., B.A.'35, Western Md. Col.; M.A.'48, Tchrs. Col., Columbia Univ.; Supvr. of Pupil Personnel, Pub. Sch., Ellicott City, Md., since 1945.

Murray, Loren L., Architect, 855 Pershing Drive, Silver Spring, Md., since 1945.

Newell, Clarence A., A.B.'35, Hastings Col.; A.M.'39, Ph.D.'43, Tchrs. Col., Columbia Univ.; Prof. of Educ. Admin., Univ. of Md., College Park, Md., since 1948.

O'Toole, James B., Jr., A.B.'28, Lynchburg Col.; M.A.'38, Columbia Univ.; Asst. Supt., Baltimore Co. Bd. of Educ., Towson, Md.

Parrott, (Mrs.) Lillian M., B.A.'24, Morgan State Col.; M.A.'49, New York Univ.; Special Asst. to the Asst. Supt. of Sch., Baltimore, Md., since 1949.

Price, Hugh Glynn, B.S.'25, Denison Univ.; M.A.'35, Univ. of Chicago; Dean, Montgomery Jr. Col., Takoma Park, Md., since 1946.

Pruitt, Eugene Watts, M.A.'26, Tchrs. Col., Columbia Univ.; Co. Supt. of Sch., Frederick, Md., since 1932.

Pullen, Thomas G., Jr., A.B.'17, M.A.'25, Col. of William and Mary; Ed.D.'41, Tchrs. Col., Columbia Univ.; LL.D.'47, Loyola Col.; State Supt. of Sch., Baltimore, Md., since 1942.

Rannels, Morris W., B.S.'38, State Tchrs. Col., Millersville, Pa.; M.Ed.'48, Univ. of Md.; Cecil Co. Supt. of Sch., Elkton, Md., since 1952.

Rasmussen, L. R., 9213 Bradford, Silver Spring, Md.

Raver, Milson C., B.Eng.'31, Johns Hopkins Univ.; Exec. Secy., Md. State Tchrs. Assn., Baltimore, Md., since 1945.

Reidy, Kathryn G., Prin., Ager Road Sch., Silver Spring, Md.

Remaley, Charles B., B.S.'35, Allegheny Col.; M.A.'49, George Washington Univ.; Prin., Sherwood H. S., Sandy Spring, Md., since 1948.

Rizer, Richard T., Asst. Supt. of Sch., Cumberland, Md.

Roberts, Clarence J., B.S.'32, M.A.'40, Tchrs. Col., Columbia Univ.; Prin., Elem. Sch., Baltimore, Md., since 1928.

Row, Howard E., B.S.Ed.'43, State Tchrs. Col., Shippensburg, Pa.; M.Ed.'48, Pa. State Col.; Regional Rep., Citizenship Educ. Project, Tchrs. Col., Columbia Univ. Address: Md. State Tchrs. Col., Towson, Md.

Sartorius, William S., A.B.'32, Amherst Col.; M.A.'33, Duke Univ.; Asst. Dir., Finance and Research, State Dept. of Educ., Baltimore, Md., since 1952.

Schmidt, William S., A.B.'29, Franklin and Marshall Col.; A.M.'36, Tchrs. Col., Columbia Univ.; Co. Supt. of Sch., Upper Marlboro, Md., since 1951.

Schneider, Fern Duey, B.S. in Ed.'32, Nebr. Wesleyan Univ.; M.A.'34, George Washington Univ.; Ed.D.'40, Tchrs. Col., Columbia Univ.; 1542 Live Oak Dr., Silver Spring, Md.

Seidel, John J., B.S.'26, Tchrs. Col., Columbia Univ.; M.A.'40, George Washington Univ.; Asst. State Supt. of Sch. for Voc. Educ., Baltimore, Md., since 1937.

Sensenbaugh, James A., B.S.'36, M.A.'40, Ed.D.'51, Columbia Univ.; Asst. Co. Supt. of Sch., Towson, Md., since 1946.

Skidmore, Howard James, B.A.'46, Western Md. Col.; M.A.'49, Univ. of Md.; Prin., Elem. and Jr. H. S., Hughesville, Md.

Smith, George F., Jr., B.A.'17, Univ. of Richmond; M.A.'21, Univ. of Pa.; Dir., Educ. Supplies and Equipment, City Sch., Baltimore, Md., since 1929.

Somers, Wilson E., Diploma and A.B.'15, Col. of William and Mary; M.A.'23, Tchrs. Col., Columbia Univ.; Rep., Educ. Dept., Charles Scribner's Sons, New York, N. Y., since 1926. Address: 3333 N. Charles St., Baltimore 18, Md., since 1946.

Sorrell, Frank J., M.A.'50, New York Univ.; Prin., Druid Jr. H. S. 137, Baltimore, Md., since 1947.

Speicher, Ross, Vicepres., Bd. of Educ., Oakland, Md., since 1951.

Stapleton, Edward G., B.S.'17, Johns Hopkins Univ.; M.Ed.'41, Univ. of Md.; Supt. of Sch., Towson, Md., since 1948.

Stein, Edwin, B.S.'33, Johns Hopkins Univ.; M.Ed.'51, Pa. State Col.; Dir. of Personnel, Bd. of Educ., Baltimore, Md., since 1948.

Stern, Bessie C., A.B.'09, Cornell Univ.; Ed.M. '21, Harvard Univ. Address: 4013 Maine Ave., Baltimore 7, Md.

Stottler, Richard H., B.S.'35, N. Y. State Col. for Tchrs. at Buffalo; M.A.'48, N. Y. Univ.; Dir. of Inst., Univ. of Md., College Park, Md.

Sylvester, Charles W., B.S. in M.E.'08, D.Sc.'48, Univ. of Md.; Asst. Supt. of Sch. in charge of Voc. Educ., Baltimore, Md., since 1922.

Taylor, J. Carey, B.S.'22, M.A.'28, D.Ed.'30, Johns Hopkins Univ.; Asst. Supt. of Sch., Baltimore, Md., since 1930.

Throckmorton, Edith M., B.S.'40, State Tchrs. Col., Shippensburg, Pa.; Longview Sch., Gaithersburg, Md.

Tremonti, Joseph B., B.S.'36, Loyola Univ.; M.A.'41, Catholic Univ. of America; Ed.D.'50, Temple Univ.; Prof. of Educ., Mt. Saint Mary's Col., Emmitsburg, Md., since 1952.

Trice, Otis M., B.A.'30, Western Md. Col.; M.Ed.'46, Univ. of Maine; Assoc. Supt. of Sch., in charge of Admin. and Supvy. Functions, Hurlock, Md., since 1936.

Truxal, Andrew Gehr, A.B.'20, A.M.'23, Franklin and Marshall Col.; B.D.'23, Theol. Sem. of the Evangelical and Reformed Church, Lancaster, Pa.; Ph.D.'28, Columbia Univ.; M.A.'36, Dartmouth Col.; Pres., Hood Col., Frederick, Md., since 1948.

*Van Zwoll, James A., A.B.'33, Calvin Col.; M.A.'37, Ph.D.'42, Univ. of Mich.; Prof. of Educ. Admin., Col. of Educ., Univ. of Md., College Park, Md., since 1948.

*Whiteside, Harold C., B.S.'24, M.A.'26, Univ. of Pa.; Vice Prin., Cambridge H. S., Cambridge, Md.

Willis, Charles W., A.B.'30, Western Md. Col.; M.A.'34, Columbia Univ.; Co. Supt. of Sch., Bel Air, Md., since 1945.

Wilson, Theodore Halbert, A.B.'07, A.M.'08, Harvard Univ.; S.T.B.'11, Union Theological Seminary; Ed.M.'28, Ed.D.'35, Harvard Univ.; Pres., Univ. of Baltimore, Baltimore, Md., since 1940.

Wilson, William O., B.S.'40, M.S.'47, Ind. Univ. Address: 4601 Stanford St., Chevy Chase, Md.

Yingling, John E., Co. Supt. of Sch., Ellicott City, Md.

Zimmerman, David W., A.B.'23, Franklin and Marshall Col.; A.M.'27, Columbia Univ.; D.Ed.'48, Johns Hopkins Univ.; Asst. State Supt. in Finance and Research, Baltimore, Md., since 1950.

MASSACHUSETTS

INDIVIDUAL MEMBERS

Abernethy, Thomas James, A.B.'17, Harvard Univ.; M.Ed.'34, Ed.D.'40, Boston Univ.; Supt. of Sch., Westfield, Mass., since 1947.

Adair, David, A.B.'28, Cedarville Col.; Supt. of Sch., Wareham, Mass., since 1948.

Anderson, Gerald W., M.A.'49, Tchrs. Col., Columbia Univ.; Supt. of Sch., Mansfield, Mass., since 1950.

Anderson, Marion, B.A.'24, M.A.'26, Ph.D.'35 State Univ. of Iowa; Ginn and Co., Boston Mass.

Anketell, Richard N., A.B.'26, Bates Col.; M.Ed.'38, Boston Univ.; Supt. of Sch., Framingham, Mass.

*Antony, Paul U., B.S.'33, Univ. of Dayton; M.A.'43, Tchrs. Col., Columbia Univ.; Prin., Franklin and Montrose Schs., Wakefield, Mass., since 1950.

Appleton, William B., A.B.'13, Harvard Univ.; Supt. of Sch., Leominster, Mass., since 1937.

Ashley, Frederick A., B.B.A.'21, Boston Univ.; Supt. of Sch., Everett, Mass., since 1932.

Austin, George R., A.B.'33, Bates Col.; Ed.M.'41, Harvard Univ.; Union Supt. of Sch., Middleboro, Mass., since 1941.

Bacon, Charles Edward, A.B.'96, Harvard Univ.; Publisher, Allyn & Bacon, Boston, Mass., since 1916.

Bailey, Hamilton R., B.S., Bates Col.; LL.B.'30, American Extension Univ.; Supt. of Sch., Seekonk, Mass., since 1950.

Bain, Winifred E., Ph.B.'24, Univ. of Chicago; M.A.'26, Ph.D.'29, Columbia Univ.; Pres., Wheelock Col., Boston, Mass., since 1940.

Baird, Paul R., A.B.'12, A.M.'15, Hamilton Col.; M.Ed.'42, Springfield Col.; Supt. of Sch., Ludlow, Mass.

Barber, Anson B., M.B.A.'31, Harvard Univ.; M.A.'35, Colo. State Col. of Educ., Greeley; Ed.D.'42, Harvard Univ.; Supt. of Sch., Attleboro, Mass.

Beal, Alice B., B.S.'26, New York Univ.; M.Ed. '36, Boston, Univ.; Asst. Supt. of Sch., in charge of Elem. Educ., Springfield, Mass., since 1950.

Bierkoe, George O., A.B.'22, Litt.D.'46, Muhlenberg Col.; B.D.'25, Lutheran Theol. Seminary; M.A.'35, New York Univ.; Pres. and Chaplain, Endicott Jr. Col., Beverly, Mass., since 1939.

Biggy, M. Virginia, B.S. in Ed.'45, Ed.M.'46, Boston Univ.; Dir. of Elem. Educ., Pub. Sch., Concord, Mass., since 1947.

Billett, Roy O., B.S.'23, M.A.'27, Ph.D.'29, Ohio State Univ.; Prof. of Educ. since 1935 and Chmn., Dept. of Educ., Grad. Sch., Boston Univ., Boston, Mass., since 1944.

Billings, Maurice P., A.B.'29, Univ. of Maine; M.Ed.'48, State Tchrs. Col., Fitchburg, Mass.; Supt. of Sch. Union 26, Townsend, Mass., since 1949.

Black, William B., B.S. in Ed.'39, Boston Univ.; M.Ed.'50, Harvard Univ.; Sch. Plant Specialist, Mass. Sch. Bldg. Assistance Commn., Boston, Mass., since 1950.

Boland, Ruth F., B.S. in Ed.'31, Boston Univ.; M.A.'41, Tchrs. Col., Columbia Univ.; Ed.D. '46, Harvard Univ.; Dir., Bur. of Child Services, Cambridge, Mass., since 1948.

Bowman, Grover C., B.A.'06, Williams Col.; M.A.'12, Yale Univ.; Ed.D.'42, R. I. Col. of Educ.; Pres., Mass. State Tchrs. Col., North Adams, Mass., since 1937.

Boyden, George H., A.B.'05, Harvard Col.; Asst. Supt. of Sch., Worcester, Mass., since 1944.

Bradley, Clifton E., B.S.'26, Colgate Univ.; M.Ed.'33, Boston Univ.; Union Supt. of Sch., Hanover, Mass., since 1943.

Brennan, Fred J., A.B.'17, A.M.'18, Clark Univ.; LL.B.'32, Northeastern Univ.; Asst. Supt. of Sch., Worcester, Mass., since 1943.

Bristol, Gilbert D., Jr., M.S.'45, Univ. of Mass.; Supt. of Sch., Abington, Mass., since 1948.

Buker, William H., A.B.'10, Bates Col.; M.A.'24, Columbia Univ.; Supt. of Sch., Holden, Mass., since 1948.

Burch, Robert L., B.A.'34, Iowa State Tchrs. Col., Cedar Falls; M.A.'39, State Univ. of Iowa; Ph.D.'49, Duke Univ.; Assoc. Prof., Sch. of Educ., Boston Univ., since 1949, and Ed., Elem. Textbooks, Ginn and Co., Boston, Mass., since 1950.

Burdick, Raymond C., A.B.'14, Alfred Univ.; A.M.'25, Columbia Univ.; Supt. of Sch., Stoneham, Mass., since 1950.

Burgess, Joseph R., B.S. in Ed.'30, State Tchrs. Col., Bridgewater, Mass.; Supt. of Sch., Sturbridge, Mass., since 1937.

Burke, Arthur E., A.B.'19, Boston Col.; Supt. of Sch., Turners Falls, Mass., since 1937.

Burke, W. Kenneth, B.S. in Ed.'22, State Tchrs. Col., Bridgewater, Mass.; Supt. of Sch., New Bedford, Mass., since 1946.

Burns, David A. J., B.S.'31, M.A. in Ed.'33, Boston Univ.; Prin., Jr. H. S., Fall River, Mass., since 1951.

Carbone, Peter F., B.B.A.'21, Boston Univ.; LL.B.'28, Suffolk Univ.; Ed.M.'38, Boston Univ.; Supt. of Sch., Salem, Mass., since 1946.

Caverly, Ernest R., A.B.'15, Harvard Univ.; A.M.'27, Columbia Univ.; D.A.O.'52, Staley Col.; Supt. of Sch., Brookline, Mass., since 1931.

Chace, Edward Kip, Ph.B.'26, A.M.'35, Brown Univ.; Supt. of Sch., Scituate, Mass., since 1951.

Chace, Frank C., A.B.'27, Ed.M.'37, Harvard Univ.; Supt. of Sch., Gardner, Mass., since 1946.

Chace, Ruth E., B.S. of Ed.'45, Boston Univ.; Prin., Sarah D. Ottiwell Sch., New Bedford, Mass., since 1945.

Chaffee, John B., Ph.B.'31, M.A.'36, Brown Univ.; Supt. of Sch., Hingham, Mass.

Christie, Lindon E., B.S.'30, Colby Col.; M.Ed. '40, Univ. of Maine; Supt. of Sch., East Bridgewater, Mass., since 1951.

Clark, A. A., Houghton Mifflin Co., Boston, Mass.

Coleman, Aura W., A.B.'28, M.Ed.'40, Bates Col.; Supt. of Sch., Marblehead, Mass., since 1948.

Conant, James Bryant, A.B.'14, Ph.D.'16, Harvard Univ.; Pres., Harvard Univ., Cambridge, Mass., since 1933.

Cotton, Dana Meserve, A.B.'28, Univ. of N. H.; Ed.M.'43, Harvard Univ.; Dir. of Placement, Grad. Sch. of Educ., since 1944, Assoc. Dir. of Summer Sch., since 1947, and Asst. to the Chmn. of the Committee on Admission in Harvard Col., Harvard Univ., Cambridge, Mass., since 1948.

Coughlan, John D., Supt. of Sch., Marlboro, Mass., since 1949.

Cox, Edwin Allerton, B.S. in Ed.'32, Boston Univ.; M.S. in Ed.'39, Univ. of Maine; Supt. of Sch., Franklin, Mass., since 1951.

Crossley, B. Alice, B.S. in Ed.'44, Ed.M.'46, Ed.D.'48, Boston Univ.; Asst. Prof. of Educ., Boston Univ., Boston, Mass.

Curtin, Thomas Joseph, A.B.'34, Harvard Col.; Ed.M.'39, Harvard Grad. Sch. of Educ.; Research Dir., Civic Educ. Project, Nahant, Mass.

Cushing, J. Stearns, Supt. of Sch., Middleboro, Mass., since 1927.

Davis, John Bradford, Jr., B.A.'44, Univ. of N. H.; M.Ed.'49, Graduate Sch. of Educ., Harvard Univ.; Exec. Secy., New England Sch. Development Council, Cambridge, Mass., since 1950.

Davis, Orrin C., B.Sc.'21, Univ. of Mass.; M.Ed.'32, Boston Univ.; Supt. of Sch., Winthrop, Mass., since 1946.

Davoren, David I., A.B.'30, Col. of the Holy Cross; M.Ed.'40, Boston Univ.; Supt. of Sch., Milford, Mass., since 1947.

Delaney, Frederick J., B.A.'35, Boston Col.; M.Ed.'42, Boston Univ.; Supt. of Sch., Wrentham, Mass., since 1951.

Desmond, John J., Jr., A.B.'09, Harvard Col.; A.M.'10, Harvard Grad. Sch.; D.Ed.'49, Suffolk Univ.; State Commr. of Educ., Boston, Mass., since 1946.

Dexter, William A., A.B.'28, Clark Univ.; A.M.'36, Univ. of Mich.; Union Supt. of Sch., Easthampton, Mass., since 1945.

Doherty, Charles E., Supt. of Sch., Richmond, Mass.

Doherty, Leo T., B.S.E.'27, Mass. Sch. of Art; Ed.M.'31, Boston Col. Graduate Sch.; Asst. Supt. of Sch., Worcester, Mass., since 1950.

Domas, Simeon J., A.B.'32, Harvard Col.; Ed.M.'36, Boston Tchrs. Col., Mass.; Specialist in Sch. Dist. Organization, Mass. Sch. Bldg. Assistance Commn., Boston, Mass., since 1950.

Donahue, Leo C., A.B.'29, A.M.'30, Ph.D.'42, Boston Col.; Ed.M.'48, Tufts Col.; Asst. Supt. of Sch., Somerville, Mass., since 1941.

Dow, Donald S., B.S.Ed.'49, Gorham State Tchrs. Col.; Supt. of Sch., Hopedale, Mass., since 1951.

Driscoll, Martina McDonald, Diploma '19, Boston Normal Sch.; LL.B.'27, Portia Law Sch.; A.B.'38, Calvin Coolidge Col.; State Supvr. of Music, Boston, Mass., since 1936.

Durrell, Donald D., A.B.'26, A.M.'27, State Univ. of Iowa; Ed.D.'30, Harvard Univ.; Dean and Prof. of Educ., Sch. of Educ., Boston Univ., Boston, Mass., since 1930.

Eaton, E. Perley, B.S.'27, Tufts Col.; M.A.'32, Boston Univ.; M.Ed.'39, Harvard Univ.; Supt. of Sch., Athol, Mass., since 1949.

Ehnes, Albert F., B.S.E.'30, State Tchrs. Col., Bridgewater, Mass.; M.S.E.'37, Boston Univ.; Supt. of Sch., Marion, Mass., since 1947.

Englesby, George H., Supt. of Sch., Dracut, Mass.

English, Fred Charles, A.B.'16, Colby Col.; Ed.M.'42, Harvard Univ.; Supt. of Sch., Amesbury, Mass., since 1934.

Erickson, Edward I., B.S.'28, Bates Col.; Ed.M. '37, Univ. of N. H.; Supt. of Sch., Methuen, Mass., since 1948.

Esten, Richard Stewart, A.B.'14, Middlebury Col.; A.M.'25, Tchrs. Col.; Columbia Univ.; Supt. of Sch., Rockland, Mass., since 1929.

Farrell, John Franklin, A.B.'18, Univ. of Mich.; M.Ed.'35, Boston Univ.; Supt. of Sch., Adams, Mass., since 1936.

Fitzgerald, Pierce J., A.B.'27, Boston Col.; Ed.M.'49, Boston Univ.; A/V Coordinator, Rindge, Cambridge, Mass., since 1952.

Fitzpatrick, John L., Diploma '25, State Tchrs. Col.; Fitchburg, Mass.; B.S. in Ed.'37, State Tchrs. Col., Hyannis, Mass.; Supt. of Sch., Chicopee, Mass., since 1946.

Fogg, Laurence A., B.S. in Ed.'43, State Tchrs. Col., Bridgewater, Mass.; Ed.M.'49, State Tchrs. Col., Fitchburg, Mass.; Union Supt. of Sch., Sterling, Mass., since 1946.

Ford, Albert F., B.S. in Ed.'30, State Tchrs. Col., Bridgewater, Mass.; Supt. of Sch., Acushnet, Mass., since 1932.

Fox, Robert L., B.Sc.'28, Mass. State Col.; M.Sc.'50, Univ. of Mass.; Supt. of Sch., Ware, Mass., since 1951.

Francis, George C., B.S. and Ed.M., Boston Univ.; Supt. of Sch., Fitchburg, Mass., 1938-52 (retired).

Galligan, Harold H., A.B.'21, Col. of the Holy Cross; A.M.'31, Brown Univ.; Supt. of Sch., Taunton, Mass., since 1949.

Gans, Leo, B.B.A.'32, Univ. of Minn.; M.A.'36, Ed.D.'41, Tchrs. Col., Columbia Univ.; Prin., Tech. H. S., Springfield, Mass., since 1949.

Gardner, Charles Warren, B.S. in Ed.'41, M.Ed.'48, Boston Univ.; Supt. of Sch., Union 30, Ashfield, Mass., since 1951.

Giaudrone, Angelo, B.A.'35, M.A.'48, State Col. of Wash.; Asst. Dir., CPEA, Harvard Univ., Cambridge, Mass., since 1952.

Gibbons, Joseph H., B.A.'33, Boston Col.; M.Ed.'36, Harvard Univ.; Supt. of Sch., Stoughton, Mass., since 1948.

Gifford, Flavel M., B.S.'20, Mass. State Col.; M.Ed.'30, Harvard Univ.; Supt. of Sch., Fairhaven, Mass., since 1939.

Gilgan, H. C., Supt. of Sch., Union 34, Avon, Mass.

Gilman, Marion C., B.S.E.'21, A.M.'22, Boston Univ.; Ed.M.'40, Tchrs. Col. of the City of Boston; Head of English Dept., Brighton H. S., Brighton, Mass., since 1950.

Glenn, John, B.S. in Ed.'34, State Tchrs. Col., Bridgewater, Mass.; M.S. in Ed.'48, Boston Univ.; Supt. of Sch., North Brookfield, Mass., since 1947.

Goodwin, A. Jerome, B.S.'28, Dartmouth Col.; M.A.'35, Columbia Univ.; Supt. of Sch., Agawam, Mass., since 1950.

Gores, Harold B., B.S.'31, State Tchrs. Col.; Bridgewater, Mass.; M.Ed.'38, Harvard Univ.; Supt. of Newton Sch., Newtonville, Mass., since 1949.

Gossard, Arthur Paul, A.B.'21, Ohio State Univ.; M.A.'26, Ph.D.'40, Univ. of Chicago; Supt. of Sch., Quincy, Mass., since 1944.

Gotschall, John H., Ed.D.'42, Harvard Univ.; Supt. of Sch., Auburn, Mass.

Goward, Paul F., B.S.'16, Dartmouth Col.; Bus. Mgr., *School Arts Magazine*, Worcester, Mass., since 1925.

Grandy, L. Munro, B.S.'30, Norwich Univ.; M.Ed.'41, Bates Col.; Supt. of Sch., Gloucester, Mass., since 1952.

Grant, Francis V., B.S.'21, Colgate Univ.; Supt. of Sch., Williamstown, Mass., since 1922.

Greenman, Richard Baker, A.B.'27, Harvard Univ.; Ed.M.'39, Boston Univ.; Supt. of Sch., Swansea, Mass., since 1946.

Grindle, Thomas S., M.Ed.'24, Harvard Univ.; Supt. of Sch., Lexington, Mass., 1924-52 (retired).

Gross, Calvin E., A.B.'40, Univ. of Calif. at Los Angeles; M.S. in Ed.'47, Univ. of Southern Calif.; Supt. of Sch., Weston, Mass.

Grout, M. A., Asst. Mgr., Holden Patent Bk. Cover Co., Springfield, Mass., since 1927.

Gunn, Mary Agnella, Ph.D.'33, State Univ. of Iowa; Assoc. Prof. of Educ., Boston Univ., Boston, Mass., since 1947.

Haggerty, Earl J., Elem. Supvr., Pub. Sch., Rockland, Mass., since 1952.

Haley, Dennis C., A.B.'15, A.M.'22, LL.D.'45, Holy Cross Col.; Ed.M.'25, Harvard Univ.; Supt. of Pub. Sch., Boston, Mass., since 1948.

Hall, Clifford R., A.B.'20, Tufts Col.; Ed.M.'21, Harvard Univ.; Supt. of Sch., Arlington, Mass., since 1942.

Hallowell, Philip M., B.S.Ed.'35, M.Ed.'47, Boston Univ.; Supt. of Sch., Shelburne Falls, Mass., since 1951.

Handy, Everett L., S.B.'34, Boston Univ.; Ed.M.'38, Ed.D.'45, Harvard Univ.; Supt. of Sch., Duxbury, Mass., since 1950.

Hapgood, Charles G., B.S.E.'31, M.A.'36, Boston Univ.; Supt. of Sch., Manchester, Mass., since 1947.

Harriman, Edwin J., B.S.'21, M.Ed.'35, Bates Col.; Supt. of Sch., Harvard, Mass., since 1952.

Haskins, Ralph Warner, B.S.'27, Mass. State Col.; A.M.'33, Tchrs. Col., Columbia Univ.; Prin., Westfield H. S., Westfield, Mass., since 1947.

Hassett, J. Frank, Ph.B.'30, Col. of the Holy Cross; M.S.'36, Univ. of Miss.; Supt. of Sch., Woburn, Mass., since 1945.

Hawkes, Franklin Powers, A.B.'17, Amherst Col.; A.M.'21, Ph.D.'27, Boston Univ.; Dir., Fair Educ. Practices, State Dept. of Educ., Boston, Mass., since 1950.

Hempel, Edward C., Ph.B.'08, Brown Univ.; M.Ed.'34, Harvard Univ.; Supt. of Sch., Orange, Mass., since 1929.

Hendershot, John B., B.S. in Ed.'30, Ed.M.'33, Boston Univ.; Supt. of Sch., Wakefield, Mass.

Hennessey, James F., A.B.'20, M.Ed.'28, Harvard Univ.; Supt. of Sch., Lawrence, Mass., since 1946.

Herlihy, J. Frank, A.B.'28, Boston Col.; Ed.M.'34, Boston Univ.; Supt. of Sch., Chelsea, Mass., since 1942.

Herman, Beaumont A., A.B.'30, A.M.'31, Harvard Univ.; Ph.D.'37, Boston Col.; Supt., Northbridge Sch., Whitinsville, Mass., since 1948.

Herrschaft, Howard G., A.B.'23, Eastern Nazarene Col.; M.A.'34, New York Univ.; Supt. of Sch., Longmeadow, Mass., since 1948.

Hetherman, Patrick J., B.S.'29, Lowell Textile Inst.; Asst. Supt. of Sch., Lowell, Mass., since 1947.

Higgins, J. Henry, A.B.'21, Boston Col.; LL.B. '26, Suffolk Univ.; M.A.'32, Boston Col.; Asst. Supt. of Sch., Peabody, Mass., since 1946.

Hill, Allen J., Diploma '09, Nebr. State Tchrs. Col., Peru; B.A.'27, Brigham Young Univ.; M.A.'28, Tchrs. Col., Columbia Univ.; Supt. of Sch., Dalton, Mass., since 1942.

Hilyard, Harry Y., Supt. of Sch., Douglas, Mass.

Holm, Lewis N., A.B.'28, Emmanuel Missionary Col.; M.S.'36, Mich. State Col.; Pres., Atlantic Union Col., South Lancaster, Mass., since 1948.

Holmes, Chester W., S.B.'16, Ed.M.'24, Harvard Univ.; Ed.D.'36, George Washington Univ.; Supt. of Sch., Malden, Mass., since 1946.

Holt, Frank E., B.S.'06, Amherst Col.; Ed.M.'29, Harvard Univ.; Supt. of Sch., Whitman, Mass., since 1922.

Hooper, Bertrand, B.S.'30, Boston, Univ.; Supt. of Sch., Medford, Mass., since 1952.

Hoyt, Herbert E., A.B.'31, M.A.'38, Bates Col.; Union Supt. of Sch., Harwich, Mass., since 1947.

Huff, Eleanor L., B.S.Ed.'43, Tchrs. Col., Framingham, Mass.; Ed.M.'50, Harvard Grad. Sch. of Educ.; Asst. Dir. Student Tchg., Lesley Col., Cambridge, Mass., since 1951.

Hunt, Albert F., Jr., Ph.B.'26, Brown Univ.; M.A.'38, New York Univ.; Supt. of Sch., Bridgewater, Mass., since 1940.

Ireland, Everett W., B.S.'11, Tufts Col.; Supt. of Sch., Somerville, Mass., since 1928.

Jarvis, Robert J., B.S.'37, M.A.'40, Tufts Col.; Union Supt. of Sch., New Salem, Mass., since 1948.

Jeffords, H. Morton, A.B.'14, Syracuse Univ.; A.M.'32, New York Univ.; Supt. of Sch., Chelmsford, Mass., since 1947.

Johndroe, M. Elizabeth, B.A.'36, Wellesley Col.; Prin., House in the Pines, Norton, Mass., since 1948.

Johnson, Carroll F., A.B.'35, Univ. of Chattanooga; M.S. in Ed.'40, Univ. of Ga.; M.A.'47, Ed.D.'50, Tchrs. Col., Columbia Univ.; Supt. of Sch., Fitchburg, Mass., since 1953.

Johnston, Ida M., Instr. in Educ., Boston Univ., Boston, Mass.

Jones, Arthur C., M.Ed.'38, Boston Univ.; Supt. of Sch., Walpole, Mass., since 1931.

Jones, Burr F., A.B.'07, Colby Col.; A.M.'12, Harvard Univ.; Supt. of Sch., Plymouth, Mass., since 1941.

Jones, Donovan S., B.S.'17, Univ. of Vt.; M.A. '37, Tchrs. Col., Columbia Univ.; Dist. Supt. of Sch., Winchendon, Mass., since 1940.

Jones, Sherman H., Prin. Architect, W. H. Jones and Son, Melrose, Mass., since 1930.

Kadesch, J. Stevens, A.B.'10, Ed.M.'30, Clark Univ.; Ed.D.'31, Tufts Col.; Supt. of Sch., Medford, Mass., 1930-52 (retired). Address: 131 Traincroft, Medford 55, Mass.

Keck, Winston B., Prin., H. S., Bridgewater, Mass.

Kelly, Francis A., A.B.'24, M.A.'25, Boston Col.; Supt. of Sch., Watertown, Mass., since 1939.

Kelly, Marcella R., B.S.'36, State Tchrs. Col., Fitchburg, Mass.; M.A.'38, Columbia Univ.; Ph.D.'45, Yale Univ.; Asst. Supt. of Sch., Holyoke, Mass., since 1945.

Kenyon, Alfred R., Supt. of Sch., Bass River, Yarmouth, Mass.

Keppel, Francis, A.B.'38, Harvard Univ.; Dean, Faculty of Educ., Harvard Univ., Cambridge, Mass., since 1948.

Kiernan, Owen B., B.S.'35, State Tchrs. Col., Bridgewater, Mass.; Ed.M.'40, Boston Univ.; Ed.D.'50, Harvard Univ.; Supt. of Sch., Milton, Mass., since 1951.

Kiley M. Marcus, B.A.'14, Clark Univ.; M.Ed. '40, Boston Univ.; Asst. Supt. of Sch., Springfield, Mass., since 1949.

King, Starr M., B.Sc.'21, Mass. State Col.; M.Ed., Harvard Univ.; Supt. of Sch., Beverly, Mass., since 1935.

Knight, Melvin C., Supt. of Sch., Hyannis, Mass.

Ladd, Harold Marden, B.S.'20, M.Ed.'37, Univ. of N. H.; Union Supt. of Sch., Monson, Mass., since 1942.

Lauritz, James D., B.E.'40, Yale Univ.; M.Ed.'47, Univ. of Chicago; Dir., Newton Jr. Col., Newtonville, Mass.

Lord, Arthur B., B.S. in Ed.'37, Boston Univ.; Union Supt. of Sch., Vineyard Haven, Mass., since 1936.

Lord, Arthur Bertelle, Jr., A.B.'35, Tufts Col.; M.Ed.'43, Boston Univ.; Supt. of Sch., Reading, Mass., since 1948.

Lynch, Lincoln D., A.B.'21, Boston Col.; Ed.M. '39, Boston Univ.; Supt. of Sch., Norwood, Mass., since 1936.

Lynch, William S., A.B.'25, Col. of the Holy Cross; A.M.'31, Boston Univ.; Supt. of Sch., Fall River, Mass., since 1945.

McAuliffe, Mary Frances, B.S. in Ed.'27, Tchrs. Col. of the City of Boston, Boston, Mass.; M.E.'28, Boston Univ.; Ph.D.'35, Boston Col.; Prin., Robert Treat Paine Sch., Dorchester, Mass., since 1941.

McCaffrey, Donald F., Supt. of Sch., Palmer, Mass.

McCarn, Robert H., B.A.'29, Holy Cross Col.; M.Ed.'48, Boston Col.; Supt. of Sch., Southbridge, Mass., since 1950.

McCartin, Vincent M., Supt. of Sch., Lowell, Mass.

McCloskey, Walter H., B.A.'29, Col. of the Holy Cross; Ed.M.'34, Harvard Univ.; Supt. of Sch., Uxbridge, Mass., since 1947.

McCook, T. Joseph, A.B.'31, Boston Col.; M.Ed.'34, Boston Univ.; Supt. of Sch., Haverhill, Mass., since 1949.

McDevitt, John W., B.A.'28, M.A.'29, Boston Col. Address: 55 School St., Waltham 54, Mass.

McFadden, Ruth B., B.S. in Ed.'34, Ed.M.'36, Boston Univ.; Asst. Supt. of Sch., New Bedford, Mass., since 1952.

McGinn, Lawrence G., Ph.B.'31, Brown Univ.; M.Ed.'44, Harvard Univ.; Deputy Supt. of Sch., Lynn, Mass., since 1945.

Mahoney, John J., A.B.'03, Ed.M.'22, Ed.D.'44, Harvard Univ.; Dir. Civic Educ. Project, Cambridge, Mass., since 1948.

Malcolm, David J., S.B.'13, Harvard Col.; Supt., Northern Berkshire Union Sch., Charlemont, Mass., since 1930.

Malin, Donald F., Pres., C. C. Birchard and Co., Boston, Mass.

Manges, Andrew J., A.B.'32, Manchester Col.; M.S. in Ed.'41, Butler Univ.; Supt. of Sch., Lincoln, Mass., since 1948.

Manley, Daniel A., B.S. in Ed.'25, State Tchrs. Col., Salem, Mass.; M.Ed.'40, Tufts Col.; Asst. Supt. of Sch., Medford, Mass., since 1952.

Mann, Gilbert C., B.S.'15, Univ. of Vt.; M.Ed.'38, Boston Univ.; Supt. of Sch., North Easton, Mass., since 1925.

Mansur, Frank L., A.B.'10, Brown Univ.; Supt. of Sch., Swampscott, Mass., since 1931.

Mapes, Elmer Stephens, A.B.'20, Alfred Univ.; A.M.'23, Cornell Univ.; Supt. of Sch., East Weymouth, Mass., since 1945.

*Marshall, John E., A.B.'36, A.M.'37, W. Va. Univ.; Administrator, Mass. Sch. Bldg. Assistance Commn., Boston, Mass., since 1948.

Martinson, Edwin A., M.A. in Ed.'33, Tufts Col.; Supt. of Sch., Billerica, Mass., since 1947.

Merriam, Burr J., Diploma '98, State Normal Sch., Oneonta, N. Y.; B.S.'16, Columbia Univ.; Ed.M.'27, Harvard Univ.; Supt. of Sch., Framingham, Mass., 1922-49 (retired). Address: 417 Main St., Wilbraham, Mass.

Merriam, Thornton W., A.B.'15, Harvard Col.; Ph.D.'34, Columbia Univ.; Dean, Springfield Col., Springfield, Mass., since 1946.

Merrill, Bert L., B.S.'24, Colby Col.; Ed.M.'46, Boston Univ.; Supt. of Sch., West Bridgewater, Mass., since 1950.

Miller, Charles A., Diploma '17, State Normal Sch., Millersville, Pa.; A.B.'23, Franklin and Marshall Col.; Ed.M.'24, Harvard Univ.; Supt. of Sch., South Hadley Falls, Mass., since 1944.

Miller, Fred W., B.S.'18, St. Lawrence Univ.; Ed.M.'27, Harvard Univ.; Supt. of Sch., Holliston, Mass., since 1924.

Mitchell, Donald P., B.S. in Ed.'40, Hyannis State Tchrs. Col.; Ed.M.'47, Harvard Graduate Sch. of Educ.; Asst. Dir., Center for Field Studies, Graduate Sch. of Educ., Harvard Univ., Cambridge, Mass., since 1950.

Mitchell, John J., B.A.'17, Seton Hall Col.; Supt. of Sch., Clinton, Mass., since 1946.

Moore, Millard C., A.B.'07, Colby Col.; Ed.M.'27, Harvard Univ.; Supt. of Sch., Southwick, Mass., since 1930.

Morgan, Jesse J., B.S.'26, Dartmouth Col.; Ed.M.'34, Harvard Univ.; Supt. of Sch., Saugus, Mass., since 1951.

Morrill, Radcliffe, A.B.'28, St. Stephen's Col.; Ed.M.'39, Harvard Univ.; Supt. of Sch., Concord, Mass., since 1950.

Mott, Arthur J., A.B.'16, Middlebury Col.; A.M.'27, Brown Univ.; Supt. of Sch., North Attleboro, Mass., since 1949.

Murphy, Helen A., B.S. in Ed.'39, M.A.'40, Ed.D.'43, Boston Univ.; Prof. of Educ., Dir. of Elem. Educ., Boston Univ., Boston, Mass.

Nelson, Edwin A., B.S.'35, Ed.M.'40, Boston Univ.; Supt. of Sch., Brockton, Mass., since 1942.

Nelson, Milton H., B.S. in Ed.'36, M.Ed.'47, Boston Univ.; Supt. of Sch., Nahant, Mass., since 1949.

Nesmith, R. A., Prescott St., South Lancaster, Mass.

Newman, Derwood A., B.S.'22, Univ. of N. H.; Ed.M.'31, Ed.D.'35, Harvard Univ.; Supt. of Sch., Needham, Mass., since 1944.

Niven, Henry A., LL.B.'11, Syracuse Univ.; Vicepres., L. G. Balfour Co., Attleboro, Mass., since 1922.

Nock, Rupert A., Ph.B.'30, Brown Univ.; Ed.M. '38, Boston Univ.; Supt. of Sch., Newburyport, Mass., since 1946.

Norris, Forbes H., A.B.'22, Manchester Col.; Ed.M.'26, Ed.D.'46, Harvard Univ.; Supt. of Sch., Winchester, Mass., since 1946.

Norton, Harold G., B.S.'32, Bates Col.; Supt. of Sch., Ayer, Mass., since 1944.

Nourse, Laurence G., A.B.'17, Dartmouth Col.; A.M.'20, Harvard Univ.; Supt. of Sch., Norton, Mass., since 1924.

O'Brien, Francis J., A.B.'16, Harvard Col.; A.M.'31, Harvard Univ.; Supt. of Sch., North Andover, Mass., since 1946.

O'Brien, Thomas F., A.B.'31, Ed.M.'41, Boston Col.; Asst. Supt. of Sch., Watertown, Mass., since 1947.

O'Connor, Mary Elizabeth, B.S. in Ed.'25, M.E.'25, Boston Univ.; Dir., Tchr. Tr., Lesley Col., Cambridge, Mass., since 1941.

Osborne, Ralph W., B.S. in Ed.'32, State Tchrs. Col., Bridgewater, Mass.; M.Ed.'39, Boston Univ.; Graduate Student, Harvard Univ. Address: 361 Harvard St., Cambridge, Mass.

O'Toole, Austin J., B.S.Ed.'31, State Tchrs. Col., Bridgewater, Mass.; M.Ed.'34, Boston Col.; Supt. of Sch. Somerset Centre, Mass., since 1946.

Owen, Lyman B., A.B.'30, A.M.'37, New York State Col. for Tchrs., Albany; Supt. of Sch., Wellesley, Mass., since 1949.

Padin, José, B.S.'07, A.M.'08, LL.D.'31, Haverford Col.; Litt.D.'32, Univ. of Puerto Rico; Ped.D.'34, Dartmouth Col.; Editor-in-Chief, D. C. Heath and Co., Boston, Mass. since 1946.

Page, John C., A.B.'08, Univ. of New Hampshire; Ed.M.'24, Ed.D.'28, Harvard Univ.; Union Supt. of Sch., West Newbury, Mass., since 1928.

Page, Richmond, B.A.'22, Harvard Univ.; B.S.'29, Columbia Univ. Address: Box 151, Winchester, Mass.

Palmer, James B., B.S.'21, Ph.D.'30, Cornell Univ.; Editor-in-Chief, Ginn and Co., Boston, Mass., since 1936.

Palmer, John C., A.B.'36, Tufts Col.; A.M.T.'42, Harvard Univ.; Dir. of Guidance, Pub. Sch., Concord, Mass., since 1951.

Parkman, Francis, A.B.'19, A.M.'29, Ph.D.'30, Harvard Univ.; Exec. Secy., Natl. Council of Independent Sch., Boston, Mass., since 1948.

Pearson, Whitman, B.S.'29, Univ. of Pa.; M.S. in Ed.'48, Boston Univ.; Supt. of Acton Sch., West Acton, Mass., since 1948.

Peck, William R., A.B.'16, M.A.'20, Col. of the Holy Cross; M.A.'30, Tchrs. Col., Columbia Univ.; Supt. of Sch., Holyoke, Mass., since 1920.

*Peebles, James F., B.S.'31, Ed.M.'40, Boston Univ.; Union Supt. of Sch., Bourne, Mass., since 1927.

Perry, Henry B., A.B.'39, Clark Univ.; Educ. Placement Officer, 308 Bay State Rd., Boston 15, Mass., since 1949.

Perry, Marvin B., A.B.'12, Univ. of Ga.; Pres., D. C. Heath and Co., Boston, Mass.

Perry, Peter F., M.Ed.'40, Boston Univ.; Supt. of Sch., Westford, Mass., since 1948.

Peterson, Carl J., Admin. Asst. to Supt. of Sch., Belchertown, Mass.

Phaneuf, Paul H., A.B.'35, Col. of the Holy Cross; M.A.'36, Univ. of N. H.; Supt. of Sch., Dracut, Mass., since 1947.

Poole, Roger K., B.S.'32, Tufts Col.; Ed.M.'33, Boston Univ.; Union Supt. of Sch., Northboro, Mass., since 1948.

Porter, Frederick W., B.S.'14, Tufts Col.; Ed.M.'27, Harvard Univ.; Supt. of Sch., Greenfield, Mass., since 1929.

Porter, Richard J., Supt. of Sch., Nantucket, Mass.

Power, Thomas F., A.B.'08, Amherst Col.; Supt. of Sch., Worcester, Mass., since 1943.

Preston, Kenneth Frank, A.B.'24, Cornell Univ.; A.M.'29, Columbia Univ.; Supt. of Sch., Great Barrington, Mass., since 1939.

Proctor, Ralph W., B.S.'21, Tufts Col.; Ed.M.'34, Boston Univ.; Supt. of Sch., Braintree, Mass., since 1946.

Pulsifer, Walter T., A.B.'27, Univ. of N. H.; Ed.M.'40, Harvard Univ.; Supt. of Sch., Union 66, West Boylston, Mass., since 1950.

Quinn, James P., Jr., B.S.'36, Tchrs. Col., Fitchburg, Mass.; Ed.M.'40, Tufts Col. Graduate Sch. Medford, Mass.; Dir. Guidance and Placement Pub. Sch., Medford, Mass., since 1951.

Rand, Harold T., B.S.'25, Univ. of N. H.; M.Ed.'32, Boston Univ.; Supt. of Sch., Melrose, Mass., since 1949.

Ray, Chester T., B.S. in Ed.'29, State Tchrs. Col., Bridgewater, Mass.; Ed.M.'40, Boston Univ.; Supt. of Sch., Mass. Superintendency Union 37, Kingston, Mass.

*Reed, Carroll T., B.A.'06, M.A.'14, Harvard Univ.; L.H.D.'35, Carleton Col.; Pres., American Assn. of Sch. Admin., 1940-41; Honorary Life Member, American Assn. of Sch. Admin. Address: Dunrovin, Orleans, Mass.

Regan, Teresa A., B.A.'25, Boston Univ.; M.Ed. '28, Harvard Univ.; Ph.D.'37, Boston Col.; Headmaster, Boston Clerical Sch., City of Boston Pub. Bus. Sch., Roxbury, Mass., since 1947.

Rice, Frederick A., A.B.'08, Cornell Univ.; Chmn. of the Bd., and Pres., Ginn & Company, Boston, Mass., since 1942.

Richardson, Herman H., A.B.'29, Dartmouth Col.; A.M.'34, Columbia Univ.; Supt. of Sch., Sharon, Mass., since 1950.

Richter, Charles O., A.B.'33, Bates Col.; M.Ed. '40, Boston Univ.; Asst. Supt. of Newton Pub. Sch., Newtonville, Mass., since 1944.

Ripley, William, Jr., Ph.B.'26, Brown Univ.; Ed.M.'43, Harvard Univ.; Supt. of Sch., Cohasset, Mass., since 1942.

Robinson, Charles M., B.S.'21, A.M.'24, Boston Univ.; Union Supt. of Sch., Westboro, Mass., since 1949.

Rogean, Edward J., B.S. in C.E.'34, Ed.M.'39, Tufts Col.; Supt. of Sch., Groton, Mass., since 1947.

Rolfe, John J., B.S. in Ed.'35, State Tchrs. Col., New Britain, Conn.; M.Ed.'38, Bates Col.; Union Supt. of Sch., North Dighton, Mass., since 1943.

Rose, Carleton F., B.S.E.'35, State Tchrs. Col., Bridgewater, Mass.; M.E.'49, Boston Univ.; Supt. of Sch., Warren, Mass., since 1951.

Ross, Charles F., B.S.'25, M.S.'41, Univ. of Mass.; Supt. of Truro, Provincetown and Wellfleet Sch., Provincetown, Mass., since 1949.

Rowe, Percy L., Ed.M.'43, Boston Univ.; Supt. of Sch., Bellingham, Mass., since 1943.

Rowell, Edwin W., A.B.'29, Ed.M.'34, Harvard Univ.; Supt., Sch. Union 1, Baldwinsville, Mass.

Roy, George C., A.B.'34, Providence Col.; Ed.M.'39, Boston Univ.; Supt. of Sch., Millis, Mass.

Russell, Edward J., A.B.'17, Col. of the Holy Cross; M.A.'27, Providence Col.; Ph.D.'50, Univ. of Ottawa; Supt. of Sch., Pittsfield, Mass., since 1949.

Sanders, William J., B.A.'28, Ph.D.'35, Yale Univ.; Supt. of Sch., Springfield, Mass., since 1950.

427

Sargent, Cyril G., A.B.'33, M.A.'36, Brown Univ.; Ed.D.'48, Harvard Univ.; Dir., Center for Field Studies and Assoc. Prof. of Educ., Harvard Univ., Cambridge, Mass., since 1949.

Savitt, Robert F., B.Ed.'46, State Tchrs. Col., Fitchburg, Mass.; M.S.'48, Univ. of Mass.; Supt. of Sch., Ipswich, Mass., since 1952.

Scanlon, Edward J., A.B.'15, Holy Cross Col., Worcester, Mass.; Ed.M.'35, Boston Univ.; Pres., State Tchrs. Col., Westfield, Mass., since 1938.

Sellig, George Arthur, Ph.B.'32, Providence Col.; M.A.'37, Columbia Univ.; Supt. of Sch., Webster, Mass., since 1941.

Serviss, Trevor K., Ph.B.'23, Univ. of Chicago; M.A.'39, Northwestern Univ.; Editor, D. C. Heath and Co., Boston, Mass., since 1946.

Simpson, Alfred Dexter, A.B.'13, Syracuse Univ.; M.A.'23, Yale Univ.; Ph.D.'27, Columbia Univ.; Paed.D.'41, Syracuse Univ.; M.A.'42, Harvard Univ.; Prof. of Educ., Harvard Univ., Cambridge, Mass., since 1948.

Smith, John Blackhall, B.S.'32, R. I. State Col.; M.Ed.'48, Boston Univ.; Supt. of Sch., Lexington, Mass., since 1952.

Somes, John, B.S.'31, Univ. of Mass.; Union Supt. of Sch., Sheffield, Mass.

Souder, Rexford S., B.S.'35, N. J. State Tchrs. Col., Glassboro; A.M.'37, Ed.D.'41, Tchrs. Col., Columbia Univ.; Supt. of Sch., Wayland, Mass., since 1952.

Spaulding, William E., A.B.'19, Harvard Univ.; Vicepres., Houghton Mifflin Co., Boston, Mass., since 1939.

Stephens, Ernest, A.B.'10, Dartmouth Col.; Ed.M.'27, Harvard Univ.; Supt. of Sch., Lynn, Mass., since 1945.

Sturke, Ralph C., B.S.'35, Univ. of Maine; Ed.M.'42, Boston Univ.; Supt. of Sch., Grafton, Mass., since 1945.

Suitor, Earl, Supt. of Sch., Hinsdale, Mass.

Sullivan, Helen Blair, Prof. of Educ., Boston Univ., Boston, Mass., since 1936.

Sullivan, Mary T., Vice Prin., David A. Ellis Sch., Roxbury, Mass.

Sweatt, Chester V., B.S.'24, Univ. of Maine; M.Ed.'41, Western Reserve Univ.; Union Supt. of Sch., Ashland, Mass., since 1947.

Sweeney, Ellen C., B.S.'36, Boston Univ.; Asst. Supt. of Sch., New Bedford, Mass., 1942-52 (retired).

Swicker, Harold B., B.A. in Ed.'21, Univ. of Maine; M.A. in Ed.'27, Tchrs. Col., Columbia Univ.; Supt. of Sch., Chester, Mass., since 1930.

Taylor, Charles G., A.B.'24, Univ. of Maine; Ed.M.'33, Harvard Univ.; Supt. of Sch., Foxboro, Mass., since 1952.

Taylor, Robert N., B.Ch.E.'24, Northeastern Univ.; Ed.M.'34, Harvard Univ.; Supt. of Sch., North Adams, Mass., since 1948.

Thibadeau, Charles Raymond, B.S.'19, Bates Col.; Ed.M.'30, Harvard Univ.; Supt. of Sch., Belmont, Mass., since 1947.

Thomas, Benjamin, Supt. of Dover-Sherborn Sch., Dover, Mass.

*Thompson, Theron Barker, B.C.E.'31, Northeastern Univ.; Ed.M.'33, C.A.G.S.'51, Boston Univ.; B.S.'38, Northeastern Univ.; Supt. of Sch., Brookfield Union 8, Mass., since 1952.

Thurston, Edmund W., B.S.'27, Boston Univ.; Ed.M.'40, Univ. of N. H.; Supt. of Sch., Westwood, Mass., since 1949.

Tilton, John Philip, A.B.'23, Colby Col.; Ed.M. '27, Ed.D.'33, Harvard Univ.; Dean, Grad. Sch., Tufts Col., Medford, Mass., since 1943.

Tobin, John M., A.B.'19, Boston Col.; LL.B.'28, Suffolk Law Sch.; Ed.M.'38, Boston Univ.; Supt. of Sch., Cambridge, Mass., since 1945.

Truell, Harold A., B.S.'30, Ed.M.'35, Univ. of N.H.; Supt. of Sch., East Longmeadow, Mass., since 1946.

Tucker, Richard D., Ph.B.'06, Brown Univ.; Supt. of Sch., South Dartmouth, Mass.

Turner, F. Sumner, A.B.'24, Dartmouth Col.; Ed.M.'32, Harvard Univ.; Supt. of Sch., Union 22, Northfield, Mass., since 1948.

Vorse, Walter J., B.S.Ed.'40, Fitchburg Tchrs. Col.; M.Ed.'48, Boston Univ.; Supt. of Sch., Lynnfield, Mass., since 1952.

Vose, James Wilson, A.B.'03, Williams Col.; Ed.M.'28, Harvard Univ.; A.M.'29, Williams Col. Address: Broadway, South Hanover, Mass.

Wales, (Mrs.) Alfreda R., B.S. in Ed.'28, State Tchrs. Col., Bridgewater, Mass.; Ed.M.'49, Harvard Graduate Sch. of Educ.; Assoc. Dir. of Tchr. Tr., Lesley Col., Cambridge, Mass., since 1948.

Warren, Thomas L., B.S. in Ed.'38, State Tchrs. Col., Bridgewater, Mass.; M.Ed.'51, Boston Univ.; Supt. of Sch., Charlemont, Mass., since 1948.

Warren, Worcester, A.B.'12, Knox Col.; A.M.'21, State Univ. of Iowa; Ph.D.'42, Yale Univ.; Prof. of Sch. Admin., Boston Univ., Boston, Mass., since 1943.

Webber, Dana O., B.S.'29, Univ. of Mass.; M.Ed.'43, Boston Univ.; Supt. of Sch., Union 33, Huntington, Mass., since 1949.

Welch, William A., LL.B.'27, Suffolk Univ.; A.B.'30, M.A.'31, Boston Col.; Supt. of Sch., Peabody, Mass., since 1933.

Wetherell, Alliston C., A.B.'30, M.Ed.'41, Bates Col.; Supt. of Sch., Sutton, Mass., since 1951.

White, Trentwell Mason, B.S.'22, A.M.'28, Norwich Univ.; L.H.D.'40, Md. Col. for Women; Pres., Lesley Col., Cambridge, Mass., since 1944.

Whitehead, John A., B.S. in Ed'38, M.Ed.'42, Boston Univ.; Supt. of Sch., Canton, Mass.

Wilcox, Calvin E., Ed.M.'32, Boston Univ.; Ph.D.'39, Yale Univ.; Supt. of Sch., Dedham, Mass., since 1941.

Williston, Arthur L., S.B.'89, Mass. Inst. of Tech. Address: 986 High St., Dedham, Mass.

Wingate, Harold C., B.A.'05, Clark Univ.; Supt. of Marshfield Sch., Egypt, Mass., since 1926.

Woodbury, E. Davis, B.S.'31, Tufts Col.; Ed.M. '41, Boston Univ.; Supt. of Sch., Natick, Mass., since 1942.

Woodward, Myrle A., B.S. in Ed.'45, M.Ed.'46, Boston Univ.; Braintree, Mass.

Wright, Stanley W., A.B.'30, M.Ed.'40, Univ. of N. H.; Supt. of Sch., West Springfield, Mass., since 1950.

INSTITUTIONAL MEMBERS

J. L. Hammett Co., 290 Main St., Cambridge 42, Mass.

Holden Patent Book Cover Co., P. O. Box 1929, Springfield, Mass.

Library, State Teachers College, Fitchburg, Mass.

Library, State Teachers College, Worcester, Mass.

Standard Electric Time Company, H. W. Anzier, Treas., Springfield, Mass.

MICHIGAN
INDIVIDUAL MEMBERS

Abbott, Warren W., A.B.'29, Western Mich. Col. of Educ., Kalamazoo; M.A.'39, Wayne Univ.; Supt. of Sch., Keego Harbor, Mich., since 1932.

MICHIGAN

Ackley, Clark R., B.S.A.'37, Univ. of Mich.; Professional Archt., Lansing, Mich., since 1936.

Ahrens, Maurice R., A.B.'25, Culver-Stockton Col.; M.A.'38, Ed.D.'47, Univ. of Denver; Asst. Supt. and Dir. of Instr., Pub. Sch., Battle Creek, Mich.

Allinder, Allen F., B.S.'29, Hillsdale Col.; M.A.'37, Univ. of Mich.; Supt. of Sch., Greenville, Mich., since 1948.

Alwood, William L., A.B.'24, Huntington Col.; A.M.'29, Univ. of Mich.; Supt. of Sch., Coloma, Mich., since 1930.

Amble, Charles, A.B., Central Mich. Col. of Educ.; Supt of Sch., Harrison, Mich., since 1927.

Ambrose, Rell Atlon, B.A.'28, Mich State Normal Col., Ypsilanti; M.A.'34, Univ. of Mich.; Supt. of Sch., Oxford, Mich., since 1942.

Amundsen, Alfred G., M.A., Univ. of Mich.; Supt. of Sch., Marlette, Mich., since 1948.

Anderson, Lester W., B.A.'40, Luther Col.; M.A.'47, Ph.D.'50, State Univ. of Iowa; Consultant, Bur. of Sch. Serv. and Asst. Prof. in Sch. of Educ., Univ. of Mich., Ann Arbor, Mich., since 1952.

Anderson, Milburn P., A.B.'26, Kalamazoo Col.; M.A.'32, Univ. of Mich.; Supt. of Twp. Sch., Berkley, Mich., since 1939.

Anger, Byron F., B.S.'43, Western Mich. Col.; Master's '52, Mich. State Col.; Supt. of Sch., Shepherd, Mich., since 1951.

Ansel, James O., Ed.D.'49, Tchrs. Col., Columbia Univ.; Assoc. Prof. of Educ., Western Mich. Col. of Educ., Kalamazoo, Mich.

Appel, Paul H., Supt., Dearborn Twp. Sch., Detroit, Mich.

Archer, Hubert G., A.B.'30, Central Mich. Col. of Educ., Mt. Pleasant; A.M.'38, Univ. of Mich.; Supt., Paw Paw Tr. Sch., Paw Paw, Mich., since 1946.

Ardis, Evart W., A.B.'34, Western Mich. Col.; M.A.'38, Northwestern Univ.; Supt. of Sch., East Detroit, Mich., since 1950.

Asbury, Thomas, Treas., Bd. of Educ., Van Dyke, Mich., since 1946.

Aschenbach, Allen D., Bd. of Educ., East Detroit, Mich.

Atkinson, William N., B.A.'25, Iowa Wesleyan Col.; M.A.'32, Ph.D.'39, State Univ. of Iowa; Acting Supt. of Sch., Jackson, Mich., since 1952.

Auble, Lee F., Supt. of Sch., Berrien Springs, Mich.

Austin, W. L., A.B.'37, M.A.'46, Mich. State Col.; Supt. of Wyoming Park Pub. Sch., Grand Rapids, Mich., since 1948.

Averill, Forrest G., A.B.'24, M.A.'28, Ed.D.'49, Univ. of Mich.; Asst. Supt. of Sch., Lansing, Mich., since 1947.

Ayers, Archie Raymond, B.S.'35, Univ. of S. C.; M.A.'39, Duke Univ.; Ph.D.'44, George Peabody Col. for Tchrs.; Pres., Detroit Inst. of Tech., Detroit, Mich.

Ayres, Frank M., A.B.'24, M.A.'26, Univ. of Mich.; Supt. of Sch., Dundee, Mich., since 1924.

Babcock, Earl H., Diploma '09, Mich. State Normal Col.; B.A.'22, M.A.'29, Univ. of Mich.; Supt. of Sch., Grand Haven, Mich., 1923-52.

Bacon, Ruth N., Co. Supt. of Sch., Port Huron, Mich.

Baker, Raymond N., A.B.'27, Olivet Col.; M.A.'41, Wayne Univ.; Supt. of Sch., Auburn Heights, Mich., since 1945.

Baker, Stuart K., A.B.'32, Central State Tchrs. Col., Mt. Pleasant, Mich.; M.A.'40, Wayne Univ.; Supt., Troy Twp. Sch. Dist., Birmingham, Mich., since 1948.

Baldwin, Donald C., B.A.'37, State Tchrs. Col., Cedar Falls, Iowa; M.A.'41, Univ. of Mich.; Supt. of Community Sch., Rochester, Mich., since 1950.

Balmes, Louis Francis, B.A.'44, M.A.'48, Univ. of Mich.; Supt. of Sch., Camden-Frontier Rural Agrl. Sch., Camden, Mich., since 1950.

Barhitte, Fay E., B.S.'33, Central Mich. Col. of Educ., Mt. Pleasant; M.S.'51, Univ. of Mich.; Supt. of Bentley Sch., Flint, Mich., since 1946.

Barr, Harold F., Supt. of James Couzens Agr. Sch., Bath, Mich.

Barr, Ralph W., A.B.'37, Western Mich. Col. of Educ.; M.A.'49, Mich. State Col.; Supt. of Sch., Comstock, Mich., since 1951.

Bartlett, Frank, B.S.'32, Mich. State Normal Col., Ypsilanti; M.A.'41, Univ. of Mich.; Supt., Twp. Sch., South Lyon, Mich., since 1946.

Bates, Austin F., Asst. Supt. of Sch., Jackson, Mich.

Bates, W. C., B.S.'30, Western Mich. Col. of Educ., Kalamazoo; M.A.'39, Univ. of Mich.; Supt. of Sch., Decatur, Mich., since 1948.

Beach, Richard H., B.S. in Ed.'34, Univ. of Fla.; M.A. in Ed.'38, Tchrs. Col., Columbia Univ.; Supt., Bangor Twp. Sch., Bay City, Mich., since 1952.

Beach, William J., B.S.'38, Central Mich. Col. of Educ.; M.A.'47, Univ. of Mich.; Supt. of Sch., Elsie, Mich., since 1951.

Beagle, Kenneth T., A.B.'39, Western Mich. Col. of Educ., Kalamazoo; M.A.'46, Univ. of Mich.; Supt. of Sch., Grand Ledge, Mich., since 1946.

Beiser, Mack J., M.A.'32, Univ. of Mich.; Supt. of Sch., Eaton Rapids, Mich., since 1948.

Bemer, C. W., A.B.'12, Albion Col.; M.A.'26, Tchrs. Col., Columbia Univ.; Supt. of Sch., Muskegon, Mich., since 1943.

Bennett, Roy G., A.B.'31, Central Mich. Col. of Educ., Mt. Pleasant; M.A.'41, Univ. of Mich.; Supt. of Sch., Charlevoix, Mich., since 1945.

Berkhof, William L., A.B.'27, Calvin Col.; M.A.'30, Univ. of Mich.; Supt. of Sch., Mount Clemens, Mich.

Best, Oakley W., A.B.'28, Central Mich. Col. of Educ., Mount Pleasant; M.A.'32, Univ. of Mich.; Supt. of Twp. Sch. Dist. 7, Dearborn, Mich., since 1949.

Bodley, Elwyn J., Supt. of Sch., Sturgis, Mich.

Bogan, G. R., B.S.'16, Mich. State Col.; A.M.'31, Univ. of Mich.; Supt. of Sch., Farwell, Mich., 1947-52.

Booker, W. R., A.B.'16, A.M.'26, Ind. Univ.; Supt. of Sch., Muskegon Hgts., Mich., since 1928.

Bordine, Kenneth T., Dir., Tchr. Educ., Central Mich. Col., Mount Pleasant, Mich.

Borgerson, Norman E., M.E.'45, Mich. State Normal Col.; Asst. Supt., State Dept. of Pub. Instr., Lansing, Mich., since 1936.

Borough, James L., B.S.'46, Western Mich. Col. of Educ.; M.S.'49, Univ. of Mich.; Supt. of Sch., Mattawan, Mich., since 1951.

Bowen, Glenn K., Supt., Taylor Twp. Sch. Dist., Inkster, Mich., since 1949.

Bowers, R. Paul, B.A.'19, Grinnell Col.; M.A.'48, Univ. of Mich.; Supt. of Sch., Bellevue, Mich., since 1949.

Boyce, Robert B., B.S.'34, Western Mich. Col. of Educ., Kalamazoo; M.A.'46, Univ. of Mich.; Supt. of Milwood Sch., Kalamazoo, Mich., since 1947.

Brablec, Carl, B.A.'30, Mich. State Normal Col., Ypsilanti; M.A.'40, Univ. of Mich.; Supt. of Sch., Roseville, Mich.

429

Bradfield, Albert L., B.S.'35, Western Mich. Col. of Educ., Kalamazoo; M.A.'40, Univ. of Mich.; Deputy Co. Supt. of Sch., Grand Haven, Mich., since 1941.

Bragg, F. J., A.B.'23, M.A.'31, Univ. of Mich.; Supt. of Sch., Otsego, Mich., since 1949.

Brake, Charles E., A.B.'20, Kalamazoo Col.; A.M.'39, Univ. of Mich.; Deputy Co. Supt. of Sch., Detroit, Mich., since 1935.

Brant, Ralph E., B.A.'27, Olivet Col.; M.A.'32, Columbia Univ.; Supt. of Sch., Ecorse, Mich., since 1948.

Brautigam, Carl W., A.B.'36, Adrian Col.; M.A.'41, Univ. of Mich.; Supt. of Sch., Vermontville, Mich., since 1948.

Brembeck, Cole S., Ph.D.'51, Univ. of Wis.; Supt. of Sch., North Muskegon, Mich., since 1951.

Brendel, Anthony J., B.S.'22, Mich. State Col.; M.A.'43, Univ. of Mich.; Supt. of Twp. Unit Sch., Grand Blanc, Mich., since 1935.

Brender, Peter E., B.C.E.'13, M. in Landscape Arch.'47, Univ. of Mich.; Brender and Van Reyendam, Ann Arbor, Mich.

Britton, Ernest R., B.S.'24, McKendree Col.; M.S.'33, Univ. of Ill.; Ed.D.'47, Tchrs. Col., Columbia Univ.; Supt. of Sch., Midland, Mich., since 1946.

Browe, Herman J., A.B.'11, M.A.'22, Univ. of Mich.; LL.B. and J.D.'24, Detroit Col. of Law; LL.D.'37, Univ. of Detroit; Deputy Supt. of Sch., Detroit, Mich., since 1942.

Brown, Kenneth Willis, B.S.'38, Alma Col.; M.A.'52, Wayne Univ.; Asst. Co. Supt. of Sch., Pontiac, Mich., since 1949.

Brozak, Joseph, Supt. of Sch., Athens, Mich.

Brundage, Lyle B., A.B.'28, Mich. State Col.; M.A.'36, Univ. of Mich.; Supt. of Sch., Morley, Mich., since 1952.

Brunelle, Leo J., Ph.B.'37, Jordan Col.; B.A.'44, Northern Mich. Col. of Educ.; M.A.'50, Univ. of Mich.; Supt. of Sch., Bark River, Mich., since 1947.

Buell, Theodore J., A.B.'39, Mich. State Normal Col., Ypsilanti; Supt. of Beecher Schs., Flint, Mich., since 1924.

Buffington, Walter, Supt. of Sch., Ferndale, Mich.

Buikema, Benjamin J., A.B.'26, Western State Tchrs. Col., Kalamazoo, Mich.; M.A.'36, Univ. of Mich.; Supt. of Sch., Grand Rapids, Mich., since 1949.

Burklund, Arthur E., B.S.'36, Western Mich. Col. of Educ., Kalamazoo; M.A.'40, Univ. of Mich.; Supt., W. K. Kellogg Consol. Agrl. Sch., Hickory Corners, Mich., since 1946.

Burt, Newell D., A.B.'32, Kalamazoo Col.; A.M.'49, Univ. of Mich.; Supt. of Sch., New Buffalo, Mich., since 1951.

Bush, W. R., A.B.'33, Central Mich. Col. of Educ., Mt. Pleasant; Supt. of Sch., Essexville, Mich., since 1948.

Bushong, James W., B.S.'34, Pacific Univ.; M.Ed.'41, Univ. of Oregon; Supt. of Sch., Grosse Pointe, Mich.

Cameron, Charles S., Supt. of Chelsea Agr. Sch., Chelsea, Mich., since 1952.

Cameron, W. C., A.B.'32, Albion Col.; M.A.'38, Univ. of Mich.; Supt. of Sch., Gladstone, Mich., since 1943.

Campbell, C. G., Pres. and Genl. Mgr., Kewaunee Mfg. Co., Adrian, Mich., since 1915.

Campbell, Clyde M., Ph.D.'42, Northwestern Univ.; Prof. of Educ., Mich. State Col., East Lansing, Mich., since 1945.

Campbell, Willis, Supt. of Sch., Case City, Mich.

Canfield, Charles R., B.S.'33, Univ. of Ill.; M.A.'40, Univ. of Mich.; Supt. of Sch., Dowagiac, Mich., since 1946.

Cantrick, George T., A.B.'14, Adrian Col.; M.A.'28, Univ. of Mich.; M.Ed.'47, Mich. State Normal Col., Ypsilanti; Supt. of Sch., Monroe, Mich., since 1932.

Carlson, Clemens E., B.S.'40, Northern Mich. Col. of Educ.; Supt. of Bessemer Twp. Sch. Dist., Ramsay, Mich., since 1944.

Carmany, Maurice G., A.B.'36, Central Mich. Col. of Educ., Mt. Pleasant; M.A.'41, Univ. of Mich.; Dir. of Pub. Relations, Mich. Educ. Assn., Lansing, Mich., since 1948.

Caswell, Gordon G., A.B.'38, Western Mich. Col. of Ed., Kalamazoo; M.A.'43, Univ. of Mich.; Supt. of Pub. Sch., Kalkaska, Mich., since 1948.

Chambers, Harold S., A.B.'22, Manchester Col.; A.M.'40, Univ. of Mich.; Supt. Godwin Heights Pub. Sch., Grand Rapids, Mich., since 1950.

Chapelle, Ernest H., A.B.'41, M.A.'45, Univ. of Mich.; Supt. of Sch., Ypsilanti, Mich., since 1933.

*Charters, W. W., A.B.'98, McMaster Univ.; B.Ped.'00, Univ. of Toronto; Ph.B.'03, Ph.D. '04, Univ. of Chicago. Address: Maple City, Mich.

Cherpes, Andrew B., B.S.'33, Mich. State Normal Col., Ypsilanti; M.E.'40, Wayne Univ.; Supt., Rural Agrl. Sch., Caledonia, Mich.

Christen, Ralph S., M.A.'30, Univ. of Mich.; Dept. Head, Wilbur Wright Sch., Detroit, Mich., since 1930.

Christian, Percy W., B.A.'26, Broadview Col.; B.S.'28, Lewis Inst.; M.A.'29, Ph.D.'35, Northwestern Univ.; Pres., Emmanuel Missionary Col., Berrien Springs, Mich.

Chubb, Malcolm, B.S.'41, Mich. State Normal Col.; Supt. of Sch., Flint, Mich., since 1951.

Clapp, Wilfred Franklin, B.A.'25, Kalamazoo Col.; M.A.'37, Univ. of Mich.; Asst. Supt., Sch. Organization and Plant, Dept. of Pub. Instr., Lansing, Mich., since 1948.

Clark, E. L., M.A.'27, Univ. of Mich.; Supt. of Sch., Mt. Morris, Mich., since 1934.

Clark, Lynn H., A.B.'23, Western Mich. Col. of Educ., Kalamazoo; A.M.'40, Univ. of Mich.; Co. Supt. of Sch., Rockford, Mich.

Clayton, C. Wesley, B.S.'41, Central Mich. Col. of Educ., Mt. Pleasant; M.A.'49, Univ. of Mich.; Supt. of Twp. Sch., North Branch, Mich., since 1948.

Close, Leo, Boyne City, Mich.

Coe, Dalton O., B.S.'46, Mich. State Normal Col.; M.A.'49, Univ. of Mich.; Supt. of Sch., Three Oaks, Mich., since 1950.

Coggins, Charles G., B.S.'35, Mich. State Normal Col., Ypsilanti; M.A.'42, Univ. of Mich.; Supt. of Sch., Holly, Mich., since 1947.

Collins, Arthur, Member, Bd. of Educ., Willow Run, Mich., since 1950.

Collins, Laurentine B., B.S.'28, M.A.'34, Tchrs. Col., Columbia Univ.; Dir., Sch.-Community Relations, Pub. Sch., Detroit, Mich., since 1943.

Conat, J. M., A.B.'25, Univ. of Mich.; Supt. of Bedford Sch., Lambertville, Mich., since 1922.

Coulter, Robert W., B.S.'47, Wayne Univ.; Supt., Twp. Sch. Dist., Port Huron, Mich., since 1949.

Courtis, Stuart A., Ph.D.'24, Univ. of Mich.; Prof. Emeritus of Educ., Univ. of Mich., since 1944. Address: 9110 Dwight Ave., Detroit 14, Mich.

Cousino, Paul Kenneth, A.B.'34, M.A.'36, Univ. of Mich.; Supt. of Consol. Sch., Warren, Mich., since 1939.

Covert, James C., A.B.'25, Mich. State Normal Col.; M.A.'30, Univ. of Mich.; Supt. of Sch., Royal Oak, Mich., since 1948.

Cowling, Robert, Bd. of Educ., Willow Run, Mich.

Cox, J. Cecil, B.A.'19, Albion Col.; M.A.'40, Univ. of Mich.; Asst. Supt. of Pub. Sch., Pontiac, Mich., since 1948.

Crandell, Warren B., M.A.'49, Mich. State Col.; B.A.'42, Adrian Col.; Supt. of Sch., Perry, Mich., since 1949.

Crawford, Carroll C., B.A.'26, Central Mich. Col. of Educ., Mt. Pleasant; M.A.'34, Univ. of Mich.; Bus. Mgr., Pub. Sch., Kalamazoo, Mich., since 1951.

Creaser, C. J., A.B.'15, M.A.'28, Univ. of Mich.; Supt. of Sch., East Tawas, Mich., since 1935.

Crothers, Clarence E., B.S.'33, Hillsdale Col.; M.A.'40, Univ. of Mich.; Supt. of Sch., Center Line, Mich., since 1951.

Crull, Howard D., B.S.'31, Western State Tchrs. Col., Kalamazoo, Mich.; M.A.'37, Univ. of Mich.; Supt. of Sch., Port Huron, Mich., since 1941.

Cushman, L. P., M.A.'44, Univ. of Mich.; Supt. of Sch., Owosso, Mich., since 1948.

Dacey, Rosemarie, M.A.'40, Wayne Univ.; Prin., Elem. Sch., Detroit, Mich., since 1944.

Daly, George, A.B.'33, Central Mich. Col. of Educ., Mt. Pleasant; M.A.'43, Wayne Univ.; Supt., Kearsley Agrl. Sch., Flint, Mich., since 1937.

Darnall, Thomas, Bd. of Educ., Melvindale, Mich.

Davis, Bernard L., A.B. and B.S.'20, Tri-State Col.; M.A.'31, Univ. of Mich.; Supt. of Sch., Hillsdale, Mich., since 1929.

DeHart, William H., A.B.'35, Central Mich. Col. of Educ., Mt. Pleasant; M.A.'40, Univ. of Mich.; Supt. of Sch., Sparta, Mich., since 1943.

De Jonge, Oliver J., A.B.'20, Hope Col.; M.A.'38, Univ. of Mich.; Supt. of Sch., Ludington, Mich., since 1945.

De Jonge, Willard, A.B.'30, Hope Col.; M.A.'49, Univ. of Mich.; Consultant, Finance and Child Accounting, State Dept. of Pub. Instr., Lansing, Mich., since 1951.

Dell, Elwyn R., B.S.'38, Western Mich. Col. of Educ., Kalamazoo; M.A.'44, Mich. State Col.; Supt. of Sch., Fremont, Mich., 1946-52.

Dent, Harold M., B.S.'42, M.A.'49, Wayne Univ.; Admin. Chmn., Cooperative Engineering Program, Genl. Motors Inst., Flint, Mich., since 1950.

Dodge, Frank E., A.B.'30, Mich. State Normal Col., Ypsilanti; M.A.'35, Wayne Univ.; Supt. of Sch., Bad Axe, Mich., since 1948.

Dominy, Gareth H., B.A.'37, Western Mich. Col. of Educ.; M.A.'47, Univ. of Mich.; Supt. of Sch., Cassopolis, Mich., since 1947.

Donaldson, Elery R., B.A.'20, Lombard Col.; M.A.'38, Univ. of Ill.; Supt. of Sch., Watervliet, Mich., since 1946.

Dondineau, Arthur, A.B.'14, A.M.'15, Univ. of Mich.; LL.D.'46, Central Mich. Col. of Educ., Mt. Pleasant; Supt. of Sch., Detroit, Mich., since 1945.

Donlin, (Mrs.) Verna Q., B.S.'30, Wayne Univ.; Prin., Stellwagen Sch., Detroit, Mich., since 1935.

Downer, Effie M., M.A.'28, Tchrs. Col., Columbia Univ.; Prof. of Educ., Wayne Univ., Detroit, Mich., since 1925.

Downing, Vernon W., A.B.'29, Western Mich. Col. of Educ., Kalamazoo; M.A.'38, Univ. of Mich.; Supt. of Sch., Manchester, Mich., since 1941.

Drevdahl, Lauritz A., A.B.'28, Alma Col.; M.A.'49, Univ. of Mich.; Supt. of Sch., Milan, Mich., since 1951.

Duckstad, John H., B.A.'24, Macalester Col.; M.A.'34, Univ. of N. Dak.; Elem. Coordinator, Pub. Sch., Ironwood, Mich., since 1950.

DuFrain, Frank J., A.B.'16, A.M.'22, Univ. of Ill.; A.M.'27, Tchrs. Col., Columbia Univ.; Supt. of Sch., Pontiac, Mich., since 1945.

Dunckel, Orville E., B.S.'21, Mich. State Col.; M.A.'26, Univ. of Mich.; Supt. of Sch., Farmington, Mich., 1939-43, and since 1946.

Dunstan, James Henry, M.A.'49, Univ. of Mich.; Supt. of Sch., Painesdale, Mich., since 1950.

Eddy, Theo V., A.B.'15, Hillsdale Col.; M.A.'28, Univ. of Mich.; Supt. of Sch., St. Clair, Mich., since 1930.

Edmonson, James Bartlett, A.B.'06, M.A.'10, Univ. of Mich.; Ph.D.'25, Univ. of Chicago; Dean., Sch. of Educ., Univ. of Mich., Ann Arbor, Mich., 1929-53 (retired). Address: 1503 Cambridge Road, Ann Arbor, Mich.

Eggersten, Claude, A.B.'30, M.A.'33, Brigham Young Univ.; Ph.D.'39, Univ. of Minn.; Assoc. Prof. of Educ., Univ. of Mich., Ann Arbor, Mich., since 1939.

Eidt, Earl S., A.B.'33, Mich. State Normal Col., Ypsilanti; M.A.'38, Univ. of Mich.; Supt., Fitzgerald Pub. Sch., Van Dyke, Mich., since 1950.

Eiker, William, A.B.'39, Mich State Normal Col., Ypsilanti; M.A.'46, Univ. of Mich.; Supt. of Twp. Sch., Romulus, Mich., since 1946.

Elkins, Clark, A.B.'35, Western Mich. Col. of Educ., Kalamazoo; M.A.'38, Univ. of Mich.; Educ. Consultant, Jam Handy Organization, Detroit, Mich., since 1942.

Elliot, Keith, B.S.'27, Western Mich. Col. of Educ., Kalamazoo; Supt., Pennfield Rural Agrl. Sch., Battle Creek, Mich., 1948-52. Address: 180 North Unio St., Battle Creek, Mich.

Elliott, Eugene B., B.S.'24, M.A.'26, Mich. State Col.; Ph.D.'33, Univ. of Mich.; LL.D.'36, Albion Col.; D.Ed.'37, Hillsdale Col.; Pres., Mich. State Normal Col., Ypsilanti, Mich., since 1948.

Elwyn, Foss, A.B.'21, De Pauw Univ.; A.M.'28, Columbia Univ.; Supt. of Sch., Sault Ste. Marie, Mich., since 1940.

Emerich, Paul H., A.B.'36, Hillsdale Col.; A.M.'41, Univ. of Mich.; Supt. of Sch., Fremont, Mich., since 1952.

Emerson, William J., A.B.'37, Central Mich. Col. of Educ., Mt. Pleasant; M.A.'40, Wayne Univ.; Co. Supt. of Sch., Pontiac, Mich., since 1949.

Filppula, T. C., B.S.'43, M.A.'48, Mich. State Col.; Supt. of Sch., Bath, Mich., since 1948.

Firestone, Harry P., M.A.'41, Univ. of Mich.; Supt., Rural Agrl. Sch., Ida, Mich., since 1943.

Fischer, Fred C., LL.B.'20, Hamilton Col. of Law; A.B.'21, M.Ed.'40 (Hon.), Mich. State Normal Col., Ypsilanti; M.A.'30, Univ. of Mich.; D.Sc.'48 (Hon.), Wayne Univ.; Co. Supt. of Sch., Detroit, Mich., since 1935.

Fitzharris, Burleson, Bd. of Educ., Willow Run, Mich.

Formsma, Russell W., A.B.'31, M.A.'32, Univ. of Mich.; Supt. of Sch., Grand Rapids, Mich., since 1950.

Frost, C. A., A.B.'33, Western Mich. Col. of Educ., Kalamazoo; M.A.'38, Univ. of Mich.; Supt., Oakleigh Jr. H. S., Grand Rapids, Mich., since 1928.

431

Fry, Lloyd C., B.A.'29, Western Mich. Col. of Educ., Kalamazoo; M.A.'42, Univ. of Mich.; Dist. Supt. of Sch., Godfrey-Lee Sch., Grand Rapids, Mich., since 1944.

Garber, V. E., B.A.'35, Emmanuel Missionary Col.; M.A.'44, Mich. State Col.; Prin., Adelphian Academy, Holly, Mich., since 1945.

Geisler, Henry, B.A.'30, Adrian Col.; M.A.'39, Univ. of Mich.; Supt. of Sch., Morenci, Mich., since 1942.

Gelston, W. L., A.B.'39, Alma Col.; M.A.'49, Univ. of Mich.; Supt. of Rural Agr. Schs., Farwell, Mich., since 1952.

Gerganoff, R. S., 206 N. Washington St., Ypsilanti, Mich.

Geyer, Eldon C., Supt. of Sch., Hamtramck, Mich.

Gilliland, V. Leland, A.B.'30, Rio Grande Col.; M.A.'43, Ohio State Univ.; Supt. of Sch., Monroe, Mich., since 1950.

Grambau, Harry G., M.A.'39, Univ. of Mich.; Supt. of Sch., Rogers City, Mich., since 1950.

Gray, Wayne, A.B.'28, Mich. State Normal Col., Ypsilanti; A.M.'38, Univ. of Mich.; Supt. of Sch., Addison, Mich., 1929–44, and since 1949.

Green, Leslie F., A.B.'35, Kalamazoo Col.; M.A.'39, Univ. of Mich.; Supt. of Sch., Clarkston, Mich., since 1951.

Gregory, Joe H., B.A.'35, Northern Mich. Col. of Educ., Marquette; M.Ed.'48, Wayne Univ.; Supt. of Gratiot Twp. Sch., Detroit, Mich., since 1947.

Grenier, Andrew, Bd. of Educ., Willow Run, Mich.

Griffin, John, B.S.'45, Morningside Col.; M.A.'50, Columbia Univ.; Supt. of Sch., Bergland, Mich., since 1950.

Grim, Edgar L., A.B.'34, Central Mich. Col. of Educ., Mt. Pleasant; M.A.'40, Univ. of Mich.; Asst. Supt. of Sch., State Dept. of Public Instr., Lansing, Mich., since 1949.

Grove, Isaac E., A.B.'32, Mich. State Normal Col.; M.A.'39, Univ. of Mich.; Co. Supt. of Sch., Monroe, Mich., since 1946.

Gucky, Joseph B., B.S.'34, Univ. of Chicago; M.A.'43, Univ. of Mich.; Supt. of Sch., Stephenson, Mich., since 1944.

Gumser, W. W., A.B.'17, Hope Col.; A.M.'26, Univ. of Mich.; Supt. of Sch., Lowell, Mich., since 1926.

Hachmuth, B. T., Supt. of Sch., Comstock Park, Mich.

Haisley, Otto W., M.A.'17, Columbia Univ.; Supt. of Sch., Ann Arbor, Mich., since 1924.

Haitema, John S., A.B.'24, Calvin Col.; A.M.'30, Ph.D.'46, Univ. of Mich.; Asst. Supt. of Public Instr., Lansing, Mich., since 1936.

Haley, Nelle, B.S.'21, A.M.'28, Tchrs. Col., Columbia Univ.; M.Ed.'44, Mich. State Normal Col., Ypsilanti; Dir. of Elem. Educ., Saginaw, Mich., since 1921.

Hall, Fred W. H., B.A.'33, Jamestown Col.; Supt. of Sch., Hart, Mich., since 1948.

Hampton, W. G., B.S.'45, Northern Mich. Col. of Educ., Marquette; A.M.'51, Univ. of Mich.; Supt. of Sch., Beaverton, Mich., since 1950.

Hanks, N. A., M.A.'32, Univ. of Mich.; Supt. of Sch., Marysville, Mich., since 1928.

Hansen, Harold O., A.B.'28, Mich. State Normal Col., Ypsilanti; A.M.'41, Univ. of Mich.; Supt., Huron Valley Sch., Milford, Mich., since 1929.

Hanson, Floyd H., B.S. in Ed., Kansas State Tchrs. Col., Emporia; M.S. in Ed., Univ. of Kansas; Bd. of Educ., East Detroit, Mich.

Hardy, Robert E., B.S.'40, Central Mich. Col. of Educ., Mt. Pleasant; M.A.'46, Univ. of Mich.; Supt., Rural Agrl. Sch., Fruitport, Mich., since 1946.

Engel, Anna M., B.S.'24, Detroit Tchrs. Col., Detroit, Mich.; M.A.'31, Univ. of Detroit; Dir., Div. of Special Educ., Pub. Sch., Detroit, Mich., since 1945.

Engle, Edward J., B.S.'39, Mich. State Normal Col.; M.A.'44, Univ. of Mich.; Supt., Lake Shore H. S., St. Clair Shores, Mich.

English, John Wesley, B.S.Ed.'36, M.A.'40, Ph.D.'51, Univ. of Mich.; Dir., Research and Statistics, Pub. Sch., Flint, Mich.

Erickson, Arthur E., A.B.'16, Gustavus Adolphus Col.; A.M.'29, Univ. of Minn.; Supt. of Sch., and Pres., Gogebic Jr. Col., Ironwood, Mich., since 1932.

Estes, King R., M.A.'42, Univ. of Mich.; Supt. of Oakwood Sch., Kalamazoo, Mich., since 1933.

Ewing, G. L., B.S.'32, Western Mich. Col. of Educ., Kalamazoo; M.A.'44, Mich. State Col.; Supt. of Sch., Mayville, Mich.

Eyler, Loren E., B.A.'29, Mich. State Normal Col., Ypsilanti; M.A.'36, Univ. of Mich.; Supt. of Sch., Carleton, Mich., since 1927.

Feaheny, Adele L., M.A.'34, Wayne Univ.; Critic-Prin., Poe Teaching-Tr. Sch., Detroit, Mich., since 1946.

Fetherston, Roy, B.A.'23, Beloit Col.; M.A.'32, Univ. of Iowa; Supt., East Grand Rapids Sch., Grand Rapids, Mich., since 1949.

Harper, R. W., A.B.'22, Albion Col.; M.A.'37, Univ. of Mich.; Supt. of Sch., Delton, Mich.

Harrington, H. L., A.B.'15, M.A.'20, Ph.D.'30, Univ. of Mich.; Asst. Supt. of Sch., Detroit, Mich., since 1942.

Harris, William C., A.B.'29, Mich. State Normal Col., Ypsilanti; M.E.'43, Wayne Univ.; Dist. Supt. of Sch., Allen Park, Mich., since 1946.

Hawes, Everett L., Asst. Supt. of Sch., East Detroit, Mich.

Hawley, William B., A.B.'38, M.A.'47, Wayne Univ.; State Dir. for Voc. Educ. and Asst. Supt. of Pub. Instr., Lansing, Mich., since 1950.

Hazel, Floyd M., B.S.'22, Mich. State Col.; M.A.'26, Univ. of Mich.; Supt., Lakeview Consol. Sch., Battle Creek, Mich., since 1922.

Hearne, Knox, Vicepres., Educ. Div., Hearne Bros., Detroit, Mich.

Hellenga, Robert Dean, A B.'47, Western Mich. Col. of Educ.; M.A.'50, Univ. of Mich.; Supt. of Sch., Ravenna, Mich., since 1951.

Hensen, E. C., A.B.'28, Mich. State Normal Col.; M.A.'39, Univ. of Mich.; Supt. of Sch., Stanton, Mich., since 1948.

Hicks, John E., A.B.'46, M.A.'46, Univ. of Mich.; Supt. of Sch., Manton, Mich., since 1951.

Highlund, Everett C., B.S.'29, Alma Col.; M.A.'38, Mich. State Col.; Supt. of Sch., Homer, Mich., since 1949.

Hilbert, Russel S., A.B.'29, Western Mich. Col. of Educ., Kalamazoo; M.A.'32, Univ. of Mich.; Supt., Redford Union Pub. Sch., Detroit, Mich., since 1948.

Holden, Ellsworth B., B.S.'23, Mich. State Col.; M.A.'34, Columbia Univ.; Educ. Consultant, Warren S. Holmes Co., Architects, Lansing, Mich., since 1947.

Holmes, Harley W., A.B.'26, Western Mich. Col. of Educ., Kalamazoo; M.A.'35, Albion Col.; Supt. of Sch., Marshall, Mich., since 1929.

Holmes, J. E., A.B.'27, Western Mich. Col. of Educ., Kalamazoo; A.M.'36, Univ. of Wyo.; Supt. of Sch., Spring Lake, Mich., since 1923.

Hood, Carl, A.B.'24, Mich. State Normal Col.; M.A.'28, Univ. of Mich.; Prof. of Educ., Mich. State Normal Col., Ypsilanti, Mich., since 1946.

Hooper, Mary L., M.E.'45, Wayne Univ.; Prin., Robinson Sch., Detroit, Mich.

Horst, Walter, M.A.'26, Univ. of Mich.; Supt. of Sch., Three Rivers, Mich., since 1936.

Hougen, Leif A., B.E.'37, State Tchrs. Col., St. Cloud, Minn.; M.A.'42, Univ. of Mich.; Ed.D.'47, Columbia Univ.; Supt. of West Bloomfield Sch., Keego Harbor, Mich.

Howard, Daisy E., B.S.'40, Mich. State Normal Col., Ypsilanti; M.A.'41, Univ. of Mich.; Co. Supt. of Sch., Flint, Mich., since 1929.

Huey, Arthur S., B.A.'35, Amherst Col.; Headmaster, The Leelanau Schs., Glen Arbor, Mich., since 1942.

Huff, Leo W., A.B.'30, M.A.'36, Univ. of Mich.; Supt. of Sch., Lincoln Park, Mich., since 1928.

Hungerford, E. J., A.B.'35, Western Mich. Col. of Educ.; M.A.'43, Univ. of Mich.; Supt. of Community Sch., Tekonsha, Mich., since 1948.

Hunter, Ballard, A.B.'31, Univ. of Ky.; Bd. of Educ., Ecorse Twp., Dist. 11, Melvindale, Mich.

Ireland, Dwight B., B.A.'26, M.A.'29, Ph.D.'38, Ohio State Univ.; Supt. of Sch., Birmingham, Mich., since 1942.

Isbister, Russell L., B.S.'32, Mich. State Normal Col., Ypsilanti; A.M.'37, Univ. of Mich.; Supt. of Twp. Sch. Dist., Plymouth, Mich., since 1951.

Jacobson, Harold E., A.B.'22, Olivet Col.; Prin., West Jr. H. S., Lansing, Mich., since 1945.

Jeffers, William G., A.B.'32, Central Mich. Col. of Educ.; A.M.'43, Univ. of Mich.; Supt. of Sch., Climax, Mich., since 1948.

Jelsch, John, A.B.'12, Albion Col.; M.A.'27, Columbia Univ.; Supt. of Sch., Iron Mountain, Mich., since 1933.

Jenema, P. J., M.S.'40, Mich. State Col.; Supt. of Sch., Wyandotte, Mich.

Jennings, D. J., M.A.'43, Univ. of Mich.; Supt. of Community Sch., Quincy, Mich., since 1930.

Jensen, Leo L., M.A.'41, Univ. of Mich.; Supt. of Sch., Saline, Mich., since 1943.

Johnsen, Albert C., B.S.'43, Western Mich. Col. of Educ., Kalamazoo; M.A.'39, Univ. of Mich.; Supt., Agrl. Sch., Chelsea, Mich., since 1938.

Johnson, Harry O., A.B.'29, Northern Mich. Col. of Educ., Marquette; M.A.'37, Univ. of Mich.; Supt. of Twp. Sch., Plymouth, Mich., since 1944.

Johnson, Ogden E., A.B.'24, Augustana Col.; M.Ed.'36, Boston Univ.; Supt. of Sch., Ishpeming, Mich., since 1942.

Johnson, William A., Sch. Bd. Secy., Marysville H. S., Marysville, Mich., since 1950.

Jones, D. Lorne, A.B.'47, Atlantic Union Col.; Asst. Prin., Cedar Lake Acad., Cedar Lake, Mich., since 1951.

*Jones, Howard Robert, B.S.'33, M.A.'36, Univ. of Minn.; Ph.D.'40, Yale Univ.; Prof. of Sch. Admin.; Sch. of Educ., Univ. of Mich., Ann Arbor, Mich., since 1951.

Kaechele, Arthur A., A.B.'28, Western Mich. Col. of Educ., Kalamazoo; M.A.'37, Northwestern Univ.; Supt. of Sch., Allegan, Mich., since 1939.

Kahl, Harris A., B.S.'32, Mich. State Col.; M.A.'47, Univ. of Mich.; Supt. of Twp. Sch., Rudyard, Mich., since 1945.

Kaufman, Jennie M., Co. Supt. of Sch., Grand Haven, Mich.

Kaulitz, Dale E., B.S.'43, M.A.'51, Mich. State Col.; Supt., Summerfield Twp. Sch., Petersburg, Mich., since 1952.

Keicher, R. Frederic, Supt. of Sch., Michigan Center, Mich.

Kennedy, Ernest Dale, A.B.'31, Central Mich. Col. of Educ.; M.A.'38, Univ. of Mich.; Asst. Exec. Secy., Mich. Educ. Assn., Lansing, Mich., since 1950.

King, Fred M., Mgr., Market Development, Wyandotte Chemicals Corp., Wyandotte, Mich.

King, Kenneth S., M.A.'43, Wayne Univ.; Supt. of Sch., Algonac, Mich., since 1947.

Kingdon, John W., M.A.'49, Univ. of Mich.; Supt. of Sch., Dimondale, Mich., since 1949.

Klein, Robert F., B.S.'41, Mich. State Normal Col., Ypsilanti; Supt., Rogers Sch., Grand Rapids, Mich., since 1949.

Kleinert, Erwin J., A.B.'32, Mich. State Normal Col., Ypsilanti; A.M.'39, Univ. of Mich.; Supt. of Sch., Rockford, Mich., since 1940.

Kolhoff, (Mrs.) Lloyd, Secy., Bd. of Educ., Berrien Springs, Mich.

Koopman, G. Robert, A.B.'22, Central Mich. Col. of Educ., Mt. Pleasant; A.M.'26, Tchrs. Col., Columbia Univ.; D.Political Sci.'48, Univ. of Palermo; Assoc. State Supt. of Pub. Instr., Lansing, Mich., since 1947.

Koppin, Paul G., Jr., Treas., Bd. of Educ., East Detroit, Mich.

Kos, James M., M.A.'42, Univ. of Mich.; Supt. of Sch., Lakeview, Mich., since 1937.

Krueger, Lawrence F., B.S.'32, Univ. of Toledo; M.A.'34, Univ. of Mich.; Supt., Pittsfield Sch. Dist. 9, Ann Arbor, Mich., since 1947.

Krueger, R. L., Pres., Bd. of Educ., Ecorse Twp. Sch. Dist. 11, Melvindale, Mich.

Krug, Marguerite Charlotte, B.S.'29, M.A.'34, Wayne Univ.; Prin., Elem. Sch., 2270 Leslie Ave., Detroit, Mich., since 1933.

Kuhn, Florence E., B.S.'29, M.S.'35, Wayne Univ.; Asst. Supt. of Sch., Detroit, Mich.

Lamb, L. H., B.S.'22, Stout Inst.; M.A.'32, Univ. of Mich. Address: 1014 S. Jefferson St., Hastings, Mich.

Lamb, T. N., B.S.'25, Ind. State Normal Sch.; B.A.'28, Goshen Col.; M.A.'31, Univ. of Mich.; Supt., Bendle Sch. Dist., Flint, Mich., since 1937.

Lamer, Peter A., B.S.'45, Western Mich. Col. of Educ.; Supt., Calhoun Agrl. Sch., Battle Creek, Mich., since 1949.

Lancaster, Earl R., B.S.'33, Adrian Col.; M.A.'40, Univ. of Mich.; Supt. of Sch., St. Johns, Mich., since 1952.

Lane, Edward M., B.C.Sc.'25, Univ. of Detroit; Secy. and Bus. Mgr., Bd. of Educ., Detroit, Mich., since 1939.

Leach, Kent W., A.B.'37, M.A.'38, Oberlin Col.; Ph.D.'52, Western Reserve Univ.; Asst. Dir., Bureau of Sch. Serv., and Asst. Prof. in Sch. of Educ., Univ. of Mich., Ann Arbor, Mich.

Leaver, C. B., Supt. of Sch., Kent City, Mich.

LeCronier, Russell, A.B.'23, Central Mich. Col. of Educ., Mt. Pleasant; A.M.'35, Univ. of Mich.; Supt. of Sch., Mt. Pleasant, Mich.

LeFevre, Harold E., A.B.'35, Mich. State Normal Col., Normal; M.A.'41, Wayne Univ.; Deputy Supt., Macomb Co. Sch., Mount Clemens, Mich.

Lemmer, John A., Ph B.'18, Univ. of Notre Dame; M.A.'25, Univ. of Mich.; Supt. of Sch., Escanaba, Mich., since 1935.

Letsinger, Kenneth Leo, A.B.'23, Wabash Col.; M.A.'32, Univ. of Ill.; Supt. of Sch., Dexter, Mich., since 1948.

433

MICHIGAN

Lewis, (Mrs.) Florence M., B.S. in Ed.'40, Southeast Mo. State Col.; A.M.'51, Univ. of Mich.; Supt., Level Park Sch., Battle Creek, Mich., since 1950.

Lewis, James A., B.S.'34, Central State Tchrs. Col., Mt. Pleasant, Mich.; M.A.'38, Univ. of Mich.; Supt. of Sch., Dearborn, Mich., since 1948.

Lewis, John W., A.B.'26, Rio Grande Col.; M.E.'40, Wayne Univ.; Dist. Supt. of Sch., St. Clair Shores, Mich., since 1942.

*Lindbergh, (Mrs.) Evangeline L. L., Honorary Life Member, American Assn. of Sch. Admin. Address: 508 Lakepointe, Detroit, Mich.

Little, E., Supt. of Sch., Onsted, Mich.

Loomis, Glenn E., A.B.'16, M.S.'25, LL.D.'47, Olivet Col.; M.A.'30, Univ. of Mich.; Supt. of Sch., Traverse City, Mich., since 1939.

*Lowrey, Harvey H., A.B.'17, Central State Tchrs. Col., Mt. Pleasant, Mich.; M.A.'21, Univ. of Mich.; Ph.D.'40, Univ. of Grand Rapids. Address: Saranac, Mich.

Lowry, Charles D., B.S.'08, A.M.'13, Northwestern Univ. Address: 1027 San Lucia Dr., S. E., Grand Rapids, Mich.

Lubbers, C. W., A.B.'25, Hope Col.; M.A.'39, Univ. of Mich.; Supt. of Sch., Plainwell, Mich., since 1941.

Lubbers, Clarence R., A.B.'24, Hope Col.; M.S.'33, Univ. of Mich.; Supt. of Sch., Coranna, Mich., since 1950.

Lubbers, Melvin B., A.B.'27, Hope Col.; M.A.'37, Univ. of Mich.; Supt. of Sch., Zeeland, Mich., 1942-52. Address: 522 E. Lincoln Ave., Zeeland, Mich.

Lundberg, Lawrence D., A.B.'17, Augustana Col.; M.A.'30, Univ. of Mich.; Asst. Supt. of Sch., Flint, Mich., since 1930.

Luyendyk, William A., A.B.'35, Univ. of Mich.; M.S.'48, Mich. State Col.; Supt. of Sch., Chesaning, Mich., since 1950.

McAlvey, Donald G., M.A.'49, Univ. of Mich.; Supt. of Sch., Almont, Mich., since 1951.

McCarthy, Julia M., M.A.'33, Univ. of Detroit; Supvg. Prin., Burt Sch., Detroit, Mich.

McCully, L. J., B.S.'36, Western Mich. Col. of Educ., Kalamazoo; Bus. Agt., Pub. Sch., Bay City, Mich., since 1943.

McDowell, James, A.B.'29, A.M.'40, Univ. of Mich.; Supt. of Sch., Tecumseh, Mich., since 1951.

McGee, D. Reed, B.S.'31, Mich. State Col.; M.A.'45, Univ. of Mich.; Supt. of Benzonia Consol. Sch., Benzonia, Mich., since 1948.

McHugh, (Mrs.) Evelyn C., Bd. of Educ., East Detroit, Mich.

McIntosh, Walter L., B.S.'37, Central Mich. Col. of Educ., Mt. Pleasant; M.A.'45, Univ. of Mich.; Supt. of Sch., Marion, Mich., since 1949.

MacDonald, C. E., M.A.'42, Univ. of Mich.; Supt. of Sch., East Lansing, Mich.

MacDonald, George, A.B.'34, Western State Tchrs. Col., Kalamazoo, Mich.; M.A.'40, Univ. of Mich.; Supt. of Sch., Parchment, Kalamazoo, Mich., since 1936.

MacNaughton, Orison A., M.A.'30, Univ. of Mich.; Supt. of Sch., Howard City, Mich., since 1924.

MacNeil, W. T., M.A.'40, Univ. of Mich.; Supt. of Sch., Munising, Mich., since 1951.

Madison, Frederick D., Wayne Oakland Bank Bldg., Royal Oak, Mich.

Manley, Frank James, B.S.'30, M.E.'37, Mich. State Normal Col., Ypsilanti; M.A.'46, Univ. of Mich.; Dir., Mott Foundation Program, since 1934 and Asst. Supt. of Sch., Flint, Mich., since 1945.

Martin, Stephen James, A.B.'23, Hillsdale Col.; M.A.'41, Univ. of Mich.; Supt. of Sch., Evart, Mich., since 1929.

Matteson, James A., Diploma '49, Central Mich. Col. of Educ.; Supt. of Twp. Sch., Frankenmuth, Mich., since 1950.

Medler, Hugh W., B.S.'33, Mich. State Normal Col., Ypsilanti; M.A.'41, Univ. of Mich.; Supt., Atherton Agr. Sch., Flint, Mich., since 1944.

Meyering, Corneil, A.B., B.S.'39, Western Mich. Col. of Educ., Kalamazoo; Supt., Maple Grove Sch., Muskegon, Mich., since 1939.

Michelson, E. S., M.A.'47, Univ. of Mich.; Research and Planning Consultant, Garfield Sch., Wyandotte, Mich., since 1950.

Millard, Cecil V., Ph.D.'37, Univ. of Mich.; Dir., Div. of Educ., Mich. State Col., East Lansing, Mich., since 1938.

Miller, Chester F., A.B.'07, A.M.'09, McKendree Col.; A.M.'18, Tchrs. Col., Columbia Univ.; Litt.D.'28, McKendree Col.; LL.D.'37, Alma Col.; Supt. of Sch., Saginaw, Mich., since 1927.

Miller, Leo E., B.S.'20, Alma Col.; M.A.'37, Univ. of Mich.; Supt. of Sch., Hudson, Mich., since 1935.

Miller, Ralph Harvey, B.S.'32, Mich. State Normal Col., Ypsilanti; M.S., P.H.'38, Univ. of Mich.; Supt. of Sch., Capac, Mich., since 1949.

Mills, Leonard D., B.S.'38, Central Mich. Col. of Educ., Mt. Pleasant; M.A.'42, Univ. of Mich.; Supt. of Sch., Caro, Mich., since 1947.

Miner, Roscoe C., B.S.'39, Mich State Normal Col.; M.A.'46, Univ. of Mich.; Supt. of Sch., Lake Odessa, Mich., since 1947.

Mitchell, S. C., Supt. of Sch., Benton Harbor, Mich., since 1923.

Mohr, Lloyd C., B.S.'16, Adrian Col.; M.A.'22, Tchrs. Col., Columbia Univ.; Supt. of Sch., South Haven, Mich., since 1920.

Morrison, (Mrs.) Helen L., B.S.'31, Wayne Univ.; Member and Treas., Bd. of Educ., Melvindale, Mich., since 1951.

Mosier, Earl E., Dean, Professional Educ., Mich. State Normal Col., Ypsilanti, Mich.

Muma, Clark, B.S.'29, Western Mich. Col. of Educ., Kalamazoo; M.A.'40, Univ. of Mich.; Supt. of Sch., Charlotte, Mich., since 1949.

Mumford, Don, Mgr., Hotel Statler, Detroit, Mich.

Munroe, William D., M.A.'42, Univ. of Mich.; Supt. of Rual Agrl. Sch., Whitehall, Mich., since 1950.

Munshaw, Carroll, A.B.'37, Calvin Col.; M.A.'41, Univ. of Mich.; Supt. of Sch., River Rouge, Mich., since 1951.

Munson, Eva, B.S.'35, Wayne Univ.; Prin., Van Zile Sch., Detroit, Mich., since 1943.

Murdock, Edward L., B.S.'31, Western Mich. Col. of Educ., Kalamazoo; M.A.'41, Univ. of Mich.; Supt. of Sch., Big Rapids, Mich., since 1951.

Murphy, H. M., A.B.'23, M.A.'27, Univ. of Mich.; Supt., Haslett Rural Agr. Sch., Haslett, Mich., since 1948.

Myers, Spencer W., A.B.'27, Hiram Col.; A.M. and M.B.A.'30, Northwestern Univ.; Ed.D.'42, Ind. Univ.; Supt. of Sch., Flint, Mich., since 1952.

Nagy, Joseph F., Head Instr., Shop Office, Henry Ford Trade Sch., Dearborn, Mich.

Nelson, Herbert R., B.A.'31, Union Col., Nebr.; M.A.'39, Univ. of Nebr.; Supt., Mich. Conference of Seventh-day Adventists, Lansing, Mich., since 1949.

434

Nelson, James K., M.A.'44, Univ. of Mich.; Supt., Sch. Dist. 1, Calumet, Mich., since 1952.

Nelson, W. A., B.A.'25, Union Col.; Educ. Secy., Lake Union Conf., Seventh-day Adventists, Berrien Springs, Mich., since 1947.

Niergarth, J. Ivan, M.A.'36, Univ. of Mich.; Supt. of Sch., St. Johns, Mich., since 1943.

Nill, Louise, B.A.'29, Wayne Univ.; M.A.'34, Univ. of Detroit; Prin., Hamilton Sch., Detroit, Mich., since 1946.

Norlin, Alvin P., M.A.'37, Univ. of Mich.; Supt. of Sch., Imlay City, Mich., since 1949.

Norman, Godfrey T., B.S.'32, Alma Col.; M.A.'46, Mich. State Col.; Supt. of Sch., Reed City, Mich., since 1948.

Norrix, Loy, Ph.D.'42, Univ. of Chicago; LL.D. '49, Western Mich. Col. of Educ.; Supt. of Sch., Kalamazoo, Mich., since 1937.

Nurnberger, T. S., A.B.'26, M.A.'29, Univ. of Mich.; Supt. of Sch., St. Louis, Mich., since 1932.

Nykerk, Glenn, A.B.'31, Hope Col.; A.M.'37, Univ. of Mich.; Supt. of Sch., Richland, Mich., since 1946.

Oehrli, R. R., B.S.'29, Mich. State Col.; M.A.'40, Univ. of Mich.; Supt. of Sch., Montague, Mich., since 1929.

O'Leary, Edwin John, B.S. in Ed.'40, M.S. in Ed.'45, Univ. of Ill.; Supt. of Sch., Garden City, Mich., since 1952.

Olsen, K. S., A.B.'27, Central Mich. Col. of Educ.; M.A.'31, Univ. of Mich.; Supt. of Sch., Garden City, Mich., since 1946.

Olson, Willard C., B.A.'20, M.A.'24, Ph.D.'26, Univ. of Minn.; Dean, Sch. of Educ., Univ. of Mich., Ann Arbor, Mich., since 1952.

Openlander, Stuart L., M.A.'42, Univ. of Mich.; Supt. of Sch., Wayne, Mich., since 1947.

Owen, J. Willis, B.S.'33, Hillsdale Col.; M.A.'40, Univ. of Mich.; Supt., Twp. Sch. Dist. 4, Dearborn, Mich.

Page, John S., A.B.'22, M.A.'24, Univ. of Mich.; M.A. in Ed.'43, Mich. State Normal Col., Ypsilanti; Supt. of Sch., Howell, Mich., since 1922.

Park, Charles B., B.S.'25, Mich. State Col.; M.A.'35, Univ. of Mich.; Supt. of Sch., Bay City, Mich.

Patterson, Fred W., A.B.'35, Mich. State Normal Col.; A.M.'52, Univ. of Mich.; Supt. of Sch., Dryden, Mich., since 1946.

Pepper, (Mrs.) Alice N., B.S.'35, Mich. State Normal Col.; M.A.'41, Univ. of Mich.; Supt. of Sch., Clayton, Mich., since 1951.

Perry, Dorothy M., D.Ed.'50, Wayne Univ.; Prin., Law Sch., Detroit, Mich., since 1952.

Peters, Clifford N., Supt. of Sch., Muskegon, Mich.

Peterson, Earl E., B.S.'29, Mich. State Col.; M.A.'37, Univ. of Mich.; Supt. of Sch., Brooklyn, Mich., since 1950.

Peterson, George E., A.B.'30, Mich. State Normal Col., Ypsilanti; M.A.'38, Univ. of Mich.; Supt. of Sch., Fenton, Mich.

Petzke, Max K., B.A.'34, Western Mich. Col. of Educ., Kalamazoo; M.A.'43, Univ. of Mich.; Supt. of Fair Plain Sch., Benton Harbor, Mich., since 1923.

Pfingst, Ralph A., A.B.'34, Western Mich. Col. of Educ., Kalamazoo; M.Ed.'45, Wayne Univ.; Supt. of Sch., Marine City, Mich., since 1944.

Phillips, A. J., A.B.'21, Albion Col.; M.A.'25, Ph.D.'33, Univ. of Mich.; Exec. Secy., Mich. Educ. Assn., Lansing, Mich., since 1936.

Phillips, F. R., M.A.'29, Univ. of Mich.; Supt. of Sch., Alma, Mich., since 1926.

Place, Earl H., A.B.'32, Hillsdale Col.; M.A.'37, Univ. of Mich.; Supt. of Sch., St. Joseph, Mich., since 1951.

Plummer, Leon A., A.B.'38, Western Mich. Col. of Educ., Kalamazoo; M.A.'46, Univ. of Mich.; Supt. of Twp. Sch., Olivet, Mich., since 1947.

Porter, Milton C., B.S.'39, Mich. State Normal Col., Ypsilanti; M.A.'46, Univ. of Mich.; Co. Supt. of Sch., Adrian, Mich., since 1947.

Purcell, Charles L., Bd. of Educ., Ecorse Twp. Sch. Dist. 1½, Melvindale, Mich., since 1949.

Purdom, Thomas Luther, A.B.'10, Centre Col.; M.A.'22, Ph.D.'25, Univ. of Mich.; Dir., Bureau of Appointments and Occupational Information, Univ. of Mich., Ann Arbor, Mich., since 1929.

Rainey, D. F., B.S.'20, Mich. State Col.; A.M.'37, Univ. of Mich.; Supt. of Sch., Goodrich, Mich.

Randels, James Wallace, M.A.'45, Univ. of Mich.; Supt. of Sch., Dye Community Sch., Flint, Mich., since 1949.

*Rankin, Paul T., A.B.'15, Mich. State Normal Col., Ypsilanti; M.A.'21, Ph.D.'26, Univ. of Mich.; M.Ed.'42, Mich. State Normal Col.; Asst. Supt. of Sch., Detroit, Mich., since 1943.

Rather, A. A., A.B.'16, M.A.'24, Univ. of Mich.; M.Ed.'40, Mich. State Normal Col., Ypsilanti; Supt. of Sch., Ionia, Mich., since 1917.

Reed, A. A., M.A.'38, Northwestern Univ.; Supt. of Sch., Nashville, Mich., since 1938.

Reed, (Mrs.) Helen Parker, B.S. in Ed.'31, M.A.'34, Wayne Univ.; Supvg. Prin., Marshall Sch., Detroit, Mich., since 1951.

Rezny, Arthur A., B.S.'32, M.S.'39, Univ. of Ill.; Dir. of Instr., Bd. of Educ., Royal Oak, Mich., since 1949.

Rich, Dwight H., A.B.'19, Kalamazoo Col.; M.A.'27, Columbia Univ.; Supt. of Sch., Lansing, Mich., since 1945.

Richard, Charles E., A.B.'21, Univ. of Dubuque; M.A.'41, Univ. of Mich.; Supt. of Sch., Watersmeet, Mich., since 1934.

Richards, George H., M.A.'49, Mich. State Col.; Supt. of Okemos Consol. Sch., Okemos, Mich., since 1951.

Richter, Arthur L., B.A.'30, Western Mich. Col.; M.A.'32, Univ. of Mich.; Supt. of Sch., Frankfort, Mich., since 1944.

Rittenhouse, Floyd Oliver, B.A.'28, Emmanuel Missionary Col.; M.A.'32, Ph.D.'47, Ohio State Univ.; Emmanuel Missionary Col., Berrien Springs, Mich., since 1952.

Robichaud, Hamilton J., A.B.'34, Northern Mich. Col. of Educ., Marquette; M.A.'41, Univ. of Mich.; Supt., Dist. 8, Dearborn Twp. Sch., Inkster, Mich., since 1942.

Robinson, Allen G., M.A.'39, Univ. of Mich.; A.B.'31, Greenville Col.; Supt. of Sch., Coopersville, Mich., since 1948.

Robinson, George A., M.A.'30, Univ. of Mich.; Supt., Sch. Dist. 8, Oakland Co., Hazel Park, Mich., since 1952.

Robinson, Miles W., B.S.'29, Western Mich. Col. of Educ., Kalamazoo; M.A.'39, Wayne Univ.; Supt. of Sch., Menominee, Mich., since 1950.

Robinson, Roy Edward, A.B.'25, Central Mich. Col. of Educ., Mt. Pleasant; A.M.'37, Univ. of Mich.; Supt. of Sch., Ferndale, Mich., since 1948.

Roe, Cleveland, A.B.'30, State Normal Col., Ypsilanti, Mich.; A.M.'35, Univ. of Mich.; Supt. of Van Buren Twp. Consol. Sch., Belleville, Mich., since 1935.

Roe, Merlin D., A.B.'39, Western Mich. Col. of Educ., Kalamazoo; M.A.'49, Wayne Univ.; Supt., Redford Twp. Sch. Dist., Detroit, Mich., since 1948.

Roesch, Winston, 143 Bostwick N. E., Grand Rapids, Mich.

Rogers, Virgil M., A.B.'20, Wofford Col.; A.M. '24, Western State Col. of Colo., Gunnison; Ed.D.'44, Tchrs. Col., Columbia Univ.; Pres., American Assn. of Sch. Admin., 1952-53; Supt. of Sch., Battle Creek, Mich., since 1945.

Rollin, Russell A., Life Certificate '21, Mich. State Normal Col.; B.S.'44, Central Mich. Col. of Educ., Mt. Pleasant; Co. Supt. of Sch., Tawas City, Mich., since 1939.

Rosenthal, Aimee A., B.S.'30, Wayne Univ.; Prin., A. L. Holmes Sch., Detroit, Mich., since 1920.

Ross, Meta M., Prin., Grayling Sch., Detroit, Mich., since 1930.

Rossman, James H., B.S.'47, Mich. State Normal Col., Ypsilanti; Supt. of Springfield Place Sch., Battle Creek, Mich., since 1948.

Rupright, Esther, B.S.'42, Mich. State Normal Col.; M.A.'44, Univ. of Mich.; Res. Dir., Special Serv., Pub. Sch., Battle Creek, Mich., since 1950.

Sangren, Paul V., A.B.'21, Mich. State Normal Col., Ypsilanti; A.M.'22, Ph.D.'26, Univ. of Mich.; Pres., Western Mich. Col. of Educ., Kalamazoo, Mich., since 1936.

Schalm, Paul A., A.B.'23, A.M.'31, Univ. of Mich.; Supt. of Sch., Clawson, Mich., since 1943.

Schickler, Clyde K., B.S.'27, Mich. State Col.; M.A.'39, Wayne Univ.; Supt. of Sch., Lapeer, Mich., since 1946.

Schipper, Julius F., A.B.'28, Hope Col.; M.A.'31, Univ. of Mich.; Supt. of Sch., Zeeland, Mich., since 1952.

Schmidt, Louis E., M.A.'37, Univ. of Mich.; Supt. of Clarenceville Sch., Farmington, Mich., since 1948.

Schmidt, R. W., B.S.'46, Western Mich. Col. of Educ., Kalamazoo; Deputy Supt. of Co. Sch., Muskegon, Mich., since 1942.

Schoenhals, Glenn, A.B.'28, Mich. State Normal Col.; M.A.'35, Univ. of Mich.; Supt. of Southfield Twp. Sch., Detroit, Mich., since 1947.

Schofield, Walter S., Bd. of Educ., Van Dyke, Mich.

Scott, Cecil G., A.B.'28, Western Mich. Col. of Educ., Kalamazoo; M.A.'40, Univ. of Mich.; Supt. of Sch., Oscoda, Mich., since 1945.

Scott, Walter W., B.S.'33, Western Mich. Col. of Educ., Kalamazoo; M.A.'44, Mich. State Col.; Supt. of Sch., Holland, Mich.

Shankland, Bernard C., M.A.'24, Tchrs. Col., Columbia Univ.; Prin. of Jr. H. S., Cadillac, Mich., since 1952.

Shattuck, Marquis E., A.B.'12, Albion Col.; M.Ed.'29, Harvard Univ.; LL.D.'47, Albion Col.; Asst. Supt. of Sch., Detroit, Mich., since 1945.

Shelters, (Mrs.) Mildred, A.B.'47, Western Mich. Col. of Educ.; Dist. Supt. of Sch., Detroit, Mich.

Shirtliff, Dan A., A.B.'40, Mich. State Normal Col.; M.A.'47, Univ. of Mich.; Supt. of Sch., Pittsford, Mich.

Shoemaker, Wayne N., A.B.'26, Kalamazoo Col.; M.A.'29, Univ. of Mich.; Supt. of Sch., Jonesville, Mich.

Shunck, William, A.B.'31, Mich. State Normal Col., Ypsilanti; M.A.'37, Univ. of Mich.; Supt. of Twp. Sch., Pontiac, Mich., since 1945.

Siefert, Edward F., Supt. of Sch., New Haven, Mich.

Simmons, William, A.B.'42, Mich. State Normal Col.; M.A.'47, Univ. of Mich.; Supt., Sch. Dist. 8, Wyandotte, Mich., since 1948.

Smart, Clifford H., M.S.'39, Wayne Univ.; Supt. of Consol. Sch., Walled Lake, Mich., since 1945.

Smith, Howard, 15226 Nehls Ave., East Detroit, Mich.

Smith, Ira M., LL.B.'09, Ind. Univ.; LL.D.'37, Ashland Col.; Registrar, Univ. of Mich., Ann Arbor, Mich., since 1925.

Smith, Max S., A.B.'31, Univ. of Denver; M.A.'35, Univ. of Mich.; Supt. of Sch., Highland Park, Mich., since 1951.

Smith, Rex Beach, A.B.'38, Western Mich. Col. of Educ., Kalamazoo; M.A.'47, Univ. of Mich.; Supt. of Sch., Holt, Mich., since 1951.

Snow, Fletcher J., Product Mgr., Sch. Div., American Seating Co., Grand Rapids, Mich.

Sodt, Harold F., B.S.'47, Mich. State Normal Col.; Supt., Jefferson Consol. Sch., Monroe, Mich., since 1948.

Spaulding, Bernard L., A.B.'28, Western Mich. Col. of Educ., Kalamazoo; M.A.'45, Univ. of Mich.; Supt., Fairview Sch., Grand Rapids, Mich., since 1941.

Speaker, Gaylord M., B.S.'31, Western Mich. Col. of Educ.; M.A.'41, Univ. of Mich.; Genl. Mgr., Oglesby Equipment Co., Detroit, Mich., since 1951.

Spink, John W., B.S.'31, Western Mich. Col. of Educ., Kalamazoo; M.A.'42, Univ. of Mich.; Supt. of Sch., Bangor, Mich., since 1945.

Spitler, H. Carl, Supt. of Sch., Petoskey, Mich.

Stackhouse, A. J., 2835 Parkwood, Trenton, Mich.

Stark, Harold C., B.S.'19, Mich. State Col.; A.M.'29, Univ. of Mich.; Supt. of Sch., Buchanan, Mich., since 1923.

Stauffer, Clair C., A.B.'36, Cen ral Mich. Col. of Educ.; M.A.'46, Univ. of Mich.; Supt. of Sch., Vestaburg, Mich., since 1928.

Stone, R. O., B.S.'34, Walla Walla Col.; Supt., Cedar Lake Acad., Cedar Lake, Mich., since 1947.

Stork, Elvin J., B.S.'32, Central Mich. Col. of Educ.; Supt., Utley Sch., Flint, Mich., since 1933.

Stout, Grover, A.B. in Ed.'28, Univ. of Mich.; Prin., Russell Sch., Detroit, Mich., since 1932.

Strayer, Floyd J., B.S.'32, Mich. State Normal Col.; A.M.'38, Univ. of Mich.; Supt. of Sch., Blissfield, Mich., since 1945.

Strolle, Roland S., A.B.'33, Northern Mich. Col.; M.A.'41, Univ. of Minn.; Consultant, State Dept. of Pub. Instr., Lansing, Mich.

Surline, Chester, Supt. of Sch., West Branch, Mich., since 1949.

Tableman, Marvin, B.S. in Ed.'40, Temple Univ.; M.A.'47, Univ. of Mich. Address: 1700 W. Rundle St., Lansing, Mich.

Taylor, C. L., A.B.'37, Central Mich. Col. of Educ., Mt. Pleasant; M.A.'48, Mich. State Col.; LL.D.'49, Central Mich. Col. of Educ., Mt. Pleasant; Deputy Supt., State Dept. of Pub. Instr., Lansing, Mich., since 1948.

Taylor, Edwin L., A.B.'27, Mich. State Normal Col.; A.M.'34, Univ. of Mich.; Supt. of Sch., Grandville, Mich., since 1950.

Taylor, William C., Supt. of Sch., Trenton, Mich.

Taylor, William H., B.S.'23, Mich. State Col.; Ed.M.'29, Harvard Univ.; Supt. of Sch., Vicksburg, Mich., since 1947.

Thomas, E. Byron, M.A.'35, Northwestern Univ.; Supt. of Sch., Coldwater, Mich., since 1948.

MICHIGAN

Thomas, John W., B.S.'27, Central Mo. State Tchrs. Col., Warrensburg; M.A.'35, Univ. of Mo.; Supt. of Sch., Wakefield, Mich., since 1938.

Thomas, William J., A.B.'34, Northern Mich. Col. of Educ.; M.A.'40, Univ. of Mich.; Supt. of Sch., Vassar, Mich., since 1951.

Thompson, Max, B.S.'29, Alma Col.; M.A.'41, Wayne Univ.; Supt. of Sch., Van Dyke, Mich., since 1950.

Thurston, Lee M., Ph.D.'35, Univ. of Mich.; State Supt. of Pub. Instr., Lansing, Mich., since 1948.

Torma, Matthew, A.B.'36, Northern Mich. Col. of Educ.; M.A.'49, Univ. of Mich.; Supt. of Twp. Sch., Ironwood, Mich., since 1938.

Totten, W. Fred, A.B.'27, De Pauw Univ.; M.A.'31, Ph.D.'43, Ind. Univ.; Pres., Flint Jr. Col., Flint, Mich., since 1950.

Tower, John O., A.B.'37, Mich. State Col.; Supt. of Sch., Grand Rapids, Mich., since 1951.

Tyndall, Russell F., B.S.'30, Mich. State Col.; M.A.'39, Univ. of Mich.; Supt. of Sch., Pigeon, Mich., since 1951.

Van Aken, Elbert W., A.B.'33, Mich. State Normal Col., Ypsilanti; M.A.'37, Univ. of Mich.; Supt. of Sch., Romeo, Mich., since 1948.

Vander Linden, Clarence, A.B.'35, Hope Col.; M.A.'46, Univ. of Mich.; Supt. of Sch., Leslie, Mich., since 1946.

Vander Ven, James H., M.A.'37, Univ. of Mich.; Supt. of Sch., Mason, Mich., since 1946.

Van Dyke, Elmer, A.B.'38, Hope College; M.A.'47, Univ. of Mich.; Supt. of Sch., Covert, Mich., since 1948.

Van Reyendam, Dirk, Archt., 410 Hammond Bldg., Detroit, Mich., since 1936.

Van Victor, Arthur, D.D.S.'29, Univ. of Mich.; Bd. of Educ., East Detroit, Mich.

Van Volkinburg, R. M., M.A.'41, Univ. of Mich.; Supt. of Pub. Sch., Grand Haven, Mich., since 1952.

Van Zanten, Charles, A.B.'23, Hope Col.; A.M. '28, Univ. of Mich.; Supt. of Sch., Shelby, Mich., since 1947.

Veldhuis, Charles Daniel, M.A.'30, Univ. of Mich.; Supt. of Sch., Hudsonville, Mich., since 1939.

Ver Beek, J. J., A.B.'26, Hope Col.; M.A.'33, Univ. of Mich.; Prof. of Educ., Dir. of Student Teaching, Hope College, Holland, Mich., since 1950.

VerMeulen, James M., A.B.'26, Hope Col.; Vicepres. and Genl. Sales Mgr., American Seating Co., Grand Rapids, Mich., since 1944.

Vescolani, Fred, Supt., Nadeau Twp. Sch., Carney, Mich.

Vredevoe, Lawrence E., A.B.'29, Hope Col.; M.A.'33, Ph.D.'42, Univ. of Mich.; Dir., Bur. of Sch. Services, and Assoc. Prof. of Sec. Educ., Univ. of Mich., Ann Arbor, Mich., since 1948.

Walkotten, George, A.B.'22, Kalamazoo Col.; M.A.'31, Tchrs. Col., Columbia Univ.; Supt. of Sch., Albion, Mich., since 1939.

Walter, Howard C., B.S.'24, Mich. State Col.; M.A.'36, Univ. of Mich.; Supt. of Sch., Hartford, Mich., since 1947.

Walther, Frederick, Bd. of Educ., East Detroit, Mich.

Waugh, L. H., B.A.'25, Western Mich. Col. of Educ., Kalamazoo; M.A.'37, Univ. of Mich.; Supt. of Sch., Saugatuck, Mich., since 1947.

Webb, Morley G., A.B.'40, Alma Col.; M.A.'46, Univ. of Mich.; Supt. of Sch., Edmore, Mich., since 1945.

Webb, Wayne L., B.S.'34, Mich. State Normal Col., Ypsilanti; M.S.'41, Univ. of Mich.; Supt. of Sch., Linden, Mich., since 1948.

Weinlander, M. A., A.B.'17, M.A.'24, Univ. of Mich.; Dist. Supt. of Schs., Wyandotte, Mich., since 1935.

Weller, Helen M., A.B.'36, Western Mich. Col. of Educ., Kalamazoo; M.A.'44, Univ. of Mich.; Supt., 800 Hubbard, N. E., Grand Rapids, Mich., since 1940.

*Wells, John Edward, Tchrs. Cert.'24, Provincial Normal, Regina, Sask.; Life Cert.'28, Northern Mich. Col. of Educ., Marquette; B.S.'32, Manchester Col.; M.A.'43, Univ. of Mich.; Supt. of Sch., Chassell, Mich., since 1951.

Wenrich, Ralph C., B.S.'31, M.S.'34, Pa. State Col.; Prof. of Voc. Educ., Univ. of Mich., Ann Arbor, Mich., since 1950.

Wetherell, Harold O., A.B.'31, Western Mich. Col. of Educ., Kalamazoo; M.A.'41, Univ. of Mich.; Supt. of City Sch., Cheboygan, Mich., since 1948.

White, L. E., B.S.'32, Western Mich Col. of Educ., Kalamazoo, Mich.; M.A.'41, Univ. of Mich.; Supt. of Sch., Boyne City, Mich., since 1945.

White, Thomas W., A.B.'32, Central Mich. Col. of Educ.; Supt. of Sch., Bridgeport, Mich., since 1942.

Whitman, Willard M., A.B.'09, Harvard Univ.; Supt. of Sch., Marquette, Mich., since 1920.

Wilde, Dorr L., A.B.'22, Western Mich. Col. of Educ., Kalamazoo; A.M.'29, Univ. of Mich.; Supt. of Sch., Manistee, Mich., since 1936.

Wilkinson, F. Foster, B.S.'31, Mich. State Normal Col., Ypsilanti; M.A.'41, Wayne Univ.; Supt., Madison Dist. Schs., Royal Oak, Mich., since 1939.

Wilkinson, Varl O., B.S.'39, Western Mich. Col. of Educ., Kalamazoo; M.A.'42, Univ. of Mich.; Supt., Twp. Sch., Portage, Mich., since 1947.

Williams, J. Gordon, A.B.'36, Western Mich. Col. of Educ.; M.A.'51, Mich. State Col.; Supt. of Sch., Yale, Mich., since 1951.

Wilson, Donald F., A.B.'27, Central Mich. Col. of Educ., Mt. Pleasant; A.M.'41, Univ. of Mich.; Supt. of Sch., Carson City, Mich., since 1948.

Wilson, R. H., A.B.'23, Alma Col.; M.A.'30, Univ. of Mich.; LL.D.'51, Alma Col.; Supt. of Sch., Alpena, Mich., since 1936.

Winger, Paul M., A.B.'27, Manchester Col.; A.M.'34, Ind. Univ.; Supt. of Sch., Niles, Mich., since 1951.

Winger, Robert M., A.B.'26, Manchester Col.; M.A.'41, Wayne Univ.; Asst. State Dir. of Vocational Educ., Lansing, Mich., since 1951.

Woodby, Wayne, A.B.'33, Central Mich. Col. of Educ., Mt. Pleasant; A.M.'37, Mich. State Col.; Supt. of Sch., Fennville, Mich., since 1948.

Yates, Gilbert Benton, A.B. in Ed.'34, M.A. in Ed.Adm.'42, Univ. of Mich.; Asst. Supt., Lakeview Consol. Sch. Dist., Battle Creek, Mich., since 1951.

Yokum, Robert W., Archt., Detroit, Mich., since 1949.

Zachrich, Alvin N., B.S.'47, Bowling Green State Univ.; M.A.'51, Mich. State Col.; Supt. of Sch., Potterville, Mich., since 1949.

INSTITUTIONAL MEMBERS

Kellogg Foundation Library, W. K. Kellogg Foundation, Battle Creek, Mich.

Library, Mich. State Normal Col., Ypsilanti, Mich.

Library, Western Mich. Col., Kalamazoo, Mich.

437

MINNESOTA

INDIVIDUAL MEMBERS

Almen, Ansgar L., B.A.'10, Gustavus Adolphus Col.; Supt. of Sch., Balaton, Minn., since 1921, and state senator since 1935.

Amdahl, L. H., B.E.'35, State Tchrs. Col., Winona, Minn.; M.S.'45, Univ. of N. Dak.; Supt. of Sch. Dist. 102, Washington Co., St. Paul Park, Minn., since 1950.

Amidon, Paul S., B.S.'24, M.A.'34, Univ. of Minn.; Educ. Consultant, 603 Foshay Tower, Minneapolis, Minn.

Amland, Harold J., B.A.'25, Luther Col.; M.A.'31, State Univ. of Iowa; Asst. Supt., Personnel-Teaching, St. Paul, Minn., since 1945.

Andersen, Hans E., B.A.'35, Hamline Univ.; M.A.'44, Univ. of Minn.; Supt. of Sch., Pine River, Minn., since 1952.

Anderson, Clifford E., B.A.'29, Gustavus Adolphus Col.; M.A.'40, Univ. of Minn.; Supt. of Sch., Slayton, Minn., since 1947.

Anderson, Edward E., B.A.'42, State Tchrs. Col., Valley City, N. Dak.; M.A.'47, Univ. of Minn.; Supt. of Sch., Evansville, Minn., since 1950.

Anderson, J. E., B.S. in Ed.'11, Univ. of Minn.; Supt. of Sch., Mankato, Minn., since 1931.

Anderson, W. O., B.S.'25, M.A.'38, Univ. of Minn.; Supt. of Independent Sch. Dist. 13, Aurora, Minn., since 1950.

Atwood, Perry M., B.A.'33, M.A.'35, Univ. of Minn.; Supt. of Sch., Staples, Minn., since 1921.

Ause, Harold B., B.A.'34, St. Olaf Col.; Supt. of Sch., Harmony, Minn.

Becker, Vernon W., B.A.'32, Union Col., (Neb.); Ed.M.'52, Colo. State Col. of Educ.; Educ. Secy., Northern Union Conference of Seventh-day Adventists, Minneapolis, Minn., since 1951.

Belsaas, Roy M., B.A.'32, St. Olaf Col.; M.A.'42, Univ. of Minn.; Supt. of Sch., Braham, Minn., since 1949.

Bergee, Arthur P., B.A.'30, Luther Col. (Iowa); LL.B.'36, American Extension Univ.; Supt. of Sch., Hector, Minn., since 1948.

Bettner, Fred, B.A.'39, Minn. State Tchrs. Col., Mankato; M.A.'46, Univ. of Iowa; Supt. of Sch., Lamberton, Minn., since 1949.

Borneman, George H., M.A.'39, Univ. of Minn.; Supt. of Sch., Tracy, Minn., since 1949.

Bossing, Nelson Louis, A.B.'17, LL.D.'48, Kansas Wesleyan Univ.; M.A.'22, Northwestern Univ.; Ph.D.'25, Univ. of Chicago; Prof. of Educ., Col. of Educ., Univ. of Minn., Minneapolis, Minn., since 1948.

Boynton, Willis A., B.S.'48, State Tchrs. Col., Mankato, Minn.; Co. Supt. of Sch., Mankato, Minn.

Bright, Farley D., B.E.'36, State Tchrs. Col., Bemidji, Minn.; M.A.'41, Univ. of Minn.; Supt. of Sch., Crookston, Minn., since 1950.

Brown, David M., B.S.'41, No. Dak. Agr. Col.; M.A.'51, Univ. of Minn.; Supt. of Sch., Hewitt, Minn., since 1948.

Butorac, Milo Matthew, B.S.'31, Creighton Univ.; M.A.'44, Univ. of Minn.; Supt. of Sch., Pierz, Minn., since 1950.

Bye, Morris, B.A.'18, Concordia Col.; M.A.'40, Univ. of Minn.; Supt. of Sch., Anoka-Hennepin Ind. Dist. No. 220, Anoka, Minn., since 1952.

Carlson, Edgar M., B.A.'30, Gustavus Adolphus Col.; B.D.'33, Augustana Theol. Sem.; Ph.D.'44, Univ. of Chicago; Pres., Gustavus Adolphus Col., St. Peter, Minn., since 1944.

Christensen, Bernhard, B.A.'22, Augsburg Col. and Theol. Sem.; Ph.D.'29, Hartford Sem. Foundation; Pres., Augsburg Col. and Theol. Sem., Minneapolis, Minn., since 1938.

Churchill, E. C., B.A.'29, State Col., Superior, Wis.; M.A.'40, Univ. of Minn.; Supt. of Sch., Cloquet, Minn., since 1948.

Clasen, Sherwood W., Prin., Pub. Sch., Freeborn, Minn.

Clauson, Donald L., Supt. of Sch., Farmington, Minn.

Cole, Alfred J., B.A.'20, St. Olaf Col.; M.A.'39, Univ. of N. Dak.; Supt. of Sch., St. James, Minn., since 1946.

Conner, Forrest E., A.B.'23, Univ. of S. Dak.; M.A.'33, Ph.D.'37, State Univ. of Iowa; Supt. of Sch., St. Paul, Minn., since 1949.

*Cook, Walter Wellman, B.A.'23, M.A.'26, Ph.D.'31, State Univ. of Iowa; Dean, Col. of Educ., Univ. of Minn., Minneapolis, Minn., since 1952.

Cooper, Harry P., Asst. Supt. of Sch., in chg. of Sec. Educ., Minneapolis, Minn.

Cordes, Raymond L., B.A.'34, Concordia Col. (Moorhead, Minn.); M.A.'48, Univ. of Minn.; Supt. of Sch., Marietta, Minn., since 1950.

Cory, N. Durward, A.B.'28, Wabash Col.; M.A.'35, Ball State Tchrs. Col., Muncie, Ind.; Supt. of Sch., Rochester, Minn., since 1948.

Crawford, Clarence L., B.A.'25, Cotner Col.; M.A.'28, Univ. of Nebr.; Ph.D.'36, Univ. of Mich.; Pres., State Tchrs. Col., Mankato, Minn., since 1946.

Cross, C. Willard, B.A.'15, Carleton Col.; Diploma '21, Union Theol. Sem.; M.A.'21, Tchrs. Col., Columbia Univ.; Supt. of Sch., Faribault, Minn., since 1935.

Currie, Archie G., B.S.'32, Univ. of N. Dak.; B.Ed.'33, Minn. State Tchrs. Col., Bemidji; Supt. of Sch., Garden City, Minn., since 1948.

Cutright, Prudence, Ph.B.'23, Univ. of Chicago; M.A.'27, Univ. of Minn.; Dept. of Educ., Macalester Col., St. Paul, Minn., since 1950.

Dahl, James Andy, B.Ed.'31, State Tchrs. Col., Moorhead, Minn.; M.A.'33, Colo. State Col. of Educ.; Supt., City Sch., Taylors Falls, Minn., since 1952.

Dahlin, C. H., B.A.'24, Gustavus Adolphus Col.; M.A.'41, Univ. of Minn.; Supt. of Sch., Dawson, Minn., since 1943.

Davidson, W. H., B.A.'32, Dakota Wesleyan Univ.; M.A.'43, Univ. of S. Dak.; Supt. of Sch., Fulda, Minn., since 1946.

Davini, William C., B.A.'36, St. John's Univ.; M.A.'40, Univ. of Minn.; Asst. Supt. of Sch., St. Paul, Minn., since 1945.

Dittes, William H., B.S.'21, Univ. of Minn.; M.A.'27, Columbia Univ.; Supt., Sch. Dist. 47, New York Mills, Minn., since 1949.

Domian, O. E., B.A.'21, Hamline Univ.; M.A.'29, Ph.D.'51, Univ. of Minn.; Dir., Div. of Field Studies, Univ. of Minn., Minneapolis, Minn., since 1951.

Dominick, Leo H., B.A.'20, M.S.'30, Univ. of N. Dak.; Supt. of Sch., International Falls, Minn., since 1949.

Dubke, Herbert P., B.S.'33, Univ. of Minn.; Supt. of Sch., N. Mankato, Minn., since 1929.

Duckstad, Norman B., B.A.'26, Luther Col.; M.A.'41, Univ. of Minn.; Supt. of Sch., Princeton, Minn., since 1949.

Durbahn, Ezra A., B.S.'16, Hamline Univ.; M.A.'22, Columbia Univ.; Supt. of Sch., Worthington, Minn., since 1937.

Eddie, George A., B.S. in Ed.'27, M.S. in Ed.'39, Univ. of N. Dak.; Supt. of Sch., Fairmont, Minn., since 1950.

Een, Andrew R., B.S.'43, Minn. State Tchrs. Col., Mankato; M.A.'51, Univ. of Minn.; Supt. of Sch., Winnebago, Minn., since 1948.

Eikenes, David S., B.A.'26, Concordia Col., Moorhead, Minn.; M.S.'41, Univ. of N. Dak.; Supt. of Sch., Warren, Minn., since 1943.

Eitreim, George W. B., A.B.'32, Augustana Col.; M.A.'40, Univ. of S. Dak.; Supt. of Sch., Sacred Heart, Minn., since 1946.

Eitreim, Harvey G., B.A.'36, Augustana Col., S. Dak.; M.S.'42, S. Dak. State Col.; Supt. of Sch., Luverne, Minn., since 1949.

Elwell, Reid B., B.S.'36, M.A.'51, Univ. of Minn.; Supt. of Sch., Grey Eagle, Minn., since 1950.

Enestvedt, Harold R., B.A.'28, St. Olaf Col.; M.A.'31, Univ. of Minn.; Supt. of Sch., St. Louis Park, Minn., since 1948.

Englund, Walter E., A.B.'11, Gustavus Adolphus Col.; Exec. Secy., Minn. Educ. Assn., St. Paul, Minn., since 1937.

Estenson, Emil, B.A.'11, Luther Col., Decorah, Iowa; M.S.'27, Univ. of N. Dak.; Supt. of Sch., Blooming Prairie, Minn., since 1938.

Fairchild, Charles A., B.E.'33, State Tchrs. Col., Bemidji, Minn.; M.A.'42, State Univ. of Iowa; Supt. of Sch., Glencoe, Minn., since 1942.

Feipel, George, Supt. of Sch., Montgomery, Minn.

Folkerds, Henry J., B.A.'32, Gustavus Adolphus Col.; M.A.'42, Univ. of Minn.; Supt. of Pub. Sch., Cokato, Minn., since 1946.

Formo, Lowell D., B.A.'41, Augsburg Col.; Supt., Consol. Sch., Alden, Minn., since 1950.

Fox, Frank J., B.E.'33, State Tchrs. Col., La Crosse, Wis.; M.A.'41, Univ. of Minn.; Supt. of Sch., Morris, Minn., since 1947.

Frey, L. M., Supt. of Sch., Marshall, Minn., since 1950.

Frisby, H. E., B.S.'34, Univ. of Minn.; Supt. of Sch., Ivanhoe, Minn., since 1936.

Gaffney, Michael R., B.S.'33, M.S.'39, Univ. of Minn.; Supt. of Sch., Graceville, Minn., since 1949.

Gough, Harry Betzer, Ph.B.'14, Hamline Univ.; M.A.'28, Univ. of Minn.; Supt. of Sch., St. Cloud, Minn., since 1930.

Gran, John Michael, B.A.'31, Col. of St. Thomas; M.A.'44, Univ. of Minn.; Prof. of Educ., St. Paul Sem. and the Col. of St. Catherine, St. Paul, Minn., since 1944.

Granskou, Clemens M., A.B.'17, St. Olaf Col.; D.D.'36, Luther Theol. Sem.; Pres., St. Olaf Col., Northfield, Minn., since 1943.

Gray, Reede, B.A.'25, Carleton Col.; M.A.'33, Univ. of Minn.; Supt. of Sch., Redwood Falls, Minn., since 1935.

Gustafson, Leslie J., B.A.'27, B.S.'28, M.A.'38, Univ. of Minn.; Supt. of Sch., Owatonna, Minn., since 1944.

Hafdal, Arthur O., B.E.'35, State Tchrs. Col., Moorhead, Minn.; M.A.'41, Univ. of Minn.; Supt. of Sch., Alexandria, Minn., since 1949.

Halverson, J. John, B.A.'20, St. Olaf Col.; M.A.'31, Univ. of Minn.; Supt. of Sch., Albert Lea, Minn., since 1943.

Halvorson, Gilman R., B.Ed.'31, State Tchrs. Col., St. Cloud, Minn.; M.A.'44, Univ. of Minn.; Supt. of Sch., Chatfield, Minn., since 1950.

Halvorson, K. L., M.A.'42, Univ. of N. Dak.; Supt. of Sch., Sauk Rapids, Minn., since 1943.

Hankerson, Marshall R., B.A.'38, Hamline Univ.; M.A.'46, Univ. of Minn.; Supt. of Sch., Medford, Minn., since 1942.

Hanson, Paul J., B.S.'27, N. Dak. Agrl. Col.; M.S.'41, Univ. of N. Dak.; Supt. of Sch., Little Falls, Minn., since 1946.

Hanson, W. E., A.B.'25, Gustavus Adolphus Col.; Supvr., Sch. Dist. Survey, State Dept. of Educ., St. Paul, Minn., since 1948.

Harbo, Alf. F., Supt. of Sch., Osseo, Minn.

Harbo, L. S., B.A.'18, Augsburg Col.; M.A.'32, Univ. of Minn.; Supt. of Sch., Austin, Minn., since 1949.

Hedegard, E. C., Supt., Consol. Dist. 19, Alberta, Minn.

Hegdal, H. G., B.A.'26, St. Olaf Col.; Supt. of Sch., St. Peter, Minn., since 1947.

Heggerston, A. I., B.A.'21, St. Olaf Col.; M.A.'30, Univ. of Minn.; Dir. of Admin. Research, Pub. Sch., Minneapolis, Minn., since 1936.

Heinemann, F. E., B.A.'16, Carleton Col.; M.A.'38, Univ. of Minn.; State Dept. of Educ., St. Paul, Minn., since 1942.

Herrmann, E. C., M.A.'40, Univ. of Minn.; Supt. of Sch., Lakefield, Minn., since 1949.

Herrmann, John M., B.A.'22, Hamline Univ.; M.A.'39, Univ. of Minn.; Supt. of Sch., New Ulm, Minn., since 1944.

Hill, Dolson W., M.A.'48, Univ. of Minn.; Supt., Tri-Mont Sch., Triumph, Minn., since 1949.

Holst, Alwyn Robert, Ed.D.'47, New York Univ.; Supt. of Sch., Norwood-Young America, Minn.

Hooker, Clifford E., M.A.'32, Univ. of Minn.; Supt. of Sch., Lakeville, Minn., since 1936.

Hughes, J. A., B.S.'19, Carleton Col.; M.A.'40, Univ. of Minn.; Supt. of Sch., Forest Lake, Minn., since 1950.

Hulin, Herman, B.A.'40, State Tchrs. Col., St. Cloud, Minn.; M.A.'43, Univ. of N. Dak.; Supt. of Sch., Long Prairie, Minn., since 1950.

Huselid, Arthur C., B.A.'26, Luther Col.; M.S.'41, Univ. of N. Dak.; Supt. of Sch., Renville, Minn., since 1949.

Ingebrigtson, Carl S., B.A.'29, Concordia Col.; M.A.'40, Univ. of Minn.; Supt. of Sch., Westbrook, Minn., since 1946.

Jacobson, Herman G., B.A.'28, Concordia Col., Minn.; M.A.'39, Univ. of N. Dak.; Supt. of Sch., Ada, Minn., since 1952.

Jedlicka, Alexander I., B.A.'07, M.A.'27, Univ. of Minn.; Supt. of Sch., Proctor, Minn., since 1918.

Jensen, Harvey D., B.A.'29, St. Olaf Col.; M.A.'34, Univ. of Wis.; Supt. of Sch., Winona, Minn., since 1949.

Jenson, Howard A., B.A.'32, Concordia Col., Moorhead, Minn.; M.S. in Ed.'43, Univ. of N. Dak.; Supt. of Sch., Litchfield, Minn., since 1945.

Johnson, Erling O., B.A.'31, Luther Col.; M.A. '38, Univ. of Minn.; Supt. of Sch., Northfield, Minn., since 1945.

Johnson, Grant, B.S.'39, M.A.'45, Univ. of Minn.; Supt. of Sch., Detroit Lakes, Minn., since 1951.

Jorgenson, Harry A., B.A.'27, Concordia Col., Moorhead, Minn.; Supt. of Pub. Sch., Bagley, Minn., since 1945.

Jorstad, L. J., B.A.'12, St. Olaf Col.; Supt. of Sch., Hayfield, Minn., since 1925.

Karow, Donald D., M.A.'42, Univ. of Minn.; Supt. of Sch., Lake City, Minn., since 1939.

Kearney, Nolan Charles, B.A.'24, M.A.'32, Ph.D.'48, Univ. of Minn.; Asst. Supt. of Sch. in charge of Research and Curriculum, St. Paul, Minn., since 1944.

Kelley, R. M., A.B.'24, B.E.'24, Univ. of Colo.; Area Dir. of Sch., Bureau of Indian Affairs, Minneapolis, Minn.

Kershaw, John H., M.A.'51, Univ. of Minn.; Supt. of Sch., Chokio, Minn., since 1950.

Kittleson, Arnold M., B.E.'35, State Tchrs. Col., Moorhead, Minn.; M.A.'45, Univ. of Minn.; Supt. of Sch., Halstad, Minn., since 1945.

Knalson, Edward H., B.A.'42, State Tchrs. Col., Minot, N. Dak.; M.A.'46, Univ. of Minn.; Supt. of Sch., Fertile, Minn., since 1949.

Knutson, S. R., B.A.'24, Luther Col.; M.S.'32, Drake Univ.; Supt. of Sch., Hutchinson, Minn., since 1940.

Kuhlman, Milton H., B.S.'24, S. Dak. State Col.; M.A.'40, Univ. of Minn.; Supt., Edina-Morningside Sch., Minneapolis, Minn., since 1950.

Kunelius, John E., B.S.'41, State Tchrs. Col., Winona, Minn.; Supt. of Sch., Waldorf, Minn., since 1949.

Larson, Allan L., M.A.'47, Univ. of Minn.; Supt. of Sch., Waubun, Minn., since 1949.

Law, Lyle B., M.A.'49, Colo. State Col. of Educ., Greeley; Supt. of Sch., Morgan, Minn., since 1947.

Lee, Edmund C., B.E.'35, Minn. State Tchrs. Col., Moorhead; M.A.'46, Univ. of Minn.; Supt. of Sch., Perham, Minn., since 1952.

Lewis, Arthur J., Jr., B.A.'40, M.A.'47, Univ. of Denver; Asst. Supt. in chg. of Elem. Educ., Minneapolis, Minn., since 1952.

Lewis, Carl Raymond, B.S.'31, N. Dak. Agrl. Col.; M.A.'42, Univ. of S. Dak.; Supt. of Sch., Rushford, Minn., since 1945.

Lindhal, F. A., B.A.'32, Gustavus Adolphus Col.; M.A.'42, Univ. of Minn.; Supt. of Sch., Sleepy Eye, Minn., since 1947.

Lindahl, John O., B.A.'20, Univ. of Minn.; Supt. of Sch., Crosby, Minn., since 1941.

Longstreet, John H., M.S. in Ed.'43, Univ. of N. Dak.; Supt. of Sch., Windom, Minn., since 1948.

McCartney, Ralph L., B.S.'30, M.A.'44, Univ. of Minn.; Supt. of Sch., Olivia, Minn., since 1947.

McPherson, W. B., B.S.'26, Jamestown Col.; M.A.'32, Univ. of Minn.; Supt. of Sch., St. Charles, Minn., since 1948.

Mahler, Herbert Alvin, B.A.'26, Hamline Univ.; M.A.'38, Univ. of Minn.; Supt. of Sch., Waterville, Minn., since 1941.

Malmquist, M. L., B.A.'23, Gustavus Adolphus Col.; Dist. Supt. of Sch., Grand Rapids, Minn., since 1943.

Matheson, Erroll J., B.E.'33, State Tchrs. Col., Moorhead, Minn.; M.E.'41, Univ. of Colo.; Dist. Supt. of Sch., Springfield, Minn., since 1941.

Michie, James K., B.A.'25, Carleton Col.; M.A.'36, Univ. of Minn.; Supt. of Sch., Hibbing, Minn., since 1946.

Mickelson, Irwin T., B.E.'36, State Tchrs. Col., Moorhead, Minn.; M.S. in Ed.'43, Univ. of N. Dak.; Supt. of Sch., Le Sueur, Minn., since 1948.

Moe, George A., B.S.'35, M.A.'39, Univ. of Minn.; Supt., Independent Sch. Dist. 21, Mountain Iron, Minn., since 1948.

Mogck, C. H., B.A.'37, Dakota Wesleyan Univ.; M.A.'44, Univ. of S. Dak.; Supt. of Sch., Benson, Minn., since 1947.

Myron, A. O., M.A.'23, Univ. of S. Dak.; Supt. of City Sch., Jackson, Minn., since 1928.

Neale, Mervin Gordon, B.S.'11, Univ. of Mo.; A.M.'17, Ph.D.'20, Columbia Univ.; Prof., Educ. Admin., Univ. of Minn., Minneapolis, Minn., since 1937.

Nelson, A. L., B.A.'32, Gustavus Adolphus Col.; M.A.'48, Univ. of N. Dak.; Supt. of Sch., Winthrop, Minn., since 1947.

Nelson, Dale G., B.S.'36, State Tchrs. Col., St. Cloud, Minn.; M.A.'49, Univ. of Minn.; Supt. of Sch., Mound, Minn., since 1948.

Nelson, Earle W., B.S.'37, Univ. of Minn.; B.S.'40, Minn. State Tchrs. Col., Winona; M.Ed.'49, Univ. of Colo.; Supt. of Sch., Okabena, Minn., since 1949.

Nelson, Myer, Supt., Independent Sch. Dist. 1, Pillager, Minn., since 1943.

Ness, R. A., B.A.'31, Augsburg Col. and Theol. Sem.; M.A.'44, Univ. of Minn.; Supt. of Sch., Hinckley, Minn., since 1948.

Nigg, William J., B.Ed.'38, State Tchrs. Col., Mankato, Minn.; M.A.'41, Univ. of Minn.; Supt. of Thomson Twp. Sch., Esko, Minn., since 1945.

Nilsen, William O., B.A.'24, St. Olaf Col.; M.A.'35, Univ. of Minn.; Supt. of Sch., Excelsior, Minn., since 1943.

Nordgaard, E. N., B.A.'23, Luther Col.; M.A.'42, Univ. of Minn.; Supt. of Sch., Glenwood, Minn., since 1928.

Noyes, William E., B.A.'11, Macalester Col.; M.A.'31, Univ. of Minn.; Supt., Tower-Soudan Schs., Tower, Minn., since 1922.

Olsen, Oluf T., M.Ed.'52, Univ. of N. Dak.; Supt. of Sch., Climax, Minn., since 1931.

Olson, Hubert G., B.A.'24, Carleton Col.; M.A.'41, Univ. of Minn.; Supt. of Bloomington Consol. Sch., Minneapolis, Minn., since 1943.

Olson, Paul B., Master's '39, Northwestern Univ.; Supt. of Schools, Watertown, Minn., since 1947.

Olson, Richard N., B.A.'27, Concordia Col.; M.S.'42, N. Dak. Agrl. Col.; Supt. of Sch., Arlington, Minn., since 1947.

Ostroot, James, B.A.'28, St. Olaf Col.; M.A.'39, Univ. of Minn.; Supt. of Sch., Granite Falls, Minn., since 1944.

Palmer, Carroll A., B.A.'31, Macalester Col.; M.A.'45, Univ. of Minn.; Supt. of Sch., Kasson, Minn., since 1947.

Pappas, James George, M.S.'48, Univ. of Minn.; Supt. of Sch., Mahnomen, Minn., since 1945.

Patchin, S. A., B.A.'14, M.A.'15, Univ. of Minn.; Dean, Hibbing Jr. Col., Hibbing, Minn., since 1946.

Pederson, A. C., B.A.'04, Luther Col. (Iowa); Supt. of Ada and Lockhart Sch., Ada, Minn., since 1925.

Pederson, C. A., B.A.'09, Luther Col., Decorah, Iowa; Supt. of Sch., Montevideo, Minn., since 1923.

Peters, Diedrich G., M.A.'41, Univ. of Minn.; Supt. of Sch., Minneota, Minn., since 1948.

Poston, Reuben Roger, B.A.'34, St. Olaf Col.; M.A.'46, Tchrs. Col., Columbia Univ.; Ed.D. '52, Univ. of N. Dak.; Supt. of Sch., Marietta, Minn., since 1952.

Purrington, L. C., B.E.'36, Minn. State Tchrs. Col., Mankato; M.A.'51, Univ. of Minn.; Supt. of Sch., Royalton, Minn., since 1950.

Putnam, Rufus A., B.S.'28, Evansville Col.; M.S.'35, Ind. Univ.; Supt. of Sch., Minneapolis, Minn., since 1950.

Rabe, W. C., Supt. of Sch., Madison, Minn.

Reeder, Ralph R., M.A.'40, Univ. of Minn.; Supt. of Sch., New Brighton, Minn., since 1951.

Reinertsen, S. G., B.A.'11, St. Olaf Col.; M.A.'21, Univ. of Colo.; Supt. of Sch., Moorhead, Minn., since 1926.

Reishus, K. P. B., B.A.'09, Luther Col.; M.S.'35, Univ. of N. Dak.; Supt. of Sch., East Grand Forks, Minn., since 1929.

Reishus, Victor L., B.A.'27, St. Olaf Col.; M.A.'39, Univ. of Minn.; Dist. Supt. of Sch., Biwabik, Minn., since 1941.

Richardson, Walter W., M.A.'38, Univ. of Minn.; B.A.'33, Univ. of S. Dak.; Supt. of Sch., North St. Paul, Minn., since 1947.

Rosa, Irvin E., B.A.'24, Carleton Col.; M.A.'31, Univ. of Chicago; Genl. Mgr., Josten Co., Owatonna, Minn., since 1944.

Rubash, Gust J., M.S.'49, Univ. of N. Dak.; Supt. of Sch., Melrose, Minn., since 1949.

Rumpel, Harry E., Ph.B.'23, Ripon Col.; M.A.'47, Univ. of Minn.; Supt. of Richfield Sch., Minneapolis, Minn., since 1944.

Rutherford, J. C., B.E.'37, State Col., Superior, Wis.; Ph.M.'44, Univ. of Wis.; Supt. of Sch., Lake Crystal, Minn.

Salmi, W. W., Co. Supt. of Sch., Duluth, Minn., since 1945.

Salzwedel, J. J., B.A.'26, Carleton Col.; M.A.'40, Univ. of Minn.; Supt. of Sch., Gaylord, Minn., since 1942.

Sandberg, William R., B.S.'40, M.A.'48, Univ. of Minn.; Supt. of Sch., Henning, Minn., since 1952.

Sater, John Albert, B.A.'30, Concordia Col., Moorhead, Minn.; M.Sc.'40, Univ. of N. Dak., Grand Forks; Supt. of Sch., Elbow Lake, Minn., since 1943.

Satterfield, K. C., B.S.'23, Iowa State Col.; M.A.'32, Univ. of Minn.; Supt. of Independent Sch. Dist. 35, Buhl, Minn., since 1949.

Sattgast, Charles R., B.S.'23, Univ. of Ill.; M.A.'26, Stanford Univ.; Ph.D.'39, Columbia Univ.; Pres., State Tchrs. Col., Bemidji, Minn., since 1938.

Schaefer, H. H., M.A.'46, Univ. of Minn.; B.E.'33, State Tchrs. Col., Mankato, Minn.; Supt. of Sch., Stewartville, Minn., since 1949.

Scheie, O. J., B.A.'21, Concordia Col. (Moorhead, Minn.); Supt. of Sch., Raymond, Minn., since 1945.

Schmidt, Edward L., B.S.'26, M.A.'36, Univ. of Minn.; Supt. of City Sch., New Prague, Minn., since 1938.

Schweickhard, Dean M., B.A.'17, Univ. of Wis.; M.A.'27, Univ. of Minn.; Ed.D.'44, Hamline Univ.; State Commr. of Educ., St. Paul, Minn., since 1943.

Scofield, R. J., B.A.'15, M.A.'27, Univ. of Minn.; Dist. Supt. of Sch., Coleraine, Minn., since 1946.

Sholy, George I., B.A.'43, Concordia Col., Moorhead, Minn.; M.A.'48, Univ. of N. Dak.; Supt., Independent Sch. Dist. 3, Hancock, Minn., since 1952.

Siewert, Rudolph W., Co. Supt. of Sch., Chaska, Minn., since 1934.

Simley, Irvin T., A.B.'11, Luther Col.; M.A.'27, Tchrs. Col., Columbia Univ.; Supt. of Sch., South St. Paul, Minn., since 1926.

Skoog, Melville, A.B.'32, Gustavus Adolphus Col.; M.A.'41, Univ. of Mo.; Supt. of Sch., Herman, Minn., since 1949.

Skustad, George A., B.A.'27, St. Olaf Col.; M.A.'34, Univ. of Minn.; Dist. Supt. of Sch., Virginia, Minn., since 1942.

Smith, James W., B.S.'15, Carroll Col.; M.A.'27, Univ. of Chicago; Supt. of Sch., Bemidji, Minn., since 1928.

Snarr, O. W., Ph.D.'41, Univ. of Chicago; Pres., State Tchrs. Col., Moorhead, Minn., since 1941.

Snyder, Jack, B.S.'29, Univ. of Ill.; M.A.'31, Univ. of Minn.; Supt. of Sch., Wayzata, Minn., since 1948.

Solyst, E. W., B.A.'35, St. Olaf Col.; M.A.'50, Univ. of N. Dak.; Supt. of Sch., Kerkhoven, Minn., since 1950.

Steffenson, Paul J., B.A.'31, St. Olaf Col.; M.A.'40, Univ. of Minn.; Supt. of Sch., Park Rapids, Minn., since 1950.

Steffensrud, E. R., M.A.'39, Univ. of Minn.; Supt. of Sch., Chisholm, Minn., since 1948.

Stensvad, Ray M., B.A.'36, St. Olaf Col.; M.A.'39, Univ. of Minn.; Co. Supt. of Sch., Two Harbors, Minn., since 1949.

Stolen, Alvin T., B.A.'18, St. Olaf Col.; M.A.'41, Univ. of Minn.; Supt. of Sch., Duluth, Minn., since 1944.

Stone, George P., M.A.'46, Univ. of Nebr.; Supt., Maplewood Acad., Hutchinson, Minn., since 1948.

Stout, Minard W., B.A.'29, Iowa State Tchrs. Col., Cedar Falls; M.A.'33, Ph.D.'43, Univ. of Iowa; Assoc. Prof. and Prin., Univ. H. S., Univ. of Minn., Minneapolis, Minn., since 1947.

Swenson, Justin W., A.B.'30, Augustana Col.; M.S.'38, Univ. of N. Dak.; Supt. of Sch., Pipestone, Minn., since 1948.

Tanglen, Leverne H., B.A.'25, Macalester, Col.; M.A.'39, Univ. of Minn.; Supt. of Sch., Hopkins, Minn., since 1944.

Temanson, Erland K., B.A.'27, Concordia Col.; Supt. of Sch., Parkers Prairie, Minn., since 1951.

Thompson, Donald W., B.S.'31, Buena Vista Col.; Master's '41, State Univ. of Iowa; Supt. of Sch. Dist. 6, Deer River, Minn.

Townsend, Basil L., B.Ed.'32, Moorhead State Tchrs. Col.; M.A.'38, Univ. of Iowa; Supt. of Hermantown Sch., Duluth, Minn., since 1951.

Tveten, T. D., B.A.'24, Luther Col. (Iowa); M.A.'41, Univ. of Minn.; Supt. of Sch., Kiester, Minn., since 1950.

*Tyler, Tracy F., A.B.'16, Doane Col.; M.A.'23, Univ. of Nebr.; Ph.D.'33, Columbia Univ.; Assoc. Prof. of Educ., Univ. of Minn., since 1939 and Asst. to the Dean of Summer Session, Minneapolis, Minn., since 1949.

Van Putten, Merinus W., B.A.'17, Hope Col.; M.A.'39, Univ. of Minn.; Supt. of Sch., Eveleth, Minn., since 1947.

Vaughan, James P., Ph.B.'07, Univ. of Wis. Address: Chisholm, Minn.

Vejtasa, Stanley A., B.S.'37, N. Dak. Agrl. Col.; M.A.'48, Univ. of Minn.; Supt. of Sch., Floodwood, Minn., since 1952.

Vitalis, Earl L., B.A.'23, Gustavus Adolphus Col.; M.A.'41, Univ. of Minn.; Supt. of Sch., Stillwater, Minn., since 1946.

Webster, Jerome O., B.A.'40, Gustavus Adolphus Col.; M.A.'51, Univ. of Minn.; Supt. of Sch., St. Clair, Minn., since 1951.

Weinberger, Maurice J., B.A.'25, Col. of St. Thomas; M.A.'42, Univ. of Minn.; Supt. of Sch., Nashwauk-Keewatin, Minn., since 1950.

Weir, Harry E., A.B.'33, Hanover Col.; M.S.'48, Univ. of N. Dak.; Supt. of Sch., Kennedy, Minn., since 1948.

Weitgenant, (Mrs.) Virgil E., Co. Supt. of Sch., Worthington, Minn., since 1945.

Wermager, Lawrence Everett, B.A.'33, Concordia Col.; M.A.'44, Univ. of Minn.; Supt., Independent Sch. Dist. 21, Fergus Falls, Minn., since 1949.

Wikre, L. M., B.A.'18, St. Olaf Col.; M.A.'31, Univ. of Minn.; Supt. of Sch., Red Wing, Minn., since 1950.

Williams, Emmet D., B.S.'47, M.A.'49, Univ. of Minn.; Supt. of Roseville Sch., St. Paul, Minn., since 1949.

Wisness, Arthur M., B.A.'14, Luther Col., Decorah, Iowa; M.A.'38, Univ. of Minn.; Supt. of Sch., Willmar, Minn., since 1929.

INSTITUTIONAL MEMBERS

Magney, Tusler & Setter, Architects & Engineers, Minneapolis, Minn.

President, State Tchrs. Col., St. Cloud, Minn.

State Teachers College, Reference Librarian, St. Cloud, Minn.

Winona State Teachers College, Winona, Minn.

MISSISSIPPI

INDIVIDUAL MEMBERS

Akers, B. T., B.A.'35, Millsaps Col.; M.A.'47, Univ. of Miss.; Supt. of Sch., Flora, Miss., since 1949.

Aldridge, Joseph Everett, B.S.'25, Miss. State Col.; M.A.'49, George Peabody Col. for Tchrs.; Prin. of Consol. Sch., Utica, Miss., since 1949.

Allen, W. D., B.A.'26, Miss. Col.; M.A.'41, La. State Univ.; Supt. of Sch., Tupelo, Miss., since 1944.

Anderson, Hal, B.S.'10, Miss. State Col.; Supt. of Sch., Corinth, Miss., since 1930.

Baker, James Bowen, B.A.'35, M.A.'40, Univ. of Miss.; Supt. of Sch., Baldwyn, Miss., since 1942.

Barnard, William Herschel, B.S. in Ed.'23, Univ. of Ala.; A.M.'27, Tchrs. Col., Columbia Univ.; Ed.D.'35, Ind. Univ.; Prof. of Educ., Miss. State Col., State College, Miss., since 1943.

Barnett, Jim C., B.S.'32, Miss. Southern Col.; M.A.'37, Univ. of Mo.; Supt. of Sch., N. Carrollton, Miss., since 1947.

Bidwell, J. R., Sales Mgr., Pathfinder Coach Div., Superior Coach Corp., Kosciusko, Miss.

Bigham, V. L., Jr., B.A.'32, Miss. Col.; M.Ed.'39, Duke Univ.; Supt. of Sch., Forest, Miss., since 1949.

Blair, Stephen Henry, B.S.'23, Miss. State Col.; M.A.'31, George Peabody Col. for Tchrs.; Supt. of Sch., Hattiesburg, Miss., since 1939.

Bond, J. E., Supt. of Sch., Picayune, Miss.

Brandon Clifford N., Sr., B.S. in C.E.'17, Miss. State Col.; M.A. in Sch. Admin.'38, George Peabody Col. for Tchrs.; Supt. of City Sch., Columbus, Miss., since 1929.

Brasfield, Stephen A., M.A.'33, George Peabody Col.; Dir. of Instr., State Dept. of Educ., Jackson, Miss., since 1950.

Bright, Leland W., B.A.'39, Miss. Col.; M.A.'47, Univ. of Miss.; Supt. of Pearl H. S., Jackson, Miss., since 1948.

Brooks, Burrow Penn, B.A.'08, Union Univ.; M.A.'32, George Peabody Col. for Tchrs.; Dean, Sch. of Educ. and Dir., Summer Sch., Miss. State Col., State College, Miss., since 1939.

Brown, B. Frank, B.L. and B.A.'09, Georgetown Col.; Supt. of Sch., Gulfport, Miss., since 1922.

Bufkin, William Ernest, B.A.'20, Millsaps Col.; M.A.'33, Tchrs. Col., Columbia Univ.; Supt. of Sch., Leland, Miss., since 1933.

Carpenter, James Albert, B.A.'32, Miss. Col.; M.A.'34, Univ. of Miss.; Supt. of Sch., Okolona, Miss., since 1948.

Caughman, J. M., M.A.'31, Univ. of Miss.; M.A.'38, George Peabody Col. for Tchrs.; Supt. of Sch., Laurel, Miss., since 1948.

Cook, R. C., Pres., Miss. Southern Col., Hattiesburg, Miss.

Cooper, Homer Vernon, B.S.'20, Miss. State Col.; M.S.'32, Univ. of Va.; Supt. of Sch., Vicksburg, Miss., since 1931.

Coulter, Bayard L., B.S.'11, Univ. of Miss.; LL.B.'14, Millsaps Col.; M.A.'28, George Peabody Col. for Tchrs.; Supt., East Forrest Sch., Petal, Miss., since 1948.

Crain, S. M., B.S.'25, Univ. of Miss.; M.A.'33, M.Ed.'40, George Peabody Col. for Tchrs.; Supt. of Sch., Clinton, Miss., since 1945.

Ditto, George W., B.S.'22, Univ. of Ala.; M.A.'27, Columbia Univ. Address: Biloxi, Miss.

Dribben, William Barnett, B.A.'29, Millsaps Col.; M.A.'38, Duke Univ.; Supt. of Pub. Sch., Greenwood, Miss.

Durrett, T. J., B.S.'30, Miss. Southern Col.; M.A.'48, Univ. of Miss.; Supt. of Sch., Philadelphia, Miss., since 1951.

Elkema, Charles E., A.B.'22, Univ. of Iowa; A.M.'40, Tchrs. Col., Columbia Univ.; Ed.D. '45, New York Univ.; Head, Dept. of Sch. Admin., Miss. Southern Col., Hattiesburg, Miss., since 1947.

Ewing, James Milton, B.S.'22, Miss. State Col.; M.A.'32, Columbia Univ.; Pres., Copiah-Lincoln Jr. Col., Wesson, Miss., since 1932.

Golding, E. B., B.A.'37, Miss. Col.; Supt. of Sch., Benton, Miss., since 1947.

Gooden, James, B.S.'22, Alcorn Col.; M.S. in Ed.'36, Northwestern Univ.; Supvr. of Colored Schs., Jackson, Miss.

Hathorn, J. C., B.S.'21, LL.D.'24, M.A.'38, Univ. of Miss.; Supt. of Sch., Grenada, Miss., since 1946.

Hayman, C. E., M.A.'42, Univ. of Miss.; Supt. of Sch., Sardis, Miss., since 1945.

Heard, Talmage H., Jr., B.A.'36, Delta State Tchrs. Col.; M.A.'49, Univ. of Ala.; Reservation Prin., Philadelphia, Miss., since 1949.

Heidelberg, Harvey Brown, B.A.'03, Millsaps Col.; M.A.'33, Univ. of Mich.; Supt. of Sch., Clarksdale, Miss., since 1905.

Hinze, Robert E., B.A.'28, Miss. Col.; M.A.'47, Univ. of Ala.; Supt. of Sch., Louisville, Miss., since 1947.

Huggins, W. Zack, B.A.'25, Miss. Col.; M.A.'40, Univ. of Ala.; Supt. of Sch., Quitman, Miss., since 1936.

Ivy, Horace M., A.B.'03, A.M.'04, Central Col., Fayette, Mo.; Ph.D.'22, George Peabody Col. for Tchrs.; Supt. of Sch., Meridian, Miss., since 1923.

Jack, William Elkin Shell, B.A.'34, Univ. of Miss.; M.A.'36, La. State Univ.; Supt. of Sch., Arcola, Miss., since 1945.

James, A. W., Supt. of Sch., Drew, Miss.

Johnson, Charles A., Jr., B.S.'32, M.S.'45, Miss. State Col.; Supt. of Sch., Starkville, Miss., since 1951.

Kethley, William Marion, B.A.'14, Miss. Col.; M.A.'25, Tchrs. Col., Columbia Univ.; LL.D.'48, Miss. Col.; Pres., Delta State Tchrs. Col., Cleveland, Miss., since 1926.

Keye, R. E., B.A.E.'38, M.A.'40, Univ. of Miss.; Supt. of Sch. and Dir., Univ. H. S., Oxford, Miss., since 1945.

Kirshman, Harry S., B.S. in Ed.'34, Ark. State Tchrs. Col., Conway; M.A.'38, George Peabody Col. for Tchrs.; Ph.D.'48, Univ. of Nebr.; Asst. Supt. of Sch., Jackson, Miss., since 1949.

Koonce, Riley J., B.S.'20, Miss. Col.; M.A.'26, Ind. Univ.; Supt. of Sch., Greenville, Miss., since 1946.

Leggett, T. E., M.Ed.'51, Univ. of Miss.; Supt. of Sch., Dublin, Miss., since 1940.

Lewis, Charles L., B.A.'35, Miss. Col.; M.A.'40, Duke Univ.; Supt. of City Sch., Amory, Miss., since 1948.

McCallister, B. D., B.Sc.'22, Miss. State Col.; M.B.A.'36, Northwestern Univ.; Supt. of City Sch., West Point, Miss., since 1936.

McKay, M. K., Supt. of Sch., Prentiss, Miss.

McKenzie, Norman B., B.S.'35, Murray State Col.; M.A.'48, George Peabody Col. for Tchrs.; Supt. of Sch., Holly Springs, Miss., since 1948.

May, Albert L., B.S.'23, M.A.'33, George Peabody Col. for Tchrs.; Pres., Perkinston Jr. Col., Perkinston, Miss.

Mayo, Robert M., B.A.'37, Millsaps Col.; M.A.'48, George Peabody Col. for Tchrs.; Co. Supt. of Educ., Jackson, Miss., since 1948.

Meadors, Reed R., B.S.'40, Miss. Southern Col.; M.A.'49, Univ. of Ala.; Supt. of Sch., Magnolia, Miss., since 1951.

Megehee, L. D., M.S.'41, Miss. State Col.; Supt. of Sch., Hazlehurst, Miss., since 1948.

Milling, C. L., B.S.'26, Miss. Southern Col.; M.A.'38, George Peabody Col. for Tchrs.; Supt. of Sch., Ruleville, Miss., since 1938.

Mitchell, Guy Clifford, B.A.'32, M.A.'33, La. State Univ.; Ph.D.'42, Univ. of Mich.; Dir. Div. of Graduate Studies, Prof. of Educ., Dir. of Bureau of Appointments, Miss. Col., Clinton, Miss., since 1947.

Murphy, Forrest W., A.B.'17, Transylvania Col.; M.S.'31, Univ. of Ill.; Ed.D.'45, Tchrs. Col., Columbia Univ.; Dean, Sch. of Educ., Univ. of Miss., University, Miss., since 1946.

Naylor, T. H., B.S., Millsaps Col.; M.A., Univ. of Miss.; Dir., Sch. Bldg. and Transportation, State Dept. of Educ., Jackson, Miss., since 1947.

Otis, Jesse R., B.S.'25, Iowa State Univ.; M.S.'32, Ph.D.'44, Cornell Univ.; Pres., Alcorn Agrl. and Mech. Col., Alcorn, Miss., since 1949.

Owings, Ralph S., A.B.'24, M.A.'35, Wofford Col.; M.A.'40, Ed.D.'49, Tchrs. Col., Columbia Univ.; Prof. of Educ. Admin., Miss. Southern Col., Hattiesburg, Miss., since 1951.

Parks, W. J., B.S.'21, Miss. Col.; M.A.'39, Univ. of Ala.; Supt. of Consol. Schs., Cleveland, Miss., since 1932.

*Phay, John E., Ed.D.'46, Columbia Univ.; M.S. in Ed.'42, Univ. of Pa.; A.B.'34, Maryville Col.; Dir., Bureau of Educ. Research, and Assoc. Prof. of Educ., Sch. of Educ., Univ. of Miss., University, Miss., since 1948.

Roebuck, Arthur Aldridge, B.A.'27, Miss. Col.; M.A.'30, Univ. of Ala.; Supt. of Sch., Aberdeen, Miss., since 1946.

Ross, Cecil L., A.M.'32, Columbia Univ.; Ph.D. '37, New York Univ.; Prof. of Educ., Univ. of Miss., University, Miss., since 1946.

Schultz, John Thomas, B.S.'25, Millsaps Col.; M.A.'39, George Peabody Col. for Tchrs.; Supt., Tunica Co. H. S., Tunica, Miss., since 1945.

Scruggs, Arthur E., B.S.'23, M.A.'33, Univ. of Miss.; Supt. of Sch., Biloxi, Miss., since 1947.

Simpson, Robert S., B.A.'30, Millsaps Col.; M.A.'35, Duke Univ.; Supt. of Sch., McComb, Miss., since 1948.

Smith, S. F., B.S.'25, M.A.'38, Univ. of Miss.; Supt. of City Sch., Columbia, Miss., since 1946.

Tanner, Luther W., A.B.'30, Transylvania Col.; M.A.'43, Univ. of Miss.; Supt. of Sch., Moss Point, Miss., since 1946.

Taylor, Robert H., M.A.'43, Univ. of Miss.; Supt. of City Sch., Winona, Miss., since 1945.

Tubb, Jackson M., B.S.'37, Miss. Southern Col.; M.A.'38, Univ. of Miss.; State Supt. of Pub. Educ., Jackson, Miss., since 1945.

Walker, Kirby P., A.B.'22, Southwestern at Memphis; M.A.'34, Univ. of Chicago; Supt. of Sch., Jackson, Miss., since 1936.

Walker, Nicholas L., B.A.'37, Miss. Col.; M.A.'45, Univ. of Miss.; Supt., Shelby Special Consol. Sch., Shelby, Miss., since 1943.

Wells, Thomas R., B.A.'23, Centre Col.; M.A.'40, Univ. of Ala.; Supt. of Sch., Pascagoula, Miss., since 1937.

Young, Fred W., A.B.'17, Univ. of Miss.; M.A.'32, George Peabody Col. for Tchrs.; Supt. of Sch., Yazoo City, Miss., since 1946.

Young, James B., B.A.'30, Univ. of Miss.; M.A.'36, Columbia Univ.; Pres., Jones Co. Agrl. H. S. and Jr. Col., Ellisville, Miss., since 1940.

MISSOURI

INDIVIDUAL MEMBERS

Acuff, Davis H., B.S. in Ed.'30, Northeast Mo. State Tchrs. Col.; M.A.'36, Univ. of Mo.; Supvr., Sec. Educ., State Dept. of Educ., Kirksville, Mo.

Adams, Arvol A., M.A.'33, Univ. of Mo.; Supt. of Sch., Bethany, Mo., since 1946.

Adams, Edward Randolph, B.S. in Ed.'18, A.M.'24, Univ. of Mo.; Supt. of Maplewood and Richmond Heights Sch., Maplewood, Mo., since 1941.

Adams, Noel T., B.A.'25, State Univ. of Iowa; M.A.'49, Northeast Mo. State Tchrs. Col.; Tchr. of Math., Princeton, Mo., since 1952.

Agee, Marple, B.S. in Ed.'41, Northeast Mo. State Tchrs. Col., Kirksville; M.Ed.'45, Univ. of Mo.; Supt. of Sch., Consol. Dist. 3, Wentzville, Mo., since 1946.

Alexander, Audrey M., B.S. in Ed.'33, Southwest Mo. State Col.; A.M.'39, Ed.D.'50, Univ. of Mo.; Supt. of Sch., Mt. Vernon, Mo., since 1941.

Allison, Eugene F., B.S.'26, Northwest Mo. State Col.; A.M.'32, Univ. of Mo. Address: P. O. Box 166, Chillicothe, Mo.

Anderson, Robert W., B.S.'24, Southwest Mo. State Col.; M.A.'25, George Peabody Col. for Tchrs.; Supt. of Sch., Neosho, Mo., since 1938.

Arnold, Marshall, B.S.'42, A.B.'46, Southeast Mo. State Col.; M.Ed.'50, Univ. of Mo.; Supt. of Sch., Marquand, Mo., since 1950.

Aslin, Neil C., B.S. in Ed.'35, Southeast Mo. State Col.; M.A. in Ed.'39, Univ. of Mo.; Supt. of Sch., Columbia, Mo., since 1947.

Bailey, J. H., M.E.'41, Univ. of Mo.; Supt. of Sch., Aurora, Mo., since 1951.

Baker, Curtis Cedric, B.S.B.A.'47, M.S. in Ed.'51, Univ. of Arkansas; Supt. of Sch., Macks Creek, Mo., since 1951.

Ballou, Richard Boyd, A.B.'31, Amherst Col.; Ed.D.'40, Harvard Univ.; Chmn., Dept. of Educ., Washington Univ., St. Louis, Mo., since 1951.

Barnard, Lloyd, B.S. in Ed.'40, Central Mo. Col.; M.E.'47, Univ. of Mo.; Supt. of Sch., St. Clair, Mo., since 1947.

Barnes, Ward E., B.S.'28, Northwest Mo. State Col.; M.A.'31, Univ. of Mo.; Supt., Normandy Consol. Sch. Dist., St. Louis, Mo., since 1947.

Bartley, Imon, B.S. in Ed.'39, Southwest Mo. State Col.; M.Ed.'44, Univ. of Mo.; Supt. of Sch., Unionville, Mo., since 1945.

Bartow, Gale T., B.S. in Ed.'49, M.A. in Sch. Admin. '52, Northeast Mo. State Tchrs. Col.; Supt. of Sch., Laclede, Mo., since 1952.

Bass, M. Reed, B.S.'24, Colo. State Col. of Agr. and Mech. Arts; Dir., The David Ranken, Jr. Sch. of Mech. Trades, St. Louis, Mo., since 1937.

Beck, Hugo E., A.B.'39, A.M.'44, Univ. of Chicago; Supt., Bayless Sch. Dist., St. Louis, Mo., since 1943.

Bell, C. M., M.E.'39, Univ. of Mo.; Supt. of Sch., Hayti, Mo., since 1944.

Bell, Clifton R., B.S.'34, Southeast Mo. State Col.; M.A.'38, Univ. of Mo.; Supt. of Sch., Farmington, Mo., since 1946.

Bell, Leslie H., B.S. in Ed.'14, A.B.'15, A.M.'31, Univ. of Mo.; Supt. of Sch., Lexington, Mo., since 1919.

Bernard, Emil H. C., B.Pd.'07, Southeast Mo. State Col.; B.Agr.'12, B.S. in Ed.'12, Univ. of Mo.; Supt., Mehlville Sch. Dist., Lemay, St. Louis, Mo., since 1913.

Beumer, Edward H., A.B. and B.S.'14, Univ. of Mo.; A.M.'24, Univ. of Ill.; Asst. Supt. of Instr., St. Louis, Mo., since 1942.

Bierbaum, Milton Wesley, A.B.'28, Central Wesleyan Col.; A.M.'38, Washington Univ.; Supt., West Walnut Manor Schs., St. Louis Co., Mo., since 1934.

Bills, Mark W., B.A.'23, DePauw Univ.; Mus.B. '35, Ph.D.'43, Univ. of Mich.; Supt. of Sch., Kansas City, Mo., since 1952.

Blackhurst, Stephen, M.A.'26, Univ. of Mo.; Supt. of Sch., St. Charles, Mo., since 1926.

Blackwell, George L., A.B.'29, Drury Col.; A.M.'30, Clark Univ.; A.M. in Ed.'46, Univ. of Kansas City; Supt. of Sch., St. Joseph, Mo., since 1943.

Bleckschmidt, H. C., M.A.'34, Washington Univ.; Asst. Supt. of Sch. in chg. of Bus. and Finance, St. Louis Co., Mo., since 1933.

Bohler, Calvin A., A.B.'28, Mission House Col.; B.S. in Ed.'31, Central Mo. Col.; M.Ed.'44, Univ. of Mo.; Supt. of Sch., Union, Mo., 1949-52.

Bolen, Homer E., B.S. in Ed.'42, Northwest Mo. State Col.; M.Ed.'45, Univ. of Mo.; Area Supvr., Mo. State Dept. of Educ., Cameron, Mo., since 1948.

Bonney, Stephen F., Supt. of Sch., Breckenridge, Mo.

Bowman, (Mrs.) Edna Davis, B.S.'34, Cumberland Univ.; M.A.'51, George Peabody Col. for Tchrs.; Supt. of Pub. Sch., Altenburg, Mo., since 1948.

Boyd, Lloyd E., B.S. in Ed.'48, Wash. Univ.; Supt. of Sch., Centerville, Mo., since 1948.

Bracken, John L., A.B.'14, Col. of Emporia; A.M.'22, Univ. of Chicago; LL.D.'49, Col. of Emporia; Pres., American Assn. of Sch. Admin., 1949-50; Supt. of Sch., Clayton, Mo., since 1923.

Bradley, Benn, M.Ed.'47, Univ. of Mo.; B.S.'38, Southwest Mo. State Col.; Supt. of Niargua Sch., Springfield, Mo., since 1950.

Brewer, C. E., B.S. in Ed.'29, Southeast Mo. State Col.; M.A.'34, Univ. of Mo.; Supt. of Sch., Esther, Mo., since 1951.

Brock, Raymond A., A.M.'34, Univ. of Mo.; Supt. of Sch., Liberty, Mo., since 1937.

Brown, Alfred, B.S. in Ed.'40, Central Mo. Col.; M.E.'47, Univ. of Mo.; Supt. of Sch., Stoutland, Mo., since 1952.

Brown, M. Dwight, Partner, Marshall & Brown, Architects and Engineers, 1016 Baltimore Ave., Kansas City 6, Mo.

Bruce, Thor W., A.B.'23, Lawrence Col.; A.M.'31, Ph.D.'35, Univ. of Ill.; Auditor, St. Louis Bd. of Educ., St. Louis, Mo., since 1947.

Bryan, Joseph G., A.B.'21, Central Mo. Col.; A.M.'27, Tchrs. Col., Columbia Univ.; Dir. of Sec. Educ., Pub. Sch., Kansas City, Mo., since 1940.

Bueker, Armin H., B.S.'28, Central Mo. Col.; A.M.'32, Univ. of Mo.; Supt. of Sch., Marshall, Mo., since 1946.

Burger, C. J., B.A.'16, Central Col., Fayette, Mo.; M.A.'29, Univ. of Mo.; Supt. of Sch., Washington, Mo., since 1930.

Burris, Carl, B.S.'21, Central Mo. Col.; A.M.'31, Washington Univ., St. Louis, Mo.; Prin., H. S., Clayton, Mo., since 1924.

Byerly, Carl L., A.B.'28, Manchester Col.; M.A.'36, Ph.D.'46, Univ. of Chicago; Dir. of Special Serv., Pub. Sch., Clayton, Mo., since 1942.

Camp, E. E., A.M.'34, Univ. of Mo.; Supt. of Sch., Monett, Mo., since 1939.

Campbell, Bernard C., B.S. in Ed.'39, Southwest Mo. State Col.; M.Ed.'43, Univ. of Mo.; Ed.D.'52, Tchrs. Col., Columbia Univ.; Supt. of Sch., Lee's Summit, Mo., since 1943.

Campbell, John Lucas, B.S.'15, Southwest Mo. State Col.; A.M.'30, Univ. of Mo.; Supt. of Sch., Carthage, Mo., since 1929.

Capps, A. G., Ph.D.'21, Univ. of Ill.; Prof. of Educ., Univ. of Mo., Columbia, Mo., since 1921.

Carpenter, W. W., Ph.D.'26, Columbia Univ.; Prof. of Educ., Univ. of Mo., Columbia, Mo.

Carter, Guy, B.S. in Ed., Southwest Mo. State Col.; M.Ed.'48, Univ. of Mo.; Supt. of Sch., Mansfield, Mo., since 1948.

Clark, Glynn E., A.B.'34, A.M.'35, Wash. Univ.; Dir. of Guid. Serv., Pub. Sch., St. Louis, Mo., since 1941.

Clarke, L. Katherine, B.A.'31, M.A.'33, State Univ. of Iowa; 254 South Brentwood, Clayton, Mo.

Clements, H. M., A.B.'28, Univ. of Kansas; M.A.'34, Univ. of Mo.; Co. Supt. of Sch., Independence, Mo., since 1940.

Cline, Hershel F., M.A.Ed.'41, Univ. of Wyo.; Supt. of Oak Grove Reorganized Sch. Dist. #6, Oak Grove, Mo., since 1935.

Cobble, Delmar A., M.Ed.'50, Univ. of Mo.; Supt. of Sch., Lutesville, Mo.

Collier, I. J., Bldg. Const. '25, Prairie View A. & M. Col.; Supt., Bldg. and Utilities, Lincoln Univ., Jefferson City, Mo., since 1941.

Cooper, C. E., B.S. in Ed.'23, Central Mo. Col.; M.Ed.'50, Univ. of Mo.; Supt. of Sch., Greenville, Mo., since 1948.

Cooper, J. V., B.S. in Ed.'36, Southeast Mo. State Col.; M.A.'41, Univ. of Wyo.; Supt., Reorganized Sch. Dist. 2, Broseley, Mo.

Coverdell, Mac E., B.S.'38, Northwest Mo. State Col.; M.E.'49, Univ. of Mo.; Supt. of Sch., Bowling Green, Mo., since 1947.

Coy, S. Clay, A.B.'31, Nebr. State Tchrs. Col., Peru; M.A.'39, Univ. of Nebr.; Supt. of Pub. Sch., Mexico, Mo., since 1950.

Crader, E. Earl, M.A.'46, George Peabody Col. for Tchrs.; Supt. of Sch., Diehlstadt, Mo., since 1928.

Crawford, William H., A.B.'31, Ohio Wesleyan Univ.; M.A.'49, Tchrs. Col., Columbia Univ.; Dean, Col. of Mortuary Science, St. Louis, Mo., since 1948.

Crow, A. L., B.S.'30, Northeast Mo. State Tchrs. Col.; M.A.'34, Univ. of Mo.; Supt. of Sch., Jefferson City, Mo. since 1945.

Croy, Wallace, M.A.'28, State Univ. of Iowa; Supt. of Sch., Tarkio, Mo., since 1947.

Cummings, Guy W., A.B.'27, William Jewell Col.; A.M.'39, Univ. of Mo.; Supt. of Sch., Palmyra, Mo., since 1942.

Cunningham, Robert N., A.B.'25, Princeton Univ.; B.A.'28, B.Litt.'29, M.A.'31, Queen's Col., Oxford Univ., England; Headmaster, St. Louis Country Day Sch., St. Louis, Mo., since 1946.

Curtin, James T., Assoc. Supt., Archdiocese of St. Louis, St. Louis, Mo.

Curtright, Willis L., M.Ed.'49, Univ. of Mo.; Supt. of Sch., LaBelle, Mo., since 1951.

Dabney, Richard S., M.A.'46, Columbia Univ.; Dir. of Special Educ., State Dept. of Educ., Jefferson City, Mo., since 1947.

Dale, Tracy E., B.S.'25, Northwest Mo. State Col.; M.A.'30, Univ. of Mo.; Asst. Commr. of Educ., Dept. of Educ., Jefferson City, Mo., since 1947.

Dawson, W. T., B.S.Ed.'49, Northwest Mo. State Col.; M.S.Ed.'51, Univ. of Southern Calif.; Supt. of Sch., Guilford, Mo., since 1951.

DeWitt, Robert Lee, M.Ed.'47, Univ. of Mo.; Supt. of Pub. Sch., Crane, Mo., since 1948.

DeWoody, George M., Eminence, Mo.

Diemer, George W., B.S. in Ed.'16, Central Mo. Col.; A.M.'26, Tchrs. Col., Columbia Univ.; Pres., Central Mo. State Tchrs. Col., Warrensburg, Mo., since 1937.

Dierker, L. J., Diploma '21, Concordia Tchrs. Col., River Forest, Ill.; B.S. in Ed.'41, Washington Univ.; Supt., Lutheran Sch., St. Louis, Mo., since 1946.

Dill, Lloyd L., M.Ed.'48, Univ. of Mo.; Supt. of Sch., Golden City, Mo.

Dille, G. E., B.S.'20, Northeast Mo. State Tchrs. Col.; M.A.'28, Tchrs. Col., Columbia Univ.; Supt. of Sch., Maryland Heights, Mo., since 1947.

Dunn, Joseph G., A.B.'38, Drury Col.; M.Ed.'47, Univ. of Mo.; Supt. of Sch., Norwood, Mo., since 1946.

Ehrhardt, Oscar A., 526 Buder Bldg., St. Louis, Mo.

Elliott, Cecil A., Supt. of Sch. Waynesville, Mo.

Ellis, J. Russell, B.S.'26, Culver-Stockton Col.; M.A.'35, Univ. of Mo.; Supt. of Sch., Canton, Mo., since 1929.

Ellison, Irvin F., B.S. in Ed.'38, Central Mo. Col.; M.A.'49, Univ. of Kansas City; Supt., Harrison Co. Reorganized Sch. Dist. R-4, Gilman, Mo., since 1950.

Englehart, George Dewey, B.S. in Ed.'25, Southeast Mo. State Col.; A.M.'29, Ed.D.'46, Univ. of Mo.; Dir. of Sch. Bldg. Serv., Div. of Pub. Sch., State Dept. of Educ., Jefferson City, Mo., since 1947.

Evans, Walter E., B.S.'30, Northeast Mo. State Tchrs. Col.; M.A.'39, Univ. of Mo.; Supt. of Sch., Fulton, Mo., since 1949.

Evans, Wendell L., A.B.'25, Central Wesleyan; M.A.'34, Univ. of Mo.; Asst. Supt., Ritenour Consol. Sch. Dist., Overland, Mo., since 1949.

Eversull, Frank L., Ph.B.'20, A.M.'27, Univ. of Chicago; Ph.D.'34, Yale Univ.; D.D.'37, Marietta Col.; Lecturer, Washington Univ., St. Louis, Mo., since 1948.

Farnham, C. W., B.S. in Ed.'38, Southwest Mo. State Col.; A.M.'41, Univ. of Mo.; Supt. of Sch., West Plains, Mo., since 1947.

Ferguson, Dee A., A.B.'31, Southwest Mo. State Col.; M.Ed.'41, Univ. of Mo.; Supt. of Sch., Cabool, Mo., since 1948.

*Flood, Thomas H., A.B., B.S.'42, Southwest Mo. State Col.; M.A.'48, Tchrs. Col., Columbia Univ.; Dean, Joplin Jr. Col., Joplin, Mo., since 1949.

Floyd, Cecil, Asst. Supt. of Sch., in chg. of Elem. Educ., Joplin, Mo.

Frasure, Glenwood, M.A.'48, Central Mo. Col.; Supt. of Sch., Buckner, Mo., since 1948.

Freeland, Henry C., B.S.'33, Northeast Mo. State Tchrs. Col.; M.A.'36, George Peabody Col. for Tchrs.; Supt., Linn Co. R-I Pub. Sch., Browning, Mo., since 1947.

Freund, Roy E., M.A.'32, Univ. of Mo.; Supt. of Sch., Warsaw, Mo., since 1945.

Friede, (Mrs.) Irma H., Graduate '08, Harris Tchrs. Col.; Member, Bd. of Educ., 1941–47, and since 1949, and Pres., Mo. Federation of Women's Clubs, St. Louis, Mo.

Garrison, Milton, B.S. in Ed.'29, Northeast Mo. State Tchrs. Col.; M.A.'32, M.Ed.'40, Univ. of Mo.; Supt., Center Pub. Sch., Kansas City, Mo., since 1944.

Ghan, Lawrence J., B.S.'34, Southwest Mo. State Col.; M.A.'41, Univ. of Mo.; Supt. of Sch., Strafford, Mo., since 1938.

Gillman, Lester, B.S.'35, Southwest Mo. State Col.; M.S.'49, Univ. of Ark.; Supt. of Sch., Marshfield, Mo., since 1951.

Glick, Arthur A., B.S. in Ed.'23, Central Mo. Col.; A.M.'37, Univ. of Mo.; Prin., Columbia Sch., St. Louis, Mo., since 1948.

Gold, Gladwyn H., B.S.'40, Southwest Mo. State Col.; M.E.'47, Univ. of Mo.; Supt. of Sch., Liberal, Mo., since 1952.

Gottmann, C. L., B.A.'33, McPherson Col.; M.A.'38, Univ. of Mo.; Supt. of Sch., Monroe City, Mo., since 1944.

Graff, Willard J., B.S.'30, Southwest Mo. State Col.; M.A.'34, Univ. of Mo.; Supt. of Sch., Springfield, Mo., since 1952.

Gray, Earl L., B.S. in Ed.'35, Central Mo. Col.; M.Ed.'38, Univ. of Mo.; Supt. of Sch., Brookfield, Mo., since 1948.

Gray, Noah E., B.S. in Ed.'47, Southeast Mo. State Col.; M.A. in Ed.'51, Wash. Univ.; Acting Supt. of Sch., Sikeston, Mo., since 1952.

Green, Harold E., M.Ed.'47, Univ. of Mo.; Supt. of Sch., New Haven, Mo., 1948-52.

Greene, Paul R., B.S. in Ed.'40, Northeast Mo. State Tchrs. Col.; M.A. in Ed.'47, Washington Univ.; Supt. of Sch., Malta Bend, Mo., since 1949.

Griffith, Madison, A.M.'35, Univ. of Mo.; Viceprin., Central Jr. H. S., Kansas City, Mo., since 1946.

Grubb, Ira E., B.S.'32, Northwest Mo. State Col.; M.A.'42, Univ. of Mo.; Supt. of Sch., Tipton, Mo., since 1942.

Guy, J. Raymond, B.S. in Ed.'31, Central Mo. Col.; M.S. in Ed.'37, Univ. of Wyo.; Supt. of Sch., Sugar Creek, Mo., since 1934.

Haberaecker, H. J., B.A.'35, M.A. in Ed.'41, Univ. of Ill.; Supt. of Sch., Clinton, Mo., since 1952.

Hageman, Tom V., B.S.Ed.'37, Central Mo. Col., Warrensburg; Supt. of Sch., Clearmont, Mo., since 1948.

Hailey, Aaron C., B.S. in Ed.'28, Southwest Mo. State Col.; M.A.'31, Univ. of Mo.; Supt. of Sch., Rolla, Mo., since 1947.

Halter, Millard M., A.B.'21, Central Wesleyan Col.; A.M.'26, Univ. of Mo.; Supt. of Sch., Wellston, St. Louis, Mo., since 1939.

Hamilton, Ralph E., B.S.'35, Southwest Mo. State Col.; Ed.M.'41, Univ. of Mo.; Supt. of Consol. Sch., Cassville, Mo., since 1950.

Hansford, Byron W., M.Ed.'47, Univ. of Mo.; Dist. Supt. of Sch., Higginsville, Mo.

Harlan, Hollis H., M.A.'49, George Peabody Col. for Tchrs.; Supt. of Sch., Canalou, Mo., since 1948.

Harpham, Elmer D., B.S. in Ed.'25, Northeast Mo. State Tchrs. Col.; A.M.'32, Univ. of Mo.; Supt. of Sch., Tuscumbia, Mo., since 1952.

*Hawkins, George L., A.B.'04, B.S.'08, Univ. of Mo. Address: 515 Fairview Ave., Webster Groves, Mo.

Hawkins, R. O., Supt. of Sch., Jackson, Mo.

Hazelbaker, N. D., Supt. of Sch., Mountain Grove, Mo.

445

Hazlett, James A., B.S. in Ed.'37, Kansas City Tchrs. Col.; M.A.'43, Univ. of Kansas City; Dir. of Research, Pub. Sch., Kansas City, Mo., since 1951.

Heagerty, Frank, B.S.'31, Southwest Mo. State Col.; M.E.'37, Ed.D.'50, Univ. of Mo.; Supt. of Sch., Lebanon, Mo., since 1943.

Heltzell, George D., A.B.'30, Drury Col.; M.Ed. '45, Univ. of Mo.; Supt. of Sch., Clinton, Mo.

Helvey, O. J., B.S. in Ed.'48, Central Mo. State Col.; M.S. in Ed.'52, Univ. of Ark.; Supt. of Sch., Pineville, Mo., since 1952.

Henderson, Barbara, B.S.'28, M.A.'29, Tchrs. Col., Columbia Univ.; Dir. of Elem. Educ., Pub. Sch., Kansas City, Mo., since 1929.

Henderson, Carl, B.S. in Ed.'32, Southwest Mo. State Col.; Ed.M.'39, Univ. of Mo.; Supt. of Sch., Moberly, Mo., since 1946.

Henderson, Perry B., B.S. in Ed.'25, Univ. of Mo.; M.A. in Ed.'32, Wash. Univ.; Prin., Glenridge Sch., Clayton, Mo., since 1927.

Hendricks, Floyd W., B.S.'25, Univ. of Ill.; M.A.'31, Univ. of Chicago; Supt. of Sch., Kirkwood, Mo., since 1947.

Hentchel, William W., B.S.'43, M.A.'48, Wash. Univ., St. Louis; Supt. of Sch., Goodman, Mo., since 1952.

Herndon, Joe, Supt. of Sch., Raytown, Mo.

Heuman, Carl C., A.B.'37, Mo. Valley Col.; M.A.'51, Univ. of Mo.; Supt. of Sch., Grain Valley, Mo., since 1948.

Hickey, Margaret, LL.D.'28, Univ. of Kansas City; Dir., Miss Hickey's Sch. for Secretaries, St. Louis, Mo., since 1933.

Hickey, Philip J., B.S.'18, M.S.'20, Univ. of Wis.; Supt. of Instr., St. Louis, Mo., since 1942.

Hill, Robert Russell, B.S. in Ed.'22, Southeast Mo. State Col.; M.A.'26, Tchrs. Col., Columbia Univ.; Ph.D.'34, George Peabody Col. for Tchrs.; Prof. of Educ., Southeast Mo. State Col., Cape Girardeau, Mo., since 1925.

Hill, Thurston S., A.B.'36, Southeast Mo. State Col.; M.Ed.'40, Univ. of Mo.; Supt. of Sch., Dexter, Mo., since 1937.

Hillyard, Robert B., Pres., Hillyard Sales Co., St. Joseph 1, Mo.

Hilpert, A. O., B.S. in Ed., Southeast Mo. State Col.; M.A., Univ. of Mo.; Supt. of Sch., Perryville, Mo., since 1948.

Hitch, A. M., A.B.'97, A.M.'34, Univ. of Mo.; LL.D.'44, Westminster Col.; Pres., Kemper Military Sch., Boonville, Mo., since 1934.

Hoech, Arthur A., B.S.'07, Central Wesleyan Col.; B.S. in Ed.'18, M.A.'31, Univ. of Mo.; Supt., Ritenour Consol. Sch. Dist., Overland, Mo., since 1920.

Hoeffken, Theodore, Ph.D.'37, Univ. of Fribourg, Switzerland; Supt. of Sch., St. Louis Province, Society of Mary, Kirkwood, Mo., since 1949.

Hoeft, Norman R., B.S.'47, M.S.'51, Univ. of Ill.; Admin. Asst., Bd. of Educ., Springfield, Mo., since 1949.

Holland, Clement, B.A.'25, St. Thomas Col.; M.A.'33, Ph.D.'41, Univ. of Minn.; Prof. of Educ., St. Louis Univ., St. Louis, Mo., since 1940.

Holman, Monroe A., M.A.'43, Univ. of Mo.; Supt. of Sch., Pattonville, Mo., since 1927.

Holman, T. L., M.Ed.'39, Univ. of Mo.; Supt. of Sch., Berkeley, Mo., since 1936.

Holstein, J. M., M.Ed.'41, Univ. of Mo.; Supt. of Sch., Stockton, Mo., since 1948.

House, Fred B., B.S. in Ed.'28, Central Mo. Col.; A.M.'34, Univ. of Mo.; Supt. of Sch., Warrensburg, Mo., since 1941.

Howard, Joseph E., B.S.'15, Central Col., Fayette, Mo.; A.M.'28, Univ. of Mo.; Prin., DeMun Sch., Clayton, Mo.

Hoy, L. B., A.M.'29, Univ. of Mo.; Supt. of Sch., Gideon, Mo., since 1916.

Inbody, R. M., B.A.'19, Univ. of Nebr.; M.S. in Ed.'36, Wash. Univ.; Dir. of Sec. Educ., Pub. Sch., St. Louis, Mo., since 1951.

Ingle, Truman L., M.A.'42, Gallaudet Col.; LL.D.'51, Westminster Col. (Mo.); Supt., Mo. Sch. for the Deaf, Fulton, Mo., since 1933.

Isley, Thurston Fayette, A.B.'28, William Jewell Col.; M.Ed.'30, Univ. of Kansas; Prof. of Educ., William Jewell Col., Liberty, Mo., since 1930.

Ittner, William B., Vicepres., William B. Ittner, Inc., St. Louis, Mo., since 1923.

Jackson, Euris J., B.S.Ed.'23, Univ. of Ill.; M.A.'32, Washington Univ.; Asst. Prin., H. S., St. Louis, Mo., since 1947.

Jackson, Marshall, B.S.'40, Southeast Mo. State Col.; M.Ed.'46, Univ. of Mo.; Supt. of Sch., St. Clair, Mo., since 1952.

Johnson, Donald W., B.S.'41, Northwest Mo. State Col.; M.A.'49, Northeast Mo. State Tchrs. Col.; Supt. of Sch., Rockport, Mo., since 1949.

Johnson, Waldo P., Pd.B.'11, Southeast Mo. State Col.; Pres., Webster Pub. Co., St. Louis, Mo., since 1924.

Jones, Barrett Lee, A.B.'17, Drury Col.; A.M.'25, Columbia Univ.; Supt. of Sch., Galena, Mo., since 1949.

Jones, C. H., Jr., A.B.'38, Southwest Mo. State Col.; M.Ed.'41, Univ. of Mo.; Supt. of Sch., Nevada, Mo., since 1947.

Jones, Leonard, B.S. in Ed.'26, Northeast Mo. State Tchrs. Col.; M.A.'29, Univ. of Mo.; Co. Supt. of Sch., St. Joseph, Mo., since 1935.

Keeling, Aubrey W., B.S.'31, Southwest Mo. State Col.; M.A.'41, Univ. of Colo.; Supt. of Sch., Purdy, Mo., since 1931.

Keith, Everett Earnest, B.S. in Ed.'29, Southwest Mo. State Col.; M.A.'32, Univ. of Mo.; Exec. Secy., Mo. State Tchrs. Assn., Columbia, Mo., since 1941.

Keith, Lowell G., B.S.'35, Southwest Mo. State Col.; M.E.'40, Univ. of Mo.; Supt. of Sch., Independence, Mo., since 1947.

Kinder, Leemon Newton, B.S. in Ed.'32, Southeast Mo. State Col., Cape Girardeau; M.A.'41, Univ. of Mo.; Supt. of Sch., Holland, Mo., since 1951.

Klein, Elmer F., B.S. in Ed.'41, Central Mo. Col.; M.Ed.'46, Univ. of Mo.; Supt. of Sch., Maryville, Mo.

Knight, George S., A.B.'31, Central Mo. Col.; Ed.M.'45, St. Louis Univ.; Graduate Sch., Univ. of Mo., Columbia, Mo.

Knight, Riley F., B.S.'27, Southwest Mo. State Col.; M.A.'45, George Peabody Col. for Tchrs.; Supt. of Sch., Steele, Mo., since 1949.

Korte, Tom D., A.B.'34, Central Col.; M.A.'39, Univ. of Mo.; Supt. of Rock Creek Sch. Dist. 36, Independence, Mo., since 1938.

Kraft, Lester M., B.S. in Ed.'49, M.A. in Ed.'50, Kirksville State Tchrs. Col., Mo.; Supt. of Sch., Perry, Mo., since 1952.

Kruse, Samuel Andrew, A.B. and B.S. in Ed.'09, Univ. of Mo.; A.M.'15, Univ. of Wis.; Ph.D.'28, George Peabody Col. for Tchrs.; Head, Dept. of Educ., Southeast Mo. State Col., Cape Girardeau, Mo., since 1915.

Kuehner, J. Ernest, B.S. in Ed.'30, Southeast Mo. State Col.; M.S. in Ed.'41, Colo. State Col., Fort Collins; Dir. of Educ., Admin. Asst. to Supt. of Sch., St. Louis, Mo., since 1948.

Lages, Charles R., B.S.'25, Southeast Mo. State Col.; A.M.'38, Colo. State Col. of Educ.; Supt. of Sch., Bismarck, Mo., since 1950.

Lane, (Mrs.) Helen Schick, B.A.'26, M.A.'28, Ph.D.'30, Ohio State Univ.; Prin., Central Inst. for the Deaf, St. Louis, Mo., since 1941.

Lange, Paul W., Ph.B.'30, M.A.'33, Ph.D.'40, Univ. of Chicago; Prin., Lutheran H. S., St. Louis, Mo., since 1946.

Larson, Richard J., B.S.'29, Univ. of Calif.; M.Ed.'36, Stanford Univ.; Prin., Sunnydale Acad., Centralia, Mo., since 1951.

Lawrence, John T., B.S.'41, Southeast Mo. State Col.; M.Ed.'46, Univ. of Mo.; Supt. of Sch., Bloomfield, Mo., since 1948.

Lee, Charles A., A.M.'32, Univ. of Mo.; D.Ed.'36, Tchrs. Col., Columbia Univ.; Prof. of Educ., Washington Univ., St. Louis, Mo., since 1935.

LeFevre, E. R., A.M.'32, Univ. of Mo.; Supt. of Sch., Paris, Mo., since 1948.

Lemasters, E. M., B.S. in Ed.'25, Northeast Mo. State Tchrs. Col.; A.M.'29, Univ. of Mo.; Supt. of Riverview Gardens Schs., St. Louis, Mo., since 1935.

Lemen, Robert F., A.B.'32, M.A.'33, Wash. Univ.; Prin., Wydown Sch., Clayton, Mo., since 1948.

Lewallen, Fred, Supt. of Sch., Chaffee, Mo.

Lindhurst, James, A.B.'29, M.A.'39, Ed.D.'49, Washington Univ.; Supt., Hancock Place Sch., St. Louis Co., Mo., since 1947.

Lott, E. B., B.S. in Ed.'30, Central Mo. Col.; M.Ed.'49, Univ. of Colo.; Supt., Faucett Consol. Sch., Buchanan Co., Mo. since 1952.

Loughead, George R., B.S. in Ed.'20, Northeast Mo. State Tchrs. Col.; M.A.'34, Univ. of Mo.; Supt. of Sch., Popular Bluff, Mo., since 1928.

Luse, Carl, M.A.'51, Northeast Mo. State Tchrs. Col.; Supt. of Sch., Cairo, Mo., since 1951.

McCluer, Franc Lewis, A.B.'16, M.A.'20, Westminster Col.; Ph.D.'28, Univ. of Chicago; Pres., Lindenwood Col., St. Charles, Mo., since 1947.

McCluer, V. C., A.B.'18, Westminster Col.; A.M.'29, Washington Univ.; Supt. of Sch., Ferguson, Mo., since 1930.

McConnell, Clyde W., M.A.'40, Columbia Univ.; Supt. of Sch., Ozark, Mo., since 1930.

McCullough, D. Ralph, B.S. in Ed.'28, Southeast Mo. State Col.; A.M.'31, Ed.D.'48, Univ. of Mo.; Supt. of Sch., Flat River, Mo., since 1952.

McDaniel, Leslie L., Supt. of Sch., Rogersville, Mo., since 1951.

McDonald, Moss, M.A.'35, Univ. of Mo.; Co. Supt. of Sch., Versailles, Mo., since 1946.

McDonald, Paul, B.S.'49, Ed.M.'51, St. Louis Univ.; Registrar, St. Louis Univ., St. Louis, Mo., since 1951.

McEachen, Howard D., A.B.'25, State Tchrs. Col., Wayne, Nebr.; A.M.'35, Univ. of Nebr.; Supt. of Instr., Shawnee-Mission H. S., Merriam, Kansas, 1944-52. Address: 4107 West 69th St., Kansas City, Mo.

McEowen, D. W., B.S. in Ed.'27, Central Mo. Col.; M.A.'36, Univ. of Mo.; Supt. of Pub. Sch., Harrisonville, Mo., since 1938.

McKee, Ernest M., B.S.'29, Northwest Mo. State Col.; M.A.'37, Univ. of Mo.; Supt. of Sch., Potosi, Mo., since 1950.

McKinley, N. F., B.S. in Ed.'24, Southwest Mo. State Col.; Supt. of Consol. Sch., Seymour, Mo., since 1931.

MacNeven, Robert W., B.S.E.'39, Tchrs. Col. of Kansas City; M.A.'46, Columbia Univ.; Dir., Pupil Services, Pub. Sch., Kansas City, Mo., since 1951.

Mallory, Dillard A., M.Ed.'46, Univ. of Mo.; Supt. of Sch., Buffalo, Mo., since 1944.

Marcellus, Ralph, B.S. in Ed.'30, Univ. of Mo.; Co. Supt. of Sch., Rollo, Mo., since 1930.

Masterson, H. Byron, B.S. in Ed.'27, Southeast Mo. State Col.; M.A.'37, State Univ. of Iowa; Supt. of Sch., Kennett, Mo., since 1945.

*Matthews, D. Boulder, B.S.'46, M.Ed.'47, Univ. of Mo.; Ed.D.'50, Tchrs. Col., Columbia Univ.; Supt. of Sch., Troy, Mo., since 1950.

Matthews, Don E., B.S.'24, Southwest Mo. State Col.; M.A.'32, Univ. of Mo.; Supt. of Consol. Sch., Linn, Mo., since 1950.

Max, David P., A.B.'26, B.S. in Ed.'26, Northwest Mo. State Col.; M.A.'30, Univ. of Mo.; Supt. of Sch., Crystal City, Mo.

Melcher, George, A.B.'98, Drury Col.; A.M.'19, Tchrs. Col., Columbia Univ.; Supt. of Sch., Kansas City, Mo., 1928-40; Supt. Emeritus, since 1940. Address: 3331 Campbell St., Kansas City, Mo.

Merick, W. A., B.S. in Ed.'35, Southeast Mo. State Col.; A.M.'45, Univ. of Mo.; Supt. of Sch., Parma, Mo., since 1939.

Mesnier, Charles J., A.B.'26, M.A.'51, Washington Univ.; Dist. Supt. of Sch., Affton, Mo., since 1933.

Miller, Albert Austin, B.S. in Ed.'41, Northeast Mo. State Tchrs. Col.; M.Ed.'49, Univ. of Mo.; Supt. of Sch., Hamilton, Mo., since 1951.

Miller, Emmett T., A.B.'15, B.S.'16, A.M.'25, Univ. of Mo.; Supt. of Sch., Hannibal, Mo., since 1931.

Mills, Leland O., B.S.'26, Southwest Mo. State Col.; M.A.'31, Univ. of Mo.; Supt., Sch. of the Osage, Lake Ozark, Mo., since 1935.

Moore, Clyde T., A.B.'28, Central Wesleyan Col.; A.M.'33, Univ. of Mo.; Supt. of Community Unit Sch. R-VI, Laddonia, Mo., since 1936.

Morgan, Frederic Evan, A.B.'19, Washington Univ.; Ed.M.'33, Harvard Univ.; LL.D.'46, Lincoln Memorial Univ.; Pres., The Principia Col., St. Louis, Mo., since 1938.

Morgan, William E., B.A.'27, M.A.'41, Washington Univ.; Vicepres. The Principia Schs. and Col., and Headmaster, Upper Sch., The Principia, St. Louis, Mo.

Morrissy, Jas. F., M.A.'34, Univ. of Mo.; Supt. of Sch., Green City, Mo., since 1940.

Nagel, Frank P., Diploma '37, Natl. Col. of Educ.; Bd. of Educ., St. Louis, Mo., since 1945.

Newton, Carl H., M.E.'51, Univ. of Miss.; Supt. of Sch., Bell City, Mo., since 1951.

Nicholas, Ivan C., B.S.'29, Northern Ill. State Tchrs. Col.; M.S.'34, Ph.D.'41, Northwestern Univ.; Supt., Sch. Dist., City of Ladue, St. Louis Co., Mo., since 1942.

Nicoletti, Pete, B.S. in Ed.'37, Southwest Mo. State Col.; M.A.'42, Univ. of Mo.; Supt. of Sch., Milan, Mo., since 1947.

Nushan, A. K., 3431 School St., St. Louis, Mo.

Oliver, Stanley C., B.S.'19, M.S.'26, Pa. State Col.; Ph.D.'33, Columbia Univ.; Prof. of Educ., Southwest Mo. State Col., Springfield, Mo., since 1929.

Parker, C. W., M.A.'37, Univ. of Mo.; Supt. of Sch., Ava, Mo., since 1938.

Parker, Carl L., B.S. in Ed.'23, Southeast Mo. State Col.; A.M.'32, Ph.D.'36, Univ. of Mo.; Supt. of Sch., Maplewood-Richmond Heights Dist., Maplewood, Mo., since 1952.

Parker, Walter W., A.B.'12, Hendrix Col.; A.M.'15, Columbia Univ.; LL.D.'29, Hendrix Col.; LL.D.'47, Central Col.; Pres., Southeast Mo. State Col., Cape Girardeau, Mo., since 1933.

Pegler, Morris L., B.S. in Ed.'48, Northeast Mo. State Tchrs. Col.; M.A.'49, Tchrs. Col., Columbia Univ.; Supt. of Sch., Augusta, Mo., since 1950.

Pepmiller, Carl Emmert, B.S. in Ed.'27, Southeast Mo. State Col.; M.A. in Ed.'34, Univ. of Mo.; Supt. of Sch., Thayer, Mo., since 1939.

Pettigrew, Maynard M., M.A.'36, Univ. of Mo.; Supt. of Sch., Boonville, Mo., since 1948.

Phelps, Lawrence E., B.S. in Ed.'35, Northwest Mo. State Col.; M.E. in Sec. Ed.'41, Univ. of Mo.; Supt. of Sch., Macon, Mo., since 1948.

Phillips, Claude Anderson, B.S.'92, Odessa Col.; A.M.'10, Univ. of Chicago; Ph.D.'20, George Peabody Col. for Tchrs.; Prof. of Educ., Univ. of Mo., Columbia, Mo., since 1924.

Philpott, Charles H., A.B.'15, A.M.'16, Ph.D.'27, Univ. of Mo.; Dir. of Educ. Curriculum Research and Development, Bd. of Educ., St. Louis, Mo., since 1947.

Plucker, Orvin L., B.A.'43, Augustana Col.; M.Ed.'48, Univ. of S. Dak.; Ed.D.'51, Univ. of Colo.; Dir., Elem. Educ., Independence, Mo., since 1951.

Pope, Dennis H., B.S. in Ed.'48, M.Ed.'48, Univ. of Mo.; Supt. of Sch., Renick, Mo., since 1948.

Potter, Charles Edward, B.S.Ed.'36, Southwest Mo. State Col.; M.S.Ed.'42, Univ. of Mo.; Admin. Asst. to Supt. of Sch., St. Louis, Mo., since 1951.

Powell, Marvin S., B.S. in Ed.'47, M.A.'52, Northeast Mo. State Col.; Supt. of Sch., Novinger, Mo., since 1951.

Prock, Samuel E., A.B.'32, Berea Col.; A.M.'40, Univ. of Mo. Address: Iberia, Mo.

Puckett, Harold G., B.S. in Ed.'26, Central Mo. Col.; M.A.'34, Univ. of Mo.; Supt. of Sch., Savannah, Mo., since 1940.

Punch, David Allen, B.S. in Ed.'46, Southeast Mo. State Col.; M.A.'50, Wash. Univ.; Supt. of Sch. Dist. R-8, St. Louis, Mo., since 1950.

Ragland, John W., M.A.'35, Univ. of Mo.; Supt. of Sch., Cole Camp, Mo., since 1932.

Rainey, Homer P., A.B.'19, Austin Col.; M.A.'23, Ph.D.'24, Univ. of Chicago; Pres., Stephens Col., Columbia, Mo., since 1947.

Reals, Willis H., A.B.'16, M.A.'21, Syracuse Univ.; Ph.D.'28, Columbia Univ.; Dean, Univ. Col., Washington Univ., St. Louis, Mo., since 1943.

Reason, Arthur W., Prin., Pub. Sch., St. Louis, Mo.

Rein, Fred H., Gen. Mgr., St. Louis Convention and Publicity Bureau, St. Louis, Mo.

Rhodes, V. Harry, LL.B.'16, Washington Univ.; Commr. of Sch. Bldgs., St. Louis, Mo., since 1948.

Riefling, B. Jeannette, B.S.'11, A.B.'13, Univ. of Mo.; A.M.'20, Columbia Univ. Address: 3907 Connecticut St., St. Louis 16, Mo.

Riley, George Arthur, A.B.'27, Southwest Mo. State Col.; M.A.'31, D.Ed.'45, Univ. of Mo.; Supt. of Sch., California, Mo., since 1945.

Rissler, S. M., A.B.'21, Central Col., Fayette, Mo.; A.M.'31, Univ. of Mo.; Supt. of Sch., Trenton, Mo., since 1937.

Rogers, B. A., B.S.'42, Southwest Mo. State Col.; M.Ed.'48, Univ. of Mo.; Supt. of Sch., Eugene, Mo., since 1946.

Rucker, D. C., D.Ed.'41, Univ. of Mo.; Dir. of Curriculum and Personnel, Bd. of Educ., Springfield, Mo., since 1935.

Rufi, John, B.S.'18, Kansas State Tchrs. Col., Emporia; M.A.'19, Ph.D.'27, Tchrs. Col., Columbia Univ.; Prof. of Educ., Univ. of Mo., Columbia, Mo., since 1928.

Ryle, Walter Harrington, B.S. in Ed.'19, Northeast Mo., State Tchrs. Col.; A.M.'27, Ph.D.'30, George Peabody Col. for Tchrs.; Pres., Northeast Mo. State Tchrs. Col., Kirksville, Mo., since 1937.

Saltzman, B. George, LL.B.'27, M.A.'40, Univ. of Colo.; Supt. of Sch., Brentwood, Mo., since 1946.

Schaefer, Norval P., B.S.'33, Southwest Mo. State Col.; M.A.'38, Univ. of Mo.; Supt. of Sch., Fredericktown, Mo., since 1944.

Schooling, H. W., B.S. in Ed.'36, Southwest Mo. State Col.; M.A. in Ed.'40, Univ. of Mo.; Supt., Sch. Dist. 74, North Kansas City, Mo., since 1949.

Schuessler, H. R., Bus. Mgr., Westminster Col., Fulton, Mo.

Schultz, Louis J., M.A.'31, State Univ. of Iowa; Supt. of Sch., Central H. S., Cape Girardeau, Mo., since 1935.

Scott, Charles, B.Pd.'15, B.S. in Ed.'25, Southeast Mo. State Col.; LL.B.'17, City Col. of Law, St. Louis, Mo.; A.M.'29, Univ. of Mo.; Supt. of Sch., Anniston, Mo., since 1945.

Scott, James Armstrong, A.B.'19, Univ. of Kansas; M.A.'20, Harvard Univ.; Dir. of Educ., Pub. Sch., St. Louis, Mo., since 1942.

Scotten, C. F., B.S. and B.S. in Ed.'24, Central Mo. Col.; M.A.'30, Ed.D.'42, Univ. of Mo.; Co. Supt. of Sch., Sedalia, Mo., since 1951.

Scruggs, Sherman D., A.B.'20, Washburn Col.; A.M.'25, Ph.D.'35, Univ. of Kansas; Pres., Lincoln Univ., Jefferson City, Mo., since 1938.

See, Otis A., M.A.'22, Tchrs. Col., Columbia Univ.; Supt. of Sch., Jennings, Mo., since 1925.

Selvidge, Morgan, M.S. in Ed.'37, Univ. of Colo.; Supt. of Sch., Eureka, Mo., since 1948.

Shaffner, Charles H., A.B.'25, Mo. Wesleyan Col.; M.A.'31, Univ. of Mo.; Supt. of Sch., Princeton, Mo., since 1928.

Sheperd, B. W., B.S. in Ed.'27, Central Mo. Col., Warrensburg; M.A.'34, Univ. of Mo.; Supt. of Sch., Maysville, Mo., since 1941.

Shores, Roscoe V., A.B.'10, Central Col.; A.M.'25, Univ. of Wis.; Deputy Supt. of Sch., Kansas City, Mo., since 1945.

Short, Claude R., M.A.'39, Univ. of Mo.; Supt. of Sch., Willard, Mo., since 1950.

Shultz, Lewis W., B.S.'29, Baker Univ.; M.A.'41, Univ. of Mo.; Supt. of Sch., Hickman Mills, Mo.

Simpson, Elvis E., M.Ed.'40, Univ. of Mo.; B.S. in Ed.'31, Southwest Mo. State Col.; Supt. of Sch., Belton, Mo., since 1947.

Sloat, Mayme Louise, Diploma, Harris Tchrs. Col.; B.S.'28, Col. Univ.; M.A.'40, Univ. Southern Calif.; Act. Asst. Prin., Southwest H. S., St. Louis, Mo., since 1952.

Smart, John R., Jr., A.B.'40, Central Col. (Fayette, Mo.); M.Ed.'45, Univ. of Mo.; Supt. of Sch., Glasgow, Mo., since 1941.

Snarr, (Mrs.) Ruth G., B.S.'43, Northeast Mo. State Tchrs. Col.; Co. Supt. of Sch., Montgomery City, Mo., since 1947.

Snell, Lois L., A.B.'31, Univ. of Ala.; M.A.'46, Tchrs. Col., Columbia Univ.; Educ. Consultant, Webster Pub. Co., St. Louis, Mo.

Snyder, Robert D., A.B.'43, Harris Tchrs. Col., St. Louis, Mo.; M.A.'46, Wash. Univ.; Supt. of Consol. Sch. Dist. 2, Clayton, Mo., since 1950.

Spratt, Elliott Cowgill, Secy., Hillyard Chemical Co., and Vicepres., Hillyard Sales Co., Eastern Div., St. Joseph, Mo., since 1925.

Spurgeon, Leslie E., B.S.'33, M.A.'37, Univ. of Mo.; Supt. of Sch., Owensville, Mo., since 1943.

Steger, Leonard Andrew, A.B.'27, Iowa State Tchrs. Col., Cedar Falls; A.M.'32, State Univ. of Iowa; Supt. of Sch., Webster Groves, Mo., since 1944.

Stephens, Claude E., M.A. in Ed.'27, Univ. of Mo., Acting Dir. of Educ., Pub. Sch., St. Louis, Mo., since 1951.

Stephens, Paul W., B.S. in Ed.'38, Mo. Valley Col.; M.E.'46, Univ. of Mo.; Supt. of Sch., Risco, Mo., since 1948.

Stinson, Jesse H., B.S. in Ed.'38, Northeast Mo. State Tchrs. Col.; M.A. in Sch. Adm.'44, Univ. of Mo.; Supt. of Sch., Butler, Mo., since 1952.

Strachan, Lexie, B.S.'20, Univ. of Oregon; A.M.'21, Stanford Univ.; Psychologist, Pub. Sch., Kansas City, Mo., since 1921.

Street, Ed, Supt. of Sch., Versailles, Mo.

Strickler, Robert E., A.B.'20, Ind. State Tchrs. Col.; M.A.'23, Univ. of Chicago; Prin., Elem. Sch., St. Louis, Mo., since 1929.

Study, Harry P., A.B.'03, Baker Univ.; A.M.'11, Boston Univ.; Supt. of Sch., Springfield, Mo., 1924-52 (retired).

Suddath, William N., M.Ed.'37, Univ. of Mo.; Supt. of Sch., Desloge, Mo., since 1939.

Sullivan, Ralph E., M.Ed.'49, Univ. of Mo.; Supt., Sch. Dist. R-2, Brunswick, Mo., since 1952.

Summitt, James Euel, A.B.'26, Union Univ.; M.A.'35, George Peabody Col. for Tchrs.; Supt. of Sch., Cardwell, Mo., since 1930.

Tallent, Ora T., B.S.'42, Southeast Mo. State Col.; M.Ed.'50, Univ. of Mo.; Supt. of Sch., Steelville, Mo., since 1950.

Taylor, Jess L., B.S.'32, Kansas State Tchrs. Pittsburg; M.A.'41, Univ. of Mo.; Supt. of Sch., Grandview, Mo., since 1948.

Taylor, Roy E., B.S.'23, State Tchrs. Col., Pittsburg, Kansas; M.S.'27, Univ. of Kansas; Supt. of Sch., Herculaneum, Mo., since 1947.

Tedlock, Randall Welden, B.S.'40, Northwest Mo. State Col.; M.A.'49, Northeast Mo. State Tchrs. Col.; Supt. of Sch., Martinsville, Mo., since 1951.

Terry, Howard M., A.B.'30, Drury Col.; A.M.'38, Ed.D.'50, Univ. of Mo.; Supt. of Sch., Bonne Terre, Mo., since 1947.

Terry, Roscoe Linn, A.B.'28, Mo. Wesleyan Col.; M.Ed.'41, Univ. of Mo.; Supt. of Sch., Memphis, Mo., since 1947.

Tetrick, James W., Master's '26, Columbia Univ.; Representative, Ginn and Co., Springfield, Mo., since 1925.

Thomas, Earl D., Ph.B.'29, M.A.'30, Univ. of Chicago; Prin., Lincoln H. S., and Dean, Lincoln Jr. Col., Kansas City, Mo.

Thomas, Raymond W., A.B. in Ed.'39, St. Louis Univ.; M.S. in Ed.'47, Univ. of Southern Calif.; Supt. of Sch., Ste. Genevieve, Mo., since 1951.

Thompson, Robert H., B.A.'31, Pd.D.'51, Mo. Valley Col.; M.A.'37, Univ. of Mo.; Supt., Mo. Sch. for the Blind, St. Louis, Mo., since 1942.

Thurman, Ewell S., B.S. in Ed.'38, Northwest Mo. State Col.; A.M. in Ed.'41, Univ. of Mo.; Prin., Bellevue Elem. Sch., Richmond Heights, Mo., since 1948.

Thurman, R. S., B.S. and M.A.'49, Univ. of Kansas City; Supt. of Sch., Hollister, Mo., since 1944.

Thurston, A. R., B.S. in Ed.'29, Central Mo. State Col.; M.A. in Sch. Admin.'39, Univ. of Mo.; Supt. of Sch., Elvins, Mo., since 1951.

Townsend, Loran George, B.S. in Ed.'25, Southwest Mo. State Col.; A.M.'31, Ph.D.'32, Univ. of Mo.; Prof. of Educ., Dir. of Summer Session, and Dean of the Faculty, Col. of Educ., Univ. of Mo., Columbia, Mo., since 1945.

Twitty, Lynn M., B.S.'34, Southeast Mo. State Col.; M.A.'42, Univ. of Mo.; Supt. of Sch., Sikeston, Mo.

Unruh, Adolph, Ph.D.'48, Univ. of Colo.; Assoc. Prof. of Educ., Washington Univ., St. Louis, Mo., since 1948.

Upchurch, Edwin R., B.S. in Ed.'47, Southeast Mo. State Col.; M.E.'50, Univ. of Mo.; Supt., Delta Consol. Sch., Delta, Mo., since 1950.

Van Sickel, J. G., A.M.'31, Univ. of Mo.; Supt. of Sch., Kirksville, Mo., since 1947.

Vogelgesang, N. D., B.S. in Ed.'25, Northeast Mo. State Tchrs. Col.; A.B.'26, Northwest Mo. State Col.; A.M.'32, Univ. of Mo.; Supt. of Sch., Fairfax, Mo., since 1951.

Vossbrink, George W., B.S. in Ed.'25, Central Mo. Col.; M.A. in Ed. and Pol. Sci.'42, Washington Univ.; Co. Supt. of Sch., Clayton, Mo., since 1951.

Walker, N. Earl, B.S.'39, Southwest Mo. State Col.; M.Ed.'49, Univ. of Mo.; Supt. of Sch., El Dorado Springs, Mo., since 1950.

Ward, Robert J., B.S. in Ed.'36, Kansas City Tchrs. Col.; M.E.'43, Univ. of Mo.; Dir., Employee Personnel, Kansas City, Mo., since 1951.

Wardlaw, H. Pat, B.S. in Ed.'38, Univ. of Ark.; M.Ed.'42, D.Ed.'48, Univ. of Mo.; Asst. Commr. of Educ., State Dept. of Educ., Jefferson City, Mo., since 1947.

Warren, Julius E., A.B.'10, Dartmouth Col.; M.A.'22, Tchrs. Col., Columbia Univ.; D.Sc. in Ed.'44, Boston Univ.; LL.D.'44, Northeastern Univ.; Supt. of Sch., University City, Mo., since 1946.

Webb, Frank J., B.S. in Ed.'29, B.S.'29, Central Mo. Col.; M.A.'38, Univ. of Mo.; Supt. of Sch., Windsor, Mo., since 1948.

Weir, Thomas A., B.S.'39, M.A.'40, Univ. of Ill.; Ph.D.'51, Ohio State Univ. Address: 4729 Oakridge Blvd., St. Louis 20, Mo.

Welch, Vernon W., B.S. in Ed.'29, Central State Col., Edmond, Okla.; M.Ed.'40, Univ. of Mo.; Supt. of Sch., Adrian, Mo., since 1944.

Whaley, Charles A., B.A.'32, William Jewell Col.; B.D.'34, Central Baptist Theol. Sem.; Ed.M. '44, Univ. of Mo.; Supt. of Sch., Wellsville, Mo.

Wheeler, Hubert, B.S. in Ed.'32, Southwest Mo. State Col.; M.A.'39, Univ. of Mo.; State Commr. of Educ., Jefferson City, Mo., since 1947.

Whitehead, Copeland, B.S. in Ed.'49, Missouri Valley Col.; M.Ed.'51, Univ. of Mo.; Supt. of Sch., Chamois, Mo., since 1951.

Whitener, Joy E., B.S. in Ed.'42, Southeast Mo. State Col.; M.Ed.'50, Univ. of Mo.; Supt. of Sch., Louisiana, Mo., since 1952.

Wiethaupt, Mervyn E., Secy. and Treas., Bd. of Educ., St. Louis, Mo.

Willett, W. J., B.S. in Ed.'28, Southwest Mo. State Col.; M.A.'32, Univ. of Mo.; State Supvr. of Sch., Greenfield, Mo., since 1944.

Wilson, Orus, B.S.'39, Southwest Mo. State Col.; M.A.'41, Univ. of Mo.; Supt. of Sch., Mountain Grove, Mo., 1947-52.

Wilson, Wallace Marvin, B.S. in Ed.'28, Southwest Mo. State Col.; M.A.'31, Ph.D.'46, Univ. of Mo.; Supt. of Sch., Camdenton, Mo., since 1949.

Windes, T. R., B.S.'29, Southwest Mo. State Col.; M.S.'38, Univ. of Wyo.; Supt. of Sch., Lamar, Mo., since 1940.

*Wood, F. Ray, B.S.'26, Southwest Mo. State Col.; A.M.'34, Univ. of Mo.; Supt. of Sch., Bolivar, Mo., since 1931.

Wood, Roi S., A.B.'27, Central Wesleyan Col.; M.A.'34, Univ. of Mo.; Supt. of Sch., Joplin, Mo., since 1944.

449

Wright, Frank Lee, A.B.'10, Kansas State Tchrs. Col.; M.A.'15, Univ. of Wis.; Ed.M.'24, Ed.D.'25, Harvard Univ.; Head, Dept. of Educ., Wash. Univ., St. Louis, Mo., since 1924.

Young, Harold L., B.S. in Ed.'37, Central Mo. Col.; M.Ed.'49, Univ. of Mo.; State Sec. Sch. Supvr., Higginsville, Mo., since 1946.

Zwingle, J. L., Pres., Park Col., Parkville, Mo.

INSTITUTIONAL MEMBERS

Kent Library, Southeast Mo. State Col., Cape Girardeau, Mo.

Lincoln University, Inman E. Page Library, Jefferson City, Mo.

Professional Library, Bd. of Educ., St. Louis, Mo.

St. Louis Public Library, St. Louis, Mo.

MONTANA

INDIVIDUAL MEMBERS

Baker, Ray G., B.S.'41, Univ. of N. Dak.; Supt. of Sch., Denton, Mont., since 1951.

Baum, C. W., Supt., Sch. Dist. 55, Roundup, Mont.

Beary, D. Hartley, B.S. in Ed.'23, Central Mo. Col.; M.Ed.'46, Mont. State Univ.; Prin., Co. H. S., Missoula, Mont., since 1945.

Bergan, K. W., B.A.'15, Luther Col.; M.A.'29, M.A.'48, Univ. of Minn.; Dir., Transportation and Indian Educ., State Dept. of Pub. Instr., Helena, Mont., since 1949.

Brockmann, Louis O., B.A.'28, M.A.'29, Ph.D.'45, Univ. of Wis.; Pres., Northern Mont. Col., Havre, Mont.

Condon, Mary M., B.A.'39, M.A.'41, State Univ. of Iowa; State Supt. of Pub. Instr., Helena, Mont., since 1947.

Cooper, A. L., B.A.'30, Intermountain Union Col.; M.E.'43, Mont. State Univ.; Supt. of Pub. Sch., Poplar, Mont., since 1946.

Cooper, D. D., B.A.'31, M.E.'39, Mont. State Univ.; Supt. of Sch., Townsend, Mont., since 1948.

Cox, Edith, Co. Supt. of Sch., Shelby, Mont. (retired). Address: 117 Central Ave., Shelby, Mont.

Cummings, Rial, B.A.'37, Mont. State Univ.; Supt. of Pub. Sch., Plains, Mont., since 1941.

Davidson, V. G., B.A.'31, State Tchrs. Col., Valley City, N. Dak.; M.E.'49, Mont. State Univ.; Prin., Park Co. H. S., Livingston, Mont., since 1949.

Dean, A. L., B.A.'30, Mont. State Univ.; Supt. of Sch., Polson, Mont.

Farnsworth, Robert B., B.A.'27, M.A.'33, State Col. of Wash.; Dist. Supt. of Sch., Great Falls, Mont., since 1946.

Fellbaum, Earl H., B.A.'33, Univ. of Mont.; M.A.'38, Univ. of Minn.; Supt. of Sch., Helena, Mont., since 1947.

Fisher, John M., B.A.'47, State Col., Superior, Wis.; M.A.'51, Univ. of Minn.; Prin., Sr. H. S., Hardin, Mont., since 1951.

Gallagher, M. C., B.A.'18, M.Ed.'42, Mont. State Univ.; Supt. of Sch., Billings, Mont., since 1937.

Gerber, Raymond A., Supt. of Sch., Sidney, Mont.

Gillespie, O. Lloyd, B.Ed.'32, State Tchrs. Col., Platteville, Wis.; M.Ed.'46, Mont. State Univ.; Supt. of Sch., Libby, Mont., since 1945.

Githens, Donald W., B.A.'34, Parsons Col.; M.A.'46, State Univ. of Iowa; Supt. of Sch., Lewistown, Mont., since 1949.

Goetz, Herbert J., B.A.'42, N. Dak. State Tchrs. Col., Dickinson; Supt., Madison Valley Consol. Sch., Ennis, Mont., since 1946.

Graham, Robert C., B.A.'25, Ed.M.'40, Mont. State Univ.; Supt. of Sch., Choteau, Mont., since 1947.

Hansen, George G., A.B.'18, A.M.'22, Ph.D.'40, Univ. of Nebr.; Supt. of Huntley Project Sch., Worden, Mont.

Harmala, Clifford A., B.S.'40, Univ. of Minn., Duluth; M.Ed.'48, Mont. State Univ.; Supt. of Sch., Dixon, Mont., since 1948.

Haynes, Charles D., B.A.'22, Univ. of Wash.; M.A.'27, Mont. State Univ.; Supt. of Sch., Hamilton, Mont., since 1933.

Hodges, Ivan H., M.E.'49, Univ. of Mont.; Supt. of Sch., Troy, Mont.

Hood, Charles E., B.S.'27, Jamestown Col.; M.A.'35, Mont. State Univ.; Prin., Co. H. S. and Jr. Col., Miles City, Mont., since 1948.

Jeffries, D. J., M.A.'51, Mont. State Univ.; Supt. of Sch., Wilsall, Mont., since 1949.

Lawson, Hazen R., Supt. of Sch., Cascade, Mont.

McCormick, Michael L., B.S.'48, Mont. State Col.; M.A.'50, Univ. of Minn.; Supt. of Sch. Dist. 44, Belgrade, Mont., since 1951.

Manning, Clarence G., A.B.'07, Morningside Col.; M.E.'44, Univ. of Mont.; Prof. of Educ., Rocky Mountain Col., Billings, Mont., since 1949.

Moe, Martin P., B.S.'27, Univ. of Minn.; M.A.'46, Univ. of Mont.; Exec. Secy., Mont. Educ. Assn., Helena, Mont., since 1933.

Naugle, Carlton E., B.A. in Ed.'49, Mont. State Univ.; Supt. of Sch., Bigfork, Mont., since 1951.

Nordgaard, Ernest J., A.B.'10, St. Olaf Col.; A.M.'27, Univ. of Chicago; Supt. of Sch., Anaconda, Mont., since 1947.

Porter, Clarence S., B.P.E.'32, Normal Col. of the American Gymnastic Union; B.A.'32, M.E.'44, Univ. of Mont.; Supt. of Sch., Missoula, Mont., since 1944.

Rafter, Wendell G., B.A.'46, Intermountain Col.; M.E.'49, State Univ. of Mont.; Supt. of Sch., Three Forks, Mont., since 1945.

Rawson, Kenneth A., A.B.'28, Upper Iowa Univ.; M.A.'35, Univ. of Colo.; Prin., Flathead Co. H. S., Kalispell, Mont., since 1948.

Rickerd, M. L., B.S.'32, Univ. of Ill.; M.A.'40, Univ. of Wyo.; Supt. of Sch., Big Sandy, Mont., since 1950.

Roeseler, W. Lyle, B.S.'26, B.S.'36, Mont. State Col.; State Supvr., Trade and Indus. Educ., State Dept. of Pub. Instr., Helena, Mont., since 1948.

Ruppel, Henry G., B.A.'20, Univ. of Mont.; M.S.'32, Oregon State Col.; Supt. of Pub. Sch., Deer Lodge, Mont., since 1950.

Seibel, Louie W., B.A.'24, State Tchrs. Col., Valley City, N. Dak.; M.A.'40, Mont. State Univ.; Supt. of Pub. Sch. and Prin. of Granite Co. H. S., Philipsburg, Mont., since 1951.

Shively, John D., M.A.'27, Univ. of N. Dak.; Supt. of Sch., Bozeman, Mont., since 1947.

Squires, Genevieve, B.E.'38, Western Mont. Col. of Educ.; Chief Deputy Supt. of Pub. Instr., Helena, Mont., since 1949.

Staehle, John F., B.A.'41, Pacific Univ.; M.A.'47, D.Ed.'51, Univ. of Oregon; Asst. Prof. of Educ., Missoula, Mont., since 1950.

Stegner, Warren E., B.S.'16, Carleton Col.; M.A.'39, Univ. of Minn.; Supt. of Sch., Havre, Mont., since 1947.

Wylie, Robert H., M.E.'49, Mont. State Univ.; Prin., H. S., Havre, Mont., since 1952.

NEBRASKA

INDIVIDUAL MEMBERS

Anderson, J. F., M.A.'40, Colo. State Col. of Educ., Greeley; Supt. of Sch., Harrisburg, Nebr., since 1937.

Bail, Philip Milo, B.A.'20, LL.D.'47, Mo. Valley Col.; M.A.'28, Ph.D.'31, State Univ. of Iowa; Pres., Univ. of Omaha, Omaha, Nebr., since 1948.

Beggs, W. K., Tchrs. Col., Univ. of Nebr., Lincoln, Nebr.

Brooks, Ralph G., Supt. of Sch., McCook, Nebr.

Burgeson, John G., B.S.'33, Ga. Tchrs. Col., Collegeboro; M.A.'39, Univ. of Colo.; Supt. of Sch., Gordon, Nebr., since 1944.

Burke, Harry A., B.A.'17, Univ. of Idaho; M.A. '28, Ed.D.'42, Stanford Univ.; Supt. of Sch., Omaha, Nebr., since 1946.

Burkhardt, Allen Paul, A.B.'25, Nebr. Wesleyan Univ.; M.A.'29, Columbia Univ.; Ph.D.'43, Univ. of Nebr.; Supt. of Sch., and Pres., Jr. Col., Norfolk, Nebr., since 1931.

Burnham, Archer L., A.B.'16, A.M.'27, Univ. of Nebr.; Ph.D.'38, Colo. State Col. of Educ., Greeley; Exec. Secy., Nebr. State Educ. Assn., Lincoln, Nebr., since 1938.

Carey, Raymond Burdette, A.B.'13, Nebr. Wesleyan Univ.; M.A.'31, Univ. of Nebr.; Supt. of Sch., Bellevue, Nebr., since 1948.

Carkoski, Chester A., B.Sc.'28, M.A.'40, Univ. of Nebr.; Supt. of Sch., Hartington, Nebr., since 1941.

Chisholm, Leslie L., Ph.D.'35, Columbia Univ.; Prof. of Educ., Univ. of Nebr., Lincoln, Nebr., since 1945.

Chittim, Harry D., B.S. in Ed.'32, M.Ed.'35, Boston Univ.; Operations Analyst (Training), Hq. Strategic Air Command, Offut A. F. Base, Omaha, Nebr., since 1944.

Christian, Ivan, A.B.'27, Nebr. State Tchrs. Col., Chadron; M.A.'41, Univ. of Wyo.; Supt. of Sch., Bayard, Nebr., since 1950.

Colson, M. R., A.B.'18, Grand Island Col.; M.A.'33, Univ. of Nebr.; Supt. of Sch., Lyman, Nebr.

Corneer, Robert, B.A.'48, Nebr. State Tchrs. Col., Kearney; M.A.'49, Univ. of Wyo.; Supt. of Sch., Stapleton, Nebr.

Crawford, Theodore R., B.Sc.'13, Hastings Col.; Rep., Scott Foresman Co., Lincoln, Nebr., since 1924.

Cushing, Herbert L., A.B.'14, Grand Island Baptist Col.; M.A.'30, Univ. of Nebr.; D.Ed. '37, Nebr. Wesleyan Univ.; Pres., Nebr. State Tchrs. Col., Kearney, Nebr., since 1936.

Decker, F. B., A.B.'30, Nebr. State Tchrs. Col., Wayne; M.A.'45, Univ. of Nebr.; State Supt. of Pub. Instr., Lincoln, Nebr., since 1951.

Downing, Lester N., B.S.'47, M.S.'49, Utah State Col.; D.Ed.'51, Colo. State Col. of Educ., Greeley; Dean of Col. and Dir. of Guidance Serv., Nebr. State Tchrs. Col., Peru, Nebr., since 1951.

Eastman, Leo E., B.E.'39, State Tchrs. Col., Moorhead, Minn.; D.E.'50, Univ. of N. D.; Dir., Campus Sch., Nebr. State Tchrs. Col., Peru, Nebr., since 1951.

Emery, Donald G., B.S.'41, Ind. Central Col.; M.S.'45, Butler Univ.; Ph.D.'49, State Univ. of Iowa; Assoc. Dean, Col. of Adult Educ., Univ. of Omaha, Omaha, Nebr., since 1951.

Exstrom, Paul E., A.B.'27, Nebr. State Tchrs. Col., Kearney; Co. Supt. of Pub. Instr., North Platte, Nebr., since 1943.

Farrow, M. G., B.S.'35, State Tchrs. Col., Wayne, Nebr.; M.A.'40, Univ. of Nebr.; Supt. of Sch., Fremont, Nebr., since 1945.

Frazer, Donald Wayne, B.S. in Ed.'40, Nebr. State Tchrs. Col., Kearney; M.A. in Ed.'50, Univ. of Nebr.; Supt., Consol. Sch., Scotia, Nebr., since 1949.

Goman, Neal S., A.B.'31, M.A.'45, Univ. of Nebr.; Pres., Nebr. State Tchrs. Col., Peru, Nebr., since 1951.

Gorman, Frank H., B.S.'24, Central Mo. Col.; M.A.'28, Ph.D.'31, Univ. of Mo.; Dean, Col. of Educ., Univ. of Omaha, Omaha, Nebr., since 1948.

Grass, Anzie Vernon, B.A.'29, Nebr. State Tchrs. Col., Peru; M.A.'37, Univ. of Colo.; Supt., Pub. Sch., Tecumseh, Nebr., since 1942.

Grubb, Neal A., B.A.'34, Wayne State Tchrs. Col., Nebr.; M.A.'41, Colo. State Col. of Educ., Greeley; Supt. of Sch., Tilden, Nebr., since 1946.

Haight, Lewis S., B.S., A.B.'04, Shurtleff Col.; Supt. of Sch., Blue Springs, Nebr., since 1951.

Hall, Edythe K., B.A.'26, MacMurray Col. for Women; M.A.'40, D.Ed.'49, Northwestern Univ.; Prin., Kellom Elem. Sch., Omaha, Nebr. since 1945.

Halsted, Albert V., B.S.'28, Univ. of Nebr.; M.S.'34, Univ. of Colo.; Supt. of Sch., Hemingford, Nebr., since 1951.

Hanson, Leonard E., M.A.'42, Colo. State Col. of Educ., Greeley; Supt. of Sch., Ogallala, Nebr., since 1950.

Hauser, W. J., A.B.'34, Nebr. State Tchrs. Col.; M.A.'38, Univ. of Nebr.; Co. Supt. of Pub. Instr., Omaha, Nebr., since 1944.

Henzlik, F. E., Ph.D.'24, Columbia Univ.; Dean and Prof. of Sch. Admin., Tchrs. Col., Univ. of Nebr., Lincoln, Nebr., since 1931.

Hill, Fred, B.S.'14, North Central Col.; M.A.'39, Univ. of Nebr.; Asst. Supt. of Sch., Omaha, Nebr., since 1944.

Humann, Emanuel D., M.A.'37, Univ. of Nebr.; Supt. of Sch., since 1945, and Co. Supt. of Sch., Aurora, Nebr., since 1947.

Kelly, Homer C., A.M.'49, Univ. of Nebr.; Supt. of Sch. and Pres., Fairbury Jr. Col., Fairbury, Nebr., since 1951.

Klasek, Bernard J., A.B.'27, Doane Col.; M.A. '39, Univ. of Nebr.; Supt. of Sch., Wilber, Nebr., since 1936.

Kline, Barton L., B.Sc.'29, Cotner Col.; M.A.'37, Univ. of Nebr.; D.Ed.'48, Colo. State Col. of Educ., Greeley; Supt. of Sch., Beatrice, Nebr., since 1946.

Krantz, B. E., Supt. of Sch., Central City, Nebr., since 1951.

Kreizenbeck, F. W., A.B. in Ed.'21, Nebr. State Tchrs. Col., Chadron; M.A. in Ed.'22, Univ. of Nebr.; Supt. of Sch., Ainsworth, Nebr., since 1947.

Lichtenberger, Allan R., A.B.'31, Nebr. State Tchrs. Col., Peru; M.A.'36, Univ. of Nebr.; Dir. of Research, State Dept. of Pub. Instr., Lincoln, Nebr., since 1949.

Lightbody, E., M.A.'34, Univ. of Nebr.; Supt. of Sch., Nebraska City, Nebr., since 1945.

Lundstrom, Glenn A., B.S., Midland Col.; M.A.'46, Univ. of Nebr.; Supt. of Sch., Blair, Nebr., since 1951.

McNickle, T. R., B.S.'28, M.A.'34, Univ. of Nebr.; Supt. of Sch., York, Nebr., since 1942.

Maehr, Martin J., B.S.'38, M.S.'41, Okla. Agrl. and Mech. Col.; Prin. of Tr. Sch., and Dir. of Tchr. Tr., Concordia Tchrs. Col., Seward, Nebr., since 1944.

Mead, Benjamin H., A.B.'25, Municipal Univ. of Omaha; M.A.'49, Stanford Univ.; Supt. of Sch., Gothenburg, Nebr., since 1948.

Miller, Dohn A., A.B.'40, McPherson Col.; M.E.'52, Univ. of Colo.; Supt. of Sch., Shickley, Nebr., since 1950.

Miller, Glenn E., A.B.'16, Univ. of Nebr.; M.A.'29, Univ. of Nebr. and Univ. of Wash.; Supt. of Sch., Lexington, Nebr., since 1935.

Morehouse, Charles O., B.A.'41, Dana Col.; M.A.'47, Univ. of Nebr.; Supt. of Sch., Elwood, Nebr., since 1944.

Morris, E. Paul, A.B.'29, Nebr. Wesleyan Univ.; M.A.'38, Univ. of Nebr.; Supt. of Sch., Kearney, Nebr., since 1947.

Morrison, L. Eugene, B.S.'42, Nebr. State Tchrs. Col., Kearney; M.A.'51, Univ. of Omaha; Supt. of Sch., Exeter, Nebr., since 1951.

Morton, William Henry, A.B.'09, York Col.; A.M.'12, Univ. of Nebr.; A.M.'23, Columbia Univ.; Ph.D.'28, Univ. of Nebr.; Dir. of Tchr. Tr., Chmn., Dept. of Sec. Educ. and Prin., Tchrs. Col. H. S., Univ. of Nebr., Lincoln, Nebr., 1927-52.

Nolte, Roy W., M.A.'35, Univ. of Mo.; Counselor, Col. of Adult Educ., Univ. of Omaha, Omaha, Nebr., since 1952.

Oakes, W. Otto, A.B.'28, Nebr. State Tchrs. Col., Peru; A.M.'38, Univ. of Denver; Supt. of Sch., North Platte, Nebr., since 1948.

Patterson, Luther L., B.A.'31, Nebr. State Tchrs. Col., Peru; M.A.'38, Univ. of Nebr.; Supt. of Sch., Cozad, Nebr., since 1951.

Pecht, Karl E., B.A.'27, Cornell Col.; M.A.'39, Univ. of Nebr.; Supt. of Sch., Loup City, Nebr., since 1944.

Pickrel, Glenn E., A.B.'36, Nebr. Central Col.; M.A.'46, Univ. of Nebr.; Supt. of Westside Community Sch., Omaha, Nebr., since 1949.

Rarick, Eugene L., A.B.'33, Nebr. State Tchrs. Col., Peru; M.A.'39, Univ. of Nebr.; Supt. of Sch., West Point, Nebr., since 1946.

Rice, John D., A.B.'24, Grand Island (Nebr.) Col.; M.A.'30, Tchrs. Col., Columbia Univ.; Ed.D.'49, Colo. State Col. of Educ.; Pres., Nebr. State Tchrs. Col., Wayne, Nebr., since 1951.

Russell, O. D., M.A.'43, Colo. State Col. of Educ., Greeley; Supt. of Sch., Overton, Nebr., since 1946.

Schindler, W. A., M.A.'37, Univ. of Nebr.; Supt. of Sch., Alliance, Nebr., since 1951.

Schroeder, Howard F., B.Sc.'24, M.A.'36, Univ. of Nebr.; Supt. of Sch., Holdredge, Nebr.

Sims, G. L., B.S.'39, Nebr. State Tchrs. Col., Kearney; M.A.'47, Univ. of Nebr.; Supt. of Sch., Albion, Nebr., since 1951.

Sinkey, L. F., M.A.'39, Univ. of Nebr.; Dean, Fairbury Jr. Col., Fairbury, Nebr., since 1949.

Smith, Leon O., B.A.'10, M.A.'18, State Univ. of Iowa; Asst. Supt. of Sch., Omaha, Nebr., since 1919.

Stoneman, Merle A., A.B.'27, Central Col. (Mo.); A.M.'34, Ph.D.'38, Univ. of Nebr.; Prof. of Sch. Admin., Univ. of Nebr., Lincoln, Nebr., since 1941.

Stout, H. G., A.B.'14, Nebr. Wesleyan Univ.; A.M.'25, Ph.D.'37, Univ. of Nebr.; Chmn., Dept. of Educ., Nebr. State Tchrs. Col., Kearney, Nebr., since 1937.

Strong, Elwood W., M.A.'46, Univ. of Nebr.; Supt. of Sch., Sutherland, Nebr., since 1947.

Thorpe, N. F., A.B.'29, Nebr. State Tchrs. Col., Peru; M.A.'38, Ph.D.'50, Univ. of Nebr.; Dir. of Tchr. Tr., and Assoc. Prof. of Sec. Educ. and Prin., Tchrs. Col. H. S., Lincoln, Nebr., since 1952.

Towne, George L., A.B.'95, Univ. of Nebr.; Pres., University Pub. Co., Lincoln, Nebr., since 1902.

Velte, Charles Henry, A.B.'14, Hastings Col.; M.A.'29, Univ. of Nebr.; Supt. of Sch., Crete, Nebr., since 1919.

Watkins, Steven N., B.S. in Ed.'31, Cotner Col.; M.A.'35, Ph.D.'45, Univ. of Nebr.; Supt. of Sch., Lincoln, Nebr., since 1950.

Watson, Raymond A., B.S. in Ed.'21, Univ. of Mo.; M.A.'28, Univ. of Chicago; Supt. of Sch., Hastings, Nebr., since 1944.

Weyer, Frank E., Ph.D.'41, Univ. of Nebr.; Dean, Hastings Col., Hastings, Nebr., since 1918.

Wilkie, Russell M., A.B.'27, Nebr. Wesleyan Univ.; M.A.'40, Colo. State Col. of Educ., Greeley; Supt. of Sch., Gering, Nebr., since 1948.

Willert, Everett W., A.B.'27, Midland Col.; M.A.'42, Univ. of Nebr.; Supt. of Sch., Wayne, Nebr., since 1949.

Willits, Kenneth C., Supt. of Sch., Franklin, Nebr.

Wiltse, Earle W., A.B.'22, Nebr. Wesleyan Univ.; A.M.'26, Columbia Univ.; Ph.D.'42, Univ. of Nebr.; Supt. of Sch., Grand Island, Nebr., since 1944.

Wrenn, Ben H., Asst. Supt. of Sch., Bellevue, Nebr.

Young, Joseph P., B.S.'25, M.A.'32, Univ. of Nebr.; Supt. of Sch., Columbus, Nebr., since 1948.

INSTITUTIONAL MEMBER

Library, Nebr. State Tchrs. Col., Chadron, Nebr.

NEVADA

INDIVIDUAL MEMBERS

Best, Robert, B.S.'36, Univ. of Nevada; Supt., Mineral Co. H. S., Hawthorne, Nevada, since 1944.

Copenhaver, Roxie, B.A.'29, Univ. of Mont.; Deputy State Supt. of Sch., Fifth Supvn. Dist., Las Vegas, Nevada, since 1943.

Corbett, Roger, B.S.'34, Univ. of Oregon; M.A.'41, Univ. of Nevada; Asst. Supt. of Sch., Reno, Nevada, since 1944.

Davis, Chester V., M.A.'34, Stanford Univ.; Exec. Secy., State Educ. Assn., Reno, Nevada, since 1952.

Dilts, Dwight F., B.A.'31, Wash. State Col.; M.A.'39, Univ. of Nevada; Retirement Clerk and Statistician, Carson City, Nevada, since 1937.

Dodson, Edwin S., B.A.'42, Univ. of Nevada; M.A.'48, Univ. of Oregon; Supt., Consol. Sch. Dist. 1, Lovelock, Nevada, since 1950.

Duncan, Glenn A., B.A.'30, Univ. of Wis.; State Supt. of Pub. Instr., Carson City, Nevada, since 1951.

Edwards, Elbert B., Supt. of Sch., Boulder City, Nevada.

Fant, John H., B.S.'31, Univ. of Nevada; Deputy State Supt. of Pub. Instr., Reno, Nevada, since 1951.

Fish, Seymour P., A.B.'28, Univ. of Utah; Supt., Clark Co. Sch., Overton, Nevada, since 1944.

Galbraith, C. Layton, B.S.'28, Utah State Agrl. Col.; M.A.'31, Stanford Univ.; Supt. of Sch., McGill, Nevada, since 1932.

Harris, George E., A.B.'24, Howard Payne Col.; Prin., H. S., Las Vegas, Nevada, since 1946.

Hawley, Albert M., A.B.'32, Davis and Elkins Col.; M.A.'51, Stanford Univ.; Prin., Stewart Indian Sch., Stewart, Nevada.

Johnson, Walter D., A.B.'31, Univ. of Nevada; Supt. of Sch., Las Vegas, Nevada, since 1946.

Lodge, Harry, A.B.'35, Wash. Missionary Col.; Educ. Supt., Nevada-Utah Conference, Reno, Nevada, since 1950.

Manning, R. H., B.S.'39, Utah State Agrl. Col; Deputy Supt., State Dept. of Educ., Carson City, Nevada, since 1951.

Perry, Donald K., Deputy State Supt. of Pub. Instr., Ely, Nevada.

Reed, Flo, B.A.'44, Univ. of Nevada; Deputy Supt., 2nd Supvn. Dist., Ely, Nevada, since 1952.

Robertson, Donald A., A.B.'23, Eureka Col.; Supt. of Sch., Carson City, Nevada, since 1944.

Traner, Fred W., A.B.'08, Beloit Col.; M.A.'20, Ph.D.'30, Univ. of Calif.; Dean, Sch. of Educ., Univ. of Nevada, Reno, Nevada, since 1937.

White, Hugh M., B.S. in Ed.'34, Univ. of Oregon; M.S. in Ed.'40, Univ. of S. C.; Supt. of Sch., Ely, Nevada, since 1939.

Wooster, Earl, A.B.'21, Univ. of Nevada; M.A. '40, Stanford Univ.; Supt. of Sch., Reno, Nevada; since 1944.

NEW HAMPSHIRE

INDIVIDUAL MEMBERS

Appleton, David, B.S.'41, Univ. of N. H.; Supt. of Sch., Supvry. Union 9, Conway, N. H.

Arnold, Dexter O., A.B.'32, Hobart Col.; M.A.'38, Syracuse Univ.; Ed.D.'51, Boston Univ.; Asst. Supt. of Sch., Concord, N. H., since 1948.

Atherton, Harlan E., B.A.'25, Yale Univ.; Ed.M. '33, Univ. of N. H.; Supt. of Sch., Concord, N. H., since 1947.

Badger, Lester B., B.S.'18, Dartmouth Col.; M.A.'31, Tchrs. Col., Columbia Univ.; Union Supt. of Sch., Peterborough, N. H., since 1946.

Bailey, Robert D., Ed.B.'32, Keene Tchrs. Col. (N. H.); Ed.M.'43, Harvard Univ.; Exec. Secy., N. H. State Tchrs. Assn., Concord, N. H., since 1950.

Beal, Raymond I., B.S.'36, Univ. of N. H.; Supt. of Sch., Portsmouth, N. H., since 1946.

Bennett, Phil A., Supt. of Sch., Woodsville, N. H.

Bowlby, Charles L., B.S.'27, City Col. of the City of New York; M.A.'44, Columbia Univ.; Supt. of Sch., Union 38, Marlboro, N. H., since 1949.

Bowley, Harold Croft, Ph.B'20, Univ. of Vt.; M.Ed.'40, Univ. of N. H.; Union Supt. of Sch., Milford, N. H., since 1939.

Brasier, Everett H., A.B.'20, Univ. of Maine; Ed.M.'31, Grad. Sch. of Educ., Harvard Univ.; Supt. of Sch., Supvy. Union 36, Ossipee, N. H., since 1945.

Buley, Hilton C., B.S.'27, Hobart Col.; M.A.'34, Cornell Univ.; Ed.D.'47, Columbia Univ.; State Commr. of Educ., Concord, N. H., since 1948.

Bushnell, Almon W., A.B.'16, Dartmouth Col.; A.M.'26, Columbia Univ.; Supt. of Sch., Meredith, N. H., since 1934.

Danforth, H. Raymond, A.B.'28, Ed.M.'37, Univ. of N. H.; Supt. of Sch., Nashua, N. H.

Danielson, Arthur W., B.S.'37, Bates Col.; M.Ed.'45, Univ. of N. H.; Supt. of Supvry. Sch. Union 56, Somersworth, N. H., since 1950.

Davidson, Arthur Ole, B.A.'31, Luther Col.; M.A.'38, Univ. of Minn.; Chairman, Dept. of Educ., Dartmouth Col., Hanover, N. H.

Davis, Wendell V., A.B.'26, Univ. of N. H.; M.Ed.'41, Bates Col.; Prin. of Sch., Salem, N. H., since 1949.

Day, John Wilman, B.S. in Ed.'37, Plymouth Tchrs. Col. (N. H.); M.S. in Ed.'49, Univ. of N. H.; Supt., Union 49, Pittsfield, N. H., since 1952.

Doe, Chester W., A.B.'10, Harvard Univ.; B.D. '13, Auburn Theol. Sem.; M.Ed.'32, Univ. of N. H.; Union Supt. of Sch., Northwood, N. H., since 1928.

Eddy, Rhoden B., B.S.'20, Colby Col.; Ed.M.'28, Harvard Univ.; Supt. of Sch., Laconia, N. H., since 1943.

Farnum, Paul E., B.S.'25, Univ. of N. H.; M.S. '36, Cornell Univ.; Chief, Div. of Admin. Serv., State Dept. of Educ., Concord, N. H., since 1940.

*Fillion, Paul Raoul, A.B.'42, Adrian Col.; Ed.M.'46, Western Md. Col.; Dir. of Educ. Finance, State Bd. of Educ., Concord, N. H., since 1950.

Flint, Gordon B., B.S.'40, M.Ed.'48, Univ. of N. H.; Supt. of Sch., Newport, N. H., since 1947.

Foote, Lewis F., B.S.'25, M.Ed.'33, Univ. of N. H.; Supt. of Sch., Goffstown, N. H., since 1944.

Fox, Gordon L., Supt. of Sch., Tilton, N. H.

Frye, John H., B.E.'31, Keene Tchrs. Col., N. H.; M.E.'40, Univ. of N. H.; Supt. of Sch., Rochester, N. H., since 1949.

Gillmore, Roy W., B.A.'15, Colby Col.; M.A.'24, Bates Col.; Supt. of Sch., Hampton, N. H., since 1930.

Gray, C. Maurice, A.B.'28, Dartmouth Col.; M.Ed.'38, Univ. of N. H.; Supt. of Sch., Union 4, Bristol, N. H., since 1946.

Hastings, Henry James, B.S. in Ed.'41, State Tchrs. Col., Fitchburg, Mass.; Supt. of Sch., Supvy. Union 27, Hudson, N. H.

Holloway, George E., Jr., Litt.B.'29, M.Ed.'33, Rutgers Univ.; Union Supt. of Sch., Pittsfield, N. H., 1946-52.

Hounsell, William B., B.A.'30, M.A.'33, Univ. of N. H.; Supt. of Sch., Supvy. Union 46, Penacook, N. H., since 1951.

Hoyt, Raymond A., B.A.'28, Ed.M.'37, Univ. of N. H.; Supt. of Sch., Exeter, N. H., since 1948.

Hyde, Harold E., B.S.'33, Hartwick Col.; M.S. '39, N.Y. State Col. of Tchrs., Albany; Ed.D. '50, New York Univ.; Pres., Plymouth Tchrs. Col., Plymouth, N. H., since 1951.

Kelley, John J., Dir., Sec. Sch. Serv., State Board of Educ., Concord, N. H.

Knightly, Albert P., B.S.'26, Ed.M.'35, Bates Col.; Union Supt. of Sch., Gorham, N. H., since 1947.

Leavitt, Russell Hall, B.S.'16, Dartmouth Col.; Ed.M.'35, Harvard Univ.; Chief, Div. of Instr., State Dept. of Educ., Concord, N. H., since 1946.

Lees, Chester C., A.B.'26, Harvard Univ.; A.M.'37, Brown Univ.; Supt. of Sch., Winchester, N. H., since 1947.

McCaffrey, Austin J., B.S.'36, Ed.M.'40, Univ. of N. H.; Supt. of Sch., Manchester, N. H., since 1947.

Mason, Howard F., B.A.'31, Dartmouth Col.; M.Ed.'39, Univ. of N. H.; Supt. of Sch., Hanover, N. H., since 1948.

Morrison, Maria P., B.S. in Ed.'33, M.S.'37, Boston Univ.; Asst. Supt. of Sch., Nashua, N. H., since 1937.

Nelson, Wm. J., B.S.'11, Trinity Col. (Conn.); Supt. of Sch., Plaistow, N. H. (retired).

Nichols, Augusta M., B.S.'29, M.Ed.'32, D.Ed. '47, Boston Univ.; Asst. Supt. of Sch., Manchester, N. H., since 1938.

Niles, Caleb H., Supt. of Sch., Berlin, N. H.

Osgood, Jonathan A., B.S.'32, M.Ed.'35, Univ. of N. H.; Supt. of Supvy. Sch. Union 55, Salem, N. H.

Parkinson, Everton H., B.A.'26, Wesleyan Univ.; Ed.M.'32, Univ. of N. H.; Supt. of Sch., Derry, N. H., since 1942.

Perham, Ronald A., Supt. of Sch., Lisbon, N. H.

Ramsay, Louis L., M.Ed.'43, Boston Univ.; Supt. of Sch., Union 14, Epping, N. H., since 1950.

Sillari, Edward Anthony, B.Ed.'37, Plymouth Tchrs. Col.; M.Ed.'49, Univ. of N. H.; Prin., H. S., Keene, N. H., since 1947.

Snell, Fred W., M.Ed.'40, Univ. of N. H.; Supt. of Sch., Franklin, N. H., since 1950.

Sterling, William C., B.A.'31, Univ. of N. H.; Ed.M.'42, Univ. of Vt.; Union Supt. of Sch., Contoocook, N. H., since 1941.

Thompson, Laurence O., A.B.'17, Ed.M.'40, Bates Col.; Supt. of Sch., Keene, N. H., since 1933.

Trafton, F. Lester, A.B.'14, Clark Col.; Ed.M.'34, Harvard Univ.; Supt. of Sch., Claremont, N. H., since 1943.

Young, Hammond, Supt. of Sch., Lebanon, N. H.

Young, Lloyd P., B.S.'22, State Tchrs. Col., Emporia, Kansas; A.M.'29, Ph.D.'31, Tchrs. Col., Columbia Univ.; Pres., Keene Tchrs. Col., Keene, N. H., since 1939.

INSTITUTIONAL MEMBER

Library, Plymouth Teachers College, Plymouth, N. H.

NEW JERSEY

INDIVIDUAL MEMBERS

Adams, J. Harry, A.M.'35, Univ. of Mich.; Supt. of Sch., Elizabeth, N. J., since 1948.

Agnone, Anthony F., M.S.'42, Pa. State Col.; Supt. of Sch., South River, N. J., since 1951.

Ahlbach, James F., B.S. in Ed.'36, Ed.D.'48, Rutgers Univ.; M.A. in Sec.Ed.'37, Tchrs. Col., Columbia Univ.; Asst. to the Dir. of Elem. Educ., Trenton, N. J., since 1952.

Alvarez, Alfonso, Jr., Architect, Upper Montclair, N. J., since 1936.

Anderson, Helen I., B.S. in Ed.'33, M.E.'42, Rutgers Univ.; Prin., Madison-Monroe Sch. No. 16, Elizabeth, N. J., since 1942.

Anderson, Roy A., B.S.'40, Newark State Tchrs. Col.; M.A.'44, Montclair State Tchrs. Col.; Admin. Asst. (in charge of business), Geo. Washington Sch., Millburn, N. J., since 1946.

Anderson, Theo. I., B.Ed.'37, Ill. State Normal Univ.; M.A.'41, Univ. of Ill.; Ed.D.'52, Tchrs. Col., Columbia Univ.; Supt. of Sch., Manasquan, N. J., since 1952.

Anibal, Earle W., Ph.B.'08, Hamilton Col.; A.M.'23, Tchrs. Col., Columbia Univ.; Supt. of Sch., Mountain Lakes, N. J., since 1932.

Antrim, G. Harold, A.B.'25, Washington and Jefferson Col.; M.A.'29, Tchrs. Col., Columbia Univ.; Supt. of Sch., Pt. Pleasant Beach, N. J., since 1930.

Archibald, John Lauren, B.S.'43, M.S.'49, Rutgers Univ.; Prin., Twp. Sch., Dutch Neck, N. J., since 1950.

Atwood, Will G., Litt.B.'10, Rutgers Univ.; Co. Supt. of Sch., Belvidere, N. J., since 1928.

Axtell, Paul H., A.B.'16, Colgate Univ.; M.A.'21, Tchrs. Col., Columbia Univ.; Ph.D.'34, New York Univ.; Supt. of Sch., Caldwell, N. J.

Bain, Harry L., A.B.'15, Union Col.; M.A.'23, Columbia Univ.; Supt. of Sch., West New York, N. J., since 1927.

Bair, Carl M., Ph.B.'09, Grinnell Col.; M.A.'30, Columbia Univ.; Co. Supt. of Sch., Toms River, N. J., since 1944.

*Bair, Carl M., Jr., B.S.'33, State Tchrs. Col., Trenton, N. J.; M.A.'43, Univ. of Conn.; Ed.D.'50, Harvard Univ.; Supt. of Sch., Glen Ridge, N. J., since 1951.

Ball, Lester B., B.E.'34, Northern Ill. State Tchrs. Col.; M.A.'38, Ed.D.'49, Northwestern Univ.; Supt. of Twp. Sch., Millburn, N. J., since 1950.

Bare, Thurman H., B.S.'26, M.A.'29, Univ. of Mo.; Ed.D.'44, Columbia Univ.; Supt. of Sch., North Plainfield, N. J., since 1946.

Barnes, (Mrs.) Mary D., B.S. in Ed.'39, M.Ed. '42, Rutgers Univ.; Elem. Prin., Elizabeth, N. J., since 1941.

Bates, Ralph F., A.B.'11, Colgate Univ.; A.M.'14, Columbia Univ.; Supt. of Sch., Chatham, N. J., since 1920.

Battaglia, Joseph C., A.B.'35, Upsala Col.; M.A.'36, Univ. of Tenn.; Prin., Peapack and Gladstone Sch., Gladstone, N. J., since 1947.

Batten, (Mrs.) Pluma B., B.S. in Ed.'28, Univ. of Pa.; Supt. of Sch., Woodstown, N. J., since 1943.

Bean, Albert M., A.B.'10, A.M.'14, Dickinson Col.; LL.D.'44, Col. of South Jersey; Co. Supt. of Sch., Camden, N. J., since 1930.

Beck, Richard T., B.S.'30, M.A.'32, Tchrs. Col., Columbia Univ.; Ed.D.'37, New York Univ.; Asst. Supt. of Sch., Jersey City, N. J., since 1947.

Behmer, John H., B.A.'25, Elizabethtown Col.; M.A.'29, Tchrs. Col., Columbia Univ.; Ed.D. '38, Rutgers Univ.; Supt. of Twp. Sch., New Market, N. J., since 1935.

Beidel, F. Douglass, B.A.'20, Lebanon Valley Col.; M.A.'31, Columbia Univ.; Supt. of Twp. Sch., Cape May Court House, N. J., since 1948.

Berman, Edward, A.B.'11, Yale Col.; M.A.'23, Tchrs. Col., Columbia Univ.; Asst. Supt. of Sch., Bayonne, N. J., since 1940.

Best, Howard R., B.A.'17, Yankton Col.; Certif. '19, Univ. of Montpelier, France; M.A.'29, Univ. of Nebr.; Ed.D.'39, Tchrs. Col., Columbia Univ.; Supt. of Sch., Cranford, N. J., since 1935.

Best, Leonard E., B.S.'16, Mass. Inst. of Tech.; Pres.-Member, Summit Bd. of Educ., Springfield, N. J.

*Bigelow, Merrill A., A.B.'18, Colby Col.; M.A.'29, Ed.D.'47, Tchrs. Col., Columbia Univ.; Prin., Franklin and Brookside Schs., Bloomfield, N. J., since 1942.

Bishop, J. Edgar, A.B.'25, A.M.'27, Susquehanna Univ.; Ed.M.'40, Pa. State Col.; Supt. of Sch., Merchantville, N. J., since 1946.

Blewitt, Catherine A., M.A.'44, Seton Hall Col.; Supvr. of Elem. Educ., Newark, N. J., since 1952.

Bogle, Frank P., A.B.'27, State Tchrs. Col., Peru, Nebr.; A.M.'38, Colo. State Col. of Educ.; Ed.D.'42, Tchrs. Col., Columbia Univ.; Supt. of Sch., Morristown, N. J.

Bolge, George Robert, B.S.'36, N. J. State Tchrs. Col., Trenton; M.Ed.'39, Rutgers Univ.; Viceprin., Central H. S., Trenton, N. J., since 1952.

Booth, Leslie A. E., B.A.'24, Univ. of New Brunswick, Canada; M.A.'38, State Tchrs. Col., Upper Montclair, N. J.; Prin., H. S., Boonton, N. J., since 1943.

Bosshart, John H., B.A.'02, Cornell Univ.; State Commr. of Educ., Trenton, N. J., 1943-52 (retired). Address: 23 Colinwood Road, Maplewood, N. J.

Bowers, Ray L., B.S.'22, Franklin and Marshall Col.; M.A.'25, Tchrs. Col. Columbia Univ.; Supt. of Sch., Lincoln Park, N. J., since 1925.

Boyer, Clarence Edwin, A.B.'19, Albright Col.; M.A.'26, Columbia Univ.; Supt. of Sch., Boonton, N. J., since 1942.

Bradford, Eugene J., B.S.'36, Ursinus Col.; M.Ed.'41, Rutgers Univ.; Supt. of Sch., Glen Rock, N. J., since 1952.

Bradford, Harmon M., B.A.'23, Boston Univ.; M.A.'36, New York Univ.; Supt. of Sch., Long Branch, N. J., since 1951.

Branom, Wayne T., B.Ed.'32, Ill. State Normal Univ.; M.S.'34, Northwestern Univ.; Ed.D.'41, New York Univ.; Supt. of Sch., Hillside, N. J., since 1944.

Brightbill, David F., A.B.'24, Elizabethtown Col.; M.A.'28, Univ. of Pittsburgh; Supt. of Sch., Gloucester City, N. J., since 1948.

Brilliantine, Dalba, B.A.'38, Wilson Col. (Pa.); M.A.'41, Columbia Univ.; Viceprin., Jr. H. S. 1, Trenton, N. J., since 1952.

Brown, Milton W., B.S.'23, Knox Col.; A.M.'26, Ph.D.'46, Univ. of Chicago; Supt. of Sch., West Orange, N. J., since 1946.

Brown, Paul R., A.B.'21, Simpson Col.; S.T.B.'24, Boston Univ.; Ed.M.'31, Rutgers Univ.; A.M.'34, Tchrs. Col., Columbia Univ.; Ed.D. '45, Rutgers Univ.; Supt. of Sch., Linden, N. J., since 1935.

Brunner, Howard B., A.B.'23, Swarthmore Col.; A.M.'28, Columbia Univ.; Supt. of Sch., Scotch Plains, N. J., since 1936.

Bulger, Mary M., B.S.'30, M.A.'34, Columbia Univ.; Prin.-in-charge, Edgewater Sch., Edgewater, N. J., since 1950.

Bunce, Edgar F., B.S.'16, M.A.'26, Columbia Univ.; Ed.D.'39, New York Univ.; Pres., N. J. State Tchrs. Col., Glassboro, N. J., since 1937.

Bunting, Eugenie McE., Member, Bd. of Educ., Cranbury, N. J., since 1944.

Burt, Roy P., B.S.'28, Rutgers Univ.; M.A.'33, New York Univ.; Supt., Saddle River Twp. Sch., Rochelle Park, N. J., since 1926.

Bustard, Joseph L., Diploma '18, N. J. State Tchrs. Col., Upper Montclair; B.S.'30, Rutgers Univ.; M.A.'33, Tchrs. Col., Columbia Univ.; Asst. State Commr. of Educ., Newark, N. J., since 1945.

Butler, Warren N., B.S.'31, M.S.'32, Pa. State Col.; Supt., Pub. Sch., Maywood, N. J.

*Byrnes, Frederick J., B.S.'37, New York State Col. for Tchrs., Albany; M.A.'47, Tchrs. Col., Columbia Univ.; Dist. Clerk, Pub. Schs., Ridgewood, N. J., since 1951.

Cassel, Lloyd S., A.B.'13, Ursinus Col.; M.A.'28, Columbia Univ.; Supt. of Sch., Freehold, N. J., since 1929.

Ceres, Anthony V., A.B.'28, Notre Dame Univ.; LL.B.'31, Ed.M.'47, Rutgers Univ.; Asst. Supt. of Sch., Perth Amboy, N. J., since 1951.

Chalmers, James F., B.S.'21, Mt. Union Col.; M.A.'23, Ohio State Univ.; Prin., H. S., Perth Amboy, N. J., since 1945.

Chase, Urban W., B.S.'33, M.A.'35, New York Univ.; Supt., Hudson Co. Sch., Jersey City, N. J.

Chauncey, Henry, A.B.'28, Harvard Univ.; Pres., Educ. Testing Serv., Princeton, N. J., since 1948.

Chittick, Murray A., B.S.'16, Rutgers Univ.; Supt. of Twp. Sch., Old Bridge, N. J., since 1929.

Christie, V. J. W., Jr., B.S.'43, N. J. State Tchrs. Col., Paterson; M.A.'48, N. J. State Tchrs. Col., Upper Montclair; Prin., Geo. Washington Sch., Wyckoff, N. J., since 1950.

Clayton, Joseph E., Co. Supt. of Sch., Freehold, N. J.

Conner, J. Harold, B.S.'35, State Tchrs. Col., Shippensburg, Pa.; Ed.M.'37, Rutgers Univ.; Supt. of Sch., Wildwood, N. J., since 1947.

Cook, J. Frederick, 97 Lincoln Park, Newark, N. J.

Curtis, Charles LaRue, B.S. in Ed.'27, M.A. in Ed.'42, New York Univ.; Supt. of Sch., Rockaway, N. J., since 1919.

Cynamon, Shepard H., B.S.'36, N. J. State Tchrs. Col., Paterson; M.A.'47, N. J. State Tchrs. Col., Upper Montclair; Supt. of Sch., Park Ridge, N. J., since 1947.

Davey, Ira H., Architect, 83 Highwood Ave., Tenafly, N. J.

Davis, B. Woodhull, B.S.'19, Wesleyan Univ.; M.S.'27, Columbia Univ.; Supt. of Sch., Princeton, N. J., since 1929.

Dee, Frank P., B.S.'34, Manhattan Col.; M.A.'48, N. J. State Tchrs. Col., Upper Montclair; Supt. of Sch., Lambertville, N. J., since 1950.

DeHart, Donald C., B.S.'29, New York Univ.; Ed.M.'36, Ed.D.'50, Rutgers Univ.; Assoc. Prof. of Educ., Rutgers Univ., Rutgers, N. J., since 1947.

Delaney, (Mrs.) Eleanor C., B.S. in Ed.'30, M.A.'39, Rutgers Univ.; Prin., Woodrow Wilson Sch., Elizabeth, N. J., since 1942.

Della Penta, Anthony H., B.S.'41, N. J. State Tchrs. Col., Newark; M.A.'44, N. J. State Tchrs. Col., Upper Montclair; Supt. of Sch., Lodi, N. J., since 1948.

DePuyt, J. Hobart, M.A.'37, Univ. of Rochester; Supt. of Sch., Hackensack, N. J., since 1950.

Dick, Margaret D., B.S.'33, M.A.'42, New York Univ.; State Helping Tchr., Phillipsburg, N. J., since 1930.

Diefenbach, Carl M., A.B.'19, Syracuse Univ.; M.A.'26, American Univ.; Supt. of Sch., Collingswood, N. J., since 1939.

Donahue, Frank L., B.S. in Ed.'35, N. J. State Tchrs. Col., Glassboro; Ed.M.'49, Temple Univ.; Supt., Lower Camden Co. Regional H. S., Clementon, N. J., since 1951.

Donley, A. L., B.S.Ed.'26, Western Mich. Col. of Educ.; M.Ed.'41, Rutgers Univ.; Supt. of Sch., Vineland, N. J., since 1944.

Douthett, Walter R., A.B.'12, Ursinus Col.; A.M.'21, Univ. of Pa.; Supt. of Sch., Darby, Pa., 1922-50 (retired). Address: 108 North Argyle St., Margate City, N. J.

Durell, Thomas J., A.B.'07, Princeton Univ.; A.M.'30, Columbia Univ.; Asst. State Commr. of Educ., Trenton, N. J., since 1940.

Easterbrook, Neil B., A.B.'23, Syracuse Univ.; Ed.M.'32, Rutgers Univ.; Supt. of Sch., Butler, N. J., since 1943.

Ebbert, Lida M., Ph.B.'08, Dickinson Col.; A.M.'21, Columbia Univ.; Prin., H. S., Linden, N. J., 1910-52 (retired).

England, Herbert K., Jr., B.A.'31, Princeton Univ.; M.S. in Ed.'33, Rutgers Univ.; M.A.'38, Tchrs. Col., Columbia Univ.; Supt. of Sch., Salem, N. J., since 1948.

Evans, Frederick W., B.S.'26, Bucknell Univ.; M.A.'40, N. J. State Tchrs. Col., Upper Montclair; Supt. of Sch., Mt. Holly, N. J., since 1952.

Ewan, S. N., Jr., B.Sc.'21, Haverford Col.; A.M.'32, Ph.D.'35, Univ. of Pa.; Supt. of Sch., Westfield, N. J., since 1947.

Faddis, Robert E., Sc.B.'24, Dickinson Col.; M.A.'34, New York Univ.; Prin., H. S., Millburn, N. J., since 1942.

Faust, Alfred S., B.S.'21, Penn State Col.; M.A.'34, Tchrs. Col., Columbia Univ.; Ed.D. '51, New York Univ.; Supt. of Sch., East Rutherford, N. J., since 1933.

*Ferguson, Harold Allen, A.B.'14, A.M.'16, Clark Univ.; Litt.D.'47, Princeton Univ.; Prin., H. S., Montclair, N. J., since 1926.

Fishack, Howard G., B.A.'21, M.A. in Pub. Adm.'22, Univ. of Mich.; Exec. Dir., Tax Survey Comm., Atlantic City, N. J., since 1947.

Fisher, Gilmore J., B.S.'25, St. Lawrence Univ.; M.A.'32, Ed.D.'44, Tchrs. Col., Columbia Univ.; Supt. of Sch., Ewing Township, N. J., since 1945.

Fisher, Leon, Supt. of Sch., Washington, N. J.

Flood, Robert A., B.S.'34, Pa. State Col.; M.S. '40, Univ. of Pa.; Supt. of Sch., Haddon Heights, N. J., since 1950.

Francis, Mary J., M.A.'38, Rutgers Univ.; Dir. of Elem. Educ., Pub. Sch., Newark, N. J., since 1949.

Freifeld, George F., B.S.'14, Wesleyan Univ.; M.A.'16, Columbia Univ.; Supt. of Sch., Roselle, N. J., since 1945.

Fries, H. C., A.B.'20, Bucknell Univ.; A.M.'22, Columbia Univ.; Supt. of Sch., South Plainfield, N. J., since 1927.

Fry, Alvin A., B.S.'26, Dickinson Col.; M.S.'32, Pa. State Col.; Ed.D.'48, Tchrs. Col., Columbia Univ.; Supt. of Sch., Lower Penn's Neck Twp., Pennsville, N. J., since 1951.

Funston, Augusta Redfield, B.S.'37, M.A.'38, New York Univ.; Prin., Pub. Sch. 37, Jersey City, N. J., since 1934.

Gallagher, Ralph P., B.S.'33, M.A.'37, Ed.D.'49, Tchrs. Col., Columbia Univ.; Supt. of Sch., Bound Brook, N. J., since 1948.

Garofalo, Domenick M., B.S.'36, N. J. State Tchrs. Col., Glassboro; M.Ed.'41, Temple Univ.; Supt. of Sch., Minotola, N. J., since 1941.

Geary, Neil J., B.S.'33, N. J. State Tchrs. Col., Paterson; M.A.'39, N. J. State Tchrs. Col., Montclair; Ph.D.'49, N. Y. Univ.; Supt. of Sch., Weehawken, N. J., since 1952.

Geiger, Vincent, B.S.'23, Pa. State Col.; M.A.'28, Tchrs. Col., Columbia Univ.; Supt. of Sch., Verona, N. J., since 1938.

Geissinger, John B., A.B.'27, Muhlenberg Col.; M.A.'29, Ph.D.'45, Univ. of Pa.; Supt. of Sch., Somerville, N. J., since 1952.

Gerace, Stephen J., Ed.M.'39, Rutgers Univ.; Supt. of Sch., Pompton Plains, N. J., since 1944.

Gibbs, Bert F., B.S.'15, Tchrs. Col., Columbia Univ.; Supt. of Sch., New Milford, N. J., since 1915.

Gifford, Nathan, B.S.'31, M.S.'34, Syracuse Univ.; Supt. of Morris Hills Regional Sch. Dist., Morris Co., Rockaway, N. J., since 1950.

Gill, J. Goodner, B.B.A.'34, Rider Col.; LL.D.'48, John Marshall Col.; Vicepres., Trustee and Registrar, Rider Col., Trenton, N. J., since 1942.

Gillespie, William K., B.S.'26, Pa. State Col.; A.M.'40, Univ. of Del.; Prin., H. S., Pompton Lakes, N. J., since 1950.

Gilliland, E. L., B.S. in Ed.'34, State Tchrs. Col., Lock Haven, Pa.; M.Ed.'37, Pa. State Col.; Supt. of Sch., Highland Park, N. J., since 1949.

Gold, Lentz D., Diploma '25, Philadelphia Museum Sch. of Indus. Art; Dir. of Fine and Indus. Arts, Pub. Sch., Atlantic City, N. J., since 1947.

Gorab, Joseph A., B.S. in Ed.'33, Ed.M.'40, Rutgers Univ.; Supt. of Sch., Totowa Boro' Memorial Sch., Paterson, N. J., since 1949.

Grant, William F., A.B.'20, Seton Hall Col.; M.A.'23, St. Peter's Col.; LL.B.'27, N. J. Law Sch.; Supt. of Sch., Harrison, N. J., since 1948.

Groezinger, Eric, A.B.'30, Westminster Col., New Wilmington, Pa.; M.A.'32, Univ. of Pa.; Co. Supt. of Sch., Flemington, N. J., since 1948.

Grover, Elbridge C., B.S.'15, Harvard Col.; M.A.'20, Tchrs. Col., Columbia Univ.; Ph.D. '25, Sch. of Educ., New York Univ.; Supt. of Sch., Fair Lawn, N. J., since 1948.

Haas, Charles A., B.S. in Ed.'32, N. J. State Tchrs Col., Trenton; M.Ed.'34, Rutgers Univ.; Asst. Dir., Middlesex Co. Voc. and Tech. H. S., Perth Amboy, N. J., since 1946.

Hacker, Ralph E., Sch. Architect, Hacker & Hacker, Fort Lee Trust Bldg., Fort Lee, N. J.

Halse, (Mrs.) Virginia A., Special Admin. Asst., Pub. Schs., Montclair, N. J., since 1946.

Hamilton, Charles Woods, B.C.S.'24, B.S. in Ed.'29, M.A.'32, New York Univ.; Exec. Asst. to the Commr., State Dept. of Educ., Trenton, N. J., since 1948.

Harney, Julia C., B.S.'18, A.M.'20, Ph.D.'31, New York Univ.; LL.D.'37, Col. of St. Elizabeth. Address: 302 Pavonia Ave., Jersey City, N. J.

Harshman, Floyd E., A.B.'14, Ohio Wesleyan Univ.; M.A.'26, Tchrs. Col., Columbia Univ.; Ph.D.'31, New York Univ.; Supt. of Sch., Nutley, N. J., since 1944.

*Hartman, Albert L., Prin., Edgemont and Watchung Schs., Montclair, N. J.

Hassard, Charles T., M.A.'27, Univ. of Pa.; Supt. of Twp. Sch., Union, N. J., since 1938.

Hehnly, Frank K., Diploma '19, State Tchrs. Col., Millersville, Pa.; B.S.'34, Ed.M.'36, Ed.D.'41, Rutgers Univ.; Supt. of Clark Twp. Sch., Rahway, N. J., since 1935.

Helmbold, John S., B.S.'30, M.S.'39, Univ. of Pa.; Supt. of Sch., Pleasantville, N. J., since 1950.

Herbst, William, M.Ed.'47, Temple Univ.; Prin., Cinnaminson Twp. Sch., Riverton, N. J., since 1948.

Herron, John S., B.S.'15, M.A.'18, New York Univ.; LL.D.'44, Seton Hall Col.; Supt. of Sch., Newark, N. J., since 1943.

Hess, Arnold M., Secy., Bd. of Educ., Newark, N. J.

Hibbs, M. Gregg, Jr., Litt.B.'28, M.Ed.'35, Ed.D.'46, Rutgers Univ.; Supt. of Sch., Red Bank, N. J., since 1949.

Hill, Harry Segner, A.B.'22, Wheaton Col. (Ill.); M.A.'27, Univ. of Pa.; Ed.D.'35, Rutgers Univ.; Supt. of Sch., Asbury Park, N. J., since 1944.

Hill, Walter Henry, B.S.'23, Gettysburg Col.; M.A.'31, Columbia Univ.; Supt. of Sch., Swedesboro, N. J., since 1923.

Hilleboe, Guy L., A.B.'20, Univ. of Minn.; A.M.'28, Ph.D.'30, Tchrs. Col., Columbia Univ.; Supt. of Sch., Rutherford, N. J., since 1938.

Hipp, Frederick L., B.S. in Ed.'33, Bowling Green State Univ.; M.S.'36, Ed.D.'39, Syracuse Univ.; Exec. Secy., New Jersey Educ. Assn., Trenton, N. J., since 1946.

Hochstuhl, Frank J., Jr., Secy. and Bus. Mgr., Bd. of Educ., Bloomfield, N. J., since 1927.

Hodgins, George W., B.A.'31, M.A.'46, N. J. State Tchrs. Col., Upper Montclair; Supt. of Sch., Paramus, N. J., since 1950.

Hoffman, Harold F., Ed.M.'34, Ed.D.'50, Univ. of Buffalo; Supt. of Sch., Leonia, N. J., since 1947.

Holbert, William R., Ph.B.'14, Lafayette Col.; M.A.'25, Univ. of Pa.; Supt. of Sch., North Arlington, N. J., since 1935.

Hollinger, John R., Diploma '10, State Tchrs. Col., West Chester, Pa.; Owner-Mgr., Madison Hotel, Atlantic City, N. J., since 1930.

Hollingsworth, Henry T., B.S.'18, Wash. Col.; M.A.'23, Columbia Univ.; LL.B'28, N. J. Law Sch.; Supt. of Sch., Bloomfield, N. J., since 1942.

Hollobaugh, E. E., B.S.'23, M.Ed.'37, Pa. State Col.; Supt. of Sch., Franklin, N. J., since 1948.

Howe, Joseph William, A.B.'28, Juniata Col.; M.A.'32, Tchrs. Col., Columbia Univ.; Ed.D. '50, Rutgers Univ.; Supt. of Sch., Burlington, N. J., since 1946.

Huber, Clyde M., A.B.'22, Pa. State Col.; A.M.'24, Ph.D.'26, Univ. of Ill.; Dean of Instr., State Tchrs. Col., Upper Montclair, N. J., since 1951.

Irwin, Forrest A., B.S.'15, Northwestern Univ.; A.M.'26, Columbia Univ.; Pres., N. J. State Tchrs. Col., Jersey City, N. J., since 1946.

Jenkins, Albion Urban, B.S.'13, A.M.'16, Columbia Univ.; Asst. Supt. of Sch., Newark, N. J., since 1944.

Jenkins, Robert E., A.B.'32, Columbia Univ.; A.M.'38, Ed.D.'47, Tchrs. Col., Columbia Univ.; Supt. of Sch., Ridgewood, N. J., since 1952.

Jochen, Albert E., Litt.B.'29, M.Ed.'32, Ed.D.'47, Rutgers Univ.; Dir., Co. Voc. and Tech. H. S., New Brunswick, N. J., since 1946.

Johnson, Burt P., B.A.'30, Univ. of N. C.; M.A.'39, Columbia Univ.; Ed.D.'47, Tchrs. Col., Columbia Univ.; Supt. of Sch., Tenafly, N. J., since 1951.

Jones, Paul R., B.S.'28, State Tchrs. Col., Mansfield, Pa.; M.A.'31, Tchrs. Col., Columbia Univ.; Supt. of Sch., Moorestown, N. J., since 1946.

Judd, Arthur M., B.S. in Ed.'40, Rutgers Univ.; Supt. of Twp. Sch., New Brunswick, N. J., since 1927.

Kelly, (Mrs.) May, Secy., Elem. Div., and Vice-pres., Advisers Assn., Columbia Scholastic Press Assn. Address: 3028 N. Harding Ave., Margate City, N. J.

Kennelly, Edward F., A.B.'25, Col. of the Holy Cross; LL.B.'29, Fordham Univ.; A.M.'38, Seton Hall Col.; Ed.D.'43, New York Univ.; Asst. Supt. of Sch., in chg. of Personnel, Newark, N. J., since 1950.

Kent, Ronald W., A.B.'13, Ind. Univ.; Ph.D.'31, New York Univ.; Dir., Essex Co. Voc. Sch., Newark, N. J., since 1944.

Kentopp, Henry Eugene, B.A.'21, Midland Col.; M.A.'30, Univ. of Wis.; D.Ed.'40, Tchrs. Col., Columbia Univ.; Supt. of Sch., East Orange, N. J., since 1936.

Kershner, T. Franklin, B.S. in Ed.'43, N. J. State Tchrs. Col., Trenton; M.Ed.'44, Temple Univ.; Supt. of Sch., Clayton, N. J., since 1948.

Klauminzer, Frederick A., B.S. in Ed.'29, M.Ed. '37, Rutgers Univ.; Supt., Vineland State Sch., Vineland, N. J.

Knight, Edward R., B.A.'40, LL.B.'41, Univ. of Wis.; M.A.'42, Ph.D.'43, New York Univ.; Headmaster, Oxford Acad., Pleasantville, N. J., since 1947.

Knight, Russell, B.S. in Ed. '32, M.Ed.'35, Rutgers Univ.; Supt. of Twp. Sch., Erlton, N. J., since 1934.

Kraus, Edwin W., B.S.'44, N. J. State Tchrs. Col., Glassboro; M.E.'47, Rutgers Univ.; Supt., Harding Sch., Kenilworth, N. J., since 1944.

Kreps, Melvin H., B.S. in Ed.'30, State Tchrs. Col., Shippensburg, Pa.; Ed.M.'36, Temple Univ.; Supt. of East Windsor Pub. Sch., Hightstown, N. J., since 1950.

Krom, Edward F., B.S.'31, Rutgers Univ.; M.A. '34, Tchrs. Col., Columbia Univ.; Supt. of Sch., Carlstadt, N. J., since 1932.

Kuhn, Ralph E., B.S.'42, N. J. State Tchrs. Col., Glassboro; Ed.M.'48, Temple Univ.; Supt., Walnut St. Sch., Delanco, N. J., since 1950.

Kuntzelman, Harvey A., B.S.'25, Wesleyan Univ.; M.Ed.'39, Rutgers Univ.; Supt. of Sch., Dover, N. J., since 1944.

Lautenschlager, Charles, B.S. in Ed.'36, N. J. State Tchrs. Col., Newark; M.Ed.'50, Rutgers Univ.; Asst. Dir. of Indus. Educ., Jersey City, N. J., since 1950.

LaVigne, Bernard E., B.S.'29, New York Univ.; M.A.'33, Tchrs. Col., Columbia Univ.; Asst. Supt. of Sch., Montclair, N. J., since 1946.

Lawrence, Edgar P., A.B.'20, Dickinson Col.; A.M.'23, Tchrs. Col., Columbia Univ.; Supvr. of Curriculum, Augusta St. Sch., Irvington, N. J., since 1952.

Leeds, Albert M., B.S. in Ed.'32, M.S. in Ed.'34, Rutgers Univ.; Supt. of Sch., Franklinville, N. J., since 1929.

Leonard, Mary A., M.A.'40, New York Univ.; Supvr. of Elem. Educ., Elizabeth, N. J., since 1944.

Libby, Herschel Scott, B.Ped.'16, Univ. of Maine; M.A.'32, Ed.D.'49, New York Univ.; Supt. of Sch., Irvington, N. J., since 1934.

Littel, Charles L., A.B.'12, Univ. of Nebr.; A.M.'26, Stanford Univ.; Ed.D.'35, New York Univ.; Pres., Bergen Jr. Col., Teaneck, N. J., since 1933.

Loser, Paul, Ph.B.'13, Litt.D.'41, Muhlenberg Col.; M.A.'25, Tchrs. Col., Columbia Univ.; Supt. of Sch., Trenton, N. J., since 1932.

Lott, Leigh M., B.A.'26, Wesleyan Univ.; M.A. '32, Univ. of Pa.; Ph.D.(Hon.)'46, Univ. of Vienna; Supt. of Sch., Hackettstown, N. J., since 1946.

Lutz, Leon C., A.B.'22, Univ. of Pa.; Supt. of Sch., Glassboro, N. J., since 1950.

Lynch, J. M., Ph.D.'38, New York Univ.; Supt. of Sch., Middlebush, N. J., since 1947.

McClellan, George B., A.B.'34, Pa. State Col.; M.Ed.'41, Temple Univ.; Ph.D.'52, Columbia Univ.; Supt. of Sch., Ridgefield, N. J., since 1948.

McDermith, Clark Wright, A.B.'29, Ill. Col.; A.M.'34, Univ. of Ill.; Ed.D.'40, Tchrs. Col., Columbia Univ.; Supt. of Sch., Passaic, N. J., since 1946.

McFeely, Thomas F., B.S.'34, Villanova Col.; LL.B.'43, John Marshall Law Col.; M.A.'44, Tchrs. Col., Columbia Univ.; Supt. of Sch., Hoboken, N. J., since 1944.

McGinnis, W. C., B.S., Univ. of Vt.; A.M., Ph.D., Columbia Univ.; Supt. of Sch., Perth Amboy, N. J., since 1930.

McGreal, Michael R., B.S.'16, Univ. of N. H.; M.A.'29, New York Univ.; Asst. Supt. in charge of Sec. Sch., Bd. of Educ., Newark, N. J., since 1945.

McHugh, Thomas F., A.M.'34, New York Univ.; Asst. Supt. of Sch., Newark, N. J., since 1944.

McLean, William, B.S.'24, Tchrs. Col., Columbia Univ.; M.A.'27, Columbia Univ.; Prin., Mt. Hebron Sch., Upper Montclair, N. J., 1922-52 (retired). Address: 190 Fernwood Ave., Upper Montclair, N. J.

McLeary, Ralph D., B.S.'24, M.A.'30, Colby Col.; Supt. of Sch., Plainfield, N. J., since 1950.

McMackin, Frank J., B.A.'13, Ph.D.'16, Columbia Univ.; Pres., Jersey City Jr. Col., Jersey City, N. J., since 1946.

Marvin, William B., Litt.B.'18, Princeton Univ.; Supt. of Sch., Cape May, N. J.

Mason, William H., Jr., B.S.'34, M.A.'36, Tchrs. Col., Columbia Univ.; Co. Supt. of Sch., Morristown, N. J., since 1941.

457

Matthews, Willard B., B.S. in Ed.'31, State Tchrs. Col., West Chester, Pa.; M.S. in Ed.'41, Univ. of Pa.; Co. Supt. of Sch., Cape May, N. J., since 1945.

Medes, E. Harold, B.S.'23, Tchrs. Col., Columbia Univ.; LL.B.'38, John Marshall Col. of Law; Supt. of Sch., Fairview, N. J., since 1946.

Merity, Howard E., A.B.'26, Seton Hall Col.; M.A.'32, Ed.D.'36, New York Univ.; Supt. of Sch., Bayonne, N. J., since 1941.

Merritt, Harold I., B.S. in C.E.'24, Cooper Union; B.S. in Genl.Ed.'29, M.A. in Ed. Adm.'34, Columbia Univ.; Supt. of Haddon Sch., Westmont, N. J., since 1938.

Mertching, (Mrs.) R. A., B.S. in Ed.'34, New York Univ.; Supt. of Sch., Oradell, N. J., since 1945.

Miller, W. A., Jr., A.B.'36, Susquehanna Univ.; M.S.'42, Bucknell Univ.; Supt. of Sch., Dunellen, N. J., since 1949.

Milligan, John Padgett, A.B.'26, Dickinson Col.; Ed.M.'32, Ed.D.'37, Rutgers Univ.; Supt. of Sch., Atlantic City, N. J., since 1950.

Mongon, John E., B.A.'31, M.A.'40, Seton Hall Col.; Co. Supt. of Sch., Mt. Holly, N. J.

Morehead, Allan, A.B.'34, A.M.'41, State Tchrs. Col., Upper Montclair, N. J.; N. J. State Tchrs. Col., Upper Montclair, N. J.

Moreland, Jerre F., A.B.'25, Univ. of Colo.; M.A.'30, Colo. State Col. of Educ.; Ed.D.'40, Tchrs. Col., Columbia Univ.; Supt. of Sch., Florence, N. J., since 1940.

Morgan, Clarence B., B.S.'42, State Tchrs. Col., Glassboro, N. J.; M.E.'48, Temple Univ.; Supt. of Twp. Sch., Gibbstown, N. J., since 1942.

Morgenroth, George W., B.S. in M.E.'28, Cooper Union; B.S. in Ed.'45, Rutgers Univ.; M.A. in Ed.'46, New York Univ.; Asst. Dir., Essex Co. Voc. Sch., Newark, N. J., since 1947.

Morris, Howard, Jr., B.S.'39, State Tchrs. Col., Trenton, N. J.; M.Ed.'47, Temple Univ.; Supt. of Sch., Verga, N. J., since 1951.

Morrison, Howard D., B.S.'26, Columbia Univ.; M.S.'33, Univ. of Pa.; Supt. of Sch. of Hamilton Twp. (P. O. Trenton 10, N. J.), since 1939.

Morrison, Robert H., B.A.'23, Mich. State Normal Col., Ypsilanti; M.A.'26, Colo. State Col. of Educ.; Ph.D.'33, Tchrs. Col., Columbia Univ.; Asst. Commr. for Higher Educ., State Dept. of Pub. Instr., Trenton, N. J., since 1945.

Moshier, Stephen W., B.S.'32, M.A.'36, Tchrs. Col., Columbia Univ.; Supt. of Sch., Hawthorne, N. J., since 1939.

Moulton, Onsville Joshua, B.A.'14, Bates Col.; Ed.M.'32, Harvard Univ.; Ed.D.'37, New York Univ. Address: Old Corlies Ave., Neptune, N. J.

Mueller, Ernest J., B.S.'43, N. J. State Tchrs. Col., Paterson; M.A.'48, N. J. State Tchrs. Col., Upper Montclair; Prin., Coolidge Sch., Wyckoff, N. J., since 1951.

Munson, Ruth W., B.S.'36, Tchrs. Col., Columbia Univ.; Prin., Jefferson Sch., Maplewood, N. J., since 1941.

Murray, Norman J. M., B.S.'37, William and Mary Col.; M.A.'49, Tchrs. Col., Columbia Univ. Address: 14 Country Club Ter., Springfield, N. J.

Muschell, Charles S., M.A.'32, Tchrs. Col., Columbia Univ.; Supt. of Sch., Westwood, N. J., since 1946.

Neulen, Leon N., A.B.'16, St. Olaf Col.; M.A.'22, Ph.D.'31, Columbia Univ.; Ped.D.'37, Temple Univ.; Supt. of Sch., Camden, N. J., since 1931.

Neulen, Lester N., B.A.'16, St. Olaf Col.; M.A. '23, Ph.D.'28, Columbia Univ.; Supt. of Twp. Sch., Teaneck, N. J., since 1928.

Newswanger, B. F., B.S.'29, New York Univ.; M.A.'33, Tchrs. Col., Columbia Univ.; Supt. of Sch., Springfield, N. J., since 1948.

Nicklas, Victor C., B.A.'17, Univ. of Pittsburgh; M.A.'23, Tchrs. Col., Columbia Univ.; Supt. of Sch., Woodbridge, N. J., since 1933.

Nicolello, Louis L. D., A.B.'29, Syracuse Univ.; M.A.'41, New York Univ.; Prin., Newark, N. J., since 1952.

Northrup, Charles M., B.S.'34, Iowa State Tchrs. Col., Cedar Falls; M.S.'49, Drake Univ. Address: 21 East 201st St., Orange, N. J.

Oberholser, Robert M., Ph.B.'12, Franklin and Marshall Col.; A.M.'24, Univ. of Pa.; Supt. of Sch., Bordentown, N. J., since 1919.

O'Brien, Richard J., B.A.'32, Seton Hall Col.; M.A.'36, Fordham Univ.; D.Ed.'45, New York Univ.; Assoc. Supt. of Sch., Jersey City, N. J., since 1949.

O'Connor, Paul D., B.S.'24, Niagara Univ.; M.A.'41, New York Univ.; Supt. of Sch., Allendale, N. J., since 1941.

Olson, Edwin C., Ph.B.'19, Yale Univ.; M.A.'32, Columbia Univ.; Supt. of Sch., Lyndhurst, N. J., since 1950.

Osborn, George H., Jr., B.A.'32, Maryville Col.; M.A.'35, N. J. State Tchrs. Col., Upper Montclair; Supt. of Twp. Sch., Hopewell, N. J., since 1952.

Parker, Albert C., M.A.'27, Columbia Univ. Address: 4547 Brown St., Union City, N. J.

Parker, Robert C. B., B.S.'30, M.A.'35, Rutgers Univ.; Supt. of Sch., Madison, N. J., since 1940.

Parks, Leonard Radcliffe, B.S. in Ed.'32, Rutgers Univ.; M.A.'47, Tchrs. Col., Columbia Univ.; Supt. of Sch., Cedar Grove, N. J., since 1937.

Partch, Clarence E., B.S. in Mech. Eng.'09, Univ. of Mich.; Ed.M.'25, Ed.D.'26, Harvard Univ.; Dean, Sch. of Educ., Rutgers Univ., New Brunswick, N. J., since 1927.

Partridge, Ernest DeAlton, B.S.'30, Brigham Young Univ.; Ph.D.'34, Tchrs. Col., Columbia Univ.; Pres., State Tchrs. Col., Montclair, N. J., since 1951.

Pate, Wylie G., B.S.'21, Washington and Jefferson Col.; M.A.'26, Univ. of Pa.; Ed.D.'36, Rutgers Univ.; Supt. of Middletown Twp. Sch., Leonardo, N. J., since 1938.

Patterson, Harry E., B.S.'29, New York Univ.; Supt. of Sch., Elberon, N. J.

Peters, Mary V., B.S.'39, N. J. State Tchrs. Col., Glassboro; Supt. of Sch., Ventnor, N. J., since 1937.

Pierce, Charles B., A.B.'32, Franklin and Marshall Col.; M.A.'37, Ph.D.'42, Univ. of Pittsburgh; Supt. of Sch., Ocean City, N. J., since 1950.

Pollack, Richard S., B.S.'31, Mass. Inst. of Tech.; M.Ed.'40, D.Ed.'42, Temple Univ.; Supt. of Sch., Sayreville, N. J., since 1945.

Pratt, Harry H., B.S.'22, Rutgers Univ.; M.Ed. '34, Temple Univ.; Supt. of Sch., Trenton, N. J., since 1950.

Preston, Everett C., B.S.'21, Mass. State Col.; M.Ed.'26, Harvard Univ.; Ph.D.'36, Tchrs. Col., Columbia Univ.; Dir., Div. of Adult Educ., State Dept. of Educ., Trenton, N. J., since 1944.

Purcell, Earl E., A.B.'18, Lafayette Col.; M.A.'29, Tchrs. Col., Columbia Univ.; Supt. of Sch., Bogota, N. J., since 1944.

Quimby, Joseph H., B.S.'35, N. J. State Tchrs. Col., Newark; M.A.'46, N. J. State Tchrs. Col., Upper Montclair; Supt. of Sch., East Paterson, N. J., since 1952.

Quin, Edwin S., B.S.'31, Fordham Univ.; M.A.'40, Columbia Univ.; Supt., H. S., Carteret, N. J., since 1948.

*Race, Stuart R., A.B.'11, Lafayette Col.; A.M.'27, New York Univ.; Supt. of Sch., Newton, N. J., since 1941.

Ragg, H. Joseph, Jr., B.Ed.'36, M.Ed.'43, Rutgers Univ.; Supt., West Milford Twp. Sch., Newfoundland, N. J., since 1948.

Ramsay, William W., B.S.'42, N. J. State Tchrs. Col., Jersey City; M.A.'48, New York Univ.; Prin. of Pub. Schs., Union Beach, N. J., since 1949.

Raubinger, Frederick M., B.S.'30, Southwest Mo. State Tchrs. Col.; M.A.'40, Ed.D.'47, Tchrs. Col., Columbia Univ.; State Commr. of Educ., Trenton, N. J., since 1952.

Reed, Roberts V. S., B.Ed.'26, R. I. Col. of Educ., Providence; M.A.'35, Tchrs. Col., Columbia Univ.; Supt. of Sch., Summit, N. J., since 1947.

Reeve, Howard, B.S.'37, M.A.'41, New York Univ.; Supt. of Sch., Little Falls, N. J., since 1937.

Reilly, Joseph G., Prin., Fairmount Sch. 4, Hackensack, N. J.

Reynolds, James E., A.B.'15, Litt.D.'47, St. Peter's Col.; Supt. of Sch., Jersey City, N. J., since 1947.

Reynolds, William W., A.B.'24, M.A.'29, Lafayette Col.; Supt. of Sch., Haddonfield, N. J., since 1944.

Rice, Harry M., A.B.'26, Ph.D.'48, Susquehanna Univ.; M.A.'31, Columbia Univ.; Prin., Sr. H. S., Bloomfield, N. J., since 1941.

Rickards, Edward S., B.S.'35, Univ. of N. C.; M.A.'42, Columbia Univ.; Supt. of Sch., Milltown, N. J., since 1949.

Ricketts, (Mrs.) Ella S., B.S.'30, M.A.'35, New York Univ.; Supt. of Sch., Belmar, N. J., since 1936.

Roberts, Allen W., B.S. in Ed.'37, N. J. State Tchrs. Col., Newark; M.Ed.'41, Rutgers Univ.; Supt. of Sch., New Providence, N. J., since 1937.

Robbins, Chester, A.B.'13, Ursinus Col.; A.M. '22, Univ. of Pa.; Asst. State Commr. of Educ., Trenton, N. J., since 1942.

Robinson, Richard J., B.A.'31, Lehigh Univ.; M.Ed.'34, D.Ed.'48, Rutgers Univ.; Asst. to the Supt. of Sch., Trenton, N. J., since 1952.

Robinson, Thomas E., B.A.'26, Lehigh Univ.; M.A.'31, Univ. of Pa.; D.Ed.'40, Rutgers Univ.; Pres., State Tchrs. Col., Glassboro, N. J., since 1952.

Rodgers, J. Harvey, A.B.'20, Franklin and Marshall Col.; Ed.M.'21, Harvard Univ.; Co. Supt. of Sch., Woodbury, N. J., since 1933.

Rowland, Maurice William, B.A.'29, Univ. of Denver; M.A.'36, Tchrs. Col., Columbia Univ.; Supt. of Sch., New Brunswick, N. J., since 1949.

Rozema, John R., Supt. of Sch., Garfield, N. J.

Ruggieri, Joseph M., M.E.'36, Rutgers Univ.; Supt. of Raritan Twp. Sch., Fords, N. J., since 1947.

Sandilos, James C., B.S. in Ed.'49, M.Ed.'50, Temple Univ.; Supvg. Prin., West Windsor Twp. Sch. Dist., Dutch Neck, N. J., since 1952.

Saunders, Carleton M., Ph.B.'29, Yale Col.; M.A.'38, Ed.D.'40, Tchrs. Col., Columbia Univ.; Supt. of Bridgewater Twp. Sch., Raritan, N. J., since 1942.

Schmerber, Louis J., B.S.'27, New York Univ.; M.A.'45, N. J. State Tchrs Col., Upper Montclair; Supt. of Sch., Paterson, N. J., since 1944.

Schneider, Edward T., B.S.'33, M.A.'36, Ed.D. '44, New York Univ.; Supt., Regional H. S. Dist. 1, Little Falls, N. J., since 1946.

Schoenly, G. Austin, Supt. of Sch., Spotswood, N. J.

Schotland, Joseph H., B.S.'16, Cooper Union Inst. of Tech.; C.E.'17, Brooklyn Polytechnic Inst.; A.M.'18, Columbia Univ.; Ph.D.'37, New York Univ.; Asst. Supt. of Sch., Newark, N. J., since 1944.

Schreiber, Ernest, B.S. in Ed.'36, State Tchrs. Col., Millersville, Pa.; M.Ed.'39, Pa. State Col.; Supt. of Sch., Audubon, N. J., since 1949.

Schultz, Joseph L., A.B.'24, George Washington Univ.; M.A.'28, Ph.D.'38, Univ. of Pa.; Supt. of Sch., Millville, N. J., since 1945.

Shambaugh, John B., B.S.'19, Franklin and Marshall Col.; Supt. of Twp. Sch., Succasunna, N. J., since 1920.

Shershin, William F., B.S.'40, Ed.M.'41, Rutgers Univ.; Supt. of Sch., Clifton, N. J., since 1950.

Shoff, Robert C., B.S. in Ed.'37, State Tchrs. Col., Millersville, Pa.; M.Ed.'42, Pa. State Col.; Supt. of Twp. Sch., Riverside, N. J., since 1949.

Shuck, Albert C., A.B.'11, A.M.'12, Dickinson Col.; Co. Supt. of Sch., Salem, N. J., since 1931.

Shue, J. Harvey, B.S.'27, Franklin and Marshall Col.; M.A.'32, Columbia Univ.; Supt. of Sch., Livingston, N. J., since 1950.

*Shugart, Lehman C., A.B.'27, Ind. Univ.; M.S.'31, Lehigh Univ.; Asst. Supt. of Sch., Elizabeth, N. J., since 1949.

Skean, A. H., B.S.'14, Muhlenberg Col.; Mgr., The Convention Bureau, 16 Central Pier, Atlantic City, N. J.

Slocum, Clyde W., M.A.'33, N. Y. State Col. for Tchrs.; Supt. of Sch., Toms River, N. J., since 1950.

Smith, Donald R., B.S. in Ed.'43, State Tchrs. Col., Trenton, N. J.; M.Ed.'51, Rutgers Univ.; Tchr., Monroe Twp. Sch., Jamesburg, N. J., since 1951.

Smith, H. Edmond, B.S.'32, State Tchrs. Col., Bloomsburg, Pa.; M.S.'38, Temple Univ.; Supt. of Palmyra Borough Sch., Palmyra, N. J., since 1952.

Smith, Hubert H., A.B.'15, Wabash Col.; M.A. '26, Tchrs. Col., Columbia Univ.; Supt. of Sch., Hammonton, N. J., since 1926.

Smith, LeRoy, Dir. of Health Educ. and Physically Handicapped Children, Trenton Pub. Sch., Trenton, N. J., since 1947.

Smith, Sampson G., B.S.'25, Ind. State Tchrs. Col., Terre Haute; M.A.'37, Tchrs. Col., Columbia Univ.; Co. Supt. of Sch., Somerville, N. J., since 1945.

Smith, Sarah K., B.S.'43, M.A.'45, Seton Hall Col.; Viceprin. of Sch., Jersey City, N. J., since 1948.

Snyder, H. Jacob, B.S.Ed.'49, State Tchrs. Col., East Stroudsburg, Pa.; Supvr., Twp. Sch., Bedminster, N. J., since 1951.

Sosted, Harold A., B.Ed.'30, State Tchrs. Col., Eau Claire, Wis.; Ph.M.'39, Univ. of Wis.; Prin., Pub. Sch., Essex Fells, N. J., since 1951.

Spencer, Paul R., B.A.'16, Univ. of Wis.; M.A. '20, Ph.D.'29, Tchrs. Col., Columbia Univ.; Prin., Central H. S., Trenton, N. J., since 1935.

Spragg, Charles L., B.S.'32, State Tchrs. Col., West Chester, Pa.; Ed.M.'40, Rutgers Univ.; Supt. of Sch., Egg Harbor City, N. J., since 1949.

Spurr, Ethel M., B.A.'19, Radcliffe Col.; M.A.'24, Columbia Univ.; Prin., The Kimberley Sch., Montclair, N. J., since 1950.

Stager, Christian, Jr., Prin., Pub. Sch., Sparta, N. J.

Stearns, Harry Lee, A.B.'22, Dickinson Col.; M.A.'29, Univ. of Pittsburgh; Ph.D.'36, New York Univ.; Supt. of Sch., Englewood, N. J., since 1944.

Steel, Charles L., Jr., B.S.'19, Muhlenberg Col.; Prin., H. S., Teaneck, N. J., since 1933.

Stover, Frank B., B.A.'31, M.A.'32, Wesleyan Univ.; Co. Supt. of Sch., Newark, N. J., since 1950.

Stover, William R., B.S. in Ed.'37, Ed.M.'40, Temple Univ.; Supt. of Sch., Pennsauken, N. J., since 1947.

Stratton, Mason A., B.S. in Ed.'28, New York Univ.; Ed.M.'46, Temple Univ.; Co. Supt. of Sch., Mays Landing, N. J., since 1946.

Straub, J. Harold, B.S. in Ed.'32, M.A.'33, Ed.D.'36, N. Y. Univ.; Co. Supt. of Sch., Paterson, N. J., since 1949.

Stuart, Harry G., B.S.'11, Muhlenberg Col.; A.M.'34, Tchrs. Col., Columbia Univ.; Supt. of Sch., Bernardsville, N. J., 1930-52 (retired).

Stumpf, Phillip Q., A.B.'21, Franklin and Marshall Col.; M.S.'47, Temple Univ.; Supt. of Sch., Paulsboro, N. J., since 1951.

Sullivan, Richard Howard, A.B.'39, Harvard Col.; A.M.'40, Harvard Univ.; Exec. Vicepres. and Treas., Educ. Testing Service, Princeton, N. J.

Sutton, Helen P., B.S.'36, M.A.'39, New York Univ.; Vicepres., J. W. Wakeman Sch., Jersey City, N. J., since 1934.

Swaim, Laura Grey, Ed.M.'38, Temple Univ.; Supt. of Sch., Maple Shade, N. J., since 1922.

Taylor, Charles H., B.S. in Ed.'38, N. J. State Tchrs. Col., Paterson; M.E.Adm. and Sup.'40, Rutgers Univ.; Supt. of Sch., Midland Park, N. J., since 1948.

Thomas, Evan H., A.B.'29, Lafayette Col.; M.Ed.'35, Rutgers Univ.; Supt. of Sch., Belleville, N. J., since 1951.

Thompson, James B., B.S.'12, Colby Col.; M.A.'27, Tchrs. Col., Columbia Univ.; Supt. of Sch., Ft. Lee, N. J., since 1933.

Threlkeld, Curtis H., B.S.'21, Northeast Mo. State Tchrs. Col.; A.M.'27, Tchrs. Col., Columbia Univ.; Supt. of South Orange and Maplewood Sch., Maplewood, N. J., since 1943.

Tink, Edmund L., B.A.'23, Lawrence Col.; M.A.'27, Ph.D.'29, Tchrs. Col., Columbia Univ.; Supt. of Sch., Kearny, N. J., since 1932.

Tomlinson, Allan, B.S. in Ed.'35, State Tchrs. Col., Shippensburg, Pa.; M.Ed.'39, Temple Univ.; Supt., Penns Grove-Upper Penns Neck Sch. Dist., Penns Grove, N. J., since 1949.

Trowbridge, John E., B.S. in Ed.'30, State Tchrs. Col., Mansfield, Pa.; Ed.M.'34, Rutgers Univ.; Prin., Cranbury Sch., Cranbury, N. J., since 1947.

Tustin, James F., A.B.'22, Dickinson Col.; A.M.'27, Tchrs. Col., Columbia Univ.; LL.B. '32, N. J. Law Sch.; Supt. of Sch., South Amboy, N. J., since 1940.

Twichell, Jack B., B.S.'32, M.A.'34, Tchrs. Col., Columbia Univ.; Mercer Co. Supt. of Sch., Trenton, N. J., since 1952.

Van Houten, Robert W., B.S. in C.E.'30, C.E.'32, Newark Col. of Engineering; Dean, Newark Col. of Engineering, Newark, N. J., since 1943, and Pres., since 1950.

Van Nuys, Jay C., Architect, 1 W. Main St., Somerville, N. J., since 1938.

Walton, L. Arthur, B.S.'20, Ursinus Col.; A.M. '24, Univ. of Pa.; Supt. of Sch., Pitman, N. J., since 1941.

Warwick, Raymond, B.S.'32, M.S.'38, Rutgers Univ.; Prin., Bradley Park Sch., Neptune, N. J., since 1932.

West, Roscoe L., A.B.'14, Ed.M.'23, Harvard Univ.; Pres., State Tchrs. Col., Trenton, N. J., since 1930.

West, William H., B.Act.'31, B.Ed. in Commerce '32, Rider Col.; M.Ed.'37, Rutgers Univ.; Supt. of Sch., Belvidere, N. J., since 1945.

Whilden, Charles Steelman, B.S. in Ed.'39, N. J. State Tchrs. Col., Glassboro; M.E.'43, Temple Univ.; Supt. of Sch., Upper Freehold Twp., Allentown, N. J., since 1952.

Wightman, Clair S., A.B.'20, Syracuse Univ.; M.A.'24, Columbia Univ.; Ph.D.'34, New York Univ.; Pres., N. J. State Tchrs. Col., Paterson, N. J., since 1937.

Wilkins, Eugene G., A.B.'26, North Texas State Col.; M.A.'29, Ph.D.'37, Tchrs. Col., Columbia Univ.; Pres., N. J. State Tchrs. Col., Newark, N. J., since 1950.

Williams, George B., Dist. Clerk, Pub. Sch., Glen Ridge, N. J., since 1938.

Wilson, Walter E., B.S.'37, N. J. State Tchrs. Col., Newark; M.S.'42, Rutgers Univ.; Supvg. Prin. of Sch., Jamesburg, N. J.

Winans, S. David, A.B.'37, Temple Univ.; B.S. in Ed.'37, N. J. State Tchrs. Col., Glassboro; Ed.M.'48, Rutgers Univ.; Supv. of Research, Div. of Higher Educ., State Dept. of Educ., Trenton, N. J., since 1947.

Winchell, Lawrence Romie, B.S.'25, City Col. of the City of N. Y.; M.A.'29, Tchrs. Col., Columbia Univ.; D.Ed.'37, Rutgers Univ.; Co. Supt. of Sch., Bridgeton, N. J., since 1942.

Wolbach, Charles A., A.B.'18, Lehigh Univ.; M.A.'24, Tchrs. Col., Columbia Univ.; Ph.D. '34, New York Univ.; Supt. of Sch., Rumson, N. J., since 1934.

Wood, John A., 3rd, B.S.'15, Princeton Univ.; Secy., Tchrs. Pension and Annuity Fund, Trenton, N. J., since 1925.

Woodbury, Kenneth Foster, B.A.'24, Univ. of Maine; M.A.'33, Tchrs. Col., Columbia Univ.; Asst. Commr. and Supv. of Bus. Affairs, State Dept. of Educ., Trenton, N. J.

Woolf, Kenneth A., A.B.'27, Lafayette Col.; M.A.'32, Ed.D.'42, New York Univ.; Supt. of Twp. Sch., Mountain View, N. J., since 1946.

Workman, David Frank, B.S.'25, M.A.'29, Franklin and Marshall Col.; M.A.'29, Tchrs. Col., Columbia Univ.; Supt. of Sch., Waldwick, N. J., since 1927.

Worrall, John R., B.S.'32, Allegheny Col.; M.Ed.'39, Univ. of Pittsburgh; H. S. Prin., Woodbury, N. J., since 1947.

Yost, Frank L., A.M.'12, Bucknell Univ.; Supt. of Sch., Orange, N. J., since 1949.

Zimmerman, Frederick, A.B.'39, Columbia Col.; M.A.'41, N. J. State Tchrs. Col., Upper Montclair; Supt. of Sch., Hohokus, N. J., since 1948.

Zimmerman, Roy R., A.B.'28, M.A.'32, Tchrs. Col., Columbia Univ.; Co. Supt. of Sch., Hackensack, N. J., since 1934.

Zorella, John W., B.S.'31, Pa. State Col.; M.Ed. '37, Rutgers Univ.; M.A.'48, Columbia Univ.; Supt. of Sch., Manville, N. J., since 1937.

INSTITUTIONAL MEMBERS

Benjamin Franklin Junior High School, Ridgewood, N. J.

Board of Education, Hackensack, N. J.

Bogota High School, Bogota, N. J.

Bridgeton Public Schools, Bridgeton, N. J.

Edgemont School, Montclair, N. J.

George Washington Elementary School, Ridgewood, N. J.

George Washington Junior High School, Ridgewood, N. J.

Hackensack Teachers Association, c/o Supt. of Sch., Hackensack, N. J.

Harrison Avenue Elementary School, Ridgewood, N. J.

Kenilworth Elementary School, Ridgewood, N. J.

Montclair High School, Montclair, N. J.

Montclair Public School Teachers Association, George Inness Jr. H. S., Montclair, N. J.

Princeton Survey, Bernice Cloutier, Librarian, Princeton Univ., Princeton, N. J.

Public Library, 5 Washington St., Newark, N. J.

Public Schools, Lyndhurst, N. J.

Ridgewood High School, Ridgewood, N. J.

Tenafly High School, Clifford L. Rall, Prin., Tenafly, N. J.

Union Street Elementary School, Ridgewood, N. J.

Watchung School, Montclair, N. J.

Willard Elementary School, Ridgewood, N. J.

NEW MEXICO

INDIVIDUAL MEMBERS

Alexander, Harold Everett, A.B.'22, Univ. of Colo.; M.A.'45, Univ. of N. Mex.; Supt. of Sch., Grants, N. Mex., since 1945.

Allbee, Lewis, A.B.'36, A.M.'40, Middlebury Col.; Ph.D. Yale Univ.; Asst. Supt. of Sch., Los Alamos, N. Mex., since 1952.

Allen, Eugene V., M.A.'39, Okla. A. & M. Col.; Supt. of Sch., Greenville, N. Mex., since 1951.

Alvis, Berry N., Supt. of Sch., Clayton, N. Mex., since 1950.

*Ambrose, Philip S., B.S.'41, Georgetown Univ.; M.A.'46, Ed.D.'49, Tchrs. Col., Columbia Univ.; Asst. Dir., Col. Instr. Center, Carlsbad, N. Mex.

Angel, (Mrs.) Tonie L., B.S. in Ed.'40, Univ. of N. Mex.; Co. Supt. of Sch., Las Vegas, N. Mex., since 1950.

Barlow, Nathan J., B.S.'24, Univ. of Utah; M.S. '46, Univ. of Southern Calif.; Dir. of Educ., State Dept. of Educ., Santa Fe, N. Mex., since 1951.

Beggs, Vernon L., M.A.'32, Ph.D.'36, Univ. of Chicago; Dir. of Sch., United Pueblos Agency, Albuquerque, N. Mex., since 1945.

Bibo, Nell Heard, B.S.'41, Central State Col., (Okla.); Educationist, United Pueblos Agency, Federal Indian Sch., Albuquerque, N. Mex., since 1945.

Bird, T. C., B.A.'25, Howard Payne Col.; M.A. '40, Univ. of N. Mex.; Supt. of Sch., Santa Fe, N. Mex., since 1946.

Burke, J. L., Jr., B.A.'29, West Texas State Col.; M.A.'33, Texas Tech. Col.; Supt. of Pub. Sch., Jal, N. Mex., since 1935.

Caton, W. Barnie, A.B.'32, N. Mex. Highlands Univ., Las Vegas; M.A.'40, Univ. of N. Mex., Supt. of Sch., Alamogordo, N. Mex., since 1947.

Clark, L. W., B.A.'30, M.A.'34, Texas Tech. Col.; Supt. of Capitan Union H. S., Capitan, N. Mex., since 1948.

Conway, C. H., M.A.'34, Univ. of N. Mex.; Supt. of Sch., Eunice, N. Mex., since 1935.

Craig, Edith, B.S. Home Ec.'28, Northeastern State Col., Tahlequah, Okla.; M.Ed.'32, Colo. A. & M. Col.; Educationist, Indian Service, Albuquerque, N. Mex., since 1934.

DeVargas, Diego, B.A.'35, N. Mex. Highlands Univ.; Supt. of Co. Sch., Santa Fe, N. Mex., since 1950.

Donaldson, (Mrs.) Martha W., B.S.'48, N. Mex. Western Col.; Co. Supt. of Sch., Roswell, N. Mex., since 1949.

Field, Benwood, B.S.'27, N. Mex. State Tchrs. Col., Silver City; M.A.'39, Univ. of N. Mex.; Supt. of Sch., Dexter, N. Mex., since 1947.

Foster, W. H., M.A.'49, George Peabody College; B.S.'32, Murray State Col. (Ky.); Supt. of Sch., Raton, N. M., since 1952.

Freeburg, Wesley, B.A.'31, N. Mex. Highlands Univ. Las Vegas; M.A.'37, Univ. of N. Mex.; Supt., Lordsburg Municipal Sch., Lordsburg, N. Mex., since 1947.

Galaz, A. C., M.A.'34, Univ. of N. Mex.; Supt. of Sch., Los Lunas, N. Mex., since 1937.

Gonzales, Clara B., B.A. in Ed.'30, Loyola Univ.; Prin., Zuni Day Sch., Zuni, N. Mex., since 1930.

Gonzales, Phillip, M.A.'46, N. Mex. Highlands Univ.; Supt. of Sch., Pecos, N. Mex., since 1950.

Hemsing, W. M., Prin., Santa Fe Indian Sch., Santa Fe, N. M.

*Hobbs, Edwin G., B.A.'25, State Tchrs. Col., Silver City, N. Mex.; M.A.'36, Univ. of N. Mex. Address: Bd. of Educ., Clovis, N. Mex.

Huff, Raymond, B.A.'21, Univ. of Texas; M.A. '30, Univ. of Colo.; Supt. of Sch., Clayton N. Mex., 1920-50. Address: c/o Pub. Sch. Clayton, N. Mex.

Hunt, Malcolm G., B.S.'31, M.A.'32, West Texas State Col.; Supt. of Sch., Portales, N. Mex., since 1943.

Jackson, Charles Everett, B.S.'34, Kansas State Tchrs. Col., Pittsburg; M.A.'41, Univ. of N. Mex.; Dir. of Curriculum and Admin. Asst., Municipal Sch., Lovington, N. Mex., since 1952.

James, Haddon W., B.S.'21, State Tchrs. Col., Emporia, Kansas; Ph.D.'23, State Univ. of Iowa; Pres. Emeritus, N. Mex. Western Col., Silver City, N. Mex., since 1952.

Karlin, Glenn C., B.S.'38, Univ. of N. Mex.; M.A.'51, N. Mex. Highlands Univ.; Prin of Jr. H. S., Raton, N. Mex., since 1952.

Koogler, Clare V., M.A.'31, N. Mex. Highlands Univ., Las Vegas; Supt. of Sch., Aztec, N. Mex., since 1935.

Langston, LaMoine, B.A.'34, N. Mex. Highlands Univ.; M.A.'39, Univ. of N. Mex.; Supt. of Sch., Farmington, N. Mex., since 1950.

Larkin, John L., M.A.'31, Univ. of Ariz.; Supt. of Sch., Tularosa, N. Mex., since 1935.

Linton, M. E., M.A.'41, Univ. of N. Mex.; Supt., Hatch Valley Municipal Sch., Dist. 11, Hatch, N. Mex., since 1951.

Lofton, Ray J., A.B'28, N. Mex. State Tchrs. Col., Silver City; M.A.'41, Univ. of N. Mex.; Supt. of Sch., Melrose, N. Mex., since 1941.

Ludi, Phillip Morris, B.A.'44, M.A.'48, N. Mex. Highlands Univ.; Supt. of Sch., Las Vegas (Town), N. Mex., since 1942.

McBride, George C., B.S.'18, Dartmouth Col.; M.A.'31, Univ. of Calif.; Supt. of Sch., Des Moines, N. Mex.

Marshall, Robert E., B.S.'20, Middle Tenn. State Col., Murfreesboro; M.A.'30, George Peabody Col. of Tchrs.; Supt. of Sch., Clovis, N. Mex., since 1945.

Mayfield, Tom J., B.A.'26, Miss. Col.; M.A.'38, Univ. of N. Mex.; City Supt. of Sch., Artesia, N. Mex., since 1947.

Medina, Edward, B.A.'42, Univ. of N. Mex.; M.A.'50, N. Mex. Highlands Univ.; Pres., Northern N. Mex. Normal Sch., El Rito, N. Mex., since 1951.

Miles, Samuel F., Prin., Mesa Sch., Los Alamos, N. Mex.

Miller, J. Cloyd, B.S. in Bus. Adm.'27, N. Mex. Col. of Agr. and Mech. Arts; M.A. in Ed.'36, Univ. of N. Mex.; Pres., Natl. Educ. Assn., 1951-52; Pres., N. Mex. Western Col., Silver City, N. Mex., since 1952.

Mills, Charles L., B.A.'29, N. Mex. Highlands Univ.; M.A.'41, Univ. of N. Mex.; Supt. of Sch., Hobbs, N. Mex., since 1947.

Milne, John, B.S.'29, Univ. of N. Mex.; M.A.'31, Tchrs. Col., Columbia Univ.; Supt. of Sch., Albuquerque, N. Mex., since 1911.

Morgan, Henry E., B.A.'26, Univ. of Kansas; M.A.'38, Univ. of N. Mex.; Supt. of Sch., Elida, N. Mex., since 1935.

Morrison, Donald B., B.S.'34, Texas Col. of Arts and Indus.; M.A.'43, Univ. of N. Mex.; Supt. of Sch., Cimarron, N. Mex.

Murphy, Irvin P., M.A.'38, Univ. of N. Mex.; Supt. of Sch., Carlsbad, N. Mex., since 1941.

Nanninga, Simon P., B.S.'16, Kansas State Tchrs. Col.; M.A.'22, Stanford Univ.; Ph.D. '25, Univ. of Calif.; Dean, Col. of Educ., Univ. of N. Mex., Albuquerque, N. Mex., since 1925.

Nunn, Earl, M.A.'43, N. Mex. Highlands Univ.; Supt. of Sch., Springer, N. Mex., since 1950.

Owens, Charles S., B.A.'30, Hardin-Simmons Univ.; M.A.'40, Texas Tech. Col.; Supt. of Sch., Gallup, N. Mex., since 1949.

Pannell, H. C., M.A.'34, Univ. of Colo.; Supt. of Sch., Lovington, N. Mex., since 1939.

Prevost, Charles O., A.B.'32, N. Mex. State Tchrs. Col., Silver City; Co. Supvr. of Rural Sch., Silver City, N. Mex., since 1938.

Rhodes, L. H., B.S.'26, West Texas State Tchrs. Col.; M.A.'31, Univ. of Colo.; Supt. of Sch., Tucumcari, N. Mex., since 1937.

Robertson, Walter J., A.B.'22, Southwestern Col.; A.M.'34, N. Mex. Highlands Univ.; Supt. of Sch., Las Vegas, N. Mex., since 1941.

Rosenberg, Samuel, B.S.S.'30, M.S.Ed.'32, City Col. of the City of New York; Reservation Prin., Jicarilla Indian Agency Sch., Dulce, N. Mex., since 1949.

Russell, John Dale, A.B.'17, A.M.'24, Ph.D.'31, Ind. Univ.; Chancellor and Exec. Secy., Board of Educ. Finance, State of N. Mex., Santa Fe, N. Mex., since 1951.

Sanchez, Adelino, A.B.'30, N. Mex. Tchrs. Col., Silver City; M.A.'40, Univ. of N. Mex.; Supt. of Sch., Belen, N. Mex., since 1943.

Shinkle, James D., B.S.'20, Central Mo. Col.; M.A.'27, George Peabody Col. for Tchrs.; Supt. of Sch., Roswell, N. Mex., since 1936.

Sloan, Katherine E., B.S.'37, Texas Col. of Arts and Industries; M.A.'51, George Peabody Col.; Sypvr. Prin. of Sch., Isleta, N. Mex., since 1945.

Stafford, W. D., A.B.'30, N. Mex. Highlands Univ., Las Vegas; M.A.'37, Texas Tech. Col.; Supt. of Sch., San Jon, N. Mex., since 1945.

Steiner, John P., A.B.'23, Southwestern Col.; M.A.'34, Univ. of Kansas; Exec. Sec., N. Mex. Educ. Assn., Santa Fe, N. Mex., since 1950.

Stinnette, Ray L., A.B.'30, M.A.'30, Colo. State Col. of Educ.; Supt. of Sch., Hot Springs, N. Mex., since 1945.

Thomas, R. N., Co. Supt. of Sch., Carlsbad, N. Mex., since 1939.

Tunnell, Hal, B.A.'41, M.A.'48, N. Mex. Highlands Univ.; Supt. of Sch., Estancia, N. Mex., since 1951.

Wegner, F. Robert, A.B.'21, Cornell Univ.; M.A.'28, N. Y. State Col. for Tchrs., Albany; Co. Supt. of Sch., Los Alamos, N. Mex., since 1946.

Wiley, Tom, Supt. of Pub. Instr., State Dept. of Educ., Santa Fe, N. Mex.

Williams, Burton T., M.S.'37, Univ. of N. Mex.; Supt. of Sch., Ft. Sumner, N. Mex., since 1945.

Wood, (Mrs.) Alice C., Supt. of Sch., Wagon Mound, N. Mex.

Wood, Charles H., B.A.'29, Montezuma Col.; M.A.'32, N. Mex. Highlands Univ.; Field Serv. Secy., N. Mex. Educ. Assn., 114 East Marcy St., Santa Fe, N. Mex., since 1952.

INSTITUTIONAL MEMBER

Library, University of New Mexico, Albuquerque, N. Mex.

NEW YORK

INDIVIDUAL MEMBERS

Ackley, E. L., A.B. and A.M.'05, Pd.B.'08, Syracuse Univ.; Supt. of Sch., Johnstown, N. Y., 1910-49 (retired). Address: 402 S. Market St., Johnstown, N. Y.

Adinoff, Rebecca, B.S.'36, M.A.'43, Columbia Univ.; Asst. Dir., Early Childhood Educ., Pub. Sch., Brooklyn, N. Y., since 1949.

Agnew, Peter L., B.B.Ed.'23, Boston Univ.; M.A.'28, Ph.D.'40, N. Y. Univ.; M.Ed.'30, Harvard Univ.; Asst. Dean, N. Y. Univ., New York, N. Y., since 1948.

Ahern, T., James, B.A.'23, Alfred Univ.; A.M.'36, New York Univ.; Supt. of Sch., Mamaroneck, N. Y., since 1942.

Akerly, Harold E., B.S.'08, Univ. of Rochester; S.B.'10, Mass. Inst. of Tech.; M.A.'33, Univ. of Rochester; Asst. Supt. of Sch., Rochester, N. Y., since 1929.

Akin, Clayton L., B.Ed.'48, Washington Univ.; M.A.'51, Columbia Univ.; AASA-CPEA Intern, 1952-53, Tchrs. Col., Columbia Univ., New York, N. Y.

Allardyce, Agnes I., Prof. of Speech and Educ., Syracuse Univ., Syracuse, N. Y.

Allen, David G., M.Ed.'38, St. Lawrence Univ.; Prin. of Dist. Sch., Cazenovia, N. Y., since 1944.

Allen, Edward E., A.B.'28, Ellsworth Col.; Ed.M.'30, Harvard Univ.; Supvg. Prin. of Sch., Akron, N. Y., since 1941.

Allen, James E., Jr., A.B.'32, Davis and Elkins Col.; Ed.M.'42, Ed.D.'45, Harvard Univ.; N. Y. State Deputy Commr. of Educ., Albany, N. Y., since 1950.

Aloysia, Mother M., Ph.D.'26, Fordham Univ.; Good Counsel Col., White Plains, N. Y., since 1923.

Alpern, Hymen, A.B.'17, City Col. of the City of New York; A.M.'21, Columbia Univ.; Ph.D.'25, New York Univ.; Prin., Evander Childs H. S., New York, N. Y., since 1934.

Ambellan, Fred, B.S.'33, N. Y. State Col. for Tchrs., Buffalo; M.A.'38, New York Univ.; Supt. of Sch., Gloversville, N. Y., since 1952.

Anderson, Walter A., B.S.'29, M.A.'31, Univ. of Minn.; Ed.D.'37, Tchrs. Col., Columbia Univ.; Chmn., Dept. of Admin. and Supvn., Sch. of Educ., New York Univ., New York, N. Y., since 1947.

Armstrong, Hubert C., B.S.'30, M.S.'31, Univ. of Wash.; Dir., Pub. Educ. Assoc., New York, N. Y., since 1951.

Armstrong, Louis W., B.S.'31, M.A.'37, Ed.D.'51, Tchrs. Col., Columbia Univ.; Assoc. in Educ. Plant Planning, State Educ. Dept., Albany, N. Y., since 1951.

Armstrong, T. H., Interstate Tchrs. Agency, Genesee Valley Trust Bldg., Rochester, N. Y.

Arnold, Dorothy Livingston, Dir., Educ. Relations and Head, Dept. of Tchr. Tr., Parsons Sch. of Design, New York N. Y., since 1934.

Atwood, Chase Carlos, B.S.'26, Temple Univ.; LL.B.'37, St. Lawrence Univ.; Jur. Sc. D.'46, Brooklyn Law Sch.; Controller, Horace Mann Sch., New York, N. Y., since 1949.

Atwood, Clinton H., B.S.'19, Colgate Univ.; A.M.'23, Syracuse Univ.; Supt. of Sch., Solvay, N. Y., since 1938.

Austin, David B., A.B.'29, Pomona Col.; M.A.'30, Claremont Col.; Ed.D.'51, Tchrs. Col., Columbia Univ.; Assoc. Prof. of Educ., Tchrs. Col., Columbia Univ., New York, N. Y.

Ayer, Roderick E., M.S. in Ed.'46, Syracuse Univ.; Supvr. Prin., Onteora Sch., Phoenicia, N. Y., since 1952.

Bailey, Richard James, A.B.'30, Univ. of Notre Dame; Ph.D.'40, N. Y. Univ.; Supvg. Prin. of Greenburgh No. 8 Sch., White Plains, N. Y., since 1947.

Bain, Howard E., A.B.'28, Houghton Col.; M.A. in Ed.'38, Cornell Univ.; Prin. Oakfield Alabama C. S., Oakfield, N. Y., since 1948.

Bair, Frederick Haigh, A.B.'12, Grinnell Col.; M.A.'17, Ph.D.'31, Tchrs. Col., Columbia Univ.; Chief, Bureau of Curriculum Development, State Educ. Dept., Albany, N. Y., since 1947.

Baisch, Carl W., M.A.'27, Univ. of Buffalo; Deputy Supt. of Sch., Kenmore, N. Y., since 1946.

Baker, Erwin L., Prin. of Sch., Sullivan Co., Jeffersonville, N. Y.

Baker, Howard E., B.S.'26, Union Univ.; M.A.'34, New York State Col. for Tchrs., Albany; Supt. of Draper Sch., Schenectady, N. Y., since 1948.

Baldwin, Clare C., B.S.'27, Univ. of Kansas; M.A.'32, Ph.D.'34, Tchrs. Col., Columbia Univ.; Asst. Supt. of Sch., New York, N. Y., since 1946.

Barber, George A., Dist. Supt. of Sch., Batavia, N. Y.

Barkan, Samuel H., B.S.'23, Col. of the City of New York; M.S.'30, N. Y. Univ.; Dir., Sch. Housing, New York City Bd. of Educ., 110 Livingston St., Brooklyn, N. Y., since 1947.

Barry, Franklyn S., B.A.'31, M.A.'42, Syracuse Univ.; Acting Supt. of Sch., Irondequoit, N. Y., since 1945, and Supt. of Sch., Cortland, N. Y., since 1947.

Bassett, Cecil A., Secy. and Mgr., of the Coop. Sch. Purchasers, Inc., Cazenovia, N. Y., since 1940.

*Beach, Norton Lewis, B.B.A.'38, Ed.M.'40, Boston Univ.; Ed.D.'48, Tchrs. Col., Columbia Univ.; Assoc. Prof. of Educ., Tchrs. Col., Columbia Univ., New York, N. Y., since 1949.

Bean, Berten B., Ph.B.'12, Alfred Univ.; M.A.'25, Columbia Univ.; Assoc. Supt. of Sch. for Elem. Educ., Buffalo, N. Y., since 1939.

Beaumont, Florence S., B.S.'37, M.A.'39, New York Univ.; Asst. Supt. of Sch., Jackson Hgts., N. Y., since 1943.

Beddow, William D., B.A.'21, Muhlenberg Col.; M.A.'33, Tchrs. Col., Columbia Univ.; Prin. H. S., Hempstead, N. Y., since 1951.

Beha, James A., B.S.'22, M.S.'29, St. Lawrence Univ.; Supt. of Sch., Frankfort, N. Y., since 1945.

Belknap, Walter, Time, Inc., 9 Rockefeller Plaza, New York N. Y.

Bell, Robert E., A.B.'23, M.A.'26, Syracuse Univ.; Ph.D.'34, New York Univ.; Dist. Supt. of Sch., Chappaqua, N. Y., since 1942.

Bentley, C. H., Prin., Newfane Central Sch., Newfane, N. Y.

Bernath, Edward J., B.S.S.'26, M.S. in Ed.'30, City Col. of the City of N. Y.; J.D.'29, New York Univ.; Asst. Supt. of Sch., New York, N. Y., since 1948.

Bible, Margaret K., 1517 Benson St., New York 61, N. Y.

Bigelow, Karl W., B.A.'20, Clark Univ.; Ph.D.'29, Harvard Univ.; L.H.D.'38, Clark Univ.; LL.D. '41, Parsons Col.; Prof. of Educ., Tchrs. Col., Columbia Univ., New York, N. Y., since 1936.

Bills, John E., A.B.'35, N. Y. State Col. for Tchrs., Albany; M.S. in Ed.'42, Cornell Univ.; Supvg. Prin., Moravia Central H. S., Moravia, N. Y., since 1949.

Blair, Mary M., Asst. Supt. of Sch., Staten Island, N. Y., since 1950.

Blakeslee, Harry K., B.S. in Ed.'31, Univ. of Ala.; M.E.'45, Univ. of Buffalo; Prin., Lewiston H. S., Lewiston, N. Y., since 1948.

Bliss, D. Everett, A.B.'34, Union Col.; M.A.'44, Cornell Univ.; Dist. Supt. of Sch., Whitesboro, N. Y., since 1949.

*Blom, Edward Charles, A.B.'11, Southeast Mo. State Tchrs. Col., Cape Girardeau; B.S. in Ed.'15, A.M.'17, Univ. of Mo.; Ph.D.'30, Columbia Univ.; Prof. of Mathematics and Physical Sci., State Tchrs. Col., Fredonia, N. Y., since 1946.

Boardman, Walter S., Ed.D.'41, New York Univ.; Supt. of Sch., Oceanside, L. I., N. Y., since 1940.

Bodley, George R., B.S.'07, Syracuse Univ.; Supt. of Sch., Fulton, N. Y., since 1922.

Bogg, Ridgley M., B.S. in Econ.'40, Univ. of Conn.; M.B.A.'49, Harvard Grad. Sch. of Adm.; Ed.D.'51, Tchrs. Col., Columbia Univ.; Auditor and Budget Dir., City Sch. Dist., Schenectady, N. Y., since 1951.

*Borgeson, F. C., A.B.'21, Univ. of Denver; M.A.'25, Tchrs. Col., Columbia Univ.; Ph.D. '27, Columbia Univ.; Prof. of Educ., New York Univ., New York, N. Y., since 1929.

Bowie, Arthur, M.A.'30, N. Y. Univ.; Asst. Supt. of Sch., Brooklyn, N. Y., since 1938.

Bradley, Allan P., M.A.'37, Syracuse Univ.; Dir., Genl. Elem. Div., New York State Col. for Tchrs., Buffalo, N. Y., since 1949.

Brasted, F. Kenneth, A.B.'35, Univ. of Fla.; A.M.'38, Tchrs. Col., Columbia Univ.; Dir., Educ. Dept., Natl. Assn. of Manufacturers, New York, N. Y., since 1948.

Braun, John C., B.S.'27, Springfield Col.; M.A. '52, Tchrs. Col., Columbia Univ.; Supvg. Prin. of Sch., Ellenville, N. Y., since 1950.

Braun, Julius C., B.S.'33, State Tchrs. Col., Buffalo, N. Y.; Ed.M.'37, Univ. of Buffalo; Supt. of Sch., Salamanca, N. Y., since 1946.

Bretsch, Glenn E., B.S.'23, M.A.'33, Cornell Univ.; Supvg. Prin., Colonie Central Schs., Albany, N. Y., since 1949.

Brighton, George W., B.S. in Ed.'37, State Tchrs. Col., Buffalo, N. Y.; Prin., Amherst Sch. 18, Snyder, N. Y., since 1947.

Bristow, William H., B.S.'20, Central Mo. State Tchrs. Col., Warrensburg; A.M.'22, Ed.D.'36, Tchrs. Col., Columbia Univ.; Dir., Bureau of Curriculum, Bd. of Educ., City of New York, Brooklyn, N. Y., since 1940.

Brokaw, Frank, A.B.'29, Hope Col.; M.S.'36, Syracuse Univ.; Supt. of Sch., Fairport, N. Y., since 1951.

Brown, Foster S., B.S.'30, M.A.'33, St. Lawrence Univ.; Dean, Cortland State Tchrs. Col., Cortland, N. Y., since 1951.

Brown, Harold S., Vicepres., D. Van Nostrand Co., Inc., New York, N. Y., since 1946.

*Brown, James E., Prin., H. S., Whitesboro, N. Y., since 1949.

Brown, Milton W., A.B.'28, Marietta Col.; Ed.M. '40, Harvard Univ.; Supt. of Sch., Lancaster, N. Y., since 1948.

Brownell, (Mrs.) Eleanor K., M.A.'46, Tchrs. Col., Columbia Univ.; Supvg. Prin., Division Ave. Sch., Levittown, N. Y., since 1945.

Bruce, William French, B.Sc.'11, M.A.'24, Ph.D. '26, Ohio State Univ.; Prof. of Educ., State Tchrs. Col., Oneonta, N. Y., since 1929.

Bruggeman, L. L., A.B.'26, Rutgers Univ.; Mgr., Eastern Div., American Book Co., New York, N. Y., since 1943.

Bruner, Herbert B., Ph.D.'25, Columbia Univ.; Prof. of Educ., New York Univ., New York, N. Y., since 1950.

Bryant, George E., B.S.'34, A.M.'37, New York Univ.; Supt. of Sch., Roslyn Hgts., N. Y., since 1943.

Buesch, Charles G., B.A.'26, North Central Col.; Prin. of Woodlawn H. S., Blasdell, Buffalo, N. Y., since 1934.

Bulger, Paul G., M.S.'42, N. Y. State Col. for Tchrs., Albany; Ed.D.'51, Tchrs. Col., Columbia Univ.; Asst. Provost, Tchrs. Col., Columbia Univ., New York, N. Y., since 1948.

Bumgardner, Walter L., B.S.'18, Pa. State Col.; Supt. of Sch., East Aurora, N. Y., since 1932.

Burger, I. Victor, B.S.'16, M.A.'29, Ph.D.'34, New York Univ.; Asst. Supt. of Sch., New York, N. Y., since 1944.

Burgess, Frank D., Superior Body Sales, Inc., Newark, N. Y.

Burke, James M., Clerk, Bd. of Educ., Whitesboro, N. Y., since 1929.

Burke, Regina C. M., B.A.'00, Hunter Col.; B.S.'24, Fordham Univ.; Assoc. Supt., New York City Sch., Brooklyn, N. Y., since 1938.

Burns, Robert, B.S.'16, M.A.'19, Ph.D.'28, Tchrs. Col., Columbia Univ.; Assoc. Prof., Sch. of Educ., Fordham Univ., New York, N. Y.

Buros, Francis C., B.S.'25, Univ. of Minn.; M.A.'29, Tchrs. Col., Columbia Univ.; Asst. Supt. of Sch., White Plains, N. Y., since 1937.

Butterworth, Julian E., A.B.'07, M.A.'10, Ph.D. '12, State Univ. of Iowa; Prof. of Rural Educ., Educ. Admin., Cornell Univ., Ithaca, N. Y., 1919-52 (retired). Adress: 101 Irving Place, Ithaca, N. Y.

Butts, R. Freeman, A.B.'31, M.A.'32, Ph.D.'35, Univ. of Wis.; Head, Dept. of Social and Philosophical Foundations since 1948, and Prof. of Educ., Tchrs. Col., Columbia Univ., New York, N. Y., since 1947.

Byrnes, John F., B.S.'20, M.A.'38, St. Lawrence Univ.; Dist. Supt. of Sch., Brushton, N. Y., since 1936.

Caine, Alfred B., B.S.'26, Univ. of Ill.; M.A.'32, Columbia Univ.; Asst. Prin. of Sewanhaka H. S., Floral Park, N. Y., since 1947.

Calhoun, Sanford H., B.S.'26, St. Lawrence Univ.; M.A.'31, Columbia Univ.; Supvg. Prin., Wellington C. Mepham H. S., Bellmore, N. Y., since 1935.

Capen, Samuel Paul, A.B. and M.A.'98, L.H.D. '21, Tufts Col.; A.M.'00, Harvard Univ.; Ph.D. '02, LL.D.'33, Univ. of Pa.; LL.D.'20, Lafayette Col.; L.H.D.'25, Hobart Col.; Sc.D.27, George Washington Univ.; LL.D.'32, Univ. of Chicago; Litt.D.'37, Clark Univ.; LL.D.'38, McMaster Univ.; Chancellor, Univ. of Buffalo, Buffalo, N. Y., 1922-50 (retired). Address: 42 Linwood Ave., Buffalo, N. Y.,

*Carey, Elizabeth B., A.B.'23, M.A.'34, New York State Col. for Tchrs., Albany; Ph.D.'49, New York Univ.; Supvr. of Elem. Educ., State Educ. Dept., Albany, N. Y., since 1940.

Carlisle, William T., B.A.'35, Henderson State Tchrs. Col., Arkadelphia, Ark.; Ed.M.'40, Univ. of Okla.; Asst., Dept. of Educ. Admin., Tchrs. Col., Columbia Univ., New York, N. Y., since 1950.

Carter, Guyon J., B.S.'10, Alfred Univ.; M.A.'24, Columbia Univ.; Dist. Supt. of Sch., Avoca, N. Y., since 1911.

*Casey, Leo Martin, B.S.'47, Manhattan Col.; M.A.'48, Ed.D.'49, Columbia Univ.; Bus. Mgr., Scotia-Granville Sch., Scotia, N. Y., since 1951.

Caswell, Hollis L., Ph.D.'29, Columbia Univ.; Dean, Tchrs. Col., Columbia Univ., New York, N. Y., since 1948.

Center, Stella Stewart, A.B.'01, George Peabody Col. for Tchrs.; Ph.B.'11, Univ. of Chicago; A.M.'13, Columbia Univ.; Litt.D.'29, Univ. of Ga.; Dir., Reading Clinic, New York Univ., New York, N. Y., since 1935.

Chisholm, J. Wilber, B.S.'29, New York Univ.; M.A.'40, Tchrs. Col., Columbia Univ.; Dist. Supt. of Sch., Mineola, N. Y., since 1936.

Cholet, Bertram, Asst. Vicepres., Higgins Ink Co., Inc., Brooklyn, N. Y.

Church, Frank E., A.B.'27, Alfred Univ.; M.A.'37, Columbia Univ.; Supvg. Prin. of Sch., East Meadow, Hempstead, N. Y., since 1932.

Church, Stanley R., M.S.'41, Syracuse Univ.; Supvg. Prin., Central Sch., Hannibal, N. Y., since 1949.

Clark, Harold F., Ph.D.'23, Tchrs. Col., Columbia Univ.; Prof. of Educ., Tchrs. Col., Columbia Univ., New York, N. Y., since 1928.

Clifford, Walter G., A.B.'32, Colgate Univ.; M.S. in Ed.'40, Cornell Univ.; Supt. of Sch., Canastota, N. Y., since 1947.

Cocking, Walter D., A.B.'13, Des Moines Col.; M.A.'23, State Univ. of Iowa; Ph.D.'28, Columbia Univ.; Prof. of Educ., New York Univ. and Chmn., Bd. of Editors, The American School Publishing Corp., New York, N. Y., since 1943.

Codding, James W., Supt. of Sch., Chazy, N. Y.

Colburn, Alfred L., B.A.'30, M.A.'37, Cornell Univ.; Supvg. Prin., Cuba Central Sch., Cuba, N. Y., since 1937.

Coleman, Georgia Avis, Supvg. Prin., Colonial and Siwanoy Sch., Pelham, N. Y., since 1916.

Collins, Evan R., A.B.'33, Dartmouth Col.; Ed.M. '38, Ed.D.'46, Harvard Univ.; Pres., New York State Col. for Tchrs., Albany, N. Y., since 1949.

Collins, Raymond L., A.B.'31, M.A.'35, N. Y. State Col. for Tchrs., Albany; Ed.D.'45, Tchrs. Col., Columbia Univ.; Supt. of Sch., Manhasset, N. Y., since 1945.

Collins, Tobias J., A.B.'26, Hamilton Col.; M.A.'34, Columbia Univ. Address: 620 River Road, Lewiston, N. Y.

*Colmey, James W., B.B.A.'46, Univ. of Texas; M.A.'47, Tchrs. Col., Columbia Univ.; Admin. Asst. to Supt. of Sch., Manhasset, N. Y.

Colton, Merrill L., Supvg. Prin., Unit Sch. Dist. #5, New Hyde Park, N. Y.

Conant, Eugene F., A.B.'30, Union Col. and Univ.; Ed.M.'34, Harvard Univ.; Supt. of Sch., Johnstown, N. Y., since 1949.

Cook, (Mrs.) Harriet P., B.A.'36, M.A.'37, Univ. of Buffalo; Dean and Dir. of Pub. Rel., Cazenovia Jr. Col., Cazenovia, N. Y., since 1945.

Corey, Stephen M., B.A.'26, Eureka Col.; M.A. '27, Ph.D.'30, Univ. of Ill.; Prof. of Educ. and Exec. Officer, Horace Mann-Lincoln Inst. of Sch. Experimentation, Tchrs. Col., Columbia Univ., New York, N. Y., since 1948.

Cornelius, Rev. Brother C., A.B.'35, Manhattan Col.; A.M.'40, N. Y. Univ.; Ph.D.'49, St. John's Univ.; M.S. in Ed.'52, Syracuse Univ.; Prin., Christian Bros. Academy, Syracuse, N. Y., since 1946.

Cornell, Ethel L., A.B.'14, Cornell Univ.; Ph.D. '19, Columbia Univ.; Educ. Research Div., State Educ. Dept., Albany, N. Y., since 1920.

Cosman, Charles B., B.S.'32, St. Lawrence Univ.; M.S.'38, Syracuse Univ.; Supvg. Prin., H. S., Islip, N. Y., since 1947.

Cottle, William E., A.B.'20, Clark Univ.; Ed.M. '28, Harvard Univ.; Supt. of Sch., Tuckahoe, N. Y., since 1949.

Coughlin, Robert M., B.S.'31, St. Lawrence Univ.; M.Ed.'41, Pa. State Col.; Supvg. Prin. of Sch., Westfield, N. Y., since 1950.

Counts, George S., Tchrs. Col., Columbia Univ., New York, N. Y.

Cousins, Anthony Frank, A.B.'29, New York State Col. for Tchrs., Albany; M.Ed.'41, St. Lawrence Univ.; Prin. of Central Sch., Crown Point, N. Y., since 1943.

Cowan, Charles Thomas, B.S.'31, New York Univ.; M.A.'37, Ed.D.'51, Tchrs. Col., Columbia Univ.; Supt. of Sch., Saranac Lake, N. Y., since 1947.

Cox, W. Kenneth, B.S.'31, Middlebury Col.; M.A.'39, N. Y. State Col. for Tchrs., Albany; Prin., Central Dist. Sch., Port Leyden, N. Y., since 1938.

*Coxe, Warren W., B.Sc.'11, Dakota Wesleyan Univ.; Ph.D.'23, Ohio State Univ.; Dir., Div. of Research, State Educ. Dept., Albany, N. Y., since 1923.

Craib, (Mrs.) Mildred Hull, B.S.'19, M.S.'35, N. Y. State Col. for Tchrs., Albany; Supt. of Sch., Second Supvy. Dist., Rensselaer Co., Berlin, N. Y., since 1931.

Craig, Gerald S., A.B.'15, Baylor Univ.; M.A.'17, Ph.D.'27, Columbia Univ.; Prof. of Natural Sciences, Tchrs. Col., Columbia Univ., New York, N. Y., since 1934.

Craig, Marjorie L., A.B.'34, Smith Col.; M.A.'35, Tchrs. Col., Columbia Univ.; Dir., Sch. Health Bureau, Health and Welfare Div., Metropolitan Life Ins. Co., New York, N. Y., since 1947.

Crist, Amy Bull, B.S.'39, M.A.'40, New York Univ.; Dist. Supt. of Sch., Montgomery, Orange Co., N. Y., since 1940.

Crittenden, Harold C., A.B.'34, Alfred Univ.; M.Ed.'40, Pa. State Col.; Prin. of Sch., Armonk, N. Y., since 1948.

Crow, Lester D., Ph.D.'27, N. Y. Univ.; Assoc. Prof. of Educ., Brooklyn Col., Brooklyn, N. Y.

Crowley, Arthur J., Diploma '13, State Tchrs. Col., Potsdam, N. Y.; Dir., Educ. Staff, *The Reader's Digest*, Pleasantville, N. Y., since 1940.

Cummings, John A., B.A.'34, St. Mary's Univ., Baltimore, Md.; Asst. Dir., Bureau of Attendance, New York City Bd. of Ed., Brooklyn, N. Y., since 1951.

Cummings, L. O., A.B.'10, Harvard Col.; A.M. '11, Harvard Grad. Sch. of Arts and Science; Ed.D.'21, Harvard Grad. Sch. of Educ.; Dean, Sch. of Educ., Buffalo, N. Y., since 1930.

Cushman, Edward B., A.B.'22, M.A.'37, Cornell Univ.; Supt. of Sch., Amsterdam, N. Y., since 1943.

*Cyr., Frank W., B.Sc.'23, Univ. of Nebr.; Ph.D.'33, Columbia Univ.; Prof. of Educ., Tchrs. Col., Columbia Univ., New York, N. Y., since 1934.

Dailey, C. Alton, A.B.'45, Seattle Pacific Col.; Bus. Mgr., Roberts Wesleyan Col., North Chili, N. Y., since 1945.

Daly, Francis J., B.S. in Ed.'41, Ed.M.'43, Boston Univ.; Ed.D.'47, Harvard Univ.; Dir. of Pupil Personnel Serv., State Dept. of Educ., Albany, N. Y., since 1951.

*Dann, George J., A.B.'96, A.M.'99, Union Col.; Pd.D.'14, New York Univ. Address: 2 Watkins Ave., Oneonta, N. Y.

Davey, Harold, M.A.'33, N. Y. State Col. for Tchrs., Albany; Supt. of Sch., Pleasantville, N. Y., since 1947.

*Davies, Daniel R., A.B.'33, Harvard Univ.; M.A.'43, Bucknell Univ.; Ed.D.'46, Columbia Univ.; Prof. of Educ. and Coordinator, Coop. Program in Educ. Admin., Tchrs. Col., Columbia Univ., New York, N. Y., since 1950.

Davis, James F., B.S.'33, Taylor Univ.; M.A.'41, Ball State Tchrs. Col., Muncie, Ind.; Supvg. Prin. of Sch., Ellicottville, N. Y., since 1941.

Davis, O. Wendell, B.S. in Ed.'31, State Tchrs. Col., Mansfield, Pa.; M.A. in Elem. Ed.'40, New York Univ.; Prin., John Lewis Childs Sch., Floral Park, N. Y., since 1948.

Davis, Paul H., Vicepres. in charge of Development, Columbia Univ. and Genl. Secy., Tchrs. Col., Columbia Univ., New York, N. Y.

*Davis, Ron W., B.A.'47, Reed Col.; M.A.'48, Tchrs. Col., Columbia Univ.; Chmn. Laboratory Practice Development, Citizenship Educ. Project, Tchrs. Col., Columbia Univ., New York, N. Y., since 1952.

Davis, W. Cecil, B.S.'26, M.S.'27, Ed.D.'46, St. Bonaventure Univ.; Supt. of City Sch., Olean, N. Y., since 1951.

Deci, F. Theodore, B.S.'28, Hobart Col.; Ed.M. '37, Univ. of Rochester; Supvg. Prin., Palmyra, N. Y., since 1950.

Demeter, Lee Harry, A.B.'39, Harvard Univ.; M.A.'41, Boston Univ.; Ed.D.'51, Tchrs. Col., Columbia Univ.; Research Assoc., Tchrs. Col., Columbia Univ., New York, N. Y., since 1950.

Densmore, David W., B.S. in Ed.'28, Univ. of Rochester; A.M.'35, Cornell Univ.; Asst. Supt. of Sch., Rochester, N. Y., since 1940.

Dietrich, Grace L., B.S. in Ed.'37, N. Y. State Col. for Tchrs., Albany; M.S. in Ed.'45, Syracuse Univ.; Supvg. Prin., Menands Sch., Menands, Albany, N. Y., since 1945.

Dingman, Erwin, A.B.'33, Mich. State Tchrs. Col., Ypsilanti; M.A.'38, Univ. of Mich.; Ph.D.'49, New York Univ.; Coordinator of Personnel, Bd. of Educ., Buffalo, N. Y., since 1951.

Dixon, James L., A.B.'22, A.M.'24, Ed.M.'31, Ed.D.'44, Rutgers Univ.; Headmaster, Kew Forest Sch., Forest Hills, N. Y., since 1941.

Dodd, John W., B.S.'20, A.M.'22, Tchrs. Col., Columbia Univ.; Ph.D.'35, New York Univ.; Supt. of Sch., Freeport, N. Y., since 1925.

Dodd, Lawrence V., B.S.'30, Susquehanna Univ.; M.A.'37, Tchrs. Col., Columbia Univ.; Supt. of Sch., Lawrence, N. Y., since 1934.

*Dodge, Harrison S., B.S. and Pd.B.'15, Syracuse Univ.; M.A.'30, Columbia Univ.; Supt. of Sch., Hornell, N. Y., since 1919.

Dodge, W. Parker, 78 Scott Ave., Castleton-On-Hudson, N. Y.

Donahue, Terence C., A.B.'28, Univ. of Notre Dame; M.A.'36, Ohio State Univ.; Ed.D.'39, Tchrs. Col., Columbia Univ.; Supt., Eastchester Sch. Dist. 1, Tuckahoe, N. Y., since 1946.

Donati, Edward P., M.A.'42, Tchrs. Col., Columbia Univ.; Admin. Asst., Sch. Dist. 16, Elmont, N. Y., since 1947.

Donnan, E. Craig, B.S.'23, Colgate Univ.; M.S.'45, Cornell Univ.; Dist. Supt., Tompkins Co. Sch., Newfield, N. Y., since 1931.

Driver, Chester S., A.B.'33, Houghton Col.; M.S.'43, Cornell Univ.; Supvg. Prin. of Sch., Marcellus, N. Y., since 1935.

Ducker, Henry Carsten, B.S.'32, M.A.'34, Ed.D.'45, New York Univ.; Supt. of Sch., Baldwin, N. Y., since 1945.

Dugan, Howard F., Vicepres., Hotels Statler Co., Inc., Hotel Statler, New York, N. Y.

Dunnan, Donald W., B.S.'33, Univ. of N. H.; M.Ed.'40, Boston Univ.; Supt. of Sch., Malone, N. Y., since 1950.

Dunsmoor, Clarence C., B.S.'22, State Univ. of Iowa; Ed.M.'34, Ed.D.'38, Harvard Univ.; Dir., Bd. of Coop. Educ. Serv., First Supvy. Dist., Westchester Co., South Salem, N. Y.

Dyer, Everett R., M.A.'38, Univ. of Rochester; Exec. Secy., N. Y. State Sch. Bds. Assn., Albany, N. Y., since 1948.

Eby, Harry K., A.B.'23, Muskingum Col.; Natl. Dir. of Sch. Relationships, Boy Scouts of America, New York, N. Y., since 1947.

Eckhoff, Harry C., B.S.'24, Central Mo. Col.; Chief, Information and Educ. Div., Personnel Serv. Directorate, Headquarters USAFE, APO 633, c/o P.M., New York, N. Y., since 1950.

Eddy, Paul Dawson, A.B.'21, A.M.'24, Univ. of Pa.; B.D.'24, Crozer Theol. Sem.; LL.D.'44, Adelphi Col.; Pres., Adelphi Col., Garden City, L. I., N. Y., since 1937.

Edinger, Paul J., M.A.'34, Syracuse Univ., Supvg. Prin. of Central Sch., North Rose, N. Y., since 1941.

Egdorf, M. F., B.S.'33, Northwest Mo. State Col.; M.S.'39, Univ. of Ill.; Supt. of Sch., Garden City, N. Y., since 1952.

Ehrenfeld, Abraham, B.A.'10, M.S.'23, City Col. of the City of New York; Ph.D.'36, New York Univ.; Asst. Supt. of Sch., 1825 Prospect Ave., New York, N. Y., since 1947.

Eldred, Arvie, A.B.'05, A.M.'21, Williams Col.; Pd.D.'25, N. Y. State Col. for Tchrs.; Exec. Secy., N. Y. State Tchrs. Assn., Albany, N. Y., 1930-51.

Elliott, Lloyd H., M.A.'39, W. Va. Univ.; Ed.D. '48, Univ. of Colo.; Assoc. Prof. of Educ., Cornell Univ., Ithaca, N. Y., since 1948.

Elsbree, Willard S., Ph.D.'28, Tchrs. Col., Columbia Univ.; Prof. of Educ., and Exec. Officer, Inst. of Field Studies, Tchrs. Col., Columbia Univ., New York, N. Y., since 1928.

Emerson, Lynn A., E.E.'11, Univ. of Minn.; Ph.D.'32, New York Univ.; Prof. of Indus. and Labor Relations, Cornell Univ., Ithaca, N. Y., since 1946.

*Engelhardt, N. L., A.B.'03, Yale Univ.; Ph.D.'18, Columbia Univ.; Pres., American Assn. of Sch. Admin., 1944-45; Honorary Life Member, American Assn. of Sch. Admin.; Educ. Consultant, Engelhardt, Engelhardt and Leggett, New York, N. Y., since 1947.

Engelhardt, N. L., Jr., B.S.'29, Yale Univ.; M.A.'37, Ph.D.'39, Tchrs. Col., Columbia Univ.; Educ. Consultant, Engelhardt, Engelhardt and Leggett, New York, N. Y., since 1947.

Epting, Roy W., B.S.'27, Colgate Univ.; M.A.'33, Columbia Univ.; Supvg. Prin. of Sch., Warwick, N. Y., since 1938.

Ernst, Frederic, A.B.'02, Col. of the City of New York; L.H.D.'41, Union Col.; Deputy Supt., New York City Sch., Brooklyn, N. Y., since 1952.

Espy, Herbert G., Ed.D.'29, Harvard Univ.; Pres., State Tchrs. Col., Geneseo, N. Y., since 1946.

Essert, Paul L., B.A.'22, Univ. of Wyo.; M.A.'30, Colo. State Col. of Educ., Greeley; Ed.D.'41, Tchrs. Col., Columbia Univ.; Prof. of Educ., and Exec. Officer, Inst. of Adult Educ., Columbia Univ., New York, N. Y., since 1947.

Essex, Don L., A.B.'17, M.A.'25, Ind. Univ.; Ph.D.'30, Tchrs. Col., and Columbia Univ.; Dir., Sch. Bldgs. and Grounds Div., State Educ. Dept., Albany, N. Y., since 1942.

Evans, (Mrs.) Nancy, AAUP Exhibits Mgr., Columbia Univ. Press, New York, N. Y.

Evenden, Edward S., Diploma '03, Oregon Normal Sch., Monmouth, Oregon; A.B.'10, A.M.'11, Stanford Univ.; Ph.D.'19, Columbia Univ.; Prof. of Educ., and Exec. Officer of Advanced Sch. of Educ., Tchrs. Col., Columbia Univ., New York, N. Y., since 1919.

Ewing, Parmer L., B.S.'30, M.S.'34, Univ. of Ill.; Ed.D.'50, New York Univ.; Supt. of Sch., White Plains, N. Y., since 1950.

Fairclough, W. W., A.B., Bowdoin Col.; A.M., Univ. of Berlin and Columbia Univ.; Supt. of Sch., Pelham, N. Y., since 1945.

Farron, Anthony T., M.A.'52, New York Univ.; Supvg. Prin., H. S., Maybrook, N. Y., since 1952.

Faust, Edwin C., B.A.'46, St. Francis Col. (Pa.); M.A.'50, Fordham Univ.; Supvg. Prin., Copiague Union Sch., Copiague, N. Y., since 1949.

*Felix, Allen O., B.A.'39, Univ. of Colo.; M.A.'48, Ed.D.'50, Tchrs. Col., Columbia Univ.; Asst. Prof. and Research Assoc., Citizenship Educ. Project, Tchrs. Col., Columbia Univ., New York, N. Y.

Fields, Harold, B.S.'11, M.A.'14, New York Univ.; Chairman, Bd. of Examiners, Bd. of Educ. for New York City Sch., Brooklyn, N. Y.

Fields, Ralph R., A.B.'29, Univ. of Ariz.; M.A.'34, Ed.D.'40, Stanford Univ.; Prof. of Educ., and Dir., Div. of Instr., Tchrs. Col., Columbia Univ., New York, N. Y., since 1948.

Finnessy, John James, A.B.'16, Univ. of Vt.; A.M.'36, Ed.D.'38, New York Univ.; Supt. of Sch., Farmingdale, N. Y., since 1949.

Fisher, Edwin L., B.S.'25, Hobart Col.; M.A.'32, Columbia Univ.; Supvg. Prin., Penfield Central Sch., Penfield, N. Y., since 1934.

Fisk, Robert S., B.A.'35, Grinnell Col.; M.A.'40, Univ. of Minn.; Ed.D.'43, Tchrs. Col., Columbia Univ.; Assoc. Prof. of Educ., Syracuse Univ., Syracuse, N. Y., since 1948.

*Fitzgerald, James A., A.B.'15, A.M.'24, Univ. of S. Dak.; Ph.D.'31, State Univ. of Iowa; Prof. of Educ., Fordham Univ., New York, N. Y., since 1939.

Fitzsimmons, Thomas A., B.S.E.'32, Rutgers Univ.; M.A.'35, Columbia Univ.; N. Y. Educ. Rep., P. F. Collier & Son, 640 Fifth Ave., New York, N. Y., since 1952.

Fletcher, Ervin R., A.B.'27, Hamilton Col.; M.A.'34, Tchrs. Col., Columbia Univ.; Supt. of Sch., Port Jervis, N. Y., since 1946.

Fletcher, (Mrs.) Eudora, M.A.'26, Fordham Univ.; Prin., Pub. Sch. 99, Brooklyn, N. Y., since 1931.

Forbes, Harold W., B.S. in M.E.'33, Clarkson Col. of Tech., Potsdam, N. Y.; M.S.'41, N. Y. State Col. for Tchrs., Albany; Supvg. Prin., Whitesboro Central Sch., Whitesboro, N. Y., since 1948.

Ford, Prentice C., B.A.'27, Univ. of Mich.; Vicepres., The American School Publishing Corp., New York, N. Y., since 1928.

Foreman, Lester B., B.S.'26, Cornell Univ.; M.A.'41, Univ. of Rochester; Dist. Supt. of Sch., Pittsford, N. Y., since 1936.

Forester, John J., B.S.'25, Washington Univ.; M.A.'28, Colo. State Col. of Educ.; Ph.D.'33, New York Univ.; Supvg. Prin., Pub. Sch., Uniondale, N. Y., since 1951.

Fox, Jesse G., A.B.'04, City Col. of the City of N. Y.; Asst. Supt., New York City Sch., Brooklyn, N. Y., since 1944.

Frasure, Kenneth Jones, B.Ed.'37, Southern Ill. Univ.; M.A.'40, Ed.M.'45, Ed.D.'48, Univ. of Ill.; Asst. Prof. of Educ., N. Y. State Col. for Tchrs., Albany, N. Y., since 1948.

Freeborn, Malcolm J., B.Arch.'30, M.S. in Ed.'47, Cornell Univ.; Dir. of Educ., George Junior Republic Assn., Inc., and Prin., Hunt Memorial Sch., Freeville, N. Y., since 1946.

French, Harold P., B.S.'24, N. Y. State Col. for Tchrs., Albany; M.S.'30, Cornell Univ.; Ph.D. '40, New York Univ.; Dist. Supt., 3rd Supvy. Sch. Dist., Albany Co., Newtonville, N. Y. (retired). Address: Box 75, Loudonville, N. Y.

French, Will, A.B.'12, Univ. of Kansas; A.M.'22, Ph.D.'33, Tchrs. Col., Columbia Univ.; Prof. of Educ., Tchrs. Col., Columbia Univ., New York, N. Y., since 1937.

Fuller, Delbert O., Ph.B.'20, Brown Univ.; M.A.'33, Columbia Univ.; Assoc. Supt., Tarrytown and North Tarrytown Pub. Sch., North Tarrytown, N. Y., since 1949.

Fundis, Fred P., A.B.'40, New York State Col. for Tchrs., Albany; M.S.'46, Cornell Univ.; Prin., Central Sch., Skaneateles, N. Y., since 1945.

Funk, Howard V., B.S.'23, Univ. of Wis.; Supt. of Sch., Bronxville, N. Y., since 1946.

Furlong, F. R., B.S.'33, M.A.'35, St. Lawrence Univ.; Supvg. Prin., Pub. Sch., Sea Cliff, N. Y., since 1941.

*Gage, Snyder J., B.A.'99, Union Col.; Ph.B.'01, New York State Tchrs. Col., Albany; Supt. of Sch., Newburgh, N. Y. since 1938.

Gates, Arthur I., A.B.'14, M.A.'15, Univ. of Calif.; Ph.D.'17, Columbia Univ.; Prof. of Educ., Tchrs. Col., Columbia Univ., New York, N. Y., since 1917.

Gatje, George H., Ch.E.'21, Rensselaer Polytech. Inst.; M.A.'24, Ed.D.'41, Columbia Univ.; Supt. of Sch., Bay Shore, N. Y., since since 1939.

Gedney, Hilan B., B.S. in Ed.'35, M.A. in Ed.'39, New York Univ.; Dir. of Elem. Educ., Oakside Sch., Peekskill, N. Y., since 1947.

Gerard, Bert S., A.B.'48, Brooklyn Col.; M.S. in Ed.'51, Hofstra Col.; Tchr., Jr. H. S., Trustee, Bd. of Educ., Uniondale, L. I., N. Y., since 1951.

Gewirtz, Max, B.A.'13, City Col. of the City of New York; Asst. Supt., New York City Sch., Long Island City, N. Y., since 1950.

Gillies, Harry W., B.S.Com.'37, M.A.Pol.Sc.'47, Northwestern Univ.; Archt., Perkins & Will, White Plains, N. Y., since 1950.

Gillis, Hugh L., A.B.'06, Cornell Univ.; Asst. Supt. of Sch., Jamestown, N. Y., since 1938.

Gilmore, John W., Lt. Comdr., U.S.S. Caperton DD650, FPO New York, N. Y.

Goble, Emerson, Mng. Editor, *Architectural Record*, 119 W. 40th St., New York 18, N. Y.

Goff, Howard L., A.B.'28, N. Y. State Col. for Tchrs., Albany; M.A.'33, Columbia Univ.; Supvg. Prin. of Sch., East Greenbush, N. Y., since 1947.

Goldwasser, David, Asst. Supt., Div. of Housing, New York City Sch., 110 Livingston St., Brooklyn, N. Y., since 1950.

Good, Harry I., B.C.S.'20, New York Univ.; B.S.'27, M.A.'31, Univ. of Buffalo; Deputy Supt. of Sch., Buffalo, N. Y., since 1937.

Goold, G. Howard, B.S.'39, Hobart Col.; M.A. '37, Cornell Univ.; Exec. Secy., New York State Tchrs. Assn., Albany, N. Y., since 1951.

Grace, Alonzo G., A.B.'17, A.M.'20, Univ. of Minn.; Ph.D.'32, Western Reserve Univ.; Head, Div. of Advanced Study, Sch. of Educ., New York Univ., New York, N. Y., since 1951.

Grafflin, Douglas G., B.A.'31, Ohio Univ.; M.A.'33, New York Univ.; Dist. Prin., Pub. Sch., Chappaqua, N. Y., since 1942.

Gragg, William L., B.S.'39, Ind. Univ.; Ph.D.'49, Cornell Univ.; Supt. of Sch., Ithaca, N. Y., since 1951.

*Graves, Frank Pierrepont, A.M.'90, A.M.'91, Columbia Univ.; Ph.D.'92, Boston Univ.; Litt.D.'97, Heidelberg Col.; LL.D.'97, Hanover Col.; Ph.D.'12, Columbia Univ.; LL.D.'20, Oberlin Col.; L.H.D.'21, Tufts Col.; L.H.D.'22, Colgate Univ.; LL.D.'22, Hobart Col.; LL.D. '22, Hamilton Col.; Litt. D.'23, Univ. of Rochester; LL.D.'26, Union Univ.; LL.D.'28, Alfred Univ.; LL.D.'29, Col. of William and Mary; LL.D.'29, Columbia Univ.; LL.D.'30, Univ. of Mo.; LL.D.'30, Syracuse Univ.; LL.D. '30, Juniata Col.; LL.D.'31, Niagara Univ.; LL.D.'33, Ohio Univ.; LL.D.'33, Fordham Univ.; Litt.D.'35, Canisius Col.; LL.D.'35, St. Bonaventure's Col.; LL.D.'36, Manhattan Col.; LL.D.'37, Univ. of Wyo.; D.C.L.'38, Ursinus Col.; LL.D.'38, George Washington Univ.; LL.D.'38, Houghton Col.; LL.D.'38, Bucknell Univ.; LL.D.'39, Wash. Col.; LL.D. '39, Boston Univ.; LL.D.'39, Western Reserve Univ.; LL.D.'39, Miami Univ.; J.U.D.'40, Univ. of Pa.; LL.D.'40, Bethany Col.; D.C.L. '40, Univ. of the South; LL.D.'40, St. John's Univ.; L.H.D.'40, Yeshiva Col.; LL.D.'40, Univ. of the State of New York; Honorary Life Member, American Assn. of Sch. Admin.; Pres., Univ. of the State of New York and State Commr. of Educ., Albany, N. Y., 1921-1940. Address: 303 Woodlawn Ave., Albany, N. Y.

Green, James H., B.S.'15, Colgate Univ.; M.A. '35, Univ. of Rochester; Supt. of Sch., Tonawanda, N. Y., since 1941.

Greenbaum, Rabbi Bernard, Prin., Yeshiva of Spring Valley, Spring Valley, N. Y.

Greenberg, Benjamin B., A.B.'06, City Col. of the City of N. Y.; M.A.'12, New York Univ.; Ed.D.'38, Tchrs. Col., Columbia Univ.; Asst. Supt. of Sch., New York, N. Y., since 1931.

Greenberg, Jacob, Ph.D.'36, New York Univ.; Assoc. Supt., New York Sch., Brooklyn, N. Y., since 1934.

Griffin, Francis E., A.B.'28, N. Y. State Col. for Tchrs., Albany; M.A.'38, Cornell Univ.; Chief, Bureau of Rural Admin. Serv., State Educ. Dept., Albany, N. Y., since 1943.

Griffiths, Daniel E., B.Ed.'40, Tchrs. Col. of Conn.; M.Ed.'49, Univ. of N. H.; Dir., Admin. Seminar Project, N. Y. State Col. for Tchrs., Albany, N. Y., since 1951.

Gross, Harry W., B.S.'27, New York Univ.; M.A.'29, Tchrs. Col., Columbia Univ.; Dist. Supt. of Sch., Mineola, N. Y., since 1941.

Gross, Lester, Pres., Chic Maid Hat Mfg. Co., Inc., 630 High St., Buffalo 11, N. Y., since 1926.

Grover, George H., Ed.D.'52, Tchrs. Col., Columbia Univ.; Dir., Health and Physical Educ., City Sch. Dist., New Rochelle, N. Y., since 1952.

Haessig, William B., B.E.'42, State Tchrs. Col., Oswego, N. Y.; M.S. in Ed.'48, Syracuse Univ.; Supvg. Prin., The Hills Sch., Huntington, N. Y., since 1949.

Hafer, Lilla D., A.B.'23, A.M.'26, Tchrs. Col., Columbia Univ.; Dir., Early Childhood Educ., New York City Sch., 110 Livingston St., Brooklyn 2, N. Y., since 1949.

Hager, Harold V., A.B.'26, Colgate Univ.; M.A.'35, Syracuse Univ.; LL.D.'45, Hartwick Col.; Supt. of Sch., Oneonta, N. Y., since 1945.

Hammond, Maurice S., B.S.'29, St. Lawrence Univ.; M.A.'33, Tchrs. Col., Columbia Univ.; Ed.D.'39, New York Univ.; Supt. of Sch., North Syracuse, N. Y., since 1950.

Handel, Elmer E., B.S. in Ed.'36, State Tchrs. Col., Buffalo, N. Y.; Prin. of the Dist., Central Sch., Orchard Park, N. Y., since 1947.

Hanson, Abel A., B.Ed.'30, Ill. State Normal Univ., Normal; M.S.'35, Univ. of Ill.; D.Ed.'41, Columbia Univ.; Genl. Secy., Tchrs. Col., Columbia Univ., New York, N. Y., since 1948.

Hardy, H. Claude, A.B.'11, Wesleyan Univ.; M.A.'21, Univ. of Rochester; M.A.'23, Syracuse Univ.; Ph.D.'31, New York Univ.; Dir. of Pub. Relations, Hartwick Col., Oneonta, N. Y.

Harney, Thomas E., B.Ed.'27, State Tchrs. Col., Superior, Wis.; M.A.'29, Univ. of Notre Dame; Supt. of Sch., Dunkirk, N. Y., since 1942.

Harris, Harold, B.S.S.'23, Col. of the City of N. Y.; M.A.'33, Columbia Univ.; Head of The Augustus Rapelye Sch., Maspeth, N. Y., since 1945.

Hartstein, Jacob I., B.A.'32, Yeshiva Col.; M.S.'33, City Col. of the City of New York; M.A.'36, Columbia Univ.; Ph.D.'45, New York Univ.; Prof. of Educ. and Dean, Grad. Sch., Yeshiva Univ., since 1944; Prof. and Head, Educ. and Psych., since 1945 and Chairman, Grad. Div., Long Island Univ., Brooklyn, N. Y., since 1950.

*Hartwell, Ernest C., B.A.'05, Albion Col.; M.A.'10, Univ. of Mich.; Pd.D.'28, N. Y. State Col. for Tchrs., Albany; D.Ed.'30, Albion Col.; Pres., Dept. of Superintendence, 1918-19; Honorary Life Member, American Assn. of Sch. Admin. Address: Box 29, Brockport, N. Y.

Hasseltine, Erwin K., B.S.'27, Middleburg Col.; M.A.'38, New York Univ.; Supvg. Prin., Katonah, N. Y., since 1944.

Hatten, Harry H., B.S. in Ed.'35, N. Y. State Col. for Tchrs., Buffalo; M.A.'48, Tchrs. Col., Columbia Univ.; Supt. of Sch., Elmira Heights, N. Y., since 1948.

Hausner, Harold S., B.S.'39, Ithaca Col.; Dist. Supt. of Sch., Mohawk, N. Y., since 1936.

Hawley, William Earl, B.S.'20, A.M.'21, Univ. of Rochester; Supt., Brighton Sch. Dist. 1, Rochester, N. Y., 1947-52 (retired).

Haynes, Andrew Francis, A.B.'30, Univ. of Rochester; M.A.'36, N. Y. Univ.; Supvg. Prin. of Sch., Fillmore, N. Y., since 1936.

Heiman, Vernon W., A.B.'29, Alfred Univ.; Dist. Prin. of Sch., Woodlawn, Buffalo, N. Y., since 1936.

Helfer, Martin A., B.S.'27, Dartmouth Col.; M.S.'37, Syracuse Univ.; Supt. of Sch., Binghamton, N. Y., since 1947.

Helmes, Charles T., M.A.'46, New York Univ.; Supvg. Prin., Lewisboro Union Free Sch., South Salem, N. Y., since 1945.

Hemstreet, A. Earle, Ph.B. and Ped.B.'11, Syracuse Univ.; M.A.'23, Columbia Univ.; Prin., Riverside Elem. Sch. 60, Buffalo, N. Y., since 1936.

Henrickson, Velma W., B.S.'26, M.A.'29, Tchrs. Col., Columbia Univ.; Prin., East Sch., Long Beach, L. I., N. Y., since 1927.

*Herber, Howard T., A.B.'25, Ursinus Col.; A.M.'26, Ph.D.'38, Tchrs. Col., Columbia Univ.; Supt. of Sch., Malverne, L. I., N. Y., since 1931.

Herrington, Walter J., A.B.'17, N. Y. State Col. for Tchrs., Albany; M.A.'23, Columbia Univ.; Supvg. Prin. of H. S., Williamsville Br., Buffalo, N. Y., since 1924.

Hetherington, Charles George, B.S.'16, Colgate Univ.; M.S.'17, Pa. State Col.; Ph.D.'34, New York Univ.; Supt. of Sch., Auburn, N. Y., since 1937.

Hewes, Earl D., Supt. of Sch., Beacon, N. Y.

Hickey, Joseph J., B.S.'42, Catholic Univ. of America; M.A.'48, Columbia Univ.; Supvg. Prin., Orangeburg Grammar Sch., Orangeburg, N. Y., since 1952.

Hicks, Alvin W., Supt., Rye Neck Sch., Mamaroneck, N. Y.

Hicks, Samuel I., A.B.'24, Univ. of Mich.; M.A.'27, Ed.D.'47, Tchrs. Col., Columbia Univ.; Supt. of Sch., Pearl River, N. Y., since 1932.

*Hill, Frederick William, B.S.'34, M.S.'35, Kansas State Col.; Ed.D.'41, Tchrs. Col., Columbia Univ.; Deputy Supt. and Bus. Admin. of Sch., Yonkers, N. Y., since 1950.

*Hodge, Lamont F., A.B.'97, A.M.'21, Pd.D.'26, Colgate Univ. Address: 448 Clinton Ave., Albany, N. Y.

Hoffman, M. Gazelle, B.A.'11, Elmira Col.; M.A.'26, Columbia Univ.; Dist. Supt. of Sch., Lewiston, N. Y., since 1915, and Lecturer, N. Y. State Tchrs. Col., Buffalo, N. Y., since 1931.

Hogue, O. Wendell, B.S.'18, Syracuse Univ.; M.A.'25, Tchrs. Col., Columbia Univ.; Supvg. Prin. of Sch., Croton-on-Hudson, N. Y., since 1934.

Holbritter, J. Albert, A.B.'43, Hobart Col.; M.A.'48, New York State Col. for Tchrs., Albany; Coordinator of Field Services, State Tchrs. Col., Plattsburgh, N. Y., since 1949.

Holden, Fox D., B.S.'20, Ed.M.'38, Univ. of Rochester; Supt. of Sch., Poughkeepsie, N. Y., since 1938.

Hollister, Harold Edmund, A.B.'17, Middlebury Col.; A.M.'36, N. Y. State Col. for Tchrs., Albany; Dist. Supt. of Sch., White Plains, N. Y., since 1941.

Hoover, W. Wendell, A.B.'42, McKendree Col.; M.A.'47, Washington Univ.; Supt. of Sch., Rye, N. Y., since 1950.

Hopke, William E., A.B.'39, M.A.'46, New York State Tchrs. Col., Albany; Ed.D.'50, Tchrs. Col., Columbia Univ.; Exec. Asst., Office of Placement and Field Relations, Tchrs. Col., Columbia Univ., New York, N. Y., since 1950.

Hopkins, Johanna Marie, Diploma '14, Brooklyn Tr. Sch. for Tchrs.; B.S.'37, M.A.'38, New York Univ.; Asst. Dist. Supt. of Sch., Jackson Hgts., New York, N. Y., since 1942.

Hopkins, L. Thomas, A.B.'10, A.M.'11, Tufts Col.; Ed.D.'22, Harvard Univ.; Prof. of Educ., Tchrs. Col., Columbia Univ., New York, N. Y., since 1929.

Horsman, Louis C., Prin., H. S., Port Jervis, N. Y.

Horton, Joseph S., M.A.'39, Albany State Col.; Supt. of Sch., Little Falls, N. Y., since 1951.

Hossfield, George L., Dir., Tchrs. Advisory Serv., Underwood Corp., New York, N. Y., since 1914.

Hostler, Amy M., B.S.'30, M.A.'34, Western Reserve Univ.; Pres., Mills Col. of Educ., New York, N. Y., since 1941.

Houseman, W. Lynn, B.S.'08, Colgate Univ.; M.A.'21, Tchrs. Col., Columbia Univ.; Supt. of Sch., Geneva, N. Y., since 1926.

Huebner, Robert H., Pres., Long Island Institutional Equipment Co., Mineola, N. Y.

Huggard, Ethel F., M.S. in Ed.'29, Col. of the City of New York; Assoc. Supt. of New York City Sch., Elem. Div., 110 Livingston St., Brooklyn 2, N. Y., since 1941.

Hughson, Arthur, A.B.'16, Col. of the City of New York; A.M.'18, Columbia Univ.; Asst. Supt. of Sch., Brooklyn, N. Y., since 1948.

Hunt, Charles Wesley, A.B.'04, Brown Univ.; A.M.'10, Ph.D.'22, Columbia Univ.; Pres., State Tchrs. Col., Oneonta, N. Y., 1933-51 (retired).

Jacobs, Charles C., A.B.'27, M.A.'30, Syracuse Univ.; Supvg. Prin. of Sch., Holland Patent, N. Y., since 1944.

Jallade, L. E., 597 5th Ave., New York, N. Y.

Jammer, George F., B.S.'19, Bucknell Univ.; M.A.'26, Columbia Univ.; Supt. of Sch., Lockport, N. Y., since 1943.

Jansen, William, B.S.'08, M.A.'13, Ed.D.'40, Tchrs. Col., Columbia Univ.; LL.D.'47, Union Col.; LL.D.'48, Gettysburg Col.; Supt., New York City Sch., Brooklyn, N. Y., since 1947.

Jarvie, Lawrence L., B.S.'28, Ohio Univ.; M.A. '32, Ph.D.'36, Ohio State Univ.; Exec. Dean for Tech. Inst. and Community Col., State Univ. of New York, Albany, N. Y.

Jean, Sally Lucas, A.M.'24, Bates Col.; Health Educ. Consultant, The Natl. Found. for Infantile Paralysis, New York, N. Y., since 1943.

Jennings, Harold M., A.B.'13, M.A.'15, Cornell Univ.; Supt. of Sch., Mt. Kisco, N. Y., since 1920.

Jensen, Richard A., A.B.'28, N. Y. State Col. for Tchrs., Albany; M.A.'38, Cornell Univ.; Supt. of Sch., North Tonawanda, N. Y., since 1946.

Johnson, Herbert F., B.S.'30, Univ. of Minn.; M.A.'34, Tchrs. Col., Columbia Univ.; Supt. of Sch., Rockville Centre, N. Y., since 1952.

Jones, Evan E., A.B.'16, Hamilton Col., Clinton, N. Y.; M.A.'25, Tchrs. Col., Columbia Univ.; Supt. of Sch., Port Chester, N. Y., since 1934.

Jones, J. Wilbert, M.S.'38, Syracuse Univ.; Supt. of Sch., Southampton, N. Y., since 1949.

Jones, Willard T., A.B.'25, M.A.'30, Syracuse Univ.; Ed.D.'42, Tchrs. Col., Columbia Univ.; Supt. of Sch., Ballston Spa, N. Y., since 1933.

Joslyn, William F., A.B.'34, Houghton Col.; Ed.M.'45, St. Bonaventure Col.; Supt., Central Sch. Dist., Penn Yan, N. Y., since 1952.

Joyce, Leo A., B.S.'23, M.Ed.'41, Canisius Col.; Supt. of Sch., Lackawanna, N. Y., since 1941.

Kaemmerlen, John T., A.B.'16, A.M.'17, New York Univ.; Supt. of Sch., Hudson, N. Y., since 1938.

Kauffman, Treva E., B.S.'11, Ohio State Univ.; M.A.'31, Columbia Univ.; State Supvr. of Home Economics Educ., State Educ. Dept., Albany, N. Y., since 1921.

Keating, J. Walter, B.Ed.'40, State Tchrs. Col., Brockport, N. Y.; M.S.'50, Cornell Univ.; Central Sch., Gorham, N. Y.

Keating, Norine B., M.A.'29, N. Y. State Col. for Tchrs., Albany; Supt. of Sch., Green Island, N. Y., since 1936.

Keeler, Donald S., A.B.'33, Colgate Univ.; M.A. '38, Columbia Univ.; Supt. of Sch., Perry, N. Y., since 1946.

Keliher, Alice Virginia, B.S.'28, M.A.'29, Ph.D. '30, Tchrs. Col., Columbia Univ.; Prof. of Educ., New York Univ., New York, N. Y., since 1945.

Kelley, Norman R., B.S.'30, Syracuse Univ.; Ed.M.'40, Univ. of Rochester; Supt. of Sch., Newark, N. Y., since 1947.

Kelsey, R. Wilfred, B.S.'33, Haverford Col.; Dir., Educ. Div., Inst. of Life Insurance, New York, N. Y., since 1940.

Kennedy, Mark, A.B.'21, M.A.'22, St. Bonaventure Col.; Lect. Glis.S.S.'29, Collegio S. Antonio, Rome, Italy; Pres., Siena Col., Loudonville, N. Y., since 1943.

Kennedy, Mary A., B.S.'26, M.A.'34, New York Univ.; Asst. Supt. of Sch., Jr. H. S. Div., 110 Livingston St., Brooklyn 2, N. Y., since 1936.

Kerlin, Oscar F., B.S.'21, Univ. of Mich.; M.S. '26, Syracuse Univ.; Supt. of Sch., Elmira,N.Y., since 1938.

Kimball, Reginald Stevens, A.B.'21, A.M.'22, Brown Univ.; Ed.M.'29, Harvard Univ.; Ed.D. '41, New York Univ.; Dir., Civil Serv. Inst., Brooklyn, N. Y., since 1945.

Kimm, Willard I., A.B.'15, Columbia Univ.; H. S. and Col. Dept., Ginn & Co., New York, N. Y.

Kimple, James A., B.A.'40, Parsons; M.A.'48, Tchrs. Col., Columbia Univ.; Asst., Inst. of Field Studies, Tchrs. Col., Columbia Univ., New York, N. Y., since 1951.

Kincaid, William Amos, A.B.'23, Ohio Univ.; M.A.'28, Ed.D.'46, Tchrs. Col., Columbia Univ.; Supt. of Sch., Hempstead, N. Y., since 1947.

King, Dana M., B.S.'21, Greenville Col.; A.M. '30, Cornell Univ.; Supt. of Sch., Hudson Falls, N. Y., since 1938.

King, John B., B.S.'31, M.A.'36, New York Univ.; Asst. Supt. of Sch., Dist. 26 and 28, New York City Sch., Brooklyn, N. Y., since 1951.

King, Lloyd W., A.B.'23, William Jewell Col.; A.M.'31, Univ. of Mo.; Exec. Secy., American Textbook Publishers Inst., New York, N. Y., since 1943.

Kirk, Lucile D. (Mrs. George W.) B.A.'19, Western Reserve Univ.; M.A.'44, Tchrs. Col., Columbia Univ.; Metropolitan New York Editor, *Parent's Magazine*, 52 Vanderbilt Ave., New York 17, N. Y., since 1936; also Pacific Coast Editor and Beauty Editor, since 1952.

Klein, Agnes Sayler, Vicepres., Grolier Society and Dir., Americana Corp., 2 West 45th St., New York 19, N. Y., since 1938.

Klein, Louis M., A.B.'25, N. Y. State Col. for Tchrs., Albany; M.A.'33, Cornell Univ.; Supt. of Sch., Harrison, N. Y., since 1936.

Krugman, Morris, B.S.'19, Polytech Inst. of Brooklyn; M.A.'25, Ph.D.28, New York Univ.; Asst. Supt. of Sch. in charge of Guid., New York City Bd. of Educ., Brooklyn 2, N. Y., since 1947.

Krum, William J., Jr., Supt. of Sch., Endicott, N. Y.

Kullman, Nathan E., Jr., A.B.'37, M.A.'41, State Col. for Tchrs., Albany, N. Y.; Coordinator of Field Services and Pub. Relations, State Tchrs. Col., Plattsburg, N. Y., since 1947.

*Kulp, Claude L., B.S.'27, Univ. of Rochester; M.A.'30, Cornell Univ.; Prof. of Educ. and Supvr. of Experimental Program in Elem. Tchr. Educ., Sch. of Educ., Cornell Univ., Ithaca, N. Y., since 1952.

Lahr, John M., B.S.'25, Alfred Univ.; M.A.'35, Cornell Univ.; Ed.D.'38, New York Univ.; Supt. of Pub. Sch., Oyster Bay, L. I., N. Y., since 1950.

Laidlaw, Arthur J., B.S.'11, M.S.'13, St. Lawrence Univ.; Supt. of Sch., Kingston, N. Y., since 1939.

Lamb, Wallace Emerson, A.B.'26, M.A.'27, Clark Univ.; Ed.D.'49, Syracuse Univ.; Supvg. Prin. of Sch., Greenport, N. Y., since 1950.

Landis, Mildred M., B.S.'35, Alfred Univ.; M.A.'41, Columbia Univ.; Ed.D.'47, Harvard Univ.; Dual Prof. of Art and Educ., Sch. of Art, Syracuse Univ., Syracuse, N. Y., since 1949.

Landry, Herbert A., B.M.E.'21, Northeastern Univ.; M.S.'30, Mass. State Col.; Ph.D.'35, New York Univ.; Admin. Research, Bd. of Educ., 110 Livingston St., Brooklyn 2, N. Y., since 1937.

Langfitt, R. Emerson, B.S. in Ed.'20, Ohio Univ.; A.M.'26, Tchrs. Col., Columbia Univ.; Ed.D. '38, New York Univ.; Prof. of Educ., New York Univ., New York, N. Y., since 1938.

Langworthy, Philip B., A.B.'34, Union Col.; M.A.'38, Ed.D.'50, Tchrs. Col., Columbia Univ.; Supt. of Sch., Hastings-on-Hudson, N. Y., since 1951.

Lant, Kenneth A., M.A.'40, Ed.D.'50, Tchrs. Col., Columbia Univ.; Supvg. Prin. of Sch., Jericho, Long Island, N. Y., since 1945.

Larsen, Roper F., B.Ed.'46, State Tchrs. Col., New Paltz, N. Y.; M.A.'48, Tchrs. Col., Columbia Univ.; Prin., Elem. Sch., Cicero, N. Y., since 1951.

Larson, Jordan L., B.A.'22, M.A.'31, State Univ. of Iowa; M.A.'51, Ed.D.'51, Tchrs. Col., Columbia Univ.; Supt. of Sch., Mt. Vernon, N. Y., since 1946.

Law, Frederick Houk, A.B.'95, Amherst Col.; A.M.'96, Columbia Univ.; Ph.D.'14, New York Univ.; Editor, Educ. Dept., *Reader's Digest*, since 1942. Address: 472 Argyle Rd., Brooklyn 18, N. Y.

Lawrence, William F., B.A.'33, Ursinus Col.; M.A.'37, Ed.D.'47, New York Univ.; Supt. of Sch., Wantagh, Long Island, N. Y., since 1952.

Lawson, Dorothy S., B.S.'20, Russell Sage Col.; M.A.'34, Tchrs. Col., Columbia Univ.; Chief, Bur. of Home Ec. Educ., State Educ. Dept., Albany, N. Y., since 1947.

Lazar, May, Ph.D.'37, Columbia Univ.; Asst. Dir., Bur. of Educ. Research, New York City Bd. of Educ., Brooklyn, N. Y., since 1946.

LeBarron, Erie H., M.A.'33, Columbia Univ.; Ed.D.'47, New York Univ.; Supt. of Sch., Hicksville, N. Y., since 1936.

Leggett, Stanton, A.B.'38, Columbia Col.; M.A.'39, Ph.D.'48, Tchrs. Col., Columbia Univ.; Educational Consultant, Engelhardt, Engelhardt, and Leggett, New York, N. Y., since 1947.

Levenson, Samuel M., B.S.'16, M.A.'20, Ph.D.'32, New York Univ.; Asst. Supt., New York City Sch., 856 Quincy St., Brooklyn 21, N. Y., since 1945.

Lewis, Charles E., M.A.'34, Cornell Univ.; Supvr. Prin. of Sch., Callicoon, N. Y., since 1939.

Lieberman, Elias, B.A.'03, Col. of the City of New York; M.A.'06, Ph.D.'11, New York Univ.; Assoc. Supt. of Sch., 110 Livingston St., Brooklyn 2, N. Y., since 1940.

Lindbloom, Ray L., A.B.'30, M.A.'37, Colo. State Col. of Educ., Greeley; Supvg. Prin., Union Free Sch. Dist. 16, Elmont, N. Y., since 1947.

Linden, Arthur V., B.S.'33, M.A.'35, Tchrs. Col., Columbia Univ.; Ed.D.'41, Arnold Col.; Assoc. Dir. of Student Personnel in charge of Field Relations and Placement, Tchrs. Col., Columbia Univ., New York, N. Y., since 1936.

Lindsey, Morton Cole, M.A.'29, New York Univ.; Supvg. Prin., Hendrick Hudson H. S., Montrose, N. Y., since 1943.

Linn, Henry H., A.B.'18, State Tchrs. Col., Peru, Nebr.; M.A.'22, Univ. of Nebr.; M.A.'26, Ph.D.'29, Tchrs. Col., Columbia Univ.; Prof. of Educ., Tchrs. Col., Columbia Univ., New York, N. Y., since 1944.

Linton, Clarence, A.B.'19, Nebr. State Tchrs. Col., Wayne; M.A.'21, Univ. of Nebr.; Ph.D.'27, Columbia Univ.; Prof. of Educ., Tchrs. Col., Columbia Univ., New York, N. Y., since 1937.

Linton, Harry J., B.S.'21, Univ. of Nebr.; LL.D.'49, Union Col. (N. Y.); Supt. of Sch., Schenectady, N. Y., since 1946.

Livengood, William W., A.B.'07, Ind. Univ.; Editor-in-Chief and Vicepres., American Book Co., New York, N. Y., since 1931.

Livingston, Melvin C., B.S.'25, Middlebury Col.; M.A.'32, Tchrs. Col., Columbia Univ.; Supt. of Sch., Mechanicville, N. Y., since 1942.

Lobaugh, Lawrence C., B.S.'27, Alfred Univ.; M.A.'42, New York Univ.; Supt. of Sch., Lindenhurst, L. I., N. Y., since 1947.

Lockhart, Raymond J., M.E.'20, Pratt Inst.; M.A.'31, New York Univ.; Supvg. Prin. of Sch., Massapequa, N. Y., since 1930.

Long, Edward W., A.B.'28, Syracuse Univ.; Prin., Dryden-Freeville Central Sch., Dryden, N. Y., since 1947.

Loomis, Harold V., A.B.'12, Syracuse Univ.; M.A.'26, Tchrs. Col., Columbia Univ.; Supt. of Sch., Ossining, N. Y., since 1932.

Lopardo, R. A., A.B.'21, Hamilton Col.; A.M.'31, Tchrs. Col., Columbia Univ.; Supt. of Sch., Utica, N. Y., since 1951.

Loretan, Joseph O., B.S. in Ed.'26, City Col. of the City of New York; M.A.'28, Ph.D.'30, Fordham Univ.; Supt., Sch. Dist. 23, 24, and Bronx Park Community Schs., Borough of the Bronx, New York, N. Y.

Lotz, Thomas M., B.S.'30, Syracuse Univ.; M.S.'39, Cornell Univ.; Supvg. Prin. of Sch., Sherburne, N. Y., since 1946.

Loveland, Gilbert, B.A.'14, M.A.'15, Northwestern Univ.; Henry Holt and Co., Inc., New York, N. Y., since 1934.

Lowe, Wayne L., Ed.'31, Harvard Univ.; Supt. of Sch., Dobbs Ferry, N. Y., since 1949.

McCleary, Edward J., B.S.'33, Fordham Univ.; M.A.'36, Columbia Univ.; Ed.D.'41, New York Univ.; Prin. Dist. Elem. & Sec. Educ., Meadow Lawn Sch., East Meadow, L. I., N. Y.

*McCormick, Felix J., B.S.'29, Bucknell Univ.; M.A.'41, State Tchrs. Col., Upper Montclair, N. J.; Assoc. Inst. of Field Studies, Tchrs. Col., Columbia Univ., New York, N. Y., since 1948.

McDonald, Everett A., Jr., BSE.'38, Fitchburg State Tchrs. Col. (Mass.); M.Ed.'45, Boston Univ.; M.A.'51, Yale Univ.; Supt. of Sch., Westbury, N. Y., since 1951.

McGuire, John P., Dist. Supt. of Sch., Huntington, N. Y.

McKee, Louis E., B.S.'40, M.S.'42, Bucknell Univ.; Supvg. Prin., H. S., Maybrook, N. Y., since 1946.

McLaughlin, Frederick C., B.S.'30, Univ. of Detroit; M.A.'38, Tchrs. Col., Columbia Univ.; D.Ed.'49, Columbia Univ.; CPEA, Tchrs. Col., Columbia Univ., New York, N. Y., since 1951.

McLaughlin, Samuel J., Ph.D.'36, New York Univ.; Prof. of Educ., New York Univ., New York, N. Y., since 1946.

*McNally, Harold J., B.S.'38, M.A.'40, Ph.D.'42, Columbia Univ.; Prof. of Educ., Tchrs. Col., Columbia Univ., New York, N. Y., since 1946.

McNamara, Anna L., B.S. in Ed.'32, M.A.'35, Fordham Univ.; Asst. Supt. of Sch., Brooklyn, N. Y., since 1948.

MacCalman, Kenneth R., A.B.'21, Elon Col.; M.A.'30, Columbia Univ.; Supt. of Sch., Nyack, N. Y., since 1932.

Mackenzie, Gordon N., B.S. and M.A.'29, Univ. of Minn.; Ed.D.'40, Stanford Univ.; Prof. of Educ., and Head, Dept. of Curriculum and Tchg., Tchrs. Col., Columbia Univ., New York, N. Y., since 1945.

MacNeill, H. J., Mgr., Crayon Div., Binney and Smith Co., New York, N. Y.

Mahoney, Rev. Charles J., A.B.'34, M.A.'36, Niagara Univ.; Ph.D.'41, Catholic Univ. of America; Supt. of Catholic Sch., Diocese of Rochester, Rochester, N. Y., since 1945.

Marshall, James, LL.B.'20, Columbia Univ.; Member, Bd. of Educ., New York City Public Sch., 1935-52 (retired). Address: 521 Fifth Ave., New York, N. Y.

Martin, Henning J., A.B.'24, Macalester Col.; M.A.'27, Tchrs. Col., Columbia Univ.; Supt. of Sch., Herkimer, N. Y., since 1940.

Martin, William H., M.S.'45, Syracuse Univ.; Supt. of Sch., Scotia, N. Y., since 1949.

Mason, Frank W., A.B.'25, Allegheny Col.; M.A.'40, N. Y. State Col. for Tchrs., Albany; Supt. of Sch., Gouverneur, N. Y., since 1949.

Meade, Mary E., A.B.'18, Hunter Col.; A.M.'26, Columbia Univ.; Ph.D.'35, Fordham Univ.; Prin., Wash. Irving H. S., New York, N. Y., since 1944.

Meeker, John B., B.A.'31, Trinity Col. (Conn.); Ed.M.'33, Rutgers Univ.; Supvg. Prin. of Sch., East Hampton, N. Y., since 1951.

Melby, Ernest O., B.A.'13, St. Olaf Col.; M.A. '26, Ph.D.'28, Univ. of Minn.; Dean and Prof. of Educ., Sch. of Educ., New York Univ., New York, N. Y., since 1945.

Melchior, William T., M.A.'22, Ph.D.'23, Tchrs. Col., Columbia Univ.; Prof. Emeritus and Dir., Bus. and Indus. Scholarships, Syracuse Univ., Syracuse, N. Y., since 1952.

Merchant, Larry, Pres., Pilsbury Pub. Inc., New York, N. Y., since 1949.

Merrall, David, Vicepres., Rhodes Sch., New York, N. Y., since 1920.

Metcalfe, Tristram Walker, Litt.D.'48, Long Island Univ.; Dean, Col. of Arts and Sciences since 1932 and Pres., Long Island Univ., Brooklyn, N. Y., since 1942.

Miller, Alexander W., A.B.'12, Harvard Univ.; A.M.'22, Columbia Univ.; Supt. of Sch., Glens Falls, N. Y., since 1927.

Miller, John L., A.B.'26, Bates Col.; Ed.M.'29, Ed.D.'46, Harvard Univ.; Supt. of Sch., Great Neck, N. Y., since 1942.

Miller, Stanton H., Asst. Dist. Prin., Corona Ave., Sch. Dist. 13, Valley Stream, N. Y.

Miller, Thomas R., B.S.'30, M.A.'31, Ph.D.'38, Syracuse Univ.; Dean, State Tchrs. Col., Oswego, N. Y., since 1948.

Miller, Victor L., M.A.'42, New York Univ.; Supvg. Prin. of Sch., Bethpage, L. I., N. Y., since 1940.

Milliken, William H., Jr., Educ. Dept., Binney and Smith Co., New York, N. Y., since 1919.

Miner, Edwin H., A.B.'27, Dartmouth Col.; A.M.'29, Univ. of Pa.; Orange Co. Community Col., Middletown, N. Y.

Moore, Clyde B., A.B.'12, Nebr. Wesleyan Univ.; B.Ed.'13, Nebr. State Tchrs. Col., Peru; A.M.'16, Clark Univ.; Ph.D.'24, Columbia Univ.; Prof. of Educ., Cornell Univ., Ithaca, N. Y., since 1925.

Moore, Thomas C., B.S.'26, Alfred Univ.; Ed.M. '42, Univ. of Buffalo; Prin., H. S., East Aurora, N. Y., since 1946.

Moore, Victor E., B.A.'29, Asbury Col.; Asst. Dir., Air World Educ., Trans World Airlines, Inc., New York, N. Y., since 1952.

Morgan, W. George, A.B.'29, Oberlin Col.; A.M.'37, Tchrs. Col., Columbia Univ.; Supt. of Sch., Owego, Tioga Co., N. Y., since 1937.

Morris, Lyle L., B.S.'20, Drake Univ.; M.A.'26, Ph.D.'30, Columbia Univ. Address: 534 N. 11th St., New Hyde Park, N. Y.

Morris, Marion P., Bristol Myers Co., New York, N. Y.

*Morrison, J. Cayce, A.B.'12, Valparaiso Univ.; M.A.'16, Ph.D.'22, Columbia Univ.; LL.D.'32, Alfred Univ.; Asst. Commr. for Research, State Educ. Dept., Albany, N. Y., since 1937.

Morse, Grant D., Ph.D.'41, New York Univ.; Supt. of Sch., Saugerties, N. Y., since 1924.

Mort, Paul R., Ph.D.'24, Columbia Univ.; Prof. of Educ., Tchrs. Col., Columbia Univ., New York, N. Y., since 1924.

Mortola, Edward J., B.A.'38, M.A.'41, Ph.D.'46, Fordham Univ.; Provost, Pace Col., New York, N. Y., since 1949.

Moseley, Thomas, A.B.'29, Occidental Col.; A.M.'30, Univ. of Southern Calif.; D.D.'40, Wheaton Col.; LL.D.'47, Bob Jones Univ.; Pres., The Missionary Tr. Inst., Nyack, N. Y., since 1940.

Mosher, Frank K., B.S.'29, M.S.'37, D.Ed.'49, Syracuse Univ.; Dist. Prin., Central Sch., Liverpool, N. Y., since 1950.

Moskowitz, David H., B.A.'13, M.A.'14, Columbia Univ.; Asst. Supt. of New York City Sch., Brooklyn, N. Y., since 1937.

Moyer, Edward, B.S.'40, Northern State Tchrs. Col., Aberdeen, S. Dak.; A.M.'41, Yale Univ.; Dist. Prin., Briarcliff H. S., Briarcliff Manor, N. Y., since 1947.

Moyle, William D., B.A.'23, Wesleyan Univ.; M.A.'29, Tchrs. Col., Columbia Univ.; Supvg. Prin., Edgemont Sch., Scarsdale, N. Y., since 1937.

Mullin, Mark J., C.M., B.A.'28, M.A.'33, St. Joseph's Col. (N. J.); Ph.L.'35, Collegium Angelicum, Rome, Italy; Dean, Sch. of Educ., Niagara Univ., Niagara University, N. Y., since 1950.

Mummert, Ira C., B.S.'17, M.A.'25, Susquehanna Univ.; M.A.'33, Columbia Univ.; Supvg. Prin. of Sch., Valley Stream, N. Y., since 1928.

Munson, Samuel K., B.H.'21, Springfield Col.; B.S.'26, M.A.'28, New York Univ.; Supt. of Sch., Sayville, L. I., N. Y., since 1950.

Murray, Cornelius B., B.S.'27, N. Y. State Col. for Tchrs., Albany; M.S.'35, St. Lawrence Univ.; Exec. Secy., N. Y. State Tchrs. Retirement Board, Albany, N. Y., since 1944.

Nelson, L. Warren, Dir., Educ. Research, Hill & Knowlton, 350 Fifth Ave., New York, N. Y.

Neuner, Elsie Flint, A.B.'18, A.M.'19, Ph.D.'22, Brown Univ.; Dir. of Instr., 131 Huguenot St., New Rochelle, N. Y., since 1939.

Nifenecker, Eugene A., B.A.'01, Col. of the City of New York.; M.A.'06, Columbia Univ.; Dir. of Reference, Research and Statistics, Pub. Sch., 110 Livingston St., Brooklyn 2, N. Y., since 1920.

Noethen, Joseph C., M.A.'40, New York Univ.; Asst. Supt., New York City Sch., 901 Classon Ave., Brooklyn 25, N. Y., since 1945.

Noon, Elizabeth F., B.S.'34, State Tchrs. Col., West Chester, Pa.; M.S.'36, Temple Univ.; Dir., Books and Teaching Aids Dept., F. A. Owen Publishing Co., Dansville, N. Y., since 1948.

*Norton, John K., A.B.'16, A.M.'17, Stanford Univ.; Ph.D.'26, Tchrs. Col., Columbia Univ.; Prof. of Educ. since 1931 and Dir., Div. of Admin. and Guid., Tchrs. Col., Columbia Univ., New York, N. Y., since 1942.

*Norton, LaVerne Allen, A.B.'31, Colgate Univ.; M.A.'35, Tchrs. Col., Columbia Univ.; Prin., Beaver River Central Sch., Beaver Falls, N. Y., since 1950.

Obermeier, Minnie, A.B.'01, Hunter Col. of the City of N. Y.; M.A.'06, New York Univ.; Asst. Supt. of N. Y. City Sch., Brooklyn, N. Y., since 1939.

Obourn, Lewis C., B.S.'32, Alfred Univ.; Supt. of Sch., East Rochester, N. Y., since 1944.

O'Brien, Frank J., A.B.'12, Holy Cross Col.; A.M.'13, Ph.D.'16, Clark Univ.; M.D.'27, Univ. of Louisville; Assoc. Supt. of Sch., 110 Livingston St., Brooklyn 2, N. Y., since 1941.

O'Connor, Edward P., B.S.'14, City Col. of the City of N. Y.; LL.B.'26, Fordham Univ.; M.A.'38, New York Univ.; Prin., Brooklyn H. S. of Automotive Trades, Brooklyn, N. Y., since 1943.

Ogden, Chauncey M., B.S.'17, Colgate Univ.; M.A.'33, New York Univ.; Supt. of Sch., Woodmere, N. Y., since 1940.

O'Keefe, Walter, Sales Mgr., Institutional Dept., Doubleday & Co., Inc., Garden City, N. Y.

Ormsby, Walter M., B.S.'26, Alfred Univ.; M.A.'30, Tchrs. Col., Columbia Univ.; Dist. Supt. of Sch., Bayport, N. Y., since 1936.

Orton, Dwayne, A.B.'26, Univ. of Redlands; M.A.'33, Col. of the Pacific; LL.D.'44, Univ. of Redlands; LL.D.'48, Tusculum Col.; Dir. of Educ., Internatl. Bus. Machines Corp., New York, N. Y., since 1942.

Osborn, Edward L., A.B.'31, M.A.'38, New York State Col. for Tchrs.; Supt. of Sch., Batavia, N. Y., since 1951.

Ostrander, Raymond H., A.B.'28, Hamilton Col.; M.A.'34, Ed.D.'49, Tchrs. Col., Columbia Univ.; Supt. of Sch., Mineola, N. Y., since 1951.

Ostwald, Ernest, Pres., Uniforms by Ostwald, Inc., Staten Island, N. Y., since 1932.

Owen, Mary E., A.B.'17, Smith Col.; A.M.'20, Univ. of Chicago; Ped.D.'49, Alfred Univ.; Editor, *The Instructor*, Dansville, N. Y., since 1946.

Painter, Fred B., B.S.'29, Black Hills Tchrs. Col.; A.M.'34, Cornell Univ.; Supt., Brighton Schs., Dist. No. 1, Rochester, N. Y., since 1952.

Panebaker, David E., B.S.'22, Gettysburg Col.; M.A.'37, New York Univ.; Supvg. Prin. of Sch., Liberty, N. Y., since 1931.

Park, John W., Diploma, State Tchrs. Col., Oswego, N. Y.; Bachelor's, New York Univ.; Master's, N. Y. State Col. for Tchrs., Albany; Supt. of Sch., Albany, N. Y., since 1942.

Patton, David H., A.B.'23, Wilmington Col.; M.A.'31, Univ. of Cincinnati; Supt. of Sch., Syracuse, N. Y., since 1945.

Payne, Carl, A.B.'26, Univ. of Rochester; M.A. '33, Tchrs. Col., Columbia Univ.; Security Mutual Life Insurance Co., Norwich ,N. Y.

Perry, Ralph W., A.B.'22, Hamilton Col.; Supvg. Prin. of Sch., New Hartford, N. Y., since 1947.

Pertsch, C. Frederick, B.A.'12, Col. of the City of N. Y.; M.A.'24, Ph.D.'36, Tchrs. Col., Columbia Univ.; Assoc. Supt., H. S. Div., Bd. of Educ. of the City of New York, 110 Livingston St., Brooklyn, N. Y.

Phelan, William F., B.A.'28, M.A.'34, Niagara Univ.; Ed.D.'49, Tchrs. Col., Columbia Univ.; Supt. of Sch., Depew, N. Y., since 1943.

Phillips, Donald K., A.B.'28, Columbia Col.; M.A.'33, Tchrs. Col., Columbia Univ.; Supt. of Sch., New Rochelle, N. Y., since 1948.

Phisterer, Isabel Dewey, A.B.'29, Smith Col.; M.A.'32, Univ. of Wash.; Pres., Cazenovia Jr. Col., Cazenovia, N. Y.

*Pickett, Ralph E., B.S.'17, Columbia Univ.; Ph.D.'24, New York Univ.; Assoc. Dean, Dir., Summer Sessions, Sch. of Educ., New York Univ., New York, N. Y., since 1940.

Pitkin, Edgar S., A.B.'31, Dartmouth Col.; M.A.'40, New York Univ.; Supvg. Prin., North Colonie Central Sch., Latham, N. Y., since 1950.

*Polley, John W., A.B.'37, Hamilton Col.; M.A.'42, N. Y. State Col. for Tchrs.; Ed.D.'50, Tchrs. Col., Columbia Univ.; Asst. Prof. of Educ., Tchrs. Col., Columbia Univ., New York, N. Y., since 1952.

Pomeroy, Edward C., B.A.'39, American International Col.; M.A.'47, Ed.D.'49, Tchrs. Col., Columbia Univ.; Assoc. Secy., American Assn. of Col. for Tchr. Educ., Oneonto, N. Y., since 1951.

Power, Leonard, B.S.'16, Central Mo. State Tchrs. Col., Warrensburg; M.A.'27, Univ. of Chicago; Ed.D.'35, Tchrs. Col., Columbia Univ.; Educ. Consultant, 511 Dobbs Ferry Rd., White Plains, N. Y., since 1936.

Powers, Edward P., M.A.'48, New York Univ.; Elem. Prin., Plainedge Sch., Hicksville, N. Y., since 1950.

Powers, Pliny H., B.S.'15, Wilmington Col.; M.A.'26, Tchrs. Col., Columbia Univ.; Ed.D. '41, New York Univ.; Deputy Chief Scout Executive, Boy Scouts of America, New York, N. Y., since 1945.

Pratt, Milford H., A.B.'27, Univ. of Rochester; A.M.'31, Columbia Univ.; Supvg. Prin., Central Sch., Barker, N. Y., since 1931.

Prestwood, E. L., A.B.'29, Columbia Univ.; M.A.'39, Lehigh Univ.; Ed.D.'51, Tchrs. Col., Columbia Univ.; Assoc. Coordinator of Coop. Program in Educ. Admin., Middle Atlantic Region, Tchrs. Col., Columbia Univ., New York, N. Y., since 1951.

*Priester, Harold F., B.A.E.'32, Univ. of Fla.; M.Ed.'40, Duke Univ.; M.A.'49, Tchrs. Col., Columbia Univ.; Admin. Asst., in charge of Bus. Affairs, Pub. Sch., Great Neck, N. Y., since 1951.

Proctor, Percy M., B.S.'10, Tufts Col.; M.A.'27, Tchrs. Col., Columbia Univ.; Supvg. Prin. of Sch., Babylon, N. Y., since 1935.

Pugh, Sterling B., A.B.'21, Syracuse Univ.; M.A.'31, Tchrs. Col., Columbia Univ.; Prin., Wash. Sch., New Rochelle, N. Y., since 1938.

Quackenbush, Neil R., B.S.'15, N. Y. State Col. for Tchrs., Albany; M.A.'30, Tchrs. Col., Columbia Univ.; Supvg. Prin. of Union Sch., East Islip, N. Y., since 1928.

Quick, Sherwood S., B.S.'38, State Tchrs. Col., Buffalo, N. Y.; M.A.'42, New York Univ.; Supvg. Prin. of Union Free Sch. Dist. 30, Valley Stream, N. Y., since 1945.

Quinn, J. William, B.S.'32, M.S.'39, Syracuse Univ.; Supvg. Prin. of Sch., New York Mills, N. Y., since 1942.

Rabinow, Barney, B.S.'33, Col. of the City of New York; M.A.'43, New York Univ.; Supvg. Prin. of Sch., Hawthorne, N. Y., since 1939.

Ralph, Richard J., A.B.'25, Hamilton Col.; Supvg. Prin., Clinton Central Sch., Clinton, N. Y., since 1943.

Rasbach, Floyd B., B.S.'26, St. Lawrence Univ.; M.A.'31, Columbia Univ.; Supt. of Sch., Rochester, N. Y., since 1947.

Rathbun, (Mrs.) Ruth C., A.B.'10, M.A. in Ed.'35, Syracuse Univ.; Dist. Supt. of Sch., Cincinnatus, N. Y., since 1926.

Redcay, Edward E., Acting Pres., State Univ. Tchrs. Col., Plattsburg, N. Y., since 1952.

Reed, Thomas M., Jr., B.S.'20, Pa. State Col.; Mgr., John J. Nesbitt, Inc., New York, N. Y., since 1930.

*Reid, Charles Frederick, A.B.'23, Colgate Univ.; A.M.'29, Ph.D.'40, Columbia Univ.; Asst. Prof., Sch. of Educ., Col. of the City of New York, New York, N. Y., since 1931.

*Reutter, E. Edmund, Jr., A.B.'44, Johns Hopkins Univ.; A.M.'48, Ph.D.'50, Tchrs. Col., Columbia Univ.; Asst. Prof. of Educ., Tchrs. Col., Columbia Univ., New York, N. Y.

Rhind, Flora M., Secy., Rockefeller Foundation, New York, N. Y.

Rhodes, Catharine I., B.A.'15, Vassar Col.; M.A.'20, Tchrs. Col., Columbia Univ.; Asst. Supt. of Sch., Mount Vernon, N. Y., since 1941.

Rice, Harvey Mitchell, A.B.'29, Concord Col.; M.A.'.3, W. Va. Univ.; Ph.D.'38, Ohio State Univ.; Pres., New York State Col. for Tchrs. at Buffalo, Buffalo, N. Y., since 1951.

Ring, Carlyle C., B.S.'22, Wesleyan Univ.; M.A.'29, Cornell Univ.; D.Ed.'40, New York Univ.; Supt. of Sch., since 1946 and Pres., Jamestown Col., Jamestown, N. Y., since 1950.

472

Riordan, Bessie B., Prin., North Syracuse Central Matty Dale Unit Schools, Syracuse, N. Y.

Riordon, Antoinette, A.B.'09, Columbia Univ.; A.M.'27, Tchrs. Col., Columbia Univ.; Asst. Supt. of New York City Sch., 223 Graham Ave., Brooklyn 6, N. Y., since 1944.

Ripson, (Mrs.) Edith T., Dir., Personnel Serv., Lewistown-Porter Central Sch. Youngstown, N. Y., since 1952.

Rising, Lee Robert, B.S.'33, Springfield Col.; Prin., Grade and H. S., Minoa, N. Y., since 1944.

Robbins, Clarence Rainold, A.B.'27, N. Y. State Col. for Tchrs., Albany; M.A.'35, Cornell Univ.; Prin., North Syracuse, N. Y., since 1933.

Roberts, Jack D., Ed.B.'38, R. I. Col. of Educ.; A.M.'42, Ed.D.'48, Tchrs. Col., Columbia Univ.; Prin., Daniel Webster Sch., New Rochelle, N. Y., since 1947.

Roberts, Lyle E., B.S.'25, N. Y. State Col. for Tchrs., Albany; M.A.'34, Cornell Univ.; Supvg. Prin., Central Sch., Newcomb, N. Y., since 1925.

Robertson, Arthur D., A.B.'26, Willamette Univ.; Educ. Coordinator, HQS, USAFE, AI&E, APO 633, c/o PM, New York, N. Y., since 1947.

Robertson, John W., B.S.'24, M.A.'32, Tchrs. Col., Columbia Univ.; Supvg. Prin., Floral Park Bellerose Sch., Floral Park, N. Y., since 1929.

Roda, Frank C., B.S.'26, M.A.'32, Tchrs. Col., Columbia Univ.; Supt. of Sch., Ogdensburg, N. Y., since 1939.

Rodgers, William Hamilton, B.A.'28, Maryville Col.; Ed.M.'37, Harvard Univ.; Asst. Supt. of Sch., Scarsdale, N. Y., since 1950.

Ronnei, Herman L., B.A.'16, Luther Col.; M.A.'30, Tchrs. Col., Columbia Univ.; Supvg. Prin. of Sch., Valhalla, N. Y., since 1930.

Rooney, Rev. Edward B., S.J., A.B.'24, M.A.'25, Woodstock Col.; Ph.D.'32, Gregorian Univ., Rome, Italy; Exec. Dir. and Natl. Secy., Jesuit Educ. Assn., New York, N. Y., since 1937.

Rose, Clayton Earl, B.S.'24, Colgate Univ.; M.A.'30, Columbia Univ.; Admin. Asst. in charge of Pub. Relations, N. Y. State Tchrs. Assn., Albany, N. Y.

Rosecrance, Francis C., A.B.'20, Lawrence Col.; Ph.D.'36, Northwestern Univ.; Assoc. Dean of Instr., Sch. of Educ., New York Univ., New York, N. Y., since 1946.

Rosen, Frances A., B.S.'39, State Tchrs. Col., Buffalo, N. Y.; Prin., Elem. Sch., East Aurora, N. Y., since 1939.

Ross, Donald H., B.A.'36, N. J. State Tchrs. Col., Upper Montclair; M.A.'46, Ed.D.'50, Tchrs. Col. Columbia Univ.; Metropolitan Sch. Study Council since 1952; Address: 525 W. 120th St., New York 27, N. Y.

Rounds, Lester E., B.A.'35, M.A.'42, Syracuse Univ.; Supvg. Prin. of Sch., Suffern, N. Y., since 1951.

Rugg, Harold, B.S.'08, C.E.'09, P.D.D.'33, Dartmouth Col.; Ph.D.'15, Univ. of Ill.; Ph.D.'37, Univ. of Tasmania, Australia; Prof. Emeritus, Tchrs. Col., Columbia Univ. Address: Woodstock, N. Y.

Russell, James E., A.B.'38, Princeton Univ.; A.M.'40, Ph.D.'50, Columbia Univ.; Asst. Exec. Officer of the Citizenship Educ. Project and Asst. Prof. of Educ., Tchrs. Col., Columbia Univ., New York, N. Y., since 1950.

Russell, William F., A.B.'10, Cornell Univ.; Ph.D.'14, Columbia Univ.; LL.D.'28, George Washington Univ.; LL.D.'28, Univ. of Pittsburgh; LL.D.'29, Colby Col.; LL.D.'29, Columbia Univ.; Ed.D.'35, Colo. State Col. of Educ., Greeley; Paed.D.'39, Sofia; F.E.I.S.'47, Edinburgh; Pres., Tchrs. Col., Columbia Univ., New York, N. Y.

Rutherford, Kenneth L., A.B.'16, Hobart Col.; M.A.'24, Tchrs. Col., Columbia Univ.; Supvg. Prin. of Sch., Monticello, N. Y., since 1928.

Ryan, Louise T., Ed.D.'50, New York Univ.; Asst. Supt. of Sch., Richmond Hill, N. Y., since 1950.

Sabin, Charles E., B.S. in Ed.'26, N. Y. State Col. for Tchrs.; Supt. of Sch., Watertown, N. Y., since 1933.

Sackett, Howard G., Dist. Supt. of Sch., Port Leyden, N. Y.

Salten, David George, B.S.'53, Washington Square Col., New York Univ.; M.A.'39, Columbia Univ.; Ph.D.'44, New York Univ.; Supt. of Sch., Long Beach, N. Y., since 1950.

*Sampson, James J., B.S. in Ed.'38, State Tchrs. Col., Salem, Mass.; M.Ed.'46, State Tchrs. Col., Bridgewater, Mass.; Ed.D.'50, Columbia Univ.; Prof. of Educ., State Univ. of New York, State Tchrs. Col., Oneonta, N. Y.

Sanborn, Philip E., A.B.'35, Colgate Univ.; M.A.'46, N. Y. Univ.; Ed.D.'52, Columbia Univ.; Supvg. Prin. of Sch., Irvington, N. Y., since 1952.

Scarborough, Truman G., B.A.E.'37, M.A.E.'47, Univ. of Fla.; Supvg. Prin., U. S. Naval Operating Base Sch., Box 50, Navy 115, c/o Fleet P. O., New York, N. Y., since 1951.

Scheller, John, Prin. Amherst Central H. S., Snyder, N. Y.

Schindele, (Mrs.) May F., Prin., Pub. Sch., Brooklyn, N. Y.

Schmidt, A. W., A.B.'20, Cornell Col.; M.A.'26, Ph.D.'32, Tchrs. Col., Columbia Univ.; Asst. Commr. for Finance and Sch. Admin. Serv., State Educ. Dept., Albany, N. Y., since 1940.

*Schreiber, Paul D., B.S.'12, Bucknell Univ.; Supt. of Sch., Port Washington, N. Y., since 1920.

Schroeder, Herbert W., B.A.'33, Gettysburg Col.; M.A.'35, Univ. of Vt.; Supvg. Prin., Cato-Meridian Central Sch., Cato, N. Y., since 1951.

Schultz, Frederick, Ph.D.'22, Univ. of Chicago; A.M.'24, Columbia Univ. Address: Box 1160, G. P. O., N. Y. City, N. Y.

Schweickhard, Philip, B.S. in Ed.'17, Univ. of Chicago; Prin., Amherst Central H. S., Snyder, N. Y., since 1930.

Scott, Julius E., A.B.'26, Ark. State Tchrs. Col., Conway; A.M.'29, Tchrs. Col., Columbia Univ.; D.Sc.'45, Alma Col.; Supt. of Sch., Peekskill, N. Y., since 1935.

Seamans, Herbert L., A.B.'13, Fairmont Col.; M.A.'28, Yale Univ.; Ed.D.'47, Stanford Univ.; Dir., Comm. on Educ. Organizations, Natl. Conference of Christians and Jews, 381 Fourth Ave., New York 16, N. Y., since 1939.

Seidlin, Joseph, Ph.D.'31, Columbia Univ.; Dean Grad. Sch., Alfred Univ., Alfred, N. Y., since 1947.

Seifert, Leland B., A.B.'34, M.S.'40, Syracuse Univ.; Prin., H. S., Haverstraw, N. Y., since 1947.

Shack, Jacob, B.A.'24, City Col. of the City of N. Y.; M.A.'28, Tchrs. Col., Columbia Univ.; Asst. Supt. of Sch., Curriculum Div., New York City Sch., Brooklyn, N. Y., since 1951.

Sharp, J. Stanley, Architect, 227 East 44 St., New York, N. Y.

Shattuck, Ralph L., B.Litt.'28, Emerson Col.; M.Ed.'45, Univ. of Buffalo; Supt. of Sch., Middletown, N. Y., since 1949.

Shaw, Archibald Boyden, B.S. in Ed.'29, State Tchrs. Col., Bridgewater, Mass.; M.Ed.'40, Boston Univ.; Supt. of Sch., Scarsdale, N. Y., since 1949.

473

Shoemaker, Elwin S., Dist. Supt. of Sch., York-ville, N. Y.

Simonson, Jacob, Prin., Food Trades Voc. H. S., New York, N. Y.

Small, William J., Pd.D.'51, Niagara Univ.; Supt. of Sch., Niagara Falls, N. Y., since 1945.

Smith, Andrew J., A.B.'25, Dickinson Col.; A.M.'40, Cornell Univ.; Supvg. Prin., Central Sch., Union Springs, N. Y., since 1931.

Smith, Calvin U., B.S.'28, St. Lawrence Univ.; M.A.'33, New York Univ.; Dist. Supt. of Sch., Painted Post, N. Y., since 1931.

Smith, Carl D., B.H.'14, Springfield Col.; Ed.M.'25, Harvard Univ.; LL.D.'41, Adrian Col.; Dir. of Educ., since 1945, and Dir. of Research and Educ., Credit Research Foundation, New York, N. Y., since 1949.

Smith, Clarence E., Ed.D.'38, Univ. of Buffalo; Prof. of Educ. Admin., Univ. of Buffalo, Buffalo, N. Y.

Smith, Dana H., Ph.B.'27, Muhlenberg Col.; M.A.'33, New York Univ.; Supvg. Prin., Pub. Sch., Bellmore, Long Island, N. Y., since 1946.

Smith, Harry Pearse, A.B.'09, A.M.'15, State Univ. of Iowa; Ph.D.'25, Columbia Univ.; Prof. Emeritus, Syracuse Univ., since 1952. Address: 856 Maryland Ave., Syracuse 10, N. Y.

Smith, Herford A., B.S.'29, M.S. in Ed.'34, N. Y. State Col. for Tchrs., Albany; Dist. Supt. of Sch., East Greenbush, N. Y., since 1934.

Smith, Homer I., B.S.'35, M.A.'46, New York Univ.; Supt. of Sch., West Hempstead, N. Y., since 1948.

Smith, Kenneth E., B.S.'21, Colgate Univ.; M.A.'27, Tchrs. Col., Columbia Univ.; Supt. of Sch., Walden, N. Y., since 1937.

Smith, Nila B., B.A.'28, Univ. of Chicago; M.E.'30, Ph.D.'33, Tchrs. Col., Columbia Univ.; Prof. of Educ., Reading Inst., New York Univ., New York, N. Y., since 1949.

Smith, R. Jackson, B.A.'36, Dartmouth Col.; B.Arch.'46, Yale Univ.; Architect, Eggers and Higgins, 100 E. 42nd Street, New York, N. Y., since 1939.

Smith, Sim Joe, A.B.'15, Trinity Univ.; LL.B.'21, Univ. of Texas; M.A.'27, Tchrs. Col., Columbia Univ.; Asst. Supt. of Sch., New Rochelle, N. Y., since 1930.

Smith, Walter R., A.B.'27, Western Md. Col.; M.A.'29, Columbia Univ.; Supt. of Sch., Glen Cove, N. Y., since 1950.

Snyder, Dudley C., B.A.'32, Pa. State Col.; M.A.'38, New York Univ.; Dist. Supvg. Prin. of Sch., Valley Stream, N. Y., since 1938.

Sorensen, Carl G., B.S.'29, Middlebury Col.; M.A.'38, New York Univ.; Supt. of Sch., Plattsburg, N. Y.

Southworth, John Van Duyn, B.A.'26, Harvard Univ.; M.A.'36, Columbia Univ.; Vicepres. and Treas., Iroquois Pub. Co., Inc., Syracuse, N. Y., since 1945.

Spacht, Charles A., A.B.'21, Univ. of Nebr.; M.A.'31, Tchrs. Col., Columbia Univ.; Elem. Prin., Mayflower Sch., New Rochelle, N. Y., since 1931.

Sparks, Fred L., Jr., B.S. in Ed.'33, Clemson Col.; M.A.'38, Gallaudet Col.; Supt., The Central N. Y. Sch. for the Deaf, Rome, N. Y., since 1946.

Spence, Ralph B., A.B.'22, Univ. of Wis.; A.M. '24, Ph.D.'27, Tchrs. Col., Columbia Univ.; Prof. of Educ. since 1937 and Exec. Officer, Advanced Sch. of Educ., since 1950, Tchrs. Col., Columbia Univ., New York, N. Y.

Spinning, James M., A.B.'13, Univ. of Rochester; Supt. of Sch., Rochester, N. Y., since 1933.

Sprague, Raymond B., B.S. in Ed.'26, Rutgers Univ.; M.A.'Ed.'30, Columbia Univ.; Supvg. Prin., North Side Sch., East Williston, L. I., N. Y., since 1925.

*Spry, Edward W., A.B.'11, A.M.'22, Univ. of Rochester. Address: Summit Road, LeRoy, N. Y.

Stanley, Ralph J., A.B.'29, N. Y. State Col. for Tchrs., Albany; M.A.'36, Cornell Univ.; Supvg. Prin. of Sch., Clarence Central Sch., Buffalo, N. Y., since 1948.

Steeves, Willard W., M.Ed.'44, St. Lawrence Univ.; Supvg. Prin. of Sch., West Winfield, N. Y., since 1947.

Stevens, Francis L., B.S.'26, Union Col.; M.A. '38, Columbia Univ.; Supvg. Prin., Burnt Hills-Ballston Lake Central Sch., Ballston Lake, N. Y., since 1938.

Stewart, Kenneth, B.C.S.'27, B.S.'36, M.A.'42, New York Univ.; Prin., Union Free Sch., Staatsburg, N. Y., since 1941.

Stewart, R. E., Mgr., Adding Machine Div., Underwood Corp., New York, N. Y.

Stokes, Charles W., B.S.'33, Harvard Univ.; M.A.'39, Ed.D.'49, Tchrs. Col., Columbia Univ.; Supvg. Prin., Mahopac Central Sch., Mahopac, N. Y., since 1951.

Storm, Harold C., B.S.'32, M.A.'34, New York Univ.; Supt., Central Sch. Dist. 1, Pough-keepsie, N. Y.

Stormer, John C., B.S.'36, N. J. State Tchrs. Col.; M.S.'39, Rutgers Univ.; Supvg. Prin., Central Sch., Earlville, N. Y., since 1945.

Story, George O., M.S.'41, N. Y. State Tchrs. Col., Albany; Supvg. Prin., Central Sch., Oriskany, N. Y., since 1946.

Stratton, J. Edward, Asst. Prin. Rye H. S., Rye, N. Y.

*Strayer, George D., A.B.'03, Johns Hopkins Univ.; Ph.D.'05, Columbia Univ.; LL.D.'25, Col. of William and Mary; Litt.D.'29, Columbia Univ.; LL.D.'30, Bucknell Univ.; LL.D.'49, Univ. of Calif.; Pres., Natl. Educ. Assn., 1918-19; Chmn., Commn. on the Emergency in Educ., of the Dept. of Superintendence and the Natl. Educ. Assn., 1918-23; Honorary Life Member, American Assn. of Sch. Admin.; Prof. Emeritus, Tchrs. Col., Columbia Univ., New York, N. Y., since 1943.

Streeter, Robert A., B.S.'25, Univ. of Pa.; M.A. '35, N. J. State Tchrs. Col., Upper Montclair; Citizenship Educ. Project, Tchrs. Col., Columbia Univ., New York, N. Y.

Strough, Lyndon H., B.S.'18, Colgate Univ.; M.A.'42, Niagara Univ.; Supt. of Sch., Rome, N. Y., since 1945.

Stuart, John Goodspeed, B.A.'49, Univ. of Denver; M.A.'52, Tchrs. Col., Columbia Univ.; Circulation Dir., The School Executive, New York, N. Y., since 1952.

Studebaker, John W., A.B.'10, Leander Clark Col.; A.M.'17, Columbia Univ.; LL.D.'34, Drake Univ.; LL.D.'38, Muhlenberg Col.; LL.D.'45, Univ. of Md.; LL.D.'48, Boston Univ.; Vicepres., Scholastic Magazines, New York, N. Y.

Studwell, Harold F., B.S.'22, St. Lawrence Univ.; M.A.'27, Columbia Univ.; Ed.D.'39, New York Univ.; Supt. of Sch., East Rockaway, N. Y., since 1925.

Suerken, Ernst Henry, A.B.'30, A.M.'31, Cornell Univ.; M.A.'42, State Tchrs. Col., Montclair, N. J.; Supvg. Prin., The Echo Hills Sch., Union Free Sch. Dist., Greenburgh, Dobbs Ferry, N. Y.

Sullivan, W. Cassell, A.B.'30, Salem Col., W. Va.; M.A.'49, Tchrs. Col., Columbia Univ.; Supvg. Prin., Union Free Sch. Dist. 7, Centerport, N. Y., since 1951.

Swartz, David J., B.A.'20, City Col. of the City of N. Y.; M.A.'22, Tchrs. Col., Columbia Univ.; Ph.D.'26, Fordham Univ.; Admin. Asst. to the Supt. of Sch., Brooklyn, N. Y., since 1947.

Sweeting, (Mrs.) Stella M., D.Ed.'39, New York Univ.; Prin., Jr. H. S., New York 11, N. Y., since 1946.

Tarr, L. Ernest, B.C.S.'28, Rider Col.; B.S.'37, M.S.'40, Syracuse Univ.; Supvg. Prin. of Sch., Wilson, N. Y., since 1945.

Taylor, Earl A., B.A.'28, M.A.'29, Univ. of Texas; Ed.D.'43, New York Univ.; Dir., Washington Square Reading Center, New York, N. Y., since 1943.

Taylor, Lee, B.A.'42, Washington Missionary Col.; M.A.'48, Northwestern Univ.; Supt. of Seventh-Day Adventist Parochial Sch., Woodside, N. Y.

Templeton, Arthur, B.S.'35, New York Univ.; M.A.'43, Ed.D.'51, Tchrs. Col., Columbia Univ.; Admin. Asst., Bd. of Educ., Yonkers, N. Y., since 1950.

Terry, Daniel R., B.A.'31, Cornell Univ.; M.A. '36, Columbia Univ.; Supvg. Prin. of Pub. Sch., Roosevelt, N. Y., since 1949.

Thomas, Harrison C., B.A.'09, Hamilton Col.; Ph.D.'19, Columbia Univ.; Asst. Supt., N. Y. City High Sch., Brooklyn, N. Y., since 1946.

Thomas, John B., M.A.'32, Tchrs. Col., Columbia Univ.; Supvg. Prin. of Sch., Riverhead, N. Y., since 1938.

Thomas, Llewyn U., M.S.'37, Pa. State Col.; Supvg. Prin. of Sch., Naples, N. Y., since 1947.

Thompson, Robert S., LL.B.'12, Univ. of Mich.; A.B.'25, Univ. of Denver; Ph.D.'30, Columbia Univ.; Dean, State Tchrs. Col., Fredonia, N. Y., since 1948.

Thomson, F. Edward, M.A.'35, N. Y. State Col. for Tchrs., Albany; Supvg. Prin., Royalton-Hartland Central Sch., Middleport, N. Y., since 1945.

Thomson, Willis I., B.A.'18, Univ. of Minn.; M.A.'27, Columbia Univ.; Prin., H. S., New Rochelle, N. Y., since 1928.

Tilroe, Dexter G., A.B.'30, Syracuse Univ.; Assoc. Supvr., State Educ. Dept., Albany, N. Y., since 1948.

*Tompkins, Clarence H., B.S.E.'45, Univ. of Tenn.; M.A.'46, Tchrs. Col., Columbia Univ.; Research Asst., Pub. Educ. Assn., New York, N. Y., since 1950.

Trapasso, Anthony J., Supvg. Prin. of Sch., White Plains, N. Y.

Treharne, Thomas O., B.S.'24, Denison Univ.; M.S.'28, Ohio State Univ.; Dist. Supt. of Sch., Troy, N. Y., since 1942.

Trippensee, Arthur E., B.A.'24, Univ. of Mich.; M.A.'32, Ph.D.'48, Yale Univ.; Supt. of Sch., Medina, N. Y., since 1935.

Turbin, Elizabeth E., B.S.'34, M.A.'36, New York Univ.; Dir. of Elem. Educ., Pub. Sch., Yonkers, N. Y., since 1944.

Turner, Francis A., B.A.'19, City Col. of the City of New York; M.A.'38, New York Univ.; Asst. Dir. of Community Educ., New York City Sch., Brooklyn, N. Y., since 1947.

Tuttle, Albert E., A.B. and Ped.B.'15, Syracuse Univ.; M.A.'22, Tchrs. Col., Columbia Univ.; Asst. Supt. of Sch., Mamaroneck, N. Y., since 1936.

Tuttle, Frederick B., A.B.'30, Ph.D.'42, Yale Univ.; Prin. of Laboratory Sch. and Dir. of Summer Session, State Univ. Tchrs. Col., Plattsburg, N. Y., since 1952.

Udall, Richard M., A.B.'23, Dartmouth Col.; M.A.'32, Tchrs. Col., Columbia Univ.; Prin., Central H. S., Valley Stream, L. I., N. Y., since 1946.

Uphill, Jared L. M., B.S., Univ. of Rochester; Diploma, State Normal Sch., Geneseo, N. Y.; Dist. Supt. of Sch., Batavia, N. Y., since 1916.

Van Arnam, D. P., Supt. of Sch., Troy, N. Y.

Van Cott, Harrison H., B.S.'06, Tchrs. Col., Columbia Univ.; M.A.'19, N. Y. State Col. for Tchrs., Albany; Ph.D.'33, New York Univ.; Chief, Bureau of Instr. Supvn. for Sec. Educ., and Dir., Div. of Sec. Educ., State Educ. Dept., Albany, N. Y.

Vanderhoef, W. Howard, B.S.'16, Colgate Univ.; M.A.'29, Columbia Univ.; Supt. of Sch., Hamburg, N. Y., since 1940.

Van Giesen, Raymond, B.S.'31, Hobart Col.; M.S. in Ed.'41, Cornell Univ.; Supvg. Prin., Fayetteville H. S., Fayetteville, N. Y., since 1937.

Van Kleeck, Edwin R., A.B.'27, N. Y. State Col. for Tchrs., Albany; A.M.'33, Cornell Univ.; Ph.D.'37, Yale Univ.; Asst. State Commr. of Educ., State Educ. Dept., Albany, N. Y., since 1941.

Van Ness, Carl Condit, A.B.'16, Columbia Univ.; Mng. Editor, Educ. Book Dept., Appleton-Century-Crofts, Inc., New York, N. Y., since 1922.

Van Wie, Claude, B.A.'21, Colgate Univ.; M.A.'35, New York State Col. for Tchrs., Albany; Supt. of Sch., Saratoga Springs, N. Y., since 1945.

Vincent, William S., A.B.'36, Col. of William and Mary; A.M.'40, Ph.D.'44, Columbia Univ.; Tchrs. Col., Columbia Univ., New York, N. Y.

Wade, John E., B.S.'97, Col. of the City of N. Y.; A.M.'02, Columbia Univ.; Supt. of New York City Sch., 1942-47 (retired). Address: 390 West End Ave., New York 24, N. Y.

*Wagner, Thomas J., A.B.'10, Franklin and Marshall Col.; A.M.'13, Tchrs. Col., Columbia Univ.; Pd.D.'23, New York Univ. Address: Croton-on-Hudson, N. Y.

Ward, Charles C., B.S.'18, Bucknell Univ.; M.A.'30, Tchrs. Col., Columbia Univ.; Ph.D. '34, New York Univ.; LL.D.'43, Bucknell Univ.; Pres., State Tchrs. Col., Plattsburg, N. Y., 1933-52.

Warren, Carl V., B.S.'23, Hamilton Col.; M.A.'32, Columbia Univ.; Supt. of Sch., Huntington, N. Y., since 1949.

Wassung, Frank R., Ph.B.'13, Ph.M.'17, Hamilton Col.; LL.B.'48, Brooklyn Law Sch.; Supt. of Sch., Garden City, N. Y., 1937-51 (retired).

Watkin, Earl P., Ph.B.'12, Ph.M.'17, Hamilton Col.; M.A.'30, Columbia Univ.; Ed.D.'39, New York Univ.; Supt. of Sch., Ilion, N. Y., since 1923.

Watson, Floyd B., A.B.'14, Cornell Univ.; Supt. of Sch., Rockville Centre, N. Y., 1933-52. Address: 262 Lakeview Ave., Rockville Centre, N. Y.

Webb, Everett S., A.B.'24, Amherst Col.; A.M.'28, Cornell Univ.; Supv. Prin. of Sch., Hartsdale, N. Y., since 1940.

*Weet, Herbert S., B.A.'99, M.A.'01, Univ. of Rochester; Pd.D.'18, New York State Col. for Tchrs., Albany; Litt.D.'33, Univ. of the State of New York; Honorary Life Member, American Assn. of Sch. Admin.; Supt. of Sch., Rochester, N. Y., 1911-34. Address: R. F. D. 3, Medina, N. Y.

Weil, Truda T., B.S.'20, M.A.'30, New York Univ.; Asst. Supt. of New York City Sch., New York, N. Y.

Weiss, Leon Jay, B.A.'28, Cornell Univ.; M.A.'30, Tchrs. Col., Columbia Univ.; M.S.'43, New York Univ.; Supt. of Sch., South Fallsburgh, N. Y., since 1946.

Welch, Earl E., B.A.'25, State Univ. of Iowa; Ph.M.'33, Univ. of Wis.; Editor-in-Chief, Silver Burdett Col., New York, N. Y., since 1940.

Wenzl, Theodore C., C.E.'31, Rensselaer Polytech. Inst., Troy, N. Y.; M.A.'36, N. J. State Tchrs. Col., Upper Montclair; Ed.D.'40, Tchrs. Col., Columbia Univ.; Chief, Bureau of Apportionment, N. Y. State Educ. Dept., Albany, N. Y., since 1945.

Westervelt, Ralph Vincent, B.S.'36, Ithaca Col.; M.A.'43, Columbia Univ.; Supvg. Prin., Guilderland Central Sch., Altamont, N. Y., since 1946.

Whalen, Frank D., A.B.'13, St. Joseph's Col.; M.A.'30, Ph.D.'33, Fordham Univ.; Asst. Supt. of Sch., New York, N. Y., since 1941.

Wheaton, Gordon A., B.S.'42, Ithaca Col.; M.A.'47, Ed.D.'51, Tchrs. Col., Columbia Univ.; Asst. to Supt. of Sch., Eastchester Pub. Sch. Dist. 1, Yonkers, N. Y., since 1947.

White, Verna, A.B.'28, Wheaton Col. (Mass.); M.A.'35, Univ. of Mich.; Ph.D. in Ed.'45, Univ. of Chicago; Assoc. Prof. and Chmn. of Com. on Selection for Div. of Tchr. Preparation, Sch. of Educ., Syracuse Univ., Syracuse, N. Y., since 1945.

*Wilber, (Mrs.) Esther R., 11 Ford Ave., Oneonta, N. Y.

Wiles, Marion Elizabeth, B.S.'29, Columbia Univ.; Ed.M.'36, Ed.D.'40, Harvard Univ.; Admin. Asst. to Supt. of Sch., Great Neck, N. Y., since 1945.

Wiley, George M., Jr., A.B.'99, A.M.'03, Union Col.; Pd.D.'20, N. Y. State Col. for Tchrs., Albany; LL.D.'20, Syracuse Univ.; L.H.D.'31, Union Col. Address: Pomona, Rockland Co., N. Y.

Wilhousky, Peter J., B.S.'36, Juilliard Sch. of Music; Asst. Dir. of Music, Bd. of Educ., New York City, Brooklyn, N. Y., since 1940.

Williamson, Pauline Brooks, Secy., American Assn. for Gifted Children, New York, N. Y., since 1947.

Willis, Benjamin C., A.B.'22, George Washington Univ.; M.A.'26, Univ. of Md.; Supt. of Sch., Buffalo, N. Y., since 1950.

Wilson, Arthur Jess, B.S.'35, M.A.'49, New York Univ.; LL.B.'40, St. Lawrence Univ.; Asst. Dir., Yonkers Evening H. S., Bd. of Educ., Yonkers, N. Y., since 1946; Dir. of Rehabilitation, Grasslands Hospital of Westchester Co., Valhalla, N. Y., since 1948.

Wilson, L. A., D.Sc.'26, Stout Inst.; LL.D.'34, Alfred Univ.; LL.D.'42, Syracuse Univ.; Commr. of Educ., State Educ. Dept., Albany, N. Y., since 1950.

Wilson, William Keith, A.B.'20, Rio Grande Col.; M.A.'24, Ph.D.'33, Ohio State Univ.; Assoc. Supvr. of Sch. in charge of Sch. Bldg. Planning, State Educ. Dept., Albany, N. Y., since 1930.

Winsor, A. Leon, Ph.D.'29, Cornell Univ.; Dir., Sch. of Educ., Cornell Univ., Ithaca, N. Y., since 1945.

Winterble, (Mrs.) Margaret R., M.A.'34, Tchrs. Col., Columbia Univ.; Research Asst., Bd. of Educ., 110 Livingston St., Brooklyn 2, N. Y., since 1930.

Wise, James Waterman, Dir., Council Against Intolerance in America, 17 E. 42nd St., New York 17, N. Y.

Wolner, Louis J., A.B.'30, M.A.'36, N. Y. State Col. for Tchrs., Albany; Supvg. Prin., H. S., Homer, N. Y., since 1933.

Woodruff, Robert B., B.S.'32, Springfield Col.; M.A.'33, St. Lawrence Univ.; Supvg. Prin. of Sch., Van Hornesville, N. Y., since 1942.

*Woollatt, Lorne Hedley, B.A.'30, B.Ed.'39, M.Ed.'44, Univ. of Saskatchewan; Ph.D.'48, Columbia Univ.; Research Assoc., Inst. of Admin. Research, Tchrs. Col., Columbia Univ., New York, N. Y., since 1946.

Worboys, Herbert J., A.B.'28, Hamilton Col.; M.A.'39, Columbia Univ.; Supvg. Prin., Honeoye Falls, N. Y., since 1929.

Workman, Robert L., B.S.'41, M.A.'46, New York Univ.; Headmaster, Lakemont Academy, Lakemont, Yates Co., N. Y., since 1952.

Wormley, Donald S., Asst. Prin., Union Free Sch. Dist. 2, Irvington, N. Y.

Wright, Harold W., M.A.'28, New York Univ.; M.A.'38, Columbia Univ.; Supvg. Prin., Sewanhaka H. S., Floral Park, N. Y., since 1947.

Wrightstone, J. Wayne, B.S.'25, Univ. of Pa.; M.A.'28, New York Univ.; Ph.D.'33, Tchrs. Col., Columbia Univ.; Dir., Bureau of Educ. Research, Bd. of Educ., 110 Livingston St., Brooklyn 2, N. Y., since 1949.

Wyckoff, Philip A., B.S.'31, Syracuse Univ.; M.Ed.'38, Cornell Univ.; Dist. Supt. of Sch., Herkimer Co., Frankfort, N. Y., since 1941.

Wynn, Dale Richard, B.S. in Ed.'39, M.S. in Ed.'46, Bucknell Univ.; Ed.D.'52, Tchrs. Col., Columbia Univ.; Coordinator of Admin. Internships, Tchrs. Col., New York, N. Y., since 1952.

*Wynstra, Stanley S., B.A., M.A. in Ed.'47, Univ. of Wash.; Ed.D.'49, Tchrs. Col., Columbia Univ.; Supt. of Sch., Yonkers, N. Y., since 1950.

York, Arthur C., B.S.'32, State Tchrs. Col., Buffalo, N. Y.; M.A.'36, Univ. of Rochester; Prin., Amherst 13 Elem. Sch., Eggertsville, N. Y., since 1941.

*Young, William E., A.B.'24, Bates Col.; M.A. '28, Ph.D.'30, State Univ. of Iowa; Dir. of Elem. Educ., State Educ. Dept., Albany, N. Y., since 1938.

Zakary, Robert F., Supvg. Prin. of Sch., Roosevelt, N. Y.

Zuckerman, George, B.A.'20, Col. of the City of New York; M.A.'25, Columbia Univ.; Ph.D.'37, New York Univ.; Asst. Supt. of New York City Sch., Brooklyn, N. Y., since 1947.

INSTITUTIONAL MEMBERS

Brooklyn College, H and Bedford Aves., Brooklyn 10, N. Y.

Christian Brothers Academy, 421 E. Willow St., Syracuse, N. Y.

Education Index, H. W. Wilson Company, 950-972 University Ave., New York 52, N. Y.

Educ. Div., Americana Corp., New York, N. Y.

Federation of Parent-Teacher Associations, c/o Supt. of Sch., Yonkers, N. Y.

Jamestown Teachers Association, c/o Madeleine C. Rogers, Jamestown H. S., Jamestown, N. Y.

Johnson City Teachers Association, H. S., Johnson City, N. Y.

Knappe and Johnson, Architects, 390 East 150th St., New York 55, N. Y.

Library, N. Y. State Tchrs. Col., New Paltz, N. Y.

Library, Port Jervis High School, Port Jervis, N. Y.

Library, Teachers College, Columbia University, 525 W. 120th St., New York 27, N. Y.

National Society for the Prevention of Blindness, 1790 Broadway, New York 19, N. Y.

New York State Association of Elementary Principals, Charles W. Joyce, Secy., 933 Sibley Tower Bldg., Rochester 4, N. Y.

New York State Library, Univ. of the State of N. Y., Order Section 3, Albany 1, N. Y.

New York State Tchrs. Col., c/o Library, Cortland, N. Y.

New York University, Washington Square Library, 100 Washington Sq. East, New York 3, N. Y.

Niagara Falls Teachers Association, Niagara St. Sch., Niagara Falls, N. Y.

Office of Development, Low Library, Columbia Univ., New York, N. Y.

Olean Public Schools, Olean, N. Y.

President, Hornell Teachers Association, Hornell, N. Y.

Research Service Department, Silver Burdett Co., 45 E. 17th St., New York 3, N. Y.

Rochester Teachers Association, Leon C. Friel, Pres., John Marshall H. S., Rochester, N. Y.

St. George Regional Branch, The New York Pub. Libr., 10 Hyatt St., Staten Island 1, N. Y.

Schermerhorn Teachers' Agency, 366 Fifth Ave., New York 1, N. Y.

School No. 16, N. Broadway, Yonkers, N. Y.

State Teachers College, Fredonia, N. Y.

State Teachers College, c/o Helen Hagger, Librarian, Oswego, N. Y.

Superintendent of Schools, Olean, N. Y.

NORTH CAROLINA

INDIVIDUAL MEMBERS

Armstrong, Ray, A.B.'18, A.M.'26, Univ. of N.C.; Supt. of Sch., Goldsboro, N. C., since 1927.

Arnold, G. H., A.B.'27, M.A.'40, Univ. of N. C.; Supt. of City Sch., Thomasville, N. C., since 1944.

Ashley, Frank L., B.S.'11, Young Harris Col.; A.M.'13, Newberry Col.; Prin., Sr. H. S., Gastonia, N. C., since 1929.

Barnes, B. N., A.B.'26, Wake Forest Col.; A.M. '31, Univ. of N. C.; Supt. of Sch., King's Mountain, N. C., since 1934.

Barnes, Edward M., A.B.'31, Livingstone Col.; A.M.'45, Univ. of Mich.; Prin., Charles H. Darden H. S., Wilson, N. C., since 1932.

Benton, Randolph, B.A.'13, Wake Forest Col.; M.A.'26, Tchrs. Col., Columbia Univ.; Co. Supt. of Sch., Raleigh, N. C., since 1940.

Blanchard, C. W., A.B.'20, Wake Forest Col.; Dir., Div. of Plant Operation, State Bd. of Educ., Raleigh, N. C.

*Boger, W. J., Jr., A.B.'22, Lenior-Rhyne Col.; A.M.'42, Univ. of N. C.; Supt. of Sch., Charlotte, N. C.

Bolmeier, E. C., B.S.'27, N. Dak. Agrl. Col.; M.A.'31, Ph.D.'37, Univ. of Chicago; Prof. of Educ., Duke Univ., Durham, N. C., since 1948.

Booth, Jean Patrick, A.B.'23, Davidson Col.; M.A.'39, New York Univ.; Supt. of Sch., Kinston, N. C., since 1945.

*Brimley, Ralph F. W., B.S.'28, N. C. State Col.; M.A.'40, Univ. of N. C.; Co. Supt. of Sch., Winston-Salem, N. C., since 1947.

Brown, C. C., Dir., Div. of Transportation, State Bd. of Educ., Raleigh, N. C.

Bruton, Lawrence Allen, A.B.'27, Elon Col.; M.A. in Ed.'47, Univ. of N. C.; Supt. of Sch., Whiteville, N. C., since 1947.

Bueck, Hieronymus, B.S.'24, M.S.'26, N. C. State Col.; Supt., City Admin. Unit, Murphy, N. C., since 1932.

Bullock, William J., A.B.'24, Duke Univ.; A.M.'27, Col. of William and Mary; Supt. of Sch., Kannapolis, N. C., since 1931.

Byers, J. W., A.B.'30, Catawba Col.; M.E.'43, Univ. of N. C.; Supt. of Sch., Asheville, N. C., since 1945.

Calhoun, D. M., A.B.'27, Davidson Col.; Co. Supt. of Sch., Elizabethtown, N. C., since 1945.

Cameron, John L., A.B.'37, Elon Col.; M.A.'47, Univ. of N. C.; Dir., Div. of Schoolhouse Planning and Surveys, State Dept. of Pub. Instr., Raleigh, N. C., since 1950.

*Campbell, O. K., A.B., Southeastern State Col., Durant, Okla.; M.A.'35, Tchrs. Col., Columbia Univ.; P.O. Box 4106, Duke Univ. Station, Durham, N. C.

Carpenter, N. H., B.A.'35, Lenoir-Rhyne Col.; M.A.'41, Duke Univ.; Supt. of Sch., Elkin, N. C., since 1945.

Carr, G. P., A.B.'30, Univ. of N. C.; Supt., Orange Co. Sch., Hillsboro, N. C., since 1951.

Carroll, Charles F., A.B.'21, M.Ed.'30, Duke Univ.; State Supt. of Pub. Instr., Raleigh, N. C., since 1952.

Carter, David V., A.B.'17, Univ. of N. C.; Co. Supt. of Sch., Clinton, N. C., since 1927.

Chappell, S. G., A.B.'27, Univ. of N. C.; M.A.'50, East Carolina Tchrs. Col.; Supt. of Sch., Wilson, N. C., since 1939.

Chewning, Charles H., A.B.'29, Wofford Col.; M.A.'42, Univ. of S. C.; Co. Supt. of Sch., Durham, N. C.

Combs, A. B., B.A.'10, M.A.'11, Wake Forest Col.; Assoc. Div. of Instructional Serv., State Dept. of Pub. Instr., Raleigh, N. C., since 1929.

Conley, Donald Hayes, B.A.'23, Duke Univ.; Co. Supt. of Sch., Greenville, N. C., since 1932.

Cooke, Dennis H., A.B.'25, M.Ed.'28, Duke Univ.; Ph.D.'30, George Peabody Col. for Tchrs.; Pres., High Point Col., High Point, N. C., since 1949.

Cope, W. Vernon, B.S.'40, Western Carolina Tchrs. Col.; Supt., Jackson Co. Pub. Sch., Sylva, N. C., since 1948.

Cromer, Voigt Rhodes, A.B.'25, Lenoir-Rhyne Col.; A.M.'27, Univ. of S. C.; B.D.'28, Lutheran Theol. Southern Sem.; S.T.M.'29, Hartford Sem. Foundation; D.D.'47, Lenoir-Rhyne Col.; Pres., Lenoir-Rhyne Col., Hickory, N. C., since 1949.

Davis, Alfred C., B.S.'36, Univ. of N. C.; Dir., Div. of Auditing and Acctg., State Bd. of Educ., Raleigh, N. C., since 1949.

Denning, J. T., B.A.'36, Atlantic Christian Col.; Co. Supt. of Sch., Southport, N. C., since 1947.

Douglas, Clarence DeWitt, A.B.'20, Duke Univ.; Controller, State Bd. of Educ., Raleigh, N. C.

Dudley, Walter R., A.B.'37, Chowan Col.; Master's '42, Univ. of N. C.; Supt. of City Sch., Red Springs, N. C., since 1944.

Dupree, J. L., B.S.'31, Wake Forest Col.; A.M.'41, Duke Univ.; Co. Supt. of Sch., Windsor, N. C., since 1946.

Eason, Francis Halstead, B.S.'36, Wake Forest Col.; M.A.'50, E. Carolina Col.; Supt. of City Sch., Franklinton, N. C., since 1951.

Edwards, (Mrs.) Ethel P., B.S.'34, George Peabody Col. for Tchrs.; Exec. Secy., N. C. Educ. Assn., Raleigh, N. C., since 1944.

Eller, C. B., B.S.'26, N. C. State Col.; Co. Supt. of Sch., Wilkesboro, N. C., since 1933.

Erwin, Charles C., B.A.'37, Univ. of N. C.; M.A.'40, Tchrs. Col., Columbia Univ.; Co. Supt. of Sch., Salisbury, N. C., since 1945.

Fields, Clyde, A.B.'32, Univ. of N. C. Woman's Col.; Supt., Alleghany Co. Sch., Sparta, N. C., since 1943.

Funderburk, Earl C., A.B.'34, M.A.'46, Univ. of N. C.; Supt. of Sch., Elizabeth City, N. C., since 1949.

Furr, C. A., A.B.'20, Loyola Univ.; A.M.'31, Univ. of N. C.; Co. Supt. of Sch., Concord, N. C., since 1939.

Garinger, Elmer H., A.B.'16, Univ. of Mo.; M.A.'21, Ph.D.'36, Tchrs. Col., Columbia Univ.; Supt. of Sch., Charlotte, N. C., since 1949.

Gibson, A. B., A.B.'26, Duke Univ.; M.A.'40, Columbia Univ.; Supt. of City Sch., Laurinburg, N. C., since 1940.

Green, Roy M., A.B.'30, Elon Col.; Co. Supt. of Sch., Danbury, N. C., since 1947.

Griffin, R. B., B.A.'25, Wake Forest Col.; Co. Supt. of Sch., Roxboro, N. C., since 1935.

Grigg, Claud, A.B.'21, M.A.'28, Duke Univ.; Supt. of Sch., Albemarle, N. C., since 1934.

Grigg, Jasper Horace, A.B.'16, Duke Univ.; Co. Supt. of Sch., Shelby, N. C., since 1926.

Guy, T. Ward, A.B.'29, Univ. of Chattanooga; Supt. of Sch., Columbus Co., Whiteville, N. C., since 1951.

*Gwynn, John Minor, A.B.'18, A.M.'27, Univ. of N. C.; Ph.D.'35, Yale Univ.; Prof. of Educ., Univ. of N. C., Chapel Hill, N. C., since 1927.

Hagaman, J. G., B.S.'34, Appalachian State Tchrs. Col.; M.Ed.'40, Duke Univ.; Supt. of Sch., Lenoir, N. C., since 1951.

Harrell, W. C., A.B.'38, High Point Col.; Co. Supt. of Sch., Gatesville, N. C., since 1947.

Helton, Sam H., B.S.'35, Appalachian State Tchrs. Col.; M.A.'45, Univ. of N. C.; Supt. of Sch., Statesville, N. C., since 1951.

Hix, David N., A.B.'25, M.Ed.'43, Duke Univ.; Co. Supt. of Sch., Oxford, N. C., since 1949.

Hough, John M., B.A.'29, Wake Forest Col.; M.A.'40, Univ. of N. C.; Supt. of Twp. Sch., Leaksville, N. C., since 1947.

Hudson, Isham B., Supt. of Sch., Onslow Co., Jacksonville, N. C.

Huneycutt, J. E., A.B.'34, M.A.'40, Univ. of N. C.; Supt. of Sch., Rockingham, N. C., since 1948.

Hurlburt, Allan S., A.B.'33, A.M.'37, Ph.D.'47, Cornell Univ.; Dir., Bureau of Educ. Research and Serv., Univ. of N. C., Chapel Hill, N. C., since 1951.

Huss, Hunter, A.B.'23, Univ. of N. C.; Co. Supt. of Sch., Gastonia, N. C.

Idol, E. D., A.B.'14, Park Col.; Co. Supt. of Sch., Greensboro, N. C., since 1945.

Inscoe, L. S., B.A.'15, Wake Forest Col.; M.A.'28, Tchrs. Col., Columbia Univ.; Co. Supt. of Sch., Nashville, N. C., since 1919.

Irwin, Harry P., Jr., A.B.'43, Univ. of Del.; M.Ed.'50, Duke Univ.; Bus. Mgr. of City Sch., Salisbury, N. C., since 1951.

Jenkins, Wade M., Dir., Div. of Textbooks, State Bd. of Educ., Raleigh, N. C., since 1945.

Johnson, Daniel Sloan, A.B.'24, M.A.'29, Duke Univ.; Supt. of City Sch., Rocky Mount, N. C., since 1949.

Johnson, O. P., A.B.'27, Duke Univ.; Supt. of Co. Sch., Kenansville, N. C., since 1935.

Joslyn, H. L., Mus.'10, Maryville Col. (Tenn.); B.S.'13, M.S.'16, N. C. State Col., Raleigh; Co. Supt. of Sch., Beaufort, N. C., since 1947.

Knox, J. H., B.S.'22, The Citadel; M.A.'38, Univ. of Chicago; Supt. of Sch., Salisbury, N. C., since 1934.

Kornegay, A. D., A.B.'33, M.A.'40, Univ. of N. C.; Supt. of Sch., Hendersonville, N. C., since 1946.

Kuykendall, R. L., A.B.'32, Catawba Col.; Prin., Griffith Sch., Winston-Salem, N. C.

Kyzer, H. M., A.B.'19, Newberry Col.; Supt. of City Sch., Hamlet, N. C., since 1939.

Lambeth, M. T., A.B.'26, Univ. of N. C.; M.A.'32, Tchrs. Col., Columbia Univ.; Supt. of Sch., Statesville, N. C., since 1947.

Larson, Fenton L., A.B.'33, Asbury Col.; M.A.'39, Univ. of N. C.; Supt. of Sch., Cherryville, N. C., since 1949.

Lentz, J. J., B.S.'34, Appalachian State Tchrs. Col.; Co. Supt. of Sch., Sanford, N. C., since 1949.

Lewis, J. Allan, A.B.'34, Lynchburg Col.; M.A., Univ. of N. C.; Co. Supt. of Sch., Wentworth, N. C., since 1946.

Littlefield, Broados E., Co. Supt. of Sch., Lumberton, N. C., since 1949.

Lockhart, John C., A.B.'12, Univ. of N. C.; Asst. Controller, Woman's Col., Univ. of N. C., Greensboro, N. C.

Lohr, B. E., B.A.'21, M.A.'22, Univ. of N. C.; Supt. of Sch., Lumberton, N. C., since 1942.

Lowder, S. Ray, A.B.'27, M.A.'46, Univ. of N. C.; Supt. of Sch., Lincolnton, N. C., since 1940.

Lowry, Roy Frank, A.B.'30, M.A.'36, Univ. of N. C.; Co. Supt. of Sch., Plymouth, N. C., since 1947.

McAllister, R. Brown, A.B.'30, Lenoir-Rhyne Col.; Supt. of Sch., Concord, N. C., since 1943.

McLamb, C. O., A.B.'36, Atlantic Christian Col.; M.A.'47, Univ. of N. C.; Prin., Pub. Sch., Walkertown, N. C., since 1948.

McSwain, Holland, A.B. in Ed.'28, Univ. of N. C.; Supt. Macon Co. Sch., Franklin, N. C., since 1951.

MacDonald, Henry J., A.B.'34, M.A.'40, Duke Univ.; Supt., City Sch., New Bern, N. C., since 1947.

MacDonald, K. A., B.S.'16, Davidson Col.; Co. Supt. of Sch., Raeford, N. C., since 1935.

Manning, James C., A.B.'23, Atlantic Christian Col.; Supt., Martin Co. Sch., Williamston, N. C., since 1931.

Milner, Charles F., A.B.'33, Guilford Col.; M.A. in Ed.'41, Univ. of N. C.; Assoc. Dir. of Extension Div., Univ. of N. C., Chapel Hill, N. C.

Moore, J. H., A.B.'25, Miss. Col.; M.A.'31, Univ. of N. C.; Co. Supt. of Sch., Elizabeth City, N. C., since 1947.

Moore, John Watson, A.B.'12, Davidson Col.; M.Ed.'32, Duke Univ.; Supt. of Sch., Winston-Salem, N. C., since 1933.

Moore, W. B., A.B. in Ed.'31, Univ. of N. C.; Co. Supt. of Sch., Trenton, N. C., since 1945.

Morgan, Roland R., B.A.'28, Berea Col.; M.A.'40, Univ. of N. C.; Supt. of Sch., Mooresville, N. C., since 1945.

Nixon, Joe R., A.B.'19, Univ. of N. C.; Co. Supt. of Sch., Lincolnton, N. C., since 1931.

Overman, W. Henry, B.A.'30, Wake Forest Col.; Co. Supt. of Sch., Halifax, N. C., since 1947.

Parham, Maston S., B.S.'32, The Citadel; M.Ed. '49, Duke Univ.; Supt. of City Sch., Morganton, N. C., since 1951.

Payne, W. D., A.B.'27, Bridgewater Col.; M.A.'41, Univ. of N. C.; Supt. of City Sch., Henderson, N. C., since 1950.

Peek, William W., B.S.'40, Western Carolina Tchrs. Col., Cullowhee; M.S.'48, Univ. of Tenn.; Supt. of Co. Sch., Marshall, N. C., since 1950.

Pendergraph, L. B., A.B.'07, Duke Univ.; Supt. of Sch., Mount Airy, N. C., since 1928.

Phillips, Guy Berryman, A.B.'13, Univ. of N. C.; M.A.'42, Columbia Univ.; Dir. of Summer Session, since 1942, and Dean, Sch. of Educ., Univ. of N. C., Chapel Hill, N. C., since 1948.

Proctor, Arthur Marcus, A.B.'10, Duke Univ.; A.M.'22, Ph.D.'30, Tchrs. Col., Columbia Univ.; Prof. of Educ., since 1923, and Dir. of Summer Session, Duke Univ., Durham, N. C., since 1947.

Proffit, G. T., A.B.'26, M.A.'33, Univ. of N. C.; Co. Supt. of Sch., Lillington, N. C.

Proffitt, Brank, B.S.'42, Western Carolina Tchrs. Col.; M.A.'49, George Peabody Col. for Tchrs.; Supt. of City Sch., Tryon, N. C., since 1951.

Pruette, Dean B., B.A.'33, Limestone Col.; M.A.'41, Univ. of N. C.; Supt. of City Sch., High Point, N. C., since 1952.

Pugh, Robert Lee, A.B.'25, Wake Forest Col.; A.M.'50, Univ. of N. C.; Supt. of Co. Sch., New Bern, N. C., since 1937.

Ready, I. Epps, A.B.'25, A.M.'29, Univ. of S. C.; Ed.D.'49, New York Univ.; Supt. of Sch., Roanoke Rapids, N. C., since 1945.

*Roland, H. M., A.B.'20, Wake Forest Col.; Co. Supt. of Sch., Wilmington, N. C., since 1936.

Rose, Junius H., A.B.'13, Duke Univ.; A.M.'26, Columbia Univ.; Supt. of Sch. and Dir. of Lab. Sch., East Carolina Tchrs. Col., Greenville, N. C., since 1920.

Rosenstengel, William E., B.S. in Ed.'23, Northeast Mo. State Tchrs. Col., Kirksville; M.A.'27, Ph.D.'31, Univ. of Mo.; Prof. of Educ., Univ. of N. C., Chapel Hill, N. C., since 1941.

Ross, C. Reid, A.B. in Ed.'29, Univ. of N. C.; Co. Supt. of Sch., Fayetteville, N. C., since 1951.

Rufty, John E., B.S.'38, Western Carolina Tchrs. Col.; M.A.'51, George Peabody Col. for Tchrs.; Supt. of Sch., Andrews, N. C., since 1952.

Ryan, W. Carson, A.B.'07, Harvard Univ.; Ph.D. and Ed.D.'18, LL.D.'32, George Washington Univ.; Kenan Prof. of Educ., Univ. of N. C., Chapel Hill, N. C., since 1940.

Sanderson, Jess O., A.B.'24, Duke Univ.; Supt. of Sch., Raleigh, N. C., since 1942.

*Schiebout, Ferdinand Conrad, Master's '48, Tchrs. Col., Columbia Univ.; Prin., H. S., Elkin, N. C., since 1950.

Scott, William Jackson, A.B.'33, M.A.'47, Univ. of N. C.; Prin., Central H. S., Mooresville, N. C., since 1945.

Seabrook, J. W., A.B.'09, Biddle Univ.; A.M.'30, Columbia Univ.; Pres., State Tchrs. Col., Fayetteville, N. C., since 1933.

Shelton, Nollie W., B.S.'31, Col. of William and Mary; M.A.'37, Univ. of N. C.; Co. Supt. of Sch., Swan Quarter, N. C., since 1941.

Sifford, James P., Co. Supt. of Sch., Albemarle, N. C.

Simpson, Evander S., A.B.'36, M.A.'43, Univ. of N. C.; Supt. of Sch., Johnston Co., Smithfield, N. C., since 1952.

Sipe, Gene C., A.B.'30, M.A.'39, Univ. of N. C.; Supt. of City Sch., Clinton, N. C., since 1947.

Smith, Benjamin L., A.B.'16, M.A.'37, Duke Univ.; Supt. of Sch., Greensboro, N. C., since 1936.

Smith, Budd E., A.B. in Ed.'31, M.A.'34, Ph.D. '42, Univ. of N. C.; Supt. of Sch., Oxford, N. C., since 1951.

Spikes, L. E., A.B.'24, M.Ed.'34, Duke Univ.; M.A.'39, Columbia Univ.; Ph.D.'42, George Peabody Col. for Tchrs.; Supt. of Sch., Burlington, N. C., since 1936.

Steere, Arthur, A.B.'35, Elon Col.; M.Ed.'42, Univ. of N. C.; Asst. Co. Supt. of Sch., Winston-Salem, N. C., since 1949.

Stumpf, Wippert A., B.S.'22, Univ. of Ill.; M.A. '34, Ph.D.'41, Univ. of Chicago; Assoc. Prof. of Educ., Dept. of Educ., Duke Univ., Durham, N. C.

Teachey, Guy B., A.B.'35, M.A.'45, Univ. of N. C.; Supt. of City Sch., Asheboro, N. C., since 1947.

Terrell, W. B., A.B.'25, Elon Col.; Co. Supt. of Sch., Warrenton, N. C., since 1948.

Veasey, Wesley F., B.A.'25, M.A.'45, Univ. of N. C.; Co. Supt. of Sch., Washington, N. C., since 1947.

Ward, Marvin M., B.S.'34, Appalachian State Tchrs. Col., Boone, N. C.; M.A.'40, Univ. of N. C.; Admin. Asst. to Supt. of Sch., Winston-Salem, N. C., since 1949.

Waters, Fred M., A.B.'16, Wabash Col.; M.A.'28, State Col. of Univ. of N. C.; Supt. of City Sch., Gastonia, N. C., since 1945.

Weaver, Lucius Stacy, A.B.'24, Duke Univ.; M.A.'32, Columbia Univ.; Supt. of Sch., Durham, N. C., since 1947.

Weaver, Philip J., A.B.'34, Duke Univ.; A.M.'37, Univ. of N. C.; Asst. Supt. of Sch., Greensboro, N. C., since 1951.

West, Edwin Arthur, A.B.'24, Davidson Col.; M.A.'40, Univ. of N. C.; Supt. of Sch., Washington, N. C., since 1946.

White, R. C., A.B.'13, Davidson Col.; Supt., Randolph Co. Sch., Asheboro, N. C., since 1949.

Workman, John H., A.B.'13, M.A.'32, Ph.D.'35, Univ. of N. C.; Head, Economics Dept., Appalachian State Tchrs. Col., Boone, N. C., since 1946.

Yount, Marvin Edward, Sr., A.B.'11, Concordia Col.; M.A.'43, George Peabody Col. for Tchrs.; LL.D.'50, Elon Col.; Co. Supt. of Sch., Graham, N. C., since 1927.

INSTITUTIONAL MEMBER

Library, East Carolina Teachers College, Greenville, N. C.

NORTH DAKOTA

INDIVIDUAL MEMBERS

Aarthun, Gabriel, B.A.'32, Concordia Col.; M.S. in Ed.'45, Univ. of N. Dak.; Supt. of Sch., Mayville, N. Dak., since 1946.

Aarthun, Martin, B.A.'35, Concordia Col.; M.S. in Ed.'48, Univ. of N. Dak.; Supt. of Sch., Grenora, N. Dak., since 1946.

Aasmundstad, P. O., B.A.'38, State Tchrs. Col., Minot, N. Dak.; M.S.'48, Univ. of N. Dak.; Supt. of Sch., McClusky, N. Dak., since 1947.

Appel, G. E., B.A.'42, State Tchrs. Col., Valley City, N. Dak.; M.S.'49, Univ. of N. Dak.; Supt. of Sch., Leonard, N. Dak., since 1942.

Arnason, A. F., B.S.'29, M.A.'35, Univ. of N. Dak.; LL.D.'48, Jamestown Col.; Commr. of Higher Educ., State Dept. of Pub. Instr., Bismarck, N. Dak., since 1943.

Arveson, Raymond G., B.A.'42, State Tchrs. Col., Mayville, N. Dak.; M.A.'48, Univ. of Minn.; Supt. of Sch., Leeds, N. Dak., since 1945.

Ashby, Clarence, B.S.'31, West Texas State Col.; M.S.'38, A. & M. Col. of Texas; Reservation Prin., Belcourt, N. D., since 1940.

Backman, Kenneth E., B.A. in Ed.'32, State Tchrs. Col., Valley City, N. Dak.; Supt. of Sch., Sanborn, N. Dak., since 1951.

Bangs, R. W., M.S.'47, Univ. of N. Dak.; Supt. of Sch., Bottineau, N. Dak., since 1949.

Bartlett, Thayer E., Educ. Field Agent, U. S. Indian Service, Fort Yates, N. Dak., since 1935.

Bensell, Arthur S., A.B.'34, Heidelberg Col.; Supt. of Sch., Elbowoods, N. Dak., since 1951.

Bishop, R. S., M.S.'47, N. Dak. Agrl. Col.; Supt. of Sch., Special Sch. Dist. 13, Hebron, N. Dak., since 1947.

Bjork, Alton J., B.A.'38, State Tchrs. Col., Valley City, N. Dak.; Ed.D.'42, Tchrs. Col., Columbia Univ.; Assoc. Prof. of Sec. Educ. and Admin., Univ. of N. Dak., Grand Forks, N. Dak., since 1946.

Calhoun, H. C., B.S.Ed.'19, Southwest Mo. Tchrs. Col.; Supt. of Sch., Wahpeton, N. Dak., since 1949.

Carlson, J. T., M.A.'40, Univ. of Wash.; Supt. of Sch., Lakota, N. Dak., since 1947.

Crank, Charles E., M.S.(Ed.)'43, Univ. of Idaho; Supt. of Sch., Garrison, N. Dak., since 1940.

Cummings, Nathan W., B.A.Ed.'28, State Tchrs. Col., Valley City, N. Dak.; Supt. of Sch., Oakes, N. Dak., since 1951.

Dalager, Paul A., B.A.'20, St. Olaf Col.; Exec. Secy., N. Dak. Educ. Assn., Bismarck, N. Dak., since 1946.

Dannewitz, David D., B.A.'38, State Tchrs. Col., Minot, N. Dak.; M.Ed.'48, Mont. State Univ.; Supt. of Sch., Tioga, N. Dak., since 1949.

Davis, Lloyd S., B.A.'45, Pacific Union Col.; Supt., Sheyenne River Acad., Harvey, N. Dak., since 1951.

Day, Erven W., Sr., B.A.'32, State Tchrs. Col., Minot, N. Dak.; M.Ed.'52, Univ. of N. Dak.; Supt. of Sch., Goodrich, N. Dak., since 1949.

Digerness, LeRoy, Supt., Sch. Dist. 8, Williston, N. Dak., since 1950.

Ensrud, H. B., B.S.'29, M.S.'37, Univ. of N. Dak.; Supt. of Sch., Grafton, N. Dak., since 1936.

Eslinger, Dan C., B.S.'32 Ellendale Normal and Indus. Col.; M.S.'49, Univ. of N. Dak., Supt. of Hazen H. S., Hazen, N. D., since 1950.

Evans, L. L., B.A.'40, State Tchrs. Col., Dickinson, N. Dak.; Supt. of Sch., Noonan, N. Dak., since 1952.

Evingson, Caroline J., B.A.'30, N. Dak. State Col.; Co. Supt. of Sch., Cass Co., Fargo, N. Dak., since 1923.

Falkenstein, George L., B.A.'31, M.S.'45, Univ. of N. Dak.; Supt. of Sch., Turtle Lake, N. Dak., since 1951.

Flaten, Alf R., B.A. in Ed.'29, State Tchrs. Col., Mayville, N. Dak.; M.S. in Ed.'50, Univ. of Idaho; Supt. of Sch., Alexander, N. Dak., since 1944.

Garvin, Rev. John E., M.A.'46, Columbia Univ.; Ed.D.'48, Tchrs. Col., Columbia Univ.; Supt., St. Mary's Central H. S. and Diocese of Bismarck, Bismarck, N. Dak., since 1950.

Gilliland, F. H., B.A.'17, M.A.'36, State Univ. of Iowa; Supt. of Sch., Devils Lake, N. Dak., since 1930.

Gludt, Clarence J., B.E.'31, State Tchrs. Col., Moorhead, Minn.; M.S.'34, Univ. of N. Dak.; Supt. of Sch., Killdeer, N. Dak., since 1941.

Gussner, William S., B.S.'26, Jamestown Col.; M.S. in Ed.'38, Univ. of N. Dak.; Supt. of Sch., Jamestown, N. Dak., since 1939.

Guthrie, James R., B.A.'37, State Tchrs. Col., Minot, N. Dak.; M.Ed.'51, Mont. State Univ.; Supt. of Sch., Mott, N. Dak., since 1951.

Hagen, Alem L., B.A.'25, Concordia Col.; M.A.'33, Univ. of Minn.; Supt. of Sch., Dickinson, N. Dak., since 1938.

Hanson, B. M., M.S. in Ed.'49, Univ. of N. Dak.; Supt. of Pub. Sch., Harvey, N. Dak., since 1949.

Haring, Richard J., M.A. in Ed. Admin.'51, Colo. State Col. of Educ.; Supt., Pub. Sch., Hazen, N. Dak., since 1952.

Havig, Leonard T., B.A.'21, St. Olaf Col.; M.A.'31, Univ. of Minn.; Supt. of City Sch., Williston, N. Dak., since 1946.

Herwick, Edwin N., B.A.'40, N. Dak. State Tchrs. Col., Valley City; Supt. of Sch., Clifford, N. Dak., since 1947.

Hilde, E. R., B.A.'32, Minot State Tchrs. Col.; Supt. of Sch., Washburn, N. Dak., since 1947.

Hill, Lyle H., B.S.'28, N. Dak. Agrl. Col.; M.Ed.'41, Univ. of Wash.; Supt. of Sch., New Salem, N. Dak., since 1943.

Hillesland, Earl F., B.S.'50, N. Dak. Agr!. Col.; Supt. of Sch., Stanton, N. Dak., since 1951.

Holstine, Garold D., B.Ed.'28, Western Ill. State Col.; M.A.'35, Ph.D.'42, State Univ. of Iowa; Dean, Sch. of Educ., Univ. of N. Dak., Grand Forks, N. Dak., since 1951.

Iverson, Irving L., B.A.'34, St. Olaf Col.; M.Ed. '41, Univ. of Mont.; Supt. of City Sch., New Rockford, N. Dak., since 1949.

James, Bernard P., B.A.'23, Drake Univ.; M.S.'39, Univ. of N. Dak.; Supt. of Sch., Napoleon, N. Dak., since 1949.

Johnson, Elmer C., B.S. in Ed.'38, Univ. of N. Dak.; Supt. of Sch., Kenmare, N. Dak., since 1929.

Jordahl, Carl W., B.A.'29, Luther Col., Decorah, Iowa; M.A.'39, Univ. of Minn.; Supt. of Sch., Lidgerwood, N. Dak., since 1944.

Juhala, R. W., B.S. in Ed.'49, State Tchrs. Col., Valley City, N. Dak.; Supt. of Pub. Sch., Taylor, N. Dak., since 1950.

Keefer, Daryle Earl, B.S.'29, M.A.'35, Ball State Tchrs. Col., Muncie, Ind.; Ph.D.'46, Northwestern Univ.; Dir. of Grad. Div., Univ. of N. Dak., Grand Forks, N. Dak., since 1951.

King, Lloyd H., B.A.'28, Jamestown Col.; M.A.'33, Univ. of Minn.; Ed.D.'50, Colo. State Col. of Educ., Greeley; Asst. Prof., Sch. of Educ., Univ. of N. Dak., Grand Forks, N. Dak., since 1952.

Kirk, Harold H., B.A.'13, Ohio Wesleyan Univ.; M.A.'26, Columbia Univ.; Supt. of Sch., Fargo, N. Dak., since 1935.

Korbel, Albin, B.A.'30, State Tchrs. Col., Valley City, N. Dak.; Supt. of Sch., Tolna, N. Dak.

Kosebud, C. R., B.S.'28, State Tchrs. Col., Valley City, N. Dak.; M.Ed.'46, Univ. of Mont.; Supt. of Sch., Rolla, N. Dak., since 1951.

Krogh, W. R., B.A.'46, State Tchrs. Col., Mayville, N. Dak.; Supt. of Sch., Casselton, N. Dak., since 1951.

Kval, Edwin E., B.S.'35, State Tchrs. Col., Ellendale, N. Dak.; M.S.'48, Univ. of N. Dak.; Supt. of Sch., Wildrose, N. Dak., since 1948.

Larsen, Levi N., B.A.'32, Jamestown Col.; M.A.'42, Montana State Univ.; Supt. of Sch., Watford City, N. Dak., since 1942.

Lee, Knute H., B.A.'35, State Tchrs. Col., Minot, N. Dak.; Supt. of Sch., Fort Yates, N. Dak., since 1945.

Lockwood, Dwight A., B.S.Ed.'48, State Tchrs. Col., Dickinson, N. Dak.; Supt. of Sch., McGregor, N. Dak., since 1949.

Lokken, Roscoe L., Ph.D.'39, State Univ. of Iowa; Pres., State Tchrs. Col., Valley City, N. Dak., since 1946.

Lura, Casper P., A.B.'27, State Tchrs. Col., Mayville, N. Dak.; A.M.'30, Ph.D.'32, State Univ. of Iowa; Pres., State Tchrs. Col., Mayville, N. Dak., since 1947.

McCrea, Minard, B.S.'36, M.S.'43, Univ. of N. Dak.; Supt. of City Sch., Valley City, N. Dak., since 1949.

McFadden, J. H., B.S. in Ed.'41, Northwestern Univ.; M.S. in Ed.'47, Univ. of N. Dak. Address: Maxbass, N. Dak.

McMillan, J. C., M.A.'26, Univ. of Chicago; Pres., State Normal and Indus. Col., Ellendale, N. Dak., since 1936.

Meinecke, Reuben, B.A. in Sec. Ed.'39, State Tchrs. Col., Valley City, N. Dak.; M.S. in Ed. '49, Univ. of N. Dak.; Supt. of Pub. Sch., Plaza, N. Dak., since 1952.

Melsted, Freeman, B.A.'40, State Tchrs. Col., Mayville, N. Dak.; Supt. of Sch., Starkweather, N. Dak., since 1952.

Miller, A. R., B.A.'28, State Tchrs. Col., Minot, N. Dak.; M.A.'36, Univ. of Minn.; Supt. of Sch., Beach, N. Dak., since 1936.

Miller, Paul A., B.A.'18, Valparaiso Univ.; M.A.'30, Univ. of N. Dak.; Supt. of City Sch., Minot, N. Dak., since 1944.

Murray, Robert J., B.S.'50, State Tchrs. Col., St. Cloud, Minn.; Prin., Standing Rock Community Sch., Fort Yates, N. Dak., since 1951.

Myhre, Olger, M.S. in Ed.'38, Univ. of N. Dak.; Supt. of Sch., Pembina, N. Dak., since 1944.

Neff, William Lee, Ed.D.'41, Stanford Univ.; Supt. of City Sch., Mandan, N. Dak., since 1944.

Noonan, James L., B.S.'48, N. Dak. Agr. Col.; M.S. in Ed.'52, Univ. of N. Dak.; Supt. of Sch., Page, N. Dak., since 1951.

Olafson, M. O., B.A.'30, St. Olaf Col.; M.S.'46, Univ. of N. Dak.; Supt. of Sch., Minto, N. Dak., since 1945.

Olson, Morris C., B.A.'31, State Tchrs. Col., Valley City, N. Dak.; M.E.'39, Mont. State Univ.; Supt. of Sch., Lisbon, N. Dak., since 1947.

Olson, Olger, M.S. in Ed.'39, Univ. of N. Dak.; B.A.'32, Concordia Col. (Minn.); Supt. of Sch., Fairmount, N. Dak., since 1941.

Pennington, J. I., B.A.'30, Hastings Col.; M.E. '40, Univ. of Colo.; Supt. of Sch., Rugby, N. Dak., since 1946.

Peterson, M. F., B.A.'33, Concordia Col. (Moorehead, Minn.); State Supt. of Pub. Instr., Bismarck, N. Dak., since 1951.

Randall, James, B.S. in Ed.'40, State Tchrs. Col., Minot, N. Dak.; M.S. in Ed.'49, Univ. of N. Dak.; Supt. of Sch., Belfield, N. Dak., since 1949.

Reich, Roland H., M.Ed.'49, Mont. State Univ.; Supt. of Sch., Wilton, N. Dak., since 1950.

Rhodes, Vaughn E., B.A.'46, N. Dak. State Tchrs. Col., Valley City; M.Ed.'52, Univ. of N. Dak.; Supt. of Sch., Sharon, N. Dak., since 1951.

Richardson, Vernon, B.A. in Ed.'42, N. Dak. State Tchrs. Col., Dickinson; Prin. of H. S., Rhame, N. Dak., since 1949.

Rindt, J. E., B.A.'41, State Tchrs. Col., Minot, N. Dak.; Supt. of Sch., Sheyenne, N. Dak., since 1949.

Roberts, John J., B.S.'29, M.A.'39, Univ. of Minn.; Supt. of Sch., Hettinger, N. Dak., since 1939.

Rogers, F. Ray, B.Pd., A.B.'17, Tri-State Col.; M.A.'23, Indiana Univ.; Supt. of Sch., Mohall, N. Dak., since 1949.

Roscoe, Henry G., M.S.'49, Univ. of N. Dak.; Supt. of Sch., Steele, N. Dak., since 1951.

Rue, Knute L., B.A.'27, Univ. of N. Dak.; M.A. '41, Univ. of Minn.; Supt. of Sch., Cavalier, N. Dak., since 1945.

Schroeder, Elroy H., B.S. in Ed.'26, M.S. in Ed.'35, Univ. of N. Dak.; LL.D.'48, Wesley Col.; Supt. of Sch., Grand Forks, N. Dak., since 1933.

Schultz, Otto C., B.S.'36, State Normal and Indus. Col.; M.S.'47, Univ. of N. Dak.; M.A. '49, Univ. of Minn.; Supt. of Sch., Buffalo, N. Dak., since 1949.

Scott, Charles E., B.A.'21, M.A.'22, Colo. Col. of Educ.; Pres., State Tchrs. Col., Dickinson, N. Dak., since 1939.

Selke, Erich, Ph.D.'32, Univ. of Minn.; Prof. of Educ., Univ. of N. Dak., Grand Forks, N. Dak., since 1936.

Simle, T. E., B.A.'30, State Tchrs. Col., Mayville, N. Dak.; M.A.'47, Colo. State Col. of Educ.; Supt. of Sch., Bismarck, N. Dak., since 1952.

Stephens, G. M., M.A.'41, Univ. of Colo.; Supt. of Sch., Riverdale, N. Dak., since 1951.

Swain, Carl C., M.A.'18, Columbia Univ.; LL.D.'40, St. Olaf Col.; Pres., State Tchrs. Col., Minot, N. Dak., since 1938.

Thordarson, T. W., M.S.'29, N. Dak. Agrl. Col.; State Dir., Dept. of Correspondence Study, Div. of Supervised Study, N. Dak. Agrl. Col., Fargo, N. Dak., since 1925.

Totdahl, A. O., B.A.'35, Luther Col.; Supt. of Sch., Beulah, N. Dak., since 1941.

Totdahl, L. J., B.A.'29, Luther Col. (Iowa); M.S.'40, Univ. of N. Dak.; Supt. of Sch., Crosby, N. Dak., since 1944.

Turner, Daniel O., B.S.A.'24, Kansas State Col. of Agr. and Applied Science; Supt. of Sch., Ashley, N. Dak., since 1947.

Urban, Wilmar A., B.A.'49, Jamestown Col.; Supt., Pub. Sch., Sentinel Butte, N. Dak., since 1952.

Van Der Hoeven, Eugene, B.S. in Ed.'46, Ohio Univ.; Supt. of Sch., Golva, N. Dak., since 1952.

Wakefield, Harold, M.S.'34, Univ. of N. Dak.; Supt. of Sch., La Moure, N. Dak., since 1928.

Wallestad, Eugene T., B.A.'40, State Tchrs. Col., Minot, N. Dak.; M.A.'48, Univ. of Minn.; Supt. of Sch., Minnewaukan, N. Dak., since 1946.

Walters, John G., B.S. in Ed.'32, State Tchrs. Col., Valley City, N. Dak.; M.S. in Ed.'37, Univ. of N. Dak.; Supt., Walsh Co. Agrl. and Tr. Sch., Park River, N. Dak., since 1942.

Westley, Harry A., M.A.'36, Mont. State Univ.; Supt. of Sch., Bowman, N. Dak., since 1941.

Wilson, Richard B., B.S.'50, State Normal and Indus. Col., N. Dak.; Prin., Monango Sch., Monango, N. Dak., since 1952.

Yvonne, Sister M., M.A.'29, Univ. of Minn.; Supt., St. John's Academy, Jamestown, N. Dak., since 1940.

Ziegenhagen, Alvin P., B.S.'30, M.S.'38, Univ. of N. Dak.; Supt. of Sch., Enderlin, N. Dak., since 1947.

Zimmerman, M. B., B.A.'18, Central Wesleyan Col.; M.S.'37, Univ. of N. Dak.; Supt. of Sch., Wahpeton, N. Dak., since 1937.

INSTITUTIONAL MEMBERS

Library, State Teachers College, Mayville, N. Dak.

Library, State Teachers College, Minot, N. Dak.

OHIO

INDIVIDUAL MEMBERS

Abel, Robert D., B.A.'38, Mount Union Col.; M.A.'47, Ohio State Univ.; Local Supt. of Sch., Berlin Heights, Ohio, since 1946.

Adell, James C., B.A.'09, Ohio State Univ.; M.A.'30, Columbia Univ.; Chief, Bur. of Educ. Research, Bd. of Educ., Cleveland, Ohio, since 1937.

Alberts, T. L., Exec. Head, Local Sch., Hanover, Ohio.

Alspach, Ninde N., B.S.'16, Ohio Wesleyan Univ.; Mgr., Goodyear Indus. Univ., Akron, Ohio, since 1944.

*Anderson, Earl William, A.B.'18, Univ. of Ill.; A.M.'25, Ph.D.'26, Tchrs. Col., Columbia Univ.; Prof. of Educ., Dept. of Educ., Ohio State Univ., Columbus, Ohio.

Armstrong, George E., B.A.'23, Ohio Wesleyan Univ.; M.A.'37, Ohio State Univ.; Supt., Centralia Sch., Chillicothe, Ohio, since 1928.

Arnold, E. J., M.A.'23, Ohio State Univ.; Supvr, Sch. Plant Rehabilitation, State Dept. of Educ., Columbus, Ohio, since 1945.

Ashman, Ward, B.S. Bus. Admin.'29, Ohio State Univ.; Exec. Secy., Sch. Employees' Retirement System of Ohio, Columbus, Ohio, since 1947.

Augspurger, R. E., A.B.'26, Bluffton Col.; M.A. '33, Ohio State Univ.; Supt. of Sch., Wapakoneta, Ohio.

Baden, Carl A., A.B.'28, Wittenberg Col.; M.A. '37, Ohio State Univ.; Co. Supt. of Sch., Greenville, Ohio, since 1945.

Bahner, W. G., A.B.'15, Wittenberg Col.; M.A.'24, Columbia Univ.; Supt., Cuyahoga Hgts. Sch., Cleveland, Ohio, since 1943.

Bailey, Thomas C., B.S.E.'39, Ohio Northern Univ.; M.A.E.'46, Ohio State Univ.; Supt., Canton South H. S., Canton, Ohio, since 1951.

Baird, Joseph L., B.Ed.'38, Univ. of Toledo; M.A.'46, Univ. of Mich.; Supt. of Sch., Maumee, Ohio, since 1952.

Baker, Homer K., B.S.'25, Miami Univ.; M.A.'31, Ohio State Univ.; Supt. of Sch., Fairborn, Ohio.

Baker, J. L., A.B.'25, Manchester Col.; M.A.'34, Ohio State Univ.; Supt. of Exempted Village Sch., Covington, Ohio, since 1946.

Baker, Joseph E., B.Arch.'36, Univ. of Ill.; Archt., Joseph Baker and Associates, Newark, Ohio.

Ball, Leonard T., A.B., Ohio Univ.; M.A.'39, Ohio State Univ.; Supt. of Exempted Village Sch., Tipp City, Ohio, since 1946.

Banning, Gail W., B.S. in Ed.'24, Ohio Univ.; M. in Ed.'33, Univ. of Pittsburgh; Supt., Mecca Sch., Cortland, Ohio, since 1934.

Barger, W. S., B.S. in Ed.'24, Ohio State Univ.; Supt. of Sch., Lucas, Ohio, since 1946.

Barker, Willard P., B.S.'31, Col. of Wooster; M.A.'46, Kent State Univ.; Supt. of Sch., Athens, Ohio, since 1949.

Barr, William Wayne, B.S. in Ed.'38, Ashland Col.; M.A. in Ed.'46, Western Reserve Univ.; Prin., Brookside H. S., Lorain, Ohio, since 1941.

Bascom, Arthur L., B.S.'24, M.A.'29, Ohio State Univ.; Exec. Head, Twp. Sch., Leavittsburg, Ohio, since 1926.

Bates, Harold S., B.S.'21, Knox Col.; A.M.'34, Columbia Univ.; D.Ed.'40, Univ. of Cincinnati; Supt. of Sch., Norwood, Ohio, since 1936.

Baumgartner, Ira, A.B.'22, Bluffton Col.; M.A.'27, Ohio State Univ.; Supt. of Sch., Sylvania, Ohio, since 1934.

Becker, Adams, Supt. of Jefferson Twp. Sch., Dayton, Ohio.

Becker, Edwin G., Vicepres., Bd. of Educ., Cincinnati, Ohio.

Beckman, Joseph M., M.A.'34, Univ. of Cincinnati; Asst. to the Supt. of Sch., Cincinnati, Ohio, since 1947.

Beery, George C., A.B.'16, M.A.'25, Ohio State Univ.; Co. Supt. of Sch., Columbus, Ohio, since 1924.

Bennett, R. M., B.S. and M.S.'45, Univ. of Ill.; Ohio and W. Va. Rep., Follett Publishing Co., 2925 Norwood Ave., Columbus 11, Ohio.

Bennett, R. Dwight, B.A.'28, Wittenberg Col.; M.A.'37, Ohio State Univ.; Supt. of Sch., Van Wert, Ohio, since 1946.

Berry, Merrill M., A.B.'19, Baldwin-Wallace Col.; A.M.'22, Ohio State Univ.; Supt. of Sch., Chillicothe, Ohio, since 1935.

Betts, Ralph W., B.A.'29, Ohio Univ.; M.A.'41, Ohio State Univ.; Supt of Sch., East Liverpool, Ohio, since 1951.

Bishop, Benjamin J., B.S. in Ed.'28, M.A.'34, Ohio State Univ.; Supt. of Sch., Holland, Ohio, since 1942.

Bixler, Lorin E., A.B.'21, Mt. Union Col.; M.A.'23, Tchrs. Col., Columbia Univ.; Ph.D. '31, Ohio State Univ.; Prof. of Educ. and Head, Dept. of Educ., Muskingum Col., New Concord, Ohio, since 1929.

Blackford, John D., B.S. in Ed.'26, A.M. in Sch. Admin.'37, Miami Univ.; Supt. of Mariemont Sch., Mariemont, Cincinnati, Ohio, since 1944.

Bliss, Walton B., A.B.'15, Heidelberg Col.; M.A. '29, Ohio State Univ.; Exec. Secy., Ohio Educ. Assn., Columbus, Ohio, since 1935.

Bloser, Robert E., A.B.'17, Ohio State Univ.; Pres., Zaner-Bloser Co., Columbus, Ohio, since 1929.

Blott, E. J., A.B.'24, M.A.'30, Univ. of Mich.; Supt., Liberty Twp. Sch., Youngstown, Ohio, since 1934.

Boda, Harold L., A.B.'25, Otterbein Col.; A.M.'30, Ohio State Univ.; Ed.D.'44, Otterbein Col.; Asst. Supt. of Sch., Dayton Ohio, since 1940.

Bode, F. H., A.B.'28, Heidelberg Col.; M.A.'34, Columbia Univ.; Supt. of Sch., Cuyahoga Falls, Ohio, since 1949.

Bodenbender, D. P., B.A.'31, Defiance Col.; M.A.'41, Univ. of Mich.; Supt. of Sch., Wooster, Ohio, since 1947.

Bodenbender, Karl R., A.B.'33, B.S.'42, Defiance Col.; M.A.'42, Miami Univ.; Supt of Exempted Village Sch., Glouster, Ohio, since 1948.

Bolen, Wilber Floyd, B.S.Ed.'31, M.A.'38, Ohio State Univ.; Supt. of Sch., Junction City, Ohio, since 1938.

Bonham, S. J., A.B.'20, Wittenberg Col.; A.M.'24, Ind. Univ.; Supt. of Sch., Niles, Ohio, since 1933.

Borst, R. M., A.M.'41, Wittenberg Col.; Asst. Co. Supt. of Sch., Springfield, Ohio, since 1948.

Bower, James Crawford, B.S.'30, M.S.'35, Ohio State Univ.; Supt. of Sch., Kenton, Ohio, since 1949.

Bowman, George A., A.B.'17, Western Reserve Univ.; M.A.'31, Columbia Univ.; LL.D.'45, Bowling Green State Univ.; Pres., Kent State Univ., Kent, Ohio, since 1944.

Bowman, Herbert L., B.S.'23, Denison Univ.; M.A.'34, Ohio State Univ.; Supt. of Sch., Bowling Green, Ohio, since 1939.

Bowman, Lawrence L., A.B.'29, Hiram Col.; M.S.'35, Univ. of Mich.; Dir., Dept. of Audio-Visual Aids, Pub. Sch., Barberton, Ohio, since 1929.

Bowsher, E. Leslie, A.B.'13, Defiance Col.; M.A.'26, Univ. of Mich.; LL.D.'37, Ashland Col.; LL.D.'42, Defiance Col.; D.Ped.'42, Bowling Green State Univ.; Supt. of Sch., Toledo, Ohio, since 1937.

Boyd, Margaret, A.B.'20, Mt. Union Col.; M.A.'28, Ohio State Univ.; Asst. Supt. of Sch., Steubenville, Ohio, since 1950.

Braden, Wallace H., B.A.'25, Col. of Wooster; M.A.'31, Ohio State Univ.; Supt. of Edgewood Sch., Ashtabula, Ohio, since 1936.

Brady, Ballard I., A.B.'29, Hiram Col.; M.A.'37, Kent State Univ.; Supt., Orange Village Sch. Dist., Chagrin Falls, Ohio.

Brand, R. G., A.B.'29, Heidelberg Col.; M.A.'37, Ohio State Univ.; Co. Supt. of Sch., Van Wert, Ohio, since 1946.

482

Briegel, Virgil J., M.A.'39, Ohio State Univ.; Supt., Exempted Village Sch., Clyde, Ohio, since 1952.

Brillhart, C. D., A.B.'16, Albright Col.; M.A.'25, Univ. of Mich.; Supt. of Sch., Napoleon, Ohio, since 1925.

Brown, Elijah H., B.S.'25, Kenyon Col.; M.A.'30, Columbia Univ.; Supt. of Sch., Fairport Harbor, Ohio, since 1925.

Brown, Francis W., A.B.'21, Univ. of Mich.; A.M.'31, Western Reserve Univ.; Supt. of Ottawa Hills Schs., Toledo, Ohio, since 1936.

Brown, H. Larry, B.S.'21, Mount Union Col.; M.A.'29, Tchrs. Col., Columbia Univ.; Supt. of Sch., Ravenna, Ohio, since 1939.

Brown, Paul V., A.M.'30, Univ. of Chicago; Supt. of Sch., Tiffin, Ohio, since 1931.

Brown, Robert S., B.A.'38, Muskingum Col.; M.A.'48, Ohio State Univ.; Supt., Springfield Twp. Sch., Akron, Ohio, since 1952.

Brown, Stephen C., A.B.'29, Adrian Col.; M.A. '41, Miami Univ. (Ohio); Supt. of City Sch., Washington Court House, Ohio, since 1949.

Bryan, William R., Secy.-Mgr., Ohio Tchrs. and Pupils Reading Circle, 1456 N. High St., Columbus 1, Ohio, since 1946.

Bube, O. E., B.S. in Ed.'37, M.A.'41, Miami Univ. (Ohio); Supt. of Sch., Milton Union Exempted Village, West Milton, Ohio, since 1951.

Bunn, Paul C., Ph.B.'09, Col. of Wooster; M.A.'22, Tchrs. Col., Columbia Univ.; Supt. of Sch., Youngstown, Ohio, since 1944.

Bunnell, C. P., Supt. of Pub. Sch., Bradford, Ohio.

Burkey, A. A., A.B.'15, A.M.'28, Ohio State Univ.; Ed.D.'36, Webster Col.; Supt. of Sch., McDonald, Ohio, 1925-52 (retired).

Burkhart, Lewis L., B.A.'38, B.S. in Ed.'40, Defiance Col.; M.A.'45, Western Reserve Univ.; Supt. of Sch., Solon, Ohio, since 1948.

Burkholder, Forrest D., A.B.'27, Bluffton Col.; M.A.'35, Ohio State Univ.; Exec. Head, Green Local Sch., Smithville, Ohio, since 1942.

Burkholder, M. H., A.B.'29, Asbury Col.; M.A. '34, Columbia Univ.; Supt. of Sch., Wadsworth, Ohio, since 1946.

Burneson, L. G., A.B.'21, Oberlin Col.; M.A.'29, Tchrs. Col., Columbia Univ.; Supt. of Sch., Westlake, Ohio, since 1924.

Burnett, Cecil M., A.B.'27, Oberlin Col.; A.M.'39, Western Reserve Univ.; Supt. of Sch., Brecksville, Ohio, since 1945.

Butterfield, E. E., Ph.B.'11, Mt. Union Col.; A.M.'24, Western Reserve Univ.; A.M.'25, Columbia Univ.; Deputy Supt. of Sch., Cleveland, Ohio, since 1947.

Byers, Carl C., B.S.'32, Otterbein Col.; M.A.'37, Ohio Univ.; Supt. of Sch., Thoreau Park Sch., Parma, Cleveland, Ohio, since 1942.

Campbell, Roald F., A.B.'30, M.A.'34, Brigham Young Univ.; Ed.D.'42, Stanford Univ.; Prof of Educ., Ohio State Univ., Columbus, Ohio.

Carmean, Byron H., A.B.'30, Ohio Univ.; M.A. '38, Ohio State Univ.; Supt. of Sch., Shelby, Ohio, since 1946.

Carr, George Eldon, A.B.'20, Ohio Univ.; A.M. '27, Ohio State Univ.; Supt. of Sch., Logan, Ohio, since 1930.

Carr, Paul A., B.S. in Ed., Ohio Univ.; Supt. of Sch., Gibisonville, Ohio, since 1943.

Christman, George E., B.Ed.'35, M.Ed.'50, Ohio Univ.; Co. Supt. of Sch., Athens, Ohio, since 1950.

Christy, Robert H., B.S.'32, Bowling Green Univ.; M.A.'40, Ohio State Univ.; Supt. of Sch., Delphos, Ohio, since 1940.

Coblentz, C. R., B.S. in Ed.'32, Miami Univ.; Co. Supt. of Sch., Eaton, Ohio, since 1923.

Coffeen, Carl, B.S.'14, Ohio Wesleyan Univ.; M.A.'36, Western Reserve Univ.; Co. Supt. of Sch., Cuyahoga Falls, Ohio, since 1935.

Conkey, B.J., A.B.'32, Defiance Col.; M.A.'47, Indiana Univ.; Supt. of Sch., Continental, Ohio, since 1950.

Conrad, M. J., B.S. in Ed.'38, Capital Univ.; M.A.'46, Ph.D.'52, Ohio State Univ.; Research Associate, Bur. of Educ. Research, Ohio State Univ., Columbus, Ohio, since 1952.

Cook, Harold H., B.A.'30, Ohio Wesleyan Univ.; M.A.'38, Ohio State Univ.; Supt. of Sch., St. Mary's, Ohio, since 1945.

Coon, M. J., A.B.'38, Bluffton Col.; M.A.'49, Ohio State Univ.; Supt. of Sch., Plymouth, Ohio, since 1951.

Cottrell, Donald P., B.A.'23, Ohio State Univ.; M.A.'27, Ph.D.29, Columbia Univ.; Dean, Col. of Educ., Ohio State Univ., Columbus, Ohio, since 1946.

Courter, Claude V., B.S.'11, D.Ed.'38, Kalamazoo Col.; M.A.'25, Univ. of Chicago; LL.D.'52, Miami Univ.; Supt. of Sch., Cincinnati, Ohio, since 1937.

Cox, Clifford C., M.S.'45, Ind. Univ.; Supt. of Sch., Pandora, Ohio, since 1943.

Crabbs, Robert W., B.S.'41, M.A.'49, Ohio State Univ.; Supt., Twin Twp. Sch., Bourneville, Ohio, since 1951.

Craig, Raymond B., B.S. in Ed.'34, M.A.'38, Ohio State Univ.; Supt., Liberty Union Sch., Baltimore, Ohio.

Crewson, Walter Samuel, M.S.'37, Univ. of Chicago; Supt. of Sch., Hamilton, Ohio, since 1948.

Cromwell, Howard R., B.S.'30, Ind. State Tchrs. Col., Terre Haute; M.S.'41, Ohio State Univ.; Supt. of Sch., Glendale, Ohio, since 1947.

Crotty, Maurice, B.S.'33, Univ. of Cincinnati; M.A.'36, Columbia Univ.; Dir.-in-Chief, Pupil Personnel Serv., Pub. Sch., Cincinnati, Ohio, since 1948.

Crouch, Charles B., A.B.'27, Muskingum Col.; M.A.'34, Ohio State Univ.; Co. Supt. of Sch., Cincinnati, Ohio, since 1948.

Crowell, Gilford W., B.S.'47, Murray State Col.; M.Ed.'49, D.Ed.'51, Univ. of Mo.; Asst. Prof. and Asst. Dir., Center for Educ. Service, Col. of Educ., Ohio Univ., Athens, Ohio, since 1951.

Cummins, Paul R., B.S. in Ed.'34, Ohio Northern Univ.; M.A. in Adm.'44, Ohio State Univ.; Co. Supt. of Sch., Lancaster, Ohio, since 1945.

Curry, Robert P., M.A.'37, Univ. of Cincinnati; Asst. Supt. of Sch., Cincinnati, Ohio., since 1948.

Daugherty, Kermit, A.B.'28, Rio Grande Col.; M.A.'37, Ohio State Univ.; Supt. of Sch., Jackson, Ohio, since 1946.

Davies, Robert O., A.B.'30, Marietta Col.; M.A.'37, Ohio State Univ.; Exec. Head, Pub. Sch., Camden, Ohio, since 1946.

Davis, Charles E., A.B.'26, Rio Grande Col.; M.A.'35, Wittenberg Col.; Pres., Rio Grande Col., Rio Grande, Ohio.

Davis, J. H., B.S.'49, Ohio State Univ.; Asst. Mgr., Ohio Tchrs. and Pupils Reading Circle, Columbus, Ohio, since 1951.

Davis, Thoburn Scott, B.A.'21, Ohio Wesleyan Univ.; M.A.'26, Tchrs. Col., Columbia Univ.; Supt. of Rocky River Sch., Rocky River, Ohio, since 1948.

Daw, Seward E., M.A.'33, Univ. of Chicago; Ph.D.'40, Univ. of Pittsburgh; Supt. of Sch., Wellsville, Ohio, since 1922.

Demyan, J. G., B.S.'30, Valparaiso Univ.; M.A. '41, Univ. of Mich.; Supt. of Sch., Defiance, Ohio, since 1949.

Dennis, Merrill L., B.S. in Ed.'19, Ohio Univ.; M.A.'37, Columbia Univ.; Supt. of Sch., Mingo Junction, Ohio, since 1937.

Devol, Gerald O., B.S. in Ed.'36, Ohio Univ.; Supt., Ward Local Sch., Carbon Hill, Ohio, since 1945.

Dickey, Lester L., A.B.'25, Ohio Wesleyan Univ.; M.A.'34, Ohio State Univ.; Supt. of Sch., Marion, Ohio, since 1948.

Diener, U. E., M.A.'30, Ohio State Univ.; Supt. of Sch., Fremont, Ohio, since 1938.

Donaldson, Howard W., A.B.'20, Hiram Col.; M.E., Kent State Univ.; Supt. of Sch., Madison, Ohio, since 1949.

Downing, Roger L., B.S. in Ed.'37, Ohio Northern Univ.; M.S. in Ed.'47, Univ. of Wis.; Supt. of Sch., Upper Sandusky, Ohio, since 1951.

Driscoll, W. A., A.B.'22, Wilmington Col.; M.A. '28, Ohio State Univ.; Co. Supt. of Sch., Dayton, Ohio, since 1933.

Duncan, Robert W., A.B.'33, M.A.'41, Ohio State Univ.; Supt. of Sch., Greenville, Ohio, since 1951.

Dungan, J. U., B.S.'19, Univ. of Ill.; A.M.'31, Univ. of Cincinnati; Supt. of Sch., Lockland, Ohio, since 1923.

Dunsmore, Philo C., B.A.'21, Mich. State Normal Col., Ypsilanti; M.A.'23, Univ. of Toledo; Asst. Supt. of Sch., Toledo, Ohio, since 1945.

Durkee, Warren M., A.B.'29, Bluffton Col.; M.A.'35, Ohio State Univ.; Supt. of Sch., Reading, Ohio, since 1946.

Durling, William J., B.S.'21, Mt. Union Col.; M.A.'32, Ohio State Univ.; Supt. of Clearview Sch., Lorain, Ohio, since 1925.

Eastman, George H., Supt. of Sch., Dalton, Ohio.

Edwards, Paul B., B.Sc.'17, M.A.'36, Ohio State Univ.; Supt. of Sch., Newark, Ohio, since 1936.

Edwards, William B., B.A.'31, Ohio Univ.; M.A.'38, Kent State Univ.; Supt., South Euclid-Lyndhurst Sch., Cleveland, Ohio.

Eibling, Harold H., B.Sc. in Ed.'26, Ohio Northern Univ.; M.A.'32, Ph.D.'50, Ohio State Univ.; Supt. of Sch., Canton, Ohio, since 1950.

Ellsworth, F. O., A.B.'29, Defiance Col.; M.S.'38, Univ. of Mich.; Supt. of Sch., Stryker, Ohio, since 1950.

Ely, Ralph, B.A.'31, Col. of Wooster; M.A. in Adm.'42, Ohio State Univ.; Co. Supt. of Sch., Wooster, Ohio, since 1948.

Essex, Martin W., B.S.'30, M.A.'34, Ohio State Univ.; D.Ped.'50, Baldwin-Wallace Col.; Supt. of Sch., Lakewood, Ohio, since 1947.

Essig, J. Fred, B.S. in Ed.'27, Kansas State Tchrs. Col., Emporia; M.A.'31, State Univ. of Iowa; Ed.D.'44, Colo. State Col. of Educ.; Asst. Supt. of Sch., Youngstown, Ohio, since 1944.

Evans, Howard R., A.B. in Ed.'25, Ind. State Tchrs. Col., Terre Haute; M.A.'28, Columbia Univ.; Ph.D.'30, Northwestern Univ.; Dean, Col. of Educ., Univ. of Akron, Akron, Ohio, since 1933.

Evans, John W., A.B.'29, Rio Grande Col.; M.A.'33, Ph.D.'51, Ohio State Univ.; Supt. of Sch., Lorain, Ohio, since 1951.

Everman, Edwin E., B.S. in Ed.'46, M.A. in Ed.'48, Ohio State Univ.; Supt., Monroe Twp. Sch., West Manchester, Ohio, since 1952.

Eyman, R. Merle, B.E.'20, M.A.'29, Ohio State Univ.; Asst. State Supt. of Pub. Instr., Columbus, Ohio, since 1945.

Farrar, O. H., M.Ed.'39, Ohio Univ.; Supt. of Sch., Mt. Gilead, Ohio, since 1948.

Fassett, Josephine, B.S.'26, M.A.'37, Univ. of Toledo; Supvr., Oregon Local Sch. Dist., Toledo, Ohio, since 1930.

Fawcett, Novice G., B.Sc.'31, LL.D.'52, Kenyon Col.; M.A.'37, Ohio State Univ.; Supt. of Sch., Columbus, Ohio, since 1949.

Feick, Kenneth G., A.B.'23, Capitol Univ.; M.A.'45, Western Reserve Univ.; Supt. of Sch., Independence, Ohio, since 1942.

Fenn, Sidney M., B.S.'16, M.A.'37, Ohio State Univ.; Supt., Exempted Village Sch., Medina, Ohio, since 1947.

Few, Ray G., B.Ph.'08, Hiram Col.; Prin., Perry Schs., Perry, Ohio, since 1918.

Finley, Lester M., B.S. in Ed.'23, Ohio State Univ.; M.A.'30, Columbia Univ.; Co. Supt. of Sch., Jefferson, Ohio, since 1938.

Fintz, John E., B.S. in Ed.'30, M.A.'33, Ohio State Univ.; Asst. Supt. of Sch., Cleveland, Ohio, since 1936.

Flesher, William R., A.B.'30, Marietta Col.; M.A.'35, Ph.D.'42, Ohio State Univ.; Head, Evaluation Div., Bureau of Educ. Research, and Prof. of Educ., Ohio State Univ., Columbus, Ohio, since 1947.

Force, Leon S., B.S. in Ed.'46, Kent State Univ.; M.Ed.'50, Univ. of Pittsburgh; Supt. of Exempted Village Sch., Sebring, Ohio, since 1950.

Ford, H. L., A.B.'19, Ashland Col.; B.Sc.'20, M.A.'27, Ohio State Univ.; Supt. of Sch., Fostoria, Ohio, since 1937.

Fordyce, Wellington G., A.B.'24, M.A.'33, Ph.D. '44, Ohio State Univ.; Supt. of Sch., Euclid, Ohio, since 1952.

Forshey, William, Supt. of Sch., Corning, Ohio.

Fowler, Myron, M.A.'37, Ohio State Univ.; Supt. of Sch., New Lexington, Ohio, since 1952.

Fowler, Robert E., A.B.'28, Muskingum Col.; M.A.'37, Tchrs. Col., Columbia Univ.; Supt., East Union Local Sch., Apple Creek, Ohio, since 1948.

Fowler, Victor M., A.B.'33, Defiance Col.; M.Ed.'44, Ohio Univ.; 100 Farregat Ave., Green Hill, Cincinnati, Ohio.

Fox, H. Clifford, A.B.'20, M.A.'22, Findlay Col.; Ph.D.'41, State Univ. of Iowa; Pres., Findlay Col., Findlay, Ohio, since 1947.

Francis, R. A., B.S. in Ed.'29, Wilmington Col.; M.A.'40, Ohio State Univ.; Supt. of Sch., Kingston, Ohio, since 1941.

Frazier, William V., Jr., B.A.'21, Ohio Wesleyan Univ.; LL.B.'24, Univ. of Va.; Vicepres., Bd. of Educ., Martins Ferry, Ohio, since 1950.

French, Robert B., A.B.'22, M.A.'31, Univ. of Mich.; Supt. of Sch., Dayton, Ohio, since 1947.

Frey, James, M.Ed.'49, Ohio Univ.; Exec. Head of Sch., Laurelville, Ohio, since 1944.

Gabriel, O. J., B.S.'25, Col. of Wooster; M.Ed. '33, Univ. of Pittsburgh; Supt. of Sch., Struthers, Ohio, since 1944.

Gallaher, Paul C., B.S. in Ed.'40, Kent State Univ.; M.Ed.'44, Univ. of Pittsburgh; Supt. of Sch., Geneva, Ohio, since 1948.

Gantz, Ralph M., A.B.'29, Otterbein Col.; M.S.'35, Univ. of Akron; Supt. of Sch., Steubenville, Ohio, since 1950.

Gantz, Theodore A., A.B.'29, Col. of Wooster; M.A.'48, Ohio State Univ.; Co. Supt. of Sch., Mt. Gilead, Ohio, since 1949.

Gates, Dale W., B.S. in Ed.'28, M.A.'38, Ohio State Univ.; Supt. of Sch., Willard, Ohio, since 1939.

OHIO

Geiger, John David, A.B.'22, Bluffton Col.;
M.A.'29, Ohio State Univ.; Supt. of Sch.,
Mt. Vernon, Ohio, since 1941.

Geognegan, Sister Barbara, Ph.D.'50, Fordham
Univ.; Supvr. of Sec. Sch., Sisters of Charity,
Mount St. Joseph, Ohio, since 1950.

Gibbens, C. A., B.S.'15, Muskingum Col.;
M.A.'25, Tchrs. Col., Columbia Univ.; Co.
Supt. of Sch., Elyria, Ohio, since 1935.

Gingery, Stanley L., A.B.'20, Ohio Wesleyan
Univ.; A.M.'27 ,Ohio State Univ.; Asst. Supt.
of Sch., Columbus, Ohio, since 1941.

Good, Frederick W., B.S. in Ed.'35, Ohio Univ.;
M.A. in Ed.'52, Ohio State Univ.; Local Exec.
of a Consolidated Sch., South Bloomingville,
Ohio, since 1946.

Good, Theodore J., B.S.Ed.'40, Ohio Univ.;
Supt. of Sch., Rockbridge, Ohio, since 1947.

Goodrich, Paul C., B.S.'48, M.Ed.'51, Miami
Univ.; Supt. of Sch., West Alexandria, Ohio,
since 1950.

Gottfried, Franklin J., B.S. in Ed.'34, Bowling
Green State Col.; M.A.'39, Ph.D.'51, Ohio
State Univ.; Asst. Supt. of Sch., Elyria, Ohio,
since 1951.

Gower, Albert E., M.A.'24, Ohio State Univ.;
Co. Supt. of Sch., Chillicothe, Ohio, since
1937.

*Graff, Ellis U., A.B.'97, A.M.'15, Lake Forest
Col.; Pres., Dept. of Superintendence, 1919-20;
Honorary Life Member, American Assn. of
Sch. Admin. Address: 103 Hudson Avenue,
Newark, Ohio.

Greene, Maxson F., Supt. of Sch., Granville,
Ohio, since 1952.

Gregg, Wilbur I., B.S.'26, Muskingum Col.;
M.A.'40, Ohio State Univ.; Supt. of Sch., St.
Clairsville, Ohio, since 1934.

Gunnett, Paul G., B.A.'29, Ohio Wesleyan Univ.;
M.A. in Sch. Adm. '35, Ohio State Univ.; Supt.
of Sch., Barberton, Ohio, since 1948.

Hadfield, Albert E., A.B.'24, Hiram Col.;
A.M.'32, Tchrs. Col., Columbia Univ.; Supt. of
City Sch., Maple Heights, Ohio, since 1938.

Halchin, John, B.S.'37, State Tchrs. Col., Edinboro, Pa.; M.Ed.'39, Pa. State Col.; Supt. of
Sch., Yellow Springs, Ohio, since 1948.

Hales, James H., Supt. of Sch., R. D. 1, Amherst,
Ohio.

Hall, Raymond Elmo, B.A.'34, Defiance Col.;
M.A.'43, Ohio State Univ.; Supt. of Sch., New
Boston, Ohio, since 1951.

Hall, Robert H., B.S.'21, M.A.'33, Ohio State
Univ.; Exec. Head of Sch., Navarre, Ohio,
since 1935.

Hallauer, William E., B.S.'22, Univ. of Ill.; Asst.
Supt., in charge of Bus. Admin., Pub. Sch.,
Toledo, Ohio, since 1950.

Hammack, W. M., B.S. in Ed.'39, Kent State
Univ.; M.Ed.'50, Univ. of Pittsburgh; Exec.
Head, Vienna Twp. Sch., Vienna, Ohio, since
1952.

Hammack, William Eberly, B.A.'31, Western
Ky. State Tchrs. Col., Bowling Green; M.A.'32,
Univ. of S. Dak.; Supt., Colerain Twp. Sch.,
Cincinnati, Ohio, since 1949.

Hammond, Granville S., A.B.'40, Otterbein Col.;
M.A.'46, Ohio State Univ.; Dir. of Instr.,
Warren City Sch., Warren, Ohio.

Hanely, Merlin C., B.S.'39, M.A.'51, Univ. of
Toledo; Supt., Troy Twp. Sch., Luckey, Ohio,
since 1946.

Hanna, Marcus A., B.S. in Ed.'31, Ohio Univ.;
M.A. in Ed.'41, Ohio State Univ.; Local Supt.
of Sch., Pickerington, Ohio, since 1943.

Harkness, Charles S., A.B.'15, Otterbein Col.;
M.A.'26, Ohio State Univ.; Co. Supt. of Sch.,
Bowling Green, Ohio, since 1934.

Harris, Walter L., B.S.'35, M.A.'41, Ohio State
Univ.; Supt. of Exempted Village Sch.,
Wellington, Ohio, since 1951.

Harry, David P., Jr., A.B.'16, Swarthmore Col.;
A.M.'22, Ph.D.'28, Tchrs. Col., Columbia
Univ.; Prof. of Educ., Graduate Sch., Western
Reserve Univ., Cleveland, Ohio, since 1937.

Hartley, Joseph J., A.B.'28, Ohio Wesleyan
Univ.; A.M.'45, Ohio State Univ.; Supt. of Sch.,
London, Ohio, since 1943.

Harvey, Albert B., A.B.'16, Bates Col.; A.M.'30,
Tchrs. Col., Columbia Univ.; Asst. Supt. of
Sch., Cleveland Heights, Ohio, since 1948.

Hatton, Otis C., B.A.'10, M.A.'27, Ohio State
Univ.; Supt. of Sch., Akron, Ohio, since 1942.

Hauenstein, W. H., A.B.'29, Muskingum Col.;
M.A.'41, Ohio State Univ.; Supt. of Sch.,
Rittman, Ohio, since 1946.

Hawke, Oscar T., A.B.'14, A.M.'17, Wittenberg
Col.; Co. Supt. of Sch., Springfield, Ohio,
since 1946.

Hayes, Paul C., B.S. in Ed.'46, Wilmington Col.;
M.A. in Adm.'48, Miami Univ.; Supt. of Sch.,
Sharonville, Ohio, since 1951.

Hearing, Odin E., B.S.'19, M.A.'38, Ohio State
Univ.; Supt. of Co. Sch., New Lexington, Ohio,
since 1928.

Heck, Arch O., B.S.'13, Hedding Col.; M.S.'14,
Univ. of Ill.; Ph.D.'24, Ohio State Univ.;
Prof. of Educ., Ohio State Univ., Columbus,
Ohio, since 1923.

Heer, Amos L., A.B. and B.Pd.'14, Tri-State Col.;
A.M.'21, Tchrs. Col., Columbia Univ.; Ph.D
'26, Ohio State Univ.; Dir. of Tchr. Tr., Kent
State Univ., Kent, Ohio, since 1927.

Heinold, Fred W., M.D.'24, Univ. of Cincinnati;
Pres., Bd. of Educ., Cincinnati, Ohio, since
1940.

Heischman, Walter B., B.S.'32, Capital Univ.;
M.A.'40, Ohio State Univ.; Supt. of Sch.,
Upper Arlington, Columbus, Ohio, since 1951.

Henning W. K., B.E.'39, M.S. Ed.'50, Ohio
Univ.; Supt. of Sch., Glenford, Ohio, since
1945.

Henry, David W., B.A.'11, Kansas State Tchrs.
Col., Emporia, Kansas; M.A.'16, Columbia
Univ.; Diploma'37, London Univ., England;
Dean, Col. of Educ., Univ. of Toledo, Toledo,
Ohio, since 1914.

Hensel, Beryl D., B.S.'39, M.A.'40, Ohio State
Univ.; Supt., Exempted Village Sch., Versailles, Ohio, since 1952.

Hentze, Louis J., Superior Coach Corp., Lima,
Ohio.

*Herrick, John H., B.A.'28, M.A.'36, Ph.D.'44,
Ohio State Univ.; Head Survey Div., Bureau
of Educ. Research, Ohio State Univ., Columbus, Ohio, since 1947.

Herron, J. Wendell, B.S.'29, Muskingum Col.;
M.Ed.'40, Univ. of Pittsburgh; Supt. of
Exempted Village Sch., Carrollton, Ohio,
since 1947.

Heskett, Dale D., B.S.'27, Muskingum Col.;
M.A.'37, Ohio State Univ.; Supt. of City Sch.,
Bedford, Ohio, since 1950.

Hibschman, Ralph O., D.Ed.'41, Ohio Northern Univ.; Dir., The Andrews Sch. for Girls,
Willoughby, Ohio, since 1929.

Hiestand, Ernest, A.B.'25, Ind. Univ.; A.M.'32,
Wis. Univ.; Exec. Head, Old Fort Sch., Old
Fort, Ohio, since 1943.

Higgins, Edwin E., B.S. in Ed.'25, Ohio Univ.;
M.A.'29, Columbia Univ.; Supt. of Sch.,
Gallipolis, Ohio, since 1936.

Hill, O. E., B.S. in Ed.'27, Ohio Univ.; M.A. in
Admin.'36, Columbia Univ.; Supt. of Sch.,
Cleveland Heights, Ohio, since 1951.

485

OHIO

Hissong, Clyde, Ph.D.'31, Ohio State Univ.; State Supt. of Pub. Instr., Columbus, Ohio, since 1945.

Hockman, Clayton M., B.A.'32, Ohio Wesleyan Univ.; Rep., Macmillan Co., 869 Montrose Ave., Columbus, Ohio, since 1937.

Hoerner, W. F., A.B.'24, Earlham Col.; M.A.'30, Columbia Univ.; Supt. of Piqua Pub. Sch., Piqua, Ohio, since 1952.

Holmes, Jay William, A.B.'16, Hiram Col.; M.A.'28, Ohio State Univ.; Prin., Wilbur Wright H. S., Dayton, Ohio, since 1940.

Holt, E. E., A.B.'26, Wilmington Col.; M.A.'36, Miami Univ.; Supt. of Sch., Springfield, Ohio, since 1948.

Hoovler, G. L., B.Sc.'48, M.A.'50, Ohio State Univ.; Supt. of Sch., Fredericktown, Ohio, since 1952.

Howell, Charles W., B.S.'11, Denison Univ.; M.A.'35, Ohio State Univ.; Supt. of Sch., St. Bernard, Ohio, since 1940.

Humbert, Gordon G., B.Sc.'29, M.A.'36, Ohio State Univ.; Supt. of Sch., Lima, Ohio, since 1947.

Hunter, James T., A.B.'38, Ashland Col.; M.A. '51, Ohio State Univ.; Agent, Macmillan Co., 229 Lindale Ave., Ashland, Ohio.

Huyck, F. S., B.S. in Ed.'23, M.A.'31, Univ. of Mich.; Supt. of Sch., Wauseon, Ohio, since 1935.

Ingham, Clyde A., A.B.'28, Baldwin-Wallace Col.; M.A.'41, Ohio State Univ.; Local Supt. of Sch., Geneva, Ohio, since 1947.

Jameson, Sanford F., A.B.'23, Ohio Northern Univ.; M.A.'35, Columbia Univ.; First Asst. Supt. of Sch., Akron, Ohio, since 1950.

Jarvis, Emerson D., A.B.'24, Franklin Col.; A.M.'30, Ind. Univ.; Ph.D.'48, Ohio State Univ.; Supt. of Sch., Bexley, Columbus, Ohio, since 1948.

Jewett, Mary E., B.S. in Ed.'34, Ohio Univ.; M.Ed., Univ. of Pittsburgh; M.A.'48, Tchrs. Col., Columbia Univ.; Elem. Sch. Prin., Youngstown, Ohio, since 1942.

Johnson, C. Montelle, B.A.'32, Defiance Col.; M.A.'48, Kent State Univ.; Supt. of Sch., Canfield, Ohio, since 1949.

Johnson, Charles W., B.S. in Ed.'18, Univ. of Cincinnati; M.A.'29, Ohio State Univ.; Ed.D. '38, Univ. of Cincinnati; Assoc. Prof. of Educ. and Chmn., Dept. of Admin. and Supvn., Univ. of Cincinnati, Cincinnati, Ohio, since 1948.

Johnson, Samuel R., A.B.'30, B.S. in Ed.'32, Wittenberg Col.; M.A.'46, Ohio State Univ.; Supt., Johnstown-Monroe Sch., Johnstown, Ohio, since 1947.

Jones, Arthur W., M.A.'38, B.S.'17, Ohio State Univ.; Supt. of Sch., Tiffin, Ohio.

Jones, Gilbert H., A.B.'10, B.S.'15, Wilberforce Univ.; Ph.B.'15, A.M.'20, Dickinson Col.; Ph.D.'20, Jena Univ., Germany; Dir., Div. of Educ., Col. of Educ. and Indus. Arts, Wilberforce Univ., Wilberforce, Ohio, since 1939.

Jones, Howard W., A.B.'20, Hiram Col.; A.M. '30, Western Reserve Univ.; Ped.D.'43, Westminster Col.; Pres., Youngstown Col., Youngstown, Ohio, since 1931.

Joseph, Elmer J., A.B.'27, Manchester Col.; M.A.'38, Ohio State Univ.; Supt., Hancock Co. Pub. Sch., Findlay, Ohio, since 1948.

Kabat, George Jule, B.E.'36, State Tchrs. Col., Winona, Minn.; M.A.'38, Univ. of Colo.; Ph.D.'47, Univ. of Md.; Dean, Col. of Educ., Ohio Univ., Athens, Ohio, since 1950.

Kauber, A. J., B.A.'29, Capital Univ.; M.A.'40, Ohio State Univ.; Prin. of Sch., Pemperville, Ohio.

Kemp, L. P., A.B.'26, Defiance, Col.; M.A.'41, Ohio State Univ.; Coordinator of Curriculum, Massillon, Ohio, since 1952.

Kennedy, Harold William, B.S.'27, M.A.'32, Ph.D.'40, Ohio State Univ.; Head, Sec. Educ. Dept., Cedarville Col., Cedarville, Ohio, since 1952.

Kerr, E. S., B.S. in Ed.'16, Ohio State Univ.; Supt. of Sch., Salem, Ohio, since 1931.

King, J. Irvine, A.B.'30, Univ. of Dubuque; M.A.'40, Ohio State Univ.; Supt. of Sch., Avon Lake, Ohio, since 1936.

Kinley, Frederick L., B.S.'16, Heidelberg Col.; M.A.'28, Ohio State Univ.; Supt. of Sch., Findlay, Ohio, since 1936.

Kinney, Dale B., B.S. in Ed.'34, Bowling Green State Univ.; M.A.'48, Ohio State Univ.; Supt., Richland Co. Sch., Mansfield, Ohio, since 1950.

Kiser, Carl C., B.S.'23, Mount Union Col.; M.A.'33, Univ. of Pittsburgh; Supt., Champion Sch., Warren, Ohio, since 1936.

Kizer, Elmer Winfield, B.S.'11, Hiram Col.; A.M.'30, Univ. of Cincinnati; Prin., Hughes H. S., Cincinnati, Ohio, since 1945.

Klay, Roy W., B.S. in Ed.'37, Ohio Univ.; M.A. '47, Ohio State Univ.; Supt. of Sch., Shreve, Ohio, since 1949.

Klein, Arthur J., B.A.'06, Wabash Col.; B.D.'09, Union Theol. Sem.; M.A.'09, Ph.D.'16, Columbia Univ.; Exec. Secy., Ohio Citizens Commn. for the Pub. Sch., Columbus, Ohio, since 1950.

Klinko, Andrew S., A.B.'27, Western Reserve Univ.; M.A.'33, Univ. of Pittsburgh; Supt. of Sch., Campbell, Ohio, since 1950.

Klohr, Paul R., A.B.'40, DePauw Univ.; Ph.D.'48, Ohio State Univ.; Dir. of Univ. Sch. and Prof. of Educ., Ohio State Univ., Columbus, Ohio, since 1952.

Klopfer, V. L., B.S.Ed.'40, Wittenberg Col.; M.A.'48, Ohio State Univ.; Supt., Bethel Local Sch., Tipp City, Ohio, since 1950.

Knapp, Thomas C., B.S.'27, M.A.'31, Ohio State Univ.; Co. Supt. of Sch., Canton, Ohio, since 1940.

Knight, N. Taylor, A.B.'26, King Col.; M.S. in Ed.'37, Univ. of Tenn.; Instr. and Asst. Coordinator of Student Field Experience, Col. of Educ., Ohio State Univ., Columbus, Ohio, since 1952.

Knight, William H., B.S.'25, Kent State Univ.; M.A.'30, Ohio State Univ.; Supt. of Sch., Canal Fulton, Ohio, since 1947.

Koeppe, John F., B.S. in Ed.'21, Kent State Univ.; M.A.'32, Western Reserve Univ.; Supt. of Sch., Berea, Ohio, since 1935.

Koeppe, Paul D., A.B.'27, Defiance Col.; M.A. '36, Columbia Univ.; Local Exec. Head of Sch., Andover, Ohio, since 1930.

Korb, O. J., B.S.'18, Kent State Univ.; M.A.'27, Tchrs. Col., Columbia Univ.; Ph.D.'38, Western Reserve Univ.; Supt. of Sch., East Cleveland, Ohio, since 1939.

*Lake, Charles H., B.A.'09, M.A.'10, LL.D.'34, Ohio State Univ.; LL.D.'44, Western Reserve Univ.; Pres., American Assn. of Sch. Admin., 1945-46; Honorary Life Member, American Assn. of Sch. Admin. Address: 3238 Chadborne Rd., Shaker Heights, Ohio.

LaMuth, Henry, B.S.'38, Ed.M.'41, Univ. of Pittsburgh; Prin., Riverside H. S., Painesville, Ohio, since 1949.

Lautenschlager, J. F., B.S. in Ed.'27, M.A. in Adm.'35, Ohio Univ.; Supt., Co. Sch., Coshocton, Ohio, since 1921.

Laws, W. Edward, B.S.'22, Denison Univ.; M.A.'33, Ohio State Univ.; Co. Supt. of Sch., New Philadelphia, Ohio, since 1936.

486

Lea, John R., B.A.'24, Col. of Wooster; M.A.'37, Ohio State Univ.; Supt. of Sch., Fredericksburg, Ohio, since 1939.

Lease, R. A., B.S.'24, M.A.'26, Univ. of Minn.; Exec. Dir., Bay View Hospital, 23200 Lake Road, Bay Village, Ohio, since 1952.

Lemasters, Austin O., B.S.'24, Ohio State Univ.; M.E.'41, Univ. of Pittsburgh; Supt. of Howland Sch., Warren, Ohio, since 1945.

Lemmon, D. C., B.A.'28, Muskingum Col.; M.A.'40, Ohio State Univ.; Supt. of City Sch., Dover, Ohio, since 1947.

Lenhart, O. W., B.S.'15, Wooster Col.; M.A.'36, Columbia Univ.; Supt. of Sch., Lowellville, Ohio, since 1933.

Lenkaitis, Lewis A., B.S.'40, Baldwin-Wallace Col.; M.A.'48, Western Reserve Univ.; Supt. of Sch., Strongsville, Ohio, since 1952.

Levenson, William B., B.S.'27, Ohio State Univ.; M.A.'32, Ph.D.'37, Western Reserve Univ.; Asst. Supt. of Sch., Cleveland, Ohio, since 1947.

*Lewis, E. E., A.B.'07, M.A.'09, Stanford Univ.; Ph.D.'20, Columbia Univ.; Prof. of Educ., Ohio State Univ., Columbus, Ohio, since 1926.

Litzenberg, E. F., A.B.'25, B.S.'27, Marion Col.; A.M.'36, Ohio State Univ.; Supt. of Columbia Local Sch., Columbia Station, Ohio, since 1946.

Locke, John F., B.S.'31, Univ. of Cincinnati; Dir., Dept. of Community Relations, Pub. Sch., Cincinnati, Ohio, since 1938.

Long, Howard H., Wilberforce State Col., Wilberforce, Ohio.

Longsworth, Robert H., A.B.'27, Adrian Col.; M.Ed.'37, Univ. of Pittsburgh; Co. Supt. of Sch., Carrollton, Ohio, since 1948.

Loos, Leonard E., A.B.'22, Wittenberg Col.; M.A.'26, Tchrs. Col., Columbia Univ.; Ph.D. '40, New York Univ.; Prin., Shore Sch., Euclid, Ohio, since 1937.

Louys, Frederick B., B.S.'27, M.A.'36, Ohio State Univ.; Supt. of Co. Sch., Warren, Ohio, since 1951.

Lower, Kenneth E., B.A.'29, Baldwin-Wallace Col.; M.A.'40, Western Reserve Univ.; Supt., Exempted Village Schs., North Olmsted, Ohio, since 1947.

Lucas, Homer C., A.B.'20, Ohio Wesleyan Univ.; Ginn & Co., Columbus, Ohio.

Lucas, Robert E., B.S. in Ed.'37, Wilmington Col.; M.A.'46, Ohio State Univ.; Elem. Supvr., State Dept. of Educ., Columbus, Ohio, since 1951.

Luther, (Mrs.) Gertrude Hawkins, Asst., Bureau of Educ. Research, Cleveland, Ohio.

McBride, James H., B.S.'35, Muskingum Col.; M.A.'40, Univ. of Colo.; Supt. of City Sch., Norwalk, Ohio, since 1949.

McBride, James L., Ph.M.'36, Univ. of Wis.; Supt. of Co. Sch., Lisbon, Ohio, since 1950.

McCarroll, Emmet F., A.B.'25, Otterbein Col.; M.A.'40, Univ. of Mich.; Supt. of Sch., Dennison, Ohio, since 1937.

McClintock, Douglas, M.A.'47, Western Reserve Univ.; Local Supt. of Sch., Kirtland H. S., Willoughby, Ohio, since 1949.

McConagha, G. A., A.B.'29, Muskingum Col.; M.A.'36, Ohio State Univ.; Supt. of Sch., Coshocton, Ohio, since 1947.

McCord, Harold C., B.S. in Ed.'26, Ohio Univ.; M.A.'34, Ohio State Univ.; Supt. of Sch., Worthington, Ohio, since 1938.

McCormick, R. L., B.S.'28, Ball State Tchrs. Col., Muncie, Ind.; M.A.'32, Columbia Univ.; Supt. of Sch., Huron, Ohio, since 1939.

McCoy, Raymond F., A.B.'34, Xavier Univ.; M.A.'35, B.E.'36, Ed.D.'39, Univ. of Cincinnati; Chmn., Dept. of Educ. and Dir., Grad. Div., Xavier Univ., Cincinnati, Ohio, since 1946.

McDermott, Harold C., M.A.'51, Univ. of Cincinnati; Supt. of Sch., Sidney, Ohio, since 1951.

McDonald, James M., B.S.'31, M.A.'37, Ohio State Univ.; Supt. of Sch., Wilmington, Ohio, since 1951.

McDonald, Ralph W., A.B.'25, Hendrix Col.; A.M.'27, Ph.D.'33, Duke Univ.; Pres., Bowling Green State Univ., Bowling Green, Ohio, since 1951.

McDougall, Richard E. C., A.B.'16, Greenville Col.; M.A.'25, Northwestern Univ.; Ph.D.'43, Ohio State Univ.; Supt. of Sch., Orrville, Ohio, since 1936.

McGlone, Orin G., B.S. in Ed.'31, M.A.'38, Ohio State Univ.; Supt., Marlboro Local Sch., Louisville, Ohio, since 1948.

McKelvey, Frederick H., A.B.'30, Univ. of Ill.; Ed.M.'36, Harvard Univ.; Dir., Univ. Center for Educ. Serv., Col. of Educ., Ohio Univ., Athens, Ohio, since 1948.

McKelvey, Herbert W., A.B.'27, Ohio Univ.; M.A.'34, Ohio State Univ.; Supt. of Sch., Portsmouth, Ohio, since 1949.

McKibben, Ralph M., M.A.'46, Ohio State Univ.; Co. Supt. of Sch., Ottawa, Ohio, since 1950.

McMahan, Corwin L., A.B.'20, Marietta Col.; M.A.'33, Ohio State Univ.; Co. Supt. of Sch., Marietta, Ohio, since 1945.

McMullen, R. F., B.A.'13, M.A.'32, Ohio State Univ.; Supt. of Sch., Loudonville, Ohio, since 1929.

McPherson, William N., B.S.'28, M.S.'37, Ind. State Tchrs. Col., Terre Haute; Supvg. Prin. of Sch., Chillicothe, Ohio, since 1950.

MacKey, Carl L., A.B.'18, Marietta Col.; M.A. '51, Univ. of Wyo.; Asst. Supt. of Sch., Sandusky, Ohio, since 1948.

Malone, E. R., B.S.Ed.'35, Ohio Northern Univ.; M.S.Ed.'42, Univ. of Akron; Exec. Head, Twp. Sch., Copley, Ohio, since 1939.

Martin, Herman M., B.S. in Ed.'32, M.A.'41, Ohio State Univ.; Supt. of Twp. Sch., Groveport, Ohio, since 1946.

Martin, Stanley E., A.B.'35, Denison Univ.; M.A.'42, Ohio State Univ.; Supt. of Sch., Granville, Ohio, since 1941.

Mattes, Milan, B.S.'23, Mount Union Col.; M.A.'39, Western Reserve Univ.; Supt. of Sch., Newton Falls, Ohio, since 1946.

Maxwell, W. T., B.S.'42, Ohio State Univ.; M.A.'50, Miami Univ.; Prin., East Elem. Sch., Greenville, Ohio.

Mayer, Lewis F., B.A.'20, Col. of Wooster; M.A.'30, Ohio State Univ.; Supt. of Sch., Fairview Park, Cleveland, Ohio, since 1921.

Metzger, D. B., Supt. of Sch., Toronto, Ohio.

Michel, Gerald H., A.B.'23, Ohio Wesleyan Univ.; M.A.'31, Columbia Univ.; Supt. of Sch., Wickliffe, Ohio, since 1945.

Mikesell, Ralph H., A.B.'30, Ohio Northern Univ.; M.A.'34, Ohio State Univ.; Supt., Exempted Village Schs., Eaton, Ohio, since 1945.

Miller, Edgar F., B.S.'25, Denison Univ.; M.A. '33, Columbia Univ.; Supt of Twp. Sch., Clyde, Ohio, since 1948.

Miller, I. J., B.S.'35, Baldwin-Wallace Col.; M.S.'42, Western Reserve Univ.; Supt. of City Sch., Bucyrus, Ohio, since 1950.

Miller, M. Hughes, A.B.'29, Muhlenberg Col.; M.A.'32, Univ. of Pa.; Mgr., Wesleyan Univ. Press Inc., 400 South Front St., Columbus, Ohio.

487

Miller, Marvin H., B.S.'30, Ohio Univ.; A.M.'37, Ohio State Univ.; Supt., Big Walnut Sch., Sunbury, Ohio, since 1950.

Miller, Paul A., B.S. in Ed.'36, Wilmington Col.; M.A.'41, Miami Univ.; Ph.D.'51, Ohio State Univ.; Supt. of Sch., Warren, Ohio, since 1951.

Miller, W. W., A.B.'22, Goshen Col.; M.A.'28, Ph.D.'39, Ohio State Univ.; Asst. Supt. of Sch., Columbus, Ohio, since 1936.

Miller, Wade E., A.B.'11, Heidelberg Col.; M.A.'16, Ohio State Univ.; Supt. of Pub. Instr., Middletown, Ohio, since 1944.

Miller, William Lawrence, A.B.'16, Muskingum Col.; M.A.'33, Univ. of Pittsburgh; Supt. of Sch., Mansfield, Ohio, since 1934.

Mills, DeWitt T., M.A.'17, Ohio State Univ.; Co. Supt. of Sch., Marion, Ohio, since 1931.

Milner, Alfred W., M.S.'42, Ohio Univ.; Supt. of Sch., Mt. Healthy, Cincinnati, Ohio, since 1942.

Moffett, V. B., A.B.'29, Wittenberg Col.; M.A. '38, Ohio State Univ.; Co. Supt. of Sch., Ashland, Ohio, since 1939.

Moore, Benjamin Arthur, B.Sc. in Ed.'19, Ohio Northern Univ.; M.A.'33, Ohio State Univ.; Asst. Dir., Ohio Scholarship Tests, State Dept. of Educ., Columbus, Ohio, since 1938.

Morgan, Thomas O., M.A. in Ed.'42, Kent State Univ.; Supt. of Sch., Tallmadge, Ohio, since 1949.

*Morris, M. Ray, B.S. in Ed.'27, Muskingum Col.; B.S. in Bus. Admin.'28, Bliss Col.; M.A.'39, Columbia Univ.; Supt. of Sch., Westerville, Ohio, since 1943.

Morrison, J. H., Supt. of Northridge Sch., Dayton, Ohio.

Munzenmayer, L. H., Ph.D.'31, Ohio State Univ.; Prof. of Educ. and Dir. of Appointments, Kent State Univ., Kent, Ohio, since 1931.

Murray, A. B., A.B.'27, Bluffton Col.; M.A.'35, Ohio State Univ.; Supt., Bluffton Exempted Village Sch., Bluffton, Ohio, since 1949.

Musgrave, Oscar L., B.A.'34, Findlay Col.; M.A.'46, Ohio State Univ.; Supt. of Sch., Lebanon, Ohio, since 1951.

Musselman, D. L., A.B.'26, Bluffton Col.; M.A.'39, Ohio State Univ.; Supt. of Sch., McConnelsville, Ohio, since 1950.

Naragon, Lloyd E., B.S.'31, Heidelberg Col.; M.A.'39, Columbia Univ.; Supt. of York Local Sch., Medina, Ohio, since 1936.

Nash, Robert L., B.A.'32, Muskingum Col.; M.A.'38, Ohio State Univ.; Prin., McGuffey Sch., Columbus, Ohio, since 1952.

Neal, Richard W., B.S. in Ed.'37, M.A. in Ed.'46, Kent State Univ.; Local Supt. of Sch., Rock Creek, Ohio, since 1943.

Nicholas, Lynn N., B.A.'29, Ohio Wesleyan Univ.; M.A.'35, Ohio State Univ.; Supt. of Sch., Elyria, Ohio, since 1949.

Nichols, Harold L., A.B.'39, Mt. Union Col.; M.A.'47, Ph.D.'52, Ohio State Univ.; Asst. Supt. of Sch., Mt. Vernon, Ohio, since 1952.

Nisonger, I. J., B.S. in Ed.'27, M.A.'36, Ohio State Univ.; Supt., Boardman Local Schs., Youngstown, Ohio, since 1950.

Nolley, Gilbert, B.S.'32, M.S.'33, Akron Univ.; Exec. Head, East Franklin Pub. Sch., Akron, Ohio, since 1937.

Nystrom, Wendell C., A.B.'14, Bethany Col.; M.A.'34, Ph.D.'37, Univ. of Kansas; Dean and Prof. of Educ., Wittenberg Col., Springfield, Ohio, since 1937.

O'Grady, John J., B.S. in Ed.'18, Univ. of Dayton; Supt. of Sch., Maria Stein, Ohio, since 1942.

Oldfather, Robert B., A.B.'25, Heidelberg Col.; M.A.'37, Ohio State Univ.; Supt. of Sch., Painesville, Ohio, since 1948.

Oman, Durling W., A.B.'27, Findlay Col., M.A.'34, Univ. of Mich.; Co. Supt. of Sch., Upper Sandusky, Ohio, since 1948.

Painter, William I., A.B.'25, Oakland City Col.; M.A.'29, Ph.D.'33, Ind. Univ.; Assoc. Prof. of Educ., Univ. of Akron, Akron, Ohio, since 1945.

Parsons, Harold F., M.A.'47, Western Reserve Univ.; Prin., Browning Jr. H. S., Willoughby, Ohio, since 1950.

Patterson, C. M., A.B.'30, James Millikin Univ.; M.A.'34, Ohio State Univ.; Supt. of Sch., Bay Village, Ohio, since 1950.

Pelley, James H., M.A.'41, Univ. of Wash.; Ed.D.'48, Tchrs. Col., Columbia Univ.; Prof. of Sch. Admin., Miami Univ., Oxford, Ohio, since 1951.

Penrod, C. C., A.B.'36, Ohio Univ.; M.A.'46, Ohio State Univ.; Exec. Head, Starr-Washington Sch., Union Furnace, Ohio, since 1948.

Porter, William, O., B.S. in Ed.'35, M.S.'39, Ohio Univ.; Co. Supt. of Sch., McConnelsville, Ohio, since 1948.

Potts, Harold M., B.S., M.Ed.'39, Ohio Univ.; Local Supt. of Fairfield Sch., Hamilton, Ohio.

Powers, Fred R., A.B.'13, Oberlin Col.; A.M.'20, Tchrs. Col., Columbia Univ.; Supt. of Sch., Amherst, Ohio, since 1918.

Pugh, Roy M., B.S.'20, Ohio Northern Univ.; M.A.'33, Ohio State Univ.; Supt., Bath-Richfield Sch., Akron, Ohio, since 1950.

Purdy, Woodrow W., A.B.'35, Otterbein Col.; M.A.'40, Miami Univ. (Ohio); Supt. of City Sch., Urbana, Ohio, since 1950.

Quick, Thomas J., B.S. in Ed.'33, M.Ed.'41, Ohio Univ.; Exec. Head of Utica-Wash. Local Sch., Utica, Ohio, since 1951.

Rader, G. L., A.B.'30, Ashland Col.; M.Ed.'40, Duke Univ.; Supt. of Sch., Hicksville, Ohio, since 1948.

Rahmann, Harry L., A.B.'36, Findlay Col.; M.A. '47, Springfield Col.; Litt.D.'48, D.D.'49, Ph.D.'50, Rockford Sem.; M.Ed.'51, Ind. Univ.; Supt. of Center Twp. Sch., Celina, Ohio, since 1947.

Rainey, Paul Rees, M.A.'30, Ohio State Univ.; Prin., H. S., Georgetown, Ohio, since 1930.

Ramseyer, John A., A.B.'29, Bluffton Col.; M.A.'34, Ph.D.'48, Ohio State Univ.; Prof. and Dir., Sch.-Community Development Study, Ohio State Univ., Columbus, Ohio, since 1951.

Rasmus, Carl J., A.B.'28, Defiance Col.; M.A.'33, Columbia Univ.; Supt. of Sch. Celina, Ohio, since 1942.

Rasor, Floyd, A.B.'26, Otterbein Col.; Asst. Co. Supt. of Sch., Dayton, Ohio, since 1934.

Raver, Virgil L., B.S.'29, Ottenbein Col.; M.A.'37, Ohio State Univ.; Supt. of Sch., Cadiz, Ohio, since 1948.

Redd, Bryan, B.S.'25, M.S.'26, M.A. in Sch. Adm.'37, Ohio State Univ.; Supt. of Sch., Somerset, Ohio, since 1951.

Reeder, Ward G., A.B.'14, Ind. Univ.; A.M.'19, Ph.D.'21, Univ. of Chicago; Prof. of Educ., Ohio State Univ., Columbus, Ohio, since 1922.

Reinbolt, F. N., B.S. in Ed.'23, Ohio State Univ.; M.Ed.'38, Univ. of Pittsburgh; Supt. of Sch., Bellaire, Ohio, since 1949.

Replogle, Laurence K., A.B.'19, Otterbein Col.; A.M.'24, Columbia Univ.; Asst. Supt. of Sch., Columbus, Ohio, since 1936.

Reynolds, R. C., Supt., Exempted Village Sch., Hubbard, Ohio.

Rice, Clarence L., B.C.E.'32, M.A.'37, Ohio State Univ.; Supt., Brooklyn City Sch., Cleveland, Ohio, since 1946.

OHIO

Rice, D. R., B.S.'15, Ohio Northern Univ.; M.A.'28, Tchrs. Col., Columbia Univ.; Supt. of Sch., Mentor, Ohio, since 1924.

Riegel, Ernest F., A.B.'28, Otterbein Col.; B.A.S.'30, George Williams Col.; M.A.'30, Univ. of Chicago; Supt. of Sch., New Lebanon, Ohio, since 1944.

Ritchie, Harry E., A.B.'20, Mt. Union Col.; M.A.'24, Univ. of Akron; Ph.D.'40, Western Reserve Univ.; Asst. Supt. of Sch., Cleveland, Ohio, since 1942.

Roberson, C. C., B.S. in Ed.'28, Oakland City Col.; M.A.'40, Ohio State Univ.; Supt. of Sch., Maumee, Ohio, 1950-52. Address: 247 Turner St., Ada, Ohio.

*Roberts, Edward D., B.A.'99, M.A.'07, Univ. of Cincinnati; M.A.'08, Tchrs. Col., Columbia Univ.; LL.D.'32, Col. of Wooster. Address: 3533 Burch Ave., Cincinnati 8, Ohio.

Roeder, Donald B., A.B.'27, Manchester Col.; M.A.'34, Ohio State Univ.; Supt. of Sch., Newcomerstown, Ohio, since 1942.

Rogge, H. W., M.A.'39, Ohio State Univ.; Supt. of Sch., Bryan, Ohio, since 1946.

Rohleder, W. C., A.B.'20, M.A.'23,, Ohio State Univ.; Supt. of Sch., Grandview Hgts., Columbus, Ohio, since 1927.

Roudebush, George E., B.S. in Ed.'18, Ohio State Univ.; M.A.'23, Tchrs. Col., Columbia Univ.; D.Ed.'40, Ohio Wesleyan Univ.; Supt. of Sch., Columbus, Ohio, 1937-49 (retired). Address: 182 W. Royal Forest Blvd., Columbus 2, Ohio.

Roush, William J., B.S.'37, Geneva Col.; M.Ed. '44, Univ. of Pittsburgh; Supt. of Sch., Cortland, Ohio, since 1945.

Routson, Martin L., B.A.'30, Wittenberg Col.; M.A.'31, Ohio State Univ.; Prin., Concord Local Sch., Troy, Ohio, since 1936.

Rummel, D. D., A.B.'30, Wittenberg Col.; M.A.'39, Ohio State Univ.; Supt. of Sch., Leetonia, Ohio.

Rupp, Allen E., B.A.'23, Ohio Wesleyan Univ.; M.A.'34, Ohio State Univ.; Supt. of Sch., Cambridge, Ohio, since 1947.

Ryan, Carl J., B.A.'16, Univ. of Dayton; M.A.'24, Ph.D.'27, Catholic Univ. of America; Supt. of Parochial Sch., Cincinnati, Ohio, since 1932.

Ryder, Harold, B.S.'21, M.S.'22, Ohio Northern Univ.; M.A.'24, Ohio State Univ.; Co. Supt. of Sch., Toledo, Ohio, since 1940.

Salisbury, Robert Kenneth, B.A.'23, M.Sc.'33, Ohio State Univ.; Supt., Exempted Village Schs., Georgetown, Ohio, since 1947.

Sanders, Herschel W., B.S. in Bus. Admin.'30, Miami Univ.; B.S. in Ed.'30, Wilmington Col.; M.A.'36, Ohio State Univ.; Asst. Co. Supt., Preble Co. Pub. Sch., Eaton, Ohio, since 1952.

Sauder, Harold C., B.S.'27, M.A.'37, Ohio State Univ.; Supt. of Jackson Local Sch., Massillon, Ohio, since 1932.

Sawmiller, R. O., B.S.'46, Iowa State Univ.; Local Exec. Head, Ridge Local Sch., Van Wert, Ohio, since 1949.

Schaaf, Olus H., B.S. in Ed., Ashland Col.; M.A., Western Reserve Univ.; Supt., Garfield Heights City Sch., Cleveland, Ohio, since 1949.

Schafer, Russell E., B.S.'21, Ohio Northern Univ.; M.A.'32, Columbia Univ.; Supt. of Sch., Alliance, Ohio, since 1942.

Scheetz, Harvey A., B.S.'29, Kent State Univ.; M.A.'33, Western Reserve Univ.; Supt. of Mayfield City Sch., Mayfield Heights, Ohio, since 1943.

Schinnerer, Mark C., A.B.'20, Ind. State Tchrs. Col., Terre Haute; A.M.'23, Tchrs. Col., Columbia Univ.; Ph.D.'43, Western Reserve Univ.; Supt. of Sch., Cleveland, Ohio, since 1947.

Schofield, F. R., B.A.'19, Western Reserve Univ.; M.A.'26, Ohio State Univ.; Co. Supt. of Sch., Chardon, Ohio, since 1927.

*Schweisberger, Harold C., B.S.'28, Wooster Col.; M.A.'49, Columbia Univ.; Local Supt., Richfield Sch., West Richfield, Ohio, since 1930. Address: Box 242, North Canton, Ohio.

Sebold, Harold, A.B.'30, [Capital Univ.; M.A. '36, Ohio State Univ.; Co. Supt. of Sch., Newark, Ohio, since 1950.

Shade, Walter E., B.S.'16, M.A.'34, Ohio State Univ.; Supt. of Sch., West Carrollton, Ohio, since 1931.

Shank, M. E., A.B.'34, Findlay Col.; M.A.'42, Ohio State Univ.; Supt. of Sch., Galion, Ohio, since 1948.

Shanks, Carl H., A.B.'27, Cedarville Col.; M.A.'38, Miami Univ.; Supt. of Sch., Wilmington, Ohio, since 1932.

Shaw, E. G., Supt. of Sch., Dayton, Ohio.

Shaw, Roger M., B.S.'36, M.S.'38, Univ. of Ill.; Ph.D.'42, Ind. Univ.; Assoc. Prof. of Educ., Kent State Univ., Kent, Ohio, since 1949.

Shepherd, Donald W., A.B.'34, Ohio Univ.; M.A.'38, Ohio State Univ.; Supt. of Sch., Barnesville, Ohio, since 1949.

Shields, C. Dallas, Sales Mgr., Superior Coach Corp., Lima, Ohio, since 1939.

Shipman, William A., B.S. in Ed.'36, M.Ed.'39, Kent State Univ.; Local Supt. of Grand Valley Schs., Orwell, Ohio, since 1946.

Shreve, John W., M.A.'40, W. Va. Univ.; Dir. of Research, Pub. Sch., Cincinnati, Ohio, since 1952.

Shull, John R., B.A.'39, Emmanuel Missionary Col.; Prin. and Bus. Mgr., Mt. Vernon Academy, Mt. Vernon, Ohio, since 1947.

Shuman, William L., A.B.'21, M.A.'29, Ohio State Univ.; Supt. of Sch., Cuyahoga Co., Cleveland, Ohio, since 1943.

Shuter, L. D., A.B.'23, Ohio Wesleyan Univ.; M.A.'41, Ohio State Univ.; Exec. Secy., State Tchrs. Retirement System of Ohio, Columbus, Ohio, since 1947.

Sibbing, Paul A., B.A.'17, Univ. of Dayton; Lic.Sc.'26, Univ. of Fribourg, Switzerland; Supvr. of Marianist Schs., Mt. St. John, Dayton, Ohio, since 1946.

Simkins, S. W., B.S.'41, Ohio State Univ.; M.E.'49, Univ. of Pittsburgh; Prin., H. S., Barnesville, Ohio, since 1952.

Sims, Cecil Melville, B.A.'14, M.A.'27, Ohio State Univ.; Supt. of Sch., Piqua, Ohio, 1944-52 (retired). Address: 404 Broadway, Piqua, Ohio.

Sims, D. D., A.B.'17, M.A.'27, Ohio State Univ.; Supt. of Sch., Port Clinton, Ohio, since 1937.

Sinclair, Roy E., B.S.'28, Mt. Union Col.; M.A. '37, Ohio State Univ.; Supt., North Central Local Sch., Sterling, Ohio.

Slade, William, Jr., B.S.'17, Middlebury Col.; M.A.'20, Tchrs. Col., Columbia Univ.; Supt. of Sch., Shaker Hgts., Ohio, since 1944.

Slager, Fred C., B.S. in Ed.'20, Ohio Northern Univ.; M.A.'22, Ph.D.'36, Ohio State Univ.; Prin., Central H. S., Columbus, Ohio, since 1944.

Slater, Paul R., A.B.'25, Geneva Col.; M.Ed.'39, Ed.D.'50, Univ. of Pittsburgh; Supt. of Twp. Sch., Brookfield, Ohio, since 1945.

Slutz, Frank Durward, A.B.'04, M.A.'06, Mount Union Col.; M.A.'11, Harvard Univ.; Litt.D. '15, Univ. of Denver; L.H.D.'28, Mount Union Col. Address: 16 Lexington Ave., Dayton 7, Ohio.

Smith, David R., B.A.'21, M.A.'22, Ohio Wesleyan Univ.; Supt. of Sch., Delaware, Ohio, since 1933.

489

Smith, Howard P., B.S.'27, Mount Union Col.; M.A.'33, Ohio State Univ.; Ph.D.'43, Univ. of Pittsburgh; Supt. of Sch., Kent, Ohio, since 1944.

Smith, L. J., B.Sc.'18, Ohio State Univ.; M.Sc. '37, Cornell Univ.; Supt. of Sch., Massillon, Ohio, since 1936.

Smith, Paul F., B.A.'32, Heidelberg Col.; M.A. '46, Ohio State Univ.; Supt. of Sch., Shadyside, Ohio, since 1946.

Smith, Robert Lyle, B.S. in Ed.'50, Youngstown Col.; M.A. in Admin.'52, Ohio State Univ.; Supt., Bristol Township Sch., Bristolville, Ohio, since 1952.

Smith, Wilbur W., B.S. in Ed.'26, Ohio State Univ.; M.A.'37, Western Reserve Univ.; Supt. of Sch., Strongsville, Ohio, since 1947.

Smith, William A., A.B.'29, M.Ed.'42, Ohio Univ.; Supt. of Sch., Pomeroy, Ohio, since 1941.

Sollars, S. K., B.A.'28, Ohio Wesleyan Univ.; M.A.'38, Ohio State Univ.; Co. Supt. of Sch., Bucyrus, Ohio, since 1948.

Specht, Clarence W., Ph.B.'28, Xavier Univ.; M.Ed.'33, Univ. of Pittsburgh; Co. Supt. of Local Sch., Fort Jennings, Ohio.

Springer, Wilbur J., B.S.'25, Mt. Union Col.; Ed.M.'32, Harvard Univ.; Supt. of Sch., Ashland, Ohio, since 1950.

Stallbohm, H. R., B.S.'26, Northeast Mo. State Tchrs. Col., Kirksville; Vicepres., Bd. of Educ., Lima, Ohio, since 1950.

Stalter, S. S., Mgr., Cincinnati Div. of American Book Co., Cincinnati, Ohio, since 1945.

Starr, Leighton P., M.A.'34, Ohio State Univ.; Supt. of Auburn Local Sch., Chagrin Falls, Ohio, since 1941.

Stebbins, Walter E., B.S. in Ed.'37, Univ. of Dayton; Supt. of Twp. Sch., Dayton, Ohio, since 1939.

Stingley, C. L., B.S.'22, Wilmington Col.; M.A.'28, Ohio State Univ.; Supt. of Washington Twp. Sch., Centerville, Ohio, since 1939.

Stone, Joseph J., B.S.Ed.'33, M.Ed.'40, Ohio Univ.; Supt. of Sch., Murray City, Ohio, since 1937.

Stover, James D., B.A.'12, M.A.'13, Princeton Univ.; Asst. Supt. of Sch., Cincinnati, Ohio, since 1929.

Streitz, Ruth, Ph.B.'21, M.A.'22, Univ. of Chicago; Ph.D.'26, Columbia Univ.; Prof. of Educ., Ohio State Univ., Columbus, Ohio, since 1938.

Streng, Arthur A., A.B.'33, Baldwin-Wallace Col.; Salesman, American Bk. Co., Warren, Ohio, since 1935.

Sullivan, Henry Lee, B.Sc. in Ed.'19, Ohio Univ.; M.A.'27, Columbia Univ.; Supt. of Sch., Marietta, Ohio, since 1928.

Summers, Donald F., B.A.'24, M.A.'31, Ohio State Univ.; Supt. of Sch., Zanesville, Ohio, since 1941.

Swasey, Fred H., B.S.'42, M.Ed.'51, Kent State Univ.; Local Supt. of Sch., Malvern, Ohio, since 1951.

Swigart, Forrest Damon, B.S.'21, Denison Univ.; M.A.'29, Ohio State Univ.; Supt. of Sch., Bellevue, Ohio, since 1942.

Swope, Mary B., Prin., Hartford and Roosevelt Sch., Canton, Ohio, since 1921.

Tanner, D. E., Supt. of Sch., Lockwood, Ohio.

Taylor, Lester G., B.S.'41, Heidelberg Col.; Local Sch. Admin., Chatfield, Ohio, 1947-52.

Tays, James T., M.A.'50, Ohio State Univ.; Exec. Head of Sch., Alexandria, Ohio, since 1952.

Teichert, John R., B.S. in Ed.'30, Wilmington Col.; Supvg. Prin. of Sch., Waverly, Ohio, since 1932.

Thompson, C. V., Co. Supt. of Sch., Troy, Ohio.

Tower, Cecil O., B.S.'27, Kansas State Tchrs. Col., Pittsburg; M.S.'29, Univ. of Toledo; Dir. of Research, Bd. of Educ., Cincinnati, Ohio, since 1946.

Townsend, Wayne L., B.S. in Ed.'37, Wilmington Col.; M.A. in Ed.'50, Univ. of Cincinnati; Supt. of Sch., New Haven, Ohio, since 1946.

Trachsel, Raymond E., B.S. in Ed.'27, Kent Univ.; M.A.'36, Ohio State Univ.; Supt. of Sch., North Canton, Ohio, since 1938.

Tyler, I. Keith, B.A.'25, Univ. of Nebr.; M.A.'30, Tchrs. Col., Columbia Univ.; Ph.D.'39, Columbia Univ.; Dir. of Radio Educ. and Prof. of Educ., Ohio State Univ., Columbus, Ohio, since 1944.

Utterback, T. V., B.S.'34, M.Ed.'50, Kent State Univ.; Prin., Fairfield Local Sch., Columbiana, Ohio, since 1945.

Van Atta, E. A., B.S. in Ed.'31, Ohio Northern Univ.; M.A.'35, Ohio State Univ.; Supt. of Sch., North Baltimore, Ohio, since 1947.

Virtue, Ross M., A.B.'24, Muskingum Col.; M.A.'35, Ohio State Univ.; Supt. of Sch., Gnadenhutten, Ohio, since 1941.

Wach, Michael, Clerk-Treas., Bd. of Educ., Cleveland, Ohio.

Waldorf, Harry B., B.S.'27, Muskingum Col.; M.A.'33, Ohio State Univ.; Supt. of Sch., Bridgeport, Ohio, since 1946.

Walker, George A., A.B. in Com.'29, Ohio Univ.; M.A in Ed.'39, Akron Univ.; Supt. of Warrensville Heights Sch., Cleveland, Ohio, since 1942.

Walls, L. Earl, B.S. in Ed.'26, Muskingum Col.; Asst. Co. Supt. of Sch., St. Clairsville, Ohio, since 1943.

Walter, Z. M., B.Sc. in Ed.'21, M.A.'23, Ohio State Univ.; Supt. of Wyoming Schs., Cincinnati, Ohio, since 1932.

Wanamaker, J. H., A.B.'30, M.S.'32, Western Reserve Univ.; City Supt. of Sch., Conneaut, Ohio, since 1952.

Warner, Rodney J., B.S.'22, M.A.'29, Ohio State Univ.; Supt. of Sch., Xenia, Ohio, since 1936.

Warnke, Robert, Supt. of Sch., Brookville, Ohio.

Watson, Charles M., B.S. in Ed.'31, M.A.'38, Ohio State Univ.; Supt. of Sch., Jefferson, Ohio, since 1945.

Watson, Kenneth A., B.S.'34, Ohio Univ.; M.A.'40, Ohio State Univ.; Local Supt. of Sch., Bellville, Ohio, since 1950.

Weagly, W. E., B.S.'25, Capital Univ.; M.A.'32, Columbia Univ.; Co. Supt. of Sch., Sandusky, Ohio, since 1939.

Webster, Rolla D., A.B.'24, Heidelberg Col.; M.A.'34, Ohio State Univ.; Co. Supt. of Sch., London, Ohio, since 1951.

Welfle, Frederick E., S.J., B.A.'22, M.A.'23, Gonzaga Univ.; M.A.'30, St. Louis Univ.; Ph.D.'40, Ohio State Univ.; Pres., John Carroll Univ., Cleveland, Ohio, since 1946.

Welty, Leo D., Exec. Head, Pub. Sch., Wooster, Ohio.

Wenger, Paul, B.A.'25, Bluffton Col.; M.A.'30, Ohio State Univ.; Supt. of Sch., Lancaster, Ohio, since 1938.

Wesley, Charles H., B.A.'11, Fisk Univ.; M.A.'13, Yale Univ.; Ph.D.'25, Harvard Univ.; Pres., Col. of Educ. and Indus. Arts, Wilberforce, Ohio, since 1942.

West, Glen C., B.S. in Ed.'17, Ohio Univ.; M.A.'28, Columbia Univ.; Co. Supt. of Sch., Celina, Ohio.

West, Herschel D., B.S.'30, Wilmington Col.; M.A.'40, Columbia Univ.; Co. Supt. of Sch., Georgetown, Ohio, since 1937.

Whinnery, Karl E., Ph.B.'12, Mt. Union Col.; M.A.'15, Univ. of Wis.; Supt. of Sch., Sandusky, Ohio, since 1939.

White, Harold A., B.A.'25, Baldwin-Wallace Col.; M.A.'29, Columbia Univ.; Co. Supt. of Sch., Medina, Ohio, since 1947.

Whitehead, Willis A., B.Arch.'30, M.A.'33, Ohio State Univ. Address: Outcalt, Guenther and Associates, Architects, 13124 Shaker Sq., Cleveland 20, Ohio, since 1949.

Whitman, William A., B.S.'20, Bowling Green State Univ.; M.A.'31, Toledo Univ.; Co. Supt. of Sch., Fremont, Ohio, since 1939.

Wical, Noel, A.B.'32, Bethany Col. (W. Va.); Educ. Writer, *The Cleveland Press*, Cleveland, Ohio, since 1946.

Wickham, Terry, A.B.'20, Heidelberg Col.; M.A.'27, Ohio State Univ.; Ped.D.'49, Catawba Col.; Pres., Heidelberg Col., Tiffin, Ohio, since 1948.

Wigton, Charles E., A.B.'19, Ohio Wesleyan Univ.; M.A.'37, Northwestern Univ.; Supt. of Sch., Oberlin, Ohio, since 1937.

Wiley, F. L., A.B. and B.S. in Ed.'05, Univ. of Mo.; A.M.'09, Tchrs. Col.; Columbia Univ.; Supt. of Sch., Cleveland Hgts., Ohio, 1923-51.

Williams, E. I. F., Ph.B.'14, Heidelberg Col.; A.M.'20, Tchrs. Col.; Columbia Univ.; Ph.D. '41, Columbia Univ.; Litt.D.'48, Heidelberg Col.; Head, Dept. of Educ. and Registrar, Heidelberg Col., Tiffin, Ohio, since 1915.

Williams, John Roger, Co. Supt. of Sch., Painesville, Ohio, since 1931.

Williams, William Wendell, B.S.'35, M.A.'36, Ohio Univ.; Ph.D.'50, Ohio State Univ.; Viceprin., Linden McKinley H. S., Columbus, Ohio, since 1949.

Wilson, Robert E., B.S. in Ed.'39, Ohio Northern Univ.; B.S. in Bus. Admin.'38, M.A.'46, Ph.D.'49, Ohio State Univ.; Asst. Supt. of Sch., Canton, Ohio, since 1951.

Wilson, W. Harmon, Vicepres., South-Western Pub. Co., 634 Broadway, Cincinnati, Ohio.

Woelfel, Norman, B.S.'23, M.A.'24, Ph.D.'33, Columbia Univ.; Prof. of Educ., and Dir., Teaching Aids Lab., Ohio State Univ., Columbus, Ohio, since 1943.

Wood, Ray G., B.S. in Ed.'22, Ohio Northern Univ.; M.A.'28, Ph.D.'35, Ohio State Univ.; Dir., Ohio Scholarship Tests and Instructional Research, State Dept. of Educ., Columbus, Ohio, since 1932.

Wood, Wilber S., B.A.'25, Otterbein Col.; M.A.'30, Ohio State Univ.; Local Supt. of Sch., Lodi, Ohio, since 1943.

Woodford, Delbert, B.S. in Ed.'31, Kent State Univ.; M.A.'44, Ohio State Univ.; Supt. of Sch., Oakwood, Dayton, Ohio, since 1946.

Woods, Arthur, B.S. in Ed.'33, Ohio Univ.; Exec. Head, Green Elem. Sch., Logan, Ohio, since 1934.

Woodside, J. Barnes, A.B.'28, Western Reserve Univ.; M.A.'34, Columbia Univ.; Supt. of Sch., Willoughby, Ohio, since 1939.

Yaple, Graydon W., A.B.'29, Colgate Univ.; M.A. in Ed.'35, Cornell Univ.; Ed.D.'48, Syracuse Univ.; Dean, Wilmington Col., Wilmington, Ohio, since 1950.

Young, Franklin M., B.S.'26, Otterbein Col.; M.A.'31, Ohio State Univ.; Supt. of Sch., Miamisburg, Ohio, since 1943.

Young, Ray A., A.B.'25, Manchester Col.; M.Ed.'45, Univ. of Cincinnati; Supt. of Exempted Village Sch., Greenhills, Cincinnati, Ohio, since 1945.

Zack, J. F., B.S.'33, Ohio Univ.; M.S.'36, Ohio State Univ.; Supvg. Prin. of Sch., Midvale, Ohio, since 1949.

Zeisert, E. E., Supt. of Sch., Phillipsburg, Ohio.

Zeller, Glenn W., M.A.'32, Ohio State Univ.; Supt. of Sch., Uhrichsville, Ohio, since 1942.

Zirbes, Laura, B.S.'25, M.A.'26, Ph.D.'28, Tchrs. Col., Columbia Univ.; Prof. of Educ., Ohio State Univ., Columbus, Ohio, since 1928.

INSTITUTIONAL MEMBERS

Antioch College Library, Yellow Springs, Ohio.

Library, Miami Univ., Oxford, Ohio.

Library, The Ohio State Univ., Columbus, Ohio.

Library, Ohio University, Athens, Ohio.

Ohio State Library, State Office Bldg., Columbus 15, Ohio.

Youngstown College Library, Youngstown Ohio.

OKLAHOMA

INDIVIDUAL MEMBERS

Abbott, Whitt K., B.S.'28, Southeastern State Col., Durant, Okla.; M.S.'41, Okla. Agrl. and Mech. Col.; Prin., Alice Robertson Jr. H. S., Muskogee, Okla., since 1947.

Allen, Paul B., A.B.'27, Okla. City Univ.; M.Ed. '36, Univ. of Okla.; Supt. of Sch., Pauls Valley, Okla., since 1943.

Allen, T. E., B.A.'33, Central State Col., Edmond, Okla.; Co. Supt. of Sch., Pawhuska, Okla., since 1943.

Anderson, Carl G., B.S.'37, Central State Col., Edmond, Okla.; M.A.'47, Univ. of Okla.; Supt. of Sch., Durant, Okla., since 1948.

Armstrong, Ira R., B.S.'30, Southeastern State Col., Durant, Okla.; M.A.'36, Okla. Agrl. and Mech. Col.; Supt. of Sch., Hugo, Okla., since 1943.

Arterbery, A. C., B.S.'27, Prairie View A. & M. Col.; Supt. of Sch., Langston, Okla., since 1947.

Avery, Henry, A.B.'29, M.'37, Phillips Univ.; Supt., City Sch., Kingfisher, Okla., since 1950.

Babb, A.R., M.Ed.'40, Okla. Univ.; Supt. of Sch., Sentinel, Okla., since 1941.

Ball, Ralph M., B.A.'31, Okla. A. & M. Col.; Archt., Oklahoma City, Okla., since 1942.

Barnes, Melvin W., A.B.'32, Greenville Col.; M.S.'34, Ph.D.'41, Univ. of Ill.; Asst. Supt. of Sch. in chg. of Instr., Oklahoma City, Okla., since 1949.

Barr, Fred, B.S.'38, Southwestern State Col., Weatherford, Okla.; M.S.'50, Univ. of Okla.; Supt. of Sch., Custer, Okla., since 1939.

Barrett, Arthur W., M.Ed.'47, Univ. of Okla.; B.S.'42, East Central State Col.; Supt. of Pub. Sch., Stratford, Okla., since 1948.

Battles, E. E., A.B.'27, Ed.M.'39, Univ. of Okla.; Ed.D.'49, Stanford Univ.; Supt. of Sch., Henryetta, Okla.

Beall, Ross H., B.S.'21, Coe Col.; M.A.'24, Ph.D.'32, State Univ. of Iowa; Prof. of Educ., Univ. of Tulsa, Tulsa, Okla., since 1938.

Boyd, Clyde, Master's'36, Phillips Univ.; Supt. of Sch., Sand Springs, Okla., since 1938.

Boyd, Jasper N., Supt. of Sch., Gans, Okla.

Boyer, D. Lee, A.B.'28, Southwestern State Col.; Ed.M.'40, Univ. of Okla.; Supt. of Sch., Balko, Okla., since 1948.

Briggs, Eugene S., B.S.'12, Central Col.; M.A.'17, Univ. of Mo.; Ph.D.'34, Columbia Univ.; LL.D. '48, Phillips Univ.; Pres., Phillips Univ., Enid, Okla., since 1938.

Brown, J. Henry, M.S.'39, Okla. Agrl. and Mech. Col.; Supt. of Sch., Coweta, Okla., since 1950.

Brown, Jack, B.A.'36, Northeastern State Col., Tahlequah, Okla.; Supt., Sequoyah Vocational Sch., Tahlequah, Okla., since 1924.

Buchanan, Hal N., B.A.'34, Southeastern State Col., Durant, Okla.; M.S.'41, Okla. Agrl. and Mech. Col.; Supt. of Sch., Cherokee, Okla. since 1947.

Buchanan, W. E., Supt. of Sch., Temple, Okla., since 1950.

Buck, Carl, B.S.'32, Southeastern State Col., Durant, Okla.; M.A.'41, Okla. A. & M. Col.; Supt. of Sch., Fox, Okla., since 1945.

Burch, Richard, M.S.'39, Univ. of Okla.; Supt. of Sch., Elk City, Okla., since 1949.

Burks, Arthur L., A.B.'18, Colo. State Col. of Educ., Greeley; M.Ed.'32, Univ. of Okla.; Supt. of Sch., Shawnee, Okla., since 1934.

Burton, Rupert Harold, B.A.'27, Central State Col., Edmond, Okla.; M.A.'32, Okla. Agrl. and Mech. Col.; Pres., Southwestern State Col., Weatherford, Okla., since 1945.

Caldwell, A. B., A.B.'16, Maryville Col.; M.A.'21, Ed.D.'36, Columbia Univ.; Dir. of Sch., Muskogee, Okla., since 1947.

Campbell, Ralph E., B.S.'33, Col. of the Ozarks; M.S.'42, Okla. Agrl. and Mech. Col.; Supt. of Sch., Talihina, Okla., since 1950.

Carr, William D., B.S.'30, Southeastern State Col., Durant, Okla.; M.A.'35, Columbia Univ.; Supt. of Sch., Cushing, Okla., since 1940.

Carter, Bruce G., A.B.'28, Okla. Baptist Univ.; M.A.'32, Ed.D.'50, Univ. of Okla.; Pres., Northwestern A. & M. Col., Miami, Okla., since 1943.

Cates, Eugene F., A.B.'36, Southwestern State Col.; Ed.M.'39, Univ. of Okla.; Supt. of Sch., Leedey, Okla., since 1940.

Cavalier, Walter A., B.A.'39, Northeastern State Col.; M.Ed.'51, Okla. Agrl. and Mech. Col.; Supt. of Sch., Davenport, Okla., since 1947.

Cawood, E. B., B.S.'30, Northwestern State Col.; M.S.'39, Univ. of Wyo.; Supt. of Sch., Waynoka, Okla., since 1940.

Cecil, Elmer P., B.S.'27, Southwestern Inst. of Tech., Weatherford, Okla.; M.Ed.'38, Univ. of Okla.; Supt. of Sch., Weatherford, Okla., since 1945.

Chambers, W. Max, A.B.'21, M.S.'29, Univ. of Okla.; Prof. Diploma '37, Tchrs. Col., Columbia Univ.; D.Ed., Colo. State Col. of Educ., Greeley; Pres., Central State Col., Edmond, Okla., since 1949.

Claiborne, Ray, M.Ed.'41, Okla. Univ.; Supt. of Sch., Hollis, Okla., since 1945.

Clark, Arthur, B.A.'31, Northeastern State Col.; M.S.'46, Okla. Agrl. and Mech. Col.; Supt. of Sch., Prague, Okla.

Clifford, Preston Jack, B.S.'41, East Central State Col.; M.A.'49, Okla. Agrl. and Mech. Col.; Supt. of Sch., Dewar, Okla., since 1946.

Clodfelter, Clifford R., M.S.'36, Okla. A. & M. Col.; Supt. of Sch., Snyder, Okla., since 1952.

Collum, M. C., B.S.'31, Southeastern State Col., Durant, Okla.; Ed.M.'37, Univ. of Okla.; Supt. of Sch., Madill, Okla., since 1938.

Cooley, John H., B.S.'32, Central State Col.; M.S.'40, Okla. A. & M. Col.; Supt. of Sch., Lamont, Okla., since 1947.

Cooper, Henry, M.A. in Ed.'41, Okla. A. & M. Col.; Supt. of Sch., Atoka, Okla., since 1945.

Cornelison, George Coy, M.Ed.'41, Okla. Univ.; Supt. of Sch., Tipton, Okla., since 1948.

Cornelius, T. M., B.S.'42, East Central State Col., Ada, Okla.; M.Ed.'51, Univ. of Okla.; Supt. of Sch., Addington, Okla., since 1948.

Costner, Elbert L., M.A.'34, Okla. Univ.; Supt. of Sch., Pateau, Okla., since 1939.

Cox, Raymond E., M.S.'40, Okla. A. & M. Col.; Supt. of Sch., Wilburton, Okla., since 1947.

Crooks, C. E., M.S.'36, Phillips Univ.; Supt. of Sch., Guthrie, Okla., since 1942.

Davis, Clarence L., B.S.'32, Southeastern State Col.; M.S.'41, Okla. A. & M. Col.; Supt. of Sch., Walters, Okla., since 1944.

Davison, O. W., A.B.'32, Central State Col., Edmond, Okla.; M.S.'37, Okla. A. & M. Col.; Ed.D.'49, Univ. of Okla.; Dir., Dept. of Adult Educ., Univ. of Okla., Norman, Okla., since 1948.

Dean, Robin R., B.S.'31, Northern Mich. Col. of Educ.; Ed.M.'52, Univ. of Okla.; Supt. of Riverside Indian Sch., Anadarko, Okla., since 1946.

De Wees, Clarence L., B.A.'31, B.S.'35, Southwestern Col.; Asst. Dir. of Finance, State Bd. of Educ., Oklahoma City, Okla., since 1947.

Dunlap, E. T., B.S.'39, Southeastern State Col., Durant, Okla.; M.S. in Ed. Adm.'41, Okla. A. & M. Col.; Pres., Eastern Okla. A. & M. Col., Wilburton, Okla.

Dunlap, Leo H., B.A.'43, Southeastern State Col. (Okla.); Supt. of Buffalo Valley Sch., Talihina, Okla., since 1943.

Duty, Richard, M.A.'39, A. & M. Col.; Supt. of Sch., Tishomingo, Okla., since 1948.

Earp, Jay B., M.A.'40, Okla. Agrl. and Mech. Col.; Supt. of Sch., Jay, Okla., since 1931.

Easley, Marvin L., B.S.'32, Southwestern State Col., Weatherford, Okla.; M.Ed.'37, Univ. of Okla.; Supt. of Sch., Erick, Okla., since 1951.

Emans, Roy H., M.E.D.'39, Univ. of Okla.; Dir. of Finance, State Dept. of Educ., Oklahoma City, Okla., since 1941.

Emerson, Earle E., B.A.'23, E. Central State Col., Ada, Okla.; M.S.'31, Okla. Agrl. and Mech. Col.; Supt. of Sch., Coalgate, Okla., since 1950.

Evans, Andy J., B.S.'32, Central State Col.; M.S.'41, Okla. Agrl. and Mech. Col.; Supt. of Sch., Tonkawa, Okla., since 1951.

Evans, E. J., M.A.'41, Okla. Agrl. and Mech. Col.; Supt. of Sch., Konawa, Okla., since 1934.

Ferguson, Leslie Guy, B.A.'24, Central State Col.; Co. Supt. of Sch., Tulsa, Okla., since 1947.

Fisher, B. B., Bachelor's '34, Central State Col.; Master's '39, Okla. A. & M. Col.; Supt. of Sch., Okeene, Okla., 1939-43 and since 1948.

Frazier, James R., B.A.'24, M.A.'32, Univ. of Okla.; Supt. of Sch., Okmulgee, Okla., since 1949.

Garrison, Harrell E., A.B.'32, Bethany-Peniel Col.; M.S.'36, Northwestern Univ.; Ph.D.'49, George Peabody Col. for Tchrs.; Pres., Northeastern State Col., Tahlequah, Okla., since 1951.

Garrison, Joseph Don, B.S.'27, M.Ed.'36, Univ. of Okla.; Supt. of Sch., Norman, Okla., 1935-40, and since 1946.

Geis, Earl L., B.A.'38, Northwestern State Col., Alva, Okla.; M. in Sch. Adm.'45, Univ. of Okla.; Supt. of Sch., Alva, Okla., since 1942.

George, N. L., B.S. in Ed.'26, Ed.M.'31, Univ. of Okla.; Ed.D.'48, Tchrs. Col., Columbia Univ.; Asst. Supt. and Bus. Mgmt. Clerk, Pub. Sch., Oklahoma City, Okla., since 1941.

Gililland, J. R., B.A.'39, Southwestern State Col.; Supt. of Merritt Pub. Sch., Elk City, Okla., since 1950.

Ginn, Hugh B., B.S.'39, Southwestern State Tchrs. Col., Weatherford, Okla.; Bus. Mgr. of Pub. Sch., Oklahoma City, Okla., since 1948.

Glasgow, M. W., A.B.'21, Univ. of Mich.; Ed.M. '32, Ed.D.'37, Univ. of Okla.; Supt. of Sch., Edmond, Okla., since 1947.

Godfrey, Garland A., B.S.'33, M.A.'36, Okla. Agrl. and Mech. Col.; Supt. of Sch., Pryor, Okla., since 1939.

Gourley, W. E., B.S.'32, Northwestern State Col.; M.Ed.'50, Phillips Univ.; Supt. of Sch., Shattuck, Okla., since 1942.

Grady, Charles E., A.M.'11, Indiana Univ.; Co. Supt. of Sch., Oklahoma City, Okla., since 1947.

Griffin, G. R., B.A.'37, Northeastern State Col.; M.A.'48, Okla. Agrl. and Mech. Col.; Supt. of Sch., Vinita, Okla., since 1949.

Griggs, Oscar C., B.S.'15, Okla. Agrl. and Mech. Col.; M.S.'28, Univ. of Okla.; Asst. Supt. of Sch., Tulsa, Okla., since 1944.

Hamilton, Oather L., A.B.'38, East Central State Col.; M.A.'50, Okla. A. & M. Col.; Supt. of Sch., Bearden, Okla., since 1943.

Hamon, Earl, M.S.'39, Okla. A. & M. Col.; Supt. of Sch., Newkirk, Okla., since 1948.

Hann, George D., A.B.'17, Okla. Baptist Univ.; M.Ed.'36, Univ. of Okla.; Supt. of Sch., Ardmore, Okla., since 1938.

Harrel, Kenneth H., B.S.'34, Central State Col., Edmond, Okla.; M.Ed.'47, Univ. of Okla.; Supt. of Sch., Fletcher, Okla., since 1933.

Harris, Al, B.S.'31, B.A.'33, Southwestern State Col.; M.A.'38, George Peabody Col. for Tchrs.; Supt. of Sch., Clinton, Okla., since 1947.

Harris, Hercel J., Supt. of Sch., Maysville, Okla.

Harris, Herman, M.Ed.'41, Okla. Univ.; Supt. of Sch., Seiling, Okla., since 1941.

Harvey, Raymond, M.S.'36, Okla. A. & M. Col.; Supt. of Sch., Bixby, Okla., since 1937.

Haynes, R. H., B.S.'33, Langston Univ.; Supt. of Sch., Tullahassee, Okla., since 1949.

Henninger, E. O., B.S.'33, Southeastern State Col. (Okla.); M.Ed.'39, Univ. of Okla.; Supt. of Sch., Jenks, Okla., 1943-52.

Herron, J. Arthur, M.Ed.'36, Univ. of Okla.; Supt. of Sch., Blackwell, Okla., since 1948.

Hodge, Oliver, B.A.'29, Univ. of Tulsa; M.Ed.'33, D.Ed.'37, Univ. of Okla.; State Supt. of Pub. Instr., Oklahoma City, Okla., since 1947.

Hoffman, Willis L., B.S.'36, Southwestern State Col.; M.A.'41, Western State Col. of Colo. Address: Lawton, Okla.

Holcomb, John E., B.S.'25, Northeastern State Col.; M.S.'32, Okla. A. & M. Col.; Supt. of Sch., Garber, Okla., since 1949.

Howell, C. M., A.B.'15, M.Ed.'36, Univ. of Okla.; Assoc. Secy., Okla. Educ. Assn., Oklahoma City, Okla.

Jennings, Al, Supt. of Sch., Jenks, Okla.

Jimerson, Fred, A.B.'25, Hendrix Col.; M.A.'39, Univ. of Okla.; Co. Supt. of Sch., Miami, Okla., since 1941.

Jinks, J. E., M.Ed.'41, Univ. of Okla.; Supt. of Sch., Quinton, Okla., since 1941.

Johns, Oliver D., A.B.'26, Okla. Baptist Univ.; M.Ed.'33, Okla. Univ.; Supt. of Sch., Seminole, Okla., since 1945.

Johnson, Rector, B.S.'33, Central State Col.; M.Ed.'38, Okla. Univ.; Supt. of Sch., Broken Bow, Okla., since 1946.

Jordan, Alphonso Milton, B.S.'31, Langston Univ.; M.A.'41, Univ. of Wichita; Supt. of Separate Sch., Douglass H. S., Wewoka, Okla., since 1940.

Jordan, Paul E., B.A.'28, M.A.'39, Okla. Univ.; Supt. of Sch., Moore, Okla., since 1946.

Kagey, J. N., Music'13, Art'13, Voice'17, Bridgewater Col. (Va.); Prin., Seneca Indian Sch., Wyandotte, Okla., since 1928.

Kirkland, Denver D., B.A.'28, Northwestern State Col., Alva, Okla.; M.Ed.'33, Univ. of Okla.; Supt. of Putnam City Sch., Oklahoma City, Okla., since 1950.

Knezevich, Stephen J., Assoc. Prof. of Educ., Univ. of Tulsa, Tulsa, Okla.

Lane, Willard R., B.S.'39, River Falls State Col.; M.S.'47, Ph.D.'51, Univ. of Wis.; Asst. Prof. of Educ., Univ. of Okla., Norman, Okla., since 1951.

Langston, Chalmer, B.A.'40, Southeastern State Col.; M.A.'51, Univ. of Okla.; Elem. Prin., Wilson, Okla., since 1948.

Lawrence, John Howard, B.S.'33, Okla. A. & M. Col.; M.Ed.'40, Univ. of Okla.; Grad. Fellow, Okla. A. & M. Col., Stillwater, Okla., since 1952.

Little, Evert T., M.Ed.'40, Univ. of Okla.; Asst. Prof. of Educ., Okla. A. & M. Col., Stillwater, Okla., since 1950.

Lockett, Victor James, B.S.'28, Central State Col., Edmond, Okla.; M.S.'33, Okla. Agrl. and Mech. Col.; Supt. of Sch., Fairfax, Okla., since 1931.

McCollom, Walter W., B.S.'29, M.S.'35, Okla. A. & M. Col.; Supt. of Sch., Glencoe, Okla., since 1951.

McCutcheon, Grover, B.S.'40, Southwestern State Col.; Supt. of Pub. Sch., Chattanooga, Okla., since 1937.

McDonald, (Mrs.) Gladys, M.A.'46, Univ. of Okla.; Dir. of Elem. Educ., Oklahoma City, Okla.

McDonald, Lee, B.S.'37, Central State Col., Edmond, Okla.; M.A.'44, Western State Col. of Colo., Gunnison; Supt. of Sch., Snyder, Okla., since 1948.

McIntosh, Daniel C., A.B.'13, A.M.'16, Ind. Univ.; B.S.'20, Iowa State Col.; Ph.D.'24, Ind. Univ.; Dean, Grad. Sch. and Prof. of Agrl. Educ., Okla. Agrl. and Mech. Col., Stillwater, Okla., since 1928.

McKee, Marvin Eugene, B.S.'31, Southwestern Inst. of Tech., Weatherford, Okla.; Pres., Panhandle Agrl. and Mech. Col., Goodwell, Okla., since 1945.

McKeel, J. N., B.S.'33, East Central State Col.; M.S.'45, Okla. A. & M. Col.; Supt. of Sch., Fittstown, Okla., since 1944.

McLean, R. H., A.B.'24, Southwestern State Tchrs. Col.; M.A.'46, Western State Col. of Colo.; Asst. Supt. of Sch., Midwest City, Okla., since 1947.

Marrs, Charles A., M.Ed.'41, Univ. of Okla.; Supt. of Sch., Skiatook, Okla., since 1949.

Martin, Ferrill, B.S.'33, Southwestern State Col.; M.Ed.'46, Univ. of Okla.; Supt. of Sch., Sayre, Okla., since 1947.

Martin, Jesse W., M.S.'38, Okla. Agrl. and Mech. Col.; Supt. of Sch., Nowata, Okla., since 1946.

Mason, Charles C., B.A.'25, Central Wesleyan Col.; M.A.'28, Washington Univ.; Ed.D.'41, Colo. State Col. of Educ., Greeley; Supt. of Sch., Tulsa, Okla., since 1944.

Moon, F. D., B.S.'29, Langston Univ.; M.A.'38, Univ. of Chicago; Supt., Douglass H. S., Oklahoma City, Okla.

Morrison, Rex O., B.A.'25, Trinity Univ.; M.Ed.'39, Univ. of Okla.; Supt. of Sch., Ada, Okla., since 1943.

Mouser, E. G., Supt. of Pub. Sch., Eugaula, Okla.

Myers, Bruce J., A.B.'22, M.Ed.'34, Univ. of Okla.; Supt. of Sch., Chickasha, Okla., since 1939.

Nash, M. A., Chancellor, Okla. State Regents for Higher Educ., Oklahoma City, Okla., since 1943.

493

Newman, Jennings B., Ed.M.'40, Univ. of Okla.; Supt. of Sch., Sapulpa, Okla., since 1951.

Nichols, B. R., M.S. in Ed.'35, Ed.D.'48, Okla. Agrl. and Mech. Col.; Supt. of Sch., Bristow, Okla., since 1942.

Nichols, Richard Clyde, M.A.'32, Univ. of Mo.; Supt. of Sch., Miami, Okla., since 1928.

Obuch, W. A., B.S.'32, Phillips Univ.; Supt. of Sch., Antlers, Okla., since 1947.

Ogle, Fred C., M.E.'34, Univ. of Okla.; Supt. of Sch., Checotah, Okla., since 1940.

Overstreet, Clarence A., B.S.'34, Southwestern Tchrs. Col., Weatherford, Okla.; M.Ed.'46, Okla. Agrl. and Mech. Col.; Supt. of Sch., Hammon, Okla., since 1945.

Parker, Bernard E., Supt. of Sch., Stafford, Okla.

*Patterson, Herbert, B.A.'08, M.A.'11, Wesleyan Univ.; M.A.'11, Ph.D.'13, Yale Univ.; Dean of Admin., Okla. Agrl. and Mech. Col., Stillwater, Okla., since 1919.

Pauly, Frank R., B.A.'17, Univ. of Okla.; M.A. '25, Ed.D.'35, Columbia Univ.; Dir. of Research, Bd. of Educ., Tulsa, Okla., since 1929.

Payne, J. Win, B.S.'32, Central State Col., Edmond, Okla.; M.S.'44, Okla. Agrl. and Mech. Col.; Supt. of Sch., Ponca City, Okla., since 1946.

Phillips, David E., A.B.'24, M.A.'35, Univ. of Okla.; Supt. of Sch., Chandler, Okla., since 1945.

Phillips, Ferman, A.B.'32, Southeastern State Col., Durant, Okla.; M.S.'38, Okla. Agrl. and Mech. Col.; Exec. Secy., Okla. Educ. Assn., Oklahoma City, Okla.

Phillips, W. T., B.A.'45, Northeastern State Col.; Supt. of Sch., Oologah, Okla., since 1949.

Pierce, George A., B.S.'32, Southeastern State Col.; M.S.'34, Okla. A. & M. Col.; Supt. of Pub. Sch., Cromwell, Okla., since 1950.

Pigg, Cloys, B.S.'39, Okla. A. & M. Col.; Supt., Pub. Sch., Texola, Okla., since 1942.

Piguet, Guss, M.S.'48, Okla. A. & M. Col.; Supt. of Sch., Ramona, Okla., since 1951.

Price, Dave D., Pres., The Economy Co., Oklahoma City, Okla.

Procter, C. Dan, B.A.'28, East Central State Col., Ada, Okla.; Ed.M.'35, Ed.D.'43, Univ. of Okla.; Pres., Okla. Col. for Women, Chickasha, Okla., since 1943.

Pugmire, D. Ross, B.S.'27, Brigham Young Univ.; M.A.'33, Tchrs. Col., Columbia Univ.; Ph.D.'37, Columbia Univ.; Prof. of Sch. Admin., Univ. of Okla., Norman, Okla., since 1947.

Quinn, (Mrs.) Lila, M.Ed.'43, Univ. of Okla.; Prin., Millard Fillmore Elem. Sch., Oklahoma City, Okla.

Richardson, James W., B.A.'17, Ind. Univ.; Ed.M.'27, Harvard Univ.; Ph.D.'40, Columbia Univ.; Prof. of Educ., Okla. A. & M. Col., Stillwater, Okla., since 1949.

Riley, Wilson M., A.B.'31, M.Ed.'35, Phillips Univ.; Supt. of Sch., Woodward, Okla., since 1947.

Rinsland, Henry Daniel, A.B.'20, A.M.'23, Univ. of Okla.; Ph.D.'35, Columbia Univ.; Prof. of Educ. and Dir., Bureau of Educ. Research, Univ. of Okla., Norman, Okla., since 1924.

Roach, Diamond, Prin., C & A Sch., Concho, Okla.

Robberson, Guy E., B.S.'38, Central State Col.; M.Ed.'46, Okla. A. & M. Col.; Supt. of Sch., Lindsay, Okla., since 1949.

Roberts, G. M., A.B.'27, M.A.'28, Univ. of Okla.; Supt. of Sch., Bartlesville, Okla., since 1947.

Rose, Oscar V., B.S.'31, East Central State Col., Ada, Okla.; Supt. of Sch., Midwest City, Okla., since 1943.

Rowe, Omer, B.S.'31, Southeastern State Col., Durant, Okla.; Co. Supt. of Sch., Ardmore, Okla., since 1946.

Russell, R. R., A.B.'27, Phillips Univ.; M.A.'34, Okla. Agrl. and Mech. Col.; Supt. of Sch., Stillwater, Okla., since 1947.

Sasser, Laurence, B.S.'31, M.S.'40, Okla. A. & M. Col.; Supt. of Sch., Hinton, Okla., since 1951.

Schubert, O. G., M.S.'40, Okla. A. & M. Col.; Supt., Union Pub. Sch., Broken Arrow, Okla., since 1946.

Self, E. R., Supt. of Sch., Mountain View, Okla.

Setzepfandt, A. O. H., B.A.'22, M.A.'23, Univ. of Iowa; Asst. Supt. in chg. of Elem. Educ., Bd. of Educ., Tulsa, Okla., since 1952.

Shackelford, Harry C., B.S.'40, Northeastern State Col.; M.S.'49, Phillips Univ.; Supt. of Sch., Laverne, Okla., since 1947.

Shaw, Homer, B.A.'30, Okla. Baptist Univ.; M.A.'35, Okla. Agrl. and Mech. Col.; Supt. of Sch., Pawnee, Okla., since 1942.

Shaw, Otto E., B.S.'27, Southeastern State Col.; M.S.'33, Okla. A. & M. Col.; Dir. of Surveys, State Dept. of Pub. Instr., Oklahoma City, Okla., since 1948.

Shepherd, Byron L., B.S.'32, M.S.'33, Kansas State Col.; Asst. Supt. of Sch. in charge of Sec. Sch., Tulsa, Okla., since 1941.

Shoemaker, John D., B.S.'26, Southwestern Inst. of Tech., Weatherford, Okla.; M.E.'32, Univ. of Okla.; Supt. of Sch., Lawton, Okla., since 1946.

Simmons, Harry D., B.S.'24, Univ. of Okla.; M.A.'27, Columbia Univ.; Supt. of Sch., Muskogee, Okla., since 1947.

Smith, Calvin T., M.Ed.'40, Univ. of Okla.; Supt. of Sch., Wewoka, Okla., since 1949.

Smith, Doyle, B.S.'41, Central State Col., Edmond, Okla.; Supt. of Sch., Maramec, Okla., since 1946.

Smith, Levia Meyers, Prin., Elem. Sch., Oklahoma City, Okla.

Smith, Willie G., M.S.'48, Okla. A. & M. Col.; Supt. of Sch., Billings, Okla., since 1950.

Sneed, Jeter D., B.S.'28, East Central Col.; M.A.'36, Tchrs. Col., Columbia Univ.; Bus. Mgr., Okla. Col. for Women, Chickasha, Okla., since 1942.

Snider, Glenn R., A.B., B.S., B.S. in Ed.'32, Central Mo. Col., Warrensburg; A.M.'38, Univ. of Mich.; Ed.D.'49, Univ. of Wyo.; Head, Dept. of Educ., Southwestern Inst. of Tech., Weatherford, Okla., since 1949.

Sorenson, Helmer E., B.E.'35, State Tchrs. Col., Eau Claire, Wis.; Ph.M.'39, Ph.D.'48, Univ. of Wis.; Prof. of Educ., Okla. Agrl. and Mech. Col., Stillwater, Okla., since 1949.

Spencer, Charles F., B.S.'28, East Central State Col., Ada, Okla.; M.A.'29, Univ. of Okla.; Ph.D.'38, Univ. of Wis.; Pres., East Central State Col., Ada, Okla., since 1949.

Spenner, George W., A.B.'42, Northwestern State Col.; M.A.'44, Phillips Univ.; Supt. of Sch., Guymon, Okla., since 1944.

Stubbs, G. T., A.B.'26, Southeastern State Tchrs. Col., Durant, Okla.; M.A.'31, Tchrs. Col., Columbia Univ.; Dir., Dept. of Pub. Sch. Serv., Okla. Agrl. and Mech. Col., Stillwater, Okla., since 1945.

Swanson, J. Chester, A.B.'26, Univ. of Richmond; M.A.'29, Ph.D.'35, Duke Univ.; Supt. of Sch., Oklahoma City, Okla., since 1950.

Sweeney, Kenneth K., M.Ed.'46, Univ. of Okla.; Supt. of Sch., Thomas, Okla., since 1939.

Taylor, Paul R., M.S. in Ed.'31, Okla. Agrl. and Mech. Col.; Supt. of Sch., El Reno, Okla., since 1935.

Teague, J. E., B.S.'29, East Central State Col., Ada, Okla.; M.S.'32, Okla. A. & M. Col.; Supt. of Byng Sch., Ada, Okla., since 1926.

Terrill, Oren M., B.S.'36, Northeastern State Col.; M.S.'41, Northeastern A. & M. Col.; Supt. of Sch., Pawhuska, Okla., since 1951.

Thompson, S. Arch, B.S.'25, Okla. A. & M. Col.; M.S.'35, Kansas State Col.; Supt. of City Sch., McAlester, Okla., since 1950.

Towry, M. Forrest, M.S.'35, Okla. A. & M. Col.; B.S.'32, Northeastern State Col.; Supt. of Sch., Anadarko, Okla., since 1951.

Tuttle, Francis T., B.S.'42, Okla. A. & M. Col.; Supt. of Sch., Gotebo, Okla., since 1951.

Van Meter, Oather E., B.A.'22, Southern Methodist Univ.; M.A.'29, Univ. of Okla.; Supt. of Sch., Bowlegs, Okla., since 1952.

Vaughn, Noel E., M.Ed.'39, Univ. of Okla.; Supt. of Sch., Healdton, Okla., since 1947.

Vickers, M. M., M.A.'50, Univ. of Okla.; Supt. of Sch., Watonga, Okla., since 1947.

Wall, Henry A., A.B.'30, Colo. State Col. of Educ.; Area Dir. of Sch., Anadarko, Okla., since 1950.

Wallace, Charles S., A.B.'25, Southwestern State Col., Weatherford, Okla.; M.S.'31, Univ. of Okla.; Ed.D.'50, Tchrs. Col., Columbia Univ.; Asst. Supt. of Sch., Oklahoma City, Okla., since 1942.

Wallace, James D., B.S.'34, Springfield Col.; Prin., Fort Sill Indian Sch., Lawton, Okla., since 1946.

Wallace, Morris S., B.A.'31, M.A.'38, North Texas State Tchrs. Col., Denton; Ed.D.'48, Tchrs. Col., Columbia Univ.; Prof. of Educ. Admin., Col. of Educ., Okla. Agrl. and Mech. Col., Stillwater, Okla., since 1949.

Waller, DeWitt, A.B.'11, Epworth Univ.; A.M. '28, Univ. of Mo.; Supt. of Sch., Enid, Okla., since 1934.

Watson, Loyd R., B.S.'25, East Central State Col.; M.S.'39, Okla. Agrl. and Mech. Col.; Supt. of Sch., Allen, Okla., since 1934.

Weil, W. E., B.A.'38, Southwestern State Col., Weatherford, Okla.; Prin., Cowden Sch., Cloud Chief, Okla., since 1952.

Welborn, Howard, Master's '47, Western State Col. of Colo.; Supt. of Sch., Medford, Okla., since 1943.

White, Clark E., B.S.'39, Southeastern State Col. (Okla.); LL.B.'42, Univ. of Okla.; Supt. of Sch., Rattan, Okla., since 1949.

White, J. Phillip, Supt. of Pub. Sch., Davis, Okla.

White, William Earl, M.A.'29, Columbia Univ.; Supt. of Sch., Haskell, Okla., since 1928.

Wickett, William, Supt. of Sch., Tulsa, Okla.

Wiemer, A. C., A.B.'23, North Central Col.; M.Ed.'44, Colo. State Col. of Educ., Greeley; Supt. of Sch., Drumright, Okla., since 1948.

Williams, A. F., A.B.'40, Southwestern Tech. Col.; M.A.'50, Phillips Univ.; Supt. of Sch., Dover, Okla., since 1946.

Willingham, Farris E., B.A.'27, East Central Col.; M.Ed.'37, Okla. Univ.; Supt. of Sch., Tecumseh, Okla., since 1927.

Wilson, Howell H., M.S.'41, Univ. of Okla.; Supt. of Sch., Collinsville, Okla., since 1943.

Wood, Dion Carlos, A.B.'31, Southeastern State Col., Durant, Okla.; M.A.'35, Univ. of Okla.; Supt. of Sch., Duncan, Okla., since 1941.

Woods, William Russell, B.S.'30, Southwestern Tchrs. Col., Okla.; M.S.'34, Kansas State Tchrs. Col., Emporia; Supt. of Sch., Canton, Okla., since 1949.

Young, W. Rankin, B.S.'22, Kansas State Tchrs. Col.; M.A.'25, Tchrs. Col., Columbia Univ.; Supt. of Sch., Cleveland, Okla., since 1934.

Younger, L. S., Supt. of Sch., Custer, Okla.

INSTITUTIONAL MEMBERS

Library, Northeastern State College, Tahlequah, Okla.

Oklahoma City Tchrs. Mutual Organization, 228 N. W. 8, Oklahoma City, Okla.

Superior Coach Sales Company, 3724 N. May, Oklahoma City, Okla.

OREGON

INDIVIDUAL MEMBERS

Adams, Warren S., B.A.'37, Nebr. State Tchrs. Col., Peru; Supt., Union H. S., Molalla, Oregon, since 1946.

Anderson, A. B., B.S.'27, N. Dak. State Col.; Supt. of Sch., Silverton, Oregon, since 1943.

Armstrong, D. Herbert, M.A.'50, Whitman Col.; Supt. of City Sch., North Bend, Oregon, since 1950.

Armstrong, Hubert E., B.A.'25, Pacific Col.; M.A.'32, Univ. of Oregon; Supt. of Sch., Newberg, Oregon, since 1944.

Bain, V. D., Asst. Supt. of Sch., Portland, Oregon.

Barr, H. M., Research Dir., Portland Pub. Sch., Portland, Oregon.

Bates, David E., B.A. in Ed.'27, Iowa State Tchrs. Col., Cedar Falls; M.A. in Adm. and Supvn.'35, Univ. of Mich.; Supt. of Sch., The Dalles, Oregon, since 1948.

Beardsley, Florence E., B.S.'30, M.S.'36, Univ. of Oregon; State Dir. of Elem. Educ., State Dept. of Pub. Instr., Salem, Oregon, since 1941.

Beck, A. L., B.S.'34, Univ. of Oregon; M.A.'37, Stanford Univ.; Asst. Sch. Bldg. Consultant, State Bd. of Educ., Salem, Oregon.

Bennett, Frank B., B.A.'21, Willamette Univ.; M.A.'33, Univ. of Oregon; Ed.D.'48, Willamette Univ.; Pres., Eastern Oregon Col. of Educ., La Grande, Oregon, since 1952.

Booth, (Mrs.) Agnes C., Diploma'23, Oregon Col. of Educ., Monmouth; Co. Supt. of Sch., Salem, Oregon, since 1939.

Bortolazzo, Julio L., B.A.'36, Santa Barbara State Col.; M.S.'39, Univ. of Southern Calif.; Ed.M.'42, Ed.D.'48, Harvard Univ.; Supt. of Oswego-Lake Grove Sch., Oswego, Oregon, since 1950.

Brogoitti, S. E., Chmn., State Bd. of Educ., Helix, Oregon.

Brown, James L., B.A.'29, Univ. of Mont.; M.Ed.'47, Univ. of Oregon; Supt., Redmond Union H. S. Dist., Redmond, Oregon, since 1952.

Buck, Edward M., B.S.'29, Whitman Col.; M.S. in Ed.'47, Univ. of Idaho; Supt. of Sch., Junction City, Oregon, since 1951.

Campbell, Don J., B.S.'30, M.S.'40, Univ. of Oregon; Supt. of Sch., Parkrose, Portland, Oregon, since 1946.

Cannon, G. O., B.S.'31, Univ. of Denver; M.Ed.'49, Univ. of Wash.; P. O. Box 3632, Portland, Oregon.

Carmichael, Jack W., B.S.'47, M.S.'49, Oregon State Col.; Supt. of Sch., Huntington, Oregon.

495

Corwin, George A., M.Ed.'46, Univ. of Oregon; Supt., Hood River Co. Sch. Dist., Hood River, Oregon.

Cox, George B., B.S. in Engr.'19, Univ. of Mo.; M.S. in Ed.'40, Oregon State Col.; Prof., and Head, Dept. of Indus. Arts and Indus. Engr., Oregon State Col., Corvallis, Oregon, since 1927.

Cox, John R., A.B.'29, Albany Col.; Prin., Union H. S., Hillsboro, Oregon, since 1938.

Cramer, John Francis, B.A.'20, M.A.'21, Willamette Univ.; M.Ed.'32, D.Ed.'37, Univ. of Oregon; Dean, Genl. Extension Div., Oregon State System of Higher Educ., Portland, Oregon, since 1944.

Daehler, Louis A., B.A.'35, Univ. of Ill.; M.Ed. '51, Oregon State Col.; Prin., Banks Union H. S., Banks, Oregon, since 1951.

Darland, D. D., Ed.D.'47, Tchrs. Col., Columbia Univ.; Dean of Students, Prof. of Educ., Pacific Univ., Forest Grove, Oregon.

Davis, G. Harland, B.S.'22, Monmouth Col.; M.Ed.'41, Oregon State Col.; Supt. of Sch., Toledo, Oregon, since 1945.

Dishaw, Harold C., B.S.'34, Albany Col.; Prin., Union H. S. 2, Sweet Home, Oregon, since 1946.

Ditto, Charles E., B.A.'41, Eastern N. Mex. Col.; M.A.'50, Univ. of Oregon; Supt., Creswell Union H. S., Creswell, Oregon, since 1951.

Doerfler, Frank P., B.A.'35, Mont. State Univ.; M.S. in Ed.'45, Univ. of Idaho; Supt., Sch. Dist. 103-C, Woodburn, Oregon, since 1949.

Dolmyer, William H., A.B.'40, Univ. of Chicago; M.Ed.'50, Oregon State Col.; Co. Supt. of Sch., Albany, Oregon, since 1950.

Dove, Eugene E., B.S.'45, M.S.'49, Univ. of Oregon; Supt.-Prin., Union H. S. Dist. 1, Vernonia, Oregon, since 1952.

Eaton, Asa T., B.A.'26, Bucknell Univ.; Supt., Jefferson Co. Sch., Madras, Oregon, since 1952.

Edwards, Jonathan W., A.B.'17, Whitman Col.; M.A.'32, Univ. of Oregon; Deputy Supt. of Sch., Portland, Oregon, since 1936.

Elliott, Edward C., Supt. of Pub. Sch., Dist. 6, Umatilla, Oregon.

Elliott, Paul S., B.A.'21, Pacific Col.; Supt. of Sch., Roseburg, Oregon, since 1944.

Emerson, D. A., B.A.'23, Univ. of Wash.; M.A.'24, State Col. of Wash.; Asst. Supt. of Pub. Instr., Salem, Oregon, since 1934.

Evans, James R., B.A.'30, State Col. of Wash.; M.S.'35, Univ. of Oregon; Supt. of Sch., Baker, Oregon, since 1946.

Ferrin, Holman B., B.S.'15, Univ. of Vt.; Supt. of Sch., Lakeview, Oregon, since 1948.

Fishback, Elton, B.S.'52, Oregon Col. of Educ.; Prin., Shasta Elem. Sch., Klamath Falls, Oregon, since 1944.

Foster, Wayne, B.S.'37, M.Ed.'46, Univ. of Oregon; Supt. of Sch., Hood River, Oregon, since 1950.

Frisbie, Chester C., B.A.'28, Univ. of Wash.; M.B.A.'38, Northwestern Univ.; Ed.D.'49, Stanford Univ.; Head, Educ. Dept., Lewis and Clark Col., Portland, Oregon, since 1950.

Fuller, William A., Jr., B.S.'48, Oregon State Col.; Supt. of Sch. and Prin., Union H. S., Harrisburg, Oregon, since 1951.

Gabbert, Donald, A.B.'32, Pacific Univ.; M.Ed. '48, Oregon State Col.; Supt., Union H. S. Dist. 2, Burns, Oregon, since 1949.

Gastineau, Gerald M., Ed.M.'51, Willamette Univ.; Supt.-Prin. of Sch., Newport, Oregon, since 1949.

Gilles, Mathilda, A.B.'45, San Francisco State Col.; Prin., Richmond Elem. Sch., Salem, Oregon, since 1946.

Goldhammer, Keith, B.A.'38, Reed Col.; M.A. '43, Univ. of Oregon; Eugene, Oregon.

Gralapp, A. L., B.A.'17, Willamette Univ.; M.A.'36, Univ. of Calif.; Supt. of Sch., Klamath Falls, Oregon, since 1942.

Grant, Leslie E., M.Ed.'51, Univ. of Oregon; Co. Supt. of Sch., Heppner, Oregon, since 1951.

Halseth, I. R., B.S. in Ed.'27, Eastern State Tchrs. Col., Madison, S. Dak.; M.S. in Ed.'36, Univ. of Wyo.; Supt. of Sch., Albany, Oregon, since 1948.

Harcombe, William F., M.S.'48, Univ. of Oregon; Supt. of Sch. and Prin., Union H. S., Elmira, Oregon, since 1947.

Hartley, Henry H., B.A.'27, Williamette Univ.; M.A.'40, Univ. of Oregon; Supt. of Sch., Nyssa, Oregon, since 1940.

Hassell, Errol, B.A.'41, Western Wash. Co. of Educ., Bellingham; M.Ed.'48, Univ. of Oregon; Supt. of Elem. Sch. Dist. 48, Beaverton, Oregon, since 1948.

Hedrick, E. H., A.B.'16, M.A.'29, Univ. of Oregon; Supt. of Sch., Medford, Oregon, since 1925.

Hines, Clarence, A.B.'25, Drury Col.; M.A.'29, Univ. of Mo.; Ed.D.'50, Univ. of Oregon; Dist. Supt. of Sch., Eugene, Oregon, since 1946.

Hogard, Winslow A., B.S. in Ed.'25, Southwest Mo. State Col.; Admin. Officer (Educ.), Bur. of Indian Affairs, Portland, Oregon, since 1948.

Holm, Martin N. B., A.B.'35, A.M.'36, Colo. State Col. of Educ.; Area Dir. of Sch., Bureau of Indian Affairs, Portland Area Office, Portland, Oregon, since 1952.

Howe, Carrol B., B.S.'36, M.S.'42, Univ. of Oregon; Co. Supt. of Sch., Klamath Falls, Oregon, since 1948.

Huff, Milton C., A.B.'28, M.A.'34, Univ. of Nebr.; Asst. Co. Supt. of Sch., Toledo, Oregon, since 1949.

Hunsaker, Ray, B.S.'40, Univ. of Oregon; Supt. of Sch., Coquille, Oregon, since 1947.

Hunter, Frederick Maurice, A.B.'05, Univ. of Nebr.; A.M.'19, Columbia Univ.; B.A.'25, Univ. of Calif.; LL.D.'30, Colo. Col.; LL.D.'32, Univ. of Colo.; LL.D.'39, Univ. of Nebr.; Pres., Natl. Educ. Assn., 1920-21; Chancellor, Oregon State System of Higher Educ., Eugene, Oregon, 1935-46, Honorary Chancellor since 1946.

Ickes, Dale J., M.Ed.'48, Univ. of Oregon; Supt. of Elem. Sch., Milwaukie, Oregon, since 1945.

Ingles, Edwin T., A.B.'29, Pacific Univ.; M.A.'35, Ed.D.'47, Univ. of Oregon; Vicepres., Pacific Univ., Forest Grove, Oregon, since 1946.

Jacob, Keith W., B.S.Ed.'39, M.S.Ed.'51, Univ. of Idaho; Supt. of Sch., Culver, Oregon.

Jacobson, Paul B., A.B.'22, Luther Col.; A.M.'28, Ph.D.'31, State Univ. of Iowa; Dean, Sch. of Educ., Univ. of Oregon, Eugene, Oregon, since 1947.

Jacoby, Harry, Master's'38, Univ. of Idaho; Supt. of Sch., Wallowa, Oregon, since 1948.

Jewell, R. E., B.A.'29, Lewis and Clark Col.; M.A.'40, Univ. of Southern Calif.; Supt. of City Sch., Bend, Oregon since 1950.

Jewett, H. P., A.B.'16, Willamette Univ.; Supt. of Sch., Central Point, Oregon, since 1924.

Johnson, Elmer R., M.A. in Sch. Admin.'48, Colo. State Col. of Educ.; Prin. of Pub. Sch., Paisley, Oregon, since 1948.

Jones, Ralph E., B.S.'27, Oregon State Col.; M.S.'37, Univ. of Oregon; Supt. of City Sch., Grants Pass, Oregon.

496

Kelly, Glenn Kuns, B.A.'16, Franklin Col.; M.A.'28, Univ. of Chicago; Supt. of Sch., Negaunee, Mich., 1948-52 (retired). Address: Genl. Delivery, Salem, Oregon.

King, James W., B.A.'27, Pacific Univ.; M.A.'35, Univ. of Oregon; Supt. of Sch., Lebanon, Oregon, since 1944.

King, Luther A., M.Ed.'36, Univ. of Oregon; Supt. of Sch., Oregon City, Oregon, since 1946.

King, William E., B.S.'21, M.A.'40, State Col. of Wash.; Co. Supt. of Sch., Pendleton, Oregon, since 1944.

Kingsley, Virgil G., B.S.'33, Linfield Col.; Supt., Union H. S., Cottage Grove, Oregon, since 1948.

Larive, Armand, M.S.'41, Univ. of Oregon; Supt. of Sch., Hermiston, Oregon, since 1947.

Leavitt, Jerome E., B.S.'38, N. J. State Tchrs. Col., Newark; M.A.'41, Sch. of Educ., New York Univ.; Asst. Prof. of Educ., Portland State Extension Center, Portland, Ore., since 1952.

Light, Floyd, B.S.'28, Oregon State Col.; Supt. of Sch., St. Helens, Oregon, since 1949.

Linn, Leland P., A.B.'21, Willamette Univ.; M.A.'33, Univ. of Oregon; Supt. of Sch., Ashland, Oregon, since 1945.

Longfellow, J. T., B.S.'15, Wash. State Col.; Dist. Supt., Lincoln Co. Sch., Toledo, Oregon, since 1949.

McCrae, Wallace W., B.S.'33, Univ. of Oregon; Supt. of Sch., Pendleton, Oregon.

Martin, George B., B.S.'30, M.A.'38, Ed.D.'44, Univ. of Calif.; Prof. and Head, Educ. Dept., since 1947, and Dir. of Grad. Study, Willamette Univ., Salem, Oregon.

Mekvold, Alf B., Co. Supt. of Sch., Medford, Oregon.

Menegat, Paul A., M.A.'30, Univ. of Oregon; Prin., Union H. S., Forest Grove, Oregon, since 1941.

Moffitt, Laurence C., B.S.'40, Univ. of Oregon; Co. Supt. of Sch., Grants Pass, Oregon, since 1945.

Neet, Al M., B.S.'46, Oregon Col. of Educ.; Supt. of Sch., Myrtle Creek, Oregon, since 1952.

Newman, Harold R., B.A.'48, Southern Idaho Col. of Educ., Albion; Dist. Supt. of Sch., Adrian, Oregon, since 1949.

Olds, Douglas V., B.S.'46, Willamette Univ.; Supt., Jefferson Pub. Sch., Jefferson, Oregon, since 1950.

Ott, (Mrs.) Alice E., B.S.'50, Univ. of Oregon; Supt. of Gilbert Sch., Portland, Oregon, since 1945.

Patton, Fred J., B.A.'24, Willamette Univ.; M.A.'35, Univ. of Oregon; Supt. of Sch., McMinnville, Oregon.

Posey, Cecil William, M.S.'40, Univ. of Oregon; Exec. Secy., Oregon Educ. Assn., Portland, Oregon, since 1948.

Powers, T. R., Jr., B.A.'28, M.A.'34, Univ. of Oregon; Supt., Lane Co. Sch. Dist. 52, Eugene, Oregon, since 1948.

Poynter, James William, B.A.'25, State Tchrs. Col., Peru, Nebr.; Supt., Elem. Sch., Hillsboro, Oregon, since 1937.

Putnam, Rex, B.A.'15, M.A.'29, Univ. of Oregon; State Supt. of Pub. Instr., Salem, Oregon, since 1937.

Rehmus, Paul A., A.B.'23, M.A.'29, Univ. of Mich.; Supt. of Sch., Portland, Oregon, since 1947.

Riggs, Lyle N., Supt. of Sch., LaGrande, Oregon.

Sabin, Owen O., B.A.'28, Parsons Col.; M.A.'37, Univ. of N. Mex.; Supt. of Sch., Milwaukie, Oregon, since 1951.

Sandin, Adolph A., B.A.'33, Central Wash. Col. of Educ., Ellensburg; M.A.'38, Univ. of Wash.; Ph.D.'43, Tchrs. Col., Columbia Univ.; Assoc. Prof., Sch. of Educ., Univ. of Oregon, Eugene, Oregon, since 1950.

Silke, Eugene H., A.B.'30, Willamette Univ.; Supt. of Sch., Springfield, Oregon, since 1940.

Sly, Cecil M., B.S.'19, State Col. of Wash.; Co. Dist. Supt. of Sch., Prineville, Oregon, since 1945.

Staley, David A., M.S.'40, Univ. of Oregon; Supt.-Prin., Union H. S., Clatskanie, Oregon, since 1947.

Stevenson, Elmo N., B.A.'27, San Jose State Col.; M.A.'29, Ed.D.'38, Stanford Univ.; Pres., Southern Oregon Col., Ashland, Oregon, since 1946.

Stewart, J. H., B.S.'38, M.E.'48, Univ. of Oregon; Supt. of Sch., Coburg, Oregon, since 1946.

Tetz, Henry E., B.S.'25, M.S.'37, Univ. of Oregon; Supt. of Sch., Monmouth-Independence, Oregon.

Thomas, Frank W., B.S.'36, Univ. of Oregon; M.Ed.'51, Oregon State Col.; Prin., H. S., Grants Pass, Oregon.

Thompson, Harry A., B.S.'38, Linfield Col.; M.S.'49, Univ. of Oregon; Supt., Gresham Union H. S., Gresham, Oregon, since 1952.

Todd, Glenn W., B.S. in Ed.'16, Kansas State Tchrs. Col., Pittsburg; M.A.'26, Univ. of Colo.; Supt. of Sch., Dist. 9, Tillamook, Oregon, since 1952.

Tope, Donald E., B.A.'28, Western State Col., Gunnison, Colo.; M.A.'29, Ph.D.'34, State Univ. of Iowa; Dir., CPEA, Univ. of Oregon, Eugene, Oregon, since 1951.

Tunnell, Chester L., B.S.'35, Linfield Col.; M.S.'40, Univ. of Oregon; Supt. of Sch., West Linn, Oregon, since 1946.

Van Loan, Wendell L., Ed.D.'42, Stanford Univ.; Supt. of Sch., Corvallis, Oregon, since 1946.

Weddle, (Mrs.) Carmalite I., M.E.'52, Willamette Univ.; Supt. of Keizer Elem. Sch., Salem, Oregon, since 1952.

Wells, Thomas A., B.A.'31, Pacific Univ.; M.Ed.'51, Oregon State Col.; Supt. of Sch., Astoria, Oregon, since 1951.

Whitworth, Sidney E., B.S.'11, Whitworth Col.; A.B.'24, A.M.'31, Univ. of Wash.; Supt. of Sch., Dallas, Oregon, since 1942.

Williams, Delos D., B.A.'31, Concordia Col.; M.E.'52, Univ. of Oregon; Supt.-Prin., Pub. Sch., Colton, Oregon, since 1948.

*Winslow, Marion B., B.A.'27, Pacific Col.; M.A.'34, Univ. of Wash.; Supt. of Sch., Coos Bay, Oregon, since 1934.

Wolf, Ray O., Supvr., Soc. Studies, Portland Oregon.

INSTITUTIONAL MEMBERS

Library, Oregon College of Education, Monmouth, Oregon.

Oregon State Library, Salem, Oregon.

University of Oregon Library, Eugene, Oregon.

PENNSYLVANIA

INDIVIDUAL MEMBERS

Abbott, E. Carlton, Ph.B.'26, Vt. Univ. and State Agrl. Col.; M.A.'33, Columbia Univ.; Ph.D.'43, Univ. of Pa.; Dist. Supt. of Sch., Lansdowne, Pa., since 1947.

Abernethy, Robert R., B.S.'21, Muhlenberg Col.; A.M.'23, Univ. of Pa.; Ed.D.'40, New York Univ.; Supt., Haverford Twp. Sch. Dist., Brookline, Havertown, Pa., since 1942.

Ableson, Eula M., B.Ped.'08, Alma Col.; Prof. of Educ., Beaver Col., Jenkintown, Pa., since 1918.

Ackley, Clarence E., A.B.'10, M.A.'13, Oberlin Col.; Ph.D.'33, Univ. of Pittsburgh; Specialist in Educ., Pa. Economy League, Inc., Harrisburg, Pa., since 1947.

Adams, Norman E., B.S.'30, Grove City; M.Ed. '41, Univ. of Pittsburgh; Supt. of Etna Boro Pub. Sch., Pittsburgh, Pa., since 1951.

Adams, Robert L., B.S.'33, State Tchrs. Col., Millersville, Pa.; M.Ed.'37, Duke Univ.; Supvg. Prin., West Lampeter Twp. Sch., Lampeter, Pa., since 1943.

*Ade, Lester Kelly, B.A.'21, Bucknell Univ.; M.A.'24, Yale Univ.; Ph.D.'31, New York Univ.; LL.D.'35, Bucknell Univ.; Litt.D.'36, Temple Univ.; L.H.D.'38, Beaver Col.; Address: 621 Market St., Williamsport 8, Pa.

Allard, J. A., B.S.'20, Pa. State Col.; M.A.'34, D.Ed.'45, Univ. of Pittsburgh; Supvg. Prin. of Moon Twp. Sch., Coraopolis, Pa., since 1928.

Amalong, Raymond H., B.S.'35, Pa. State Col.; M.Ed.'44, Univ. of Pittsburgh; Head, Dept. of Educ., Thiel Col., Greenville, Pa., since 1946.

Ammerman, Homer B., B.S. in Ed.'30, Pa. State Col.; M.S. in Ed.'38, New York Univ.; Co. Supt. of Sch., Honesdale, Pa., since 1946.

Anderson, John D., A.B.'16, Univ. of Rochester; M.A.'30, Ph.D.'41, Univ. of Pittsburgh; Supt. of Sch., Butler, Pa., since 1946.

Anderson, Robert R., Diploma '08, State Tchrs. Col., Millersville, Pa.; Supvg. Prin. of Sch., Brackenridge, Pa., since 1919.

Angotti, Lewis P., B.S.'35, State Tchrs. Col., California, Pa.; M.Ed.'49, Univ. of Pittsburgh; Supvg. Prin. of Sch., Ellsworth, Pa., since 1949.

Annunciata, Sister Mary, R.S.M., Ph.D.'42, Univ. of Notre Dame; Dean, College Misericordia, Dallas, Pa., since 1946.

App, Isaac D., B.S.'05, M.S.'11, Ed.D.'40, Susquehanna Univ.; Co. Supt. of Sch., Harrisburg, Pa., since 1922.

Arnold, William E., A.B.'21, Ky. Wesleyan Col.; M.A.'27, Columbia Univ.; Ph.D.'32, Ohio State Univ.; Prof. of Educ., Univ. of Pa., Philadelphia, Pa., since 1935.

Artman, William Edgar, B.S.'33, State Tchrs. Col., Bloomsburg, Pa.; M.Ed.'46, Pa. State Col.; Supvg. Prin., Juniata Valley Sch., Alexandria, Pa., since 1952.

Ashby, Lloyd W., A.B.'26, Hastings Col.; M.A. '35, Ed.D.'50, Tchrs. Col., Columbia Univ.; Prin., Cheltenham Twp. H. S., Elkins Park, Pa., since 1950.

Asper, William W., A.B.'37, Lafayette Col.; M.Ed.'42, State Col.; Supvg. Prin. of Sch., Jonestown, Pa., since 1946.

Aurand, O. H., B.S.'21, Susquehanna Univ.; M.A.'32, D.Ed., Tchrs. Col., Columbia Univ.; Prof. of Educ., Pa. State Col., State Col., Pa., since 1950.

Azarias, Brother, F.S.C., A.B.'24, A.M.'27, La Salle Col.; Ed.D.'51, Univ. of Pa.; Head, Dept. of Educ., La Salle Col., Philadelphia, Pa., since 1947.

Bailey, Helen Cheyney, B.S. in Ed.'19, M.S. in Ed.'31, Univ. of Pa.; Supt. of Sch., Philadelphia, Pa., since 1951.

Baily, Carl S., A.B.'19, Wash. and Jefferson Col.; Supt., Swissdale Sch. Dist., Pittsburgh, Pa., since 1934.

Bair, Medill, B.S.'35, State Tchrs. Col., Trenton N. J.; M.A.'39, Tchrs. Col., Columbia Univ.; Supt. of the Pennsbury Schs., Fallsington, Pa.

Baird, Betty, B.S.'31, Lock Haven State Tchrs. Col., Pa.; M.A.'31, Columbia Univ.; Asst. Co. Supt. of Sch., Lock Haven, Pa., since 1931.

Baker, A. F., B.S.'29, M.A.'31, Univ. of Pittsburgh; Supvg. Prin. of Twp. Sch., Bridgeville, Pa., since 1929.

Bamberger, Russell Elwood, B.S.'24, M.S.'25, Gettysburg Col.; Supvg. Prin. of Glen-nor Jr.-Sr. H. S., Glenolden, Pa., since 1945.

Barner, Robert P., A.B.'16, Univ. of Pittsburgh; A.M.'27, Columbia Univ.; Supt. of Sch., Rochester, Pa., since 1934.

Barnett, Ralph E., B.S.'29, Juniata Col.; M.Ed. '35, Pa. State Col.; Asst. Co. Supt. of Sch., Somerset, Pa., since 1942.

Barnhart, Charles J., B.S.'39, State Tchrs. Col., Slippery Rock, Pa.; M.Ed.'47, Univ. of Pittsburgh; Supvg. Prin., Blawnox Sch. Dist., Springdale, Pa., since 1947.

Bartholonew, Richard H., A.B.'28, M.Ed.'42, Pa. State Col.; Supvg. Prin. of Sch., Athens, Pa., since 1949.

Battle, Elizabeth G., B.S. in Ed.'26, Marrywood Col.; Supt. of Sch., Pittston, Pa., since 1938.

Baugher, R. R., Supvg. Prin. of Pub. Sch., Slatington, Pa.

Bay, James Campbell, A.B.'12, Oberlin Col.; A.M.'16, Columbia Univ.; Ph.D.'27, New York Univ.; Supt. of Sch., Easton, Pa., since 1922.

Bazard, Walter S., A.B.'16, Washington and Jefferson Col.; Ed.M.'32, Univ. of Pittsburgh; Supvg. Prin. of Har-Brack Union H. S., Brackenridge, Pa., since 1947.

Beahm, W. I., B.S.'29, Elizabethtown Col.; M.Ed.'40, Temple Univ.; Supvg. Prin of Sch., Mount Joy, Pa., since 1946.

Beamer, Henry G., M.A.'32, Univ. of Pittsburgh; Supt. of Sch., East Pittsburgh, Pa., since 1946.

Bean, Harold J., B.S.'26, Univ. of Pa.; Dir. of Curtis Voc. Plan, Curtis Circulation Co., Philadelphia, Pa.

Beattie, Alfred W., B.S.'22, Allegheny Col.; M.A.'24, Ph.D.'31, Univ. of Pittsburgh; Co. Supt. of Sch., Pittsburgh, Pa., since 1948.

Beck, John E., B.S. in Ed.'40, State Tchrs. Col., California, Pa.; M.Ed.'50, Univ. of Pittsburgh; Supvg. Prin., South Connellsville Borough Sch. and Connellsville Twp. Sch., South Connellsville, Pa., since 1948.

Beckett, Verona Elsey, B.S. in Ed.'28, M.S. in Ed.'32, Temple Univ.; Supvg. Prin., Kane Sch., Germantown, Philadelphia, Pa., since 1927.

Bedison, G. V., B.S.'35, Geneva Col.; Ed.M.'40, Univ. of Pittsburgh; Supvg. Prin. of Sch., Leetsdale, Pa., since 1946.

Beierschmitt, Gerald A., A.B.'25, Holy Cross Col.; A.M.'35, Bucknell Univ.; Supt. of Sch., Mt. Carmel, Pa., since 1934.

Bell, J. Ellis, B.S.'22, Westminster Col., New Wilmington, Pa.; M.A.'28, Tchrs. Col., Columbia Univ.; Supt. of Sch., Ellwood City, Pa., since 1938.

Bell, Lewis Wheeler, M.A.'36, Columbia Univ.; Supvr. Prin. of Sch. Duncannon, Pa., since 1948.

Bell, Requa W., A.B.'16, William Jewell Col.; A.M.'26, Univ. of Okla.; Supvg. Prin. of Sch., Jenkintown, Pa., since 1938.

Berkey, Harry D., B.S.'31, State Tchrs. Col., Indiana, Pa.; Ed.M.'38, Univ. of Pittsburgh; Supt. of Sch., Arnold, Pa., since 1950.

Bertin, Eugene P., B.A. (Jurisprudence)'17, Bucknell Univ.; M.A. (Comparative Lit.)'25, Harvard Univ.; Asst. Exec. Secy., Pa. State Educ. Assn., Harrisburg, Pa., since 1947.

*Betts, Emmett Albert, B.S.'25, Des Moines Univ.; M.A.'28, Ph.D.'31, State Univ. of Iowa; Dir. of Reading Clinic, Temple Univ., Philadelphia, Pa., since 1945.

Biemesderfer, Daniel L., A.B.'21, Franklin and Marshall Col.; M.A.'31, Univ. of Pa.; Litt.D. '43, Muhlenberg Col.; Pres., State Tchrs. Col., Millersville, Pa., since 1943.

Bingeman, Joseph Wade, B.S. in Ec.'27, Franklin and Marshall Col.; M.A.'34, Columbia Univ.; D.Ed.'44, Temple Univ.; Supvg. Prin., East Donegal Sch., Maytown, Pa., since 1937.

Birch, Jack W., Ph.D.'51, Univ. of Pittsburgh; Dir. of Spec. Educ., Pub. Sch., Pittsburgh, Pa., since 1948.

Blakley, William J., A.B.'29, Westminster Col.; M.Ed.'37, Univ. of Pittsburgh; Supvg. Prin., Jefferson Twp. Sch., Large, Pa., since 1950.

Bluebaugh, Ralph D., B.A.'40, Washington and Jefferson Col.; Master's'47, Univ. of Pittsburgh; Supvg. Prin., Chartiers Twp. Sch. Dist., Washington, Pa., since 1947.

*Boehm, Charles H., A.B.'23, Franklin and Marshall Col.; A.M.'26, Tchrs. Col., Columbia Univ.; Ed.D.'49, Rutgers Univ.; Co. Supt. of Sch., Doylestown, Pa., since 1940.

Bohern, Karl, Ed.D.'46, Univ. of Pittsburgh; Supt. of Sch., Clairton, Pa., since 1950.

Bolan, H. S., Supt. of Sch., Lebanon, Pa.

Bond, Horace Mann, A.B.'23, Lincoln Univ.; A.M.'26, Ph.D.'36, Univ. of Chicago; Pres., Lincoln Univ., Lincoln University, Pa., since 1945.

Boniface, Mother Mary, B.A.'21, Col. of New Rochelle; M.A.'39, Catholic Univ. of America; Pres., Rosemont Col., Rosemont, Pa., since 1946.

Boughner, W. L., Supvg. Prin. of Sch., West Elizabeth, Pa.

Bounds, Clyde E., B.S.'19, Washington Col.; M.A.'27, Univ. of Pa.; Supt. of Sch., Windber, Pa., since 1941.

Boyer, Phillip A., Ph.D.'20, Univ. of Pa.; Assoc. Supt. of Sch., Philadelphia, Pa. (retired, 1952). Address: The Ballinger Co., 121 N. Broad St., Philadelphia 7, Pa.

Boyle, Joseph E., A.B.'25, Mt. St. Mary's Col.; M.Ed.'36, Pa. State Col.; Supt. of Sch., Mahanoy City, Pa., since 1942.

Braden, C. B., Supvg. Prin. of Sch., Daisytown, Pa.

Brady, Edward A., B.A.'18, Dickinson Col.; M.A.'36, Bucknell Univ.; Supt. of Sch., Minersville, Pa., since 1941.

Bredlinger, LeRoy R., B.S.'46, State Tchrs. Col., West Chester, Pa.; M.S.'49, Univ. of Pa.; Supvg. Prin., Lower Pottsgrove Twp. Sch. Dist., Sanatoga, Pa., since 1949.

Brenner, Frank E., A.B.'31, Pa. State Col.; M.Ed.'44, Temple Univ.; Supvg. Prin. of Sch., Cornwall, Pa., since 1951.

Brewer, Karl M., B.A.'33, M.Ed.'38, Pa. State Col.; Supt. of Sch., Du Bois, Pa., since 1942.

Brinton, Charles A., B.S.'21, Haverford Col.; M.A.'40, Univ. of Pa.; Supvg. Prin., Clifton Heights, Pa., 1935-50. Address: R. D. 1, Biglerville, Pa.

Broad, Lambert E., A.B.'27, Lehigh Univ.; A.M.'31, Univ. of Pittsburgh; Prin., Mining and Mech. Inst., Freeland, Pa., since 1934.

Brocker, Robert John, Sch. Arch. and Engr., Coulter Bldg., Greensburg, Pa., since 1922.

Brown, Cardin D., B.S.'35, State Tchrs. Col., Kutztown, Pa.; M.Ed.'40, Pa. State Col.; Supvg. Prin., Plymouth-Whitemarsh Twp. Sch., Norristown, Pa., since 1944.

Brown, Robert, Supt. of Sch. Dist. 4, Philadelphia, Pa.

Bruce, David Harry, M.A.'38, Ph.D.'44, Univ. of Pittsburgh; Supt., West Mifflin Boro Sch. Dist., West Mifflin, Pa., since 1944.

Bruggeman, Ednamae, A.B.'34, Allegheny Col.; M.A.'44, Univ. of Pittsburgh; Educ. Consultant, Scott Foresman & Co., Pittsburgh, Pa.

Bryan, Charles H., B.S.'34, State Tchrs. Col., California, Pa.; Supvg. Prin., East Bethlehem Twp. Sch. Dist., Fredericktown, Pa., since 1949.

Bryan, Fred E., B.S.'33, State Tchrs. Col., California, Pa.; M.A.'37, Columbia Univ.; D.Ed. '52, Univ. of Pittsburgh; Supt. of Sch., Uniontown, Pa., since 1950.

Bulick, Samuel B., B.S.'17, Susquehanna Univ.; Ed.M.'33, Univ. of Pittsburgh; Ph.D.'45, Webster Col.; Supt. of Sch., Greensburg, Pa., since 1941.

Burkard, William E., B.S.'17, M.A.'25, Ph.D., Univ. of Pa.; Assoc. Supt. of Sch., Philadelphia, Pa., since 1951.

Burke, P. J., Diploma '13, State Tchrs. Col., East Stroudsburg, Pa.; Cert. '23, Wharton Sch. of Accts. and Finance, Univ. of Pa.; B.A.'26, Univ. of Scranton; M.A.'36, Bucknell Univ.; Supt., Mt. Carmel Twp. Sch., Locust Gap, Pa., since 1933.

Burkhart, J. Paul, A.B.'27, Albright Col.; M.A.'30, Columbia Univ.; Co. Supt. of Sch., Carlisle, Pa., since 1946.

Burkholder, W. Clay, B.S.'35, Juniata Col.; M.Ed.'41, Pa. State Col.; Co. Supt. of Sch., Lewistown, Pa.

Burton, Frank L., A.B.'20, Westminster Col., New Wilmington, Pa.; M.A.'28, Univ. of Pittsburgh; D.Ped.'45, Westminster Col.; Supt. of Sch., New Castle, Pa., since 1942.

Butterweck, Joseph S., B.S. in Ed.'22, M.A.'24, Univ. of Pa.; Ph.D.'26, Columbia Univ.; Dir., Div. of Secondary Educ. and Prof. of Educ., Temple Univ., Philadelphia, Pa., since 1926.

Butts, James E., A.B.'20, Juniata Col.; A.M.'25, Columbia Univ.; Co. Supt. of Sch., Hollidaysburg, Pa., since 1942.

Cameron, Donald L., B.A.'33, Juniata Col.; M.Ed.'47, Pa. State Col.; Supvr. of Special Educ. for Somerset Co. Sch., Somerset, Pa., since 1948.

Campbell, A. L., B.S.'30, State Tchrs. Col., Slippery Rock, Pa.; M.Ed., Univ. of Pittsburgh; Supvg. Prin., Apollo Area Jt. Sch., Apollo, Pa., since 1950.

Campbell, Charles M., A.B.'33, Grove City Col.; M.Ed.'41, Univ. of Pittsburgh; Supvg. Prin., Mt. Oliver Sch., Pittsburgh, Pa., since 1951.

Carson, Thomas E., Jr., B.S.'31, Bethany Col.; Ed.M.'34, Ph.D.'44, Univ. of Pittsburgh; Supvg. Prin. of North Allegheny Joint Sch., Pittsburgh, Pa., since 1948.

Carter, E. Frank, B.S.'33, State Tchrs. Col., California, Pa.; M.A. in Ed.'37, Univ. of Pittsburgh; Supt. of Rostraver Twp. Sch., Belle Vernon, Pa., since 1938.

Carter, R. Glenn, A.B.'32, Pa. State Col.; M.Ed.'38, Univ. of Pittsburgh; Dist. Supt. of Twp. Sch., Franklin, Pa., since 1948.

Cartwright, John S., A.B.'26, Cornell Univ.; A.M.'40, New York Univ.; Supt. of Sch., Allentown, Pa., since 1950.

Carvolth, R. T., B.S.'21, M.A.'34, Bucknell Univ.; Supt., Blakely Borough Sch., Peckville, Pa., since 1942.

Cassler, George W., B.S.'20, Susquehanna Univ.; M.S.'31, Pa. State Col.; Asst. Supt., Allegheny Co. Sch., Pittsburgh, Pa., since 1943.

Champlin, Carroll D., A.B.'14, A.M.'15, Haverford Col.; Ph.D.'25, Univ. of Pittsburgh; Prof. of Educ., Pa. State Col., State College, Pa., since 1926.

Chandler, Paul G., B.A.'14, Ky. Wesleyan Col.; M.A.'20, Ph.D.'30, Columbia Univ.; Pres., State Tchrs. Col., Clarion, Pa., since 1937.

Chapman, Ernest T., Diploma '11, Ashland Col.; B.S.'26, Univ. of Pittsburgh; Supt. of Sch., New Kensington, Pa., since 1924.

Christman, Paul Snyder, B.S.'19, M.Sc.'21, Ped.D.'50, Franklin & Marshall Col.; Supt. of Sch., Schuylkill Haven, Pa., since 1931.

Church, W. H., D.Ed.'42, Univ. of Pittsburgh; Supt. of Sch., McKees Rocks, Pa., since 1926.

Clark, A. G., B.S.'28, Muskingum Col.; M.A.'38, Ph.D.'48, Univ. of Pittsburgh; Supvg. Prin. of Avonworth Sch., Ben Avon, Pittsburgh, Pa., since 1946.

Claude, John, Special Rep., Sch. Sales, Rockwell Manufacturing Co., Pittsburgh, Pa., since 1946.

Clipman, William Henry, Jr., A.B.'19, Washington and Jefferson Col.; M.A.'27, Bucknell Univ.; Supt. of Sch., Charleroi, Pa., since 1946.

Coates, Robert H., B.S. in Ed.'30, M.S. in Ed.'37, Temple Univ.; Special Asst. to the Dir., Div. of Sch. Extension, Bd. of Educ., Philadelphia, Pa., since 1947.

Cober, John G., B.S. in Ed.'38, State Tchrs. Col., Indiana, Pa.; M.Ed.'46, Univ. of Pittsburgh; Supvg. Prin. O'Hara Twp. Sch., Pittsburgh, Pa., since 1947.

Cobley, Herbert F., M.A. in Ed.'47, Lehigh Univ.; Assoc. Supt., Bloomsburg Sch. Dist., Bloomsburg, Pa.

Cocklin, Warren H., B.S.'23, Franklin and Marshall Col.; A.M.'31, Univ. of Pa.; Supt., Upper Merion Twp. Sch., King of Prussia, Pa., since 1944.

Cogley, Jesse W., Jr., A.B.'27, Westminster Col., Pa.; M.Ed.'37, Univ. of Pittsburgh; Supvg. Prin. of Sch., Patton, Pa., since 1947.

Cole, E. W., Headmaster, Shady Side Academy, Pittsburgh, Pa.

Cole, John S., Ph.B.'26, Muhlenberg Col.; M.A.'31, New York Univ.; Supvg. Prin. of Twp. Sch., Easton, Pa., since 1921.

Coleman, Arthur Prudden, B.A.'20, Wesleyan Univ.; M.A.'22, Ph.D.'25, Columbia Univ.; Pres., Alliance Col., Cambridge Springs, Pa., since 1950.

Colton, Harold John, A.B.'24, Thiel Col.; A.M.'29, Columbia Univ.; Ph.D.'39, Univ. of Pittsburgh; Supvg. Prin. of Sch., Bridgeville, Pa., since 1931.

Cooper, E. Newbold, S.B.'21, Haverford Col.; M.A.'25, Univ. of Pa.; Ed.D.'47, Rutgers Univ.; Vicepres., Girard Col., Philadelphia, Pa., since 1949.

Cornelius, Clair R., A.B.'37, Juniata Col.; M.Ed. '42, Pa. State Col.; Supvg. Prin. of Sch., Osceola Mills, Pa., since 1946.

Cottrell, Elmer B., B.P.E.'19, M.P.E.'24, Springfield Col.; B.S.'28, Ed.D.'36, Univ. of Pittsburgh; Chief, Health and Phys. Educ., State Dept. of Pub. Instr., Harrisburg, Pa., since 1947.

Cowan, I. Newton B.S.'30, Franklin and Marshall Col.; M.E.D.'41, Temple Univ.; Supvg. Prin., Hatfield Jt. Consol. Sch., Hatfield, Pa., since 1951.

Craig, James C., B.S.'33, Carnegie Inst. of Tech.; M.A.'37, Univ. of Pittsburgh; Assoc. Prof. of Elem. Educ., Univ. of Pittsburgh, Pittsburgh, Pa., since 1950.

Craig, Sam B., B.A.'23, Litt.D.'51, Centre Col.; M.A.'25, Litt.D.'51, Gallaudet Col.; M.A.'27, George Washington Univ.; Supt., Western Pa. Sch. for the Deaf, Pittsburgh, Pa., since 1946.

Craven, Samuel D., B.S.'35, Univ. of Pa.; M.Ed.'41, Temple Univ.; Supvg. Prin., Borough Sch. Dist., Folcroft, Pa., since 1949.

Cressman, Paul L., B.S.'25, Univ. of Pittsburgh; Ed.D.'34, Pa. State Col.; Dir., Bureau of Instr., State Dept. of Pub. Instr., Harrisburg, Pa., since 1936.

Crouthamel, E. Merton, A.B.'14, Juniata Col.; M.Ed.'36, Temple Univ.; Supvg. Prin. of Sch., Souderton, Pa., since 1922.

Crumbling, C. S., B.S., Albright Col.; M.S., Cornell Univ.; Supt. of Twp. Sch., Laureldale, Pa., since 1946.

Culler, Ned, B.S.'29, M.Ed.'37, Pa. State Col.; Ed.D.'45, Univ. of Pittsburgh; Supt. of Sch., Connellsville, Pa.

Cushman, Charles Leslie, A.B.'21, Grinnell Col.; Ph.D.'27, State Univ. of Iowa; Assoc. Supt. of Sch., Philadelphia, Pa., since 1943.

Daldy, A. Cyril, B.A.'22, Oxford Univ., England; Mgr. of Sch. and Col. Serv., Sun Oil Co., Philadelphia, Pa., since 1946.

Dalton, Clyde E., B.S.'35, State Tchrs. Col., West Chester, Pa.; A.M.'38, Tchrs. Col., Columbia Univ.; Supvg. Prin. of Sch., Marcus Hook, Pa., since 1945.

Daum, Henry F., Bus. Mgr., Sch. Dist of Abington Twp., Abington, Pa.

Davidson, Robert L. D., A.B.'31, Dickinson Col.; Ed.M.'37, Ed.D.'47, Temple Univ.; Asst. Dean, Community Col., Temple Univ., Philadelphia, Pa., since 1945.

Davies, Gordon T., B.S.'33, State Tchrs. Col., Edinboro, Pa.; M.Ed.'39, Pa. State Col.; Supvg. Prin. of Sch., Johnsonburg, Pa., since 1948.

Davies, Gwilym D., B.A.'34, M. of Ed.'46, Univ. of Pittsburgh; Supervising Prin., Millersburg Boro. Sch., Millersburg, Pa., since 1952.

Davies, Marcus W., B.S.'27, Waynesburg Col.; Ed.M.'36, Univ. of Pittsburgh; Supvg. Prin. of Sch., Coraopolis, Pa., since 1949.

Davis, Bennett H., B.S.'32, State Tchrs. Col., W. Chester, Pa.; M.Ed.'48, Temple Univ.; Supvg. Prin. of Sch., Linwood, Pa., since 1948.

Davis, Clyde M., B.S.'34, Temple Univ.; Supvg. Prin., New Hope-Solebury Sch., New Hope, Pa., since 1942.

Davis, Donald P., B.A.'20, M.A.'30, Ph.D.'35, Univ. of Pittsburgh; Field Rep., U. S. Office of Educ., Main Capitol Bldg., Harrisburg, Pa., since 1945.

Davis, Earle C., B.S.'27, New York Univ.; M.Ed.'33, Univ. of Pittsburgh; Supvg. Prin. of Sch., North East, Pa., since 1927.

Davis, Frank Garfield, Ph.B.'11, Bucknell Univ.; M.A.'24, Columbia Univ.; Ph.D.'30, New York Univ.; Head, Dept. of Educ., Bucknell Univ., Lewisburg, Pa., since 1924.

Dean, Clarence, B.S.'37, M.E.'43, Univ. of Pittsburgh; Prin., Homeville Jr. H. S., West Mifflin, Pa., since 1939.

Decker, Henry B., Ed.M.'49, Temple Univ.; Asst. Regional Supt., Delhaas H. S., Bristol, Pa., since 1950.

Deery, Edward B., B.S. in Elem. Ed.'38, Muskingum Col.; M.S. in Ed.'40, Temple Univ.; Supt. of Sch., Darby, Pa., since 1950.

Delahunty, Kenneth R., A.B.'31, Westminster Col.; M.Ed.'37, Penn State Col.; Supvr. Prin., Hickory Twp. Sch. Dist., Sharon, Pa., since 1952.

Denniston, A. Bruce, B.S.'25, M.A.'28, Ed.D.'42, Univ. of Pittsburgh; Supt. of Sch., Altoona, Pa., since 1950.

Derr, LaRue C., M.A. in Ed.'42, Temple Univ.; Supvg. Prin. of Sch., Highspire, Pa., since 1947.

Dessenberger, Vernon H. W., Ed.M.'40, Temple Univ.; Supvg. Prin., Sharon Hill Sch. Dist., Sharon Hill, Pa., since 1949.

500

Diehl, Fred W., M.S. in Ed.'35, Bucknell Univ.; Co. Supt. of Sch., Danville, Pa., since 1918.

Dieruff, Louis E., Ph.B.'29, Muhlenberg Col.; Secy., Bus. Mgr., Pub. Sch., Allentown, Pa., since 1948.

Dimmick, Earl A., A.B.'16, Albright Col.; M.A.'25, Ed.D.'37, Univ. of Pittsburgh; LL.D.'46, Albright Col.; LL.D.'48, Univ. of Pittsburgh; Supt. of Sch., Pittsburgh, Pa., 1945-51.

Dolbear, Frank T., M.Ed.'32, Pa. State Col.; Supvg. Prin. of Sch., Tunkhannock, Pa., since 1935.

Donaldson, W. H., M.Ed.'38, Univ. of Pittsburgh; Co. Supt. of Sch., Washington, Pa., since 1946.

Donato, Robert V., B.A.'38, Pa. State Col.; M.S.'45, Univ. of Pa.; Supt. of Ridley Twp. Sch. Dist., Folsom, Pa., since 1950.

Donohue, Francis J., A.B.'34, M.A.'36, Fordham Univ.; Ph.D.'44, Univ. of Mich.; Head, Dept. of Educ., Villanova Col., Villanova, Pa., since 1949.

Douds, Howard C., M.A.'37, Univ. of Pittsburgh; Supvg. Prin. of Sch., Verona, Pa., since 1944.

Duckrey, James Henry, A.B.'23, Univ. of Pa.; M.S.'27, Ed.D.'39, Temple Univ.; Pres., Cheyney State Tchrs. Col., Cheyney, Pa., since 1951.

Duda, Stanley R., M.E.'48, Univ. of Pittsburgh; Prin., Emerson Sch., Duquesne, Pa., since 1948.

Dugan, John E., A.B.'26, A.M.'29, Princeton Univ.; Ed.D.'32, Rutgers Univ.; Head, Dept. of Educ., Beaver Col., Jenkintown, Pa., since 1946.

Dumbauld, George W., M.A.'38, Tchrs. Col., Columbia Univ.; A.B.'29, Susquehanna Univ.; Asst. Co. Supt. of Sch., Uniontown, Pa., since 1938.

Dunmire, Burt, B.A.'41, Thiel Col.; Ed.M.'47, Univ. of Pittsburgh; Supt., Kittanning Borough Sch. Dist., Kittanning, Pa., since 1952.

Dunn, James C., B.S.'24, Pa. State Col.; M.Ed. '34, Univ. of Pittsburgh; Supvg. Prin. of Sch., McDonald, Pa., since 1950.

Eberhart, Guy F., B.S.'36, W. Va. Univ.; M.Ed. '47, Univ. of Pittsburgh; Supvg. Prin. of Sch., Somerset, Pa., since 1951.

*Eck, Lee, A.B.'26, Albright Col.; M.S.'31, Lebanon Valley Col.; Supvg. Prin. of Sch., Richland, Pa., since 1926.

Eckles, Port, A.M.'24, Univ. of Pittsburgh; Supt. of Sch., Homestead, Pa., since 1922.

Eichler, George A., A.B.'14, Muhlenberg Col.; M.A.'28, Ed.D.'34, Pa. State Col.; Supt. of Sch., Northampton, Pa., since 1930.

Elliott, Alvin W., B.S. in Ed.'34, State Tchrs. Col., Slippery Rock, Pa.; Ed.M.'43, Univ. of Pittsburgh; Supvg. Prin. of Center Twp. Sch., Monaca, Pa., since 1939.

Emerich, David J., B.S.'32, State Tchrs. Col., Millersville, Pa.; Ed.M.'48, Temple Univ.; Supvg. Prin. of Sch., Hummelstown, Pa., since 1950.

Emery, Charles P., M.A.'41, Univ. of Pa.; Supvg. Prin. of Sch., Downingtown, Pa., since 1946.

Engle, Carl R., B.S.'36, State Tchrs. Col., Kutztown, Pa.; M.S.'47, Univ. of Pa.; Supvg. Prin., Hill Street Sch., Upland, Pa., since 1949.

English, O. H., B.S. in Ed.'29, M.A.'32, D.Ed.'42, Univ. of Pittsburgh; Supt. of Twp. Sch., Abington, Pa., since 1950.

Engstrom, G. Evan, A.B.'18, Allegheny Col.; M.Sc.'37, Pa. State Col.; Supt. of City Sch., Tarentum, Pa., since 1942.

Erdly, Calvin V., B.S.'20, Susquehanna Univ.; M.S.'33, Pa. State Col.; Pd.D.'43, Susquehanna Univ.; Supt. of Sch., Lewistown, Pa., since 1938.

Eshelman, Arthur W., B.S.'27, Elizabethtown Col.; M.A.'31, Columbia Univ.; Supvg. Prin. of Twp. Sch., Paradise, Pa., since 1935.

Eshelman, Walter W., A.B.'30, Elizabethtown Col.; LL.B.'31, Blackstone Inst.; A.M.'33, Columbia Univ.; Ed.D.'41, New York Univ.; Supvg. Prin. of Twp. Sch., Ft. Washington, Pa., since 1945.

Evans, William C., A.B.'19, Lebanon Valley Col.; Ed.M.'41, Univ. of Pittsburgh; Supvg. Prin. of Sch., Dillsburg, Pa., since 1947.

Farley, Eugene Shedden, B.S.'21, Pa. State Col.; M.A.'27, Ph.D.'33, Univ. of Pa.; Pres., Wilkes Col., Wilkes-Barre, Pa., since 1936.

Faust, Beaver S., A.B.'29, Susquehanna Univ.; A.M.'39, Univ. of Pittsburgh; Juniata Co. Sch., Mifflintown, Pa.

Faust, J. Frank, B.Sc.'15, Susquehanna Univ.; M.A.'28, Columbia Univ.; Ed.D.'35, Pa. State Col.; Supt. of Sch., Chambersburg, Pa., since 1940.

Ferguson, Arthur W., B.S.'12, Univ. of Pa.; A.M.'20, Lafayette Col.; Ph.D.'24, Univ. of Pa.; Supt. of Sch., York, Pa., since 1930.

First, William H., B.S.'30, Allegheny Col.; M.S.'38, Univ. of Chicago; Supvg. Prin. of Sch., California, Pa., since 1940.

Fisher, Marshall, A.B.'31, Westminster Col., New Wilmington, Pa.; M.Ed.'40, Univ. of Pittsburgh; Supt. of Sch., Titusville, Pa., since 1947.

Fisher, W. H., Formerly Secy.-Bus. Mgr., Allentown Sch. Dist., Allentown, Pa.

Flanagan, John C., B.S.'29, M.A.'32, Univ. of Wash.; Ph.D.'34, Harvard Univ.; Prof. of Psych., Univ. of Pittsburgh, since 1946, and Dir. of Research, American Inst. for Research, Pittsburgh, Pa., since 1947.

Flegal, Edwin J., A.B.'35, Juniata Col.; M.A.'46, Tchrs. Col., Columbia Univ.; Supvg. Prin., Joint Sch., Portage, Pa., since 1948.

Ford, Thomas H., Ph.B.'14, Dickinson Col.; A.M.'25, Univ. of Pa.; Litt.D.'36, Albright Col.; Supt. of Sch., Reading, Pa., since 1933.

Fowler, Burton P., A.B.'07, Syracuse Univ.; A.M.'25, Tchrs. Col., Columbia Univ.; Ped.D. '39, Syracuse Univ.; Prin., Germantown Friends Sch., Germantown, Philadelphia, Pa., since 1941.

Francis, Thomas, B.S.'28, Pa. State Col.; M.A.'33, Columbia Univ.; Co. Supt. of Sch., Scranton, Pa., since 1926.

Franklin, Samuel P., A.B.'19, Union Col. (Ky.); M.A.'21, Northwestern Univ.; S.T.B.'24, Boston Univ.; Ph.D.'25, State Univ. of Iowa; Dean, Sch. of Educ., Univ. of Pittsburgh, Pittsburgh, Pa., since 1943.

Frantz, K. D., Supvg. Prin., Rice Ave. Union H. S., Girard, Pa.

Fretz, Floyd C., B.S.'27, M.Ed.'30, Univ. of Pa.; Supt. of Sch., Bradford, Pa., since 1936.

Fritz, J. Elias, B.S.'31, Franklin and Marshall Col.; Supvg. Prin., E. Lampeter Twp. H. S., Lancaster, Pa., since 1948.

Fromuth, Carl L., B.S. in Ed.'23; M.Ed.'32, Temple Univ.; Supt., Dist. #1, Pub. Sch., Philadelphia, Pa., since 1952.

Fruth, Jacob Richard, A.B.'32, Geneva Col.; M.A.'41, Duke Univ.; Supvr. Prin. of Sch., Freedom, Pa., since 1951.

Furjanic, Frank S., Pres., Sch. Board, Pittsburgh, Pa., since 1949.

Gable, Martha A., Ed.B.'29, Ind. Univ.; Ed.M. '35, Temple Univ.; Asst. Dir., Sch.-Community Relations, Bd. of Educ., Philadelphia, Pa., since 1949.

501

PENNSYLVANIA

Gallagher, Joseph D., A.B.'26, Univ. of Pa.; M.A.'37, New York Univ.; Supt. of Hazle Twp. Sch., Hazleton, Pa., since 1938.

Garber, Lee O., B.S.'20, Ill. Wesleyan Univ.; M.S.'26, Univ. of Ill.; Ph.D.'32, Univ. of Chicago; Assoc. Prof. of Educ., Univ. of Pa., Philadelphia, Pa., since 1949.

Gayman, Harvey E., B.S.'16, Cornell Univ.; M.A.'33, Columbia Univ.; Exec. Secy., Pa. State Educ. Assn., Harrisburg, Pa., since 1939.

Gehman, A. L., A.B.'09, Franklin and Marshall Col.; A.M.'18, Tchrs. Col., Columbia Univ.; Supt. of Springfield Twp. Sch., Chestnut Hill, Philadelphia, Pa., since 1922.

Gehring, C. H., B.A.'39, Moravian Col.; M.A.'50, Lehigh Univ.; Prin., Fountain Hill Jr. H. S., Bethlehem, Pa., since 1947.

Geiges, Ellwood A., B.S.'16, M.S.'23, Temple Univ.; Ed.D.'45, Columbia Univ. and Temple Univ.; Supt. of Sch., Norristown, Pa., since 1945.

Geigle, Ralph C., A.B.'35, Susquehanna Univ.; M.A.'40, Columbia Univ.; Ed.D.'50, George Wash. Univ.; Supvg. Prin., Susquenita Joint Sch., Duncannon, Pa., since 1952.

Geiss, Newton W., A.B.'15, Muhlenberg Col.; A.M.'23, Univ. of Pa.; Co. Supt. of Sch., Reading, Pa., since 1946.

Gemmill, Charles W., A.B.'18, Lebanon Valley Col.; A.M.'25, Tchrs. Col., Columbia Univ.; Supvg. Prin. of Sch., New Cumberland, Pa., since 1927.

Gerlach, H. K., B.S.'33, Elizabethtown Col.; M.S. in Ed. Adm.'38, Univ. of Pa.; Supvg. Prin., Southern Lancaster Co. Joint Sch., Quarryville, Pa., since 1951.

Getty, R. F., B.S.'21, Susquehanna Univ.; M.Ed.'35, Pa. State Col.; Supt. of Sch., Huntingdon, Pa., since 1949.

Gill, J. A., B.S.'28, M.Ed.'36, Univ. of Pittsburgh; Prin., Elem. Sch., West Mifflin, Pa., since 1947.

Gilland, Thomas M., A.B.'09, Ursinus Col.; A.M.'26, Tchrs. Col., Columbia Univ.; Ph.D. '35, Univ. of Chicago; Dir. of Student Tchg. and Placement, State Tchrs. Col., California, Pa., since 1931.

Glasser, Robert J., M.Ed.'52, Pa. State Col.; Supvg. Prin., Warriors Mark-Franklin Sch., Warriors Mark, Pa., since 1952.

Gockley, Clarence M., Diploma '17, State Tchrs. Col., West Chester, Pa.; B.S.'30, Muhlenberg Col.; M.A.'40, Lehigh Univ.; Supt. of Sch., Whitehall Twp., Hokendauqua, Pa., since 1938.

Grebe, M. Alice, Diploma '18, Keystone State Normal Sch., Kutztown, Pa.; B.S.'32, Univ. of Pa.; Supvg. Prin. of Sch., Schwenksville, Pa., since 1935.

*Greenawalt, William C., A.B.'07, A.M.'12, Franklin and Marshall Col.; Supt. of Sch., Olean, N. Y., 1920-40. Address: 418 W. Market St., Orwigsburg, Pa.

Greth, Morris S., Acting Pres., Muhlenberg Col., Allentown, Pa.

Griffith, Edward D., A.B.'19, Lafayette Col.; M.A. '31, Univ. of Pa.; Eastern Mgr., Lyons and Carnahan, Wilkes-Barre, Pa., since 1943.

Griffith, H. T., B.S.'29, State Tchrs. Col., Millersville, Pa.; M.Ed.'34, Ed.D.'49, Pa. State Col.; Supt. of Sch., Steelton, Pa., since 1950.

Grim, Paul H., B.S.'27, Albright Col.; Supvg. Prin. of Sch., Pottstown, Pa., since 1940.

Grizzell, E. Duncan, B.A.'15, Yale Univ.; M.A.'19, Ph.D.'22, Univ. of Pa.; Dean, Sch. of Educ., since 1948, and Prof. of Educ., Univ. of Pa., Philadelphia, Pa., since 1929.

Groner, Earl F., B.S. in Ed.'32, State Tchrs. Col., East Stroudsburg, Pa.; M.A.'42, New York Univ.; Dist. Supt. of Sch., Stroudsburg, Pa., since 1950.

Grose, C. Herman, B.S.'16, W. Va. Wesleyan Col.; A.M.'27, Ph.D.'40, Univ. of Pittsburgh; Ped.D.'40, W. Va. Wesleyan Col.; LL.D.'50, Allegheny Col.; Pres., State Tchrs. Col., California, Pa., since 1952.

Gross, Ira C., B.S.'15, M.S.'17, Susquehanna Univ.; Supvg. Prin. of Southmont Sch., Johnstown, Pa., since 1934.

Grover, Arlton G., B.S.'31, M.E.'45, Univ. of Pittsburgh; Supvg. Prin., Harmony Twp. Sch. Dist., Ambridge, Pa., since 1950.

Grumbling, H. Virgil, B.S.'30, State Tchrs. Col., Indiana, Pa.; M.A.'38, Univ. of Pittsburgh; Pd.D.'51, Waynesburg Col.; Supt. of Sch., Oil City, Pa., since 1946.

Gruver, E. M., B.S.'24, Gettysburg Col.; M.Ed. '39, Temple Univ.; Supvg. Prin. of Conewago Joint Sch. System, East Berlin, Pa., since 1948.

Guerrier, Joseph A., B.S. in Ec.'29, M.E.'36, Duquesne Univ.; Supvg. Prin. of Sch., Natrona, Pa., since 1946.

Gustin, Seth, A.B.'27, Susquehanna Univ.; M.A.'34, Columbia Univ.; Supvg. Prin., Jt. Consol. Sch., Mercer, Pa., since 1948.

Haas, Francis B., B.S.'13, Temple Univ.; M.A.'22, Univ. of Pa.; Pd.D.'25, Temple Univ.; LL.D. '34, Juniata Col.; Litt.D.'39, Bucknell Univ.; LL.D.'42, Univ. of Pittsburgh; State Supt. of Pub. Instr., Harrisburg, Pa., since 1939.

Haas, Frederick P., B.S.'49, Temple Univ.; Prin., Elem. Sch., Norwood, Pa.

Hackenberg, J. L., A.B.'20, Susquehanna Univ.; A.M.'29, Pa. State Col.; Supt. of Sch., Shamokin, Pa., since 1946.

Hackman, Arthur A., B.S.'31, State Tchrs. Col., Millersville, Pa.; M.A.'37, Columbia Univ.; Supvg. Prin., East Hempfield Twp. Sch., Landisville, Pa., since 1937.

Halderman, J. L., B.S.'22, Pa. State Col.; M.S.'32, Univ. of Pa.; Doctor's '45, Temple Univ.; Supvg. Prin., Springfield Twp. Sch., Springfield, Pa., since 1952.

Hallman, Mildred B., Prin., Franconia Consol. Sch., Souderton, Pa.

Handwork, Cora Lacey, Ph.B.'14, Dickinson Col.; M.S.'37, Univ. of Pa.; Supvg. Prin. of Sch., Birdsboro, Pa., since 1933.

Hanley, William M., B.S.'36, State Tchrs. Col., California, Pa.; Ed.M.'38, Univ. of Pittsburgh; Supvg. Prin., Albert Gallatin Joint Sch. System, Point Marion, Pa., since 1951.

Hardy, H. W., Supvg. Prin. of Twp. Sch., Derry, Pa.

Hare, H. Frank, B.S. in Ed.'24, M.S. in Ed.'34, Univ. of Pittsburgh; Sc.D. in Ed. (Hon.)'44, Gettysburg Col.; Supt. of Sch., Phoenixville, Pa.

Harman, Allen C., B.A.'26, Ursinus Col.; Ed.M. '34, Temple Univ.; Ph.D.'47, Univ. of Pa.; Asst. Co. Supt. of Sch., Willow Grove, Pa., since 1941.

Hartman, Joseph A., B.S.'26, Grove City Col.; A.M.'37, Ph.D.'49, Univ. of Pittsburgh; Supt. of Sch., Greenville, Pa., since 1950.

Hartz, Robert E., A.B.'16, Lebanon Valley Col.; Supvg. Prin. of Sch., Palmyra, Pa., since 1927.

Harvey, John A., Supvg. Prin. of Sch., Saegertown, Pa.

Harvey, Randolph B., A.B.'31, Susquehanna Univ.; M.A.'33, New York Univ.; Supt. of Sch., Coaldale, Pa., since 1939.

Hayes, Lynn, M.A.'43, New York Univ.; Supvg. Prin. of Sch., Pittsburgh, Pa., since 1948.

502

Hays, Jo, Diploma '18, State Tchrs. Col., Shippensburg, Pa.; A.B.'23, Pa. State Col.; Ed.M.'30, Harvard Univ.; Supvg. Prin. of Sch., State College, Pa., since 1927.

Heaton, Kenneth L., A.B.'24, Ind. Univ.; A.M.'26, Boston Univ.; Ph.D.'31, Univ. of Chicago; Richardson, Bellows, Henry and Co., Inc., Philadelphia, Pa.

Heckman, Oliver S., B.A.'22, Lebanon Valley Col.; M.A.'26, Univ. of Ill.; Ph.D.'39, Duke Univ.; Supvg. Prin., Neshaminy Sch., Langhorne, Pa.

Hedge, John W., Supt. of Sch., Bethlehem, Pa.

Heintzelman, Norman H., Ed.M.'37, Temple Univ.; Supvg. Prin., Jr. H. S., Malvern, Pa., since 1935.

Helmlinger, John D., B.A.'21, Allegheny Col.; Elem. Supvg., Stowe Twp. Pub. Sch., McKees Rocks, Pa., since 1949.

Hendricks, Howard L., B.S.'35, State Tchrs. Col., Mansfield, Pa.; M.S.'41, Bucknell Univ.; Supvg. Prin. of Sch., Millersburg, Pa., 1948-52.

Henninger, Arthur H., M.A.'30, Columbia Univ.; Supt., Schuylkill Co. Sch., Pottsville, Pa., since 1945.

Henry, Albert L., B.S.'33, State Tchrs. Col., Clarion, Pa.; M.Ed.'37, Pa. State Col.; Supvg. Prin. of Twp. Sch., Bradford, Pa., since 1948.

Henshaw, J. Harry, B.S.'22, Grove City Col.; M.S.'32, M.S. in Ed.'33, Pa. State Col.; Supt. of Sch., Hollidaysburg, Pa., since 1946.

Herbein, William B., Ph.B.'27, Muhlenberg Col.; M.A.'33, Univ. of Pa.; Asst. Co. Supt. of Sch., Topton, Pa., since 1946.

Herman, Thomas Jefferson, A.B.'12, Susquehanna Univ.; M.A.'25, Tchrs. Col., Columbia Univ.; Supvg. Prin. of Foster Twp. Sch., Freeland, Pa., since 1930.

Herr, Benjamin B., A.B.'11, D.Pd.'49, Franklin and Marshall Col.; A.M.'19, Columbia Univ.; Prin., J. P. McCaskey Sr. H. S., Lancaster, Pa., since 1937.

Hervey, E. Frances, Pres., Phila. Tchrs. Assn., Philadelphia, Pa.

Herzog, Webster Carl, Diploma '19, State Tchrs. Col., West Chester, Pa.; A.B.'23, Dickinson Col.; A.M.'31, Univ. of Pa.; Asst. Co. Supt. of Sch., West Chester, Pa., since 1934.

Hess, Glenn C., B.S. in Ed.'37, State Tchrs. Col., Indiana, Pa.; Ed.M.'39, Ed.D.'49, Univ. of Pittsburgh; Supvg. Prin., Richland Twp. Sch. Dist., Johnstown, Pa., since 1946.

Hetra, John, A.B.'26, Westminster Col.; M.Ed. '39, Univ. of Pittsburgh; Supt. of Sch., Farrell, Pa., since 1946.

Hibbs, Ben, Editor, *The Saturday Evening Post*, Philadelphia, Pa.

Hibschman, John A., B.Sc.'25, Franklin and Marshall Col.; Supvg. Prin., Lower Alsace Twp. Sch., Stony Creek Mills, Pa., since 1936.

Hickes, Roy M., B.S.'29, State Tchrs. Col., Indiana, Pa.; M.Ed.'34, Pa. State Col.; Ed.D.'51, Univ. of Pittsburgh; Supt. of Sch., Carnegie, Pa., since 1951.

Hickey, John M., B.S.'34, State Tchrs. Col., Edinboro, Pa.; Ed.M.'38, Ph.D.'45, Univ. of Pittsburgh; Supt. of Sch., Erie, Pa., since 1950.

Hill, Leslie P., A.B.'03, M.A.'04, Harvard Univ.; Pres. Emeritus, Cheyney State Tchrs. Col., Cheyney, Pa. Address: 46 Lincoln Ave., Yeadon, Pa.

Hinkle, Thomas L., Ph.B.'33, Muhlenberg Col.; M.S.'38, Bucknell Univ.; Supt. of Sch., Hazleton, Pa., since 1939.

Hoch, Reagan I., A.B.'20, Franklin and Marshall Col.; A.M.'27, Bucknell Univ.; Prin., Sr. H. S., Lock Haven, Pa., since 1929.

Hoelzle, Norman F., B.S.'23, Westminster Col.; M.Ed.'41, Duquesne Univ.; Asst. Supt. of Penn Twp. Sch., Pittsburgh, Pa., since 1933.

Hoke, Franklin L., Supvg. Prin., Sch. Dist. of Lower Moreland Twp., Huntingdon Valley, Pa.

Holt, Alfred S., B.Ed.'29, Keene Tchrs. Col., Keene, N. H.; M.Ed.'39, Pa. State Col.; Prin., Pub. Serv. Inst., Dept. of Pub. Instr., Harrisburg, Pa., since 1943.

Hood, Miller C., B.S.'41, State Tchrs. Col., Indiana, Pa.; M.Ed.'46, Univ. of Pittsburgh; Supvg. Prin., Everett Southern Joint Sch., Everett, Pa., since 1950.

Hooper, Laura, B.A.'18, Univ. of S. Dak.; Ph.D.'35, Yale Univ.; Dir., Illman Carter Unit for Kdgn.-Elem. Tchrs., Sch. of Educ., Univ. of Pa., Philadelphia, Pa., since 1946.

Hornbeck, James Wilford, M.A.'35, Washington and Jefferson Col.; Supvg. Prin., Plum Twp. Sch., Unity, Pa., since 1950.

Horsman, Ralph D., B.S.'29, M.Ed.'34, Ph.D.'40, Univ. of Pittsburgh; Supt. of Sch., Mt. Lebanon, Pittsburgh, Pa., since 1946.

Hottenstein, Gerald G., B.S.'38, Albright Col.; M.S. in Ed.'43, Univ. of Pa.; Supvg. Prin., North Wales Sch. Dist., North Wales, Pa., since 1952.

Houk, Dale W., A.B.'24, Park Col.; M.A.'33, Ed.D.'40, Univ. of Pittsburgh; Pres., State Tchrs. Col., Slippery Rock, Pa., since 1948.

Houseal, George M., B.S.'35, Millersville State Tchrs. Col.; M.S.'41, Temple Univ.; Prin., Harrison Jr. H. S., Lebanon, Pa., since 1951.

Hoyer, Louis P., M.S.'35, Temple Univ.; LL.D. '48, Drexel Inst. of Tech.; D.S.'49, Temple Univ.; LL.D.'49, Gettysburg Col.; Supt. of Sch., Philadelphia, Pa., since 1943.

Hozempa, A. J., A.B.'32, Univ. of Scranton; M.A.'38, Bucknell Univ.; Supvg. Prin. of Sch., Edwardsville, Pa., since 1951.

Hudson, Donald B., A.B.'35, Juniata Col.; A.M.'41, Duke Univ.; Supvg. Prin. of Sch., Union City, Pa., since 1951.

Hudson, J. H., B.S.'23, Geneva Col.; M.Ed.'35, Univ. of Pittsburgh; Supvg. Prin. of Sch., Mars, Pa., since 1935.

Hughes, M. V., A.B.'32, Susquehanna Univ.; A.M.'37, New York Univ.; Supvg. Prin. of Sch., Plains, Pa., since 1934.

Hughes, Ralph C., B.S.'20, Univ. of Chicago; Ed.M.'31, Univ. of Pittsburgh; Supvg. Prin. of Sch., Turtle Creek, Pa., since 1948.

Hughes, Ray O., A.B.'00, Brown Univ.; A.M.'24, Univ. of Pittsburgh; L.H.D.'41, Brown Univ. Address: 5517 Beverly Pl., Pittsburgh, Pa.

Hulton, John G., A.B.'18, Franklin Col.; M.Ed. '38, Univ. of Pittsburgh; LL.D.'44, St. Vincent Col.; Supt. of Sch., Latrobe, Pa., since 1929.

Hummer, William R., B.S.'46, West Chester State Tchrs. Col., Pa.; M.S.'48, Univ. of Pa.; Supvg. Prin., Lower Providence Twp. Sch. Dist., Norristown, Pa.

Hurley, Paul F., B.S.'48, Pa. State Tchrs. Col., Shippensburg; M.Ed.'51, Pa. State Col.; Supvg. Prin., Green Park Union Sch. Dist., Loysville, Pa., since 1952.

Husted, Inez M., M.A.'35, Ed.D.'39, Tchrs. Col., Columbia Univ.; Co. Supvr. of Special Educ., Wilkes-Barre, Pa., since 1939.

Illick, Montford E., B.S.'23, Lafayette Col.; M.A.'35, Lehigh Univ.; Supvg. Prin. of Sch., Hellertown, Pa., since 1928.

Ingraham, William W., B.S.'43, State Tchrs. Col., Lock Haven, Pa.; M.A.'49, Rutgers Univ.; Asst. Regional Supt., Yardley, Pa., since 1949.

Ingram, Evan W., A.B.'20, Bucknell Univ.; M.Ed.'39, Univ. of Pittsburgh; First Assoc. Supt. of Sch., in charge of Instr., Pittsburgh, Pa., since 1946.

Irons, Harold S., B.S. in Ed.'18, Ohio Univ.; M.A.'33, Ohio State Univ.; D.Ed.'42, Univ. of Pittsburgh; Supvg. Prin. of Sch., Sewickley, Pa., since 1943.

Jacks, Thomas A., Ph.B.'27, Muhlenberg Col.; M.A.'34, Tchrs. Col., Columbia Univ.; Prin., Harrison Morton Jr. H. S., Allentown, Pa., since 1946.

Jacques, L. Eugene, B.A.'37, M.Ed.'41, D.Ed.'52, Univ. of Pittsburgh; Supvg. Prin., Jersey Shore Borough Sch., Jersey Shore, Pa., since 1952.

Jewell, Ralph H., B.A.'29, Pa. State Col.; M.Ed.'39, Univ. of Pittsburgh; Supt. of Sch., Midland, Pa., since 1942.

Johnson, (Mrs.) Estella Scott, B.S.'34, State Tchrs. Col., Cheyney, Pa.; M.S. in Ed.'37, Univ. of Pa.; Admin. Asst. and Tchr., State Tchrs. Col., Cheyney, Pa., 1943-45 and since 1946.

Johnson, Lester F., A.B.'19, D.Sc.Ed.'49, Dickinson Col.; M.S.'38, Univ. of Pa.; Pres., York Jr. Col., York, Pa., since 1941.

Johnson, Royce Oliver, B.S.'45, State Tchrs. Col., Lock Haven, Pa.; M.Ed.'47, Univ. of Pittsburgh; Supvg. Prin., Lawrence Twp. Sch., Clearfield, Pa.

Johnston, David A., B.S.'29, Franklin and Marshall Col.; M.A. in Ed.'33, Cornell Univ.; Supvg. Prin. of Twp. Sch., 422 Price St., West Chester, Pa.

Johnston, Ernest Milton, B.S.'25, Grove City Col.; M.A.'32, Univ. of Pittsburgh; Supvg. Prin. of Sch., Ebensburg, Pa., since 1929.

Johnston, G. W., B.S.'29, Geneva Col.; Supvg. Prin. of Sch., New Castle, Pa., since 1932.

Jones, Charles S., B.S.'29, Bucknell Univ.; M.S.'43, Univ. of Pa.; Supvg. Prin., Hatboro Sch. Dist., Hatboro, Pa., since 1952.

Jones, D. Paul, A.B.'29, Washington and Jefferson Col.; Ed.M.'36, Univ. of Pittsburgh; Supvg. Prin., Forest Hills Jr. H. S., Pittsburgh, Pa., since 1940.

Jones, Henry S., M.A.'35, Bucknell Univ.; Supt. of Sch., Plymouth, Pa., since 1926.

Jones, Lloyd M., A.B.'22, Univ. of Wichita; M.A.'27, Ph.D.'35, Columbia Univ.; Prof. of Physical Educ., Pa. State Col., State College, Pa., since 1940.

Judy, Byron R., M.Ed.'35, Pa. State Col.; Supvg. Prin., West Fallowfield Twp. Sch., Cochranville, Pa., since 1927.

Kealy, Sister M. Eugenia, Ph.D.'30, Catholic Univ. of America; Pres., Marywood Col., Scranton, Pa., since 1949.

Kearney, Walter A., B.S.'34, M.Ed.'41, Pa. State Col.; Dir. of Educ. Placement, Sch. of Educ., Pa. State Col., State College, Pa., since 1949.

Keat, Donald B., B.S.'22, Lafayette Col.; M.A. '33, Lehigh Univ.; Supt., Borough Sch. Dist., Bangor, Pa., since 1951.

Keefauver, Lloyd C., A.B.'15, A.M.'24, Sc.D. (Hon.)'45, Gettysburg Col.; Dist. Supt. of Borough Sch., Gettysburg, Pa., since 1926.

Keffer, (Mrs.) Sadie R., Secy., Sch. Bd., Clairton H. S., Clairton, Pa.

Kehrli, Edwin H., M.A.'28, Columbia Univ.; Co. Supt. of Sch., Tunkhannock, Pa., since 1934.

Keim, Edwin B., B.S.'34, State Tchrs. Col., West Chester, Pa.; M.S.'40, D.Ed.'51, Univ. of Pa.; Admin. Asst., Kennett Consol. Sch., Kennett Square, Pa., since 1945.

Keim, Merle L., A.B.'27, Dickinson Col.; A.M. '32, Tchrs. Col., Columbia Univ.; Supvg. Prin. of Sch., Annville, Pa., since 1951.

Kelly, Thomas J., Ed.D.'51, Univ. of Pittsburgh; Supvg. Prin. of Sch., Pitcairn, Pa., since 1951.

Kennedy, John B., Ph.B.'22, Dickinson Col.; M.A.'30, Bucknell Univ.; Supt. of Sch., Kingston, Pa., since 1942.

Kerl, Jules J., B.S.'26, New York Univ.; M.A.'30, Columbia Univ.; Supvg. Prin. of Sch., Forest City, Pa., since 1925.

Kerschner, E. E., A.B.'23, A.M.'32, Univ. of Pa.; Supvg. Prin. of Sch., Ambler, Pa., since 1935.

Ketler, Frank C., A.B.'11, Grove City Col.; A.M.'29, Ph.D.'31, Tchrs. Col., Columbia Univ.; Supt. of Sch., Elkins Park, Philadelphia, Pa., since 1932.

Kindred, Leslie W., A.B.'28, A.M.'34, Ph.D.'38, Univ. of Mich.; Prof. of Educ., Temple Univ., Philadelphia, Pa., since 1940.

Kirkpatrick, George W. R., A.B.'26, Ursinus Col.; M.A.'32, Univ. of Pa.; Prin., Jr. H. S., Bala-Cynwyd, Pa., since 1939.

Klonower, Henry, B.S.'15, M.A.'20, Univ. of Pa.; Pd.D.'36, Ursinus Col.; D.F.A.'50, Moore Inst. of Art, Science, and Indus.; LL.D.'51, Waynesburg Col.; Dir., Tchr. Educ. and Certification, State Dept. of Pub. Instr., Harrisburg, Pa., since 1920.

Koch, Carl R., M.A.'36, New York Univ.; Supt. of Sch., Mechanicsburg, Pa.

Koch, Raymond H., A.B.'28, Lebanon Valley Col.; M.A.'34, Univ. of Pittsburgh; Supt. of Sch., Hershey, Pa., since 1942.

Kolpien, Maurice E., B.S.'26, Allegheny Col.; M.Ed.'36, Harvard Univ.; Co. Supt. of Sch., Erie, Pa., since 1941.

Koopman, Philip U., A.B.'31, Central State Tchrs. Col., Mt. Pleasant, Mich.; A.M.'32, Univ. of Mich.; Ed.D.'41, Columbia Univ.; Asst. Dist. Supt. of Sch., Ardmore, Pa., since 1940.

Kopp, John W., B.S.'29, Albright Col.; M.A.'36, New York Univ.; Supvg. Prin. of Sch., Cambridge Springs, Pa., since 1949.

Kost, Michael R., Secy., Braddock Hills Sch. Dist., Braddock, Pa.

Krah, W. Edward, B.S.'31, M.S.'36, Temple Univ.; Prin., Elem. Sch., North Hills, Pa., since 1924.

Kramer, Frank H., B.A.'14, Gettysburg Col.; A.M.'16, Ph.D.'20, Univ. of Pa.; Prof. of Educ., Gettysburg Col., Gettysburg, Pa., since 1921.

Kurtz, John R., B.S.'16, Bucknell Univ.; Supt. of Sch., Vandergrift, Pa., since 1932.

Kurtz, Paul, A.B.'29, Juniata Col.; M.Ed.'36, Pa. State Col.; Asst. Supt., Blair Co. Sch., Hollidaysburg, Pa., since 1943.

Kurtz, Ray A., B.S.'32, Elizabethtown Col.; M.S.'39, Pa. State Col.; Supvg. Prin., South Lebanon Twp. Sch., Lebanon, Pa., since 1945.

Kurtz, Stanley M., Ph.B.'24, Muhlenberg Col.; M.A.'29, Univ. of Pa.; Supvg. Prin. of East Greenville Sch., since 1933, and Supvg. Prin. of Red Hill Sch., since 1947. Address: East Greenville, Pa.

Kutz, William C., A.B.'24, Franklin and Marshall Col.; A.M.'28, Tchrs. Col., Columbia Univ.; Ed.D.'47, Pa. State Col.; Supvg. Prin. of Sch., West Lawn, Pa., since 1935.

Landis, Robert C., Diploma '10, Keystone Tchrs. Col.; Ph.B.'18, Muhlenberg Col.; A.M.'29, Univ. of Pa.; Supt. of Sch., Conshohocken, Pa., since 1926.

Landis, Stanley K., M.S. in Ed.'47, Univ. of Pa.; Asst. Co. Supt. of Sch., West Chester, Pa., since 1950.

Landis, William H., Jr., B.S.'28, Washington and Jefferson Col.; M.Ed.'39, Univ. of Pittsburgh; Supvg. Prin. of Derry Borough Sch., Derry, Pa., since 1947.

Lathrop, Cecil D., B.S.Ed.'33, State Tchrs. Col., Mansfield, Pa.; M.Ed.'38, Pa. State Col.; Supvg. Prin., Dimock-Springville Jt. Sch., Dimock, Pa., since 1944.

Lauer, John Edwards, B.S.'30, Franklin and Marshall Col.; M.A.'37, New York Univ.; Supt. of Sch., Lansford, Pa., since 1938.

Lawson, James H., B.S.'16, Univ. of Chicago; Ed.D.'34, Univ. of Pittsburgh; Supt. of Sch., McKeesport, Pa., since 1935.

LeCron, Wilbur R., M.A.'28, Univ. of Pittsburgh; Ed.D.'38, Pa. State Col.; Supt. of Sch., Ashland, Pa., since 1942.

Leech, Carl G., A.B.'07, Franklin and Marshall Col.; A.M.'10, Ph.D.'32, Univ. of Pa.; Co. Supt. of Sch., Media, Pa., since 1925.

Lengel, D. H. H., Diploma '17, State Tchrs Col., Kutztown, Pa.; B.S.'25, Muhlenberg Col.; Ed.M.'30, Harvard Univ.; Supt. of Sch., Pottsville, Pa., since 1949.

Liggitt, Earle O., B.S.'17, Muskingum Col.; A.M.'27, Ph.D.'42, Univ. of Pittsburgh; Dist. Supt. of Sch., Munhall, Pa., since 1938.

Liggitt, William A., A.B.'39, Col. of Wooster; M.Litt.'41, Ph.D.'50, Univ. of Pittsburgh; Dean of Men, Kutztown State Tchrs. Col., Kutztown, Pa., since 1951.

Lindsey, James L., Supvg. Prin. of Sch., Shinglehouse, Potter, Pa.

Linton, John H., A.B.'25, Ohio Wesleyan Univ.; M.A.'32, Univ. of Pittsburgh; Supt., Penn Twp. Sch., Pittsburgh, Pa., since 1946.

Lissfelt, Elmer A., A.B.'27, A.M.'30, Univ. of Pittsburgh; A.M.'31, Univ. of Pa.; Supvg. Prin., Upper Moreland Twp. Sch. Dist., Willow Grove, Pa., since 1947.

Little, Marsby C., B.S.'28, Gettysburg Col.; M.A.'32, Tchrs. Col., Columbia Univ.; Supt. of Sch., Waynesboro, Pa., since 1945.

Litts, John C., B.S.'34, State Tchrs. Col., East Stroudsburg, Pa.; M.S.'37, Bucknell Univ.; Co. Supt. of Sch., Stroudsburg, Pa., since 1946.

Lloyd, R. Todd, A.B.'28, Geneva Col.; M.Ed.'41, Univ. of Pittsburgh; Supt. of Sch., Shippensburg, Pa.

Logan, Arthur P., Secy., Bus. Mgr., Pub. Sch., Erie, Pa., since 1949.

Long, Charles M., A.B.'32, Tarkio Col.; A.M. '38, Colo. State Col. of Educ., Greeley; Dept. of Educ., Pa. State Col., State College, Pa.

Long, Clarence M., B.S.'31, State Tchrs. Col., California, Pa.; M.A.'34, D.Ed.'42, Univ. of Pittsburgh; Dir. of Lab. Sch. and Tchr. Tr. and Placement, State Tchrs. Col., Slippery Rock, Pa., since 1950.

Long, Edwin B., A.B.'19, Dickinson Col.; A.M.'25, Tchrs. Col., Columbia Univ.; Ed.D. '44, Pa. State Col.; Supt. of Bellevue Sch., Pittsburgh, Pa.

Look, Arnold Evert, B.Th.'17, Southern-Baptist Theol. Sem.; B.A.'19, McMaster Univ.; M.A.'20, Univ. of Pa.; B.D.'20, M.Th.'22, Crozer Theol. Sem.; Ph.D.'27, Yale Univ.; Pres. and Prin., Ellis Country Sch., Newtown Square, Pa., since 1931.

Low, Luther W., A.B.'39, Washington-Jefferson Col.; M.Ed.'47, Univ. of Buffalo; Supvg. Prin. of Jt. Consol. Sch., West Middlesex, Pa., since 1948.

Lumley, John M., A.B.'28, Muhlenberg Col.; M.Ed.'46, Pa. State Col.; Co. Supt. of Sch., Dushore, Pa., since 1938.

Lunger, Earl C., Supvg. Prin. of Sch., Avella, Pa.

McAndrew, Mary B., B.A.'23, Marywood Col.; M.A.'36, Columbia Univ.; Supt. of Sch., Carbondale, Pa., since 1934.

McCleary, Eugene E., Prin., Glenside Weldon Jr. H. S., Glenside, Pa.

McConnel, Clarence H., Diploma '17, Muncy Normal Sch.; B.S.'36, Pa. State Col.; M.S.'42, Bucknell Univ.; Co. Supt. of Sch., Williamsport, Pa., since 1947.

McCormick, George A., A.B.'25, Muskingum Col.; M.Ed.'34, D.Ed.'46, Univ. of Pittsburgh; Dist. Supt. of Sch., Pottstown, Pa.

McCracken, Theo O., Litt.B.'25, Grove City Col.; M.Ed.'46, Pa. State Col.; Supvg. Prin., Turnpike Sch. System, Mildred, Pa.

McDonald, Samuel E., B.S.'29, M.A.'35, Univ. of Pittsburgh; Supt. of Sch., Coatesville, Pa., since 1950.

McFadden, Elton, B.S.'31, State Tchrs. Col., Slippery Rock, Pa.; M.E.'42, Univ. of Pittsburgh; Supvg. Prin., Neville Sch., Pittsburgh, Pa., since 1943.

McKee, Margaret G., B.S.'29, M.A.'33, Univ. of Pittsburgh; Asst. Co. Supt. of Sch., Pittsburgh, Pa., since 1942.

McKee, William B., B.S.'40, State Tchrs. Col., Slippery Rock, Pa.; Master's '44, Univ. of Pittsburgh; Supvg. Prin., Wesleyville Pub. Sch., Wesleyville, Pa., since 1943.

McKelvey, Eugene M., M.Ed.'40, Univ. of Pittsburgh; Asst. Co. Supt. of Sch., Greensburg, Pa., since 1947.

McLean, David S., B.S.'31, M.A.'33, Columbia Univ.; Supt. of Sch., Radnor Twp., Wayne, Pa.

McMillan, Chandler B., B.S.'30, Grove City Col.; M.S.'36, Pa. State Col.; D.Ed.'48, Univ. of Pittsburgh; Supt. of Sch., Beaver, Pa., since 1950.

McMullen, J. Willard, A.B.'21, Univ. of Del.; M.A.'35, Univ. of Pa.; Supvg. Prin. of Sch., Oxford, Pa., since 1923.

McNerney, Chester T., B.S.'39, M.S.'45, Ph.D., Ind. Univ.; Assoc. Prof. of Educ., Pa. State Col., State College, Pa.

McNitt, Ernest B., B.C.S.'35, M.Ed.'41, Univ. of Pittsburgh; Supt. of Sch., New Brighton, Pa., since 1943.

Mack, Melvin G., B.S.'34, Franklin and Marshall Col.; M.S. in Ed.'45, Univ. of Pa.; Supvg. Prin., Palisades Joint Schs., Pleasant Valley, Bucks Co., Pa., since 1944.

Madden, Neil S., A.B.'42, Grove City Col.; M.Ed.'50, Univ. of Pittsburgh; Prin., Rice Ave. Union H. S., Girard, Pa., since 1952.

Magill, Frank, A.B.'22, Juniata Col.; Co. Supt. of Sch., Huntingdon, Pa., since 1946.

Maher, Rev. Robert J., B.A.'33, M.A.'35, St. Vincent Col.; Supt. of Parochial Sch., Diocese of Harrisburg, Columbia, Pa., since 1947.

Manwiller, Charles E., M.A.'27, Ph.D.'34, Univ. of Pittsburgh; Dir. of Research, Pub. Sch., Pittsburgh, Pa., since 1940.

Marsh, Paul N., B.S.'16, Pa. State Col.; M.Ed. '36, Univ. of Pittsburgh; Supt. of Pub. Sch., Ford City, Pa., since 1950.

Marshall, Loyal S., A.B.'15, Geneva Col.; Supvg. Prin. of Sch., Springdale, Pa., since 1922.

Martin, August, B.S.'25, Muhlenberg Col.; M.S.'31, Pa. State Col.; Supvg. Prin. of Sch., West Hazleton, Pa., since 1936.

Martin, J. A., B.S.'18, Pa. State Col.; M.A.'36, Tchrs. Col., Columbia Univ.; Supvg. Prin. of Sch., Shavertown, Pa., since 1932.

Mast, J. Earl, B.S. in Ed.'31, State Tchrs. Col., Millersville, Pa.; M.E.'38, Temple Univ.; Supvg. Prin. of Twp. Sch., Lima, Pa., since 1941.

Mateer, Kenneth H., B.S.'29, State Tchrs. Col., Shippensburg, Pa.; M.A.'41, Univ. of Pa.; Supvg. Prin., Willistown Twp. Sch., Paoli, Pa., since 1948.

Mathewson, Clinton A., A.B.'30, M.A.'33, Washington and Jefferson Col.; Supt. of Sch., Canonsburg, Pa., since 1938.

Maxwell, C. W., B.S.'38, S. C. State A. & M. Col.; Pres., William Penn Bus. Inst., 1530 Lombard St., Philadelphia, Pa., since 1947.

Maxwell, Charles Frederick, A.B.'09, Lafayette Col.; M.A.'34, Univ. of Pittsburgh; Ed.D.'41, Washington and Jefferson Col.; c/o Co. Sch., Greensburg, Pa.

Maxwell, Paul L., B.S.'26, Grove City Col.; Ed.M.'40, Univ. of Pittsburgh; Supt. of Sch., Pittsburgh, Pa., since 1951.

Means, William J., B.S.'38, Calif. State Tchrs. Col.; M.Ed.'41, Univ. of Pittsburgh; Prin., North Union H. S., Uniontown, Pa., since 1945.

Meisberger, D. T., A.B.'30, Susquehanna Univ.; M.A.'35, Bucknell Univ.; Supt. of Coal Twp. Sch., Shamokin, Pa., since 1940.

Merkel, Ralph S., M.S.'49, Univ. of Pa.; Supvg. Prin. of Sch., Mertztown, Pa., since 1946.

Metcalf, Charles O., B.S.'30, Ursinus Col.; M.S. in Ed.'36, Univ. of Pa.; Supvg. Prin., Bellwood-Antis Sch., Bellwood, Pa., since 1952.

Metzgar, James H., B.S. in Ed.'31, Univ. of Pittsburgh; Supvg. Prin., Salem Twp. Sch., Slickville, Pa., since 1936.

Meyer, Nathan G., A.B.'22, Elizabethtown Col.; A.M.'28, Tchrs. Col., Columbia Univ.; Ed.D. '40, New York Univ.; Dir., Student Tchg. and Placement, State Tchrs. Col., East Stroudsburg, Pa.

Michener, Howard A., B.S. Ed.'37, Ursinus Col.; M.Ed.'48, Temple Univ.; Supvg. Prin., Limerick Twp. Sch., Royersford, Pa., since 1948.

Miller, Frank M., A.B.'27, Pa. State Col.; M.A.'31, Stanford Univ.; Ph.D.'42, Univ. of Pittsburgh; Asst. Supt. of Sch., Erie, Pa., since 1950.

Miller, Franklin A., B.S.'25, M.S.'31, Ph.D.'48, Univ. of Pittsburgh; Assoc. Prof. of Educ., Pa. State Col., State College, Pa., since 1949.

Miller, Fred E., B.S.'30, State Tchrs. Col., Clarion, Pa.; M.Ed.'49, Univ. of Pittsburgh; Supvg. Prin., Union Joint Sch., Rimersburg, Pa., since 1941.

Miller, Frederic K., A.B.'29, Lebanon Valley Col.; M.A.'31, Ph.D.'48, Univ. of Pa.; Head, Dept. of History, since 1939, and Acting Pres., Lebanon Valley Col., Annville, Pa., since 1950.

Miller, Homer F., B.S.'35, Clarion State Tchrs. Col.; Ed.M.'49, St. Bonaventure Univ.; Supvg. Prin., Foster Twp. Sch., Bradford, Pa., since 1951.

Miller, Kenneth W., B.S.'33, State Tchrs. Col., California, Pa.; M.E.'40, Univ. of Pittsburgh; Supt. of Sch., Bellefonte, Pa., since 1949.

Miller, Norman, B.S.'25, Ed.M.'28, Harvard Univ.; Ed.D.'46, New York Univ.; Supt. of Sch., Tyrone, Pa., since 1939.

Miller, Walter Daniel, B.S. in Ed.'29, State Tchrs. Col., Lock Haven, Pa.; M.Ed.'47, Temple Univ.; Supvg. Prin. of Twp. Sch., Bristol, Pa., since 1948.

Milliette, Earl B., Bd. of Educ., Philadelphia, Pa.

Millikin, Robert C., A.B.'15, Waynesburg Col.; M.A.'30, Columbia Univ.; D.Paed.'47, Waynesburg Col.; Assoc. Supt. of Sch. in charge of Sec. Educ., Pittsburgh, Pa., since 1946.

Mitman, T. O., A.B.'10, Lafayette Col.; Supvg. Prin. of Sch., Mauch Chunk, Pa., since 1935.

Moll, Clarence R., B.S.'34, Ed.M.'37, Temple Univ.; L.H.D. (Hon.)'49, Pa. Military Col.; Dean of Admissions and Student Personnel and Prof. of Educ., Pa. Military Col., Chester, Pa., since 1947.

Moll, Richard M., Diploma '05, State Normal Sch., Kutztown, Pa.; A.B.'15, Lebanon Valley Col.; A.M.'25, Univ. of Pa.; Asst. Co. Supt. of Sch., Robesonia, Pa., since 1928.

Montgomery, W. Walter, B.S.'27, Waynesburg Col.; Ed.M.'38, Univ. of Pittsburgh; Supvg. Prin. of Borough Sch., Waynesburg, Pa., since 1946.

Moore, Dale H., B.A.'22, M.A.'23, McGill Univ.; B.D.'25, Congregational Col., Montreal; D.Th. '32, United Theol. Col., Montreal; LL.D.'47, Franklin and Marshall Col.; D.Sc.Ed.'47, Lafayette Col.; Pres., Cedar Crest Col., Allentown, Pa., since 1942.

Moore, Harry H., B.S.'31, Pa. State Tchrs. Col.; M.Ed.'34, Ed.D.'50, Univ. of Pittsburgh; Dist. Supt. of Sch., Franklin, Pa., since 1950.

Moore, J. Layton, A.B.'23, Wesleyan Univ.; Supvg. Prin. of Sch., Ridley Park, Pa., since 1926.

Morgan, Hugh C., A.B.'15, Dickinson Col.; A.M.'20, Tchrs. Col., Columbia Univ.; Supvg. Prin. of Sch., West Grove, Pa., since 1930.

Morrison, S. F. W., A.B.'18, Lebanon Valley Col.; M.A.'27, Columbia Univ.; Supt. of Sch., Clearfield, Pa., since 1931.

Morrow, J. Andrew, Co. Supt. of Sch., Towanda, Pa., since 1922.

Moser, William G., M.A.'46, Lehigh Univ.; Supvg. Prin. of Sch., Pennsburg, Pa., since 1949.

Mowls, J. Nelson, B.S. in Ed.'24, Kent State Univ.; A.M.'28, Ph.D.'37, Univ. of Pittsburgh; Supt. of Sch., Grove City, Pa., since 1946.

Muir, (Mrs.) Josephine Mang, A.B.'29, Pa. Col. for Women; M.Ed.'39, Univ. of Pittsburgh; Supvg. Prin. of Sch., East McKeesport, Pa., since 1949.

Musmanno, Neal V., B.A.'36, Pa. State Col.; M.Litt.'39, Univ. of Pittsburgh; Prin., Stowe H. S., McKees Rocks, Pa., since 1949.

Mutch, Heber R., A.B.'23, Lebanon Valley Col.; M.Ed.'48, Temple Univ.; Supvg. Prin., Southern Jt. Sch. Dist., Glen Rock, Pa., since 1951.

Myers, C. Randall, B.S.'40, State Tchrs. Col., Slippery Rock, Pa.; M.Ed.'44, Univ. of Pittsburgh; Supvg. Prin. of Indiana Twp. Sch., Pittsburgh, Pa., since 1945.

Myers, Edward T., B.S. in Ed.'23, Temple Univ.; M.S.'28, Ph.D.'30, Univ. of Pa.; Dist. Supt. of Sch., Philadelphia, Pa., since 1946.

Myers, F. Lee, A.B.'30, Juniata Col.; M.Ed.'38, Pa. State Col.; Supvg. Prin., Freeport Area Joint Sch., Freeport, Pa., since 1947.

Mylin, Arthur P., Ph.B.'12, Pd.D.'33, Franklin and Marshall Col.; Co. Supt. of Sch., Lancaster, Pa., since 1922.

Nagle, Arthur J., Ph.B.'25, Muhlenberg Col.; M.A.'35, Columbia Univ.; Prin. of Raub Jr. High & Elem. Sch., Allentown, Pa., since 1945.

Neagley, Ross Linn, B.S. in Ed.'29, State Tchrs· Col., Shippensburg, Pa.; M.A.'33, Columbia Univ.; Ed.D.'38, Temple Univ.; Prof. of Educ., Temple Univ., Philadelphia, Pa., since 1949.

Neidig, Joseph Shine, Supt. of Sch., Quakertown, Pa.

Nelson, Arnold C., B.S. in Ed.'27, Pa. State Col.; M.S. in Ed.'33, Univ. of Ill.; Dist. Supt. of Sch., Ridgway, Pa., since 1935.

Newcomer, J. Carman, A.B.'17, Juniata Col.; Supt. of Twp. Sch., McClellandtown, Pa., since 1934.

Neyhart, Amos Earl, B.S. in Indus. Eng.'21, M.S.'34, Pa. State Col.; Admin. Head, Inst. of Pub. Safety, Pa. State Col., State College, Pa., since 1938.

Nietz, John A., A.B.'14, Ohio Northern Univ.; M.A.'19, Ohio State Univ.; Ph.D.'33, Univ. of Chicago; Prof. of Educ., Univ. of Pittsburgh, Pittsburgh, Pa., since 1926.

Nitrauer, Harvey L., A.B.'28, M.A.'40, Lebanon Valley Col.; Supvg. Prin. of Sch., Myerstown, Pa., since 1946.

Nitrauer, W. E., A.B.'25, Lebanon Valley Col.; A.M.'30, Columbia Univ.; Supvg. Prin. of Manheim Twp. Sch., Neffsville, Pa., since 1942.

Noble, William E., B.A.'23, M.A.'29, Washington and Jefferson Col.; Ph.D.'45, Univ. of Pittsburgh; Supvg. Prin. of Sch., Claysville, Pa., since 1931.

Norris, Clarence T., B.A.'37, Pa. State Col.; M.Ed.'42, Univ. of Pittsburgh; Co. Supt. of Sch., Tarentum, Pa.

Norton, Warren P., A.B.'15, Brown Univ.; A.M.'23, Tchrs. Col., Columbia Univ.; Supt. of Sch., Meadville, Pa., since 1928.

Nusbaum, Louis, B.S.'08, Ped.D.'30, Temple Univ.; Pres., Philadelphia Pub. Sch. Retired Employees' Assn., Philadelphia, Pa., since 1947.

Orr, Gerald R., Supvg. Prin. of Sch., New Kensington, Pa.

Orr, Will W., A.B.'26, Erskine Col.; B.D.'31, Pittsburgh-Xenia Theol. Sem.; D.D.'39, Sterling Col.; D.Litt.'49, Carroll Col. (Wis.); Pres., Westminster Col., New Wilmington, Pa., since 1949.

Ott, Arthur R., B.S.'23, Franklin and Marshall Col.; M.Ed.'37, Temple Univ.; Prin., Manheim Twp. H. S., Neffsville, Pa., since 1942.

Ovsiew, Leon, M.A.'47, Ed.D.'52, Tchrs. Col., Columbia Univ.; Lecturer on Educ., Sch. of Educ., Univ. of Pa., Philadelphia, Pa., since 1952.

Owen, Ralph Dornfeld, B.A.'05, Northwestern Col.; M.A.'11, Harvard Univ.; Ph.D.'22, Univ. of Wis.; Prof. of Educ., Graduate Div., Tchrs. Col., Temple Univ., Philadelphia, Pa., since 1925.

Paynter, William Robert, A.B.'30, Pa. State Col.; M.Ed.'37, Univ. of Pittsburgh; Supvg. Prin., Baldwin Twp. Sch., Pittsburgh, Pa., since 1951.

Pearce, Milton O., B.S.'25, M.S.'29, Temple Univ.; Dist. Supt. of Pub. Sch., Philadelphia, Pa., since 1950.

Pearsall, Carl C., B.S.'24, M.A.'26, Univ. of Pittsburgh; Supt. of Twp. Sch., Irwin, Pa., since 1934.

Pebly, Harry E., A.B.'17, Thiel Col.; M.Ed.'35, Univ. of Pittsburgh; Supt. of Sch., Sharpsville, Pa., since 1927.

Pegg, Harold J., AB.'25, Gettysburg Col.; M.A.'34, Univ. of Wash.; Prin., Theodore Roosevelt Jr. H. S., Altoona, Pa., since 1938.

Perry, Edgar C., B.S.'23, Pa. State Col.; M.A.'29, Univ. of Pa.; Ed.D.'52, Univ. of Pittsburgh; Supt. of Sch., Indiana, Pa., since 1938.

Phillips, Raymond V., A.B.'34, Iowa State Tchrs. Col.; M.Ed.'49, Temple Univ.; Asst. Dir., Tchr. Placement Bur., Temple Univ., Philadelphia, Pa., since 1948.

Potter, William Matthew, B.A.'33, M.Ed.'46, Ph.D.'48, Univ. of Pittsburgh; Supt. of Sch., Wilkinsburg, Pittsburgh, Pa., since 1950.

Pownall, Harry V., B.S.'32, State Tchrs. Col., Millersville, Pa.; M.S.'43, Temple Univ.; Supvg. Prin., Salisbury Twp. Sch., Gap, Pa., since 1943.

Preisler, Kenneth L., A.B.'25, Susquehanna Univ.; A.M.'35, Bucknell Univ.; Supt. of Sch., Columbia, Pa., since 1942.

Preston, Thomas Francis, B.S. in M.E.'17, M. in Ed.'38, Univ. of Pittsburgh; Voc. Dir., H. S., Monessen, Pa.. since 1936.

Prutzman, Stuart E., B.A.'23, Pa. State Col.; M.A.'29, Columbia Univ.; Co. Supt. of Sch., Mauch Chunk, Pa.

Puderbaugh, J. Frank, A.B.'17, Dickinson Col.; M.A.'27, Columbia Univ.; Supt. of Sch., Lock Haven, Pa., since 1929.

Puff, Clinton M., A.B.'26, Maryville Col.; Ed.M.'32, Ph.D.'50, Univ. of Pittsburgh; Supt. of Sch., Scottdale, Pa., since 1942.

Quackenbush, Everett A., B.S.'07, St. Lawrence Univ.; Dir., Bureau of Sch. Admin., State Dept. of Pub. Instr., Harrisburg, Pa., since 1940.

Quigley, Joseph S., A.B.'18, Pa. State Col.; Ed.M.'41, Univ. of Pittsburgh; Asst. Supvg. Prin. of Sch., Brackenridge, Pa., since 1951.

Quivey, G. M., A.B.'31, M.A.'36, Univ. of Pittsburgh; Supt. of Twp. Sch., Canonsburg, Pa.

Raab, George Edward, A.B.'40, Franklin and Marshall Col.; M.S. in Ed.'46, Ed.D.'49, Univ. of Pa.; Asst. Dir., Illman-Carter Unit; Prin., Illman Sch. for Children; Assoc. in Educ., Univ. of Pa., Philadelphia, Pa., since 1946.

Ramage, Oleta, A.B.'30, M.A.'32, Univ. of Calif., Berkeley; Supvg. Prin., Concord Twp. Sch., Glen Mills, Pa., since 1951.

Ramsey, V. P., Supvg. Prin., Patton Twp. Sch. Dist., Turtle Creek, Pa.

Ranck, A. Norman, A.B.'27, Franklin and Marshall Col.; M.Ed.'37, Temple Univ.; Supvg. Prin., Manor Twp. and Millersville Borough Sch., Millersville, Pa., since 1943.

Rank, Allen W., A.B.'21, Princeton Univ.; M.A.'33, Columbia Univ.; Supvg. Prin. of Sch., Wyomissing, Pa., since 1948.

Rannells, Emilie, A.B.'20, Ohio Univ.; M.S.W. '36, Univ. of Pa.; Asst. Dir., Div. of Pupil Personnel and Counsel, Bd. of Educ., Philadelphia, Pa., since 1942.

Rausch, Herbert S., B.E.'09, Keystone Normal Sch., Kutztown, Pa.; B.S.'17, M.A.'19, Susquehanna Univ.; Supvg. Prin. of Sch., Girardville, Pa., since 1921.

Rausch, Mary D., Ph.B.'26, Muhlenberg Col.; M.A.'31, Tchrs. Col., Columbia Univ.; Supvg. Prin., Garber-Horne Elem. Sch., Allentown, Pa., since 1927.

Reed, Margaret, A.B.'13, Wellesley Col.; A.M.'25, Columbia Univ.; Prin., William Penn H. S., Philadelphia, Pa., since 1950.

Reese, James E., B.S.'36, Ursinus Col.; M.A. in Ed.'49, Lehigh Univ.; Prin of Central Jr. High Sch., Allentown, Pa., since 1951.

Reilly, Rev. Edward M., Diocesan Supt. of Sch., Philadelphia, Pa.

Reist, Norman I., B.S.'21, Ottawa Univ.; M.A. '26, Univ. of Kansas; Supvg. Prin. of Sch., Wilmerding, Pa., since 1937.

Reiter, M. R., A.B.'27, Muhlenberg Col.; M.S.'39, Univ. of Pa.; Supt. of Sch., Morrisville, Pa., since 1940.

Remaley, J. W. Crane, A.B.'27, Ph.D.'35, Univ. of Pittsburgh; M.S.'31, Pa. State Col.; Assoc. Prof. of Educ., Pa. State Col., State College, Pa., since 1949.

Reynolds, O. Edgar, Diploma '14, Ill. State Normal Univ.; A.B.'16, Univ. of Ill.; M.A.'17, Ph.D.'27, Columbia Univ. Address: 430 E. Main St., Annville, Pa.

Rhodes, Harry K., B.S.'39, State Tchrs. Col., Edinboro, Pa.; Supvg. Prin. of Dist. Sch., Erie, Pa., since 1933.

Rice, Harold R., B.S. in A.A.'34, B.S. in Ed.'34, M.Ed.'42, Univ. of Cincinnati; Ed.D.'44, Columbia Univ.; Pres., Moore Inst. of Art, Science and Indus., Philadelphia, Pa., since 1951.

Rice, Ralph Samuel, B.Sc.'25, M.Sc.'30, D.Ed. '35, Pa. State Col.; Supvg. Prin. of North Hills Joint Schs., West View, Pittsburgh, Pa., since 1948.

Rickert, Glennis H., A.B.'22, Susquehanna Univ.; M.A.'28, Tchrs. Col., Columbia Univ.; Supt. of Sch., Kane, Pa., since 1932.

Riegle, H. Edgar, A.B.'31, Gettysburg Col.; M.E.'50, Pa. State Col.; Asst. Co. Supt. of Sch., York, Pa., since 1950.

Ritenour, Jesse J., M.Ed.'39, Univ. of Pittsburgh; Supvg. Prin., Hempfield Twp. Sch. Dist., Greensburg, Pa., since 1942.

Roberts, Henry E., B.S.'29, Pa. State Col.; Ed.M.'39, Univ. of Pittsburgh; Supvg. Prin., Scott Twp. H. S., Carnegie, Pa., since 1946.

Roberts, Stephen W., A.B.'27, Broaddus Univ.; B.S.'32, Bucknell Univ.; M.A.'35, N. Y. Univ.; Headmaster, Perkiomen Sch., Pennsburg, Pa. since 1951.

Rockey, H. S., Supvg. Prin. of Sch., Brookville, Pa.

Roddy, Joseph Stockton, Jr., B.S.'32, M.S.'34, Univ. of Pa.; Supvg. Prin. of Sch., Narberth, Pa., since 1951.

Rodemoyer, William Edward, B.S.'34, Geneva Col.; Ed.M.'48, Univ. of Pittsburgh; Supvg. Prin. of Sch., Zelienople, Pa., since 1947.

Roeder, J. N., A.B.'17, Franklin and Marshall Col.; A.M.'23, Tchrs. Col., Columbia Univ.; Ph.D.'33, New York Univ.; Supt. of Sch., Palmerton, Pa., since 1926.

Rogers, R. C., M.A.'29, New York Univ.; Supvg. Prin., Shaler Twp. Sch., Glenshaw, Pa., since 1931.

Rohrbach, Quincy A. W., A.B.'22, Franklin and Marshall Col.; A.M.'24, Ph.D.'25, Univ. of Pa.; LL.D.'34, Univ. of Pittsburgh; Pres., State Tchrs. Col., Kutztown, Pa., since 1934.

Rometo, Albert R., B.A.'33, Washington and Jefferson Col.; M.E.'42, Univ. of Pittsburgh; Supvg. Prin., East Deer-Frazer Union Sch., Creighton, Pa., since 1949.

Rosenkrance, Robert A., A.B.'27, Wheaton Col., Ill.; M.A.'40, Tchrs. Col., Columbia Univ.; Supvg. Prin. of Sch., West Reading, Pa., since 1950.

Roth, Samuel S., B.S., H.Ed.'28, State Tchrs. Col., Slippery Rock, Pa.; B.S.'32, M.S.'34, Duquesne Univ.; Supvg. Prin. of Twp. Sch., McKees Rocks, Pa., since 1949.

*Rowland, Albert Lindsay, A.B.'08, Temple Univ.; M.A.'11, Ph.D.'14, Univ. of Pa. Address: 10 Surrey Rd., Oak Lane, Philadelphia 26, Pa.

Ryder, Paul T., B.S. in Ed.'32, Univ. of Pa.; M.A.'34, Pa. State Col.; Asst. Co. Supt. of Sch., Honesdale, Pa., since 1949.

Saul, Marie A., A.B.'26, Carnegie Inst. of Tech.; M.A.'32, Univ. of Pittsburgh; Assoc. Supt. of Elem. Educ., Pittsburgh, Pa., since 1945.

Sauvain, Walter Howard, A.B.'24, Univ. of N. Dak.; A.M.'25, Ph.D.'34, Columbia Univ.; Prof. of Educ., Bucknell Univ., Lewisburg, Pa., since 1936.

Savage, Edward H., B.S.'33, State Tchrs. Col., California, Pa.; M.Ed.'38, Univ. of Pittsburgh; Supvg. Prin. of Twp. Sch., Uniontown, Pa., since 1937.

Sawyer, W. C. "Tom", B.A.'20, Univ. of Redlands; M.A.'24, Univ. of Chicago; Dir., Awards Programs, Freedoms Foundation, Valley Forge, Pa., since 1950.

Saylor, Charles F., B.A.'27, M.A.'31, Univ. of Pittsburgh; Supt. of Sch., Jeannette, Pa., since 1951.

Saylor, Clyde T., Co. Supt. of Sch., West Chester, Pa.

Schaffer, Anna M., Assoc. Supvg. Prin., North Allegheny Joint Schs., Pittsburgh, Pa.

Schlegel, Albert G. W., B.A.'20, Moravian Col.; M.A.'27, Ed.D.'35, Pa. State Col.; Supt. of Sch., Milton, Pa., since 1950.

Schmehl, Kermit H., Ph.B.'25, Muhlenberg Col.; M.S.'37, Univ. of Pa.; Prin., Muhlenberg Twp. H. S., Laureldale, Pa., since 1946.

Schricker, John A., B.S.'34, M.Ed.'37, Univ. of Pittsburgh; Supvg. Prin., Twp. Sch., Lyndora, Pa., since 1950.

Seegers, J. Conrad, A.B.'13, Muhlenberg Col.; A.M.'16, Columbia Univ.; Ph.D.'30, Univ. of Pa.; Litt.D.'40, Muhlenberg Col.; Dean, Tchrs. Col., Temple Univ., Philadelphia, Pa. 1948-50.

Shafer, Robert K., B.S.'36, State Tchrs. Col., Kutztown, Pa.; M.A.'39, New York Univ.; Supvg. Prin. of Twp. Sch., Buckingham, Pa., since 1945.

Shaffer, Sanford B., Supvg. Prin. of Sch., Wilkinsburg, Pa.

Sheely, W. Edward, A.B.'28, Franklin and Marshall Col.; M.Ed.'45, Pa. State Col.; Supt. of Pub. Sch., Hanover, Pa., since 1950.

Shellenberger, William B., B.S.'35, State Tchrs. Col., Shippensburg, Pa.; M.Ed.'43, Pa. State Col.; Supt., Bensalem Twp. Sch. Dist., Cornwells Heights, Pa., since 1950.

Shenk, Harry W., A.M.'33, Gettysburg Col.; Asst. Co. Supt. of Sch., York, Pa., since 1938.

Sherman, C. A., B.S.'33, State Tchrs. Col., Slippery Rock, Pa.; Ed.M.'36, Ed.D.'44, Univ. of Pittsburgh; Supvg. Prin. of Sch., Aspinwall, Pa., since 1944.

Shimko, Michael J., A.B.'31, Scranton Univ.; M.A.'50, Bucknell Univ.; Supvg. Prin., Larksville, Kingston, Pa., since 1949.

Showalter, Addison H., A.B.'19, A.M.'20, Franklin and Marshall Col.; A.M. in Ed.'22, Univ. of Pa.; Supt. of Sch., Chester, Pa., since 1950.

Shupe, Thomas R., B.S.'32, Grove City Col.; M.Ed.'42, Univ. of Pittsburgh; Supvg. Prin., East Washington Sch. Dist., Washington, Pa., since 1950.

Simmons, J. Blair, B.S. in Ed.'32, Geneva Col.; Ed.M.'36, Univ. of Pittsburgh; Supvg. Prin., Borough Twp. Sch., Vanport, Pa., since 1943.

Simpson, R. Leslie, B.S.'35, Westminster Col.; M.Ed.'39, Univ. of Pittsburgh; Supvg. Prin. of Sch., Blairsville, Pa., since 1950.

Singleton, J. Robert, B.S.'38, Franklin and Marshall Col.; M.Ed.'49, Temple Univ.; Supvg. Prin., Shippenville-Elk Joint Sch., Shippenville, Pa., since 1950.

Smaltz, Harold A., B.Sc.'28, Susquehanna Univ.; Supvg. Prin., Hughestown Boro. Sch., Pittston, Pa., since 1947.

Smith, Charles C., A.B.'12, Lebanon Valley Col.; A.M.'19, Columbia Univ.; Supt. of Sch., Bridgeport, Pa., since 1932.

Smith, David L., B.S.'43, Lock Haven State Tchrs. Col., Pa.; M.Ed.'46, Univ. of Pittsburgh; Supvg. Prin., Adams Twp. Sch. Dist., Sidman, Pa., since 1947.

Smith, Harvey A., A.B.'14, Franklin and Marshall Col.; A.M.'22, Univ. of Pa.; Ph.D.'30, Columbia Univ.; Supt. of Sch., Lancaster, Pa., since 1938.

Smith, J. Edward, A.B.'27, Geneva Col.; A.M.'30, Ed.D.'42, Univ. of Pittsburgh; Regional Supt., Central Bucks Joint Sch., Doylestown, Pa.

Smith, John, Supt. of Sch., Nanticoke, Pa., since 1950.

Smith, Lawrence D., A.B.'26, Geneva Col.; M.A.'34, Ph.D.'43, Univ. of Pittsburgh; Supt. of Sch., Beaver Falls, Pa., since 1948.

Smith, Ralph C., A.B.'30, Pa. State Col.; M.Ed. '35, Bucknell Univ.; Asst. Supt., Lycoming Co. Pub. Sch., Williamsport, Pa.

Smith, Ralph Richards, B.S. in Ed.'24, M.A.'27, Univ. of Pa.; Supt. of Sch., Lansdale, Pa., since 1926.

Snively, Donald L., B.S. in Ed.'37, State Tchrs. Col., Shippensburg, Pa.; M.S. in Ed.'41, Univ. of Pa.; Supvg. Prin. of Sch., Upper Providence Twp., Media, Pa., since 1947.

Snoke, James S., B.S. in Ed.'30, State Tchrs. Col., Shippensburg, Pa.; M.A.'38, D.Ed.'44, Univ. of Pittsburgh; Asst. Supt. of Sch., Allegheny Co., Pittsburgh, Pa., since 1946.

Snyder, H. Austin, B.S. in Ed.'32, State Tchrs. Col., Mansfield, Pa.; M.Ed.'35, Pa. State Col.; Supt. of Borough Sch., Sayre, Pa., since 1946.

Snyder, Lewis N., A.B.'16, Gettysburg Col.; A.M.'24, Univ. of Pa.; Ed.D.'47, Temple Univ.; Supvg. Prin. of Sch., Perkasie and Sellersville, Pa., since 1929.

Snyder, Warren P., B.S.'20, Muhlenberg Col.; M.S.'32, Temple Univ.; Supt of Sch., Bristol, Pa., since 1936.

Spaid, G. Marlin, B.A.'30, Susquehanna Univ.; M.S. in Ed.'40, Cornell Univ.; Supvg. Prin. of Boro Sch., Lititz, Pa., since 1951.

Spancake, Fred Arthur, M.Ed.'38, Pa. State Col.; Supvg. Prin., Logan Twp. Sch., Altoona, Pa., since 1947.

Speg, William M., A.B.'33, Lebanon Univ.; M.A. '34, Columbia Univ.; Supvg. Prin. of Sch., Harrisburg, Pa., since 1951.

Spitler, Franklin C., B.A.'34, Pa. State Col.; M.Ed.'38, Temple Univ.; Elem. Supvr., Baldwin Twp. Sch., Pittsburgh, Pa.

Sproul, C. D., B.S.'32, Juniata Col.; M.Ed.'38, Pa. State Col.; Supvg. Prin. of Sch., Bedford, Pa., since 1948.

Squier, Lester B., B.S.'30, State Tchrs. Col., Mansfield, Pa.; M.Ed.'35, Pa. State Col.; Supvg. Prin., Twp. Sch., Lehman, Pa., since 1948.

Squires, Howard G., Ed.D.'47, Univ. of Pittsburgh; Supt. of Sch., Ambridge, Pa., since 1950.

Stabley, Elwood C., A.B.'24, Lebanon Valley Col.; M.A.'31, Univ. of Pa.; Supvg. Prin. of Sch., Unionville, Pa., since 1936.

Stapleton, R. B., B.S.'14, Bucknell Univ.; M.A. '30, Columbia Univ.; Supt. of Sch., Tamaqua, Pa., since 1948.

Starr, James G., B.S.'27, Lebanon Valley Col.; M.S.'38, Univ. of Pa.; Asst. Co. Supt. of Sch., Lebanon, Pa., since 1951.

Stassen, Harold E., B.A.'27, LL.B.'29, Univ. of Minn.; Pres., Univ. of Pa., Philadelphia, Pa., since 1948.

Stauffer, Carryl E., B.S.'29, Franklin and Marshall Col.; M.A.'37, Columbia Univ.; Supvg. Prin., Warwick Sch. Dist., Elverson, R.D. 1, Pa.

Stauffer, Charles J., B.S.'31, Albright Col.; M.Ed.'36, Pa. State Col.; Supt. of Boro Sch., Shenandoah, Pa., since 1951.

Steckel, A. D., Ph.B.'26, Muhlenberg Col.; M.A.'35, Univ. of Pa.; Supvg. Prin. of Sch., Sinking Spring, Pa., since 1933.

Stengle, F. E., A.M.'30, Lebanon Valley Col.; A.M.'33, Univ. of Pa.; Supt. of Sch., Collingdale, Pa., since 1934.

Stetson, G. Arthur, B.S.'19, Allegheny Col.; M.A.'27, Tchrs. Col., Columbia Univ.; D.Ed. '41, Univ. of Pittsburgh; Supt. of Sch., West Chester, Pa., since 1938.

Stevens, Elmer S., B.S.'41, Mansfield State Tchrs. Col., Pa.; M.S.'47, Univ. of Pa.; Supvg. Prin., Whitpain Twp. Sch. Dist., Blue Bell, Pa., since 1951.

Stewart, David H., B.S.'15, Pa. State Col.; A.M.'25, Columbia Univ.; Ph.D.'35, Univ. of Pittsburgh; Supt. of Sch., Dormont, Pittsburgh, Pa., since 1936.

Stewart, William A., M.Ed.'40, Univ. of Pittsburgh; Supvg. Prin., Cranberry Twp. Sch. Dist., Seneca, Pa., since 1942.

Stock, L. V., M.S.'31, Gettysburg Col.; Supvg. Prin., Upper Adams Joint Sch. Dist., Biglerville, Pa., since 1937.

Stover, Burd D., B.S.'36, State Tchrs. Col., West Chester, Pa.; M.S.'41, Univ. of Pa.; Ed.D.'52, Tchrs. Col., Columbia Univ.; Prin., Highland and Green Ave. Schs., Lansdowne, Pa., since 1951.

Stover, Kermit M., B.S. in Ed.'33, State Tchrs. Col., Lock Haven, Pa.; M.Ed.'37, Duke Univ.; Supvg. Prin., South Middleton Twp. Sch. Dist., Boiling Springs, Pa., since 1948.

Strattan, J. Maurice, B.S. in Ed.'31, M.Ed.'34, Temple Univ.; Ed.D.'49, Univ. of Pa.; Supt., Tredyffrin-Easttown Sch. Dist., Berwyn, Pa., since 1952.

Strine, Huber D., A.B.'20, Lebanon Valley Col.; A.M.'24, Columbia Univ.; Supvg. Prin., Spring Garden Twp. Sch., York, Pa., since 1938.

Sukel, Andrew S., B.A.'28, Washington and Jefferson Col.; M.A.'39, Pa. State Col.; Supt. of Pub. Sch., Donora, Pa., since 1950.

Sutherland, Lawrence R., B.S.'32, State Tchrs. Col., California, Pa.; M.Ed.'40, Pa. State Col.; Asst. Co. Supt. of Sch., Washington, Pa., since 1944.

Swan, Ralph C., B.S.'31, State Tchrs. Col., Shippensburg, Pa.; M.Ed.'36, Pa. State Col.; Co. Supt. of Sch., New Bloomfield, Pa., since 1944.

Swank, Paul A., B.S.'33, Susquehanna Univ.; M.Ed.'39, Temple Univ.; Prin., Shamokin Area Joint Jr.-Sr. H. S., Shamokin, Pa., since 1952.

Swartz, David L., B.A.'37, Juniata Col.; M.Ed. '40, Pa. State Col.; Dist. Supt. of Sch., Carlisle, Pa.

Swartz, Harvey E., A.B.'21, A.M.'23, Franklin and Marshall Col.; Co. Supt. of Sch., York, Pa., since 1938.

Sweitzer, Ralph L., B.S.'28, Grove City Col.; M.S.'37, Pa. State Col.; Supvg. Prin., Otto Twp. Sch. Dist., Duke Center, Pa., since 1945.

Swinehart, George B., A.B.'15, Ursinus Col.; M.S.'41, Univ. of Pa.; Supvg. Prin. of Sch., Boyertown, Pa., since 1917.

Swope, Charles S., A.B.'25, Dickinson Col.; A.M.'31, Univ. of Pa.; Pd.D.'41, Dickinson Col.; Pres., State Tchrs. Col., West Chester, Pa., since 1935.

*Tanger, Fredrick E., B.S.'34, State Tchrs. Col., Millersville, Pa.; M.A.'36, Ed.D.'51, Tchrs. Col., Columbia Univ.; Supt. of Borough Sch. Dist., Media, Pa., since 1950.

Templin, R. J. W., Sc.B.'16, A.M.'19, Bucknell Univ.; Supt. of Sch., West Pittston, Pa., since 1923.

Tennyson, Harry L., B.S.'26, Wash. and Jefferson Col.; M.A.'33, Tchrs. Col., Columbia Univ.; Ed.D.'49, Univ. of Southern Calif.; Supt. of Sch., Lehighton, Pa., since 1951.

Thomas, Harold Prescott, B.S.'20, Colgate Univ.; Ed.M.'25, Ed.D.'32, Harvard Univ.; Head, Dept. of Educ., since 1932, Dir. of Summer Sessions since 1935, and Dir., Genl. Col., Lehigh Univ., Bethlehem, Pa., since 1942.

Thomas, Maurice J., B.A.'25, Univ. of Wash.; M.A.'26, Ed.D.'43, Columbia Univ.; Prof. of Educ., Univ. of Pittsburgh, Pittsburgh, Pa., since 1948.

Thomas, Victor F., Jr., B.S.'30, M.Ed.'37, Univ. of Pittsburgh; Supvg. Prin. of Sch., Bessemer, Pa., since 1948.

Thompson, Donald C., B.S.'33, Grove City Col.; M.Ed.'39, Pa. State Col.; Supvg. Prin., Albion Area Sch., Albion, Pa., since 1941.

Todd, G. Raymond, B.S.'31, Ursinus Col.; Ed.M.'36, Temple Univ.; Supvg. Prin., Lower Saucon Twp. Sch., Bethlehem, Pa., since 1950.

Tollinger, William P., A.B.'27, Swarthmore Col.; M.A.'30, Univ. of Pa.; Supt. of Wilson Borough Sch., Easton, Pa., since 1946.

Trabue, M. R., B.A.'11, Northwestern Univ.; M.A.'14, Ph.D.'15, Columbia Univ.; Dean, Sch. of Educ., Pa. State Col., State College, Pa., since 1937.

Tracy, Edward, Ph.B.'34, Brown Univ.; M.A.'43, Harvard Univ.; Prin. of H. S., Easton, Pa., since 1951.

Trevaskis, John L., A.B.'30, Westminster Col.; M.Ed.'36, Univ. of Pittsburgh; Supvg. Prin. of Castle Shannon Sch., Pittsburgh, Pa., since 1947.

Truby, Charlotte C., M.A.'28, Univ. of Pittsburgh; Prin., Lemington Elem. Sch., Pittsburgh, Pa., since 1932.

Turnbull, (Mrs.) Margaret Allen, B.S.'45, M.Ed.'47, Univ. of Pittsburgh; Supvg. Prin. of Sch., Fair Oaks, Pa., since 1947.

Tyson, John H., Diploma '12, State Tchrs. Col., West Chester, Pa.; B.S. in Ed.'20, M.A.'22, Univ. of Pa.; Supt. of Twp. Sch., Upper Darby, Pa., since 1943.

*Ulrich, Foster G., A.B.'30, Lebanon Valley Col.; M.Ed.'40, Temple Univ.; Co. Supt. of Sch., Lebanon, Pa.

Ungemach, Dena D., B.S., A.M., Univ. of Pa.; Head, Science Dept., Overbrook Sr. H. S., Philadelphia, Pa.

Veltri, John B., B.S. in Ed.'32, Duquesne Univ.; M.S. in E.'37, Univ. of Pittsburgh; Supvg. Prin. of Sch., Sharpsburg, Pa., since 1940.

Wahl, John B., B.S.'32, Pa. State Col.; M.Ed.'41, Univ. of Pittsburgh; Supvg. Prin., Conway Sch., Conway, Pa., since 1948.

Waldman, John L., Ed.D.'30, Temple Univ.; Assoc. Supt. of Pub. Sch., Philadelphia, Pa., since 1950.

Walker, Paul H., M.Ed.'42, Univ. of Pittsburgh; Supt. of Twp. Sch., Leisenring, Pa., since 1950.

Weaver, Martin E., B.A.'29, M.A. in Ed.'38, Univ. of Pittsburgh; Supvg. Prin. of Twp. Sch., Library, Pa., since 1944.

Weaver, W. Donald, B.S.'30, Grove City Col.; M.Ed.'37, Pa. State Col.; Supt. of Twp. Sch., DuBois, Pa., since 1942.

Webster, Wayne C., B.S. in Ed.'30, State Tchrs. Col., Mansfield, Pa.; M.Ed.'35, Pa. State Col.; Co. Supt. of Sch., Montrose, Pa., since 1946.

Weidner, Henry J., B.S.'31, Muhlenberg Col.; M.A.'42, Lehigh Univ.; Prin., South Mountain Jr. H. S., Allentown, Pa., since 1947.

Weiss, Emalyn R., A.B.'31, Goucher Col.; M.A.'33, Univ. of Pa.; Co. Supvr. of Special Educ., Reading, Pa., since 1941.

Welch, Carl F., B.S.'34, State Tchrs. Col., Edinboro, Pa.; M.Ed.'41, Univ. of Pittsburgh; Supvg. Prin., Joint Consol. Sch., Stoneboro, Pa., since 1947.

Wenger, Ethel M. B., M.A.'34, Univ. of Pa.; Supvr. of Special Educ., Butler, Pa., since 1946.

Wenger, Henry, M.S.'39, Univ. of Pa.; Supvg. Prin. of Sch., Fredericksburg, Pa., since 1932.

Wentz, Howard A., B.S. in Ed.'29, Lebanon Valley Col.; M.Ed.'43, Temple Univ.; Supvg. Prin. of Sch., Wallingford, Pa., since 1942.

Werley, Marvin O., Ph.B.'31, Muhlenberg Col.; M.S. in Ed.'36, Univ. of Pa.; Supvg. Prin. of Sch., Pine Grove, Pa., since 1947.

Wetter, Allen H., B.S. in Ed.'21, M.S. in Ed.'29, Temple Univ.; Asst. to the Supt. of Sch. in charge of Sch.-Community Relations, Bd. of Educ., Philadelphia, Pa., since 1946.

Wetzel, Jacob F., A.B.'25, A.M.'30, Susquehanna Univ.; Supvg. Prin. of Sch., Centre Hall, Pa., since 1925.

Whipple, Carl E., B.S.'25, M.S.'30, Pa. State Col.; Ed.D.'40, Univ. of Pittsburgh; Supt. of Sch., Warren, Pa., since 1949.

Whitney, Nelle R., Supvg. Prin. of Sch., Jefferson, Pa.

Wiley, Roy William, B.S.'18, Grove City Col.; M.A.'28, Ed.D.'38, Univ. of Pittsburgh; Supt. of Sch., Johnstown, Pa., since 1946.

Williammee, John T., Jr., B.S.'24, Bucknell Univ.; M.S.'32, Penn State Col.; Supvg. Prin. of Sch., Canton, Pa., since 1942.

Williams, David E., A.B.'29, Westminster Col., Pa.; M.Ed.'47, Univ. of Pittsburgh; Supvg. Prin., Kennedy Twp. Sch., McKees Rocks, Pa., since 1946.

Williams, Russell L., B.S. in Ed.'34, Lebanon Valley Col.; M.S. in Ed.'39, Bucknell Univ.; Supvg. Prin. of Sch., Prospect Park, Pa., since 1945.

Williams, Thomas Stuart, B.S.'21, M.A.'37, Bucknell Univ.; Supvg. Prin. of Sch., Luzerne, Pa., since 1934.

Williams, Walter R., B.S.'19, Pa. State Col.; M.Ed.'41, Univ. of Pittsburgh; Supvg. Prin. of Sch., West Brownsville, Pa., since 1946.

Williamson, LaRue C., A.B.'31, M.Ed.'36, Pa. State Col.; Supvg. Prin., Muncy-Muncy Creek Union Sch. Dist., Muncy, Pa., since 1949.

Wills, Merlin Vincent, A.B.'27, M.A.'30, Univ. of Pittsburgh; Asst. Co. Supt. of Sch., Greensburg, Pa., since 1950.

Wilson, James S., B.S.'26, Grove City Col.; M.E.'35, Univ. of Pittsburgh; Supvg. Prin., Millcreek Sch. Dist., Erie, Pa., since 1942.

Wilson, Lytle Murray, B.S.'27, Bucknell Univ.; M.A.'31, Univ. of Pittsburgh; Supt. of Sch., Aliquippa, Pa., since 1937.

Wilson, Roy D., B.S.'40, Juniata Col.; M.Ed.'46, Pa. State Col.; Asst. Co. Supt. of Sch., Lewistown, Pa., since 1950.

Witmeyer, Paul E., A.B.'15, Lebanon Valley Col.; M.A.'23, Columbia Univ.; Ed.D.'38, New York Univ.; Ped.D.'45, Lebanon Valley Col.; Prof. of Educ., Bucknell Univ., Lewisburg, Pa., since 1952.

Wylie, Clarence C., Supvg. Prin. of Sch., Ligonier, Pa.

Yeager, Howard J., B.A.'11, Franklin and Marshall Col.; M.A.'23, Lehigh Univ.; Supt. of Sch., Emmaus, Pa., since 1930.

Yeager, William A., A.B.'14, Ursinus Col.; A.M.'18, Ph.D.'29, Univ. of Pa.; Prof. of Educ. and Dir. of Courses in Sch. Admin., Univ. of Pittsburgh, Pittsburgh, Pa., since 1934.

Yeich, Edwin B., A.B.'20, Franklin and Marshall Col.; A.M.'25, Univ. of Pa.; Prin. of H. S., West Reading, Pa., since 1928.

Yoakam, Gerald A., B.A.'10, M.A.'19, Ph.D.'22, State Univ. of Iowa; Prof. of Educ. and Dir. of Courses in Elem. Educ., Univ. of Pittsburgh, Pittsburgh, Pa., since 1923.

Yozviak, Michael H., Supvg. Prin., Hanover Twp. Pub. Sch., Wilkes-Barre, Pa.

Zahn, D. Willard, B.S. in Ed.'22, M.S. in Ed.'30, Temple Univ.; Assoc. Supt. of Sch., Philadelphia, Pa.

Zorger, Clarence E., Ph.B.'15, Franklin and Marshall Col.; A.M.'31, Columbia Univ.; D.Ped. '46, Franklin and Marshall Col.; Supt. of Sch., Harrisburg, Pa., since 1942.

Zuerner, Frank Dewitt, A.M.'30, Univ. of Pittsburgh; LL.D.'36, Westminster Col.; Supt. of Sch., North Braddock, Pa.

INSTITUTIONAL MEMBERS

Administration Library, 160 Sch. Admin. Bldg., Bellefield Ave. at Forbes St., Pittsburgh, Pa.

Community Activities, State Tchrs. Col., Bloomsburg, Pa.

Drexel Institute of Technology, Philadelphia, Pa.

Educational Test Bureau, Educ. Publishers, Inc., 3433 Walnut St., Philadelphia 4, Pa.

Free Library of Philadelphia, Periodical Dept., Middle City W. Dist., Philadelphia 3, Pa.

John J. Nesbitt, Inc., State Rd. and Rhawn St., Holmesburg, Philadelphia, Pa.

Wayne Iron Works, H. B. Wood, Vicepres., Wayne, Pa.

PUERTO RICO

INDIVIDUAL MEMBERS

Downing, Ronald A., B.S. in Ed.'39, Ohio Northern Univ.; Supt. of Sch., Ramey Air Force Base, P. R., since 1951.

Duprey, Luis A., A.B.Ed.'39, Univ. of Puerto Rico; Supt. of Sch., Moca, P. R., since 1947.

Garcia, Ramón, B.A. in Ed.'36, Univ. of Puerto Rico; M.A.'40, Columbia Univ.; Supt. of Sch., Rio Piedras, P. R.

Gil, Pedro, B.A.'17, Univ. of Puerto Rico; Dir., Veterans Educ. Div., Dept. of Educ., San Juan, P. R.

Lopez-Alvarez, Jose R., B.A.'35, Univ. of Puerto Rico; Dist. Supt. of Sch., Mayaguez, P. R., since 1941.

Villaronga, Mariano, B.S.'29, Univ. of Puerto Rico; Ed.M.'41, Harvard Univ.; Commr. of Educ., San Juan, P. R., since 1949.

INSTITUTIONAL MEMBER

Puerto Rico Tchrs. Assn., San Juan 6, P. R.

RHODE ISLAND

INDIVIDUAL MEMBERS

Bosworth, Clarence W., A.B.'09, A.M.'10, Brown Univ.; Supt. of Sch., Cranston, R. I., since 1935.

Bray, Marion B., B.E.'13, R. I. Col. of Educ., Providence; Supvg. Prin. of Sch., Providence, R. I., since 1928.

Brittan, Olive C., B.Ed.'34, State Tchrs. Col., Bridgewater, Mass.; M.Ed.'52, R. I. Col. of Educ.; Asst. Prin., Lincoln Memorial Jr. H. S., Lonsdale, R. I.

Calcutt, Earl F., B.B.A.'29, A.M.'37, Boston Univ.; Supt. of Sch., Central Falls, R. I., since 1947.

Callahan, William L., A.B.'12, Col. of the Holy Cross; Ed.M.'26, Harvard Univ.; Ed.D.'39, Catholic Tchrs. Col., Providence, R. I.; Supt. of Burrillville Schs., Harrisville, R. I., since 1949.

Casey, J. Edward, A.B.'31, A.M.'41, Boston Col.; Ed.M.'47, Ed.D.'52, Harvard Univ.; Assoc. Prof. of Educ. and Psych., Univ. of R. I., Kingston, R. I., since 1952.

Clark, James, B.A.'30, Dartmouth Col.; Ed.M. '40, Boston Univ.; Supt. of Sch., Coventry, R. I., since 1951.

Cole, Archie R., B.A.'29, M.A.'39, Bates Col.; Supt. of Sch., East Greenwich, R. I.

Conlon, James E., B.B.A.'24, Boston Univ.; Supt. of South Kingstown Sch., Peace Dale, R. I., since 1947.

Crosby, Percy R., B.S.'12, Univ. of N. H.; A.M. '19, Ph.D.'26, Brown Univ.; Supt. of Pub. Sch., Pawtucket, R. I., since 1949.

Davis, Hiram A., B.S.'22, Norwich Univ.; Supt. of Sch., Wickford, R. I., since 1930.

DeMoranville, Aaron F., Diploma '25, R. I. Col. of Educ., Providence; A.B.'30, A.M.'34, N. Y. State Col. for Tchrs., Albany; Supt. of Sch., Johnston, R. I., since 1938.

Dullea, Bernard C., B.A.'31, Boston Col.; M.A.'32, Boston Univ.; Supt. of Sch., Charlestown, R. I., since 1950.

Farrell, Edmund J., Ph.B.'30, Brown Univ.; Asst. Supt. of Sch., Pawtucket, R. I., since 1949.

Farrin, Leon M., A.B.'15, Ed.M.'26, Harvard Univ.; Supt. of Sch., Woonsocket, R. I., since 1935.

Fitzgerald, Edward J., B.S.'27, Norwich Univ.; Supt. of Sch., Bristol, R. I., since 1946.

Gaige, William C., A.B.'32, Oberlin Col.; A.M.'35, Univ. of Chicago; Pres., R. I. Col. of Educ., Providence, R. I., since 1952.

Grant, Alfred E., B.S.'23, Tufts Col.; Ed.M.'30, Harvard Univ.; Asst. Supt. of Sch., Cranston, R. I., since 1932.

Hanley, James Lawrence, A.B.'19, Boston Col.; A.M.'20, Brown Univ.; LL.B.'27, Northeastern Univ.; Ed.M.'32, Harvard Univ.; Ed.D.'37, Catholic Tchrs. Col., Providence, R. I.; D.Ped.'41, Bryant Col.; LL.D.'45, Boston Col.; Supt. of Sch., Providence, R. I., since 1937.

Harkins, John M., A.B.'08, Bates Col.; Supt. of Sch., Warren, R. I., since 1941.

Howard, Marie R., M.E.'49, R. I. Col. of Educ., Providence; Prin., Elem. Sch., since 1941 and Supvg. Prin., Providence, R. I., since 1948.

Jacobs, Henry L., D.B.A.'35, Bryant Col.; D.Ed.'47, R. I. Col. of Educ.; Pres., Bryant Col., Providence, R. I., since 1916.

La Perche, Raymond C., B.Sc.'22, R. I. State Col.; Supt. of Smithfield Schs., Georgiaville, R. I., since 1938.

Leonard, Charles B., Ph.B.'29, Brown Univ.; Supt. of Foster and Scituate Sch., North Scituate, R. I., since 1949.

Leonard, (Mrs.) Newton P., A.B.'16, Mt. Holyoke Col.; D.Ed.'52, Bryant Col.; Pres., Natl. Congress of Parents and Tchrs., since 1952; Address: 341 Sharon St., Providence, R. I.

Leonard, Wardwell C., Ph.B.'18, A.M.'41, Brown Univ.; Supt. of Sch., Tiverton, R. I., since 1944.

McGuire, James L., A.B.'13, The Catholic Univ. of America; Supt. of Sch., North Providence, R. I., since 1931.

McMahon, Katherine B., B.Ed.'47, R. I. Col. of Educ., Providence; Supt. of Sch., Little Compton, R. I., since 1949.

MacKay, Charles B., Ph.B.'16, A.M.'24, Brown Univ.; Supt. of Sch., Warwick, R. I., since 1949.

Martin, Edward R., B.S.'35, Providence Col.; M.Ed.'49, R. I. Col. of Educ.; Supt. of Sch., East Providence, R. I., since 1951.

*Miller, Anthony J., Ed.M.'33, Boston Univ.; Supt. of Sch., Jamestown, R. I., since 1943.

Mitchell, Clovis W., B.S.'08, R. I. State Col.; Supt., Gloucester Schs., Harmony, R. I., since 1940.

Nevins, Vincent, B.S. in Ed.'33, State Tchrs. Col., Bridgewater, Mass.; Ed.M.'41, Boston Univ.; Supt. of Sch , Lonsdale, R. I.

Nikula, Peter E., B.S. in Ed.'50, M.S. in Ed.'52, State Tchrs. Col., Fitchburg, Mass.; Supt. of New Shoreham Sch. Dist., Block Island, R. I., since 1951.

Noble, M. C. S., Jr., A.B.'21, Univ. of N. C.; M.A.'22, Ed.D.'24, Harvard Univ.; Assoc. Prof. of Educ. and Psych., R. I., State Col., Kingston, R. I., since 1948.

Norton, Bernard F., B.S.'27, Providence Col.; Supt. of Sch., Valley Falls, R. I., since 1935.

Nugent, Henry F., A.B.'31, Providence Col.; Ed.D.'40, Catholic Tchrs. Col., Providence; State Supvr. of Adult Educ., State Dept. of Educ., Providence, R. I., since 1936.

O'Brien, George J., A.B.'21, Holy Cross Col.; M.A.'32, Brown Univ.; Asst. Supt. of Sch., Providence, R. I., since 1945.

Oldham, James R. D., A.B.'97, Brown Univ.; Supt. Emeritus of Sch., East Providence R. I., since 1945. Address: 66 Don Ave., Rumford, R. I.

Pelton, Frank M., A.B.'28, A.M.'31, Cornell Univ.; Ph.D.'34, New York Univ.; Prof. of Educ. and Dir. of Summer Sch., R. I. State Col., Kingston, R. I., since 1945.

Pezzullo, Thomas J., B.A.'38, Univ. of Ariz.; Asst.-Supt. of Sch., Johnston, R. I., since 1946.

Porter-Shirley, Carl H., B.S. in Ed.'27, State Tchrs. Col., Bridgewater, Mass.; M.Ed.'30, R. I. Col. of Educ.; Supt. of Sch., Newport, R. I.

Potenza, Robert A., Ph.B.'36, Boston Col.; Supt. of Sch., Slatersville, R. I.

Quinn, Edmund A., B.S.'24, Providence Col.; A.M.'31, Brown Univ.; Dir. of Curriculum Research, Admin. Bldg., 20 Summer St., Providence, R. I., since 1949.

Quinn, Maisie E., B.Ed.'37, R. I. Col. of Educ.; Supt. of Sch., West Warwick, R. I., since 1938.

Robinson, William P., Jr., A.B.'35, Providence Col.; M.Ed.'50, R. I. Col. of Educ.; D.Ed.'50, Catholic Tchrs. Col. of Providence; Supvr. of Tchr. Certification, State Dept. of Educ., Providence, R. I., since 1948.

Searle, Roger L., Supt. of Sch., Shannock, R. I.

Smith, Elmer R., Ph.B.'26, A.M.'28, Brown Univ.; Asst. Supt. of Sch., Providence, R. I., since 1949.

Snell, Hayward, A.B.'30, Clark Univ.; Ed.M.'46, Harvard Univ.; Supt. of Sch., Middletown, R. I., since 1946.

Sturtevant, Clarence E., B.S.'25, Middlebury Col.; M.A.'31, Tchrs. Col., Columbia Univ.; Supt. of Sch., Barrington, R. I., since 1945.

Thomas, L. Ralston, B.S.'13, Haverford Col.; Ed.M.'24, Harvard Univ.; Sc.D.'43, R. I. Col. of Pharmacy and Allied Sciences; Headmaster, Moses Brown Sch., Providence, R. I., since 1924.

Trowt, B. C., Supt. of Sch., Narragansett, R. I., since 1933.

Varieur, Francis J., B.B.A.'34, Bryant Col.; Ed.M.'43, R. I. Col. of Educ., Providence; Asst. Supt. of Sch., Pawtucket, R. I., since 1949.

Walsh, Michael Francis, B.A.'22, Col. of the Holy Cross; Ed.D., Catholic Tchrs. Col., Providence, R. I.; Dir. of Educ., State Dept of Educ., Providence, R. I., since 1947.

Whelan, Joseph A., Ed.B.'42, Ed.M.'51, R. I. Col. of Educ.; Acting Supt. of Sch., North Providence, R. I., since 1952.

Wilcox, Edward F., B.S.'36, R. I. State Col.; E.B.'38, R. I. Col. of Educ., Providence; Supt. of Sch., Ashaway, R. I., since 1949.

SOUTH CAROLINA

INDIVIDUAL MEMBERS

Alford, George R., B.S.'31, Univ. of Okla.; Ed.M.'48, Univ. of S. C.; Supt. of Sch., Lake View, S. C., since 1943.

Anderson, Jesse T., B.A.'14, Furman Univ.; M.A.'42, Univ. of S. C.; State Supt. of Educ., Columbia, S. C., since 1947.

Anderson, John Hugh, A.B.'14, Wofford Col.; M.A.'32, Tchrs. Col., Columbia Univ.; Supt. of Parker Sch. Dist., Greenville, S. C., since 1935.

Anderson, M. T., Prin., Sr. H. S., Greenville, S. C.

Anderson, W. R., A.B.'23, Presbyterian Col. of S. C.; M.A.'31, Emory Univ.; Supt. of Pub. Sch., Clinton, S. C., since 1945.

Barbare, Ralph, A.B.'26, M.A.'31, Univ. of S. C.; Dir., Winthrop Tr. Sch., Winthrop Col., Rock Hill, S. C., since 1949.

Barnett, John H., B.S.'23, Furman Univ.; Supt. of Sch., Marietta, S. C., since 1938.

Beam, J. Paul, B.A.'21, Furman Univ.; Th.B.'38, Southern Baptist Theol. Sem.; M.A.'39, Duke Univ.; Dir., Union Co. Sch., Union, S. C., since 1952.

Betchman, H. B., A.B.'22, Clemson and Newberry Col.; Supt. of Sch., Summerton, S. C., since 1925.

Blakely, Charles B., B.A.'24, Erskine Col.; M.A.'45, Univ. of S. C.; Co. Supt. of Educ., Chester, S. C., since 1949.

Blanding, James D., A.B.'25, The Citadel; M.A.'34, Peabody Col.; Supt. of Sch., Sumter, S. C., since 1951.

Brissie, S. C., A.B., Furman Univ.; M.A., Univ. of S. C.; Supt. of Sch., Woodruff, S. C., since 1945.

Brockman, Myron E., A.B.'03, Furman Univ.; Supt. of City Sch., Chester, S. C., 1920-52 (retired). Address: P. O. Box 374, Chester, S. C.

Busbee, Cyril B., B.S.'28, M.A.'38, Univ. of S. C.; Supt. of Brookland-Cayce Sch., West Columbia, S. C., since 1943.

Cain, Ralph H., B.S.'26, Clemson Col.; M.A.'43, Cornell Univ.; Supt. of D. A. R. Sch., Tamassee, S. C., since 1926.

Carmichael, William Boyd, A.B.'37, Wofford Col.; M.Ed.'50, Univ. of S. C.; Dillon Co. Supt. of Educ., Dillon, S. C., since 1950.

Coates, James Pierce, A.B.'11, M.A.'26, Univ. of S. C.; Secy., S. C. Educ. Assn., Columbia, S. C., since 1925.

Coble, Parks M., B.A.'36, M.A.'43, Furman Univ.; Supt. of Sch. Area 1, Horry Co., Conway, S. C., since 1952.

Coker, Homer, Supt., Pub. Sch., Saint Stephen, S. C.

Coleman, J. H., A.B.'25, M.A.'42, Furman Univ.; Supt. of Sch., Honea Path, S. C., since 1925.

Cross, J. Russel, Supt., Cross Area Sch., Cross, S. C.

Crout, James McBride, B.A.'37, Wofford Col.; M.Ed.'47, Univ. of S. C.; Supt., Batesburg-Leesville Sch. System, Batesburg, S. C., since 1946.

Crow, E. R., A.B.'15, Furman Univ.; A.M.'24, Univ. of S. C.; Dir., State Educ. Finance Comm., Columbia, S. C.

Crow, Orin F., A.B.'17, Univ. of S. C.; A.M.'25, Ph.D.'31, George Peabody Col. for Tchrs.; Dean, Sch. of Educ., Univ. of S. C., Columbia, S. C., since 1930.

Denmark, Annie Dove, Diploma in Piano'04, Meredith Col.; A.B.'25, Anderson Col.; Litt.D.'41, Furman Univ.; Pres., Anderson Col., Anderson, S. C., since 1928.

Dixon, C. A., Supt. of Sch., Loris, S. C.

Doggette, James Carlisle, Sr., A.B.'27, Univ. of S. C.; Supt. of Sch., York, S. C., since 1948.

Dorman, Paul M., B.A.'28, Furman Univ.; Supt., Spartanburg Co. Sch. Dist. 6, Fairforest, S. C., since 1942.

Dowling, Thomas I., B.S.'24, M.S.'25, Univ. of S. C.; M.A.'33, Columbia Univ.; Supt. of Sch., Dist. 50, Greenwood, S. C., since 1952.

Dubose, Frank E., A.B. in Ed.'29, Univ. of S. C.; Supt., East Clarendon Sch., Turbeville, S. C.

East, J. K., B.S.'35, Berry Col.; Supt. of Sch., Blacksburg, S. C., since 1946.

Faulk, Joseph Hampton, B.A. in Ed.'32, M.A. in Ed.'37, Univ. of S. C.; Prin., Jenkins Jr. H. S., Spartanburg, S. C., since 1945.

Fort, Arthur H., A.M.'24, Wofford Col.; Prin., Jr. H. S., Anderson, S. C., since 1945.

Foy, G. N., A.B.'34, Newberry Col.; M.A.'47, Univ. of S. C.; Supt. of Sch., Joanna, S. C., since 1929.

Frampton, G. C., Co. Supt. of Educ., Charleston, S. C.

Garrett, Gordon H., B.S.'28, The Citadel; M.A. '37, Duke Univ.; Supt. of Cooper River Sch. Dist. 4, North Charleston, S. C., since 1936.

Gault, Marvin G., A.B.'19, Erskine Col.; M.A.'43, George Peabody Col. for Tchrs.; Supt. of City Sch., Bamberg, S. C., since 1948.

Gettys, R. H., A.B.'33, Erskine Col.; Supt. of Sch., Westminster, S. C., since 1951.

Gray, Wil Lou, B.A.'03, Columbia Col.; M.A.'10, Columbia Univ.; LL.D.'47, Wofford Col.; Dir., Opportunity Sch., West Columbia, S. C., since 1947.

Green, Albert, A.B.'39, Univ. of S. C.; B.D.'42, Yale Univ.; Co. Supt. of Educ., Georgetown, S. C., since 1948.

Grier, Boyce M., A.B.'16, Erskine Col.; M.A.'28, Univ. of Ga.; Litt.D.'41, Erskine Col.; Ph.D. '47, George Peabody Col. for Tchrs.; Pres., Lander Col., Greenwood, S. C., since 1948.

Hair, A. B., Jr., B.S.'22, Clemson Col.; Supt. of Sch., Williamston, S. C., since 1938.

Hanberry, T. J., M.S.'32, State Univ. of Iowa; Dean, Benedict Col., Columbia, S. C., since 1950.

Harllee, John M., A.B.'17, Wofford Col.; M.A. '34, Univ. of S. C.; Supt. of Sch., Florence, S. C., since 1946.

Harman, H. Odelle, A.B.'29, M.A.'36, Univ. of S. C.; Supt. of Sch., Lexington, S. C., since 1939.

Harmon, Price K., A.B.'21, Newberry Col.; M.A.'39, Univ. of S. C.; Supt. of Sch., Newberry, S. C., since 1946.

Harrell, M. M., Prin., Donaldson Elem. Sch., Greenville, S. C.

Hawkins, Sewell C., A.B.'39, M.Ed.'51, Univ. of S. C.; Supvr. of Certification, State Dept. of Educ., Columbia, S. C.

Hawthorne, Mark Fant, A.B.'28, Furman Univ.; M.Ed.'40, Duke Univ.; Supt. of Sch., Anderson, S. C., since 1945.

Hendrix, J. H., Area Supt., Union Co. Sch., Lockhart, S. C.

Herndon, J. E., Supt. of Sch., Fountain Inn, S. C.

Hoole, W. H., A.B.'36, Col. of Wooster; M.A.'37, N. Y. State Col. for Tchrs., Albany; Ed.M.'48, Univ. of S. C.; Supt. of Sch., Society Hill, S. C., since 1940.

Hursey, Mertin, B.A.'29, Univ. of S. C.; Supt., Co. Sch. Dist. 1, Chesterfield, S. C., since 1944.

Jolly, Thomas Claude, Jr., B.S.'17, M.A.'32, Univ. of S. C.; Supt. of Sch., Union, S. C., since 1924.

Kellett, J. N., A.B.'26, Wofford Col.; Supt. of Sch., Seneca, S. C., since 1945.

Kinard, T. G., A.B.'29, Newberry Col.; M.A.'44, Univ. of S. C.; Supt. of Sch., Clover, S. C., since 1945.

King, Morris A., B.Ed.'39, Univ. of Ga.; M.A.'46, Tchrs. Col., Columbia Univ.; Prof. of Educ., Lander Col., Greenwood, S. C., since 1952.

Kirk, F. M., B.S.'26, Col. of Charleston; M.A.'46, Univ. of S. C.; Supt. of Sch., Summerville, S. C., since 1946.

Lake, Robert Campbell, A.B.'13, Lenoir-Rhyne Col.; M.A.'35, Univ. of S. C.; Supt. of Sch., Whitmire, S. C., since 1924.

Lee, B.D., B.A.'25, M.A.'36, Wofford Col.; Supt. of Sch., Gaffney, S. C., since 1949.

Lockwood, Charles Madden, A.B.'16, Furman Univ.; M.A.'38, Univ. of S. C.; Supt. of City Sch., Johnston, S. C., since 1951.

Loggins, W. F., M.A.'28, Columbia Univ.; Ed.D.'45, New York Univ.; Supt. of Sch., Greenville, S. C., since 1940.

McArthur, Laurin Currie, Jr., A.B.'39, A.M.'42, Univ. of S. C.; Ed.D.'50, Tchrs. Col., Columbia Univ.; Dir. of Elem. Educ., City Sch., Orangeburg, S. C., since 1950.

McCormac, D. Leon, A.B.'25, M.A.'30, Univ. of S. C.; Dir., Div. of Instr., State Dept. of Educ., Columbia, S. C., since 1952.

McCracken, Joseph Glenn, B.S.'38, Wake Forest Col.; M.A.'42, Univ. of N. C.; Supt. of Sch., Spartanburg, S. C., since 1950.

McDaniel, Olin K., A.B. in Ed.'14, Univ. of S. C.; M.A. in Sch. Admin.'40, George Peabody Col. for Tchrs.; Supt. of City Sch., Beaufort, S. C., since 1934.

McKnight, Loramer, M.A.'43, Univ. of S. C.; Supt., Mt. Zion Inst., Winnsboro, S. C.

Mabry, T. E., A.B.'25, Erskine Col.; M.S.'34, Univ. of Ga.; Supt., Sch. Dist. 4, Inman, S. C.

Mangum, G. C., A.B.'39, Wofford Col.; M.A.'47, Univ. of S. C.; Supt. of Sch., Ridgeland, S. C., since 1950.

Marshall, Harris Andrew, A.B.'31, Furman Univ.; M.A.'42, Duke Univ.; Supt. of Sch., Orangeburg, S. C., since 1952.

*Martin, Charles J., A.B.'30, Presbyterian Col.; M.Ed.'47, Univ. of S. C.; Asst. Supt., Co. Sch. Dist., Greenville, S. C., since 1951.

Martin, J. V., A.B.'26, Presbyterian Col.; M.A.'39, Univ. of S. C.; Supt. of Sch., Dillon, S. C., since 1936.

Mellette, J. R., A.B.'30, Wofford Col.; M.Ed.'52, Univ. of S. C., Supt. of Sch., Timmonsville, S. C., since 1939.

Mims, Sallie Kate, 1312 Augusta St., Greenville, S. C.

Mobley, Robert A., Supt., Colleton Co. Sch. Dist. 2, Walterboro, S. C.

Moffat, Sam S., A.B.'33, Erskine Col.; M.A.'40, Univ. of Ga.; Supt. of City Sch., Abbeville, S. C., since 1946.

Moore, Hilda M., 228 E. Park Ave., Greenville, S. C.

Myers, Govan T., A.B.'32, Wofford Col.; M.A.'41, Ph.D.'51, Univ. of N. C.; Supt. of City Sch., Lancaster, S. C., since 1951.

Nelson, T. M., Prin., Parker Sch., Greenville, S. C.

Nixon, Drury M., B.A.'20, Furman Univ.; Supt., Dist. 5 H. S. of Spartanburg Co., Lyman, S. C., since 1950.

O'Sheasy, Edward A., B.S.E.'39, Mass. State Tchrs. Col., Fitchburg; M.E.'51, Boston Univ.; Supt., James Island Sch. Dist. 3, Charleston, S. C., since 1946.

513

Pinson, B. S., B.A.'20, Furman Univ.; M.S.'33, Univ. of S. C.; Supt., Thornwell Orphanage Sch., Clinton, S. C., since 1927.

Poats, Ella, B.A.'33, Converse Col.; M.A.'48, Emory Univ.; Asst. to Supt. of City Sch., Spartanburg, S. C., since 1948.

Rice, Spencer M., B.A.'32, M.A.'38, Wofford Col.; Diploma '47, Tchrs. Col., Columbia Univ.; Prin., H. S., Spartanburg, S. C., since 1942.

Richards, A. J., B.S.'17, Clemson Agrl. Col.; M.A.'39, Univ. of S. C.; Supt. of Sch., Heath Springs, S. C., since 1949.

Richards, J. G., Jr., A.B.'09, Davidson Col.; Supt. of Sch., Camden, S. C., since 1917.

Robison, J. D., A.B.'13, Erskine Col.; Dir., S. C. Sch. Bk. Commn., Columbia, S. C., since 1938.

Rogers, George Calvin, B.S.'10, The Citadel; M.A.'28, Columbia Univ.; Supt. of Sch., Charleston, S. C., since 1946.

Sadler, James K., B.S.'28. Clemson Col.; Bus. Admin.'30, Columbia Univ.; Bus. Mgr., City Sch., Greenville, S. C., since 1946.

Sanders, Horace K., B.A.'22, M.Ed.'46, Univ. of S. C.; Supt., Socastee Sch., Myrtle Beach, S. C., since 1948.

Silcox, Willard A., B.S.'33, Col. of Charleston; Dir. of Athletics, Col. of Charleston, Charleston, S. C., since 1939.

Sims, Henry R., A.B.'13, LL.D.'45, Wofford Col.; Pres., Winthrop Col., Rock Hill, S. C., since 1944.

Smith, Arthur, B.A.'29, Furman Univ.; M.Ed.'40, Duke Univ.; Supt. of Sch., Bennettsville, S. C., since 1950.

Sneed, Henry L., Jr., A.B.'36, Erskine Col.; M.A.'43, Univ. of S. C.; Supt., Chester City Area Sch., Chester, S. C., since 1952.

Southerlin, William Broadus, B.A.'29, Furman Univ.; M.A.'43, Univ. of S. C.; Supvr., Schoolhouse Planning, State Educ. Finance Commn., Columbia, S. C., since 1948.

Southwell, J. L., B.A.E.'37, M.A.'40, Univ. of Fla.; Bus. Mgr., Sumter Sch. Dist. #17, Sumter, S. C.

Spann, J. H., Jr., B.S.Ed.'37, M.A.'41, Univ. of S. C.; Supt. of Sch., Myrtle Beach, S. C., since 1950.

Stackhouse, Esther, Co. Supt. of Educ., Marion, S. C.

Stoddard, Hugh T., A.B.'30, M.A.'37, Univ. of S. C.; Supt. of Sch., Co. Dist. 2, Sumter, S. C., since 1952.

Stoudemire, Emory Blair, A.B.'23, Newberry Col.; Supt. of Sch., Walhalla, S. C., since 1926.

Sullivan, Walter Caswell, A.B.'17, A.M.'18, Univ. of S. C.; Supt. of Sch., Rock Hill, S. C., since 1938.

Taylor, T. L., Supt. of Mountain View Sch., RFD 1, Taylors, S. C.

Togneri, Louis M., B.S.'32, Ed.M.'48, Univ. of S. C.; Supt. of Sch., Graniteville, S. C., since 1945.

Ulmer, T. H., A.B.'24, Furman Univ.; M.A.'44, George Peabody Col. for Tchrs.; Supt. of Sch., Hartsville, S. C., since 1950.

Varn, Guy L., A.B.'27, Wofford Col.; M.A.'42, Univ. of S. C.; Supt. of Sch., Columbia, S. C., since 1951.

Ward, W. H., A.B.'14, Furman Univ.; Dir., Extension Div., Univ. of S. C., Columbia, S. C., since 1937.

Washington, William Harold, B.S.'20, Clemson Col.; M.S.'22, Iowa State Col.; Dean, Sch. of Educ., Clemson Col., Clemson, S. C., since 1934.

Weldon, William Heathley, A.B.'29, Presbyterian Col.; M.A.'41, Furman Univ.; Supt. of Sch. Dist. 9, Manning, S. C., since 1949.

White, Henry A., A.B.'31, M.A.'40, Univ. of S. C.; Supt. of City Sch., Georgetown, S. C., since 1946.

Williams, C. E., B.S.'31, Furman Univ.; M.A.'43, Univ. of S. C.; Supt., St. Andrews Parish Sch., Charleston, S. C., since 1941.

Williams, Eugene Allen, A.B.'20, Furman Univ.; Ed.M.'46, Univ. of S. C.; Supt., Baron DeKalb Sch., Westville, S. C., since 1943.

Wood, Herbert A., B.S.'37, Clemson Agrl. Col.; M.Ed.'48, Univ. of S. C.; Prin., Brookland-Cayce H. S., Cayce, S. C., since 1945.

Woodson, Camillus C., A.B.'28, Benedict Col.; M.A.'44, Univ. of Mich.; Prin., Carver H. S., Spartanburg, S. C., since 1932.

Wright, C. K., A.B.'24, George Peabody Col.; M.A.'27, Univ. of S. C.; Supt. of Sch., Laurens, S. C., since 1952.

Younginer, James W., B.S.'35, Wofford Col.; M.A.'52, Univ. of Ga.; Supt., Chesterfield Co. Sch. Dist. 3, McBee, S. C., since 1949.

INSTITUTIONAL MEMBER

Clemson College Library, c/o Cornelia A. Graham, Librn., Clemson, S. C.

SOUTH DAKOTA

INDIVIDUAL MEMBERS

Baumann, Lester H., B.A.'32, State Tchrs. Col., Valley City, N. Dak.; M.A.'37, Northwestern Univ.; Supt. of Sch., Yankton, S. Dak.

Berger, Harry S., B.S. in Ed.'19, Northeast Mo., State Tchrs. Col., Kirksville; M.A. in Ed.'29, Univ. of Mo.; Supt. of Sch., Deadwood, S. Dak., since 1928.

Bergquist, Ernest B., B.A.'02, Gustavus Adolphus Col.; M.A.'30, Univ. of Minn.; Supt. of Sch., Rapid City, S. Dak., since 1929.

Bogard, Herman, A.B.'15, Morningside Col.; Ph.M.'31, Univ. of Wis.; Supt., Indian Sch., Flandreau, S. Dak., since 1941.

Delzell, Mark W., A.B.'25, Nebr. State Tchrs. Col., Peru; M.A.'28, Columbia Univ.; Ph.D. '46, Univ. of Nebr.; Dean, Sch. of Educ., Univ. of S. Dak., Vermillion, S. Dak., since 1951.

Douglas, E. L., B.S.'38, Eastern Ky. State Col.; M.E.'50, Univ. of S. Dak.; Supt. of Sch., Lennox, S. Dak., since 1950.

Ehlers, O. K., B.A.'28, Concordia Col.; Supt. of Sch., Wakpala, S. Dak., since 1949.

Fort, Lyman M., B.A.'13, Univ. of Ill.; M.A.'28, Univ. of Colo.; LL.D.'34, Dakota Wesleyan Univ.; Supt. of Sch., Sioux Falls, S. Dak., 1944-52. Address: c/o Pub. Sch., Sioux Falls, S. Dak.

Freeman, H. S., B.A.'19, LL.D.'50, Morningside Col.; M.A.'34, Univ. of Minn.; State Supt. of Pub. Instr., Pierre, S. Dak., since 1949.

Hald, Robert E., B.S. in Ed.'38, Northern State Tchrs. Col., Aberdeen, S. Dak.; M.A.'45, Univ. of Minn.; Supt. of Sch., Clark, S. Dak.

Headley, John W., B.S.'31, Eastern State Normal Sch., Madison, S. Dak.; M.A.'34, Ed.D.'41, Colo. State Col. of Educ., Greeley; Pres., South Dakota State Col., Brookings, S. Dak.

Holgate, Clare H., B.S.'28, Dakota Wesleyan Univ.; M.S.'41, Univ. of Wis.; Supt. of Sch., Aberdeen, S. Dak., since 1951.

Holgate, E. L., B.A.'30, Dakota Wesleyan Univ.; M.E.'45, Univ. of S. Dak.; Supt. of Sch., Mobridge, S. Dak., since 1948.

Hunkins, Ralph V., B.A.'14, Univ. of Nebr.; M.A.'21, Univ. of Chicago; D.Litt.'36, Dakota Wesleyan Univ.; Supt. of Sch., Lead, S. Dak., since 1922.

Iverson, H. W., A.B.'25, Augustana Col.; M.A. '41, Univ. of S. Dak.; Supt. of Sch., Groton, S. Dak., since 1938.

Jonas, Russell E., B.S. in Ed.'31, Northern State Tchrs. Col., Aberdeen, S. Dak.; M.A.'34, Ph.D.'36, State Univ. of Iowa; Pres., Black Hills Tchrs. Col., Spearfish, S. Dak., since 1942.

Kramer, J. Howard, B.A.'24, Univ. of S. Dak.; M.A.'30, State Univ. of Iowa; Ed.D.'43, Colo. State Col. of Educ., Greeley; Pres., Southern State Tchrs. Col., Springfield, S. Dak., since 1945.

Lindsey, Mervin E., B.A.'24, Huron Col.; M.A.'34, Univ. of Colo.; Supt. of Sch., Custer, S. Dak., since 1924.

Lovinger, Warren C., B.A.'42. M.A.'44, Mont. State Univ.; Ed.D.'47, Columbia Univ.; Pres., Northern State Tchrs. Col., Aberdeen, S. Dak., since 1951.

Lundy, Andrew M., B.A.'37, Augustana Col.; M.A.'47, Univ. of S. Dak.; Supt. of Sch., Gettysburg, S. Dak.

Marquette, Harvey E., B.S.'26, S. Dak. State Col. of Agrl. and Mech. Arts; M.A.'33, Univ. of Minn.; Supt. of Sch., Milbank, S. Dak., since 1946.

Mikkelsen, E. C., B.A.'28, Yankton Col.; M.A. '36, Univ. of S. Dak.; Supt. of Sch., Spearfish, S. Dak., since 1945.

Miller, Dwight D., M.A.'30, Univ. of Ill.; Supt. of Sch., Watertown, S. Dak., since 1940.

Morgen, Fred S., B.S. in Ed.'26, Northern State Tchrs. Col., Aberdeen, S. Dak.; M.S. in Ed.'40, Univ. of Wyo.; Supt. of Sch., Pollock, S. Dak., since 1936.

Nesset, Novalf, B.A.'44, State Tchrs. Col., Valley City, N. Dak.; Reservation Prin., Cheyenne Agency, S. Dak., since 1950.

Newman, Harvey H., B.A.'38, Univ. of Colo.; M.A.'43, Univ. of S. Dak.; Supt. of Sch., Webster, S. Dak., since 1945.

Newport, K. K., Reservation Prin., Rosebud, S. Dak., since 1933.

Pyles, Albert T., B.A.'35, Fairmont State Tchrs. Col.; Reservation Prin., Pine Ridge, S. Dak., since 1947.

Reynolds, Merton L., B.S.'27, S. Dak. State Col. of Agrl. and Applied Arts; M.A.'40, Univ. of Minn.; Supt. of Sch., Pierre, S. Dak., since 1948.

Schunk, Harold W., B.S.'31, Southern State Tchrs. Col.; Educ. Specialist, Cheyenne Agency, S. Dak., since 1951.

Skarda, Edward W., B.S.'35, Univ. of Minn.; M.A.'40, Univ. of S. Dak.; Supt. of Sch., Sioux Falls, S. Dak., since 1950.

Slocum, James F., B.A.'30, Yankton Col.; M.A.'41, Univ. of S. Dak.; Supt. of Sch., Huron, S. Dak., since 1950.

Smith, R. J., Reservation Prin. of Sch., Ft. Thompson, S. Dak.

Sonstegard, Ansel P., M.A.'43, Univ. of S. Dak.; Supt. of Sch., Redfield, S. Dak., since 1950.

Strand, F. A., B.A.'23, St. Olaf Col.; M.A.'37, Leland Stanford Jr. Univ.; Exec. Secy., S. Dak. Educ. Assn., Sioux Falls, S. Dak., since 1952.

Thompson, Floyd, B.A.'40, Huron Col.; M.E.'48, Univ. of S. Dak.; Supt. of Sch., Madison, S. Dak., since 1952.

Truax, (Mrs.) Grace Greves, B.A.'37, Augustana Col.; Special Lecturer, Augustana Col., Sioux Falls, S. Dak., since 1932.

Uecker, Lloyd T., B.A.'26, M.A.'37, Univ. of S. Dak.; Supt. of Sch., Mitchell, S. Dak., since 1947.

Vanden Berge, H. O., B.A.'31, Yankton Col.; M.E.'47, Univ. of S. Dak.; Supt. of Sch., Vermillion, S. Dak., since 1947.

Voss, Edward F., B.S.'18, S. Dak. State Col.; M.A.'26, Tchrs. Col., Columbia Univ.; Supt. of Sch., Chester, S. Dak., since 1951.

White, C. E., M.A.'40, Univ. of S. Dak.; Supt. of Sch., Canton, S. Dak., since 1948.

Woodward, Harry R., A.B.'16, Litt.D.'42, Dakota Wesleyan Univ.; A.M.'29, Stanford Univ.; Supt. of Sch., Hot Springs, S. Dak., since 1922.

INSTITUTIONAL MEMBER

Library, General Beadle State Teachers College, Madison, S. Dak.

TENNESSEE

INDIVIDUAL MEMBERS

Alexander, Philip Wade, B.S.'24, M.A.'26, Ph.D.'39, George Peabody Col. for Tchrs.; Dean, East Tenn. State Col., Johnson City, Tenn., since 1946.

Anderson, Robert C., B.S.'42, Ala. Polytech. Inst.; M.A.'47, Univ. of N. C.; Ph.D.'50, New York Univ.; Dir. of the Graduate Sch., Memphis State Col., Memphis, Tenn., since 1950.

Armour, Quinnie, B.S.'29, Union Univ.; M.A.'37, George Peabody Col. for Tchrs.; Supt., Hardeman Co. Sch., Bolivar, Tenn., since 1940.

Arrants, John H., A.B.'16, M.S.'32, Univ. of Tenn.; Supt. of Sch., Johnson City, Tenn., since 1946.

Baker, Roy N., B.S.'34, Memphis State Col.; M.A.'44, George Peabody Col. for Tchrs.; Pres., Bethel Col. and the Cumberland Presbyterian Theol. Sem., McKenzie, Tenn., since 1944.

Ball, Ernest C., B.S.'26, Memphis State Col.; M.A.'36, George Peabody Col. for Tchrs.; Supt. of Sch., Memphis, Tenn., since 1935.

Barksdale, James A., M.A.'36, Univ. of Colo.; Commr. of Educ., State Dept. of Educ., Nashville, Tenn., since 1950.

Barnes, George H., B.S.'28, Univ. of Ill.; Supt. of Co. Sch., Memphis, Tenn., since 1951.

Bass, F. E., Exec. Secy., Tenn. Educ. Assn., Nashville, Tenn., since 1950.

Bass, W. A., B.A.'28, Univ. of Tenn.; M.A.'28, Univ. of Chicago; Supt. of Sch., Nashville Tenn., since 1938.

Bates, Creed F., A.B.'14, Univ. of Chattanooga; A.M.'24, Columbia Univ.; Prin., H. S., Chattanooga, Tenn.

Benjamin, Harold, A.B.'21, A.M.'24, Univ. of Oregon; Ph.D.'27, Stanford Univ.; Chairman, Div. of Foundations of Educ., George Peabody Col. for Tchrs., Nashville, Tenn.

Black, Charles R., B.A.'25, Maryville Col.; M.A.'49, Univ. of Tenn.; Supt. of Sch., Harriman, Tenn., since 1938.

Black, R. E., B.S.'26, Union Univ., Tenn.; Co. Supt. of Sch., Alamo, Tenn., since 1949.

Bohannon, Oliver T., B.S.'39, Tenn. Polytech. Inst.; Co. Supt. of Sch., Cookeville, Tenn., since 1943.

Bower, Thomas C., B.S.'35, M.S.'41, Univ. of Tenn.; Supt. of Sch., Cleveland, Tenn.

Broughton, P. M., A.B.'30, Union Col. (Ky.); M.A.'48, Univ. of Ky.; Prin., H. S., Jellico, Tenn., since 1949.

Brown, Glennon C., B.A.'28, Bridgewater Col.; M.S.'47, Univ. of Tenn.; Co. Supt. of Sch., Greeneville, Tenn., since 1948.

515

TENNESSEE

Buckner, J. Guy, A.B.'30, Carson-Newman Col.; Supt. of Sch., Lenoir City, Tenn., since 1943.

Byrom, J. Marvin, B.S.'30, Middle Tenn. State Tchrs. Col.; M.S.'40, Univ. of Tenn.; Co. Supt. of Sch., Lynchburg, Tenn., since 1948.

Crider, Basil J., B.S.'34, Murray State Col.; M.A.'48, George Peabody Col. for Tchrs.; Supt. of Pub. Sch., Bells, Tenn., 1936–44, and since 1946.

Crouch, J. Willard, B.S.'39, State Tchrs. Col.; Co. Supt. of Sch., Jamestown, Tenn., since 1948.

Davis, Mack Parker, A.B.'34, Carson-Newman Col.; M.Ed.'42, Univ. of Tenn.; Dir., East Tenn. State Col. Training Sch. and Exec. Secy., East Tenn. Educ. Assn., Inc., East Tenn. State Col., Johnson City, Tenn., since 1947.

Deen, Pearl, A.B.'23, Univ. of Tenn.; M.A.'29, George Peabody Col.; Elem. Prin., Grahamwood Sch., Memphis, Tenn., since 1944.

Denton, J. C., B.S. in Ed.'48, Bethel Col. (Tenn.); Supt., Carroll Co. Sch., Huntingdon, Tenn., since 1950.

Derryberry, Everett, A.B.'28, Univ. of Tenn.; B.A.'32, M.A.'32, Oxford Univ., England; Pres., Tenn. Polytech. Inst., Cookeville, Tenn., since 1940.

Derthick, Lawrence G., B.A.'27, Milligan Col.; M.A.'30, Univ. of Tenn.; Supt. of Sch., Chattanooga, Tenn., since 1942.

Dossett, Burgin E., A.B.'22, Univ. of Tenn.; M.A.'24, Harvard Univ.; LL.D.'47, Bob Jones Univ.; Pres., East Tenn. State Col., Johnson City, Tenn., since 1949.

Dowtin, J. V., A.B.'26, Bethel Col.; B.S.'29, M.A.'40, George Peabody Col. for Tchrs.; Prin., H. S., Kenton, Tenn., since 1943.

Doyle, Mildred E., B.S. in Ed.'40, M.Ed.'44, Univ. of Tenn.; Co. Supt. of Sch., Knoxville, Tenn., since 1946.

Dugger, Thomas A., Jr., B.S.'34, East Tenn. State Col.; M.S.'49, Univ. of Tenn.; Supt. of Sch., Elizabethton, Tenn., since 1946.

Emerson, Don N., B.S.'31, Milligan Col.; M.A.'47, George Peabody Col. for Tchrs.; Supt. of Sch., Franklin, Tenn., since 1947.

Evans, W. E., Prin. of H. S., Knoxville, Tenn.

Finchum, Ralph N., B.A.'28, M.S.'36, Univ. of Tenn.; Supt. of City Sch., Clinton, Tenn., since 1947.

Fitzgerald, N. E., B.S. in Ed.'15, B.S. in Agr.'17, Univ. of Tenn.; M.S.'26, Cornell Univ.; Dean, Col. of Educ., Univ. of Tenn., Knoxville, Tenn., since 1943.

Frost, Norman, A.B.'09, Oberlin Col.; M.A.'13, Ph.D.'21, Tchrs. Col., Columbia Univ.; Prof. of Rural Educ., George Peabody Col. for Tchrs., Nashville, Tenn., since 1917.

Furney, Charles Phillip, M.A.'43, Kent State Univ.; Prin., Elem. Sch., Oak Ridge, Tenn., since 1944.

Gilliland, John W., A.B.'27, Southwest Mo. State Tchrs. Col., Springfield; M.A.'31, Univ. of Mo.; Ed.D.'49, New York Univ.; Prof. of Educ. Admin., Univ. of Tenn., Knoxville, Tenn., since 1949.

Goddard, V. F., B.A.'13, Maryville Col.; M.A.'28, Univ. of Mich.; Supt. of Sch., Alcoa, Tenn., since 1924.

Goslin, Willard E., B.S.'22, Northeast Mo. State Tchrs. Col., Kirksville; M.A.'29, Univ. of Mo.; LL.D. (Hon.)'49, Occidental Col.; Pres., American Assn. of Sch. Admin., 1948–49; Chmn., Div. of Educ. Admin. and Community Development, George Peabody Col. for Tchrs., Nashville, Tenn., since 1951.

Graff, Orin B., B.S.'29, Ohio Northern Univ.; M.A.'34, Ph.D.'41, Ohio State Univ.; Head, Dept. of Educ. Admin. and Supvn., Col. of Educ., Univ. of Tenn., Knoxville, Tenn., since 1944.

*Grove, Robert N., B.S.'39, State Tchrs. Col., Millersville, Pa.; M.A.'48, Ed.D.'50, Tchrs. Col., Columbia Univ.; Admin. Asst. Supt. of Sch., Chattanooga, Tenn., since 1949.

Hamilton, Milton, B.S.'38, Murray State Tchrs. Col., Murray, Ky.; Co. Supt. of Sch., Union City, Tenn., since 1939.

Harper, R. A., B.S. in Ed.'26, Southeast Mo. State Tchrs. Col., Cape Girardeau; M.A.'31, Univ. of Mo.; Supt. of Sch., Maryville, Tenn., since 1944.

Headden, Harmon C., B.S.'30, State Tchrs. Col., Memphis, Tenn.; M.A.'31, Columbia Univ.; Pres., Tenn. Equipment and Supply Co., Nashville, Tenn., since 1948.

Hill, Henry H., A.B. and M.A.'21, Univ. of Va.; Ph.D.'30, Tchrs. Col., Columbia Univ.; Pres., American Assn. of Sch. Admin., 1946–47; Pres., George Peabody Col. for Tchrs., Nashville, Tenn., since 1945

Hobgood, Baxter E., M.A.'38, George Peabody Col. for Tchrs.; Supt. of Sch., Murfreesboro, Tenn., since 1945.

Hodges, Theron H., Supvr. of Resource Educ., 225 Memorial Bldg., Nashville, Tenn.

Holt, A. D., Ph.D.'37, Tchrs. Col., Columbia Univ.; Pres., Natl. Educ. Assn., 1949–50; Admin. Asst. to the Pres., Univ. of Tenn., Knoxville, Tenn., since 1950.

Human, W. D., B.S.'33, Tenn. Polytech. Inst.; Supt., Morgan Co. Sch., Wartburg, Tenn., since 1948.

Hyder, Gretchen, B.A.'22, Milligan Col.; M.A. '29, George Peabody Col. for Tchrs.; Assoc. Prof. of Educ., East Tenn. State Col., Johnson City, Tenn., since 1938.

Inman, William O., B.S.'25, M.A.'48, George Peabody Col. for Tchrs.; Supt. of Sch., Paris, Tenn., since 1933.

Jeffords, Dexter M., B.A.'42, Syracuse Univ.; M.A.'47, Tchrs. Col., Columbia Univ.; Bus. Dir., Pub. Sch., Oak Ridge, Tenn., since 1950.

Johnston, (Mrs.) Eula A., M.A.'38, Tchrs. Col., Columbia Univ.; Co. Supvr. of Sch., Chattanooga, Tenn., since 1925.

Jones, William Clarence, B.S.'22, East Texas State Tchrs. Col., Commerce; M.A.'25, Colo. State Col. of Educ., Greeley; Ph.D.'31, George Peabody Col. for Tchrs.; Dean of Admin., George Peabody Col. for Tchrs., Nashville, Tenn., since 1949.

Kennedy, G. T., B.S.'37, Memphis State Col., Memphis, Tenn.; M.A.'49, George Peabody Col. for Tchrs.; Co. Supt. of Sch., Decaturville, Tenn., since 1948.

Lee, Robert E., B.S.'27, State Col.; M.A.'38, George Peabody Col. for Tchrs.; Supt., City Sch., Tullahoma, Tenn., since 1935.

Lindman, Erick Leroy, A.B.'31, Whitman Col.; M.A.'39, Ph.D.'48, Univ. of Wash.; Prof. of Sch. Adm. and Finance, Geo. Peabody Col., Nashville, Tenn., since 1952.

Lowe, Everette C., Prin., Wynn H. S., Hebersham, Tenn.

McCharen, W. K., B.A.'26, Univ. of Miss.; M.A.'33, B.S. in L.S.'39, Ph.D.'47, George Peabody Col. for Tchrs.; Dir., Peabody Demonstration Sch., George Peabody Col. for Tchrs., Nashville, Tenn.

McClurkin W. D., A.B.'29, Hendrix Col.; M.S.'34, Univ. of Ark.; Ph.D.'40, George Peabody Col. for Tchrs.; Dir., Div. of Field Serv., George Peabody Col. for Tchrs., Nashville, Tenn.

516

McKee, Clinton O., B.A.'36, Univ. of Tenn.;
M.A.'39, M.Ed.'41, George Peabody Col. for
Tchrs.; Asst. Prof. of Educ., Austin Peay State
Col., Clarksville, Tenn., since 1952.

Mackey, A. B., A.B.'25, Eastern Ky. State Tchrs.
Col., Richmond; M.A.'26, George Peabody Col.
for Tchrs.; LL.D.'41, Northwest Nazarene
Col.; Pres., Trevecca Nazarene Col., Nashville, Tenn., since 1936.

Maddox, J. C., A.B.'30, Murray State Tchrs.
Col., Murray, Ky.; M.A.'38, George Peabody
Col. for Tchrs.; Supt. of City Sch., Union City,
Tenn., since 1949.

May, Daniel, B.A.'19, Vanderbilt Univ.; Pres.,
Bd. of Educ., Nashville, Tenn., since 1950.

Moore, C. H., A.M.'17, George Peabody Col. for
Tchrs.; Supt. of Sch., Clarksville, Tenn.,
since 1927.

Moore H. Claude, B.S. in Ed.'29, Univ. of Tenn.;
M.S. in Sch. Adm.'41, George Peabody Col.
for Tchrs.; Co. Supt. of Sch., Dyersburg, Tenn.,
since 1945.

Moss, J. E., B.S.'26, Univ. of Tenn.; M.A.'28,
George Peabody Col. for Tchrs.; Co. Supt. of
Sch., Nashville, Tenn., since 1949.

Nants, J. S., A.B.'09, Ind. Univ.; M.A.'10, Columbia Univ.; Asst. Supt. of Sch., St. Louis,
Mo., 1942-52. Address: Gleason, Tenn.

New, Wilson, B.S. in Ed.'11, Valparaiso Univ.;
M.S. in Ed.'33, Univ. of Tenn.; Supt. of Sch.,
Knoxville, Tenn., since 1949.

Newport, Lamar, M.S.'40, Univ. of Tenn.;
Bursar, since 1943 and Acting Pres., since 1948,
Memphis State Col., Memphis, Tenn.

Parrott, (Mrs.) Lagretta C., B.A.'28, Univ. of
Tenn.; Co. Supt. of Sch., Newport, Tenn.,
since 1944.

Pickel, T. Wesley, Asst. Dir., Schoolhouse
Planning and Transportation, State Dept. of
Educ., Nashville, Tenn., since 1943.

Pierce, Truman M., Ph.D.'46, Columbia Univ.;
Prof. of Educ. and Dir., CPEA, George Peabody Col. for Tchrs., Nashville, Tenn.

Pinkston, M. L., B.A.'38, Bethel Col.; M.A.'47,
George Peabody Col.; Supt. of City Sch.,
Greeneville, Tenn., since 1948.

Pullias, Athens Clay, B.A.'31, LL.B.'32, Cumberland Univ.; B.D.'34, Vanderbilt Univ.; Pres.,
David Lipscomb Col., Nashville, Tenn., since
1946.

Ray, Dennie Ezell, Sr., B.S.'26, A.M.'38, George
Peabody Col. for Tchrs.; Supt. of Sch., Jackson, Tenn., since 1946.

Robinson, Ross N., A.B.'15, Carson-Newman
Col.; A.B.'19, Univ. of Tenn.; A.M.'21, Tchrs.
Col., Columbia Univ.; Supt. of Sch., Kings-
port, Tenn., since 1924.

Robison, R. M., B.A.'24, Southwestern at
Memphis; M.A.'31, George Peabody Col. for
Tchrs.; Dean, Memphis State Col., Memphis,
Tenn., since 1946.

Sandborn, William C., B.S.'36, Madison Col.;
M.A.'38, George Peabody Col.; Dean of Madison Col., Madison College, Tenn., since 1952.

Shannon, W. A., B.S.'39, Middle Tenn. State
Col., Murfreesboro; M.A.'49, George Pea-
body Col. for Tchrs.; Exec. Secy., Tenn. Sch.
Bds. Assn., Nashville, Tenn., since 1949.

Shoulders, W. B., M.S.'37, Univ. of Tenn.; Dir.,
Div. of Equalization, State Dept. of Educ.,
Nashville, Tenn., since 1942.

Smith, G. Hobart, B.S.'28, Lincoln Memorial
Univ.; M.S.'33, Univ. of Tenn.; Co. Supt. of
Sch., Jacksboro, Tenn., since 1940.

Smith, J. Millard, B.S.'29, Memphis State Col.;
M.A.'30, George Peabody Col. for Tchrs.;
Pres., Memphis State Col., Memphis, Tenn.
since 1950.

Smith, Q. M., Pres., Middle Tenn. State Col.,
Murfreesboro, Tenn.

Smith, S. L., B.A.'11, Southwestern; M.A.'18,
George Peabody Col. for Tchrs.; D.Ed.'32,
Southwestern; Provost Emeritus, George Peabody Col. for Tchrs., Nashville, Tenn., since
1947.

Smotherman, Bealer, B.S.'33, Middle Tenn.
State Col.; M.A.'40, Ed.D.'52, George Peabody Col. for Tchrs.; Asst. Prof. of Sch. Admin.,
Middle Tenn. State Col., Murfreesboro, Tenn.,
since 1952.

Steele, A. J., B.S.'35, Union Univ.; Supt. of Sch.,
McKenzie, Tenn., since 1944.

Story, Bascom Howard, A.A.'32, Weatherford
Jr. Col.; B.S.'34, North Texas State Col.;
M.A.'42, Southwest Texas State Col.; Ed.D.
'49, Univ. of Texas; Dir., Sch. of Educ., Memphis State Col., Memphis, Tenn., since 1951.

Taylor, John F., M.S.'50, Univ. of Tenn.;
Supvr., Co. Sch., Jacksboro, Tenn., since 1948.

Turner, W. E., A.B.'24, M.S.'31, Univ. of Tenn.;
State Dir., Div. of Negro Educ., State Dept. of
Educ., Nashville, Tenn., since 1930.

Turpen, H. H., B.S.'38, Middle Tenn. State Col.;
M.A.'49, George Peabody Col. for Tchrs.;
Asst. Supt. of City Sch., Nashville, Tenn.

Upperman, Harry Lee, A.B.'22, M.A.'28, Syracuse Univ.; D.D.'29, Simpson Col.; Pres.,
Baxter Sem., Baxter, Tenn., since 1923.

Vaughan, William Hutchinson, A.B.'23, Georgetown Col.; A.M.'27, Ph.D.'37, George Peabody Col. for Tchrs.; Registrar, and Dir. of
Admissions, George Peabody Col. for Tchrs.,
Nashville, Tenn., since 1946.

Wallen, A. B., B.S.'37, East Tenn. State Col.;
M.A.'41, Columbia Univ.; Supt. of City Sch.,
Morristown, Tenn., since 1949.

Waters, George Hugh, B.A.'33, Vanderbilt Univ.;
M.A.'40, George Peabody Col. for Tchrs.;
General Supvr. of Sec. Educ., Pub. Sch.,
Nashville, Tenn., since 1944.

Wheeler, Arville, A.B.'26, Centre Col.; M.A.'35,
Univ. of Chicago; Ph.D.'39, Cornell Univ.;
Prof. of Educ., George Peabody Col. for
Tchrs., Nashville, Tenn., since 1947.

Wicke, Myron F., A.B.'30, Baldwin-Wallace
Col.; A.M.'34, Ph.D.'41, Western Reserve
Univ.; Secy., Dept. of Higher Educ., Methodist
Bd. of Educ., Nashville, Tenn., since 1949.

Williams, Margaret, B.A.'31, Southwestern at
Memphis; M.A.'44, George Peabody Col. for
Tchrs.; Dir. of Personnel and Research, City
Sch., Memphis, Tenn., since 1948.

Windrow, J. E., M.A.'25, Ph.D.'37, George
Peabody Col. for Tchrs.; Dir. of Pub. Serv.,
George Peabody Col. for Tchrs., Nashville,
Tenn., since 1947.

Wirth, Fremont P., Ph.D.'25, Univ. of Chicago;
Prof., George Peabody Col. for Tchrs.;
Nashville, Tenn., since 1926.

Wright, Kenneth Albert, M.S. in Ed.'38, Cornell
Univ.; Pres., Southern Missionary Col.,
Collegedale, Tenn., since 1943.

INSTITUTIONAL MEMBERS

Library, East Tenn. State Col., Johnson City,
Tenn.

Library, George Peabody College for Teachers,
Nashville 4, Tenn.

Library, Middle Tenn. State Col., Murfreesboro,
Tenn.

TEXAS
INDIVIDUAL MEMBERS

Abshier, Clyde, B.S.'31, Sam Houston State
Tchrs. Col., Huntsville, Texas; M.A.'36,
Univ. of Mo.; Supt., Deer Park Independent
Sch. Dist., Deer Park, Texas, since 1940.

517

TEXAS

Adams, E. W., Supt. of Sch., Henderson, Texas, since 1946.
Adams, J. C., B.S.'27, Sam Houston State Tchrs. Col., Huntsville, Texas; M.S.'39, Agrl. and Mech. Col. of Texas; Supt. of Independent Sch. Dist., Kirbyville, Texas, since 1948.
Akridge, R. W., B.A.'36, M.A.'40, Southwest Texas State Tchrs. Col., San Marcos; Supt., Independent Sch. Dist., Cedar Bayou, Texas, since 1946.
Allen, Howard A., B.A.'16, Morningside Col.; M.A.'46, Texas Christian Univ.; Prin., W. H. Adamson H. S., Dallas, Texas, since 1935.
Allenson, Frank W., M.A.'39, Southwest Texas State Tchrs. Col., San Marcos; Supt. of Sch., Brenham, Texas, since 1942.
Allison, Glenn L., B.A.'33, M.A.'39, Texas Tech. Col.; Supt. of Sch., Oklaunion, Texas, since 1948.
Alves, H. F., B.A.'27, Southwest Texas State Tchrs. Col., San Marcos; M.A.'28, Univ. of Texas; Dir., Cooperative Program in Sch. Admin., Univ. of Texas, Austin, Texas, since 1950.
Alvis, James C., B.S.'31, Southwestern State Tchrs. Col., Okla.; M.S.'43, North Texas State Col., Denton; Supt. of Sch., Bandera, Texas, since 1945.
Anderson, A. M., M.A.'47, East Texas State Tchrs. Col., Commerce; Supt. of Sch., Longview, Texas, since 1949.
Anderson, J. A., M.A.'32, Univ. of Colo.; Supt. of Sch., Lufkin, Texas.
Andrews, Wallace C., B.S.'42, Univ. of Texas; Supt. of Sch., Gregory, Texas, since 1944.
Appleby, Kent, B.A.'34, Howard-Payne Col.; Supt. of Sch., Clifton, Texas, since 1942.
Armstrong, Vernon L., M.S.'46, North Texas State Col.; Research Assoc., Southwestern Coop. Study in Sch. Admin., Univ. of Texas, Austin, Texas, since 1951.
Arnaud, E. E., B.A.'35, M.A.'42, St. Mary's Univ. of San Antonio; Supt.; Edgewood Sch. Dist., San Antonio, Texas, since 1948.
Ashburn, G. L., B.S.'10, Baylor Univ.; Prin., Woodrow Wilson H. S., Dallas, Texas, since 1927.
Ashworth, Robert K., B.A.'34, East Texas State Tchrs. Col.; M.A.'39, Southern Methodist Univ.; Supt. of Sch., Kilgore, Texas, since 1952.
Avinger, W. H., M.A.'43, Univ. of Texas; Supt. of Sch., Plainview, Texas, since 1949.
Awalt, A. B., B.S.'28, Univ. of Texas; Frankston ISD, Frankston, Texas.
Bailey, John F., A.B.'23, Baylor Univ.; M.A.'31, Univ. of Colo.; Supt. of Sch., Breckenridge, Texas, since 1939.
Bailey, Orris G., B.S.'34, M.S.'43, N. Texas State Tchrs. Col., Denton; Jr.-Sr. H. S. Supvr. of Science and Math., Houston, Texas, since 1949.
Baines, Alberta, 5022 Madalyn, Houston, Texas.
Baker, Harry C., M.A.'30, Univ. of Texas; Supt. of Sch., Tabasco Community Independent Sch. Dist., La Joya, Texas, since 1948.
Baker, Marvin P., B.A.'28, M.A.'33, Univ. of Texas; Pres., Panola Co. Jr. Col., Carthage, Texas, since 1951.
Baker, Oscar J., M.Ed.'39, Univ. of Texas; Supt. of Sch., Dickinson, Texas, since 1946.
Baker, (Mrs.) Vallie, M.A.'47, Stephen F. Austin State Col.; Elem. Supvr. of Sch., Carthage, Texas, since 1948.

Ballew, Harvey C., M.S.'39, North Texas State Col., Denton; Supt. of Independent Sch. Dist., Lampasas, Texas, since 1949.
Balusek, Frank J., B.S.'36, Southwest Texas State Tchrs. Col., San Marcos; M.Ed.'39, Univ. of Texas; Asst. Supt., Dir. of Elem. Educ., Bay City, Texas, since 1946.
Banks, Buford C., B.A.'30, Southwestern Univ.; M.A.'48, Texas Col. of Arts and Indus.; Supt. of Sch., Robstown, Texas, since 1947.
Barber, William G., B.S.'45, M.A.'49, East Texas State Tchrs. Col., Commerce; Supt. of Sch., Electra, Texas, since 1949.
Barker, Ernest A., M.A.'32, George Peabody Col. for Tchrs.; Supt. of Sch., Honey Grove, Texas, since 1934.
Barnett, Harold R., B.S.'37, Univ. of Mo.; M.A.'46, West Texas State Col., Canyon; Supt. of Sch., Independent Sch. Dist., Knox City, Texas, since 1951.
Barron, John F., B.A.'31, Southwest Texas Tchr. Col.; M.A.'39, Texas Col. of Arts and Indus.; Supt., Independent Sch. Dist. 80 and Pres., Texas Southwest Col., Brownsville, Texas, since 1945.
Beard, John L., Univ. of Texas, '48; Supt. of Sch., Irving, Texas, since 1949.
Beard, Roy J., Star Engraving Co., Houston, Texas.
Betts, Floyd G., B.A.'26, Southwestern Univ.; M.A.'26, Southern Methodist Univ.; Pres., Port Arthur Col., Port Arthur, Texas, since 1950.
Betts, J. D., B.S.'30, East Texas State Tchrs. Col., Commerce; M.S.'40, Agrl. and Mech. Col. of Texas; Dist. Supt. of Sch., Gladewater, Texas, since 1949.
Bickers, W. T., Jr., B.B.A.'47, Baylor Univ.; Bus. Mgr., Orange, Texas, since 1951.
Billingsley, Herman F., M.Ed.'42, Univ. of Texas; Supt. of Sch., Brookeland, Texas, since 1939.
Bird, Arthur Otis, B.S.'30, M.A.'42, Southwest Texas State Tchrs. Col., San Marcos; Supt. of Sch., Gonzales, Texas, since 1936.
Bishop, John L., M.A.'35, Univ. of Colo.; Prin., Sr. H. S., San Angelo, Texas, since 1944.
Black, Ernest Howard, B.A.'19, Univ. of Okla.; M.A.'29, Columbia Univ.; Ed.D.'47, Univ. of Houston; Supt. of Sch., Lamarque, Texas, since 1944.
Bland, Earl, B.S.'36, Stephen F. Austin State Col.; M.A.'48, Sul Ross State Tchrs. Col.; Supt. of Sch., Marathon, Texas, since 1945.
Blankenship, William Clayton, M.S.'37, Southern Methodist Univ.; Supt. of Sch., Big Spring, Texas, since 1928.
Bledsoe, A. T., B.A.'39, Sam Houston State Tchrs. Col., Huntsville, Texas; M.Ed.'48, Univ. of Houston; Supt. of Sch., Sweeny, Texas, since 1949.
Boone, J. D., B.A., M.A., Univ. of Texas; Supt. of Pub. Sch., Alto, Texas, since 1945.
Boone, James L., Sr., B.S. in Rural Ed.'37, Agrl. and Mech. Col. of Texas; M.S. in Ed.'40, Univ. of Houston; Supt. of Sch., Needville, Texas, since 1947.
Bost, Edward Lawson, A.B.'36, Trinity Univ.; M.E.'50, Texas Christian Univ.; Supt. of Sch., Maypearl, Texas, since 1946.
Boswell, Grover C., B.A.'26, East Texas State Tchrs. Col., Commerce; M.A.'33, Simmons Univ.; LL.D.'39, Texas Wesleyan Col.; Pres., Ranger Jr. Col., and Supt. of Sch., Ranger, Texas, since 1941.
Boyd, Roy, B.S.'26, M.S.'38, North Texas State Col., Denton; Co. Supt. of Sch., Lubbock, Texas, since 1943.

518

Boynton, S. G., Supt., Pub. Sch., San Saba, Texas.

Bracken, W. Earl, B.S.'28, Ursinus Col.; M.S.'37, Temple Univ.; West Jr. H. S., Waco, Texas.

Bradford, W. R., M.A.'42, Texas Tech. Col.; Supt. of Sch., Iowa Park, Texas, since 1920.

Bray, Lem, B.S.'43, Texas Wesleyan Col.; M.S.'50, North Texas State Col.; Supt. of Pub. Sch., Ozona, Texas, since 1950.

Breazeale, Albert H., B.A.'31, North Texas State Tchrs. Col., Denton; M.A.'36, Univ. of Texas; Supt. of Sch., Canadian, Texas, since 1948.

Brewer, C. F., B.S.'40, Texas Christian Univ.; Supt., White Settlement Sch., Ft. Worth, Texas, since 1932.

Briesemeister, A. J., M.A.'37, Univ. of Texas; Supt. of Sch., Seguin, Texas, since 1949.

Bringhurst, Nancy, B.A.'35, M.A.'40, Univ. of Texas; Consultant in Special Educ., Dallas Independent Sch. Dist., Dallas, Texas, since 1950.

Brinson, Elzo B., B.S.'40, Daniel Baker Col.; Co. Supt. of Sch., Comanche, Texas, since 1949.

Brodhead, E. A., M.A.'40, Southern Methodist Univ.; Supt. of Sch., Sonora, Texas, since 1950.

Brooks, B. R., B.A.'31, M.A.'41, Univ. of Texas; Supt. of Sch., Texas City, Texas, since 1949.

Brooks, Ercell W., B.A.'30, West Texas State Col.; M.A.'39, Baylor Univ.; Asst. Supt. of Sch., San Angelo, Texas, since 1949.

Brotherton, L. H., B.S.'34, M.A.'39, West Texas State Col.; Supt. of Sch., Gruver, Texas, since 1944.

Brown, A. E., B.S.'35, Ed.M.'39, Univ. of Okla.; Supt. of Sch., Wheeler, Texas, since 1952.

Brown, Mortimer, B.B.A.'25, Univ. of Texas; M.A.'31, Tchrs. Col., Columbia Univ.; Ph.D. '41, Univ. of Texas; Supt. of Sch., El Paso, Texas, since 1951.

Brown, Ray D., A.B.'30, Southwestern Univ.; M.A.'39, Southern Methodist Univ.; Supt. of Sch., Greenville, Texas.

Brown, Robert H., B.A.'33, Southwest Texas State Tchrs. Col., San Marcos; Supt. of Pub. Sch., Runge, Texas, since 1946.

Buckley, J. L., B.A.'28, Baylor Univ.; M.A.'37, Univ. of Texas; Supt. of Sch., Lockhart, Texas, since 1945.

Buckner, D. U., B.A.'21, Trinity Univ.; M.A.'29, Univ. of Texas; Supt. of Sch., Pharr, Texas, since 1941.

Budd, Harrell, B.A.'16, Guilford Col.; M.A.'25, Univ. of Texas; Prin., Trinity Heights Sch., Dallas, Texas.

Burleson, Sidney Jean, B.A.'36, Howard Payne Col.; M.A.'50, Univ. of Texas; Supt. of Lake View Sch., San Angelo, Texas, since 1950.

Burnett, Clinton E., B.A.'25, M.A.'35, Univ. of Texas; Supt. of Sch., Harlingen, Texas.

Burton, Floyd H., B.S.'30, Sam Houston State Tchrs. Col., Huntsville, Texas; M.Ed.'38, Univ. of Texas; Ed.D.'48, Univ. of Houston; Supt. of Sch., Humble, Texas, since 1942.

Busby, Elden B., A.B.'30, Abilene Christian Col.; M.A.'31, Texas Christian Univ.; Ed.D.'48, Stanford Univ.; Asst. Supt. of Sch. in charge of Genl. Admin., Fort Worth, Texas, since 1946.

Butler, W. H., M.Ed.'50, Stephen F. Austin State Tchrs. Col., Nacogdoches; Supt. of Sch., Saratoga, Texas, since 1948.

Calhoun, Theodore C., B.S.'29, Bishop Col.; M.A.'41, Univ. of Mich.; Prin., Kealing Jr. H. S., Austin, Texas, since 1940.

Campbell, William B., A.B.'13, Shaw Univ.; A.M.'40, Univ. of Mich.; Prin., Anderson H. S., Austin, Texas.

Cannon, W. F., B.S.'28, North Texas State Tchrs. Col., Denton; M.A.'35, Texas Tech. Col.; Supt. of Sch., Grapevine, Texas, since 1938.

Carmichael, W. R., M.S.'36, Texas Agrl. and Mech. Col.; Supt. of Sch., Bryan, Texas, since 1949.

Carrick, W. O., B.S.'39, Sul Ross State Tchrs. Col., Alpine; Supt. of Sch., Wheeler, Texas, since 1945.

Carroll, John S., B.A.'30, San Diego Col.; M.A.'32, Univ. of Southern Calif.; Ph.D.'40, Yale Univ.; Head, Dept. of Educ., Texas Tech. Col., Lubbock, Texas.

Carroll, Monroe S., A.B.'21, Baylor Univ.; A.M.'26, Brown Univ.; Ph.D.'37, Univ. of Chicago; Dean, Baylor Univ., Waco, Texas, since 1948.

Carruth, Irby B., B.A.'27, West Texas State Tchrs. Col., Canyon; M.A.'32, Univ. of Chicago; Supt. of Sch., Austin, Texas, since 1950.

Carter, O. Dan, A.B.'41, M.A.'48, Baylor Univ.; Supt. of Pub. Sch., Navasota, Texas, since 1949.

Cassell, Mabel, M.A.'36, Columbia Univ.; Dir. of Curriculum, Pub. Sch., Houston, Texas, since 1941.

Center, Leslie R., M.A.'30, Tchrs. Col., Columbia Univ.; Prin., James S. Hogg Jr. H. S., Houston, Texas, since 1937.

Chambers, H. H., M.A.'27, Univ. of Texas; Supt. of Sch., Grand Prairie, Texas, since 1950.

Chandler, C. O., B.A.'34, Sam Houston State Tchrs. Col., Huntsville, Texas; M.A.'45, Univ. of Houston; Supt. of Sch., Orange, Texas, since 1947.

Chapman, Gerald B., M.A.'47, Stephen F. Austin Tchrs. Col., Nacogdoches, Texas; Supt. of Sch., Rusk, Texas, since 1943.

Cleveland, Ernest D., B.A.'23, Baylor Univ.; M.A.'40, Southern Methodist Univ.; Supt. of Sch., Palestine, Texas, since 1950.

Clifton, H. Lee, B.S.'32, East Texas State Tchrs. Col., Commerce; M.S. in Ed.'38, Univ. of Southern Calif.; Supt. of Pub. Sch., Bee-ville, Texas, since 1950.

Clifton, Leldon, M.A.'47, Hardin-Simmons Univ.; Supt., Sheffield Independent Sch. Dist., Iraan, Texas, since 1951.

Cochran, J. Chester, B.S.'29, Sul Ross State Tchrs. Col., Alpine, Texas; M.A.'31, Ed.D.'50, Univ. of Texas; Prof. of Educ. and Field Representative, Univ. of Houston, Houston, Texas, since 1943.

Codwell, John E., B.S.'27, Howard Univ.; M.A. '38, Ph.D.'48, Univ. of Mich.; Prin., Sr. H. S., Houston, Texas, since 1945.

Coers, Walter C., M.A.'33, George Peabody Col. for Tchrs.; Supt. of Sch., Los Fresnos, Texas, since 1950.

Coles, J. E., M.A.'46, Sam Houston State Tchrs. Col., Huntsville; Supt. of Sch., Grandfalls, Texas, since 1945.

Columkille, Sister M., B.A.'13, M.A.'14, Ph.D. '23, Catholic Univ. of America; Pres., Incarnate Word Col., San Antonio, Texas, since 1923.

Colvert, C. C., B.S.E.'29, M.S.'30, Univ. of Ark.; Ph.D.'37, George Peabody Col. for Tchrs.; Chmn., Dept. of Educ. Admin., and Prof. and Consultant in Jr. Col. of Educ., Univ. of Texas, Austin, Texas, since 1944.

Cook, C. F., Supt. of Sch., Spur, Texas.

TEXAS

Copass, Benjamin A., B.A.'26, Baylor Univ.; M.A.'37, Texas Christian Univ.; Supt. of Sch., Nacogdoches, Texas, since 1947.

Cornette, James P., A.B.'29, Ky. Wesleyan Col.; M.A.'30, Univ. of Va.; Ph.D.'38, George Peabody Col. for Tchrs.; Pres., West Texas State Tchrs. Col., Canyon, Texas, since 1948.

Cosper, Cecil, B.S.'47, M.Ed.'48, La. State Univ.; Admin. of Tchr. Educ. and Assoc. Prof. of Educ., Wayland Col., Plainview, Texas, since 1951.

Couch, (Mrs.) O. D., 1832 Maryland, Houston 6, Texas.

Courtney, L. C., B.S.'26, Sam Houston State Tchrs. Col., Huntsville, Texas; Supt., Aldine Independent Sch. Dist., Houston, Texas, since 1944.

Covin, Fred, M.S.'46, East Texas State Tchrs. Col.; Supt. of Sch., Pittsburg, Texas, since 1946.

Cowan, S. P., Supt. of Sch., Temple, Texas.

Cowan, Weldon, B.S.'36, East Texas State Tchrs. Col.; M.S.'48, North Texas State Col.; Supt. of Sch., Muenster, Texas, since 1949.

Cowley, Herman A., Prin., Maple Lawn Sch., Dallas, Texas.

Cox, James R., B.S.'35, M.S.'49, North Texas State Tchrs. Col.; Denton; Supt. of Sch., Panhandle, Texas, since 1951.

Cox, Larue, B.A.'22, Howard Payne Col.; M.A. '26, Univ. of Texas; Roanoke, Texas, since 1952.

Cox, W. C., B.S.'29, East Texas State Tchrs. Col., Commerce; M.E.'35, Southern Methodist Univ.; Supt. of Sch., Munday, Texas, since 1946.

Craver, D. T., M.S.'41, East Texas State Tchrs. Col., Commerce; Supt.; Chapel Hill Sch., Tyler, Texas, since 1941.

Crowson, Clifton, B.S.'29, M.S.'42, Sam Houston State Tchrs. Col., Huntsville, Texas; Supt., Independent Sch. Dist., Trinity, Texas, since 1940.

Cryer, Curtis A., B.A.'26, M.A.'27, Univ. of Okla.; Supt. of Sch. and Pres., Frank Phillips Col., Borger, Texas, since 1942.

Culpepper, Sam B., B.A.'27, Howard Payne Col.; M.A.'37, Baylor Univ.; Dir. of Field Serv., Texas State Tchrs. Assn., Austin, Texas, since 1950.

Cunningham, Noah, B.S.'39, Texas Tech. Col.; Supt., Independent Sch., Whiteface, Texas, since 1950.

Curlee, J. R., B.S.'35, Texas Col. of Arts and Indus.; M.Ed.'41, Univ. of Colo.; Supt. of Sch., Sour Lake, Texas, since 1948.

Darby, Ezelle E., B.S.'28, Southwest Texas State Tchrs. Col.; M.E.'47, A. & M. Col. of Texas; Prin. of H. S., Caldwell, Texas, since 1946.

Davis, A. L., B.S.'37, M.S.'49, East Texas State Col.; Supt. of Sch., Hedley, Texas, since 1948.

Davis, Ralph M., B.A.'32, M.A.'38, Austin Col.; Supt. of Sch., Burkburnett, Texas, since 1943.

Davis, W. C., M.A.'38, Univ. of Calif.; Supt. of Sch., Memphis, Texas, since 1935.

Dean, Guy D., A.B.'94, Iuka Normal Inst.; LL.B.'03, Univ. of Miss.; M.A.'40, George Peabody Col. for Tchrs.; Co. Supt. of Sch., Uvalde, Texas, since 1942.

Dennard, E. N., A.B.'27, Lon Morris Col.; B.A.'29, Trinity Univ.; M.A.'37, Southern Methodist Univ.; Supt. of Sch., Waco, Texas, since 1950.

De Pena, Fernando, B.A.'39, Texas Col. of Arts and Indus.; Supt. of Independent Sch. Dist., San Diego, Texas, since 1947.

Denton, Lynn C., M.A.'50, East Texas State Tchrs. Col.; Supt. of Sch., Blossom, Texas, since 1939.

Dickenson, S. V., M.A.'44, Texas Christian Univ.; Supt. of Sch., Godley, Texas, since 1939.

Dickson, Bryan, B.B.A.'23, Univ. of Texas; M.A.'35, Southern Methodist Univ.; Supt. of Sch., San Angelo, Texas, 1940-52.

Dillard, Frank G., A.B.'32, M.A.'39, Oglethorpe Univ.; Supt. of Sch., Overton, Texas, since 1950.

Dillehay, Claude H., A.B.'16, Baylor Univ.; M.A.'17, Brown Univ.; Supt. of Sch., Bonham, Texas, since 1949.

Dinsmore, B. M., M.A.'29, Southern Methodist Univ.; Co. Supt. of Sch., Wichita Falls, Texas, since 1944.

Dodson, P. J., B.A.'25, Baylor Univ.; M.A.'35, Univ. of Texas; Supt. of Sch., Bastrop, Texas, since 1931.

Dodson, Walter Lawrence, M.A.'27, Univ. of Texas; Supt. of Sch., Kilgore, Texas, since 1932.

Dominy, E. L., B.S., Sam Houston State Tchrs. Col., Huntsville, Texas; M.Ed., Southern Methodist Univ.; Prin. of Sch., Lancaster, Texas.

Donner, Arvin N., B.S.'27, M.A.'28, Ph.D.'37, State Univ. of Iowa; Dean, Col. of Educ., Univ. of Houston, Houston, Texas, since 1945.

*Dorsey, Julius, M.A.'19, George Peabody Col. for Tchrs.; Address: 5316 Waneta Drive, Dallas 9, Texas.

Douglas, Dale, A.B.'37, Howard Payne Col.; M.S.'48, North Texas State Col.; Supt., Pleasant Grove Indep. Sch. Dist., Dallas, Texas, since 1946.

Douglas, N. L., B.S.'47, Howard Payne Col.; Supt. of Sch., Hale Center, Texas, since 1947.

Douglas, Omer R., M.S.'49, North Texas State Col.; Prin. of H. S., Brownfield, Texas, since 1949.

Downing, Avery R., B.S.'37, North Texas State Col.; M.S.'47, East Texas State Col.; Asst. Supt. of Sch., Waco, Texas, since 1951.

Duran, John, B.S.'35, Stephen F. Austin State Col.; M.Ed.'39, Univ. of Texas; Supt. of Sch., Joinerville, Texas, since 1951.

Dusek, C. O., B.S.'41, Univ. of Texas; M.E.'47, Univ. of Houston; Supt. of Sch., Crosby, Texas, since 1947.

Dyer, Jesse J., M.A.'41, West Texas State Tchrs. Col.; Co. Supt. of Sch., Wheeler, Texas, since 1949.

Ebey, George W., Deputy City Supt. of Sch., Houston, Texas, since 1952.

Echols, Wilburn O., B.S. in Bus. Admin.'40, Southern Methodist Univ.; M.S. in Ed.'47, East Texas State Tchrs. Col.; Supt. of Sch., Olney, Texas, since 1952.

Edgar, James Winfred, B.A.'28, Howard Payne Col.; M.A.'38, Ed.D.'48, Univ. of Texas; State Commr. of Educ., Texas Educ. Agency, Austin, Texas, since 1950.

Edwards, Ted E., M.A.'49, Hardin-Simmons Univ.; Admin. Asst., Dept. of Educ., Texas Tech. Col., Lubbock, Texas, since 1950.

Eilers, William, Jr., B.S.'37, M.Ed.'41, Univ. of Texas; Prin., Thomas A. Edison Jr. H. S., San Angelo, Texas, since 1949.

Ellison, C. E., M.Ed.'39, Univ. of Texas; Supt. of Sch., Big Lake, Texas, since 1941.

Evans, E. B., Pres., Prairie View A. & M. Col., Prairie View, Texas.

Evans, Leslie P., B.A.'32, Howard Payne Col.; M.A.'40, Ph.D.'48, Univ. of Texas; Assoc. Prof. of Educ., Texas Christian Univ., Fort Worth, Texas, since 1948.

520

Everett, Cecil M., B.A.'41, East Texas State Tchrs. Col.; Supt. of Sch., Sumner, Texas, since 1943.

Everitt, William James, B.A.'32, St. Mary's Univ. of San Antonio; M.Ed.'41, Univ. of Texas; Supt. of Sch., Pleasanton, Texas, since 1942.

Fagg, R. C., B.S.'32, North Texas State Tchrs. Col.; Denton; M.A.'34, Southern Methodist Univ.; Supt. of White Oak Pub. Sch., Longview, Texas, since 1949.

Farquear, Floyd E., B.S.'20, Miami Univ.; M.A.'21, Univ. of Chicago; D.Ed.'42, Univ. of Texas; Chmn., Dept. of Educ., Texas Western Col. of the Univ. of Texas, El Paso, Texas, since 1942.

Farrington, William G., Bd. of Educ.; 1661 Tanglewood Ave., Houston 5, Texas.

Faseler, Walter L., B.A.'34, Southwest Texas State Tchrs. Col., San Marcos; M.A.'46, Univ. of Texas; Coordinator of Sec. Educ., Independent Sch. Dist., Pasadena, Texas.

Ferguson, Garland P., Prin., Union Grove Sch. Dist. 42, Gladewater, Texas.

Ferguson, W. A. Supt. of Pub. Sch., Winnsboro, Texas.

Ferrell, D. H., B.A.'25, M.Ed.'37, Univ. of Texas; Prin., Robert E. Lee Elem. Sch., Port Arthur, Texas, since 1947.

Fite, George K., M.S.'50, East Texas State Tchrs. Col.; Supt. of Sch., Lindale, Texas, since 1952.

Fletcher, Deane D., M.A.'39, West Texas State Tchrs. Col., Canyon; Supt. of Sch., Eagle Lake, Texas, since 1950.

Fly, Murry H., B.S.'15, East Texas Normal Sch.; B.A.'21, M.A.'29, Univ. of Texas; Pres., Odessa Col., Odessa, Texas, since 1946.

Foreman, Mary, B.S.'37, M.A.'49, W. Texas State Tchrs. Col., Canyon; Co. Supt. of Sch., Memphis, Texas, since 1943.

Fortescue, Z. T., M.A.'27, Univ. of N. C.; Supt. of Sch., Port Arthur, Texas, since 1944.

Foster, Henry L., B.A.'26, Southwest Texas State Tchrs. Col., San Marcos; M.A.'40, Colo. State Col. of Educ., Greeley; Supt. of Sch., Longview, Texas, since 1923. (Retired June 1952.)

Foster, Inez, M.A.'28, Tchrs. Col., Columbia Univ.; Asst. Supt. of Sch., Elem. Div., San Antonio, Texas, since 1947.

Fox, Louis William, B.S. in C.E.'15, Univ. of Texas; Dir. of Voc. Educ., Pub. Sch., San Antonio, Texas, since 1917.

Freshour, Jack, M.A.'47, Southwest Texas State Col.; Supt. of Sch., Rio Hondo, Texas, since 1939.

Galyean, Elmo L., B.S.'36, North Texas State Col.; M.Ed.'43, Southern Methodist Univ.; Dir. of Research and Records, Texas State Tchrs. Assn., Austin, Texas, since 1950.

Gardner, J. F., Supt. of Sch., Ennis, Texas.

Garland, C. J., B.A.'26, M.A.'37, Univ. of Texas; Supt. of Sch., Eagle Pass, Texas, since 1946.

Garlin, R. E., B.A.'20, M.A.'21, Ph.D.'27, Univ. of Texas; Prof. of Educ., Texas Tech. Col., Lubbock, Texas, since 1927.

Gary, Enos G., B.A.'07, M.A.'24, Univ. of Texas; Prin., Brackenridge H. S., San Antonio, Texas, since 1928.

Gary, R. W., B.S.'38, Stephen F. Austin State Tchrs. Col., Nacogdoches, Texas; M.S.'46, Univ. of Houston; Dir. of Pupil Serv. and Statistics, Beaumont Independent Sch. Dist., Beaumont, Texas.

Gay, E. A., B.A.'30, Southwestern Univ.; M.A.'39, Southwest Texas State Tchrs. Col., San Marcos; Supt. of Sch., George West, Texas, since 1947.

Gentry, George H., B.A.'26, Baylor Univ.; M.A.'33, Univ. of Texas; Dist. Supt. of Sch. and Pres., Lee Jr. Col., Baytown, Texas, since 1946.

Gentry, W. J., B.S.'33, M.A.'48, Sam Houston State Tchrs. Col., Huntsville, Texas; Supt. of Independent Sch. Dist., Elkhart, Texas, since 1948.

Gerber, Joe N., Ed.B.'34, Ill. State Normal Univ., Normal; M.S.'35, Univ. of Ill.; Ph.D.'41, George Peabody Col. for Tchrs.; Dean of the Jr. Div., Stephen F. Austin State Col., Nacogdoches, Texas, since 1950.

Gerron, J. F., M.A.'41, North Texas State Tchrs. Col., Denton; Supt. of Sch., Archer City, Texas, since 1941.

Gibson, Joe A., B.A.'24, Hardin-Simmons Univ.; M.A.'41, Texas Tech. Col.; Supt. of Sch., Canyon, Texas, since 1952.

Gifford, C. T., B.A.'30, Stephen F. Austin State Tchrs. Col.; M.A.'44, Sam Houston State Tchrs. Col.; Supt. of Sch., Livingston, Texas.

Gilbert, Lloyd E., B.A.'35, M.A.'40, East Texas State Tchrs. Col., Commerce; Supt. of Sch., Dayton, Texas, since 1945.

Gilmer, Ira T., A.B.'05, LL.B.'10, M.A.'36, Univ. of Miss.; Supt. of Sch., Graham, Texas, since 1924.

Gladden, John W., B.S.'25, North Texas State Col.; M.A.'49, Sam Houston State Tchrs. Col.; Supt. of Sch., East and Mt. Houston Independent Sch. Dist., Houston, Texas, since 1950.

Glass, Herman A., B.A.'26, West Texas State Tchrs. Col, Canyon; M.A.'33, Univ. of Chicago; Dir. of Textbook Div., State Dept. of Educ., Austin, Texas, since 1937.

Glaze, F. M., B.A.'35, Daniel Baker Col.; Supt., Independent Sch. Dist., Alief, Texas, since 1949.

Goettee, James H., B.S.'33, Sam Houston State Tchrs. Col., Huntsville, Texas; M.Ed.'37, Univ. of Texas; 1514 Godwin St., Houston, Texas.

Golden, Joe Bob, B.S.'30, West Texas State Tchrs. Col., Canyon; M.E.'39, Southern Methodist Univ.; Supt. of Sch., Vernon, Texas, since 1949.

Gourley, Charles E., B.S.'34, Northwestern State Col.; M.A.'51, Phillips Univ.; Supt. of Sch., Higgins, Texas, since 1948.

Graham, George L., B.S.'40, West Texas State Tchrs. Col., Canyon; Supt. of Sch., Hereford, Texas, since 1946.

Graham, Leon R., M.A.'36, Southern Methodist Univ.; Transportation Officer, Texas Educ. Agency, Austin, Texas.

Grandy, C. W., A.B.'26, Peru State Col.; A.M.'39, Univ. of Nebr.; Supt. of Sch., Muleshoe, Texas, since 1949.

Graves, M. W., M.A.'45, West Texas State Col.; Co. Supt. of Sch., Stinnett, Texas, since 1948.

Gray, Hob, B.A.'18, Daniel Baker Col.; M.A.'25, Tchrs. Col., Columbia Univ.; Ph.D.'30, Univ. of Texas; LL.D.'48, Southwestern Univ.; Assoc. Prof. of Sec. Educ., since 1933, and Dir., Tchr. Placement Serv., Univ. of Texas, Austin, Texas, since 1946.

Gray, J. D., B.S.'38, Sam Houston State Tchrs. Col., Huntsville, Texas; M.A.'46, Colo. State Col. of Educ.; Supt. of Sch., Pearland, Texas, since 1947.

Green, Raymond K., B.A.'33, Daniel Baker Col.; M.A.'40, Texas Tech. Col.; Supt. of Sch., Santa Anna, Texas, since 1947.

Greene, Pat H., M.A.'32, Univ. of Texas; Supt., Clear Creek Consol. Independent Sch. Dist., Webster, Texas, since 1948.

521

Griffin, L. H., M.S.'43, Texas Agrl. and Mech. Col.; Supt. of Pub. Sch., Hooks, Texas, since 1950.

Griffin, W. O., M.A.'40, Baylor Univ.; Prin., South Jr. H. S., Waco, Texas, since 1948.

Griggs, Joseph R., B.A.'32, M.A.'39, Texas Tech. Col.; Ed.D.'43, Univ. of Texas; Dir., Demonstration Sch., Sam Houston State Tchrs. Col., and Supt. of Sch., Huntsville, Texas, since 1945.

Grisham, Noel, B.A.'44, Abilene Christian Col.; M.A.'48, East Texas State Tchrs. Col., Commerce; Supt. of Pub. Sch., Odell, Texas, since 1945.

Guinn, John A., B.A. and M.A.'29, Ph.D.'39, Univ. of Texas; Pres., Texas State Col. for Women, Denton, Texas, since 1950.

Hackney, V. H., B.A.'31, M.A.'49, Southern Methodist Univ.; Supt. of Sch., Marshall, Texas, since 1949.

Hadley, William M., B.S., M.A., Univ. of Ala.; Supt. of Sch., Alice, Texas, since 1952.

Hagler, J. W., M.S.'47, East Texas State Tchrs. Col., Commerce; Co. Supt. of Sch., Longview, Texas, since 1951.

Hall, Roy Maxwell, Sr., A.B.'37, Piedmont Col.; M.Ed.'47, Emory Univ.; Ed.D.'51, Syracuse Univ.; Assoc. Prof. of Educ. Admin. and Assoc. Dir., Southwest Coop. Program in Educ. Admin., Univ. of Texas, Austin, Texas, since 1952.

Hall, W. E., B.S.'42, North Texas State Col., Denton; M.Ed.'49, Univ. of Texas; Supt., West Oso Independent Sch. Dist., Corpus Christi, Texas, since 1948.

Hamilton, John Woodrow, B.A.'36, Okla. City Univ.; M.Ed.'42, Univ. of Okla; Supt. of Sch., Seymour, Texas, since 1945.

Hamilton, T. D., B.S.'29, Sul Ross State Tchrs. Col., Alpine, Texas; Supt. of Sch., Andrews, Texas, since 1939.

Hancock, Dee, M.A.'50, Texas Tech. Col.; Supt. of Sch., Shallowater, Texas, since 1948.

Hancock, W. E., B.A.'27, Univ. of Texas; Supt. of Pub. Sch., Quanah, Texas, since 1945.

Hanes, W. T., M.A.'38, Texas Tech. Col.; Supt. of Sch., Cameron, Texas, since 1945.

Hanks, J. M., B.S.'32, Southwest Texas State Tchrs. Col., San Marcos; Supt. of Sch., Ysleta, Texas, since 1929.

Harbour, B. F., B.A.'27, North Texas State Col.; M.A.'34, Univ. of Texas; Supt. of Sch., Ganado, Texas, since 1949.

Hare, J. Malvin, B.S.'37, Agrl. and Mech. Col. of Texas; Supt. of Sch., Caldwell, Texas, since 1946.

Harris, Robert E., B.S.'23, Agrl. and Mech. Col. of Texas; M.A.'50, Southwest Texas State Tchrs. Col.; Co. Supt. of Sch., Lockhart, Texas, since 1935.

Hart, G. S., Master's, '40, Sam Houston State Tchrs. Col., Huntsville, Texas; Supt. of Sch., Channelview, Texas, since 1943.

Hartman, H. R., M.A.'40, North Texas State Tchrs. Col.; Supt. of Sch., Spearman, Texas, since 1948.

Harvin, Edwin L., B.A.'21, Baylor Univ.; M.A.'26, Univ. of Texas; Pres., Del Mar Col., Corpus Christi, Texas, since 1946.

Haskew, Laurence D., B.Ph.'26, Emory Univ.; M.A.'34, Univ. of Chicago; Ph.D.'41, Univ. of Ga.; Dean, Col. of Educ., Univ. of Texas, Austin, Texas, since 1947.

Hedrick, Wyatt C., Archt. and Engineer, 904 Fort Worth Ave., Dallas 8, Texas.

Henderson, Paul G., B.S.'31, M.S.'48, East Texas State Tchrs. Col., Commerce; Supt. of Sch., Princeton, Texas, since 1944.

Hendricks, Jake J., B.A.'24, North Texas State Tchrs. Col., Denton; M.A.'29, Univ. of Texas; Educ. Rep., The Macmillan Co., Austin, Texas, since 1949.

Hensley, R. G., B.S.'35, M.A.'40, Stephen F. Austin State Tchrs. Col., Nacogdoches; Prin., Spring Hill H. S., Longview, Texas, since 1945.

Hereford, C. S., B.A.'32, Southwestern Univ.; M.A.'43, Univ. of Texas; Supt. of Sch., Mexia, Texas, since 1946.

Herndon, Franklin C., B.A.'24, Southwest Texas State Tchrs. Col., San Marcos; M.A.'38, Colo. State Col. of Educ., Greeley; Supt., Lamar Sch. Dist., Rosenberg, Texas, since 1934.

Herndon, H. W., B.S. and M.A.'40, Southwest Texas State Tchrs. Col., San Marcos; Supt. of Sch., Odem, Texas, since 1942.

Hershey, Paul W., B.S.'36, Lebanon Valley Col.; Co. Supt. of Sch., Galveston, Texas, since 1951.

Hill, J. Davis, M.A.'38, West Texas State Tchrs. Col., Canyon; Supt. of Sch., Galveston, Texas, since 1946.

Hillyer, Ruth, B.A.'32, Baylor Univ.; M.A.'49, Univ. of Texas; Tchr., Sr. H. S., San Angelo, Texas, since 1942.

Hinds, Walton, Ph.D.'34, Webster Univ.; Supt. of Sch., Galena Park, Texas, since 1937.

Hines, Ben B., M.A.'36, Southern Methodist Univ.; Dist. Supt. of Sch., Kaufman, Texas, since 1942.

Hinson, Y. L., B.A.'27, Univ. of Texas; M.A.'40, Stephen F. Austin State Tchrs. Col., Nacogdoches, Texas; Prin., Dowling Jr. H. S., Beaumont, Texas, since 1946.

Hodges, H. A., M.A.'27, Univ. of Texas; Dir., Pan American Col., Edinburg, Texas, since 1948.

Hodges, R. L., M.A.'42, Texas Christian Univ.; Supt. of Lake Worth Sch., Fort Worth, Texas, since 1950.

Hollenshead, M. R., B.A.'30, Trinity Univ.; M.A.'38, Univ. of Texas; Asst. Supt. of Sch., El Paso, Texas, since 1946.

Holmes, C. D., B.S.'35, Abilene Christian Col.; M.E.'48, Texas Tech. Col.; Supt. of Sch., Stratford, Texas, since 1947.

Holmes, L. A., M.A.'45, Baylor Univ.; Supt. of Sch., Belton, Texas.

Horn, Thomas D., Ph.D.'47, State Univ. of Iowa, Assoc. Prof., Dept. of Curriculum and Instr.; Col. of Educ., Univ. of Texas, Austin, Texas.

Howell, E. J., B.S.'22, M.S.'32, Agrl. and Mech. Col. of Texas; Pres., Tarleton State Col., Stephenville, Texas, since 1948.

Hudspeth, Ben H., M.A.'41, George Peabody Col. for Tchrs.; Supt. of Sch., Atlanta, Texas, since 1945.

Hudspeth, Sam A., M.A.'41, Southwest Texas State Tchrs. Col.; Supt. of Sch., Skidmore, Texas, since 1951.

Huff, Z. T., A.B.'25, Baylor Univ.; A.M.'29, Columbia Univ.; Ph.D.'36, Univ. of Texas; Dean, Howard Payne Col., Brownwood, Texas, since 1938.

Huffman, R. L., B.S.'31, M.S.'38, East Texas State Tchrs. Col., Commerce; Supt. of Sch., Mansfield, Texas, since 1944.

Hughes, (Mrs.) Roy, B.S.'37, West Texas State Tchrs. Col., Canyon; Co. Supt. of Sch., Vernon, Texas, since 1947.

Humphrey, Joe R., B.A.'25, Trinity Univ.; M.A.'31, Ed.D.'38, Columbia Univ.; Chief, School Plant Section, Texas Educ. Agency, Austin, Texas, since 1950.

Hunt, Andrew William, B.A.'31, M.A.'33, Baylor Univ.; Ph.D.'41, Univ. of Texas; Prof. and Head, Dept. of Educ. and Psych., McMurry Col., Abilene, Texas, since 1949.

Hunter, Fred W., M.A.'37, Austin Col.; Supt. of Sch., Beaumont, Texas, since 1951.

Hutchinson, Joe C., M.A.'38, Texas Tech. Col.; Supt. of Sch., Littlefield, Texas, since 1945.

Hynds, Ray H., Supt. of Sch., Port Isabel, Texas.

Irons, W. C., Supt. of Sch., Quitman, Texas.

Irvin, William Buel, A.B.'21, Simmons Col.; M.A.'27, Simmons Univ.; Ed.D.'39, Univ. of Texas; Supt. of Sch., Highland Park, Texas, since 1944.

Jackson, Eugene, Bus. Mgr., Pub. Sch., Galveston, Texas.

Jackson, Frank M., B.A.'28, Southwestern Univ.; Co. Supt. of Sch., San Angelo, Texas, since 1939.

James, William Alonzo, B.A.'94, M.A.'95, Univ. of Texas; Prin. Emeritus, Ball H. S., 2327 Ave. M, Galveston, Texas, since 1940.

Jennings, Morris S., B.B.A.'31, M.B.A.'38, Univ. of Texas; Supt. of Sch., South San Antonio, Texas, since 1943.

Jenson, J. Justin, M.S.'40, Univ. of Houston; Supt., Barbers Hill Independent Sch. Dist., Mont Belvieu, Texas, since 1932.

Johnson, Lee, B.A.'24, Simmons Univ.; M.S.'38, Univ. of Southern Calif.; Supt. of Sch., Phillips, Texas, since 1946.

Johnson, Leroy W., B.S.'24, North Texas State Tchrs. Col., Denton; M.A.'29, Univ. of Colo.; Supt. of Sch., Stamford, Texas, since 1928.

Johnson, R. H., B.S.'29, Sam Houston State Tchrs. Col., Huntsville, Texas; Co. Supt. of Sch., Palestine, Texas, since 1943.

Johnson, T. H., A.B.'23, Baylor Univ.; M.A.'35, Univ. of Texas; Supt. of Sch., Taylor, Texas, since 1947.

Jones, J. T., M.A.'40, Texas Christian Univ.; B.S.'33, North Texas State Col., Denton; Supt. of Sch., Olton, Texas, since 1948.

Jones, J. W., B.A.'30, West Texas State Tchrs. Col., Canyon; M.A.'39, Texas Tech. Col.; Supt., Sligo Independent Sch. Dist., Denver City, Texas, since 1940.

Jones, L. O., B.S.'41, Sam Houston State Tchrs. Col., Huntsville, Texas; Supt. of Sch., Buffalo, Texas, since 1947.

Jones, M. E., B.S., North Texas State Col.; M.A.'40, Univ. of N. Mex.; Supt. of Sch., Hearne, Texas, since 1948.

Jones, R. E. L., A.B.'23, Southwestern Univ.; Supt. of Sch., Fort Hood, Texas, since 1947.

Jones, Theron M., M.A.'36, George Peabody Col.; Supt. of Sch., Deport, Texas, since 1950.

Jordan, W. L., M.A.'37, Baylor Univ.; Supt. of Sch., Crockett, Texas, since 1939.

Justiss, Thomas S., M.A.'37, Univ. of Texas; Supt. of Sch., Paris, Texas, since 1946.

Kaderli, Fred, B.A.'24, Southwest Texas State Tchrs. Col., San Marcos; M.A.'28, Univ. of Texas; Supt. of Sch., San Marcos, Texas, since 1937.

Kavanaugh, Allen, B.A.'35, East Texas State Col.; M.A.'41, West Texas State Tchrs. Col.; Supt. of Sch., New London, Texas, since 1949.

Key, Billy, B.A.'38, M.A.'42, Texas Tech. Col.; Supt. of Sch., Sundown, Texas, since 1946.

Kimbrough, B. D., B.S.'35, A.B.'38, M.A.'39, East Texas State Tchrs. Col.; Supt. of Sch., Rockwall, Texas, since 1948.

Kinard, Knox, B.A.'31, West Texas State Tchrs. Col.; M.A.'41, Univ. of Texas; Supt. of Sch., Pampa, Texas, since 1945.

King, James D., M.S.'39, Southern Methodist Univ.; Supt. of Sch., Brownwood, Texas, since 1947.

Kirk, Jerry R., B.A.'47, Southwestern State Col.; M.Ed.'52, West Texas State Col.; Supt. of Sch., Muleshoe, Texas, since 1952.

Koerth, Alexander, Prin., Stephen F. Austin Sch., Port Arthur, Texas.

Kruse, M. F., M.S.'44, North Texas State Col.; Supt. of Sch., West, Texas, since 1946.

Landolt, C. D. "Cap", B.A.'32, M.A.'35, Austin Col.; Supt. of Sch., Sherman, Texas, since 1947.

Landrum, C. R., M.A.'48, Southwest Texas State Tchrs. Col., San Marcos; Supt. of Pub. Sch., Cotulla, Texas, since 1948.

Landrum, H. M., D.Ed.'49, Univ. of Houston; Supt., Spring Branch Indep. Sch. Dist., Houston, Texas, since 1941.

Lane, Jack, M.A.'39, Southwest Texas State Tchrs. Col., San Marcos; Supt. of Pub. Sch., Poth, Texas, since 1935.

Langwith, J. E., A.B.'13, Southwestern Univ.; M.A.'29, Southern Methodist Univ.; Supt. of Sch., Terrell, Texas, since 1923.

*Lanier, Raphael O'Hara, A.B.'22, D.Ped.'44, Lincoln Univ.; M.A.'28, Stanford Univ.; D.H.L.'47, Univ. of Liberia, Monrovia, Liberia; Pres., Texas Southern Univ., Houston, Texas, since 1946.

Larsen, A. R., Macmillan Co., Dallas, Texas.

Lasater, Ira L., B.S.'38, M.S.'47, North Texas State Tchrs. Col.; Supt. of Sch., Winters, Texas, since 1944.

Laughlin, Frances, B.A.'31, M.A.'32, State Univ. of Iowa; Asst.; Pupil Personnel Serv., Pub. Sch., Port Arthur, Texas, since 1935.

Laycock, Huelyn W., M.A.'49, West Texas State Col.; Supt. of Sch., White Deer, Texas, since 1951.

Lee, Umphrey, B.A.'14, Trinity Univ.; M.A.'16, Southern Methodist Univ.; D.D.'28, Trinity Univ.; Ph.D.'31, Columbia Univ.; Litt.D.'40, Southwestern; LL.D.'42, Ohio Wesleyan Univ.; Pres., Southern Methodist Univ., Dallas, Texas, since 1939.

Le Fevers, Riley, B.A.'30, M.A.'34, Univ. of Texas; Supt., Santa Fe Independent Sch. Dist., Alta Loma, Texas, since 1951.

Lemmons, Charles A., B.S.'35, M.A.'38, Southwest Texas State Tchrs. Col., San Marcos, Supt. of Sch., LaGrange, Texas, since 1946.

Lindsey, Charles A., Supt. of Pub. Sch., Albany, Texas.

Lipscomb, Roland Arthur, B.S.'30, N. Texas State Tchrs. Col., Denton; Supt. of Sch., Wink, Texas, since 1946.

Little, Alfred T., M.S.'46, East Texas State Tchrs. Col.; Supt. of Sch., Emory, Texas, since 1948.

Lockey, J. H., Dist. Supt. of Sch., Liberty, Texas.

Loftin, James Otis., M.A.'25, Colo. State Col. of Educ., Greeley; Pres., San Antonio Col., San Antonio, Texas, since 1941.

Loos, Alfred J., A.B.'10, Grinnell Col.; Dist. Prin., Cumberland Sch., since 1942, and Prin., William B. Travis Sch., Dallas, Texas.

Lowe, J. Ray, M.S.'41, East Texas State Tchrs. Col., Commerce; Supt. of Sch., Athens, Texas, since 1946.

Lowman, Harmon, B.A.'24, Southwest Texas State Tchrs. Col., San Marcos; M.A.'25, Univ. of Texas; Ph.D.'30, Univ. of Chicago; Pres., Sam Houston State Tchrs. Col., Huntsville, Texas, since 1942.

Loyd, Doyal T., B.S.'28, North Texas State Tchrs. Col., Denton; Supt. of Sch., East Mountain, Gilmer, Texas, since 1933.

Lux, Clara, M.A.'39, Baylor Univ.; Prin., Bell's Hill Elem. Sch., Waco, Texas, since 1944.

Lyon, Robert E., B.S.'36, Southwest Texas State Tchrs. Col.; M.A.'41, Baylor Univ.; Supt. of Independent Sch., Riesel, Texas, since 1947.

McCollum, Kenneth Dillard, B.S.'34, M.A.'38, Southwest Texas State Tchrs. Col.; Supt., Harlandale Independent Sch. Dist., San Antonio, Texas, since 1942.

McCollum, T. E., B.A.'28, Hardin-Simmons Univ.; M.A.'40, Texas Tech. Col.; Supt. of Sch., McAllen, Texas, since 1947.

McCord, Weldon, B.S.'36, East Texas State Col.; Supt. of Sch., New Boston, Texas, since 1949.

McDaniel, B., M.A.'28, Univ. of Texas; Supt. of Sch., Denison, Texas, since 1937.

McDonald, Leslie C., B.S.'21, Southwest Texas State Tchrs. Col., San Marcos; M.A.'30, Ph.D.'34, Univ. of Texas; Dir. of Attendance and Census, Pub. Sch., Houston, Texas, since 1945.

McDonald, T. H., M.Ed.'37, Univ. of Texas; Supt. of Sch., Mesquite, Texas, since 1950.

McGuire, B. H., M.A.'44, Univ. of Texas; Supt. of Sch., Woodville, Texas, since 1945.

McKay, Robert H., M.A.'37, Southern Methodist Univ.; Asst. Supt. of Sch., in charge of Admin., Dallas, Texas.

McNiel, Joe B., B.A.'29, North Texas State Tchrs. Col., Denton; M.A.'33, Southern Methodist Univ.; Supt. of Sch., Wichita Falls, Texas, since 1947.

McPherson, E. W., A.B.'27, Baylor Univ.; M.S.'47, North Texas State Col., Denton; Supt. of Sch., Nocona, Texas, since 1945.

Macon, Carl, B.A.'31, Howard Payne Col.; M.A.'49, Eastern N. Mex. Univ.; Supt. of Sch., Morton, Texas, since 1945.

Malish, William, B.A.'43, Southwestern Univ.; Supt. of Sch., Thrall, Texas, since 1946.

Marcom, O. W., B.A.'36, M.A.'49, Texas Tech. Col.; Supt. of Sch., Levelland, Texas, since 1947.

Marecek, Peter S., A.B.'32, Howard Payne Col.; Supt. of Sch., Pawnee, Texas, since 1936.

Martin, Edwin D., A.B.'23, Abilene Christian Col.; M.S.'27, Texas Agrl. and Mech. Col.; Ed.D.'41, Colo. State Col. of Educ.; Asst. Supt., Research and Pupil Accounting, Houston, Texas, since 1950.

Martin, Leland L., B.S.'34, M.E.'39, Texas Tech. Col.; Supt. of Sch., Crane, Texas, since 1940.

Martin, Quintin M., B.A.'26, M.A.'38, Univ. of Texas; Supt., Independent Sch. Dist., Carthage, Texas, since 1927.

Martin, W. E., M.A.'41, Sam Houston State Tchrs. Col., Huntsville, Texas; Asst. Supt. of Sch., Kountze, Texas.

Mason, Byron D., M.A.'36, Stephen F. Austin State Tchrs. Col., Nacogdoches, Texas; Supt., Leverett's Chapel Independent Sch. Dist., Overton, Texas, since 1937.

Mason, J. Marcus, B.S.'40, Sam Houston State Tchrs. Col., Huntsville, Texas; Co. Supt. of Sch., Crockett, Texas, since 1946.

Mathews, Charles F., Dir., Curricular Serv., Midland, Texas.

Mathews, Clarke A., B.S.'27, Texas Agrl. and Mech. Col.; M.A.'37, Univ. of Texas; Supt. of Sch., Nederland, Texas, since 1946.

Matthews, Benjamin Albion, B.A.'27, Southwestern Univ.; M.A.'30, Southern Methodist Univ.; Prin., Boude Storey Jr. H. S., Dallas, Texas.

Matthews, J. C., B.A.'25, North Texas State Col.; M.A.'28, Ph.D.'32, George Peabody Col. for Tchrs.; Pres., North Texas State Col., Denton, Texas, since 1951.

Mauldin, W. D., B.A.'33, Hardin-Simmons Col.; M.A.'38, Univ. of Texas; Supt. of Sch., Jacksonville, Texas, since 1950.

Maxwell, Stapp N., B.S.'35, M.S.'40, Texas A. & M. Col.; Asst. Supt. of Sch., Alvin, Texas, since 1949.

Meacham, W. A., M.A.'37, Colo. State Col. of Educ., Greeley; Asst. Supt. of Sch., Fort Worth, Texas, since 1931.

Meek, J. Aaron, B.A.'37, West Texas State Tchrs. Col., Canyon; Prin., Sam Houston Sch., Pampa, Texas, since 1927.

Merrell, J. B., B.S.'34, M.S.'38, North Texas State Tchrs. Col., Denton; Supt. of Sch., Stephenville, Texas, since 1944.

Meyer, A. M., A.B.'20, M.A.'25, Ind. Univ.; Ph.D.'33, George Peabody Col. for Tchrs.; Pres., Amarillo Col., Amarillo, Texas, since 1946.

Meyers, W. H., B.S.'27, M.S.'35, Texas A. & M. Col.; Dean, Alvin Jr. Col., Alvin, Texas, since 1939.

Miller, Fred, B.A.'41, Howard Payne Col.; Supt. of Sch., Abernathy, Texas, since 1947.

Miller, Homer L., B.S.'35, North Texas State Col., Denton; M.Ed.'49, Texas Univ.; Supt. of Sch., Coahoma, Texas, since 1952.

Miller Oscar E., B.A.'32, M.A.'36, Univ. of Texas; Asst. Dist. Supt. of Sch. in charge of Jr. and Sr. Sch., San Antonio, Texas, since 1947.

Miller, Vincent W., B.S.'29, Sam Houston State Tchrs. Col., Huntsville, Texas; M.A.'35, Univ. of Colo.; Supt. of Sch., Pasadena, Texas, since 1945.

Miller, W. A., M.A.'40, Univ. of Texas; Supt. of Sch., Odessa, Texas, since 1949.

Mills, Hubert Lawrence, Diploma '11, Sam Houston State Tchrs. Col., Huntsville, Texas; LL.B.'15, Houston Law Sch.; LL.D.'31, Southwestern Univ.; Ph.D.'32, Webster Univ.; Bus. Mgr., Pub. Sch., Houston, Texas, since 1922.

Mills, Robert E., M.A.'43, Sam Houston State Tchrs. Col., Huntsville, Texas; Supt. of Sch., Sabinal, Texas, since 1946.

Mize, Gilbert, B.A.'32, Sul Ross State Tchrs. Col., Alpine, Texas; M.A.'39, Texas Tech. Col.; Supt. of Sch., Perryton, Texas, since 1948.

Moffett, F. L., B.S.'24, Sam Houston State Tchrs. Col., Huntsville, Texas; M.S.'29, Texas Agrl. and Mech. Col.; Supt. of Sch., Center, Texas, since 1926.

Monroe, Frank, B.S.'33, West Texas State Tchrs. Col., Canyon; M.A.'41, Colo. State Col. of Educ., Greeley; Supt. of Sch., Midland, Texas, since 1941.

Moore, Elmer J., B.A.'30, M.A.'40, Texas Tech. Col.; Supt. of Sch., Shamrock, Texas, since 1945.

Moore, Hollis A., B.S. in Ed.'27, Southwest Mo. State Tchrs. Col., Springfield; M.A.'32, Univ. of Mo.; D.Ed.'47, Univ. of Texas; Supt. of Sch., Tyler, Texas, since 1951.

Moore, J. D., B.S.'34, M.S.'38, N. Texas State Tchrs. Col., Denton; Pres., Victoria Col., Victoria, Texas, since 1948.

Moore, Joe Preston, B.S.'25, North Texas State Tchrs. Col., Denton; M.A.'28, Colo. State Col. of Educ., Greeley; LL.D.'48, Texas Christian Univ.; Supt. of Sch., Fort Worth, Texas, since 1946.

Moorman, J. M., M.S.'45, Texas Agrl. and Mech. Col.; Supt. of Sch., Hempstead, Texas, since 1950.

Moreland, William E., M.A.'36, Columbia Univ.; LL.D.'45, Southwestern Univ.; Supt. of Sch., Houston, Texas, since 1945.

Morgan, R. S., B.A.'31, Southwest Texas State Tchrs. Col., San Marcos; M.A.'36, Univ. of Texas; Supt. of Sch., Bishop, Texas, since 1952.

Morris, John T., B.S.'33, M.S.'40, North Texas State Tchrs. Col.; Supt. of Sch., O'Donnell, Texas, since 1951.

Morris, M. B., B.A.'34, Univ. of Texas; M.A.'42, Colo. State Col. of Educ., Greeley; Supt. of Sch., Uvalde, Texas, since 1947.

Morton, Ohland, A.B.'25, Southeastern Okla. Tchrs. Col.; M.A.'29, Univ. of Okla.; Ph.D.'39, Univ. of Texas; Supt. of Sch., Edinburg, Texas, since 1952.

Moseley, W. H., M.A.'46, North Texas State Col.; Co. Supt. of Sch., McKinney, Texas, since 1950.

Moses, Elsie, President, Fort Worth Council of Administrative Women in Education, Fort Worth, Texas.

Moses, J. L., B.S.'28, Sam Houston State Tchrs. Col., Huntsville, Texas; M.S.'35, Texas Agrl. and Mech. Col. System; Dir. of Tchr. Tr. in Voc. Educ., Sam Houston State Tchrs. Col., Huntsville, Texas, since 1938.

Moss, F. P., M.A.'26, Austin Col.; 310 Lindsey St., San Marcos, Texas.

Moss, Hubert H., M.S.'35, North Texas State Col.; Co. Supt. of Sch., Gainesville, Texas, since 1946.

Mossman, Hobart F., M.A.'36, Northwestern Univ.; LL.D.'49, Morningside Col.; Pres., Hockaday Sch., Dallas, Texas, since 1946.

Mulkey, O. C., B.A.'30, East Texas State Tchrs. Col.; M.A.'37, George Peabody Col.; Elem. Supvr., Denison, Texas, since 1947.

Murphy, M. D., B.S.'32, Texas Christian Univ.; M.A.'41, Southern Methodist Univ.; Supt. of Sch., Cleburne, Texas, since 1950.

Muse, E. W., B.A.'13, Texas Christian Univ.; Prin., Stephen F. Austin Sch. and San Jacinto Sch., Dallas, Texas (retired).

Nash, Walter C., B.S.'23, M.S.'50, East Texas State Tchrs. Col., Commerce; A.B. and M.A.'28, Austin Col.; Co. Supvr. of High Schs., Bonham, Texas, since 1949.

Neale, D. E., Southern Mgr., Lyons and Carnahan, 501 Elm Street, Dallas, Texas, since 1916.

*Nelson, Charles R., B.A.'35, Eastern Wash. Col. of Educ., Cheney; M.A.'43, Ed.D.'50, Tchrs. Col., Columbia Univ.; Asst. Supt. of Elem. Sch., Houston, Texas, since 1950.

Nelson, George K., B.S.'36, Southwest Texas State Tchrs. Col.; M.Ed.'50, Univ. of Houston; Supt. of Tidehaven Sch., Blessing, Texas, since 1942.

Newman, Stacy A., Jr., Master's '48, East Texas State Tchrs. Col.; Supt. of Sch., Bells, Texas, since 1951.

Nicholas, H. H., M.E.'45, Texas Tech. Col.; Supt., Ralls, Texas, since 1950.

Nixon, J. W., B.S.'34, Sul Ross State Tchrs. Col., Alpine, Texas; Supt. of Sch., Laredo, Texas, since 1945.

Norwood, Pat H., B.A.'25, East Texas State Tchrs. Col.; M.A.'28, George Peabody Col. for Tchrs.; Ph.D.'47, Univ. of Texas; Dir. of Pub. Serv. and Prof. of Educ., Southwest Texas State Tchrs. Col., San Marcos, Texas, since 1939.

Norwood, W. Howard, B.A.'16, Univ. of Texas; M.A.'36, Tchrs. Col., Columbia Univ.; Supt. of Sch., Corsicana, Texas, since 1931.

Notley, Llewellyn, M.A.'33, Univ. of Texas; Supt. of Sch., Teague, Texas, since 1920.

Nuckols, Bert R., M.S.'41, West Texas State Col.; Co. Supt. of Sch., Pampa, Texas, since 1951.

*Oberholtzer, Edison Ellsworth, Ph.B.'10, M.A. '15, Univ. of Chicago; LL.D.'21, Univ. of Tulsa; Ph.D.'34, Columbia Univ.; Pres., Dept. of Superintendence, 1934-35; Honorary Life Member, American Assn. of Sch. Admin.; Pres. Emeritus, Univ. of Houston since 1950. Address: 1708 W. Alabama St., Houston 6, Texas.

Odell, Newell H., B.A.'43, Howard-Payne Col.; M.A.'52, Hardin-Simmons Univ.; Supt. of Sch., Childress, Texas, since 1952.

Ogg, James T., B.S.'27, Stephen F. Austin State Tchrs. Col., Nacogdoches, Texas; M.Ed.'41, Univ. of Texas; Supt. of Pine Tree Sch., Greggton, Texas, since 1946.

Ogg, Terrell W., B.S.'35, Stephen F. Austin State Tchrs. Col., Nacogdoches, Texas; M.Ed.'42, Univ. of Texas; Supt. of Brazosport Independent Sch. Dist., Freeport, Texas, since 1946.

Oliver, Horace, B.B.A.'28, Sul Ross State Tchrs. Col., Alpine, Texas; M.S., Texas Univ.; Supt. of Sch., Ft. Hancock, Texas, since 1946.

Otto, Henry J., Ph.D.'31, Univ. of Minn. Address: Col. of Educ., Univ. of Texas, Austin, Texas.

Owens, C. M., A.A.'33, Lon Morris Col.; B.S.'35, M.A.'39, Sam Houston State Tchrs. Col., San Marcos, Texas; Supt., Independent Sch. Dist., Livingston, Texas, since 1951.

Owens, H. A., M.E.'52, Texas Tech. Col.; Supt. of Sch., Petersburg, Texas, since 1950.

Owensby, Jesse A., Supt. of Sch., Hamshire, Texas.

Parnell, John F., B.A.'20, Union Univ.; M.A.'35, Peabody Col.; Supt. of City Sch., Jasper, Texas, since 1924.

Parrish, J. D., B.S.'37, Univ. of Texas; M.S.'49, East Texas State Tchrs. Col.; Co. Supt. of Sch., Daingerfield, Texas, since 1941.

Parsons, Floyd W., M.A.'45, Univ. of Texas. Address: 1210 Polk St., Beeville, Texas.

Pearce, J. J., M.A.'43, Southern Methodist Univ.; Supt. of Sch., Richardson, Texas, since 1946.

Pearson, H. D., B.S.'34, M.E.'49, East Texas State Tchrs. Col.; Supt. of Sch., Garland, Texas, since 1945.

Peay, Austin L., M.A.'41, Baylor Univ.; Supt. of Sch., Kenedy, Texas, 1948-52. Address: Box 893, Elsa, Texas.

Pena, William M., B.S.'42, B.Arch.'48, Agrl. and Mech. Col. of Texas; Partner in Caudill, Rowlett and Scott, Box 1351, College Station, Texas, since 1948.

Perry, Oliver Floyd, B.A.'29, Southwestern Univ.; Supt. of Sch., Round Rock, Texas, since 1938.

Perry, W. C., B.S.'38, Southwest Texas State Tchrs. Col., San Marcos; M.A.'43, Baylor Univ.; Supt. of Sch., Meridian, Texas, 1943-52.

Peters, J. V., M.S. in Ed.'46, Univ. of Idaho; Pres., Southwestern Jr. Col., Keene, Texas, since 1946.

Peters, Joe, Prin., T. G. Terry Sch., Dallas, Texas.

Petty, J. C., M.Ed.'47, Univ. of Texas; Supt. of Sch., Burnet, Texas, since 1948.

Phipps, Raymond W., B.Ed.'33, Eastern Ill. State Tchrs. Col., Charleston; M.A.'35, Ohio State Univ.; Dir., Adult Educ., 1500 Louisiana St., Houston 3, Texas, since 1949.

Pipes, Wesley O., A.B. and M.A.'26, Baylor Univ.; Prin., North Dallas H. S., Dallas, Texas, since 1945.

525

Porter, T. N., B.S.'26, North Texas State Col., Denton; Asst. Supt. of Sch., Austin, Texas, since 1951.

Portwood, Thomas B., B.S.'19, Kansas State Tchrs. Col., Emporia; A.M.'22, Columbia Univ.; D.Litt.'47, Trinity Univ.; Supt. of Sch., San Antonio, Texas, since 1946.

*Proffer, Robert L., B.S.'35, M.S.'37, North Texas State Col.; Asst. Prof. of Educ. Admin. and Government at North Texas State Col., Denton, Texas, since 1949.

Pryor, Guy C., B.A.'29, North Texas State Tchrs. Col., Denton; M.A.'36, Southern Methodist Univ.; Supt. of Sch., Grand Saline, Texas, since 1946.

Railsback, H. F., M.A.'38, Texas Tech. Col.; Supt. of Sch., Dalhart, Texas, since 1950.

Randolph, W. H., Dir., South Texas Colleges, Houston, Texas.

Raynes, L. F., B.S.'37, East Texas State Tchrs. Col.; Supt. of Sch., Crandall, Texas, since 1946.

Reagan, G. H., Prin., Lida Hooe Sch., Dallas, Texas.

Reed, J. Herman, B.A.'41, M.Ed.'50, East Texas State Tchrs. Col.; Supt. of Pub. Sch., Duncanville, Texas, since 1951.

Reynolds, C. A., M.A.'46, Sul Ross Col.; Supt. of Pub. Sch., Brady, Texas, since 1951.

Reynolds, James W., B.A.E.'30, Ark. State Tchrs. Col., Conway; M.A.'34, State Univ. of Iowa; Ph.D.'45, Univ. of Chicago; Prof. of Jr. Col. Educ., Univ. of Texas, Austin, Texas, since 1948.

Reynolds, Roland, B.B.A.'32, M.B.A.'37, Univ. of Texas; Supt. of Sch., Franklin, Texas, since 1946.

Rhodes, J. E., B.S.'34, North Texas State Tchrs. Col.; M.E.'39, Southern Methodist Univ.; Supt. of Sch., Van, Texas, since 1930.

Richardson, Frank W., B.A.'28, East Texas State Tchrs. Col.; M.A.'31, Southern Methodist Univ.; Supt. of Sch., Henrietta, Texas, since 1934.

Richardson, L. S., B.S.'45, M.E.'48, Texas Agrl. and Mech. Col.; Supt. of Sch., College Station, Texas, since 1949.

Riley, Richard F., Supt. of Sch., Anahuac, Texas.

Roach, Truett A., M.A.'33, Baylor Univ.; Supt. of Sch., Victoria, Texas, since 1947.

Robbins, Edward T., B.B.A.'26, Univ. of Texas; M.S.'33, Agrl. and Mech. Col. of Texas; Dist. Supt. of Sch., Alamo Heights, Texas, since 1947.

Roberts, Charles T., B.A.'36, East Texas State Tchrs. Col.; M.Ed.'47, Univ. of Colo.; Supt. of Sch., Wellington, Texas, since 1949.

Roberts, L. A., B.S.'27, North Texas State Tchrs. Col.; M.A.'29, Southern Methodist Univ.; Co. Supt. of Sch., Dallas, Texas, since 1951.

Robertson, Rankin, B.S. in Ed.'33, Texas Col. of Arts and Indus.; Supt. of Sch., Bloomington, Texas, since 1944.

Robinson, Lyman B., B.S.'28, North Texas State Tchrs. Col.; B.A. and M.A.'32, Austin Col.; Supt. of Independent Sch., Whitesboro, Texas.

Robinson, Wm. J., B.S.'39, State Tchrs. Col., Millersville, Pa.; M.Ed.'41, Ph.D.'49, Temple Univ.; Dir. of Research, Dallas Independent Sch. Dist., Dallas, Texas, since 1949.

Rodgers, John O., B.A.'35, Southwestern Univ. (Texas); M.A.'40, Univ. of Texas; Supt., Williamson Co. Sch., Georgetown, Texas, since 1942.

Rogers, Charles M., A.B.'13, Miss. Col.; M.A.'31, Texas Tech. Col.; Supt. of Sch., Amarillo, Texas, since 1935.

Rogers, J. C., Jr., B.A.'32, Stephen F. Austin Tchrs. Col., Nacogdoches; M.A.'40, Univ. of Texas; Supt. of Sch., West Columbia, Texas, since 1946.

Rogers, T. Guy, M.A.'27, Univ. of Texas; Prin., Thomas Jefferson H. S., San Antonio, Texas, since 1932.

Rogers, W. C., Supt., Chapel Hill Independent Sch. Dist., Tyler, Texas.

Ross, (Mrs.) Cecil, B.A.'49, M.A.'50, East Texas State Tchrs. Col.; Dir., Off-Campus Activities, East Texas State Tchrs. Col., Commerce, Texas, since 1950.

Rowland, K. H., M.Ed.'41, Texas Tech. Col.; Supt. of Pub. Sch., Baird, Texas, since 1949.

Schiebel, Walter J. E., B.S. in M.E.'16, M.A.'32, Univ. of Rochester; Prin., N. R. Crozier Tech. H. S., Dallas, Texas, since 1932.

Scott, (Mrs.) Florence J., M.A.'40, Univ. of Texas; Dist. Supt. of Sch., Roma, Texas, since 1948.

Scott, J. S., Sr., A.B.'17, New Orleans Col., New Orleans, La.; B.D.'20, D.D.'40, Gammon Theol. Sem., Atlanta, Ga.; D.D.'27, Wiley Col.; Pres., Wiley Col., Marshall, Texas, since 1948.

Selby, R. A., M.A.'34, B.A.'29, Univ. of Okla.; Asst. Supt. of Sch., Amarillo, Texas, since 1950.

Self, Lester D., Supt. of Sch., Silsbee, Texas.

Sellars, David K., B.B.A.'24, M.Ed.'35, Univ. of Texas; Coordinator of Instr., Fort Worth, Texas, since 1938.

Sellers, Mary, Prin., James Stephen Hogg Sch., Dallas, Texas.

Shea, James T., B.A.'15, M.A.'24, Univ. of Detroit; Dir. of Curriculum and Research, Bd. of Educ., San Antonio, Texas, since 1922.

Shelby, Thomas Hall, Dean, Div. of Extension, Univ. of Texas, Austin, Texas.

Shelton, P. W., B.A.'25, M.A.'38, Baylor Univ.; Supt. of LaVega Pub. Sch., Waco, Texas, since 1929.

Sigler, E. A., B.S.'28, North Texas State Tchrs. Col.; Supt. of Sch., Plano, Texas, since 1927.

Sikes, L. B. T., Supt. of Sch., Calvert, Texas.

Silk, Charles E., M.S.'48, North Texas State Col.; Co. Supt. of Sch., Denton, Texas, since 1943.

Silk, W. O., B.S.'35, North Texas State Col.; M.S., Austin Col.; Supt. of Sch., Frisco, Texas, since 1949.

Sims, (Mrs.) G. M., Dir., Pupil Personal Serv., Port Arthur, Texas.

Singletary, Frank L., B.S.'35, Stephen F. Austin State Tchrs. Col., Nacogdoches, Texas; M.Ed.'42, Southern Methodist Univ.; Supt. of Sch., Troup, Texas, since 1948.

Singletary, James D., B.S.'44, N. Y. State Col. for Tchrs. at Buffalo; A.M.'46, Ph.D.'50, Univ. of Chicago; Prof. and Head of the Dept. of Educ., Prairie View A. & M. Col., Prairie View, Texas, since 1950.

Singleton, Con, Pub. Sch. Tchr., Houston, Texas.

Singleton, Gordon G., Diploma '19, Cambridge Univ., England; B.S.'19, Univ. of Ga.; M.A.'24, Tchrs. Col., Columbia Univ.; Ph.D.'25, Columbia Univ.; D.Litt.'40, Baylor Univ.; Sch. of Educ., Baylor Univ., Waco, Texas.

Slayton, R. E., M.A.'39, Univ. of Texas; Supt. of Sch., Longview, Texas, since 1952.

Smith, E. M., M.A.'39, Univ. of Texas; Supt. of Pub. Sch., Sinton, Texas, since 1947.

526

Smith, E. W., B.S.'32, Texas Col. of Arts and Indus.; M.A.'36, Colo. State Col. of Educ., Greeley; Supt. of Sch., Fort Stockton, Texas, since 1947.

Smith, W. H., M.S.'47, East Texas State Tchrs. Col.; Supt. of Sch., Hawkins, Texas, since 1936.

Snow, Deskin D., B.S.'25, Southwest Texas State Tchrs. Col.; Co. Supt. of Sch., Corpus Christi, Texas, since 1929.

South, Olaf G., Supt. of Sch., Sweetwater, Texas, since 1952.

Sowers, R. M., B.S.'33, Sam Houston State Tchrs. Col., Huntsville, Texas; M.S.'38, Agrl. and Mech. Col. of Texas; Supt., Independent Sch. Dist., Hardin, Texas, since 1945.

Spann, Rubert W., B.S.'36, Panhandle A. & M. Col. (Okla.); M.S. in Adm.Ed.'43, Okla. A. & M. Col.; Supt. of Springlake Sch., Earth, Texas, since 1951.

Sparks, Robert Burdette, M.A.'26, Univ. of Chicago; Prin., Robert E. Lee H. S., Baytown, Texas, since 1931.

Spears, Otis, M.Ed.'50, Texas Tech. Col.; Supt. of Sch., Tahoka, Texas.

Speer, James B., Sr., B.S.'29, West Texas State Col.; M.A.'33, Texas Tech. Col.; Ed.D.'45, Univ. of Texas; Dir., Tchr. Educ., Pan American Col., Edinburg, Texas.

Spencer, Ray, B.S.'36, M.S.'42, East Texas State Tchrs. Col.; Asst. Supt. of Sch., Texas City, Texas, since 1951.

Stafford, R. E., B.A.'29, Howard Payne Col.; M.Ed.'41, Univ. of Texas; Supt. of Sch., Three Rivers, Texas, since 1949.

Stanfield, M. E., Asst. Supt. of Sch., Snyder, Texas.

Stevens, Archie, B.S.'40, Daniel Baker Col.; Supt. of Sch., Stinnett, Texas, since 1948.

Stevens, Rudolph Harroll, B.S.'27, Southwest Texas State Tchrs. Col.; M.S.'34, Univ. of Chicago; Supt. of Sch., Boling, Texas, since 1950.

Stilwell, H. W., B.A.'09, M.A.'19, Univ. of Texas; LL.D. Southwestern Univ.; Supt. of Sch. and Pres., Texarkana Col., Texarkana, Texas, since 1920.

Stone, Frank, B.S.'36, M.S.'51, East Texas State Tchrs. Col.; Supt. of Sch., Powderly, Texas, since 1944.

Strevell, Wallace H., A.B.'29, M.A.'37, N. Y. State Col. for Tchrs., Albany; Ed.D.'48, Tchrs. Col., Columbia Univ.; Chmn., Dept. of Educ. Admin., Univ. of Houston, Houston, Texas, since 1951.

Strickland, Chester O., M.A.'39, Univ. of Texas; Supt. of Sch., Denton, Texas, since 1947.

Stringer, D. D., B.S.'28, East Texas State Tchrs. Col.; Bus. Mgr., Port Neches Pub. Sch., Port Neches, Texas, since 1952.

Stroble, M. D., M.Ed.'36, Univ. of Texas; Supt. of Sch., Poteet, Texas, since 1939.

Stroh, M. Margaret, B.S.'12, Susquehanna Univ.; A.M.'25, Ph.D.'27, Columbia Univ.; Natl. Exec. Secy., Delta Kappa Gamma Society, Austin, Texas, since 1945.

Summers, J. Wyatt, A.A.'25, Rusk Jr. Col.; B.S.'30, Stephen F. Austin State Tchrs. Col., Nacogdoches, Texas; M.A.'44, Sam Houston State Tchrs. Col., Huntsville, Texas; Supt. of Sch., Mount Pleasant, Texas.

Swim, Keith D., M.A.'49, Colo. State Col. of Educ.; Supt. of Independent Sch. Dist. 903, St. Jo, Texas, since 1950.

Swinburn, W. V., B.S.'33, North Texas State Col.; M.Ed.'35, Texas Tech. Col.; Supt. of Sch., Tulia, Texas, since 1947.

Tallman, Pearle, A.B.'20, Iowa State Tchrs. Col., Cedar Falls; M.A.'28, Columbia Univ.; Asst. Supt. of Sch., Houston, Texas, since 1941.

Tarter, C. W., M.A.'36, Texas Tech. Col.; Supt. of Sch., Lamesa, Texas, since 1952.

Tate, Albert M., M.A.'34, Univ. of Texas; Supt. of Sch., Marlin, Texas, since 1942.

Tate, D. M., B.A.'29, Austin Col.; M.A.'49, East Texas State Tchrs. Col.; Supt. of Sch., Clarksville, Texas, since 1944.

Taylor, James E., B.S.'33, Sam Houston State Tchrs. Col., Huntsville, Texas; M.S.'40, Texas Agrl. and Mech. Col.; Supt. of Sch., Katy, Texas, since 1946.

Teltschik, Alfred E., M.Ed.'49, Univ. of Houston; Supt. of Sch., Yorktown, Texas, since 1948.

Tennyson, Charles H., B.S.'25, East Texas State Tchrs. Col.; M.A.'36, Southern Methodist Univ.; Exec. Secy., Texas State Tchrs. Assn., Austin, Texas.

Thomas, W. G., Jr., M.A.'47, Texas Christian Univ.; Supt. of Birdville Sch., Ft. Worth, Texas, since 1943.

Thomas, Willet S., B.A.'26, Abilene Christian Col.; M.A.'41, Southern Methodist Univ.; Supt. of Sch., Holiday, Texas, since 1935.

Thompson, G. E., A.B.'32, Trinity Univ.; M.Ed. '42, Univ. of Texas; Supt. of Sch., Kermit, Texas, since 1948.

Travis, Walter F., B.S.'38, West Texas State Tchrs. Col., Canyon; M.Ed.'41, Texas Tech. Col.; Supt. of Sch., Dumas, Texas, since 1944.

Tunnell, Lenore M., A.B.'34, M.A.'43, Texas Tech. Col.; Co. Supt. of Sch., Tahoka, Texas, since 1939.

Turner, Robert L., M.S.'39, North Texas State Col.; Supt. of Pub. Sch., Carrollton, Texas since 1945.

Ullrich, Felix H., B.S.'24, Univ. of Wis.; M.A.'29, Ph.D.'37, Univ. of Texas; Chmn., Dept. of Educ., Trinity Univ., San Antonio, Texas, since 1942.

Umstattd, James Greenleaf, B.S. in Ed.'18, M.A.'24, Univ. of Mo.; Ph.D.'30, Univ. of Minn.; Litt.D.'46, Univ. of Bordeaux, France; Prof. of Sec. Educ., Univ. of Texas, Austin, Texas, since 1938.

Vardy, P. L., Jr., B.A.'29, M.A.'37, Texas Tech. Col.; Dist. Supt. of Sch., Slaton, Texas, since 1947.

Vaughter, Sam, B.A.'29, East Texas State Tchrs. Col.; M.A.'41, Hardin-Simmons Univ.; Supt. of Sch., Haskell, Texas, since 1946.

Vestal, R. S., Supt. of Sch., Dimmitt, Texas.

Vincent, Joseph J., B.S.'23, La. State Univ. and A. and M. Col.; M.A.'29, Univ. of Texas; Supt., South Park Sch., Beaumont, Texas, since 1947.

Vineyard, Ray, B. S.'36, West Texas State Tchrs. Col.; M.A.'39, Colo. State Col. of Educ.; Prin., South Ward Sch., Dumas, Texas, since 1951.

Voelcker, Herbert, B.S.'09, Agrl. and Mech. Col. of Texas; Sr. Partner, Herbert Voelcker and Assts., Architects, 1202 Dennis, Houston 4, Texas, since 1945.

Wadzeck, G. B., B.S.'33, McMurry Col.; M.E.'47, Texas Tech. Col.; Supt. of Sch., San Angelo, Texas, since 1952.

Waldrip, Rankin C., B.S.'37, M.S.'39, North Texas State Col.; Supt. of Sch., Brookshire, Texas, since 1949.

Walker, Ewell D., A.B.'19, Austin Col.; Asst. Supt. in charge of Personnel, Dallas, Texas, since 1945.

Walker, Merle, M.Ed.'47, Univ. of Texas; Supt. of Sch., Idalou, Texas, since 1947.

TEXAS

Wallace, Howard D., M.A.'45, Stephen F. Austin State Col.; Supt., Carlisle Independent Sch., Price, Texas, since 1951.

Ward, R. P., B.A.'24, M.A.'26, Univ. of Texas; Supt., Consol. Independent Sch. Dist., and Pres., Edinburg Regional Col., Edinburg, Texas, since 1931.

Ware, Thomas L., M.A.'39, Baylor Univ.; Prin., H. S., Waco, Texas.

Watson, Roy James, B.S.'30, East Central State Tchrs. Col., Ada, Okla.; M.A.'41, Stephen F. Austin State Tchrs. Col., Nacogdoches, Texas; Supt. of Pub. Sch., Palmer, Texas, since 1950.

Webb, J. O., B.A.'14, Southwestern Univ.; M.A.'24, Univ. of Texas; Asst. Supt. of Sch. in charge of Sec. Educ., Houston, Texas, since 1935.

Welch, A. G., A.B.'24, M.A.'25, Mercer Univ.; Supt. of Sch., Alvin, Texas, since 1939.

Wells, A. E., B.A.'31, Abilene Christian Col.; M.A.'36, Colo. State Col. of Educ., Greeley; Supt. of Sch., Abilene, Texas, since 1951.

Wheat, Hubert L., B.S.'39, East Texas State Tchrs. Col.; Supt. of Sch., Winnie, Texas, since 1942.

White, Frank E., B.A.'29, Sam Houston State Tchrs. Col., Huntsville, Texas; M.A.'36, Univ. of Texas; Supt. of Sch., Groveton, Texas, since 1939.

White, John W., B.A.'34, Univ. of Texas; M.A. '46, North Texas State Col.; Supt. of Pub. Sch., Roby, Texas, since 1947.

*White, Warren Travis, B.A.'26, M.A.'31, Univ. of Texas; LL.D.'52, Baylor Univ.; Pres., American Assn. of Sch. Admin., 1950-51; Supt. of Sch., Dallas, Texas, since 1945.

White, William Richardson, A.B.'17, Howard Payne Col.; Th.D.'24, D.D., Th.M.'27, South-western Baptist Theol. Sem.; D.D.'30, Baylor Univ.; Pres., Baylor Univ., Waco, Texas, since 1948.

Whitehurst, H. O., M.A.'45, Southern Methodist Univ.; Supt. of Sch., Groesbeck, Texas, since 1931.

Whitley, Ray H., M.A.'43, Southwest Texas State Tchrs. Col.; Supt. of Sch., Pecos, Texas, since 1945.

Whittlesey, James T., A.B.'17, Emory Univ.; M.A.'20, Southern Methodist Univ.; Prin., Forest Ave. H. S., Dallas, Texas, since 1944.

Wildman, E. L., B.S.'34, M.A.'44, Southwest Texas State Tchrs. Col.; Supt. of Sch., Kerr-ville, Texas.

Wilemon, Tirey C., M.A.'49, Southern Methodist Univ.; Supt. of Sch., Waxahachie, Texas, since 1935.

Wilkerson, Walter D., M.A.'23, Baylor Univ.; Supt. of Sch., Conroe, Texas, since 1949.

Wilkes, Lowell L., B.A.'12, M.A.'30, Univ. of Texas; Supt. of Sch., Hubbard, Texas, since 1927-52.

Williams, Dana, B.S.'40, M.S.'45, Stephen F. Austin State Tchrs. Col., Nacogdoches, Texas; Supt. of Sch., Gladewater, Texas, since 1950.

Williams Ed E., B.A.'29, McMurry Col.; M.A. '42, Hardin-Simmons Univ.; Supt. of Sch. Colorado City, Texas, since 1942.

Williams, Frank L., B.A.'29, M.A.'36, Hardin-Simmons Univ.; Ed.D.'45, Univ. of Texas; Asst. Supt. in charge of Instr., Pub. Sch., Dallas, Texas, since 1949.

Williams, Nat, M.A.'42, Univ. of Texas; Supt. of Sch., Lubbock, Texas, since 1951.

Williams, R. L., B.A.'25, Abilene Christian Col.; M.A.'39, Ed.D.'43, Univ. of Texas; Supt. of Sch., Corpus Christi, Texas, since 1951.

Wilson, J. D., Supt. of Independent Sch. Dist., Hillsboro, Texas.

Wilson, Roy P., B.S.'28, M.S.'49, North Texas State Col.; Supt. of Sch., Gainesville, Texas, since 1945.

Wimbish, W. R., B.A.'30, Abilene Christian Col.; M.A.'36, Univ. of Texas; Supt. of Pub. Sch., Arlington, Texas, since 1941.

Wisseman, Charles Louis, B.A.'27, M.A.'28, Southern Methodist Univ.; Ph.D.'32, New York Univ.; Dir. Sch. of Educ., Southern Methodist Univ., Dallas, Texas, since 1948.

Woods, Quata, B.S.'32, North Texas State Col.; M.Ed.'52, Southern Methodist Univ.; Prin., Obadiah Knight Sch., Dallas, Texas, since 1942.

Wooldridge, W. C., B.S.'41, M.S.'49, East Texas State Tchrs. Col.; Co. Supt. of Sch., Paris, Texas, since 1947.

Wooten, E. A., Supt. of Sch., Dumas, Texas, since 1952.

Wranosky, Ernest J., M.A.'43, Texas Col. of Arts and Indus.; Supt., Flour Bluff Independent Sch. Dist., Corpus Christi, Texas, since 1946.

Wright, J. Herbert, B.A.'18, Southern Methodist Univ.; M.A.'39, Univ. of Calif.; Asst. Supt. in chg. of Personnel, Pub. Sch., Houston, Texas, since 1945.

Wright, N. O., B.S.'30, N. Texas State Col.; M.S.'46, E. Texas State Tchrs. Col.; Supt. of Sch., Farmersville, Texas, since 1934.

Wroten, Joe G., B.A.'35, La. Polytech. Inst.; Supt. of Sch., Pettus, Texas, since 1950.

Yarbrough, Cecil L., M.A.'39, Southern Methodist Univ.; Supt. of Sch., Snyder, Texas, since 1952.

Young, F. J., B.A.'31, McMurry Col.; M.A.'39, Univ. of Texas; Supt. of Sch., Seminole, Texas.

Zevely, Claud, Prin. of Elem. Sch., Pampa, Texas.

INSTITUTIONAL MEMBERS

W. H. Adamson High School, Dallas, Texas.

Ascher Silberstein School, Dallas, Texas.

Baylor University Library, Box 307, B. U. Station, Waco, Texas.

N. R. Crozier Technical High School, Dallas, Texas.

Cumberland School, Dallas, Texas.

Estill Library, Sam Houston State Tchrs. Col., Huntsville, Texas.

Forest Avenue High School, Dallas, Texas.

James B. Bonham School, Henderson and Manett Sts., Dallas, Texas.

James Stephen Hogg School, Dallas, Texas.

Jefferson County Education Association, c/o C. E. Doyle, Beaumont, Texas.

John Henry Brown School, Dallas, Texas.

Library, Hardin-Simmons Univ., Abilene, Texas.

Library, Southwest Texas State Tchrs. Col., Box 695, San Marcos, Texas.

Library, Stephen F. Austin State Tchrs. Col., Nacogdoches, Texas.

Library, Texas State College for Women, Denton, Texas.

Library, West Texas State Teachers College, Canyon, Texas.

Lida Hooe School, Dallas, Texas.

Maple Lawn School, Dallas, Texas.

North Dallas High School, Dallas, Texas.

Obadiah Knight School, Dallas, Texas.

Richard Lagow School, Dallas, Texas.

Sam Houston School, Dallas, Texas.

San Jacinto School, Dallas, Texas.

Stephen F. Austin School, Dallas, Texas.

Stephen J. Hay School, Dallas, Texas.

Sunset High School, Dallas, Texas.

T. G. Terry School, Dallas, Texas.

Texas Southern University, 3200 Cleburne St., Houston, Texas.

Trinity Heights School, Dallas, Texas.

Trinity University Library, Mrs. Theresa R. Simms, Librn., San Antonio, Texas.

University of Houston Library, St. Bernard at Wheeler, Houston, Texas.

William B. Travis School, Dallas, Texas.

William Lipscomb School, Dallas, Texas.

Woodrow Wilson High School, Dallas, Texas.

UTAH

INDIVIDUAL MEMBERS

Ash, Cecil L., B.S.'32, Brigham Young Univ.; Prin., Lehi Elem. Sch., Lehi, Utah, since 1938.

Ball, W. N., B.S.'37, M.S.'42, Brigham Young Univ.; Supt. of South Summit Sch. Dist., Kamas, Utah.

Barnett, Maurice C., B.S.'40, M.S.'49, Brigham Young Univ.; Supt. of Sch., South Sanpete Sch. Dist., Manti, Utah, since 1951.

Barnett, Owen Lee, B.S.'23, M.S.'27, Brigham Young Univ.; Assoc. Prof. of Educ. Admin., Brigham Young Univ., Provo, Utah, since 1950.

Bateman, E. Allen, A.B.'17, Univ. of Utah; M.A.'29, Univ. of Chicago; Ph.D.'40, Columbia Univ.; State Supt. of Pub. Instr., Salt Lake City, Utah, since 1945.

Bates, A. Parley, B.S.'30, Utah State Agrl. Col.; M.S.'35, Univ. of Calif.; Co. Supt. of Sch., Ogden, Utah, since 1943.

Bates, Louis A., B.S.'28, Univ. of Utah; M.S.'38, Univ. of Southern Calif.; Prin., Sr. H. S., Payson, Utah, since 1936.

Beckstead, Reed H., Asst. Supt., Jordon Sch. Dist., Midvale, Utah.

Bennion, M. Lynn, B.S.'26, M.S.'32, Univ. of Utah; Ed.D.'36, Univ. of Calif.; Supt. of Sch., Salt Lake City, Utah, since 1945.

Blight, Alexander, B.S.'35, Brigham Young Univ.; M.S.'39, Univ. of Southern Calif.; Dist. Supt. of Sch., Eureka, Utah, since 1939.

Boyce, George A., B.S.'21, Trinity Col., (Conn.); M.A.'26, Cornell Univ.; Ed.D.'41, Tchrs. Col., Columbia Univ.; Supt. of Sch., Brigham City, Utah, since 1949.

Brockbank, Wallace W., M.S.'49, Brigham Young Univ.; Supt., Nebo Sch. Dist., Spanish Fork, Utah, since 1950.

Chipman, R. S., B.S.'26, M.S.'51, Brigham Young Univ.; Dist. Supt. of Sch., Coalville, Utah, since 1947.

Christensen, Dean C., B.A.'38, M.A.'48, Utah State Agr. Col.; Supt. of Co. Sch., Duchesne, Utah, since 1950.

Christensen, J. A., Prin., Sr. H. S., Nebo Dist., Spanish Fork, Utah.

Christensen, Louis W., B.S.'29, Brigham Young Univ.; M.S.'42, Univ. of Utah; Dist. Supt. of Sch., Morgan, Utah, since 1943.

Cornaby, Leslie H., M.S.'51, Brigham Young Univ.; Prin., Jr. H. S., Spanish Fork, Utah, since 1947.

*Eastmond, Jefferson N., B.S.'47, M.S.'48, Brigham Young Univ.; Ed.D.'50, Tchrs. Col., Columbia Univ.; Asst. Prof. of Educ., Utah State Agrl. Col., Logan, Utah, since 1951.

Evans, Carl R., B.A.'16, Univ. of Utah; M.A.'30, Univ. of Cincinnati; Supt. of Juab Sch., Nephi, Utah, since 1947.

Eyre, Sherman G., B.S.'39, Utah State Agrl. Col.; Supt., Garfield Co. Sch. Dist., Panguitch, Utah, since 1950.

Fawley, Paul C., A.B.'29, Ind. Central Col.; M.A.'34, Mont. State Univ.; Ed.D.'49, Ind. Univ.; Assoc. Prof. of Educ. Admin., Col. of Educ., Univ. of Utah, Salt Lake City, Utah, since 1949.

Frye, Clifford L., B.S.'35, Utah State Agrl. Col.; Co. Supt. of Sch., Huntington, Utah, since 1947.

Gardner, G. Grant, B.S.'33, M.S.'47, Brigham Young Univ.; Asst. Supt., Nebo Sch. Dist., Spanish Fork, Utah, since 1950.

Gibson, L. Dale, B.S.'49, M.S.'50, Univ. of Utah; Supt. of Sch., Daggett Co., Manila, Utah, since 1949.

Gourley, David, B.S.'15, M.S.'35, Brigham Young Univ.; Supt. of Granite Sch. Dist., Salt Lake City, Utah, since 1944.

Hall, Martha, Supvr., Indian Educ., U. S. Indian Serv., Brigham City, Utah.

Hanks, C. Lynn, B.S., Brigham Young Univ.; Prin., Jr. H. S., Springville, Utah, since 1946.

Harmon, Mont, B.S.'35, M.A.'43, Utah State Agr. Col.; Supt., Carbon Co. Sch., Price, Utah, since 1948.

Harrington, J. Genevieve, A.B.'27, State Col. of Educ.; Dept. Head, Intermountain Indian Sch., Brigham City, Utah, since 1950.

Harris, Sterling Richard, B.S.'24, Utah State Agrl. Col.; Supt. of Sch., Tooele, Utah, since 1940.

Hartvigsen, Elmer J., B.S.'31, Utah State Agrl. Col.; M.S.'45, Univ. of Utah; Co. Supt. of Sch., Farmington, Utah, since 1945.

Jacobsen, Ernest A., A.B.'20, M.A.'23, Brigham Young Univ.; Ed.D.'37, Univ. of Oregon; Dean, Sch. of Educ., Utah State Agrl. Col., Logan, Utah, since 1929.

Law, Reuben D., Ed.D.'41, Univ. of Southern Calif; Dean, Col. of Educ., Brigham Young Univ., Provo, Utah, since 1946.

Lundell, Harold M., Supt., Uintah Sch. Dist., Vernal, Utah.

McAffee, Boyd, B.S.'40, M.S.'49, Brigham Young Univ.; Prin., Grandview Elem. Sch., Provo, Utah, since 1949.

Madsen, Louis Linden, B.S.'30, Utah State Agrl. Col.; Ph.D.'34, Cornell Univ.; Pres., Utah State Agrl. Col., Logan, Utah, since 1950.

Merrill, Ray S., B.S.'24, Utah State Agrl. Col.; M.A.'30, Stanford Univ.; Prin., Elem. Sch., Pleasant Grove, Utah, since 1936.

Miller, George L., B.S.'42, M.S.'49, Brigham Young Univ.; Prin., Wasatch Primary Sch., Provo, Utah, since 1949.

Miller, William P., B.S.'36, Utah State Agrl. Col.; M.S.'42, Univ. of Utah; Ed.D.'49, Stanford Univ.; Asst. State Supt. of Pub. Instr., Salt Lake City, Utah, since 1951.

Mitchell, David R., A.B.'11, Brigham Young Univ.; Supt. of Sch., American Fork, Utah, since 1938.

Moffitt, J. C., B.S.'26, M.S.'29, Brigham Young Univ.; Ph.D.'40, Univ. of Chicago; Supt. of Sch., Provo, Utah, since 1937.

Moody, Milton E., B.S.'27, Brigham Young Univ.; Supt., Wash. Co. Sch., St. George, Utah, since 1929.

Morgan, Samuel, B.S.'19, Utah State Agrl. Col.; Asst. Supt., Davis Co. Sch. Dist., Farmington, Utah, since 1946.

Morril, A. Reed, A.B.'28, M.S.'38, Brigham Young Univ.; Ed.D.'48, Univ. of Oregon; Assoc. Prof. of Sch. Admin., Brigham Young Univ., Provo, Utah, since 1948.

UTAH

Mower, J. F., M.S.'49, Brigham Young Univ.; Prin., Jr. H. S., Provo, Utah, since 1931.

Neilson, Emil K., M.S.'48, Brigham Young Univ.; Prin., Franklin Sch., Provo, Utah, since 1932.

Olsen, Marion J., M.S.'47, Brigham Young Univ.; Prin., Maeser Sch., Provo, Utah, since 1941.

Orton, F. A., Supt., Bldg. and Grounds, Sandy, Utah.

Parratt, J. Easton, B.A.'27, Univ. of Utah; M.A.'28, Univ. of Chicago; Supt. of Sch., Murray, Utah, since 1950.

Pearce, D. R., B.S.'26, Brigham Young Univ.; Dist. Supt. of Sch., Beaver, Utah, since 1947.

Peterson, Arthur E., B.S.'32, Univ. of Southern Calif.; Dist. Supt. of Sch., Sandy, Utah, since 1945.

Runyan, Norma C., B.A.'32, Southeastern State Col., Durant, Okla.; M.A.'46, Tchrs. Col., Columbia Univ.; Educ. Specialist, U. S. Bureau of Indian Affairs, Intermountain Indian Sch., Brigham City, Utah, since 1949.

Smith, Dasil A., A.B.'15, M.A.'23, Univ. of Utah; Assoc. Prof. of Educ., Univ. of Utah, Salt Lake City, Utah, since 1947.

Smith, T. O., B.S.'27, M.S.'31, Univ. of Utah; Ed.D.'48, Univ. of Southern Calif.; Supt. of City Sch., Ogden, Utah, since 1950.

Staheli, Harvey R., M.S.'41, Brigham Young Univ.; Prin., Sch., Provo, Utah, since 1929.

Stutz, Rowan C., M.S.'51, Brigham Young Univ.; Supt. of Sch., Heber, Utah, 1951-52.

Theurer, Lloyd M., B.S.'28, Utah State Agrl. Col.; Co. Supt. of Sch., Logan, Utah, since 1946.

Thornton, James W., B.S.'17, Utah State Agrl. Col.; M.A.'40, Northwestern Univ.; Prin., Farrer Jr. H. S., Provo, Utah, since 1931.

Tregeagle, Delbert V., B.S.'32, M.S.'34, Brigham Young Univ.; Prin., Provo H. S., Provo, Utah, since 1947.

Vest, H. Grant, M.S.'38, Brigham Young Univ.; Dist. Supt. of Sch., Logan, Utah, since 1948.

Victor, Wilma L., B.S.'41, Milwaukee State Tchrs. Col.; Elem. Dept. Head, Intermountain Indian Sch., Brigham City, Utah, since 1949.

Walker, Paul K., B.S.'33, Brigham Young Univ.; Prin., H. S., Springville, Utah, since 1946.

Weight, Kenneth E., B.S.'22, M.S.'28, Brigham Young Univ.; Co. Supt. of Sch., Brigham City, Utah, since 1947.

West, Allan M., B.S.'32, Utah State Agr. Col.; Exec. Secy., Utah Educ. Assn., Salt Lake City, Utah, since 1946.

West, Franklin Lorenzo, B.S.'04, Utah State Agrl. Col.; Ph.D.'11, Univ. of Chicago; Commr. of Educ., Church of Jesus Christ of Latter-Day Saints, Salt Lake City, Utah, since 1934.

Whitlock, Loyd G., B.A.'47, M.A.'48, Brigham Young Univ.; Ed.D.'51, Univ. of Colo.; Dir., Pupil Personnel, City Sch., Provo, Utah, since 1947.

Wright, Ianthus, Supt. of Sch., Cedar City, Utah.

INSTITUTIONAL MEMBER

Library, Univ. of Utah, Salt Lake City, Utah.

VERMONT

INDIVIDUAL MEMBERS

Adams, Frank R., Diploma '12, State Normal Sch., Bloomsburg, Pa.; B.A.'18, Dickinson Col.; Supt. of Sch., St. Johnsbury, Vt., since 1935.

Allen, Harlan B., B.S.'16, M.A.'19, Union Col.; Ph.D.'39, New York Univ.; Dist. Supt. of Sch., Brattleboro, Vt.

Amsden, Clarence F., B.S. in Ed.'31, M.A. in Ed.'41, Univ. of Vt.; Dist. Supt. of Sch., Woodstock, Vt., since 1943.

Anderson, Raymond, A.M.'37, Ed.D.'43, Sch. of Educ., New York Univ.; Dist. Supt. of Sch., Swanton, Vt., since 1940.

Ashland, Homer Butler, Ph.B.'24, M.Ed.'39, Univ. of Vt.; Supt. of Sch., Rutland, Vt., since 1948.

Bigelow, Edwin Lawrence, A.B.'13, Middlebury Col.; A.M.'26, Columbia Univ.; Dist. Supt. of Sch., Manchester Center, Vt., since 1926.

Bole, Lyman W., B.S.'19, Cornell Univ.; M.Ed. '39, Univ. of Vt.; Supt. of Sch., Springfield, Vt., since 1940.

Bole, Rita L., A.B.'20, Middlebury Col.; M.A.'36, Tchrs. Col., Columbia Univ.; Pres., State Tchrs. Col., Lyndon Center, Vt., since 1927.

*Boothby, Arthur Z., Ped.B.'00, N. Y. State Col. for Tchrs., Albany; B.S.'16, A.M.'20, Tchrs. Col., Columbia Univ. Address: Weston, Vt.

Boright, Charles P., B.S. in Ed.'28, M.Ed.'42, Univ. of Vt.; Dist. Supt. of Sch., Randolph, Vt., since 1946.

Bountress, George W., B.S.Ed.'40, Pa. State Tchrs. Col., East Stroudsburg; M.Ed.'42, Univ. of N. H.; Dist. Supt. of Sch., Essex Junction, Vt., since 1952.

Bullis, Jerome Q., B.S.'30, Univ. of Vt.; Dist. Supt. of Sch., Ludlow, Vt., since 1945.

Butler, N. Richard, B. of Mech. Eng.'29, Northeastern Univ.; Ed.M.'39, State Tchrs. Col., Hyannis, Mass.; Supt. of Sch., Bellows Falls, Vt.

Byrne, Thomas J., B.S.'22, Dartmouth Col.; Ed.M.'33, Harvard Univ.; Supt. of Sch., Windsor South-East Dist., Windsor, Vt., since 1935.

Clowse, Eugene H., Ph.B.'09, M.A.'49, Univ. of Vt.; Supvg. Prin. of Sch., Richmond, Vt., since 1915.

Codding, Ernest M., B.S. in Ed.'31, M.Ed.'42, Univ. of Vt.; Dist. Supt. of Sch., North Troy, Vt., since 1947.

Currier, Roland E., B.S.'26, Bates Col.; M.S. in Ed.'36, Univ. of Maine; Supt. of Essex-Orleans Sch. Dist., Island Pond, Vt., since 1946.

Dopp, Raymond D., B.S.'37, M.A.'38, Univ. of Vt.; Supt., Rutland-Northeast Sch. Dist., Pittsford, Vt., since 1948.

Dyer, Daniel B., B.S.'24, Ed.M.'43, Univ. of Vt.; Dist. Supt. of Sch., Concord, Vt., since 1950.

Fiske, Fremont, Diploma '31, State Normal Sch., Johnson, Vt.; B.S. in Ed.'42, Boston Univ.; M.A.'46, Tchrs. Col., Columbia Univ.; D'st. Supt. of Sch., Waterbury, Vt., since 1947.

Fussell, Clyde G., A.B.'25, A.M.'26, Middlebury Col.; Ed.M.'38, Univ. of N. H.; Supt. of City Sch., Barre, Vt., since 1952.

Gallagher, Walter D., B.S.'25, Middlebury Col.; M.A.'35, Columbia Univ.; Dist. Supt. of Sch., Northfield, Vt., since 1945.

Garvin, J. Stewart, A.B.'18, Westminster Col., New Wilmington, Pa.; Ed.M.'41, Univ. of Vt.; Dist. Supt. of Sch., South Ryegate, Vt., since 1924.

Goodrich, Ralph W., B.S.'32, Univ. of N. H.; M.A.'45, Univ. of Conn.; Dist. Supt. of Sch., Middlebury, Vt., since 1948.

Gunn, James, B.S.'31, Springfield Col.; M.Ed. '45, Univ. of Vt.; Dist. Supt. of Sch., Jacksonville, Vt., since 1949.

Haggerty, Tobin, Supt., Franklin-Northeast Sch. Dist., Richford, Vt.

530

Heath, Allan J., B.S.'23, Univ. of Mass.; M.A.'42, Univ. of Vt.; Supt. of Sch., Bennington, Vt., since 1944.

Holden, Arthur John, Jr., S.B. in C.E. and Bus. Adm.'23, Ed.M.'29, Harvard Univ.; Ed.D.'43, Columbia Univ.; State Commr. of Educ., Montpelier, Vt., since 1949.

Hoxie, Irwin H., B.S.'28, M.Ed.'40, Univ. of Vt.; Dist. Supt. of Sch., East Hardwick, Vt., since 1947.

Hoyt, Eugene G., B.S.'34, Middlebury Col.; M.E.'47, Univ. of Vt.; Dist. Supt. of Sch., Hartford, Vt., since 1950.

Hunt, Lyman Curtis, A.B.'12, Univ. of Vt.; M.A.'38, Columbia Univ.; Supt. of Sch., Burlington, Vt., since 1922.

Keniston, Harry A., Dist. Supt. of Sch., Barton, Vt., since 1952.

King, Thomas C., B.A.'40, M.S.'41, Ft. Hays Kansas State Col.; Ed.D.'50, Harvard Univ.; Dean, Col. of Educ. and Nursing, Univ. of Vt., Burlington, Vt.

Lawton, Albert D., A.B.'16, Dartmouth Col.; Dist. Supt. of Sch., Essex Junction, Vt., 1935-52.

Lull, Robert D., Jr., A.B.'35, Dartmouth Col.; M.E.'51, Univ. of Vt.; Supt. of Sch., Chittenden West Dist., South Burlington, Vt., since 1948.

McClelland, Donald W., A.B.'11, M.A.'25, Univ. of Vt.; Supt. of Sch., Montpelier, Vt., since 1944.

Maloney, Edwin T., B.A.'11, Middlebury Col.; Dist. Supt. of Sch., Jericho, Vt., since 1935.

Martin, Wallace A., Dist. Supt. of Sch., Bethel, Vt.

Maynard, Addie E., B.S. in Ed.'32, Boston Univ.; M.A.'42, Tchrs. Col., Columbia Univ.; State Helping Tchr., 10 Church St., Essex Junction, Vt.

Montague, Harry N., B.S.'28, M.E.'39, Univ. of Vt.; Supt. of Sch., Brattleboro, Vt., since 1951.

Moore, Milton G., B.S.'26, Univ. of Conn.; M.Ed.'37, Univ. of Vt.; Dist. Supt. of Sch., Bristol, Vt., since 1950.

Moulton, Lloyd W., B.S.'27, Dartmouth Col.; M.A.'35, Tchrs. Col., Columbia Univ.; Dist. Supt. of Sch., Vergennes, Vt., since 1947.

Nason, Charles P., A.B.'31, Univ. of Maine; M.Ed.'42, Univ. of Vt.; Dist. Supt. of Sch., Chester, Vt., since 1945.

Oulton, Arthur C., B.S. in Ed.'36, State Tchrs. Col., Fitchburg, Mass.; Ed.M.'40, Boston Univ.; Dist. Supt. of Sch., Poultney, Vt., since 1947.

Parker, A. Courtney, A.B.'19, Dartmouth Col.; M.A.'22, Columbia Univ.; Supt. of Orange-Windsor Sch. Dist., South Royalton, Vt., since 1927.

Pelkey, W. Harry, B.S.'28, Tchrs. Col., Columbia Univ.; M.S.'42, Univ. of Vt.; Supt. of Sch., Windham Central Dist., Newfane, Vt., since 1947.

Perrin, Justus Newton, 3rd, A.B.'26, Middlebury Col.; M.E.'42, Univ. of Vt.; Dist. Supt. of Sch., Orange-Washington Union Sch. Dist., Barre, Vt., since 1952.

Phelps, Edson E., A.B.'29, Dartmouth Col.; Ed.M.'41, Boston Univ.; Dist. Supt. of Sch., Johnson, Vt., since 1951.

Roberts, Llewellyn, A.B.'29, Middlebury Col.; M.Ed.'40, Univ. of Vt.; Dist. Supt. of Sch., Danville, Vt., since 1943.

Sargent, Theodore D., B.S. in Ed.'34, M.S. in Ed.'42, Univ. of Vt.; Dist. Supt. of Sch., Orwell, Vt., since 1947.

Spencer, Rupert J., B.S.'29, Norwich Univ.; M.Ed.'42, Univ. of Vt.; Dist. Supt. of Sch., Morrisville, Vt., since 1947.

Stefaniak, Edward W., B.S.'34, Middlebury Col.; M.A.'41, Columbia Univ.; Supt. of Sch., Alburg, Vt., since 1951.

Stiles, Frank O., B.S.'23, M.E.'39, Univ. of Vt.; Dist. Supt. of Sch., Fair Haven, Vt., since 1940.

Taplin, Winn L., B.S.'18, Iowa State Col.; M.A.'35, Univ. of Vt.; M.A.'43, Yale Univ.; Dir. of Educ. Planning, State Dept. of Educ., Montpelier, Vt., since 1947.

*Threlkeld, A. L., B.Pd.'11, Northeast Mo. State Tchrs. Col., Kirksville; B.S.'19, Univ. of Mo.; A.M.'23, Tchrs. Col., Columbia Univ.; LL.D.'30, Univ. of Denver; Ed.D.'32, Univ. of Colo.; LL.D.'35, Colo. Col.; Pres., Dept. of Superintendence, 1936-37; Honorary Life Member, American Assn. of Sch. Admin.; Supt. of Sch., Montclair, N. J., 1937-50 (retired). Address: South Londonderry, Vt.

Wagner, Leon E., B.S.'39, Boston Univ.; M.A. '42, Univ. of Vt.; Supt. of Sch., Bennington, Vt., since 1948.

Wakefield, Urban C., A.B.'31, Ohio Northern Univ.; M.Ed.'41, Univ. of Vt.; Dist. Supt. of Sch., Lyndonville, Vt., since 1946.

Wells, Lynford L., Ph.B.'26, M.Ed.'40, Univ. of Vt.; Dist. Supt. of Sch., Newport, Vt., since 1940.

Whitcomb, Fay G., B.S.'33, Springfield Col.; Dist. Supt. of Sch., Bradford, Vt., since 1948.

Wiggin, Joseph A., Exec. Secy., Vt. Educ. Assn., Montpelier, Vt.

INSTITUTIONAL MEMBER

Director of Libraries, Univ. of Vermont, State Agrl. Col., Burlington, Vt.

VIRGINIA

INDIVIDUAL MEMBERS

Adams, L. D., B.S.'32, Va. Polytech. Inst.; M.S.'38, Univ. of Pa.; Dir. of Instr., Pub. Sch., Richmond, Va., since 1950.

Alvey, Edward, Jr., B.A.'23, M.A.'28, Ph.D.'31, Univ. of Va.; Dean, Mary Washington Col. of the Univ. of Va., Fredericksburg, Va., since 1934.

Beazley, William Raymond, M.S.'37, Univ. of Va.; Div. Supt. of Co. Sch., Covington, Va., since 1946.

Bell, M. H., A.B.'30, Lynchburg Col.; M.A.'41, Univ. of Va.; Supt. of Sch., Harrisonburg, Va., since 1947.

Bishop, Leon W., Diploma '10, Pratt Inst., Brooklyn, N. Y.; Asst. Supvr., Sch. Bldgs., State Dept. of Educ., Richmond, Va., since 1925.

Bobbitt, Robert W., A.B.'12, Univ. of N. C.; M.A.'24, Tchrs. Col., Columbia Univ.; Co. Supt. of Sch., Keysville, Va., since 1925.

Bonner, Oscar Trent, B.S.'30, Birmingham-Southern Col.; M.A.'39, Univ. of Va.; Div. Supt. of Sch., Danville, Va., since 1948.

Brann, R. E., B.A.'25, Univ. of Richmond; M.A. '32, Univ. of Va.; Div. Supt., Lancaster and Northumberland Co. Sch., Heathsville, Va., since 1945.

Braun, Edward J., A.B.'22, Baldwin-Wallace Col.; M.A.'31, Ph.D.'41, Univ. of Wis.; Asst. Supt. of Sch., Arlington, Va., since 1949.

Brewbaker, John J., A.B.'18, Roanoke Col.; A.M.'39, Univ. of Va.; Supt. of Sch., Norfolk, Va., since 1949.

Buck, J. L. Blair, Ph.B.'06, Yale Univ.; Ed.M.'26, Harvard Univ.; Ph.D.'42, Univ. of Mich.; Coordinator of Tchr. Educ., State Dept. of Educ., Richmond, Va., since 1940.

Bussinger, C. M., B.S.'32, William and Mary Col.; M.A., Columbia Univ.; Supt. of Pub. Sch., Nottoway, Va., since 1951.

Byrd, Rawls, A.B.'18, Col. of William and Mary; M.A.'25, Columbia Univ.; Supt. of Sch., Williamsburg, Va., since 1928.

Cale, Paul H., B.A.'31, Univ. of Richmond; M.A.'37, Univ. of Va.; Div. Supt. of Co. Sch., Charlottesville, Va., since 1947.

Camden, Arthur Jordan, A.B.'28, Roanoke Col.; M.A.'33, Univ. of Va.; LL.B.'36, La Salle Extension Univ.; Div. Supt. of Sch., Amherst, Va., since 1941.

Carper, M. L., B.S.'27, Roanoke Col.; A.M.'37, Univ. of Chicago; Supt. of Sch., Martinsville, Va.

Cassell, Hugh K., B.S.'31, Mercer Univ.; M.Ed. '38, Duke Univ.; Div. Supt. of Co. Sch., Staunton, Va., since 1947.

Charlton, Gladys G., B.S.'35, Madison Col.; A.M.'40, Columbia Univ.; Dir., Elem. Educ., Pub. Sch., Norfolk, Va., since 1944.

Chittum, E. W., A.B.'33, Washington and Lee Univ.; M.A.'41, George Peabody Col. for Tchrs.; Div. Supt. of Co. Sch., Norfolk, Va., since 1949.

Combs, Morgan LaFayette, A.B.'17, Univ. of Richmond; A.M.'22, Univ. of Chicago; Ed.M. '26, Ed.D.'27, Harvard Univ.; Pres., Mary Washington Col. of the Univ. of Va., Fredericksburg, Va., since 1928.

Cox, Frank W., A.B.'24, Col. of William and Mary; M.A.'31, Univ. of Va.; Co. Supt. of Sch., Princess Anne, Va., since 1933.

Critzer, Frank J., A.B.'25, A.M.'32, Univ. of Va.; Co. Supt. of Sch., Pulaski, Va., since 1939.

Cummings, A. G., B.S.'27, M.S.'34, Univ. of Va.; Div. Supt. of Sch., Bedford, Va., since 1932.

Daniel, Robert Prentiss, A.B.'24, Va. Union Univ.; A.M.'28, Tchrs Col., Columbia Univ.; Ph.D.'32, Univ. of Chicago; LL.D.'49, Va. Union Univ.; LL.D.'49, Morris Brown Col.; Pres., Va. State Col., Petersburg, Va., since 1950.

DeHaven, Foy E., A.B.'26, King Col.; M.A.'37, Univ. of Va.; Supt. of Sch., Radford, Va., since 1942.

Deierhoi, William Hansen, B.A.'12, Col. of William and Mary; M.A.'24, Columbia Univ.; Asst. Supt. of Sch., Richmond, Va., since 1945.

Driscoll, Irving S., B.S.'30, William and Mary Col.; M.S.'36, Univ. of Va.; Div. Supt. of Sch., Buckingham, Va., since 1949.

Ellis, Fendall R., A.B.'31, Col. of William and Mary; M.A.'35, Univ. of Va.; Co. Supt. of Sch., Wytheville, Va., since 1945.

Ellison, John Malcus, A.B.'25, Va. Union Univ.; A.M.'27, Oberlin Col.; Ph.D.'33, Drew Univ.; Pres., Va. Union Univ., Richmond, Va., since 1941.

Fears, Macon F., A.B.'33, M.A.'40, Col. of William and Mary; Div. Supt. of Sch., Victoria, Va., since 1943.

Fisher, A. F., B.S.'30, Roanoke Col.; M.S.'38, Univ. of Va.; Deputy Clerk, Bd. of Educ., Roanoke, Va., since 1949.

Foster, Talmadge D., B.S.'24, M.A.'27, Col. of William and Mary; Co. Supt. of Sch., Waverly, Va., since 1925.

Fray, John Joseph, B.S. in Ed.'29, Roanoke Col.; Co. Supt. of Sch., Rustburg, Va., since 1921.

Gayle, Thomas Benton, B.S.'23, Va. Polytech. Inst.; Div. Supt. of Sch., Fredericksburg, Va., since 1925.

Glenn, F. Berkeley, A.B.'29, Col. of William and Mary; M.S.'41, Univ. of Tenn.; Supt. of Sch., Waynesboro, Va., since 1946.

Godbey, S. T., A.B.'21, M.A.'23, Roanoke Col.; M.A. in Ed.'24, Univ. of Va.; Supt. of Sch., Montgomery Co., Christiansburg, Va., since 1949.

Graves, Cecil C., Div. Supt., Page Co. Pub. Sch., Luray, Va.

Greene, E. S. H., A.B.'31, M.A.'35, Col. of William and Mary; Div. Supt. of Sch., Chesterfield, Va., since 1937.

Haga, Alonzo B., B.A.'31, Randolph Macon Col.; M.A.'37, Univ. of Va.; Div. Supt. of Co. Sch., Boydton, Va., since 1949.

Hall, L. T., B.A.'11, Univ. of Richmond; M.A.'40, Col. of William and Mary; Div. Supt. of Sch., Windsor, Va., since 1922.

Hamilton, Thomas T., B.A.'23, Wake Forest Col.; M.A.'30, Columbia Univ.; Dir. of Sec. Educ., State Dept. of Educ., Richmond, Va., since 1949.

Hass, C. Glenn, B.A.'37, Denver Univ.; M.A.'46, Stanford Univ.; Assoc. Supt. and Dir. of Instr., Pub. Sch., Arlington, Va., since 1952.

Healy, Joseph Ewart, B.A.'10, Col. of William and Mary; M.A.'25, Tchrs. Col., Columbia Univ.; Supt., Va. Sch. for the Deaf and the Blind, Staunton, Va., since 1939.

Hook, Paul Garland, B.A.'28, Elon Col.; M.A.'34, Univ. of Va.; Supt. of Sch., Clifton Forge, Va., since 1941.

Howard, Dowell J., State Supt. of Public Instr., Richmond, Va.

Jarman, A. M., B.S. and M.S.'20, Univ. of Va.; Ph.D.'32, Univ. of Mich. Address: 1872 Winston Ave., Charlottesville, Va.

Jenkins, Floyd Franklin, B.A.'18, Col. of William and Mary; M.A.'31, Columbia Univ.; Dir., Div. of Research & Planning, State Bd. of Educ., Richmond, Va.

Johnson, Preston Clarence, B.S.'17, Univ. of Pa.; Ed.M.'38, Ed.D.'39, Temple Univ.; Prof. of Educ., Va. State Col., Petersburg, Va., since 1939.

Johnston, King, A.B.'20, Emory and Henry Col.; M.A.'27, Columbia Univ.; Co. Supt. of Sch., Pearisburg, Va., 1936-52.

Kay, Floyd Sale, A.B.'24, Univ. of Richmond; M.A.'39, Univ. of Va.; Div. Supt., Rockbridge Co. Pub. Sch., Lexington, Va., since 1949.

Kindred, Robert B., A.B.'37, Santa Barbara State Col.; Dist. Supt. of Sch., Lancaster, Calif., 1946-52. Address: 3165 Kensington Ave., Arlington, Va.

Kyle, Clyte John Madison, B.S.'24, Col. of William and Mary; M.A.'29, George Peabody Col. for Tchrs.; Div. Supt. of Sch., Orange, Va., since 1949.

Kyle, Roy E., B.S.'24, Col. of William and Mary; M.A.'31, George Peabody Col. for Tchrs.; Div. Supt. of Sch., Hillsville, Va., since 1938.

Lacy, R. L., B.A.'18, Univ. of Richmond; M.A.'32, Tchrs. Col., Columbia Univ.; Div. Supt. of Sch., Halifax, Va., since 1934.

Lamberth, Edwin L., B.A.'28, Col. of William and Mary; M.A.'38, Univ. of Va.; Asst. Supt. of Sch., Norfolk, Va., since 1949.

Lancaster, Dabney S., B.A.'11, Univ. of Va.; M.S.'15, Va. Polytech. Inst.; LL.D.'43, Univ. of Richmond; Pres., Longwood Col., Farmville, Va., since 1946.

Lawson, William F., Jr., B.A.'26, M.A.'37, William and Mary Col.; Supt. of Co. Sch., Cheriton, Va., since 1950.

Lindsay, C. Alton, B.S.'27, Col. of William and Mary; M.A.'40, Univ. of Va.; Div. Supt. of Schools, Hampton, Va., since 1942.

Long, Raymond V., M.A.'14, Columbia Univ.; Commr., Div. of Planning and Economic Development, 301 State Finance Bldg., Richmond, Va.

McIlwaine, Thomas J., A.B.'14, Hampden-Sydney Col.; Co. Supt. of Sch., Farmville, Va., since 1918.

McQuilkin, Dwight Eggleston, A.B.'05, A.M.'06, W. Va. Univ.; A.M.'08, Harvard Univ.; L.H.D. '49, Roanoke Col.; Supt. of Sch., Roanoke, Va., since 1918.

Mapp, A. J., Supt. of Pub. Sch., Portsmouth, Va.

Martin, Charles Knox, Jr., A.B.'32, Southwest Mo. State Col.; M.A.'35, Univ. of Mo.; Ph.D. '39, Yale Univ.; Pres., Radford Col., Woman's Div. of Va. Polytech. Inst., Radford, Va., since 1952.

Mauck, J. Leonard, B.S.'29, Emory and Henry Col.; M.A.'40, Univ. of Virginia; Co. Supt. of Sch., Marion, Va., since 1948.

Meade, John David, A.B.'31, Randolph-Macon Col.; M.A.'37, Univ. of Va.; Supt. of Sch., Petersburg, Va., since 1943.

Miller, G. Tyler, B.S.'23, Va. Military Inst.; Pres., Madison Col., Harrisonburg, Va., since 1949.

Moron, Alonzo G., Ph.B.'32, Brown Univ.; M.A.'33, Univ. of Pittsburgh; LL.B.'47, Harvard Univ.; Pres., Hampton Inst., Hampton, Va., since 1949.

Munro, Paul Merritt, A.B.'10, Emory Univ.; M.A.'22, Ed.D.'41, Tchrs. Col., Columbia Univ.; Supt. of Sch., Lynchburg, Va., since 1945.

Nash, Ethel H., M.A.'44, Columbia Univ.; Prin. of Sch., Fredericksburg, Va., since 1924.

Nelson, Robert Oliver, A.B.'20, Erskine Col.; M.A.'30, George Peabody Col. for Tchrs.; Ph.D.'41, Univ. of Ga.; Supt. of Sch., Newport News, Va., since 1946.

Nininger, R. Douglas, A.B.'28, Bridgewater Col.; M.A.'43, Univ. of Va.; Div. Supt. of Sch., Roanoke Co., Salem, Va., since 1945.

Painter, Hunter M., B.A.'16, Roanoke Col.; M.A.'26, Univ. of Va.; Div. Supt. of Sch., Fincastle, Va., since 1933.

Pence, Wilbur S., M.A.'42, Tchrs. Col., Columbia Univ.; Supt., Rockingham Co. Sch., Harrisonburg, Va., since 1950.

Picott, J. Rupert, A.B.'32, Va. Union Univ.; M.Ed.'40, Temple Univ.; Exec. Secy., Va. Tchrs. Assoc., Richmond, Va., since 1944.

Ramsey, Benjamin Sterling, A.B.'27, A.M.'45, Duke Univ.; Asst. Supt. of Sch., Martinsville, Va., since 1946.

Ramsey, Harold W., A.B.'27, M.A.'40, Col. of William and Mary; Co. Supt. of Sch., Rocky Mount, Va., since 1927.

Reid, Ray E., B.S.'26, M.A.'36, Col. of William and Mary; Asst. Supt. of Pub. Instr., State Dept. of Educ., Richmond, Va.

Rushton, E. W., A.B.'26, Litt.D.'50, Wofford Col.; M.A.'40, Univ. of S. C.; Asst. Supt. of Sch., Roanoke, Va., since 1952.

Rutter, T. Edward, B.S.E.'29, Franklin and Marshall Col.; M.A.'36, Tchrs. Col., Columbia Univ.; Supt. of Sch., Arlington, Va., since 1952.

Sanford, T. R., Jr., B.S.'27, Univ. of Richmond; M.A.'33, New York Univ.; Supt. of Sch., Hilton Village, Va., since 1933.

Savage, W. R., Jr., Supt. of Sch., Suffolk, Va.

Scarborough, William Acree, A.B.'19, Randolph-Macon Col.; M.A.'21, Univ. of Pa.; Co. Supt. of Sch., Dinwiddie, Va., since 1923.

Schmitt, Irvin H., M.A.'37, State Univ. of Iowa; Supt. of Sch., Falls Church, Va., since 1949.

Shelburne, C. C., B.S.'27, M.S.'34, Univ. of Va.; Admin. Asst., Henrico Co. Sch., Richmond, Va.

Shelburne, L. F., M.A.'14, Univ. of Va.; Supt. of Sch., Staunton, Va., since 1925.

Shelburne, S. J., B.A.'14, Lynchburg Col.; Co. Supt. of Sch., Jonesville, Va., since 1925.

Showalter, John F., Ph.D.'45, Univ. of Nebr.; Admin. Asst. to the Supt. of Sch., Richmond, Va.

Simpson, John Childs, A.B. and A.M.'11, LL.D.'48, Randolph-Macon Col.; Pres., Stratford Col., Danville, Va., since 1930.

Smith, Charles William, B.A.'30, Howard Col.; M.A.'46, Col. of William and Mary; Supt. of, City Sch. and Prince George Co., Hopewell Va., since 1946.

Smith, Stanley Vernon, A.B.'42, Univ. of Buffalo; M.A.'47, Cornell Univ.; Supvr. of Research, Co. Sch., Arlington, Va., since 1951.

Stiles, Lindley J., A.B.'35, M.A.'39, Ed.D.'45, Univ. of Colo.; Dean, Dept. of Educ., Univ. of Va., Charlottesville, Va., since 1949.

Story, William J., Jr., A.B.'34, Elon Col.; M.Ed. '49, Col. of William and Mary; Supt. of Sch., South Norfolk, Va., since 1949.

Sulfridge, Hugh L., B.A.'16, Col. of William and Mary; M.A.'29, Columbia Univ.; Supt. of Sch., Charlottesville, Va., since 1949.

Sutherland, J. Hoge T., B.A.'21, Washington and Lee Univ.; M.A.'40, Univ. of Va.; Co. Dir. of Instr., Liberty Academy, Bedford, Va., since 1943.

Van Pelt, Joseph Benjamin, B.A.'26, Randolph-Macon Col.; M.A.'38, Univ. of Va.; Supt. of Sch., Bristol, Va., since 1945.

Vaughan, W. A., B.A.'20, Univ. of Richmond; M.A.'30, Univ. of Va.; Div. Supt. of Co. Sch., Bowling Green, Va., since 1921.

*Waller, J. Flint, B.A.'16, Univ. of Va.; M.A.'28, Ph.D.'32, Columbia Univ. Address: Route 4, Staunton, Va.

Weisiger, Louise P., B.A.'15, Sweet Briar Col.; M.A.'31, Ed.D.'45, Tchrs. Col., Columbia Univ.; Dir. of Research, Pub. Sch., Richmond, Va., since 1946.

Whitehead, William M., B.S.'32, M.A.'35, New York Univ.; LL.D.'50, Va. State Col.; Supt., Va. State Sch., Hampton, Va., since 1940.

Will, Edwin E., B.A.'31, Bridgewater Col.; M.A.'42, Univ. of Va.; Co. Supt. of Sch., Warm Springs, Va., since 1949.

Willett, Henry I., B.A.'25, Col. of William and Mary; M.A.'30, Columbia Univ.; Supt. of Schools, Richmond, Va., since 1946.

Williams, Robert F., B.A.'29, Roanoke Col.; M.A.'32, Columbia Univ.; Exec. Secy., Va. Educ. Assn., Richmond, Va., since 1946.

Williams, Thomas C., B.S.'15, Va. Military Inst.; M.A.'38, George Washington Univ.; Supt. of Sch., Alexandria, Va., since 1933.

Wise, Henry A., B.S.'98, Va. Polytech. Inst.; M.A. and LL.B.'05, Centre Col.; M.A.'11, Univ. of S. C.; Div. Supt. of Sch., Accomac, Va., since 1929.

Woodson, Wilbert T., A.B.'16, Col. of William and Mary; Div. Supt. of Sch., Fairfax, Va., since 1929.

INSTITUTIONAL MEMBERS

Johnston Memorial Library, Va. State Col., Petersburg, Va.

Library, Longwood College, Farmville, Va.

533

WASHINGTON
INDIVIDUAL MEMBERS

Allen, Wendell C., Ed.D.'42, Tchrs. Col. Columbia Univ.; Asst. State Supt. of Pub. Instr., Olympia, Wash., since 1950.

Anderson, Homer T., B.A.'39, Eastern Wash. Col. of Educ., Cheney; B.E.'43, State Col. of Wash.; Supt., Bethel Sch. Dist. 403, Kapowsin, Wash.

Anderson, Loran E., B.A. in Ed.'35, Eastern Wash. Col. of Educ.; B.E.'46, Whitworth Col.; Supt. of Sch., Otis Orchards, Wash., since 1949.

Ayars, Albert L., B.A., B.Ed.'39, M.A.'42, State Col. of Wash.; Supt. of Pub. Sch., Sunnyside, Wash., since 1949.

Baker, L. D., M.A.'29, Wash. State Col.; Supt., Highline Pub. Sch., Seattle, Wash., since 1941.

Barbee, F. L., Life Diploma '31, Wash. State Col.; Supt. of Sch., Tekoa, Wash., since 1949.

Beardsley, W. H., B.S.'16, Wash. State Col.; Supt. of Sch., Bothell, Wash., since 1942.

Beeler, Harold B., B.A.'40, Univ. of Wash.; Dir. of Instr. and Curriculum, Sch. Dist. 17, Port Angeles, Wash., since 1951.

Blankenship, Alden H., B.A.'33, M.A.'38, Univ. of Wash.; Ed.D.'43, Tchrs. Col., Columbia Univ.; Supt. of Sch., Tacoma, Wash., since 1950.

Bloom, Edward F., B.A.'27, M.A.'34, Univ. of Wash.; Supt. of Sch., Aberdeen, Wash., since 1938.

Bloom, William H., A.B.'27, M.A.'39, Univ. of Wash.; Supt. of Sch., Centralia, Wash., since 1948.

Bohrnsen, William F., B.A.'34, Eastern Wash. Col. of Educ.; M.A.'42, Univ. of Wash.; Supt. of Sch., Hoquiam, Wash., since 1949.

Brock, Frank M., B.S.'41, Western Wash. Col. of Educ.; Asst. Supt. and Bus. Mgr., Pub. Sch., Seattle, Wash., since 1943.

Burns, H. Lyle, B.A.'32, Wash. State Col.; Supt. of Sch., Steptoe, Wash., since 1948.

Cady, Donald I., B.A.'26, Univ. of S. Dak.; M.A.'36, Univ. of Wash.; Supt., South Central Sch. Dist. 406, Seattle, Wash., since 1936.

Campbell, Ernest W., A.B.'18, LL.B.'22, Univ. of Wash.; Asst. Supt. of Sch., Seattle, Wash., since 1940.

Carter, Gordon L., B.S. in Ed.'35, M.E.'46, Univ. of Wash.; Supt. of Sch., Sedro-Woolley, Wash., since 1948.

Castles, William I., B.A.'35, Mont. State Univ.; M.A.'47, Univ. of Wash.; Supt., Mt. Baker Sch. Dist. 507, Deming, Wash., since 1948.

Chandler, Joe A., B.A.'25, Wash. State Col.; Exec. Secy., Wash. Educ. Assn., Seattle, Wash., since 1940.

Clausen, Melvin F., B.A. in Ed.'49, Univ. of Wash.; Supt., Elem. Sch. Dist. 314, Sultan, Wash., since 1942.

Cooper, Joyce, M.A.'42, Univ. of Wash.; Tchrs. Col., Columbia Univ.; Asst. Supt. in chg. of Instr., State Dept. of Pub. Instr., Olympia, Wash., since 1951.

Crabb, John J., B.S.'26, Whitman Col.; M.A. in Ed.'47, Univ. of Wash.; Supt. of Central Valley Consol. Sch. Dist. 356, Greenacres, Wash., since 1940.

Cramblitt, DeFore, A.B.'27, Linfield Col.; M.E.'44, Univ. of Kansas; Co. Supt. of Sch., Port Orchard, Wash., since 1952.

Crogstad, L. J., B.A.'24, Wash. State Col.; Supt. of Valley Sch., Menlo, Wash., since 1933.

Cronquist, George L., B.A. in Ed.'41, Col. of Puget Sound; Prin., Edgemont Sch., Tacoma, Wash., since 1947.

Crosby, Lydia F., Co. Supt. of Sch., Kelso, Wash.

Crow, Lanche R., B.A.'28, Wash. State Col.; Prin., H. S., Oak Harbor, Wash., since 1943.

Croy, Donald C., B.A.'30, Univ. of Wash.; Supt. of Sch., Toutle, Wash., since 1947.

Crum, J. Wesley, B.S.'36, Seattle Pacific Col.; M.S.'38, Ph.D.'50, Univ. of Wash.; Prof. of Educ., Central Wash. Col. of Educ., Ellensburg, Wash., since 1949.

Curtis, George R., M.A. in Ed.'34, Col. of Puget Sound; Supt., University Place Sch., Tacoma, Wash., since 1927.

Dahlke, Florence, B.A.'43, Eastern Wash. Col. of Educ., Cheney; Co. Supt. of Sch., Waterville, Wash., since 1943.

Dennis, R. G., A.B.'30, Univ. of Wash.; Supt. of Pub. Sch., Kelso, Wash., since 1951.

Dieckmann, Werner C., B.A.'40, Univ. of Wash.; Dir. of Sec. Educ., State Dept. of Pub. Instr., Olympia, Wash., since 1947.

Dimmitt, L. M., B.A.'23, M.A.'33, Univ. of Wash.; Co. Supt. of Sch., Seattle, Wash., since 1945.

Duncan, Clifford A., M.A.'44, Univ. of Wash.; Supt. of Sch., Camas, Wash., since 1949.

Duyff, E. A., B.A.'33, Univ. of Wash.; Supt. of Sch., Coupeville, Wash., since 1951.

Edwards, Harry O., B.S.'23, M.S. in Ed.'41, Univ. of Idaho; Supt. of Sch., Darrington, Wash., since 1946.

Elias, L. J., B.A.'28, State Tchrs. Col., Valley City, N. Dak.; M.A.'39, Univ. of Washington; Ph.D.,'49, State Col. of Washington; Dean, Olympic Jr. Col., Bremerton, Wash., since 1949.

Ellwanger, L. C., B.A.'27, Kansas State Tchrs. Col., Pittsburgh; M.Ed.'41, Univ. of Okla.; Supt., Ahtanum Valley Sch., Yakima, Wash., since 1947.

Erickson, Ed. K., B.A.'39, B. of Ed.'44, M.A.'46, State Col. of Wash.; Supt. of Sch., Issaquah, Wash., since 1948.

Estes, John F., B.Ed.'22, Univ. of Wash.; Supt. of Pub. Sch. Dist. 118, Riverside, Wash., since 1952.

Farmer, George S., B.A.'26, M.A.'32, State Col. of Wash.; B.A.'37, Eastern Wash. Col. of Educ.; Prin., Queen Anne H. S., Seattle, Wash., since 1951.

Fleming, Samuel E., B.A.'07, Wabash Col.; Supt. of Sch., Seattle, Wash., since 1945.

Forry, (Mrs.) Grace M., Supt. of Co. Sch., Goldendale, Wash.

Fox, Ernest R., B.A. of Ed.'41, Eastern Wash. Col. of Educ., Cheney; B. of Ed.'46, Wash. State Col.; Supt. of Sch., Okanogan, Wash., since 1949.

Frasier, Clark Melville, A.B.'22, A.M.'29, Colo. State Col. of Educ., Greeley; Dir., Student Tchg. and Summer Sessions, Eastern Wash. Col. of Educ., Cheney, Wash., since 1930.

Furgeson, Paul F., B.A.'24, Univ. of Wash.; Supt. of City Sch., Wenatchee, Wash., since 1948.

Gaiser, Louis W., B.S.'21, Whitman Col.; Supt. of Sch., Chewelah, Wash., since 1930.

Gaiser, Paul F., B.A.'17, Whitman Col.; M.A.'23, State Col. of Wash.; Ph.D.'32, Univ. of Wash.; Pres., Clark Jr. Col., Vancouver, Wash., since 1931.

Ganfield, Jack F., B.A.'40, Seattle Pacific Col.; Counselor, Magnolia Elem. Sch., Seattle, Wash., since 1951.

Gilbert, Wilbur B., B.S.'36, Wash. State Col.; Supt. of Sch., Oak Harbor, Wash., since 1951.

Glann, John D., B.A.'26, M.A.'40, Wash. State Col.; Supt. of Sch., Port Angeles, Wash., since 1945.

Goold, H. R., B.S.'08, Northwestern Univ.; M.A.'22, Univ. of Wash.; Prof. of Educ., Col. of Puget Sound, Tacoma, Wash., since 1950.

Griffith, Harold C., M.A.'48, State Col. of Wash.; Supt. of Sch., Twisp, Wash., since 1945.

Haggard, W. W., B.A.'17, Maryville Col.; M.A.'27, Univ. of Mich.; Ph.D.'37, Univ. of Chicago; Pres., Western Wash. Col. of Educ., Bellingham, Wash., since 1939.

Hall, Robert C., B.A.'24, Univ. of Wash.; Supt., Fife Pub. Sch. Dist. 88, Tacoma, Wash., since 1937.

Halstead, Harry G., State Dir. of Voc. Educ., State Bd. for Voc. Educ., Olympia, Wash., since 1940.

Hamilton, Ross E., Dir., Educ. for Handicapped Children, State Dept. of Pub. Instr., Olympia, Wash., since 1949.

Hanawalt, Paul B., A.B.'18, Col. of Puget Sound; M.A.'25, Univ. of Wash.; Supt. of Sch., Puyallup, Wash., since 1930.

Hansen, Herbert, B.A. in Ed.'26, M.A. in Ed.'33, Univ. of Wash.; Supt. of Sch., Castle Rock, Wash., since 1941.

Hazen, Oliver M., B.A.'27, Univ. of Wash.; Supt. of Sch., Renton, Wash., since 1936.

Heimbigner, Roy R., B.A.'46, Eastern Wash. Col. of Educ.; Elem. Prin., Thornton, Wash., since 1950.

Helgesen, Borghild, Admin. Asst. to the State Supt. of Pub. Instr., Olympia, Wash., since 1941.

Hendel, Douglas, B.A.'28, Col. of Puget Sound; Supt., South Kitsap Sch. Dist. 402, Port Orchard, Wash.

Hills, Earle C., B.A.'30, Univ. of Wash.; B.A.'37, Eastern Wash. Col. of Educ.; Supt. of Sch., Mead, Wash., since 1939.

Hitchcock, John B., B.A.'40, B.Ed.'41, M.A.'49, State Col. of Wash.; Supt. of Sch., Rosalia, Wash., since 1950.

Holman, Hayes, B.S.'29, East Texas State Tchrs. Col.; M.A.'37, Univ. of Colo.; Supt., Valley Sch., White Salmon, Wash., since 1945.

Homburg, J. George, M.Ed.'40, State Col. of Wash.; Supt., Cape Flattery Sch. Dist. 401, Neah Bay, Wash., since 1950.

Howard, Ray W., B.A.'31, M.A.'40, Univ. of Wash.; Supt., Shoreline Dist. Sch., Seattle, Wash., since 1944.

Howe, Homer, B.A.'32, M.A.'33, Univ. of Wash.; Supt. of Peninsula Sch., Gig Harbor, Wash., since 1942.

Hudtloff, A. G., B.S.'20, M.A.'30, Univ. of Wash.; Supt., Clover Park Sch., Tacoma, Wash., 1928-51. Address: 5214 Steilacoon Blvd., S.W., Tacoma, Wash.

Huffman, Vern L., B.S.'49, McPherson Col.; Supvg. Prin., Consol. Sch. Dist. 13, Malott, Wash., since 1951.

Hunt, Ernest R., M.A.'29, Univ. of Wash.; Supt. of Sch., Lake Stevens, Wash., since 1931.

Hussey, Clifton A., A.B.'32, A.M.'38, Whitworth Col.; Co. Supt. of Sch., Spokane, Wash., since 1947.

Ingman, Kenneth, B.S.'40, Univ. of Wash.; Supt. of Sch., Trout Lake, Wash., since 1949.

Jacobs, Hugh L., B.A.'31, Spokane Univ.; M.A.'45, State Col. of Wash.; Supt. of Sch., Woodland, Wash., since 1944.

Jaeger, Herman F., M.A.'40, Univ. of Chicago; Dist. Supt. of Sch., Pasco, Wash.

Jahr, Armin George, M.A.'37, Univ. of Minn.; Rt. 3, Box 471, Bremerton, Wash.

Janeway, Harold L., Supt. of Sch., Peshastin, Wash., since 1943.

Jarrell, Cleo, B.A.'38, Central State Col., Edmond, Okla.; B.Ed.'47, Col. of Puget Sound; Supt., Boistfort Consol. Sch., Dist. 234, Klaber, Wash., since 1948.

Johnson, Carl G., B.A.'24, State Col. of Wash.; Supt. of Sch., Battle Gound, Wash., since 1938.

Johnson, Clifford M., B.Ed.'44, Western Wash. Col. of Educ.; Supt. of Sch., Issaquah, Wash., since 1952.

Johnson, Jasper H., B.A.'41, M.Ed.'52, Univ. of Wash.; Grad. Student, Univ. of Wash., Seattle, Wash., 1952-53.

Johnson, Morton A., B.A.'27, Col. of Puget Sound; M.A.'50, Univ. of Wash.; Supt., Lake Wash. Sch., Kirkland, Wash., since 1940.

Johnson, Paul W., M.A.'39, Univ. of Wash.; Supt. of Sch., Goldendale, Wash., since 1932.

Johnson, William Arild, B.S. in Arch.'31, State Col. of Wash.; Sch. Archt., First Natl. Bank Bldg., Everett, Wash., since 1928.

Jones, Arthur D., B.S.'29, Whitman Col.; Supt. of Sch., Walla Walla, Wash., since 1950.

Katterle, Zeno B., Ed.D.'47, State Col. of Wash.; Prof. of Educ. and Acting Dean, Sch. of Educ., State Col. of Wash., Pullman, Wash., since 1952.

Kinkade, Herbert J., B.A.'44, Eastern Wash. Col. of Educ.; Supt. of Co. Sch., Wenatchee, Wash., since 1946.

Knutson, (Mrs.) Rachel Royston, B.S. in Ed.'35, Western Wash. Col. of Educ., Bellingham; Classroom Tchr., 506 Seaboard Bldg., Seattle, Wash., since 1944.

Kolste, Luther Norman, A.B.'27, St. Olaf Col.; M.A. in Ed.'42, Gonzaga Univ.; Supt., Sch. Dist. No. 506, Nooksack, Wash.

Kramer, Herman J., B.A.'29, M.A.'35, Univ. of Ore.; Supt. of Sch., Wapato, Wash., since 1944.

Krangnes, Bert A., B.A.'30, Col. of Puget Sound; Supt. of Sch., Colton, Wash., since 1949.

La Coste, John A., M.A.'47, State Univ. of Iowa; Supt. of Sch., Republic, Wash., since 1948.

Lacy, Susan M., M.A.'34, State Col. of Wash.; Dir. of Elem. Educ., State Dept. of Pub. Instr., Olympia, Wash., since 1945.

Lamka, Dewane E., A.B.'40, B.Ed.'44, Col. of Puget Sound; Supt. of Sch., Rochester, Wash., since 1952.

Laughbon, Wendell B., B.A.'36, Univ. of Wash.; Supt., Sch. Dist. 7, Dupont, Wash., since 1938.

Lavin, Leila, Asst. Supt. of Sch., Spokane, Wash.

Loree, G. Ira, B.A. in Ed.'38, Univ. of Wash.; Supt., Skagit Co. Sch., Mt. Vernon, Wash., since 1947.

McClure, Clarence Ray, B.S.'26, Col. of Idaho; Supt. of Sch., Grandview, Wash., since 1949.

McFadden, C. B., B.A.'36, State Col. of Wash.; Supt. of Sch., Moses Lake, Wash., since 1944.

McGlade, Chas. A., B.A.'25, M.A.'37, State Col. of Wash.; Supt. of Sch., Everett, Wash., since 1948.

McIntire, Gordon, B.A.'40, Northeastern State Col., Tahlequah, Okla.; Supt. of Sch., Concrete, Wash., since 1951.

McNamara, Eugene J., M.A.'14, Univ. of Wash.; Supt. of Sch., Longview, Wash., since 1929.

McNurlin, Charles A., B.S.'48, Univ. of Wash.; Supt., Pub. Sch., Lester, Wash., since 1950.

Mahaffey, Audley F., Supt., Consol. Sch., Dist. 90, Moxee City, Wash.

Mallery, K. P., A.B.'28, Marietta Col.; M.A.'35, Ohio State Univ.; Supt. of Sch., Dist. 201, Sunnyside, Wash.

535

Manning, Philip C., B.S.'30, M.S.'38, Univ. of Idaho; Supt., Sch. Dist. 400, Casey, Wash., since 1946.

Marsden, Thomas E., B.A.'35, M.A.'36, Wash. State Col.; Supt. of Sch., Sequim, Wash., since 1946.

Martin, M. L., B.A.'26, M.A.'33, Wash. State Col.; Supt. of Sch., Yakima, Wash., since 1947.

Miles, Joe E., B.S.'15, State Col. of Wash.; Co. Supt. of Sch., Ellensburg, Wash., since 1947.

Milligan, Scott, B.S.'30, M.Ed.'36, Univ. of Oregon; Asst. Supt., Sch. Dist. 122, Longview, Wash., since 1947.

Mills, Gilbert C., A.B.'35, M.Ed.'51, Univ. of Wash.; Supt. of Sch., Marysville, Wash., since 1948.

Milroy, John D., B.S.'39, Col. of Puget Sound; M.A.'46, Columbia Univ.; Supt. of Sch., Langley, Wash., since 1951.

Moore, W. Lyndle, B.A.'35, York Col.; M.A.'39, Univ. of Wash.; Supt. of Sch., Zillah, Wash., since 1952.

Muncaster, T. H., B.A.'25, M.A.'35, State Col. of Wash.; Asst. Supt. of Sch., Everett, Wash., since 1948.

Mundt, Edna, B.A.'41, Eastern Wash. Col. of Educ.; Tchr., since 1946, and Pres., Seattle Grade Tchrs. Club, Seattle, Wash., since 1951.

Murray, James M., M.S. in Ed.'38, Univ. of Idaho; Supt. of Sch., Hay, Wash., since 1950.

Nelson, Carl A., B.A.'23, M.A.'31, Washington State Col.; Supt. of Sch., Dayton, Wash., since 1926.

Newland, Ernest E., B.S.'31, M.A.'40, Univ. of Wash.; Supt., Sch. Dist. 19, Omak, Wash., since 1949.

Olafson, Erling K., B.A.'26, St. Olaf Col.; B.A. '40, Western Wash. Col. of Educ.; B.D.'31, Pacific Theol. Sem.; Supt. of Sch., Cusick, Wash., since 1951.

Olmsted, Keith, B.A.'35, M.A.'36, State Col. of Wash.; Dist. Supt. of Sch., Sprague, Wash., since 1948.

Olson, H. C., B.A.'26, M.A.'35, Univ. of Mont.; Supt. of Sch. Dist. 404, Eatonville, Wash., since 1949.

Opstad, E. R., A.B.'28, Univ. of Wash.; Dist. Supt. of Sch., Snoqualmie, Wash., since 1944.

Overstreet, Ira M., B.S.'37, Univ. of Wash.; M.S.'51, Wash. State Col.; Supt. of Sch., Raymond, Wash., since 1951.

Pasnick, George R., B.S.'33, Univ. of Wash.; Dir., Sch. Finance and Admin. Research, State Dept. of Pub. Instr., Olympia, Wash., since 1947.

Pence, Clarence O., B.A.'32, Wash. State Col.; B.A.'35, Eastern Wash. Col. of Educ.; Supt. of Sch., Millwood, Wash.

Peterson, Tillman, B.A.'08, Luther Col.; M.A.'21, Univ. of Wash.; Supvr. of School Dist. Organi-ation, Old Capitol Bldg., Olympia, Wash.

Phillips, Ned, B.A.'26, Wash. State Col.; Supt. of Sch., Naches, Wash., since 1940.

Phipps, Wendell T., B.S.'31, Oregon State Col.; B.A.'36, Eastern Wash. Col. of Educ.; Supt., Union H. S., Mt. Vernon, Wash., since 1951.

Pierce, (Mrs.) Mary C., B.A.'33, Eastern Wash. Col. of Educ.; M.A.'42, State Col. of Wash.; Co. Supt. of Sch., Ritzville, Wash., since 1943.

Poffenroth, Ella, B.Ed.'47, Eastern Wash. Col. of Educ.; Co. Supt. of Sch., Okanogan, Wash., since 1951.

Powers, Francis F., B.A.'23, Ph.D.'28, Univ. of Wash.; M.A.'27, Univ. of Oregon; Dean, Col. of Educ., Univ. of Wash., Seattle, Wash., since 1939.

Pugh, Ralph W., M.S.'36, Univ. of Idaho; Supt., Springdale Consol. Sch. Dist. 192, Springdale, Wash., since 1948.

Rhodes, Chester V., B.A. in Bus. Admin.'31, Col. of Puget Sound; Supt. of Sch., Chehalis, Wash., since 1949.

Richards, Ralph R., B.A.'28, Seattle Pacific Col.; M.A.'29, Univ. of Wash.; Supt. of Sch., Entiat, Wash., since 1950.

Ross, J. Alan, Ph.D.'43, Yale Univ.; Prof. of Educ., Western Wash. Col. of Educ., Belling-ham, Wash., since 1948.

Saale, Charles W., Ph.D.'47, State Univ. of Iowa; Chmn. Educ. and Psych. Div., Central Wash. Col. of Educ., Ellensburg, Wash., since 1947.

Schwartz, Henry F., B.S.'27, Mont. State Col.; M.Ed.'47, Mont. State Univ.; Supt., Sch. Dist. 14, Nespelem, Wash., since 1952.

Selby, Kenneth E., B.A.'25, M.A.'28, Univ. of Wash.; Asst. Supt. of Sch., Seattle, Wash., since 1945.

Shangle, C. Paine, B.A.'10, Univ. of Oregon; M.A.'11, Univ. of Wis.; Supt. of Sch., Belling-ham, Wash., since 1933.

Shaw, John A., B.A.'18, Wash. and Jefferson Col.; Supt. of Sch., Spokane, Wash., since 1943.

Simpson, J. Olen, B.A.'32, Univ. of Wash.; Supt. of Sch., Mukilteo, Wash., since 1947.

Smith, W. Virgil, LL.B.'10, Univ. of Mo.; A.B.'20, A.M.'30, Univ. of Wash.; Asst. Supt. of Sch., Seattle, Wash., since 1929.

Smith, Walter Irvine, A.B.'11, Union Col.; M.S.'17, Whitman Col.; Ed.D.'34, George Wash. Univ.; Head, Dept. of Sec. Educ., Walla Walla Col., College Place, Wash.

Sovde, Obert J., B.A.'42, Pacific Lutheran Col.; B.E.'48, Col. of Puget Sound; Supt. of Sch., Orting, Wash., since 1951.

Spencer, (Mrs.) Evelyn, Chmn., South Whidbey Bd. of Sch. Dirs., Langley, Wash., since 1949.

Stamper, Lyman D., B.S.'41, Univ. of Idaho; B.Ed.'50, Wash. State Col.; Supt. of Sch., Grand Coulee, Wash., since 1951.

Stansfield, Joseph W., B.A.'20, Trinity Col.; M.A.'39, Univ. of Wash.; Supt. of Sch., Coulee Dam., Wash., since 1938.

Steinke, E. L., M.A.'37, State Col. of Wash.; Supt. of Consol. Sch. Dist. 119, Selah, Wash., since 1946.

Stephens, Thomas Lindley, B.A.'39, Central Wash. Col. of Educ.; B.Ed.'49, M.S.'49, State Col. of Wash.; Supt. of Sch., Brewster, Wash., since 1952.

Stewart, Lyle, A.B.'24, Simpson Col.; A.M.'30, Ph.D.'52, Univ. of Wash.; Asst. Supt. of Sch., Seattle, Wash., since 1945.

*Strayer, George D., Jr., B.S.'27, Princeton Univ.; M.A.'28, Ph.D.'34, Tchrs. Col., Colum-bia Univ.; Prof. of Educ., Univ. of Washington, Seattle, Wash., since 1949.

Strom, Walter, B.A.'38, Central Wash. Col. of Educ.; M.P.H.'45, Univ. of Mich.; Prin. of Sch., Roslyn, Wash., since 1934.

Studebaker, Robert S., B.A.'39, Univ. of Wash.; Supt. of Sch., Mercer Island, Wash., since 1945.

Sutter, Fred J., B.A.'49, Pacific Lutheran Col.; Supt., Woodland Sch., Puyallup, Wash., since 1950.

Temby, J. H., B.A.'28, State Col. of Wash.; Supt. of Sch., Creston, Wash., since 1949.

Thordarson, T. Roy, B.A. in Ed.'29, M.A.'49, Univ. of Wash.; Supt. of Pub. Sch., Bellevue, Wash., since 1947.

Tucker, George E., B.A.'25, Pacific Univ.; Supt., Lindbergh Consol. Sch. Dist. 340, Valleyford, Wash., since 1949.

Upton, Rolland H., A.B.'26, M.S.'37, Seattle Pacific Col.; Ed.D.'46, Univ. of Southern Calif.; Supt. of Sch., Auburn, Wash., since 1948.

Wanamaker, (Mrs.) Pearl A., B.A.'22, Univ. of Wash.; Pres., Natl. Educ. Assn., 1946-47; State Supt. of Pub. Instr., Olympia, Wash., since 1941.

Watson, Charles Hoyt, A.B.'18, A.M.'23, Univ. of Kansas; LL.D.'41, Whitworth Col.; Pres., Seattle Pacific Col., Seattle, Wash., since 1926.

Wendt, Julius A., B.A.'29, Mont. State Univ.; Supt. of Sch., Cathlamet, Wash., since 1937.

Westling, Norman L., B.A.'40, Univ. of Wash.; Supt. of Broadway Sch. Dist., Yakima, Wash., since 1944.

Weyermann, O. F., M.Ed., Univ. of Wash.; Supt., Sch. Dist. 49, Chimacum, Wash.

Willard, Clayton E., B.A.'25, Linfield Col.; M.A.'37, Univ. of Wash.; Supt. of Sch., Sumner, Wash., since 1948.

Willis, David E., Ed.D.'48, Tchrs. Col. Columbia Univ.; Assoc. Prof. of Educ., Acting Dir. of Summer Session, State Col. of Washington, Pullman, Wash., since 1948.

Woodward, C. Warren, B.A.'35, Univ. of Wash.; Supt. of Sch., Napavine Dist. 14, Napavine, Wash., since 1951.

Wright, P. A., B.A.'24, Univ. of Wash.; Supt. of Sch. Dist. 400, Richland, Wash., since 1948.

Wyngarden, John L., B.A. in Ed.'29, Univ. of Wash.; Supt. of North Kitsap Sch. Dist. #400, Poulsbo, Wash., since 1950.

INSTITUTIONAL MEMBERS

Library, Central Washington College of Education, Ellensburg, Wash.

Library, College of Puget Sound, Tacoma, Wash.

Library, State Col. of Wash., Pullman, Wash.

President's Office, Eastern Wash. Col. of Educ., Cheney, Wash.

Seattle Grade Teachers Club, 3043 Arcade Bldg., Seattle 1, Wash., Edna Mundt, Pres.

Spokane Public Library, Gladys S. Puckett, Librarian, Spokane, Wash.

The State College of Washington Library, Acquisition Dept., Serial Section, Pullman, Wash.

Washington Educ. Assn., Dept. of Admin. and Supvn, A. D. Whitenack, Treas., Vancouver, Wash.

Whitworth College, Mrs. R. Strun French, Librarian, Spokane, Wash.

WEST VIRGINIA

INDIVIDUAL MEMBERS

Andre, Lloyd W., T. and I. Cert.'45, W. Va. State Dept. of Voc. Educ.; Supt. of Bldgs. and Maintenance, Wheeling, W. Va., since 1950.

Archer, Charles H., A.B.'26, Concord State Col., Concord, W. Va.; Co. Supt. of Sch., Princeton, W. Va., since 1935.

Baldwin, Robert Dodge, A.B.'13, Princeton Univ.; A.M.'16, Columbia Univ.; Ph.D.'26, Cornell Univ.; Prof. of Educ., W. Va. Univ., Morgantown, W. Va., since 1931.

Bird, Ralph S., B.S.'34, Morris Harvey Col.; M.Ed.'40, Duke Univ.; Prin., H. S., Matoaka, W. Va., since 1947.

Bobbitt, James S., M.A.'35, W. Va. Univ.; Asst. Supt., Mercer Co. Sch., Princeton, W. Va., since 1935.

Bruffey, James B., A.B.'25, A.M.'39, W. Va. Univ.; Asst. Supt., Randolph Co. Sch., Elkins, W. Va., since 1944.

Bryson, George W., M.A.'34, Univ. of Ky.; Supt. of McDowell Co. Sch., Welch, W. Va., since 1935.

Cartright, Roy B., A.B.'33, Marshall Col.; A.M.'40, W. Va. Univ.; Co. Supt. of Sch., Sutton, W. Va., since 1944.

Coffindaffer, Wade H., A.B.'25, Salem Col.; A.M.'37, W. Va. Univ.; Asst. Co. Supt. of Sch., Clarksburg, W. Va., since 1935.

Colabrese, Felix A., B.S. in Ed.'36, M.A. in Ed.'38, West Va. Univ.; Asst. Supt., Tucker Co. Sch., Albert, W. Va.

Cox, Floyd B., A.B.'18, M.A.'21, W. Va. Univ.; Co. Supt. of Sch., Morgantown, W. Va., since 1930.

Cramblet, Wilbur Haverfield, B.A.'10, Bethany Col.; A.M.'11, Ph.D.'13, Yale Univ.; LL.D.'45, Univ. of Pittsburgh; Pres., Bethany Col., Bethany, W. Va., since 1934.

Creasy, James L., A.B.'33, Glenville State Col.; M.A.'40, W. Va. Univ.; Co. Supt. of Sch., Martinsburg, W. Va., since 1949.

Davis, John W., A.B.'11, A.M.'20, Morehouse Col.; Litt.D.'31, State Col., Orangeburg, S. C.; LL.D.'39, Wilberforce Univ.; LL.D.'40, Howard Univ.; Pres., W. Va. State Col., Institute, W. Va., since 1919.

Dickason, Henry Lake, B.A.'13, M.A.'14, Ohio State Univ.; Pres., Bluefield State Col., Bluefield, W. Va., since 1936.

Dowdy, Glenn, A.B.'31, Concord Col., Athens, W. Va.; M.A.'35, Columbia Univ.; Co. Supt. of Sch., Union, W. Va., since 1944.

Duncan, H. L., A.B.'24, Fairmont State Col., Fairmont, W. Va.; M.A.'27, George Peabody Col. for Tchrs.; Dir. of School Plant Planning, State Dept. of Educ., Charleston, W. Va., since 1946.

Elbin, Paul N., Ph.D.'32, Columbia Univ.; Pres., State Col., West Liberty, W. Va., since 1935.

Flinn, Virgil L., A.B.'20, W. Va. Univ.; M.A.'28, Ohio State Univ.; LL.D.'44, Morris Harvey Col.; Co. Supt. of Sch., Charleston, W. Va., since 1937.

Floyd, Troy, Jr., Co. Supt. of Sch., Williamson, W. Va.

Gibson, A. J., A.B.'16, W. Va. Univ.; M.A.'20, Columbia Univ.; State Supvr. of H. S., State Dept. of Educ., Charleston, W. Va., since 1933.

Harrah, D. D., B.A.'33, Marshall Col.; M.A.'41, W. Va. Univ.; Asst. Supt., Greenbrier Co. Sch., Lewisburg, W. Va., since 1943.

Humphrey, Joe C., B.A.'30, Southwestern Univ. (Texas); M.A.'31, Southern Methodist Univ.; Ed.D.'52, George Peabody Col. for Tchrs.; Academic Dean, Shepherd Col., Shepherdstown, W. Va., since 1952.

Hyde, Richard E., A.B.'21, W. Va. Univ.; A.M. '24, Columbia Univ.; Ph.D.'29, Univ. of Pittsburgh; Exec. Secy., State Tchrs. Retirement Bd., Charleston, W. Va., since 1941.

Idleman, H. L., A.B.'29, Univ. of Ky.; A.M.'39, Univ. of W. Va.; Co. Supt. of Sch., Keyser, W. Va., since 1941.

Losh, Laurence, M.A.'38, W. Va. Univ.; Asst. Co. Supt. of Sch., Kingwood, W. Va., since 1948.

Lovenstein, L. K., B.S.'22, Davis-Elkins Col.; M.A.'40, W. Va. Univ.; Admin. Asst. Supt. of Co. Sch., Charleston, W. Va., since 1946.

McCarty, Clyde R., A.B.'20, Salem Col. (W. Va.); M.A.'37, W. Va. Univ.; Asst. Co. Supt. of Sch., Clarksburg, W. Va., since 1939.

McGuffie, Jeannette, A.B.'30, M.A.'36, W. Va. Univ.; Genl. Supvr., Mineral Co. Sch., Keyser, W. Va., since 1947.

McHenry, J. P., A.B.'29, W. Va. Univ.; M.Ed.'36, Univ. of Pittsburgh; Co. Supt. of Sch., Wheeling, W. Va., since 1935.

Maddy, Irvin S., A.B.'30, Concord Col.; M.A.'34, W. Va. Univ.; Prin. of H. S., Hinton, W. Va., since 1948.

Montgomery, John Fleshman, A.B.'29, Hampden-Sydney Col.; A.M.'32, Univ. of Southern Calif.; Ph.D.'50, Duke Univ.; Co. Supt. of Sch., Lewisburg, W. Va., since 1943.

Newman, Winifred H., A.B.'29, Marshall Col.; M.A.'36, W. Va. Univ.; Asst. Co. Supt. of Sch., Charleston, W. Va., since 1940.

Nine, E. Grant, A.B.'25, Davis and Elkins Col.; A.M.'35, W. Va. Univ.; Prin., Scott H. S., Madison, W. Va.

Peregoy, C. G., A.B.'23, Wash. Col.; A.M.'32, W. Va. Univ.; Prin., Woodrow Wilson H. S., Beckley, W. Va., since 1933.

Potts, Louis Roberts, B.A. and B.S. in Ed.'16, M.A.'35, Ohio State Univ.; LL.B.'25, Columbus, Ohio, Col. of Law; Co. Supt. of Sch., Moundsville, W. Va., since 1935.

*Purdy, Ralph D., A.B.'29, Asbury Col.; M.A.'33, Univ. of Ky.; Acting Dir., Research and Field Serv., Marshall Col., Huntington, W. Va.

Randolph, Jackson K., A.B.'36, Salem Col.; M.A.'46, W. Va. Univ.; Co. Supt. of Sch., West Union, W. Va., since 1948.

Rapking, Aaron, Jr., B.S.'36, W. Va. Wesleyan Col.; M.S.'46, W. Va. Univ.; Dir., Research and Pub. Relations, W. Va. Educ. Assn., Charleston, W. Va., since 1950.

Rohrbough, R. Virgil, A.B.'33, Fairmont State Col., Fairmont, W. Va.; M.A.'42, W. Va. Univ.; Co. Supt. of Sch., Grafton, W. Va., 1942-47 and since 1949.

Rutan, Olen, M.A.'35, Univ. of Pittsburgh; Co. Supt. of Sch., Wellsburg, W. Va., since 1927.

Saundle, J. S., A.B.'29, W. Va. State Col.; M.A.'45, Atlanta Univ.; Asst. Co. Supt. of Sch., Bluefield, W. Va., since 1934.

Shannon, E. S., A.B.'23, Morris Harvey Col.; M.A.'30, Univ. of N. Mex.; Co. Supt. of Sch., Parkersburg, W. Va., since 1949.

Smith, Glen, M.A.'37, Univ. of Pittsburgh; Asst. Co. Supt. of Sch., Wellsburg, W. Va., since 1947.

Smith, Rex M., M.A.'39, W. Va. Univ.; Asst. Supt. of Co. Sch., Morgantown, W. Va., since 1947.

Spencer, Myles A.B.'41, Glenville State Col.; M.A.'48, W. Va. Univ.; Co. Supt. of Sch., Spencer, W. Va., since 1949.

Springer, A. G., M.A.'37, W. Va. Univ.; Asst. Co. Supt. of Sch., Keyser, W. Va., since 1948.

Thompson, French W., A.B.'97, Ark. Col.; B.D.'02, Presbyterian Theol. Sem.; D.D.'20, Daniel Baker Col.; Pres., Greenbrier Jr. Col., Lewisburg, W. Va., since 1925.

Trent, W. W., A.B.'12, W. Va. Univ.; A.M.'21, Tchrs. Col., Columbia Univ.; Ped.D.'31, Salem Col.; LL.D.'41, Marshall Col.; State Supt. of Free Sch., Charleston, W. Va., since 1933.

Trussler, Brown, A.B.'36, W. Va. Wesleyan Col.; M.A.'40, W. Va. Univ.; Supt., Upshur Co. Sch., Buckhannon, W. Va., since 1951.

Upton, Arthur V. G., A.B.'23, W. Va. Wesleyan Col.; A.M.'37, W. Va. Univ.; Ped.D.'38, W. Va. Wesleyan Col.; Co. Supt. of Sch., Clarksburg, W. Va., since 1939.

Watson, Paul W., A.B.'24, A.M.'32, W. Va. Univ.; Co. Supt. of Sch., Kingwood, W. Va., since 1935.

Whiting, Gregory W., A.B.'17, Fisk Univ.; M.A.'34, Tchrs. Col., Columbia Univ.; Dean and Acting Head, Dept. of Educ., Bluefield State Col., Bluefield, W. Va., since 1937.

Williams, Fountie N., A.B.'35, Salem Col.; M.A.'38, W. Va. Univ.; Prin., Broadway Jr. H. S., Clarksburg, W. Va., since 1943.

Wilmoth, Stark, B.S.'31, M.A.'38, West Va. Univ.; Supt. of Sch., Elkins, W. Va., since 1943.

Wolford, Jason, A.B.'25, Berea Col.; A.M.'39, W. Va. Univ.; Co. Supt. of Sch., Parsons, W. Va., since 1950.

Woods, Roy C., A.B.'18, M.S.'20, William Penn Col., Iowa; M.A.'24, Ph.D.'27, State Univ. of Iowa; Prof. of Educ., Marshall Col., Huntington, W. Va., since 1927.

INSTITUTIONAL MEMBERS

James E. Morrow Library, Marshall Col., Huntington, W. Va.

Parkersburg Teachers Association, Carnegie Library, Parkersburg, W. Va.

WISCONSIN

INDIVIDUAL MEMBERS

Ambruster, John Rea, B.S.'17, M.S.'28, Univ. of Ill.; Prin., Pub. Sch., Greendale, Wis.

Amundson, Elden M., Supvg. Prin. of Sch., Waterloo, Wis.

Antholz, H. J., Ph.B.'26, Univ. of Chicago; Supt. of Sch., Spooner, Wis., since 1921.

Austin, Edward C., B.E.'36, State Tchrs. Col., Milwaukee, Wis.; Supt. of Sch., Burlington, Wis., since 1947.

Ballentine, Will G., Supt. of Sch., Menomonie, Wis., since 1920.

Balliette, Ralph E., Ph.B.'23, Ph.M.'27, Univ. of Wis.; Supt. of Sch., Platteville, Wis., 1933-52 (retired).

Bannerman, G. W., B.A.'23, Lawrence Col.; M.A.'32, Univ. of Chicago; Supt. of Sch., Wausau, Wis., since 1947.

Bardwell, Richard W., A.B.'10, Univ. of Ill.; M.A.'22, Univ. of Chicago; Ph.D.'39, Univ. of Wis.; Dir., Voc. and Adult Sch., Madison, Wis., since 1948.

Barkley, Mathew, Ph.B.'29, M.E.'39, Marquette Univ.; Supt. of Sch., West Milwaukee, Wis.

Batho, Marshall G., Diploma '25, State Tchrs. Col., River Falls, Wis.; B.S.'31, State Univ. of Iowa; M.Ph.'34, Univ. of Wis.; 23 Craig Ave., Madison 5, Wis.

Bauer, Harold C., B.A.'25, Central Col.; M.A.'36, Univ. of Minn.; Supt. of Sch., Fond du Lac, Wis.

Becker, Eric T., B.S.'39, State Tchrs. Col., Oshkosh, Wis.; M.S.'47, Univ. of Wis.; Supt. of Sch., Beaver Dam, Wis., since 1952.

Behrens, Catherine M., A.B.'28, Ill. Col.; M.S.'39, Univ. of Mich.; Pres., Wis. Educ. Assn., Madison, Wis.; Tchr., Jr. H. S., Kenosha, Wis., since 1942.

Benka, Paul A., Secy., Bd. of Educ., Cudahy, Wis.

Bick, Kenneth F., Ph.B.'28, M.A.'36, Univ. of Wis.; Prin., Jr.-Sr. H. S., Janesville, Wis., since 1946.

Bingham, Vernon A., B.C.S.'24, N. Y. Univ.; Member, Bd. of Educ., Kenosha, Wis., since 1951.

Bjorge, John A., B.E.'34, State Tchrs. Col., La Crosse, Wis.; Ph.M.'44, Univ. of Wis.; Supt. of Sch., Whitewater, Wis., since 1950.

Boebel, Theodore H., M.A.'38, Northwestern Univ.; Supt. of Sch., Kaukauna, Wis., since 1944.

Brittelli, Len, B.S.'42, State Tchrs. Col., Whitewater, Wis.; M.S.'48, Univ. of Wis.; Supt. of Sch., Boscobel, Wis., since 1948.

Brown, Douglas M., B.S.'40, State Tchrs. Col., Superior, Wis.; M.S.'48, Univ. of Wis.; Supt. of Sch., Portage, Wis., since 1951.

Brown, Winston D., B.A.'33, Univ. of Wis.; M.A.'39, Marquette Univ.; Co. Supt. of Sch., Waukesha, Wis., since 1941.

Bruce, Walter R., Ph.M.'34, Univ. of Wis.; Supt. of Sch., Oconto, Wis., since 1950.

Bruce, William C., A.B.'01, A.M.'10, Marquette Univ.; Editor, American School Board Journal, Bruce Pub. Co., Milwaukee, Wis., since 1920.

Bruce, William R., B.A.'15, Lawrence Col.; M.A.'26, Univ. of Wis.; Supt. of Sch., Sparta, Wis., since 1935.

Burnkrant, Eugene George, B.A.'35, Dartmouth Col.; M.Ed.'41, Univ. of Vt.; Supt. of Sch., Plymouth, Wis., since 1949.

Carlson, Paul A., Ph.D.'21, Ph.M.'31, Univ. of Wis.; Dir. of Comml. Educ., State Tchrs. Col., Whitewater, Wis., since 1917.

Christenson, Christine A., B.E.'42, State Tchrs. Col., Oshkosh, Wis.; Co. Supt. of Sch., Marinette, Wis., since 1927.

Clemens, Paul B., Ph.B.'22, Ph.M.'27, Univ. of Wis.; Asst. Supt. of Sch., Milwaukee, Wis., since 1923.

Compton, Herold R., B.E.'36, State Tchrs. Col., River Falls, Wis.; M.A.'48, Univ. of Wis.; Supt. of Sch., Chilton, Wis., since 1949.

Cornell, Harvey H., M.A.'48, Univ. of Wis.; B.E.'45, Central State Tchrs. Col., Stevens Point, Wis.; Supt. of City Sch., Algoma, Wis., since 1950.

Cravillion, Ira, B.E.'40, State Tchrs. Col., Oshkosh, Wis.; Co. Supt. of Sch., Juneau, Wis., since 1945.

Crawford, Stuart B., Prin. of Union Free H. S., Hollandale, Wis.

Cupery, Nicholas P., B.A.'32, Hope Col.; M.Ph. '39, Univ. of Wis.; Supt. of Sch., Shawano, Wis., since 1948.

Davis, Dale F., B.S.'39, State Tchrs. Col., Platteville, Wis.; M.A.'46, Univ. of Wis.; Supt. of Sch., Sheboygan Falls, Wis., since 1947.

Dawson, Lawrence, Supt. of Sch., River Falls, Wis.

DeLong, Homer E., B.A.'29, Milton Col.; M.A.'35, Univ. of Wis.; Supt. of Sch., Eau Claire, Wis. since 1950.

Denman, G. E., Ph.B.'27, Ripon Col.; M.A.'32, State Univ. of Iowa; Supt. of Sch., Green Bay, Wis., 1935-52 (retired).

Diehl, Margaret, B.E.'45, State Tchrs. Col., Whitewater, Wis.; Co. Supt. of Sch., Kenosha, Wis., since 1948.

Dimick, Donald E., Supt. of Sch., Mount Horeb, Wis.

Dodsworth, Orvus L., B.S.'38, State Tchrs. Col., La Crosse, Wis.; M.Ph.'46, Univ. of Wis.; Supt. of Sch., Medford, Wis., since 1948.

Dorr, Charles H., B.A.'28, M.A.'32, Univ. of Wis.; Supt. of Sch., Milton, Wis., since 1928.

Dosch, Ralph H., B.E.'34, State Tchrs. Col., Whitewater, Wis.; M.A.'43, Northwestern Univ.; Supt. of Sch., New Holstein, Wis., since 1942.

Dunwiddie, Walter Rockwood, B.S.'16, M.S.'27, Univ. of Wis.; Supt. of Sch., Port Washington, Wis., since 1926.

Edwards, Conan S., John Edwards Sch., Port Edwards, Wis.

Eggold, E. F., A.B.'39, Valparaiso Univ.; M.A.'44, Marquette Univ.; Prin., Lutheran H. S., Milwaukee, Wis., since 1949.

Evans, Ewart O., A.B.'11, Carroll Col.; A.M.'29, Univ. of Wis.; Supt. of Sch., Monroe, Wis., since 1927.

Falk, Philip H., B.A.'21, M.A.'28, Ph.D.'35, Univ. of Wis.; Supt. of Sch., Madison, Wis., since 1939.

*Fowlkes, John Guy, A.B.'16, Ouachita Col.; A.M.'20, Ph.D.'22, Tchrs. Col., Columbia Univ.; Dir. of Summer Sessions since 1942, and Dean of Sch. of Educ., Univ. of Wis., Madison, Wis., since 1947.

Frailey, Charles U., M.S.'47, Univ. of Wis.; Dir. of Research, Wis. Educ. Assn., Madison, Wis., since 1952.

Fredrick, Hattie, Supvr., Rock Co. Sch., Jonesville, Wis.

Fryklund, Verne C., A.B.'23, Colo. Col. of Educ., Greeley; M.A.'27, Univ. of Mo.; Ph.D.'33, Univ. of Minn.; Pres., The Stout Inst., Menomonie, Wis.

Fuszard, Melvin C., B.A.'30, M.A.'37, Univ. of Wis.; Supt. of Sch., Lake Mills, Wis., since 1936.

Gegan, M. J., M.A.'42, Lawrence Col.; Supt. of Sch., Menasha, Wis., since 1944.

Gerritts, J. R., Supt. of Sch., Kimberly, Wis.

Glynn, R. P., Prin., Union Free H. S., Frederic, Wis.

Gordon, Laurin P., B.E.'32, State Tchrs. Col., Stevens Point, Wis.; Ph.M.'37, Univ. of Wis.; Supt. of Sch., Mt. Horeb, Wis., since 1942.

Gregg, Russell T., B.S.'28, A.M.'29, Ph.D.'34, Univ. of Ill.; Prof. of Educ., Dept. of Educ., Univ. of Wis., Madison, Wis., since 1945.

Grosenick, Gilbert H., B.Ed.'35, State Tchrs. Col., Oshkosh, Wis.; Ph.M.'44, Univ. of Wis.; Supt. of Sch., Richland Center, Wis., since 1950.

Halmstad, Robert N., M.S.'41, Univ. of Wis.; Supt. of Sch., Chippewa Falls, Wis., since 1952.

Hein, Reinhard G., B.A.'26, M.A.'32, Univ. of Wis.; Supt. of Sch., Waukesha, Wis., since 1949.

Heine, Oliver C., B.A.'35, Valparaiso Univ.; M.A.'43, Univ. of Wis.; Supvg. Prin., Milwaukee, Wis., since 1948.

Helms, Stanley B., M.A.'44, Univ. of Iowa; Supt. of Sch., Elkhorn, Wis.

Herrell, Francis, B.Ed.'30, State Tchrs. Col., Eau Claire, Wis.; Ph.M.'40, Univ. of Wis.; Supt. of Sch., Bloomer, Wis., since 1948.

Himmelmann, Frank M., B.S.'38, State Tchrs. Col., Milwaukee, Wis.; M.A.'41, Northwestern Univ.; Dir., Campus Laboratory Sch., Wis. State Col., Milwaukee, Wis.

Holt, Fred R., B.S.'34, M.S.'38, Univ. of Wis.; Supt. of Sch., West Bend, Wis., since 1948.

Holtz, Roger B., B.A.'32, Carroll Col.; M.A.'41, Univ. of Wis.; Supt. of Sch., Watertown, Wis., since 1945.

Huenink, Derwin J., B.A.'26, Hope Col.; M.A. '37, Univ. of Wis.; Supt. of Sch., Chetek, Wis., since 1943.

Jenson, Theodore J., Ph.B.'28, Univ. of Chicago; M.S.'31, Ph.D.'52, Univ. of Wis.; Supt. of Sch., Shorewood, Wis., since 1946.

Johnson, Leslie W., B.E.'28, State Tchrs. Col., Winona, Minn.; M.A.'34, Tchrs. Col., Columbia Univ.; Supt. of Sch., Superior, Wis., since 1949.

Johnston, Fred N., B.A.'26, Ill. Col.; M.A.'33, Northwestern Univ.; Supt. of Sch., Beloit, Wis., since 1949.

Jones, George E., Diploma '15, State Tchrs. Col., La Crosse, Wis.; Ph.B.'30, Ph.M.'37, Univ. of Wis.; Supt. of Sch., Mayville, Wis., since 1940.

Jones, James A., A.B.'21, M.A.'26, Ripon Col.; Supt. of Pub. Sch., North Fond du Lac, Wis., since 1929.

Jones, John E., Ph.B.'31, Marquette Univ.; Ph.M.'38, Univ. of Wis.; Supt. of Sch., Cudahy, Wis., since 1938.

Jordan, Arthur F., Diploma '24, B.Ed.'31, Wis. State Tchrs. Col., Whitewater; M.Ed.'52, Tufts Col.; Supt. of Sch., La Crosse, Wis., since 1952.

Jutta, Sister M., A.B.'17, Catholic Univ. of America; A.M.'29, Marquette Univ.; Dean, Alverno Col., Milwaukee, Wis., since 1936.

Keller, F. W., B.E.'32, State Tchrs. Col., Platteville, Wis.; M.A.'44, Univ. of Wis.; Supt. of Sch., Sturgeon Bay, Wis., since 1947.

Kellogg, E. G., B.E.D.'31, State Tchrs. Col., Oshkosh, Wis.; M.A.'40, Univ. of Minn.; Supt. of Sch., West Allis, Wis., since 1950.

Kies, Michael S., Diploma '24, State Tchrs. Col., Milwaukee, Wis.; Ph.B.'33, M.E.'47, Marquette Univ.; Co. Supt. of Sch., Milwaukee, Wis., since 1941.

Klaus, Roland A., B.A.'20, Lawrence Col.; M.A.'27, Univ. of Wis.; Supt. of Sch., Edgerton, Wis., since 1929.

Kleinpell, Eugene H., B.A.'25, State Univ. of Iowa; M.A.'36, Univ. of Chicago; Ph.D.'36, Ohio State Univ.; Pres., State Tchrs. Col., River Falls, Wis., since 1946.

Klontz, Vernon E., B.A.'17, Univ. of Wis.; A.M.'29, Univ. of Chicago; Supt. of Sch., Janesville, Wis., since 1933.

Knudtson, H. G., B.S.'38, State Tchrs. Col., Eau Claire, Wis.; Ph.M.'43, Univ. of Wis.; Supt. of Sch., Two Rivers, Wis., since 1952.

Kruschke, Walter F., Ph.B.'20, Ph.M.'40, Univ. of Wis.; Supt. of Sch., Rhinelander, Wis., since 1928.

Kujath, H. E., M.A.'39, Northwestern Univ.; Supt. of Sch., Waupun, Wis., since 1947.

Lake, Ernest G., B.A.'29, Univ. of Mont.; Ed.M. '38, Ed.D.'43, Harvard Univ.; Supt. of Sch., Racine, Wis., since 1951.

Lamers, William M., A.B.'22, A.M.'23, Ph.D.'29, Marquette Univ.; Asst. Supt. of Sch., Milwaukee, Wis., since 1942.

Lanphere, Milo M., B.E.'35, State Tchrs. Col., La Crosse, Wis.; Supvg. Prin., Pub. Sch., Stratford, Wis., since 1946.

Lauritzen, A. E., B.A.'29, Upper Iowa Univ.; M.A.'38, Univ. of Colo. Address: 111 Winn Terrace, Beaver Dam, Wis.

Leamer, Emery W., A.B.'09, Univ. of Nebr.; A.M.'19, Univ. of Chicago; Dir. of Tr., State Tchrs. Col., La Crosse, Wis., since 1925.

Lee, Howard D., B.S.Ed.'37, Univ. of Ill.; M.A.Ed.'47, Univ. of Chicago; Prin., Atwater Elem. Sch., Shorewood, Wis., since 1948.

Leistikow, Gordon R., B.A.'27, Macalester Col.; M.A.'39, Columbia Univ.; Supvg. Prin. of Sch., Winneconne, Wis., since 1935.

Leopold, Mollie, B.E.'31, Wis. State Col.; M.A.'39, Col. Univ.; Pres., Natl. League of Tchrs. Assn.; Tchr., Keefe Ave. Sch., Milwaukee, Wis., since 1933.

Lewis, R. F., B.A.'15, M.A.'28, Univ. of Wis.; First Asst. State Supt. of Pub. Instr., Madison, Wis., since 1949.

Loofboro, Paul M., B.A.'28, Milton Col.; M.A.'40, Univ. of Wis.; Supt. of Sch., New London, Wis., since 1952.

Luther, Earl W., Ph.B.'30, Ph.M.'35, Univ. of Wis.; Supt. of Sch., South Milwaukee, Wis.

Luther, James F., M.E.'39, Univ. of Wis.; Supt. of Sch., Fort Atkinson, Wis.

Lynn, Delford H., M.Ed.'47, Marquette Univ.; Supvg. Prin., State Graded Sch., West Allis, Wis., since 1947.

McConagha, Glenn L., Ph.D.'42, Ohio State Univ.; Dir., U. S. Armed Forces Inst., Madison, Wis., since 1949.

McKean, E. J., M.A.'23, Univ. of Wis.; Supt. of Sch., Tomah, Wis., since 1922.

McKenna, John C., B.A.'28, M.A.'31, State Univ. of Iowa; Supt. of Sch., Evansville, Wis., since 1934.

MacLachlan, F. G., Ph.B.'33, Ph.M.'45, Univ. of Wis.; Supt. of Sch., Park Falls, Wis., since 1945.

Mann, John P., B.A.'22, Ripon Col.; M.A.'27, Univ. of Wis.; Supt. of Sch., Appleton, Wis., since 1944.

Marshall, Richard J., B.Ed.'31, Central State Tchrs. Col.; Ph.M.'39, Univ. of Wis.; Supt. of Sch., Jefferson, Wis., since 1947.

Maurer, Harold R., B.S.'24, Col. of Wooster; M.A.'30, Ohio State Univ.; Supt. of Sch., Kenosha, Wis., since 1949.

Mennes, Harold B., A.B.'27, St. Olaf Col.; Ph.M.'37, Univ. of Wis.; Supt. of Sch., Neenah, Wis., since 1946.

Moldenhauer, Albert, B.S.'36, Wis. State Col., Eau Claire; M.Ph.'42, Univ. of Wis.; Supt. of Sch., Stoughton, Wis., since 1950.

Moser, Robert P., B.S.'39, M.S.'40, Univ. of Wis.; Supt. of Sch., Columbus, Wis., since 1949.

Murphy, John Howard, B.S.'25, Univ. of Wis.; M.A.'32, Univ. of Minn.; Supt. of State Colony, Chippewa Falls, Wis., since 1952.

Murphy, Joseph E., M.A.'32, Univ. of Mich.; Supt. of Sch., Hurley, Wis., since 1904.

Nemick, (Mrs.) J. A., Bd. of Educ., Fond du Lac, Wis.

Newlun, Chester O., Ph.B.'24, Ph.M.'26, Univ. of Wis.; Ph.D.'29, Columbia Univ.; Pres., State Tchrs. Col., Platteville, Wis., since 1943.

Nichols, Walter S., Ph.B.'25, Marquette Univ.; Ph.M.'38, Univ. of Wis.; Asst. Supt. of Sch., Milwaukee, Wis., since 1947.

Nicholson, Alfred S., B.S.'30, Princeton Univ.; M.A.'50, Columbia Univ.; Prin., Country Day Jr. Sch., Milwaukee, Wis.

Normington, Roy T., B.Ed.'23, Central State Tchrs. Col., Stevens Point, Wis.; M.A.'30, Tchrs. Col., Columbia Univ.; Supt. of Sch., Reedsburg, Wis., since 1936.

O'Brien, George M., B.A.'24, M.A.'31, Univ. of Wis.; Sales Mgr., Lab. Equip. Div., Hamilton Mfg. Co., Two Rivers, Wis., since 1952.

Olson, Harry E., B.E.'35, State Tchrs. Col., Platteville, Wis.; Ph.M.'36, Univ. of Wis.; Supt. of Sch., Oconomowoc, Wis., since 1944.

Paukert, Harold L., Master's '38, Univ. of Wis.; Supvg. Prin. of Sch., Kohler, Wis., since 1946.

Peterson, LeRoy, B.A.'28, Hastings Col.; M.A.'30, Ph.D.'32, Univ. of Wis.; Assoc. Prof. of Educ., Univ. of Wis., Madison, Wis., since 1948.

Philemon, Sister Mary, Head of Dept. of Educ., Mount Mary Col., Milwaukee, Wis.

Plenzke, O. H., A.B.'14, Lawrence Col.; A.M.'24, Univ. of Wis.; Exec. Secy., Wis. Educ. Assn., Madison, Wis., since 1933.

Ploetz, Walter, Supt. of Sch., Phillips, Wis.

Pollock, Vernon O., B.Ed.'29, State Tchrs. Col., Whitewater, Wis.; M.A.'37, Univ. of Iowa; Supt. of Sch., Lake Geneva, Wis., since 1948.

*Potter, Milton Chase, Ph.B.'95, Albion Col.; M.A.'05, Univ. of Chicago; Litt.D.'13, Univ. of Denver; M.Pd.'14, Mich. State Normal Col., Ypsilanti; Pres., Dept. of Superintendence, 1932-33; Honorary Life Member, American Assn. of Sch. Admin.; Supt. Emeritus of Sch., Milwaukee, Wis., since 1943. Address: 2725 N. Prospect, Milwaukee 11, Wis.

Powell, Harley J., B.A.'29, State Univ. of Iowa; M.A.'30, Univ. of Wis.; Supt. of Sch., Wauwatosa, Wis., since 1942.

Rawson, Kenneth O., B.A.'32, M.A.'37, Univ. of Wis.; Supt. of Sch., Clintonville, Wis., since 1945.

Ray, George R., Mgr., The Parker Tchrs. Agency, Madison, Wis.

Rilling, Walter E., B.A.'22, North Central Col.; Secy.-Bus. Mgr., Bd. of Sch. Dir., Milwaukee, Wis., since 1938.

Rohde, Richard R., B.S.'39, Oshkosh State Col., Wis.; M.Ph.'45, Univ. of Wis.; Supt. of City Sch., Barron, Wis., since 1951.

Rothwell, Angus B., B.E.'29, State Tchrs. Col., Superior, Wis.; M.A.'32, Columbia Univ.; Supt. of Sch., Manitowoc, Wis., since 1949.

Schneider, Marcella, Pres., Natl. League of Tchrs. Assn. Address: 3035 W. Wisconsin Ave., Milwaukee 8, Wis.

Schumann, Walter A., Ph.B.'35, Univ. of Chicago; Ph.M.'42, Univ. of Wis.; Supt. of Sch., Menomonee Falls, Wis., since 1943.

Senty, Walter B., B.S.'16, North Central Col.; M.A.'26, Univ. of Wis.; Asst. State Supt. of Pub. Instr., Madison, Wis., since 1940.

Sizer, Woodrow J., B.A.'37, Ripon Col.; M.S.'48, Univ. of Wis.; Supt. of Sch., Mayville, Wis., since 1952.

Smith, Floyd, Ph.M.'34, Univ. of Wis.; Supt. of Sch., Wisconsin Rapids, Wis., since 1936.

Smith, Henry Earl, Ph.B.'20, Ph.M.'28, Univ. of Wis.; Supt. of Sch., Sheboygan, Wis., since 1934.

Spangler, Chester W., B.S.'39, State Tchrs. Col., La Crosse, Wis.; M.S.'47, Univ. of Wis.; Supt. of Sch., Horicon, Wis., since 1950.

Spies, Jacob, B.A. in Commerce '24, Univ. of Wis.; Dir. of Voc. and Adult Educ., Sheboygan, Wis., since 1943.

Tall, Henry M., B.A.'25, Univ. of Chicago; M.A.'41, Univ. of Colo.; Supt. of Sch., Onalaska, Wis., since 1944.

Theisen, W. W., B.Sc.'07, Univ. of Nebr.; Ph.D.'17, Columbia Univ.; Asst. Supt. of Sch., Milwaukee, Wis., since 1922.

Theodine, Sister Mary, Ph.D.'47, Catholic Univ. of America; Pres., Viterbo Col., La Crosse, Wis., since 1947.

Thorson, Clarence, B.E.'36, Central State Col., Stevens Point, Wis.; Ph.M.'42, Univ. of Wis.; Supt. of Sch., Cedarsburg, Wis., since 1949.

Tinkham, Glenn D., B.S.'21, Ph.M.'36, Univ. of Wis.; Supt. of Sch., Marshfield, Wis., since 1947.

Tipler, Harry A., B.S.'23, Carroll Col.; M.S.'30, Univ. of Wis.; Supt. of Sch., Oshkosh, Wis., since 1946.

Tyler, Harry E., A.B.'20, Doane Col.; M.A.'27, Univ. of Nebr.; Chief, Curriculum Section, U. S. Armed Forces Inst., Madison, Wis., since 1952.

Vincent, Harold Sellew, A.B.'23, Greenville Col.; A.M.'32, Ohio State Univ.; Supt. of Sch., Milwaukee, Wis., since 1950.

Vincent, Paul M., M.A.'21, Univ. of Wis.; Supt. of Sch., Stevens Point, Wis., since 1923.

Wandrey, Fred H., B.E.'29, State Tchrs. Col., River Falls, Wis.; M.A.'39, State Univ. of Iowa; Supt. of Pub. Sch., Green Bay, Wis., since 1952.

Waterpool, W. F., B.A.'20, Lawrence Col.; Ph.M.'26, Univ. of Wis.; Supt. of Sch., Marinette, Wis., since 1940.

Waterstreet, E. F., Ed.B.'31, State Tchrs. Col., Oshkosh, Wis.; M.A.'38, Northwestern Univ.; Supvg. Prin. of Sch., Kewaunee, Wis., since 1946.

Watson, George E., B.A.'21, LL.D.'49, Lawrence Col.; M.A.'33, Univ. of Wis.; State Supt. of Pub. Instr., Madison, Wis., since 1949.

Werwath, Karl O., B.S. in E.E.'36, Milwaukee Sch. of Engineering; Pres., Milwaukee Sch. of Engineering, Milwaukee, Wis., since 1948.

Wicklund, Arnold D., B.A.'29, Northland Col.; M.A.'39, Univ. of Minn.; Supt. of Sch., Nekoosa, Wis., since 1947.

Wileman, Charles H., B.A.'26, Milton Col.; M.A.'34, Univ. of Wis.; Supt. of Sch., Delavan, Wis., since 1950.

Williams, Robert C., Ph.B.'14, Central Col.; M.A.'29, Ph.D.'38, State Univ. of Iowa; Pres., Wis. State Col., Whitewater, Wis., since 1946.

Willson, Gordon L., B.A.'25, M.A.'35, Univ. of Wis.; Supt. of Sch., Baraboo, Wis., since 1936.

Winther, Adolph I., B.A.'30, Augsburg Col.; Ph.M.'38, Ph.D.'48, Univ. of Wis.; Dir. of Tr. and Placement, State Tchrs. Col., Whitewater, Wis., since 1945.

Wolf, C. R., B.A.'23, Ripon Col.; M.A.'37, Univ. of Wis.; Supt. of Sch., Berlin, Wis., since 1951.

Zeiler, Edward J., Ph.B.'29, M.A.'32, Univ. of Chicago; Supt. of Sch., Whitefish Bay, Milwaukee, Wis., since 1952.

Zielanis, Stanley W., M.S., Univ. of Wis.; Supt. of Sch., Kiel, Wis., since 1948.

Zuill, Frances L., B.S.'20, M.A.'21, Tchrs. Col., Columbia Univ.; Dir. of Home Economics, Univ. of Wis., Madison, Wis., since 1939.

INSTITUTIONAL MEMBERS

Lawrence College, H. A. Brubaker, Librarian, Appleton, Wis.

Library, State Teachers College, Milwaukee, Wis.

Library, State Tchrs. Col., Stevens Point, Wis.

Library, State Tchrs. Col., Superior, Wis.

Library, State Tchrs. Col., Whitewater, Wis.

Racine Public Library, Fred Wezeman, Libn., 701 Main St., Racine, Wis.

State Tchrs. Col., Eau Claire, Wis.

State Teachers College, Library, La Crosse, Wis.

WYOMING

INDIVIDUAL MEMBERS

Bell, Karl D., B.Ed.'41, Western Mont. Col. of Educ., Dillon; M.Ed.'44, Mont. State Univ.; Supt. of Sch., Sheridan, Wyo., since 1950.

Belnap, Ralph A., M.A.'49, Univ. of Wyo.; Supt. of Sch., Lovell, Wyo., since 1951.

Bernard, John V., M.S. in Ed. Adm.'33, Colo. Agrl. and Mech. Col.; Supt. of Sch., Green River, Wyo., since 1948.

Bowen, Chet H., Supt., Campbell Co. H. S., Gillette, Wyo.

Breeden, Leo P., A.B.'38, M.A.'45, Colo. State Col. of Educ.; Supt. of Sch., Wheatland, Wyo., since 1947.

Bush, E. J., B.S.'21, Mont. State Col.; M.S.'37, Univ. of Wyo.; Supt. of Sch., Thermopolis, Wyo., since 1935.

Gingles, Roy, A.B.'34, Nebr. State Tchrs. Col.; A.M.'40, Univ. of Wyoming; Supt. of Pub. Sch., Torrington, Wyo., since 1950.

Goins, Jesse L., A.B.'25, Univ. of Wyo.; A.M.'31, Univ. of Chicago; Supt. of Sch., Cheyenne, Wyo., since 1938.

Humphrey, George Duke, B.A.'29, Blue Mountain Col.; M.A.'31, Univ. of Chicago; Ph.D.'39, Ohio State Univ.; Pres., Univ. of Wyo., Laramie, Wyo., since 1945.

Kraus, Frank G., B.S.'29, Univ. of N. Dak.; M.S.'43, Univ. of Wyo.; Supt. of Sch., Cody, Wyo., since 1941.

Kurtz, Clyde W., B.A.'25, M.A.'37, Univ. of Wyo.; Supt. of Sch., Evanston, Wyo., since 1941.

Lindell, George E., A.B.'17, Bethany Col.; M.S.'40, Univ. of Wyo.; Dir. of Distributive Educ., Cheyenne, Wyo., since 1947.

Metcalf, John L., B.S.'28, Brigham Young Univ.; Supt. of Consol. Sch. Dist. 19, Afton, Wyo., since 1935.

Morgan, Dean C., B.S.'21, Springfield Col.; M.A.'35, Wyoming Col.; Supt. of Sch., Casper, Wyo., since 1935.

Paulsen, F. Robert, B.S.'47, Utah State Agr. Col.; M.S.'48, Univ. of Utah; Supt. of Sch., Cokeville, Wyo., since 1951.

Quigg, James C., B.A.'28, State Tchrs. Col., Eau Claire, Wis.; M.A.'33, Univ. of N. Dak.; Supt. of Sch., Greybull, Wyo., since 1939.

Reusser, Walter C., A.B.'20, Upper Iowa Univ.; M.A.'23, Ph.D.'29, State Univ. of Iowa; Dean, Div. of Adult Educ. and Community Serv. and Prof. of Educ. Admin., Univ. of Wyo., Laramie, Wyo., since 1924.

Richard, C. W., A.B.'28, Nebr. State Tchrs. Col., Wayne; M.A.'29, Univ. of Nebr.; Supt. of Sch., Powell, Wyo., since 1947.

Rollins, J. Leslie, B.S.'37, Brigham Young Univ.; Supt. of Sch., Lyman, Wyo., since 1945.

Schaub, Roy, Jr., A.B.'48, Colo. State Col. of Educ.; Supt. of Sch., Pinedale, Wyo., since 1950.

Schwiering, Oscar C., A.B.'09, Iowa Wesleyan Col.; M.A.'16, Univ. of Wyo.; Ph.D.'32, New York Univ.; Dean, Col. of Educ., Univ. of Wyo., Laramie, Wyo., since 1939.

Stevens, Theodore B., Litt.B.'25, Rutgers Univ.; M.A.'32, New York Univ.; Supt. of Sch. Dist. 2, Buffalo, Wyo., since 1950.

Stolt, Edna B., B.A.'23, Colo. State Col. of Educ., Greeley; State Supt. of Pub. Instr., Cheyenne, Wyo., since 1947.

Thayer, J. E., B.A.'25, M.A.'27, Univ. of Wyo.; Supt. of Sch., Laramie, Wyo., since 1945.

Thompson, Edward Merle, A.B.'12, Nebr. Wesleyan Univ.; A.M.'29, Colo. State Col. of Educ., Greeley; Supt. of Sch., Rock Springs, Wyo., since 1925.

Thompson, R. W., B.A.'28, M.A.'38, Univ. of Wyo.; Supt., Fremont Co. Voc. H. S., Lander, Wyo., since 1938.

Watson, Frank R., B.E.'30, Pioneer State Tchrs. Col., Wisconsin; Supt., Elem. Sch., Worland, Wyo., since 1926.

Willey, Ivan R., M.A.'40, Univ. of Wyo.; Supt. of Sch., Superior, Wyo., since 1946.

OTHER NATIONS
CANADA
INDIVIDUAL MEMBERS

Baird, Norman B., B.A.'33, Pd.D.'45, Univ. of Toronto; Supt. of Sch., and Bus. Admin., Welland, Ontario, Canada, since 1950.

Boulanger, Trefflé, Dir. of Educ., The Montreal Catholic Sch. Comm., 117 St. Catherine St. W., Montreal, Canada, since 1942.

Brown, Clifton G., B.A.'13, Univ. of Toronto; M.A.'34, Univ. of Wash.; Municipal Inspector of Sch., 2800 McKay Ave., South Burnaby, B. C., Canada, since 1936.

Brown, Corbin A., B.A.'24, Queen's Univ., Kingston, Canada; A.M.'27, Columbia Univ.; B.Paed.'32, D.Paed.'48, Univ. of Toronto; Registrar, Ontario Dept. of Educ., Toronto, Ontario, Canada, since 1945.

Campbell, H. L., B.A.'28, Univ. of British Columbia; M.Ed.'38, Univ. of Wash.; Asst. Supt. of Educ., Dept. of Educ., Victoria, B. C., Canada.

Desaulniers, Omer-Jules, D.Ped.'41, Laval Univ., Quebec City, Canada; Supt. of Educ. for the Province of Quebec, Quebec City, Canada, since 1945.

DuCap, Wilfrid, Dir. of Sch. Supplies, The Montreal Catholic Sch. Commn., 117 St. Catherine St., Montreal 18, Quebec, Canada.

Flemington, William Thomas Ross, O.B.E., B.A.'22, M.A.'23, Mt. Allison Univ.; B.Paed.'30, Univ. of Toronto; D.D.'43, Queen's; D.D.'47, Victoria; F.R.S.A.'47,; Pres., Mt. Allison Univ., Sackville, N. B., Canada, since 1945.

Flower, George E., M.A.'49, McGill Univ.; Dir., Canadian Educ. Assn.-Kellogg Project in Educ. Leadership, 206 Huron St., Toronto 5, Ontario, Canada, since 1952.

Goldring, Cecil C., B.A.'18, Queen's Univ.; M.A.'20, D.Ped.'24, Univ. of Toronto; Supt. of Sch., Toronto, Canada, since 1932.

Japp, Robert, M.A.'27, B.Ed.'29, Univ. of St. Andrews, Scotland; M.A.'30, McGill Univ., Montreal; Educ. Officer, 3460 McTavish St., Montreal, Canada, since 1942.

Le Borgne, Gaétan, Architect's Degree '43, Univ. of Montreal; Architect, Montreal Catholic Sch. Commn., 117 St. Catherine St., West, Montreal, Province of Quebec, Canada.

Lent, George G., B.A.'38, St. Francis Xavier Col.; M.A.'47, Tchrs. Col., Columbia Univ.; Inspector of Sch., Educ. Office, Port Hawkesbury, Nova Scotia, Canada, since 1950.

Linteau, J. O., Comptroller, The Montreal Catholic Sch. Commn., 117 St. Catherine St., West, Montreal 18, Quebec, Canada, since 1949.

McCordic, William J., B.A.'40, Univ. of Toronto; Bus. Admin., East York Bd. of Ed., 670 Cosburn Ave., Toronto 6, Ontario, Canada, since 1950.

MacCorkindale, H. N., B.A.'13, Univ. of Toronto; Supt. of Sch., 1595 W. Tenth Ave., Vancouver, B. C., Canada, since 1933.

MacDiarmid, F. E., Dir. and Chief Supt. of Educ., Fredericton, New Brunswick, Canada.

MacKenzie, W. H., B.A.'33, Mount Allison Univ.; M.A.'42, Ed.D.'42, Columbia Univ.; Supt. of Sch., Saint John, New Brunswick, Canada, since 1945.

MacLeod, Clare R., B.A.'42, Univ. of Western Ontario; B.Paed.'45, Univ. of Toronto; Insp. and Asst. Supt. of Pub. Sch., Bd. of Educ., Windsor, Ontario, Canada, since 1950.

Morgan, Ewart H., M.A. in Ed.'34, Univ. of Manitoba; Asst. Supt. of Sch., Winnipeg, Manitoba, Canada, since 1947.

Page, Joseph L., B.Ped.'41, Univ. of Montreal; Dir. of Schoolhouse Construction Serv., Dept. of Educ., Province of Quebec, Parliament Bldgs., Quebec City, Quebec, Canada, since 1949.

Phimister, Z. S., B.A.'30, Queen's Univ.; B.Paed.'34, Univ. of Toronto; Supt. and Chief Inspector of Pub. Sch., Toronto, Ontario, Canada, since 1945.

Ritter, Archibald C., B.A.'33, Queen's Univ., Canada; B.Paed.'40, Univ. of Toronto; Dir. of Educ., Kingston, Ont., Can., since 1950.

Scace, Muriel, B.A.'28, Univ. of British Columbia; Dir., Educ. Reference and Sch. Serv., and Asst. Dir. of Curriculum, Dept. of Educ., Victoria, B. C., Canada, since 1934.

Sharp, R. F., B.A.'32, Univ. of British Columbia; Pd.D.'40, Univ. of Toronto; Asst. Supt., 1595 W. 10th Ave., Vancouver, B. C., Canada, since 1951.

Sommerville, Thomas, M.A.'15, Glasgow Univ., Scotland; Dir. of Educ. and Secy.-Treas., Montreal Protestant Central Sch. Bd., 3460 McTavish St., Montreal, Quebec, Canada, since 1945.

Wheable, Geoffrey Alfred, B.A.'21, Queen's Univ.; LL.D.'44, Univ. of Western Ontario; Supt. of Sch., London, Ont., Can., since 1925.

Worrell, Henry G., B.A.'40, Sir George Williams Col.; Bursar, Sir George Williams Col., 1441 Drummond St., Montreal 25, Quebec, Canada, since 1947.

INSTITUTIONAL MEMBER

Summer School of Education, Bank of Montreal Bldg., Victoria, B. C., Canada.

ENGLAND

Alexander, W. P., Secy., Assn. of Educ. Com., 10 Queen Anne St., London, W. 1, England.

Dent, Harold Collett, B.A.'22, Univ. of London; Editor, *The Times Educational Supplement*, The Times, Printing House Square, London, E. C. 4, England, since 1940.

Ford, Edith A., Dartmouth House, 37 Charles St., London W. 1, England.

Frost, T., Education Offices, Rosslyn Rd., Barking, Essex, England.

Pritchard, Mervyn W., M.A.'32, Manchester Univ., England; Ministry of Educ., Curzon St., London, W. 1., England.

Savage, Sir Edward Graham, B.A.'06, Cambridge Univ.; Educ. Officer, London Co. Council, The Co. Hall, Westminster Bridge, London S. E. 1, England, since 1940.

FRANCE

Beatty, Willard Walcott, B.S.'13, M.A.'22, Univ. of Calif.; Ed.D.'37, Reed Col.; Deputy Dir., Dept. of Educ. in charge of Fundamental Educ. Tr. Centers, UNESCO, 19 Ave. Kléber, Paris 16, France, since 1951.

GERMANY

Borders, Ferman N., Prin., Karlsruhe, Germany. Address: APO 403, U. S. Army, c/o P. M., New York, N. Y.

IRAN

Greenawalt, George L., M.A.'29, Tchrs. Col., Columbia Univ.; Adviser on Educ. Materials, Point Four Educ. Party T.C.A., c/o American Embassy, Tehran, Iran, since 1952.

Irvine, John Richard, Bd. of Foreign Missions of the Presbyterian Church in the U. S., c/o American Mission, Tehran, Iran, since 1952.

IRELAND

Brownell, R. S., Exec. Dir., Ministry of Educ., Netherleigh, Massey Ave., Belfast, Ireland.

ITALY

Pritschet, Andrew G., B.A.'38, State Tchrs. Col., Minot, N. Dak.; M.S.'47, Univ. of Idaho; Educ. Specialist, United States Government, Naples, Italy, since 1952. Address: Navy No. 510, FPO New York, N. Y.

JAPAN

Fuwa, Osamu, Supt. of City Sch., Bd. of Educ., City Hall, Kyoto, Japan.

Hamada, Shigemasa, Supt., Osaka Prefectural Sch., Osaka, Japan.

Nakamura, Shinichi, LL.B.'31, Tokyo Univ.; Supt., Kanagawa Prefectural Bd. of Educ., Kaigan-dori, Yokohama Bldg., Yokahoma, Japan, since 1931.

MEXICO

Cain, Henry L., B.S.'24, LL.D.'44, Centenary Col.; M.A.'27, Baylor Univ.; Pres., Mexico City Col., Chiapas 138, Mexico City, Mexico, since 1940.

Cundiff, Roger F., Supt., The American Sch. Foundation, Porfirio Diaz 200, Tacubaya, Mexico, D. F., since 1951.

NICARAGUA

Lund, John, A.B.'13, Clark Univ.; M.A.'14, Columbia Univ.; Ph.D.'38, Yale Univ.; Specialist in Sch. Admin., Institute of Inter-American Affairs, c/o American Embassy, Managua, Nicaragua.

PAKISTAN

Haq, A. F. M. Abdul, B.A.'28, M.A.'29, Dacca Univ., Pakistan; Asst. Dir. of Pub. Instr., East Bengal, Pakistan, since 1948.

PARAGUAY

Packer, Paul C., A.B.'18, State Univ. of Iowa; M.A.'21, Univ. of Mich.; Ph.D.'23, Columbia Univ.; Dir. of Educ. Program in Paraguay, Inst. of Inter-American Affairs, c/o American Embassy, Asuncion, Paraguay, S. A., since 1950.

PHILIPPINES

Bernardino, Vitaliano, B.S.E.'33, Natl. Univ., Manila, Philippines; M.A.'38, Univ. of Philippines; Div. Supt. of Sch., and Secy.-Treas., Philippine Assn. of Sch. Supts., Malolos, Bulacan, Philippines, since 1943.

Cayco, Florentino, A.B.'21, Ind. Univ.; M.A.'22, Tchrs. Col., Columbia Univ.; Pres., Arellano Univ., 252 Plaza Arellano, Sampaloc, Manila, Philippines, since 1937.

Drag, Francis L., B.A.'30, Chico State Col.; M.A.'42, Ed.D.'47, Stanford Univ.; Basic Educ. Specialist, Mutual Security Agency, Manila, P. I., since 1952. Address: APO 928, c/o P.M., San Francisco, Calif.

Fair, Eugene R., B.S. in Ed.'30, Northeast Mo. State Tchrs. Col., Kirksville; M.A.'30, Tchrs. Col., Columbia Univ.; Ph.D.'38, State Univ. of Iowa; Chief Cultural Officer, American Embassy, Manila, Philippine Republic, since 1953. Address: APO 928, c/o Postmaster, San Francisco, Calif.

Guiang, Pedro G., B.A.E.'26, M.A.E.'27, Ph.D. '34, State Univ. of Wash.; Div. and City Supt. of Sch., Cebu City, Cebu, Philippines, since 1946.

Putong, Cecilio, B.S.E.'20, Western Ill. State Col.; M.A.'21, Columbia Univ.; Ph.D.'37, Univ. of Chicago; Undersecretary of Educ., P.N.C. Bldg., Corner Ayala-Taft, Manila, Philippines, since 1949.

SCOTLAND

Anderson, John Dunlop, Invermay, Milngavnie, Glasgow, Scotland.

Frizell, J. B., Dir. of Educ., 14 Giles St., Edinburgh, Scotland.

VENEZUELA

Wilson, Woodrow B., B.S.'37, Southwest Texas State Tchrs. Col.; Supt. Sch., Barcelona, Venezuela, S. A., since 1949.

543

INDEX OF NAMES

545

SUBJECT INDEX

Curriculum, improvement of: action research, 119-24; adjustment to school size, 91-93; administrative evaluation, 157-59; arithmetic program, 138-39; citizenship project, 172-75; classroom origin of, 88-89; classroom teacher's role in, 102; consultants' role in, 104; county approaches to, 133-36; county-wide programs for, 93-96; curriculum revision needed periodically, 20; discovering pupil interests and needs, 225-27; English, 151-53; evaluation of, 235-38; extension to a 12-grade system, 162-69; from theory to practice, 104-106; functional mathematics, 159-62; getting resources for, 227-29; guiding pupil activities for, 232-35; in small city, 124-27; individual school approach to, 89-90; inservice growth approach to, 87; life adjustment education, 176-78; meeting needs of people, 17; occupational education, 147-51; open-mindedness study, 116-19; organizing for curriculum improvement, 80; parent and lay participation, 103-104; planning, 222-25; preparation of guides, 131-32; primary block plan, 113-15; principal's role in, 100-101; pupil's role in, 103; purpose of curriculum change, 107-109; reading-readiness programs, 109-12, 115; regional planning, 97-98; remedial reading clinic approach, 136-37; school-community emphasis, 127-30; special-interest beginning on curriculum improvement, 90-91; statewide programs, 97, 159-62; steering committee in Illinois, 169-72; superintendent's role in, 98-100; systemwide approach, 82-87; teacher cooperation in, 241-42; teachers association role in, 102-103; teacher's role in, 219-42; use of guides for, 229-32; use of polls and surveys in, 283; use of test results in, 337-38. *See also* Curriculum, development of.

Curriculum, organization of: bases for agreement on curriculum organization, 77-78; basis of curriculum choices, 55; basic curriculum issues, 70; broad fields curriculum, 61-64; classroom experiences, 76; core curriculum, 64-68; correlation, 62; courses of study and guides, 72-73; criticism of core curriculum, 66; experience curriculum, 68; fusion, 62; general formula of, 55; integration, 62-64; nonschool experiences, 75; objections to subject emphasis, 60-

61; organization of experience, 71; organizational patterns, 57-58; pupil-teacher planning, 69; school experiences, 76-77; subject curriculum, 59; values of core curriculum, 66; unit plans, 73-75.

Curriculum guides: teachers' list of, 155-56; use of, 229-30.

Curriculum laboratories: description of, 201-202.

Curriculum resources: budget for, 212-16; courses of study, 230-31; curriculum guides, 229-30; curriculum laboratories, 201-202; development of, 207-10; individuals and community groups, 228-29; list of, 227; long range planning, 210-17; Metropolitan School Study Council, 187; production of, 85-86; purchasing agent for, 211-12; special bureaus, 227; tables of expenditures for, 214-15; textbooks, 231-32; use of local resources, 124-27.

Discipline: parents' opinions on, 284.

Drop-out studies: use in curriculum evaluation, 347-48.

Education: and social advancement, 27-30; content of, 42-44.

Educational Policies Commission: publications of, cited, 30, 75, 79, 101, 106, 275; quoted, 101.

Emotions: development of, 44-45.

English: curriculum improvement in, 151-53.

Evaluation: administrative evaluation of curriculum improvement, 157-59; and social change, 343-46; as an aid to instruction, 236-37; comprehensiveness of, 323-29; construction of standardized tests, 328-29; coordination of, 329-34, definition of, 310-11; effectiveness of administrator, 351-54; essentials of a program of, 312-13; interpretation of results of, 334-38; local achievement and standard norms, 335; objectives of, 312-13; of teacher-parent workshops, 130; of ultimate objectives, 313-17; pupil's role in, 339-41; teachers' role in, 338-39; use of anecdotal records in, 333-34; use of drop-out studies in, 347-48; use of follow-up studies in, 348-49; use of opinion surveys in, 349, 353; use of paper-pencil tests in, 332-33; use of tests in, 321-23, 351-52.

Exhibits: as teaching aids, 204.

Social studies: an approach to curriculum improvement, 131-32; cooperation among professional groups, 178-79; in a core program, 163-66.

Society: debate over new principles of education, 12; dynamic society, 10; education underlies social progress, 29; education under state control, 12-13; equality of opportunity, 14, 22; faith in education, 9; group living, 18; growth of public schools, 14-16; home obligations to child, 23; human resources, 9; increased leisure time, 14; keeping in touch with needs of people, 17; leisure time, 19; meeting needs of people, 17; new inventions, 15; social forces affect scope of education, 16; specialization, 18; speed and tension, 19; technological changes, 19.

State programs: Florida Program for Improvement of Schools, 159-62; Illinois Secondary School Curriculum Program, 159-62.

Studies: *See* Surveys.

Superintendent: as a leader, 80; effectiveness, 351-54; role in curriculum development, 98-100.

Surveys: and parent-teacher associations, 255-57; as public relations technics, 283-85; by citizens committees, 255-57, 283-85; list of instruments of, 350; of high-school graduates, 348-49; of office occupations, 144-47; of opinion, 349-51, 353; of school drop-outs, 347-48.

Tables: expenditures for instructional materials, 214-15; references to attacks on public schools, 286.

Teacher, classroom: and development of a class curriculum, 221-41; as an individual, 219-21; cooperation in curriculum improvement, 241-42; role in curriculum development, 102, 219-42, 246-48; role in curriculum evaluation, 338-39; role in public relations, 278-79.

Teacher, visiting: role in curriculum development, 248-50.

Teachers associations: programs for curriculum revision, 153-57; role in curriculum development, 102-103, 178-79.

Teaching aids: community resources, 207-10, 228-29; cooperation between educators and publishers, 192-95; criteria for, 191, 199-200; currently available aids, 183-86; exhibits, 204; expenditures for, 212-17; free and inexpensive, 184-86; homemade, 202; human resources, 209-10; lay participation in selection of, 198-99; museums, 208; need for improved materials, 188-95; newer materials, 186-88; organization for use of, 204-207; school camps and farms, 209; selection of, 196-200; selection of as inservice education, 200-204; special bureaus, 227-28; study council materials, 187; tables of expenditures, 214-15; textbooks, 71-72; unsolved problems, 190; use of library, 205-206.

Teaching units: *See* Units of work.

Television and radio: and the curriculum, 271-72; and school-community relations, 305-309; arguments for and against, 270-71; constructive approach to, 271; effects of, 270; publicity programs in Cleveland, 307-309.

Tests: construction of standardized tests, 328-29; improvement of, 332; limitations of, 330-32; paper-pencil tests, 332-33; use in curriculum improvement, 235-36, 337-38; use in curriculum evaluation, 321-23, 351-52.

Textbooks: adoptions by state departments of education, 198; as aids to instruction, 71-72.

Three R's: and public relations, 289-95; in the early schools, 13-14; reply to criticism of, 295.

U. S. Office of Education: Life Adjustment Education, 176-78; publications of, cited, 79, 143, 176, 177, 184, 243; referred to, 143, 176-77.

Units of work: characteristics of a unit, 73-74; planning a unit, 239-41; unit plans, 73-75; using courses of study, 230-31.

Vocational education: in curriculum improvement, 147-51; occupational efficiency, 25-26.

Workshops: in Dade County (Fla.), 135; Garrett County, Md., 164-66; in La Mesa-Spring Valley, 127; in Manhattan Project, 128-29; in Oak Ridge, 128-29; parent participation in, 128-29.

Writing: an essential learning, 39.

POLICIES

INSTRUCTION

PUPIL PLANNING